Magill's Cinema Annual 2006

Magill's Cinema Annual 2006

25th Edition
A Survey of the Films of 2005

Hilary White, Editor

Jim Craddock and Michael J. Tyrkus, Contributing Editors

A VideoHound® Reference

Detroit • New York • San Francisco • San Diego • New Haven, Conn. • Waterville, Maine • London • Munich

Magill's Cinema Annual 2006

Project Editor
Hilary White

Editorial
Tom Burns, Jim Craddock, Michael J. Tyrkus

Editorial Support Services
Wayne Fong

Composition and Electronic Prepress
Gary Leach, Evi Seoud

Manufacturing
Rhonda Dover

For more information, contact
The Gale Group, Inc.
27500 Drake Rd.
Farmington Hills, MI 48331-3535
Or you can visit our Internet site at
http://www.gale.com

ISBN 1-55862-577-1
ISSN 0739-2141

Printed in the United States of America
10 9 8 7 6 5 4 3 2 1

Contents

Preface

Magill's Cinema Annual 2006 continues the fine film reference tradition that defines the VideoHound series of entertainment industry products published by Gale. The twenty-fifth annual volume in a series that developed from the 21-volume core set, *Magill's Survey of Cinema,* the *Annual* was formerly published by Salem Press. Gale's twelfth volume, as with the previous Salem volumes, contains essay-reviews of significant domestic and foreign films released in the United States during the preceding year.

The *Magill's* editorial staff at Gale, comprising the VideoHound team and a host of *Magill's* contributors, continues to provide the enhancements that were added to the *Annual* when Gale acquired the line. These features include:

- More essay-length reviews of significant films released during the year
- Obituaries and book review sections
- Trivia and "fun facts" about the reviewed movies, their stars, the crew, and production
- Quotes and dialogue "soundbites" from reviewed movies, or from stars and crew about the film
- More complete awards and nominations listings, including the American Academy Awards®, Golden Globe, New York Critics Awards, Los Angeles Film Critics Awards, and others (see the User's Guide for more information on awards coverage)
- Box office grosses, including year-end and other significant totals
- Publicity taglines featured in film reviews and advertisements

In addition to these elements, the *Magill's Cinema Annual 2006* still features:

- An obituaries section profiling major contributors to the film industry who died in 2005
- An annotated list of selected film books published in 2005
- Nine indexes: Directors, Screenwriters, Cinematographers, Editors, Art Directors, Music Directors, Performers, Subject, and Title (now cumulative)

COMPILATION METHODS

The *Magill's* editorial staff reviews a variety of entertainment industry publications, including trade magazines and newspapers, as well as online sources, on a daily and weekly basis to select significant films for review in *Magill's Cinema Annual. Magill's* staff and other contributing reviewers, including film scholars and university faculty, write the reviews included in the *Annual.*

MAGILL'S CINEMA ANNUAL: A VIDEOHOUND REFERENCE

The *Magill's Survey of Cinema* series, now supplemented by the *Annual,* is the recipient of the Reference Book of the Year Award in Fine Arts by the American Library Association. Gale, an award-winning publisher of reference products, is proud to offer *Magill's Cinema Annual* as part of its popular VideoHound(R) product line, which includes *VideoHound's Golden Movie Retriever* and *The Video Source Book.* Other Gale film-related products include the four-volume *International Dictionary of Film and Filmmakers, Women Filmmakers & Their Films,* the *Contemporary Theatre, Film, and Television* series, and the four-volume *Schirmer Encyclopedia of Film.*

ACKNOWLEDGMENTS

Thank you to Gary Leach for his typesetting expertise, and Wayne Fong for his invaluable technical assistance. The *VideoHound* staff is thanked for its contributions to this project. Also, the following producers, distributors, and publicists for their invaluable assistance: Susan Norget at Susan Norget Publicity and Marketing; Graham Leggat at the Press Office of the Society of Lincoln Center; Ronald Ramsland at New Yorker Films; Sarah Mardock at Sony Pictures Classics; Roderigo Brandao at Kino International; The Press Office of the Tribeca Film Festival. We at *Magill's* would also like to acknowledge the accomplishments of freelance reviewer James Welsh, who has been a contributor for *Magill's* for 20 years and has recently received a lifetime achievement book award from the Southwest Pop Culture Conference in Albuquerque.

The Year in Film: An Introduction

Five years into the twenty-first century marked another amazing year in film. Big budget Hollywood blockbusters were bigger and better than ever, counting entries from the illustrious Star Wars and Harry Potter franchises among its number. There was also Peter Jackson's much-heralded remake of *King Kong* to look forward to, a film adaptation of the children's classic *The Chronicles of Narnia: The Lion, the Witch and the Wardrobe,* and remarkable new films from heavy-hitting directors Steven Spielberg (*Munich*) and Woody Allen (*Match Point*). Meanwhile, director Ang Lee's quiet western/love story, *Brokeback Mountain,* starring two of Hollywood's hottest leading men as frustrated lovers, cleaned up at most of the award ceremonies. Paul Haggis' *Crash,* winning the Academy Award® for Best Film, was another small film tackling a controversial subject that prevailed. The year also yielded a wide crop of astonishing independent movies, documentaries, and foreign films that explored important subjects, from terrorism and the Middle East to corporate corruption and sexual harassment.

Not surprisingly, George Lucas's much anticipated *Star Wars: Episode III—Revenge of the Sith* stormed the box office and ended up on top. This final prequel, (supposedly) marking the end of the six-part *Star Wars* series, went out with a bang, taking in $380.3 million by the end of 2005. A distant second was the latest installation in the Harry Potter series, *Harry Potter and the Goblet of Fire,* which trailed by nearly $100 million with a $286 million chunk of the $8.9 billion 2005 box office receipts. Under the direction of Mike Newell, Harry stayed on top even as he, and the uber-successful franchise, matured.

While sequels held sway over much of last year's top ten, many of the biggest box office winners of 2005 were original films. Disney's *The Chronicles of Narnia: The Lion, the Witch and the Wardrobe* finished third with $281 million domestically, shaping up to have the potential for becoming its own franchise. The Spielberg-helmed Tom Cruise vehicle *War of the Worlds* also cracked the top five list of highest-grossing films, with $234 million. Another big screen, action spectacle sat in fifth place, Peter Jackson's *King Kong,* which grabbed $214 million of moviegoer's dollars.

Rounding out the top ten-grossing films of 2005 was the summer hit *Wedding Crashers* ($209 million); *Charlie and the Chocolate Factory* ($206 million); *Batman Begins* ($205 million); *Madagascar* ($193 million); and *Mr. & Mrs. Smith* ($186 million).

It was not big box office and big budgets, however, that impressed The Academy of Motion Picture Arts and Sciences. Three of the five nominees for Best Picture, including *Capote, Crash,* and *Good Night, and Good Luck* had budgets well under $10 million; while *Brokeback Mountain* was produced for $14 million. *Brokeback,* which took in a mere $15 million by the end of 2005, benefited from the slew of awards and award nominations it garnered, which amped its gross to more than $75 million by March 2006. As well as crowned the winner by many critical bodies, the film also made most critics personal top ten lists. Star Heath Ledger, co-star Jake Gyllenhaal, and Michelle Williams all scored Oscar® nominations as well as receiving numerous nominations and awards from other award-giving bodies.

Aside from Spielberg's *Munich,* a nearly three-hour political thriller addressing the massacre of Israeli athletes at the 1972 Munich Olympics, all the other Oscar®-nominated films were small, character-driven dramas. *Munich,* with a reported budget of $75 million was also the only Oscar® contender fully financed by a major Hollywood studio. All the films, however, showed high profits in relations to their production costs. In addition to small budgets, each of the Oscar®-nominated films grossed under $80 million domestically. The smallest of them all, *Crash,* surprisingly took the Oscar® for Best Picture over *Brokeback Mountain* which was favored due to its Golden Globe win for Best Picture. An ensemble drama about Los Angeles dealing with racism, *Crash,* directed and co-written by Paul Haggis, also won Best Original Screenplay. Director Ang Lee, however, took the Oscar® for Best Director and *Brokeback Mountain* also won Best Adapted Screenplay and Best Original Score.

Though it featured an intelligent and thoughtful screenplay and direction, Bennett Miller's *Capote* was overshadowed by the towering performance of Philip Seymour Hoffman, depicting author Truman Capote as he researched and wrote his non-fiction novel *In Cold Blood.* Hoffman was given a host of best actor awards, culminating in the Best Actor Oscar®. The George Clooney-directed and co-written *Good Night, and Good Luck,* a political drama about the downfall of Senator Joseph McCarthy mainly praised for the black-and-white cinematography of Robert Elswit, also earned Oscar® nominations in many other categories, including Best Director for Clooney, Best Original Screenplay, and Best Actor for star David Strathairn and even earned Best Picture Awards from the National Board of Review, USA and the Venice Film Festival. Mr. Clooney, however, took home an Oscar® for Best Supporting Actor for his critically acclaimed performance in Stephen Gaghan's political thriller about Middle Eastern oil, *Syriana.* Rob Marshall's beautiful *Memoirs of a Geisha* won Academy Awardsr for Best Cinematography, Art Direction and Costume Design.

Winning the Best Actress Oscar® this year was Reese Witherspoon for her portrayal of June Carter Cash in James Mangold's biographical drama *Walk the Line,* which took the Golden Globe for Best Film, Musical or Comedy. Witherspoon and co-star, Joaquin Phoenix who portrayed the legendary Johnny Cash, both won Golden Globe Awards for performance while Phoenix was also a nominee for a Best Actor Oscar®. Rachel Weisz took the Best Supporting Actress Oscar® for her performance in *The Constant Gardener,* a film about corporate corruption and murder. Other noteworthy, talked-about performances of the year included Oscar® nominee Felicity Huffman as a pre-operative transsexual in *Transamerica;* former Oscar® winner Charlize Theron, nominated for a Best Actress Oscar® and co-star Frances McDormand, nominated for a Best Supporting Actress Oscar®, both for *North Country,* a fictionalized account of the first major successful sexual harassment case in the U.S.; Judi Dench, for her turn in *Mrs. Henderson Presents;* Keira Knightley for *Pride & Prejudice;* Terrence Howard for his turn as a pimp in *Hustle & Flow* (which won for Best Original Song); Amy Adams in *Junebug;* Maria Bello and William Hurt for David Cronenberg's *A History of Violence;* Catherine Keener for *Capote;* and, of course, Andy Serkis' amazingly realistic performance as the embodiment of the King of the Apes in *King Kong.* In addition to his acclaimed role in *Broke-*

back Mountain, Ledger also showed amazing versatility in 2005, appearing as the consummate womanizer *Casanova* and an underrated and remarkable turn as a free-wheeling surf-shop owner in *Lords of Dogtown.*

Although Oscar shunned mass-audience appeal films, moviegoers nonetheless had the usual pick of sequels and remade classics to choose from. *Bad New Bears* struck out critically but fared somewhat better at box office, recouping its $30 million budget with $2 million to spare. *Son of the Mask,* with its bloated $75 million budget, was rightfully shunned by critics and audiences alike, bringing in only $17 million during it's domestic run. John Carpenter had a hand in remaking his own 1980 classic *The Fog* with predictably lesser results, while he had nothing to do with the somewhat better remake of his 1976 *Assault on Precinct 13. Guess Who* was a lame attempt at a new millennium version of *Guess Who's Coming to Dinner*; while Herbie was marginally more successful in his attempted comeback in the 2000s with *Herbie: Fully Loaded.* Mining 1960s television, Hollywood also came up with a bedraggled *Bewitched* and a horrible *The Honeymooners.* Going back even further in time for better material, Jane Austen-fever apparently struck Hollywood *and* Bollywood with *Pride & Prejudice* appearing in 2005 alongside India's *Bride and Prejudice.* Hollywood also tapped Broadway for inspiration, bringing the Tony-Award winning musicals *Rent* and *The Producers* to the big screen with dubious results. Both were met with lukewarm reviews and neither came close to recouping their budgets.

Other than *Batman Begins,* most superhero and comic book fare was hum-drum. *Sky High* was an exception. *Aeon Flux, Constantine, Fantastic Four, Elektra,* and the video game-inspired *Doom* failed critically and were met with disappointment by most audiences.

Documentaries fared far better, led by the Academy Award-winning French nature film, *March of the Penguins.* The touching look at the annual trek of the Emperor penguins, when released, became the second-highest grossing documentary after *Fahrenheit 9/11,* taking in $77 million. *Enron: The Smartest Guys in the Room,* a documentary/cautionary tale about corporate greed won the Independent Spirit Award for Best Documentary and also received an Oscar® nod. Oscar® contender *Murderball,* a documentary about quadriplegics who engage in brutal wheelchair rugby, was critically acclaimed as was *Gunner Palace,* a documentary about soldiers living in one of Saddam Hussein's bombed-out palaces during the Iraq War. *Grizzly Man* was Werner Herzog's fascinating and much-talked-about look at one man's deadly obsession with grizzly bears.

Foreign films also flourished, including the six-hour Italian epic tracing the lives of two brothers, *The Best of Youth.* Other notable foreign films included the Greek epic, *The Weeping Meadow;* the French/Chinese *Balzac and the Little Chinese Seamstress;* the well-received *Breakfast on Pluto* from Great Britain; Fatih Akin's *Head-On* from Turkey and Germany; and the Oscar®-nominated *Paradise Now* a controversial film from France, Germany, The Netherlands and Israel which focused on the lives of two suicide bombers in the Middle East. Japanese animator Hayao Miyazaki's *Howl's Moving Castle* also made many critics top ten lists.

Among the surprise hits of the year was *The 40 Year Old Virgin,* a comedy which was co-written by and starred Steve Carell which grossed over $100 million and launched the comedian into the major leagues (he was ranked second in *Entertainment Weekly's* 2005 Entertainers of the Year). Another comedy, *Wedding Crashers,* proved a massive hit with audiences, breaking the $200 million mark ($209 million to be exact). *Crashers,* which earned the title of second-highest-grossing R-rated comedy of all time also kept star Vince Vaughn busy in a year where he also appeared in *Mr. & Mrs. Smith, Be Cool,* and *Thumbsucker.* Sadly, Douglas Adams passed away before he was able to see his cult classic *The Hitchhiker's Guide to the Galaxy* finally come to the big screen. Independent films like performance artist Miranda July's small, quirky *Me and You and Everyone We*

Know was at the top of many illustrious critics top ten lists for 2005 as was Jim Jarmusch's *Broken Flowers,* starring Bill Murray, and Phil Morrison's delightful *Junebug,* exploring an eccentric Southern family.

Horror ranged from the downright horrific, like co-producers Sam Raimi and Rob Tapert outing their closet-dwelling nightmare of a *Boogeyman,* to the truly terrifying, such as the supernaturally eerie *The Exorcism of Emily Rose.* Another in a seemingly endless *Exorcist* franchise included *Dominion: The Prequel to the Exorcist* (not to be confused with last year's *Exorcist: The Beginning*), which wasn't able to scare up much box office or critical acclaim. Many also thought producer/distributor Lion's Gate should've thrown back *The Devil's Rejects,* Rob Zombie's sequel to *House of 1,000 Corpses.* Sequel *Ring 2* was bad horror and a bad sequel. The Australian zombie horror *Undead* and American remake *Amityville Horror* were unremarkable while *House of Wax* merely served to legitimize Paris Hilton as a viable media presence. *Saw II* proved to be a horror sequel to reckon with in terms of profitability, grossing $85 million or about 21 times its less-than $4 million budget.

Children, again, had their beloved Harry Potter and the gorgeous *Narnia* as well as other children's literature classics adapted for the big screen. Among the best was *Wallace & Gromit: The Curse of the Were-Rabbit,* which won the Academy Awardr for Best Animated Feature. Winnie the Pooh showed up in *Pooh's Heffalump Movie* and Disney had another success with the animated *Chicken Little.* Bringing Charles Dickens to the older set, Roman Polanski's *Oliver Twist* was a worthy entry, as was Jon Favreau's space fantasy *Zathura* and Carroll Ballard's excellent *Duma,* about a boy and his cheetah. Lesser kid pics included Robert Rodriguez's disappointing *Adventures of Shark Boy & Lava Girl in 3-D,* which was universally panned by critics but earned nearly $40 million at the box office.

Sadly, the world lost the groundbreaking comedian/actor Richard Pryor in 2005. Hollywood also mourned the deaths of longtime screen favorites Anne Bancroft, writer/actor/director Ossie Davis, Sandra Dee, Bob Denver, James Doohan, Barbara Bel Geddes, Virginia Mayo, Don Adams, Geraldine Fitzgerald, Eddie Albert, Debralee Scott, Barney Martin, Nipsey Russell, Simone Simon, Vincent Schiavelli and such behind-the-screen talents as producer and sometime director Ismail Merchant; playwright Arthur Miller; producer Anthony Patrick Adams; producer of all eight *Halloween* films, Moustapha Akkad; director/producer Robert Wise; producer Sid Luft; art director and production designer John Box; animation artist Vance Gerry; art director Alexander Golitzen; and makeup artist Bob Schiffer. These and other celebrated talents who passed away in 2005 are profiled in the Obituaries section at the back of this book.

We at *Magill's* look forward to another exciting year in film and preparing the next edition of *Magill's Cinema Annual.* As always, we invite your comments, questions, and suggestions. Please direct them to:

Hilary White, Editor
Magill's Cinema Annual
Thomson Gale
27500 Drake Road
Farmington Hills, MI 48331-3535
Phone: (248) 699-4253
Toll-Free: (800) 347-GALE (4253)
Fax: (248) 699-8054

Contributing Reviewers

Laura Abraham
Freelance Reviewer

Michael Adams
Graduate School, City University of New York

Vivek Adarkar
Long Island University

Richard Baird
Freelance Reviewer

Michael Betzold
Freelance Reviewer

David L. Boxerbaum
Freelance Reviewer

Beverley Bare Buehrer
Freelance Reviewer

Tom Burns
Freelance Reviewer

David E. Chapple
Freelance Reviewer

Peter N. Chumo II
Freelance Reviewer

Jim Craddock
Freelance Reviewer

Beth Fhaner
Freelance Reviewer

David Flanagin
Freelance Reviewer

Jill Hamilton
Freelance Reviewer

Nick Kennedy
Freelance Reviewer

Eric Monder
Freelance Reviewer

David Metz Roberts
Freelance Reviewer

John C. Tibbetts
Freelance Reviewer

Christine Tomassini
Freelance Reviewer

Michael J. Tyrkus
Freelance Reviewer

James M. Welsh
Salisbury State University

Michael White
Freelance Reviewer

User's Guide

ALPHABETIZATION

Film titles and reviews are arranged on a word-by-word basis, including articles and prepositions. English leading articles (A, An, The) are ignored, as are foreign leading articles (El, Il, La, Las, Le, Les, Los). Other considerations:

Acronyms appear alphabetically as if regular words.

Common abbreviations in titles file as if they are spelled out, so *Mr. Death* will be found as if it was spelled *Mister Death.*

Proper names in titles are alphabetized beginning with the individual's first name, for instance, *Gloria* will be found under "G."

Titles with numbers, for instance, *200 Cigarettes,* are alphabetized as if the numbers were spelled out, in this case, "Two-Hundred." When numeric titles gather in close proximity to each other, the titles will be arranged in a low-to-high numeric sequence.

SPECIAL SECTIONS

List of Awards. An annual list of awards bestowed upon the year's films by the following associations: Academy of Motion Picture Arts and Sciences, Directors Guild of America Award, Golden Globe Awards, Los Angeles Film Critics Awards, National Board of Review Awards, National Society of Film Critics Awards, New York Film Critics Awards, the Screen Actors Guild Awards, and the Writer's Guild Awards.

Obituaries. Profiles major contributors to the film industry who died in 2005.

Selected Film Books of 2005. An annotated list of selected film books published in 2005.

INDEXES

Film titles and artists are arranged into nine indexes, allowing the reader to effectively approach a film from any one of several directions, including not only its credits but its subject matter.

Directors, Screenwriters, Cinematographers, Editors, Art Directors, Music Directors, and *Performers* indexes are arranged according to artists appearing in this volume, followed by a list of the films on which they worked.

Subject Index. Films may be categorized under several of the subject terms arranged alphabetically in this section.

Title Index. The title index is a cumulative alphabetical list of films covered in the twenty-five volumes of the *Magill's Cinema Annual,* including the films covered in this volume. Films reviewed in past volumes are cited with the year in which the film was originally released; films reviewed in this volume are cited with the film title in bold with a bolded Arabic numeral indicating the page number on which the review begins. Original and alternate titles are cross-referenced to the American release title in the Title Index. Titles of retrospective films are followed by the year, in brackets, of their original release.

SAMPLE REVIEW

Each *Magill's* review contains up to sixteen items of information. A fictionalized composite sample review containing all the elements of information that may be included in a full-length review follows the outline on the facing page. The circled number preceding each element in the sample review designates an item of information that is explained in the outline on the next page.

1. **Title:** Film title as it was released in the United States.
2. **Foreign or alternate title(s):** The film's original title or titles as released outside the United States, or alternate film title or titles. Foreign and alternate titles also appear in the Title Index to facilitate user access.
3. **Taglines:** Up to ten publicity taglines for the film from advertisements or reviews.
4. **Box office information:** Year-end or other box office domestic revenues for the film.
5. **Film review:** A signed review of the film, including an analytic overview of the film and its critical reception.
6. **Reviewer byline:** The name of the reviewer who wrote the full-length review. A complete list of this volume's contributors appears in the "Contributing Reviewers" section which follows the Introduction.
7. **Principal characters:** Listings of the film's principal characters and the names of the actors who play them in the film.
8. **Country of origin:** The film's country or countries of origin.
9. **Release date:** The year of the film's first general release.
10. **Production information:** This section typically includes the name(s) of the film's producer(s), production company, and distributor; director(s); screenwriter(s); cinematographer(s) (if the film is animated, this will be replaced with Animation or Animation direction, or it will not be listed); editor(s); art director(s); production designer(s); music composer(s); and other credits such as visual effects, sound, costume design, and song(s) and songwriter(s).
11. **MPAA rating:** The film's rating by the Motion Picture Association of America. If there is no rating given, the line will read, "Unrated."
12. **Running time:** The film's running time in minutes.
13. **Reviews:** A list of brief citations of major newspaper and journal reviews of the film, including publication title, date of review, and page number.
14. **Film quotes:** Memorable dialogue directly from the film, attributed to the character who spoke it, or comment from cast or crew members or reviewers about the film.
15. **Film trivia:** Interesting tidbits about the film, its cast, or production crew.
16. **Awards information:** Awards won by the film, followed by category and name of winning cast or crew member. Listings of the film's nominations follow the wins on a separate line for each award. Awards are arranged alphabetically. Information is listed for films that won or were nominated for the following awards: American Academy Awards®, British Academy of Film and Television Arts, Directors Guild of America, Golden Globe, Los Angeles Critics Association Awards, National Board of Review Awards, National Society of Film Critics Awards, New York Critics Awards, Writers Guild of America, and others.

THE GUMP DIARIES ①
(Los Diarios del Gump) ②

Love means never having to say you're stupid.

— Movie tagline ③

Box Office: $10 million ④

In writer/director Robert Zemeckis' *Back to the Future* trilogy (1985, 1989, 1990), Marty McFly (Michael J. Fox) and his scientist sidekick Doc Brown (Christopher Lloyd) journey backward and forward in time, attempting to smooth over some rough spots in their personal histories in order to remain true to their individual destinies. Throughout their time-travel adventures, Doc Brown insists that neither he nor Marty influence any major historical events, believing that to do so would result in catastrophic changes in humankind's ultimate destiny. By the end of the trilogy, however, Doc Brown has revised his thinking and tells Marty that, "Your future hasn't been written yet. No one's has. Your future is whatever you make it. So make it a good one."

In *Forrest Gump,* Zemeckis once again explores the theme of personal destiny and how an individual's life affects and is affected by his historical time period. This time, however, Zemeckis and screenwriter Eric Roth chronicle the life af a character who does nothing but meddle in the historical events of his time without even trying to do so. By the film's conclusion, however, it has become apparent that Zemeckis' main concern is something more than merely having fun with four decades of American history. In the process of re-creating significant moments in time, he has captured on celluloid something eternal and timeless—the soul of humanity personified by a nondescript simpleton from the deep South.

The film begins following the flight of a seemingly insignificant feather as it floats down from the sky and brushes against various objects and people before finally coming to rest at the feet of Forrest Gump (Tom Hanks). Forrest, who is sitting on a bus-stop bench, reaches down and picks up the feather, smooths it out, then opens his traveling case and carefully places the feather between the pages of his favorite book, *Curious George.*

In this simple but hauntingly beautiful opening scene, the filmmakers illustrate the film's principal concern: Is life a series of random events over which a person has no control, or is there an underlying order to things that leads to the fulfillment of an individual's destiny? The rest of the film is a humorous and moving attempt to prove that, underlying the random, chaotic events that make up a person's life, there exists a benign and simple order.

Forrest sits on the bench throughout most of the film, talking about various events of his life to others who happen to sit down next to him. It does not take long, however, for the audience to realize that Forrest's seemingly random chatter to a parade of strangers has a perfect chronological order to it. He tells his first story after looking down at the feet of his first bench partner and observing, "Mama always said that you can tell a lot about a person by the shoes they wear." Then, in a voice-over narration, Forrest begins the story of his life, first by telling about the first pair of shoes he can remember wearing.

The action shifts to the mid-1950's with Forrest as a young boy (Michael Humphreys) being fitted with leg braces to correct a curvature in his spine. Despite this traumatic handicap, Forrest remains unaffected, thanks to his mother (Sally Field) who reminds him on more than one occasion that he is no different from anyone else. Although this and most of Mrs. Gump's other words of advice are in the form of hackneyed cliches, Forrest, whose intelligence quotient is below normal, sincerely believes every one of them, namely because he instinctively knows they are sincere expressions of his mother's love and fierce devotion. ⑤

John Byline ⑥

CREDITS ⑦

Forrest Gump: Tom Hanks
Forrest's Mother: Sally Field
Young Forrest: Michael Humphreys
Origin: United States ⑧
Language: English, Spanish
Released: 1994 ⑨
Production: Liz Heller, John Manulis; New Line Cinema; released by Island Pictures ⑩
Directed by: Scott Kalvert
Written by: Bryan Goluboff
Cinematography by: David Phillips
Music by: Graeme Revell
Editing: Dana Congdon
Production Design: Danny Nowak
Sound: David Sarnoff
Costumes: David Robinson
MPAA rating: R ⑪
Running time: 102 minutes ⑫

REVIEWS ⑬

Entertainment Weekly. July 15, 1994, p. 42.
The Hollywood Reporter. June 29, 1994, p. 7.
Los Angeles Times. July 6, 1994, p. F1.
New York Times Online. July 15, 1994.

QUOTES ⑭

Forrest Gump (Tom Hanks): "The state of existence may be likened unto a receptacle containing cocoa-based confections, in that one may never predict that which one may receive."

TRIVIA (15)

Hanks was the first actor since Spencer Tracy to win back-to-back Oscars for Best Actor. Hanks received the award in 1993 for his performance in *Philadelphia.* Tracy won Oscars in 1937 for *Captains Courages* and in 1938 for *Boys Town.*

AWARDS (16)

Academy Awards 1994: Film, Actor (Hanks), Special Effects, Cinematography

Nomination:

Golden Globes 1994: Film, Actor (Hanks), Supporting Actress (Field), Music

A

A LOT LIKE LOVE

There's nothing better than a great romance...to ruin a perfectly good friendship.
—Movie tagline

Box Office: $21.8 million

Seven years ago Emily (Amanda Peet) and Oliver (Ashton Kutcher) met on a flight to New York City. Actually, "met" may not be the right word. They join the Mile-High Club on the plane without even knowing each other's name or exchanging a word between them. Oliver tries to start up a conversation with her as they wait for the baggage, but she's a hard, cynical rock-and-roll babe and blows him off. Later they bump into each other again, but Emily just uses Oliver as an excuse not to go to the Guggenheim museum with her parents. They share a few drinks in a bar, Oliver gives her a scrap of paper with his parents phone number on it, and then they part ways.

Three years later, in Los Angeles, Emily is an aspiring actress who has just been dumped by her boyfriend. However, it is New Year's Eve and she is desperately phoning everyone in her little black book to find a date. Having no success, Emily then comes across that scrap of paper containing Oliver's name and his parent's phone number. On a lark she phones and is pleasantly surprised to find that he is at his mother's. So they have their one-night date and the next day Emily awakens to find that Oliver has left for San Francisco where his Internet diaper sales business is located.

Now it is two years after that and Oliver, who is in San Francisco, has been left by his girlfriend while in L.A. Emily, who is now a photographer, is re-meeting Ben Miller (Jeremy Sisto) whom she originally met at a friend's wedding. In a funk Oliver looks up Emily and the two share a loving night sleeping in a car in a national park. The next day, however, Oliver has to go to New York City to make a presentation in the hopes of getting some venture capital to expand his business.

One year later, Oliver's business has gone bust and he has moved back to Los Angeles. There he passes an art gallery filled with Emily's photographs. Because his life is in ruins, he is reluctant to see her again but eventually he gets up his nerve, gets a guitar and serenades her with a little Bon Jovi. Emily, however, is now engaged to Ben. Once again they part ways.

Six months later Emily has broken up with Ben but her friend runs into Oliver getting fitted for a suite for a wedding which she assumes is his. Will this couple never get together?

Initially *A Lot Like Love*'s leading characters are a lot like jerks. They are not pleasant people. They're childish, self-indulgent users of other people who are prone to doing anti-social things with food. As the movie progresses, the characters should presumable progress, but only Amanda Peet's Emily seems to accomplish a degree of adulthood. Ashton Kutcher's Oliver seems permanently stuck in adolescence. Whether this is due to the plot as written by first-time screenwriter Colin Patrick Lynch or Kutcher's seemingly limited acting style is unclear. Running the emotional gamut from silly to doofus, Kutcher has yet to show any real acting range in his movies. In fact, because of Kutcher, one gets the distinct impression that a more accurate title for this movie might be *Dude, Where's My Girlfriend?*

Perhaps with a more mature or able actor in the Oliver role *A Lot Like Love* could have had the potential to be another of director Nigel Cole's excellent films. His *Calendar Girls* (2003) and *Saving Grace* (2000) were entertaining and amusing sentimental comedies. But then they featured "adult" actors who knew their craft. Unfortunately, unlike his previous films, *A Lot Like Love* seems a lot more like fluff than his other films.

Because the lives of Emily and Oliver only intersect after some personal upheaval for one or the other of them, the story starts to feel strained. Their meetings and partings begin to seem like contrived coincidences and the time they spend together is marked by an incredible and unnatural passivity. They are obviously in love with each other more than they are with any of the other interested parties the two hook up with, but they are totally incapable of doing anything about it. In most romantic comedies this lack of connectedness between the main characters would be caused by a lot of silly misunderstandings, but this excuse is used only once at the very end. The rest of the time it is strictly due to character inertia. And it gets really annoying.

Beverley Bare Buehrer

CREDITS

Oliver Martin: Ashton Kutcher
Emily Friehl: Amanda Peet
Michelle: Kathryn Hahn
Jeeter: Kal Penn
Ellen Martin: Taryn Manning
Brent Friehl: James Read
Christine: Molly Cheek
Peter: Gabriel Mann
Graham Martin: Ty Giordano
Nicole: Aimee Garcia
Gina: Ali Larter
Diane Martin: Amy Aquino
Ben Miller: Jeremy Sisto
Stephen Martin: Holmes Osborne
Stewardess: Lee Garlington
Airline attendant: Linda Hunt
Carol Martin: Melissa van der Schyff
Origin: USA
Language: English
Released: 2005
Production: Armyan Bernstein, Kevin J. Messick; Beacon Production; released by Buena Vista
Directed by: Nigel Cole
Written by: Colin Patrick Lynch
Cinematography by: John de Borman
Music by: Alex Wurman
Sound: Steve Nelson
Music Supervisor: Laura Z. Wasserman, Diane Stata
Editing: Susan Littenberg
Art Direction: Denise Hudson
Costumes: Alix Friedberg
Production Design: Tom Meyer
MPAA rating: PG-13
Running time: 95 minutes

REVIEWS

Boxoffice Online. April, 2005.
Chicago Sun-Times Online. April 22, 2005.
Entertainment Weekly Online. April 20, 2005.
Los Angeles Times Online. April 22, 2005.
New York Times Online. April 22, 2005.
Premiere Magazine Online. April 21, 2005.
Variety Online. April 20, 2005.

QUOTES

Emily Friehl: "Honestly, if you're not willing to sound stupid you don't deserve to be in love."

THE ADVENTURES OF SHARKBOY AND LAVAGIRL IN 3-D

Smaller heroes. Just as super.
—Movie tagline
Everything that is...or was...began as a dream.
—Movie tagline

Box Office: $39 million

The story behind *The Adventures of Sharkboy and Lavagirl in 3-D* is arguably more interesting than the movie itself. The genesis of the film came from seven-year-old Racer Rodriguez, who came up with the characters of Sharkboy and Lavagirl. His father, who is known to most as the director of the *Spy Kids* series as well as adult fare like *Sin City*, encouraged his son to think further about the characters, and they would use the results to make a family film. (The film is truly a family affair. In addition to Racer's input, Rodriguez brothers Rebel and Rocker have acting roles in the movie.) This makes for a nice back story, but does not make for the most carefully developed screenplay. Ty Burr, movie critic for *The Boston Globe* put it thusly: "Look, my kids are geniuses too, but I don't let them write the reviews."

The story may not be that interesting (or logical), but the elder Rodriguez tries his hardest to dress up the visuals so that the story will look more thrilling than it actually is. His first step was to film parts of the movie in 3-D. Oddly, he did not use the newest and best 3-D technology, but the old-fashioned kind with the cardboard glasses with red and blue lenses. Those who watched the film in the theater were given the glasses, and instructions flashed on during the movie directing viewers when to put them on or take them off. Besides the glasses-on glasses-off process being rather cumbersome, especially for younger viewers, the 3-D effects themselves were nearly universally panned for being muddy and dull.

The DVD version of the movie lacked the 3-D effects and it helped the film. Rodriguez makes his movies in a home studio full of the latest in special effect technology and knows how to make a film full of eye-popping images. Most of the scenes involve characters interacting with a computer-generated world, so the landscapes are limited only by Rodriguez's imagination. His imagination is, as usual, in overdrive, so characters float down a sea of milk in the Land of Milk and Cookies, ride a wild Train of Thought and fight monsters made of ice cubes.

Far less interesting is why the characters are in such stunningly rendered lands. Max (Cayden Boyd) is a young Texas boy who escapes from the realities of his fighting parents (Kristin Davis and David Arquette) and the school bully, Linus (Jacob Davich), by obsessing over his dream journal. Two of his favorite characters, Sharkboy (Taylor Lautner) and Lavagirl (Taylor Dooley), leave his dreams and come to Max's school after their home, Planet Drool, starts going dark. It seems that Max is losing his dreams, so that they are disappearing, or something along those lines.

On Planet Drool, Max must contend with his fantasy versions of his real-life friends, enemies and family. Mr. Electric (George Lopez) is a scary villain who looks a lot like Max's teacher, Mr. Electricidad. School bully Linus becomes the evil Minus who tries to take over Planet Drool. And Max's school crush, Marissa (Sasha Pieterse), looks a lot like the planet's heroine, the Ice Princess. Also in there are plenty of play-on-words, such as a ride down the Stream of Consciousness or a brainstorm producing an actual storm of brains. And there is a somewhat muddled moral in there, too. It is something along the lines that being a dreamer is good, but the dreamer must also dream unselfish dreams.

Reviewers were not particularly enchanted by it all. Dana Stevens of *The New York Times* wrote, "There's a reason children aren't allowed to vote, drive or make movies with multimillion-dollar budgets. Lively and imaginative as their inner worlds may be, the very young still lack the discipline and maturity to shape them into coherent and compelling stories." Ty Burr of *The Boston Globe* wrote, "*Adventures* sounds like a grand old time—a hip fusion of Nickelodeon attitude, the wittier children's books, and retro kitsch culture. In fact, it's a nearly unwatchable combination of the worst elements of all three." Roger Ebert of *The Chicago Sun-Times* took issue to Rodriguez's use of 3-D. "*The Adventures of Sharkboy and Lavagirl in 3-D* is an innocent and delightful children's tale spoiled by a disastrous decision to film most of it in lousy 3-D," he wrote. Bob Strauss of *The Los Angeles Daily News* was a rare critic who liked the film, calling it "Like a Saturday-morning cartoon by Salvador Dali" and "still brimming with the kind of funky, anything-can-happen creativity that we've come to expect from Rodriguez productions."

Jill Hamilton

CREDITS

Max's Mom: Kristen Davis
Max's Dad: David Arquette
Mr. Electric/Tobor/Ice Guardian/Mr. Electricdad: George Lopez
Sharkboy: Taylor Lautner
Lavagirl: Taylor Dooley
Max: Cayden Boyd
Linus/Minus: Jacob Davich
Marissa/Ice Princess: Sasha Pieterse
Sharkboy's Dad: Rico Torres
Sharkboy (age 5): Rebel Rodriquez
Sharkboy (age 7): Racer Rodriguez
Lug: Rocket Rodriguez
Origin: USA
Language: English
Released: 2005
Production: Elizabeth Avellan, Robert Rodriguez; Troublemaker Studios; released by Dimension Films
Directed by: Robert Rodriguez
Written by: Robert Rodriguez
Cinematography by: Robert Rodriguez
Music by: John Debney, Graeme Revell
Sound: Edward Novick
Editing: Robert Rodriguez
Art Direction: Jeanette Scott
Costumes: Nina Proctor
MPAA rating: PG
Running time: 94 minutes

REVIEWS

Boxoffice Online. June, 2005.
Chicago Sun-Times Online. June 9, 2005.

Entertainment Weekly Online. June 8, 2005.
Los Angeles Times Online. June 10, 2005.
New York Times Online. June 10, 2005.
Variety Online. June 3, 2005.
Washington Post Online. June 9, 2005, p. WE38.

QUOTES

Sharkboy: "Normally when you snooze, you lose. But when Max snoozes, he wins."

TRIVIA

A Big Kahuna Burgers fast food bag can be seen in the film when Max is on the dock before he runs into Sharkboy. Big Kahuna is actually a fictional burger joint used in many of Rodriguez's films as well as those of friend, director Quentin Tarantino.

AEON FLUX

The future is flux.
—Movie tagline

Perfect - Future - Shock.
—Movie tagline

Box Office: $24.5 million

When Charlize Theron and Sophie Okonedo, two very good actresses, are playing a pair of assassins infiltrating the headquarters of the director of a totalitarian society of the future, they don't just run across the gardens of the perimeter. As kick-ass rebel terminatrix Aeon Flux and her protege and sidekick Sithandra, Theron (who's proven her acting chops with an Oscar for *Monster*) and Okonedo (who was so moving in *Hotel Rwanda*)—or, more specifically, their body doubles—flip, spin, jump, and fly through the air, for no apparent reason. In the process, they are attacked by giant seed pods on trees in the garden that spray bullet-like seeds at them. And, just to make things more interesting, when the seeds hit certain patches of grass (but not *all* patches of grass), they turn into literal *blades* of grass—sharp pointed carpets ideal for impalement. Of course, the scene ends with Aeon Flux spread-eagled across a planted terrace of lethal grass, hanging on by her toes, and Sithandra rescuing her and dropping the deadpan line: "Better keep off the grass."

Inspired by an animated sci-fi action series that ran on MTV in the 1990s, *Aeon Flux* might have been an enjoyably over-the-top romp if it had kept its tone tongue-in-cheek. Certainly the sequence with the two superheroines somersaulting across the barrier gardens is ridiculously overdone. The problem is, though, that this feature, directed by John Sayles protege Karyn Kusama, takes itself far too seriously. It's a deadly combination: a cartoon romp that gets strangled by its own gravity.

And what are Theron, whose socially conscious *North Country* came out just a few months before *Flux,* and Okonedo—not to mention the compelling Martin Csokas and both Frances McDormand and Pete Postlewaithe in throwaway roles—doing in this film? Let's hope the upfront money was good, because despite a lot of promotion, the film flopped at the box office, killed by bad word-of-mouth. Full of hysterically overwrought scenes and leaden dialogue, *Aeon Flux* might have been interesting to some only to see how Theron fit into the heroine's skin-tight outfits. But even those fans might be disappointed when, after a few different getups in the opening half-hour, Theron is stuck in the same black body suit for the rest of the film. It's as if Emma Peel never had a wardrobe change.

It won't be giving away much to reveal the plot, because *Aeon Flux* is one of those movies that simply has its characters tell you everything's that happening in frequent dumps of exposition. The script (by Phil Hay and Matt Manfredi, based on Peter Chung's original series) can't seem to sustain periods of tension longer than a few minutes before revealing what's up. And what's up is very serious business indeed: After a modern plague called simply "the industrial disease," human civilization has been confined to a large walled city, with nothing beyond it but a desolate jungle of presumably life-threatening disease. Four hundred years after this plague, the survivors are ruled by a seemingly ruthless Director, Trevor Goodchild (Czokas). After witnessing the murder of her sister Una (Amelia Warner), Aeon is ready to seek revenge. She is the most powerful warrior among the rebel Monicans, who are at war with Goodchild and his directorate. Aeon receives orders from the mysterious Handler (McDormand) to move against Goodchild.

But after Aeon and Sithandra penetrate the defenses of the leaders, and Aeon has a rather easy time getting a chance to shoot Trevor to death, she hesitates, bedeviled by a gauzy memory of a kiss. It's as if a Terminator movie is interrupted by a commercial for mouthwash. Eventually, they sleep together, and Goodchild's evil brother Oren (Jonny Lee Miller) plots a coup to take over leadership of the ruling council, who are identified by wearing suits with very wide lapels and by meeting in summits on oversized red chairs.

Though Kusama tries mightily to muddle the picture with bizarre intimations of mind control, it's not hard to guess what is eventually revealed: that Trevor is actually a benevolent dictator who's trying to reconstitute the human race through cloning and other experiments. After many snippets of dialogue in which Aeon ponders openly why she doesn't really know who she is and why she feels so strange, Trevor tells her she's part of his science experiment (along with most everyone else, including her sister). His mission is designed to restore human beings to fertility, because that was taken away through the side effects of the vaccine that vanquished the "industrial disease." But even clones, it seems, have romantic ties that remain strong; love is in the DNA.

Not only is this plot as clunky and ludicrous as it sounds, it gets worse. Why the Monicans and the other clones don't understand they're not fertile is unexplained, and in the climax Oren reveals that nature, not just his brother's experiment, is bringing back fertility anyway. This would end seven generations in which Postlewaithe's character, The Keeper, is flying around in an airborne jellyfish that finds couples to artificially impregnate, birth, and raise the clones of those who die. Pete's in charge of the DNA bank.

All this heavy, leaden plot weighs down the film's action sequences, keeping them from achieving the kind of camp giddiness that might have lifted this awful movie from the sludge of its recycled ideas and strained concepts. Kusama tries so hard to package the story in confusing trickery that all the fun goes out of the enterprise through too much effort. Gadgets and gimmicks abound, but they don't provide much entertainment because all of them are egregious and none connected to the story itself. Theron makes some effect to inject passion and angst into her character, but it's overcome by her cartoonish slick jet-black hairdo with bangs that frame and fall into her face, while her sister appears like a recycled Princess Leia. Aeon has narrow escapes, heavy-artillery fights, and plenty of chances to demonstrate advanced karate moves. But none of this high energy amounts to more than lifeless, weightless dazzle. There's a lot of sound and fury signifying nothing.

The unintentionally hilarious but oh-so-full-of-itself story line and the wooden characters suffocate any opportunity for audience involvement, and Kusama further distances viewers by staging too many scenes as if they were hallucinatory drug trips. Neither the ideas here nor the execution are particularly new or inspiring: certainly, we've seen this kind of action heroine many, many times. Aeon is a cliche in more ways than one, including the fact that she is a physically unstoppable fighter who has a soft spot in her heart for the man she's supposedly trying to defeat.

The showdown at the end that features Trevor, Oren, Aeon, and Sithandra all under a cross-fire of potential snipers is the worst sequence of all. While guns are trained and there is no reason for shooting not to begin, the principals are locked in another expository dump, with the brothers engaging in a painful philosophical discussion. The plotting of this film is so amateurish and the dialogue so poor that the action never has a chance to get off the ground, much less land on its feet. You sometimes feel as if you are the victim of those pod seeds, shooting inane visuals and dialogue at the audience.

Michael Betzold

CREDITS

Aeon Flux: Charlize Theron
Trevor Goodchild: Marton Csokas
Oren Goodchild: Jonny Lee Miller
Sithandra: Sophie Okonedo
Handler: Frances McDormand
Keeper: Pete Postlethwaite
Una Flux: Amelia Warner
Claudius: Nikolai Kinski
Freya: Caroline Chikezie
Origin: USA
Language: English
Released: 2005
Production: Gale Anne Hurd, David Gale, Gary Lucchesi, Gregory Goodman, Martha Griffin; Lakeshore Entertainment, Valhalla Motion Pictures, MTV Films; released by Paramount
Directed by: Karyn Kusama
Written by: Phil Hay, Matt Manfredi
Cinematography by: Stuart Dryburgh
Music by: Graeme Revell
Sound: Manfred Banach
Editing: Peter Honess, Plummy Tucker, Jeff Gullo
Art Direction: Dave Warren, Sarah Horton
Costumes: Beatrix Aruna Pasztor
Production Design: Andrew McAlpine
MPAA rating: PG-13
Running time: 95 minutes

REVIEWS

Boxoffice Online. December, 2005.
Entertainment Weekly Online. December 2, 2005.
Los Angeles Times Online. December 5, 2005.
New York Times Online. December 3, 2005.
Premiere Magazine Online. December 2, 2005.
Variety Online. December 3, 2005.
Washington Post Online. December, 2005.

QUOTES

Aeon: "I had a family once, I had a life. Now all I have is a mission."

TRIVIA

Michelle Rodriguez was originally cast as Aeon Flux when the film was announced in 2003.

ALONE IN THE DARK

Evil awakens.
—Movie tagline

Box Office: $5.1 million

Angry killer lizards, Tara Reid as an intelligent anthropological expert, all the evil of the "dark" world being successfully held back from the good world by a flimsy door. Such are the premises one must accept in *Alone in the Dark.* With the release of the movie, January successfully kept its reputation for being the month in which studios unleash their most undesirable product.

In the movie, Edward Carnby (Christian Slater) is an orphan who has grown-up and has a strong suspicion that his memory gaps have something to do with a terrible thing happening back at the orphanage. He is a former worker for the government's super-secret Bureau 713. Bureau 713, as is laboriously explained in some very lengthy scrolling text at the beginning of the film, is dedicated to studying an ancient tribe called the Abskani. It seems the tribe spread a bunch of artifacts over the globe to ensure that no one ever opened the door—hidden in an old mine—that leads to the dark world. (No one in the modern world seems to notice that the door could probably be easily opened by even the most marginally competent locksmith.)

The evil Professor Hudgens (Matthew Walker), himself a former employee of Bureau 713, is searching for the artifacts so that he can unlock the door and rule the world, or something like that. It is up to Edward, who has become a paranormal investigator, to stop him. He enlists the help of his estranged girlfriend, Aline Cedrac (Reid), and the two must do much shooting of machine guns at angry attacking creatures. If it all sounds a bit like a video game, it's because it is. The movie is spun off from an old Atari game, and is as clunky as the original Atari system.

It is hard to say which is worse, the acting or the story. There is much to be said about the acting, especially Reid's. She is completely unbelievable as someone of intelligence, despite her pointed wearing of glasses and hair pulled into a bun. Perhaps it is the way she pronounces Newfoundland as New-FOUND-Land, or maybe it is the way that she does not appear to have the foggiest notion of what the lines she is mouthing actually mean. Stephen Dorff, in the uncoveted role of Commander Richards, the head of Bureau 713, tries hard enough, but his efforts seem sort of pitiful, given the movie he is in. And Slater seems to think it is the 1980s and he is still box office gold. His wardrobe, consisting of tank tops and a trench coat, does nothing to modernize him.

But the story is pretty bad, too. In the first few minutes, there is a car chase in which glass on a storefront is broken not one, but two times. Director Uwe Boll apparently cannot resist the filmic cliché of a chase going through an ethnic food market because he places an Istanbul-like market down a Los Angeles side street. The monsters are not scary and, for a time, there are also some zombies for Edward and friends to contend with. Slater has to say lines like, "I just killed John. I had to. He was one of them." The hows and whys of what is actually going on is so muddled that it is hard to feel much of a sense of terror, or interest. Slater's voiceover narration is supposed to clear up confusing plot points, but making this film understandable would probably require an accompanying five-hour lecture.

Critics could muster no kind words for the film. Peter Hartlaub of *The San Francisco Chronicle* wrote, "Every casting decision, camera angle, special effect and sound seems created as a dare to leave the theater." Stephen Holden of *The New York Times* wrote, "Bad movies are a dime a dozen, but every so often, an out-and-out stinker like *Alone in the Dark* slinks into the marketplace. This horror film…is so inept on every level, you wonder why the distributor didn't release it straight to video, or better, toss it directly into the trash." Janice Page of *The Boston Globe* wrote, "Think of the lamest horror movie you've ever seen. Now think of Tara Reid in the lamest horror movie you've ever seen. See how much worse it could have been? That, folks, is the level of pee-yew we're talking when we evaluate *Alone in the Dark.*"

Jill Hamilton

CREDITS

Edward Carnby: Christian Slater
Aline Cedrac: Tara Reid
Cmdr. Burke: Stephen Dorff
Professor Hudgens: Matthew (Matt) Walker
Agent Miles: Will Sanderson
John Houghton: Darren Shahlavi
Sister Clara: Karin Konoval
James Pinkerton: Ed Anders
Fischer: Frank C. Turner
Capt. Chernick: Mark Acheson
'80s Sheriff: Craig Bruhnanski
Deputy Adams: Kwesi Ameyaw
Krash: Catherine Lough Haggquist

Origin: USA, Canada, Germany
Language: English
Released: 2005
Production: Shawn Williamson; Boll KG Prods.; released by Lions Gate Films
Directed by: Uwe Boll
Written by: Elan Mastai, Michael Roesch, Peter Scheerer
Cinematography by: Mathias Neumann
Music by: Bernd Wendlandt
Sound: Tim Richardson
Editing: Richard Schwadel
Art Direction: Tania Richard
Costumes: Martha Livingstone
Production Design: Tink
MPAA rating: R
Running time: 96 minutes

REVIEWS

Boxoffice Online. January, 2005.
Entertainment Weekly Online. February 2, 2005.
Los Angeles Times Online. January 28, 2005.
New York Times Online. January 28, 2005.
Variety Online. January 27, 2005.
Washington Post Online. January 28, 2005, p. WE38.

QUOTES

Edward Carnby: "Being afraid of the dark is what keeps most of us alive."

AWARDS

Nomination:

Golden Raspberries 2005: Worst Actress (Reid), Worst Director (Boll).

THE AMITYVILLE HORROR

Katch 'em, kill 'em.
—Movie tagline

Box Office: $64.5

After all the years of rip-offs and sequels, most people probably already know the plot of *The Amityville Horror,* but for those who don't, it goes like this. The blended family created by the recent marriage of contractor George Lutz (Ryan Reynolds) to Kathy (Melissa George), the widowed mother of three children, is looking for a home to call their own. They find an ideal house, a large, waterfront Dutch colonial at 112 Ocean Avenue with a price that is just too good to pass up. Eventually a skittish realtor tells them that the reason the house is such a good buy is because one year earlier, at 3:15 am on November 13, 1974 voices finally convinced the previous owner's eldest son, Ronnie DeFeo, to "kill them"...and he did: his mother, father, and siblings. But as George notes, "Houses don't kill people, people kill people," so the Lutzes decide to move in anyway with high hopes—which just happens to be the name of the house—and a big mortgage.

It only takes the house 28 days to convince the Lutzes that they have made a bad investment. Gradually a perpetually cold George has been descending into madness, chopping a lot of wood to keep himself warm, and using his ax on more than logs. Youngest daughter Chelsea (Chloe Grace Moretz) is also acting a bit odd. She is convinced there is a young girl named Jodie living in her closet and Jodie may not have Chelsea's best interests at heart as is indicated when she does things like lead Chelsea onto the peak of the house's roof. Kathy, in a desperate attempt to save her family and their investment, calls in a priest, Father Callaway (Philip Baker Hall) to bless the house, but he is no match for what evil lurks behind those trademark "eye" windows.

Explaining that evil, however, is something that this latest version of the story does in some detail. It seems that not only is the house built on an Indian burial ground—the previous version's explanation—but those Indians are buried there because there was a monstrous Colonial torturer, Reverend Jeremiah Katchem, who had built an entire chamber of horrors underneath it. Finding these chambers and reliving Katchem's actions is what finally sends George over the edge and down the path to killing his family too, just as Ronnie DeFeo did a year earlier. Kathy, however, will save the day when she loads the family into a boat and runs off leaving all the family's possessions behind, never to return.

The original 1979 version of *The Amityville Horror* starred James Brolin as George and Margot Kidder as Kathy and a scenery-chewing Rod Steiger as the out-of-his-league priest. It was a modest hit as most horror films are prone to be, but is not listed amongst the greats of the genre. So why remake it? Because, as previously mentioned, horror films are prone to be modest hits, even bad ones, and this is especially true in the era of DVDs and videos.

This current version of *The Amityville Horror* at least manages to benefit from several factors. For one thing, although it sticks fairly closely to the original story, by being about a half-an-hour shorter in its running time, it is more tightly told. (Whether or not the film and all its predecessors are "based on a true story" as we are told in an opening caption or on the imagination of the original book's author Jan Anson, is not something to be argued here.)

The film also benefits from better special effects. They are not only more sophisticated, they are also more subtle. This doesn't mean the film is less scary, but in fact it is quite chilling. There are many sudden frights that actually work, and with one exception, they're not the cheating frights filmmakers often use to fool the audience. There is also a general feeling of eeriness to this version of the story with some frightening things being seen only by the audience and not at all by the characters in the film. (There are many indications that the makers of the 2005 *Amityville* are playing to *The Ring*'s audience and have borrowed many of its techniques.)

As directed by Andrew Douglas, whose previous work consists primarily of television commercials, and written by Scott Kosar, who is best known for writing the remake of another horror film, *The Texas Chainsaw Massacre,* the 2005 version of *The Amityville Horror* is a nominal improvement over the original.

Beverley Bare Buehrer

CREDITS

George Lutz: Ryan Reynolds
Kathy Lutz: Melissa George
Billy Lutz: Jesse James
Michael Lutz: Jimmy Bennett
Lisa: Rachel Nichols
Father Callaway: Philip Baker Hall
Chief of Police: Rich Komenich
Scott Kosar
Ronald Defeo: Brendan Donaldson
Realtor: Annabel Armour
Chelsea Lutz: Chloe Grace Moretz
Jodie Defeo: Isabel Conner
Snitch: Jose Taitano
ER Doctor: David Gee
Officer Greguski: Danny McCarthy
Librarian: Nancy Lollar
Origin: USA
Language: English
Released: 2005
Production: Michael Bay, Andrew Form, Brad Fuller; Platinum Dunes; released by MGM
Directed by: Andrew Douglas
Cinematography by: Peter Lyons Collister
Music by: Steve Jablonsky
Sound: Jim Stuebe
Editing: Christian Wagner, Roger Barton
Art Direction: Marco Rubeo
Costumes: David Robinson
Production Design: Jennifer Williams
MPAA rating: R
Running time: 89 minutes

REVIEWS

Boxoffice Online. April, 2005.
Entertainment Weekly Online. April 20, 2005.
Los Angeles Times Online. April 15, 2005.
New York Times Online. April 15, 2005.
Premiere Magazine Online. April 14, 2005.
Variety Online. April 14, 2005.

QUOTES

George Lutz: "Houses don't kill people. People kill people."

TRIVIA

The reproduction of the Amityville House's notorious exterior was constructed in Silver Lake, Wisconsin. However, many of the interiors were built on a temporary sound stage in an empty building in Buffalo Grove, Illinois.

ARE WE THERE YET?

24 hours. 350 miles. His girlfriend's kids. What could possibly go wrong?
—Movie tagline

Box Office: $82.3 million

Hollywood is supposedly a hotbed of progressive values, but it was not looking so progressive when *Are We There Yet?* came out. There was a major article in *The Los Angeles Times* wondering if the movie could possibly be successful. Was it because the premise—a sort of half-baked combination of *Planes, Trains and Automobiles* and *Johnson Family Vacation*—was too dumb to attract viewers? Or was it that it was an Adam Sandler reject? No, the hand-wringing was over the fact that star Ice Cube was not white. It seems improbable that in 2005, studios would still be unsure whether white people would go see a film starring nonwhite actors, but that was the case. (And sadly, in previous years, white people indeed would avoid films with largely African-American casts.)

Whether it was the considerable charm of Ice Cube or some sort of mass enlightenment is hard to say, but *Are We There Yet?* did just fine. The film topped the box office charts and pretty much guaranteed that a studio would be willing to take another such "chance."

It is odd that *Are We There Yet?* would be a breakthrough film because the thing is really not that good. Were it not for Cube, the film would be notable only for being so utterly unnoticeable. It is boilerplate family comedy—exactly the kind of bland, semi-gross family fare that one would expect from director Brian Levant, who was also responsible for *Snow Dogs, The Flintstones,* and *Jingle All the Way.*

Nick (Cube) is the owner of a sports memorabilia store in Portland, Oregon. For some unexplained reason, he hates children. As he tells his coworker (Jay Mohr), "Kids are like cockroaches, except you can't squish them." When he sees Suzanne (Nia Long), a gorgeous party-planner who works across the street, he falls in love at first sight. After he finds out that she has two kids, though, he decides that she should remain just a friend. Perhaps he should have stuck with this decision because her children, young Kevin (Philip Daniel Bolden) and big sister Lindsey (Aleisha Allen), are some of the most hellacious children to ever grace the screen. The kids still hold onto hope that their divorced parents will get back together, so they make life miserable for any man who tries to date their mom. One hapless fellow bearing flowers is subjected to a vicious attack that includes a dousing with glue and an unleashing of marbles.

Nick is set up to be the next victim when he reluctantly agrees to take the kids up to visit their mom on a business trip in Vancouver. Perhaps he should have canceled the trip after Kevin plants a knife on him and he is barred from taking a plane. Or maybe he should have canceled after Kevin's aggressive dawdling makes them miss the train. It is quite definitely a bad decision to drive them up in his brand new, beloved SUV. Surely no one in the audience doubts that by the end of the film, that SUV will be badly mutilated. And indeed it is.

In one really bad day of car travel, Nick fights a crazed deer, cleans up projectile vomit and watches Kevin urinate on a horrified woman. He suffers through Kevin's feigned asthma attack and Lindsey's karaoke version of "Respect." In their most heinous trick—and there are many—the kids hold up a "Help!" sign out the car window, leading a vigilante truck driver to believe that they have been kidnapped. Somehow Cube finds this all appealing and ends up bonding with the kids. By the end of the day, he is ready to chuck his old bachelor life for a life with these kids. If nothing else, credit should go to Cube and his fine acting for making this seems like a reasonable decision.

Most reviewers did not care for the film, but had good things to say about Cube, calling him "charming," "a real movie star" and "effortlessly likable." Wesley Morris of *The Boston Globe* called him an "asset" and wrote, "He's so genuinely good with the effortless Long that you wish the two would just run off and make a real romantic comedy." And Stephanie Zacharek of *Salon.com* wrote, "If only there were more movie projects worthy of him." Kevin Thomas of *The Los Angeles Times* wrote, "Its star Ice Cube remains characteristically amiable, but this thuddingly miscalculated comedy is way beneath him." Lou Lumenick of *The New York Post* called the film a "vulgar, grating alleged 'family' comedy."

Jill Hamilton

CREDITS

Nick Persons: Ice Cube
Suzanne Kingston: Nia Long
Marty: Jay Mohr
Al: M.C. Gainey
Lindsey Kingston: Aleisha Allen
Kevin Kingston: Philip Daniel Bolden
Voice of Satchel Paige: Tracy Morgan
Miss Mable: Nichelle Nichols
Origin: USA
Language: English
Released: 2005
Production: Dan Kolsrud, Ice Cube, Matt Alvarez; Cube Vision; released by Sony Pictures Entertainment
Directed by: Brian Levant
Written by: Steven Banks, Claudio Grazioso, J. David Stem, David N. Weiss
Cinematography by: Thomas Ackerman
Music by: David Newman
Sound: Darren Brisker
Music Supervisor: Spring Aspers
Editing: Lawrence Jordan
Art Direction: Kevin Humenny
Costumes: Gersha Phillips
Production Design: Steven Lineweaver
MPAA rating: PG
Running time: 91 minutes

REVIEWS

Boxoffice Online. January, 2005.
Chicago Sun-Times Online. January 21, 2005.
Entertainment Weekly Online. January 19, 2005.
Los Angeles Times Online. January 21, 2005.
New York Times Online. January 21, 2005.
Variety Online. January 17, 2005.

THE ARISTOCRATS

No Nudity, No Violence, Unspeakable Obscenity.
—Movie tagline

Box Office: $6.3 million

"In all of art, it's the singer not the song," says *The Aristocrats* filmmaker Penn Jillette. The title of the film is the punch line of the sole joke told by the one hundred or so comedians featured in the film. The beginning of the filthy, ages-old joke historically only told by comedians to other comedians, is basically always the same: A guy walks into a talent agent's office and says he has an act, a family act. The punch line, given after the man is queried about what such an act is called, is always the same too: The Aristocrats. It's when the agent asks the man to describe said family act that the joke, always improvised and extremely perverse in nature, takes on the different personalities of the person telling it. As evidenced by the nonstop retelling in this 87 minute documentary, the variations on the grotesque theme are endless, leading the comparisons made in the film to the comic equivalent of a Miles David jazz riff.

A few of the comedians, some well-known, other less-so, pointedly asked fellow *Aristocrats* filmmaker and director Paul Provenza why he would want to devote an entire film to that one very filthy, very hackneyed joke that is mainly used as a mental stretching exercise among comedians. It becomes clear as the film progresses, why. The way in the which the comedian chooses to tell the joke, what he says, and how far he goes—not to mention how long he can stretch it out (the longest is reportedly 90 minutes)—is like a sort comic Rorshach test. Then there is much analysis of the joke itself and whether it is, in fact, even funny; accounts of famous tellings of the joke; when the comedian first heard the joke and how they reacted; and comparisons of variations of the joke.

Some of the funniest versions include Kevin Pollock doing an imitation of Christopher Walken telling the joke; Steven Banks a.k.a. "Billy the Mime" does a hilarious mime version of the joke in the middle of a public boardwalk; a magician tells it using the aid of a deck of cards; and Mario Cantone mimics Liza Minelli telling it. Then there's the editorial staff of *The Onion* who all participate in a brainstorming session over what could be the funniest possibilities of the various parts of the joke, opening debating which bodily fluid or pornographic sex act would work best. The film shows Robin Williams in San Francisco with his version and Monty Python alum Eric Idle doing it in some foreign language. Sarah Silverman's deadpan version has her imagining her family was the actual family featured in the joke. Perceived in the public as squeaky clean, Bob Saget does an especially twisted version that even causes him to break mid-way through, only to return more disgusting than ever. Drew Carey has a special snaps-up flair at the end of his. Everyone from Carrot Top to Carrie Fisher, Rip Taylor to Taylor Negron, Andy Dick to Andy Richter (who tells the joke to his infant son), has their own special twist. And it is the then-pregnant female comedian Judy Gold who more than topped her male counterparts with one of the most disgusting versions involving her unborn child. A specially rendered *South Park* version with Cartman telling the joke gives an emphatic "no" to the aforementioned question about whether or not the joke is, indeed, funny.

What many agree is the most famous version, however, is when Gilbert Gottfried pulled out the joke as a last-ditch effort to redeem himself during the Friars Club Roast of Hugh Hefner. After being booed and chastised for telling a premature 9/11 joke, Gottfried quickly began to tell the titular joke, to the shock and awe of the mostly comedian-filled audience who were literally rolling on the floor in laughter and wondering how far he would, indeed, take it.

Many comedians return throughout the film, including George Carlin who called "The Aristocrats" the Tourette's syndrome of jokes and the film sometimes becomes a bit tedious in its relentless obscenity. Reportedly in use since vaudeville days, there are also reverse versions of the joke where a very tame family act is given an outrageously pornographic name. Robin Williams tells a version where a musician gives his beautiful songs disgusting names. This immediately prompts memories of the scene from *This Is Spinal Tap* where the Christopher Guest's Nigel Tufnel plays a beautiful piano melody and when asked the name of the lovely piece, tosses out "Lick My Love Pump." An infinitely more tame moniker than any that would used in this film which touts the tagline: "No Nudity No Violence Unspeakable Obscenity."

Hilary White

CREDITS

Origin: USA
Language: English
Released: 2005
Production: Peter Adam Golden; Mighty Cheese
Directed by: Paul Provenza
Music by: Gary Stockdale
Editing: Paul Provenza
MPAA rating: Unrated
Running time: 87 minutes

REVIEWS

Boxoffice Online. July, 2005.
Chicago Sun-Times Online. August 12, 2005.
Entertainment Weekly Online. July 27, 2005.
Los Angeles Times Online. July 29, 2005.
New York Times Online. July 29, 2005.
Premiere Magazine Online. July 29, 2005.

Variety Online. February 22, 2005.
Washington Post Online. August 12, 2005, p. WE32.

QUOTES

Joe Franklin: "A man walks into a talent agent's office and says that he has an act...."

THE ASSASSINATION OF RICHARD NIXON

The mad story of a true man.
—Movie tagline
Power is a state of mind.
—Movie tagline

Whatever the intention of this grim, political film, it gives the lie to those in the second Bush administration who claimed after the 9/11 attacks on the Twin Towers in New York City and on the Pentagon in Washington, D.C., that a hijacked commercial airplane could be used as a terrorist weapon was unimaginable. Not only was this imaginable, it nearly happened 27 years before September 11, 2001. No matter that the earlier attack was the work of a loner lunatic rather than an international terrorist plot. The plan of attack was the same, to hijack an airplane and fly it into the White House, in hopes of killing the President of the United States. Fortunately, neither the plot nor the plane ever got off the ground. The film's end credits explain that the film was "inspired by a true story." But not one that Condoleezza Rice or other White House advisors apparently had ever heard of.

Of course, President Richard Nixon was not assassinated, but the image and memory of Nixon and what he seemed to represent motivates the would-be assassin, Samuel J. Bicke (Sean Penn in yet another eccentric, troubled, virtuoso performance as an anguished loner). The film begins on February 22, 1974, with Sam Bicke in his parked car at Baltimore-Washington International Airport. Sam shaves in his car and prepares himself for his coming ordeal in what appears to be a kind of suicide ritual. He puts a brace on his leg that is intended to conceal a loaded revolver that he takes out of the glove box. As Sam begins his walk from the airport parking lot, the film has two flashbacks, the first "Two Weeks Earlier," when Sam begins preparing recorded tapes he intends to send to the composer Leonard Bernstein to introduce himself and to explain his actions: "Tell them my reasons. Tell them why...My name is Sam Bicke, and I consider myself a grain of sand," but Sam wants "to show the powerful that even the least grain of sand has in him the power to destroy them." Why does Sam choose Bernstein? That mystery is never explained. Sam is irrational, a "strange man," as his brother describes him later on. The Bernstein dialogue runs throughout the film in voice-over. "Explain to me Mr. Bernstein," Sam says while driving to his ex-wife's home, for example, "All I want is a piece of the American dream."

The second flashback, "One Year Earlier," contextualizes the irrational and violent behavior that is to come later. Sam is working as a salesman in a store that sells office furniture. He hates his job and his boss, Jack Jones (played by Jack Thompson), who gives Sam fatherly, professional advice to help improve his sales skills and self-improvement books such as Dale Carnegie's *How to Win Friends and Influence People*, and Norman Vincent Peale's *The Power of Positive Thinking*. The boss intercepts Sam's awkward exchange with a customer who doesn't think he wants to buy naugahide furniture by telling the sucker that the chair at issue is really naugahide-coated leather. Sam's boss also introduces the Nixon motif, by calling Nixon "the greatest salesman in the world. He sold the whole country, 200 million people, on himself, twice. He made a promise; he didn't deliver; and then he sold us." The film begins with images of Nixon making a political speech behind the credits, and Nixon is constantly seen on television trying to lie his way our of the Watergate scandal. Sam believes that Nixon represents everything that is wrong with America. Hence Sam's motive for the planned assassination.

The problem is that Sam is programmed to fail at everything he attempts. His marriage with Marie (Naomi Watts) is falling apart. Sam has been separated from his wife and children for over a year. Sam has a scheme that would put him into business with his friend Barney selling tires from a refurbished school bus. Sam wants to patent the idea and needs a loan to start the business. The key figure Sam has to "sell" on this idea is Tom Ford (Nick Searcy), who listens politely to Sam but is not really convinced that Sam's scheme will work. Sam's head is filled with self-improvement formulas and clichés, such as "The salesman who believes is the salesman who receives." Ultimately, Sam believes, but he doesn't receive.

Sam is expecting a letter that will give him the go-ahead for his tire business scheme. Instead, he gets a notice that Marie's divorce proceedings will be finalized. Sam loses interest in his job, then he loses his job as well. Devastated by Marie leaving, he broods and nurses his desperation. The day after the divorce papers arrive, Sam calls his ex-wife at 3 a.m. and gets the man she is sleeping with, who gives the telephone to Marie, who refuses to talk. After she hangs up on him, Sam cries. The next day he melts down at work and quits his job. Significantly, he quits as Nixon on television is proclaiming, memorably, "I am not a crook." In this miserable frame of mind, Sam hatches his cockeyed plot to hijack an airplane and fly it into the White House in his attempt to assassinate Nixon. Sam also fails in his attempt to join the Black Panthers. He makes a fool of himself by telling the local Panther leader that he wants to be a "Zebra," ("you know, black and white"), but the Panther leadership is neither impressed nor amused, even though Sam leaves a donation of $107 for the cause. The film fully establishes a pattern of failure in everything Sam attempts.

The least that can be said about writer-director Niels Mueller's debut film is that it is narrowly and closely focused, but that is the film's major drawback as well as its main advantage. The focus is racked on Sam Bicke's dismal trajectory towards failure and insanity. Mueller could not have found an actor better qualified to play Sam Bicke than Sean Penn, who overwhelms all the others, in this case, notably Naomi Watts, who plays his wife, Marie, Don Cheadle who plays his friend and would-be partner, Barney, and Michael Wincott, who plays his older brother, Julius Bicke. By and large, this is a one-man show, and Sean Penn's talent is almost up to the challenge. In his *New Yorker* review, David Denby described the film as having "the character of a passionately enlarged footnote." "The hard-nosed question for films about losers" to be asked here, Denby notes, is 'Why should we care?' and the answer in this case lies in Mueller's idiosyncratic idea of who Sam is—an idea executed by Sean Penn with the lucidity that he always brings to the roles of desperate men. Penn's performance is both chilling and spooky, but the vehicle pales in comparison to greater works about exploited and frustrated salesmen, such as Arthur Miller's *Death of a Salesman* and David Mamet's *Glengarry, Glenn Ross*. On the other hand, the plot might also be described as *Death of a Salesman* meets *Taxi Driver*, particularly since the name of the protagonist, Sam Bicke, echoes that of Travis Bickle in Scorsese's 1976 film. The tagline for the Sean Penn film was "The mad story of a true man," but the line might be reversed and still make sense: "The true story of a mad man," even if some details have been changed.

James M. Welsh

CREDITS

Samuel Bicke: Sean Penn
Bonny Simmons: Don Cheadle
Marie Bicke: Naomi Watts
Jack Jones: Jack Thompson
Julius Bicke: Michael Wincott
Harold Mann: Mykelti Williamson
Tom Ford: Nick Searcy
Martin Jones: Brad Henke
Receptionist: Lily Knight
Businesswoman: Tracy Middendorf
Mae Simmons: April Grace
Marie's mother: Eileen Ryan
Sammy Jr.: Jared Dorrance
Origin: USA
Language: English
Released: 2005
Production: Alfonson Cuaron, Jorge Vergara; Anhelo Producciones
Directed by: Niels Mueller
Written by: Niels Mueller, Kevin Kennedy
Cinematography by: Emmanuel Lubezki
Music by: Steven Stern
Sound: Jose Antonio Garcia
Editing: Jay Cassidy
Costumes: Aggie Guerard Rodgers
Production Design: Lester Cohen
MPAA rating: R
Running time: 95 minutes

REVIEWS

Boxoffice Online. January, 2005.
Chicago Sun-Times Online. January 14, 2005.
Entertainment Weekly Online. January 5, 2005.
Los Angeles Times Online. December 29, 2004.
New York Times Online. December 29, 2004.
The New Yorker. January 10, 2005, p. 87-89.
Premiere Magazine Online. January 4, 2005.
Variety Online. May 17, 2004, p. WE41.
Washington Post Online. January 21, 2005, p. WE41.

QUOTES

Samuel Bicke: "Certainty is the disease of kings."

ASSAULT ON PRECINCT 13

Unite and fight.
—Movie tagline

Box Office: $20 million

Proving once again that Hollywood's fascination with its own past is not a recent phenomenon is the action-thriller *Assault on Precinct 13*. The first of two remakes of John Carpenter classics this year (the other being *The Fog*), this story traces its lineage to the Hawks-Wayne Western collaborations *Rio Bravo*, *Rio Lobo*, and *El Dorado*. The basic story of a small, disparate, and not always cooperative group holding off a larger, implacable force has even been effectively explored in the horror genre in *Night of the Living Dead* and *From Dusk Till Dawn*.

This particular iteration of the story is set in the industrial, wintry landscape of Detroit, moving it from the original's L.A. locale and creating an entirely different, if not original, enemy. Detroit seems to be the new venue of choice for tales of urban decay and corruption within the law enforcement community. Witness the excellent *Narc* and the *Sons of Katie Elder* remake *Four Brothers*. It is hard to argue with the city's effectiveness as a symbol for these ills, since the desolation of the winter setting in all these films plays into the city's national reputation.

Director Richet and scripter DeMonaco waste no time in introducing us to the major players, or in telling us pretty much all we need to know about them. Crime lord Marion Bishop (Laurence Fishburne) is meeting with what we quickly learn is a contact from inside the Detroit police force in the back of a church during a service. He is calm, menacingly so, in the face of an ultimatum about the divvying up of the proceeds of his deal with the cops. When he coolly refuses, the cop soon learns the depth of Bishop's capacity for ruthless violence. His escape is short-lived, however, and Bishop is taken into custody (although you'd hardly know it by looking at his face, whose expression barely changes).

Sgt. Roenick (Ethan Hawke) has an equally auspicious, and much more urgent introduction. The audience first sees him in full-on undercover, motor-mouthed junkie/dealer mode, regaling his potential customer with the joys of his "product." In a flash, the deal goes bad, resulting in a gunshot wound in the leg for him, and the deaths of his entire undercover team. Nothing in the original is as visually or viscerally exciting as this scene (the murder of the little girl may be more emotionally jolting, but isn't treated differently than any other violent act in Carpenter's film) but, unfortunately, nothing in the remake is, either.

When we see Roenick next, eight months later, he's been relegated to desk duty at the soon-to-be-closed Precinct 13, overseeing the last of the packing with what's left of the skeleton staff on New Year's Eve. He is trying to hide his addiction to painkillers and booze from the department shrink, Alex Sabian (Maria Bello), whose diagnosis is that he's hiding behind his injury and desk to avoid putting himself in the position of making life-or-death decisions. She tells him so only after he steals her chart on him and reads it as she's leaving. The rest of the staff is intent on finishing the packing in time to celebrate the new year and leave the building behind in the morning. Jasper (Brian Dennehy) is the requisite crusty old-timer, counting the days until retirement. Receptionist Iris (Drea De Matteo) is the flirty sexpot, complete with fishnet stockings, stilettos, and a thing for bad boys.

As the party begins at Precinct 13, the dead cops' colleagues in an elite anti-gang unit, led by the stoic Marcus Duvall (Gabriel Byrne), decide that Bishop (named for the acting head of Precinct 13 in the original) cannot live to see the inside of a courtroom. Because of the holiday and the lateness in the day, Bishop can't be arraigned and make bail, but he also avoids being held in the custody of the cops who want him dead. Instead, he is piled onto a bus for a trip to lockup, along with a motley assortment of colorful fellow prisoners. Yet more introductions ensue as they enter the bus. Leguizamo lands (or, perhaps, creates) the showiest role as Beck, a twitchy, conspiracy-theory spouting junkie who's easily the most unpredictable of the bunch. The rest of the cannon-fodder cast includes Smiley (Ja Rule), a con man who refers to himself in the third person and Anna (Aisha Hinds), a female gangbanger who claims complete innocence. The bus guards round out the group, but they are dispatched almost as quickly as the guards in the original once the siege begins.

Once en route, the bus is quickly imperiled, and then rerouted to the precinct by the raging blizzard. Alex has, likewise, returned because of the storm. Roenick and the others are not pleased to greet the busload of prisoners, but they get everyone settled and re-start the party, until a fight between two of the prisoners coincides with masked intruders breaking into the cell area. Once the attack is repulsed and the bus guards are dead, theories abound about the identity of the intruders. Jasper believes Bishop's gang is trying to bust him out. Bishop tells Roenick that it's the cops coming to kill him.

When a close encounter with one of the outsiders confirms Bishop's story, they realize that not one of them will be allowed to live, and that they must form an uneasy truce in order to survive. In this point, the remake draws out the drama a little more than the original did. After fending off an initial onslaught, the group engages in a Mexican Standoff that Tarantino would've enjoyed filming before Bishop and Roenick calm their respective troops into grudging cooperation. In the original, that cooperation never seemed anything but unanimous and permanent.

As the siege deepens, an officer from the precinct makes it through the blockade, getting wounded in the process. He represents another gun to the survivors, but also introduces the possibility of traitors in the group's midst, the suspicion voiced by the fast-talking Beck.

Roenick vouches for him and everyone calms down until an unlocked door heightens those suspicions once again. Richet does a good job of keeping the tension high within the walls, while keeping enough action going to give the audience some relief. Separate plans to get someone out to get help result in some heart-thumping moments as the number of survivors dwindles. As expected, Beck and Smiley see a chance to fend for themselves, with rather predictable results. A plan is quickly hatched to take advantage of the distraction. Anna, the only one left who can hotwire a car, and Alex, who can't be relied on to handle a weapon, are chosen to try to sneak out and get help. This is also unsuccessful, and leads to the most surprising moment of the film: the ease with which the nominal female lead is dispatched, reflecting the shocking moment (and catalyst) of the original when the aforementioned little girl is shot.

Probably the biggest similarity between the two films is the cold ruthlessness with which the violence is handled. The gang members in Carpenter's film barely register emotion, while the bad cops in the remake are just as coolly efficient. The reaction of those inside is a study in contrasts. Bishop and Roenick, as the leaders, remain calm (after Roenick dramatically climbs out of his self-pity and substance dependence), while the other criminals take a certain delight in being given free rein to take on the invading cops. The rest range from various degrees of hysteria to grim determination to survive.

Carpenter's work, with Watergate and Vietnam still fresh, gave the "bad guys" inside more honor and dignity than some of the cops, most notably the warden in the prologue and the outgoing commander at the precinct. Richet's idea of political commentary is having old guard cops as the bad guys, both inside and out. Bishop makes no bones about his allegiance to himself, and acts on this philosophy when given the chance. When Jasper reveals his true colors, not only is it no surprise, but it ironically shows the bad guys as, most likely, nostalgic for the good old days of '70s, when abusing suspects and other random acts of unkindness were, for them, the norm. In the end, the characters who started out bad, whether they showed it right away or not, are never proven otherwise.

The relatively big-name cast is not really given much to work with, aside from Hawke's Roenick who gets to show an actual range of emotion. Fishburne effectively channels Morpheus from *The Matrix* for his cool, in-control villain. Bello acquits herself well, but won't be focusing on this work over *A History of Violence* when discussing her resume.

Once the situation inside the precinct becomes untenable, some major weaknesses in plotting are exposed. Jasper suddenly "remembers" a sewer leading out of the building, leading to the group leaving the dramatically important setting. This not only leads to the clichéd reveal of Jasper's allegiance, but leads the group into the geographically impossible (if earlier establishing shots are to believed) FOREST a few yards away from the building. Any dramatic credibility the film had established up to this point is deflated, especially with Detroit-area audiences.

The mixed reviews this remake received are deserved, as it has all the inherent strengths (solid casting, well-choreographed action) and weaknesses (pedestrian plotting, clichés aplenty, too few developed characters) of the modern urban crime/action thriller. The bigger problem is that it didn't bring anything new to the original or the genre, except maybe a disturbing fascination with lethal head shots and a lousy sense of geography.

Devotees of the original most likely won't like the updating, preferring the down-and-dirty, straight ahead style that film displayed. But then, younger viewers, or those coming to that film for the first time after seeing this one, may ask what all the fuss was about back then.

Jim Craddock

CREDITS

Sgt. Jake Roenick: Ethan Hawke
Marion Bishop: Laurence "Larry" Fishburne
Jasper O'Shea: Brian Dennehy
Iris Ferry: Drea De Matteo
Alex Sabien: Maria Bello
Marcus Duvall: Gabriel Byrne
Smiley: Ja Rule
Capra: Matt Craven
Beck: John Leguizamo
Ray Ray: Fulvio Cecere
Kahane: Currie Graham
Gil: Dorian Harewood
Rosen: Kim Coates
Tony: Hugh Dillon
Milos: Titus Welliver
Anna: Aisha Hinds
Origin: USA
Language: English
Released: 2005
Production: Pascal Caucheteux, Jeffrey Silver, Stephane Sperry; Liaison Films, Biscayne Pictures; released by Rogue Pictures
Directed by: Jean-Francois Richet
Written by: James DeMonaco
Cinematography by: Robert Gantz

Music by: Graeme Revell
Sound: David Lee
Music Supervisor: John Houlihan
Editing: Bill Pankow
Art Direction: Nigel Churcher
Production Design: Paul Denham Austerberry
MPAA rating: R
Running time: 109 minutes

REVIEWS

Boxoffice Online. January, 2005.
Chicago Sun-Times Online. January 19, 2005.
Entertainment Weekly Online. January 19, 2005.
Los Angeles Times Online. January 19, 2005.
New York Times Online. January 19, 2005.
Premiere Magazine Online. January 21, 2005.
Variety Online. January 13, 2005.
Washington Post Online. January 21, 2005, p. WE41.

QUOTES

Rosen: "Your eyes are red. You been smokin' crack?"
Beck: "Your eyes are glazed. You been eatin' donuts?"

ASYLUM

Passion knows no boundaries.
—Movie tagline
Passion. Possession.
—Movie tagline

Dreary, erotic thriller from *Young Adam* director David Mackenzie suffers from an overdose of melodrama, improbable and overwrought plotting, and stiff, heavy-handed performances. A steamy, forbidden 1950's romance between a bored British housewife and a dangerous but sensual mental patient set against the backdrop of the titular asylum sinks under a series of clichés and foggy motivations in Patrick Marber (*Closer*) and Chrysanthy Balis' script adapted from a novel by Patrick McGrath.

It's nighttime, and the relatively strong first act opens with the aptly dark and foreboding asylum's newly appointed deputy superintendent Dr. Max Raphael (Hugh Bonneville) arriving on the grounds with his wife Stella (Natasha Richardson) and young son Charlie (Gus Lewis) slyly observed by the ever-watchful Dr. Peter Cleave, played deliciously by Ian McKellen. A longtime member of the institution's staff, Cleave has been passed over for Max's new position and one can guess that the less-than-amused Dr. will continue to keep a watchful eye on his new superior, waiting for any slip-ups that might occur.

The fact that Stella and Edgar share a common and very obvious contempt for one another also becomes very clear in the opening scenes. The very soul of proper British propriety, Max is concerned only with appearances—scolding his wife for not mingling more with the other doctor's wives instead preferring to chat up Cleave. Another example of clichéd British repression, Cleave, is a bachelor, Stella discovers, who finds love a "dangerous sport" and admits "I'm not sure I have the stomach for it." Cleave is also in charge of treating the asylum's most dangerous patients.

One of these is Cleave's "pet" patient Edgar Stark (Marton Csokas). Perhaps in a calculated move, Cleave sets Martin out to renovate a dilapidated glass conservatory very near the lodging of Max and his wife. Playing on the grounds, Charlie stumbles upon the quiet, gentle Edgar and the two become friends. A jarringly strange and abrupt cut shows Edgar entering Stella's house carrying in a bloodied Charlie, whom despite the nosy housekeepers accusations, he has rescued from a tree fall. This coincides with the asylum's annual ball, which allows male and female inmates to mingle and Stella, dressed in a sexy black sheath, accepts Edgar's offer to dance with him (as Cleave looks sinisterly on, of course). Just as her namesake in Tennessee Williams' *A Streetcar Named Desire,* Stella falls for the rugged, lower-class hunk of mental instability who she learns was a sculptor in his former life. She also learns that Edgar, whose official diagnosis is severe personality disorder with features of morbid jealousy, not only killed his wife, but then cut out her eyes and gouged up her face. Nevertheless, Stella wastes no time in seducing the willing Edgar and many wordless, steamy sex scenes in the glass house ensue.

Edgar is the also the object of Cleave's obsession and despite the major "progress" Cleave claims he's made, is in no hurry to release his most handsome patient, much to Edgar's chagrin. One day, while Stella and Edgar are enjoying a tryst in the bedroom of her house, they are unexpectedly interrupted by Stella's mother-in-law Brenda (Judy Parfitt). He's able to sneak out unnoticed by the cranky matron only to be discovered by a confused and hurt Charlie. Edgar sees his chance to escape from the asylum in the trunk of the car Brenda and Charlie are riding in and heads to London. Charlie tells Brenda that he saw Edgar in his mommy's bedroom and that he also saw his escape. The asylum investigates and although Stella denies her involvement with Edgar, Cleave immediately gleans the truth and it is clear Max will be dismissed—though not right away in order to avoid bad press after Edgar's escape.

It is here the movie begins its serious foray into melodrama and sheer absurdity. Several clandestine meetings in London which Stella explains to the gullible Max are "shopping trips," (an explanation Cleave, naturally, does not buy) reveal another side to the proper wife and mother as she is shown boozing and engaging in other hedonistic behavior with Edgar in the dingy artist's loft he shares with his assistant Nick (Sean Harris). Given an ultimatum to leave Max, Stella inexplicably decides to abandon her family and live in the seedy side of town with her deranged lover and Nick. Things quickly turn ugly, with Edgar immediately jealous of her growing friendship with Nick and, at the same time, so engrossed in his sculpting that he has no time to engage in the animalistic lovemaking they used to so often enjoy. Stella becomes just as bored with her boho life as she did in her life with Max, accusing Edgar of becoming just like her husband. Edgar then becomes violent, slapping her around and choking her. Still, the smitten Stella is unable to leave him.

She's rescued from her dubious fate when the police track her down and arrest her, also dragging Edgar back to the asylum. Her husband, now officially dismissed, takes her and Charlie to his new post in far-off Wales where they can enjoy anonymity and a plethora of sheep. Edgar manages to escape, again, and track her down in this remote, rural locale where they meet and she tells him that while she still loves him, she cannot leave Charlie again. Edgar is again found and dragged back to the waiting Cleave. Estranged from Max, Stella is inexplicably still mooning around for the abusive Edgar when she takes Charlie to a nearby river to play and when he falls in, Stella sits frozen, watching as he drowns, presumably half-wishing him dead so she may be with Edgar again and half in some sort of catatonic dream state. Even more improbably, someone rushes out of the secluded woods to witness the whole thing and rush into the water to try and save the unfortunately deceased child. Stella wakes up from her reverie to be appropriately horrified at what has occurred, rushing in to the water wailing.

For some reason, she is shuttled off to the very asylum Max was fired from and where, conveniently, Edgar is still incarcerated. Cleave, of course, becomes the doctor treating her. In one of the film's most laughable devices, Cleave has taken his obsession with Edgar and transferred it to Stella. With the film all but spelling out that heretofore Cleave was a homosexual with a clearly sexual interest in Edgar, whatever credence the movie had is completely gone at this point. Cleave keeps the longing lovers separated at the asylum and asks Stella to marry him, which would fulfill the asylum's ridiculous conditions of letting her free provided she is properly "supervised." Despite the fact, which she points out, that she is still married to Max, she accepts the ring he gives her and decides to take Cleave up on his offer. Cleave tells Edgar Stella is now a resident there and engaged to him prompting one of the film's only sensible lines at this point, "What would she want with an old queen like you?"

The film comes full circle as the annual ball arrives and the familiarly black-sheathed Stella, despite her claims to the contrary, is desperately looking forward to seeing Edgar. The fiendish Cleave tells Edgar he can go to the ball but lies, staying Stella does not want to see him. When the disappointed Stella finds Edgar isn't coming, she doffs the doctor's ring and purposefully climbs the many flights of stairs to the top of the asylum and balletically dives to her death. That can't stop the trite, melodrama, however, which allows her to utter the fateful, final words to the distraught Cleave: "Leave me alone."

Hilary White

CREDITS

Stella Raphael: Natasha Richardson
Dr. Peter Cleave: Ian McKellen
Edgar Stark: Marton Csokas
Max Raphael: Hugh Bonneville
Brenda Raphael: Judy Parfitt
Nick: Sean Harris
Charlie: Gus Lewis
Mrs. Straffen: Wanda Ventham
Dr. Jack Straffen: Joss Ackland
Origin: Ireland, Great Britain
Language: English
Released: 2005
Production: Mace Neufeld, Laurence Borg, David E. Allen; Mace Neufeld; released by Paramount Classics, Seven Arts Pictures
Directed by: David Mackenzie
Written by: Patrick Marber, Chrys Balis
Cinematography by: Giles Nuttgens
Music by: Mark Mancina
Sound: Brendan Deasy
Editing: Colin Monie, Steven Weisberg
Costumes: Consolata Boyle
Production Design: Laurence Dorman
MPAA rating: R
Running time: 90 minutes

REVIEWS

Boxoffice Online. August, 2005.
Chicago Sun-Times Online. August 19, 2005.

Entertainment Weekly Online. August 10, 2005.
Los Angeles Times Online. August 12, 2005.
New York Times Online. August 12, 2005.
Variety Online. February 11, 2005.

B

THE BAD NEWS BEARS

Baseball has rules. Meet the exceptions.
—Movie tagline

Disorganized. Disrespected. Dis Summer.
—Movie tagline

When the original *Bad News Bears* came out in 1976, it was a big hit not only because it was an underdog sports story, but also because of its lively, mischievous spirit. The kids were losers, the coach (Walter Matthau) drank, and the littlest team member cursed like a sailor. Richard Linklater, the indie director of films like *Slackers,* and writers Glenn Ficarra and John Requa (who penned *Bad Santa)* do not change the formula much (the original's screenwriter, Bill Lancaster, is still listed as the main screenwriter), but the movie does not have the same wild, anarchy-fueled spirit of the original. It is difficult to say why. Perhaps the sight of a pint-sized kid spewing creative obscenities is no longer the comedy goldmine it once was. Or maybe the memories of a movie thirty years previous have grown rosier over the passage of time. Whichever, the latest *Bad News Bears* is still an enjoyable diversion.

Linklater's laid-back direction and Billy Bob Thornton's lazy southern manner work well together in the retelling of the familiar tale. Morris Buttermaker (Thornton), a former minor league player who played briefly in the majors, gets offered a little league coaching gig by Liz Whitewood (Marcia Gay Harden). Whitewood has sued the league to allow the supremely untalented Bears to play. Buttermaker, who makes his main income from pest extermination, hates children and just about anything else that causes him to interrupt his drinking, but accepts the job for the paycheck.

The team includes original characters like the aforementioned foul-mouthed Tanner Boyle (Timmy Deters, sporting the blonde bowl cut of the original), fat kid Engelberg (Brandon Craggs) and weakling Timmy Lupus (Tyler Patrick Jones), plus new members, wheelchair-bound Matthew Hooper (Troy Gentile) and nerdy smart kid Prem Lahiri (Aman Johal). When Buttermaker first sees them play, he tells them they "look like Helen Keller at a pinata party." Giving up on them immediately, he puts them to work making him martinis and spraying toxic clouds of rat poison under houses. When two of the boys start spraying poisonous ant killer at each other, Buttermaker barks, "Stop it. That s--t's expensive."

But whether it is love of the game, bonding with the kids or just a desire to beat obnoxious fellow coach Roy Bullock (Greg Kinnear), Buttermaker starts taking his job seriously. He recruits fast pitcher Amanda (Sammi Kane Kraft), his daughter from a former marriage; and the local tough kid, Kelly Leak (Jeffrey Davis). The Bears may have a coach who takes them to Hooters and is a self-described "drunken a--hole," but they are a family of sorts. And, as they continue to practice, they are also a team that starts winning games.

Thornton shades his Buttermaker differently than Matthau and both interpretations work fine. Thornton's Buttermaker is more sexual. He often sports a busty companion and, when forced to find a sponsor for team uniforms, signs up a local gentlemen's club. Several critics called Thornton's performance a PG-rated version of his role in *Bad Santa.* The key child actors are not quite up to Thornton's level. Kraft is fine enough but does not have the same kind of fierce anger that Tatum O'Neal put into the role. And "bad boy"Kelly Leak seems about as bad a one of the Backstreet Boys. Kinnear is tightly-wound as winning coach Bullock. In one scene, he roughly shoves his son on the pitcher's mound for throwing a bad ball. "He could have hurt somebody!" says Bullock, weakly, trying to explain away his own violence.

Critics split about fifty-fifty on the merits of *Bad News Bears.* Ty Burr of *The Boston Globe* wrote, "The setup is maximized for glorious political incorrectness—and yet the movie isn't funny." Manohla Dargis of *The New York Times* wrote, "Filled with small, cute kids and large, goofy laughs and buoyed by fine supporting work from Greg Kinnear and Marcia Gay Harden, [Linklater's] latest effort won't rock your movie world, but the fact that he manages to keep the freak flag flying in the face of our culture of triumphalism is a thing of beauty." Michael Wilmington of *The Chicago Tribune* called it, "a good movie, not the disgraceful, witlessly modernized rip-off we have grown to expect from remakes." Glenn Whipp of *The Los Angeles Daily News* wrote, "Faithful to the point of irrelevancy, Richard Linklater's remake of *Bad News Bears* is an OK enough time passer, but given the talent involved, it should have been much, much better."

Jill Hamilton

CREDITS

Morris Buttermaker: Billy Bob Thornton
Roy Bullock: Greg Kinnear
Liz Whitewood: Marcia Gay Harden
Timmy Lupus: Tyler Patrick Jones
Amanda Whurlitzer: Sammi Kraft
Tanner Boyle: Timmy Deters
Toby Whitewood: Ridge Canipe
Mike Engelberg: Brandon Craggs
Kelly Leak: Jeff Davies
Joey Bullock: Carter Jenkins
Garo Daragebridadian: Jeffrey Tedmori
Matthew Hooper: Troy Gentile
Miguel Aguilar: Carlos Estrada
Jose Agila: Emmanuel Estrada
Kenneth "K.C." Harris: Kenneth "K.C." Harris
Prem Lahiri: Aman Johal
Origin: USA
Language: English
Released: 2005
Production: J. Geyer Kosinski, Richard Linklater; Detour Filmproduction; released by Paramount Pictures
Directed by: Richard Linklater
Written by: Glenn Ficarra, John Requa, Bill Lancaster
Cinematography by: Rogier Stoffers
Music by: Ed Shearmur, Randall Poster
Sound: Edward Tise
Editing: Sandra Adair
Art Direction: David Lazan
Costumes: Karen Patch
MPAA rating: PG-13
Running time: 111 minutes

REVIEWS

Boxoffice Online. July, 2005.
Chicago Sun-Times Online. July 22, 2005.
Entertainment Weekly Online. July 20, 2005.
Los Angeles Times Online. July 22, 2005.
New York Times Online. July 22, 2005.
Premiere Magazine Online. July 26, 2005.
Variety Online. July 17, 2005.
Washington Post Online. July 22, 2005, p. WE33.

QUOTES

Morris Buttermaker: "You guys swing like Helen Keller at a piñata party."

TRIVIA

Buttermaker solicits a local business called Chico's Bail Bonds to sponsor the team, the same business that sponsored the team in the original film.

THE BALLAD OF JACK AND ROSE

In *The Ballad of Jack and Rose*, writer/director Rebecca Miller has created a startlingly beautiful film with rare intelligence and more than a fair share of courage. The daughter of famous playwright Arthur Miller and photographer Inge Morath has a taste of her father's ear and her mother's eye. The stigma that art house or indie films look like the black and white, French subtitled, bizarre angled film from a college dormitory are nowhere to be seen in Miller's vision. With an astounding ensemble, led by none other than chameleon (and Miller's husband) Daniel Day-Lewis as Jack, we are swept away by the film's story of forbidden love and unusual hope.

The Ballad of Jack and Rose takes place in 1986 in a former island commune, "somewhere off the East Coast." There, Jack and 16-year-old daughter Rose (Camilla Belle) have spent their days shielded from the "real world." Jack and Rose have developed an almost symbiotic relationship, which throughout the film veers dangerously towards incest. Meanwhile a developer (Beau Bridges) is building new homes nearby the former commune. Jack, who has a fatal heart condition, has been shouting threats, vandalizing the homes, and even firing a shotgun to warn off construction workers.

Early in the film, Jack tells Rose the story of an ox and a house, and it appears that Rose wants to consummate their relationship. She has had no other man to really even look at (aside from mild-mannered flower man Jason Lee) let alone explore sexuality with. Rose seems to believe that the natural step is to become her father's lover.

Jack, for all his arrogance and manipulation, begins to feel pangs of guilt and decides to try "an experiment." Like a mad Prospero conjuring up revenge for his enemies, he whisks away to offer his girlfriend Kathleen (Catherine Keener) a home. This "experiment" will in effect serve three purposes for Jack: a caretaker, a lover, and a mother for his daughter.

Hell hath no Fury, Rose has other ideas. The new family of Kathleen and her two teenage sons Rodney (Ryan McDonald) and Thaddius (Paul Dano) are not welcome. "How long have you been lying to me?" screams Rose, whose jealousy over her father's lover is more than apparent. To get back at "the experiment," Rose practically throws herself at every man in sight, from the boys to the flower man. The events that unfold create a beautifully spun tale of comedy and tragedy.

Every performance is a knockout. The always dependable Catherine Keener tries new ground as an overly sensitive woman who seeks out losers with cash. Underneath this exterior though, there lies a salesman as ruthless as David Mamet would have her. Ryan McDonald supplies a straightforward, honest performance as and overweight hairdresser who attempts to calm down the disastrous "experiment." Paul Dano (who should also be seen in the blistering indie film *L.I.E.* starring Brian Cox, 2001) creates a wounded dangerous young teen. Beau Bridges rounds out the support with a genuinely flustered and practical developer.

But the heart of the film is the intensely natural and courageous performances of Daniel Day Lewis and Camilla Belle. Daniel Day Lewis forces us to love this bizarre Scottish hippie who manipulates everything in his life. Camilla Belle has a strange beauty and makes her inconsistent character a joy to watch from scene to scene. Underneath their performances, scored mainly by old Bob Dylan songs and with beautiful cinematography, there is a love created out of pain. They must both let go of what severed their lives, the mother of which they occasionally speak. In one of the films greatest moments, Rose plays an old film inside her tree house. She stares at her guilt ridden father as her mother dances on the canvas of the past, a memory that will, hopefully, save their dangerous relationship.

Richard Baird

CREDITS

Jack Slavin: Daniel Day-Lewis
Kathleen: Catherine Keener
Rose Slavin: Camilla Belle
Marty Rance: Beau Bridges
Gray: Jason Lee
Red Berry: Jena Malone
Thaddius: Paul Franklin Dano
Miriam Rance: Susanna Thompson
Rodney: Ryan McDonald
Origin: USA
Language: English
Released: 2005
Production: Lemore Syvan, Melissa Marr, Graham King, Jonathan Sehring, Caroline Kaplan; Initial Entertainment Group, Elevation Pictures; released by IFC Films
Directed by: Rebecca Miller
Written by: Rebecca Miller
Cinematography by: Ellen Kuras
Music by: Michael Rohatyn
Sound: Shawn Holden
Editing: Sabine Hoffman
Art Direction: Mark Ricker, Pierre Rovira
Costumes: Jennifer von Mayrhauser
MPAA rating: R
Running time: 138 minutes

REVIEWS

Boxoffice Online. March, 2005.
Chicago Sun-Times Online. April 1, 2005.
Entertainment Weekly Online. March 23, 2005.
Los Angeles Times Online. March 25, 2005.
New York Times Online. March 25, 2005.
Premiere Magazine Online. March 24, 2005.
Variety Online. January 26, 2005.
Washington Post Online. April 1, 2005, p. WE43.

AWARDS

L.A. Film Critics 2005: Actress (Keener).

BALZAC AND THE LITTLE CHINESE SEAMSTRESS

(Balzac et la petite tailleuse Chinois) (Xiao cai feng)

French novelist Honore de Balzac (Cousin Bette) plays no role in *Balzac and the Little Chinese Seamstress,* but one wishes he did. This coming-of-age story of two Chinese boys who learn about the wonders of Western literature is rudimentary and routine.

Director Sijie Dai bases his tale on his own best-seller (also known as and he does adequate work with an impressive production, yet the lack of complexity, or even genuine reflection, is disappointing at best.

Balzac and the Little Chinese Seamstress takes place in China in 1971 as the Maoist "Cultural Revolution" grips the country. Two urban teenagers, Luo (Kun Chen) and Ma (Ye Liu), are dispatched to a mountain mining region when their parents realize they are acquiring too great a Western education. Thus, the boys are forced to learn about Maoist and communist philosophy, in addition to doing menial physical chores.

When the Luo and Ma visit a large town on a break from their "rehabilitation," both of them become smitten with the granddaughter (Zun Zhou) of the local tailor (Zhijun Cong), whom they nickname "the little seamstress." During the same trip, the boys uncover a valise containing forbidden tomes by Western writers, including Flaubert and Balzac, and they expend hours reading aloud to the little seamstress in a secret hideaway. They also find a violin and learn to play Mozart on it.

In time, Luo and the little seamstress fall in love, but they must part from one another when Luo and Ma are summoned back to the mountain village by their headmaster (Shuangbao Wang). Later, the little seamstress discovers she is pregnant and has to decide weather to keep the baby. Meanwhile, the boys recall their sojourn and the young woman who helped change their lives. Much later, Ma moves to France where he watches China change from afar.

Balzac and the Little Chinese Seamstress is helmed by a Fujian-born director, cast with Chinese actors, and subtitled in English but spoken strictly in Mandarin, yet the impetus of the project is more Western than Eastern. In terms of any theme or thesis, Balzac tries to posit that Western culture is superior to Eastern culture, implying there is (or was) little Asian or Chinese culture apart from the deadly agitprop of the communists. And similar to most stories from the West about boys growing up, the narrative is linear (here may be an indirect homage to Balzac, if not Truffaut's *400 Blows*). In terms of craftsmanship, the film is purely conventional Hollywood (scenes are "broken down" into long, medium and close-up shots, music cues the action on-screen, and the editing is seamless).

By comparison, Zhang Ke Jia's Zhantai (also known as Platform), which bridged the 1970s and 1980s, presents a far more complicated view by depicting both group and personal reactions to the cultural transformations during and after "the Cultural Revolution." (Zhantai was finished in 2000 while Balzac was completed in 2001 and both films had French financial backing, which would explain the denouement of the latter.)

Contrasting another 2001 release, Alfonso Cuaron's *Y tu mama tambien,* Balzac offers a much simpler outlook on sexuality, despite the basically parallel "coming-of-age" and "menage a trois" love plots. Feminists may protest the fact that the boys never even bother to know the name of the little seamstress—and the viewer doesn't get to, either. In this way, the title of the film (and Sijie Dai's novel) is outright offensive, let alone pro-Western.

The sumptuous settings and attractive widescreen cinematography make *Balzac and the Little Chinese Seamstress* easy on the eye (Jean Marie Dreujou's photography is often stunning), and Pujian Wang's score makes the film easy on the ear. Nevertheless, discriminating audiences looking for a radical perspective should stay away from this polite, traditional bourgeois text.

Not surprisingly, Western critics embraced Balzac. A.O. Scott in the *New York Times* on July 29, 2005 called the film, "tender, touching…" Jonathan Curiel in the *San Francisco Chronicle* on September 2, 2005 wrote, "…the movie is explosive without going over the top, humorous without being absurd, romantic without being melodramatic." Peter Bradshaw's May 9, 2003 review in *The Guardian* was even more enthusiastic: "With a mood not far from *Cinema Paradiso,* the movie is full of humanity and pathos, and likeable performances from the three principals."And Ty Burr, in a relatively recent September 16, 2005 *Boston Globe* piece, wrote: "In the end, it's a lovely little movie about very big things, and the smallness both illuminates it and keeps it from greatness,"though even Burr admitted *Balzac and the Little Chinese Seamstress,* " plays very much like a French film that merely happens to be set in China."

Eric Monder

CREDITS

Ma: Liu Ye

Four Eyes: Wang Hongwei

Little Chinese Seamstress: Ziiou Xun

Luo: Chen Kun

Village Head: Wang Shuangbao

Old Tailor: Chung Zhijun

Origin: China, France

Language: Chinese, French

Released: 2002

Production: Lise Fayolle; TF-1 Films; released by Bac Distribution

Directed by: Dai Sijie
Written by: Dai Sijie, Nadine Perront
Cinematography by: Jean-Marie Drejou
Music by: Wang Pujian
Sound: Wu Lala, Nilas Nacgelen
Editing: Luc Barnier, Julia Gregory
Costumes: Tong Huamiao
Production Design: Cao Jumping
MPAA rating: Unrated
Running time: 111 minutes

REVIEWS

Boxoffice Online. July, 2005.
Chicago Sun-Times Online. September 30, 2005.
New York Times Online. July 29, 2005.
Variety Online. May 17, 2002.
Washington Post Online. August 12, 2005, p. WE33.

BATMAN BEGINS

Box Office: $205.3 million

If films absolutely must be made from comic books, graphic novels, and television series, Christopher Nolan's *Batman Begins* is the way to do it. Nolan, the admirable director of *Following* (1998), *Memento* (2000), and *Insomnia* (2002), treats the Batman legend with just the right blend of reverence and humor. Tim Burton's *Batman* (1989) and *Batman Returns* (1992) offered, as usual with Burton, an effective mixture of the gothic and the comic, with outsized villains like Jack Nicholson's Joker. With *Batman Forever* (1995) and *Batman & Robin* (1997), Joel Schumacher nearly killed the franchise with a heavy-handed overdose of camp. Nolan eliminates camp altogether and offers only a modicum of the gothic while emphasizing the mythic qualities that attract audiences to such heroic characters.

As with Peter Parker of *Spider-Man* (2002) and *Spider-Man 2* (2004), Bruce Wayne (Christian Bale) is a flawed, tortured hero. As an eight-year-old (Gus Lewis), he sees a homeless man (Richard Brake) murder his parents (Linus Roache and Sara Stewart) and blames himself for their deaths. As an adult, he journeys to Asia to become a criminal so that he can better understand the criminal mind. Bruce is rescued from prison by the mysterious Henri Ducard (Liam Neeson), under whose tutelage he undergoes extensive martial-arts training in the Himalayas. Ducard wants him to join the vigilante ninja army run by Ra's Al Ghul (Ken Watanbe) to fight evil by being evil. Bruce declines, in a spectacular fight scene, and returns home to Gotham City after seven years of exile.

Bruce has two more mentors, Alfred (Michael Caine), the butler who raised him after the deaths of his parents, and Lucius Fox (Morgan Freeman), an inventor working for the Wayne Enterprises. With their help and the training regimen he learned from Ducard, Bruce transforms himself into the masked crime-fighter Batman. Around an hour of *Batman Begins* elapses before Bruce dons the famous costume, as Nolan and co-writer David S. Goyer slowly establish the protagonist and his quest.

Batman first sets out against Carmine Falcone (Tom Wilkinson), who runs organized crime in Gotham City, buying off judges and policemen, having his enemies murdered. One of the many clever touches in *Batman Begins* is having Falcone superseded by an even more dangerous villain, Dr. Jonathan Crane, aka Scarecrow (Cillian Murphy), who plans to release a hallucinogenic substance that will drive everyone in Gotham City mad. Scarecrow then turns out to be the pawn of a surprise supervillain.

In addition to Alfred and Lucius, Batman is aided by two people who do not know his real identity: Jim Gordon (Gary Oldman), a policeman who consoled young Bruce after his parents were killed, and Rachel Dawes (Katie Holmes), an assistant district attorney who was Bruce's childhood friend. Rachel's irritation at the playboy façade Bruce cultivates is one of the film's few tired devices. Another cliché is the young slum boy Batman befriends who shows up later to be saved by Rachel.

By delving into Bruce's insecurities and fears, by giving him conflicted motives, and by having him slowly learn how to be Batman—not everything works perfectly the first few times out—Nolan and Goyer, whose credits include *Dark City* (1998) and *Blade* (1998), provide a greater depth than is usual for such superheroes. These quirky flaws also make Bruce/Batman closely resemble the protagonists of Nolan's three previous films, each of whom might also be seen as having two identities. The main character in *Following* even has the Batman symbol on the door of his apartment.

While *Memento* and *Insomnia* have a few noirish action scenes, Nolan has his first shot here at big-scale action and handles it quite well. The showdown at Ra's Al Ghul's mountain lodge is well choreographed by Robert G. Godwin and edited by Lee Smith, though as with all such martial-arts battles, realism goes out the window. The climactic action sequence on Gotham City's monorail is even better, though similar to the one in *Spider-Man 2*.

As always, Nolan handles his actors very well. As with Michael Keaton in the Tim Burton films, Bale is not an obvious choice to play Batman. Bale has slowly progressed from adolescent roles to the other extreme, playing villains in *American Psycho* (2000) and *Shaft* (2000). Regaining the sixty pounds he lost for *The Machinist* (2004), Bale is a more athletic Batman than the other actors who have played the role. His using a raspier voice as Batman makes the superhero seem even more of a threat. His hawk face, however, works against him a bit in expressing the character's sensitive side.

Caine and Freeman are very good, but their roles are underwritten. Neeson gives the film's best performance as an edgier character than he usually plays. The casting-against-type of Wilkinson and Murphy as villains and Oldman as a good guy is also quite effective. Wilkinson's Damon Runyonesque accent is delightful, and Murphy's pretty-boy looks make his villainy only more slimy. Mark Boone Junior, the motel manager in *Memento*, is menacing as a sleazy, corrupt cop. Rutger Hauer is rescued from the straight-to-cable underworld as an oily corporate executive. Holmes, alas, has little presence in the film's token female role. Seeming much too young, she would be hard to believe as a law student, much less as a crusading prosecutor.

Nolan and Goyer try so hard to resist falling into the camp trap of their predecessors that *Batman Begins* at times seems a tad solemn. When Gordon sees the Batmobile and exclaims, "I'd like to have one of those," the humor is slightly jarring but welcome. Batman also gets off two or three quips at the expense of the bad guys.

Batman Begins features the atmospheric cinematography of Wally Pfister, who also shot *Memento* and *Insomnia*. He makes the Himalayas both beautiful and threatening. Nathan Crowley's production design accentuates the decay Gotham City, at the mercy of Falcone, has fallen into. The grime, graffiti, and perpetual rain or dripping water recall Ridley Scott's *Blade Runner* (1982), to which the mood and style of *Batman Begins* owes a large debt.

Almost any work of art employing myth opens itself to a wide variety of interpretations. According to *The Washington Post*, *Batman Begins* has been embraced by political conservatives for several reasons. Supposedly, it shows the virtues of individual initiative over entrenched bureaucracies. Such initiative, however, is part of the definition of superheroes, and Gotham City's police and courts are not ineffective bureaucracies but corrupted by Falcone. Conservatives have also praised the film as being pro-business, but Hauer's Earle cares only about power, not the welfare of his company or the stockholders. He is also unaware that the company has created a dangerous weapon. Bruce replaces him as the CEO of Wayne Enterprises with Lucius, a scientist.

At the other extreme, *Batman Begins* has been viewed as criticizing the George W. Bush administration's actions in Iraq because the film's ultimate villain sees destroying Gotham City as the only means of eradicating its evil. Yet the primary purpose of this plot element seems to be to validate Batman's method of dealing with one bad guy at a time as virtuous and heroic.

Batman Begins is a much more traditional adventure yarn than the Burton and Schumacher films, owing less to the comic books created by Bob Kane than to Frank Miller's Dark Knight graphic novels. The film's darker, less comic tone thus invites it to be seen as more seriously than what it really is: an intelligent, extremely well-made, yet still simplistic morality tale about conquering one's fears. While not a perfect film, *Batman Begins* is smarter and more entertaining than its summer of 2005 blockbuster competitors such as *Mr. and Mrs. Smith*, *Star Wars: Episode III—Revenge of the Sith*, and *War of the Worlds*. Its main virtue is that its ideas never interfere with the action at its true center.

Michael Adams

CREDITS

Bruce Wayne/Batman: Christian Bale
Alfred: Michael Caine
Ra's Al Ghul: Ken(saku) Watanabe
Dr. Jonathan Crane: Cillian Murphy
Carmine Falcone: Tom Wilkinson
Lucius Fox: Morgan Freeman
Rachel Dawes: Katie Holmes
Jim Gordon: Gary Oldman
Ducard: Liam Neeson
Earle: Rutger Hauer
Flass: Mark Boone Jr.
Thomas Wayne: Linus Roache
Bruce Wayne (age 8): Gus Lewis
Origin: USA
Language: English
Released: 2005
Production: Charles Roven, Emma Thomas, Larry J. Franco; Syncopy; released by Warner Bros.
Directed by: Christopher Nolan
Written by: Christopher Nolan, David S. Goyer
Cinematography by: Wally Pfister
Music by: Hans Zimmer, James Newton Howard
Sound: Peter Lindsay
Editing: Lee Smith
Art Direction: Sue Whitaker, Paul Kirby, Dominic Masters, Peter Francis
Costumes: Lindy Hemming
Production Design: Nathan Crowley

MPAA rating: PG-13
Running time: 141 minutes

REVIEWS

Boxoffice Online. June, 2005.
Chicago Sun-Times Online. June 13, 2005.
Entertainment Weekly Online. June 15, 2005.
Los Angeles Times Online. June 14, 2005.
New York Times Online. June 15, 2005.
Premiere Magazine Online. June 17, 2005.
Variety Online. June 3, 2005.
Washington Post Online. June 17, 2005, p. WE33.

QUOTES

Bruce Wayne: "My anger outweighs my guilt."

TRIVIA

In one scene, Bruce Wayne pulls up at a swank hotel in a Lamborghini Murciélago. Although named for a famous bull, the word murciélago also means "bat" in Spanish.

AWARDS

Nomination:
Oscars 2005: Cinematog.
British Acad. 2005: Sound, Visual FX
Golden Raspberries 2005: Worst Support. Actress (Holmes).

THE BAXTER

A romantic comedy for anyone who's ever been dumped.
—Movie tagline

Imagine if a classic screwball comedy such as *The Awful Truth* or *His Girl Friday* focused not on Cary Grant but on Ralph Bellamy, the perennial wrong man, the guy whom the heroine finally dumps so that she can be with the man with whom she clearly shares a destiny. The wrong man in such movies is typically decent and nice looking but dull, the man a woman is willing to settle for only because Mr. Right seems just out of reach. In modern romantic comedies, he is Bill Pullman in *Sleepless in Seattle*. In *The Baxter*, writer-director Michael Showalter creates a charming, good-hearted, little tale that flips the formula on its head, telling the story from this character's point of view.

Showalter himself plays Elliot Sherman, an accountant who bears a history stretching back to high school of always losing the girl. A self-proclaimed "Baxter" (the term, he tells us in voice-over, that his grandmother coined for the wrong man), Elliot is polite but predictable and has difficulty connecting with women, even when one who is perfect for him, Cecil Mills (Michelle Williams), shows up as an office temp. Their passion for reading the dictionary (Elliot is particularly fond of the letter G) obviously sets them apart as geeks, but Elliot is immediately attracted to the blonde, glamorous Caroline Swann (Elizabeth Banks), to whom he quickly becomes engaged. What she sees in Elliot is not obvious—the heart of their courtship actually takes place offscreen—but it does not matter because the tradition that Showalter is paying homage to takes it for granted that the leading lady will initially be with the reserved, socially awkward fellow.

Showalter does not imitate the Ralph Bellamy type, who was merely dull and safe, but plays Elliot as very mannered; his forced attempts at humor are not very funny, and his stiff body language and formal, clipped pronunciation make him seem clueless. Banks epitomizes refinement without descending into snobbery, while Williams's mousy turn as Cecil speaks volumes for all the bright but quietly unassuming women who tend to go unnoticed.

Everything gets complicated when Caroline's old boyfriend, Bradley Lake (Justin Theroux), reenters the picture and gradually starts insinuating his way back into her life. Theroux is no Cary Grant and actually makes a bit of an odd suitor—he is unshaven and somewhat unkempt, certainly not dashing in the conventional sense, but he is a globetrotting scientist who can sweep a girl off her feet with his wealth, spontaneity, sensitivity, and easygoing charm.

Perhaps *The Baxter*'s most appealing quality is its resolutely old-fashioned sense of humor. In the film's most hilarious sequence, after a distraught Cecil has a fight with her boyfriend and spends the night with a sympathetic Elliot, she is forced to hide when Caroline arrives the following morning with the gay wedding planner, the preposterously named Benson Hedges (Peter Dinklage, practically stealing his scenes with a funny mix of self-importance and flirtatiousness). After he leaves, a distraught Caroline, furious that Elliot has put no thought into the pending nuptials, throws a fit and comes close to discovering Cecil hiding under a blanket on the bed. Since only the dullest woman would not sense someone cowering right next to her, the scene could easily be dismissed as corny, but somehow the physical comedy works within the film's overall atmosphere as a throwback to another era. Banks plays great comic rage, and Showalter's befuddled looks and panic work well in the context of the slightly artificial world he has created.

And yet, if the screwball antics and the characters themselves are often broad, there is genuine heart in the tender scenes between Cecil and Elliot, two sweet souls slightly out of step with the rest of the world who clearly belong together. An aspiring singer-songwriter, Cecil is shy about performing her own material onstage, but Elliot tries to encourage her dream. In return, she sees into his soul and is able to get to the source of his dilemma as she analyzes his prom night, when he failed to ask his date to dance: "You've got to be willing to take risks," she tells him. It is a simple diagnosis, but it speaks to Elliot's reluctance to break out of his set ways. A Baxter, she sees, becomes a hero only when he asserts himself.

The situation does not get easier when Bradley ends up on a date with Caroline and Elliot. From a hip, out-of-the-way restaurant where Elliot fails miserably in his attempt to act like a regular to a dance club where Bradley shows off his skills as a break-dancer and accidentally kicks him, nothing seems to go right for the hapless Elliot, whose woes climax at the wedding when Bradley barges in to proclaim his devotion to Caroline just when vows are about to be exchanged. What would be the triumphant ending in other romantic comedies is, of course, the big defeat for the protagonist of this film, but it is also the best thing that could have happened to him.

Elliot fell for the rich, beautiful society girl (as most men would) when what he really needed was the adorable office temp. He practically races across New York City to win Cecil before it is too late, and, in a cute throwaway during the film's credits, Cecil's boyfriend declares, in voice-over, his own beleaguered status as the guy who got rejected, thus transforming Elliot into a romantic hero triumphing over a fellow Baxter.

With the appealing dorkiness and stunted adolescence of its protagonist, the ultimate loser in lover who finally becomes a winner, *The Baxter* could be seen as the indie cousin of the summer smash, *The 40 Year Old Virgin*. But *The Baxter* trods its own unique path, eschewing raunch and bodily functions in favor of a gentler sensibility, which may be why *The Baxter* received a much smaller release. If Showalter's directorial debut does not fit in with contemporary comedy, however, it also does not quite exhibit the madcap spirit of the best films in the old screwball tradition. That may be because focusing on a Baxter instead of a fast-talking, quick-witted hero cannot help but diminish the sheer energy we expect from the genre. Nonetheless, there are enough funny situations as well as Showalter and Williams's sweet rapport to make *The Baxter* a delight.

Peter N. Chumo II

CREDITS

Elliot Sherman: Michael Showalter
Caroline: Elizabeth Banks
Cecil Mills: Michelle Williams
Bradley Lake: Justin Theroux
Wendal: Zak Orth
Ed: Michael Ian Black
Stella: Catherine Lloyd Burns
Benson Hedges: Peter Dinklage
Dan Abbott: Paul Rudd
Origin: USA
Language: English
Released: 2005
Production: Galt Niederhoffer, Daniela Taplin Lundberg, Celine Rattray, Reagan Silber; IFC Films; released by IFC Films
Directed by: Michael Showalter
Written by: Michael Showalter
Music by: Theodore Shapiro, Craig (Shudder to Think) Wedren
Sound: Tom Paul, Eric Milano
Music Supervisor: Glen Caplin
Editing: Sarah Flack, Jacob Craycroft
Costumes: Jill Newell, Jill Kliber
Production Design: Mark White
MPAA rating: PG-13
Running time: 91 minutes

REVIEWS

Boxoffice Online. September, 2005.
Chicago Sun-Times Online. September 9, 2005.
Entertainment Weekly Online. August 24, 2005.
New York Times Online. August 26, 2005.
Premiere Magazine Online. September 9, 2005.
Variety Online. May 4, 2005.
Washington Post Online. September 16, 2005, p. C05.

BE COOL

Everyone is looking for the next big hit.
—Movie tagline

Box Office: $55.8 million

The only thing cool about *Be Cool* is that it is not entitled *Be Cool: Get Shorty II*. Sequels have a well-deserved reputation for poor quality and half-hearted efforts and adaptations of Elmore Leonard crime novels also have a spotty history, but *Be Cool* stands out for its numbing ineptitude.

When last seen in *Get Shorty* (1995), Chili Palmer (John Travolta), the semi-reformed Brooklyn gangster, had achieved his goal of producing a Hollywood film. As *Be Cool* opens, Chili has a bad taste in his mouth from being forced to make (as if producers really make films) a sequel to *Get Leo,* as the film within the film is called. Driving through Los Angeles with a sleazy record producer, Tommy Athens (James Woods), Chili bemoans the necessity of sequels to successful films, making clear from the beginning that the makers of *Be Cool* are winking at the audience.

Travolta does the same winking at the beginning of *Swordfish* (2001), ridiculing the lack of realism in films similar to *Swordfish.* That self-mockery works, though it represents that depressing film's highpoint. For the same technique to score in *Be Cool,* the film must at least be adequate. Because it is not, *Be Cool* begins by shooting itself in the foot.

Because he perceives the film industry as "too corporate," Chili wants to switch to music, as if it is not guilty of the same sins. At least the world of popular music acknowledges its corruption more openly. Everyone involved in it, according to *Be Cool,* wants to be a gangster, or should that be gangsta? Because most of the characters carry guns and pull them out at the merest provocation, *Be Cool* is actually more like a Western than a crime film.

After Athens is murdered by a Russian mobster (Alex Kubik) over a debt, Chili tries to become the manager of a young singer, Linda Moon (Christina Milian), Athens has recommended. Linda is already managed by Raji (Vince Vaughn), who fancies himself a black pimp, despite being white and Jewish, and Linda's contract is owned by the sleazy recording executive Nick Carr (Harvey Keitel), who knew Chili back in Brooklyn. Somehow—the plot is extremely difficult to follow, for those who want to make the effort—Chili, Raji, Nick, and the Russians become entangled with sleazy hip-hop producer Sin LaSalle (Cedric the Entertainer). Bodies pile up, though the film is so slovenly thrown together that there are no consequences for some of the deaths.

Leonard's 1999 novel is not as good as the 1990 *Get Shorty,* but he makes the reader care about the fates of Chili and Linda. No such luck here. Some reviews complained about Travolta's lack of effort, but the problem is not the actor but the script by Peter Steinfeld, also responsible for another dismal sequel, *Analyze That* (2002). In *Get Shorty,* Chili grows, finding new outlets for his talents. In *Be Cool,* he is simply the master of ceremonies for a display of conflicting tones. Leonard's readers want to see Linda succeed, but *Be Cool* seems to forget about her for stretches at a time. Milian is pleasant, though her overly emotive Mariah Carey-like singing is rather generic. It is embarrassing to see Chili express unreserved delight for her talent. He could travel a block in Los Angeles and find someone just as good.

Even more embarrassing is Uma Thurman as Athens' widow, Edie. Again the problem is not the performer but the material. Edie is an empty-headed blonde and nothing more. After the *Kill Bill* films (2003-2004), Thurman deserves better. Keitel is also humiliated in yet another poorly written role that even requires him to rap. A rather obvious in-joke has Nick return telephone messages from Marty and Robert, a reminder of how far away Keitel is from his days with Scorsese and De Niro.

Danny DeVito is on hand again as diminutive superstar Martin Weir, but his part is really a cameo, much smaller than that of Aerosmith's Steven Tyler, playing himself. Tyler warns Chili that he has no interest in being in a film. He should have listened to his own advice.

Cedric the Entertainer is not as bombastic as usual, and rapper Andre 3000 has a few good moments as the dumbest of LaSalle's henchmen. As a gay bodyguard, The Rock displays more skill than in his action films. Because his character is constantly being humiliated—by both the other characters and the script—the audience finds itself rooting for him.

Raji, not Chili, is really the film's main character, appearing on screen more often than anyone else and having twice as many lines, with his rapid-fire, pseudo-jive patter. More than any of the other performers, Vaughn is trying to give a performance, but the script presents Raji as non-threatening comic relief only for him suddenly to beat to death an incompetent hit man (the late Robert Pastorelli, in his final role) with a baseball bat. Then Raji goes back to being a clown. Such jarring shifts in tone appear throughout Leonard's works, as he expertly blends humor and violence, but this murder is unintentionally unsettling.

Be Cool lurches awkwardly not only from scene to scene but even within scenes, as if the actors are making up their lines and the plot as they go along. These dead spots are surprising because director F. Gary Gray's previous effort, *The Italian Job* (2003), hurtled forward with a ruthless efficiency.

Apparently to remind reviewers that Travolta and Thurman previously appeared in a much better film, Gray and Steinfeld have them dance, as they do in *Pulp Fiction* (1994). The dance begins with an extra almost bumping into Chili and proceeds to cut back and forth between the dancers and a stage performance by the Black Eyed Peas and Sergio Mendes. Not only is the rhythm established by Thurman and Travolta disrupted, but Gray does not keep their entire bodies within the frame to show their smooth moves.

In *Get Shorty,* Chili convinces producer Harry Zimm (Gene Hackman) to set aside a project entitled *Mr. Lovejoy* to make *Get Leo.* In *Be Cool,* Chili drives by a billboard announcing that Zimm has finally made *Mr.*

Lovejoy while his former partner was occupied with a dumb sequel. Zimm's star is Tom Hanks, which must have seemed a good idea at the time, but after *The Ladykiller* (2004), *The Terminal* (2004), and *The Polar Express* (2004), Hanks has lost much of his luster. His decline, though perhaps momentary, recalls how far Travolta has fallen since the apex of his career in the mid-1990's. There is nothing cool about any of this.

Michael Adams

CREDITS

Chili Palmer: John Travolta
Edie Athens: Uma Thurman
Raji: Vince Vaughn
Sin LaSalle: Cedric the Entertainer
Dabu: Andre Benjamin
Joe Loop: Robert Pastorelli
Linda Moon: Christina Milian
Hy Gordon: Paul Adelstein
Marla: Debi Mazar
Darryl: Gregory Alan Williams
Nick Carr: Harvey Keitel
Elliot Wilhelm: Dwayne "The Rock" Johnson
Martin Weir: Danny DeVito
Tommy Athens: James Woods
Origin: USA
Language: English
Released: 2005
Production: Danny DeVito, Michael Shamberg, Stacey Sher, David Nicksay; Jersey Films, Double Feature Films; released by MGM
Directed by: F. Gary Gray
Written by: Peter Steinfeld
Cinematography by: Jeffrey L. Kimball
Music by: John Powell
Sound: Douglas B. Arnold
Music Supervisor: Mary Ramos
Editing: Sheldon Kahn
Art Direction: Lauren E. Polizzi
Costumes: Mark Bridges
Production Design: Michael Corenblith
MPAA rating: PG-13
Running time: 112 minutes

REVIEWS

Boxoffice Online. March, 2005.
Chicago Sun-Times Online. March 4, 2005.
Entertainment Weekly Online. March 2, 2005.
Los Angeles Times Online. March 4, 2005.
New York Times Online. March 4, 2005.
Premiere Magazine Online. March 4, 2005.
Variety Online. February 25, 2005.
Washington Post Online. March 4, 2005, p. WE41.

QUOTES

Chili Palmer: "I hate sequels."

TRIVIA

This was Robert Pastorelli's last film.

BEAUTY SHOP

Beauty Shop is the feminine counterpart and spinoff of 2004's *Barbershop 2: Back in Business.* Hairstylist Gina Norris (Queen Latifah) briefly appeared in *Barbershop* to basically set up this film. The widowed Gina has moved from Chicago to Atlanta so her musically talented, 11-year-old daughter Vanessa (charmingly played by Paige Hurd) can attend a prestigious performing arts school. Gina is living with her mother-in-law Paulette (Laura Hayes) and party girl sister-in-law Darnelle (Keisha Knight Pulliam) while working at an upscale salon owned by the self-absorbed Jorge (Kevin Bacon—complete with Eurotrash accent, blonde highlights and orange fake tan). Gina's well-liked by her clients but a jealous Jorge pushes her buttons one too many times, so Gina up and quits, vowing to open her own shop.

Which she does, buying out a storefront shop in a working-class black neighborhood in southwest Atlanta. First order of business is to get the shop, which Darnelle proclaims looks like someone "swallowed the seventies and threw it up in here," into presentable shape. Second is to get her stylists into presentable shape, including the holdovers from the previous business: sassy and pregnant Ida (Sherri Shepard), truth-talking beauty Chanel (Golden Brooks), and Ms. Josephine (Alfre Woodard), an Afrocentric, New Agey, Maya Angelou-quoting woman of a certain maturity. Into the mix comes country bumpkin Lynn (Alicia Silverstone with an accent as wide as the Mississippi), a friend of Gina's and a former shampoo girl at Jorge's who's looking for her big break. Lynn is made to feel out of place because she's "really, really white."

And Gina's beauty shop has some other problems—the electrical system needs a complete overhaul she can't afford but, wouldn't you know it, a handsome African immigrant, crack electrician, and jazz-playing pianist named Joe (Djimon Hounsou) lives right above the shop. Can love be in the air? Maybe that's just the hair conditioner that everybody's sniffing because Gina's styling secret is the homemade conditioner the girls dub "hair crack," which can fix any disaster. And the first hair disaster comes in the form of wealthy, white Terri (Andie MacDowell), a former client of Gina's whose unhappy marriage is causing her hair to fall out. She relaxes amidst all the you-go-girl conviviality and a plate of collard greens served up by eccentric vendor Catfish Rita (Sheryl Underwood). In fact, she relaxes so much and chows down on so many collard greens that Terri develops an enviable "back" that she begins to shake once she dumps her two-timing louse. Another neighborhood character is peewee playa, Willie (Lil JJ), who's always filming ladies booties for his music video when not trying to hustle candy to Gina's clients.

Gina's got some more business hiccups: she gets fined by an officious state board examiner, which conversely leads her to hiring hunky ex-thug James (Bryce Wilson) to do braiding in the salon. He's popular with his female clients although his fellow stylists suspect his masculinity (he puts his pinkie up while drinking his cappuccino and carries a man bag). Darnelle also winds up at the shop, working to pay off her bail money when Gina has to pick her up at the police station, and finally gets a little maturity going. Meanwhile, another of Jorge's clients—superficial "Botox Barbie" Joanne (Mena Suvari)—comes to Gina's, which really gets Jorge's curls in a frizz. He prances into Gina's offering to give her her old job back should something happen to her shop. Gee, can you guess what happens next? Yep, poor Gina's shop is trashed and she tells a sympathetic Joe she just can't take the money worries anymore.

Of course, before this happens we find out that James isn't gay and has a thing for Lynn, who gets accepted by the other stylists when she doesn't try so hard; and Gina and Joe get together; and Willie accidentally films Jorge paying off the state board examiner. Then everyone pitches in to fix up the shop again, Gina gets a second helping of can-do spirit and some appropriate revenge on Jorge, and her business gets a big boost when radio DJ Hollering Helen (Adele Given) gives the shop an on-air shout-out for rescuing her from a hair catastrophe (it's that miracle conditioner again). And they all cut and dyed and crimped and ironed and braided happily ever after.

Beauty Shop is mildly amusing as it meanders its way to a happy conclusion. If you are a fan of the *Barbershop* movies, you'll notice a lot of similarities—particular with characters: Terri and Eddie are now Chanel and Ms. Josephine, ex-thug Ricky is ex-thug James, white guy Isaac is white girl Lynn, and Gina is a sort of Calvin—ever-practical as she tries to keep both her workers and clients under control while running a struggling business (although Gina's seems to be very popular very quickly). And you can't complain too stridently when the talent onboard is Queen Latifah (who also produced), Woodard, Hounsou, Bacon, MacDowell, and the many others, including a cameo by Della Reese. The sassy salon talk is frequently funny (with just a touch of female-centric raunch) but it's still so predictable. You're actually surprised when the film ends because you think "Is that all there is?" And that's really it.

Christine Tomassini

CREDITS

Gina: Queen Latifah
Lynn: Alicia Silverstone
Terri: Andie MacDowell
Ms. Josephine: Alfre Woodard
Joanne: Mena Suvari
Mrs. Towner: Della Reese
Chanel: Golden Brooks
Vanessa: Paige Hurd
Rochelle: Lisa Ray McCoy
Darnelle: Keisha Knight Pulliam
James: Bryce Wilson
Jorge Christophe: Kevin Bacon
Joe: Djimon Hounsou
DJ Helen: Adele Givens
Paulette: Miss Laura Hayes
Willie: L'il JJ
Ida: Sherri Shepherd
Denise: Kimora Lee Simmons
Catfish Rita: Sheryl Underwood
Origin: USA
Language: English
Released: 2005
Production: David Hoberman, Robert Teitel, George Tillman Jr., Queen Latifah, Shakim Compere; State Street Pictures, Mandeville Films; released by MGM
Directed by: Bille Woodruff
Written by: Kate Lanier, Norman Vance, Jr
Cinematography by: Theo van de Sande
Music by: Christopher Young
Sound: Nick Shaffer, Erin Rettig, Mark Coffey
Music Supervisor: Barry Cole
Editing: Michael Jablow
Art Direction: Kevin Kavanaugh
Costumes: Sharen Davis
Production Design: Jon Gary Steele
MPAA rating: PG-13
Running time: 105 minutes

REVIEWS

Boxoffice Online. March, 2005.
Chicago Sun-Times Online. March 30, 2005.

Entertainment Weekly Online. March 30, 2005.
Los Angeles Times Online. March 30, 2005.
New York Times Online. March 30, 2005.
Premiere Magazine Online. April 1, 2005.
Variety Online. March 28, 2005.
Washington Post Online. April 1, 2005, p. WE45.

BECAUSE OF WINN-DIXIE

Discover what happens when you go looking for a miracle and a miracle comes looking for you.
—Movie tagline

When Wayne Wang announced he was bringing to the screen Kate DiCamillo's beloved children's book about a lonesome ten-year-old Southern cutie pie who meets a charming and genial dog, it seemed like a departure to many, but not to the director himself. "I generally make movies about something that is missing in our lives, empty places that we're trying to fill," Wang noted. "I am always attracted to stories about people longing for and finding deep contact with others, about lonely people struggling for some sense of connection."

Because of Winn-Dixie is a generally agreeable, soothing, but, to some, a tad syrupy family film which captures a fair amount of the book's charm but not quite enough depth of feeling. This seems due in large part to the casting of young AnnaSophia Robb, who is good throughout at chirpy enthusiasm but less able to poignantly and convincingly convey things which are deeper and more complex. She plays protagonist India Opal Buloni, who spends a great deal of time wondering why her mother walked out on her and her father seven years before, never to make contact again. Opal aches to learn more about her mother and the reason she deserted them, but her wistfully distracted albeit loving father (eminently likeable Jeff Daniels) remains loath to get anywhere near the subject. Tamping down his sorrows deep inside himself, the man predominantly concentrates upon his job of being a minister. To emphasize his focus, he is referred to simply as Preacher throughout most of the film, even by his own daughter. Opal says he seems like a turtle tucked inside his shell.

Opal's lonesomeness is compounded when her father uproots them for a move to the small Florida town of Naomi, site of his new post at the Open Arms Baptist Church. (It is actually just a convenience store with folding chairs set up for services.) They live in a trailer park. Forlorn, friendless, and in unfamiliar surroundings, it is enough to make anyone want their mama all the more. Everything changes, however, after Opal observes a large, scruffy, smelly and rambunctious stray wreaking havoc in the local Winn-Dixie supermarket. The dog upsets just about everything in sight, including the truly livid store manager. The man huffs and puffs about sending it off to the pound, but an amused Opal, sensing the animal is in need of someone as much as she is, steps in and claims to be its owner. She christens him Winn-Dixie, and trots off to sing the messy mutt's praises to her father. (The dogs used in the film were actually pure-bred Picardy Shepherds.) "Winn-Dixie wasn't lost," a grateful Opal insists. "He found me." Grown-ups in the audience will know that Winn-Dixie will transform the child's life, and they will also foresee the initial misgivings (her father's) and strenuous objections (the trailer park owner's) of adults who will eventually thaw and embrace the fur-covered godsend.

Early on, Opal gazes at a map she has drawn of the town, sighs, and says to Winn-Dixie, "Kind of lonely, isn't it?" It is at that point that the dog sets off to remedy the situation, barking ala Lassie for Opal to follow him. The dog and the film meander from place to place, allowing both chipper Opal and the audience to make the acquaintance of some of Naomi's most solitary figures. They are an eccentric bunch. There is Otis (singer Dave Matthews, in his feature film debut), a guitar-strumming, hard-luck pet store clerk who seems to do better amongst animals than with people. (The small shop itself is a little odd, too, stocking such things as ducks, geese, chickens, pigs, and goats.) Genteel Miss Franny (Eva Marie Saint), a Southern Belle turned spinster librarian, who is gathering dust along with her books. The woman almost swoons with fright upon first glimpsing Opal's prodigious pet, recalling the harrowing day she had to hurl a copy of *War and Peace* at a bear that came into the library. Miss Franny insists the beast took the tome with him back into the woods, and has been teased by townspeople about this implausible incident ever since. Gloria Dump (Cicely Tyson), even more unfortunately named than young Miss Buloni, is a reclusive, blind former alcoholic who local children swear is a witch. The visits with these people are mutually beneficial, with everyone glad to have someone to talk with who takes the time to really listen. Opal learns a lesson or two about life and the universality of heartache and feelings of emptiness, and hits upon an idea to make her own little dent in this problem: throwing a party which would bring together Naomi's loneliest. (It is lucky the town's fire marshal did not also show up considering the fête's amazing number of candles, lights, and lanterns, making it look like Martha Stewart may have also had a hand in festooning Gloria's yard.) Things are looking up in Naomi, and no one will miss the significance of Opal's previously drab, desolate drawing of the town now being suffused with color.

As a big deal was made earlier in the film about Winn-Dixie being wildly phobic about thunderstorms and likely to run away should one occur, adults in the audience will not be the least bit surprised when just such a storm arrives during the all-important get-together causing Winn-Dixie to hightail it out of there. However, it soon seems like this dogged do-gooder may have merely disappeared in order to further advance his healing agenda. While Opal and her father search for the pet both have now fallen in love with, long pent-up emotions about another disappearance—her mother's and his wife's—are released which lead to new understanding and closeness. Shared concern for Winn-Dixie has also helped cement newly-forged bonds between the diffident partygoers, and even the neighborhood boys who had taunted and teased Opal turn from hurtful to helpful. That accomplished, Winn-Dixie returns of his own volition, and a final scene in which everyone is holding hands and singing is all about blissful togetherness. They are rejoicing because they have all found much more that night than a lost, beloved dog.

A pleasantly enjoyable film which makes only a fleeting impression, *Because of Winn-Dixie* is Wang's fourth film based on a popular work of fiction. It is also his latest film concerning a daughter's feelings about her mother, a subject the director has dealt with before in works like *Dim Sum: A Little Bit of Heart* (1981), *The Joy Luck Club* (1993), and *Anywhere but Here* (1999). Made on a budget of $14 million, *Because of Winn-Dixie* grossed $32.6 million and will doubtlessly do well on DVD with parents in search of wholesomeness. In the film, various characters are offered one of Miss Franny's Littmus Lozenges and asked what the candy tastes like to them. The lozenges are sweet but tinged with sadness, as sorrow was somehow added during the making of the sugary confection. Only those people who can relate to melancholy can actually taste it and feel moved as a result, while others detect no richness in flavor beyond mere sweetness and are left unimpressed or even desirous of spitting it out. Reaction to *Because of Winn-Dixie* itself was similar, with some people finding it heartwarming and affecting, while others were either left unimpressed or gagging on its sugary content.

David L. Boxerbaum

CREDITS

Preacher: Jeff Daniels
Gloria Dump: Cicely Tyson
Miss Franny: Eva Marie Saint
Amanda Wilkinson: Courtney Jines
Sweetie Pie Thomas: Elle Fanning
Opal: Anna Sophia Robb
Otis: Dave Matthews
Dunlap Dewberry: Nick Price
Stevie Dewberry: Luke Benward
Origin: USA
Language: English
Released: 2005
Production: Trevor Albert, Joan V. Singleton; released by 20th Century-Fox
Directed by: Wayne Wang
Written by: Joan Singleton
Cinematography by: Karl Walter Lindenlaub
Music by: Rachel Portman
Sound: Steve Aaron
Editing: Deidre Slevin
Art Direction: Monroe Kelly
Costumes: Hope Hanafin
Production Design: Donald Graham Burt
MPAA rating: PG
Running time: 105 minutes

REVIEWS

Boxoffice Online. February, 2005.
Chicago Sun-Times Online. February 18, 2005.
Entertainment Weekly Online. February 16, 2005.
Los Angeles Times Online. February 18, 2005.
New York Times Online. February 18, 2005.
Premiere Magazine Online. February 17, 2005.
Variety Online. February 8, 2005.
Washington Post Online. February 18, 2005, p. C01.

TRIVIA

Soon after this movie was released, supermarket chain Winn-Dixie filed for bankruptcy and closed most of its stores throughout the country.

BEE SEASON

Words may define us, but it's love that connects us.
—Movie tagline

Family isn't just about talking. It's about understanding.
—Movie tagline

Box Office: $1.1 million

If nothing else, *Bee Season* is one of the more innovative American movies of recent years. On the surface it appears to be a standard family drama about how a girl's entrance into serious spelling-bee competition seems to exacerbate tensions between parents and children. What's unique is not the conflict—that's pretty standard fare—

but the themes and the material. From start to finish, *Bee Season* is openly and frankly spiritual, as each of its main characters pursues individual quests to get closer to the divine.

This sort of *Spellbound* for mystics is a real gamble as a film, because most of the "action" is interior, taking place not just inside the mind or heart, but deep in the soul. And, unlike too many Hollywood movies that delve into religious themes only to whitewash or satirize then, to its credit *Bee Season* doesn't condescend to pass judgment. It's respectful and keenly observant, but still puzzling and difficult to embrace.

Does it work or fall flat? It depends on the openness of the viewer. For me, it does both. It reaches for deep themes and almost touches them, but stumbles on its own ambitions. Its vision of the divine is a bit pedestrian, limited and literal, and it never offers a coherent explanation for its central points. But it's still an intriguing film.

Based on a novel by Myra Goldberg that should by all rights have been unfilmable, *Bee Season* is a directorial collaboration of David Siegel and Scott McGehee, who worked together on the 2001 thriller *The Deep End.* Richard Gere, whose own well-known spiritual yearnings may have attracted him to the part, plays Saul Naumann, a teacher of religious studies at the University of California at Berkley. Saul is a deeply religious Jew, but not a conventional one: he is engaged in a quest for mystic revelations. His wife, Miriam (Juliette Binoche), is a laboratory scientist (but the film gives us no information about her work) who is a convert to Judaism from Catholicism (she must have changed her first name too when she converted). Their children are Aaron (Max Minghella), a high school student who is serious about classical music and his own religious studies in Judaism; and Eliza (Flora Cross), an 11-year-old girl who seemingly can't get the attention of her father, until she suddenly becomes a spelling champion.

The family dynamics are set up with little subtlety. Saul is a seemingly perfect father —he's kind, loving, intelligent, and he even cooks—and the children are little angels. Dinner-table conversations tend toward deep religious inquiry, the children study Hebrew together, and after dinner son and father retire to play classical music on bass and violin. It seems to be an ideal family, held together by strong bonds of love and faith, but also open to new ideas and frank discussion.

Eliza's need for her father's attention is revealed with a rather clunky plot device. When she is invited by her school principal to compete in a citywide spelling championship, she puts the letter of invitation under her father's home office door. It gets lost in a mess and never opened. When her father doesn't say anything about the letter, Eliza asks Aaron to drive her to the bee. It's hard to imagine that, in such a family as this, Eliza wouldn't just announce her achievement at the dinner table.

When dad finds out, the focus of his attention turns toward his daughter. Saul, it seems, is not only interested in spelling as an intellectual achievement, he believes that unlocking the secrets to the power of letters is a way of getting close to God, and he has even written his own translation of a Kabala mystic's instructions on how to do just that. He opens up his world to Eliza, and in doing so creates some sibling rivalry. Again, the conflict is made painfully obvious. Whereas Eliza used to be tucked into bed while father and son loudly practiced music together in another room, now Aaron is told to quiet down his playing so the spelling champ can get some rest.

Aaron responds to his father's withdrawal of attention by rebelling in a way that will prove the most potent at arousing his religious dad's wrath. He first stumbles into a Catholic church and takes communion, and then is recruited by a stunning blonde co-ed, Chali (Kate Bosworth) into a Krishna temple. The girl appears by magic, Hollywood-movie-style.

Meanwhile, mother Miriam is becoming rapidly unglued. Haunted by memories of the sudden death of her parents in an auto accident when she was a young girl, she starts making mysterious ventures into strange residences, and becomes increasingly emotionally distant and distraught. The film spends far too much time tracking her puzzling mental disease, the parameters of which are barely discernible, meanwhile teasing Saul with the suggestion that she is being unfaithful to him.

Taking Eliza as his student, Saul not only drills her on words—though there is relatively little of that kind of preparation—he reveals to her a mystical pathway to communicating more directly with God. In her he sees powers that he wishes he had but has never been able to fully plumb. When Eliza has to spell a word, she closes her eyes and the word takes visual shape inside her head. Siegel and McGehee make this come to life by using incarnations of the word—a bird turning to an origami bird, sprouting plants spelling out letters—to suggest she is being aided by extrasensory perception or perhaps divine inspiration.

It's interesting but tough to swallow whole, particularly since the filmmakers seem to have a rather limited grasp of how to suggest divine revelation or inspiration. They play on themes suggested by Saul in an earlier lecture about the potential power of human beings to put back together the shards of a broken universe. When Miriam's illness is revealed, the literal way she has taken Saul's instructions seems more than a bit absurd, and the explanation for her actions doesn't track—we learn she's been disturbed for years, so why has she only recently been exhibiting signs of her affliction?

Gere plays Saul as such an insufferably saintly guy that when he is accused of being a control freak, it seems an unfair accusation, even though it's obviously true. The family conflicts seem a bit overcooked. Saul may be unbearably good—when Gere is goaded, he barely gets angry—but he doesn't seem to be the ogre his son accuses him of being, repeatedly, in the film's last half-hour. And throughout the conflict, Eliza's role of the healing force in the family seems all the more intellectualized because her character is never given room to stretch and roam and be a kid. Cross, in her debut, is quite understated, but we never get a sense of who Eliza really is, other than a sort of willing vessel for God and her father to work through. If she had a stronger personality or her own inner conflicts, her climactic decision would have more impact.

Gere seems to be playing the same role he's played repeatedly in recent years—the quiet, sensitive, brilliant man who's plagued and put upon by a world that eludes him. The beautiful and accomplished Binoche struggles mightily to give some weight to a character who's more of the embodiment of a concept than an actual human being. Minghella carries his coming-of-age conflict with quiet intensity, but in the end the major problem with this film is that the characters seem to be created to embellish themes rather than to have an appeal of their own.

As for the spelling competition, for all the superficial visual attention to the play of words and letters, the film seems otherwise rather uninterested in its central subject. Of course, the documentary *Spellbound* has already told us everything we need to know. But even so, in this film the competitions seem to race by in rather perfunctory and predictable fashion and serve merely as a backdrop.

The meat of this movie is, irreducibly, about the quest for divine connection, and it is this theme, and the delicate and powerful way it's treated, that makes *Bee Season* worth seeing. The film raises as many questions about this quest as it answers, and the ending will leave viewers with room for many interpretations, but that's fine. Inner struggles are difficult to visualize on film, however, especially spiritual ones, and the directors don't entirely succeed. Does Saul learn a lesson in the end about ego being an impediment in the quest for the divine? It appears so. Is that the message of the film? It's hard to say. The combination of a rather limited visual depiction of the divine with a rather murky explication of each character's spiritual and emotional progress makes the film both intriguing and frustrating.

Take away the spiritual dimension of the film, and *Bee Season* becomes quite pedestrian, a rather predictable interplay of the controlling dad, the disturbed mother, and two siblings vying for attention. That there's no real conflict between the siblings keeps the film from seeming truly disturbing—the friendship of the kids is what ends up holding the family together, and that's nice. But in the end *Bee Season* mistakes the concoction of conflict for real drama, and while it tries to probe the supernatural it often falls far short of being inspirational. For those intrigued by such matters, however, *Bee Season* is at the least a welcome relief from films that treat the spiritual as either forbidden territory, a killing ground, or a comic swamp.

Michael Betzold

CREDITS

Saul Naumann: Richard Gere
Miriam Naumann: Juliette Binoche
Eliza Naumann: Flora Cross
Aaron Naumann: Max Minghella
Chali: Kate (Catherine) Bosworth
Origin: USA
Language: English
Released: 2005
Production: Albert Berger, Ron Yerxa; Bona Fide; released by 20th Century-Fox
Directed by: Scott McGehee, David Siegel
Written by: Naomi Foner
Cinematography by: Giles Nuttgens
Sound: Nelson Stoll
Editing: Lauren Zuckerman
Art Direction: Michael E. Goldman
Costumes: Mary Malin
Production Design: Kelly McGehee
MPAA rating: PG-13
Running time: 104 minutes

REVIEWS

Boxoffice Online. November, 2005.
Chicago Sun-Times Online. November 11, 2005.
Entertainment Weekly Online. November 9, 2005.
Los Angeles Times Online. November 11, 2005.
New York Times Online. November 11, 2005.
Premiere Magazine Online. November 11, 2005.
Variety Online. September 6, 2005.

TRIVIA

Dakota Fanning was originally set to play Eliza, but directors then selected Flora Cross due to her resemblance to Juliette Binoche.

THE BEST OF YOUTH

(La Meglio Gioventu)

The possibilities were endless...
—Movie tagline

Filled with psychology and symbolism but also simplicity; politics and history, but essentially a poignant family drama, director Marco Tullio Giordana's engrossingly realistic six-hour epic follows the lives of two brothers. The film's main protagonists, the brothers' divergent personalities send their lives in wildly different directions, perhaps embodying the duality of Italy itself during the often-turbulent 37 year history the movie spans. Written by Sandro Petraglia and Stefano Rulli, *The Best of Youth* (*La meglio gioventu*) was originally a made-for-Italian-TV miniseries which eventually got a theatrical release in Italy in 2003 before making its way to a limited release in the US in 2005 to universal critical acclaim.

The Animals' version of "House of the Rising Sun" plays over the opening credits, amid orange over-saturated images of black-and-white newspaper headlines of 1960's Italy, where the film opens. The color orange, the fruit, and the representative sun are all predominant images throughout the film and may have a double meaning, as well. Orange represents health and warmth but is also the color of political opposition, one of the themes the film addresses. In the summer of 1966, however, times are relatively simple for the Carati brothers, Nicola (Luigi Lo Cascio) and Matteo (Alessio Boni), who are studying for their exams at school. Matteo is the family's prodigy: blue-eyed and handsome but intense and brooding with a love of poetry who is studying literature. Nicola, shown studying at the outset with his long-time friend Carlo (Fabrizio Gifuni), is a medical student who, while not as naturally gifted as his brother, is more playful and interactive with the rest of the family. Rounding out the middle-class Carati clan is their charismatic father Angelo (Andrea Tidona), nurturing mother Adriana (Adriana Asti), 8-year-old little sister Francesca (Nila Carnelutti) and an older sister, a lawyer living away from home, Giovanna (Lidia Vitale).

Nicola, Matteo, Carlo and friend Berto (Giovanni Scifoni) are typical Italian teenagers: going to dances, trying to get girls, and planning their long-awaited summer trip to Norway after their college exams. The first in the film's many unforeseen events, Matteo's life takes a complicated turn when he takes a part-time job at a psychiatric hospital and meets a patient named Giorgia (Jasmine Trinca). Giorgia is beautiful but extremely disturbed and, perhaps for this reason, Matteo feels a connection to the girl. After observing the physical traces of abuse and electroshock therapy on her body, Matteo smuggles her out of the hospital. On the eve of their vacation, Carlo and Berto are shocked to find the obviously unbalanced and unwanted guest that Matteo insists on bringing along. Nicola sides with his brother and they agree to meet their two friends in a few days, after he and Matteo can drop Giorgia off with her family in her hometown.

Things don't go very well for the brothers and their female companion, however, and a local priest who recognizes Giorgia informs the boys that her father has long since moved out of town. They board a train the next day and meet Giorgia's unsympathetic stepmother and her obnoxious brood along with her father, who insists she go back to the hospital, despite the brothers' charges that they are seriously mistreating her there. While the boys are busy reformulating a new plan, Giorgia is picked up by the police who, claiming she is alone, is taken back to the hospital. The despondent Matteo admits to Nicola that he purposely failed his exams and that he no longer intends to go to Norway either before departing alone on a train. Impulsively, Matteo joins the Italian army where he seeks order and discipline and, the filmmakers suggest, a place where he no longer has to make decisions that have messy, far-reaching consequences such as the one he made involving Giorgia. From now on, Matteo will merely take orders.

The alternating and contrasting scenes show Nicola's solo adventures in Norway and Matteo's experiences in the army. While Nicola grows his hair and beard long, Matteo is shorn of his long hair. Nicola dances naked with the Allen Ginsberg-spouting hippies near a waterfall while Matteo suffers the brutal basic training and is hazed by his army cohorts. Nicola forms an attachment with a beautiful Norwegian girl while Matteo forms a bond with his army buddy Luigino (Paolo Bonanni). Their lives, however, intersect during the winter floods in Florence of 1966. Nicola returns to Italy as a volunteer, helping his countrymen spare precious artifacts of their history and meets Matteo there, whose is doing his duty as a serviceman in the same regard. There, Nicola meets and falls in love with Giulia (Sonia Bergamasco), a beautiful blond, blue-eyed music student who is also politically radical and eventually becomes a member of the Red Brigade. They decide to move to Turin where Nicola will continue his medical studies—he plans to specialize in psychiatry in honor of Giorgia and in hopes of revamping the entire psychiatric system in Italy. Carlo goes along as well, where they meet Vitale (Claudio Gioe), who they will remain lifelong friends with. As love blooms, however, the two idealists Nicola and Giulia move in together and have a daughter, Sara (Sara Pavoncelo, aged 5, and Greta Cavuoti, aged 8).

Matteo and Luigi have left the army to join the police and are sent to Turin to quell a Red Brigade rebellion where Luigi is attacked by a rioter and left partially paralyzed. An enraged Matteo nearly kills his attacker and is told to take time off the force and leave town. His interest in photography leads him to Mafia-infested Sicily, where no one else wants to go, to become a crime scene photographer. Along the way he encounters Mirella (Maya Sansa) at a café. A beautiful librarian who also has an interest in photography, Matteo, still an avid reader, encourages her to work at the library in Rome where he has often visited and loves. Matteo rushes off, giving Mirella the name "Nicola" when she asks who he is. They meet up several years later where she is, indeed, working at the library he suggested in Rome and he is now working there as a policeman. He takes her out on a date but the emotionally unavailable Matteo cannot get close to anyone and pushes her away.

Nicola is having problems of his own, as well. Giulia, who has long given up her beloved piano, has become increasingly involved in the Red Brigade underground and eventually, even her love for Nicola and Sara cannot stop her from leaving them to go on these terrorist missions. She changes her identity and appearance, but often longs to see the daughter she abandoned. She meets with Francesca (Valentina Carnelutti), now grown up with children of her own and married to Carlo who has become a high ranking member of the Bank of Italy, to warn her that Carlo is next on the Brigade's hit list, no longer content to assassinate political targets. Carlo refuses to leave Italy however, stating that then the terrorists then will have won. Nicola further learns from Francesca that Giulia wishes to see Sara and arranges a meeting. Nicola, in fact, does not bring Sara to see her long-absent mother but instead arranges for the police to arrest her in order that she is stopped from killing anyone or being killed herself, which she has thus far avoided. Nicola brings Sara to prison to meet her mother but the troubled Giulia withdraws farther and farther from her family, her passions, and the world.

Tragedy has also struck the boys' mother when their father is diagnosed with a fatal illness. Upon arriving home, Matteo learns that his mother has visited his paraplegic friend Luigi all these years, inspiring him to not only survive, but thrive, despite his disability. Indeed, Luigi has met a beautiful girl and is to be married. Matteo is shocked to learn that his mother cared for his friend as she did and is despondent to see his father looking so ill. Matteo, pulling farther away from everyone, leaves a happy family gathering on New Year's Eve and, desperate for human connection, phones Mirella. Spurned by Matteo earlier when she tracked him down at the station after finding out his real identity, a deeply hurt Mirella refuses to answer the phone and Matteo is at a loss to leave a message. While celebratory fireworks erupt outside his tiny apartment, Matteo throws himself over the balcony to his death.

By far, the most complex and enigmatic character in the film is that of Matteo. There is a vague and mysterious reference by Adriana that she was not as good a mother to Matteo as her other children. And there are numerous references to Matteo's sexual confusion, which may help explain some of his emotional suffering in a more repressive time and place in history. His father constantly asks him encouragingly about girls, as Matteo never seems to bring any around. While Nicola is anxious to bring back a girl to Carlo's beach house at the beginning of the film, Matteo looks bored dancing with his girl. When the boys visit a prostitute, she remarks to Nicola that Matteo is "strange"—a euphemism of the time for homosexual. Several people, including his family, friends, and employer, remark that he is odd. After his death, Nicola compares Matteo to Achilles, a mighty Greek warrior whose love for fellow warrior and lover Patroclus spurred Achilles—who vowed never to fight again—to avenge his death. This somewhat mirrors the relationship between Matteo and his army buddy Luigi, who nearly killed Luigi's attacker in the raids, causing his discharge. Later in the film, Matteo is shown with what is clearly a transvestite prostitute whom he divulges his real name to, unlike with Mirella. However, in the production notes, director Giordana states definitively that Matteo does fall in love with Giorgia but is afraid of the complications of such an entanglement and, perhaps, afraid of women themselves. He also falls for Mirella and their steamy love scene in his car in the rain is the sole moment we see Matteo engaged in any physical intimacy at all during the entire film.

In that moment of intimacy, something beautiful emerges in the form of a child, Andrea (Francesco La Macchia). Born after Matteo's death, Andrea possesses Matteo's beautiful eyes but his mother's sunny disposition. Mirella has gone on to become a successful photographer and Nicola stumbles onto one of her showings that displays a picture of Matteo. With the urging of Giorgia, now under Nicola's care and on the verge of independence, Nicola tracks down Mirella to find out what her relationship with Matteo was and finds he has a nephew. He brings Adriana to meet her grandson and the two bond until her death. Meanwhile, Nicola has bonded with Mirella but both are wary of getting involved due to the memory of Matteo. Carlo and Vitale urge their friend to find happiness with Mirella, which he does in the film's happy ending. The final scenes in 2003 show the now teenage Andrea (Riccardo Scamarcio) taking his girlfriend to the places his uncle/father visited in Norway that his real father tragically missed. Even Giulia is allowed some measure of happiness after emerging from prison, reuniting with the now grown-up Sara (Camilla Filippi) whom she plays the organ for in a church.

Many of the film's characters are indelible. Matteo and Giulia are probably the most engaging. Both are psychologically disturbed, denying themselves pleasure, and are very alike. Both need the structure of an organization that tells them what to do as to avoid any messy, emotionally-based decisions that threaten them. While they are interesting characters, the emotional heart of the film is embodied by Nicola, an optimist who believes in the basic goodness of people and the ability to enact social change.

The thoughtful and beautiful screenplay explores themes that are as varied as the numerous characters: marriage (the older Carati's complain "no one wants to get married anymore"), Italy as beautiful but a "dinosaur," the country's problems with the Mafia, unemployment, Italy's transformation to a consumerist society, poetry, literature, morality, psychiatry, and love. Many events from the country's history are woven in, including the bombing that killed one of Sicily's most famous anti-Mafia crusaders, Giovanni Falcone, where Mirella goes to photograph the scene and Giovanna, now a magistrate, goes to serve. Citing such diverse influences in Italian cinema as Lucino Visconti (*The Damned*) as well as Roberto Rossellini, Giordana ensures that the family is what ultimately drives this sweeping drama.

Many of the actors studied at the same drama school and were friends in real life: factors which influenced the director who cast his actors to underscore the reality of the relationships (he had already worked with the wonderful Lo Cascio in the Mafia drama *I cento passi* known in the US as *One Hundred Steps*). Superbly acted and directed, the soundtrack is period appropriate and which Giordana chose to infuse with the main theme from the Truffaut masterpiece *Jules and Jim,* perhaps echoing the fact that Matteo and Nicola both fell in love with the same women as in the Truffaut film—first Giorgia and later Mirella and a film which also spans decades in the lives of its characters. Decades that seem to fly by in *Best of Youth's* 366 minutes that take us from Rome to Turin and Palermo to Tuscany in an important period of Italy's history.

Hilary White

CREDITS

Nicola Carati: Luigi Lo Cascio
Adriana Carati: Adriana Asti
Matteo Carati: Alessio Boni
Giorgia: Jasmine Trinca
Giulia Monfalco: Sonia Bergamasco
Carlo Tommasi: Fabrizio Gifuni
Mirella Utano: Maya Sansa
Francesca Carati: Valentina Carnelutti
Angelo Carati: Andrea Tidona
Giovanna Carati: Lidia Vitale
Sara Carati: Camilla Filippi
Sara Carati (8 years old): Greta Cavuoti
Sara Carati (5 years old): Sara Pavoncello
Vitale Micavi: Claudio Gioe
Origin: Italy
Language: Italian
Released: 2003
Production: Angelo Barbagallo; RAI
Directed by: Marco Tullio Giordana
Written by: Sandro Petraglia, Stefano Rulli
Cinematography by: Roberto Forza
Editing: Roberto Missiroli
Art Direction: Jorg Baumbarten
Costumes: Elisabetta Montaldo
Production Design: Franco Ceraolo
MPAA rating: R
Running time: 383 minutes

REVIEWS

Boxoffice Online. March, 2005.
Entertainment Weekly Online. March 9, 2005.
New York Times Online. October 11, 2003.
Variety Online. June 10, 2003.

BEWITCHED

Be warned. Be ready.
—Movie tagline

Everyone knows Los Angeles is its own world, and its inhabitants who work in the entertainment industry have difficulty separating their world from the reality of the world they sometimes attempt to portray. And when ideas are short, the entertainers make up stories about themselves and their world.

It would be hard to imagine more solid proof that the business of show business is running out of fresh ideas than the movie *Bewitched.* Hollywood has long been in the habit of remaking its old movies, or foreign films, or classic tales again and again, in hopes of milking familiar stories for new profits. Recently, the industry has gotten into the mode of making movies out of old TV shows. It started with a few of the better old shows, such as *Mission Impossible* and *Rocky and Bullwinkle,* and having ruined them, the moguls are clutching at everything from *The Beverly Hillbillies* to *Charlie's Angels* to *The Dukes of Hazzard* to *McHale's Navy.* Anything for an idea that might hook in an audience on sheer name recognition.

Thus, we have *Bewitched,* a lighter-than-air remake of a lighter-than-air TV series about a witch married to a "regular guy." A popular long-running sitcom in the 1960s, the show searched for laughs by concocting situations where Samantha had to reconcile her magical powers with life as the apparently normal wife of haplessly mortal Darrin. It came complete with a meddling witch of a mother-in-law, Endora, and a standard set of plot points concerning tight domestic situations that Samantha can't help using her powers to escape from.

Would anyone other than Nora Ephron consider this as fodder for romantic comedy? Ephron, who hasn't ever matched the success of *Sleepless in Seattle,* had at her disposal one of the finest actresses of our era, Nicole Kidman, and one of the funniest comics, Will Ferrell. Unfortunately, the result is neither dramatically nor comically satisfying.

Signaling the unsuitability of the original material for a screenplay, Ephron writes a script that provides the pleasantly self-referential meta-entertainment focus that Hollywood industry types love. So this remake becomes a movie about an overrated actor on the downslide, Jack Wyatt (Ferrell), who has to take the thankless role of Darrin on an updated version of the television series in order to rescue his career (and perhaps reawaken the interest of his wife, who's divorcing him for an underwear model). Kidman plays the unfortunately named Isabel Bigelow, a "real" witch who is struggling with the dilemma of becoming normal. She's just moved to the San Fernando Valley, which signals some measure of desperation in Hollywood insider code, and she wants to find someone who really loves her rather than simply a man she can control. She is, in short, a needy powerful woman, but Kidman plays her, according to Ephron's wishes, as a rather clueless ditz who hates herself for constantly using witchcraft as a shortcut for living the way mortals do: she is always tempted to rescue herself from her ineptness at life's tasks by casting a spell or working magic.

The movie strives for satire for a good hour or so, gently sending up the foibles of egomaniacal actors, and Ferrell has several choice opportunities to strut his comic stuff. But there is way too much angst amidst what should be unalloyed silly fun. Jack tricks Isabel into thinking he needs her, but really she's just a prop for the retooled version of *Bewitched,* which centers around Darrin. In scenes played out on sound stages before test audiences, Isabel isn't even given any lines as Samantha, which seems more than a little absurd. Predictably, Isabel gets angry and tries to wreak vengeance, and Jack gets his comeuppance, several times more than is needed.

Ephron seems to want to be above making jokes that involve Isabel's sorcery, at least for awhile, and the success of her efforts to make this into a romantic comedy center around Isabel's overactive conscience. This woman is certainly high maintenance: she worries that she's tricking Jack into wanting her, is angry that he is tricking her, wants to be normal but can't give up her powers, and wants to confess and be accepted for who she is. It's hard not to take all this complicated anguish as shorthand for the emotional turmoil of a career woman stuck in the throes of romantic fantasy.

Even harder to fathom than Ephron's expectation that audiences in the real world will care a whit about this fantasy woman's dilemma is the idea that a person who longs for normality would have an iota of feeling for a cad such as Jack. Ephron deals with this problem by having Isabel wonder this out loud herself, but of course there's no real explanation—it's love, after all, or what passes for it on a sound stage.

In the end, Ephron's efforts to pump some feminine emotional turmoil into a film about actors remaking an old television series—which itself was a comic fantasy and nothing more—run out of steam. As a remotely believable character, Isabel is about as far removed from the real world as possible, so why should we care about her? And we certainly don't give a fig about Wyatt; in fact, the movie gets its energy mainly from Farrell's over-the-top riffs on narcissism. So finally, with no other recourse, Ephron lets Isabel do some of her magic tricks, even riding off on a broom, but the movie drags on and on to a ridiculous romantic denouement.

This is a trifle about a trifle, done in a trifling way. You get the acrid smell of talented people sniffing around the remains of a dead entertainment property. What a waste! The wastefulness includes Michael Caine as Isabel's skirt-chasing father, who pops in and out of scenes to give his daughter unwanted advice on behaving badly, and Shirley MacLaine (who else?) as the actress playing the new Endora. MacLaine looks awful and performs even more badly. And there's a veritable platoon of underwritten comic sidemen and women, some playing roles so minor they almost disappear. The dependably hilarious Jason Schwartzman comes through as Jack's agent, while Steve Carrell riffs boldly on Paul Lynde's Uncle Albert, from the original *Bewitched,* but Stephen Colbert and David Alan Greer all but disappear, while

Kristin Chenoweth chews up scenery and other minor characters pop in and out willy-nilly, to no good purpose.

Presumably, everyone had a good time using their considerable talents on nothing at all. They're all having fun at the expense of the moviegoing public who are shilling out nine or ten bucks a pop to see a writer-director who can't decide whether to pay homage to, poke fun at, or deconstruct and reconstruct a minor piece of television sitcom history. Kidman had an easy ride pretending to be an updated Elizabeth Montgomery, and she's cute when she twitches her nose, and that's about all there is to this travesty. This film is so flimsy most of it has been forgotten by the time the closing credits end. In Hollywood, they'll love it, because it's all about their own world of make-believe. The rest of us get another peek behind the curtain, and we come away learning to avoid movie remakes of mediocre TV shows at all costs.

Michael Betzold

CREDITS

Isabel Bigelow: Nicole Kidman
Jack Wyatt: Will Ferrell
Iris Smythson: Shirley MacLaine
Nigel Beigelow: Michael Caine
Richie: Jason Schwartzman
Nina: Heather Burns
Larry: Jim Turner
Jim Fields: David Alan Grier
Uncle Arthur: Steven Carell
Gladys Kravitz: Amy Sedaris
Abner Kravitz: Richard Kind
Stu Robison: Stephen Colbert
Maria Kelly: Kristin Chenoweth
Joey Props: Michael Badalucco
Aunt Clara: Carol(e) Shelley
Origin: USA
Language: English
Released: 2005
Production: Douglas Wick, Lucy Fisher, Penny Marshall, Nora Ephron; Lucy Fisher, Douglas Wick, Penny Marshall; released by Sony Pictures Entertainment
Directed by: Nora Ephron
Written by: Nora Ephron, Delia Ephron
Cinematography by: John Lindley
Music by: George Fenton
Sound: David MacMillan
Editing: Tia Nolan
Art Direction: Steve Arnold
Costumes: Mary Zophres
Production Design: Neil Spisak
MPAA rating: PG-13
Running time: 100 minutes

REVIEWS

Boxoffice Online. June, 2005.
Chicago Sun-Times Online. June 24, 2005.
Entertainment Weekly Online. June 24, 2005.
Los Angeles Times Online. June 24, 2005.
New York Times Online. June 24, 2005.
Premiere Magazine Online. June 17, 2005.
Variety Online. June 16, 2005.
Washington Post Online. June 24, 2005, p. WE34.

QUOTES

Isabel Bigelow changing a tarot card into a Visa Platinum Card to pay at Bed, Bath, and Beyond: "That was my last thing as a witch!"

TRIVIA

Jim Carrey was asked to play Jack Wyatt/Darrin Stephens, but declined due to other commitments.

AWARDS

Nomination:

Golden Raspberries 2005: Worst Remake/Sequel, Worst Actor (Ferrell), Worst Director (Ephron), Worst Screenplay.

BEYOND THE ROCKS

Presumed lost to the graveyard of cinema history, *Beyond the Rocks* signifies an auspicious rediscovery. This 1922 silent film costarring Gloria Swanson and Rudolph Valentino isn't a classic but it is nicely crafted entertainment, as well as the sole pairing of two mesmerizing screen icons.

Beyond the Rocks was unearthed a few years ago when a Dutch film collector died and left his archive to the Nederlands Filmmuseum. There were so many reels to analyze, the museum didn't even realize what it had right away! With the assistance of Milestone Film & Video, the museum restored the partly damaged footage and added a new musical soundtrack for the 2005-06 re-release.

Beyond the Rocks couldn't possibly measure up to the hype surrounding the finding. Clearly, the picture is not another Street Angel or even a Flesh and the Devil in the romantic melodrama genre. For a passionate love story, *Beyond the Rocks* is pretty torpid and derivative stuff—using the sort of narrative device common in romance novels and many other motion pictures of the era.

Jack Cunningham's adaptation of Elinor Glyn's 1904 novel concerns Theodora (Swanson), the youngest sibling in a destitute English household. In order to help her family with their money woes, Theodora reluctantly weds a rich but older, unattractive man, Josiah (Robert Bolder). But during her honeymoon, Theodora reunites with a young, good-looking man, Lord Bracondale (Valentino), who had helped her during a recent boating accident. Theodora tries to resist Bracondale's advances, but she can't help herself and she plunges into an affair, albeit a platonic one. Much later, when Josiah discovers Theodora has cheated on him (at least in thought), he is furious. But after Josiah is shot by mercenaries on a trip to the North African desert, he tells her his dying wish is for her to be happy and to marry Bracondale.

The extraordinary aspect about *Beyond the Rocks* in 1922 was that two mega-stars hardly ever appeared opposite each other. The idea of Hollywood teamings came later, while most screen vehicles of the early 1920s (and before) were built around a single star attraction. Curiously, Swanson was forced by Paramount Pictures to pair up with Valentino as "punishment" for demanding greater artistic control over her films (no wonder she soon quit the studio to star in and produce her own movies).

Too bad the Swanson-Valentino combination generates so little heat. At least, what the duo lacks in sexual frisson, it makes up for in sheer star power—an odd form of chemistry, but chemistry nonetheless. The Swanson-Valentino moments are over-the-top and outdated in style, but these cinema legends demonstrate why they were worshipped all over the world. Contemporary audiences seeking more "realistic" performances will appreciate the more restrained work by some of the supporting cast, including Robert Bolder as the cuckolded husband and Alec B. Francis as Theodora's father (actually, Valentino is quite subdued and natural, nothing like his Latin lover image, in his scenes apart from Swanson).

The lavish production is adequately directed by Sam Wood (*Goodbye Mr. Chips* [1939], *Kings Row* [1941], *For Whom The Bell Tolls* [1943]), who integrates into the narrative imaginative historical flashbacks and fancy special effects in a highly skilled manner for the time. Wood, a Cecil B. DeMille disciple, is aided immeasurably by the great cinematographer Alfred Gilks (*Little Miss Marker* [1934], *Ruggles of Red Gap* [1935]). The only objections to the otherwise fine restoration work is that the sound effects are too noisy and the new score (by Dutch composer Henny Vrienten) sounds like New Age music and is overly modernist and melancholy at times.

Qualified enthusiasm greeted this 1922 film in 2005. Phil Hall in *Film Threat* wrote, "...is *Beyond the Rocks* a classic? I am not entirely certain whether it deserves that title, but I can guarantee the film is a deliriously entertaining riot of soapy melodrama, gaudy production values, and high-octane star power from its romantic leads: Gloria Swanson and Rudolph Valentino, appearing together for the first and only time." Keith Ulrich in the November 2005 *Slant Magazine* was a bit harsher: "It wouldn't be the first time that two extreme movie personalities cancelled each other out; ultimately, the best moments of *Beyond the Rocks* are those that isolate the actors within their own negative space, emphasizing silent cinema's spiritual power through gesture and close-up (Swanson projects outwards, her liveliness simultaneously repelling and attracting the audience, while Valentino draws us closer into envious contemplation—how appropriate that their characters' love revolves around a narcissus flower.) It is these intimate, isolationist sequences that offset *Beyond the Rocks*' soggy, submissive melodrama and act as a pressure-cooker undercurrent that explodes in the film's lunatic climax..." Finally, A.O. Scott's 2005 *New York Times* review summed up the consensus: "The restoration is impressive, though a new score, by the Dutch composer Henny Vrienten, has too many moments that sound both anachronistic and at odds with the emotions displayed on screens. These emotions are gratifyingly simple and emphatic, and the film, while not quite a masterpiece, is a vibrant reminder of the boldness and ingenuity of early cinema. The stars glow with mischievous, hammy life, and the sets and backdrops—rocky coastline, jagged mountains, wind-swept desert—are marvels of illusion."

While no masterwork, *Beyond the Rocks* is a terrific emblem of the early Hollywood star system and the type of creation that enchanted moviegoers in a bygone time. Like it or not, all movie buffs should cheer that the film is no longer "lost."

Eric Monder

CREDITS

Theodora Fitzgerald: Gloria Swanson
Lord Bracondale: Rudolph Valentino
Lady Bracondale: Edythe Chapman
Capt. Fitzgerald: Alec B. Francis
Morelia Winmarleigh: Gertrude Astor
Mrs. McBride: Mabel van Buren
Lady Anningford: June Elvidge
Josiah Brown: Robert Bolder

Lady Ada Fitzgerald: Helen Dunbar
Sir Patrick Fitzgerald: Raymond Blathwayt
Lady Wensleydon: F.R. Butler
Origin: USA
Language: English
Released: 1922
Production: Jesse L. Lasky; Paramount
Directed by: Sam Wood
Written by: Jack Cunningham
Cinematography by: Alfred Gilks
MPAA rating: Unrated
Running time: 81 minutes

REVIEWS

New York Times Online. October 5, 2005.

TRIVIA

A copy of this film, long considered lost, was discovered in a private collection on April 2004 in Haarlem (The Netherlands). The film was restored by the Amsterdam Film Museum and screened in the U.S. in 2005 with English dialogue screens in place of the original Dutch ones.

BOOGEYMAN

You though it was just a story...but it's real.
—Movie tagline

Box Office: $46.3 million

Boasting a boogeyman that should have stayed in the closet, this horror offering from producers Sam Raimi and Rob Tapert (who also produced the American version of the Japanese *The Grudge*) would also have been better off tucked away in some out-of-the-way wardrobe. More than doubling its budget of $20 million in box office receipts, this film merely proves the popularity of the genre far outweighs mediocre acting, flat-out bad writing and worse reviews.

The bland star of this insipid affair is Barry Watson (most notably of TV's *7th Heaven*) who plays the twenty-something Tim. Tim has been afraid of closets since as an 8-year-old (played by Aaron Murphy) he was unlucky enough to witness his father being dragged into one by, what else, the boogeyman. The ensuing 15 years of psychiatry have taught him otherwise, however, and he now believes his father merely abandoned him and was not, in fact, the victim of a fictitious, closet-dwelling monster's bloodlust. His irrational fear of closets remains, however, evident in the glass-fronted refrigerator and doorless cupboards of his apartment. When his bitchy blonde girlfriend Jessica (Tory Mussett) asks that he fetch her coat after a party, Tim gets a deer-in-the-headlights look while staring down the doorknob of the dreaded storage facility.

Raised by his Uncle Mike after his estranged mother (Lucy Lawless in a virtual cameo) had a mental breakdown, Tim is beckoned home for her funeral, coinciding with a prophetic nightmare featuring his mom. Tim meets up with his former psychologist (Robyn Malcolm) who convinces him to return to his childhood home for one night to face his demons. With his shockingly unfeeling girlfriend in tow, Tim does just that where every little noise and movement scares the bejesus out of him. He is also "visited" by a strange little girl named Franny (Skye McCole Bartusiak) who talks to Tim on the playground at night, a clear sign she is not a normal little girl who would most definitely be in bed by dark.

Tim's girlfriend becomes a victim of the closet demon early on, allowing him to better get to know the film's real female protagonist and much more suitable love interest, his old neighbor Kate (a competent Emily Deschanel). She is brunette and smart and sympathetic unlike Jessica, and the two join up to find out what happened in the house. Jessica is actually abducted by the boogeyman at a cheap motel which lays out the film's supposition that many closets are connected to an otherworldly dimension inhabited by said boogeyman and that also involves time travel. It's all a bit heavy for a humble horror flick that doesn't bother to elaborate on the amazing closet world mysteries or much else in the plot, for that matter. The mystery of who the monster is and why it chooses to victimize Tim's dad and menace Tim afterward is never addressed. When the boogeyman is finally revealed whatever mystery or suspense the movie had completely evaporates. The real mystery may be why Lawless (of TV's *Xena: Warrior Princess*) agreed to this unflattering role (she's hideously aged) other than the fact she's married to producer Tapert.

Director Stephen Kay (*Get Carter* [2000]) injects some highly Japanese-influenced style and eerie moodiness which might be enough to placate some viewers and there are suspenseful sounds and shots aplenty as Tim's navigates the creepy old house that took his father. Hard core horror fans, however, will find this mainly a no-fright zone with the film's opening scene—Tim's father tucking him in and assuring him there are no lurking monsters before getting sucked up into the closet— the film's fright highlight.

Hilary White

CREDITS

Tim: Barry Watson
Kate: Emily Deschanel
Franny: Skye McCole Bartusiak
Tim's Mother: Lucy Lawless
Uncle Mike: Philip Gordon
Young Tim: Aaron Murphy
Dr. Matheson: Robyn Malcolm
Jessica: Tory Mussett
Boogeyman: Andrew Glover
Tim's Father: Charles Mesure
Pam: Jennifer Rucker
Origin: USA
Language: English
Released: 2005
Production: Sam Raimi, Robert Tapert; Ghost House Pictures; released by Sony Pictures Entertainment
Directed by: Stephen Kay
Cinematography by: Bobby Bukowski
Music by: Joseph LoDuca
Sound: Tony Johnson
Editing: John Axelrad
Art Direction: Jennifer Ward, Nick Bassett
Costumes: Jane Holland
Production Design: Robert Gillies
MPAA rating: PG-13
Running time: 86 minutes

REVIEWS

Boxoffice Online. February, 2005.
Entertainment Weekly Online. February 9, 2005.
Los Angeles Times Online. February 7, 2005.
New York Times Online. February 5, 2005.
Premiere Magazine Online. February 10, 2005.
Variety Online. February 4, 2005.

QUOTES

Tim: "One, two, three, four, five, SIX."

BORN INTO BROTHELS: CALCUTTA'S RED LIGHT KIDS

Box Office: $3.5 million

Purportedly a documentary about the children of prostitutes in the Sonagachi red-light district of Calcutta, this film, directed by Zana Briski and Ross Kauffman, is at its best when it allows the eight children (ages vary from 10 to 14 years) to document their own lives with the point-and-shoot cameras placed into their hands in 1998 by documentary filmmaker Zana ("Aunt Zana") Briski, a former *Baltimore Sun* photojournalist, and her co-director, "Uncle" Kauffman. As such, it's a strangely divided experience for viewers. On the one hand, we are told that unless rescued, these kids are destined to become prostitutes themselves, yet we see little of that life and even less of their imminent indoctrination into it. The activities of the mothers remain (thankfully) unseen and obscure, but the indoctrination is cultural and insidious. Their leisure time consists of browbeating and insulting the children with highly graphic insults and curses. The fathers don't seem to do anything, in particular, except to lie around in drug-induced states. The kids, meanwhile, when they're not scrubbing pots and remaining discreetly behind the drapes that conceal their mothers' professional activities, are left to themselves. To be fair, we are told from the beginning that this is a world where cameras are discouraged and where lives transpire behind closed doors and drawn curtains. Thus, this is not a likely opportunity for the prying lenses of the documentarians. Despite the film's suggestive title, there are no scenes of a graphic sexual nature.

On the other hand, we watch in growing fascination as the kids take their cameras, with a minimum of instruction from Auntie Zana, to the streets. She teaches them how to shoot photographs, however, giving them encouragement and positive feedback, and she then leads them to discuss and think about what, exactly, makes a photograph successful. As the children learn how to load film, frame photographs, point and shoot, they also learn how to see their world in new ways. Avijit is the first talented one, with an industry and grasp of image surpassing his friends. Not far behind are Suchitra, a 14-year old ready to "join the line" (as the euphemism suggests), the intrepid Puja, Gour, and the others. Titles introduce each child, with accompanying montages of their photographs interspersed throughout the narrative. The images are tantalizing in their skewed angles, fleeting glimpses, happy accidents (one, in particular, reveals a hand suddenly placed against the lens to block out the image). The kids themselves are precocious in their assessments of their work. With a precociously practiced hand, they peer at the contact sheets, mark with crayons the selected images, and assess the pictorial qualities in them.

Auntie Zana intends to use these pictures to get the kids out of the ghetto and into boarding schools and becomes a formidable advocate. She's everywhere, arguing with parents, talking to school authorities, wrangling with bureaucrats. Because the kids bear the stamp of their prostitute mothers, they are marginalized and ostracized. A fascinating montage sequence documents her attempts to get the necessary paperwork done and visas completed to travel abroad so the children might take their pictures to fancy art galleries and exhibitions. Negotiating India's unwieldy bureaucracy is not at all easy. Here, amidst the teeming chaos of the streets is the gridlock of a tightly restrictive and oppressive bureaucracy but Briski is up to the challenge. Somehow she manages to get most of the photographers to their exhibitions (except Avijit, who's a tough case to handle), and, in the best scenes in the film, they delightedly confront their own images, talk to the press, and sign autographs. But their celebrity is a sometime thing. As the concluding series of titles inform us, many of the children have to go back to the ghetto, and only a few succeed in going on to school. The *Baltimore Sun* reviewer conceded that the film "acknowledges that even some of Briski's chosen few may never leave the red-light district." But the *Sun* also reported that a "precious remnant used new skills to save themselves."

Some viewers might find the film's cultural context wanting and complain that the corrupt environment seems mystifying to Western viewers. What about the boys, for instance? Nothing is said about their own future in prostitution, though they will probably, as one reviewer speculated, drift into gangsterism and the drug trade. Moreover, most of what the actual practice of prostitution involves remains obscure, and, at times, quite irrelevant. And some may protest that too much of the film belongs to Auntie Zana, who is constantly at the center of things; hers is the dominant consciousness of the process and of the film itself. We see Auntie Zana throughout and listen to her narrative voice. And we watch, perhaps skeptically, as she herds the kids around, on and off buses, to the galleries, to the schools. Why these particular kids? How did she come to find them? It seems strange that she's shocked and angered by requests to get HIV tests for the kids before they are permitted to travel. And eventually we begin to wonder just who she is, who is supporting her, where the money comes from, and how is she able to communicate her English to them. Although there must be interpreters around, they remain strangely unseen. Who is paying for them? One, therefore, suspects Auntie Zana's discussions in English to the kids may have been staged, since they could not possibly understand her.

A feature story by Sumathi Reddy that appeared in the *Baltimore Sun* on March 4, 2005 helps to answer such questions. Reddy explained that Briski first went to Calcutta for five months, then returned to Maryland to work as director of photography for *Baltimore* magazine. Two years later she then returned to Calcutta, "initially intending to document the lives of the women" who lived in the Sonagachi district, until her attention was diverted to the children instead.

The concluding section of the film takes up the story of Avijit. After a promising start as a photographer, Avijit drifts into apathy and insolence, but Auntie Zana seems determined to save him before it's too late. She secures him a trip with his photographs to the World Press Photo Foundation event in Amsterdam. Invited to serve on the Children's Jury, he understandably seems to perk up. But this mini-narrative dwindles away as quickly as it arrives. A concluding title relates the fates of the children. Apparently 12-year-old Avijit, who has a good eye and a clear talent for photography, goes back to school. In fact, the *Baltimore Sun* reported that by 2005 "all but one" of the eight children "is now involved in some type of schooling" and that their continued education will be paid for with the money that their photography earns. So what at first appears to be dismal and depressing turns positive and upbeat and hopeful tribute to the human spirit. Small wonder, then, that the Motion Picture Academy was charmed.

Rather too much of the relevant background behind Auntie Zana is left unknown in the film itself, however, and viewers wanting context may wait in vain for information about the prostitution trade in Calcutta and the awful details about how children are recruited into it. All of this notwithstanding, *Born Into Brothels* effectively testifies to the natural resilience and ebullience of the children. No innocents these, they know exactly what's going on in their world; yet, they accept it with a heartbreaking casualness. Even the abuse of their mothers is met with a stoic acceptance, as when the shy, 14-year-old Suchitra is pressured by her mother to join "the line."

Born Into Brothels was so much more than just another depressing Third World documentary about dead-end kids that it was nominated for a Best Documentary Academy Award, which it went on to win. As Ann Hornaday wrote in her *Washington Post* review, the film is "filled to bursting with ravishing images, not just those created by the children—whose work demonstrates real sophistication and artistic flair—but of the young photographers themselves," who "glow with pride and joy and hope" when told that a gallery wants to exhibit their work. "Those feelings are contagious," Hornaday noted, which made the film's postscript "—wherein viewers learn a little of what befalls these indomitable young heroes—all the more heartwarming, heartbreaking, and, finally, deeply haunting."

In general, Western reviews tended to be favorable, but in Southern Asia the documentary "was criticized as patronizing and individualistic." Baltimore reviewer Michael Sragow described Briski's distinct photographic style as follows: "She seems to regard image-making as the poetic condensation of information. After you see it, the idea that this documentary doesn't sufficiently explore its social-political context becomes laughable." *Born Into Brothels* became a serious Oscar contender in 2004 after Michael Moore withdrew his politically loaded *Fahrenheit 9/11* from consideration for Best Documentary, after deciding that his controversial documentary about the war in Iraq should either win as Best Picture or not at all. Maybe it's just as well that Moore created the opening that allowed this worthy documentary to gain the respect and recognition it deserved.

John C. Tibbetts and James M. Welsh

CREDITS

Origin: USA, India
Language: English
Released: 2004
Production: Ross Kauffman, Zana Briski
Directed by: Zana Briski, Ross Kauffman
Written by: Zana Briski, Ross Kauffman
Cinematography by: Zana Briski, Ross Kauffman
Music by: John McDowell
Sound: Dave Baruch
Editing: Ross Kauffman, Nancy Baker
MPAA rating: R
Running time: 85 minutes

REVIEWS

Baltimore Sun. March 4, 2005, p. C1, C5.
Boxoffice. December, 2004.
New York Times. December 8, 2004.
Premiere Magazine. 2004.
Variety. March 2, 2004.
Washington Post. February 18, 2005, p. C1, C5.

AWARDS

Oscars 2004: Feature Doc
Nomination:
Directors Guild 2004: Feature Doc.

BREAKFAST ON PLUTO

From the director of *The Crying Game,* Neil Jordan, comes another boy-who-would-be-girl movie, *Breakfast on Pluto.* Set mainly in the 1970s, Jordan revisits transvestites in Great Britain and the dangers of the I.R.A. found in his controversial 1992 film, whose protagonist (Stephen Rea, who also appears in this film) was a member of the radical, political group. In contrast, eternally optimistic *Pluto* protagonist, Patrick "Kitten" Braden, abhors politics, dubbing it "serious, serious, serious" as bombs, riots and violence rage around the oblivious youth. The film is told as a novel with chapters, which gets a bit tedious when it ends at 35.

The ambitious comedy/drama follows the orphaned Irish Patrick, played with zest by the pretty, androgynous Irish Cillian Murphy (*Red Eye*), on a quest to find his mother during the turbulent 1960s and 1970s in Great Britain. However, written by Jordan and Patrick McCabe based on McCabe's novel, the superficial Patrick, who is endearing due to the fact that he is always himself, is also hindered by the fact that he never grows during his and the film's journey. Add in the fantasy sequences and a sugary, period appropriate pop soundtrack that features songs like Morris Albert's "Feelings" and Bobby Goldsboro's "Honey," and you get the feel of this likeable but ingratiatingly frothy, bittersweet story.

Set in the fictional Irish town of Tryeelin, the orphaned baby Patrick is left on the steps of the rectory of Father Bernard (Liam Neeson) by his mother Eily Bergin (Eva Birthistle) who used to work for the priest. It is suggested that a liaison between the father and his mum resulted in his birth. Raised by a strict foster mother who doesn't understand him, she is horrified to find the young Patrick (played by Conor McEvoy) trying on her frocks and shoes one day, threatening to parade him through the town in disgrace. "Promise?" the cheeky, self-assured youth replies. His character retains such endearing self-assuredness despite protests from his Catholic school superiors —who strongly object to his story that he's the product of an illicit affair between Father Bernard and his pretty housekeeper—and throughout his ensuing quest for his real mother and real love. Demanding to be called "Kitten," he's not a full-time drag queen, but sometimes enhances his already somewhat feminine looks with makeup and flamboyant clothing and doesn't try in any way to hide the fact that he is a man. He's merely himself in a society that doesn't have room for his kind of individuality. Retreating into a fantasy world in his mind, he does, however, find friendship with three other social misfits: Irwin (Emmet Lawlor McHugh, and later Laurence Kinlan) Laurence (Seamus Reilly), who has Down's syndrome, and a girl named

Charlie (Bianca O'Connor, later Ruth Negga) who will all show up later in Patrick's life.

The adventures really begin for Patrick as a teenager. A group of marijuana-smoking druid mystics save him from a gang of bullies, and it is they who introduce him to the concept of magical spaceways leading to "breakfast on Pluto." Patrick's horizon's sufficiently broadened by this supernatural experience, he tours with a glam-rockabilly band singer, the macho Billy Hatchet (Gavin Friday) who falls for the teen, putting himself onstage with the other Mohawks dressed as a Indian squaw with disastrous results. Hatchet then puts his young lover up in a trailer in the remote countryside where he operates his gun-running business for the I.R.A. Completely oblivious to the inherent danger of it all, Patrick simply gets rids of the stash of weapons he finds, incurring the wrath of the I.R.A.

Patrick leaves Billy and makes his way to London in the quest to find his natural mother, whom he calls the "Phantom Lady" and whose only clue is that she resembles *South Pacific* star Mitzi Gaynor, a fact mentioned many times throughout the movie. The curly-haired youth casually prostitutes himself for money until finding legit work as a costumed character at a children's theme park and also begins working for, and sleeping with, a kindly middle-aged magician Bertie (Stephen Rea), as his assistant. The two are happy until fate unexpectedly draws Patrick another way when childhood buddy Irwin, now an I.R.A. sympathizer, shows up and Patrick willingly goes along with him.

Unfortunately in a London pub when it is bombed by the I.R.A., police suspect Patrick as the cross-dressing bomber with headlines screaming "Transvestite Terrorist!" Taken into custody and brutally interrogated for days, Patrick is released a free man. His good friend Charlie reappears, he reconciles with his real father in a touching scene, and he even meets his biological mum while posing as a telecom surveyor but doesn't tell her his real identity. Things seem to be looking up for the resilient transvestite, but he still hasn't changed a whit by the film's perfunctory semi-happy ending.

There are several reasons to enjoy the film. The film is gorgeously lensed by Declan Quinn with top notch production design and the script is laced with black Irish wit. Bryan Ferry appears briefly. And the fantasy sequences, especially Patrick's spy fantasy featuring Chanel No. 5, are certainly highlights. The "talking" robins whose comments appear in subtitle quoting Oscar Wilde, are not. Garnering numerous comparisons to a modern-day *Candide*, Murphy's sunny-at-all-costs Patrick looks good in a dress and has a certain je ne sais quoi. Patrick is, nonetheless, a candle in the wind, going whichever way life pulls him and giving us little reason to care.

Hilary White

CREDITS

Patrick "Kitten" Braden: Cillian Murphy
Father Bernard: Liam Neeson
Bertie: Stephen Rea
John Joe: Brendan Gleeson
Ely Bergin: Eva Birthistle
Mosher: Liam Cunningham
Mr. Silky String: Bryan Ferry
Billy Hatchet: Gavin Friday
PC Wallis: Ian Hart
Irwin: Laurence Kinlan
Ma Braden: Ruth McCabe
Inspector Routledge: Steven Waddington
Charlie: Ruth Negga
Patrick: Conor McEvoy
Laurence: Seamus Reilly
Elly's Boy: Sid Young
Origin: Ireland, Great Britain
Language: English
Released: 2005
Production: Alan Moloney, Neil Jordan, Stephen Wooley; Pathe Pictures, Bord Scannan na hEireann, Parallel Films, Number 9 Films; released by Sony Pictures Classics
Directed by: Neil Jordan
Written by: Neil Jordan, Patrick McCabe
Cinematography by: Declan Quinn
Sound: Brendan Deasy
Editing: Tony Lawson
Costumes: Eimer Ni Mhaoldomhnaigh
Production Design: Tom Conroy
MPAA rating: R
Running time: 135 minutes

REVIEWS

Boxoffice Online. December, 2005.
Chicago Sun-Times Online. December 23, 2005.
Entertainment Weekly Online. November 16, 2005.
Los Angeles Times Online. December 2, 2005.
New York Times Online. November 16, 2005.
Premiere Magazine Online. November 18, 2005.
Variety Online. September 4, 2005.
Washington Post Online. December 23, 2005, p. C05.

QUOTES

Patrick "Kitten" Braden: "If I wasn't a transvestite terrorist, would you marry me?"

BRIDE AND PREJUDICE

Bollywood meets Hollywood...and it's a perfect match.
—Movie tagline

Box Office: $6.6 million

In her bold Bollywoodish comedy-musical *Bride and Prejudice,* globally rooted Indian expatriate filmmaker Gurinder Chadha brings to life a little known facet of a film culture that only recently has managed to capture world attention. For all its indiscriminate espousal of western motifs, Bollywood (Bombay-based Hollywood) remains bound to codes of dramatic representation that go back centuries. These dictates prescribe that the aim of all forms of drama is to create 'mysterious delight' for the audience through song, dance and women (read nymphs). Thus, on one level, Chadha's film, despite the inspiration it draws from the Jane Austen classic, has to be excused its slight narrative content in the light of its melodic departures from it.

Starting with *Bhaji on the Beach* (1993) and continuing through *What's Cooking?* (reviewed in the 2001 volume) and *Bend It Like Beckham* (reviewed in the 2003 volume), Chadha has shown herself to be acutely conscious of social prejudice made more painful within a domestic setting. Here the eponymous prejudice becomes the stuff of elite chatter and nothing more. Consequently, the powerful social realism of her earlier efforts is missing, along with the emotional melodramatic quotient integral to every traditional Bollywood film. Thus, for all her honest intentions, Chadha's departure from her filmic home turf cannot but appear vacuous mindless entertainment. Even so, she deserves to be commended for allowing the 'real artificiality' of Bollywood full rein, unlike Canadian expatriate Deepa Mehta's *Bollywood Hollywood* (2002), which was content to merely mock it.

Things get off to a spirited start as the Indian yuppie Balraj (Naveen Andrews), his American counterpart, Darcy (Martin Henderson) and Kiran (Indira Verma), Balraj's sister, fly in from London into the holy city of Amritsar in North India for the wedding of Balraj's friend. As the festivities get under way, Balraj is besotted by Jaya (Namrata Shirodkar), the eldest of four sisters (read nymphs) awaiting marriage prospects. Allowing his machismo to blend with the local fervor, Balraj leads the males in the customary dancing. In so doing, he advances his own prospects in Jaya's eyes. Darcy, though smitten by Lalita (Aishwarya Rai), the beautiful of the sisters and the smartest one around for miles, keeps his attraction under control. The two younger sisters, the dancer Maya (Meghna Kothari) and the sexy Lakhi (Peeya Rai Chowdhary) are shunted into the background.

Before the first complication can strike this bountiful upper crust world, Chadha regales her audience with a lavish resplendent production number by which she evokes the classic Hollywood musical of *Brigadoon* (1954) vintage. As the girls are shopping with the bride-to-be, an entire arcade bursts into song, offering them everything from sweets to jewelry. By collectivising the air of prosperity, Chadha is cleverly tapping into the newfound affluence of the Indian upper middle class, brought about not just through channels of trade with the west but through hi-tech outsourcing.

Persuaded by Darcy to keep his head on his shoulders, in the light of the fact that both have to return to their busy lifestyle, Darcy lets his passion cool. What comes in between Darcy and Lalita hitting it off is the latter's smarts by which she defends the economic backwardness of her country with such retorts as "What was America like after 60 years of independence?" At first her cold response to Darcy's overtures appears a ploy in her coquettishness, but then we see her start taking herself seriously, perhaps too seriously to be convincing.

Wisely, the film whisks everyone off to Goa, on India's western coast, where Darcy is thinking of buying a hotel. However, this brief jaunt distances Lalita even further from Darcy owing to the arrival literally out of nowhere of John (Daniel Gillies), a childhood friend of Darcy's, now turned beachcomber, who clambers out of the Arabian Sea. Amidst the picturesque settings and beach frolic, John tells Lalita that plans are in place for an arranged marriage that Darcy's mother has in mind for him when he returns to America. Lalita now begins to see Darcy, who has been spouting progressive notions, as a "hypocrite."

When everyone returns to Amritsar things worsen for the girls. Now the assault takes the form of the sycophant Kohli (Nitin Chandra Ganatra), a recently turned millionaire from Los Angeles who has come looking for a wife. His credo, "No Life Without Wife," provides the excuse for a smashing musical number in which the girls mock all that he represents. Kohli on his part eyes Jaya but is then prepared to settle for Lalita, who also spurns him.

This is where the film's storyline becomes sloppy. Balraj and Darcy, whom we have been led to believe as being amongst the main characters, are now relegated to the status of background extras. They soon return to London for business reasons. Lalita's spirits rise when John comes to visit, but she has to share him with Lakhi before he too has to hit the pilgrim trail. For all practical (read marital) purposes, the girls are back at square one.

A pleasant twist then ensues as Kohli finds a fiancée in Chandra (Sonali Kulkarni), a friend of Lalita's. He then invites Lalita and her family to L.A. for the wedding. In the west, Lalita falls in love all over again with Darcy (to the lilting strains of a Bollywood-style chase-around-the-trees musical number). She then falls out of love when she learns that he was responsible for persuading Balraj not to marry Jaya. Eventually Darcy apologizes and Balraj decides to wed his love at first sight. The only dilemma that looms at this stage is to get Lakhi out of the clutches of John, whom Darcy exposes as "a nasty piece of work". After a chase through London, Darcy and John fight it out in front of a theater screen showing a Bollywood movie.

The film ends with a bang-up wedding celebration in Amritsar as Balraj weds Jaya and Darcy weds Lalita, each couple atop a decorated elephant, a symbol affirming the triumph of Indian tradition over the racy glamour of the west.

Vivek Adarkar

CREDITS

Lalita Bakshi: Aishwarya Rai
Will Darcy: Martin Henderson
Mr. Bakshi: Anupam Kher
Raj: Naveen Andrews
Johnny Wickham: Daniel Gillies
Miss Bingley: Indira Varma
Willi's mother: Marsha Mason
Mrs. Bakshi: Nadira Babbar
Jaya Bakshi: Namrala Shirodkar
Maya Bakshi: Meghnaa
Lucky Bakshi: Peeya Rai Choudhuri
Origin: USA
Language: English
Released: 2004
Production: Deepak Nayar, Gurinder Chadha; Nayar Chadha; released by Miramax, Pathe
Directed by: Gurinder Chadha
Written by: Gurinder Chadha, Paul Mayeda Berges
Cinematography by: Santosh Sivan
Sound: John Hayes
Editing: Justin Krish
Art Direction: Mark Scruton, Nitish Roy
Costumes: Ralph Holes, Eduardo Castro
Production Design: Nick Ellis
MPAA rating: PG-13
Running time: 110 minutes

REVIEWS

Boxoffice Online. February, 2005.
Chicago Sun-Times Online. February 11, 2005.
Entertainment Weekly Online. February 9, 2005.
Los Angeles Times Online. February 11, 2005.
New York Times Online. February 11, 2005.
Premiere Magazine Online. February 10, 2005.
Variety Online. October 6, 2004.
Washington Post Online. February 11, 2005, p. WE44.

QUOTES

Lalita Bakshi: "You should be stirring your husband's dinner not trouble."

TRIVIA

Dubbed "The Queen of Bollywood" and Miss World of 1994, this is Aishwarya Rai's (Lalita) first movie entirely in English.

THE BRIDGE OF SAN LUIS REY

Five Lives Bound By One Fate.
—Movie tagline

The greatest legacy that *The Bridge of San Luis Rey* may well leave upon the movie world is the nearly universal reaction it is bound to illicit from patrons seeing it on a video store shelf. A look at the box reveals that it is based upon the acclaimed Pulitzer prize-winning Thornton Wilder novel and stars Robert De Niro, Kathy Bates, Gabriel Byrne, Geraldine Chaplin, F. Murray Abraham and Harvey Keitel. You can almost hear the collective response. How can it be that a film with such an illustrious cast got so little attention? Was it a case of poor marketing, or does the film deserve its obscurity? Unfortunately, it is the latter case. On RottenTomatoes.com, a Web site that compiles critical reviews, one lone reviewer gave it a positive rating.

Where did it go wrong? It is probably not the story since it had already been successfully filmed two previous times. The 1927 novel was made into an Oscar-winning silent film in 1929 and again in 1944. And it is not the costume and set design which was overseen by production designer was Gil Parrondo. Eighteenth-century Peru, or at least the 2005 interpretation of it, is recreated in fine fashion up there on the screen. The elaborate, curly wigs for the men, the dandyish clothes and the period furniture are recreated in loving detail. Perhaps watched with the sound off, *The Bridge of San Luis Rey*, might be a more enjoyable film.

The movie focuses on the Inquisition of Brother Juniper (Byrne), a Franciscan monk who studied the collapse of the bridge of San Luis Rey that killed five people. He had been walking behind the five ill-fated folks and could have easily been one of the victims. Was he spared by the grace of God or was it just happenstance? He takes it upon himself to investigate the question scientifically, and spends years interviewing those who knew the victims, looking for some sort of connection. His book detailing his findings has been deemed heretical by the Archbishop of Lima (De Niro).

In flashbacks, very slow and plodding flashbacks, we learn about the Marquesa (Bates), a wealthy woman who pines for her daughter, Dona Clara (Emilie Dequenne). The daughter has moved across the sea to Spain and never answers her mother's voluminous letters. Uncle Pio (Keitel) is a theater owner who has raised a great and vain actress La Perichole (Pilar Lopez de Ayala). La Perichole is having an affair with the viceroy of Peru (Abraham), though she does not love him. With so much time in the film when so little is happening, it seems that other seemingly important characters could have been more developed. Surely Pepita (Adrianna Dominguez), a nun sent by the Abbess (Chaplin) to work for the Marquesa, must have a more interesting story that simply wanting to return to the convent, but it is not apparent here. The same goes for the mysterious twin brothers, Manuel and Esteban (Mark and Michael Polish), who share a secret language.

The film could have been a lot more interesting. It has suspense, history and interesting philosophical questions, but the plodding direction, miscast actors and difficult-to-follow screenplay quickly negate anything good about the film. The fault must lie mostly on the shoulders of Mary McGuckian who wrote and directed the film. Perhaps she was cowed by her illustrious cast and unable to give them any constructive direction. This might explain why none of the cast bothers speaking with an accent though they are supposed to be denizens of 18th century Peru. (Oddly, De Niro accents a few words like "Luis" which somehow makes it all worse.) De Niro is especially bad and seems like he was transported straight from a gangster movie and had no time to adjust to his new character.

Put plainly, critics were bored out of their gourds. Stephen Holden of *The New York Times* wrote, "Dragged down by a stuffy screenplay clotted with generic period oratory, overdressed to the point that the actors seem physically impeded by their ornate costumes, and hopelessly muddled in its storytelling, the movie is edited with a haphazardness that leaves many dots unconnected." Philip Wuntch of *The Dallas Morning News* gave the film a C- grade and wrote, "Viewers will give thanks that there weren't more casualties with stories to be told. Unlike the bridge, the movie unravels at a very slow pace." Jack Matthews of *The New York Daily News* wrote, "...so dully written and executed that you'll be wishing the production had collapsed instead of the swaying bridge of San Luis Rey." And Desson Thomson of *The Washington Post* was also stirred to thoughts of death, writing, "After watching this movie...I was moved only to find my own bridge to leap from." And that one positive review was from Liz Braun of *The Toronto Sun* who wrote, "It is an intense philosophical undertaking that examines questions of faith, fate and chance."

Jill Hamilton

CREDITS

Archbishop of Lima: Robert De Niro
Viceroy: F. Murray Abraham
Dona Maria: Kathy Bates
Brother Juniper: Gabriel Byrne
Abbess: Geraldine Chaplin
Dona Clara: Emilie Dequenne
Pepita: Adriana Dominguez
Uncle Pio: Harvey Keitel
La Perichola: Pilar Lopez de Ayala
Captain Alvarado: John Lynch
Manuel: Mark Polish
Esteban: Michael Polish
Origin: Spain, Great Britain, France
Language: English
Released: 2005
Production: Samuel Hadida, Michael Cowan, Denis O'Dell; Spice Factory, Kanzaman, Davis Films
Directed by: Mary McGuckian
Cinematography by: Javier Aguirresarobe
Music by: Lalo Schifrin
Sound: Peter Glossop
Editing: Sylvie Landra
Costumes: Yvonne Blake
MPAA rating: PG
Running time: 120 minutes

REVIEWS

New York Times Online. June 10, 2005.
Variety Online. January 11, 2005.
Washington Post Online. June 9, 2005, p. WE38.

BROKEBACK MOUNTAIN

Love is a Force of Nature.
—Movie tagline

Box Office: $10.2 million

Prior to its release, *Brokeback Mountain* received considerable publicity as "the gay cowboy movie." With almost unanimous critical acclaim, it has transcended this misleading label by revealing itself as a compelling look at loss and unfulfilled lives. *Brokeback Mountain* also has similarities to previous films from director Ang Lee and screenwriter Larry McMurtry, working here with frequent collaborator Diana Ossana.

In 1963 Wyoming, the taciturn Ennis Del Mar (Heath Ledger) and the slightly more outgoing Jack Twist (Jake Gyllenhaal) tend a flock of one-thousand sheep belonging to Joe Aguirre (Randy Quaid). After several weeks on Brokeback Mountain, the pair, because of freezing temperatures, violate Aguirre's orders and share a tent. Before they quite know what is happening, they engage in sexual intercourse.

Both Ennis and Jack swear they are not "queer." Ennis has a fiancée waiting for him down below. Yet they continue having sex. When Aguirre summons them to leave camp a month early, the tormented Ennis takes out his frustrations, not for the last time, by punching Jack, who returns to his home in Texas. Four years later, they are reunited and continue their affair on "fishing trips" over almost two decades. Ennis's wife, Alma (Michelle Williams), is confused after seeing the two men kissing, while Jack's wife, Lureen (Anne Hathaway), remains oblivious to the relationship and her husband's true nature.

Brokeback Mountain ends with considerable sadness. While many films, notably the vile *Terms of Endearment* (1983), adapted by McMurtry from his novel, use a character's death as cheap emotional shorthand, *Brokeback Mountain* does not. Though the film explores the complex nature of homosexuality in a time and place hostile to gays, it also deals with such universal themes as the failure to be an individual, to live one's life on one's own terms. The death of one of the characters brings such themes into sharp focus.

Such themes are not so obvious to some. In a year full of politically controversial films such as *Munich* and *Syriana, Brokeback Mountain* has been criticized by conservative commentators and groups as pro-gay propaganda. Reviewers and other components of the entertainment media have been attacked for attempting to force their social views on an unwilling populace. After originally rating the film L (limited adult audience), the United States Conference of Catholics Bishops reclassified it as O (morally offensive) following complaints from pro-family organizations. Ironically, no one seems to object to Neil Jordan's thoroughly delightful and shamefully neglected *Breakfast on Pluto* (2005), whose gay protagonist never questions his sexual identity.

Wags have called *Brokeback Mountain* the gay *Gone with the Wind* (1939). While they intend to suggest that it is the first great Hollywood film with a homosexual theme, they diminish it by comparing it to the campy, though immensely popular, historical pageant that is Scarlett O'Hara. Some reviewers compared *Brokeback Mountain* to George Stevens' *Giant* (1956), another lumbering, overblown soap opera. The closest "classic" film to *Brokeback Mountain* may be *Casablanca* (1942), with its themes of miscommunication and lost love.

Brokeback Mountain is based upon a short story by E. Annie Proulx published in *The New Yorker* a year before the 1997 hate-crime murder of Matthew Shepard in Wyoming, but it has some similarities to films adapted by McMurtry from his novels: *Hud* (1963), *The Last Picture Show* (1971), and *Terms of Endearment.* The latter has, in addition to a supposedly poignant death, a difficult love, between mother and daughter, examined over several years. *Hud* has a similar background, set on a Texas cattle ranch, but its hero is being condemned by a conservative community for daring to be an individual, though of the heartless bastard variety. *Brokeback Mountain* most resembles *The Last Picture Show* with its look at the conventionality of small-town Texas morality in the 1950's. The stifled, dead-end lives of its protagonists are close to those of Ennis, Jack, and their wives. Then there is the Western television miniseries *Lonesome Dove* (1989), again adapted by McMurtry from his novel, with its contrasting garrulous and laconic heroes. Some have referred to *Brokeback Mountain* as "Lonesome Love."

Few reviewers have pointed out that Lee's second film, *The Wedding Banquet* (1993), also has a homosexual theme, though one decidedly more lighthearted than *Brokeback Mountain.* A gay Manhattan landlord from Taiwan, under pressure from his parents, marries a Chinese tenant so she can obtain her green card. Neither have the thematic and stylistic similarities between *Brokeback Mountain* and Lee's biggest success, *Crouching Tiger, Hidden Dragon* (2000), been much explored. That film presents two pairs of ill-fated lovers and a constantly reiterated theme of being true to one's destiny. The lovers played by Ziyi Zhang and Chen Chang fight and love, just like Ennis and Jack. The romantic interlude in the Mongolian desert has shots of majestic scenery much like the mountain sequences in *Brokeback Mountain,* beautifully photographed by Rodrigo Prieto. Lee has also directed a more traditional Western, the Civil War era *Ride with the Devil* (1999).

Lee rebounds from the ignominious failure of *The Hulk* (2003) to make one of his best films. As with *Eat Drink Man Woman* (1994), *Sense and Sensibility* (1995), and *Crouching Tiger, Hidden Dragon,* Lee shows he is a master at framing shots, pacing a film, and understanding the dynamics within a small group of people. The film builds slowly to the protagonists' first embrace, establishing the characters and their boredom with their job. When they finally make love, the action makes dramatic sense, and Lee shoots the scene as less an act of passion than of desperation, the need to make contact with another human being. Ennis has mentioned his fiancée, but she remains unseen until the wedding ceremony, which begins with a close-up of the extremely uncomfortable groom, to accentuate his emotional isolation, before the camera pulls back to reveal the rest of the wedding party. Alma's response to seeing her husband embracing Jack is staged to make the audience sympathetic to her situation.

Brokeback Mountain is not without flaws. Unlike Alma, Lureen is presented unsympathetically, especially as she ages from a young beauty to a tired middle-aged woman in a frightful dyed-blonde bouffant. This hairstyle seems anachronistic for the 1980's, but Lee may be suggesting that these characters are trapped in the past emotionally. Lureen's pompous father (Graham Beckel) is another cliché, and the film comes close at times to the kind of condescension to the characters that keeps *The Last Picture Show* from being the masterpiece some see it as. On the other hand, Cassie, the young woman (Linda Cardellini) who pursues Ennis after his divorce, appears to be the kind of bimbo men pick up in bars, but she turns out to have more substance and understanding.

As always, Lee excels at directing his cast. Williams handles Alma's confusion with subtlety, showing frustration slowly build until it explodes in a confrontation with Ennis after their divorce. As Jack's parents, Roberta Maxwell and Peter McRobbie economically convey a one-sided relationship in which the wife never gets to speak her piece. While Gyllenhaal's too-sensitive, sad-puppy look can be a limitation in other roles, it fits Jack perfectly, and Gyllenhaal is given several opportunities to show his range, as when Jack stands up to his bullying father-in-law.

Lee selected Ledger after seeing his performance as Billy Bob Thornton's suicidal son in *Monster's Ball* (2001). That role is similar to Ennis because both men are unable to articulate complex emotions. Ennis resembles the laconic Western heroes played by Gary Cooper and Randolph Scott who let their actions speak for them. But Ennis is not this kind of cowboy, with no chance to shoot it out with outlaws or gunslingers to resolve his conflicts. Ennis rejects Jack's plea to share a ranch because a neighbor who lived with another man was tortured and killed when he was a boy. Through keeping his jaw tense and his eyes cast down, Ledger creates a memorable character, a coiled spring of emotions, who can find no way out of his dilemma. With minor adjustments, Ledger makes Ennis slightly different in his interactions with Jack, Alma, Cassie, and his eldest daughter (Kate Mara). It is a masterful performance without which the film could not succeed.

Michael Adams

CREDITS

Ennis Del Mar: Heath Ledger
Jack Twist: Jake Gyllenhaal
Cassie: Linda Cardellini
Lashawn Malone: Anna Faris
Lureen Newsome: Anne Hathaway
Alma: Michelle Williams
Joe Aguirre: Randy Quaid
L.B. Newsome: Graham Beckel
Monroe: Scott Michael Campbell
Alma Jr., age 19: Kate Mara
Jack's Mother: Roberta Maxwell
John Twist: Peter McRobbie
Randall Malone: David Harbour
Origin: USA
Language: English
Released: 2005
Production: Diana Ossana, James Schamus; released by Focus Features, River Road Productions
Directed by: Ang Lee
Written by: Larry McMurtry, Diana Ossana
Cinematography by: Rodrigo Prieto
Music by: Gustavo Santaolalla
Sound: Drew Kunin
Music Supervisor: Kathy Nelson
Editing: Geraldine Peroni, Dylan Tichenor
Art Direction: Laura Ballinger, Tracey Baryski
Costumes: Marit Allen
Production Design: Judy Becker
MPAA rating: R
Running time: 134 minutes

REVIEWS

Boxoffice Online. December, 2005.
Chicago Sun-Times Online. December 16, 2005.
Entertainment Weekly Online. November 30, 2005.
Los Angeles Times Online. December 9, 2005.
New York Times Online. December 9, 2005.
Premiere Magazine Online. December 9, 2005.
Variety Online. September 3, 2005.
Washington Post Online. December 16, 2005, p. C01.

QUOTES

Ennis Del Mar: "Bottom line is...we're around each other an'...this thing, it grabs hold of us again...at the wrong place...at the wrong time...and we're dead."

TRIVIA

Playing in only five US theaters during its first weekend of release, the film set a record for the highest per-screen gross of any non-animated movie in history.

AWARDS

Oscars 2005: Adapt. Screenplay, Director (Lee), Orig. Score

British Acad. 2005: Adapt. Screenplay, Film, Support. Actor (Gyllenhaal)

Directors Guild 2005: Director (Lee)

Golden Globes 2006: Director (Lee), Film—Drama, Screenplay, Song ("A Love That Will Never Grow Old")

Ind. Spirit 2006: Director (Lee), Film

L.A. Film Critics 2005: Director (Lee), Film

Natl. Bd. of Review 2005: Director (Lee), Support. Actor (Gyllenhaal)

N.Y. Film Critics 2005: Actor (Ledger), Director (Lee), Film

Writers Guild 2005: Adapt. Screenplay

Nomination:

Oscars 2005: Actor (Ledger), Cinematog., Film, Support. Actor (Gyllenhaal), Support. Actress (Williams)

British Acad. 2005: Actor (Ledger), Cinematog., Film Editing, Support. Actress (Williams)

Golden Globes 2006: Actor—Drama (Ledger), Support. Actress (Williams), Orig. Score

Ind. Spirit 2006: Actor (Ledger), Support. Actress (Williams)

Screen Actors Guild 2005: Actor (Ledger), Support. Actor (Gyllenhaal), Support. Actress (Williams), Cast.

BROKEN FLOWERS

Sometimes life brings some strange surprises.
—Movie tagline

Box Office: $13.7 million

Bill Murray plays the ironically named Don Johnston, an "over-the-hill Don Juan" who reluctantly embarks on a journey to find out which of his old flames may have sent him an anonymous letter saying he fathered a child twenty years ago. The combination of quirky, avante garde director Jim Jarmusch—a specialist in portraying outsiders—and quirky, avante garde Murray—a specialist in playing them—should result in a more compelling cinematic experience than this somewhat staid, laconic affair. Here, Murray's likeable languor—so familiar and eminently watchable in films like *Rushmore, Lost in Translation* and *The Royal Tenenbaums*—begins to border on depression and despite the obvious references to his womanizing ways, it barely seems possible coming from a practically immobile introvert who sits on his plastic-covered sofa staring at a TV that is turned off. Despite some genuinely tender and funny moments, Don begins his journey reluctantly and ends it the same way, seemingly unchanged by the film's intentionally ambiguous and wholly unsatisfying conclusion. A study in regret, the camera languishes on Murray's wizened, wistful face for far too long and far too often, trying to wring the movie's meaning from those shots alone. It's too big a job, even for Murray, to carry the weight of a film on his face.

A former computer mogul, Don lives with his current girlfriend Sherry, played by Julie Delpy, who is in the process of leaving him as the film begins. "I'm like your mistress, except you're not even married" she complains as he not even half-heartedly tries to get her to stay. Clearly Don has commitment issues—evidenced in more detail during his journey—peppered with a healthy dose of regret. It seems he would like to care, but just can't seem to muster the enthusiasm. Before exiting with her suitcases, she hands him a pink envelope addressed to him that he promptly ignores until his Ethiopian neighbor Winston (Jeffrey Wright) discovers it and the mystery begins. Adding Winston to the mix, Jarmusch returns to films like his *Down by Law* and *A Stranger in Paradise* where it takes an enthusiastic foreigner that truly appreciates American culture to show the restless American native what really matters in life.

The note tells Don he fathered a child nearly twenty years ago and that his son may now be trying to find him. Somewhat of an amateur sleuth, Winston begins by analyzing the fuzzy postmark and the type—which he believes was done on an old-fashioned typewriter rather than a computer. He persuades Don to give him a list of all his old girlfriends from that period in his life which comes down to roughly five candidates. Although Winston has three jobs, five children (Jarry Fall, Korka Fall, Saul Holland, Zakira Holland and Niles Lee Wilson) and wife Mona (Heather Alicia Simms) to support, he still manages time to book the trip for Don where his will visit his five-exes looking for clues. Look for anything pink, Winston commands, and a typewriter. And, most importantly, bring them pink flowers to gauge their reaction, he specifies.

The journey starts pleasantly enough with ex number one: Laura (Sharon Stone) who is very happy to see Don, as evidenced later when he spends the night with her. Laura is a NASCAR widow whose husband died in a blaze of glory on the track. Her daughter Lolita (Alexis Dziena) lives up to her literary name by promptly trying to seduce Don from the moment he walks through the door—prancing around naked and offering him her Popsicle. And a glimpse of her pink Swarovski crystal-embellished cell phone provides an enticing clue. Definitely the most amusing of the ex-girlfriend vignettes, Stone provides just the right amount of warmth and humor (she has no idea why Don is amused at her daughter's name nor does Lolita, for that matter) in a refreshing turn.

Don's not so lucky in a visit with his next ex, Dora (Frances Conroy) , a flower child turned suburban matron married to a prefab mansion mogul Ron (Christopher McDonald) and living in a "prime example." This meeting with Dora is painful, for both of them. She seems unhappy with her structured life and all-business husband and Don seems to feel for her too. "Did I give you that necklace?" he inquires of the pearl strand she's wearing. Dora: "No." Don: "I should have." Dinner with Dora and Ron is an especially strained affair and despite a plethora of pink in the house, Don quickly rules out Dora as a candidate, as he finds out she is unable to have children after an awkward exchange over the meal.

His exes getting increasingly hostile as he continues his journey, he then meets with Carmen (Jessica Lange), an "animal communicator" who is extremely busy and extremely reluctant to see Don as is her surly, protective assistant (Chloe Sevigny). She agrees to a few minutes with him between "clients," just long enough to be understandably suspicious of his visit and inform him she's not the mother of his love child. By the time Don gets to his last living ex (the fifth has died at the journey's start), things are really looking grim: tight-lipped and angry Penny (Tilda Swinton) lives out in the country in a dilapidated house surround by menacing men and motorcycles. As Don asks to see her, her Hell's Angel-type boyfriend instead beats Don up and throws him out, landing near a pink typewriter that is part of the odds and ends strewn around the grounds. Only the gravesite of his final ex is a more grim experience, despite a minor flirtation with the sympathetic Sun Green (Pell James) who sells him the flowers he lays there.

There are some funny and touching moments, especially those with Winston. When he sneaks outside with Don to smoke a cigarette and his daughter catches him saying "Daddy, you're not supposed to be smoking," Winston retorts slyly, "Oh, no, no. This is just some assorted herbs. Some cheeba." Don humorously backs him up with "Yep, it's just cannabis sativa." Winston also burns a CD for Don for some background music for the trip, which becomes the film's soundtrack as well featuring great tunes from Ethiopian jazz musician Mulatu Astatke. Other tracks include ballads from The Greenhornes, featuring British songstress Holly Golightly, both which complement the subtle rhythms of Don's journey.

In addition to his five exes (the broken flowers of the title?), everything in Don's life seems broken—in sharp contrast to his neighbor Winston who has a rich full life complete with a loving, caring wife. Perhaps a story about Winston would have been the more fulfilling one as it is hard to get excited or care about Don whose thin connection to life seems just as narrow at the film's end. At any rate, the contrast between the two men is the most interesting and seems like the most fun. Although some of the interactions with the women in his past are interesting, they are far too brief to invest any real emotion in.

Nearing the end of his journey, Don has one more chance at redemption when he encounters a vagabond kid with a backpack who looks like he's on a quest of some sort. He buys the kid a sandwich, and one for himself, and gives the kid a bit of "fatherly" advice. All seems to be going well, until Don strongly insinuates he's the kid's father which sends the youth tearing away from the odd, obviously delusional stranger. Any chance Don had of redemption has died as the kid ridicules him in his departure leaving Don just as broken as he was at the start.

Hilary White

CREDITS

Don Johnston: Bill Murray
Winston: Jeffrey Wright
Laura: Sharon Stone
Dora: Frances Conroy
Carmen: Jessica Lange
Penny: Tilda Swinton
Sherry: Julie Delpy
The Kid: Mark Webber
Carmen's assistant: Chloe Sevigny
Ron: Christopher McDonald
Lolita: Alexis Dziena
Will: Larry Fessenden
Dan: Chris Bauer
Sun Green: Pell James
Mona: Heather Alicia Simms
Rita: Brea Frazier
Origin: USA, France
Language: English
Released: 2005
Production: Jon Kilik, Stacey Smith; Five Roses; released by Focus Features
Directed by: Jim Jarmusch
Written by: Jim Jarmusch
Cinematography by: Frederick Elmes
Sound: Drew Kunin
Editing: Jay Rabinowitz
Art Direction: Sarah Frank
Costumes: John Dunn

Production Design: Mark Friedberg
MPAA rating: R
Running time: 105 minutes

REVIEWS

Boxoffice Online. August, 2005.
Chicago Sun-Times Online. August 5, 2005.
Entertainment Weekly Online. August 3, 2005.
Los Angeles Times Online. August 5, 2005.
New York Times Online. August 5, 2005.
Premiere Magazine Online. August 5, 2005.
Variety Online. May 17, 2005.
Washington Post Online. August 5, 2005, p. WE30.

QUOTES

Sherry: "I'm like your mistress, except you're not even married."

TRIVIA

Jim Jarmusch, who reportedly finished the script in two and a half weeks, said he wrote the role exclusively for Bill Murray.

BROTHERS

(Brodre)

Worthy of its win for the Audience Award for World Dramatic Cinema at the Sundance Film Festival, Danish filmmaker Susanne Bier and writer Anders Thomas' intense psychological drama involving the shifting fates of two brothers also snagged a slew of nominations at Denmark's Bodil Awards and a Best Actress Award there for star Connie Nielsen. Bier and Thomas, who first collaborated on the equally dramatic Dogme feature *Open Hearts* (2002), have captured in *Brothers* (a.k.a. *Brodre*) the powerful emotions involved in the tragedy of a soldier and his family after he is sent to Afghanistan.

Reportedly requesting that the actors use very little makeup, Biers is intent on capturing raw feeling, evident in the frequent use of extreme close-ups. She also uses quite a bit of cross-cutting to show the parallels in the lives of the main characters but, true to her Dogme roots, which favors natural settings and light, stays away from too much filmic gimmickry to let the faces tell the story. And it is a powerful story, at that.

Michael (Ulrich Thomsen) is a major in the Danish arm of the United Nations forces being sent on a mission to Afghanistan. Michael is also a doting husband to the beautiful Sarah (a luminous Nielsen) and father of two girls, the older, sassier brunette Natalia (Sarah Juel Werner) and angelic, blond little Camilla (Rebecca Logstrup). He is the pride of his family, favored by his parents Henning and Else (Bent Mejding and Solbjorg Hojfeldt, respectively) over his younger brother Jannik (Nikolaj Lie Kaas), an out-of-work alcoholic recently released from prison for bank robbery.

A proud soldier, Michael tells the lesser-ranking soldiers to believe in their mission overseas, as he obviously does, and once in Afghanistan is given the task of rescuing a helpless radar operator captured after an assault. Biers cross-cuts from his ride in the jeep to Sarah riding a downtown bus, he, surrounded by armed soldiers in turrets, she, surrounded by children at school. Michael and his troops board a helicopter which is abruptly shot down over the water followed by a dramatic explosion and plume of black smoke. Crosscut to Sarah in the calm water of her bath interrupted by soldiers at the door who wordlessly communicate Michael was killed which is evident by the grief on Sarah's face. A drunken Jannik, who has borrowed Michael's car, shows up at the door unaware of his brother's fate and who retreats to the comfort of his parents house where he consoles his grieving mother and father.

The funeral is a perfunctory affair punctuated by a fight afterward between Jannik and his angry father who lost his favorite son and is now left with the neer-do-well youngest. It is also after the funeral that Sarah prophetically remarks that she can't quite believe Michael is dead because she would feel it deep down and she doesn't. With good cause, apparently, because we then see Michael face-down in a bloody heap captured by foreign guerilla soldiers. He is thrown in a makeshift cell with the very soldier he was sent to save—the radar operator Niels Peter (Paw Henriksen). The much stronger and adept solider, Michael buoys the frightened boy's hopes, promising him they will make it out of there alive so that Niels can see his wife and infant son.

Fate has a cruel blow in store for Michael, however. Proving to the guerillas that he can be useful to them, demonstrating how a stolen weapon worked, they discover Niels is useless and order Michael to kill him in order to stay alive himself. A gritty scene shows a heavily conflicted Michael, forced at gunpoint, to bludgeon the young soldier to death in order that he himself could return home to his own family.

In the time Michael has spent as a captive, Sarah and the girls have begun to come to terms with Michael's "death" with the unexpected help of Jannik. At his father's urging, Jannik makes himself useful and bringing in a few carpenters, helps finish the family's near unusable kitchen. Jannik begins to clean up his act, bonding with the children who appreciate his light-hearted ways in their time of grief. Sarah and Jannik bond over the loss of Michael as well, whom they both loved, and share a clandestine kiss which they both regret.

When Michael is rescued by British soldiers, he denies seeing Niels Peter at the camp when queried about other captives. After a phone call where Sarah learns of his imminent return, Michael is met at the airport by his ecstatic family. They all notice him acting strangely, however, but he won't refuses to tell Sarah what really happened there. Later, out of guilt, he informs his sympathetic superior he did, in fact, see Niels at the camp but falls short of admitting anything else. He even visits Niels wife and son, giving her hope that he is still alive, saying Niels had been moved to another camp just before the rescue.

The tension builds at home as Jannik's jovial presence fuels Michael's jealousy at his newly close relationship with his wife and daughters. Assured by Jannik and Sarah that nothing more than a kiss passed between them, the building grief and guilt over his actions mix with his insecurity about Sarah's fidelity, especially after a tense family dinner where Natalia lies that her mother and Jannik have been "shagging" because she resents her fathers change in demeanor and misses having fun with Jannik. Michael eventually explodes, going on a liquor-fueled rampage in their house. He destroys the newly finished kitchen and threatens to kill Sarah and the girls. Sarah calls Jannik and the police before fleeing with her frightened daughters. He is arrested and imprisoned after an armed show-down with police, although Jannik explains he'll get a light sentence due to his clean record and "bag full of medals." The loyal and sympathetic Sarah visits him in prison where she issues an ultimatum: tell her what happened or she'll walk away forever. Michael breaks down in the film's final scene with the beginnings of the confession that surely follows.

Thomas's revisits themes from his excellent screenplay for the recent *Wilbur Wants to Kill Himself* (2002, released in the U.S. in 2004) in which two very different brothers—one unbalanced and suicidal and one stable and married—virtually switch places due to unforeseen events. They also both love the same woman who loves them back in different ways, as clearly Michael and Jannik both love Sarah and she them. Thomsen's excellent performance and riveting blue eyes perfectly convey his pent-up anguish that eventually is violently released while the gorgeous Nielsen displays impressive equanimity in the face of even the most out-of-control situations. And Kaas is thoroughly charming, convincing as the bad boy with a heart of gold.

Hilary White

CREDITS

Sarah: Connie Nielsen
Michael: Ulrich Thomsen
Jannik: Nikolaj Lie Kaas
Origin: Denmark
Language: Danish
Released: 2005
Production: Sisse Graum Jorgensen, Peter Aalbaek Jensen; Zentropa Entertainment; released by Nordisk
Directed by: Suzanne (Susanne) Bier
Written by: Anders Thomas Jensen
Cinematography by: Morten Soborg
Music by: Johan Soderqvist
Sound: Per Streit
Editing: Pernille Bech Christensen
Art Direction: Viggo Bentzon
Costumes: Signe Sejlund
MPAA rating: R
Running time: 110 minutes

REVIEWS

Boxoffice Online. May, 2005.
Chicago Sun-Times Online. May 19, 2005.
Entertainment Weekly Online. May 11, 2005.
Los Angeles Times Online. May 13, 2005.
New York Times Online. May 6, 2005.
Premiere Magazine Online. May 6, 2005.
Variety Online. January 10, 2005.
Washington Post Online. June 3, 2005, p. WE47.

TRIVIA

Although Connie Nielsen is actually Danish, director Susanne Bier instructed Nielsen to take Danish lessons. Bier thought her accent sounded more Swedish after living in the U.S. for many years and not speaking Danish in everyday life.

THE BROTHERS GRIMM

Eliminating Evil Since 1812.
—Movie tagline

No curse we can't reverse. No spell we can't break. No demon we can't exterminate.
—Movie tagline

Fall Under The Spell.
—Movie tagline

Once Upon A Time.
—Movie tagline

This Isn't The Way To Grandmother's House.
—Movie tagline

Who's The Fairest Of Them All.
—Movie tagline

If You Go Down To The Woods Today You'll Never Believe Your Eyes.
—Movie tagline
And They Lived Happily Ever After.
—Movie tagline

Box Office: $37.9 million

It seemed like a promising idea: the fanciful master of the fantastic and grotesque, Terry Gilliam, making a film about how the Brothers Grimm got their start. The premise is that the famous purveyors of frightening children's tales got their start as tricksters who conned townspeople into paying them to protect them against monsters they concocted, but who ended up getting embroiled in some inexplicable mysteries themselves. It sounds better in print than it plays in film.

Gilliam's main problem in *The Brothers Grimm* is one of tone. He's not willing to make the film completely wacky, a la his former troupe, Monty Python, and he stumbles precariously along the gap between the absurd and the melodramatic. It's neither funny enough nor fantastic enough nor dramatic enough to work as a coherent piece, but it's certainly entertaining, as the viewer is never certain what to expect next. And, like all Terry Gilliam films, it's unique and wild, though it falls far short of being as visionary or disturbing as *Brazil* or *Twelve Monkeys,* Gilliam's most fantastic and challenging works. There's nothing too challenging in this idle romp through the fantasy forest.

The idea that the Grimm brothers made money off inventing remarkable threats to ignorant villagers is strange in itself. In Gilliam's concept, these soon-to-be-famous fablemongers don't really have a grasp of the bizarre and supernatural, they're freelance magicians and fakes, moving from place to place and inciting fears that they then extinguish. The opening sequences show how they use their rudimentary "special effects" to create a frightening barn monster, and then vanquish it heroically. In reality the "monster" is just one of their underlings in a fright suit.

Heath Ledger and Matt Damon play Jake and Will Grimm respectively, with Jake being the brains of the operation and the more serious of the two and Will supplying the chutzpah and the baloney. Damon seems to flounder in his part, unsure whether to milk it for laughs, and he's the odd man out when Jake becomes romantically entangled with a powerful villager, Angelika (played by Lena Headey). The brothers go to the village after having been set up themselves by a regional potentate who doesn't like the way they're ruining his stranglehold on the citizenry. Then they become mixed up with some real enchanted woods and a strange power within them.

Ledger plays his role with superb wide-eyed wonder, falling for trap after trap but rebounding to take on each new challenge and showing the bravery his brother lacks. Damon's Will is supposed to be the chronicler among the pair, with Ledger's Jake the action man. The brothers more often seem confused than in synch, and even their sibling rivalry and infighting is tone-deaf. As actors, Damon and Ledger clash rather than sizzle.

The Brothers Grimm, along with the mysterious Angelika, make several forays into the demonic woods, and eventually find and discover the secrets of an enchanted tower. Legend has it that a queen has been locked up there and placed under a spell. Whether this is the story of a benign Rapunzel or a Wicked Witch isn't entirely clear nor consistent. Gilliam mixes up several strains of fables, as if to challenge the viewer to decipher the familiar stories of the Grimms and interpret them in new ways. When the forest itself becomes the enemy, we get moving and malevolent trees, and it's all done with an odd mixture of intentionally clunky effects and gee-whiz wonder.

Most viewers will be left wondering what Gilliam was going for—humor, mystery, majesty, suspense, or some sort of ill-fitting satire. The film has many of these elements mashed together in an oddball stew. It's not always clear what's at stake, or what exactly is the goal the protagonists must overcome, and these questions get murkier and murkier as the film progresses. Despite some canny moments of revelation and visual surprises, *The Brothers Grimm* gets stuck amid its middling effects and flounders around in a swamp of indecipherable plot points.

It's a rollicking good ride nonetheless, because Gilliam is not a director who is content with playing out the string—there's always a new trick or surprise around the corner. It's just that the elements don't add up to much that makes a lasting impression, or even an immediate impact. It's not always clear whether Gilliam intends to tweak the notion of childish gullibility or make a social statement of some sort by posing the Grimms as some sort of political heroes against petty tyrants.

Surprisingly, Gilliam descends into melodrama, and many critics accused him of capitulating to studio imperatives by toning down his satire and making his vision and themes mawkish. The many moments of Gilliam magic are lost in a muddled patchwork of a film. The original premise that the brothers are con artists, and the initial references to many twists of their fairy tales, are eventually submerged into a sinking ship of a plot that offers few rewards besides the momentary entertainment of surprising twists and turns.

Instead of turning fairy tales on their heads, Gilliam shakes the fun out of them and then leaves viewers dazzled but puzzled—and ultimately bored, because bold visual strokes cannot substitute for a compelling story. Of course, the Brothers Grimm ought to know that better than anyone else. And so should Terry Gilliam. What was he thinking? It's hard to say. But there's at least a unique edge to his ideas and vision, however muted it may be in this film.

Michael Betzold

CREDITS

Wilhelm Grimm: Matt Damon
Jacob Grimm: Heath Ledger
Mirror Queen: Monica Bellucci
Delatombe: Jonathan Pryce
Angelika: Lena Headey
Cavaldi: Peter Stormare
Gregor: Jan Unger
Origin: USA, Czech Republic
Language: English
Released: 2005
Production: Charles Roven, Daniel Bobker; Mosaic Media Group, Daniel Bobker; released by Dimension Films
Directed by: Terry Gilliam
Written by: Ehren Kruger
Cinematography by: Newton Thomas (Tom) Sigel
Music by: Dario Marianelli
Music Supervisor: Maggie Rodford
Art Direction: Frank Walsh
Costumes: Gabriella Pescucci, Carlo Poggioli
Production Design: Guy Hendrix Dyas
MPAA rating: PG-13
Running time: 118 minutes

REVIEWS

Boxoffice Online. August, 2005.
Chicago Sun-Times Online. August 26, 2005.
Entertainment Weekly Online. August 24, 2005.
Los Angeles Times Online. August 26, 2005.
New York Times Online. August 26, 2005.
Premiere Magazine Online. August 24, 2005.
Variety Online. August 20, 2005.
Washington Post Online. August 26, 2005, p. WE33.

QUOTES

Will Grimm: "We're here to save your land from evil enchantments."
Sasha: "Papa, they're famous!"
Will Grimm: "Right you are, son! The famous Brothers Grimm! Look at this strapping young man."
Father: "*He* is my daughter."
Will Grimm: "And a fine wife he'll make some lucky man."

TRIVIA

The "hand forest" scene in this film was originally written for *Time Bandits* (1981) and almost used in *Brazil* (1985).

C

CAPOTE

Box Office: $11.2 million

In the role of a lifetime, Philip Seymour Hoffman gives the performance of his career as the diminutive literary giant Truman Capote in this spare, compelling drama. The story centers on the six-year period that sent the flamboyant writer to Kansas to research a crime that was originally intended to be a story for *The New Yorker* but instead, led to his invention of the "nonfiction novel," *In Cold Blood*, his sudden rise to fame, and his unlikely bond with killer Perry Smith that, ultimately, proved his undoing. In his first dramatic feature film, director Bennett Miller shows a surprising visual maturity, with a restrained and taut style that perfectly compliments the finely-tuned script by Dan Futterman (adapted from Gerald Clarke's book), and Hoffman's riveting presence. Friends since childhood, Miller, Futterman, and Hoffman's simpatico is evident, with *Capote* garnering a host of awards and nominations. And Hoffman, whose nuanced, pitch-perfect performance virtually channels the voice and mannerisms of the title character without resorting to caricature, gives the performance of the year.

In 1959, the *Breakfast at Tiffany's* author found himself engrossed in a *New York Times* story about two ex-cons who murdered the Clutter family in Holcomb, Kansas after a bungled, attempted robbery of $10,000 they believed was somewhere in the home. His *New Yorker* editor William Shawn (Bob Balaban) quickly green-lights Truman's story that hinges on the idea that this tragic event underscores the wildly dichotomous yet concurrent aspects of life in America: conservative home life and family vs. insidious crime and violence.

Boarding a train bound for the Great Plains state along with his childhood friend and fellow writer Nelle Harper Lee (Catherine Keener), the fey lisping Truman with his high-pitched Southern drawl causes a minor stir with his arrival in the small, prairie town. As he queries the police and residents involved with the case, he meets the man who led the hunt for the drifters Perry Smith (Clifton Collins Jr.) and Dick Hickock (Mark Pellegrino) responsible for the Clutter murders, Kansas Bureau of Investigation agent Alvin Dewey (Chris Cooper). Capote, who initially doesn't set out to tell the story of these two murderers, displays his unique brand of callousness early on, quipping that he's uninterested as to whether they are actually caught. Although Dewey is less than impressed with Truman, the self-serving author quickly seizes upon Dewey's starstruck wife Marie (Amy Ryan) as an ally, pumping her for information about the case over jovial dinners where the charming and loquacious Truman casually name-drops a slew of his celebrity acquaintances. It is the first of many calculated moves which illustrate the all-consuming drive and naked ambition of the workaholic Capote.

After a chance meeting with Perry Smith, Truman quickly realizes this is more than a mere story about how murder affects a small town, but an in-depth character study of two psychotic criminals. He becomes obsessed with Smith, bribing a prison warden to gain 24/7 access to the troubled loner. Although on the surface the two men seem polar opposites, underneath the sociopathic killer and the narcissistic writer are both social misfits of a kind, with Truman poignantly observing, "It's as if Perry and I grew up in the same house, and he stood up and went out the back door while I went out the front." Perry, seriously wooed by the ambitious Truman who visits him constantly, begins to trust Truman implicitly although he will still not talk about the details of the day of the murder, something Truman desperately needs to finish what has now become a novel. With each visit to Smith and their growing attachment to one another, we see Truman's doom in the making. His half feigned affection designed to gain the trust of a killer is also half real. Despite Truman's deepening affection, which may even be love, for Smith, he remains clearly intent on using the private confessions of the naïve killer for his own benefit, bragging about his dealings with Smith at the swank, cocktail parties where he holds court in New York. The filmmakers do not shy away from the ferocity of Truman's intent as he is shown emotionally manipulating the simple-minded Smith and his continually putting off Smith's pleas for a new lawyer for the appeal process which may have saved his life. As Truman himself says throughout the six years of grueling research while awaiting the final outcome of the various trials: he needs an execution to finish the story the way he intends.

Capote does, in fact, exact Smith's shocking confession about the murders. "I thought he was a very nice, gentle man" Smith says of Clutter patriarch Herb, continuing, "I thought so right up until I slit his throat." The film flashes back to the murders, which indeed, leave no doubt as to the guilt of both Smith and Hickock. Truman's visits lessen and then end altogether, ignoring Smith's frequent, plaintive letters. The writer gets his wished for outcome—Smith and Hickock are graphically executed in a harrowing hanging scene—but at a price he had not expected to pay. The movie reiterates the fact that Capote never finished another book after *In Cold Blood* and who eventually descended into alcoholism, shunned by his famous New York socialite friends.

Surrounding Capote in the film are the various voices of reason, embodied by the down-to-earth Lee, Shawn, and Truman's longtime companion, writer Jack Dunphy (Bruce Greenwood). Keener, especially, as Truman's under appreciated companion, underscores the selfish aspects of the man by her character's modesty in everything from her plain manner of dress to the way she generously allows him his temper tantrum during the launch of her own famous book, *To Kill a Mockingbird,* which he dismisses contemptuously.

In an especially effective scene, the tables are turned on the normally self-possessed author as a trembling, overwrought Capote visits the composed, gum-chewing Hickock and Smith just before their hanging. And the scenes where Capote interviews Smith in prison are among the most gripping, with Truman staring down the killer in various close-ups and tenderly recalling moments from his childhood he thinks Perry might relate to. The filmmakers certainly have not set out to sugarcoat the baser traits Capote possessed and the author displays a great deal of what could be termed "moral flexibility." However, a savvy script, deft direction and a sensitive portrayal by Hoffman wisely imbue the tortured artist with enough sympathetic characteristics to keep him from becoming a monster.

Hilary White

CREDITS

Truman Capote: Philip Seymour Hoffman
Nelle Harper Lee: Catherine Keener
Alvin Dewey: Chris Cooper
Jack Dunphy: Bruce Greenwood
William Shawn: Bob Balaban
Mary Dewey: Amy Ryan
Dick Hickock: Mark Pellegrino
Perry Smith: Clifton Collins Jr
Origin: USA
Language: English
Released: 2005
Production: Caroline Baron, William Vince, Michael Ohoven; Infinity Media, A-Line Pictures, Cooper's Town Prods; released by Sony Pictures Classics, United Artists
Directed by: Bennett Miller
Written by: Dan Futterman
Cinematography by: Adam Kimmel
Music by: Mychael Danna
Sound: Leon Johnson
Editing: Christopher Tellefsen
Art Direction: Gordon Peterson
Costumes: Kasia Walicka-Maimone
Production Design: Jess Gonchor
MPAA rating: R
Running time: 114 minutes

REVIEWS

Boxoffice Online. September, 2005.
Chicago Sun-Times Online. October 21, 2005.
Entertainment Weekly Online. September 28, 2005.
Los Angeles Times Online. September 30, 2005.
New York Times Online. September 27, 2005.
Premiere Magazine Online. September 30, 2005.
Variety Online. September 2, 2005.
Washington Post Online. October 21, 2005, p. C01.

QUOTES

Truman Capote: "I have 94 percent recall of all conversation. I tested it myself."

TRIVIA

Shot in 36 days, the filmed opened on September 30—Capote's birthday.

AWARDS

Oscars 2005: Actor (Hoffman)
British Acad. 2005: Actor (Hoffman)
Golden Globes 2006: Actor—Drama (Hoffman)
Ind. Spirit 2006: Actor (Hoffman), Screenplay
L.A. Film Critics 2005: Actor (Hoffman), Screenplay, Support. Actress (Keener)
Natl. Bd. of Review 2005: Actor (Hoffman)
N.Y. Film Critics 2005: First Feature
Natl. Soc. Film Critics 2005: Actor (Hoffman), Film
Screen Actors Guild 2005: Actor (Hoffman)
Broadcast Film Critics 2005: Actor (Hoffman)

Nomination:

Oscars 2005: Adapt. Screenplay, Director (Miller), Film, Support. Actress (Keener)
British Acad. 2005: Adapt. Screenplay, Director (Miller), Film, Support. Actress (Keener)
Directors Guild 2005: Director (Miller)
Ind. Spirit 2006: Cinematog., Film
Screen Actors Guild 2005: Support. Actress (Keener), Cast
Writers Guild 2005: Adapt. Screenplay
Broadcast Film Critics 2005: Support. Actress (Keener).

CASANOVA

A partially true story about lies told, virtue lost and love found.
—Movie tagline

He won every woman's heart. She won his.
—Movie tagline

There's no greater adventure than true love.
—Movie tagline

2005's protean film star, Heath Ledger, shuffled through a pantheon of disparate characters from the gay, laconic, macho Wyoming cowboy in *Brokeback Mountain* to an iconic Jim Morrison-esque, washed-out surf shop inebriate in *Lords of Dogtown.* He takes the self-assured lead in yet another character diversion as Giacomo Casanova, flourishing in Venice during the apogee of his seductive prowess. Casanova's seeming insouciance and magnetism resonate soundly with the ornate florid plumage of a baroque time. To dismiss Giovanni Giacomo Casanova as a wanton libertine satyr is to ignore his resolute tune of renaissance.

The real Casanova's 13-volume memoirs record Venice as his place of birth into a family of thespians. Hunted by the Inquisition, his eclectic career included that of a magician, violinist, spy, diplomat, secretary to a Cardinal, lawyer, inventor of the French royal lottery, and of course, author.

Narrowly escaping the grip of Inquisition forces from the bed of a young nun (who thought the consequential sentence of eternal damnation for fornicating with Casanova to be a bargain), Giacomo races along rooftops and hides in an intellectual hall where he is instantly smitten when his eyes fall on Francesca Bruni (Sienna Miller) who is a cross dresser for the feminist cause. As well as being a master at sword fighting, Francesca publishes pamphlets promoting women's equal rights under a male nom de plume. Under the protection of Venice's Doge, Casanova is ordered to settle down into the sacramental institution of matrimony. He selects a nubile virgin, Victoria (Natalie Dormer) but she is promised to Francesca's brother, Giovanni. (At the film's conclusion, Giovanni Bruni assumes Casanova's identity thus postulating in this tale that the historical figure was actually two men).

Intent on keeping the love of his life, Giovanni challenges Casanova to a duel. Francesca impersonates her brother and proves to be the more accomplished, superior swashbuckling virtuoso. In a nod to the Shakespearean use of identity confusion and gender deception coupled with convoluted plot intricacies, the cool Francesca is engaged to Papprizzio (Oliver Platt), a bacon mogul who carries the self-lampooning title of "The Lard King of Genoa." To complicate matters further for this Venetian man of licentious adventure, the Inquisition authorities implement a relentless agent, Bishop Pucci, as the ultimate judge and executioner for profligates. Played with cold, edgy stoicism, Jeremy Irons dons a hilarious orange flat-topped wig complete with a curly mullet.

Numerous subplots adorn this colorful, light romantic comedy including Casanova's use of a tactic employed in Cyrano de Bergerac by secretly reading Francesca's unpublished work in order to present himself as a progressive male. (Thus far, the evasive Francesca has proved to be immune to Casanova's Quixotic overtures).

Upon finally winning her over during a balloon ride heist, the pair are caught and sentenced to be hanged by the nefariously self righteous Puccini who has caught up with Casanova's guile and craft for disguise. At the last minute, his mother and her troupe of actors portray themselves as Vatican officials bearing a papal seal exonerating the couple of all charges as it is the Pope's birthday.

The remaining subplots are seamlessly sewn together in the improvised tradition of commedia dell' arte with

Giovanni continuing the Casanova legend and seen as an old man writing his memoirs in Dux, Bohemia where his last years were spent consigned as a secretary and librarian at the Castle of Count von Waldstein.

David Metz Roberts

CREDITS

Giacomo Casanova: Heath Ledger
Francesca Bruni: Sienna Miller
Bishop Pucci: Jeremy Irons
Papprizzio: Oliver Platt
Andrea Buni: Lena Olin
Lupo: Omid Djalili
Donato: Stephen Greif
Dalfonso: Ken Stott
Giovanni Bruni: Charlie Cox
The Doge: Tim McInnery
Bernardo Guardi: Phil Davies
Vittorio: Paddy Ward
Casanova's Mother: Helen McCrory
Tito: Leigh Lawson
Victoria: Natalie Dormer
Origin: USA
Language: English
Released: 2005
Production: Mark Gordon, Leslie Holleran, Betsy Bears; Touchstone Pictures, Mark Gordon Company; released by Buena Vista
Directed by: Lasse Hallstrom
Written by: Jeffrey Hatcher, Kimberly Simi
Cinematography by: Oliver Stapleton
Music by: Alexandre Desplat
Sound: Ivan Sharrock, Michael Kirchberger
Editing: Andrew Mondshein
Costumes: Jenny Beavan
Production Design: David Gropman
MPAA rating: R
Running time: 108 minutes

REVIEWS

Boxoffice Online. December, 2005.
Chicago Sun-Times Online. December 23, 2005.
Los Angeles Times Online. December 23, 2005.
New York Times Online. December 23, 2005.
Variety Online. September 3, 2005.
Washington Post Online. December, 2005.

QUOTES

Judge: "Your are charged with heresy, with a novice."
Casanova: "She was hardly a novice."

THE CAVE

There are places man was never meant to go.
—Movie tagline

Beneath heaven lies hell, beneath hell lies...
—Movie tagline

Box Office: $14.9 million

No one expects a film like *The Cave* to be "Masterpiece Theater," but there are certain qualities such a film should have. For example, there should be good-looking protagonists. Said protagonists should be killed off by the evil creature/force/madman, etc... in approximately the reverse order of attractiveness. There should be a lot of suspense, possibly some gore. And the creature must be frightening.

The Cave is successful on some of these counts, less so on others. The movie fares the highest in the good-looking actor department. Cole Hauser, Morris Chestnut, Eddie Cibrian and Piper Perabo are part of a daring diving team that is so collectively attractive that, if the diving business ever becomes slow, they could easy form their own soap opera cast.

Writers Michael Steinberg and Tegan West obviously understand the conventions of the genre because they know who to kill off, and in what order. That means that middle-aged scientist Dr. Nicolai (Marcel Iures) is going to be removed from the script early on and that handsome, dimpled Tyler (Cibrian) will be around awhile. Top Buchanan (Chestnut) somehow manages to avoid the usual plight of African-American actors in horror films by not being the first to be killed.

Even the premise is not that bad. The movie begins thirty years previous with a team of adventurers exploring a Romanian forest. They stumble upon an ancient cave and an abbey decorated with mosaics of ominous creatures. Bad things happen to the team. In the present day, Dr. Nicolai invites the team of divers to explore the cave to search for different forms of life. Unfortunately for the team, that is just what they will find.

The brave and good-looking divers head four miles into the cave at which time one of the less handsome members of their team is mysteriously killed. Adding to an already bad day, the cave out gets closed up by an avalanche. The comely Kathryn (Lena Headey) studies the local fauna in the cave and discovers a mysterious parasite that mutates its host. Still, the team is undeterred. "We can't wait for the rescue team. We are the rescue team!" heartily barks manly team leader Jack (Hauser).

This is also the point in which the screenwriters could have used a rescue team because it is exactly at this point in the plot when the movie turns, of all things, dull. Since the movie takes place in a cave, the shots are dark and have a sameness about them. The director does not give a good sense of where things are in the cave and where people are headed. Perhaps this was to induce a sense of claustrophobia or confusion, but the result is action that is not engaging. When the creature attacks, it is difficult to see what is going on. There are just a lot of noises and quick edits. Again, this does not seem mysterious, but rather, uninteresting. Those hoping to see a severed arm or whatnot will be disappointed.

Finally, the creature itself seems cobbled together from the prop departments of movies that came before. It is kind of a pterodactyl type thing that sees its prey using sonar. Once it sinks its teeth into someone, it starts to change that person into a killing creature like itself. The most horrifying thing about all this is the acting that it causes Hauser to do. After he is attacked by the creature, he starts feeling a little sick. As the parasite continues to infest his body, he gets reptilian eyes, paler face make-up and his acting gets more and more comical. As his character gets sicker, Hauser shows this transition by opening his eyes wider, getting a spookier look on his face and jerking his head about like a bird. It is possibly one of the worst performances of the year. And, as unintentionally comical as it is, it is not enough to save this film.

Critics said that *The Cave* did not scare them one bit. Teresa Wiltz of *The Washington Post* wrote, "*The Cave* isn't just a bad movie, it's a very, very, very bad movie, so bad that it can't even redeem itself by turning into high camp." Kathy Cano Murillo of *The Arizona Republic* wrote that the film "crawls along painfully. It lacks action, suspense, a secure plot and, most important, the scare factor." Wesley Morris of *The Boston Globe* wrote, "It's ultimately just a rigorous personal training film made by people who don't seem to like movies, or the people who go to them. With nary a shot lasting longer than five seconds, it's not edited so much as blended."

Jill Hamilton

CREDITS

Jack: Cole Hauser
Top Buchanan: Morris Chestnut
Tyler: Eddie Cibrian
Dr. Nicolai: Marcel Iures
Kim: Daniel Dae Kim
Kathryn: Lena Headey
Charlie: Piper Perabo
Briggs: Rick Ravanello
Strode: Kieran Darcy-Smith
Origin: USA
Language: English
Released: 2005
Production: Richard Wright, Michael Ohoven, Tom Rosenberg, Gary Lucchesi, Andrew Mason; Lakeshore Entertainment, Cinerenta-Cinebeta, City Productions; released by Sony Pictures Entertainment, Cineblue
Directed by: Bruce Hunt
Written by: Michael Steinberg, Tegan West
Cinematography by: Emery Ross
Music by: Johnny Klimek, Reinhold Heil
Sound: Ruth Mac
Editing: Brian Berdan
Art Direction: Vlad Vieru, Peter Pound, Corvin Cristian
Costumes: Wendy Partridge
Production Design: Pier Luigi Basile
MPAA rating: PG-13
Running time: 97 minutes

REVIEWS

Boxoffice Online. August, 2005.
Entertainment Weekly Online. August 31, 2005.
Los Angeles Times Online. August 26, 2005.
New York Times Online. August 26, 2005.
Premiere Magazine Online. August 26, 2005.
Variety Online. August 25, 2005.

QUOTES

Kathryn: "At first, I thought it couldn't survive outside of a cave environment. Now, I'm not sure. I think it wants to get out."

TRIVIA

The film was shot primarily in Romania, which boasts some 12,000 registered caves.

CHARLIE AND THE CHOCOLATE FACTORY

The Factory Opens July 2005.
—Movie tagline

Willy Wonka—Is semi-sweet and nuts.
—Movie tagline

Charlie—Is lucky to be there.
—Movie tagline

Mike—Thinks candy is a waste of time.
—Movie tagline

Veruca—Is a very bad nut.
—Movie tagline

Violet—Keeps her eyes on the prize.
—Movie tagline

Augustus—Is what he eats.
—Movie tagline

Box Office: $206.4 million

Whether the world really needed another remake of the Roald Dahl book about an eccentric candy maker with a loathing for ill-mannered children is debatable. But Tim Burton thought so. The story first told by Dahl in the book *Charlie and the Chocolate Factory* and then brought to the screen in the 1971 film *Willy Wonka & the Chocolate Factory* is a gooey, sticky confection in the hands of master fantasist Burton, reunited here with Johnny Depp. The remake—which uses Dahl's original title and perhaps is closer to his original concept than the 1971 version that starred Gene Wilder—bears some similarities to the first Burton-Depp collaboration, *Edward Scissorhands.*

Burton's always happy to immerse himself in the bizarre dark side of father-son relationships, and so in Charlie Burton concocts a back story for Willy Wonka. It's rather thin and unsurprising, however: Christopher Lee was Willy's stern dentist dad, and having such a villain as your father is enough to send any boy half-mad, ala *Scissorhands.* But what's particularly uninspiring about Burton's biographical filler is that it's so predictable—father, a dentist, denies son candy; son develops insatiable craving for candy; his career is an act of rebellion. Ho hum. It's awfully pedestrian, and where's the mother?

Burton displays more of a natural affinity for the actual Dahl storyline. The author, who likes to present children in all their wickedness and their parents in all their perfidy, saw no need to explain why Wonka was so eccentric. This film, however, with its grand swelling dramatic score and sweeping panoramas, especially in the opening scenes, seems to hint that something important's going on. As a result, Dahl's little fable about foibles seems bloated, kind of like Augustus Gloop, the insatiable fat kid who is one of the five who win a chance to tour Wonka's factory.

In nearly every way, in fact, Burton's concoction is just like Wonka's factory—extravagant, sugary, fanciful, and not easily consumed in moderation. Luckily, Dahl is the perfect author for Burton's palette—with the author's affinity for warped, off-kilter characters and ridiculous behavior; with his thin candy-coated shell of sweet morality wrapped around a tale that verges on the sinister and the sarcastic. Unfortunately, Burton himself falls too hard for Dahl's sentimental excesses.

But that's not before audiences are treated to a very pleasurable ride. *Charlie and the Chocolate Factory* is fun to watch—not only for Burton's lavish visuals and his oddball humor, but for the characters, who are a mixture of charming and alarming. We spend a very leisurely first act with the Bucket family—Charlie (Freddie Hightower), his parents (Helena Bonham Carter and Noah Taylor, who are given little to do), and his four grandparents, who together total 381 years of age and spend all their time in a big bed in the middle of the one-room family shack. Our tour guide is Grandpa Joe (David Kelly), who once worked at Wonka's factory and tells Charlie how it grew from a little shop to an empire, then was wounded by spies who stole its recipes, and finally became an automated, forbidding place run by a recluse.

When Wonka announces to the world that he's hidden "golden tickets" in candy bars that will entitle five lucky children to get a tour of his factory, and one of them to win a special undisclosed grand prize, not only do chocolate sales rise, but the world goes into a frenzy, this tale being written at a time when the world apparently had nothing better to do. In fact, a very precocious child watching this film today might ask: why all the big fuss about a factory tour? No one's been inside the factory since the workers were dismissed years before, and the appeal of the prize is not apparent.

Nonetheless, four odious children each win a ticket, but not through luck. Augustus Gloop (Philip Wiegratz), a stereotypical German overeater, wins one because he eats so much chocolate the odds are stacked in his favor. Veruca Salt (Julia Winter) wins one because her tycoon father buys up every Wonka bar he can find and gets his nut factory employees to unwrap them. Violet Beauregarde (AnnaSophia Robb) wins one because of sheer entitlement—she's a winner, a trophy daughter of a suburban trophy mom. And Mike Teavee (Jordan Fry) is so smart he figures out how to crack the code—he's a video game player extraordinaire, and though he hates chocolate, he somehow deduces where a winning ticket can be found.

Charlie is the only kid who succeeds in getting a ticket through sheer luck—or perhaps it's through sheer heart. Burton gives us not one, but two, false tugs of emotion and disappointment before Charlie finds a ten-pound note in the street and buys a third bar at a corner shop, unwrapping the last lucky ticket. He picks Grandpa Joe to accompany him on the tour. And they join the other four, each with a parent, as they meet Wonka.

The success of the first Wonka film, such as it was (it didn't do that well at the box office but has enjoyed a long and successful video afterlife), was due primarily to Wilder's winning antics. Wilder, of course, was adept at playing a likeable loony. Johnny Depp is not. The success of Charlie depends much on Depp, who is big box office and the screen's leading heartthrob. Depp appeals to almost every female above the age of infancy.

Depp's portrayal of Willie Wonka caused the greatest divide among critics, who gave a mixed reception overall to Charlie and the Chocolate Factory. Some hailed his performance as another indication of his wry range, some disdained it as overly mannered, and some were puzzled by it. Wearing a black hat, a red cape, and purple gloves, with his face made up as a mask of white punctured by inconsistently painted pink or red lips, Depp plays Wonka as a self-absorbed twit. With the gloves and the oddball remarks of a true eccentric, Depp as Wonka reminded some critics too much of Michael Jackson. Others were delighted by his deadpan humor.

There are wry moments as Depp's Wonka pretends not to hear Mike Teavee's criticisms, or reacts childishly to questions, or feigns false concern as, one by one, the contenders fall into trouble, tempted by their own moral failings. Depp relies heavily on a sing-songy, almost infantile delivery, but it's not clear whether he's intending his personality to be one of a knowing misanthrope deliberately pretending stupidity, or of someone who just has a few screws loose. That lack of clarity in his character makes all the difference as we lurch into a disappointing ending that is as schmaltzy in tone as the rest of the film studiously tries to avoid. Is Wonka's reconciliation with his father believable? Is his transformation into a family-tolerant member of society sufficiently motivated? Not hardly, and Depp doesn't help by making his Willie Wonka a little too much like a scrubbed-up version of Adam Sandler, playing dumb and then dumber.

This won't matter to those who take delight in Burton's amazing sets, and his many eccentric touches, from Oompah Loompah dinners of mashed green caterpillars to squirrels shucking nuts for the candy bars. Undoubtedly his most inspired choice in this movie—and the one thing that saves it from its perilous teetering on the cliffs of repetitive boredom —is the casting of Deep Roy to play every one of the digitally reproduced Oompah Loompahs. Roy is not only a hilarious comic actor, he can dance and sing deadpan ditties with the best of them.

At times it seems as if Burton and Depp are playing with the leftover language of the 1960s, the era Dahl's books emerged from. Certainly that's true in the crazy Oompah Loompah dance numbers—Danny Elfman's music is classic spoofery for Dahl's original lyrics. And Depp is always winking and saying things like "keep on truckin'." At times Depp seems to be channeling some old TV kid show hosts, with his gee-whiz comments and high-pitched little laughs.

But the main problem with *Charlie and the Chocolate Factory* is that Burton overreaches, making the wickedly satirical little story into a grandiose big deal. Dahl's delightful works can hardly bear full-length movie treatment—they're small and wonderful pinpricks at pretension, nothing more—and the story almost collapses under the weight of the expectations for an overproduced, overpriced remake. Neither Burton nor Depp will suffer from this excursion—it has wide appeal, and just the right knowing smirks—but it won't be remembered as either one's finest hour.

Michael Betzold

CREDITS

Willy Wonka: Johnny Depp
Charlie Bucket: Freddie Highmore
Grandpa Joe: David Kelly
Violet Beauregarde: Anna Sophia Robb
Oopmpa Loompas: Deep Roy
Dr. Wonka: Christopher Lee
Mrs. Bucket: Helena Bonham Carter
Mr. Bucket: Noah Taylor
Mr. Salt: James Fox
Mrs. Beauregarde: Missi Pyle
Veruca Salt: Julia Winter
Mike Teavee: Jordan Fry
Augustus Gloop: Philip Wiegratz
Mrs. Gloop: Franziska Troegner
Mr. Gloop: Harry Taylor
Mr. Teavee: Adam Godley
Grandma Josephine: Eileen Essell
Grandma Georgina: Liz Smith
Grandpa George: David Morris
Narrator: Geoffrey Holder (Narrated)
Origin: USA, Great Britain
Language: English
Released: 2005
Production: Richard D. Zanuck, Brad Grey; Zanuck Company, Plan B; released by Warner Bros.
Directed by: Tim Burton
Written by: John August
Cinematography by: Philippe Rousselot
Music by: Danny Elfman
Sound: Tony Dawe
Editing: Chris Lebenzon
Art Direction: Sean Haworth, James Lewis, Andy Nicholson, David Allday, Matthew Gray, Francois Audouy
Costumes: Gabriella Pescucci
Production Design: Alex McDowell
MPAA rating: PG
Running time: 115 minutes

REVIEWS

Boxoffice Online. July, 2005.
Chicago Sun-Times Online. July 15, 2005.
Entertainment Weekly Online. July 13, 2005.
Los Angeles Times Online. July 15, 2005.
New York Times Online. July 15, 2005.

Premiere Magazine Online. July 15, 2005.
Variety Online. July 8, 2005.
Washington Post Online. July 15, 2005, p. WE31.

QUOTES

Grandma Georgina: "Nothing's impossible, Charlie."

TRIVIA

This film marks the fourth Burton-Depp collaboration in 15 years.

AWARDS

Nomination:

Oscars 2005: Costume Des.
British Acad. 2005: Costume Des., Makeup, Visual FX
Golden Globes 2006: Actor—Mus./Comedy (Depp).

CHEAPER BY THE DOZEN 2

This Christmas, you better watch out!
—Movie tagline
Same Big Family...Even Bigger Adventure.
—Movie tagline

Cheaper by the Dozen is a filmic example of the old children's game "operator." In that game, a child whispers a secret to another who whispers it to the next kid and so on. Hilarity ensues as the secret is revealed to have mutated from, say, "Shells in the sand" to "Shelly's underpants." Sadly, hilarity does not ensure in *Cheaper by the Dozen 2* which is quite far removed from the original 1948 book by Frank and Ernestine Gilbreth. The book detailed life growing up in a twelve-child family run by a father who was a world-renowned efficiency expert and eager to apply his efficiency principles to child rearing. A subsequent movie starring Myrna Loy was a faithful adaptation of the story. In the 2003 version, nary a thing was intact from the original source except for the fact of a family containing twelve children. Even the family's name had been changed from Gilbreth to the blander Baker. (As in Baker's dozen. Anybody?)

In the 2005 sequel, the same lowest common denominator philosophy applies. Why make a movie about a father who taught his children, even when they were in the single digits, to read Latin, touch type and multiply large numbers in their heads, when a movie can be made in which a dad gets hit in the crotch? The answer might have something to do with money. The 2003 *Cheaper* was a successful family-friendly hit so here director Adam Shankman and writer Sam Harper serve up more of the same. It is the kind of slapstick-heavy, lowbrow film that works well during the holiday season. It is the kind of movie that kids, grandma, and various other relatives could all view together, trauma-free, at the local Megaplex.

In this installment Tom Baker (Steve Martin) and wife Kate (Bonnie Hunt) gather their brood for a family vacation to the picturesque Lake Winnetka. Tom is sad that his family is growing up and the older kids are starting to move on and he wants one last chance to do something all together as a family. Even pregnant Nora (Piper Perabo) and sullen Lorraine (Hilary Duff) agree to come along.

Once at the lake, the family discovers that their old cabin is now even older and still infested with a rat that performs such hilarious stunts as stealing shoes. Tom's old rival, Jimmy Murtaugh (Eugene Levy), lives across the lake in a huge spread that he calls The Boulders. Jimmy has a seemingly perfect family, with successful children who attend Ivy League schools and a trophy wife, Sarina (Carmen Electra).

The Murtaughs have eight children which means that, combined with the Bakers' twelve, there are a lot of child actors not getting much of a storyline. Sarah (Alyson Stoner) gets the biggest chunk of plot as a tomboy who develops an unbidden crush on Eliot Murtaugh (Taylor Lautner). In other unoriginal plot news, big brother Charlie (Tom Welling) develops an unbidden crush on a Murtaugh, Anne, (Jaime King). A lower-tier story line is that Lorraine is looking for an apartment and she seems to be pretty grouchy. Below that, the kids do not get much plot to work with. Most viewers would probably be hard pressed to even name six of the children. After Lorraine, there's Charlie, Nora and, er, that one kid with glasses who sets off the fireworks at the fancy country club.

Perhaps the worst part of the film is that, even though so many talented actors are in it, it is still so awful. Martin, in particular, is a disappointment. In recent years, he has seemed all too eager to trade in audience goodwill to make a dollar. Perhaps younger viewers will never even be aware that the manic dad in *Cheaper* is capable of such inventive, hilarious fare as *The Jerk.*

Critics were not horribly enchanted by the film. Ty Burr of *The Boston Globe* wrote, "Noisy, silly, gratingly upbeat, and piously sentimental, *Cheaper by the Dozen 2* is what passes for family entertainment these days." Laura Kern of *The New York Times* wrote, "This is a tiresome film, full of repetitive, misfired jokes, false emotions and caricatures." And Peter Hartlaub of *The San Francisco Chronicle* wrote that the film "is less a movie than random scenes from *The Brady Bunch* recreated by better actors and strung together to feature-film length."

Jill Hamilton

CREDITS

Tom Baker: Steve Martin
Jimmy Murtaugh: Eugene Levy
Kate Baker: Bonnie Hunt
Charlie Baker: Tom Welling
Nora Baker-McNulty: Piper Perabo
Sarina Murtaugh: Carmen Electra
Anne Murtaugh: Jaime (James) King
Lorraine Baker: Hilary Duff
Sarah Baker: Alyson Stoner
Bud McNulty: Jonathan Bennett
Jake Baker: Jacob Smith
Jessica Baker: Liliana Mumy
Kim Baker: Morgan York
Henry Baker: Kevin G. Schmidt
Mark Baker: Forrest Landis
Eliot Murtaugh: Taylor Lautner
Origin: USA
Language: English
Released: 2005
Production: Ben Myron, Shawn Levy; 21 Laps; released by 20th Century-Fox
Directed by: Adam Shankman
Written by: Sam Harper
Cinematography by: Peter James
Music by: John Debney
Sound: Glen Gauthier
Music Supervisor: Buck Damon
Editing: Christopher Greenbury, Matthew Cassel
Art Direction: Peter Grundy
Costumes: Joseph G. Aulisi
Production Design: Cary White
MPAA rating: PG
Running time: 94 minutes

REVIEWS

Chicago Sun-Times Online. December 21, 2005.
Entertainment Weekly Online. December 21, 2005.
Los Angeles Times Online. December 21, 2005.
New York Times Online. December 21, 2005.
Variety Online. December 20, 2005.
Washington Post Online. December 21, 2005.

QUOTES

Kate Baker: "Honey you actually bought that shirt?"

Tom Baker: "Hey every dad is entitled to one hideous shirt, and one horrible sweater. It's part of the dad code."

AWARDS

Nomination:

Golden Raspberries 2005: Worst Actress (Duff), Worst Support. Actor (Levy).

CHICKEN LITTLE

Chicken Little. Movie Big.
—Movie tagline

This time the sky really is falling.
—Movie tagline

When it comes to saving the world, it helps to be a little chicken.
—Movie tagline

A hero will emerge.
—Movie tagline

The end is near.
—Movie tagline

Box Office: $130.2 million

Chicken Little is Disney's first in-house, computer-generated animated feature, a clever, energetic movie that showcases some very funny sequences and bright characterizations voiced by a talented cast. The screenplay, credited to Steve Bencich, Ron J. Friedman, and Ron Anderson from a story by director Mark Dindal and Mark Kennedy, is inspired by the old tale of the chicken who unwittingly scares his community into thinking that the sky is falling, but the writers use it only as a framework for a moving story of father-son bonding and an alien-invasion adventure that owes more to H.G. Wells than the fairy tales that usually inspire Disney's animated films.

When we first meet Chicken Little (voiced by Zach Braff), a cute, little fellow with a head almost as big as his body, he believes that the sky has fallen on him, and he is ringing the bell in the city hall to get everyone's attention. Causing confusion on the streets of Oakey Oaks, he quickly becomes an embarrassment and the town laughingstock. Everyone surmises it must have been an acorn that hit Chicken Little, and even his own father, Buck Cluck (voiced by Garry Marshall), is ashamed of him. The joy of *Chicken Little* often lies in the very funny throwaway gags; Buck, for example, rattles off a litany of ways his son's scare has been immortalized and commercialized—from collectible spoons and commemorative plates to billboards and bumper stickers.

Chicken Little fares no better at school, although he is friends with the other unpopular kids, including Abby

Mallard (voiced by Joan Cusack), who is taunted as an "ugly duckling" by Foxy Loxy (voiced by Amy Sedaris), clearly the most popular girl in school and leader of the clique of cool kids. Then there is the ironically named Runt of the Litter (voiced by Steve Zahn), a huge, insecure pig who can barely fit in his school desk, and Fish Out of Water (voiced by Dan Molina), who lives on land but whose head resides in a diver's helmet.

Unlike some animated features that overindulge in pop culture references to show off how hip they are, *Chicken Little* uses them to develop the characters. A proponent of pop psychology, Abby Mallard is constantly urging Chicken Little to communicate with his dad and seek "closure," a word she learned from such teen magazines as *Modern Mallard* and *Cosmoduck*. Runt is prone to integrating old pop songs into his dialogue, and his love for disco energizes him during the film's climax.

Chicken Little tries to win his father's respect by taking up baseball, a sport in which he excelled, but, given his size, Chicken Little is a benchwarmer who does not get his chance to hit until many of his teammates are injured. When he hits a home run to win the championship game, he becomes the hero (not only putting away the old acorn scandal but winning his father's love as well).

Unfortunately, just when it seems that everything is finally going Chicken Little's way, a piece of the sky falls on him again. A scene in which he tries to hide this from his father and distract him from the subject is hilarious, just one example of the screenplay's sharp banter. Soon, however, it is learned that the piece of the sky is really a part of a spaceship, and suddenly the film turns into an invasion story, with creatures that could almost fit in this year's *War of the Worlds*. Chicken Little, with the help of Abby and Runt, tries to rescue Fish when it looks like he has been captured. In the course of their mission, however, they stumble upon an orange, furry, three-eyed creature named Kirby, who has been separated from his alien parents. In the midst of aliens wreaking havoc, Chicken Little finally wins his father's trust, and soon they are trying to return Kirby to his parents aboard the ship. It turns out that the aliens are not hostile but are merely coming to collect acorns since Earth, apparently, is the only planet that has them.

The traditional rendering of *Chicken Little* is a cautionary tale against the spread of unfound panic. But this movie redeems the character by showing that he is right all along. Although the sky is not falling, Chicken Little is onto something real from the outset. Nonetheless, the revelation of the alien visit is something of a letdown, not because it is a departure from the usual version but because the action-adventure sequences are the least original aspect of the movie. Indeed, it feels very formulaic, after establishing an entertaining group of characters, to resort to a science-fiction finale, even if the invasion is really a search for a lost son. *Chicken Little* is at its most imaginative not in action scenes that we have seen variations of before but in its character interactions and the humorous details—Chicken Little's use of soda pop as a means of jet propulsion, a sheep teacher leading his students in translating words into mutton (they all sound like "baa"), the unpopular kids surviving a vicious game of dodgeball, and a baseball announcer's wry and sarcastic play-by-play commentary.

The film ends on a high note with a smart, good-natured parody of the way Hollywood transforms a true story into popular entertainment. A year has passed, and a movie has been made of Chicken Little's exploits, in which he is a tall, muscular superhero known as Commander Little, Abby Mallard has been turned into a slinky love interest, and Runt is not a nervous sidekick but rather a brave fighter. Chicken Little and his pals love the adaptation, thus suggesting that even a humble guy likes to think of himself as the brawny, confident hero with amazing powers and a Clint Eastwood persona.

While all of the screenplay's plot turns may not be smooth and the triumph-of-the-underdog story is familiar, there is still much wit, many delirious laughs, and just enough heart to make *Chicken Little* a success. Perhaps Disney on its own has a ways to go before it can hope to match the storytelling sophistication and sheer imagination of Pixar, but its first foray into CG animation is a delight. As a notable aside, *Chicken Little* was projected in a special format known as Disney Digital 3-D in select movie theaters, which enhanced the fun by bringing the action, especially the sports sequences and the invasion scenes, right into the audience.

Peter N. Chumo II

CREDITS

Chicken Little: Zach Braff (Voice)
Buck Cluck: Garry Marshall (Voice)
Abby Mallard: Joan Cusack (Voice)
Runt of the Litter: Steve Zahn (Voice)
Fox Loxy: Amy Sedaris (Voice)
Mayor Turkey Lurkey: Don Knotts (Voice)
Dog Announcer: Harry Shearer (Voice)
Mr. Woolenworth: Patrick Stewart (Voice)
Principal Fetchit: Wallace Shawn (Voice)
Melvin — Alien Dad: Fred Willard (Voice)
Tina — Alien Mom: Catherine O'Hara (Voice)

Ace: Adam West (Voice)
Alien Cop: Patrick Warburton (Voice)
Origin: USA
Language: English
Released: 2005
Production: Randy Fullmer; released by Buena Vista
Directed by: Mark Dindal
Written by: Steve Bencich, Ron J. Friedman, Ron Anderson
Music by: John Debney
Editing: Dan Molina
Production Design: David Womersley
MPAA rating: G
Running time: 82 minutes

REVIEWS

Boxoffice Online. November, 2005.
Chicago Sun-Times Online. November 4, 2005.
Entertainment Weekly Online. November 2, 2005.
Los Angeles Times Online. November 4, 2005.
New York Times Online. November 4, 2005.
Premiere Magazine Online. November 4, 2005.
Variety Online. October 30, 2005.
Washington Post Online. November 4, 2005, p. C01.

QUOTES

Chicken Little: "I put on five ounces this year. I've really bulked up."

TRIVIA

Disney's first wholly computer-animated feature film.

THE CHORUS
(Les Choristes)

Box Office: $3.6 million

France's *The Chorus* (*Les Choristes*)—topping the box office in France in 2004 and garnering a best foreign language film Academy Award nomination in 2005—with it's story of orphaned and troubled children getting a second chance through the healing power of music, has provoked such trite adjectives as "heart-warming" and "inspirational." And this simple but effectively heartstring-tugging story about an upbeat music teacher who comes to an all boys reform school in rural, post-war France is indeed inspirational; the effect he has on the troubled children who desperately need his help, suitably heartwarming. Very much in the *Mr. Holland's Opus* vein, *The Chorus* is only the second film from director Christophe Barratier who is, however, the accomplished producer of such films as *Winged Migration, Himalaya,* and *Caravan,* working alongside actor/director Jacques Perrin. A loose remake of Jean Dreville's *La cage aux rossignols* (U.S. title: *A Cage of Nightingales* [1947]) Barratier and writer Philippe Lopes-Curval have created a film that is, while not terribly original or daring, is successful in its modest intent to uplift.

The opening scene introduces a famous conductor, Pierre Morhange (Jacques Perrin), returning to France for his mother's funeral. Pepinot (Didier Flamand), a former classmate Morhange has not seen in 50 years, unexpectedly shows up on his doorstep holding a diary kept by their beloved, late music teacher, Clement Mathieu (Gerard Jugnot). Cut to the day in January 1949 when Mathieu, the school's new music teacher arrives at Fond de l'Etang, (which literally translates as "bottom of the pond" or "rock bottom") a kindly, stout, round-faced man and failed composer. He is introduced to the children by its principal, M. Rachin (Francois Berleand), a cold disciplinarian who keeps the 60 attendant boys in line by any means necessary and often banishes them to solitary confinement as punishment.

Mathieu is suitably appalled at the harsh conditions he finds under Rachin's reign of terror. The sympathetic music teacher is kind to the boys, who act out as a way of protesting their oppressive living conditions, but realizes he must find his own brand of discipline to keep them in line. Once this is accomplished nearly a third of the way into the film, it is then that Mathieu begins forming his children's choir which will afford the boys a healthy, creative outlet. The fact that it enrages the easily enraged Rachin may also be a motivation for Mathieu and the boys, as well, as they all detest the fascist headmaster.

Among the boys is the aforementioned Pepinot (Maxence Perrin, Jacques Perrin's real life son), a loveable moppet, orphaned by the war who patiently waits once a week at the gate for a visitor that never comes. Pierre Morhange (Jean-Baptiste Maunier) has a mother that loves him very much, in fact, but as a single parent Violette (Marie Bunel) must put in as much time as she can at the restaurant where she works to support Pierre and therefore, Pierre must stay at school. Pierre is the focus of the story: a troublemaker with the blond hair and face of an angel. He resists Mathieu's attempts to help him get over his resentment toward his mother, fueled by the fact that the children tease him about her actually being a prostitute because she is so young and beautiful. As the defiant Pierre constantly refuses Violette's visits, the concerned music teacher steps in, meeting with her himself to ease her fears about her son. This leads to more visits (and more lies from Mathieu) and the teacher quickly falls for Violette, who we find out later, heartbreakingly does not return his unspoken feelings.

Pierre's resistance is steadily worn down by the fun all the boys seem to be having singing in the choir while he sulks around silently. Mathieu discovers Pierre not only looks like an angel but has the voice to match, as the boy secretly sings when he think no one is around. Pierre does, in fact, join the chorus as its star soloist and mends his relationship with his proud mother.

A subplot involving a particularly violent youth, who probably should have been sent to prison instead of Fond l'Etange, has an outraged Rachin having the boy arrested and thrown out for stealing a large sum of money (which in fact was never stolen as it is later revealed). The extremely disgruntled youth sets fire to the school at an unfortunate moment when Mathieu has led all the children on an unapproved field trip. Despite saving the lives of the children, Mathieu is nonetheless dismissed by the evil Rachin amid his loyal choir's protests. In a touching final scene, the orphan Pepinot begs to go along with his teacher who finally cannot resist and the two board a bus and ride off into the sunset.

Despite its clichés and obvious emotional manipulations, *The Chorus* is beautifully shot and well told tale that, at 97 minutes, says exactly was it needs to say and no more. The emotional heart of the film, Jugnot's wonderfully expressive face and humorous affect is wonderfully effective and Maunier's subtle performance, especially mature.

Hilary White

CREDITS

Clement Mathieu: Gerard Jugnot
Rachin: Francois Berleand
Pierre Morhange as an adult: Jacques Perrin
Violette Morhange: Marie Bunel
Chabert: Kad Merad
Pierre Morhange as a child: Jean-Baptiste Maunier
Pepinot as an adult: Didier Flamand
Maxence: Jean-Paul Bonnaire
Langlois: Phillippe Du Janerand
Pepinot as a child: Maxence Perrin
Origin: France, Switzerland, Germany
Language: French
Released: 2004
Production: Jacques Perrin, Arthur Cohn, Nicolas Mauvernay; Pathe Renn; released by Miramax
Directed by: Christophe Barratier
Written by: Christophe Barratier, Philippe Lopes-Curval
Cinematography by: Carlo Varini
Music by: Bruno Coulais
Editing: Yves Deschamps
Art Direction: Jean-Pierrce Gaillot, Bernard Ducrocq
Production Design: Francois Chauvaud
MPAA rating: PG-13
Running time: 95 minutes

REVIEWS

Boxoffice Online. January, 2005.
Chicago Sun-Times Online. January 28, 2005.
Entertainment Weekly Online. January 12, 2005.
Los Angeles Times Online. December 22, 2004.
New York Times Online. January 14, 2005.
Premiere Magazine Online. January 19, 2005.
Variety Online. February 23, 2004.
Washington Post Online. January 28, 2005, p. WE36.

TRIVIA

The Chorus was the number one movie at the French box-office in 2004, with more than 8.6 million admissions.

THE CHRONICLES OF NARNIA: THE LION, THE WITCH AND THE WARDROBE

The beloved masterpiece comes to life December 9.
—Movie tagline

Evil Has Reigned For 100 Years...
—Movie tagline

Box Office: $165 million

For the many fans of C.S. Lewis's *Narnia* books, there could only be an odd mix of trepidation and excitement at the prospect that at least some of the classic seven-story children's fantasy series would finally make the transition to the big screen. That mix of fear and giddy delight is exactly evocative of the feeling stirred up by reading these odd and unique books. Fans could hardly imagine anything more cinematic than Lewis's vivid descriptions of a make-believe world ruled by a cantankerous but gentle lion, inhabited by talking animals and half-human, half-animal creatures of classical mythology, and full of breathtaking terrain. But lovers of Lewis also could rightly feel fearful that, with Disney Studios in on the game, the bite and punch of the Narnia tales might become as packaged and defanged as the wit of A.A. Milne did when Disney took over his *Winnie the Pooh* books.

Timing was also a problem for the debut movie of Walden Media, an independent group which partnered with Disney after purchasing rights to the Narnia properties from Douglas Gresham, Lewis's stepson. *The Chronicles of Narnia: The Lion, the Witch and the Wardrobe* came hard on the heels of the deserved mega-success of *The Lord of the Rings* trilogy, another big-budget fantasy spectacle inspired by books also written in the mid-twentieth century by another tweedy British professor, J.R.R. Tolkien, a friend of C.S. Lewis. (It's fitting that Tolkien and Lewis would nearly compete beyond death for film audiences, since in life they competed for fame and acclaim.) And then there's the competition from the *Harry Potter* franchise, a modern, more accessible series of tales that borrows heavily from the fantasies of Tolkien, Lewis, and many others.

Narnia fans are not as big a demographic market as Harry Potter readers, being that only a minority of adults and children living today have read the C.S. Lewis books. And while the Narnia books have outsold Tolkien's, Tolkien's *The Hobbit* and *The Lord of the Rings* achieved cult status among Baby Boomers of the 1960s, who took the tales to heart as part of the counter-culture revolution.

The final concern was the pre-release marketing that emphasized the allegorical appeal of Lewis's tales to Christians. Cannily, Walden and Disney attempted to reach out to church groups to try to repeat some of the success that catapulted Mel Gibson's *The Passion of the Christ* into one of the biggest box-office successes in history. That strategy ran the risk of turning off other audiences who weren't familiar with the Narnia stories by making them seem as if they were pitches for conservative Christianity. They are anything but; in fact, Lewis's exotic blend of mysticism and Christian orthodoxy is too powerful and unique to pigeonhole, and it can't readily be called into the service of any religious agenda. Though the allegory at the center of *The Lion, the Witch and the Wardrobe* is perfectly clear—the regal lion Aslan is certainly a stand-in for Jesus as he gives his life for the sin of an imperfect human—there are so many pagan myths and characters intertwined in the rest of the story that it's clear Lewis was ecumenical when it came to the morality of his tales, which touch on themes of honor, trust, betrayal, and passion, and well as sin and redemption.

Happily, the concerns proved mostly unfounded. With *Shrek*'s Andy Adamson at the helm for his first live-action feature, and with Gresham on board making sure the stories were faithful to Lewis's intent, the first of a planned multi-film series made a huge debut at the box office, and all the back-and-forth about the Christian underpinnings of the story was blown away in the grandeur of the canvas and the execution. Still, to measure up to Peter Jackson's epic *Rings* work was a tall order, especially when *Narnia* debuted just a week before Jackson's blockbuster follow-up, *King Kong*.

Like the *Rings* trilogy, *The Lion, the Witch and the Wardrobe* was shot in New Zealand, Adamson's home, except for some sequences that had to be redone in the Czech Republic because of uncooperative weather. And *Rings* enlisted some of the fantastic creature-realization services of WETA, the New Zealand special-effects company that figured so heavily in *Rings* and in *Kong*. But most of the CG work was done by George Lucas's Industrial Light and Magic.

The result is a pleasant blend of the fantastic and the human. The story follows the adventures of four British siblings, who during the bombing of London in World War II are relocated to the countryside home of a professor uncle. While playing hide-and-seek, the youngest, Lucy (Georgie Hensley), hides in a wardrobe and, behind a gaggle of fur coats, stumbles into the enchanted land of Narnia. She returns and has to convince her older brothers and sister that her fantasy is real, and eventually all four children go to Narnia, and the adventure takes full force.

The Lion, the Witch and the Wardrobe is actually the second installment in Lewis's seven-part series about Narnia, but most of the action of the first book, *The Magician's Nephew,* which involves the professor's discovery of Narnia as a child, does not take place in Lewis's fantasy world, and so it's not as appealing to film. In this tale, the Pevensee children are separated by the war from both their parents—the father is a soldier, and the mother has sent them away from London—and they are not happy about becoming involved in their own war in Narnia. And though you can certainly read the story as a Christian allegory, it is also instructive to consider it as an alternate-world version of World War II.

In Lewis's story, in fact, the villain is a heartless fascist, the White Witch (Tilda Swinton), who has conquered Narnia and turned it into a land of endless winter, a hundred years' worth of it by the time Lucy arrives on the scene. Lucy first learns of the witch when she meet a faun, Tumnus (James McEvoy), who befriends her but then confesses he plans to turn her in to the witch's authority, because the witch has put a price on the head of human visitors. We eventually learn that's because there's a prophecy that four people—"sons of Adam and daughters of Eve," in Narnia parlance—will appear, and with the help of Aslan, eventually sit on the four thrones in the Narnian capital of Car Paravel.

Aslan is on the move, it's rumored, after his absence of 100 years, and the four children are ensnared unwittingly in the political intrigues and prophecies of Narnia. The second youngest, Edmund (Skandar Keynes), follows Lucy on her second visit, and falls into the clutches of the White Witch, who woos him with candy and false promises in hopes of using him as bait to lure the other children. When older siblings Susan (Anna Popplewell) and Peter (William Moseley) eventually join the others in Narnia, they are befriended by two beavers, who tell them what's up. But Edmund betrays them, wandering off to the witch's castle and, under threat of torture, betraying the whereabouts and plans of his siblings and Aslan.

What follows is a breathless pursuit of the children by ruthless hounds sent by the Witch, and finally an escape into the solace of Aslan, who has gathered an army of centaurs, minotaurs, animals, and other creatures who have remained faithful to the true lineage of Narnia and are awaiting the return of their proper rulers. But when Edmund is rescued and delivered to Aslan, a false moment of reunion and hope is eventually shattered. According to the rules of "Deep Magic" which govern Narnia, sacrifice must be paid for Edmund's traitorous acts.

What follows is unsparing: The Witch's gruesome retribution, a dark triumph of evil, and a tremendous battle between two armies that can't help but be reminiscent of the massive battles in *Lord of the Rings.* And, though the rest of the film does not have the complexity, drama and depth of the *Rings* movies—few movies do—the battle is equal to Jackson's epochal fights, though not nearly as long and involved. But it's just as fascinating to see the half-human, half-animal forms, and other fantastic creatures, go to war. It's a great payoff for the film.

Until then, Adamson sometimes struggles with descents into cloying preoccupation with the perils of the children, but that's not all bad, for the Pevensees and the challenges they face are the heart of the story. Of the four actors who play the children, only Popplewell *(The Girl with the Pearl Earring)* has previous film experience, but all of them, selected in a global casting call, do a wonderful job of hesitatingly embracing their new challenges. Actually, the charming Hensley, as Lucy, shows no hesitancy, and it's this girl's curiosity, courage, and heart that provide a radiant focus to the movie. And Edmund's weaknesses, also typical of children, are equally convincingly portrayed. And this is part of Lewis's genius: Though his work is written for children, it is not watered down for them, and it is often tough stuff; the stories chronicle a world where innocence must come to grips with evil, death, torture, betrayal, and other failings of the world, including the protagonists' own imperfections.

Another essential is Aslan, and Adamson doesn't stumble with the CG lion: he's totally acceptable as authentic, and wonderfully regal and vulnerable. He's pictured just as Lewis envisioned him: a kind, gentle, but untamed creature, whose passion, heart, and majesty are thrilling, but whose downfall is heartbreaking. Voiced with quiet authority by Liam Neeson, Aslan fulfills the stories' promise and is a memorable character.

But, astoundingly, considering the computerized wizardry and the talking-animal and precocious-children-in-peril competition she's up against, Swinton's White Witch is easily this film's most impactful character. Swinton and Adamson wisely avoided witch cliches in making this unique villain icy and ruthless: she's like a Nordic queen, and Swinton's stunningly heartless, conniving, and treacherous performance makes her all the more chilling. Cunning and vicious by turns, Swinton's Witch is a formidable villain, intelligent and totally amoral, and not laughably stupid as some children's movie villains are. Swinton's fantastic and fanciful performance is a treacherous delight to behold. Swinton herself saw her character as "the ultimate white-supremacist Goth," in her words, and with her snake-like hair wrapped up in coiled braids, and her ice-princess makeup and Amazon costumes, she realizes that description, while utterly avoiding the excesses that make too many villains buffoonishly evil.

The only serious missteps among the film's characters are Mr. and Mrs. Beaver, who lapse into the kind of moronic banter that you find in too many kids' movies that feature comic talking-animal couples. Yes, Lewis's story indulged in something similar with the beaver couple, but nothing so blatantly sit-comish, and their bravery gets lost in too much of this repartee. In a well-realized icy river sequence of peril—the only major scene added to the film that isn't in Lewis's book—Mr. Beaver's jokes about his wife's cooking rob the scene of the gravitas it needs.

Because of Disney's legacy, it is not an easy chore to make talking animals into something other than sappy, cute, or wisecracking characters, but apart from the Beavers, Adamson pulls it off (though besides Aslan, there are precious few other animals allowed dialogue scenes). The Beavers just seem to be imports from another, much poorer film, as does a renegade scene halfway in when the four children are on a ridge: the green-screened background is amateurishly cropped. Otherwise the CG imagery ranges from adequate to outstanding.

Overall, the film spends too much time with the children's scenes of heartbreak, loss, and reunion, lingering too long on hugs and tears. While there is no doubt that Lewis and his Narnia tales allow sentiment, they shouldn't descend into sentimentality: every precious redemptive scene is earned by equally dramatic conflict and challenges. More work with animal characters, even greater screen time for the fantastic creatures, and a little more attention to the grandeur of the Narnian landscape would have balanced the film better on the knife-edge of terror and tenderness that Lewis concocted.

As the film was a resounding success, the planned series of sequels will undoubtedly unfold, but they will face a challenge to match this opening. It's also still up in the air, as well, as to whether sentimentality will drench Lewis's harshly earned moments of tender triumph, or soften the hard edges of his stories. In *The Lion, the Witch and the Wardrobe,* this is the real battle: whether to make the film so tender and beautiful that its horror is masked. But the scenes of Aslan's sacrifice are as troubling, dark, and terrifying as anything in the Harry Potter series, and almost as dark as Tolkien's darkest terrors. All in all, considering all the pitfalls of committing Lewis's Narnia stories to the screen, this first installment is a commendable triumph. The debate about the film's message, and the degree of religious faith that is part of Lewis's concoction, will continue, but a close examination of the film should produce the same verdict as a close examination of the book: a fantasy that people of all beliefs can fully engage in and enjoy.

Michael Betzold

CREDITS

White Witch: Tilda Swinton
Susan Pevensie: Anna Popplewell
Mr. Tumnus: James McAvoy
Professor Kirke: Jim Broadbent
Father Christmas: James Cosmo
Mrs. Pevensie: Judy McIntosh
Mrs. MacReady: Elizabeth Hawthorne
Lucy Pevensie: Georgie Henley
Edmund Pevensie: Skander Keynes
Peter Pevensie: William Moseley
Ginarrbrik: Kiran Shah
Aslan: Liam Neeson (Voice)
Mr. Beaver: Ray Winstone (Voice)
Mrs. Beaver: Dawn French (Voice)
Mr. Fox: Rupert Everett (Voice)
Wolf: Sim Evan-Jones (Voice)
Gryphon: Cameron Rhodes (Voice)
Philip the Horse: Philip Steuer (Voice)
Vardan: Jim May (Voice)
Origin: USA
Language: English
Released: 2005
Production: Mark Johnson, Philip Steuer; Mark Johnson; released by Buena Vista, Walt Disney Pictures, Walden Media
Directed by: Andrew Adamson, Ann Peacock
Written by: Andrew Adamson, Christopher Markus, Stephen McFeely
Cinematography by: Donald McAlpine
Music by: Harry Gregson-Williams
Sound: Tony Johnson
Editing: Sim Evan-Jones, Jim May
Art Direction: Jeff Thorp, Karen Murphy, Jules Cook
Costumes: Isis Mussenden
Production Design: Roger Ford
MPAA rating: PG
Running time: 139 minutes

REVIEWS

Boxoffice Online. December, 2005.
Chicago Sun-Times Online. December 8, 2005.
Entertainment Weekly Online. December 7, 2005.
Los Angeles Times Online. December 7, 2005.
New York Times Online. December 9, 2005.
Premiere Magazine Online. December 9, 2005.
Variety Online. December 4, 2005.
Washington Post Online. December 9, 2005, p. C01.

QUOTES

Susan Pevensie: "Are you saying we should believe her story?"
Professor Kirke: "Why not?"
Susan Pevensie: "Well, it can't be real, logically."
Professor Kirke: "Logic? What are they teaching them at these schools?"

TRIVIA

Director Andrew Adamson wanted a genuine reaction to the Narnia forest set from Georgie Henley (Lucy) so he blindfolded her and carried her on set, then started to film.

AWARDS

Oscars 2005: Makeup
British Acad. 2005: Makeup
Nomination:
Oscars 2005: Sound, Visual FX
British Acad. 2005: Costume Des., Visual FX
Golden Globes 2006: Song ("Wunderkind"), Orig. Score.

CINDERELLA MAN

When America was on its knees, he brought us to our feet.
—Movie tagline

Box Office: $61.6 million

"You are the champion of my heart, James J. Braddock," Renee Zellweger says as Mae, the long-suffering, iconic wife of the man who would eventually become a world champion boxer. Such a noble thought is just too big to be captured in a screenplay, Stuart Klawans marveled in his *Nation* review: such a fine sentiment, he wrote, somewhat cynically, "was made to be cut out of the film and played on television to bring in the coppers from all decent men and their decent women." That surely was the scheme, but it failed. The public saw through the maudlin sentimentality of this Depression era fantasy about life, love, struggle, and second chances. However, *Cinderella Man* did not have a fabled happy ending for director Ron Howard and screenwriters Cliff Hollingsworth and Akiva Goldsman. By the second week of its release, *Cinderella Man* had only grossed $34.6 million, a 47 percent drop since opening and a puny return on the $88 million budget required to make the picture. It fell far short of being a Blockbuster, but Universal Pictures still had faith in their product and planned to release it again later in the year, desperately hoping for Oscar consideration, no doubt. But there is no evidence that this ploy worked. The film dropped off the *Variety* charts over the summer, never to return.

So what went wrong? How could they lose, especially in the early summer of a year of remarkably bad movies, a year famous for its dwindling box office receipts, a year begging to be saved by an overly long monkey movie remake? Conventional wisdom has it that the summer is not the time for serious films, but *Cinderella Man* was also a warm and fuzzy, fact-based melodrama involving a courageous fellow battling to hold hearth and home together. Moreover, could there have been a better choice of an actor to play James J. Braddock (1905-1974) than Russell Crowe, who had performed so well for Ron Howard in *A Beautiful Mind* (2001)? *A Beautiful Mind* was a huge success; it generated nearly $140 million for Ron Howard and producer Brian Glazer, which is not bad at all for a biopic about an academic from Princeton University, and also got Academy Award attention (8 nominations and 4 Oscars). The most successful movie of 2004, of course, had also been another boxing movie, Clint Eastwood's *Million Dollar Baby*, a favorite with the Academy Awards (7 nominations and 4 Oscars) that earned a respectable $96 million, and, earlier still, in 2001, Will Smith had earned an Oscar nomination for *Ali*. *New Republic* reviewer Stanley Kauffmann wrote, correctly, that Ron Howard was certainly "well equipped to direct this tonic tale," but speculated that Howard's knowledge of how movie manipulation works, that "inside view, has slightly blinkered him about the outside view: he doesn't always sense when the audience is aware of movieness." In other words, he has lost his sense of what the audience may consider true or false, and how could viewers value what may not seem convincing?

The story begins about 1928. Jim Braddock's boxing career is on the rise as the economy is tanking, until he injures his hand in 1930. Will he ever box again? When he goes back into the ring, he gets beaten to a pulp. How, then, is he going to support his family? When he is lucky, Braddock gets picked to work the docks at Weehawken, New Jersey, and using a stevedore's hook eventually helps him to build strength in his injured hand. There is an underdeveloped subplot introduced involving a comrade of Braddock's on the docks named Mike (played by English actor Paddy Considine) who helps Braddock fool the watchful and nasty dock foreman and who is clandestinely campaigning for union workers while living in a Hooverville hovel in Central Park; but the melodramatic strands are quickly lost and the subplot goes nowhere. As *The Wall Street Journal* remarked, "it's anyone's guess what he's up to, and why his character is so sketchy." (The man turns up missing? Was skullduggery afoot? Was there an opportunity missed to make a political point? How tolerable are the loose ends?) Fully aware of these problems, *The Wall Street Journal* reviewer still went on to conclude that this film represented director Ron Howard's "best work so far."

When Jim Braddock doesn't find work, he hits rock bottom and is forced to swallow his pride and panhandle, looking for charity from those who run the fight game, including his former manager, Joe Gould, wonderfully and memorably played by Paul Giamatti. Gould offers Braddock $250 to fight a heavyweight, who is sure to beat him. For *New Yorker* reviewer Anthony Lane, Braddock's match in 1934 against Corn Griffin (played by an actual heavyweight boxer, Art Binkowski) is the highlight of the film, "not the championship slugfest against Max Baer (Craig Bierko) in 1935." Max Baer is the villain of the film, a boxer who, as Desson Thomson wrote in *The Washington Post*, "doesn't just win fights, he kills people." He is portrayed as a vulgar playboy who rudely taunts and insults Braddock and his wife in public. What a cad!

This is a by-the-numbers formula sports biopic all the way as our hero, dockworker and ex-prizefighter Jim Braddock with a heart as big as the Ritz fights Depression unemployment and family starvation to make a come back against World Champ Max Baer. Jim is soft spoken and gentle and is fighting for his family, as well as his self respect. Max is loutish and brash and is fighting for—well, he is apparently fighting for the two bimbos back in his hotel room. *New York Times* book reviewer Jay Jennings praised ESPN anchor Jeremy Schaap's book, *Cinderella Man: James J. Braddock, Max Baer, and the Greatest Upset in Boxing History* (2005) as a "helpful corrective to the mawkish biopic from Ron Howard." *Washington Post* reviewer Stephen Hunter editorialized that Max Baer "was as beloved as any heavyweight in history, was seen as a friendly, clownish kind of guy, and when a fighter died after a fight with him, he was so upset he quit boxing for several months." Compare that account with the impression conveyed by Howard's film.

Film reviewers in general were more generous in evaluating the film. *Washington Post Weekend* reviewer Desson Thomson considered Howard's fable "a powerful piece of Americana, about a come-from-behind winner who makes a perfect metaphor for America's down-but-not-out spirit of the times." *New Republic* reviewer Stanley Kauffmann, who knows as much about screen acting as any living critic, praised Russell Crowe for an "astonishing" performance: "Even at his biggest moments he seems both convincing and somewhat reticent." Kauffmann also singled out Paul Giametti, whom he considered "gifted enough to make us feel that acting is a kind of afterthought: first comes the verity of the man in question." Anthony Lane of *The New Yorker* wrote that *Cinderella Man* was softened by "the unstoppable decency of the director," adding, "what hardens it is the glower of Russell Crowe, who instinctively grasps the irony of trying to sell a fairytale on the back of legalized violence—of men in a desperate age who all but murdered for a living."

Some films may be considered important because of what they effectively reveal, say, the inner life of a mentally disturbed genius in the case of Russell Crowe's John Nash in *A Beautiful Mind*, but *Cinderella Man* has nothing of that complexity or significance to reveal. The later film is significant because of its failure at the box office in the public arena, because it was a clearly mendacious attempt to exploit and manipulate popular sentiment, and because, despite its employment of a perfectly competent director and at least two more than competent actors, it fell far short of its intended goals. A goofy little film called *Dreamer* (starring Dakota Fanning) did a better job of replicating the success of *Seabiscuit* in 2004, but, then, in its fable of successful second chances, it did not attempt to humanize the horse.

Although Ron Howard has worked mighty hard to ratchet up the suspense and dramatic edge of this pugilistic melodrama lifted from the headlines of yesteryear, it is obviously a foregone conclusion that Braddock will defeat Baer in the 15th round of the 1935 title fight. To compensate, Howard factors in a restaurant confrontation where Max insults Mae and she flings a cocktail glass in his face before the viewer finally gets to old Madison Square Garden, filled with all those screaming Jersey fight-fans. There's plenty of flashbulb-popping editing and freeze-frames to punctuate the obvious action. Then we've got brave Jim Braddock himself, vulnerable with cracked ribs and a chronically damaged right hand, but a guy who believes in himself and in second chances. All the components are there, and yet, somehow, they are not enough. Maybe we've seen this picture too many times. Maybe there's just not enough conflict set up between Jim and his opponents. Maybe Russell Crowe's performance is too muffled and soft-spoken, with too many shots of the cuddly kids back home who might have to be sent off to live with relatives and too many loving clinches with ever-faithful, ever-loving Mae. Maybe we're not sure just how it is that a washed-up fighter can suddenly turn a corner and fight effectively enough to win the championship. At any rate, something went seriously awry here in this "brave" movie packed with Republican family values and optimism and hope.

James M. Welsh and John C. Tibbetts

CREDITS

Jim Braddock: Russell Crowe
Mae Braddock: Renee Zellweger
Joe Gould: Paul Giamatti
Max Baer: Craig Bierko
Mike Wilson: Paddy Considine
Jimmy Johnston: Bruce McGill
Joe Jeanette: Ron Canada
Ford Bond: David Huband
Jay Braddock: Connor Price
Rosemarie Braddock: Ariel Waller
Howard Braddock: Patrick Louis
Sara: Rosemarie DeWitt
Lucille Gould: Linda Kash
Sporty Lewis: Nicholas (Nick) Campbell
Jake: Gene Pyrz
Origin: USA
Language: English
Released: 2005
Production: Brian Grazer, Ron Howard, Penny Marshall; Brian Grazer; released by Universal Pictures
Directed by: Ron Howard
Written by: Cliff Hollingsworth, Akiva Goldsman
Cinematography by: Salvatore Totino
Music by: Thomas Newman
Sound: John J. Thomson
Editing: Mike Hill, Dan Hanley
Art Direction: Peter Grundy, Dan Yarhi
Costumes: Daniel Orlandi
Production Design: Wynn Thomas
MPAA rating: PG-13
Running time: 144 minutes

REVIEWS

Boxoffice Online. June, 2005.
Chicago Sun-Times Online. June 2, 2005.

Entertainment Weekly Online. June 1, 2005.
Los Angeles Times Online. June 3, 2005.
New York Times Online. June 3, 2005.
Variety Online. May 19, 2005.
Washington Post Online. June 3, 2005, p. C01.

QUOTES

Jim Braddock: "have to believe...that when things are bad...I can change them."

TRIVIA

Russell Crowe, who lost more than 50 pounds for the role, dislocated his shoulder while training for the film's boxing sequences, delaying filming by two months. Professional boxers were hired to play Braddock's opponents and told to land punches as close to Crowe's body as possible. However, they sometimes couldn't pull back in time and Crowe also suffered from several concussions and cracked teeth.

AWARDS

Screen Actors Guild 2005: Support. Actor (Giamatti)

Broadcast Film Critics 2005: Support. Actor (Giamatti)

Nomination:

Oscars 2005: Film Editing, Makeup, Support. Actor (Giamatti)

British Acad. 2005: Orig. Screenplay

Golden Globes 2006: Actor—Drama (Crowe)

Screen Actors Guild 2005: Actor (Crowe)

Writers Guild 2005: Orig. Screenplay

Broadcast Film Critics 2005: Actor (Crowe), Director (Howard), Film.

COACH CARTER

It begins on the street. It ends here.
—Movie tagline

Box Office: $67.2 million

Inspirational teacher movies have been around for a long time and have not changed much over the years. The basic formula goes: new teacher takes over an unruly, usually low-income class of students and works magic. There is a reason the formula has stuck around for such a long time. It is satisfying to watch one person, armed with only pluck and a philosophy, turn a class around. The unruly classes, in a sense, represent seemingly intractable social problems. If one teacher can solve a class's problem, then maybe our social problems are not as daunting as they seem. Such a teacher appeals to our sense that a hero or inspirational figure might come in to save the day. *Coach Carter* is satisfying in this sort of way. With a firm sense of vision and a commanding and sure voice, Ken Carter (Samuel L. Jackson) handles such problems as gangs, unmotivated kids, and mouthing off. Moviegoers were anxious for such inspiration and helped *Coach Carter* debut as the number one movie.

The story is based on the true tale of Coach Ken Carter who locked out his winning high school basketball team in 1999 after they failed to meet academic standards. Here, Carter, a former basketball star at Richmond High in California, returns to his old school to coach the team. On the first day, he has the players sign a contract stating, among other things, that they will wear coats and ties on game days and maintain a C grade average. Carter, somberly intoning, "I see a system that's designed for you to fail," informs his players that they are more likely to end up in prison than college. He insists that they all address each other as "Sir" explaining, "You will have my respect until you lose it." Carter handles any infraction, from being late to saying something disrespectful, in the manner of gym teachers since time began—by assigning push-ups, laps, and "suicides."

After giving lots of inspirational speeches and assigning enough push-ups, Carter wins the respect of the team. But after he cancels a game when the players do not meet their academic goals, he faces the wrath of the principal (Denise Dowse) and the community. They think that basketball is the only success that these guys will ever have, so it should not be taken away. Carter, who post-high school become a successful sports equipment retailer, argues that he is giving the players something better—life skills.

Director Thomas Carter (no relation to Coach Carter) touches on the stories of the players enough to give the Coach something to work with. Timo Cruz (Rick Gonzales) challenges the coach and gets kicked off the team. But he is secretly hungering to be back on the team because he fears his alternative as a drug dealer. The coach's son, Damien (Robert Ri'chard), is an A-student who transfers from his private school so that he can play on his dad's team. Star player Junior Battle (Nana Gbewonyo), a hero on the court, is functionally illiterate. The best drawn side story involves good guy Kenyon Stone (Rob Brown) and his girlfriend, Kyra (Ashanti). Kyra is pregnant and happy about it, but Kenyon wonders how the pregnancy will affect their lives and his plans for school. All of it is secondary to the coach and his players in the gym. Whether barking out orders, giving heartfelt speeches or getting into a power struggle with an errant kid, Jackson uses his commanding presence to make it all seem more interesting that it otherwise might have been.

Critics described the film as conventional, but did not have much worse to say about it. Wesley Morris of

The Boston Globe called the story, "from-the-heart but unoriginal." Stephanie Zacharek of *Salon.com* wrote, "*Coach Carter* is one of those highly effective conventional pictures that remind us that conventionality isn't always a bad thing. There's a reason the *To Sir With Love*-style role-model picture has become a fixture; even when we know these movies are bad, we often feel stirred by them." Critics who did not like the film had good things to say about Jackson and his performance. Owen Gleiberman of *Entertainment Weekly* gave the movie a C+ and wrote, "Jackson rules the movie with his joyful inflections," and Bob Strauss of *The Los Angeles Daily News* wrote, "Few actors have the wicked humor and smoldering presence that Jackson brings to any party, and boy are they needed here."

Jill Hamilton

CREDITS

Coach Ken Carter: Samuel L. Jackson
Damien Carter: Robert Ri'chard
Tonya: Debbi (Deborah) Morgan
Timo Cruz: Rick Gonzalez
Worm: Antwon Tanner
Principal Garrison: Denise Dowse
Kenyon Stone: Rob Brown
Kyra: Ashanti
Junior Battle: Nana Gbewonyo
Jason Lyle: Channing Tatum
Maddux: Texas Battle
Origin: USA
Language: English
Released: 2005
Production: Brian Robbins, Mike Tollin, David Gale; released by MTV Films, Tollin/Robbins Productions
Directed by: Thomas Carter
Written by: Mark Schwahn, John Gatins
Cinematography by: Sharon Meir
Music by: Trevor Rabin
Sound: Robert L. Sephton
Music Supervisor: Jennifer Hawks
Editing: Peter E. Berger
Art Direction: Tim Beach
Costumes: Debrae Little
Production Design: Carlos Barbosa
MPAA rating: PG-13
Running time: 137 minutes

REVIEWS

Boxoffice Online. January, 2005.
Chicago Sun-Times Online. January 14, 2005.
Entertainment Weekly Online. January 12, 2005.
Los Angeles Times Online. January 14, 2005.
New York Times Online. January 14, 2005.
Premiere Magazine Online. January 14, 2005.
Variety Online. January 9, 2005.
Washington Post Online. January 14, 2005, p. WE31.

TRIVIA

Based on the life of Coach Carter, who benched his team due to their poor academic performance in 1999.

THE CONSTANT GARDENER

Love. At any cost.
—Movie tagline

The focus of *The Constant Gardener,* one of the best films of 2005, is twofold: a growing problem resulting in numerous deaths, and a growing love which results from one of them. The problem concerns the destitute and dying of Africa, or, more to the point, a lack of concern for them. It is both the shameful turning of a blind eye and the even more shameful practice of preying upon those who do not have a prayer. Pharmaceutical companies, delightedly drowning in colossal earnings, sell drugs to those parts of the world where there is money to be made after first subjecting those in Africa, whom they feel have little to lose anyway, to risky testing. Thus, those who cannot afford to increase profits are unconscionably profited upon, used as human guinea pigs to try out what the companies hope will be the West's next big seller. Expendable people make for expedient, less expensive research. Government officials look the other way or even clear the way for robust, healthy business ventures despite the ill-gotten gains. The 2001 John Le Carré novel upon which the film was based is outraged fiction rooted in outrageous fact, and "by comparison with the reality," the author wrote, "my story was as tame as a holiday postcard."

The film is very much also about a man who comes to know, appreciate, and love his wife most deeply after her demise. Justin Quayle (Ralph Fiennes) is a gentlemanly mid-level British diplomat stationed in Kenya. He is a kind, decent, exceedingly well-mannered and placid sort of fellow who spends his free time absorbed in the solitary pursuit of gardening. The reserved man's younger wife, Tessa (Rachel Weisz), is his opposite, a gutsy, passionate, highly vocal and fiercely determined social and political activist. She is wonderfully, zealously alive, and *The Constant Gardener* begins with her death.

Fiennes is excellent throughout, and Weisz is equally effective in the many flashbacks which detail the characters' relationship. After Tessa is found brutally murdered while traveling with local Dr. Arnold Bluhm (Hubert Kounde), the British High Commission's Head of Chancery Sandy Woodrow (Danny Huston) comes to inform Justin that she is dead and Arnold is nowhere to be found. It is speculated that he had killed her in a crime of passion and then disappeared. In a close up, one sees that Justin is shaken but trying hard to preserve that decorously-stiff upper lip. Despite the fact that he has just lost the love he once called a "wonderful gift," he still remembers to thank Sandy for delivering the terrible news. "It was good of you to tell me," Justin says. "It couldn't have been easy." The film then flashes back to the day the couple met. While reading a lecture written by another diplomat who could not be present, Justin is vigorously questioned by this pretty, pointed and potent woman. While the others in attendance find Tessa a bit much and walk out, he cannot help but be filled with admiration for her intelligence and fearless ferocity. Shortly thereafter they are seen in bed together, kissing and laughing and generally having a magnificent time, all the while bathed in a bright white light. The content, mood and look of the scene could not be more different than what follows, as Justin, now in a much darker place, is identifying Tessa's battered and charred remains in a morgue. Sandy, who accompanied him there, vomits.

In further scenes from their past, viewers see how Tessa had asked Justin to take her with him to his post in Africa, and how surprised and flattered he looked that she would agree to go there as his wife. (It might be noted here that there was a greater age difference between the two in the book than the nine-year gap between the actors.) He says they hardly know each other. "You can learn me," she replies. Those watching learn about her as well, as Tessa, soon pregnant, is seen delightedly dedicated to and appreciated by those in this bleak locale. There are a number of telling scenes which exhibit her boundless, whatever-it-takes determination to affect a positive change. At a fancy dinner party attended by members of the High Commission and the Kenyan Health Ministry, Tessa throws caution and proper etiquette to the wind by boldly asking questions of the guests. Sandy tells Justin he should rein her in, but Justin knows that would be like trying to break a beautiful, fire-snorting horse, a task which would not only be virtually impossible but also rather sad. Later, in the hospital after losing her baby, Tessa's mind is on a sickly teenaged mother whose death is being hastened in the name of research and development. (Tessa even acts as a wet nurse to try and help the poor soul.) In another scene, she is unsuccessful in convincing Justin to stop the car and pick up the girl's family as they trudge along the road. He says with reasoned, detached practicality that they cannot get intimately involved in the lives of all these needy people, but all Tessa knows is that these are three she feels she can help. Lastly, Tessa gets Sandy to contact his superior, Sir Bernard Pellegrin (wonderful Bill Nighy), concerning the disturbing evidence she has amassed about the concealed dangers of a new tuberculosis wonder drug called Dypraxa. Sandy refuses to show her the secret (and decidedly unfavorable) response, saying it could ruin him if he does. Tessa gets her hands on it with a titillating promise to the love-struck man of a tryst, a pledge she has absolutely no intention of fulfilling. Again: whatever it takes.

It is not surprising that drug thugs wanting to suppress the report found it imperative to stop the seemingly unstoppable Tessa and Dr. Bluhm. (His horrifically mutilated corpse is eventually found.) What they clearly did not count on was sedate Justin picking up the torch to finish the job. As he does, it is like the flowering of one of the plants he tends, a slow but sure blossoming which reveals wonderful attributes previously unseen. It is intriguing and suspenseful to watch Justin's journey of discovery, traveling through Europe, the Sudan, and then finally back to Kenya, all the time followed (and at one point beaten) by those who threaten to silence him too. He daringly asks questions and painstakingly pours over endless communications, and as the dangerous network of cooperative malfeasance Tessa had gotten too close to comes clearly into view, so—for the very first time—does a complete portrait of the woman he loved, not only what he loved about her but also all the things he had missed. Justin comes to realize with relief that his jealous suspicions about Tessa and Arnold were unfounded (the doctor was gay), and neither was she unfaithful with smitten Sandy. Justin's courageous mission to bring the truth to light is clearly not only fueled by grief and a growing sense of outrage but by a sweet sense of duty to Tessa, a need to make amends. He feels he failed her, his detachment causing her to go instead to Sandy, who then betrayed her trust and helped bring about her death. Justin feels he owes her. For once in his life, "proper channels" be damned.

There are numerous moments of import and interest during Justin's transformative travels, but two are especially touching and meaningful. After garnering new insights concerning his wife and what she was up against from revealing communications sent by Tessa to her cousin Arthur "Ham" Hammond (top-notch Richard McCabe), Justin is seen sobbing through the glass of a window, overcome by deep admiration, regret and despair. It is a striking image, palpably capturing his pain through the pane. After getting his hands on a copy of Tessa's suppressed report from Dr. Marcus Lorbeer (Pete Postlethwaite) in southern Sudan, the two dash onto an airplane to narrowly escape a thunderous and deadly border raid. A young child runs along with them, and Justin unsuccessfully tries to take her along to safety. His newfound, passionate concern and outrage echo Tessa and that day in the car. A child's life is at stake, he cries, and "this is one we can help here!" He has gone from being temperate to having a temper, from dignified to indignant, from love for his wife to deep devotion for her and her work. Both literally and figuratively, Justin has come a long way.

As *The Constant Gardener* approaches its climax, one wonders exactly how Justin's journey will end but senses that it will end him. Stating wistfully that he has no home now because Tessa was his home, he mails the report to Ham so that the lid can be blown off the conspiratorial doings and change affected. It is deliciously done at Justin's memorial service back in England, with an especially startled, embarrassed, and hopefully ruined Pellegrin in attendance. In the end, viewers see Justin travel back to the exact spot where Tessa expired. He sits serenely as the henchmen who killed her come now for him. His work is done. He is at peace. He is ready and eager to go home.

Made on a budget of $25 million, *The Constant Gardener* grossed $33.5 million and received a slew of positive reviews. As awards season got underway, the film quickly started racking up nominations. It was directed by Brazilian Fernando Meirelles in an energized style similar to but more controlled and assured than his Oscar-nominated helming of *City of God* (2002), which focused on youth gangs in the slums of Rio de Janeiro. Here he makes Africa and its landscape come vividly alive with shots of children's faces, brightly-colored garb, crowded shantytowns, and reddish-brown, dusty earth. *The Constant Gardener* is a thriller, but a touching one. It contains excitement, intrigue, and provocative social and political commentary, but at the heart of the story is a heart.

David L. Boxerbaum

CREDITS

Justin Quale: Ralph Fiennes
Tessa Quayle: Rachel Weisz
Sandy Woodrow: Danny Huston
Sir Bernard Pellegrin: Bill Nighy
Lorbeer: Pete Postlethwaite
Arthur Hammond: Richard McCabe
Tim Donohue: Donald (Don) Sumpter
Gloria Woodrow: Juliet Aubrey
Arnold Bluhm: Hubert Kounde
Ghita Pearson: Archie Panjabi
Sir Kenneth Curiss: Gerard McSorley
Origin: Great Britain
Language: English
Released: 2005
Production: Simon Channing Williams; Potboiler Production; released by Focus Features
Directed by: Fernando Meirelles
Written by: Jeffrey Caine
Cinematography by: Cesar Charlone
Music by: Alberto Iglesias
Sound: Stuart Wilson
Editing: Claire Simpson
Art Direction: Denis Schnegg
Costumes: Odile Dicks-Mireaux
Production Design: Mark Tildesley
MPAA rating: R
Running time: 129 minutes

REVIEWS

Boxoffice Online. August, 2005.
Chicago Sun-Times Online. August 31, 2005.
Entertainment Weekly Online. August 24, 2005.
Los Angeles Times Online. August 31, 2005.
New York Times Online. August 31, 2005.
Premiere Magazine Online. August 24, 2005.
Variety Online. August 15, 2005.
Washington Post Online. August 31, 2005, p. C01.

QUOTES

Sir Bernard Pellegrin: "Some very nasty things can be found under rocks, especially in foreign gardens."

TRIVIA

Ralph Fiennes operated the camera for Justin's point-of-view shots in the film.

AWARDS

Oscars 2005: Support. Actress (Weisz)
British Acad. 2005: Film Editing
Golden Globes 2006: Support. Actress (Weisz)
Screen Actors Guild 2005: Support. Actress (Weisz)

Nomination:

Oscars 2005: Adapt. Screenplay, Film Editing, Orig. Score
British Acad. 2005: Actor (Fiennes), Actress, Adapt. Screenplay, Cinematog., Director (Meirelles), Film, Sound, Orig. Score
Golden Globes 2006: Director (Meirelles), Film—Drama
Writers Guild 2005: Adapt. Screenplay
Broadcast Film Critics 2005: Film, Support. Actress (Weisz).

CONSTANTINE

Hell wants him. Heaven won't take him. Earth needs him.
—Movie tagline

The wager between heaven and hell is on Earth.
—Movie tagline

Box Office: $75.5 million

Constantine is based on a series of graphic novels from DC Comics/Vertigo. The character of John Constantine was created by Alan Moore in 1985 for an issue of "The Swamp Thing" and became its own series in 1987 with writer Jamie Delano. In the novels, John Constantine is an occult magician—a drinker, a womanizer, and a chain smoker who was born in Liverpool and whose appearance was modeled on singer Sting. This means he's blonde and British and nothing at all like Keanu Reeves who plays him in this movie. Which also happens to be set in a noirish L.A. where there seems to be more rain than sun. Maybe that has something to do with all the demons that are suddenly making an appearance. *Constantine* is upfront about its Christian iconography so if you know your bible, it might be a little easier to follow (though the film certainly plays fasts and loose with its religious mythology).

But before we get to the demons, we have a little prequel. In Mexico, a scavenger (Jesse Ramirez) is digging around the ruins of a church when he finds the Spear of Destiny wrapped in a Nazi flag. We already know that "He who possesses the Spear of Destiny holds the fate of the world in his hands." The Spear possesses the scavenger and he heads for the border with it. A brand also appears on his wrist that looks like a cross within a circle (or maybe it's an X, it's a little hard to see clearly).

Back in L.A., John Constantine is called upon to perform an exorcism on a young Asian girl. This is business as usual for John, an antisocial antihero who dresses like a reserve member of the *Reservoir Dogs* team—slim black suit, white shirt, skinny black tie, and trench coat since the weather usually sucks. John's a cynical chain smoker with terminal lung cancer and a frustrated young sidekick named Chaz (Shia LaBoeuf), who wants to take a more active role in demon dispatching. John seems inexplicably put out by this particularly demon even after he successful sends it back to hell.

Next we see conflicted loner detective Angela Dodson (Rachel Weisz) going to confession. Her identical twin—Isabel—is confined to a Catholic mental hospital because she hears voices. Isabel jumps from the roof, through a skylight, and lands in the hospital's pool (water is a big theme here). Isabel also has the same brand as the Mexican scavenger. Angela goes to the scene of her sister's death but refuses to believe that Isabel committed suicide because they are devout Catholics and suicide is a mortal sin that will condemn Isabel's soul to hell. She wants her sister to have a Catholic burial but cannot persuade the priest to agree. Constantine is having his own problems in that department: he's trying to persuade the androgynous archangel Gabriel (played by the androgynous Tilda Swinton) that all his demon dispatching should earn him points for good behavior and a chance to get into heaven. For some reason we are yet unaware of, this is not about to happen. As Gabriel tells John succinctly: "You're fucked."

John's worried about the unusual demon traffic and asks his crazy psychic friend, Father Hennessey (Pruitt Taylor Vince), to "listen to the ether." Hennessey picks up a story about Isabel's suicide. Meanwhile, Angela is watching the security tape of Isabel's suicide and hears her sister call out "Constantine." Constantine has more problems when he is attacked by a bug demon. He goes to Papa Midnite's (Djimon Hounsou) occult club for some answers but his fears are dismissed: "Demons stay in hell. Angels in heaven. The great détente of the original superpowers." Only half-breeds are allowed on the earthly plane as influence peddlers. One of these demonic messengers is Balthazar (Gavin Rossdale).

Angela goes to Constantine for some answers but dismisses his stories of demons, until she sees some herself. She wants to know if Isabel's soul is indeed in hell and John goes to visit. (This involves a freakish scene where he sticks his feet in a pan of water and holds a cat.) It's a smoky, burning, orange apocalypse: John gets chased by demons and does see Isabel. He brings back her hospital bracelet as proof for Angela and explains his powers to her: "When I was a kid I could see things—things humans aren't supposed to see." These visions drive him crazy and, as a teenager, John commits suicide—"officially I was dead for two minutes"—goes to hell but comes back. Now, he deals with the half-breed demons and when they break the rules, "I send their sorry ass straight back to hell." This does not make him popular; in fact, John has been told that Satan himself would come out of hell to personally collect John's soul upon his death.

Angela admits that both she and Isabel could also see things as children but Angela denied it as she grew up while Isabel never did (hence the mental hospital). Hennessey is driven to his death by Balthazar but not before carving the mysterious circle and cross into his palm. John's friend Beeman (Max Baker) manages to interpret the symbol for John before his own demise: Satan has a son named Mammon who wants to forge his own hellish kingdom on earth but in order to cross into the earthly plane he needs to possess a powerful psychic and have some divine assistance. Naturally, Angela's the psychic, especially after she makes her own little trip into hell. John goes after Balthazar and learns that the Spear of Destiny, which has Jesus' blood on it, will be the weapon to release Mammon with Angela as, uh, the incubator. Angela is pulled away from John and lands in the pool of the mental hospital (water is the universal conduit between the earthy and unearthly realms).

After taking another little side trip to hell, John sees the Spear of Destiny in the scavenger's hands and that he has gone to the mental hospital. John and Chaz follow and vanquish a bunch of half-breed demon guards. Angela has been possessed by Mammon but John thinks he's exorcised the demon until an unseen presence kills Chaz. Made corporeal, Gabriel is revealed to be Mammon's heavenly helper, justifying his actions by saying that mankind is only at its best under the worse possible conditions: "those of you who survive the reign of hell on earth will be worthy of God's love." Gabriel shuts John out of the room and takes the Spear of Destiny to kill Angela and release Mammon when time suddenly stops.

John has slit his wrists to die again—and Satan (played by a white suit-wearing Peter Stormare) comes personally to collect his soul as John anticipated. But first John informs Satan that Gabriel is about to release Mammon into the human world. Satan is not happy (the kid is overstepping his place). He pulls Angela out of a surprised Gabriel's grasp: "Looks like somebody doesn't have your back anymore." (Gabriel gets his, losing his wings and becoming human.) Constantine asks Satan to release Isabel's soul from hell and he obliges—this coupled with John's suicidal sacrifice makes him worthy of entrance into heaven. But Satan isn't having it; he pulls John back, literally pulls the cancer from his lungs, and informs him that John is going to live and have another chance to prove that he really does belong in hell.

John and Angela have a final meeting. He gives her the Spear of Destiny to hide and she walks away. John looks out over the city, pulls out a stick of gum, and says: "I guess there's a plan for all of us. I had to die—twice—just to figure that out. Like the book says, he works his works in mysterious ways. Some people like it, some people don't."

Which pretty much sums up how a viewer will feel about the movie. Francis Lawrence is a first-time feature director who got his start in music videos and *Constantine* has a lot of visual flair. It also has a lot of story (although it boils down to one man's search for salvation). But for some reason, it's just not very involving. And that can't just be laid at the feet of the enigmatic Reeves, whose dry-voiced blankness suits the character (or at least the film version of the character). Weisz, who previously appeared with Reeves in the ineffectual 1996 thriller *Chain Reaction,* is stuck in a role that's little more than damsel-in-distress. Swinton's frankly scary but she's only got a couple of scenes and Stormare makes the devil into a perverse hambone. Maybe all the exposition that's needed for the story to make any sense just slows everything down. Anyway, if you do manage to sit through *Constantine* be sure to stay through all the end credits and you'll get a short bonus scene. John goes to visit Chaz's grave and places his cigarette lighter upon it, as he turns away, Chaz rises up as an angel. At least someone got his heavenly reward.

Christine Tomassini

CREDITS

John Constantine: Keanu Reeves
Angela Dodson/Isabel Dodson: Rachel Weisz
Midnite: Djimon Hounsou
Beeman: Max Baker
Father Hennessy: Pruitt Taylor Vince
Gabriel: Tilda Swinton
Satan: Peter Stormare
Chas: Shia LeBeouf
Balthazar: Gavin Rossdale
Detective Weiss: Jose Zuniga
Vermin Man: Larry Cedar
Origin: USA
Language: English
Released: 2005
Production: Donner/Shuler-Donner Productions, Benjamin Melnicker, Michael Uslan, Erwin Stoff, Lorenzo di Bonaventura, Akiva Goldsman; Donners' Company, 3 Arts Productions, Batfilm Prods, Weed Road Pictures; released by Warner Bros.
Directed by: Francis Lawrence
Written by: Kevin Brodbin, Frank Cappello
Cinematography by: Philippe Rousselot
Music by: Brian Tyler, Klaus Badelt
Sound: Willie Burton
Editing: Wayne Wahrman
Art Direction: David Lazan
Costumes: Louise Frogley
Production Design: Naomi Shohan
MPAA rating: R
Running time: 120 minutes

REVIEWS

Boxoffice Online. February, 2005.
Chicago Sun-Times Online. February 18, 2005.
Entertainment Weekly Online. February 16, 2005.
Los Angeles Times Online. February 18, 2005.
New York Times Online. February 18, 2005.
Premiere Magazine Online. February 18, 2005.

Variety Online. February 7, 2005.
Washington Post Online. February 18, 2005, p. WE41.

QUOTES

John Constantine: "What if I told you that God and the devil made a wager, a kind of standing bet for the souls of all mankind?"

TRIVIA

In the comic book *Hellblazer* on which the movie is based, the character of John Constantine is from Liverpool. In this movie, Constantine is from Los Angeles.

CRASH

You think you know who you are. You have no idea.
—Movie tagline
Live your life at the point of impact.
—Movie tagline
Moving at the speed of life, we are bound to collide with each other.
—Movie tagline

Box Office: $53.4 million

Crash is of a similar ilk as *Short Cuts* and *Magnolia*—films that feature vignettes of various lives in Los Angeles. Or more specifically, lives that are entangled with one another in ironic, artistic and meaningful ways—all accompanied by good lighting and an appropriate soundtrack.

Crash is full of contrasts. There are bursts of hateful anger and horrible things are said, but the film, helped quite a bit by Paul Haggis' graceful direction and Mark Isham's peaceful soundtrack, manages to seem almost meditative. People who say terribly racist things turn out to be nice guys otherwise. Nice, mild-mannered folks perform appalling acts. The movie has a certain realism in reflecting the harsh ways in which people may behave, but it is all filmed in a dreamy, allegorical fashion.

The story begins with Graham (Don Cheadle), a police detective, at a car crash site. Graham seems like an intelligent, moral guy but in a subsequent scene, he is mocking his Latina girlfriend, Ria (Jennifer Esposito), and refusing to learn exactly what country she is from. Such is the modus operandi of Paul Haggis, who also wrote the screenplay for the award-winning *Million Dollar Baby.* Characters are complex, with their good and bad parts coexisting side by side.

Anthony (Chris Bridges aka rapper Ludacris), an angry black man, is always annoying his friend Peter (Larenz Tate) with his constant complaints about racism. As they walk down a crowded street and see people clutching their purses tighter, he comments bitterly, "We're the only black people, surrounded by a sea of over-caffeinated white people—why aren't we the ones who are scared?" He makes a good point, and that makes it all the more shocking when it turns out that Anthony actually is the kind of thug people imagine him to be. Perhaps it is this kind of unexpectedness that made the film so well-liked. Most movies a) do not touch the subject of racism and b) if they do, the good and bad people are clearly delineated.

In one particularly memorable scene, unabashedly racist cop Officer Ryan (Matt Dillon) pulls over a SUV occupied by African-American TV producer Cameron (Terrence Howard) and his wife Christine (Thandie Newton). The couple is coming home from a party and a tipsy Christine had been performing a sexual act on her husband. Ryan immediately accuses the couple of stealing the car, then submits them to humiliating scrutiny. He lingers during his search of Christine and fondles her in an inappropriate way. Cameron and Ryan's rookie partner, Hansen, (Ryan Phillippe) look on horrified, cowed by Ryan's power and his abuse of it. The moment, already uncomfortable, becomes even more cringe-inducing by the way Haggis lets it play out in painfully slow real time.

Other lives explored are those of a city district attorney, Rick, (Brendan Fraser) and his wife, Jean (Sandra Bullock). After the two are carjacked, Rick despairs that the criminals were African-American. He fears that the event will paint him as either racist or soft on crime. Jean, who is unhappy with her own pampered life, takes the incident as cause to let her racism run rampant. She has all the locks in her house changed, then becomes convinced that the Mexican locksmith, Daniel (Michael Pena), is going to return and rob her. Iranian shopkeeper Farhad (Shaun Toub) becomes certain that everyone is trying to cheat him and feels that he needs to fight back to save himself and his family.

Some of the dialogue seems a bit writerly, such as when a character comments "It's the sense of touch. I think that we miss that touch so much that we crash into each other just so we can feel something." But the whole is presented in such an artful manner that an occasional overwrought moment does not much matter.

Crash was one of the more acclaimed films of the year. David Denby of *The New Yorker* wrote, "*Crash* is hyper-articulate and often breathtakingly intelligent and always brazenly alive." Roger Ebert of *The Chicago Sun-Times* wrote, "Not many films have the possibility of making their audiences better people. I don't expect *Crash* to work any miracles, but I believe anyone seeing it is likely to be moved to have a little more sympathy for people not like themselves." A. O. Scott of *The New York Times* gave the film a negative review, writing "*Crash* writes its themes in capital letters—Race, Class, Life, Fate—and then makes them the subjects of a series of speeches and the pivot points for a succession of clumsy reveals...[It's a] movie full of heart and devoid of life; crudely manipulative when it tries hardest to be subtle; and profoundly complacent in spite of its intention to unsettle and disturb."

Jill Hamilton

CREDITS

Anthony: Ludacris
Jean Cabot: Sandra Bullock
Graham Walters: Don Cheadle
Officer Ryan: Matt Dillon
Ria: Jennifer Esposito
Flanagan: William Fichtner
Rick Cabot: Brendan Fraser
Cameron Thayer: Terrence DaShon Howard
Christine Thayer: Thandie Newton
Officer Tom Hanson: Ryan Phillippe
Peter: Larenz Tate
Karen: Nona Gaye
Daniel: Michael Pena
Graham's Mother: Beverly Todd
Lt. Dixon: Keith David
Farhad: Shaun Toub
Shaniqua: Loretta Devine
Origin: USA
Language: English
Released: 2005
Production: Cathy Schulman, Bob Yari, Mark R. Harris, Don Cheadle, Bobby Moresco, Paul Haggis; Harris Communications, Apollo Proscreen, Bull's Eye Entertainment; released by Lions Gate Films
Directed by: Paul Haggis
Written by: Paul Haggis, Robert Moresco
Cinematography by: James Muro
Music by: Mark Isham
Sound: Richard Van Dyke
Editing: Hughes Winborne
Art Direction: Brandee Dell'aringa
Costumes: Linda Bass
Production Design: Laurence Bennett
MPAA rating: R
Running time: 100 minutes

REVIEWS

Boxoffice Online. May, 2005.
Chicago Sun-Times Online. May 5, 2005.
Entertainment Weekly Online. May 4, 2005.
Los Angeles Times Online. May 6, 2005.
New York Times Online. May 6, 2005.
Premiere Magazine Online. May 5, 2005.
Variety Online. September 21, 2004.
Washington Post Online. May 6, 2005, p. C01.

AWARDS

Oscars 2005: Film, Film Editing, Orig. Screenplay
British Acad. 2005: Orig. Screenplay, Support. Actress (Newton)
Ind. Spirit 2006: First Feature, Support. Actor (Dillon)
Natl. Bd. of Review 2005: Breakthrough Perf. (Howard)
Screen Actors Guild 2005: Cast
Writers Guild 2005: Orig. Screenplay

Nomination:

Oscars 2005: Director (Haggis), Song ("In the Deep"), Support. Actor (Dillon)
British Acad. 2005: Cinematog., Film, Film Editing, Sound, Support. Actor (Cheadle, Dillon)
Directors Guild 2005: Director (Haggis)
Golden Globes 2006: Screenplay, Support. Actor (Dillon)
Screen Actors Guild 2005: Support. Actor (Cheadle), Support. Actor (Dillon).

CRY_WOLF

Box Office: $10 million

Written by director Jeff Wadlow and producer Beau Bauman, *Cry_Wolf* had a unique and auspicious beginning. As the winner of the first Chrysler Million Dollar Film Festival, Wadlow triumphed over several hundred competitors for a million-dollar grant to turn a completed script into a feature film. But then something appeared to have gone awry between this victory and the movie's release date. For some reason, Rogue Pictures withheld this teen thriller from critics before its opening (usually a sign that a film is awful and even embarrassing). The result, however, turns out to be a pleasant surprise. *Cry_Wolf,* anchored not only by a clever premise and a tricky, complex script but also by two appealing lead actors, builds suspense and keeps the audience guessing through some surprising twists, delivering far more than one would expect from this often stale genre.

The opening scene actually plays with our genre expectations as we see one of the most familiar of horror clichés—a pretty blonde girl being chased through the woods by a maniac and finally stumbling and falling to the ground before she is killed. But how she meets her fate is ingenious; the killer finds her by ringing her cell phone, a hint of the unique spin the movie will offer on old conventions and the way contemporary technology will figure as a key plot device.

Julian Morris stars as Owen, an English transfer student to an exclusive boarding school called Westlake Preparatory Academy. On his first day, he meets Dodger (Lindy Booth), a smart, cute redhead who takes an immediate interest in him and brings him into her clique, a kind of liars' club, which steals away to the chapel at midnight to play a game based on deceiving each other. With everyone's eyes closed, Dodger marks one person as the wolf (the rest are sheep), and then, through rounds of questions and accusations, the wolf tries to keep his identity a secret while the others try to identify him. Owen, whom Dodger designates as the wolf, outwits everyone and thus distinguishes himself in her eyes. The group represents a range of ethnicities and types, such as Lewis (Paul James), the black guy with dreadlocks, and Randall (Jesse Janzen), the cool dude with multiple piercings, but, apart from Dodger and Owen, the characters do not have very distinct personalities.

Dodger wants to take the game to a higher level by concocting a lie that will scare the whole school, and she and Owen lead the gang in sending out a mass e-mail warning everyone that the murder of local girl Becky (Erica Yates), the victim from the film's beginning, was the work of a serial killer known as the Wolf, a madman wielding a hunting knife and wearing an orange ski mask and camouflage jacket, who will strike again but this time at the school itself.

Soon strange events begin to occur. Owen receives threatening instant messages on his computer and wonders if Dodger is having fun or if the killer is taunting him. Then his roommate, Tom (Jared Padalecki), finds his half of the room ransacked. Randall goes away for a long weekend and does not return. Most ominous of all, someone dressed as the Wolf stalks Dodger and Owen in the library.

Given the setup, one is led to believe that *Cry_Wolf* is going to be a standard slasher flick with the killer picking off one by one the kids who have started the rumor, as if their penchant for crying wolf has provoked Becky's killer to stalk them. But that is not the formula the film follows. For a while, the screenplay toys with our expectations, teasing us with suspicious characters, such as the young journalism teacher, Mr. Walker (rock star Jon Bon Jovi), who has been having an affair with Dodger, and the mysterious groundskeeper, who always seems to be lurking at the edge of the action. The narrative, however, also takes a while to get going and fills time dangling red herrings, such as a knife planted in Owen's bag to get him into trouble and his frightening encounter with the Wolf that turns out to be a joke played by Mercedes (Sandra McCoy), one of his friends.

Then comes Halloween, when the Wolf starts his killing spree. Seeing the various members of his liars' club being attacked, Owen finally takes refuge in Mr. Walker's office, where he finds a gun. When the teacher arrives, Owen believes that he is the Wolf, and a struggle over the weapon ends in Mr. Walker being shot dead. But in the film's first clever twist, it turns out that all the other deaths that night did not happen. They were a hoax perpetrated by Owen's gang, the culmination of an elaborate practical joke designed to scare him.

In the film's second big twist, Owen pieces together the bigger picture. Because Becky was sleeping with Mr. Walker, Dodger killed her and then engineered the Wolf prank so that it would climax with Owen killing Mr. Walker in self-defense without drawing any suspicion to herself. If one thinks about the ending too much, it seems far-fetched. After all, Dodger had to fool a lot of people and rely on a very elaborate scheme coming together perfectly, especially all the make-believe killings going off like clockwork on Halloween night. And yet, when the truth is revealed, it not only fits with what has gone before but is consistent with the character and makes so many details take on a deeper meaning, from Dodger picking Owen in the first place because "You're a good guy, you're predictable" (qualities she terms his "weakness"), to her description of the original game's objective—"Avoid suspicion, manipulate your friends, eliminate your enemies"—which might as well be her personal credo as well.

Given its critical reception (more indifference than outright hostility) and the lack of faith of its distributor, *Cry_Wolf* is surprisingly well done, and Booth, concealing several layers of motivations as Dodger, stands out among the ensemble. While the story may appear to revolve around a masked maniac, this is not, ultimately, a typical horror film but rather a suspenseful thriller of deception and gamesmanship. It may take a while to find its rhythm, but Wadlow's feature debut is ultimately more intelligent than other films of this genre and deserving of a wider audience than it received.

Peter N. Chumo II

CREDITS

Dodger: Lindy Booth
Tom: Jared Padalecki
Regina: Kristy Wu
Lewis: Paul James
Owen: Julian Morris
Mercedes: Sandra McCoy

Mr. Walker: Jon Bon Jovi
Mr. Matthews: Gary Cole
Randall: Jesse Janzen
Headmistress Tinsley: Anna Deavere Smith
Origin: USA
Released: 2005
Production: Beau Bauman; Hypnotic; released by Rogue Pictures
Directed by: Jeff Wadlow
Written by: Jeff Wadlow, Beau Bauman
Cinematography by: Romeo Tirone
Music by: Michael Wandmacher
Sound: Glenn Morgan
Music Supervisor: Julianne Jordan
Editing: Seth Gordon
Art Direction: Julie Smith
Costumes: Alysia Raycraft
Production Design: Martina Buckley
MPAA rating: PG-13
Running time: 90 minutes

REVIEWS

Entertainment Weekly Online. September 21, 2005.
Los Angeles Times Online. September 17, 2005.
New York Times Online. September 17, 2005.
Variety Online. September 18, 2005.

CURSED

What doesn't kill you makes you stronger.
—Movie tagline

Box Office: $19.3 million

There's something very appropriate about the title of director Wes Craven's latest film, *Cursed,* as it surely does seem to be jinxed. Craven, along with scriptwriter Kevin Williamson, broke new ground with their horror film *Scream* in 1996 and set the bar higher for every fright film to come after it. Unfortunately, not only can't *Cursed* come close to the bar, it seems intent on slithering so far underneath it that one can imagine only a brief life-span for it in theaters before it heads off to video stores.

In development since 2000, *Cursed* was just four weeks from its scheduled wrap date when it was shut down. During an 11-week hiatus the film was re-written to the point that more than half the film had to be re-shot when production began again. Between the re-write and the delay, several original cast members—many of whom appeared in a substantial amount of already-shot footage—were either written out or had to be replaced because of scheduling conflicts. Gone were Mandy Moore, Skeet Ulrich, Omar Epps, and Corey Feldman. But the studio still wasn't done with the film, because Miramax then wanted it re-edited for a PG-13 rating and demanded improved special effects. By the time they were all done, the hoped for August 2003 release date had turned into February of 2005.

The film that finally did reach theaters cost $40 million to make and $25 million to promote, but in the traditional sign that the studio has lost faith in a film, critics were not allowed to screen it in advance. In fact, it is said that *Cursed* bears so little resemblance to what was originally imagined by Craven and written by Williamson that both have distanced themselves from the final product. It is also said that the original script involved a serial killer who turned out to be a werewolf and three friends coming together to combat it, but what resulted after all that meddling is a cheesy, by-the-numbers werewolf film that could have been written by a couple of high school students.

Briefly, the plot goes like this: Ellie Myers (Christina Ricci) and her brother Jimmy (Jesse Eisenberg) live together because their parents have died. Jimmy is a smart, awkward, shy kid who is the perfect target for the high school bully (*The Gilmore Girls'* resident bad boy Milo Ventimiglia). Ellie is a harried producer for Craig Kilborn's television show who has to placate Scott Baio's pushy publicist (Judy Greer) on the one hand while balancing her current love interest, Jake Taylor (Joshua Jackson), who is himself harried trying to get a new movie-themed Hollywood nightclub opened.

It's not long before Ellie and Jimmy have an encounter with a werewolf who manages to injure them just enough to turn them into werewolves too, although they don't realize it at first. Soon Ellie becomes extraordinarily sexually attractive and can smell blood at a thousand paces and Jimmy is putting the school bully in his place in the very public arena of the wrestling team tryouts. Now the search is on to find out who Ellie and Jimmy's werewolf "benefactor" is before they officially turn, for if they can kill him or her first, they will be saved from their lycanthropic future.

The basic plot for *Cursed* is incredibly uninspired and contains none of the clever pop-culture satire one has come to expect from Williamson (who was also responsible for 1998's *The Faculty* and 1997's *I Know What You Did Last Summer*) and none of the quality frights one expects from Craven (who also brought us the *Nightmare on Elm Street* series). This latest endeavor has a very stale and hackneyed feel to it. Its pace is slow, the plot un-engaging, and the dialogue positively laughable. For a horror film it commits the unforgivable sin of not being scary or intense, and after the new paradigm set by *Scream* it also commits the sin of omission in that it seems to have no sense of humor about itself. (Unless one counts the unintentionally bad CGI werewolf special effects or the cameo by Portia de Rossi as a gypsy.)

Cursed fails to hit any of the right notes for a modern horror film, or an old-fashioned one for that matter.

Beverley Bare Buehrer

CREDITS

Ellie: Christina Ricci
Jake: Joshua Jackson
Jimmy: Jesse Eisenberg
Joanie: Judy Greer
Bo: Milo Ventimiglia
Brooke: Kristina Anapau
Zela: Portia de Rossi
Becky: Shannon Elizabeth
Jenny: Mya
Scott Baio (Cameo)
Origin: USA
Language: English
Released: 2004
Production: Kevin Williamson, Marianne Maddalena; Outerbanks Entertainment; released by Dimension Films
Directed by: Wes Craven
Written by: Kevin Williamson
Cinematography by: Robert McLachlan
Music by: Marco Beltrami
Sound: Jim Stuebe
Music Supervisor: Ed Gerrard
Editing: Patrick Lussier
Art Direction: Jeff Knipp
Costumes: Alix Fridberg
Production Design: Bruce Miller
MPAA rating: PG-13
Running time: 97 minutes

REVIEWS

Boxoffice Online. February, 2005.
Entertainment Weekly Online. March 2, 2005.
Los Angeles Times Online. February 28, 2005.
New York Times Online. February 26, 2005.
Variety Online. February 25, 2005.

QUOTES

Joanie: "I guess there's no such thing as safe sex with a werewolf."

TRIVIA

A figure of Freddy Krueger can be seen in the background of the wax museum. Freddy was created by director Wes Craven in his *A Nightmare on Elm Street.*

D

DARK WATER

Some mysteries were never meant to be solved.
—Movie tagline

Dark water conceals darker secrets.
—Movie tagline

Box Office: $25.4 million

Dark Water is one of those films that is so atmospheric that one can actually smell the dank rot and mildew. Whether this contributes to the film's suspense as opposed to just the general discomfort of the viewer is highly subjective.

Dahlia Williams (Jennifer Connelly) should take some time to smell the mold before she commits to renting apartment 9F in a building on Manhattan's neighboring Roosevelt Island. The agent, Mr. Murray (John C. Reilly), is so unctuous—if not a bit sleazy—in his desire to rent the place that he is not about to point out to her the dark spot oozing on the bedroom ceiling. But Dahlia, who is going through a messy separation from her husband Kyle (Dougray Scott), cannot afford to live anywhere else. So despite dark hallways, an unfriendly super Mr. Veek (Pete Posthelwaite), and an elevator with a mind of its own, Dahlia puts down a deposit and moves in with her six-year-old daughter Ceci (Ariel Gade).

While Dahlia now at least has a roof over her head, her problems are not over. She has to find a job, enroll Ceci in school, get the recalcitrant Mr. Veek to fix the leak in her ceiling, and stave off the hostile attacks of her husband. The first two fall into place fairly easily and Mr. Veek even makes a half-hearted attempt at the leak, but as Kyle's hostility mounts Dahlia is forced to get legal advice in the form of Jeff Platzer (Tim Roth). Mr. Platzer is somewhat of an enigma himself. He seems to work out of his car—although he does claim that his offices are being painted—and makes excuses about being reluctant to leave his family on his night out, only to see that he is at the movies by himself.

Kyle, who fears losing Ceci, complains that Dahlia had a terrible childhood. That she had an abusive father and was abandoned by her alcoholic mother. That she now suffers from crippling migraines and paranoid delusions. Of course this last comment sets the audience up for an interesting mystery, and it is a mystery masterfully played out by Jennifer Connelly. As Ceci finds herself with an imaginary friend, and footsteps run across the floor overhead in the empty apartment, and Dahlia finds dark water coming out of her faucets, we wonder if she's really experiencing the supernatural in her apartment or if she's losing her mind.

Dark Water is based on the Japanese film by Hideo Nakata and a story by Koji Suzuki, both of whom were responsible for the original film that became America's *The Ring.* Just like the recent *The Grudge* these three Japanese films were remade for Western audiences. Also similar to the other two, *Dark Water* presents the ghostly in the form of a child, but unlike the other two this latest remake seems less Byzantine. It is interesting to note, though, that all three have that deep feeling of malice that has become a hallmark of the growing genre of American translations of Japanese films.

This latest reworking of a Japanese horror film is also the first film in English for director Walter Salles who has won critical acclaim for last year's *Motorcycle*

Diaries and 1998's *Central Station*. And like the latter, *Dark Water*, too, explores the relationship between a child and its mother. And between Salles sensitive direction and Connelly's fine acting, we do come to care about this mother who is tortured by demons from without and within.

Even the supporting roles in this film are performed with gusto. John C. Reilly takes a role that could have been simply villainous and actually manages to make it amusing. And the chameleon-like Tim Roth plays Dahlia's lawyer like a knight in dull armor who forgot where he parked his horse. While the craggy-faced Pete Posthelwaite brings a real sense of wariness if not outright danger to his super. But of all the "characters" in *Dark Water*, perhaps none is as malignant as is the damp and oppressive environment of that apartment on Roosevelt Island, where, by the way, it never stops raining. Apartment 9F never feels like that home we all need as a safe haven in this world. Instead it becomes another place of danger and feeds feelings of alienation and isolation.

While the atmosphere is appropriately menacing and while the acting is uniformly superior, *Dark Water* is not all that it could be. It seems to move slowly and provides a plot very similar to those we've experienced before and while the film feels creepy, there really aren't any true scares in it. It does attempt to apply some psychology to the supernatural, but the ending still seems like a let down.

Beverley Bare Buehrer

CREDITS

Ceci: Ariel Gade
Dehlia Williams: Jennifer Connelly
Mr. Murray: John C. Reilly
Jeff Platzer: Tim Roth
Veeck: Pete Postlethwaite
Kyle: Dougray Scott
Teacher: Camryn Manheim
Natasha/Young Dahlia: Perla Haney-Jardine
Young Dahlia's teacher: Debra Monk
Dahlia's mother: Elina Lowensohn
Mary: Jennifer Baxter
Origin: USA
Language: English
Released: 2005
Production: Bill Mechanic, Roy Lee, Doug Davison; Pandemonium/Vertigo Entertainment; released by Buena Vista
Directed by: Walter Salles
Written by: Rafael Yglesias
Cinematography by: Alfonso Beato
Music by: Angelo Badalamenti
Sound: Glen Gauthier
Editing: Daniel Rezende
Art Direction: Andrew Stearn, Nicholas Lundy
Costumes: Michael Wilkinson
Production Design: Therese DePrez
MPAA rating: PG-13
Running time: 120 minutes

REVIEWS

Boxoffice Online. July, 2005.
Chicago Sun-Times Online. July 8, 2005.
Entertainment Weekly Online. July 6, 2005.
Los Angeles Times Online. July 8, 2005.
New York Times Online. July 8, 2005.
Premiere Magazine Online. July 7, 2005.
Variety Online. July 7, 2005.
Washington Post Online. July 8, 2005, p. C01.

QUOTES

Dahlia: "If you ever need me, I'll be right here."

THE DEAL

To The Victor Goes The Oil.
—Movie tagline
The stakes don't get any higher.
—Movie tagline

There is no question about the contemporary societal and political relevance of *The Deal*. The United States of America is engaged in a bitter three year war with The Confederacy of Arab States. Oil imports from the nation have been banned during the war. Gas prices have swelled to an average price of six dollars per gallon and the president is in a political meltdown. The search is underway for alternative sources of oil. Undoubtedly, the framework for the narrative touches very near to the contemporary western consciousness. However, why not call a spade a spade? The Confederacy of Arab States? This ridiculous, anti-inflammatory, politically conscious moniker converts an otherwise salient, current issue into a mockery. The United States is an actual nation. Other countries mentioned in the film are authentic. Russia is not called The Post Communist Republic of North Eastern Asia. Kazakhstan is not called The Ex-Soviet Mountainous Federation. Why is it that writer Ruth Epstein chose to create a name for a bogus nation that encapsulates the entire Middle East from Afghanistan to Lebanon to Yemen? An artistic license is one thing. An agenda is another.

After one discovers this fact, the rest of the film seems wholly trivial, which it is. The montage during credit sequence at the beginning of the film establishes the global state of affairs that will pervade the narrative of *The Deal.* Short clips of war footage mixed with clips of downtown Manhattan mixed with clips burning oil wells mixed with clips of Washington D.C. automatically verify the political mood that will dominate the film. It is a simple associative exercise in establishing the connection between oil, politics, business and war. Noam Chomsky would certainly be proud.

The first scene involves the frantic CEO of Condor, a corporate energy giant, seeking out Jared Tolson (Robert Loggia), the company's owner, in order to express his apprehension about an undisclosed transaction. Tolson assures him that there is nothing to worry about and that everything is proceeding just fine. Warning bells are already going off in my mind. Following the opening montage, in which the link between politics, business and war is made so apparent, such casual assurances must trigger a certain sense of distrust for such creatures. The result was subtle, yet effective. Then, as soon as the delicate choice was made, it was squashed. Tolson gives Rich, the CEO, further reassurance with a hug and a gaze just past the camera that made it all too apparent that he would be the villain of the narrative and exuding a distinct Lifetime Movie of the Week feel. This choice would only serve as the first in a string of instances of either over-acting or over-directing that gives *The Deal* an amateur feel throughout.

The plot itself is no exception to this trend of obviousness. The CEO is, of course, murdered by an unknown assailant. Tolson, a close friend of the President of the United States, contacts Tom Hanson (Christian Slater), a former friend of the recently deceased to help finish the deal that he had been working on before his death. Condor has been working on an agreement to ship oil from Kazakhstan to the U.S. Tolson asks Hanson to pitch the deal to his board and for a fairness opinion for a fee of $25 million. Hanson, working for the powerful, yet struggling Wall Street business management company, Dulaney and Strong, accepts the offer, as it will be profitable and successful for himself as well as his business. Hanson, however, is not in the "oil patch" and Tolson assumes he will not perform due diligence and will simply allow the deal to pass. Hanson starts to investigate at the same time that he manages two love interests: Anna (Angie Harmon), a member of the Russian mafia posing as a businesswoman, and Abbey Gallagher (Selma Blair), a "tree hugger" who is working on a plan to package alternative energy tax credits and sell them to businesses. Hanson ends up asking too many questions and ends up having his life threatened by the Russian mafia who is working with Tolson on the oil deal. Hanson finds out that there is no oil in the area of Kazakhstan in question. On the day of the pitch, Abbey is kidnapped by Anna and her comrades and Hanson is blackmailed into pitching the deal to the Condor board and giving a false fairness report. Meanwhile, Abbey escapes using the powers of seduction. Together they go to the FBI/SEC Ethics Task Force where Hanson admits his wrongdoings. A corrupt senator, however, further covers up the breaches of the law and frees Hanson. In the end, there is no justice, but a perpetuation of the lies that maintains the power structure. "History is a set of lies agreed upon" is the quote placed at the beginning of the movie, and in an obvious manner, should have been placed at the end.

Slater gives an awkward, whiny performance and shares little connection with anyone in the film besides Loggia, who plays a caricature. Blair is boring and could use some serious vocal training. Colm Feore and Angie Harmon give fine, if not short-lived performances.

Nick Kennedy

CREDITS

Tom: Christian Slater
Abbey: Selma Blair
Prof. Roseman: John Heard
Anna: Angie Harmon
John Cortland: Kevin Tighe
Janice: Francoise Yip
Hank: Colm Feore
Jared Tolson: Robert Loggia
Jerome: Philip Granger
Shane: Jim Thorburn
Hank: Ruth Epstein
Origin: USA
Language: English, Russian
Released: 2005
Production: Harvey Kahn, Ruth Epstein, Chris Dorr; Front Street Films, Clean Slate Prods.; released by Front Street Films
Directed by: Harvey Kahn
Cinematography by: Adam Sliwinski
Music by: Christopher Lennertz
Sound: Philip MacCormick
Music Supervisor: Christopher Violette
Editing: Richard Schwadel
Art Direction: Andrew Deskin, Kristina Lyne
Costumes: Katia Stand
MPAA rating: R
Running time: 107 minutes

REVIEWS

Boxoffice Online. June, 2005.
Chicago Sun-Times Online. June 17, 2005.

Los Angeles Times Online. June 17, 2005.
New York Times Online. June 17, 2005.
Variety Online. May 25, 2005.
Washington Post Online. June 16, 2005, p. WE36.

QUOTES

Jared Tolson: "That's how the game is played! Just make the deal!"

DEAR FRANKIE

One of the best-kept secrets of 2003 for mature adult viewers, the film *Dear Frankie,* was not released in the United States until 2005. This modest, independent film scripted by Andrea Gibb and first shown at the Edinburgh and Cannes film festivals in 2004, was the first feature film directed by Shona Auerbach, who had six years of experience directing commercials and who had previously directed an award-winning short, *Good Seven.* The secret of Auerbach's success depends on a very warm, human story, involving Frankie Morrison (Jack McElhone), a deaf boy who lives with his mother, Lizzie Morrison (Emily Mortimer) and grandmother (Marie Riggans). They have all just moved to Greenock, which is very near to Port Glasgow, Scotland, on the River Clyde a few miles from Glasgow proper. Frankie is nine years old and his mother has long since separated from his drunken, abusive father. She leaves with her son and her mother, who helps her maintain her resolution to become a single parent to protect herself and the boy. But the mother feels guilty and also knows the boy needs a father. Lizzie has therefore fabricated a story leading the boy to believe his father is a sailor gone to sea, working on the *HMS Accra.* She writes letters to "Dear Frankie" that the boy believes come from his father at sea, via a postal drop box in Glasgow. Lizzie feels guilty about this deception, but she also values the letters, since they provide the only means she has of listening to her son's "voice."

The major plot complication comes when Frankie discovers that the ship on which his father supposedly works is soon due to dock in Port Glasgow. Frankie, of course, will expect to see his father. Lizzie puzzles over how to resolve this dilemma. In desperation, Lizzie even goes to a pub one night to scout for likely surrogate father figures; but the barmaid, and several of the male pub patrons, wrongly assume she is a working prostitute. Thoroughly humiliated, Lizzie leaves the pub. She is later comforted by her friend, Marie (Sharon Small), who works at a fish-and-chips shop. Marie knows a man whom, she has reason to believe, will pretend to be Frankie's father in order to assist Lizzie. Lizzie is desperate enough to accept this offer, but she wants to know nothing about the man's history or background. What she does not know, therefore, is that the "Stranger" (Gerard Butler) is actually Marie's brother.

The Stranger arrives on schedule for a day's outing with Frankie (for which he is paid, by Lizzie), and he even brings Frankie a gift book about maritime creatures; the two of them get along quite well, so the Stranger asks if he can come back the next day, the day before his ship is to leave. Lizzie is at first reluctant, being mistrustful of men in general, but she finally gives in; and the next day the three of them go out on the town. Lizzie and Frankie meet the stranger quayside at the ship; as the Stranger heads for the gangplank to meet them, he slips what appears to be a bribe to a crewman, hinting to the viewer that he is not really in the merchant marine. After a happy evening of dining and dancing, the Stranger tucks an exhausted Frankie into bed. Frankie gives him a seahorse he has carved out of wood and asks if the "father" will come again, to which the Stranger can only truthfully say "I don't know." As the Stranger leaves the house, Lizzie lingers for a tender kiss and a cautious embrace. She later discovers the Stranger has returned the money she paid him. Though somewhat short of a happy ending, the possibility of his return exists. But the film is not yet over.

Meanwhile, it transpires that Frankie's real father, Davey (Cal Macaninch), is mortally ill in hospital, and his sister has been trying to locate Lizzie through a "missing person" ad in the newspaper, an ad Lizzie's mother had earlier seen but kept from her. When Lizzie finally discovers the ad, Lizzie meets her sister-in-law and finally agrees to see her sick husband, who, in turn, demands to see Frankie. But Lizzie simply cannot forgive the man, and after an ill-tempered response from the husband, Lizzie runs away. She will not give her husband a second chance and is determined to protect Frankie from him at any cost. As she tells the Stranger on their last night out, "Frankie wasn't born deaf. It was a present from his daddy." Lizzie does tell Frankie that his father is very sick, however, and soon expected to die. Frankie draws a picture of a seahorse and writes his father a note, which Lizzie takes to the hospital, along with a picture of the boy, before her husband dies.

So, end of story? Not quite. Since Frankie knows his father is now dead, Lizzie goes to the post office to close out the postal box. She finds a letter Frankie has written and mailed on his own to the Stranger, thanking him for the book, telling him he hopes they will meet again, and explaining that he knows the Stranger was not his father. It turns out that Frankie was a whole lot more perceptive than his mother or the viewers might have imagined. The conclusion is still open-ended, but not really cheapened by sentimentality.

"My biggest challenge," director Shona Auerbach confided in an interview appended to the film's Miramax DVD release, "was proving myself as a first-time director." Besides directing the feature, Auerbach also served as director of photography, with her husband working as camera operator. Moreover, she had an excellent working relationship with producer Caroline Wood and the screenwriter Andrea Gibb, who also plays a waitress in the film's dancehall scene towards the conclusion. In general, the casting (by Des Hamilton) was especially miraculous, and perfect. Moreover, the plotting and characterization is perfectly executed. The fish-and-chips seaside atmosphere is pleasantly evoked, and the film's more emotional moments, as when Frankie takes his mother and the Stranger to a hillside overlooking the river, are embellished by music, in the instance just cited, the lyrics of Irish folksinger Damien Rice, registering with heart-breaking intensity.

Reviewing the film in Britain for *Sight & Sound* (January 2005), Stephen Dalton agreed that the performances were "generally solid," but thought they "sometimes appear to belong in separate films." Emily Mortimer had proved herself capable of a passable Scots accent in the film *Young Adam*, in which she had also appeared with young Jack McElhone, who plays Frankie "with a believable but never overworked air of cute innocence." The reviewer thought that Gerard Butler, who would also later star as the Phantom in Joel Schumacher's *The Phantom of the Opera* (2004), was too sinister in playing the Stranger and surrogate father. That's debatable, though the actor does appear rather too sophisticated for an itinerant seafarer. The *Sight & Sound* review oddly faults the film for "undercutting its contemporary setting with anachronistic echoes of 1950s kitchen sink drama" and faults the director for lacking "the will, the skill or the brazen cynicism to deliver a shamelessly manipulative crowd-pleaser in the vein of *Billy Elliot* or *The Full Monty*," both of which films proved so popular that they were later adapted to the stage. Others, however, might just as easily (and reasonably) praise Shona Auerbach for her good sense and restraint.

James M. Welsh

CREDITS

Lizzie: Emily Mortimer
Frankie: Jack McElhone
Nell: Mary Riggans
Marie: Sharon Small
Davey: Cal Macaninch
Serious Girl: Sophie Main
Miss MacKenzie: Katy Murphy
Ricky Monroe: Sean Brown
Catriona: Jayd Johnson
Headmistress: Anna Hepburn
The Stranger: Gerard Butler
Origin: Great Britain
Language: English
Released: 2004
MPAA rating: PG-13
Running time: 102 minutes

REVIEWS

Boxoffice Online. March, 2005.
Chicago Sun-Times Online. March 11, 2005.
Entertainment Weekly Online. March 9, 2005.
Los Angeles Times Online. March 4, 2005.
New York Times Online. March 4, 2005.
Variety Online. May 3, 2004.
Washington Post Online. March 11, 2005, p. WE34.

D.E.B.S.

They're crime-fighting hotties with killer bodies.
—Movie tagline

D.E.B.S. means to be a cutting edge satire of girl-power entertainment like *Alias* and *Charlie's Angels*. It is a good idea, and the time would be right for such a film, but writer and director Angela Robinson was not the right person to make it. Her idea of satire is to simply to repeat the clichés of the genre. This does not make the film the knowing, winking spoof that it wishes to be, but rather makes it seem like just another entry—and not a particularly interesting one—into the comely-women-fighting-crime genre. The film is filled with familiar elements like secret spy agencies, bosses who appear via holographic communication, and hidden lairs. Perhaps the humor in *D.E.B.S.* is so dry and subtle as to be barely detectable, but it becomes harder to believe that there is a high-level comedy mastermind behind the film when the dialogue is rife with clunkers like, "Knock 'em dead—but not really!"

The one sliver of originality in the film is that the striking-looking dark-haired nemesis that Amy (Sara Foster) falls for is a woman instead of the usual man. It is a nice touch, and credit goes to Robinson for not treating the affair leeringly. But, it is one of the few parts of the film in which Robinson seems to have found the right balance.

Amy was recruited to the D.E.B.S., which stands for Discipline, Energy, Beauty and Strength, after earning a perfect score on the hidden portion of the SAT. This secret test measures aptitude for lying, cheating and killing. Amy was sent to the training college where she lives in a sorority-like house surrounded by a force field. Her best friend is Max (Meagan Good), an ambitious spy who is jealous of Amy's natural abilities. Also hanging around and wearing frighteningly short skirts are Janet (Jill Ritchie), a tepid goody-goody and Dominique, a French girl who is, well, French. So sketchily are these characters drawn that the word "character" is perhaps too strong to suggest what they are. Besides the short skirt-wearing, for example, Dominique's personality pretty much consists solely of smoking a lot of cigarettes. She also offers pseudo-French insights spoken in a world-weary voice such as, "You can't deny the nature of the heart. It is madness to try."

Amy is writing her thesis on the notorious Lucy Diamond (Jordana Brewster). According to legend, no one has survived an encounter with the criminal mastermind. When Amy runs into Lucy after a spying session gone wrong, Amy is both frightened and awed by Lucy. Lucy, in turn, shows her interest by letting Amy live. Amy, who has just dumped her handsome, but boring boyfriend, Bobby (Geoff Stults), finds herself being courted by Lucy. Lucy shows up at the D.E.B.S. house and takes Amy to a secret night spot. Lucy, who secretly yearns to leave the D.E.B.S. and go to art school, soon sneaks away with Lucy for a rendezvous.

For a spy film, there is very little action. And for a comedy, there is very little humor. What the movie is left with is a mildly interesting affair between a lovelorn criminal and a bland spy, lots of shots of girls wearing short plaid skirts and several scenes of Dominique smoking. It is not nearly enough to hang a whole movie on.

D.E.B.S. was expanded from a short film that played at Sundance in 2003. The film was a big hit, and perhaps the whole thing should have ended there on a high note. The decision to make a feature film seems to be motivated by the possibility of making money rather than a new flash of creative inspiration. It is as though Robinson was offered the job of making the film and was too embarrassed to admit that she did not have any further ideas for it.

The movie had its fans but it was largely unloved. Stephen Holden of *The New York Times* wrote, "The film has no idea how to develop its one-joke premise. The tepid love scenes are as erotically charged as a home movie of a little girl hugging her Barbie doll, and the satire as cutting as the blunt edge of a plastic butter knife." Bob Strauss of *The Los Angeles Daily News* wrote, "It's not easy to make an unwatchable movie about too-skinny girls in too-short skirts packing big guns. Somehow, though, *D.E.B.S.* gets it all wrong. The film does everything else related to moviemaking—action, acting, visual ideas, dialogue—badly, too." Carina Chocano of *The Los Angeles Times* liked it a lot more and wrote, "*D.E.B.S.* is not exactly the freshest sock in the hamper but as a teen romance with a Sapphic twist it's unselfconsciously sweet and genuine."

Jill Hamilton

CREDITS

Amy: Sara Foster
Lucy Diamond: Jordana Brewster
Max: Meagan Good
Dominique: Devon Aoki
Janet: Jill Ritchie
Mrs. Peatree: Holland Taylor
Mr. Phipps: Michael Clarke Duncan
Scud: Jimmi Simpson
Ninotchka: Jessica Cauffiel
Bobby: Geoff Stults
Origin: USA
Language: English
Released: 2004
Production: Angela Sperling, Jasmine Kosovic; released by Sony Pictures Entertainment
Directed by: Angela Robinson
Written by: Angela Robinson
Cinematography by: M. David Mullen
Music by: Steven Stern
Costumes: Frank Helmer
Production Design: Chris Miller
MPAA rating: PG-13
Running time: 91 minutes

REVIEWS

Boxoffice Online. March, 2005.
Chicago Sun-Times Online. March 25, 2005.
Entertainment Weekly Online. March 22, 2005.
Los Angeles Times Online. March 25, 2005.
New York Times Online. March 25, 2005.
Premiere Magazine Online. April 1, 2005.
Variety Online. January 21, 2004.

QUOTES

Lucy: "So, you're an assassin, huh?"
Ninotchka: "Da."
Lucy: "How does that work? "
Ninotchka: "It's mostly freelance."

DERAILED

They Never Saw It Coming.
—Movie tagline

In the indispensable *Halliwell's Film Guide,* the late British critic Leslie Halliwell describes a certain type of film as a "thick ear." Such a film may be worth watching or even reasonably entertaining, but it has serious defects of characterization, plotting, and logic. *Derailed* is a thick ear, a convoluted tale of blackmail whose unpleasant aspects overwhelm even the holes in its plot.

Charles Schine (Clive Owen) is a restless Chicago advertising executive. Things are not going well at work, and he and his wife, Deanna (Melissa George), are trapped in a bored suburban marriage. The center of Charles' life is his daughter, Amy (Addison Timlin), who remains spunky despite rejecting three kidney transplants. Her medical condition dominates the Schines.

Then one day on the train into the city, Charles meets Lucinda Harris (Jennifer Aniston), a married investment banker. After their relationship slowly develops, they end up in a seedy hotel to consummate their affair only to be interrupted by the thief Philippe LaRoche (Vincent Cassel). Philippe takes their money, knocks Charles out, and rapes Lucinda. Afterward, Charles wants to report the attack to the police, but Lucinda argues that they cannot disrupt their families with the lurid truth. Then Philippe begins blackmailing Charles, eventually taking the money he and Deanna have saved to meet Amy's medical bills. When Charles accidentally discovers he has been scammed, he sets out for revenge.

It is somewhat unfair to single out *Derailed* for exploiting a sick child and introducing such elements as rape and abortion into what is supposed to be an entertainment because a glut of films and novels unfortunately do the same in an apparent effort to introduce sociological relevance into thrillers. Still, these qualities, added to some rather graphic violence, distract from what should be the film's virtues. In an early scene, Amy asks for help with an English assignment, and Charles tells her to write that the unnamed novel is one in which everything is not as it seems. *Derailed* could be entertaining because of the complexities of its plot, with numerous twists and turns, though any half-alert viewer can see most of them coming.

The predictability of these so-called surprises contributes to the film's thick-ear quality, but it also has a classic howler, in which a briefcase containing $100,000 miraculously appears. There is no way this money would be in this location at this time. The filmmakers are just hoping the audience will not object to the stupidity of this development.

Another problem is Aniston. It is admirable for her to try to stretch beyond her image as America's sweetheart, but she does not have what it takes to be a femme fatale. She is both too nice and too bland. Fans watching *Derailed* just because Aniston is in it will be disappointed that she is on screen only fifteen or twenty minutes. George, in a thankless, underwritten role, is also miscast because she is too young to be Amy's mother. It is also a bit unusual that Charles is British yet is full of 1960's baseball trivia. While Owen is allowed to keep his native accent, Brits Tom Conti, as Charles' boss, David Morrisey, as another scam victim, and William Armstrong, as an accountant, as well as Aussie George, use American voices.

Owen gives the film some needed integrity. Viewers will give Charles some sympathy just because Owen is likeable. Owen is good at displaying Charles' deep guilt, as well as his determined resolve for revenge. Since his breakthrough roles in *Croupier* (1998) and *Gosford Park* (2001), Owen has made some questionable choices, indicating uncertainty about whether he is a leading man, an action hero, or a character actor. *Derailed* is another unfortunate choice.

Another thing that can keep some thick ears going is having a likeable villain. While Philippe is despicable, Cassel is charismatic. Philippe is meant to be both frightening and fascinating, and Cassel, who seems to be having a grand time being evil, provides these qualities. Rapper RZA has some good moments as Charles' work friend, though some of his dialogue is impenetrable. It is a bit sad to see Conti, a great actor, reduced to taking a mere payday. However, Giancarlo Esposito, one of the most reliable character actors around, provides the investigating cop with shades of sensitivity and depth missing from the script by Stuart Beattie, adapting a novel by James Siegel. It is hard to believe that this is the same screenwriter who wrote *Collateral* (2004).

Swedish director Mikael Håfström, a specialist in thrillers and horror films, making his first American effort, keeps things moving along reasonably well. Cinematographer Peter Biziou, who shot the similar but duller *Unfaithful* (2002), and editor Peter Boyle give *Derailed* a surface much slicker than its deadly soul deserves.

Michael Adams

CREDITS

Charles Schine: Clive Owen
Lucinda Harris: Jennifer Aniston
LaRoche: Vincent Cassel
Deanna Schine: Melissa George
Det. Church: Giancarlo Esposito
Sam Griffin: David Morrissey
Candy: Georgina Chapman
Jerry the Lawyer: Denis O'Hare
Elliot Firth: Tom Conti

Amy Schine: Addison Timlin
Dexter: Xzibit
Winston Boyko: The RZA
Origin: USA
Language: English
Released: 2005
Production: Lorenzo di Bonaventura; di Bonaventura Pictures; released by Weinstein Company
Directed by: Mikael Hafstrom
Written by: Stuart Beattie
MPAA rating: R
Running time: 110 minutes

REVIEWS

Boxoffice Online. November, 2005.
Chicago Sun-Times Online. November 11, 2005.
Entertainment Weekly Online. November 9, 2005.
Los Angeles Times Online. November 11, 2005.
New York Times Online. November 11, 2005.
Premiere Magazine Online. November 11, 2005.
Variety Online. November 5, 2005.
Washington Post Online. November 11, 2005, p. C01.

DEUCE BIGALOW: EUROPEAN GIGOLO

For the women of Europe…The price of love just got a lot cheaper.
—Movie tagline

Same ho. New low.
—Movie tagline

Box Office: $22.3 million

In his most recent "man whore" film, *Deuce Bigalow: European Gigolo*, Rob Schneider delivers cruder and more thoroughly politically incorrect comedy than in the first one. It's hard to believe there would be legions of fans clamoring for this sequel since six years had passed since the original Deuce Bigalow. With the first film Rob Schneider set off a "man bitch" phenomenon which seemed at the time to surely spur a sequel. But why wait six years for this new film? This is a question no one seems able to answer.

Director Mike Bigelow's film is tedious, outrageous, and feeble at the same time. This second film in the now classic "man whore" series, while filled with public urination, a woman who spits wine through her windpipe, and a Russian aristocrat with a penis for a nose, doesn't really top the first film in terms of laughs. Also, although Deuce is a gay hustler there aren't really any sex scenes; the scene in which Deuce wears a diaper is the closeest since there is partial nudity.

Deuce is summoned to Amsterdam by his friend, T.J. Hicks (Eddie Griffin) because there has been a rash of male prostitute killings. Deuce drops everything except the artificial leg of his dead girlfriend, Kate, and runs to the land of hookers and aggressive pot smoking. He is easily lured into this move by a bit of trouble with biting dolphins in California, which is never really explained. T.J. is living on his own pimp boat which includes a figurehead of his torso on the front, and harbors a thinning stable of male gigolos. One might think a national union of male prostitutes would be enough to carry a movie and offer a series of laughs but it just never quite happens.

Through the drug haze a plot really does happen. European, suave male gigolo, Heinz Hummer is found dead in an alley. T.J. decides to use Deuce as bait, ultimately leading Deuce back into his job of male gigolo. Deuce carries on his work of male prostitution as he begins dating women in an attempt to uncover the killer. Each date gets predictably more disgusting than the last. Although he is reluctant to pull out his "twatsicle" and get back to work he is committed to finding the killer.

On the other side of the plot we have a rude cop, Gasper Voorsboch (Jeroen Krabbe) who, as we may have guessed, finds Deuce annoying. Luckily for Deuce, however, his niece does not agree with Gasper and falls for Deuce. Of course, the niece Eva (Hanna Verboom) is an insanely obsessive-compulsive.

There are some very funny points in this sequel, but ultimately we lose interest when the jokes start to be monotonous and obvious. No group of people is left untouched. It is 80 minutes of blue humor and gay jokes losing steam fast as it continues. There are really only so many jokes about farting, sexual positions, and homosexuality an audience can handle. In this film, they take it too far or at least too long—like 70 minutes too long. There are no subtle jokes in *Deuce* and it starts to feel obvious and uncomfortably harried, much like Schneider himself.

Laura Abraham

CREDITS

Deuce Bigalow: Rob Schneider
T.J. Hicks: Eddie Griffin
Gaspar Voorsboch: Jeroen Krabbe
Heinz Hummer: Til Schweiger
Eva: Hanna Verboom
Greta, the Hunchback Girl: Dana Min Goodman
Svetlana: Miranda Raison
Chadsworth Buckingham III: Douglas Sills

Gian-Carlo: Charles Keating
Rodrigo: Carlos Ponce
Antoine: Oded Fehr
Javier Sandooski: Adam Sandler
Earl McManus: Norm MacDonald
Frenchman: Fred Armisen
Origin: USA
Language: English
Released: 2005
Production: Jack Giarraputo, Adam Sandler, John Schneider; Happy Madison Productions; released by Sony Pictures Entertainment
Directed by: Mike Bigelow
Written by: Rob Schneider, David Garrett, Jason Ward
Cinematography by: Marc Felperlaan
Music by: James L. Venable
Music Supervisor: Michael Dilbeck
Editing: Peck Prior, Sandy Solowitz
Art Direction: Hemmo Sportel, Marco Rooth, Hemmo Sportel
Costumes: Linda Bogers
Production Design: Benedict Schillemans
MPAA rating: R
Running time: 75 minutes

REVIEWS

Boxoffice Online. August, 2005.
Chicago Sun-Times Online. August 12, 2005.
Entertainment Weekly Online. August 10, 2005.
Los Angeles Times Online. August 12, 2005.
New York Times Online. August 12, 2005.
Variety Online. August 11, 2005.
Washington Post Online. August 11, 2005, p. WE35.

TRIVIA

Disney had originally distributed *Deuce Bigelow: Male Gigolo* (1999), the first film under Adam Sandler's Happy Madison production company, but due to creative difference with Disney, Happy Madison moved to Columbia to produce this sequel and Sony to distribute it. Disney wanted a PG-13 sequel while Adam Sandler and Rob Schneider sought an R-rating, like the original. This was the first film to use an official Happy Madison logo.

AWARDS

Golden Raspberries 2005: Worst Actor (Schneider)

Nomination:

Golden Raspberries 2005: Worst Picture, Worst Remake/Sequel, Worst Screenplay.

THE DEVIL'S REJECTS

A Tale Of Murder, Mayhem and Revenge.
—Movie tagline

Death walks behind. Hell waits ahead.
—Movie tagline

The new film by Rob Zombie.
—Movie tagline

This summer, go to Hell...
—Movie tagline

Go to Hell!
—Movie tagline

Box Office: $17 million

Rob Zombie launched into the horror genre with his 2003 cult hit premiere, *House of a 1,000 Corpses.* This brainchild and lead singer for the former heavy metal band, White Zombie, continues his uncontained reverence for horror pictures with its successor (he insists it isn't a sequel), *The Devil's Rejects.* Whereas its predecessor is a loosely plotted, heterogeneous jumble of stories with blatant thefts from such cult classics as *The Texas Chainsaw Massacre, The Devil's Rejects* attempts to format a more cohesive plot construction, by adding to the further misadventures of carnage by the Firefly clan and their ultimate demise set to Lynyrd Skynyrd's seminal anthem, "Free Bird."

The film begins with a massive police raid surrounding a rotting farmhouse located in a nonspecific area in the south. A bloody gun battle results in the capture of the clan's matriarch, Mother Firefly (Leslie Easterbrook, a staple of the *Police Academy* film series) and the escape of the sadistic homicidal sibling pair, Otis Driftwood (Bill Moseley) and the vivacious, femme fatale Baby (played by the director's wife, Sheri Moon Zombie). After baiting a Good Samaritan woman, they commandeer her car and plan for a rendezvous with their evil father, Captain Spalding (Sid Haig whose character is reminiscent of the real life serial killer, John Wayne Gacy who once was employed to entertain children as a clown).

Hot on their trail is head Sheriff Wydell (William Forsythe) who is harbors a vendetta against the Fireflys as they are responsible for the murder of his brother. Wydell realizes the degenerate family name themselves after movie characters played by the late Groucho Marx. Recruiting the expertise of a local film critic who is an avid Marx aficionado, Wydell attempts to gain clues about the clan's insidious drive to slaughter. In a scene influenced by Quentin Tarantino, the sheriff and critic engage in a humorous dispute after the critic laments the fact that Groucho's death had gone virtually unnoticed in 1977 as it was overshadowed by the death of Elvis. As it turns out, Wydell holds Elvis with religious veneration and threatens the film buff's life if he continues to degrade the name of The King.

Otis and Baby agree to meet their father at a roadside hotel where they "kill" time by continuing with their pathological predilection for torture and murder. Creative in their psychological terrorization of innocents, the hotel's maid is chased by a traumatized victim who is wearing a human mask and is pulverized by a Mack Truck.

Assisted by two bounty hunters, Wydell (who forewent due process and brutally stabbed Mother Firefly in the station's basement detention cage) the movie's climax results in a plot twist with the snapping of Wydell's neck by the horribly burned family member, Tiny, who reemerges from the film's opening where he is seen dragging a corpse and goes unnoticed as he is hidden from the convergence of lawmen. The only good guys in the film are the family's victims; the main cast is a feuding set of amoral characters.

In Roger Ebert's surprising three star rating of the movie, he offers this insight: "At the end, when we get mellow flashbacks to the characters sharing a laugh in happier days, we are reminded of all those movies that attempt to follow a sad ending with a happy one, and we have to admire the brutality with which Zombie skewers that particular cliché."

David Metz Roberts

CREDITS

Sheriff Wydell: William Forsythe
Captain Spaulding: Sid Haig
Baby: Sheri Moon
Otis: Bill Moseley
Rufus Firefly: Tyler Mane
Mother Firefly: Leslie Easterbrook
Tiny: Matthew McGrory
Charlie Altamont: Ken Foree
Clevon: Michael Berryman
Rondo: Danny Trejo
Nurse: Rosario Dawson
Casey: Deborarh Van Valenburg
Roy Sullivan: Geoffrey Lewis
Gloria Sullivan: Priscilla Barnes
Wendy Banjo: Kate Norby
Officer Ray Dobson: Dave Sheridan
Adam Banjo: Lew Temple
Candy: Elizabeth (E.G. Dailey) Daily
Billy Ray Snapper: Diamond Dallas Page
George Wydell: Tom Towles
Susan: P.J. Soles
Coggs: Chris Ellis
Abbie: Mary Woronov
Morris Green: Daniel Rocbuck
Dr. Bankhead: Duane Whitaker
Sheriff Ken Dwyer: Steve Railsback
Jimmy: Brian Posehn
Origin: USA, Germany
Language: English
Released: 2005
Production: Michael Ohoven, Andy Gould, Mike Elliott, Marco Mehlitz, Rob Zombie; Cinelamda; released by Lions Gate Films
Directed by: Rob Zombie
Written by: Rob Zombie
Cinematography by: Phil Parmet
Music by: Rob Zombie, Tyler Bates
Sound: Buck Robinson
Editing: Glenn Garland
Art Direction: Timothy "TK" Kirkpatrick
Costumes: Yasmine Abraham
Production Design: Anthony Tremblay
MPAA rating: R
Running time: 101 minutes

REVIEWS

Boxoffice Online. July, 2005.
Chicago Sun-Times Online. July 22, 2005.
Entertainment Weekly Online. July 20, 2005.
Los Angeles Times Online. July 22, 2005.
New York Times Online. July 22, 2005.
Variety Online. July 22, 2005.
Washington Post Online. July 22, 2005, p. WE34.

QUOTES

Captain J.T. Spaulding: "I'm gonna have to be taking your car today. See I have some top secret clown business that supersedes any plans that you might have for this here vehicle."

DIARY OF A MAD BLACK WOMAN

Time heals the heart. Faith heals the rest.
—Movie tagline

Get ready to meet a real straight shooter.
—Movie tagline

Box Office: $50.4 million

Diary of a Mad Black Woman is a strange bird—a movie that is somehow both completely predictable and unpredictable. What is predictable about it are the scenes that are borrowed from, or at least heavily influenced by, familiar movies. There are homages, or thefts some might argue, from *The Nutty Professor, Misery, An Officer and a Gentleman* and even *Mommie Dearest.* What is unpredictable is how it is all thrown together. In one scene in which Helen McCarter (Kimberly Elise) and her grandmother, Madea (Tyler Perry), are discovering the clothes of her husband's mistress, Madea finds a wire hanger and blurts out, Faye Dunaway-style, "No more wire hangers!" It is funny enough, but completely out of left field.

Diary of a Mad Black Woman is full of such moments. It is a genre unto itself—a broad comedy, soap opera drama, Christian redemption tale. In the beginning of the film, Helen and her wildly successful attorney husband, Charles (Steve Harris) are attending a dinner in his honor. At the ceremony, he plays the role of devoted husband, but when the couple gets home, Charles orders her out of the car and announces that he will be gone for the night. On the evening of their 18th anniversary, Charles informs Helen that he has a longtime mistress and two sons. He hires a U-Haul truck and sends Helen off into the night. The truck is driven by the handsome Orlando (Shamar Moore), but Helen has too much on her mind to notice that he is her dream man, or as the movie does not shy away from saying, her "knight in shining armor."

Since Helen signed a prenuptial agreement, she is penniless and has nowhere to go but grandma Madea's house in the Atlanta "ghetto." The beautiful white house with the ample wraparound porch does not exactly look ghetto, but perhaps it is one of those things for a moviegoer to use suspension of belief. Orlando, who sports braids neatly tied back by a series of bandanas color-coordinated to his outfits, says all kinds of sincere, loving things to Helen, waiting for her to realize that he is the one. Moore, who plays Orlando, is a soap opera actor, and Orlando is somewhat like a soap opera character come to life.

The movie was written by Tyler Perry, a wildly popular playwright. His plays, about African-Americans dealing with issues of Christianity and relationships, are favorites on the theater circuit. The irrepressible Tyler not only plays Madea, but her randy brother, Joe, and Helen's cousin, Brian. Perry's performance is uneven at best. His straight-talking, gun-toting Madea is funny and a crowd-pleaser, but she is more of a cartoon character than a real person. Her make-up is not terribly believable and it is pretty obvious that the actor playing her is neither old nor female. It is disconcerting to have a serious dramatic scene in the film, interrupted by this big drag queen-like character. Conversely, Perry is wonderful as cousin Brian. He is a wise, good-humored man who sticks with his family and tries desperately to find the proper way to deal with his junkie wife.

The Christian message of the film sneaks into the film slowly. Helen's diary entry about Orlando goes on about how "fine" he is, then segues into how happy she is to have found a man who is "strong, beautiful, sensitive and...Christian." Later, it is much more blatant, with a final scene in church where the power of the Lord inspires a junkie to clean up and a paralyzed man to walk.

Ultimately, the awkwardness and shifts in tone are too much for *Diary* to handle. It is hard to feel sympathy for Helen, for example, after watching the way she treats her ex-husband after he is paralyzed in a shooting. Helen forces her captive ex to listen to her litany of complaints about his poor behavior. That is understandable. But later she starves him while his sits helpless and crying at the other end of the table. By the end of a scene where she watches as he almost drowns in a hot tub, it is difficult to think that she is merely getting her fair revenge. Still, it is a credit to Perry's skill that a film that contains such off-key scenes still manages to be entertaining in a Movie of the Week-kind of way.

Most critics did not like *Diary,* but it had a few fans. One such fan was Ruthe Stein of *The San Francisco Chronicle* who wrote, "Raucous and overwrought, the movie is still a hoot to watch and even more fun to talk back to, as everyone around me did at will during a sneak preview." In the opposite camp, Wesley Morris of *The Boston Globe*, wrote, "Blows to the head are delivered with more subtlety than the message of *Diary of a Mad Black Woman.*" Stephanie Zacharek of *Salon* wrote "If He does exist, He surely deserves a much better movie than this one."

Jill Hamilton

CREDITS

Helen McCarter: Kimberly Elise
Charles McCarter: Steve Harris
Orlando: Shemar Moore
Debrah: Tamara Taylor
Myrtle: Cicely Tyson
Brenda: Lisa Marcos
Tiffany: Tiffany Evans
Brian/Madea/Uncle Joe: Tyler Perry
Origin: USA
Language: English
Released: 2005
Production: Reuben Cannon; Diary of a Woman; released by Lions Gate Films
Directed by: Darren Grant
Written by: Tyler Perry
Cinematography by: David Claessen

Music by: Tyler Perry, Elvin D. Ross
Sound: Jim Hawkins
Editing: Terilyn Shropshire
Costumes: Keith Lewis
Production Design: Ina Mayhew
MPAA rating: PG-13
Running time: 116 minutes

REVIEWS

Boxoffice Online. February, 2005.
Chicago Sun-Times Online. February 25, 2005.
Entertainment Weekly Online. February 23, 2005.
Los Angeles Times Online. February 25, 2005.
New York Times Online. February 25, 2005.
Variety Online. February 22, 2005.
Washington Post Online. February 25, 2005, p. WE41.

QUOTES

Helen: "I'm not bitter! I'm mad as hell!"

DIRTY LOVE

got dumped?
—Movie tagline

Dirty Love had the notable achievement of being one of the year's worst reviewed movies. On www.rottentomatoes.com, a web site that collects critics' reviews, it was difficult to find a critic who would admit to even the slightest feeling of fondness toward the film.

The writer and star of such loathed material was Jenny McCarthy, who formerly had a sketch comedy show on MTV. Her husband at the time, John Asher, directed the film. McCarthy's shtick has always been combining her bombshell looks with a hearty dose of gross-out humor and utter lack of vanity. There is not a bodily function that the former *Playboy* model is too squeamish to joke about. Perhaps that fearlessness had something to do with the poor reception the movie received. Most gross-out comedies are written by men, and their gross-out segments follow well-trod territory. In a way, the supposed outrageousness of such material is fairly well contained to specific topics. McCarthy, on the other hand, makes jokes about supersized maxi-pads and menstruation. Maybe her brand gross-out humor was a little too gross for most. About one such menstruation-based scene, Roger Ebert of *The Chicago Sun-Times* wrote, "McCarthy follows it with a scene where the cops strip-search her and she's wearing a maxi pad that would be adequate for an elephant. She doesn't need to do this. It's painful to see a pretty girl, who seems nice enough, humiliating herself on the screen. I feel sorry for her." Did Ebert also note the Farrelly brothers good looks in his review of *There's Something About Mary*? Did he find Jim Carrey too attractive to act stupid in *Dumb and Dumber*?

In the film, Rebecca (McCarthy) is devastated when she discovers the guy she thought was "the one," Richard (Victor Webster), having sex with another woman. Rebecca decides that her best coping plan is to make Richard jealous. She starts going on a set of dates that all end up horribly, usually with their most embarrassing moment happening right in front of Richard and his new girl.

Rebecca is aided in her plans by her buddies Michelle (Carmen Electra), a body waxer who thinks she is straight from the 'hood, and Carrie (Kam Heskin), an actress so dim she barely seems to exist in the real world. Also by Rebecca's side is John (Eddie Kaye Thomas), her long time nice guy friend who is secretly in love with her. John knows that he is the kind of steady loyal guy that Rebecca could use in her life and tries desperately to convince her of it.

What is good about the film is McCarthy's lack of fear of looking foolish. It is difficult to imagine a thing she would not do on-screen if she thought it could get a laugh. This adds an edginess to her comedy. With her, there really is the sense that anything could happen. What is bad about the film is that it is just not funny enough. Director Asher does not seem to know the fundamentals of filmmaking. In an early scene, McCarthy is standing on a street reacting to the news of Richard's unfaithfulness. She grimaces, she stomps around, she shrieks to the heavens. This is the point Asher should yell, "Cut!" But he does not and McCarthy seems at a loss at what to do. So she gamely shrieks, yells, etc... some more. What could have been funny, or at least mildly amusing, becomes something almost painful. It is not the duty of the audience to be mentally editing the movie. And, perhaps there was not much of a budget for the film, but Asher has nothing in his creative toolbox to disguise that fact. It looks like a poorly shot cable sitcom.

As mentioned, critics despised the film. Bob Strauss of *The Los Angeles Daily News* was one of the kinder reviewers and wrote, "Some of this is so outrageous you can't help but laugh. Yet director John Asher stages most of it with such flat presentation and inept timing that most of the jokes shrivel up and die right before our eyes." Stephen Holden of *The New York Times* wrote, "Even by the standard of its bottom-feeding genre, *Dirty Love* clings to the gutter like a rat in garbage. Ms. McCarthy compensates for her utter lack of comedic skills by making clown faces and emitting earsplitting 'omigod's' after each humiliation." Kyle Smith of *The New York Post* wrote, "Jenny McCarthy's giddy charm is wasted by screen writer Jenny McCarthy." And Ebert of *The Sun-Times* wrote, "*Dirty Love* wasn't written and directed, it was committed. Here is a film so pitiful, it doesn't rise to the level of badness."

Jill Hamilton

CREDITS

Rebecca: Jenny McCarthy
Michelle: Carmen Electra
John: Eddie Kaye Thomas
Richard: Victor Webster
Carrie: Kam Heskin
Kevin: Lochlyn Munro
Madame Belly: Kathy Griffin
Mandy: Jessica Collins
Origin: USA
Language: English
Released: 2005
Production: Trent Walford, Jenny McCarthy, John Asher
Directed by: John Mallory Asher
Written by: Jenny McCarthy
Cinematography by: Eric Wycoff
Sound: Randy Lawson
Editing: Warren Bowman
Art Direction: Clare Brown
Costumes: Paula Elins
Production Design: Frank Bollinger
MPAA rating: R
Running time: 95 minutes

REVIEWS

Boxoffice Online. September, 2005.
Chicago Sun-Times Online. September 23, 2005.
Los Angeles Times Online. September 23, 2005.
New York Times Online. September 23, 2005.
Variety Online. March 1, 2005.

QUOTES

Rebecca: "It's not bubblegum, you don't chew it!"

AWARDS

Golden Raspberries 2005: Worst Picture, Worst Actress (McCarthy), Worst Director (Asher), Worst Screenplay

Nomination:

Golden Raspberries 2005: Worst Support. Actress (Electra).

DOLLS

Deliberately paced and beautifully shot, Takeshi Kitano's *Dolls* brings three classic tales of, love, loss, and tragedy from the puppet stage to the screen. These stories are steeped in Japanese culture where sacrifice and love go hand in hand, most of the time with tragic results. Kitano takes these age-old themes and places them in contemporary Japan. Based on the classical Japanese tradition of Bunraku (Puppet) Theater, *Dolls* is Kitano's most contemplative and artistic work to date. The film takes its title from one of the three main forms of Japanese Theater begun centuries ago. Developed at the same time as its live-action sister form of theater known as Kabuki, Bunraku delves in similar themes using three foot puppets controlled by a brightly dressed master, with two aids dressed from head to toe in black on his sides. The master controls the head while the other two control movement of the rest of the puppet body. The movements are realistic, and with the accompaniment of music provided by a stringed instrument known as a Samisen, and narration and dialogue provided by another man, the audience can sometimes find themselves drawn into the stories, forgetting that they are watching puppets and believing them to be sentient beings. Knowing this, Kitano opens the film on an actual performance of a Bunraku play before smoothly segueing into the films main narrative.

In the first story we are introduced to Matsumoto (Hedetoshi Nishijima) who is planning to marry his sweetheart Sawako (Miho Kanno). However, Matsumoto's parents, insist that he marry the daughter of the company's boss, instead. It is basically a merger of wealth more than love though, as it would insure his promotion in the company and social status for his family. Matsumoto, feeling responsibility for his parents and the company, reluctantly breaks the engagement with Sawako, and on the morning of the wedding he receives a phone call informing him that Sawako has attempted suicide, leaving her alive but severely brain-damaged.

Matsumoto leaves the wedding to be by her side and when he sees her, makes the fateful decision to take her out of the hospital and be her caretaker. Cut off from his job, his parents abandoning him ironically stating that "he made his own decision." Matsumoto realizes his mistake, but we're not sure if the parents have as well. With no money, they eventually become homeless and Matsumoto and Sawako wander the landscape tied together by a length of red rope and are dubbed the "bound beggars" by the passersby.

In the second story we meet Hiro (Tatsuya Mihashi), an elderly former yakuza boss, who although retired, is still being hunted by assassins. He hides out in a house, flanked by bodyguards and begins to reflect on his life. In flashbacks we learn that when he was a young man he was a factory worker who would meet his lover Kyoko (Chieko Matsubara) every Saturday for lunch on the same park bench. One day he tells her that he doesn't have enough money to take care of her properly, so he must go away for awhile to find wealth, after which he promises to return to her. She promises him that she will come to this bench with two lunches everyday, waiting for his return. But he got caught up in the yakuza life and the years passed by he never was able to return to her. Now, he makes the fateful decision to return to the park to reflect on his tragic mistake, where he is surprised to find his former love still waiting for him on the bench, two lunches in her lap. But she doesn't recognize him, and he is too guilt ridden to tell her. She decides to share her lunch with him anyway. Hoping that he may be able to start over with her, he continues to join her for lunch several more times. But the hand of fate, always ready to remind us that we cannot outrun our past, and there are consequences to our decisions, the choices we make, is always watching.

The third story center around the relationship between a beautiful pop singer named Haruna (Kyoko Fukuda) and her number one fan Nukui (Tsutomu Takeshige), a borderline stalker. Nukui in lives in a small apartment filled with pictures of Haruna, which he dances in front of, while her music plays in his headphones. He attends every public appearance where she meets with her fans, signing autographs. But he is very shy and never gets a chance to meet her. All this changes though, when he finds out one night that she has been in a terrible car accident. He visits her home with flowers, but her mother tells him that Haruna is now retired form music and will not come out of the house. Turns out she has suffered a disfigurement from the accident and doesn't want to be seen by the public. Nukui takes drastic measures in order to get a meeting with her by cutting out his own eyes. She agrees to meet the now blind Nukui in a park, where they begin to have an odd relationship. But fate steps in once again with tragic results.

In all three segments, Kitano is reminding the audience that they are watching a live-action version of a Bunraku, as the stories are all told in a meditative and melancholy state and a slow pace that moves the characters along as leaves blown by a gentle breeze. Kitano places an objective camera on his subjects observing them for long periods of time, allowing the audience to speculate on their thoughts and motivations and use their own imaginations to fill in the blanks. This is a hallmark of the Bunraku Theater and Kitano understands that perfectly. Throughout the film we contemplate the choices we make and the strings that bind us to the consequences resulting from them. Are we all just puppets of our choices? Or do we consciously make those choices knowing the tragic outcome is inevitable? Is Fate the ultimate puppeteer?

David E. Chapple

CREDITS

Hiro: Tatsuya Mihashi
Woman in the park: Chieko Matsubara
Sawako: Miho Kanno
Matsumoto: Hidetoshi Nishijima
Haruna: Kyoko Fukada
Nukui: Sebastian Blenkov
Origin: Japan
Language: Japanese
Released: 2002
Production: Masayuki Mori, Takio Yoshida; Office Kitano, A Bandai Visual, Tokyo FM, TV Tokyo
Directed by: Takeshi "Beat" Kitano
Written by: Takeshi "Beat" Kitano
Cinematography by: Katsumi Yanagijima
Music by: Joe Hisaishi
Sound: Senji Horiuchi
Editing: Takeshi "Beat" Kitano
Costumes: Yohji Yamamoto
Production Design: Norihiro Isoda
MPAA rating: Unrated
Running time: 113 minutes

REVIEWS

Entertainment Weekly. December 8, 2004.
Variety. September 9, 2002.

DOMINION: PREQUEL TO THE EXORCIST

Set predominantly in British East Africa after World War II, this "prequel" is a fine fusion of substance and style. Paul Schrader's competent film depicts a single battle in the raging war between good and evil.

The narrative centers on Father Lenkester Merrin (Stellan Skarsgård), his journey to personal understanding and his clash with an ancient, supernatural power. The film opens during the war where we see Merrin with his Dutch parishioners during the German Army's retreat. An unknown member of the town has murdered a German soldier. The leader of the German brigade encounters the townspeople in the town square. He solicits the help of Merrin to uncover the murderer. Merrin makes it clear he is unaware of the criminal's identity. The German officer presents Merrin with a choice. He may either submit ten members of his flock for execution or everyone in the town will be killed. When Merrin refuses, the officer kills a random, innocent female. The priest realizes that the officer's intents are grave. Reticently, Merrin chooses ten of his parishioners for execution. The guilt of his decision plagues Merrin, who abandons the priesthood and turns his focus toward archaeological pursuits.

We next find Merrin in British-controlled Africa, supervising an archaeological dig. The Vatican has sent an envoy, Father Francis (Gabriel Mann), to tend to any religious artifacts and to ensure their safety. The dig proves highly successful. An ancient Church of Saint Michael is discovered in pristine condition which leads Merrin to believe that it was buried purposefully immediately after its construction was concluded. There is an outcast that lives in and around the town near the dig. He is a physical and apparently mental cripple named Cheche (Billy Crawford). Merrin's selfless spirit urges him to help the boy and to bring him into the care of the town doctor, Rachel (Clara Bellar), a Polish Jew who saw time in a relocation camp. The church is now completely unearthed and accessible to Merrin who brings Father Francis to see his discovery and his magnificence. Merrin detects that there is a chamber under the church which is accessible through what appears to be a sarcophagus. They pry the lid aside and an immortal supernatural power is released. The order of nature is turned on its head. The cows eat the hyenas. A native baby is born covered in maggots. Friends turn on each other. The British soldiers and the natives begin to feud. And, most importantly, a demonic spirit inhabits the body of the innocent Cheche, whose body undergoes an incredulous healing process. Father Francis believes that Cheche has the spirit of Jesus within him and decides to baptize him in the Church of Saint Michael. Then, literally, all hell breaks loose. The demon in Cheche makes its identity known and Francis deems an exorcism necessary. On his way to recover his book of rituals, he is mortally wounded by the natives. Merrin rediscovers his faith and triumphs over the demon and frees Cheche from its grasp. The spirit then inhabits a hyena, setting up the narrative of the sequels.

For the most part, the film is a cinematic success. The shots of the African village at night are particularly effective in their framing. The church itself is beautifully visualized, harmonious and full of light. The delivery of the maggot-covered baby is particularly gruesome, yet realistically visceral in its animatronic realization. In contrast, the computer-assisted renderings of the hyenas and the snake are specifically unimpressive. They protrude from the otherwise realistic style and detract from the significance of the symbolism. Only the possessed Cheche is stunning when modified by computer enhancement. His visual rendering is startling, yet gorgeous; very apt for the great deceiver.

Billy Crawford falters, however, in his portrayal of the "evil" Cheche. Scarcely believable deliveries and annoyingly exaggerated verbal stresses only serve to undercut the thoughtful development of the narrative. Concurrently, Clara Bellar offers an amateurish and underdeveloped character. While repression is expected from a victim of a Nazi relocation camp, such a character needs not be boring. She may have been beaten into submission, but I felt as though I was during her performance.

On the other hand Gabriel Mann and Stellan Skarsgård offer fine performances. Mann's Father Francis exhibits a true spiritual devotion which never borders on fervor. He is a victim of the evils of man despite his selflessness and charitable will. Mann is subtle and casual, yet highly substantive despite being forced to deliver lines such as "Satan is real." Skarsgård's Father Merrin is an apt anchor for the film. Skarsgård is a wonderfully expressive actor who can speak a paragraph with a glance. His performance is inspired and his recital of the exorcism ritual is an incantation for the ages.

Nick Kennedy

CREDITS

Lankester Merrin: Stellan Skarsgard
Father Francis: Gabriel Mann
Rachel Lesno: Clara Bellar
Chuma: Andrew French
Jomo: Israel Adurama
Emekwi: Eddie Osei
Kessel: Antoine Kamerling
Major Granville: Julian Wadham
Sebituana: Ilario Bisi-Pedro
Origin: USA
Language: English
Released: 2005
Production: James G. Robinson; Morgan Creek Productions
Directed by: Paul Schrader
Written by: William Wisher, Caleb Carr
Cinematography by: Vittorio Storaro
Music by: Trevor Rabin, Dog Fashion Disco
Editing: Tim Silano
Art Direction: Marco Trentini, Andy Nicholson
Costumes: Luke Reichle
Production Design: John Graysmark
MPAA rating: R
Running time: 116 minutes

REVIEWS

Boxoffice Online. May, 2005.
Chicago Sun-Times Online. May 19, 2005.

Los Angeles Times Online. May 20, 2005.
New York Times Online. May 20, 2005.
Variety Online. March 18, 2005.

TRIVIA

John Frankenheimer dropped out of directing the Exorcist prequel (then known as *Exorcist: Dominion*) in June 2002, one month before his death in July 2002. Paul Schraeder then signed on to the project later that year.

DOMINO

I Am a Bounty Hunter.
—Movie tagline

Based on a true story...sort of.
—Movie tagline

Heads You Live...Tails You Die.
—Movie tagline

Box Office: $10.1 million

The real Domino Harvey was messed up and out of control, and so is the movie based upon her life. Born in England to actor Laurence Harvey and model Pauline Stone, she was a troubled ball of fire, equally addicted to drugs and adrenaline. Domino was a lost soul who eventually found her calling in the dicey world of bounty hunting. The assertion right up front that the film is based upon a true story is followed by the words "sort of," and there is more truth in that admission than in much of what follows. Director Tony Scott, a friend of Domino's for more than a decade, had spent all of those years thinking her life story would make a wonderful film, but was unable to find an approach he liked. Unfortunately in *Domino* he is less interested in telling that story than he is in using it as a jumping-off point in creating a feverishly bizarre, gleefully hyper-violent, maddeningly complicated, and borderline incoherent tale utilizing a ceaseless, distracting onslaught of hyperbolic, flashy visual trickery. Domino served as a consultant on the film, and her family and friends insist that, contrary to numerous published reports, she was not put out by the direction it took. Maybe she was simply thrilled and flattered to be the inspiration for a kick-ass, star-studded motion picture, and relished its mad-hatter potency. It would be fascinating to know for sure, but Domino was found lying in her bathtub shortly after the film wrapped, dead from what was ruled as an accidental overdose of heavy-duty painkillers. At the time, she faced serious charges of drug possession and trafficking which she vehemently denied. She was only thirty-five years old.

What Scott serves up does far more to make viewers' heads swim than to truly understand what went on in hers. Indeed, the description of a character in the film as having "the attention span of a ferret on crystal meth" is an apt description of what the bewildering film itself is like. It zigzags back and forth between various points in time. Images flash, shake, twist and turn, overlap, move in slow motion, and a host of other things due to the manic, flamboyant tricks Scott uses with an alarming lack of discretion. Cutting is sometimes so rapid-fire as to be seizure-inducing. Various choices concerning color saturation and lighting are curious. Gunfire roars. Blood spatters and body parts get bashed in or blown off. Bombs explode in tremendous fireballs. Careening vehicles become airborne and helicopters plunge to the ground, both crashing spectacularly. If multiple angles can be shown, all the better. It seems all about showing off, a flaunting and flexing of one's filmmaking muscles well beyond the point where it aids in storytelling. In addition to the voice-over narration by up-and-comer Keira Knightley as Domino, words pop up on the screen to identify people and places, explain relationships and complicated plans, translate Spanish, and make sure every word is caught of phone conversations originating from a specially designed bubble submerged in a mobster's swimming pool. Sometimes identities and occurrences previously shown are later retracted by the narrator as incorrect and replaced onscreen by new ones. Apparently there was recognition that audiences would have a hard time keeping track of who is who and what is what in all this confusion without some helpful assistance.

Before things get quite so out of hand, Scott and screenwriter Richard Kelly give a sketchy and somewhat tweaked version of how things went awry for Domino herself. It is the most interesting part of the film, although there is more recounting of excessive behavior than delving seriously and deeply into root causes. Viewers learn about her famous father's death when she was just a small child, and how she was sent to boarding school so her mother (renamed Sophie Wynn to avoid legal trouble and played by Jacqueline Bissett) could get back to gold digging. (She ended up marrying Peter Morton, founder and chairman of the Hard Rock Café and related ventures.) Domino detested her mom's lavish and pretentious Beverly Hills lifestyle, being infinitely more rough-and-tumble than hoity-toity. At one point she is seen wielding nunchucks, at another she is bashing in a snotty sorority sister's nose, leading to expulsion from school.

Eventually, Domino stumbles upon a career as a bounty hunter, allowing her to "live the nasty" but "not do time for it." She pays $99 in cash for instruction, a seminar that turns out to be a scam run by bail bondsman Claremont Williams (Delroy Lindo) and bounty hunters Ed Mosbey (Mickey Rourke) and Choco (Edgar

Ramirez). They merely want to make off with the students' money during an initial coffee break, but Domino stops—and impresses—them by gustily blocking their getaway car and expertly hurling a knife into their windshield. It turns out to be the very weird beginning to a job interview, and she is hired on the spot.

"Nothing scares me," Domino declares, and says that the job is "her destiny." She clearly relishes the excitement that awaits behind each door they approach. "Heads you live, tails you die," is how she sums up her very lively livelihood. She does, indeed, show herself to be fearless and willing to do whatever it takes to bring people in, getting necessary information at the end of a gun barrel or, on one occasion, lapdancing it out of them.

Both Ed and (especially) Choco think she is a hot number, and as played by the fetching Knightley (in one scene only in underwear and topless in another), she is rather alluring. The actress is more lovely than the real, rather androgynous Domino. Reedy, talented Knightley attacks the role but is not completely convincing, even while screaming and swearing at the top of her lungs, giving good, hard stares through her bangs, and blowing cigarette smoke disdainfully at FBI investigator Taryn Miles (Lucy Liu).

Hope for anything cogent and truly illuminating about this intriguing creature vanishes as the film's excessively bombastic and mind-taxing elements completely take over. "The further out there, the more abstract, the better," Scott enthused incorrectly. He has a peculiar producer named Mark Heiss (Christopher Walken) and his trusty assistant Kimmie (Mena Suvari) recruit Domino and her cohorts for a reality TV show called *The Bounty Squad,* hosted by *Beverly Hills, 90210* has-beens Ian Ziering and Brian Austin Green (roughly playing themselves). The bounty hunters are shadowed by the TV crew in the film's second half, during which *Domino* speeds ahead like a runaway, narcotic-powered locomotive liable at any second to jump its twisting, turning track. Amongst the convolution and carnage are the following: the FBI; the California DMV; the Las Vegas mob and their offspring; reformed nymphomaniacs; thieves sporting Halloween masks of grinning recent First Ladies; an Afghan driver/explosives expert referred to as "the cat-eating alien;" cousins Lashandra (Macy Gray), Lashindra (Shondrella Avery) and Lateesha (Mo'Nique); Lateesha's humorous lesson on "Jerry Springer"about interracial couplings which produce such things as Blacktinos and Hispanese; a granddaughter of Claremont and Lateesha's who gets a lifesaving operation they can ill-afford thanks to bad money used for a good cause; death and destruction high atop the Stratosphere hotel and casino; the tossing-about of a shot-off arm with a safe's combination tattooed upon it; and a babbling preacher who appears in the desert and tries unsuccessfully to tie a strand or two of this mess together. It is overwhelming, overheated, overseasoned overkill. Domino states, "I'll never tell you what it all meant." All right then, but it sure would have been appreciated.

Walk on the Wild Side, the title of a 1962 Laurence Harvey film, might have been used as a subtitle for *Domino*, apropos if still something of an understatement. Made on a budget of $50 million, Scott's filmonly succeeded in grossing about a fifth of that. Most reviews were peppered with words like "incoherent," "overwrought" and "perplexing." "The experience of the movie," wrote William Arnold in the *Seattle Post-Intelligencer*, "is like having someone hit you on the side of the head with a brick for two hours." Some, like Roger Ebert and Richard Roeper, at least admired its raw energy. The film's most memorable shot is actually its last, a brief, haunting image of the real Domino Harvey smiling not long before her death. The way her life turned out was so regrettable. The same can be said for the film that bears her name.

David L. Boxerbaum

CREDITS

Domino Harvey: Keira Knightley
Ed Moseby: Mickey Rourke
Choco: Edgar Ramirez
Claremont Wiliams: Delroy Lindo
Lateesha Rodriguez: Mo'Nique
Taryn Mills: Lucy Liu
Mark Heiss: Christopher Walken
Kimmie: Mena Suvari
Lashandra Davis: Macy Gray
Sophie Wynn: Jacqueline Bisset
Drake Bishop: Dabney Coleman
Himself: Brian A(ustin) Green
Himself: Ian Ziering
Anthony Cigliutti: Stanley Kamel
Burke Beckett: Peter Jacobson
Lester Kincaid: T.K. Carter
Frances: Kel O'Neill
Lashindra Davis: Shondrella Avery
Locus Fender: Lew Temple
Wanderer: Tom Waits
Alf: Rizwan Abbasi
Origin: USA
Language: English
Released: 2005
Production: Samuel Hadida, Tony Scott; Scott Free, Davis Films; released by New Line Cinema

Directed by: Tony Scott
Written by: Richard Kelly, Steve Barancik
Cinematography by: Dan Mindel
Music by: Harry Gregson-Williams
Sound: Art Rochester
Editing: William Goldenberg, Christian Wagner
Art Direction: Drew Boughton, Keith Neely
Costumes: B.
Production Design: Chris Seagers
MPAA rating: R
Running time: 128 minutes

REVIEWS

Boxoffice Online. October, 2005.
Chicago Sun-Times Online. October 14, 2005.
Entertainment Weekly Online. October 12, 2005.
Los Angeles Times Online. October 14, 2005.
New York Times Online. October 14, 2005.
Premiere Magazine Online. October 14, 2005.
Variety Online. October 6, 2005.
Washington Post Online. October 14, 2005, p. C01.

QUOTES

Domino Harvey: "I've been training since I was twelve. Knives, guns, throwing stars. You name it, and I can fight with it. I'm a hard worker. I'm a hard worker and a fast learner. Nothing scares me. I'm not afraid to die."

TRIVIA

Ed Moseby, the character played by Mickey Rourke, is based on real-life bounty hunter Zeke Unger. Claremont Williams III, played by Delroy Lindo, is also based on a real-life figure—bail-bondsman Celes King III, Domino Harvey's real boss. Both men served as technical advisors on the film.

DON'T MOVE

(Non ti muovere)

Noted actor-turned-director Sergio Castellito's politically charged erotic melodrama from Italy, *Don't Move* (*Non ti Muovere*) draws on his country's filmic tradition of neorealism for its gritty impact but shies away from any compassionate omniscience. Castellito casts himself as his film's protagonist, but proves too much of a romantic to allow his narrative to stray from his own character, with the result that his film, for all its emotional richness, emerges as more of a narcissistic venture than a revelatory one.

As a skilled surgeon in a large hospital, the middle-aged Timoteo (Castellito), or Timo as he's affectionately known, is shaken to find his own teenage daughter Angela (Elena Perino) brought in unconscious with her skull severely fractured in a traffic accident. The jolt makes him recall not just his immediate domestic past but an affair he had around the time of her birth with an impoverished waifish floozy, Italia (Penelope Cruz), whom we see eking out an existence in an abandoned dwelling on the periphery of an urban sprawl. Timo's path crosses hers when his car breaks down and she's kind enough to allow him to use her phone. Such is his sexual arousal that he overpowers her in an act of savagery that, on a higher social plane, would be called rape.

Castellito as director then juggles around three narrative trajectories: Timo's lustful secret dalliance with Italia; his lackluster home life around that time with his wife Elsina (Claudia Gerini, who looks a cross between Sharon Stone and Maria Bello); and his own frantic attempts in the present to save Angela's life.

Timo's elite partying with Elsina appears increasingly meaningless to him. When he returns to Italia, it becomes clear that he plans to use her for the whore she is; he even leaves money before he leaves. It is only after their next bout of lovemaking that we see a glimmering of affection from her along with his need for the same; he leaves her more money and she even cooks him a meal. This leads to his wanting a baby from Elsina, who is too preoccupied with her career in publishing to even think of it. We then see a sudden reversal of sentiment with Italia as Timo pulls her skirt over her face and slaps her, after which he apologizes. This is where Timo's inner conflict takes on a social dimension as he comes to represent a moneyed class with political connections for whom the disenfranchised remain a faceless multitude to be exploited. In the present, Timo relates the news about Angela's accident via phone to Elsina in London. She wails in grief at the other end but we don't see her.

As the three narrative trajectories progress, they revolve around Timo and his desire—on the sexual and filial planes—for the three most important women in his life. After an attempt to leave Italia, Timo is drawn back to her, as if helpless. He raises her status to that of a call girl and even takes her with him to a medical convention. It is on a hotel bed that we see the sex between them as suffused by a romantic passion. Curiously, this changes his relationship with Elsina. Now he demands much less as a husband, his sexual and emotional needs having been met by Italia, with the result that it is Elsina who now initiates the sex. When Italia falls ill, she is diagnosed as pregnant. She breaks down and apologizes but Timo decides to treat her himself where she lives. Soon Elsina too becomes pregnant. As if to play upon the ironies of fate, the film cuts to Timo in the present, frantically trying to prevent

Angela from succumbing to a hemorrhaging. He starts to weep as he spouts some of the memories they have shared until he finally manages to restore her to a stable condition.

At this point in the film it becomes clear that though Timo loves Italia, he cannot keep juggling his fast-paced life as a surgeon of repute with the shadow life he has been enjoying with her. It is because of this that Italia is forced to do what she does, yet it is through Timo that we come to know of it. He is shattered when he learns that she has had an abortion, since he had been hoping to father a boy. This prompts a flashback of Timo recalling Angela losing a judo tournament and venting her disappointment at him for his wanting her to be like a boy.

Timo's two lives intersect when Italia catches a glimpse of Elsina in an advanced state of pregnancy. It is at night in the middle of city traffic in pouring rain. Timo excuses himself from Elsina and chases Italia. When he catches up with her, it is in a filthy alley. As she lashes out at him in rage, he has his way in the midst of discarded crates. Later in a café Timo says that he feels that she will never forgive him. Italia answers, "God will never forgive us."

This foreboding on Italia's part comes true in the final section of the film as Timo, after Elsina has given birth to Angela, is spurred to run away with his forbidden love. The film soars to poetic heights as Italia triumphantly bids her past farewell. Against the background of an emotional refrain from an Italian pop song, the camera sweeps in an aerial shot of luxury apartment buildings under construction around Italia's decrepit shack, thereby affirming the film's political resonance. Their idyllic escape, however, proves short-lived as Italia's health gives way and she's unable to recover from complications resulting from her abortion.

In the present, Timo manages to save Angela's life. In the film's closing moments, we see a wiser Timo but one whose lyrical alter ego is still longing for that dream goddess he has yet to meet.

Vivek Adarkar

CREDITS

Italia: Penélope Cruz
Timoteo: Sergio Castellitto
Elsa: Claudia Gerini
Nora: Lina Bernardi
Ada: Angela Finocchiaro
Manlio: Marco Giallini
Alfredo: Pietro De Silva
Raffaella: Vittoria Piancastelli
Angela: Elena Perino
Pino: Renato Marchetti
Duilio: Gianni Musi
Language: Italian
Released: 2004
Production: Riccardo Tozzi, Giovanni Stabilini, Marco Chimenz; Medusa; released by Medusa
Directed by: Sergio Castellitto
Written by: Sergio Castellitto, Margaret Mazzantini
Cinematography by: Gianfilippo Corticelli
Music by: Lucio Godoy
Sound: Mario Iaquone
Editing: Patrizio Marone
Costumes: Zaira De Vincentiis
Production Design: Francesco Frigeri
MPAA rating: Unrated
Running time: 117 minutes

REVIEWS

Boxoffice Online. March, 2005.
Entertainment Weekly Online. March 16, 2005.
Los Angeles Times Online. March 18, 2005.
New York Times Online. March 11, 2005.
Variety Online. March 12, 2004.

DOOM

Box Office: $28 million

While the video game on which this movie is based caused quite a stir when it was released in 1993 due to its graphic violence and huge popularity, 12 years later, this violence-packed movie version is not likely to cause much of a sensation let alone stir up much in the way of ticket sales beyond die-hard game fans. In fact, the film recouped a mere $28 million of its $70 million budget by the end of 2005. While it is long on gore-filled violence, intimidating-looking monsters, and perilous action it is proportionally slim on relatable characters, character development, convincing dialogue, adequate lighting, and basic plot aspects that traditionally make up what is termed a decent film.

At the heart of *Doom* is a seven-man commando team led by the aptly named Sarge (Dwayne "The Rock" Johnson), a tough customer who must lead their latest search-and-destroy mission. It is the year 2026, and this group of Marines, known as the Rapid Response Tactical Squad (RRTS), is sent to the site of a recently discovered portal in the American desert that leads to an ancient city on the planet Mars. A team of genetic scientists studying the portal have been destroyed by an unknown malevolence and Sarge's job is to find out what and get rid of it, along with teammates John "The Reaper" Grimm (Karl Urban), Destroyer (Deobia Oparei), Mac (Yao Chin), Duke (Razaaq Adoti), Goat (Ben Daniels), Portman (Richard Brake) and The Kid (Al Weaver).

The Reaper's sister is a comely blond anthropologist Samantha Grimm (Rosamund Pike) who works at Olduvai Research Station on Mars set up to study Martian life on the planet. She has succeeded in reconstructing a humanoid female Martian skeleton and her child and has constructed an interesting hypothesis about the original Martians. Her theory supposes that the humanoid Martians were actually super-human, and instead of sporting a mere 23 chromosomes that humans possess, they were able to bioengineer a 24th chromosome. Like a Spinal Tap amplifier, the Martians then have the enviable ability to go "one higher," endowing them with super strength, super intellect, and the ability to heal at rapid rates. However, not all Martians adapted well to their extra chromosome and somehow morphed into death-defying monsters instead. This unfortunate side effect forced the normal, super-Martians to build a portal to Earth to flee from the monster-Martians and where, they presumably settled to form Earth society. The carnivorous and very dimly lit monsters, still stuck on Mars, are happy to find the human researchers which they enjoy graphically obliterating. In addition to mere monsters, the film also finds a way to incorporate zombies as well, as the people that survive the Martian attacks somehow become carnivorous flesh-eaters too.

Many of Sarge's team members have suffered such a fate. Luckily most of the violence takes place in the shadowy periphery where costly, high tech special effects may be spared. The human drama consists of a rigid reunion between Samantha and brother John, who clash in their basic life view (science and reason vs. kill or be killed). The two actors are capable in their roles, while The Rock, normally oozing charm and charisma, is hindered by his one-dimensional, unlikable character. Gamers will appreciate the fact that near the film's end, the "First Person Shooter" mode of the video game kicks in, and enjoys moments of black humor amid the endless violence.

Polish Cinematographer turned director Andrzej Bartkowiak is no stranger to action films, lensing such movies as *Dante's Peak, Jade,* and *Lethal Weapon 4* and directing *Romeo Must Die* and *Exit Wounds.* Perhaps *Doom* might have benefited more from Bartkowiak holding the camera rather than directing.

Hilary White

CREDITS

Sarge: Dwayne "The Rock" Johnson
John Grimm: Karl Urban
Samantha Grimm: Rosamund Pike
Goat: Ben Daniels
Duke: Raz Adoti
Pinky: Dexter Fletcher
Portman: Richard Brake
The Kid: Al Weaver
Origin: USA
Released: 2005
Directed by: Andrzej Bartkowiak
Written by: Wesley Strick, David Callaham
Cinematography by: Tony Pierce-Roberts
Running time: 113 minutes

REVIEWS

Chicago Sun-Times Online. October 21, 2005.
Entertainment Weekly Online. October 19, 2005.
New York Times Online. October 21, 2005.
Variety Online. October 20, 2005.

AWARDS

Nomination:
Golden Raspberries 2005: Worst Actor (Johnson).

DOWNFALL

(Der Untergang)

April 1945, a nation awaits its...
—Movie tagline

Box Office: $5.5 million

Since the end of WWII, there have been many cinematic attempts to understand Nazis, if not humanize them. *Downfall* (aka *Der Untergang*) is yet another example of this type of drama—and it is no more or less successful than its predecessors.

While pop culture portraits of Adolph Hitler and the Nazis are predominantly one-dimensional, several texts over the decades have offered more nuanced and serious views. The problem with these latter portrayals is that they risk being alienating and offensive to audiences. This is a no-win situation for any artist, however, since one-dimensional depictions of evil usually are also offensive (or just laughable), too.

At least, director Oliver Hirschbiegel deserves credit for trying. *Downfall* is based on both Traudl Junge's memoirs (*Bis zur letzten Stunde*) and the documentary, *Blind Spot: Hitler's Secretary,* in which Junge recounts her experiences as Adolph Hitler's last secretary (from 1942 to 1945). The dramatization of Junge's life could never match up to what Junge herself relates so memorably in the 2002 film, but at least *Downfall* earnestly refrains from exploiting the obvious.

Following Junge's chronicle (and Joachim Fest's supplemental biography of her), *Downfall* tells the story of Junge (Alexandre Maria Lara) during her last days of work for the German dictator (in April 1945), as she is taken down to the bunker, where de Fuhrer (Bruno Ganz), his lover Eva Braun (Juliane Kohler), and Hitler's top commanders all face imminent defeat by the Russians and the Allied Expeditionary Force. Junge observes that Hitler remains optimistic about the Nazi victory, despite his apparent doom, though he is outraged when some of his supporters—including Himmler and Goring—defect in order to save their own lives. Others, including Joseph Goebbels (Ulrich Matthes) stay by Hitler's side, even if it means eventual suicide.

As reality sets in, Hitler begins to crack up. He lashes out at those around him and becomes paranoid and depressed. Meanwhile, Eva Braun tries to cheer up her boyfriend and Goebbels' wife, Magda (Corinna Harfouch), kills her children in a moment of panic. Finally acknowledging the inevitable, Hitler kills himself with a gunshot to his head. When the Allied soldiers open the bunker, they find just a few survivors, including Traudl Junge.

Past cinematic versions of Hitler's last days have had similar problems balancing public perceptions and expectations with the humanization of unspeakably bad people. G.W. Pabst got it mostly right with The Last 10 Days (1955), by also incorporating Junge's recollections and featuring a performance so complex and interesting by Albin Skoda as Hitler, it inspired Bruno Ganz to take the role in *Downfall* after initially refusing it. Hitler—*The Last 10 Days* (1973) starring Alec Guiness and *The Bunker* (1983) starring Anthony Hopkins were in the same mode but more theatrical, almost comically so, and Hans-Jürgen Syberberg's *Hitler, a Film From Germany*(1978) was deliberately strange and surreal, though maybe the best way to approach the highly charged topic.

In any case, *Downfall* works overtime not to be campy or one-dimensional. It also keeps the Nazis from being objects of pity or identification (unlike *Max*, the 2002 story of Hitler as a youth, among a few other Hitler films). Hirschbiegel doesn't get stuck in the bunker, either. He expands the action to above the ground action and events surrounding the demise of the Third Reich, which may not be as claustrophobically dramatic but provides a welcome distancing technique. The production values are at a high level, from Rainer Klausmann's agile cinematography to Bernd Lepel's authentic-looking set design. Many of the performances stand out, including Corinna Harfouch's frightening Mme. Goebbles (particularly in the scene where she poisons her children) and Juliane Kohler's desperately upbeat Eva Braun. For a film told from the point of view of Traudl Junge, Alexandre Maria Lara doesn't get much to do (see Blind Spot for Junge's real-life recitation). And Bruno Ganz gives an interesting performance, especially in his scenes of mental disintegration, but he is never really convincing if only because he just doesn't look or sound like Adolph Hitler, despite the fact the Swiss-born Ganz studied a rarely heard 10-minute recording by Hitler in his last days in the bunker.

Responses to *Downfall* were understandably mixed. Kenneth Turan's February 25, *2005 Los Angeles Times* review stated, "*Downfall*...demands our attention despite its drawbacks. One of the five best foreign-language Oscar nominees, and conceivably the winner, it is more mainstream movie of the week than work of art. But the reality it confronts is so gripping, we cannot turn away. This may not be the most sophisticated retelling of what happened while Berlin burned, but what a story it is." A.O. Scott's February 18, 2005 *New York Times* review concurred, "...*Downfall* shifts its gaze back and forth between the crumbling military situation on the ground in Berlin and the bizarre domestic situation in the bunker underneath it, combining high wartime drama with a sense of mundane detail that verges on the surreal. It is fascinating without being especially illuminating, and it holds your attention for its very long running time without delivering much dramatic or emotional satisfaction in the end." And J. Hoberman's *Village Voice* piece summed up the paradox of the film and the viewing the film: "*Downfall* may be grimly self-important and inescapably trivializing. But we should be grateful that German cinema is more inclined to normalize the nation's history than rewrite it."

Eric Monder

CREDITS

Adolf Hitler: Bruno Ganz

Traudl Junge: Agustin Lara

Magda Goebbels: Corinna Harfouch

Joseph Goebbels: Ulrich Matthes

Albert Speer: Heino Ferch

Dr. Schenck: Christian Berkel

Werner Haase: Matthias Habich

Hermann Fegelein: Thomas Kretschmann

Heinrich Himmler: Ulrich Noethen

Otto Guensche: Goetz Otto
Eva Braun: Juliane Koehler
Peter, the Hitler Youth Kid: Donevan Gunia
Origin: Germany
Language: German
Released: 2004
Production: Bernd Eichinger; released by Constantin Film
Directed by: Oliver Hirschbiegel
Written by: Bernd Eichinger
Cinematography by: Rainer Klausmann
Music by: Stephan Zacharias
Sound: Roland Winke, Michael Kranz
Editing: Hans Funck
Art Direction: Elena Zhukova
Costumes: Claudia Bobsin
Production Design: Bernd Lepel
MPAA rating: R
Running time: 155 minutes

REVIEWS

Boxoffice Online. February, 2005.
Chicago Sun-Times Online. March 11, 2005.
Entertainment Weekly Online. February 16, 2005.
Los Angeles Times Online. February 25, 2005.
New York Times Online. February 18, 2005.
Variety Online. September 15, 2004.
Washington Post Online. March 11, 2005, p. WE37.

TRIVIA

Bruno Ganz studied Parkinson's patients in a Swiss hospital to prepare for his role as Hitler.

DREAMER: INSPIRED BY A TRUE STORY

Writer/director John Gatins reportedly found inspiration for the film *Dreamer* in the true story of a horse named Mariah's Storm. The animal suffered a terrible leg injury but recovered to go on to win several major races a few years later. That is actually the extent to which *Dreamer: Inspired by a True Story* is actually based on real events. Gatins took the story of the horse and created a gentle tale of family relationships, healing, and personal triumph, choosing a very familiar plot structure and equally familiar character types. There is no shortage of movies about a girl and her horse, nor are there only a few stories about horses (and riders) who manage to beat the odds and win huge races. On that level, *Dreamer: Inspired by a True Story* accomplishes nothing new or unique. Yet the film does not aspire to be much more than a family-oriented, competently told story that touches the heart and shares simple but not insignificant themes about love, faith, and courage. In that respect, the film succeeds, aided in no small part by the performance of its child star, Dakota Fanning.

Fanning plays Cale Crane, the young daughter of horse trainer Ben Crane (Kurt Russell). Ben has had to sell off much of his farm to cover his debts, much to the frustration of his crusty father Pop Crane (Kris Kristofferson), and now he owns no horses of his own but trains the animals for a rich, arrogant stable owner named Palmer (David Morse). One day at the track, Palmer decides to race a filly named Soñador (Spanish for "dreamer") against Ben's advice. Sadly vindicating Ben's misgivings, the horse breaks a leg in the race. When Palmer orders the filly to be put down, young Cale intercedes and persuades her father to save the animal. Ben is fired by Palmer and takes Soñador as his severance pay. What happens next is no real surprise: Ben and Cale set out to help the horse mend, which eventually they do.

As Cale and the horse bond, Ben grows closer to his daughter, and even Pop starts talking to his son more. One day when Ben and Pop watch Cale and Soñador speeding across the grass, Ben hatches the idea of racing the horse again. In fact, they wind up entering Soñador in the Breeders' Cup, where the horse is ridden by Manolin (Freddy Rodriquez), a friend and fellow trainer. The rest of the plot takes a predictable but rousing path towards a triumphant conclusion.

Dakota Fanning handles the role of Cale with an understated believability and innate charm that makes the character thoroughly endearing. Fanning's performance is as nuanced and subtle as any adult actor, showing such a range of talent that she stands out even among some good performances by the rest of the cast. Kurt Russell, too, plays Ben with an effective mixture of devotion, restraint, and earnestness that makes the relationship between Ben and Cale one of the strongest points of the film.

The film avoids some of the pitfalls that are common to this type of movie. It does not try too hard to play to emotions and does not overdo the sentimental aspects of the story, nor does it overplay the characterizations. Consequently, the emotion that arises out of the story seems genuine, and even though in the end it is largely a "feel-good" movie, *Dreamer* does not come across as manipulative or saccharine. While it is not a film that merits any awards, *Dreamer: Inspired by a True Story* is a movie that accomplishes what it sets out to do and does so with skill. As such, it is a competently made movie with appeal for both children and adults.

David Flanagin

CREDITS

Ben Crane: Kurt Russell
Cale Crane: Dakota Fanning
Pop Crane: Kris Kristofferson
Lilly Crane: Elisabeth Shue
Balon: Luis Guzman
Manolin: Freddy Rodriguez
Palmer: David Morse
Prince Sadir: Oded Fehr
Bill Sellers: Ken Howard
Origin: USA
Language: English
Released: 2005
Production: Mike Tollin, Brian Robbins; Tollin/Robbins Productions, Hunt Lowry; released by DreamWorks
Directed by: John Gatins
Written by: John Gatins
Cinematography by: Fred Murphy
Music by: John Debney
Sound: Elliott L. Koretz
Editing: David Rosenbloom
Art Direction: Scott Plauche
Costumes: Judy Ruskin Howell
Production Design: Brent Thomas
MPAA rating: PG
Running time: 98 minutes

REVIEWS

Boxoffice Online. October, 2005.
Chicago Sun-Times Online. October 21, 2005.
Entertainment Weekly Online. October 19, 2005.
Los Angeles Times Online. October 21, 2005.
New York Times Online. October 21, 2005.
Variety Online. September 11, 2005.
Washington Post Online. October 21, 2005, p. WE44.

QUOTES

Teacher: "Cale Crane? Are you working on your creative writing project?"
Cale Crane: "Yes, ma'am."
Teacher, not believing her: "What is it about?"
Cale Crane: "It's about a king…in a castle…and a magic horse."

TRIVIA

Kurt Russell bought co-star Dakota Fanning a real Palamino horse, which she named Goldie.

THE DUKES OF HAZZARD

Cousins. Outlaws. Thrillbillies.
—Movie tagline

Box Office: $80.3 million

The Dukes of Hazzard is based on the TV show of the same name. The series was mainly about cousins Bo and Luke Duke riding around in their orange 1969 Dodge Charger, The General Lee, jumping over riverbeds and such. The show, while not a big hit with critics, was popular enough to run six years from its debut in 1979. Writer John O'Brien also wrote the script for the TV-show-turned film *Starsky and Hutch*, so he had experience in such matters. But while that film had the advantage of Ben Stiller and Owen Wilson wringing out the last dregs of whatever humor it had, this one is stuck with Seann William Scott and Johnny Knoxville. Both actors can be funny when given the right material, but they are not yet good enough to make something from nothing.

In his review of *The Dukes of Hazzard*, *Boston Globe* critic Wesley Morris wrote, "The real trouble is that the movie can't determine what type of dumb it would like to be. Raucous? Juvenile? Ironic and knowingly dumb? Is it good-natured? Mean?" In the absence of a clear idea, O'Brien and director Jay Chandrasekhar try a little bit of everything. There are scenes of the General Lee jumping over things (shown in slow-motion, naturally). There are a few shots of cousin Daisy (Jessica Simpson) wearing the famously short shorts that she is wont to wear. There is the lewd suggestion that Bo (Scott) is much more attracted to his car than any female. And the word "Yeee-haw" is spoken often. But there are also moments of clever humor that stick out all the more since they are so random and unexpected. When Bo and Luke (Knoxville) take the General Lee with its confederate flag-topped roof into Atlanta, they get stuck in traffic and catch a lot of flak from fellow drivers offended by the flag. It is nice that the film has some good jokes, but it could have used a whole lot more of them.

The plot for the movie seems like it could have been a lost episode of the TV series. Luke and Bo's usual life of delivering moonshine for Uncle Jesse (Willie Nelson) is interrupted when they happen upon Boss Hogg's (Burt Reynolds) evil plan to seize all the land in Hazzard Country then start strip-mining the place. Hogg's scheme entails hosting a big NASCAR race during the public hearings about the mines. Apparently everyone in Hazzard is so enamored of NASCAR that this will effectively round up every person in the county.

It is hard to say what, exactly, the Duke boys do to foil this plan, but it seems to involve a lot of car chases. Many police cars were harmed in the making of this movie and, from the amount of cars that are demolished, it would appear that Hazzard County has one of the largest police fleets around. Or did have, at least, before the mayhem. When car chases do not do the trick, Cousin Daisy shows up in a tiny outfit to charm a law enforcement official or two. Simpson looks the part of Daisy, but she is one of the most awkward actresses to hit the big screen in quite a while. In her few scenes, she smiles tightly and seems concerned with the logistics of constantly smiling and speaking lines of dialogue at the same time. She reads her lines like a Miss America contestant telling the judges about her plans for world peace.

Perhaps Simpson is in the movie that she deserves, but surely that cannot be true for Reynolds and Nelson. It was clever casting that put the former *Smokey and the Bandit* on the other end of the car chase, but it is not a good sign that *Smokey* was a far better film. In his fancy cream-colored suits, Reynolds looks dressed for a good time, but any one of his 1970s-era appearances on *The Tonight Show* was far more entertaining than anything here. Nelson brings his laid-back country charm to the role, but he is not given much to do except tell old, bad jokes. And Knoxville, despite the lameness of his role, exudes a kind offbeat charm that hints that he might be good in the sort of parts that Jack Nicholson once took.

It is not the biggest surprise in the world that critics did not have many nice things to say about the film. Melissa Rose Bernardo of *Entertainment Weekly* gave the film a C- grade and wrote, "This dumbed-down transfer of the high-octane TV series is about as much fun as a speed bump." And Roger Ebert of *The Chicago Sun-Times* called it "a lame-brained, outdated wheeze." Desson Thomson of *The Washington Post* was the rare critic who would admit to liking the *Dukes*, writing, "the movie is more charmingly lowbrow than screamingly funny, and it doesn't seem the slightest bit interested in straying from the formula of screeching cars, barroom brawls and other southern clichés."

Jill Hamilton

CREDITS

Luke Duke: Johnny Knoxville
Bo Duke: Seann William Scott
Boss Hogg: Burt Reynolds
Uncle Jesse: Willie Nelson
Sheriff Roscoe P. Coltrane: M.C. Gainey
Enos: Michael Weston
Pauline: Lynda Carter
Cooter: David Koechner
Daisy: Jessica Simpson
Deputy Cletus: Jack Polick
Jimmy: Steve Lemme
Dil Driscoll: Michael Roof
Katie Johnson: Nikki Griffin
Laurie Pullman: Alice Greczyn
Billy Prickett: James Roday
Sheev: Kevin Heffernan
Gov. Applewhite: Joe Don Baker
Annette: Jacqui Maxwell
Origin: USA
Language: English
Released: 2005
Production: Bill Gerber; Bill Gerber; released by Warner Bros.
Directed by: Jay Chandrasekhar
Written by: Jay Chandrasekhar, Jonathan Davis
Cinematography by: Lawrence Sher
Music by: Nathan Barr
Sound: David Alvarez
Music Supervisor: Nic Harcourt
Editing: Lee Haxall
Art Direction: Chris Cornwell
Costumes: Genevieve Tyrrell
Production Design: Jon Gary Steele
MPAA rating: PG-13
Running time: 105 minutes

REVIEWS

Boxoffice Online. August, 2005.
Chicago Sun-Times Online. August 5, 2005.
Entertainment Weekly Online. August 2, 2005.
Los Angeles Times Online. August 5, 2005.
New York Times Online. August 5, 2005.
Premiere Magazine Online. August 5, 2005.
Variety Online. July 31, 2005.
Washington Post Online. August 5, 2005, p. WE30.

QUOTES

Bo Duke: "I'm never gettin' out of this car again! I'm gonna eat in it, I'm gonna sleep in it, and I'm gonna make sweet love to it!"

TRIVIA

Filming began November 8, 2004, almost 26 years to the day that shooting began for "One Armed Bandits," the first episode of the original TV series *The Dukes of Hazzard* in 1979.

AWARDS

Nomination:

Golden Raspberries 2005: Worst Picture, Worst Remake/Sequel, Worst Support. Actor (Reynolds), Worst Support. Actress (Simpson), Worst Director (Chandrasekhar), Worst Screenplay.

DUMA

Some friendships are wilder than others.
—Movie tagline

Perhaps the saddest thing about Carroll Ballard's

heartstring-tugging adventure drama about a boy and his orphaned pet cheetah is that so few people were able to see it. Grossing a mere $860,000 during its "test run" in San Antonio, Phoenix, and Sacramento and limited release in New York and Los Angeles, this wonderful family film from the director of *Fly Away Home* (1996) and *The Black Stallion* (1979) deserved a national release from distributor Warner Brothers. With details still murky about a DVD release date, the highly-acclaimed *Duma* will have to settle for renewed life on the art house circuit.

Caroll Ballard once again revisits the familiar themes of children, animals, and sweeping landscapes in a story loosely based on the book *How It Was with Dooms* by wildlife photographer Carol Cawthra Hopcroft and her son Xan about their real-life experiences with their pet cheetah on an African farm. Ballard, however, dials up the drama somewhat lacking in the true but tame little story, injecting more adventure, peril, and pathos along the way.

Duma, the Swahili word for cheetah, is an adorable little orphaned cheetah cub who wanders off of a South African game reserve and onto a highway where he is rescued by the young Xan (Alexander Michaletos in his film debut) and his father Peter (Campbell Scott). They bring him home to join the family on their little farm, which includes mother Kristin (Hope Davis), where they all fall in love with the lost little cheetah. These are the salad days, with Xan forming a deep bond with his tawny, black-spotted buddy on the veld and making up the emotional springboard on which the rest of the film will be launched.

Xan, however, is made aware that there will come a day when Duma will have to return to his natural habitat in the wild. The day comes sooner than expected, however, when Peter suddenly dies and Kristin is forced to lease the little farm and move to an apartment in the big city to seek work. Xan decides that this is the time to aid his now fully-grown, furry friend in his return to the wilderness, and sets off in a passenger motorbike with Duma in tow.

The duo end up breaking down in a most unfortunate place, the unforgiving Kalahari Desert. With their supply of food and water quickly dwindling, Xan and Duma seek shelter inside a airplane wreck nearby. Hoping to be miraculously rescued, the pair instead are met by a native African tribesman called Ripkuna (Eamonn Walker) whose motives where the two are concerned are far less noble. Rip is also out to survive, scouring the abandoned diamond mines where he once made his living for anything left behind and contemplating turning in the boy and his cheetah for a reward. It's not long, however, before Rip is feeling far cozier about his new traveling companions and the three form a highly unlikely alliance in their quest to survive.

Many of the film's highlights stem from the trio's exciting but often perilous adventures. Macguyver-like, they are able convert the broken down bike into a wind-driven vehicle. Ballard conjures up a powerful image from another classic children's tale in the scene where they board a homemade raft to cross a crocodile-infested stream.

Ballard maintains a nice mix of drama to keep both children and adults entertained. The harsh realities of life, such as poverty and death, mix with the joyous freedom of youth and the pleasure and simplicity of the wild. The politics of the troubled region is also addressed but easily mixes with another of the film's themes: unlikely friendships.

Filmed on location in 75 South African locales, a large part the film's success is due to the casting of lead Michaletos, who seems like a natural interacting with the host of cheetahs of all ages used to make the film because he did, in fact, grow up in South Africa with pet cheetahs, who are less aggressive than other big cats. With no computer effects, utilizing only real cats (under the guidance of trainer Jules Sylvester) it is no small feat that Ballard successfully manages to team a child and a wild animal in nearly every scene of this engrossing and irresistible epic.

Hilary White

CREDITS

Rip: Eamonn Walker

Peter: Campbell Scott

Kristin: Hope Davis

Xan: Alexander Michaletos

Origin: USA

Language: English

Released: 2005

Production: John Wells, Hunt Lowry, Gaylord, Kristin Harris, Stacy Cohen; John Wells, Gaylord Films; released by Warner Bros.

Directed by: Carroll Ballard

Written by: Karen Janszen

Cinematography by: Werner Maritz

Editing: T.M. Christopher

Costumes: Jayne Forbes

Production Design: Johnny Breedt

MPAA rating: PG

Running time: 100 minutes

REVIEWS

Boxoffice Online. August, 2005.
Chicago Sun-Times Online. August 5, 2005.
Variety Online. April 29, 2005.

THE DYING GAUL

The Roman statue entitled The Dying Gaul is from the 3rd century B.C., depicting a wounded Celtic warrior lying the ground, supported by one arm, awaiting death. It is intended to convey the anguish of defeat, which destroys the spirit rather than the flesh. Apt symbolism for Craig Lucas's directorial debut, based on his play, which tells the story of a struggling screenwriter who seriously compromises himself to land a $1 million deal with a corrupt Hollywood executive. Writer of such auspicious films as *Longtime Companion, Reckless,* and *The Secret Lives of Dentists,* Lucas doesn't confine the classic imagery to the title, however, ramming his message home by quoting *Moby Dick* in the picture's opening, "Woe to him who seeks to please rather than appall." Strong direction, aided by solid performances by a wonderful cast, this revenge tragedy's too deliberate plotting eventually becomes it's own undoing.

"The Dying Gaul" is also the name of the script within the film, penned by Robert (Peter Sarsgaard) and sought by Paramount executive Jeffrey (Campbell Scott). Jeffrey offers the hard-up writer $1 million in 1995 dollars for his script, with the stipulation that he turn the homosexual couple in the script, a highly personal tale based on Robert and his former lover and agent Malcolm (Bill Camp) who agonizingly died of AIDS, into an infinitely more salable man and a woman, who does not die of AIDS. "Most Americans hate gay people," Jeffrey states bluntly. Initially refusing, it's an offer the seriously in-debt Robert cannot refuse and with a few keystrokes, the script's Maurice quickly becomes Maggie. Guilt-ridden at what he's done, he also must come up with the mounting child support payments to his ex-wife. And there's also Jeffrey's promise of getting Gus Van Sant to direct.

The Faustian deal complete, Jeffrey takes Robert home for dinner with his attractive and witty wife Elaine (Patricia Clarkson). A former screenwriter, Elaine now lives a more placid existence in her large Malibu estate with their two children and strikes up an immediate friendship with Robert. And although Jeffrey disapproves of homosexuality in his professional life, he embraces it warmly in his personal life as a practicing bisexual, and makes quick work of seducing Robert. Desired by both husband and wife, Robert makes regular visits to the Malibu compound for heartfelt talks with Elaine and randy romps with the duplicitous Jeffrey, who claims to still love his wife.

Elaine finds that Robert has enjoyed visiting sex chat rooms since Malcolm's death, the disembodied "voices" making up what he imagines could be the afterlife. She extracts the name of his favorite gay chat room, posing as man online and striking up a regular conversation with him. It is here that Robert confesses to his online buddy to having an affair with his married boss. Elaine is devastated and the film takes a most disturbing, and incredulous, turn at this point. Instead of making Jeffrey the object of her revenge, she inexplicably turns her wrath on the much-put-upon writer.

Although confessing to be a casual Buddhist, Elaine has no proof that Robert actually believes in the supernatural and so it is somewhat of a contrivance that she then reenters Robert's chat room as "Archangel" and convinces him that it is, in fact, Malcolm speaking to him from the beyond. In her quest to better infiltrate the tortured mind of poor Robert, she even goes so far as to steal files from his psychiatrist.

Both Clarkson and Sarsgaard laudably throw themselves into the conceit, aided by tense background music by Steve Reich. Robert becomes more and more unnerved by the chat room communiqués and Sarsgaard's wrenching emotional explosions are palpable. Clarkson's rainbow of facial expressions as she taps away on her computer are gripping. For his part, Scott makes his odious character more fun to watch than he should be.

The *Medea*-like ending has Elaine finally getting revenge against her husband too. Confronting Robert about the affair and hinting that she is, in fact, Archangel before packing her kids up and pointedly telling her housekeeper that she wants to drive. The police show up later looking for someone to identify the bodies, saying her car ran into a wall. The fact that she most likely intended to smash into the wall taking the kids with her is clear but the reasons behind it remain murky. Also, there is another unclear factor about whether she was poisoned by Robert or Jeffrey with arrowroot and if she knew this or not or, in fact, allowed herself to be poisoned.

Despite stellar performances from the three leads, the overwrought material, murky plotting, and implausible character arcs heartily strain credulity. And the characters themselves all become so thoroughly unsympathetic that there's no one left to root for in the end. As Jeffrey states in the movie "No one goes to the movies to have a bad time or to learn anything."

Hilary White

CREDITS

Elaine: Patricia Clarkson
Jeffrey: Campbell Scott
Robert: Peter Sarsgaard
Origin: USA
Language: English
Released: 2005
Production: Campbell Scott, George Van Buskirk
Directed by: Craig Lucas
Written by: Craig Lucas
Cinematography by: Bobby Bukowski
Music by: Steven Reich
Sound: Kevin Sorenson, David Waelder
Music Supervisor: Linda Cohen
Editing: Andy Keir
Art Direction: G. Victoria Ruskin
Costumes: Danny Clicker
Production Design: Vincent Jefferds
MPAA rating: R
Running time: 105 minutes

REVIEWS

Boxoffice Online. November, 2005.
Chicago Sun-Times Online. November 4, 2005.
Entertainment Weekly Online. November 9, 2005.
Los Angeles Times Online. November 4, 2005.
New York Times Online. November 4, 2005.
Premiere Magazine Online. November, 2005.
Variety Online. January 23, 2005.
Washington Post Online. November 4, 2005, p. C05.

TRIVIA

The film is dedicated to writer/director Craig Lucas's best friend, playwright Tony Kushner (*Angels in America*).

E

THE EDUKATORS

(Die Fetten Jahre sind vorbei)

Your Days Of Plenty Are Numbered.
—Movie tagline

Taking on the gulf between the haves and the have-nots, the protest against globalization, and the romantic possibility of a youth-led revolution, *The Edukators* works more like a left-wing polemic than an engaging narrative. Directed by Hans Weingartner from a screenplay he cowrote with Katharina Held, this work of radical idealism from Germany begins promisingly but soon grows stagnant and preachy as the filmmakers choose familiar liberal platitudes and shallow conflict over what could have been a complex treatment of serious social issues.

Jan (Daniel Brühl) and Peter (Stipe Erceg) are longtime friends and young rebels who engage in creative protests to disrupt the comfortable lives of the rich. They break into the homes of the well-to-do, rearrange the furniture, and leave odd notes (signed "The Edukators") with ominous warnings such as "Your Days of Plenty are Numbered" and "You have too much money." While Peter is not above pilfering a watch, the highly principled Jan does not believe in stealing; he simply wants to shake the rich out of their complacency by making them see how easily their private space of privilege can be invaded.

Jule (Julia Jentsch), Peter's girlfriend, a waitress in a fancy restaurant who has to put up with the obnoxious rich, is being evicted at the same time Peter is planning a trip to Barcelona. She must stay behind to clean up her apartment and gets help from Jan, who begins to fall for her and tells her about his and Peter's secret identities and clandestine pranks. A fierce advocate for the oppressed, he sympathizes with her plight when he learns that she owes an enormous debt to a wealthy man, Hardenberg (Burghart Klaussner), for totaling his Mercedes.

Pretty soon Jan and Jule are wrecking her former apartment instead of cleaning it, and she is persuading him to take her to Hardenberg's home, where they pull off some edukator-style shenanigans, even going so far as to toss the sofa into the swimming pool. But when they later return to retrieve a jacket, Hardenberg comes home. Jule calls Peter for help, and the trio, panicking and not knowing what to do since they are not hardcore criminals at heart, end up kidnapping Hardenberg and taking refuge in a remote cabin.

At this point, the film devolves into a talky, dull standoff between youthful ideals and middle-age compromise. Jan, the thinker of the group, details his political critique, which includes calling for the cancellation of Third World debt and decrying the false promises of capitalism, only to find out that Hardenberg, in his own youth, was himself a political radical who lived on a commune. While the hostage and his captors, who generally treat him with civility, discover some common ground, the whole situation of them bonding feels like a cliché, but, then again, so is much of the rhetoric, although Brühl's passion goes far in making Jan a real person and not just a mouthpiece. But political speeches that drive home a litany of basic leftist points are no substitute for a narrative in which the ideas are worked out through action.

Moreover, because Weingartner is obviously committed to his protagonists' point of view, he offers no substantive challenge to their beliefs—Hardenberg's debates with Jan are very mundane—or their questionable methods. The edukators never have to face the possibility that their world view may be simplistic or at least as limited in its own way as that of the people they despise.

Not only is *The Edukators* obvious in its politics, but it is decidedly unexciting as a thriller. There is no real threat that Hardenberg is going to overpower Jan and Peter. Even when Hardenberg appears to escape, he does not go very far. Peter discovers him enjoying a quiet moment in nature, so ennobled has he supposedly become by spending time with people who remind him of his own bohemian past and his latent desire to flee the rat race and move to the country.

The only other possible source of conflict and suspense in the film is the love triangle—the question of what will happen when Peter discovers that Jan and Jule are two-timing him. Peter picks up clues along the way to their attraction, and Hardenberg confirms his suspicions. But after the romance is exposed and the boys fight, everything is patched up too neatly. Neither political nor romantic conflicts are ultimately very complex in this screenplay. By the end, the three are even sharing a bed, although the precise nature of their relationship is not spelled out.

The hostage tale itself does not come to a dramatic head. It merely ends when the kidnappers deposit Hardenberg back at his home with the understanding that he will not send the law after them. Supposedly a new man, he even waives the debt Jule owes him.

But in the film's climactic twist ending, Hardenberg has not been redeemed and does indeed send the police after his abductors. They, however, have outwitted him and fled, leaving behind a note declaring "Some People Never Change." Reminiscent of a key episode in *The Silence of the Lambs*, the editing in this sequence delays the revelation that the edukators are not in the barren apartment the police are breaking into but rather in another location far away. The cutting may be clever, but the ending ultimately just confirms the simple-minded prejudices the film is built upon; the capitalist, even if he seems reformed, will ultimately betray the ideals buried deep within him, and the young will see the betrayal coming a mile away.

The Edukators has a provocative setup that flirts with saying something serious about class conflict and contemporary protest or perhaps the difficulty of meaningful protest in an age when there is no mass movement to channel youthful outrage. But it does not find a compelling framework to express such ideas. Constantly telling rather than showing and relying on leftist sloganeering to rally the audience to its point of view, the film fails to ignite our imagination with subject matter that should have been thought provoking and controversial.

Peter N. Chumo II

CREDITS

Jan: Daniel Bruhl
Jule: Julia Jentsch
Peter: Stipe Erceg
Hardenberg: Burghart Klaussner
Origin: Germany, Austria
Language: German
Released: 2004
Production: Antonin Svoboda, Hans Weingartner; Coop99, Y3 Film
Directed by: Hans Weingartner
Written by: Hans Weingartner, Katharina Held
Cinematography by: Matthias Schellenberg, Daniela Knapp
Music by: Andreas Wodraschke
Sound: Stefan Soltau
Editing: Andreas Wodraschke, Dirk Oetelshoven
Costumes: Silvia Pernegger
Production Design: Christian M. Goldbeck
MPAA rating: R
Running time: 126 minutes

REVIEWS

Boxoffice Online. July, 2005.
Entertainment Weekly Online. July 27, 2005.
Los Angeles Times Online. July 29, 2005.
New York Times Online. July 22, 2005.
Variety Online. May 17, 2004.
Washington Post Online. August 5, 2005, p. WE31.

QUOTES

Jan: "I've got news for you, Corporate Man: your days are numbered!"

TRIVIA

Director Hans Weingartner makes a cameo appearance as one of the protesters at the beginning of the film.

ELEKTRA

Looks can kill.
—Movie tagline

She was left for dead. Now she's back with vengeance.
—Movie tagline

Born to fight. Trained to kill.
—Movie tagline

Before she can find peace she will wage war.
—Movie tagline

Box Office: $24.4 million

Elektra is yet another dreary and dull comic book adaptation. The character was first created by Marvel Comics writer Frank Miller in 1980 as the romantic interest-turned-nemesis of Daredevil and later spun off into her own series. The same thing happened in the movies: Jennifer Garner played the role in 2003's execrable *Daredevil* and was rewarded with her very own spin-off. Maybe she liked the costume, maybe she liked kicking butt, and maybe she actually liked the script although it sure must have read better than what appears on screen.

The plot—such as it is—begins with a voiceover nattering on about a battle between good and evil and a warrior who could tip the balance by deciding which side she'll be on. Hey, if she had chosen evil, the movie might have been a lot more fun. Anyway, Elektra is an emotional mess. She's supposed to be this stone-cold assassin in red, which she demonstrates by wiping out her latest hit for hire in the opening scene without changing the grimace on her face. But back home, she compulsively cleans and likes things laid out just so because she suffers from obsessive-compulsive disorder; Elektra also has insomnia and nightmares about finding the body of her murdered mother when she was a little girl (and daddy was an abusive jerk) so she's got a lot of unresolved family issues too.

All this anger might be useful considering her line of work but it got Elektra tossed out of the compound of sensei master Stick (Terence Stamp) when she was learning all her martial arts tricks because all that violence was just screwing up her spiritual growth. Stick and his band are the good guys. The bad guys are an organization called the Hand, who mostly look like a bunch of Japanese suits who sit around a conference table and are led by Roshi (Cary-Hiroyuki Tagawa). Roshi has his own problems since he's being challenged by his son Kirigi (Will Yun Lee) for control. The Hand is out to obtain the "treasure," no matter what the obstacle (that would be Elektra of course).

Elektra has a slick agent named McCabe (Colin Cunningham) who sets up her hits and takes care of her money. She agrees to another assignment that sends Elektra to a lavish vacation home on an island where she meets her neighbors—bratty, 13-year-old Abby Miller (Kirsten Prout) and her hunky single dad, Mark (Goran Visnjic), who are hiding something. Cold-hearted Elektra immediately bonds with motherless Abby and can't go through with the kill when she discovers that the Millers are her targets. A couple of the Hand's ninja assassins show up instead and when Elektra kills them, they dissolve into green smoke. Elektra takes the Millers to Stick for protection but he refuses her and they wind up at McCabe's farmhouse. Kirigi and his creepy minions are given the chance to capture the Millers because the "treasure" turns out to be Abby, who's a little martial arts prodigy with powers that could rival Elektra's with the proper training.

McCabe gets killed and everybody winds up fighting in the woods where a couple of bad guys bite the dust and Stick finally comes to the rescue, taking Elektra and the Millers back to his compound. Elektra has more nightmares and realizes that Kirigi is her mother's killer (who knows why he did it). Elektra and Kirigi have a psychic one-on-one and agree to meet for a showdown at the scene of the crime, Elektra's abandoned childhood home. Naturally he cheats and brings his remaining crew and Abby decides to follow Elektra. Elektra gets distracted by her own fears during the fights and nearly gets herself and Abby killed but manages to pull herself together and save the day. (She even gets to resurrect Abby from the dead, the same way that Stick resurrected her, which proves that she's learned to use her powers for good.) Elektra says good bye and good luck to Mark and Abby, gets an "attagirl" from Stick, and walks away a much happier ex-assassin.

Jennifer Garner is used to wearing weird costumes and fighting bad guys (and having family issues); she did it for five seasons on ABC's *Alias* and we all rooted for Sydney Bristow to save the day once again. Garner makes you want to root for her—she's a very appealing actress and though she can perform her stunts with apparent ease, *Elektra* is just a really silly showcase for her talents. The other characters are like game boards pieces to be moved around as director Rob Bowman sees fit; you don't actually care about any of them (the bad guys are either bland or have comic book traits that will remind you of other, similar characters). Well, at least the Elektra character brought Garner some personal happiness since it introduced her to *Daredevil* star Ben Affleck (who did a cameo in a deleted scene in this film) and they've since married and become parents. A much more satisfying outcome than *Elektra* could ever provide.

Christine Tomassini

CREDITS

Elektra: Jennifer Garner
Stick: Terence Stamp

Mark: Goran Visnjic
Roshi: Cary-Hiroyuki Tagawa
Abby: Kirsten Prout
Kirigi: Will Yun Lee
Origin: USA
Language: English
Released: 2005
Production: Arnon Milchan, Gary Foster, Avi Arad; New Regency Pictures, Horseshoe Bay; released by 20th Century-Fox
Directed by: Rob Bowman
Written by: Zak Penn, Stuart Zicherman, Raven Metzner
Cinematography by: Bill Roe
Music by: Christophe Beck
Sound: Michael Williamson
Music Supervisor: Dave Jordan
Editing: Kevin Stitt
Art Direction: Eric Norlin
Costumes: Lisa Tomczeszyn
Production Design: Graeme Murray
MPAA rating: PG-13
Running time: 97 minutes

REVIEWS

Boxoffice Online. January, 2005.
Chicago Sun-Times Online. January 14, 2005.
Entertainment Weekly Online. January 12, 2005.
Los Angeles Times Online. January 14, 2005.
New York Times Online. January 14, 2005.
Premiere Magazine Online. January 18, 2005.
Variety Online. January 12, 2005.
Washington Post Online. January 14, 2005, p. WE31.

QUOTES

Elektra: "I'm not a good person to get involved with."

TRIVIA

Ben Affleck reprised his *Daredevil* role, filming a cameo as Matt Murdock but was cut from the final film.

ELIZABETHTOWN

It's a heck of a place to find yourself.
—Movie tagline

Box Office: $26.8 million

For the better part of a decade, Drew Baylor's life was all about creating an athletic shoe with which the public would fall head over heels in love. Unfortunately, it ended up being rejected by millions instead of making them. Drew's shoes cost the Nike-esque company he worked for almost $1 billion, a staggering, unforgivable loss that gets him the boot. While being focused did not pay off for him, it certainly would have made *Elizabethtown* more successful. The version screened at the Toronto Film Festival made clear the need for further editing to streamline, tighten, and clarify. However, the final cut, like the road trip Drew takes late in the film, feels all over the map as it endeavors to cover a lot of ground.

The film, the latest from talented writer/director Cameron Crowe, starts out in promising fashion. In voiceover, Drew speaks of "a disaster of mythic proportions." Enduring the uncomfortable, knowing "last looks" of coworkers as he makes the solemn trek to meet with his boss, Phil (enjoyable Alec Baldwin), Drew repeatedly assures them he is okay despite knowing he is a dead man walking at Mercury Worldwide Shoes. The fact that Drew had barely suppressed the urge to leap to his death during the helicopter ride there make his assertions of "I'm fine" rather unconvincing. A flashback shows merry Mercury personnel dancing ecstatically amidst falling confetti in anticipation of a profit bonanza from Drew's Spasmotica shoes. It provides a stark contrast to the glum, ruinous present, revealing just how far the mighty have fallen.

Phil tries to maintain a Zen-like calm as he reveals that Drew's debacle has cost the company $972 million, bankrupted their global environment project ("We could have saved the planet," he sighs, "but..."), and caused one bigwig to proclaim the shoes so repugnant that a horrified public will likely opt for bare feet for some time to come. "I cry a lot lately," shares Phil. In a matter of days, an article will let the world know all about the fiasco, and Drew is clearly overwhelmed and embarrassed, a perplexed pariah. Soon the other shoe drops, as his downfall causes girlfriend Ellen Kishmore (Jessica Biel) to not want to kiss him anymore.

With both his professional and personal lives suddenly and completely crumbled at his feet, Drew returns to his apartment to commit suicide. Before he is successful in doing so, his sister Heather (Judy Greer) calls with news that their father has died suddenly of a heart attack while visiting relatives in his hometown of Elizabethtown, Kentucky. Keeping his own bad news to himself, the family's dazed pride and joy dutifully catches the redeye from the West Coast. He will retrieve his father's corpse and then get right back to making himself into one.

On that fateful plane trip, Drew meets Claire Colburn (Kirsten Dunst), a cute, bubbly busybody of a flight attendant. She is incessantly perky and attentive to the aircraft's sole passenger, sensing his situation calls for some infectious, chirpy cheer. While Claire's persistent, playful gregariousness will strike some as upbeat charm, others will find her rather grating and even a little bit creepy. One thing that certainly irritates is her curious habit of pretending to take snapshots with an imaginary camera.

The most engaging sequence in *Elizabethtown* is the all-night phone marathon during which Drew and Claire begin to get to know each other. However, a lot of her banter both here and elsewhere, meant to be clever and meaningful but sometimes merely baffling, sounds too obviously from the screenwriter's purposeful pen. Examples from throughout the film include, "I'm hard to remember, but impossible to forget," "Men see things in a box, and women see things in a round room," "Sadness is easy because its surrender. I say make time to dance alone with one hand waving free." Claire repeatedly pops up in town for more talky encounters (apparently having a highly flexible work schedule). Unfortunately, the connection between Claire and Drew seems to merely persist instead of palpably and compellingly intensifying into love. The audience may be curious to see what grows from this unusual coupling, but that is not the same as caring. It certainly does not help that Bloom's performance is bland, lacking depth and emotional resonance.

Despite receiving directions from experienced-traveler Claire for driving from Louisville to Elizabethtown early on in the film, Drew gets lost. This unfortunate inability to stay on course can be viewed as a sign of things to come for *Elizabethtown* itself. Extraneous, sketchy subplots are introduced which distract and detract from the burgeoning relationship between the two protagonists. Upon arriving in the Norman Rockwellian town, Drew is uncomfortable being lauded by the bustling throng of decent, small-town, whimsical family members and assorted other folk. These characters, who could be descendants of similar folk in films by Frank Capra, would clearly love and accept Drew no matter what befell him in the big city. There is Uncle Dale Baylor (Loudon Wainwright), who worries about the parenting skills of his son Jessie (Paul Schneider), a single father to ear-piercing shrieker Samson. Jessie yearns for the days when he performed with a band called Ruckus which once played on a bill with Lynyrd Skynyrd. Bill Banyon (Bruce McGill) is also present, a jokey, untrustworthy blowhard whom Drew's mother Hollie (Susan Sarandon) detests since he swindled money out of her and her husband years before. Drew must deal over the phone with his reeling mom, whose grief and shock manifests itself in a manic desire to learn (among other things) cooking, plumbing, car repair, tap dancing and stand-up comedy. Hollie feels her late spouse's kin resent her, as if she lured him away to live with the way-out people way out West. There is some tension between Drew's family and the bucolic relatives about whether the deceased should be cremated or buried, and where. The bizarre memorial service, during which a flaming bird swoops out over the startled mourners, will ignite little interest and illicit minimal emotion. Sure, Jessie reunites with Ruckus during the event and is thrilled to be back in his element. Yes, Hollie feels the healing embrace of her husband's family after a mildly-humorous monologue garners their affectionate applause. The tap dance she does accompanied by "Moon River" (the song being more enjoyable than her steps) says a fond farewell to her husband as she rededicates herself to life. Good for her. It is just that all these elements are maddeningly peripheral to the heart of the film, of little interest and import, and make *Elizabethtown* feel repeatedly sidetracked. Even those who were not particularly fond of quirky Claire will welcome her spirited return to try and get the film back on course and hopefully give it some traction.

Claire speaks to Drew about the "courage to fail big and stick around—that's true greatness to me." As for his grief, she instructs him to wallow a little more and then finally "discard and proceed." Claire sends Drew off (with his father's urn lovingly restrained by a seat belt) on a road trip designed to heal his soul, guided by a book she has painstakingly (and maybe a tad scarily) prepared, chock full of detailed maps, extensive, meaningful instructions for specific stops, and, this being a Cameron Crowe film, a slew of apropos CD tunes. While this rambling journey was longer in earlier cuts of the film, it still drags, and is not as impactful as it should be. However, visits to the site of Martin Luther King's assassination and the 1995 Oklahoma City bombing, effectively put his crushing shoe catastrophe in proper perspective. Claire appears at one of his stops (again, when does she work?), at which point Drew, his demons exorcised through her redemptive intervention, gratefully hugs and kisses his sunny savior. The film ends, however, with a rather weak coda asserting the life-affirming glory of struggle and risk-taking.

Made on a budget estimated at $57 million, *Elizabethtown* labored to gross even half of that. Crowe has stated that the film may be his most personal, as he was called upon to fly out to his own father's Kentucky hometown when the elder Crowe died suddenly of a heart attack. The producer/writer/director remembers being warmly embraced by a swarm of unfamiliar relatives. While having numerous people around during a difficult time may be a godsend, the cramming of numerous storylines into the running time of a single film is not nearly as welcome. "How many times did your junior high school English teacher tell you to pick a theme and stick to it when writing?" asked *People*'s Leah Rozen. "*Elizabethtown* tries to tell too many stories...short-shrifting them all."Most critics did not warmly embrace the film. A number of reviewers noted similarities between it and Zach Braff's *Garden State* (2004), where viewers will find something more worthwhile than exists in *Elizabethtown.*

David L. Boxerbaum

CREDITS

Drew Baylor: Orlando Bloom
Claire Colburn: Kirsten Dunst
Hollie Baylor: Susan Sarandon
Heather Baylor: Judy Greer
Ellen Kishmore: Jessica Biel
Phil: Alec Baldwin
Jessie Baylor: Paul Schneider
Uncle Dale: Loudon Wainwright III
Bill Banyon: Bruce McGill
Aunt Dora: Paula Deem
Origin: USA
Language: English
Released: 2005
Production: Tom Cruise, Paula Wagner, Cameron Crowe; Cruise-Wagner Productions, Vinyl Films; released by Paramount Pictures
Written by: Cameron Crowe
Cinematography by: John Toll
Music by: Nancy Wilson
Sound: Jeff Wexler
Editing: David Moritz
Art Direction: Beat Frutiger
Costumes: Nancy Steiner
Production Design: Clay A. Griffith
MPAA rating: PG-13
Running time: 120 minutes

REVIEWS

Boxoffice Online. October, 2005.
Chicago Sun-Times Online. October 14, 2005.
Entertainment Weekly Online. October 12, 2005.
Los Angeles Times Online. October 14, 2005.
New York Times Online. October 14, 2005.
Premiere Magazine Online. October, 2005.
Variety Online. September 5, 2005.
Washington Post Online. October 14, 2005, p. C05.

QUOTES

Claire Colburn: "I'm hard to remember, but I'm impossible to forget."

TRIVIA

The part of Claire was originally written with Kirsten Dunst in mind. Dunst had already committed to *The Village* (2004) but then dropped that film to audition for and win the part in this film instead.

EMILE

Writer/director Carl Bessai crafts a hauntingly lovely film which nicely showcases the considerable talents of lead Ian McKellen as a lonely scientist returning from London to his long-forgotten boyhood home of Canada to accept an honorary doctorate from the University of Victoria. Emile, who arranges to stay with his niece Nadia (Deborah Kara Unger) and her daughter Maria (Theo Crane), is literally haunted by his past with images of his two bickering brothers and their life on a farm in Saskatchewan appearing before his eyes, and whose other secret regrets are also vividly reenacted in onscreen "flashbacks" that are seamlessly woven into the present narrative throughout the film. The separate, yet connected, narratives eventually dovetail into the present, forcing both Emile and Nadia to come to terms with their past.

Wanting to reconnect with his niece, whom he has not seen since she was a child, and with no other living relatives, Emile is graciously taken in by Nadia a few days before accepting his honorary degree. It is quickly shown that there is tension between the two, one that Emile is quicker to dismiss and eagerly attempts to play the role of caring uncle. Despite her gracious invitation to house Emile, Nadia is somewhat cold towards him and seems bitter towards life in general. Freshly separated from Maria's father, an emotionally raw Nadia is in the process of unpacking in their new home as Emile arrives. Maria, unhappy with her parents split as well as the unwelcome move to Victoria from Vancouver, is curious about Emile at first, gradually warming to the kindly older man who seems to be reaching out to her.

The flashbacks begin almost from the start—some of a young girl in slow motion shots, some of Emile's two rugged-looking brothers Carl and Freddy (Chris William Martin and Tygh Runyan, respectively)—with Emile always portrayed by Ian McKellen despite the bygone era. Thus, the flashback "memories" are a bit confusing at first—the elderly Emile interacting with his young brothers and speaking with his familiar British accent despite his Canadian roots. It is explained that he chose to "speak the Queen's English" but it does slightly remove him from the scenes of the past occurring around him in the future. The flashbacks make it clear that Emile has guilt about leaving his brothers behind on the dilapidated farm to study abroad in London, their parents having died sometime previous. Although his younger brother Freddy showed promise as a writer, someone had to stay behind to mind the farm and it obviously wasn't the ambitious Emile. This caused a rift between the brothers that never mended.

Back in the present, Emile awkwardly interacts with the living residents of the house with just about as much success as the dead ones. Eventually, however, he does begin to bond with Maria and a painter/handyman Tom (Ian Tracey) that the obstinately independent Nadia initially ordered off the premises becomes a friendly face around the place as well. While Emile's efforts to seek atonement from Nadia, who is actually Carl's daughter, seem futile, it is later shown in flashback how badly he actually betrayed her. Orphaned as a little girl when her parents died in an auto accident, Nadia spent her children in an orphanage waiting for Emile to come and claim her, thinking he never appeared at all. Emile recalls how he, in fact, showed up at the orphanage and lied about his fitness to care for her to protect his career and own way of life. Emile's regrets and guilt over this and the fate of his brothers come to a head as he receives his award in a touching and hopeful acceptance (in more ways than one) speech attended by Nadia, Maria, Tom, as well as the ghosts of his past.

The riveting turn by McKellen is echoed by all the supporting actors. A subtle, nuanced performance by McKellen is hardly surprising but he hasn't had the chance to play such a rich, realistic lead role in film since 1998's *Gods and Monsters*. Unger embues her character with the kind of substance she has shown in earlier films, including *Stander* (2003) and *A Love Song for Bobby Long* (2004), never going too far with the kind of bitterness that would certainly be understandable but not as sympathetic for such a character. Crane, who also doubles as the young Nadia in flashbacks, proves she certainly has appeal and loads of potential as a young actress while Tracey, who has a lengthy resume of characters roles, lightens the mood with his simple character, devoid of the emotional baggage so apparent everywhere else in the house.

Filmed on location in Canada and England, the film fully utilizes the beautiful, natural surroundings and light which nicely contrast the stylized flashback segments and echoes the duality of the characters and narrative structure.

Hilary White

CREDITS

Emile: Ian McKellen
Nadia: Deborah Kara Unger
Freddy: Tygh Runyan
Taxi Driver: Frank Borg
Maria/Nadia (age 10): Theo Crane
Carl: Chris William Martin
Superintendent: Nancy Sivak
Tom: Ian Tracey
Alice: Janet Wright
Origin: Canada, Great Britain
Language: English
Released: 2003
Production: Carl Bessai, Jacquelyn Renner; Emile Productions Inc., Raven West Films Ltd., Meltemi Entertainment; released by Castle Hill Productions Inc.
Directed by: Carl Bessai
Written by: Carl Bessai
Cinematography by: Carl Bessai
Music by: Vincent Mai
Sound: Nicole Thompson, Brad Hillman
Editing: Julian Clarke
Art Direction: Nancy Mossop
Costumes: Lara Lupish
Production Design: Dina Holmes
MPAA rating: R
Running time: 96 minutes

REVIEWS

Los Angeles Times Online. February 4, 2005.
New York Times Online. March 4, 2005.
Variety Online. September 25, 2003.

TRIVIA

On location British Columbia, Ian McKellen developed a passion for Beaver Tails, a long donut with sugar on it, and subsequently requested his character have a line referring to "beaver tails," which, indeed, found its way into the movie.

ENRON: THE SMARTEST GUYS IN THE ROOM

It's Just Business.
—Movie tagline

Box Office: $4.1 million

There exists a pervasive misquote that dogmatically declares money to be the root of all evil. The actual quote does not hold monetary systems as the architect of evil, but places responsibility on the *love* of money: "For the love of money is a root of all sorts of evil..." 1 Timothy 6:10 in the New Testament (New American Standard version). If it were not a true tale of avarice, greed, amorality, and metastatic corruption, this film could serve as a modern day parable of biblical proportions. Kenneth Turan of the Los Angeles Times illuminates: "*Enron: The Smartest Guys in the Room,* is a horror flick for adults. It's a chilling, completely fascinating documentary that reveals the face of unregulated greed in a way that's every bit as terrifying as Lon Chaney's unmasking in *The Phantom of the Opera*. Maybe more so, because everything here is true."

Written and directed by Alex Gibney, *Enron* depicts the rapid, unballasted rise and headlong plunge into corporate oblivion of the Houston-based, titular company. At its precipice, Enron was the seventh largest corporation in the United States and attained such a rank by an intricate Ponzi scheme that would result in 20,000 employees losing their jobs, $2 billion in pension plans lost, and leaving the state of California $30 billion in debt.

The beginning of Enron's plummet started with the company manufacturing fictitious favorable returns in order to maintain the ascent of their stock. The film employed a strategy known as mark-to-market accounting. This system posits that a company could claim a deal's potential earnings as the current value on the day the deal was contracted. An example of Enron's use of this tactic resulted in its claiming $53 million of profit on a venture failing to generate any income.

The framers of this financial monstrosity were CEO Jeff Skilling and Chairman Ken Lay. As an advocate for federal deregulation, Lay helmed the company's future by operating on the notion that energy could be converted into stocks and bonds. The film holds the company accountable for California's 2000-2001 false energy crisis. No shortage of energy actually existed. The company simply took advantage of the state's recently deregulated energy market. The result was the state enduring rolling blackouts with as much as 50 percent of its industry powering down at some point. The film eerily depicts recordings of company traders joking about "Grandma Millie," the conjectural victim of the orchestrated blackouts.

The film theorizes that this led to the recall of Governor Gray Davis (on October 7th, 2003, Gray Davis became the second governor to be recalled in American history) and the creation of the fortuitous, gubernatorial platform for political hopeful Arnold Schwarzenegger.

The documentary is based upon the best-selling book, *The Smartest Guys in the Room: The Amazing Rise and Scandalous Fall of Enron* by Bethany McLean and Peter Elkind. Gibney implements his musical forte throughout the film. At its opening, an aerial shot pans over Enron's finely contoured Houston skyscraper to the Tom Wait's tune "What's He Building in There?" What did they build? An empire founded on fabrication that devoured lives. One company lineman from Portland, Oregon stated his retirement fund was worth $248,000 before Enron bought out his employer and raped it of all its assets. His retirement nest egg dwindled to a net worth of $1,200. Prior to Enron's fall and the focus of inquiries by both houses of Congress, the Rev. James Nutter of the Palmer Memorial Episcopal Church counseled numerous company employees, offering an insight into the spiritual bankruptcy of the greedy corporate feudal lords directly pillaging its innocent vassals on every plane.

David Metz Roberts

CREDITS

Origin: USA

Language: English

Released: 2005

Production: Alex Gibney, Jason Kilot, Susan Motamed; HDNet Film; released by Magnolia Pictures

Directed by: Alex Gibney

Written by: Alex Gibney

Cinematography by: Maryse Albert

Music by: Matt Hauser

Sound: Martin Czembor

Editing: Alison Elwood

MPAA rating: Unrated

Running time: 110 minutes

REVIEWS

Boxoffice Online. April, 2005.

Chicago Sun-Times Online. April 28, 2005.

Entertainment Weekly Online. April 20, 2005.

Los Angeles Times Online. April 29, 2005.

New York Times Online. April 22, 2005.

Premiere Magazine Online. April 21, 2005.

Variety Online. February 8, 2005.

Washington Post Online. April 29, 2005, p. WE46.

AWARDS

Ind. Spirit 2006: Feature Doc.

Writers Guild 2005: Feature Doc

Nomination:

Oscars 2005: Feature Doc.

Broadcast Film Critics 2005: Feature Doc.

EROS

Three visionary directors. One erotic journey.
—Movie tagline

The anthology or compendium film has a spotty history. *Dead of Night* (1945), a collection of five macabre films, remains the best and best-known of the compilations of short films by different directors exploring a general theme. The most notable such collection since *Dead of Night* is *New York Stories* (1989), with a dreadful contribution by Francis Ford Coppola, a good one by Woody Allen, and a great one by Martin Scorsese, all very similar to what occurs with *Eros*.

The three films composing *Eros* not only look at love and sex but two of them are intended as a tribute to ninety-two-year-old Michelangelo Antonioni, who helped pave the way for explorations of such topics with *L/Avventura* (1960), *La Notte* (1961), *L'Eclisse* (1962), and *Blow-Up* (1966). Antonioni is also an old hand at the anthology film, having contributed episodes to *L'Amore in Citta* (1953) and *I Tre Volti* (1965). Unfortunately, his effort in *Eros* is the weakest of the three films.

The first, longest, and best is "The Hand," by Wong Kar-Wai. Set in Hong Kong in the early 1960's, it is the story of the masochistic devotion of Zhang (Chang Chen), a young tailor, to one of his clients, Miss Hua (Gong Li), a glamorous prostitute. On his first visit to Miss Hua, Zhang must wait outside her bedroom and hears her making love to a customer. As years pass, Zhang is tormented by hearing her with other men. When Miss Hua's fortunes decline as she grows older, Zhang takes pity but cannot help her.

As with all of Wong's stylish films, "The Hand" is concerned primarily with character and mood. "The Hand" is almost a miniature version of Wong's *In the Mood for Love* (2000), with men in carefully tailored black suits, women in slit skirts, dark hallways, and rainy streets. With his usual collaborator, Christopher Doyle, widely considered the greatest current cinematographer, Wong uses lighting to reveal the depths of emotions of his characters, as Zhang retreats from his disappointment into shadows.

"The Hand" also emphasizes texture, with the characters constantly touching cloth and flesh. One remarkable slow-motion shot shows Miss Hua adjusting her hair after being roughed up by a client, as if putting a strand back into place can restore her deteriorating world to what it had once been.

Li, one of the world's greatest actresses, captures Miss Hua's complex character perfectly in this scene. Ironically, Li is at her most beautiful when Miss Hua lies on her deathbed, without makeup and with her hair hanging down for the first time, as Li and Wong show that what had previously been seen was only a façade. Stripped of her artificial glamour, Miss Hua's true self is exposed. Chen's role consists mostly of staring longingly and showing disappointment. He matches Li's quiet intensity when Zhang caresses a dress he has made for his unrequited love.

Allen's effort in *New York Stories* resembles the stories he contributes to *The New Yorker*, and Steven Soderbergh's "Equilibrium" is like an Allen story. Set in Manhattan in the 1950's, it presents an advertising executive, Nick Penrose (Robert Downey, Jr.), who visits a psychiatrist, Dr. Pearl (Alan Arkin), because a recurring dream has made him lose his equilibrium. In the dream, Nick watches an attractive woman (Ele Keats) take a bath and dress. He is uncertain who the woman is and what significance the dream has. While he talks, Dr. Pearl watches someone in a building across the street. Many such comic stories have trick endings, but Soderbergh cleverly gives at least three twists to his, all very satisfying.

Downey essentially acts as Arkin's straight man as Dr. Pearl begins his voyeuristic adventure concerned that his patient will catch him only to become more bold, moving his chair from behind Nick to the window and exchanging opera glasses for larger binoculars. Whatever he is seeing is much more important than Nick's petty problems. Arkin usually plays either bumbling nebbishes, as in *The In-Laws* (1980), or sentimentalized, pathetic little men, as in *13 Conversations about One Thing* (2001). It is a delight finally to see him have so much fun with a role, as Dr. Pearl moves gingerly about behind Nick's back like a cartoon character.

The other most notable aspect of "Equilibrium" is the cinematography of Peter Andrews, a pseudonym used by Soderbergh. The Dr. Pearl scene is photographed in grainy black and white, somewhat recalling the visual style of Antonioni's early films. The dream sequence ends with the woman dressing in blue in a blue room. The way the sensual shades of blue complement each other seems almost a tribute to Doyle's distinctive use of color. When a non-dream version of the same room appears at the end of "Equilibrium," the contrast between an idealized world and reality is remarkable.

Antonioni's "The Dangerous Thread of Things," written by his longtime collaborator Tonino Guerra, lacks the sensitivity and melancholy of "The Hand" and the humor and irreverence of "Equilibrium." Cloe (Regina Nemni) and Christopher (Christopher Buchholz), a bored couple in Tuscany, bicker and wander about the landscape. Christopher encounters Linda (Luisa Ranieri), a beautiful neighbor, and they make love. Linda then walks along a beach dancing in the nude, Cloe does the same, and the two women meet and stare at each other. Other than Ranieri's being remarkably comfortable with her nudity, there is nothing memorable about "The Dangerous Thread of Things." It is almost a parody of Antonioni's treatment of ennui in his best films.

The film's theme song is also a tribute to the director, with "Michelangelo Antonioni" sung in Italian by the Brazilian singer Caetano Veloso. While "Equilibrium" is amusing and well made, it seems to have little connection to the world of Antonioni, not known for his sense of humor. "The Hand," however, perfectly captures the pain and emptiness that love creates in Antonioni at his best.

Michael Adams

CREDITS

Miss Hua ("The Hand"): Gong Li
Zhang ("The Hand"): Chang Chen
Master Jin ("The Hand"): Tin Fung
Zhao ("The Hand"): Zhou Jianjun
Nick Penrose ("Equilibrium"): Robert Downey Jr.
Dr. Pearl ("Equilibrium"): Alan Arkin
Cecilia ("Equilibrium"): Ele Keats
Christopher ("The Dangerous Thread of Things"): Christopher Buchholz
Cloe ("The Dangerous Thread of Things"): Regina Nemni
Linda ("The Dangerous Thread of Things"): Luisa Ranieri
Origin: USA, France, Italy, Luxembourg
Language: English, Italian
Released: 2004
Production: Jacques Bar, Domenico Procacci, Raphael Berdugo, Stephane Tchal Gadjieff, Wong Kar-wai; Roissy, Cite Films, Fandango, Delux Productions, Block 2 Pictures Inc.; released by Warner Independent Pictures
Directed by: Wong Kar-Wai, Steven Soderbergh, Michelangelo Antonioni
Written by: Wong Kar-Wai, Steven Soderbergh, Michelangelo Antonioni
Cinematography by: Tonino Guerra, Christopher Doyle, Marco Pontecorvo
Music by: Peer Raben, Enrica Antonioni, Vinicio Milani, Chico O'Farrill
Sound: Paul Ledford, Claude Letessier, Georges Prat, Tu Duu-chih
Editing: Mary Ann Bernard, Claudio Di Mauro, Chiara Andreussi, William Chang
Art Direction: Alfred Yau Wai-ming
Costumes: William Chang, Milena Canonero, Carin Berger
Production Design: Philip Messina, Stefano Lucci, William Chang
MPAA rating: R
Running time: 104 minutes

REVIEWS

Boxoffice Online. April, 2005.
Chicago Sun-Times Online. April 8, 2005.
Entertainment Weekly Online. April 6, 2005.
Los Angeles Times Online. April 8, 2005.
New York Times Online. April 8, 2005.
Variety Online. September 17, 2004.
Washington Post Online. April 8, 2005, p. WE46.

EVERYTHING IS ILLUMINATED

Leave Normal Behind.
—Movie tagline

Box Office: $1.7 million

The acclaimed novel *Everything Is Illuminated* (2002), by Jonathan Safran Foer, is an intricately assembled metafictional text characterized by interwoven layers of narrative, shifting from one mode to another and shifting between several eras of the past and the present, ultimately bringing everything together to explore themes concerning the ways in which the past and the present are connected, the ways the former sheds light on the latter, and the need to reconcile the two. Some of the narrative is told through letters while other pieces are bits of a novel-in-progress, glimpses into the past that are often touched with magic realism. Consequently, *Everything Is Illuminated* is a novel that many might have considered un-filmable.

At the very least, filming it would involve the far-from-simple task of developing a strategy for translating the many layers of the book into a narrative that would make sense on screen. That actor Liev Schreiber would choose to adapt the novel to the screen as his directorial debut might seem surprising, but it also suggests an admirable ambition and a certain amount of courage on his part. Schreiber's chosen method for translating the book to the medium of film was essentially to trim the majority of the historical narratives from the novel and concentrate on the outer framework of the multi-layered text, the narrative thread set in the present. Some flashback sequences to World War II are retained, but almost half of the book has been excised. Some devoted readers of the book might label this as an "easy way out," a way to avoid dealing with the complexities of handling the more difficult elements of the text, but at the same time, understanding the nature of film structure and the very different demands of the medium leads to the conclusion that the novel could not simply be filmed as written. Schreiber's strategy is a logical one, but ultimately on screen it is semi-successful, resulting in a film that moves from whimsical comedy to pathos but clearly lacks some of the depth that exists on the page in the missing elements of the book.

Elijah Wood plays Jonathan, a young Jewish American who sets out on a quest in the Ukraine to find the woman who saved his grandfather from the Nazis. Wearing huge, thick-rimmed eyeglasses that seem to exaggerate the size of his eyes, Jonathan is almost stoically obsessed with collecting relics from the past, which he keeps in Ziploc bags. Arriving in the Ukraine, he enlists the aid of Heritage Tours to help him find the village where his grandfather lived, Trachimbrod. Jonathan's primary guide is Alex (Eugene Hutz), a "translator" whose constant botching and twisting of the English language provides much of the humor in the film ("Many girls want to be carnal with me because I'm such a premium dancer," he says) and who is fascinated by American culture. (Alex also serves as narrator for the film, which is appropriate considering the fact that, in the novel, the letter portions are written from Alex to Jonathan.) Alex is partnered with his grumpy grandfather (Boris Leskin), a vaguely prejudiced old man who claims to be blind yet drives the trio around in a tiny car, accompanied by his "seeing eye bitch," a dog named Sammy Davis Jr. Jr. Unfortunately, Alex and his grandfather do not know where Trachimbrod is, and the town does not appear on any maps, so their road journey is literally a search for the unknown. Ultimately they do find the woman Jonathan is searching for, in a lone house sitting enigmatically at the center of a thick field of sunflowers.

The first third of the movie is filled with hilarious comedy arising from Jonathan's initial interactions with Alex and his grandfather. Later, however, as their road trip progresses, the tone of the film shifts into a more somber atmosphere of quiet contemplation and ultimately pathos and revelation. The climax of the story involves an unexpected twist that is meant to reflect on one of the most important themes of the film, but oddly enough it is in this climax that the movie departs most extensively from the book.

To some extent the shift in mood works, partly because the most interesting characters, Alex and especially the grandfather, are ultimately drawn into the thread that ties everything together. Additionally, Schreiber manages to evoke enough emotional resonance over the course of the trio's journey that the eventual destination delivers a genuinely moving impact. Still, something seems to be missing, as if the film attempts to "connect the dots" without engaging in a deeper, fully realized exploration of the themes it wants to convey. *Everything Is Illuminated* is an effective, meaningful film and workable effort at translating its source material onto the screen, but unfortunately the illumination it reveals only seems to touch the surface.

David Flanagin

CREDITS

Jonathan Safran Foer: Elijah Wood
Alex: Eugene Hutz
Grandfather: Boris Leskin
Lista: Laryssa Lauret
Origin: USA
Language: English
Released: 2005
Production: Marc Turtletaub, Peter Saraf; Big Beach; released by Warner Independent Pictures
Directed by: Liev Schreiber
Written by: Liev Schreiber
Cinematography by: Matthew Libatique
Music by: Paul Cantloni
Sound: Petr Forejt
Music Supervisor: Sue Jacobs
Editing: Craig McKay
Art Direction: Martin Vackar
Costumes: Michael Clancy
Production Design: Mark Geraghty
MPAA rating: PG-13
Running time: 104 minutes

REVIEWS

Boxoffice Online. September, 2005.
Chicago Sun-Times Online. September 23, 2005.
Entertainment Weekly Online. September 14, 2005.
Los Angeles Times Online. September 16, 2005.
New York Times Online. September 16, 2005.
Premiere Magazine Online. September 15, 2005.
Variety Online. September 4, 2005.

QUOTES

Alex: "Make sure to secure the door when I am gone. There are many dangerous people who wanna take things from Americans, and also kidnap them. Good night!"

THE EXORCISM OF EMILY ROSE

What happened to Emily?
—Movie tagline

Box Office: $75 million

Directed by Scott Derrickson, *The Exorcism of Emily Rose* is a hybrid thriller incorporating two genres: horror and courtroom drama. Based on the true story of a young German woman, Anneliese Michel, who died of mysterious complications following an extensive period of exorcism by the Catholic Church. An ensuing investigation and trial led to a negligent manslaughter conviction of two priests.

The opening of the film shows the arrest of Father Richard Moore (Tom Wilkinson) who is later charged by the district attorney's office for criminal negligence. The archdiocese hires a law firm to defend him. His lawyer, Erin Bruner (an always excellent Laura Linney), is a Carl Sagan thumping skeptic, and for her, the case is another stepping stone for partnership in her firm. Initially, the prosecution offers Moore a deal: plead guilty to reckless endangerment and complete six years from a 12-year sentence. Moore denies the offer and insists (much to Bruner's chagrin) on telling the story of Emily Rose, played by Jennifer Carpenter (who adds pine tingling dimension to her role with one of the most convincing blood-curdling screams in horror). The prosecution wishes to avoid a negative public perception that Father Moore is being placed on trial for his faith and so they hire wooden, calculating Methodist lawyer, Ethan Thomas (Campbell Scott) who is a teetotaler, Sunday school teacher and sings at his church's choir.

The detail of Emily Rose's nightmare are told in flashback sequences from the courtroom. Thomas procures the testimony of medical experts to solidify his stance that Emily Rose was the victim of epilepsy, psychosis, or both: not demon possession. Bruner asserts that Emily may have been possessed. The stage is set: a charged holy man, a Christian prosecutor, and a hard, agnostic serving as the defense in a legal arena that is not equipped by jurisprudence to prove or disprove the existence of supernatural phenomenon.

Emily's story begins with her departure from her small, rural hometown to college as an incoming freshman. One night at 3:00 a.m., she smells a strange odor and hears odd noises. She also sees objects moving about on their own in her dorm room. An invisible weight bears down on her. Olfactory, auditory, visual, and tactile hallucinations? The encounters mount with increasing frequency and she is eventually hospitalized and diagnosed as being mentally ill. Prescribed anti-psychotic medication does not prevail and the visions continue to haunt her. She also scares a boy she is just getting involved with when, again one night at 3:00 a.m., he sees her wide-eyed and horrifically contorted on the floor.

No longer able to maintain her course load, Emily returns home where her disturbing behavior escalates to the point where she is now acting bizarrely, eating spiders and the like. Her family believes the root cause of her affliction is due to demonic possession rather than mental illness. After taking her case, skeptic Bruner is also beginning to experience odd events. Appliances activate on their own accord, her watch stops at...yes, 3:00 a.m.

Slowly losing the battle to the prosecution, who contends that Emily died of a psychotic, epileptic disorder that was exacerbated by the priest's intervention, a psychiatrist who witnessed the exorcism comes to the aid of the defense and presents an audiotape recording of its events. On the night of the exorcism, Emily is tied down to a bed, taunting her rescuers in bouts of rage, speaking in tongues, and inciting the family's cats to run into the room and attack Father Moore. She breaks free, jumps out the window and isolates herself in the family barn. Here she discloses that she is possessed by six separate demonic entities comprising one name: Legion. The prosecution again weakens the defense by claiming that Emily could have learned the languages she is heard speaking on the audio are ones she learned in Catechism school and could train her vocal chords to mimic several voices speaking at once. The real possibility, however implausible, seems to seal the Father's fate.

Falling on the a last resort which she believes will fail, Erin calls Father Moore to the stand. He reads a letter Emily addressed to him prior to her death. In it, she describes another vision, this one not demonic, but that of the Virgin Mary who reveals to Emily (who is in a state of astral projection) that the demons will not abandon her earthly vessel but that she *can* leave this Earth to escape torment. If she decides to stay, Mary continues, it will give evidence to the world that God and Satan are real. She decides to remain alive. Despite the letter, Moore is found guilty but he is sentenced to time served and released.

Open about his faith, it appears the film's Virgin Mary vision is actually Derrikson's. But it provokes the viewer to consider that influencing people to believe in the supernatural is an easier endeavor than convincing them to believe in a specific, supernatural, and in this case, religious order.

David Metz Roberts

CREDITS

Erin Bruner: Laura Linney
Father Richard Moore: Tom Wilkinson
Ethan Thomas: Campbell Scott
Emily Rose: Jennifer Carpenter
Karl Gunderson: Colm Feore
Jason: Joshua Close
Dr. Mueller: Kenneth Welsh
Dr. Cartwright: Duncan Fraser
Ray: JR Bourne
Judge Brewster: Mary Beth Hurt

Dr. Briggs: Henry Czerny
Dr. Adani: Shohreh Aghdashloo
Origin: USA
Language: English
Released: 2005
Production: Tom Rosenberg, Gary Lucchesi; Firm Films; released by Sony Pictures Entertainment
Directed by: Scott Derrickson
Written by: Scott Derrickson, Paul Harris Boardman
Cinematography by: Tom Stern
Music by: Christopher Young
Sound: Rob Young
Editing: Jeff Betancourt
Art Direction: Sandra Tanaka
Costumes: Tish Monaghan
Production Design: David Brisbin
MPAA rating: PG-13
Running time: 114 minutes

REVIEWS

Boxoffice Online. September, 2005.
Chicago Sun-Times Online. September 9, 2005.
Entertainment Weekly Online. September 7, 2005.
Los Angeles Times Online. September 9, 2005.
New York Times Online. September 9, 2005.
Premiere Magazine Online. September 9, 2005.
Variety Online. September 1, 2005.
Washington Post Online. September 9, 2005, p. C01.

QUOTES

Father Moore: "Once you see the darkness, I think you hold onto it the rest of your life."

TRIVIA

Based on the true story of Anneliese Michel, a young woman who lived in Germany in the 1970s and shared the same fate as the film's Emily Rose.

F

THE FAMILY STONE

Feel The Love.
—Movie tagline

The Family Stone, written and directed by Thomas Bezucha, is a very odd Christmas movie, a rough mixture of mean-spiritedness, screwball comedy, and sentimentality that is hard to reconcile into a coherent and satisfying whole. The star son of a liberal New England family brings home for Christmas his fiancée, who is made to feel unwelcome or, at the very least, uncomfortable from the start. Since it is never clear why we should side with the Stone clan against the hapless outsider, much of the film is a series of unfunny, cringe-inducing jokes.

Sarah Jessica Parker tamps down her usually effervescent personality to play the repressed Meredith Morton, who is engaged to Everett (a dull Dermot Mulroney). From the outset, Meredith is depicted as unattractive, both physically and socially. She wears her hair back in a tight bun (just in case we cannot see that she is stiff), which gives her face a harsh look. She is very awkward meeting people, offering a firm handshake to her future in-laws instead of a big hug, which they prefer. Aside from Amy (Rachel McAdams), Everett's sister, who is nasty and gossiping about Meredith before she arrives, everyone else is supposed to be seen as nice and even virtuous. The patriarch of the family is Kelly (Craig T. Nelson), who is a great support to his wife, Sybil (Diane Keaton), who is dying of cancer and is meant to be a sympathetic character but is really smug and manipulative. Ben (Luke Wilson) is the easygoing, genial pothead son who lives in Berkeley, while Thad (Ty Giordano) is the gay, deaf son who brings his partner, Patrick (Brian White), home for the holidays. Everybody is fine with Thad's homosexuality and treats Patrick, who is black, as one of the family. But Bezucha turns these characters into too-good-to-be-true paragons of political correctness—a loving, gay, interracial couple dealing with a disability and having heroic ambitions to adopt a child. Another daughter, Susannah (Elizabeth Reaser), brings her little girl, but they barely register, and the film could have lost them without anyone noticing.

Meredith's major fault seems to be that she is socially inept and uptight. She bores everyone with the long story of how she and Everett met, shouts at Thad because apparently she has no conception of what it means to be deaf, and generally cannot seem to connect with the family, although she is hardly given a chance. Because she has a sense of propriety and is uncomfortable sleeping with Everett in his childhood bedroom—something the freewheeling Stones cannot understand—she ends up displacing Amy from her bedroom to the sofa. Amy retaliates by setting out to embarrass Meredith during a game of charades and make her look like a racist. Finally taking a room at a nearby inn, Meredith calls her sister, Julie (Claire Danes), to stay with her for moral support.

Sybil may not be as blatantly rude as Amy but nonetheless embodies a mix of unpleasant qualities. Supposedly an endearing, open free spirit, she recalls, with an off-putting, casual vulgarity, the first time Amy had sex (as if it were hip or cute for a mom to embarrass her daughter by bringing up something so personal). At the same time, Sybil is not so open-minded when it comes to judging others, breaking a promise to give her mother's ring to Everett just because she believes that Meredith is not good for her son. Thus, when Kelly tells Ben about his mother's hopeless medical condition and he cries with his father, as genuine as the emotion may be for Ben, the scene comes across as a manipulative way of getting us to feel that Sybil is really at heart a good person who will be sorely missed.

But even as a group, the Stones have a blind spot that the screenplay cannot acknowledge. There is a certain hypocrisy in the way they are so supportive of Thad that everyone seems to have learned sign language (the signing actually becomes so excessive that it looks like a badge of honor to show how great and accommodating they are) yet are unwilling to give a break to Meredith, who is obviously nervous meeting everyone on their turf. And yet *The Family Stone* is not a satire of liberal hypocrisy or even a good-natured jab at the way socially progressive folks sometimes make snap judgments about others and are unable to recognize their own narrow-mindedness; on the contrary, we are actually supposed to think that the Stones are wacky, well-meaning bohemians.

Perhaps the most painful scene is a conversation during which Meredith raises questions about the roots of homosexuality and, the more she has to clarify her intent, the worse she sounds, even though it seems clear that she is not prejudiced, just tactless in bringing up the subject at the dinner table. But of course she has to be made to feel like a bigot and flee in shame.

Ben comes to Meredith's rescue and takes her out to a bar, where she finally loosens up, drinking and dancing, which is clearly a step in the right direction for her, even if it is indulging the cliché of the uptight woman literally and figuratively letting her hair down and thus becoming more fun. But what follows is completely unbelievable and inconsistent with the characters we have seen thus far as Ben falls for Meredith almost instantaneously. At the same time, Everett takes a liking to Julie, although this is a bit more understandable given Julie's striking beauty and his lack of chemistry with Meredith.

A flurry of misunderstandings and reversals ensues to tie everything up neatly. Meredith wakes up in Ben's bed (she erroneously believes that they had sex), and Sybil finally gives up the prized ring, only to have Everett try it on Julie's finger and get it stuck there (a ham-fisted way of telling us, as if we could not figure it out, whom he should be with and providing yet one more humiliation for the beleaguered Meredith). Then the climax heads for screwball hijinks; thinking Ben had sex with Meredith, Everett chases him around the house, while Meredith, Sybil, and Amy make a mess in the kitchen, splattering food and falling all over themselves, ultimately laughing together as if they are all friends. But this screwball silliness feels forced and has practically no comic energy. To make this Christmas morning seem stranger, all of these shenanigans follow a quietly poignant evening when Susannah, probably the most decent of the Stones (although it may help that we barely know her), is watching Judy Garland in *Meet Me in St. Louis*, a touching moment that sums up what she is feeling about her own family. The screenplay thus makes jarring tonal changes to form a rather scattered, unfocused take on this family. It is hard to know if Bezucha wants us to be moved by the Stones, amused by them, or appalled at their behavior.

The saddest thing about *The Family Stone* is that it is filled with very appealing actors who are struggling to make something genuine out of comedic clichés and a confused script. Parker creates a real character out of the stock prig and makes Meredith's discomfort and earnestness painful to watch. Wilson has a natural, relaxed quality as the laid-back Ben but cannot make his attraction to Meredith plausible. And McAdams, so impressive in a series of major movies these past two years, does what she can with the challenge of making Amy into someone we can like in the end even though she is the most dreadful Stone.

And yet not only does Ben win Meredith and Everett get Julie, but Amy seems to be redeemed when, thanks to Meredith's intervention, Amy is able to reignite a spark with an old beau. At Christmas a year later, Sybil has passed away, but the family carries on and gathers around the tree. A framed photograph of a young Sybil pregnant with Amy, which was a gift the year before from Meredith, hangs on the wall. It is probably a tribute to Sybil, but it more effectively serves as a reminder of Meredith's goodness, which this family does not deserve.

While everyone seems to have the happy ending they want, we are left to wonder if it is really a triumph for Meredith and Julie to be part of the Stone family. Have the Stones really changed and become less judgmental and hostile? Perhaps that is what Bezucha wants us to believe. But the film's bizarre mix of romantic comedy, pratfalls, and trumped-up poignancy leaves the viewer wondering, even at the conclusion, what we are to make of this family and why anyone would want to join it. Bezucha should have decided what he really wanted to say about these characters and made either a dark satire skewering family and the holiday spirit or a lighthearted celebration of a lovable, eccentric family and an outsider trying to make a good impression.

Peter N. Chumo II

CREDITS

Julie Morton: Claire Danes
Sybil Stone: Diane Keaton
Amy Stone: Rachel McAdams
Everett Stone: Dermot Mulroney
Kelly Stone: Craig T. Nelson
Meredith Morton: Sarah Jessica Parker
Ben Stone: Luke Wilson
Thad Stone: Ty Giordano
Patrick Thomas: Brian White
Trousdale: Elizabeth Reaser
Brad Stevenson: Paul Schneider
Origin: USA
Language: English
Released: 2005
Production: Michael London; Fox 2000 Pictures, Michael London; released by 20th Century-Fox
Directed by: Thomas Bezucha
Written by: Thomas Bezucha
Cinematography by: Jonathan Brown
Music by: Michael Giacchino
Sound: Jeff Wexler
Editing: Jeffrey Ford
Art Direction: Timothy "TK" Kirkpatrick
Costumes: Shay Cunliffe
MPAA rating: PG-13
Running time: 102 minutes

REVIEWS

Boxoffice Online. December, 2005.
Chicago Sun-Times Online. December 16, 2005.
Entertainment Weekly Online. December 14, 2005.
Los Angeles Times Online. December 16, 2005.
New York Times Online. December 16, 2005.
Premiere Magazine Online. December 22, 2005.
Variety Online. December 12, 2005.
Washington Post Online. December 16, 2005, p. C01.

QUOTES

Ben Stone, to Meredith: "You have the freak flag...you just don't fly it."

TRIVIA

The role eventually played by Luke Wilson was a part that Billy Crudup, Johnny Knoxville, and Aaron Eckhart were all expected to fill at one time before all eventually dropped out.

AWARDS

Nomination:

Golden Globes 2006: Actress—Mus./Comedy (Parker).

FANTASTIC FOUR

Prepare for the fantastic.
—Movie tagline

Box Office: $154 million

Since their debut in November 1961, *The Fantastic Four* have been known as the "first family" of Marvel Comics, a quirky quartet that helped usher in the Silver Age of comic book publishing. Created by Stan Lee and Jack Kirby, the FF has become one of the comic industry's longest running series, largely due to its potent blending of a tried-and-true science fiction premise with character-driven humor and pathos. However, given its high pedigree, perhaps it's ironic that a comic such as *The Fantastic Four*—which frequently billed itself as "The World's Greatest Comic Magazine!"—has had such a sordid history when it comes to film adaptations.

In 1994, legendary B-movie icon Roger Corman financed the first *Fantastic Four* movie ever produced, allegedly budgeted at a mere one million dollars. The ramshackle, poorly lit film was never released to theatres or video, though it quickly became one of the most notorious bootleg movies of all time. After a decade of watching grainy VHS copies of Corman's *FF*, comic fans were elated when it was announced that 20th Century Fox was producing a big-budget *Fantastic Four* feature for 2005, particularly after the release of such faithful and well-crafted Marvel adaptations as Bryan Singer's *X-Men* and Sam Raimi's *Spider-Man* films. Unfortunately, *Fantastic Four* failed to attract the same level of talent that brought Spidey and Wolverine to the big-screen and instead settled for director Tim Story (*Barbershop, Taxi*) and screenwriters Mark Frost and Michael France, who were apparently out of their depth when it came to translating the magic of Lee and Kirby onto celluloid. In the words of noted critic Roger Ebert, "the really good superhero movies, like *Superman, Spider-Man 2* and *Batman Begins*, leave *Fantastic Four* so far behind that the movie should almost be ashamed to show itself in the same theaters."

Story's film takes several liberties with the origin of the Fantastic Four, which is understandable given some of the more charmingly-dated details of their 1961 debut. As the movie opens, Reed Richards (Ioan Gruffudd) is a bankrupt scientific genius who has teamed up with his best friend, ex-military pilot Ben Grimm (Michael Chiklis), to pitch a business opportunity to their multi-billionaire, former MIT classmate, Victor Von Doom (Julian McMahon). Despite their past rivalry, Reed wants to use Doom's corporate space station to study clouds of cosmic radiation, ostensibly because they might reveal the origins of evolution of Earth. Doom agrees to Reed's proposal, mostly for the possibility of lucrative patents and the chance to show off his new girlfriend, Reed's former flame, Sue Storm (Jessica Alba). However, Doom requires Reed and Ben to use his personal pilot for the space mission, Sue's reckless brother Johnny (Chris Evans), who has a past history with Ben. And thus, the five of them head into outer space, moving toward a fateful collision with a cloud of cosmic rays.

Things go wrong on the space station, and the five main characters are hit with galactic radiation that imbues them with super-human abilities—powers that mirror their personalities in fairly obvious fashions. Reed spreads himself too thin, so he gains the ability to stretch his body like elastic. Sue worries about Reed not noticing her and, as such, is now able to turn become invisible. Hardened, gruff Ben has his skin turn into an unbreakable, stone-like substance, and hot-headed Johnny discovers that he can make his body ignite into a living flame. Von Doom also gets super-powers—a major change from his comic book origins—as his skin turns into living metal and he discovers that he can shoot electricity from his fingertips.

The deus ex machina that gives the FF their amazing powers is one of the most familiar plot devices in graphic literature, and Story gets his leads into outer space as soon as he possibly can. However, once the main characters are back on Earth, the film's narrative begins to flounder, particularly since the screenwriters no longer have the Fantastic Four's iconic origin story to draw from. After the barrage of cosmic rays, the crew wakes up in a Von Doom-controlled medical facility, where their new abilities first manifest. While most of the group are disturbed by their strange powers—except for Johnny, who is endlessly amused by his ability to create flame—Ben Grimm has the worst of it, transforming from a normal human being into a freakish, stone-covered goliath. (Chiklis's make-up is one of the stronger aspects of the film's design.) He breaks out of the hospital, headed for New York to find his fiancée, and Reed, Sue, and Johnny follow after him.

When Ben finally reaches his fiancée's apartment, she's horrified by his appearance, and Ben skulks off to the Brooklyn Bridge to brood in solitude. This segues into the film's first major action sequence, in which Ben's attempts to save a suicidal jumper leads to a major traffic accident with explosions and a runaway fire truck, while at the same time, giving the individual members of the Fantastic Four an opportunity to show off their powers in public for the first time. Unfortunately, Story is remarkably unskilled at staging FX-heavy action scenes, and the chaos on the bridge looks unusually cheap and lackluster for a big-budget Hollywood superhero movie. And while directing a multi-car pile-up might be harder than it looks, Story also fails at making the audience believe any of the smaller character moments on the bridge, particularly in an insulting sequence in which the director inexplicably forces Alba to strip down to her underwear in front of a crowd of onlookers. The moment is ostensibly about Sue Storm trying to become invisible, but it has no relevance to the plot and comes across as a near-sadistic attempt to cash in on Ms. Alba's well-documented sex appeal.

After Reed, Sue, Johnny, and Ben are "outed" on the Brooklyn Bridge, the media dubs them "The Fantastic Four," and the attention-hungry Johnny gives the group their superhero nicknames—Mr. Fantastic, Invisible Girl ("Invisible *Woman*," Sue protests), the Human Torch, and The Thing. Reed then takes the FF back to his own personal skyscraper, The Baxter Building, where he sequesters them in his roof-top laboratory to try to figure out how to rid them of their confusing new powers. (FF creator Stan Lee makes a cameo as the Baxter Building's mailman, Willie Lumpkin.) This leads to a humorous montage in which Story puts the group through test after test, mining as many laughs as possible from Johnny overheating, Ben not knowing his own strength, and Reed stretching to reach something on the other side of the room.

Meanwhile, Victor Von Doom has been causing havoc with his powerful space-born abilities. When his corporate board of directors tries to seize control of Von Doom Industries, Doom responds by electrocuting the head board member in a water-soaked parking garage. As Doom recognizes his body's ongoing transformation—his skin peels off, revealing a layer of metal underneath—his thirst for power grows and he realizes that the only people who could possibly stand in his way are the similarly-powered Fantastic Four.

Doom begins his quest to break up the Fab Four by targeting the morose Ben. While Johnny loves his ability to "Flame on!" (using his powers to show off at televised moto-cross event) and Reed and Sue rekindle their past romance, Ben feels like the odd man out, trapped inside the body of a living statue. Even his encounter with Alicia Masters (Kerry Washington), a kindly blind sculptor, fails to cheer Ben out of his depression. Doom eventually convinces Ben that Reed isn't trying hard enough to cure his condition—leading to a massive fight between the old friends—and uses his new electro-abilities to super-power the cosmic ray simulator that Reed built to restore Ben's humanity. When Ben emerges from the machine without his rocky exterior, his euphoria fades quickly as he realizes that Doom only wanted to eliminate the most powerful member of the Fantastic Four.

Doom captures Mr. Fantastic (who was weakened from testing Ben's machine on himself) and freezes him with liquid nitrogen, following that up by sending a heat-seeking missile after the Human Torch. Johnny eventually shakes off the projectile, and Reed is rescued by Sue and Ben, who re-exposed himself to the cosmic rays in order to become The Thing once more. As The Thing yells "It's Clobberin' Time!" and tackles Doom, it begins a full-fledged street fight, with the Fantastic Four stretching their abilities to their limits to take down the seemingly limitless power of Doctor Doom. That might sound exciting, but the screenwriters have an amazing ability to take the fantastic and make it mundane. In between the action sequences, not much happens in *Fantastic Four.* Doom has no master scheme, aside from "Destroy Reed Richards." The FF don't really save innocents or battle evil-doers. They mostly just sit in the Baxter Building and complain.

The cast is serviceable at best, with McMahon chewing the scenery as he tries to sell his evil monologues, while Gruffudd and Alba awkwardly flirt despite a fairly obvious age gap. The strongest aspect of the ensemble is the tempestuous relationship between Evans and Chiklis. Evans does an able job at selling Johnny's hot-headed temper, and his verbal sparring with Chiklis is one of the movie's few highlights.

The film's final climatic battle is particularly problematic, not just because of Story's ineptitude with action and special effects, but also because of the sterling precedent of the Academy Award-winning 2004 Pixar CGI-animated feature, *The Incredibles*. While *The Incredibles* was undoubtedly inspired by Lee and Kirby's original *Fantastic Four* (it concerns a family of superheroes—one can stretch, one can turn invisible, etc), it presented the familiar tale in such a well-told, visually-stunning fashion that Story's film seems almost redundant in comparison. *The Incredibles* trumps Story's *Fantastic Four* in every conceivable way and, even die-hard comic book fans will be better served by watching Brad Bird's animated marvel than trying to slog through Tim Story's live-action mess.

Tom Burns

CREDITS

Reed Richards: Ioan Gruffudd
Sue Storm: Jessica Alba
Ben Grimm: Michael Chiklis
Johnny Storm: Chris Evans
Victor Von Doom: Julian McMahon
Alicia Masters: Kerry Washington
Willie Lumpkin: Stan Lee
Debbie McIlvane: Laurie Holden
Origin: USA, Germany
Language: English
Released: 2005
Production: Bernd Eichinger, Avi Arad, Ralph Winter; Constantin Film, Marvel Enterprises, Bernd Eichinger; released by 20th Century-Fox
Directed by: Tim Story
Written by: Mark Frost, Michael France, Simon Kinberg
Cinematography by: Oliver Wood
Music by: John Ottman
Sound: Eric J. Batut
Music Supervisor: Dave Jordan
Editing: William Hoy
Art Direction: Don MacAulay
Costumes: Jose I. Fernandez
Production Design: Bill Boes
MPAA rating: PG-13
Running time: 105 minutes

REVIEWS

Boxoffice Online. July, 2005.
Chicago Sun-Times Online. July 8, 2005.
Entertainment Weekly Online. July 6, 2005.
Los Angeles Times Online. July 8, 2005.
New York Times Online. July 8, 2005.
Premiere Magazine Online. July 8, 2005.
Variety Online. July 7, 2005.
Washington Post Online. July 8, 2005, p. WE39.

QUOTES

Susan Storm: "You were at 4,000 Kelvin. Any hotter, and you're approaching super nova."
Johnny Storm: "Sweet!"
Susan Storm: "No, Johnny, not sweet. That's the temperature of the sun."

TRIVIA

The film has some 900 special effects shots.

AWARDS

Nomination:
Golden Raspberries 2005: Worst Actress (Alba).

FEVER PITCH

A Comedy About The Game Of Love.
—Movie tagline

Box Office: $42 million

Perhaps the strangest match-up in *Fever Pitch* is not between its lead characters, Lindsey (Drew Barrymore) and Ben (Jimmy Fallon), but between the movie's creative team. The film was loosely based on the book by Nick Hornsby, writer of the witty novels-turned-films *About a Boy* and *High Fidelity.* The screenplay was written by longtime Hollywood team Lowell Ganz and Babaloo Mandel, who were behind such crowd-pleasers as *Splash* and *City Slickers.* And the film was directed by Peter and Bobby Farrelly, who famously found new uses for bodily excretions in films like *There's Something About Mary* and *Dumb and Dumber.* Add in the factors of Fallon, who, after years of prominence on *Saturday Night Live,* surely has his own ideas of what constitutes comedy, and Barrymore, who runs her own production company, and it is hard to guess exactly how such a collaboration would end up.

In short, it ends up quite well. Somehow everyone balances each other out. The gross edge of the Farrelly's is muted, maybe, by the more mainstream tastes of Ganz and Mandel. And the tendency toward Hollywood cliché is avoided, perhaps, by Hornsby's dry British sense of humor. *Fever Pitch* is not quite up to the level of the two other Hornsby-based films, but compared to the rest of the films it shared multiplexes with, it is not half bad.

The Hornsby novel detailed a fan's love of soccer. In the film, the sport has been switched to baseball. The fan is Ben, a rumpled high school teacher who worships the Boston Red Sox. Ben, who was introduced to the game as an 8-year-old, is as devoted to the game as he was as an excitable young boy. When Lindsey first sees Ben's room filled with all sorts of Red Sox paraphernalia, including a phone shaped like a baseball mitt, she comments, correctly, "This is not the room of a man. It is the room of a boy."

The dilemma of the movie is that Lindsey, a high-powered executive and self-described workaholic, does not know whether the boyish Ben is right for her. She can accept that he makes less money than her, but there is the issue of that bedroom decor. And his choice to stay in town to attend a game, rather than go on a last minute trip to Paris with her. Lindsey sees Ben as being Winter Guy, the kind, fun, lovable boyfriend she has during the off-season, and Summer Guy, the sort of guy who will not make any plans starting spring training time.

Perhaps it is that Fallon is so charming, or maybe it is the way his character is written, but Ben's love of baseball does not seem like the kind of relationship deal-breaker that it is supposed to be in the film. It is more like a bit of a personality quirk. Yes, Ben turns down the Paris trip, but later he gives up on a really good game to go out with Lindsey. Despite all his collectibles he never seems like one of those kinds of borderline crazy fans. Yes, he and his friends actually smell their season tickets when they arrive in the mail, and yes, Ben forces his friends to have a dance-off for the best tickets, but his love of the game seems more cute than addict-like. In fact, Ben's fandom is almost a positive. His continued devotion to a team that until recently was so unrewarding, makes him seem like the kind of boyfriend that would stick around when things got rough.

The Red Sox's real life surprise winning season forced the filmmakers to come up with a new, happier ending. It would be interesting to see the old script, featuring a losing Red Sox, but the new ending works. The movie conveys the sense of shock and joy that longtime Red Sox fans must have felt after finally winning after so many years.

Fever Pitch is sweet, but never in a cloying way. When Ben gives Lindsey a speech of all the things that he likes about her, one item on the list is that, "I like that you talk out of the side of your mouth. It's kind of like you're an adorable stroke victim." The movie is not hilarious, but it is clever. It is not devastatingly romantic, but it is charming. It is light, amiable, and eager-to-please.

Critics split almost 50-50 on *Fever Pitch.* Wesley Morris of *The Boston Globe* called the film "effortlessly entertaining" but warned, "For women in these parts who this week are starting to lose their men to NESN, ESPN, and Fenway Park itself, the movie may play like a particularly painful documentary." Lou Lumenick of *The New York Post* wrote, "This is basically an Adam Sandler movie without Adam Sandler (or his edge; the metrosexual Fallon has none)—a pleasant way to kill a couple of hours." And Manohla Dargis of *The New York Times* called the film, "thoroughly winning if not especially good."

Jill Hamilton

CREDITS

Ben: Jimmy Fallon
Lindsey: Drew Barrymore
Robin: KaDee Strickland
Molly: Ione Skye
Kevin: Willie Garson
Doug Meeks: James B. Sikking
Maureen Meeks: JoBeth Williams
Al: Jack Kehler
Uncle Carl: Lenny Clarke
Lana: Siobhan Fallon
Sarah: Marissa Janet Winokur
Troy: Evan Helmuth
Artie: Scott Severance

Steve: Zen Gesner
Origin: USA
Language: English
Released: 2005
Production: Alan Greenspan, Gil Netter, Drew Barrymore, Nancy Juvonen, Amanda Posey; Gil Netter, Flower Films, Alan Greenspan, Wildgaze Films; released by 20th Century-Fox
Directed by: Peter Farrelly, Bobby Farrelly
Written by: Lowell Ganz, Babaloo Mandel
Cinematography by: Matthew F. Leonetti
Music by: Craig Armstrong
Sound: John J. Thomson
Music Supervisor: Tom Wolfe, Manish Raval
Editing: Alan Baumgarten
Art Direction: Brandt Gordon
Production Design: Maher Ahmad
MPAA rating: PG-13
Running time: 98 minutes

REVIEWS

Boxoffice Online. April, 2005.
Chicago Sun-Times Online. April 8, 2005.
Entertainment Weekly Online. April 6, 2005.
Los Angeles Times Online. April 8, 2005.
New York Times Online. April 8, 2005.
Premiere Magazine Online. April 8, 2005.
Variety Online. April 3, 2005.
Washington Post Online. April 8, 2005, p. WE45.

QUOTES

Lindsey Meeks: "If you love me enough to sell your tickets, I love you enough not to let you."

TRIVIA

The Opening Day sequence was filmed on September 4, 2004 with Stephen King throwing out the first pitch. The Red Sox lost the game, ending a ten-game winning streak which King was blamed for in the *Boston Globe.*

FIRST DESCENT

The story of the snowboarding revolution.
—Movie tagline

Filmmakers Kemp Curley and Kevin Harrison's extreme sports documentary traces the history of snowboarding while simultaneously putting the sport in viewers' faces, following five of the world's best pro freestyle snowboarders for two weeks in the remote Alaskan mountains. A bit of a hard sell of the relatively new sport that becomes somewhat repetitious during its overly long 110 minutes, *First Descent* is nonetheless full of the icy thrills and colorful personalities that have rocketed the sport from virtual obscurity to an Olympic sport.

Five of snowboarding stars are featured including veterans Nick Perata, Shawn Farmer, Norway's Terje Haakonsen, who have all had their "first descents," riding the untouched powder of the backcountry mountains. 18-year-old sensations Shaun White, who hails from Carlsbad, Ca. and Hannah Teter of Belmont Vt. have never traversed the near vertical, virgin Alaskan peaks. Outrunning avalanches and navigating the often snowless, jagged terrain of the Chugach Mountains near Valdez where the boarders are helicoptored in, the power of the film lies in the segments featuring these top athletes showcasing their considerable skills. There are amazing stunts, harrowing crashes, near disasters, and broken bones. When the dual narrative is folded in containing the relatively dry facts involved in the sport's history, including archival footage and interviews with insiders, it tends to slow down the momentum it has built. Ditto the repetitious observations and philosophy of the snowboarder mentality.

Looked askance by snobby skiers strapped onto two boards in the 1970s, snowboarders gained an edgy, youthful image that still remains amid the now mainstream sports exploding popularity, complete with wealthy stars and corporate sponsorships. With a nod to snowboarding's roots in surfing as well as the skateboarding culture explored in Stacy Peralta's groundbreaking documentary *Dogtown and Z-Boys,* more might have been made of the connections that are given little screen time.

While the history of the sport in America is what the filmmakers focus on, they note the sport is much more popular in other countries. A highlight is watching the footage of a spectacular snow-stunt show in a Tokyo arena that involves laser light displays and riotous fans.

Although not as sophisticated as Stacy Peralta's aforementioned skateboarding documentary or his superior homage to big wave surfing, *Riding Giants,* that *First Descent* patterns itself after, it is the first to take a good look at what is also the film's tagline: the story of the snowboarding revolution.

Hilary White

CREDITS

Origin: USA
Language: English
Released: 2005
Production: Kevin Harrison, Kemp Curley; MD Films, Transition Production, Embassy Row/Live Planet/Davie-Brown Entertainment; released by Universal

Directed by: Kevin Harrison
Written by: Kevin Harrison, Kemp Curley
Cinematography by: Scott Duncan
Music by: Mark Mothersbaugh
Sound: John D'Aquino
Music Supervisor: Christopher Covert
Editing: Kemp Curley
MPAA rating: PG-13
Running time: 110 minutes

REVIEWS

Boxoffice Online. December, 2005.
Chicago Sun-Times Online. December 2, 2005.
Entertainment Weekly Online. November 30, 2005.
Los Angeles Times Online. December 2, 2005.
New York Times Online. December 2, 2005.
Variety Online. December 1, 2005.
Washington Post Online. December 2, 2005, p. C05.

FLIGHTPLAN

If Someone Took Everything You Live For...How Far Would You Go To Get It Back?
—Movie tagline

Box Office: $88.9 million

Not being able to ascertain whether something is real or only being imagined is surely terrifying in real life, but it is a pleasurable experience while watching mysterious, suspenseful thrillers like *Flightplan*. In the film, a woman, shaken by the sudden death of her husband just days before, walks onto a plane along with her six-year-old daughter to accompany his body back to the United States from Germany. During the flight, she wakes up to find that her youngster has vanished. A thorough search of the plane comes up empty, but how can anyone disappear from a sealed tube hurtling aloft at almost 40,000 feet? No one among the passengers and crew can recall actually seeing the little girl board, and soon evidence seems to suggest that, contrary to the horrified woman's exceedingly vehement protestations, no such child came with her onto the plane. The woman is grief-stricken over the loss of her husband and taking anxiety medication as a result. Is she hallucinating? The film aims to be something in the vein of *The Lady Vanishes* (1938). The question of whether there is actually a girl to be found is left enjoyably up in the air through part of *Flightplan*, but too-clear clues to the answer come much too soon. Despite its lofty plans for Hitchcockian emulation, such things keep this otherwise worthwhile film from reaching such rarified heights.

That *Flightplan* comes as close as it does is due in no small part to the casting of the immensely capable, manifestly intelligent, and always engaging Jodie Foster as the film's protagonist, Kyle Pratt. (The part, originally that of a father hell-bent on finding his supposedly-missing child, was rewritten but curiously not renamed.) Foster, contentedly enjoying motherhood in real life, has not been seen onscreen since 2002, when she played another recently-single mom who rises to the occasion with amazing guts and ingenuity to garner her daughter's safety in *Panic Room*.

From the start, the actress paints a compelling and sympathetic portrait of a woman at once strong and shattered. Foster effectively conveys Kyle's devastation over her husband's fatal rooftop plunge. The woman has obviously been blindsided and continues to reel, and her battle to remain in control could clearly go either way. Kyle is shown taking a walk with her husband through dark, snowy, deserted streets, and the tender, dreamlike quality of the scene makes one think that it might be a cherished memory until a single line of footprints reveals that the woman is very much alone.

The grieving widow's saving grace is her daughter Julia (newcomer Marlene Lawston). Kyle is shown curled up in bed with the sleeping child the night before their departure, lost in loving devotion as she strokes Julia's face. It is wholly understandable then that Kyle should fly into intense panic upon the girl's first brief disappearance just prior to boarding the plane. The camera spins around the frantic mother, visually underscoring her dizzying nervous overload. She cannot lose Julia, too.

It is revealed that Kyle is a jet propulsion engineer who helped design the gargantuan, multi-level E-474 aircraft which will be transporting them home overnight. (The fictitious 700+ capacity, cutting edge marvel was actually a 300-foot set constructed on a 27,000 square-foot soundstage.) The camera takes viewers on a tour of the plane's long, luxurious interior, which is empty when Kyle and Julia get on. While watching out the window as the casket is being brought to the plane, the solemn girl blows on the pane and, with a little finger, draws a heart. It looks like Kyle's is breaking.

Once the plane has taken off into a pitch-black sky, mother and daughter fall fast asleep. Sometime later, Kyle wakes up to find Julia gone. Perhaps she is in the bathroom, or has ventured off with some newfound playmates. Searches are undertaken, during which Kyle uses her expert knowledge of the colossal airliner to prod and guide the professional but disbelieving crew's investigation. Announcements are made, but still no Julia. "She can't have gone too far," soothes one flight attendant, and yet the child cannot be located. Incredulous and with mounting anxiety, Kyle senses that she is entering her second nightmare in less than a week. Questions are asked of the passengers, and no one can honestly say that they ever laid eyes on the child. Then Kyle is told that, according to the manifest, no Julia Pratt was ever checked onto the plane. Flight Attendant Stephanie (Kate Beahan) is sure that seat 26A was unoccupied when she did a headcount before takeoff. Reaching into the pocket where she put both their boarding passes, Kyle is shocked to find only her own. Uneasy, suspicious looks pass between the crewmembers. Obviously, they are thinking they have a nut on their hands.

Demanding help, Kyle dashes to the cockpit door and starts pounding on it, always a no-no but an action which will certainly bring a prompt, strong response since the September 11th terror attacks. Air Marshall Gene Carson dutifully pounces on her and ensures the flight's safety. However, as portrayed by Peter Sarsgaard, he also does significant harm to *Flightplan*. There is clearly something sinister behind his hooded eyes, highlighted further by the use of close-ups, which lets audience members in on the truth of the situation way too quickly out of the gate. Keeping viewers in a quandary, continually changing their minds on the question of whether this distraught mother is in reality traveling alone, would have been delicious, unsettling fun. However, with Sarsgaard's too-obvious performance, that enjoyable limbo is short-lived, and while Kyle would like to know exactly what is going on as soon as possible, those watching would have preferred being kept in the dark a lot longer. So even when solid, fair-minded Capt. Rich (effective Sean Bean) gently announces shocking word that Kyle's husband supposedly hurtled off that roof with Julia in tow, viewers will remain confident that the mother has indeed somehow lost her daughter and not her mind.

Once *Flightplan* has tipped its hand too early and made clear to those watching that what is happening results from criminal, not crazy, behavior, the film descends to more conventional altitudes. There, it remains nicely aloft by continuing to do a number of things right. Director Robert Schwentke, cinematographer Florian Ballhaus, and production designer Alexander Hammond purposefully create an unsettling sense of claustrophobic confinement which makes Kyle's plight seem all the more harrowing and dire: no one on board believes her, and there is nowhere else to turn for help. As she is seen searching the cabin, she is constricted in the frame by a low ceiling above and a sea of puzzled passengers on either side, her surroundings dimly lit and often suffused with an eerie, bluish glow. The fact that there is no cutting away to anywhere else during the flight emphasizes Kyle's being cut off from further assistance. She is far from helpless, however, and viewers will root for her when she sticks to her guns, refuses to be stifled, and increasingly takes matters into her own startlingly-capable hands. She is an admirably sharp, agile, resourceful, intrepid, fiercely determined mother-on-a-mission. Adding complexity to the characterization, however, there is at least one moment when Kyle, exhausted and at a loss, seems to briefly wonder if they might all be right about her. Her fellow passengers have their own varied opinions on the subject, and the soundtrack is effectively sprinkled with whispered assessments and hushed speculation as Kyle ventures among them. *Flightplan* also rather daringly offers up some male Arab passengers for our—and Kyle's—suspicions, false bait which sheds little light on the mystery but an interesting amount on our post-9/11 fears.

Eventually Kyle comes to realize that Gene is behind it all. After the plane makes an emergency landing and is evacuated except for Kyle, Gene and accomplice Stephanie, it is time to do battle. His far-fetched but sufficiently repugnant and diabolical plans are blown to bits along with Gene himself. (The fireball looks exceedingly fake.) Amidst stirring, triumphant music, Kyle strides towards the shocked and sheepish crew and passengers with Julia, rescued by the tenacious mother from a remote nook in the nose, cradled safe and sound in her arms.

With a reported budget of $55 million, *Flightplan* grossed over $87 million. Critical reaction was mixed. The film is a promising English feature debut for the German director. It is also the first major script penned by Peter A. Dowling, who wrote it along with Billy Ray. While Foster is her usual skillful self, Sarsgaard has come off much better in films like Ray's *Shattered Glass* (2003), where the actor is tremendous rather than transparent.

David L. Boxerbaum

CREDITS

Kyle: Jodie Foster
Carson: Peter Sarsgaard
Fiona: Erika Christensen
Captain Rich: Sean Bean
Stephanie: Kate Beahan
Therapist: Greta Scacchi
Estella: Judith Scott
Obaid: Michael Irby
Elias: Brent Sexton
Julia: Marlene Lawston
Brittany Loud: Haley Ramm
Anna: Stephanie Faracy
Origin: USA
Language: English
Released: 2005
Production: Brian Grazer; released by Buena Vista

Directed by: Robert Schwentke
Written by: Billy Ray, Peter A. Dowling
Music by: James Horner
Sound: Robert Eber
Editing: Florian Ballhaus
Art Direction: Kevin Ishioka
Costumes: Susan Lyall
Production Design: Alexander Hammond
MPAA rating: PG-13
Running time: 93 minutes

REVIEWS

Boxoffice Online. September, 2005.
Chicago Sun-Times Online. September 23, 2005.
Entertainment Weekly Online. September 23, 2005.
Los Angeles Times Online. September 23, 2005.
New York Times Online. September 23, 2005.
Premiere Magazine Online. September 23, 2005.
Variety Online. September 22, 2005.
Washington Post Online. September 23, 2005, p. C01.

QUOTES

Julia: "Are we there yet?"

TRIVIA

The role played by Jodie Foster was originally written for Sean Penn. The original character's name, Kyle, was kept.

THE FOG

Box Office: $29.5 million

The Fog, one of the recent, umpteenth remakes in horror cinema, is another, almost proverbial illustration of why originals should not be tampered with or redone. This idea is perhaps best exemplified by Gus Van Sant's remake of the 1960 Hitchcock classic, *Psycho.* Van Sant's 1998 version was a shot-by-shot redux maintaining the script's dialogue. Shot in color, the film was a failure and proved that brilliant filmmaking is a nebulous, ineffable quality that can only be housed and harnessed by those possessing genius. The most horrifying component to director Rupert Wainwright's remake is how successful he is at performing a cinematic lobotomy on the John Carpenter's 1980 original thriller. Carpenter was a master in setting a mood. His *The Fog* was as atmospheric as it was unpredictable.

Wainwright sets the scene with a campfire ghost story on the beach, it is learned that shipwrecked sailors were murdered by the island townspeople of Antonio Bay but not before the victims cursed the town with a vow of vengeance a hundred years hence. The night the story is told is the 100th anniversary of the brutal slayings. The mystery lies in motive. Are the ghostly mariners enraged at the whole island or only the descendents of their murderers? Wainwright takes the plot and fleshes it out, applying it to a formula that eliminates any sense of mystery that consigns the rest of the picture to a predictable, tedious and plodding bore. The murderers are Antonio Bay's founding fathers and their motive was one of financial greed. The victims were both passengers and crew of the clipper ship that was sunk off the island's coast for nefarious purposes.

Nick Castle (Tom Welling from television's *Smallville*) is one of the descendents of the murderers who ekes out a living as a charter boat captain with a hired mate, Spooner (DeRay Davis), who serves as the movie's comic relief. During an outing, they unknowingly hook their anchor onto a bag full of personal effects from the sunken ship that opens a Pandora's Box as the vengeful spirits are released from their frigid watery limbo and unleash terror and death on the sleepy coastal community. On this weekend, the town is dedicating a statue of the four founding fathers of the settlement of this island off the Oregon coast (inexplicably transported from the California coast in the original). The Island's sole radio station, KAB, is located atop a lighthouse that is owned, run and managed by a feisty, bemused Stevie Wayne. Selma Blair's portrayal of Wayne is at best a contrived attempt at channeling Adrienne Barbeau who played the sassy DJ in the original. Stevie and Nick have been heeding the fever of island love in the absence of Nick's girlfriend, Elizabeth Williams (Maggie Grace from TV's *Lost*), but who has returned unannounced presumably to repair a strained relationship with her mother. Elizabeth is also plagued by haunting nightmares of burning and drowning which was the dismal fate of the clipper ship's passengers.

Nick and Elizabeth resume their WB romance with the mesmerizing chemistry of two frigid mannequins. Meanwhile, Spooner and a buddy have borrowed Nick's boat, the Sea Grass to serenade bimbos on a cruise of nautical bacchanalia. The CGI fog, opaque and ominous, is reminiscent of the rolling sandstorm utilized in *The Mummy.* Spooner is the only survivor of the carnage raised by the gloomy, seemingly sentient fog. At KAB, Stevie encounters strange doings as a music box commandeers the airwaves as well as the shrill screams of the trapped passengers of a century ago. Light is shed on the portentous situation when Elizabeth discovers an 1871 journal of Patrick Malone, one of the founding fathers. After nearly drowning in an aquarium filled with sea grass, she seeks out Patrick's descendent, Father Malone, who is guilt ridden with the knowledge of the malfeasance that occurred by the settlement's forebears.

As the civic festivities commence in commemoration of the town's birth and prosperity, the fog blankets the town and creates a blackout. Being a single mother, Stevie sends out a plea over the airwaves to save her son after she failed to do so, narrowly escaping death from the murderous wraiths swamped within the soupy fog. The boy has absconded to his room after his nanny succumbed to rapid aging and decaying into dust. Nick saves him from a similar fate. But another image has appeared on the bay and the phantom ship, the Elizabeth Dane, sails in.

The main characters converge at the town hall. Once the truth is brought to the surface, Elizabeth Williams has an epiphany on the supernatural scale: she is the reincarnation of one of the victims. This illumination causes her to join her spectral husband and with justice and revenge having been exacted, the ghosts, ship, and fog roll away from the island and return to Davy Jones's locker.

Despite its intent, this foggy redux has a fright level on par with *Wallace & Gromit: The Curse of the Were-Rabbit.* The tight, clean mastery of the original as well as its beautiful cinematography are lost in the fog. It is befuddling to wonder why John Carpenter co-produced this feature when his distinguished premiere, while not on the same echelon as his venerable work, *Halloween*, had a conviction and delivery that surpasses the remakes and sequels that are being churned out at an exponential rate in Hollywood. 2005's *The Fog* is a glaring example that saturating an imitation with CGI and gore is no substitute for style and passion.

David Metz Roberts

CREDITS

Nick Castle: Tom Welling
Elizabeth Williams: Maggie Grace
Stevie Wayne: Selma Blair
Spooner: DeRay Davis
Tom Malone: Kenneth Welsh
Kathy Williams: Sara Botsford
Captain Blake: Rade Serbedzija
Father Malone: Adrian Hough
Origin: USA
Language: English
Released: 2005
Production: Debra Hill, David Foster, John Carpenter; released by Sony Pictures Entertainment
Directed by: Rupert Wainwright
Written by: Cooper Layne
Cinematography by: Nathan Hope
Music by: Graeme Revell
Sound: John Taylor
Music Supervisor: Budd Carr, Nora Felder
Editing: Dennis Virkler
Art Direction: Catherine Schroer
Costumes: Monique Prudhomme
Production Design: Michael Diner, Graeme Murray
MPAA rating: PG-13
Running time: 100 minutes

REVIEWS

Boxoffice Online. October, 2005.
Entertainment Weekly Online. October 19, 2005.
Los Angeles Times Online. October 17, 2005.
New York Times Online. October 15, 2005.
Variety Online. October 14, 2005.

QUOTES

Stevie Wayne: "What kind of fog goes against the wind?"

TRIVIA

Tom Welling's character, Nick Castle, is named after the actor who played Michael Myers in John Carpenter's *Halloween* (1978).

THE 40 YEAR OLD VIRGIN

A comedy about the moments that touch us in ways we've never been touched before.
—Movie tagline

Better Late Than Never.
—Movie tagline

The Longer You Wait, The Harder It Gets.
—Movie tagline

Box Office: $109.3 million

In the age of erectile dysfunction drugs for impotent, middle-aged men surrounded by a culture glutted with inordinate, lascivious imagery, Internet escort services, and Howard Stern's occasional port star hookup drives for the compromised male, it seems implausible that cloistered away in this sexually rapacious society is a 40-year-old virgin. This, however, is the fertile comic premise that this hilarious, runaway hit film of the summer successfully mines to the hilt as well as firmly launching the film career of Comedy Central's Steve Carell, making him a bona fide movie star.

Bearing a dreamy, doe-eyed expression and exuding innocence, Andy Stitzer (believably played by Carell) has learned to manage an unplanned life of chastity. As the story unfolds, we learn that his undefiled, virginal state has been due more to a series of unfortunate mishaps during his sexually formative years, rather than by choice. At one point during his youth, Stitzer simply dropped out the competitive sexual arena to avoid any additional failure and subsequent shame and heartache. Stitzer's life has become a programmed sequence of predictability and structure. He follows a rigid, daily routine and boards his mountain bike, pants tightly wrapped to avoid grease stains, riding to the electronics store where he works. He dutifully watches *Survivor* with the elderly couple living above his unit at the apartment complex where he lives.

Andy's coworkers, however, are not so friendly to this odd man who works in the back room. While Andy's peers at work easily converse about their wild weekends in Tijuana, Andy recounts the highlight of his weekend: making an egg salad sandwich. The guys reluctantly invite awkward misfit Andy to their poker night as they have any empty seat to fill. Overflowing with bawdy, testosterone-filled banter boasting of their sexual conquests, Andy's sexual preference is questioned when he compares a woman's breast to a bag of sand. Once the truth is learned, rather than castigating him, his maladjusted colleagues take Andy under their respective wings.

His team of sexual gurus include David (Paul Rudd), a hopeless romantic who is mired in the trenches of unrequited love due to a former girlfriend who has long since moved on. Cal (Seth Rogen), is an average-looking everyman who nonetheless seems to have no problem attracting women. He seems the most comfortable and least troubled of the group with his festive lifestyle and gives practical, bachelor-sagacious advice to Andy, such as only dating drunk women and a deceptively simple way of seducing females by answering a woman's questions with questions. The former bit of advice results in one of the film's funniest scenes, as the thoroughly wasted, serial clubber Nicky (Leslie Mann) regurgitates a strawberry daiquiri, squarely hitting the unsuspecting Andy with the volatile splatter, while the latter bit of advice succeeded in piquing the interest of a bookstore clerk. But when push comes to shove, her outré sexual endeavors were just a tad out of Andy's league. The last of Stitzer's triad of seduction coaches is Jay (Romany Malco) who likens himself to an irresistible womanizer, frequently straying out of the confines of monogamy.

As the film unspools, Stitzer engages in a trek of self-discovery, including a masturbation interlude where he "courts" himself to the melodic tune of the 1980's Lionel Richie hit, "Hello." In one of the film's more memorable scenes, David and Cal banter back and forth in a "I know you're gay because..." duel, trading a creative volley of barbs while playing one of Andy's gory, gladiatorial video games. When Cal queries him as to how he knows he gay, David's retorts include, "Because you macramed yourself a pair of jeans shorts" or "Because you like the movie *Maid in Manhattan.*" A must-see, extended version of this scene, reportedly completely improvised, can be found on the DVD.

Perhaps the film's most talked-about scene, however, occurs after the stylish, metrosexual Jay convinces Andy he needs to get his chest waxed. The extremely hirsute Carell felt it was important to film for the waxing to be performed live on camera to get the most natural reaction to the pain possible. Against the better judgment of many on the set, including the waxers who urged him to trim his hair down first or at least have some topical pain cream applied, Carell did it his way with the hilariously painful results obvious onscreen, graphically showing his pores oozing blood while alternately shouting a variety of creative expletives alongside more tame exclamations, including "Yoooooow, Kelly Clarkson!" Again the unrated DVD version of this scene is also a must-see.

Andy's many faux pas with women become a thing of the past when he meets an attractive single mother and grandmother, Trish (played with convincing natural verve by Catherine Keener). A bit odd herself, Trish owns a store across from Andy's workplace that only contains things she sells for people on eBay. As their relationship progresses, Andy becomes more self-assured as Trish, though not knowing his secret, doesn't pressure him for sex and prefers to take things slowly herself.

Along with Andy's extensive video game library, Andy's hobbies include collecting superhero dolls of antiquity. Among them is a vintage Steve Austin's boss, Oscar Goldman, from the 1970's TV show, *The Six Million Dollar Man.* When Trish convinces him to sell this highly valuable collection of memorabilia on eBay so that he can fulfill his dream of buying his own electronics store, Andy is initially elated, with the cash pouring in. He panics, however, feeling that he is losing his sense of self in the process and afraid of the day, that eventually comes, where he and Trish must consummate their relationship. He breaks it off with the confused Trish but the two quickly reconnect in the film's penultimate scene where he crashes his bike, the truth comes out, and they joyfully reunite in the middle of the road.

Directed by Judd Apatow with a screenplay by Apatow and Carell, *The 40 Year Old Virgin* is well-crafted and filled with great performances by all, including another wonderful comic gem of a character fleshed out by Jane Lynch as Andy's boss Paula and Gerry Bednob as a profanity spewing Indian salesman. Perhaps the film's only misstep is the final scene. The ensemble cast engages in a rousing musical version of "Aquarius," in a song and dance fantasy sequence after Andy and Trish's wedding followed by their post-coital bliss (yes, Andy saved himself for marriage). Otherwise, the film takes no shortcuts and preserves characterization and plot development while maintaining its comic intent.

David Metz Roberts

CREDITS

Andy: Steven Carell
Trish: Catherine Keener
David: Paul Rudd
Jay: Romany Malco
Beth: Elizabeth Banks
Nicky: Leslie Mann
Paula: Jane Lynch
Cal: Seth Rogen
Marla: Kat Dennings
Origin: USA
Language: English
Released: 2005
Production: Judd Apatow; released by Universal
Directed by: Judd Apatow
Written by: Steven Carell, Judd Apatow
Cinematography by: Jack N. Green
Music by: Lyle Workman
Sound: David MacMillan
Editing: Brent White
Art Direction: Tom Reta
Costumes: Debra McGuire
MPAA rating: R
Running time: 116 minutes

REVIEWS

Boxoffice Online. August, 2005.
Chicago Sun-Times Online. August 19, 2005.
Entertainment Weekly Online. August 17, 2005.
Los Angeles Times Online. August 19, 2005.
New York Times Online. August 19, 2005.
Premiere Magazine Online. August 19, 2005.
Variety Online. August 12, 2005.
Washington Post Online. August 19, 2005, p. WE37.

QUOTES

Andy Stitzer: "I'm a virgin. I always have been."

TRIVIA

The scene in which Steve Carell has his chest hair waxed had to be done in one take, as his chest hair was actually ripped out during filming. Carell told director Judd Apatow it would be funnier if it was real.

AWARDS

L.A. Film Critics 2005: Actress (Keener)
Nomination:
Writers Guild 2005: Orig. Screenplay.

FOUR BROTHERS

Jerimiah Mercer will take the law into his own hands.
—Movie tagline
Angel Mercer wants to know who killed his mother.
—Movie tagline
Jack Mercer will do violence to get justice.
—Movie tagline
Bobby Mercer is not the kind of man who asks twice.
—Movie tagline
They came home to bury mom...and her killer.
—Movie tagline

Box Office: $74.5 million

It is a very cold day in November when four adopted brothers, Bobby (Mark Wahlberg), Angel (Tyrese Gibson), Jeremiah (Andre Benjamin) and Jack (Garrett Hedlund), return to their home in Detroit to bury their mother Evelyn Mercer (Fionnula Flanagan). Evelyn has spent her life being a foster mother, ushering children into adoptive homes, but these four boys, two white and two black, were considered so far gone that no one would take them in. Consequently, she adopted them and they feel they owe her a debt even though their lives have not turned out as well as she had hoped for them and they have gone in different directions.

Evelyn, however, has not died an ordinary death. She has been shot during the robbery of the corner convenience store. As the four mourn and get to know each other again over a makeshift Thanksgiving dinner, older brother Bobby decides to avenge their mother's death. Although ex-Marine Angel is in on the action as is youngest brother and rock star wannabe Jack, it is Jeremiah who is reluctant to undertake such an illegal activity, even on behalf of their beloved mother. Jeremiah is the one Mercer brother who has made a stable life for himself: a wife and two daughters, a successful career in the auto industry and its unions, and now he's setting out on his own to gentrify warehouses into expensive condos. But he will eventually go along with their plan. After all, he is a Mercer brother.

Although the police, especially their boyhood friend Lieutenant Green (Terrence Howard), tells them to leave the matter to the authorities, the boys soon discover that their mother's death was no accident. It was a contract killing and the robbery was just a cover-up for Evelyn's murder. As they investigate further they will be led to the doorsteps of Detroit's underworld kingpin Victor Sweet (Chiwetel Ejiofor) and even into suspecting their own brother Jeremiah.

Like several of director John Singleton's previous works, notably his Oscar-nominated debut film *Boyz N the Hood* (1991) and his recent *2 Fast 2 Furious* (2003), "brotherhood" often just means men who are brought together by circumstances and race is only of peripheral interest. In fact, in this his latest film, the fact that the four brothers are of mixed race seems totally irrelevant. They act like brothers, fighting and teasing each other while still being comfortable in each other's company.

This belief in a multi-ethnic brotherhood is made easier by Singleton's astute casting choices. There is a real feeling of street smarts combined with a hardscrabble early life in the fine acting of Wahlberg, Gibson, Benjamin and Hedlund. They feel damaged yet salvageable. We may not agree with what they do, but the actors make it so we can understand it.

The fact that we are chilled by their actions is brought home even more clearly by the excellent sense of atmosphere Singleton creates in the cold and hostile world of a Midwest winter. This is especially true in one of the two memorable action sequences that appear in the film. We've seen plenty of car chases, but this one, executed on a dark night in the middle of a snowy blizzard, is terrifying to anyone who has ever had to drive even slowly in those conditions. The other action sequence of note is a gun battle that takes place in the clarity of daylight as masked gunmen besiege the Mercer home. It is fast-paced and tightly filmed with dizzying hand-held camerawork. Both of these scenes are filled with energy and tension and help to make *Four Brothers* a highly watchable vengeance film.

In the end, however, the story is basically ridiculous. Not even the great Motown soundtrack can distract a viewer from the fact that these men are essentially allowed to work undisturbed and totally outside of the law. They threaten, beat up, shoot, and even douse people with gasoline with no real repercussions. By the time we reach the final confrontation on a bleak and frozen lake with nothing in sight for miles and miles, watching Bobby stride into the scene from some totally unknown location is almost laughable.

Of course in this genre of film it is expected that the hero must have a psychologically satisfying man-to-man battle with the villain, but this one is so over the top that all one can think of is all those hokey showdowns in movie westerns from days gone by. Could Wahlberg be this generation's John Wayne? Or perhaps this is just some trick of the imagination because *Four Brothers* just seems so much like an urban rendition of Henry Hathaway's 1965 western *The Sons of Katie Elder* which starred Mr. Wayne. Sometimes it's just better not to think so much and just enjoy the performances and the action.

Beverley Bare Buehrer

CREDITS

Bobby Mercer: Mark Wahlberg
Jeremiah Mercer: Andre Benjamin
Angel Mercer: Tyrese Gibson
Jack Mercer: Garrett Hedlund
Det. Fowler: Josh Charles
Victor Sweet: Chiwetel Ejiofor
Evelyn Mercer: Fionnula Flanagan
Lt. Green: Terrence DaShon Howard
Sofi: Sofia Vergara
Camille Mercer: Taraji P. Henson
Councilman Douglas: Barry (Shabaka) Henley
Robert Bradford: Kenneth Welsh
Origin: USA
Language: English
Released: 2005
Directed by: John Singleton
Written by: David Elliot, Paul Lovett
Cinematography by: Peter Menzies Jr.
MPAA rating: R
Running time: 109 minutes

REVIEWS

Boxoffice Online. August, 2005.
Chicago Sun-Times Online. August 12, 2005.
Entertainment Weekly Online. August 10, 2005.
Los Angeles Times Online. August 12, 2005.
New York Times Online. August 12, 2005.
Variety Online. August 8, 2005.
Washington Post Online. August 12, 2005, p. C05.

QUOTES

Jack, leaving, after threatening to set a group of teens on fire: "Thank you very much, I hope you all have a lovely evening!"

TRIVIA

The television show that can be seen in the background of the bowling alley is *Pimp My Ride.* (2004)

FUN WITH DICK AND JANE

See Dick Run.
—Movie tagline

This Christmas, one family is living the American Dream a little differently.
—Movie tagline

Box Office: $29.1 million

Fun with Dick and Jane, directed by Dean Parisot and written by Judd Apatow and Nicholas Stoller, is a remake of the 1977 comedy about an upper-middle-class, suburban couple who turn to crime when sudden unemployment robs them of their high standard of living. Starring George Segal and Jane Fonda, the original film was a light romp with a kernel of social commentary about a couple facing the consequences of their conspicuous consumption. The new version, set in the year 2000, pretends to be a corporate satire for the Enron generation (a slew of credits at the end thanks many malefactors of various corporate scandals), but it really plays as a vehicle for Jim Carrey's physical comedy, buffoonery, and silly disguises. We know that we are in trouble when Carrey's Dick Harper, an executive on the verge of a big promotion, sings and dances spastically in an elevator to R. Kelly's "I Believe I Can Fly," during which appears the credit telling us the film is produced by Carrey himself, probably the best clue as to what its tone will be.

Dick is an executive at Globodyne Enterprises, whose vague corporate function is "a consolidator of media properties." When he is promoted to vice president of communications, he finds himself having to defend his superiors' shady practices, which he knows nothing about, on a financial news talk show. In a funny exchange, he is ambushed by Ralph Nader, one hint of the serious subtext this film could have had. Globodyne's stock plummets, and the company crumbles, but, while everyone loses his job, the CEO, Jack McCallister (Alec Baldwin), gets out with his wealth intact. But Dick does not act like a man who is worried about having just lost his job even though his wife, Jane (Téa Leoni), in the middle of his recent success, quit her own job at a travel agency to spend more time with their son; on the contrary, Dick enjoys horsing around the house, jumping over the banister, doing a somersault, and just plain goofing off. From these unimaginative scenes, the screenplay betrays its inability to create, even in a comedic context, a character in the middle of a real crisis.

Dick's meager efforts at getting a job befitting his experience prove futile, but one funny scene, a great metaphor for the cutthroat economy, has competing job applicants all racing to get to an interview first and even trying to knock each other out along the way. But when Dick sets his sights lower, his reentrance into the job market—a short stint as a greeter at a Wal-Mart kind of company called Kostmart—does not generate many laughs. The situation quickly gets more desperate. Because all of their savings was in Globodyne stock, the Harpers are wiped out, but at least some of the gags charting their decline are mildly amusing, from paying the maid in appliances to piling on the food at an all-you-can-eat salad bar to running through the neighbor's sprinkler for a quick shower. But Dick's farcical attempt to fit in with illegal immigrants looking for day work only to get deported to Mexico by the INS and then rescued by his wife is a labored set piece. Moreover, such incidents feel tailored for Carrey's broad, silly antics, not the corporate striver he is supposedly playing.

At the same time, the character of Jane is shortchanged. Her one big moment is an anemic retread of a cute scene from the original film; as the lawn and plants are being repossessed, she pretends that she is ordering them removed as a way to save face in front of the gawking neighbors. Like's Dick's attempts at menial work, Jane's are just as flat, from facing embarrassment at having to teach an exercise class to having her face swell up as a Botox tester. The original film featured a dryly humorous scene in which Jane asks her wealthy father for help, only to be turned down and congratulated for having the opportunity of hard times teaching her family a lesson in self-reliance. There is no parallel in the remake, probably because such a scene would pin some of the blame for the Harpers' misfortune on their own extravagant spending (something the remake cannot do if it is laying the blame at the feet of a corrupt corporate honcho), but it also would have been too smart and witty for this film's tone and, perhaps even more important, would have detracted from Carrey's screen time.

When the family is on the verge of losing its house, Dick turns to crime, becoming a stickup man with his son's water pistol. But the targets are not very amusing. A bungled attempt at a convenience store, for example, is no substitute for the hilarious failed robbery of a pharmacy in the original movie. Then once Dick and Jane get the hang of robbing, it is all about disguises, wearing ski masks and ordering iced mochas while emptying out the register at a coffee shop, donning Bill and Hillary Clinton costumes at a sushi restaurant, dressing as Sonny and Cher (Carrey is Cher!) at a car dealership. The filmmakers put more energy into coming up with disguises for this ersatz Bonnie and Clyde than in making the robberies fun and entertaining.

The original movie may not be a piercing social satire, but it has great comic moments taking shots at some facets of American culture, such as frustrated customers applauding Dick and Jane's robbery of the phone company or these suburban outlaws targeting a phony evangelist who preaches Christianity as a way to wealth. The remake's only nod in this direction is the way it lampoons the familiar fat cats who profit at the expense of the little guy (a very easy target), especially in Baldwin's smarmy CEO, a variation on his character in this year's *Elizabethtown.* One scene of him enjoying a vacation while justifying himself to a TV camera mimics a famous news clip of President Bush, but that is an easy jab and the extent of the screenplay's foray into political humor.

Other pointed jokes are subordinated to Carrey's clown persona. When Dick thinks that he is about to be indicted and goes nuts, dancing like a puppet in an exclusive club (ironically called The Champion Club), it is less a testament to his powerlessness in the corporate world than one more piece of physical business that Carrey gets to indulge in. While he has played real characters in the past, Carrey here is not merging his own brand of comedy with the character to create a once successful man facing unemployment and the attendant loss of self-esteem; instead, Carrey gives us shtick that is completely inconsistent with his character of a big executive.

Dick and Jane's last caper, revenge on Jack himself, is at once too technical and complicated and not very much fun—with the help of disgraced CFO Frank Bascombe (Richard Jenkins), who took the fall for Jack and now wants to settle the score, they concoct a plan involving surreptitiously switching forms at a bank so that a huge transfer of Jack's funds will be made into an account they are setting up. In short, it is a dull, tedious climax, but at least, in the course of the scheme, Carrey gets to hang from the ceiling and do a pratfall. Dick's big coup is finally tinged with the feeling of benevolence as he and Jane end up transferring $400 million into a pension relief fund for former Globodyne employees. The filmmakers seem to be playing it safe or are unwilling to make the heroes seem like they are out just for themselves, even though that is supposedly the whole point of the story up till now. After all, Dick's attempt to compete with his friends and colleagues and acquire more possessions obviously drives him from the outset, and yet this sudden reversal is not based on some change in the Harpers' values, some believable transformation in character that is an outgrowth of their suffering and a newfound empathy—it just happens. The end of the 1977 version has a thoroughly satisfying ending, with Dick and Jane cleaning out his former boss's safe (containing the company's slush fund), which leads to him resigning and Dick being rewarded as the next president of the company.

Despite the fact that it never achieved widespread popularity, acclaim, or even cult status and is probably unknown to many people seeing the remake, the original *Fun with Dick and Jane* is a comic delight. Surely the times are now ripe for a bright satire of corporate greed and middle-class consumerism, and, in an age of constant movie remakes, this is one that clearly could have been done in a clever way that resonates with contemporary economic frustrations and anxieties. But the filmmakers have not thought through what such a comedy might look like in 2005, instead creating a vanity project that caters to Carrey's knack for mugging for the camera.

Peter N. Chumo II

CREDITS

Dick Harper: Jim Carrey
Jane Harper: Tea Leoni
Jack McCallister: Alec Baldwin
Frank Bascombe: Richard Jenkins
Veronica Cleeman: Angie Harmon
Garth: John Michael Higgins
Joe: Richard Burgi
Oz Peterson: Carlos Jacott
Billy Harper: Aaron Michael Drozin
Blanca: Gloria Garayua
Origin: USA
Language: English
Released: 2005
Production: Brian Grazer, Jim Carrey; Columbia Pictures, Imagine Entertainment, Brian Grazer, JC 23 Entertainment, Bart/Palevsky; released by Sony Pictures Entertainment
Directed by: Dean Parisot
Written by: Judd Apatow, Nicholas Stoller
Cinematography by: Jerzy Zielinski
Music by: Theodore Shapiro, Randall Poster
Sound: Lee Orloff
Editing: Don Zimmerman
Art Direction: Troy Sizemore, Greg Hooper
Costumes: Julie Weiss
Production Design: Barry Robison
MPAA rating: PG-13
Running time: 90 minutes

REVIEWS

Boxoffice Online. December, 2005.
Chicago Sun-Times Online. December 21, 2005.
Entertainment Weekly Online. December 23, 2005.
Los Angeles Times Online. December 21, 2005.
New York Times Online. December 21, 2005.
Variety Online. December 20, 2005.
Washington Post Online. December 21, 2005, p. C01.

QUOTES

Jane Harper: "We might be in a little bit of a pickle, Dick."

TRIVIA

Cameron Diaz was originally cast as Jane but had to bow out due to scheduling conflicts.

G

GEORGE A. ROMERO'S LAND OF THE DEAD

(Land of the Dead)

The Legendary Filmmaker Brings You His Ultimate Zombie Masterpiece.
—Movie tagline

Box Office: $20.5 million

After waiting 20 years since his last film, zombie aficionados and fans of director George A. Romero finally have a fourth installment in the series he began in 1968 with the low-budget classic *Night of the Living Dead.* In that film the undead had one-track minds that were obsessed only with eating the living. But by 2005, the zombies have evolved under Romero's tutorship. They reason (hey, this jackhammer could break a window!), they organize (let's get the gang together and storm the livings' protected city), heck, they even show emotion like anger and revenge (did you just see those guys riding into town, killing us and in general treating us badly? Let's go teach them a lesson!) They are no longer just machines that eat whoever happens to fall into their clutches, now they can plot ways to come and get the living no matter where they hide or how safe they think they are.

The humans in the unnamed but well-protected city of *George A. Romero's Land of the Dead* are just about to piss off the zombies and discover their new abilities. This city, however, contains two classes of humans. One group, the most wealthy and privileged, living in a gleaming tower of light called Fiddler's Green. It offers them everything from good food to a relaxed atmosphere, just like they enjoyed before the zombies took over all the land they can see from their penthouses. All the land, that is, except that which is at the base of this luxurious skyscraper. Because acting as a buffer between these favored elite living the good life and the undead zombies outside the electrified fences is another group, the poor but still human who can only dream of what life must be like in Fiddler's Green and fear the un-death that lurks beyond the fence.

Fiddler's Green is controlled by a man named Kaufman (Dennis Hopper), a tyrannical CEO type guy who not only protects the whole city from the zombies but also eliminates anyone living who objects to his tactics. Kaufman is responsible for organizing and paying for the services of those trained few living in the slums who will venture beyond the city's protection in order to make raids for food, drugs, alcohol or anything else the city needs. The leader of these scavengers is Riley (Simon Baker). Riley's second-in-command is Cholo (John Leguizamo) who has been doing Kaufman's dirty work on the side and expects to be rewarded with membership into the exclusive elite. Riley is also aided in his work by a facially-scarred Charlie (Robert Joy) who is totally loyal to Riley and eventually by a young, army-trained, prostitute Slack (Asia Argento) whom he saves from being eaten by zombies at one of the slums seedier amusement areas. The diamond in the city's protective arsenal, though, is an armored super-vehicle called Dead Reckoning.

It is while on one of these raids for Kaufman that Riley notices that the zombies seem to becoming more sentient. That they're trying to live "normal" lives. And that one of them in particular, a gas-station attendant with the name "Big Daddy" on his uniform, is especially adept at communicating with other zombies and figuring things out in general. And he's pissed at how his fellow zombies are being treated by Riley's raiders.

Back at the city, Cholo presents Kaufman with champagne and cigars from his latest assault and demands what he is owed for his extra-curricular activities on the CEO's behalf and for admittance into his ivory tower. When Kaufman refuses, Cholo steals Dead Reckoning and threatens to blow Fiddler's Green up unless he gets his money. (Although why money has any value in this world is beyond this viewer.) So now Kaufman has Riley go after Cholo and bring back his armored prize. At the same time, however, Big Daddy has figured out that zombies don't breath and can avoid the electrified fences and guard towers by walking under the water that surrounds the city on three sides (did he see *Pirates of the Caribbean*?). So while Riley is out hunting Cholo, zombies break into the city. And while zombies use the poor who live in the slums for appetizers, those in Fiddler's Green attempt to escape and become the zombie's main course.

Director Romero has uniquely set the most squeamish of horror scenes against a backdrop of pointed political and social commentary aimed at the decade in which the film was released. Racism was the topic of the first film, and consumerism deflated in the second, 1978's *Dawn of the Dead,* while 1985's *Day of the Dead* went after the military and sexism. It should be pretty obvious that this latest installment, after skipping the decade of the '90s, is aiming for several aspects of modern American society. The obliviousness of the wealthy to the plight of the poor, their obvious dependence upon these poor but total denial about what goes on outside their own protected world. And the way the living exploit the un-dead can't help but make one think about third-world countries where rich nations ride in, take what they want and ignore the wake of economic and political destruction they leave behind. In fact, one might even be able to make the case that in this latest zombie film the living have become less human, less caring, while it's actually the zombies who start caring for each other and become more human. How's that for a twisted horror tale?

The result of all this is that director Romero has delivered another intriguing chapter in the zombie mythology he has had such a big part in creating. Yes, the film's gore may be hard to swallow at times, but Romero has invested it with a degree of perverse playfulness and intellectual interest that make it a well-done bit of summer entertainment.

Beverley Bare Buehrer

CREDITS

Riley: Simon Baker
Cholo: John Leguizamo
Slack: Asia Argento
Charlie: Robert Joy
Kaufman: Dennis Hopper
Big Daddy: Eugene C. Clark
Butcher: Boyd Banks
Pretty Boy: Joanne Boland
Motown: Krista Bridges
No. 9: Jennifer Baxter
Pillsbury: Pedro Miguel Arce
Butcher: Boyd Banks
Chihuahua: Phil Fondacaro
Phone booth zombie: Simon Pegg
Origin: France, Canada, USA
Language: English
Released: 2005
Production: Mark Canton, Bernie Goldman, Peter Grunwald; Bernie Goldman; released by Universal
Directed by: George A. Romero
Written by: George A. Romero
Cinematography by: Miroslaw Baszak
Music by: Reinhold Heil, Johnny Klimek
Sound: Robert Fletcher
Editing: Michael Doherty
Art Direction: Arvinder Grewal
Costumes: Alex Kavanagh
Production Design: Arvinder Grewal
MPAA rating: R
Running time: 93 minutes

REVIEWS

Boxoffice Online. June, 2005.
Chicago Sun-Times Online. June 24, 2005.
Entertainment Weekly Online. June 29, 2005.
Los Angeles Times Online. June 24, 2005.
New York Times Online. June 24, 2005.
Premiere Magazine Online. June 23, 2005.
Variety Online. June 19, 2005.
Washington Post Online. June 24, 2005, p. C01.

QUOTES

Kaufman: "In a world where the dead are returning to life, the word 'trouble' loses much of its meaning."

TRIVIA

Impressed with Simon Pegg and Edgar Wright's British zombie comedy *Shaun of the Dead* (2004), George A. Romero asked the duo to appear in this film as the "photo booth" zombies in the carnival/bar-room sequence.

GET RICH OR DIE TRYIN'

At the end of the day, what will you hang on to?
—Movie tagline

Live In Your Dreams Or Die In Someone Else's.
—Movie tagline
Inside Every Man Is The Power To Choose.
—Movie tagline

Box Office: $30.7 million

I sensed a strange feeling of déjà vu while watching *Get Rich or Die Tryin'*. Haven't I seen this somewhere before? The formula seems so familiar. Take one of hip-hop's hottest international superstars, mix in a critically acclaimed director, and voila: a mega-blockbuster film that will entertain and teach life lessons for generations to come. Right? Wrong! Not quite. 50 Cent portrays a man immersed in the turmoil of gang life, drugs and the violence-ridden slums of Queens. The opening scene involves a brutal robbery attempt that goes dreadfully wrong, which leads to the legendary gun battle that left 50 Cent filled with lead and scarred for life. What follows is a nauseating journey replete with gang warfare, drug dealing, and, above all, mediocre acting. All of which lead up to the anticlimactic ending involving the heinously inevitable rise to fame for our hero.

Hero, you say? Well, at least that's how director Jim Sheridan decided to portray this story of a poor misguided youth ignored by society and loathed by his enemies. From an early age, "young" Marcus Jackson (Marc John Jeffries) had ambitions of becoming a rapper despite his mother's prostitution and dope dealing habits. When his mother is gunned down in cold blood as part of a citywide turf war, young Marcus is cared for by his loving grandparents. Bursting at the seams with what most psychologists would describe as teen angst, young Marcus rejects the guidance of his grandparents and begins selling cocaine. The most disturbing thing about this decision is that he doesn't make this choice based on the necessity to survive. Rather, he makes this choice to enable himself to wear the right shoes, drive the right cars and garner the respect he feels is due to him. As he grows older, Marcus (now 50 Cent) decides to try his hand as an entrepreneur and heads up his own crew that ventures into the lucrative industry of crack dealing. Instantly, he finds himself living by one motto: "Getting paid and getting laid." Unfortunately, as the majority of drug dealers do, Marcus then finds himself jailed (wrongly convicted, of course) and searching for answers to his shattered life. He befriends an inmate by the name of Bama (Terrance Howard) who convinces Marcus that he has raw talent as a lyricist, and that all he needs is a guiding hand. From that point on Bama becomes Marcus's manager, leading him to what eventually will become his calling in life.

One of the major weaknesses of this film is the portrayal of Marcus Jackson as just a nice guy caught up in bad circumstances. With a fistful of crack in one hand and a 9-millimeter blazing in the other, such a portrayal becomes a little tough to swallow. The reason audiences would want to watch this movie was to see how the real 50 Cent became the international rap sensation that he is today. Sadly his rap career is more of an afterthought. Instead of showing a compelling story of an underdog battling his way to the top against all odds, the film focuses more on the inequities of the modern dope dealing game and all of the wickedness and immorality that such an existence engenders. In the end, this film winds up another cliché gangster flick focusing on street life but falling far short of other classics that have set the mark like *Goodfellas* and *Scarface*. Perhaps the emphasis on gang life was inevitable. After all, Terence Winter, who has done extensive writing for *The Sopranos,* wrote the screenplay. Walking out of the theatre I couldn't shake the feeling that I had somehow been short changed. Is it too late to get my money back?

Nick Kennedy and Jeff Sullivan

CREDITS

Marcus: Curtis "50 Cent" Jackson
Bama: Terrence DaShon Howard
Charlene: Joy Bryant
Levar: Bill Duke
Majestic: Adewale Akinnuoye-Agbaje
Keryl: Omar Benson Miller
Grandma: Viola Davis
Justice: Tory Kittles
Young Marcus: Marc John Jefferies
Slim: Leon
Grandpa: Sullivan Walker
Odell: Russell Hornsby
Antwan: Ashley Walters
Katrina: Serena Reeder
Junebug: Mpho Koaho
Origin: USA
Language: English
Released: 2005
Production: Jimmy Iovine, Paul Rosenberg, Chris Lighty, Jim Sheridan; MTV Films, Shady, Aftermath, Interscope; released by Paramount
Directed by: Jim Sheridan
Written by: Terence Winter
Cinematography by: Declan Quinn
Music by: Quincy Jones, Gavin Friday, Maurice Seezer
Sound: Bruce Carwardine
Music Supervisor: John Houlihan, Sha Money XL
Editing: Conrad Buff, Roger Barton
Art Direction: Dennis Davenport
Costumes: Francine Jamison-Tanchuck

Production Design: Mark Geraghty
MPAA rating: R
Running time: 134 minutes

REVIEWS

Boxoffice Online. November, 2005.
Chicago Sun-Times Online. November 9, 2005.
Entertainment Weekly Online. November 9, 2005.
Los Angeles Times Online. November 9, 2005.
New York Times Online. November 9, 2005.
Premiere Magazine Online. November 11, 2005.
Variety Online. November 5, 2005.
Washington Post Online. November 9, 2005, p. C01.

QUOTES

Marcus: "Rule number five...Show no love. Love will get you killed."

TRIVIA

Bono introduced Jim Sheridan to 50 Cent after Sheridan expressed his desire to meet and work with 50.

GOOD NIGHT, AND GOOD LUCK

We will not walk in fear of one another.
—Movie tagline

In A Nation Terrorized By Its Own Government, One Man Dared to Tell The Truth.
—Movie tagline

Box Office: $22.9 million

Good Night, and Good Luck chronicles the battles of legendary journalist Edward R. Murrow (David Strathairn) and his producer Fred Friendly (George Clooney) against popular culture and CBS during the 1950s. To capture the essence of the era, the movie was filmed in high-contrast black and white and uses tight shots on the faces of the cast as they exchange knowing looks. Also, in place of an instrumental score, a jazz singer (Dianne Reeves) punctuates critical scenes, contributing to an atmosphere that effectively captures the period.

Murrow was famous for his World War II reporting from rooftops during the London Blitz, and now Murrow and Friendly are responsible for *See It Now*, one of television's first news magazine series. Supporting the series is a devoted team of journalists, including Don Hewitt (Grant Helsov), Palmer Williams (Tom McCarthy), Charlie Mack (Robert John Burke), Eddie Scott (Matt Ross), and the secretly married Joe and Shirley Wershba (Robert Downey, Jr. and Patricia Clarkson).

Senator Joseph McCarthy of Wisconsin had become politically powerful at the time from his relentless pursuit of Communists; McCarthy is ruining lives and crushing careers of anyone he feels might be connected to the Communist Party. He has used the infant medium of television to capture the attention of the nation and spread his Red-baiting. The anti-Communist hysteria he embodies is so pervasive that proof of misdeeds is not required; a mere accusation can doom someone.

Murrow wants to cover what Friendly calls "the little picture," a national story brought down to an individual level, and finds a perfect example in a Detroit newspaper. He sends Joe Wershba to Detroit to interview U.S. Air Force reservist Lieutenant Milo Radulovich, who had been discharged for being a security risk. Neither Radulovich nor his attorney knew why the soldier was kicked out because the charges against him were sealed and not revealed at the proceedings. He is told he can keep his commission if he denounces and discontinues his association with suspected Communists—his father and sister. Radulovich refuses the offer.

CBS's number two man, Sig Mickelson (Jeff Daniels), opposes airing the program because its sponsor, ALCOA (the Aluminum Company of America), is a military contractor and might take offense at the indictment of the armed forces. When ALCOA pulls its sponsorship of the episode, Murrow and Friendly personally pay for the advertising. Murrow used *See It Now* to champion the right of Radulovich to view the Air Force's evidence. Thus began a media war with Senator McCarthy—a war that the Senator would ultimately lose.

After the program, McCarthy and his supporters attack. Murrow and his team read the first attack in a column by McCarthy supporter Jack O'Brian against CBS newscaster and Murrow friend Don Hollenbeck (Ray Wise). Hollenbeck was already emotionally wounded from his wife having left him and comes to Murrow for help. Murrow cannot help his friend—he is busy defending himself against an envelope of accusations given by a McCarthy aide to William Paley (Frank Langella), the head of CBS, via Joe Wershba.

With nervous support from Paley, Murrow airs another program. This program uses newsreels of Senator McCarthy to point out the half-truths, circular logic, and misstatements that constitute his demagogic technique. In the closing editorial, before his signature sign-off of "Good night, and good luck," Murrow challenges his audience to confront the fear that grips the nation.

Suddenly the Secretary of the Air Force reviews Radulovich's case and reinstates him, but McCarthy's attacks continue. *See It Now* reports on the Senate's Permanent Subcommittee on Investigations hearing into Annie Lee Moss, a clerk in the Pentagon, accused by McCarthy of being a Communist spy. Meanwhile, the effects of character assassination are felt in the newsroom when Hollenbeck commits suicide.

Murrow had invited McCarthy to appear on his show to respond to the criticism. McCarthy uses his appearance to attack Murrow without any supporting evidence, but the rebuttal exposes the Senator's methods and swings public opinion in the opposite direction. Finally, the Army and the Senate take steps against McCarthy, culminating in Army counsel Joseph Welsh saying to Senator McCarthy, "Have you no sense of shame?" and the ultimate censure of McCarthy by the Senate.

The same series of broadcasts that began McCarthy's fall also begin Murrow's reigning in by CBS. Management feels that Murrow lost his reportorial objectivity and has become the news. Murrow's courting of controversy could hurt business prospects, so Paley moves *See It Now* out of its evening timeslot.

Rather than casting Senator McCarthy as a character, director Clooney has McCarthy himself speak through archival footage viewed in the newsroom. The effect is startling, allowing the contemporary audience to feel the savageness of McCarthy's rhetoric.

As co-writer and director, Clooney seems to aspire to follow Murrow's example by using his story to reflect on contemporary events. He reminds us of a fearless citizen and issues his own warning: we are complicit if we say nothing against the stripping of our civil liberties.

Clooney also uses his film to illustrate what good journalism should be. In *Good Night, and Good Luck*, Murrow spoke truth to power; his example prompts one to wonder whether, in contemporary society, many journalists seem too intimidated to challenge powerful politicians. Clearly the director is using this powerful look inside a newsroom to ask important questions about the directions that have been taken in the field of journalism in the years since the setting of this story.

There is also an educational value to the film that is not insignificant. In an era in which studies have shown a decreasing understanding of history and political science (including Constitutional law) among younger generations, the events that unfold in *Good Night, and Good Luck* serve to remind the viewers of our Constitutional civil liberties. Learning from the past so that we are not doomed to repeat it may sound like a cliché, but one does not have to look far to see how valid that exhortation may be.

The spirit of the movie is best captured in the words that Murrow used to close his broadcast on the techniques of Senator Joseph McCarthy:

> This is no time for men who oppose Senator McCarthy's methods to keep silent, or for those who approve. We can deny our heritage and our history, but we cannot escape responsibility for the result...We proclaim ourselves, as indeed we are, the defenders of freedom, wherever it continues to exist in the world, but we cannot defend freedom abroad by deserting it at home. The actions of the junior Senator from Wisconsin have caused alarm and dismay amongst out allies abroad, and given considerable comfort to our enemies. And whose fault is that? Not really his. He didn't create this situation of fear: he merely exploited it—and rather successfully. Cassius was right. "The fault, dear Brutus, is not in our stars, but in ourselves." Good night, and good luck.

David Flanagin and Donna Wood-Martin

CREDITS

Edward R. Murrow: David Strathairn
Shirley Wershba: Patricia Clarkson
Fred Friendly: George Clooney
Sig Mickelson: Jeff Daniels
Joe Wershba: Robert Downey, Jr.
William Paley: Frank Langella
Don Hollenbeck: Ray Wise
Charlie Mack: Robert John Burke
John Aaron: Reed Edward Diamond
Jesse Zousmer: Tate Donovan
Don Hewitt: Grant Heslov
Palmer Williams: Tom McCarthy
Eddie Scott: Matt Ross
Natalie: Alex Borstein
Jimmy: Peter Jacobson
Don Surine: Rob Knepper
Jazz Singer: Dianne Reeves
Millie Lerner: Rose Abdoo
Stage manager: John David (J.D.) Cullum
Col. Anderson: Glenn Morshower
Origin: USA, Great Britain, France, Japan
Language: English
Released: 2005
Production: Grant Heslov; released by Warner Independent Pictures
Directed by: George Clooney
Written by: George Clooney, Grant Heslov
Cinematography by: Robert Elswit
Sound: Edward Tise
Music Supervisor: Allen Sviridoff

Editing: Stephen Mirrione
Art Direction: Christa Munro
Costumes: Louise Frogley
Production Design: James Bissell
MPAA rating: PG
Running time: 93 minutes

REVIEWS

Boxoffice Online. October, 2005.
Chicago Sun-Times Online. October 21, 2005.
Entertainment Weekly Online. October 5, 2005.
Los Angeles Times Online. October 7, 2005.
New York Times Online. September 23, 2005.
Premiere Magazine Online. October 6, 2005.
Variety Online. September 1, 2005.
Washington Post Online. October 7, 2005, p. C01.

QUOTES

Edward R. Murrow: "Freddie, every time you light my cigarette, I know you're lying to me."

TRIVIA

Rosemary Clooney's band and her song arrangements plays throughout the production. Rosemary Clooney is director/star George Clooney's aunt.

AWARDS

Ind. Spirit 2006: Cinematog.
L.A. Film Critics 2005: Cinematog.
Natl. Bd. of Review 2005: Film

Nomination:

Oscars 2005: Actor (Strathairn), Art Dir./Set Dec., Cinematog., Director (Clooney), Film, Orig. Screenplay
British Acad. 2005: Actor (Strathairn), Director (Clooney), Film, Film Editing, Orig. Screenplay, Support. Actor (Clooney)
Directors Guild 2005: Director (Clooney)
Golden Globes 2006: Actor—Drama (Strathairn), Director (Clooney), Film—Drama, Screenplay
Ind. Spirit 2006: Actor (Strathairn), Director (Clooney), Film
Screen Actors Guild 2005: Actor (Strathairn), Cast
Writers Guild 2005: Orig. Screenplay
Broadcast Film Critics 2005: Actor (Strathairn), Director (Clooney), Film, Screenplay, Cast.

THE GREAT RAID

The Most Daring Rescue Mission Of Our Time Is A Story That Has Never Been Told.
—Movie tagline

Box Office: $10.1 million

John Dahl is not a director you would expect to film a straightforward war story about a forgotten raid during the Allied campaign against Japan in the Pacific during World War II. Dahl earned his reputation earlier in his career as a director of latter-day film noir such as the cult hits *Kill Me Again* and *Red Rock West.* He followed those up with *The Last Seduction,* a highly acclaimed noir thriller about a femme fatale in the classic style.

Dahl seemed to tire of these kind of films, and he turned his attention to science fiction in the much-panned *Unforgettable* before returning to gangland-style dramas with *Rounders.* The easily forgettable *Joy Ride* followed, and that was his only film in seven years before he released *The Great Raid* in 2005, a film that went quickly or straight to video, depending on the market.

The Great Raid is a down-the-middle historical drama about the American military's most daring and successful wartime raid ever, the rescue of more than 500 prisoners of war being held by the Japanese in the Philippine village of Cabanatuan. It's an incident that's never gotten much attention and has never been the subject of a film. Dahl uses a meticulously researched, thoroughly detailed script by Carlo Bernard to tell a fascinating war story about unsung heroes risking their lives to save brutalized prisoners from certain death.

More than half a century after the Pacific campaign, it's been largely forgotten that the Japanese committed many atrocities against American soldiers who were left behind in the Philippines after General Douglas MacArthur's forced retreat in 1942. While the U.S. concentrated its forces on the European front, hundreds of American prisoners were tortured and killed. The Japanese had little respect for troops who surrendered and they looked for any excuse to tempt the American prisoners into fleeing or attempting escapes so that they could then be shot and killed.

Dahl sets up the story with a long exposition that relies on stock footage, and he ends it with actual newsreel clips of the rescued soldiers. In between he takes few risks with a true-to-life story of the Sixth Ranger Battalion, a highly trained group of American soldiers who hadn't seen previous war action and mostly was composed of farm boys. The story is told through the narration of the Ivy League-trained Lieutenant Colonel Henry Mucci (Benjamin Bratt), a strategist who was picked by MacArthur to lead the raid.

The young leader of the daring raid is demanding of those feeding him intelligence and also cautious, and meticulous in getting every part of the plan in place. He is assisted by a less patient and more impassioned Captain Prince (James Franco), who is eager to rescue the prisoners because he has seen too many of his comrades die needlessly in the conflict.

The movie spends a lot of time with the soldiers preparing for and plotting the raid, but it intercuts with many gripping scenes of the desperate prisoners in the camp. They don't know they're going to be rescued, but they are hearing rumors of MacArthur's return and trying to keep up hope. Their captors flee, but they are wary of leaving because they fear it's a trick—that the Japanese are waiting in the woods to shoot them.

Many have stayed alive for several years largely because a nurse who was married to a now-dead American military leader has obtained and smuggled drugs to the POW camps. Based in Manila, Margaret Utinsky (Connie Nielsen) is the leader of a small underground cell of resisters, who include people of many nationalities besides Filipinos. Utinsky is especially interested in maintaining supplies of quinine to treat the malaria of Major Gibson (Joseph Fiennes), the remaining top officer at the Cabanatuan POW camp, because she seems to be in love with him.

Gibson carries on a running friendly quarrel with Captain Redding (Martin Csokas), who keeps threatening to try to escape the camp. Redding also continues to assure Gibson that Margaret is a memory worth preserving. Gibson refrained from having an affair with Margaret while her husband was alive, and since then they have been separated. Gibson is unsure of where he stands in Margaret's eyes, but Redding continually assures him that she is obviously interested in him, even though their love has never had a chance to bloom, and Redding assures Gibson that if Gibson doesn't pursue Margaret after he's released, he will.

The POW's captors are eventually replaced by special forces who are even more brutal. They intervene with other Japanese intelligence assets in Manila to shut down the pipeline of medicines. Their commander, Major Nagai (Motoki Kobayashi), tells Gibson that if he will only reveal the names of members of the resistance, he will be allowed medicine and will live. He refuses. Meanwhile, the Japanese are putting the squeeze on Margaret's resistance group in Manila.

Dahl intercuts between the three prongs of his drama: the resistance group and their activities in Manila, the dying Major Gibson and the other prisoners of war, and Mucci and Prince and their increasingly intense plans for the raid. It's an interesting stew of wartime angst and tension, and the script and dialogue keep the plot boiling even when the action is scarce. Dahl isn't interested in skewing or sensationalizing the story, and he keeps the movie on-target as the tensions build. When the raid finally happens, it's a bittersweet triumph mixed with tragedy. Dahl stages plenty of pyrotechnics as the Americans move in during the delicate operation, but there's also much confusion as weapons are fired from many directions.

This is not an epic war movie by any stretch of the imagination, it's just a small, well-told tale that illuminates a forgotten corner of World War II. History buffs will love it, but it should be entertaining for anyone who does not demand spectacular overstatement. There's no discernible point of view to mar the story—it's not an excessively war-is-hell film, nor does it engage in egregious cheerleading for military action. *The Great Raid* simply shows us what happened on four days in January 1945 in the Philippines. The closest to noir it gets is in the figure of Nielsen's Margaret, who is shot like a real femme fatale though she's simply a heart-of-gold heroine.

Michael Betzold

CREDITS

Lt. Colonel Mucci: Benjamin Bratt
Captain Prince: James Franco
Margaret Utinsky: Connie Nielsen
Major Gibson: Joseph Fiennes
Captain Redding: Marton Csokas
Captain Fisher: Robert Mammone
Mina: Natalie Mendoza
Major Nagai: Motoki Kobayashi
Pajota: Cesar Montano
1st Sgt. Sid "Top" Wojo: Maximillian Martini
Cpl. Aliteri: James Carpinello
2nd Lt. Riley: Craig McLachlan
Gen. Kreuger: Dale Dye
Sgt. Valera: Paolo Montalban
Yamada: Gotaro Tsunashima
Origin: USA
Language: English
Released: 2005
Production: Marty Katz, Lawrence Bender; released by Miramax Films
Directed by: John Dahl
Written by: Carlo Bernard, Doug Miro
Cinematography by: Peter Menzies, Jr.
Music by: Trevor Rabin
Sound: Paul Brincat
Editing: Pietro Scalia, Scott Chestnut
Art Direction: Michael Rumpf
Costumes: Lizzy Gardiner
Production Design: Bruno Rubeo
MPAA rating: R
Running time: 132 minutes

REVIEWS

Boxoffice Online. August, 2005.
Chicago Sun-Times Online. August 12, 2005.

Entertainment Weekly Online. August 10, 2005.
Los Angeles Times Online. August 12, 2005.
New York Times Online. August 12, 2005.
Variety Online. August 3, 2005.
Washington Post Online. August 11, 2005, p. WE35.

TRIVIA

Originally shot in 2002, the film was set for a US theatrical release in 2003 and then in 2004. It was finally released in August, 2005, when the Disney and Miramax divorce was completed and numerous films like this one under the Miramax and Dimension label were able to be released in theaters.

THE GREATEST GAME EVER PLAYED

Box Office: $15.3 million

Disney's *The Greatest Game Ever Played* is more than the feel-good story of Francis Ouimet's U.S. Open victory over Harry Vardon in 1913, it is the tale of the duo's near parallel rise to golf prominence by breaking through the class system that dominated golf at the turn of the century.

Harry Vardon is the six-time British Open champion, considered by many to be England's greatest golfer ever. In the film, Harry Vardon (James Paxton and later Stephen Dillane) is introduced to the game when his family home on the Channel Island of Jersey is redeveloped to become a golf course. Vardon naturally becomes intrigued by the game and becomes one of England's most unlikely champions, rising above his modest roots with undeniable skill in the gentlemen's game. He became the game's first international superstar, showcasing his skills in matches and exhibitions around the world. It is on one of these exhibitions that a young Francis Ouimet (Matthew Knight and later Shia LaBeouf) sees Vardon play and becomes fascinated with the man and his game.

Francis Ouimet grew up across the street from the sight of his most memorable victory, the Brookline Country Club near Boston. The young Francis took a job as a caddy, against the wishes of his father Arthur (Elias Koteas), and it is here that he learns the game. Ouimet is the most unlikely challenger for the U.S. Open title, he is a 20-year-old former caddie playing against the legendary Harry Vardon and some of the finest players of the era. Ouimet's most unlikely victory served as the catalyst for the golfing revolution in America, bringing the game to the masses.

The game of golf is as popular as ever, receiving a shot in the arm from Tiger Woods and his amazing play. Golf is a game filled with a rich tradition and a history rich with larger than life characters. In spite of this, Hollywood seems unable to capitalize on the current popularity of golf. Bill Paxton, directing his second feature film (*Frailty* [2001]), uses computer-generated special effects and dramatic camera work that while technically impressive, add little to the story. The spirit of the film lies in the rags-to-riches characters and the heartfelt performance of Dillane as Vardon, the pauper in a gentleman's game.

Victoria Nelson

CREDITS

Francis Ouimet: Shia LaBeouf
Harry Vardon: Stephen (Dillon) Dillane
Arthur Ouimet: Elias Koteas
Mary Ouimet: Marnie McPhail
Ted Ray: Stephen Marcus
Lord Northcliffe: Peter Firth
John McDermott: Michael Weaver
Eddie Lowery: Josh Flitter
Sarah Wallis: Peyton List
Young Harry: James Paxton
Young Francis: Matthew Knight
Stedman Comstock: Len Cariou
Alec Campbell: Luke Askew
Origin: USA
Language: English
Released: 2005
Production: Larry Brezner, Mark Frost, David Blocker; Morra, Brezner, Steinberg & Tenenbaum Entertainment, Inc.; released by Buena Vista
Directed by: Bill Paxton
Written by: Mark Frost
Cinematography by: Shane Hurlbut
Music by: Brian Tyler
Sound: Peter Sullivan, Mark Ormandy, Paul Poduska
Editing: Elliot Graham
Art Direction: Pierre Perrault
Costumes: Renee April
Production Design: Francois Seguin
MPAA rating: PG
Running time: 115 minutes

REVIEWS

Boxoffice Online. September, 2005.
Chicago Sun-Times Online. September 30, 2005.
Entertainment Weekly Online. September 28, 2005.
Los Angeles Times Online. September 30, 2005.
New York Times Online. September 30, 2005.

Premiere Magazine Online. September 30, 2005.
Variety Online. September 18, 2005.
Washington Post Online. September 30, 2005, p. WE39.

QUOTES

Eddie Lowery: "Read it, roll it, hole it."

GRIZZLY MAN

In nature, there are boundaries.
—Movie tagline

One man spent the last 13 years of his life crossing them.
—Movie tagline

Box Office: $3.1 million

Fascinating, appalling, perplexing, touching, and at times flat out hilarious, Werner Herzog's *Grizzly Man* is a documentary like no other. The dichotomy between the downbeat German director—whose flat, bass narration echoes the doom that will eventually come—and his high-pitched, manic, almost pixie-like subject, Timothy Treadwell, is spellbinding. A man literally obsessed with bears, Treadwell's stunning accomplishment of filming nearly 100 hours of footage during his 13 seasons living among wild bears in Alaska is what veteran filmmaker Herzog seems most impressed with. What audiences are most likely to appreciate is the curiosity that is Timothy Treadwell, a social misfit, former actor and non-scientist whose fascination with bears led him back to the Alaskan wilderness one too many times where his own video camera, lens cap still in place, filmed his and his girlfriend's demise at their hands.

This final piece of Treadwell's footage, essentially an audio track, that graphically records Treadwell and his girlfriend Amie Huguenard being killed and eaten by an unfamiliar bear is undoubtedly a controversial issue the film must address. It is, of course, a compelling piece of Treadwell's vast acreage of footage but Herzog is a very respectable filmmaker with a proper respect for the victims. He bridges this thorny issue by listening to the audio through headphones in front of close Treadwell friend Jewel Palovak, who founded the organization Grizzly People with Timothy. He describes some of what he has heard—Timothy screaming for Amie to flee, Amie trying to scare away the bear attacking him by banging pans together—then wisely advises Palovak, whom he entrusts the tape to, to never listen to it and destroy it.

Treadwell began his summer visits to Alaska's Katmai National Park and Reserve around 1990 and ended them in 2003, the year of his death, at age 46. Early footage shows the slight, blond bear lover with the bowl haircut espousing his love for the creatures, who frolic in the distance. He names all the bears he has grown to know over the years, and speaks of and to them like old friends: there's Rowdy, Mr. Chocolate, Satin, Wendy and Melissa. His intentions are clearly noble: he aims to protect the bears. What is unclear is how his presence among them at a national park, where they are clearly safe, is accomplishing that goal. To illustrate this point, Herzog uses footage which shows a paranoid and enraged Treadwell tracking what he believes are poachers, but turn out to be nothing of the sort. In all his 13 years, this seems to be the only threatening event that humans pose among the bears in that park.

Treadwell did capture some amazing footage of the bears and the adorable foxes he lived among, who followed him around like pets. Still, no matter how interesting the creatures are who surround him, Treadwell is still the most interesting subject of his own footage. A Long Island native, Treadwell recounts how he once faked an Australian accent and entire life history. Of the many peculiarities evident in his exhaustive footage, Treadwell was wont to become overly emotional about his furry friends. "I will die for these animals!" he constantly emotes. There are several unintentionally funny moments, such as Treadwell waxing rhapsodic about a pile of Wendy's freshly laid dung or emotionally lamenting a dead bee ("I love you Mr. Bee!"), which actually turns out to be alive. And when food is scarce and the bears resort to cannibalism, as they are wont to do, his horrific screams decry, "Melissa is eating her babies!" He frequently changed the color of the ever-present bandana he wore around his head and vainly worries about how his hair looks. Obviously intent on eventually editing the footage for mass public viewing, Timothy obsessively did take after take of the same "shot," changing only the color of his bandana for purposes of "continuity." At times speaking like the host of a nature show and at times using the camera as a kind of video diary, the style of Timothy's "narration" varied as much as the temperamental nature-lover himself. Herzog starts out using the footage of the very much upbeat and likeable Treadwell but later a darker, more troubled man emerges during his various rants. He rants at a fly he finds in the eye of one of his deceased fox friends and then, in turn, unexpectedly rants at a fox who steals his favorite hat. But his scariest outburst is a particularly violent, profanity-laced rant against park officials who obviously don't understand his "work."

A self-styled loner, he was often not alone in the wilderness and cut out footage of others that accidentally appeared in front of the camera. Among them was a helicopter pilot familiar with Timothy who remarked after his death, "He was treating them like people in bear costumes. He got what he deserved. The tragedy is, he took the girl with him." Amie is seen only twice in the footage, her face never clearly filmed. Although his friends and family more often saw the good in what he was trying to do in regard to the bears, the pilot speaks for many others of the opinion that he had no business mixing with these wild and dangerous creatures in their element.

There are several poignant moments as Treadwell speaks into the camera, his confessional. How he overcame his alcoholism, his problems with women and what he feels are his shortcomings, the frank observations about himself emerge. He admits that with his somewhat feminine, high voice and outsider status, some people thought he was homosexual. Heartbreakingly, Treadwell says he almost wishes he were; that it would be easier than figuring out what women want from him. He's a bit of a milksop, he acknowledges, and women want someone tougher, but that's just not him and he can't change. His relationship with bears seems healthy in comparison.

In September, at the start of the hibernation season, Treadwell, accompanied by Huguenard, left the park for to return to Los Angeles. Treadwell, however, had an argument with an employee at Air Alaska and decided to cancel the trip and return again to the "Grizzly Maze" with Amie in tow. With all the bears that he knew in hibernation, Treadwell began filming a strange, more vicious bear than his old friends. Shots of this bear fishing, which is believed to be the one that killed him, are taken just a few hours before it attacked the couple.

As unbelievably (some might say foolishly) optimistic about his relationship with the bears as he was, Treadwell knew the dangers he faced and spoke of them early in the film. "If I show weakness, I'm dead. They will take me out, they will decapitate me, they will chop me up into bits and pieces..." he says, unknowingly portending his own fate. Herzog also includes a prophetic clip from one of Treadwell's appearances on late-night television where David Letterman jokingly asks if we will "read a news item one day that you have been eaten by one of these bears?" Sadly, the answer turns out to be yes; the bear that killed and ate him, was shot and killed.

Herzog, who in previous work such as *Fitzcarraldo* and *Aguirre, the Wrath of God,* has delved into the subject of madness, clearly is fascinated with his strange subject while showing respect for his heedless optimism. Near the end, however, Herzog counters Treadwell's normally chirpy, upbeat observations about life as he intones in his thick German accent, "I believe the common character of the universe is not harmony, but hostility, chaos and murder."

Hilary White

CREDITS

Origin: USA
Language: English
Released: 2005
Production: Erik Nelson; Real Big Prod.; released by Lions Gate Films
Directed by: Werner Herzog
Cinematography by: Peter Zeitlinger
Music by: Richard Thompson
Sound: Ken King, Spence Palermo
Editing: Joe Bini
MPAA rating: R
Running time: 103 minutes

REVIEWS

Boxoffice Online. August, 2005.
Chicago Sun-Times Online. August 12, 2005.
Entertainment Weekly Online. August 10, 2005.
Los Angeles Times Online. August 12, 2005.
New York Times Online. August 12, 2005.
Premiere Magazine Online. August 5, 2005.
Variety Online. January 26, 2005.
Washington Post Online. August 12, 2005, p. WE32.

QUOTES

Timothy Treadwell: "Nobody friggin' knew that there are times when my life has been on the precipice of death!"

TRIVIA

Out of respect for the late couple, director Werner Herzog declined to feature the audio tape that records the last moments of Timothy Treadwell and Amie Huguenard as they're killed by grizzly bears, although he is shown listening to the tape with headphones on.

AWARDS

Directors Guild 2005: Feature Doc. (Herzog)
L.A. Film Critics 2005: Feature Doc.
N.Y. Film Critics 2005: Feature Doc.
Natl. Soc. Film Critics 2005: Feature Doc
Nomination:
Ind. Spirit 2006: Feature Doc.
Broadcast Film Critics 2005: Feature Doc.

GUESS WHO

Some in-laws were made to be broken.
—Movie tagline

His daughter's Mr. Right just turned out to be...Mr. White.
—Movie tagline

Box Office: $68.8 million

There was a noticeable lack of resemblance between 2005's *Guess Who* and the movie it was purportedly a remake of, 1967's *Guess Who's Coming to Dinner.* The older film, earnestly dealing with the issues of bringing home a date of a different race, starred Katharine Hepburn, Spencer Tracy, and Sidney Poitier. *Guess Who* reverses the races, shuns earnestness in pursuit of light comedy, and counts as a star Ashton Kutcher. More than one critic suggested that *Guess Who's* true forebear was not *Guess Who's Coming to Dinner* but rather *Meet the Parents.*

The date of the wrong color in *Guess Who* is Simon (Kutcher), a white stockbroker who is rapidly rising up the corporate latter. He lives in a tastefully decorated apartment in Manhattan with his comely artist girlfriend, Theresa (Zoë Saldaña). Theresa is bringing Simon home to meet her parents, Percy Jones (Bernie Mac) and Marilyn (Judith Scott), on the occasion of their 25th wedding anniversary and renewal of their vows. She has neglected to tell her African-American parents that Simon is white.

Perhaps to justify its existence as an offspring of one of the best known films on race, the writers, David Ronn, Jay Scherick, and Peter Tolan, sprinkle the film with a few references to race relations, and some of them are quite funny. When Simon shows up at the Jones household, Percy immediately rushes up to the African-American taxi driver (Michael Epps) to welcome him to the family. And when Theresa's outspoken younger sister (Kellee Stewart) catches a glimpse of Simon, she gasps, "Are we being audited?" Later, Percy is revealed to be a huge fan of NASCAR, perhaps the whitest sport on the planet. And there is even a moment when the subject of race becomes uncomfortable and a little edgy. At a dinner with Theresa's family, Simon is goaded into telling some racist jokes. At first the family laughs, but at some point, they become offended and the dinner turns hideously awkward.

But, for the most part, race is just something to hang story lines on. Equally important to the plot is the fact that Simon has just lost his job and has not yet told Theresa. It is doubtful that the filmmakers thought that race relations were so rosy in 2005 that there was not enough material there to make a movie. There is plenty of fuel for a very funny or maybe scorchingly controversial film, but director Kevin Rodney Sullivan seems content to leave that to Spike Lee. Sullivan is determined to make a bland light comedy, and he does just that.

The saving grace of *Guess Who* is the combination of Mac and Kutcher. On a talk show, Kutcher described the movie as a love story between his character and Mac's, and in a way it is. While Simon and Theresa's relationship is barely explored, the minute changes in Simon and Percy's relationship are detailed extensively. It is like a cop buddy movie without the squad car. Mac is good at playing cranky and Kutcher is good at being awkward. Together they make scenes like the one in which they ride in a car uncomfortably listening to overly-appropriate songs like *Ebony and Ivory* funnier than they should be. Their performances make *Guess Who* an enjoyably light film.

Most critics found the movie to be neither thought-provoking nor funny. Kevin Crust of *The Los Angeles Times* wrote, "The film feels more like a remake of the 1970s TV sitcom 'The Jeffersons'—minus its caustic wit...It says something about the timidity of the corporate-dominated entertainment industry that a contemporary film lacks the audacity of a 30-year-old sitcom." Wesley Morris of *The Boston Globe* wrote, "Those looking for extraneous plot entanglements will be thrilled to discover that the screenplay has plenty...But if you're looking for a meaningful consideration of the intricacies that come with introducing your white boyfriend to your black family, you're probably eating nachos at the wrong multiplex." Mick LaSalle of *The San Francisco Chronicle* was kinder to the movie and wrote, "*Guess Who* is all in fun and succeeds on its own terms."

Jill Hamilton

CREDITS

Percy Jones: Bernie Mac
Simon Green: Ashton Kutcher
Theresa Jones: Zoë Saldaña
Marilynn Jones: Judith Scott
Howard Jones: Hal Williams
Reggie: RonReaco Lee
Keisha Jones: Kellee Stewart
Dante: Robert Curtis Brown
Liz Klein: Nicole Sullivan
Polly: Jessica Cauffiel
Kimbra: Kimberly Scott
Lisa: Denise Dowse
Naomi: Niecy Nash
Sydney: Sherri Shepherd
Jerry McNamara: David Krumholtz
The Cab Driver: Mike Epps
Origin: USA
Language: English

Released: 2005
Production: Jenno Topping, Erwin Stoff, Jason Goldberg; 3 Arts Productions, Tall Trees, Katalyst Films; released by Sony Pictures Entertainment
Directed by: Kevin Rodney Sullivan
Written by: Peter Tolan, Jay Scherick, David Ronn
Cinematography by: Karl Walter Lindenlaub
Music by: John Murphy
Sound: Kevin O'Connell, Greg P. Russell
Editing: Paul Seydor
Art Direction: Gary Kosko
Costumes: Judy Ruskin Howell
Production Design: Paul Peters
MPAA rating: PG-13
Running time: 105 minutes

REVIEWS

Boxoffice Online. March, 2005.
Chicago Sun-Times Online. March 25, 2005.
Entertainment Weekly Online. March 23, 2005.
Los Angeles Times Online. March 25, 2005.
New York Times Online. March 25, 2005.
Premiere Magazine Online. April 1, 2005.
Variety Online. March 23, 2005.

GUNNER PALACE

Some war stories will never make the nightly news.
—Movie tagline

400 American soldiers carry out their mission from a bombed-out pleasure palace once owned by Saddam Hussein. This is their story.
—Movie tagline

On the harsh streets of Adhamiya, District 18 of Baghdad, the Second Battalion, Third Field Artillery Regiment, First Armored Division of the United States Army patrols the streets. This is not a story concocted in a Beverly Hills apartment, but a gripping documentary directed by Peter Epperlein and Michael Tucker during a nine month period following major combat operations in Iraq. It is an intensely moving and emotional piece replete with stunning scenes of this vibrant city wracked by immense turmoil, mayhem, confusion and disorder. *Gunner Palace* tells their story.

Their residence is a bombed-out palace first constructed for Saddam Hussein's first wife and used by Uday Hussein for lavish, spectacular parties. It is complete with a "love shack" fit for Scarface, vaulted ceilings, a grand staircase, numerous dazzling chandeliers, a large swimming pool and fully stocked fishing pond. To its former inhabitants, it was a pleasure palace. To its new inhabitants, it is a fortress, a citadel.

Each soldier finds ways to cope with the bleak, harsh realities of contemporary urban combat in one of the fiercest neighborhoods in the most dangerous city in Iraq. Music is one outlet. The soundtrack to *Gunner Palace* is composed and executed almost entirely by the troops themselves. Besides "The Ride of the Valkyries," "Home on the Range" and "My Girl," the music of *Gunner Palace* consists of some of the harshest, gangster-style rap imaginable. Unlike most mainstream rap, however, these lyrics are based on the day to day engagements of real soldiers witnessing acts of real brutality and the real struggle to stay alive on real mean streets. They are infused with the ruggedness and starkness of the texture of bloody warfare. The beats come from the side of a Humvee, not a sampling machine. In addition to the free flowing soldier rap, SPC Stuart Wilf, a soldier who deals with the gruesomeness of war with his guitar and his wit. Mixing classical style guitar and heavy metal with a breed of sarcasm fostered by desensitization, Wilf becomes a hero of the struggle; a wandering spirit who has found a scary home in an unfriendly and unforgiving landscape. His riffs provide the backbone of this intense cinematic triumph.

Tragic in its nature, the members of the Second Battalion must survive staring in the face of a bitter disconnect between appearance and reality, brilliantly highlighted by Epperlein and Tucker. The theme of mixed messages runs throughout the film. At the beginning, we are met with a statement by Donald Rumsfeld importing that the shops in Baghdad are open for business. Immediately following, we find ourselves in the middle of a firefight and a shaky camera following a soldier along an unidentified Baghdad street with every single shop locked, gated, boarded, closed. We discover that these types of infantry soldiers have been trained to stop a Russian advance, not play the role of policeman, politician, social worker. We hear an Armed Forces Radio Network broadcast about the Abu Ghraib schools being opened while staring at a young Iraqi boy addicted to huffing gasses. We hear about the new Armed Forces Student Loan Program while we hear mortar fire in the background. These soldiers are trying to stay alive, not pay off their college financial aid. We meet Mohammed "Mike" Tyson, an Iraqi informant who has just made an arrest of an insurgent. Later, we discover that Tyson has been arrested by the U.S. Army for taking pictures of U.S. soldiers and selling them to an insurgent group. Nothing is as it seems. We find out that the biggest fear of the members of the Second Battalion is the IED, the Improvised Explosive Device. It can be hidden almost anywhere. It could be in a plastic bag or a gutter. Appearance may not be reality. We hear another message from Rumsfeld proclaiming that terrorists are afeard now that the Iraqi government is on its feet. Immediately we see members of an Iraqi civil council standing up on their feet and arguing forcibly with each other. Another radio broadcast states that more Iraqis are coming forward with "useful information." Then we hear from a gate guard who has people coming up to him all the time with information about weapons caches, insurgent cells and a variety of other reports. He finds it difficult to pick out who is "sort-of telling the truth." We see a group of Iraqi children running after a Humvee. Some are smiling. Some are spitting and throwing rocks. We hear of the improved policy of "Horizontal Fusion" instated by the Department of Defense to allow for better intelligence sharing between agencies directly prior to a string of raids where nothing is found but women and children. We hear that the ICDC (Iraqi Civil Defense Corps) will soon take over many security responsibilities. But we see that they can barely march and are adept at very little involving combat training. We discover from another radio broadcast that eighty-seven billion dollars has been appropriated to properly equip troops. Then we hear from SPC Wilf, "Part of our eighty-seven billion dollar budget provided for us to have some secondary armor put on top of our thin-skinned Humvees. This armor is made in Iraq, and it's high quality... metal... and it will probably slow down the shrapnel so that it stays in your body instead of going clean through. And that's about it!"

Gunner Palace strikingly and effortlessly exemplifies what so many producers and directors have attempted to achieve: the disconnect between appearance and reality. And yet, as Tucker states, "Unlike a movie, war has no end."

Nick Kennedy

CREDITS

Origin: USA

Language: English

Released: 2004

Production: Michael Tucker, Petra Epperlein; Nomados Films; released by Palm Pictures

Directed by: Michael Tucker, Petra Epperlein

Cinematography by: Michael Tucker

Sound: Chris Muller

MPAA rating: PG-13

Running time: 85 minutes

REVIEWS

Boxoffice Online. March, 2005.
Chicago Sun-Times Online. March 11, 2005.
Entertainment Weekly Online. March 2, 2005.
Los Angeles Times Online. March 4, 2005.
New York Times Online. March 4, 2005.
Variety Online. September 15, 2004.
Washington Post Online. March 4, 2005, p. WE42.

H

HAPPILY EVER AFTER

(Ils se Marient et Eurent Beaucoup D'Enfants)

Yvan Attal's sprightly but vacuous soufflé from France, *Happily Ever After,* attempts to pull the homely comforting rug implied by its title from beneath the feet of its Parisian yuppie romantics trapped by matrimony. The original French title, which translates as "They Married and Had Lots of Children," is no doubt intended as an ironic quip on the wishes of their parents. Attal however seems resolved on overturning more than an outdated idea of marital bliss.

In its unassuming way, the film reflects the slow Americanization of French cultural life and more remarkably, how Attal's generation seems to thrive on absorbing this change instead of resisting it. As writer-director, Attal proves honest to the point of discarding his national pride and allowing the very dramatic fabric of his film, or whatever little there is of it, to be woven around contemporary American-style rock music.

Attal emerges as unique in another respect as well. Whereas his contemporary French brethren seem to need the backbone of serious dramatic motifs to justify their comedy, Attal seems quite content to embrace the benevolent universe of an American TV sitcom, along with its concomitant glibness. Presenting his film at this year's Museum of Modern Art's "New Directors New Films" showcase, Attal claimed to be a stranger to it, as if it were a work in progress that he was as excited as his audience to be viewing. For his modesty, Attal deserves to be cut some slack in the matter of keeping his narrative thrust on a frothy level.

Attal's previous effort to be seen on these shores, *My Wife Is An Actress* (reviewed in the 2002 volume), which also starred him and his wife Charlotte Gainsbourg in lead roles, comes off better in comparison largely because it revolved around the eponymous wife and favored her with a clever twist at the end. Here his subject matter, in keeping with the vision of a sitcom, is more diffuse.

Attal stakes out his antinomies in the first few sequences. Though married to each other, Vincent (Attal), a car salesman, and Gabrielle (Gainsbourg), a real estate broker, comb the singles bar scene pretending to be strangers so as to energize their sex through contact with strangers. Gabrielle gets to play the emasculating siren while Vincent becomes her cool last-minute rescuer. The next morning we see them as just another harried married couple with a boisterous little son. Georges (Alain Chabat), Vincent's closest buddy and manager of a luxury hotel, dreams of partaking in the licentious life within the walls of his workplace but is saddled with an even worse home life. Married to Nathalie (Emmanuelle Seigner), a rabid feminist, Georges cannot even watch the news on TV in peace without her anti-sexist wrath raining down on him. In a willful attempt at role reversal, their son, armed with a toy vacuum cleaner, runs amok in a hilarious scene as Georges tries to unwind. Fred (Alain Cohen), their only bachelor buddy, becomes the object of envy as he juggles his sexual conquests in Vincent and George's presence with the aid of a cell phone.

As a counterpoint to the above male machismo, we see Gabrielle by herself in a music superstore where her path repeatedly crosses that of Mr. Tall, Dark and Handsome (Johnny Depp in a cameo) who is also by himself. They both find themselves moved by the magnificent strains of "Creep" by Radiohead and quite independently, choosing the same CD. Even though Gabrielle is spurred to run after him in the crowd, she is frozen by her own awkwardness and walks out of the store alone.

From here on, the film takes a picaresque turn, each episode fizzling out its emotional quotient before it can produce a dramatic situation or dilemma. There's a prolonged food fight between Vincent and Gabrielle as well as the perennial ranting between Georges and Nathalie but the anger which is resolved through love play doesn't point to anything more than a stasis that takes the characters back to where they started.

An emotional high point is reached in the sequence when Gabrielle accompanies her son to school. The little boy strikes up a friendship with a kindly woman on the bus who seems to provide him in those few moments with what Gabrielle cannot. After dropping him off, Gabrielle heads for a café where she breaks down. This inspires her to take off on a vacation with her son, where she resists advances by the swimming pool, but then she and her son are soon back in Paris. While she's away, Vincent has a lackluster affair with Geraldine (Stephanie Murat), a beautiful masseuse but it doesn't seem to do anything for either him or the film.

The triangle Vincent finds himself a part of does give Attal, as writer-director, a chance for a clever plot gambit. Gabrielle and Chloe (Chloe Combret), her friend from work, are seated at a restaurant table next to Geraldine and her Mother (Aurore Clement). Vincent first calls Geraldine on her cell phone after which he calls Gabrielle on her cell. The latter ends up spilling the contents of her purse and as she leaves, she forgets her phone, which still has Vincent at the other end. Geraldine notices the phone, picks it up, hears Vincent's voice, and returns it to Gabrielle who has rushed back for it. The result is that Geraldine gets to know her lover's wife and how much Vincent loves her without Gabrielle knowing that she's her husband's lover.

This results in Geraldine breaking off with Vincent over the silliest of reasons. Vincent then gets another jolt from Fred who, as co-worker, gets a raise because he's going to be a father out of wedlock. Fred then throws the film's original French title at Vincent and adds that it is all "fairy tale b.s."

Now all it takes is Elvis singing "Can't Help Falling in Love" (rendered in its entirety on the soundtrack) for Vincent to fall back in love with Gabrielle, after the two move to a house in the country. It is there that we see Georges and Fred accepting their henpecked status and Vincent secretly making up with Geraldine via his cell phone. Since the male dilemmas don't seem to have caused much pain, their resolution doesn't carry any weight either.

For his coda, Attal returns to the lyricism he evoked in the superstore sequence. This time, a coincidence brings Gabrielle and Mr. TDH together as broker and buyer. She comes to know that he's alone, has no children and lives a quiet life. The building elevator carrying them keeps ascending into a fantasy realm of clouds, sky and bright sunshine. As they kiss, it becomes clear, to them and us, that their rapture will not include getting married and having lots of children.

Vivek Adarkar

CREDITS

Vincent: Yvan Attal
Gabrielle: Charlotte Gainsbourg
Georges: Alain Chabat
Nathalie: Emmanuelle Seigner
Fred: Alain Cohen
Stranger: Johnny Depp
Vincent's mother: Anouk Aimee
Vincent's father: Claude Berri
Origin: France
Language: English, French
Released: 2004
Production: Claude Berri; Hirsch, Pathe Renn, TF-1 Films; released by Pathe Distribution
Directed by: Yvan Attal
Written by: Yvan Attal
Cinematography by: Remy Chevrin
Sound: Didier Sain, Jean-Paul Hurier, Jean Goudier, Marc Doisne
Editing: Jennifer Auger
Costumes: Jacqueline Bouchard
Production Design: Katia Wiszkop
MPAA rating: Unrated
Running time: 100 minutes

REVIEWS

Los Angeles Times Online. May 6, 2005.
New York Times Online. April 8, 2005.
Variety Online. August 24, 2004.

HAPPY ENDINGS

All's well that ends swell.
—Movie tagline

Everybody wants one.
—Movie tagline

Box Office: $1.3 million

Don Roos' dramedy *Happy Endings* (his first ensemble film since 1998's *The Opposite of Sex*) opens on the character of Mamie (Roos wrote the role specifically for Lisa Kudrow), hysterically crying and running down the street straight into the path of a car. The first of many title cards appears, reassuring the audience that "She's not dead. No one dies in this movie, not on-screen. It's a comedy, sort of." The sort-of comedy then goes back to Los Angeles in 1983 where we see a 17-year-old Mamie (Halle Hirsch) moving into a new house after her mother's remarriage. She's also acquired a cute British stepbrother, 16-year-old Charley (Eric Jungmann). Mamie soon seduces Charley and gets pregnant. She tells everyone she got an abortion; instead she has the baby and gives him up for adoption.

Nineteen years later, Mamie is a fretful and distracted abortion counselor whose Mexican immigrant boyfriend, Javier (Bobby Cannavale), is a massage therapist in Beverly Hills. The adult Charley (British comedian Steve Coogan) is running the failing family restaurant and is in a five-year relationship with Gil (David Sutcliffe). Gil's best friend Pam (Laura Dern) is the mother of adorable toddler Max with her partner Diane (Sarah Clarke). Gil donated sperm but the women have always insisted that Gil is not Max's biological father; Charley, suddenly, has deep suspicions that they have been lying.

The restaurant has a karaoke night where Jude (Maggie Gyllenhaal) is persuaded to sing and she turns out to be a decent torch singer, besides which she has a real presence with a don't-give-a-damn attitude. Otis (Jason Ritter), who works there, tells Jude that his band needs a temporary replacement singer. His dad, Frank (Tom Arnold), is a wealthy widower who supports his son's endeavors. They have a communication problem, which includes the fact that Otis is still denying that he's gay though it seems obvious to everyone else. Jude knows a mark when she sees one.

Nicky (Jesse Bradford) arranges a meeting with Mamie and informs her he knows all about the son she gave up, including who and where the teenager is now. In return for the information, the director wannabe wants to shoot the reunion so he can use it to get into film school. When Mamie refuses, Nicky storms out and she follows him to a motel. She later goes back with Javier and they break into his room; when Nicky catches them, Javier and Mamie devise a new documentary scenario by pretending that Javier is a sex worker who offers his wealthy female clients massages with "happy endings."

Jude invites herself over and spends the night with a nervous Otis. She makes a big deal of the situation the next morning after meeting Frank and later, after Frank hears the band at the restaurant, plays up the fact that she has no money and no place to stay. Good-hearted Frank, who's attracted to Jude, offers her the use of the pool house. Jude then blatantly tells Otis she's going to sleep with his father and blackmails him into silence by saying she won't reveal that he's gay. Jude's a cynical opportunist but at least she knows what she wants and how to get it unlike most everyone else in the film.

Neurotic Charley keeps harping on the fact that little Max could be Gil's biological child even after Gil asks him to drop the subject. Instead, Charley lies to Pam that Gil has a serious hereditary disease, hoping that she will spill the secret. Instead, Gil finds out about Charley's scheming but now his suspicions are also aroused. Meanwhile, Mamie has paid for Nicky's camera and deluxe editing software so they can start filming, using her essentially empty home as a backdrop. Nicky does his first interview with Javier but Mamie is appalled at its inanity. Nicky's volatile, delusional, and untalented but Mamie is still drawn to him because he's as lost as she is. She also gets more and more drawn into working on the documentary.

However, Mamie becomes very uncomfortable when they stage a fake massage session with Javier's friend, Shauna (Tamara Davies). Thanks to some footage Javier was unaware Nicky was shooting, she also learns that he has a green card marriage and then finds out the wife is Shauna. Nicky finishes his documentary and has a screening for Mamie and Javier; he's included the part about Javier's marriage, which starts a massive argument with them all. Since his documentary will not be finished, Nicky informs Mamie that he will tell her nothing about her son.

Gil has decided he needs a paternity test but before he can arrange it, Pam and Diane inform him that they already had a DNA test done and he is not Max's father. They have taken out a restraining order so Gil won't be able to see Max anymore. To make the situation worse, Pam informs Charley that the reason they actually decided against using Gil's sperm is that Pam discovered Gil was going to leave Charley because he was having an affair. Charley's devastated and breaks up with Gil.

Jude has insinuated herself into Frank's life and is enjoying both the perks of his free-spending ways and taunting Otis. A mistake since the young man is so appalled when they become engaged that he reveals everything to his father. Frank might not be comfortable with the fact that Otis is gay but he loves his only child and doesn't reject him. Jude, who discovers she's pregnant, becomes a client of Mamie's when she decides to have an abortion. She plays the pregnancy card before Frank kicks her out, then denies it and goes through with the procedure.

Six months later, Charley has moved in with Mamie and found a new romance with his doctor. Frank meets Mamie when they get into a fender bender and Otis discovers that his bandmate, Alvin (Ramon de Ocampo), is also gay and the two fall in love. Mamie decides to sell her house and start over but decides she must speak to Nicky one last time. She tracks him through his license plate and goes to his parents' house only to learn that his real name is Ronnie and he has moved to New York. She meets his younger brother, Tom (Eric Jungmann again), and realizes that Nicky knew about her son because the boy is Tom. She starts crying, runs out of the house, and this is where we came in.

However, it's not quite the end of the story; since Roos likes happy endings we learn what happens to the characters: Mamie and Frank get married; she tells Charley about the whole pregnancy/baby issue and they eventually do meet Tom. Charley is happy with his doctor, Otis is happy with his bandmate, Gil resumes his friendship with Pam, Javier remains married to Shauna, Nicky doesn't become a filmmaker and marries a woman who reminds him of Mamie, but no one knows what happened to Jude. She is shown singing in a supper club but who knows if this is real or not.

This is a crowded picture and Roos (who does more screenwriting than directing) doesn't yet have the skills of Robert Altman in keeping all his characters in meaningful play. The plots meander as the characters stumble around, ignoring the messes they make while trying to do their best. The title cards, which are primarily seen at the beginning and end of *Happy Endings*, are something of a distraction (although the information they impart can be amusing) and Roos likes his camera tricks—there are a number of split screens and shots that fill only corners. However, the characters aren't that interesting. Kudrow does a good job but Mamie is a sad sack who distances herself from emotional ties and Bradford's Nicky is plain creepy. Gyllenhaal is a joy though; no matter how despicable Jude may be, at least she's determined enough to go after what she needs—she acts rather than let herself be acted upon. Arnold's Frank is a sweet guy probably well aware that Jude is a gold-digger, but he can handle that—what he refuses to put up with is that she hurt his son. And family means all even to this generally self-absorbed crowd.

Christine Tomassini

CREDITS

Frank: Tom Arnold
Nicky: Jesse Bradford
Javier: Bobby Cannavale
Diane: Sarah Clarke
Charley: Steve Coogan
Pam: Laura Dern
Jude: Maggie Gyllenhaal
Mamie: Lisa Kudrow
Otis: Jason Ritter
Gil: David Sutcliffe
Mamie at 17: Hallee Hirsh
Charley at 16/Tom: Eric Jungmann
Miles: Johnny Galecki
Origin: USA
Language: English
Released: 2005
Production: Holly Wiersma, Mike Paseornek; Lions Gate Films; released by Lions Gate Films
Directed by: Don Roos
Written by: Don Roos
Cinematography by: Clark Mathis
Sound: Benjamin Patrick
Music Supervisor: Nicole Tocantins
Editing: David Codron
Costumes: Peggy Anita Schnitzer
Production Design: Richard Sherman
MPAA rating: R
Running time: 128 minutes

REVIEWS

Boxoffice Online. July, 2005.
Chicago Sun-Times Online. July 15, 2005.
Entertainment Weekly Online. July 13, 2005.
Los Angeles Times Online. July 15, 2005.
New York Times Online. July 15, 2005.
Premiere Magazine Online. 2005.
Variety Online. January 20, 2005.
Washington Post Online. July 15, 2005, p. C05.

QUOTES

Mamie: "Nothing says 'I love you' like blackmail."

TRIVIA

The film boasts Tom Arnold's first sex scene.

AWARDS

Nomination:
Ind. Spirit 2006: Support. Actress (Gyllenhaal).

HARRY POTTER AND THE GOBLET OF FIRE

"Difficult times lie ahead, Harry."
—Movie tagline

Dark And Difficult Times Lie Ahead.
—Movie tagline
On November 18 Everything Will Change.
—Movie tagline

Box Office: $263 million

Anyone having the patience to sit for 13 minutes through the seemingly endless final credits for the latest Harry Potter sequel adapted by British director Mike Newell will be rewarded by the news that "no dragons were injured in the making of this motion picture." Dragons? Yes, there are four of them linked to the Tri-Wizard competition into which heroic young Harry is coerced by sinister powers beyond his ken. Actually, Harry is too young to compete in this tournament and therefore does not volunteer by dropping his name into the magical "goblet of fire" used to select potential "champions", but when Professor Dumbledore draws the names for the competition, Harry's name is somehow drawn, and not merely "as if" by magic. It seems Harry's tutor, Alastor "Mad Eye" Moody (Brendan Gleeson), who is not exactly whom he seems to be, has finagled the rules and the selection process. Three sorcery schools are to compete, each represented by a potential "champion". Harry is three years too young for the competition and the Hogwarts candidate, Cedric Diggory (Robert Pattinson), has already been chosen; but, no matter. Harry is also in the game, which is disturbingly dangerous and consists of three tasks: 1) Recovering a golden egg, which contains clues for the next task, but which is protected by a flying dragon; 2) an underwater rescue mission; and, 3) a search through an amorphous and collapsing maze in order to discover the trophy cup. But skullduggery (of course!) is afoot here, and at the end of the maze, Harry is forced to confront a resurrected Lord Voldemort (Ralph Fiennes, not looking so fine as he usually does), which leads to a spectacular duel between Harry and the feared Lord of Darkness. Harry needs (and gets) some last-minute spiritual assistance from departed friends and relatives, but Voldemort escapes, no doubt to return for the next sequel.

As should now be obvious, increment Number 4 is darker and more "mature," as if to match the growing maturity of that first generation of J.K. Rowling's readers. Rowling nudged her readers towards a darker purpose in last year's *The Prisoner of Azkaban* (2004), but *The Goblet of Fire* is darker still. Director Mike Newell has been given a second chance at the Potter franchise after he had declined the opportunity to direct *The Philosopher's Stone* (called *The Sorcerer's Stone* in America), the first Potter adaptation, and perhaps the dullest because of its plodding and constant fidelity to the original story. *The Sorcerer's Stone* though written by Steve Kloves (who seems to have a lock on the franchise as screenwriter) was directed by Chris Columbus in 2001 and earned Oscar nominations for art direction, costume design, and the John Williams score. Clearly, none of Rowling's 100 million tot readers would be confused or disappointed, but adults would be less than enchanted by the paint-by-numbers approach. Apparently pleased with the box-office revenues of *The Sorcerer's Stone*, Warner Brothers allowed the reliable Chris Columbus to direct the first sequel, *The Chamber of Secrets* in 2002.

Critically, Mexican director Alfonso Cuaron breathed new life into the Potter franchise with the next sequel, *Azkaban*, even if, as *Variety* reported, box-office slipped with each subsequent episode. In the case of Potter, however, the slippage was tolerable because the numbers were so outrageously high: *Harry Potter and the Sorcerer's Stone* touched the ceiling with $974 million; *Chamber of Secrets* slipped to $879 million; Cuaron's *Prisoner of Azkaban*, though a critical success, dropped to a still respectable and impressive $749 million (according to *Variety*).

Mike Newell, the first English director to helm Harry, and his screenwriter, Harry Potter regular Steve Kloves, condensed Rowling's 700-plus page novel to just under two and one-half hours. Newell returns in part to the copybook ethic that informed the first Harry Potter film but avoids being engulfed by what film critic Tom Leitch has called "the Persistence of Fidelity." *Washington Post* reviewer Desson Thomson feared that some of the Rowling faithful might be disappointed by missing details from the source novel, such as events occurring (or not occurring) in the maze "that figures in a climactic scene in the movie [a maze that] has no hidden creatures—an obvious departure from Rowling's story." Thomson regarded such omissions a "necessary evil," however, adding: "Movies work on a leaner diet and, if they didn't, I'd still be watching *Goblet of Fire*."

In *The Goblet of Fire* the maturing characters, learning how to experience love and jealousy, make this sequel inherently more interesting than they appeared in the earlier increments, while, at the same time, earning it a PG-13 rating. Newell's stylish and admirable economy of pacing improves the picture throughout. The opening Quidditch World Cup match, for example, is contained and trimmed so that the story can get on with the larger challenge of Harry's nemesis, Lord Voldemort redux, with his entourage of hooded "Death Eaters." So, after a brisk 15-minute Quidditch prologue, viewers are quickly enroute to Hogwarts to prepare for the Tri-Wizard Tournament that consumes the major portion of this sequel.

The production design is quite splendid and delights the eye as much as Patrick Doyle's music delights the ear. Patrick Doyle, Kenneth Branagh's regular composer, is new to the series and skillfully incorporates the previous John Williams scores, while adding his own musical magic. The arrival and departure of the students from competing schools of wizardry and witchcraft are unforgettable. The French female students, dressed in blue uniforms and capes, from Beauxbatons arrive by a carriage floated in by flying horses and are ushered into the Great Hall of Hogwarts by their mentor, the tall and elegant Madame Olympe Maxime (Frances de le Tour). It turns out that this Amazonian bon-bon has a yen for Hogwarts Groundskeeper Rubeus Hagrid (Robbie Coltrane), who proudly wears a necktie in her honor (even though this potentially amusing subplot goes nowhere). The third contingent for the tournament brings in some fine young men from Durmstrang (presumably in Bulgaria), supporting their champion Viktor Krum (Stanislav Ianevski). These Middle-Europeans arrive on an antique sailing ship that emerges magically from beneath the loch leading to Hogwarts (and looking a whole lot like Scotland). The Beaubatons beauty Fleur Delacour (Clemence Poesy) seems to have a yen for Harry, who saves the life of her sister during the second phase of the competition.

Though rather too often too petulant, Emma Watson's Hermione Granger is absolutely radiant for the film's Grand Ball scene, where screentime involving her character passes pleasantly, though rather too quickly. *Variety* reviewer Todd McCarthy was well pleased with Daniel Radcliffe's budding adolescent Harry ("he rises to the occasion with a more dimensional and nuanced performance" than in previous outings); but *Variety* also complained that Rupert Grint's Ron Weasley "seems caught at an unappealingly awkward stage," which could, of course, be merely a consequence of growing up. The *Washington Post* reviewer praised the scene where Ron Weasley is forced to dance with Maggie Smith's Professor McGonagall. When he is instructed by her to "put your hand on my waist," it's clear from the appealingly awkward expression on Ron's face that "He'd just as soon perform the fox trot with Medusa."

Central casting has rounded up as many of the rest of the usual Potter suspects as possible, though we see rather less of them than might be expected. Maggie Smith's Professor Minerva McGonagall passes in and out of the frame, but we see a great deal more of Michael Gambon's Headmaster Albus Dumbledore and Brendan Gleeson's Moody. (The original Dumbledore was played by the now deceased Richard Harris in 2001 and 2002; Gambon, who took over the role with *The Prisoner of Azkaban* in 2004, is an agreeable substitute.) Brendan Gleeson is very well suited for the classroom at the Hogwarts School since before becoming an actor in 1990 he actually taught secondary school in Dublin; but *Washington Post* reviewer Desson Thomson was ready to grant Gleeson "a golden shoplifting award for the way he plunders scenes." Gleeson's character becomes the dominant academic in this sequel. On the other hand, Gary Oldman's Sirius Black is reduced to a dying ember that lights up the scene, briefly, a momentarily glowing performance. Alan Rickman comes and goes as Severus Snape. Miranda Richardson, who had worked with Mike Newell on other films, puts in a few turns as the amusingly irritating (and well-named) tabloid hack gossip columnist Rita Skeeter.

But overall the villains are most memorable here. The truly gifted character actor Timothy Spall is at his repulsively deferential best as Wormtail, Lord Voldemort's servant. Voldemort himself, who in diminished form resembles the hairless, chest-crashing reptilian beast from Ridley Scott's *Alien* (1979), has to be truly repulsive because he is the personification of Evil, but his ratlike image and bad manners will surely give little kids the creeps and the willies. *New Yorker* reviewer Anthony Lane neatly described the Ralph Fiennes Voldemort as "looking like the English Patient on steroids." (In the first Potter film, Voldemort, doubling as Professor Quirrell, was played by Ian Hart.)

Anthony Lane's *New Yorker* review praised director Mike Newell for doing a "more coherent job than his predecessors," who "tended to linger over the early setups and then scramble toward a confusing climax, whereas Newell measures out the magic with some aplomb," even though Newell is unable to contain "the slightly tired sadism that is creeping into the cracks of the Potter franchise." Lane discerns a blurring of the line between ordinary people, the unimaginative "Muggles," in other words, and the extraordinary community of Wizards, the "unspoken apartheid of the J.K. Rowling world." Likewise, Desson Thomson of *The Washington Post* was impressed by the way the film allows Harry to "negotiate the terrors of adolescence," as when he attempts to "muster the courage to ask the attractive Cho Chang (Katie Leung) to the school ball." The good news, then, about *Harry Potter and the Goblet of Fire* is the way the story has been humanized, proving, as at least one reviewer suggested, that just as boys will be boys, wizards will be boys, too, if they are wizards of a certain age. There was little doubt that this picture would make a ton of money at the box office. The only question was, how much? By the end of 2005 *Harry Potter and the Goblet of Fire* had earned nearly $771 million worldwide. *Variety* had predicted a "modest dip" in box-office performance, but after only six weeks on the market, the picture had surpassed revenues for its Harry Potter predecessor. Dave McNary of *Variety* reported on January 2, 2006, that *Goblet of Fire* became "the 11th film of all time...to eclipse half a billion dollars in foreign grosses." Hence, the saga continues, comfortably and profitably.

James M. Welsh

CREDITS

Harry Potter: Daniel Radcliffe
Ron Weasley: Rupert Grint
Hermione Granger: Emma Watson
Rubeus Hagrid: Robbie Coltrane
Lord Voldemort: Ralph Fiennes
Albus Dumbledore: Michael Gambon
Alastor "Mad-Eye" Moody: Brendan Gleeson
Lucius Malfoy: Jason Isaacs
Sirius Black: Gary Oldman
Rita Skeeter: Miranda Richardson
Severus Snape: Alan Rickman
Minerva McGonagall: Maggie Smith
Wormtail: Timothy Spall
Madame Olympe Maxime: Frances De La Tour
Igor Karkaroff: Pedja Bjelac
Argus Filch: David Bradley
Filius Flitwick: Warwick Davis
Draco Malfoy: Tom Felton
Cornelius Fudge: Robert Hardy
Moaning Myrtle: Shirley Henderson
Barty Crouch: Roger Lloyd Pack
Arthur Weasley: Mark Williams
Viktor Krum: Stanislav Ianevski
Cedric Diggory: Robert Pattinson
Fleur Delacour: Clarence Poesy
Barty Crouch Junior: David Tennant
Fred Weasley: James Phelps
George Weasley: Oliver Phelps
Ginny Weasley: Bonnie Wright
Cho Chang: Katie Leung
Neville Longbottom: Matthew Lewis
Padma Patil: Afshan Azad
Parvati Patil: Shefali Chowhury
Origin: USA
Language: English
Released: 2005
Production: David Heyman; Heyday Films; released by Warner Bros.
Directed by: Mike Newell
Written by: Steven Kloves
Cinematography by: Roger Pratt
Music by: Patrick Doyle
Sound: David Crozier
Editing: Mick Audsley
Art Direction: Mark Bartholomew, Al Bullock, Alan Gilmore, Gary Tomkins, Alexandra Walker
Costumes: Jany Temime
Production Design: Stuart Craig
MPAA rating: PG-13
Running time: 157 minutes

REVIEWS

Boxoffice Online. November, 2005.
Chicago Sun-Times Online. November 18, 2005.
Entertainment Weekly Online. November 16, 2005.
Los Angeles Times Online. November 17, 2005.
New York Times Online. November 17, 2005.
Premiere Magazine Online. November 17, 2005.
Variety Online. November 9, 2005.
Washington Post Online. November 18, 2005, p. C01.

QUOTES

Dumbledore: "The Goblet of Fire! Anyone wishing to submit themselves to the tournament merely write their name upon a piece of parchment and throw it in the flame before this hour on Thursday night. Do not do so lightly! If chosen, there's no turning back. As from this moment, The Triwizard Tournament has begun!"

TRIVIA

Alfonso Cuarón was offered the chance to direct this installment in the series, but declined as he would still be working on *Harry Potter and the Prisoner of Azkaban* (2004). Mike Newell, (*Four Weddings and a Funeral* and *Donnie Brasco*) who turned down an offer to direct the first Harry Potter film, is the series' first British director.

AWARDS

Nomination:

Oscars 2005: Art Dir./Set Dec.
British Acad. 2005: Makeup, Visual FX.

HEAD-ON

(Gegen die Wand)

Faith Arkin's much celebrated punk fable from Germany, *Head-On,* throws a refreshing light on today's neoimmigrant experience by unconcealing its violent and profligate substratum amongst the Turkish immigrant community in today's Hamburg. In writer-director Arkin's hands, the rootless romantic duo, who provide the film with its frenetic spin, do not possess a gender as much as a particular species of animus.

The gen-xer Sibel (Sibel Kekilli), a young Turkish hair stylist, looks lithe and feminine but can tear into the most violent of urban males with the same fury with which she ingests lines of white powder. The equally self-destructive Cahit (Birol Unel), also a Turk and a punk rock refugee, ekes out a drunkard's existence on the periphery of the club scene. He bears a striking resemblance to Mick Jagger and not coincidentally embodies the ideal set forth in the Rolling Stones anthem "Street Fighting Man." Where Arkin's film, for all its verve, falters is in embracing retrogressive traditional values as the way out of the neoimmigrant quagmire.

The film's cultural anchor, that provides a frame for its narrative, and to which the film keeps returning, as if it were a Greek chorus, is a Turkish musical ensemble that is performing romantic folk ballads on the banks of the Bosphorus in Istanbul with the dome of St. Sofia looming in the distance, almost as if it were beckoning the lost young souls home.

We are introduced to Cahit as he and his rotund uncle Seref (Guven Kirac) collect empty bottles from the floor of a club. In flashes we witness a typical night in Cahit's life: beer, cursing an old flame, the seductive and voluptuous Maren (Catrin Striebeck), yanking a German patron off a barstool for a chance remark, and more beer. The jag ends with Cahit smashing his car into a wall head-on, after which he finds himself in hospital. Dr. Schiller (Hermann Lausse) offers him kindly advice: "You don't have to die to end your life." Schiller suggests that Cahit start a new life in Africa as a social worker, but the advice falls on deaf ears. After being discharged, he's accosted by Sibel, who is there because of a suicide attempt. She pleads with him to marry her, purely for convenience, because he's a Turk and her family will not accept any other nationality. "Once we're married, I'll be out of your life!" she promises.

Cahit cannot believe what he's hearing. When they meet in a bar that night, Sibel smashes a beer bottle and slashes her wrists with it so as to prove her desperation. When Cahit finally relents, things proceed in a traditional manner as Seref serves as a go-between and approaches Sibel's parents. While her two brothers remain wary of Cahit, her father offers his blessings and Cahit kisses his hand.

The wedding takes place in a civil ceremony, for which Selma (Meltem Cumbul), Sibel's supportive cousin, flies in from Istanbul. As per custom, when the bride and groom are left alone to consume the food, Cahit introduces Sibel to the white powder, which she takes to like a fish to water.

As could be foreseen, their conjugal union gets off to a rocky start. Inside Cahit's pigsty of an apartment, when Sibel wants to know the name of his first wife, he shows her the door; she in turn storms out and spends her wedding night with the bartender in her customary hangout. The next morning, she returns to Cahit, smiling, in her wedding dress. In the scenes that follow, she openly pursues other men she finds on the club scene while Cahit has violent bouts of sex with Maren.

At this point, Akin's narrative strategy hits a snag. Since neither Cahit nor Sibel take their marital status seriously, much less its concomitant emotional bonding, their scenes lack the substratum of an ideal, whether romantic or political. Their scenes of everyday life suffer even more because of this, so that the action feels as repetitive as dance steps. It is only in the frank loveplay, which borders on the sensationalistic, and in Cahit's outbursts of violence, that the film comes alive. After one such flareup, Sibel nurses Cahit's wounds, after which their sensuality gives way to their making love for the first time.

When Sibel, asserting the freedom she has always claimed for herself, takes up with Nico (Stefan Gebelhoff), a handsome barfly, it arouses Cahit's jealousy, especially after Nico keeps taunting him one night. Cahit lifts an ashtray and strikes him with it, resulting in his accidental death. The event spills over into the tabloids and results in Sibel's family disowning her.

While Cahit languishes in prison, Sibel, after a failed attempt to slash her wrists, flies to Istanbul and is able to find a job in a luxury hotel with Selma's influence. At night she scours the bar scene looking for the white powder. Not finding any, she settles for smoking opium instead. Unable to keep to Selma's work ethic, while at the same time having to ward off sexual assaults, her violent streak surfaces in a street fight in which she is repeatedly kicked. With a bloodied face, she abuses the families of the males who are walking away. One of them then stabs her and stops, fearing that she is dead. A cabbie comes along to take her to hospital.

When Cahit is released from prison, he flies to Istanbul and catches up with a Sibel who is now completely changed as the responsible mother of a four year old daughter and living with a boyfriend. Cahit and Sibel make love once again, but she cannot follow where he's headed, to the small town which is his birthplace.

After all their nonconformist punk ways, the wounds inflicted on Cahit and Sibel in the new country, the film seems to say, can only be healed by the old.

Vivek Adarkar

CREDITS

Cahit Tomruk: Birol Unel
Sibel Guner: Sibel Kekilli

Maren: Catrin Striebeck
Seref: Guven Kirac
Selma: Meltem Cumbul
Yilmaz Guner: Cem Akin
Birsen Guner: Aysel Iscan
Yunus Guner: Demir Gokgol
Nico: Stefan Gebelhoff
Dr. Schiller: Hermann Lause
Lukas: Adam Bousdoukos
Ammer: Ralph Misske
Huseyin: Mehmet Kurtulus
Origin: Germany, Turkey
Language: German
Released: 2004
Production: Ralph Schwingel, Stefan Schubert; Wueste; released by Timebandits Films
Directed by: Fatih Akin
Written by: Fatih Akin
Cinematography by: Rainer Klausmann
Sound: Kai Luede
Editing: Andrew Bird
Production Design: Tamo Kunz
MPAA rating: Unrated
Running time: 118 minutes

REVIEWS

Boxoffice Online. January, 2005.
Los Angeles Times Online. January 28, 2005.
New York Times Online. January 21, 2005.
Variety Online. February 16, 2004.
Washington Post Online. February 25, 2005, p. WE39.

HEIGHTS

Box Office: $1.1 million

Heights is a six-degrees-of-separation kind of movie told in intersecting episodes that all take place within a 24-hour period in New York City. Based on a one-act play written by Amy Fox and on the screenplay written by Fox and first-time director Chris Terrio, it follows the lives of several characters whose lives and relationships will be challenged and even turned upside down within that one day.

The over-arching character of Diana Lee (Glenn Close) ties the characters together. She is a famous Oscar-winning actress currently appearing on stage in *Macbeth*. She is also teaching master classes at Julliard and casting for an off-Broadway play she is directing. Diana has an open relationship with her husband so her eye wanders to hunky stage hands and artsy actors. However, she is also upset that her husband is having an affair, and apparently is in love with, her understudy. One actor who has caught Diana's attention, however, is Alec (Jesse Bradford) who auditions for Diana's play and sees this as his big break even though Alec has an indirect and risky relationship to Diana of which the actress is not aware.

Diana's daughter is Isabel (Elizabeth Banks), a wedding photographer who dreams of having a greater career. Isabel is engaged to Jonathan (James Marsden) who has a secret Isabel doesn't know about. He took a class in London from the famous photographer Benjamin Stone who has taken nude photos of him. This in itself wouldn't be so bad except Stone is known for having homosexual affairs with all his subjects, none of whom speak fondly of him. Unfortunately for Jonathan, *Vanity Fair* has commissioned an article on the artist and the author, Peter Stone (John Light), is contacting all Benjamin's ex lovers, including Jonathan for background information on the photographer.

However, Isabel also has a past, but it's not a secret one. Part of it includes a writer for the *Times* Magazine who offer her a job on assignment in Eastern Europe. But the job starts immediately and she has a wedding in her near future. Isabel's secret may be that she's not sure if she really wants to pass on a great photographic career and marry Jonathan.

Connections come together that night at Diana Lee's birthday party when she is given a catalog of the Peter Stone exhibit and sees a photo of her daughter's fiancée in it. Now relationships and life goals are reexamined and one more relationship will be revealed and another created.

While *Heights* may be an interesting character study that is well acted and neatly told, it is also a low-key film where brooding is the norm of existence for its inhabitants. When Glenn Close's character screams to her Julliard class, "we have forgotten passion," it would appear that director/writer Terrio and writer Fox may have been the people to whom she was really referring. Maybe they should have listened to her a little more carefully.

Beverley Bare Buehrer

CREDITS

Diana: Glenn Close
Isabel: Elizabeth Banks
Jonathan: James Marsden
Alec: Jesse Bradford
Marshall: Thomas Lennon
Mark: Matthew Davis

Liz: Isabella Rossellini
Peter: John Light
Rabbi Mendel: George Segal
Henry: Eric Bogosian
Jesse: Michael Murphy
Origin: USA
Language: English
Released: 2004
Directed by: Chris Terrio
Written by: Amy Fox
Cinematography by: Jim Denault
Music by: Martin Erskine, Ben Butler
Editing: Sloane Klevin
Art Direction: Diane Lederman
Costumes: Marina Draghici
Production Design: Marla Weinhoff
MPAA rating: R
Running time: 93 minutes

REVIEWS

Boxoffice Online. June, 2005.
Los Angeles Times Online. June 17, 2005.
New York Times Online. June 17, 2005.
Variety Online. January 25, 2005.

TRIVIA

Mia Farrow was originally cast as Liz, but had to back out due to prior stage commitments.

HENRI LANGLOIS: THE PHANTOM OF THE CINEMATHEQUE

(Le Fantome D'henri Langlois)

Henri Langlois (1914-1977) is arguably the most important person in the history of film not directly involved in filmmaking. His painstaking creation of the Cinematheque Francaise in Paris helped preserve thousands of films that would otherwise not have survived the ravages of time and war. The availability of these films and Langlois' championing of film as art was a major influence on film history and criticism, especially the auteur theory, and on French New Wave directors.

Jacques Richard's 2004 documentary *Henri Langlois: Phantom of the Cinematheque* traces the development of the Cinematheque Francaise through archival footage of Langlois and his supporters as well as recent interviews with filmmakers, curators, scholars, critics, and bureaucrats. Langlois' quest began in the 1930's with a film club devoted to showing his beloved silent films. His uncanny ability to find and preserve rare films slowly led to the embryo of a national film library. Langlois was helped in this enterprise by several friends, including director Georges Franju and documentary filmmaker Jean Rouch. The humble Rouch never mentions his contribution during his warm reminiscences about Langlois. Neither does anyone mention that film libraries were evolving in other countries at the same time, notably Iris Barry's achievements at New York's Museum of Modern Art.

Richard effectively weaves footage from Langlois' many filmed interviews into the narrative. Langlois, who evolved from a tall, thin youth to an obese middle-aged man with long, uncontrollable hair, offers delightful recollections about his World War II experiences. During the German occupation, he traded films with a sympathetic Nazi, lying about the contents of the harmless films he was giving the enemy.

As engrossing as *Henri Langlois: Phantom of the Cinematheque* is, Richard does not present the full story, being limited to the information conveyed by existing footage and the memories of the interviewees. One of Langlois' most significant achievements was showing his countrymen many of the films they were unable to see during the war. Future film scholars and directors first saw such American films as *Citizen Kane* (1941) at the Cinematheque. Because Langlois' odd policy was to show the films in his collection only once, these screenings, in those days long before videocassettes and DVDs, were often the only chance to see a film.

Being exposed to many films by the same directors in a short period helped critic Andre Bazin and his followers to arrive at the auteur theory, which proposes that the best directors have distinctive styles, revisit favorite themes, and impose their personalities on their work. Auteur critics such as Claude Chabrol, Jean-Luc Godard, and Francois Truffaut were to become internationally acclaimed directors heavily influenced by American films. Langlois' contribution to this evolution is only hinted at in Richard's film. Bazin and the auteur theory are never even mentioned.

Of the generation of French filmmakers indebted to Langlois, only Chabrol, Claude Berri, and Jean Charles Tacchella appear in new interviews, though Godard, Jacques Rivette, Erich Rohmer, and others are seen in archival footage, as are such Hollywood directors as Alfred Hitchcock, Nicholas Ray, and Raoul Walsh. Chabrol, who specializes in dour crime films that often lack the wit of Hitchcock, his main influence, is unexpectedly charming. Langlois had a forty-year relationship with Mary Meerson, widow of art director

Lazare Meerson, but Chabrol cannot envision the overweight, eccentric couple having sex.

The largest section of *Henri Langlois: Phantom of the Cinematheque* is devoted to the efforts of the French government of Charles de Gaulle to fire Langlois in 1968. The government had long offered meager financial support to the Cinematheque, with the institution, which had moved several times into increasingly larger quarters, flourishing through the energies of Langlois and Meerson, who essentially sacrificed their lives to it. Because Langlois kept poor records and his unconventional behavior made him appear disorganized, culture minister Andre Malraux, the novelist best known for *Man's Fate* (1934), decided to replace him with a more traditional bureaucrat.

The de Gaulle government was shocked when filmmakers, actors, artists, academics, and students rallied to Langlois' support with demonstrations that grew increasingly rowdy. Chabrol recalls with considerable amusement that the police appointed him spokesman for the protestors. Richard expertly employs newsreel footage and still photographs to convey the chaos of the weeks of protest, during which Godard was slightly injured by a blow to the face.

Langlois prevailed, though Richard fails to point out that the Langlois protests gave students and others the incentive to demonstrate against other government policies, leading to the nationwide violence of May 1968 that brought down the government. Bernardo Bertolucci shows the connection between these events in *The Dreamers* (2004), but Philippe Garrel, who appears in Richard's film, does not even mention Langlois in *Regular Lovers* (2005), his numbingly tedious account of the May protests.

One of the highlights of *Henri Langlois: Phantom of the Cinematheque* is Langlois' amusement at being called upon to represent the government in bestowing the French Legion of Honor upon Hitchcock. Another is his intense pleasure at receiving an honorary Academy Award in 1974.

Showing and preserving films was not enough for Langlois, and after surviving his crisis, he added a museum to the Cinematheque, acquiring Scarlet O'Hara's dress from *Gone with the Wind* (1939), the mother's skeleton head from *Psycho* (1960), and other costumes, props, and production sketches. After his death, this collection was neglected, and some of it was later destroyed in a fire. The actual fire occurred in another part of the building, and firefighters bombarded the museum with water for no apparent reason. The commentators suggest that the conspiracy against Langlois refused to rest. At times, the first is less a celebration of Langlois than an attack upon French bureaucracy.

Henri Langlois: Phantom of the Cinematheque is fascinating and entertaining, despite some loud, bizarre techno pop during the opening and closing credits, but Richard seems to rely upon the viewer having some background knowledge about the subject for it all to make complete sense. Dipping into Richard Roud's *A Passion for Films: Henri Langlois and the Cinematheque Francaise* (1983), *Henri Langlois: First Citizen of Cinema* (1994) by Glenn Myrent, who appears in the film, or the sections devoted to the Langlois affair in Antoine de Baecque and Serge Toubiana's excellent biography *Truffaut* (1999) will help fill in the gaps. A new Cinematheque Francaise, designed by Frank Gehry, opened in Paris on September 28, 2005. A square in the city has been named for Langlois.

Michael Adams

CREDITS

Language: French
Released: 2004
Directed by: Jacques Richard
Cinematography by: Jerome Blumberg
Music by: Nicolas Baby, Liam Farell
Sound: Francois Didiot
Editing: Fabrice Radenac
MPAA rating: Unrated
Running time: 128 minutes

REVIEWS

New York Times Online. October 12, 2005.
Variety Online. June 2, 2004.

HERBIE: FULLY LOADED

He's back!
—Movie tagline

Box Office: $66 million

Herbie: Fully Loaded came during a summer when there was apparently a dearth of fresh ideas in Hollywood. It seems like the plethora of reality shows on TV would have created a surplus of underemployed writers brimming with great concepts ready to burst forth on-screen, but instead the summer brought a batch of stale remakes of such fare as *The Dukes of Hazzard* .

For its part, Disney was just following a pattern that was working for the studio. Putting Lindsay Lohan in remakes of *The Parent Trap* and *Freaky Friday* made them some money so there was no reason to believe that the same magic would not happen again. The difference with *Herbie* was two-fold. First, *Parent Trap* and *Freaky Friday* were clever and seemed at least marginally inspired by creative thought. Second, those movies were fondly remembered, but did anyone besides Don Knotts still hold a soft spot in their hearts for the hammy 1960s and 70's-era Bug?

Disney's plan was only marginally successful. The popularity of Lohan, boosted by her frequent appearances in the pages of tabloids, helped the film open at number four at the box office, making almost $13 million dollars. Word of mouth was not in the film's favor, however, and in its sixth week, the film only made about $650,000.

In the film, Lohan plays another of her plucky heroines, Maggie Peyton. Maggie comes from a racing dynasty, but because she is female, she is not being groomed to race. Instead, her bumbling brother, Ray Jr. (Breckin Meyer), is about to run the family business into the ground with his poor showings in races. Things start to change when Maggie's father, Ray Sr. (Michael Keaton), gives her $75 to buy a summer car from the junkyard. Herbie, who despite his auspicious past has apparently been left for junk, does everything he can to get Maggie's attention. He sputters oil on people, starts up unexpectedly and slams his doors on folks he does not like. Such humor is either the attraction or repulsion of the film, depending on the viewer's age.

Maggie and her possessed car have various adventures through the movie's hour and 41 minutes. Maggie reconnects with a cute auto mechanic, Kevin (Justin Long) and their relationship follows the dictates of the film's G rating. The bad guy is racing star, Trip Murphy (Matt Dillon), who Maggie angers by beating him in an impromptu street race. So cartoonish is Dillon's character that at the end of the film he is actually dragged away by men in white coats, yelling, "It's possessed, I tell ya!" and loaded up into what the audience may only assume is the modern day version of the crazy wagon. He also has to say many career low-reaching lines like, "I'm going to exterminate that bug." Along the way, Maggie learns to trust in her abilities, her dad realizes that girls can be good drivers, and the audience learns that cars are seemingly capable of lustful feelings. Michael Keaton is another of this film's victims, forced to give fatherly dating advice to Herbie and another comely auto. There is also much mugging by Herbie, who was played by 36 different Volkswagen Beetles. One or another of these Bugs drive on two wheels, pout when upset, and make coy faces. The one nod to the present day is the presence of NASCAR and accompanying cameos by Jeff Gordon and Jimmie Johnson.

Critics were split on the film, with the edge going to those who did not care for it. Ty Burr of *The Boston Globe* was disturbed by the excessive product placement and utter averageness of the film. "Fully Loaded is only interesting on a grown-up level because it isn't just a remake of a Disney movie from the past—it is a Disney movie from the past," he wrote. Peter Hartlaub of *The San Francisco Chronicle* wrote, "The movie is old-school Disney from the Fred MacMurray years, with upstanding moral young people, villains who are more bumbling than scary and the only sexual innuendoes coming between two automobiles." Kenneth Turan of *The Los Angeles Times* wrote that the film, "is that modern rarity, a genial, sweet-natured family film, G-rated and proud of it, an old-fashioned Disney film to the core." Stephen Holden of The New York Times called the film "the perfect silly movie for a silly season that in recent years has forgotten how to be this silly."

Jill Hamilton

CREDITS

Maggie Peyton: Lindsay Lohan
Trip Murphy: Matt Dillon
Kevin: Justin Long
Ray Peyton Jr.: Breckin Meyer
Ray Peyton Sr.: Michael Keaton
Charisma: Jill Ritchie
Sally: Cheryl Hines
Larry Murphy: Thomas Lennon
Crash: Jimmi Simpson
Crazy Dave: Jeremy Roberts
Origin: USA
Language: English
Released: 2005
Production: Robert Simonds; released by Buena Vista
Directed by: Angela Robinson
Written by: Robert Ben Garant, Alfred Gough, Miles Millar, Thomas Lennon
Cinematography by: Greg Gardiner
Music by: Mark Mothersbaugh
Sound: Steve Nelson
Music Supervisor: Howard Paar
Editing: Wendy Greene Bricmont
Art Direction: David Lazan
Costumes: Frank Helmer
Production Design: Daniel Bradford
MPAA rating: G
Running time: 101 minutes

REVIEWS

Boxoffice Online. June, 2005.
Chicago Sun-Times Online. June 22, 2005.

Entertainment Weekly Online. April 19, 2005.
Los Angeles Times Online. June 22, 2005.
New York Times Online. June 22, 2005.
Variety Online. June 19, 2005.
Washington Post Online. June 22, 2005, p. C01.

QUOTES

Maggie Peyton seeing Herbie with a lovestruck expression after he sees a brand new Volkswagen Beetle: "Herbie, she's too young for you."

TRIVIA

Maggie salvages Herbie from a junkyard for $75, the original price Jim Douglas (Dean Jones) offered to pay for "cheap, honest transportation" in *The Love Bug* (1968).

HIDE AND SEEK

Come out come out whatever you are.
—Movie tagline

If you want to know the secret, you have to play the game.
—Movie tagline

Box Office: $51.1 million

Hide and Seek pairs up a couple of prolific actors at opposite ends of their careers in an effective if standard-issue psychological horror film that has become a huge success in video replay after a mediocre run at the box office. Robert De Niro, who's been slumming of late in the *Analyze This* and *Meet the Parents/Fockers* comedies, takes a role that stretches him a little more. And Dakota Fanning, one of the busiest pre-teens in current cinema, plays another threatened waif—but this time with a pleasingly dicey edge of menace.

Under the stewardship of director John Polson, *Hide and Seek* proceeds in highly conventional fashion, with character and plot cues signalled by snatches of a cliched score, swelling to warn us of the approach of menace, whether real or imagined. Fanning's eyes are enhanced so that they look like the wide, glistening eyes of a kid with psychic or devilish powers, and the accomplished young actress plays her with a creepiness that bespeaks an acting prodigy.

There's nothing more than standard-issue B-movie drama here, but there's barely a misstep in execution. De Niro plays David, a child psychologist in what is hinted to be a marriage in trouble. His wife (Amy Irving) kills herself in a bathtub a couple minutes into the movie. The fact that De Niro is plenty old enough to be Amy Irving's father or Fanning's grandfather isn't factored in, of course; this is Hollywood, where you can never be too old to be the leading man. Later on, a character played by Elisabeth Shue practically throws herself at him; De Niro's still handsome enough to make this believable, but barely.

Right from the start, Fanning's character, Emily, looks sinister in the way that possessed or psychic children in such movies always are. She's bug-eyed and says little, glowering menacingly. Fanning gives the character perhaps more depth than the script should allow. She's very skilled at giving off intoxicating and exasperating bite-size pieces of information. Her character is key to the entire plot, and it's crucial that she strikes the right tone, maintaining the appearance of both a threat and victim. Fanning is masterful at it, and to the extent the movie works, it works largely because of her performance.

The plot creaks its way through a host of stereotypical situations. David has been mentor to Katherine (Famke Janssen), a young psychologist, and Emily is apparently her patient and certainly her friend; Katherine gives Emily a music box to remember her by (a device that's been used an endless number of times). After his wife's death, David takes Emily off to a small town in upstate New York, and you know it's a creepy place as soon as you see a shot of the village welcome sign. We are introduced to a host of sinister-seeming characters: the local policeman (a Barney Fife kind of guy, who is strangely familiar with Emily), the owner of the home that David and Emily are renting (very creepy, making weird overtures to Emily), and the couple next door, who have just recently had their own daughter die (the husband is especially creepy, and David warns him to stay away from Emily after he finds them playing outside the house together). These comprise the usual circle of suspects for what we know will be increasingly violent and terrifying encounters.

There's also Shue, a recent divorcee (conveniently enough) with her own daughter, who believes starting something new is the best way to heal the wounds. And most fans of the genre will not be surprised to learn that Emily prefers the company of an imaginary friend, Charlie, who seems to be able to open windows and write messages on shower curtains and tub walls, and who is very upset at David for the death of Emily's mother.

Australian director Polson (*Swimfan, Sirens*) takes this rather trite material and plays it out slowly and deftly, with just the right amount of teasing revelation parceled out. There's nothing too inventive about his choice of shots or his pacing, but almost everything in the film works toward the plot goal, so the movie is at least straightforwardly faithful to the genre. It gets a bit slow toward the middle, but the mystery continues to deepen—who is Charlie and why is he sending such horrible messages and doing such spooky things? At the climax, the revelations come rather quick and hard, and the answer to Charlie's identity shouldn't fool most perceptive fans of thrillers. Polson seems to want to throw a kitchen's sink of terror at audiences during this climax, moving the action to a flooded cave location that has not figured at all in the rest of the plot, and trying to mix in too many menacing traits for the villain. Everything else, though, works marvelously well. *Hide and Seek* has no great aspirations, but it succeeds quite well in what it intends to accomplish.

Along the way, De Niro makes hay playing David weary and quiet, with nary a hint of a crack in his facade. A less veteran actor might have wanted to add some tell-tale ticks or twitches, but De Niro is happy to let David's personality and behavior speak for himself. This performance is a relief after his many recent self-referential and noisy comic and dramatic performances, and it's more in keeping with the entire body of this great actor's work. This film won't be included among his greatest, far from it, but at least he's no longer sending up his own past glories. He's content with a competent workaday turn.

The real mystery is how young Fanning can sleep at night after a couple of years of playing terrified, vulnerable children in *Man on Fire* and *War of the Worlds.* Fanning is already amassing an impressive body of work before she's even hit her teens. You wish that Polson had toned down her bug-eyed creepiness just a tad in this film, but Fanning knows how to milk emotions out of her plight as well or better than most of her much more mature acting colleagues. That bodes well for her future, and she is certainly getting plenty of choice roles. How many actresses can say they've co-starred with Tom Cruise and Robert De Niro in the same year?

Michael Betzold

CREDITS

David Callaway: Robert De Niro
Emily Callaway: Dakota Fanning
Katherine: Famke Janssen
Elizabeth: Elisabeth Shue
Alison Callaway: Amy Irving
Sheriff Hafferty: Dylan Baker
Laura: Melissa Leo
Steven: Robert John Burke
Mr. Haskins: David Chandler
Amy: Molly Grant Kallins
Origin: USA
Language: English
Released: 2005
Production: Barry Josephson; Josephson Entertainment; released by 20th Century-Fox
Directed by: John Polson
Written by: Ari Schlossberg
Cinematography by: Darius Wolski
Music by: John Ottman
Sound: Tom Nelson
Editing: Jeffrey Ford
Art Direction: Dennis Bradford, Emily Beck
Costumes: Aude Bronson-Howard
Production Design: Steven Jordan
MPAA rating: R
Running time: 100 minutes

REVIEWS

Boxoffice Online. January, 2005.
Chicago Sun-Times Online. January 28, 2005.
Entertainment Weekly Online. January 26, 2005.
Los Angeles Times Online. January 28, 2005.
New York Times Online. January 28, 2005.
Premiere Magazine Online. January 28, 2005.
Variety Online. January 27, 2005.
Washington Post Online. January 28, 2005, p. WE39.

QUOTES

Dr. Katherine Carson: "It's not unusual for a child to create an imaginary friend."

TRIVIA

For the first time in 70 years, 20th Century Fox shipped prints of *Hide and Seek,* without the final reel, which was shipped separately to ensure the final ending would not be revealed. Security guards then hand-delivered the individually numbered reel to theaters showing the film.

HIGH TENSION

(Haute tension)

Hearts will bleed.
—Movie tagline

Box Office: $3.7 million

A French horror film inspired by '70s American classics like *The Texas Chain Saw Massacre* and *Halloween, High Tension* is a mundane slasher flick completely undone by the most illogical twist ending in recent memory. Directed by Alexandre Aja from a screenplay he cowrote with Grégory Levasseur, *High Tension* is full of grisly murders, buckets of blood, and repetitious scenes of the young heroine being chased by a fearsome killer whose only motive appears to be destruction for its own sake.

High Tension revolves around two girlfriends, Marie (Cécile de France) and Alex (Maïwenn), whose plan to study for exams is upended by a madman's killing spree. While the movie is a French import, some of the dialogue is dubbed (very badly) in an obvious concession to young American moviegoers, the target demographic for this kind of film and one that abhors subtitles. Thus, Alex has been transformed into an American for the American release, and when Marie is with Alex and her family, they speak English. It is a jarring and silly choice, especially given the fact that there is very little dialogue in the film as a whole.

But the movie's overarching problem is not the dubbing but a lack of imagination. *High Tension* has a by-the-book plot in which a generic, nameless killer (Philippe Nahon) invades the family farmhouse and summarily kills Alex's father (decapitation), mother (razor to the throat), and little brother (gunshot in the cornfield). Alex is abducted, shackled and gagged, and taken away in a rusty truck, which the tough Marie, who eludes the killer's rampage, is able to stow away in so that she can engage him in a game of cat and mouse.

Aja maintains a modicum of suspense but seems to be more interested in shocking the audience with gruesome murders and plenty of gore (so much that about one minute of film had to be trimmed to secure an R rating in America). A stop at a gas station, for example, culminates in the clerk getting an ax in his chest—practically a prerequisite for the genre—but such a scene feels like a contrived way of upping the body count. Moreover, while the killer has no reason to leave an even bigger trail of carnage, the plot needs the murder so that the police can later view the store's video recording and find out the identity of the killer.

This revelation turns out to be a ludicrous, nonsensical plot twist. On the tape, we (along with the police) discover that Marie killed the clerk. Then, in a series of flashbacks, we see that she was really the one who killed Alex's family as well. It turns out that the male killer does not really exist at all but stands for some kind of physical manifestation of Marie's lesbian fixation on Alex. This plot turn, however, cheats the audience. If Marie is the killer, what are we to make of scenes of her hiding under the bed as Alex's family is slaughtered or in the back of the killer's truck as she seeks to rescue her friend? How can Marie engage him in a chase after stealing the gas attendant's car? None of this really happened, rendering the majority of what we have seen a big lie.

In the beginning, Marie tells Alex about a dream in which she discovered that she was chasing herself, a seemingly throwaway incident that becomes the key to the film, a roundabout way of foreshadowing that Marie is the real killer. Other early scenes, like one of Marie berating her friend's choice of men and another of Marie surreptitiously watching Alex showering, clue us in to her lesbian attraction, but nothing suggests that Marie is a psychotic killer. More important, because their friendship means nothing to us, Marie's unrequited love means even less.

If a filmmaker is going to fool the audience, then he at least needs to follow narrative and physical logic. Alfred Hitchcock, for example, did not show Mother as a real, living person interacting with characters besides Norman in *Psycho*—everything in that film could have happened—whereas Aja creates practically an entire movie that, in retrospect, is filled with impossible scenes.

Even if one tries to discount the dishonesty at the film's core, *High Tension* does nothing exciting or original with the genre up to the big reversal. Indeed, it indulges all the clichés of the maniac-on-the-loose formula. When the killer is chasing the heroine through the woods with a buzz saw (by this time, Aja is intercutting shots of the male killer with shots of Marie to show that they are the same person), the link to *The Texas Chain Saw Massacre* is obvious. The deranged heroine herself is a cliché since repressed sexual desire and lesbian killers are staples of the thriller, and Marie, sporting a short, androgynous haircut and wielding a big, phallic-looking piece of wood with barbed wire on the end, fits the stereotype perfectly.

In the climactic showdown, Alex turns on Marie (after all, Alex knows from the beginning that Marie is the killer) and is finally able to stab her with a crowbar. But somehow Marie survives and ends up in a mental institution, where the movie began. Of course, in the opening scene, we did not realize where Marie was, but her hypnotic repetition of the words "I won't let anyone come between us anymore" should have been a clue to her nature. Since her sexual impulses are hinted at from the outset, the film's big secret is not a complete shock. Indeed, the screenplay's trajectory possesses a certain psychological coherence, if only Aja had expressed it in a way that actually worked dramatically.

When awful dubbing is the least of a movie's problems, that movie has to be in big trouble. *High Tension* is ugly and finally pointless, managing to fail on two different levels—as a routine slasher film, it slavishly repeats old conventions and, in its ridiculous surprise ending, completely loses whatever credibility it may have mustered with die-hard genre fans.

Peter N. Chumo II

CREDITS

Marie: Cecile de France
Alexia: Maiwenn Le Besco

The Killer: Philippe Nahon
Jimmy: Franck Khalfoun
Alexia's father: Andrei Finti
Alexia's mother: Oana Pellea
Tom: Marco Claudiu Pascu
Origin: France
Language: English, French
Released: 2003
Production: Alexandre Arcady, Robert Benmussa; Europacorp, Alexandre Films; released by Europacorp
Directed by: Alexandre Aja
Written by: Alexandre Aja, Gregory Levasseur
Cinematography by: Maxime Alexandre
Music by: Francois Eudes
Sound: Pierre Andre, Didier Lozahic, Emmanuel Augeard
Production Design: Gregory Levasseur
MPAA rating: R
Running time: 91 minutes

REVIEWS

Chicago Sun-Times Online. June 9, 2005.
Entertainment Weekly Online. June 8, 2005.
Los Angeles Times Online. June 10, 2005.
New York Times Online. June 10, 2005.
Premiere Magazine Online. June 9, 2005.
Variety Online. July 8, 2003.
Washington Post Online. June 10, 2005, p. C04.

QUOTES

Marie: "I won't let anyone come between us any more."

TRIVIA

To prepare for the physically demanding role, Cecile de France trained with a Thai boxer.

A HISTORY OF VIOLENCE

Everyone has something to hide.
—Movie tagline

Tom Stall had the perfect life...until he became a hero.
—Movie tagline

Box Office: $31.1 million

A History of Violence is one of those films that fester in the subconscious for days as the mind tries to distill a personal meaning. While the film may initially seem like a simple meditation on the effects of violence on small-town America, it is actually an intense and superbly well-made study of the human predisposition towards violence. Director David Cronenberg has crafted not only an engaging thriller but also a biting commentary on the construct of aggression and the effects of an accompanying loss of identity.

Tom Stall (Viggo Mortensen) leads the quintessential midwestern American life. He is the well-liked proprietor of the local diner in Millbrook, Indiana, who is married to the beautiful and adoring Edie (Maria Bello). Their perfect family unit is rounded out by son Jack (Ashton Holmes) and daughter Sarah (Heidi Hayes). Tom lives, as one character observes, the "American Dream." This envious life begins to change, however, when he thwarts an attempted robbery at the diner in an unexpectedly violent manner. Now a reluctant hero, Tom's exploits become a national story. He is subsequently confronted by the mysterious Carl Fogarty (Ed Harris), who says that Tom is not who he claims to be and that he might have a less-than-honorable past. Despite Tom's adamant denials, Fogarty begins to shadow members of the family. When finally confronted by Tom's wife, Fogarty suggests that she ask Tom "how come he's so good at killing people." Suddenly the Stall's idyllic existence is shattered as Edie begins questioning whether Tom is in fact hiding some secret past, and the entire family is thrown into a downward spiral of distrust and uncertainty. The family unit begins to disintegrate as Tom wrestles with the true nature and purpose of his identity.

Exceptional performances by both Mortensen and Bello make the Stalls an engaging couple. Both turn in some of their finest work to date. Mortensen's Tom is an empathetic everyman turned uncomfortable hero. The character's fall from grace is made all the more poignant by Mortensen's understated performance. Bello's devoted wife is the perfect blend of passion and hesitance as her confidence in the man she loves is shaken. Equally impressive are Holmes and Hayes as the Stall children. Ed Harris is intriguing as the deplorable Fogarty, and William Hurt delivers one of his more unnervingly honest performances. The high caliber of acting in the film clearly solidifies Roger Ebert's claim in the *Chicago Sun-Times* that "this is not a movie about plot, but about character." Of course the success of each is predicated on the other. The symbiotic relationship between character and plot is the perfect vehicle for the film's motifs; when characters are thrust into unfamiliar and disquieting situations, the viewer is forced to experience the film likewise.

Loosely adapted from the graphic novel by John Wagner and Vince Locke, Josh Olson's engaging script is a well-constructed pseudo-revenge tale that refrains from the usual violent fantasies associated with the genre. This is an emotional story that proves as traumatic for the viewer as it is for the characters. When Fogarty arrives and Tom's identity is questioned, Tom suddenly finds himself at odds with the life he is living. The schism of identity is a theme that director Cronenberg has examined in many of his films. In the narratives of such films as *Naked Lunch*, *Spider*, or *Videodrome*, exposition is delivered from the point of view of a protagonist whose believability is suspect. Whether it's Bill Lee's drug-induced Interzone in *Naked Lunch*, or Dennis Cleg's schizophrenic recollections in *Spider*, or even Max Renn's sadomasochistic fantasies in *Videodrome*, all of these films question the perception of identity by subverting an already established reality. What makes Cronenberg's use of this tack in *A History of Violence* so disconcerting is Tom's idealized character and life. Consequently, when the happy equilibrium of Tom's existence is disturbed and his identity begins to unravel, the uneasiness felt by the viewer stems not from a fondness for Tom or a steadfast belief in his character, but from an uncertainty of one's own moral fiber. In this way, as they watch their adopted lives crumble, the viewer's feelings of confusion and loss mirror the Stall's.

Cronenberg depicts Millbrook as the kind of pastoral town that in some way appeals to every American. This serves to make the disintegration of the Stall's life all the more tragic for a viewer who has so readily identified with them. The town itself is given an ethereal quality by the production design of Carol Spier; yet there is something a bit off in this midwestern hamlet (while the film is set in middle-America, it was actually shot in Canada). It is almost too perfect. However, as the film shifts from its storybook beginning to an edgier, dark tone, we see a corresponding change in the look of the film (and characters for that matter). The photography of longtime Cronenberg collaborator Peter Suschitzky is highly effective at creating a believably enticing world and then just as easily deconstructing it.

On the surface, *A History of Violence* examines what Kenneth Turan describes in the *Los Angeles Times* as the "corrosive effects of violence." However, Cronenberg is also exploring the predisposition for violence within all of us and, as Turan postulates further, "how that affects both individuals and the culture as a whole." This forces the consideration of the question Desson Thomson poses in the *Washington Post*: "Is killing excused by moral imperative?" The answer to that question is as personal and obtuse as Tom Stall's crisis of identity. Ultimately the film settles on two conclusions, as noted by Lisa Schwarzbaum in *Entertainment Weekly*: "violence begets violence" and "perception is reality."

Michael J. Tyrkus

CREDITS

Tom Stall: Viggo Mortensen
Edie Stall: Maria Bello
Richie Cusack: William Hurt
Leland Jones: Stephen McHattie
Sheriff Sam Carney: Peter MacNeill
Carl Fogarty: Ed Harris
Jack Stall: Ashton Holmes
Sarah Stall: Heidi Hayes
Origin: USA
Language: English
Released: 2005
Production: Chris Bender, JC Spink; Benderspink; released by New Line Cinema
Directed by: David Cronenberg
Written by: Josh Olson
Cinematography by: Peter Suschitzsky
Music by: Howard Shore
Sound: Glen Gauthier
Editing: Ronald Sanders
Art Direction: James McAteer
Costumes: Denise Cronenberg
Production Design: Carol Spier
MPAA rating: R
Running time: 96 minutes

REVIEWS

Boxoffice Online. September, 2005.
Chicago Sun-Times Online. September 23, 2005.
Entertainment Weekly Online. September 28, 2005.
Los Angeles Times Online. September 23, 2005.
New York Times Online. September 23, 2005.
Variety Online. May 16, 2005.
Washington Post Online. September 23, 2005, p. C04.

QUOTES

Carl Fogarty: "You should ask Tom…how come he's so good at killing people? "

TRIVIA

The names given to the bad guys at the beginning of the film, Leland and Orser, are a reference to character actor Leland Orser, the perpetrator of "Lust" in 1995's *Se7en.*

AWARDS

L.A. Film Critics 2005: Support. Actor (Hurt)

N.Y. Film Critics 2005: Support. Actor (Hurt), Support. Actress (Bello)

Natl. Soc. Film Critics 2005: Director (Cronenberg), Support. Actor (Harris)

Nomination:

Oscars 2005: Adapt. Screenplay, Support. Actor (Hurt)

British Acad. 2005: Adapt. Screenplay

Golden Globes 2006: Actress—Drama (Bello), Film—Drama

Writers Guild 2005: Adapt. Screenplay

Broadcast Film Critics 2005: Support. Actress (Bello).

HITCH

The cure for the common man.
—Movie tagline

Box Office: $177 million

Ty Burr of *The Boston Globe* wrote that silly Hollywood romances exist "because they feel good and because they make us forget about death." Perhaps moviegoers were not lining up for *Hitch* specifically to quell their thoughts of death, but *Hitch* sold a lot of tickets. In addition to temporarily stifling their feelings of mortality, moviegoers saw a movie that was nice-looking, modestly witty, and featured the formidable charms of Will Smith in what, it is hard to believe, was his first romantic comedy lead.

In the film, Alex Hitchens (Smith), known to all as Hitch, is a date doctor in New York City. His services, which are secret and by referral only, involve giving nerdy men the right moves to win the woman of their dreams. The film, written by Kevin Bisch and directed by Andy Tennant, takes great pains to point out that Hitch's business is in no way sleazy. His clients are all genuinely nice guys who want to settle down, but just do not know how to behave around a woman. When one guy tries to enlist Hitch's help in charming a woman for a one-night stand, Hitch refuses and punches him for good measure.

Hitch's latest challenge is a nebbishy accountant, Albert (Kevin James), who has his heart set on one of his firm's clients, the lovely Allegra (Amber Valletta). Allegra is famous and beautiful, but Hitch's magic is so potent that she will start noticing Albert and even falling for him. Hitch's advice, which probably would not retain its potency in the real world, includes acting really nice to the woman's best friend and standing up straight.

The reason Hitch knows so much about how to behave around a woman is because he, too, was once one of these nerdy guys. When his first love dumped him for being too clingy, he made a point of learning exactly how to act to keep a woman interested. He uses his knowledge in his own relationships but takes care never to fall in love so he does not get hurt again. Thus, according to movie conventions, he is ripe to fall in love. And, as it happens, so is Sara (Eva Mendes), a gossip columnist with a paper called *The New York Standard.* Sara, who is gorgeous, is disdainful of the multitude of men who are always trying to pick her up. Instead of getting involved with romance, she throws herself into work.

Naturally, these two must meet and, conveniently, they do. The personal charm of the actors playing these roles makes the film seem a lot better than it might have been. When the two meet in a bar, they banter about how Hitch might be behave were he indeed picking her up. It is a rare romantic comedy that allows itself to slow down and enjoy its characters using and enjoying witty language. Best are the scenes in which Hitch's well-laid dating plans go awry. When he takes Sara jet-skiing in the New York Harbor his boat runs out of gas and he accidentally kicks Sara in the head. On another date, Hitch has an allergic reaction to some restaurant food and his face swells up hideously. One critic called Smith's willingness to look so deformed "brave." Perhaps brave is too strong a word, but there is a certain enjoyment in seeing someone as suave as Smith looking so bad. Less successful and too cute are scenes in which Hitch addresses the camera directly to explain the movie. This movie is not the sort that needs any sort of explanation.

Moviegoers liked the film and critics, perhaps exhausted by the onslaught of bad movies unleashed in January, did too. Carla Meyer of *The San Francisco Chronicle* wrote, "*Hitch* has served up a duo we didn't know we were missing: well-drawn, sharp, gorgeous characters of color in a big-budget romantic comedy." Critics who did not care for the movie generally made a point that Smith was indeed charming. David Ansen of *Newsweek* called Smith "a natural" and wrote, "He breezes though the role with his characteristic mix of playful braggadocio and sweet self-deprecation." Owen Gleiberman of *Entertainment Weekly* gave the film a C, but wrote that Smith "certainly shows a gift for modulation." He wrote, "Far from coasting, he plays a world expert at romance by ratcheting his charm up and down in supple, exacting degrees."

Jill Hamilton

CREDITS

Hitch: Will Smith

Sara: Eva Mendes

Allegra: Amber Valletta

Ben: Michael Rapaport

Max: Adam Arkin
Albert: Kevin James
Casey: Julie Ann Emery
Origin: USA
Language: English
Released: 2005
Production: James Lassiter, Will Smith, Teddy Zee; Overbrook Entertainment; released by Sony Pictures Entertainment
Directed by: Andy Tennant
Written by: Kevin Bisch
Cinematography by: Andrew Dunn
Music by: George Fenton
Sound: T.J. O'Mara
Editing: Troy Takaki, Tracey Wadmore-Smith
Art Direction: Patricia Woodbridge
Costumes: Marlene Stewart
Production Design: Jane Musky
MPAA rating: PG-13
Running time: 119 minutes

REVIEWS

Boxoffice Online. February, 2005.
Chicago Sun-Times Online. February 11, 2005.
Entertainment Weekly Online. February 9, 2005.
Los Angeles Times Online. February 11, 2005.
New York Times Online. February 11, 2005.
Premiere Magazine Online. February 11, 2005.
Variety Online. February 4, 2005.
Washington Post Online. February 11, 2005, p. WE44.

QUOTES

Hitch: "May you never lie, steal, cheat or drink. But if you must lie, lie in each other's arms. If you must steal, steal a kiss. If you must cheat, cheat death. And if you must drink, drink with your friends."

TRIVIA

The fire station shown at the beginning of the film is Hook and Ladder No. 8, the same firehouse used in *Ghostbusters* (1984).

THE HITCHHIKER'S GUIDE TO THE GALAXY

Don't Panic!
—Movie tagline

Don't leave Earth without it.
—Movie tagline

The most astonishing adventure in the universe begins when the world ends.
—Movie tagline

Everything you need to know about out there, is in here.
—Movie tagline

The answers to what's out there are in here.
—Movie tagline

Losing your planet isn't the end of the world.
—Movie tagline

Box Office: $51 million

Go to any comic book or science fiction convention in the world, stop the first person you see, and ask, "What's the answer to life, the universe, and everything?" Without a doubt, you'll be greeted with a resounding chorus of "42," an oddly humorous non sequitur that speaks to the universal popularity of the late Douglas Adams' 1979 cult classic novel *The Hitchhiker's Guide to the Galaxy.* One of the most famous works of sci-fi absurdism of the past twenty-five years, *The Hitchhiker's Guide* has spawned four sequels, plays, video games, a BBC television and radio adaptation, as well as endless web pages and fan clubs. Hollywood producers have been attempting to adapt Adams' best-selling novel since its initial publication—Adams once famously complained that Ivan Reitman wanted to turn the *Hitchhiker's* movie into "*Star Wars* with jokes"—but none succeeded until Hammer & Tongs, a UK production house known for their music videos, were chosen by Touchstone Pictures to bring the *Hitchhiker's Guide* to the big-screen in 2005.

Fortunately, Hammer & Tongs' director Garth Jennings meshed well with Adams' uniquely skewed sensibilities (the *Hitchhiker's* screenplay was authored by Adams and *Chicken Run* scribe Karey Kirkpatrick), and the result was one of the most bizarrely compelling comedies ever released by the Disney Corporation. And while every aspect of the film, from set design to sound editing, works as a loving tribute to Adams' innovative creation (the author died unexpectedly just before the film began production), that unfettered reverence speaks to both the *Hitchhiker's Guide's* greatest strength and its greatest weakness—Jennings' occasionally slavish devotion to Adams' original text.

Still, it's hard to fault a movie that opens with a chorus line of singing dolphins, acting out a Busby Berkeley-style musical number called "So Long and Thanks for All the Fish." The scene is a marvelous expansion of a two-sentence joke from the opening of Adams' novel, and it truly speaks to Jennings' understanding of the *Hitchhiker's* sense of humor. Once the dolphins stop singing, we're introduced to Arthur Dent (Martin Freeman), a beleaguered English everyman who wakes up to find that the local government is trying to tear down his house to make room for a new expressway. Arthur lies in front of the bulldozers in protest, until his oddball friend Ford Prefect (Mos Def) arrives and urgently announces that he must take Arthur to the local pub. After gaining Arthur's house a temporary reprieve, the two friends head into town, where Arthur moans about losing the girl of his dreams, Tricia (Zooey Deschanel), whom he met at a costume party weeks earlier.

After a few drinks, Ford unleashes a major revelation—he is not a struggling actor, as he's always claimed. He's actually an alien researcher for an intergalactic travel guidebook (think of *Fodor's* for the Universe) called *The Hitchhiker's Guide to the Galaxy*. And if that wasn't strange enough, Ford just found out that the planet Earth is scheduled to be demolished to make room for a hyperspace expressway. The disbelieving Arthur returns to his now-destroyed house in time to witness a fleet of Vogon construction ships blanket the sky. After making an announcement (in which the Vogon captain chides humanity for not keeping up on galactic current affairs), the Vogons blow up the Earth, with Ford and Arthur "hitchhiking" off of the planet on a Vogon transporter beam at the last possible second.

It sounds like the plot of a Michael Bay action spectacular, but Adams and Kirkpatrick's script presents the Earth's destruction as such a blatant result of unrepentant bureaucracy that it's hard not to laugh. At this point, we're introduced to the *Hitchhiker's Guide* as both a physical object and as a narrator—Jennings uses the interactive guidebook as a means to convey narrative information and allow actor Stephen Fry (the voice of the Guide) to read passages verbatim from Adam's novel. His narration is also accompanied by cartoons by the UK animation firm Shynola, which gleefully bring Adams' text to life.

After their hitchhike, Ford and Arthur find themselves on one of the construction ships, where they're quickly captured the Vogon security forces. The Vogons represent one of the *Hitchhiker's Guide's* most inspired examples of character design; the Jim Henson Company created the aliens to resemble over-inflated slimy balloons with ridiculously small arms and faces. After Prostetnic Vogon Jeltz tortures Ford and Arthur with a poetry reading—a recurring joke from the original novel—the two friends are thrown off the ship into the vacuum of space. Amazingly, they're somehow rescued at the last minute by a bizarre sphere-shaped spaceship called the Heart of Gold. As Ford and Arthur debate the unlikelihood of their rescue, they meet Marvin the Paranoid Android (brilliantly deadpan-voiced by Alan Rickman), a robot with a built-in personality disorder, who orders both men to accompany him to the bridge.

On the bridge, Ford and Arthur discover another amazing coincidence—the ship is piloted by Tricia (who now calls herself Trillian) and Ford's cousin, Zaphod Beeblebrox (Sam Rockwell), the President of the Galaxy. The Heart of Gold, again, speaks to Jennings' skill with design. While such a space-faring tale could have been overladen with computer-generated imagery, Jennings uses more practical effects—for example, Marvin is just actor Warwick Davis in a iMac-inspired robot suit. Also, while Zaphod had two heads and three arms in Adams' novel, Jennings comes up with fairly clever reasons to keep the extra appendages hidden and, thus, keeps the actors from being overwhelmed by the FX.

An unrepentant egomaniac, Zaphod stole Trillian from Arthur on a visit to Earth and is now on the run from the authorities after stealing the Heart of Gold. He swiped the ship because it's powered by an Infinite Improbability Drive, a quantum engine that takes the ship through every conceivable point in the universe at the same time to reach its location. Zaphod is searching for a planet called Magrathea, where a super-computer called Deep Thought was built to calculate the Ultimate Answer to Life, the Universe, and Everything. When Deep Thought answered "42," another computer was built to calculate the Ultimate *Question* to Life, the Universe, and Everything. Zaphod wants the Question for fame and fortune, and Trillian is just along for the ride.

However, without proper coordinates, the Heart of Gold can't find Magrathea, and when Zaphod hits the Infinite Improbability Drive, the ship inexplicably arrives at Viltvodle VI, the home planet of Zaphod's most hated political rival, Humma Kavula (John Malkovich), a new character created by Adams especially for the movie. Kavula offers to give Zaphod the coordinates for Magrathea, but only if he brings back the Point-of-View Gun (a gun that makes others share your opinions), another creation of Deep Thought's. After giving Kavula Zaphod's second head as insurance, the Heart of Gold crew returns to the ship, only to be ambushed by Vogons. The Vogons kidnap Trillian and take her back to their home planet, Vogshere, and the still-smitten Arthur insists they mount a rescue. This leads to one of the film's more hilarious sequences, in which Arthur uses his experience negotiating English governmental bureaucracy to save Trillian from the paperwork-obsessed Vogons.

Once they've escaped Vogsphere, Arthur and his compatriots finally reach Magrathea. While Trillian, Ford, and Zaphod try to obtain the Question from Deep Thought, Arthur encounters a Magrathean scientist named Slartibartfast (Bill Nighy), who explains to him the origins of the planet Earth—it was a custom-made, planet-sized computer built by Deep Thought to calculate the Ultimate Question. Now that the Vogons have destroyed the Earth, the last remnants of the Question reside in Arthur's brain, and two inter-dimensional beings (posing as white mice) will stop at nothing to have it. And to make matters worse, the Vogons have tracked Zaphod and the Heart of Gold to Magrathea and they've landed with guns blazing.

The Vogsphere and Point-of-View Gun subplots are two of the biggest diversions from the original *Hitchhiker's* text and, as such, both storylines feel oddly tacked on and unnecessary. Jennings also introduces a romance between Arthur and Trillian which he presents in such a sentimental, Richard Curtis-esque fashion that it completely clashes with the self-aware satire of Adams' comedic voice. This clash of narrative voices is a consistent thread throughout the *Hitchhiker's Guide,* particularly because the screenwriters so frequently quote large passages from the original novel. While the quoted text is well written and reminds viewers why so many have embraced Adams' novels, it doesn't sound like movie dialogue. And it's hard to establish believable conflict when you have two characters reading books at each other.

Despite Jennings' difficulties at balancing new material with the canonical Adams text, the actors do a truly skillful job at imbuing their characters with life and personality. Known best from the BBC series *The Office,* Freeman has amazing depth as an intergalactic straight man, and Def brings an unusual and wholly original sense of timing to Ford Prefect. As Zaphod, Rockwell acts for the cheap seats, screaming, laughing, and squawking as he plays the President of the Galaxy as an unholy mixture between Elvis and George W. Bush.

And while the ending of *Hitchhiker's Guide* is particularly unsatisfying—multiple dangling plot threads are virtually ignored—it also oddly resembles the tone of Adams' *Hitchhiker* novels, which specialized in unresolved story tangents. On a whole, Adams fans will adore Jennings' lovingly-rendered film version of *The Hitchhiker's Guide to the Galaxy*, while casual viewers will, at the very least, appreciate the quirkiness and originality of every aspect of the production. While *Hitchhiker's Guide* might not be the most coherent sci-fi movie in recent memory, it's definitely one of the most interesting.

Tom Burns

CREDITS

Arthur Dent: Martin Freeman
Ford Perfect: Mos Def
Zephod Beeblebrox: Sam Rockwell
Trillian: Zooey Deschanel
Humma Kavula: John Malkovich
Slartibartfast: Bill Nighy
Marvin: Warwick Davis
Ghostly Image: Simon Jones
Questular Rontok: Anna Chancellor
Barman: Albie Woodington
Gag Halfrunt: Jason Schwartzman
Fook: Dominique Jackson
Lunkwill: Jack Stanley
Voice of Marvin: Alan Rickman (Voice)
Eddie the Computer: Thomas Lennon (Voice)
Voice of Deep Thought: Helen Mirren (Voice)
Narrator: Stephen Fry (Voice)
Jeltz: Richard Griffiths (Voice)
Kwaltz: Ian McNeice (Voice)
Origin: Great Britain, USA
Language: English
Released: 2005
Production: Gary Barber, Roger Birnbaum, Jay Roach, Jonathan Glickman, Nick Goldsmith; Everyman Pictures, Barber Birnbaum; released by Buena Vista
Directed by: Garth Jennings
Written by: Douglas Adams, Karey Kilpatrick
Cinematography by: Igor Jadue-Lillo
Music by: Joby Talbot
Editing: Niven Howie
Costumes: Sammy Sheldon
Production Design: Joel Collins
MPAA rating: PG
Running time: 110 minutes

REVIEWS

Boxoffice Online. April, 2005.
Chicago Sun-Times Online. April 28, 2005.
Entertainment Weekly Online. April 30, 2005.
Los Angeles Times Online. April 29, 2005.
New York Times Online. April 29, 2005.
Premiere Magazine Online. April 29, 2005.
Variety Online. April 23, 2005.
Washington Post Online. April 29, 2005, p. WE45.

QUOTES

Vogon Kwaltz: "Attention, people of Earth. I regret to inform you that in order to make way for the new hyperspace express route, your planet has been scheduled for demolition. Have a nice day."

TRIVIA

This film marks the ninth incarnation of the *Hitchhiker's Guide,* which previously appeared as a radio series, a record album, a novel, a television series, a computer game, a stage show, a comic book, and a towel.

THE HONEYMOONERS

Dream big. Scheme bigger.
—Movie tagline

Box Office: $12.8 million

Any remake of a show as well-remembered as Jackie Gleason's *The Honeymooners* is bound to be subject to undue scrutiny. No matter what, it would be impossible to create a remake that would be able to please all of the show's fans. What is surprising about this version, directed by John Schultz, is that it does not even seem to try. That means, if nothing else, that it does not require a viewer to be at all familiar with the series. It is equally displeasing to *Honeymooners* fans, non-fans, and people who have never heard of the series.

Ralph Kramden (Cedric the Entertainer, taking the Gleason role) is still a bus driver and he still verbally spars with wife Alice (Gabrielle Union in the Audrey Meadows role), but his frequent threats of sending Alice "to the moon" have been replaced by a romantic offer to take her there. No one is advocating the return of the verbal abuse, but without that, the focus is on Ralph and his zany get-rich-quick schemes. Whatever movie a film is, or is not, based on, the idea of trying to get rich by selling animal print "man purses" is not going to be that funny.

The dynamic between Ralph and Alice is less ripe for comedy than for couples' counseling. Alice is trying to save money for her dream of buying a house—preferably one not next to a railroad track, as their present apartment is. Meanwhile Ralph wastes what little savings they have on his harebrained ideas. Worse, he does not consult her about his plans, so she is unaware that their hard-earned savings are gone. Union's Alice seems like a sap. Why would such a woman waste her time on a schlub such as Ralph? Making boneheaded business moves is one thing; wasting tens of thousands of dollars, repeatedly, on schemes like the pet cactus or Y2K survival kit starts to head toward the territory of pathology.

The money that Ralph is wasting in this installment (which hopefully will remain the only installment) was earmarked for a down payment on a charming duplex that Alice wants to buy with neighbors Ed Norton (Mike Epps) and his wife, Trixie (Regina Hall). They need to come up with a down payment of $20,000 quickly or else a mean developer, William Davis (Eric Stoltz), will buy up the building and build pricey condos. Ralph, naturally, tries to come up with the money by trying new schemes involving a racing greyhound found in a dumpster and trolley bought at an auction. The results make for a film that lasts only 90 minutes, but seems a lot longer.

The movie's failures do not lie with the actors. They all tackle their roles with great enthusiasm, but it somehow never all comes together. Cedric the Entertainer is sweetly blustery as the eternally optimistic Ralph. Epps has played the dimwitted sidekick roll plenty of times and does a repeat performance of his usual shtick. Union and Hall are good when they are together, especially during their snappy verbal jousts with Davis over the house. Also good is Carol Woods as Alice's mother. She does nothing to disguise her disgust of her daughter's choice in husbands and she does a good job dressing down her son-in-law. Less successful is John Leguizamo as dog trainer, Dodge. His peripheral character takes up way too much screen time and is quickly annoying.

It was hard for *The Honeymooners* to find any fans among movie critics. Amy Biancolli of *The Houston Chronicle* was clear in her distaste for the movie and awarded it one out of a possible four stars. "A film like *The Honeymooners* is enough to plunge one into a state of pitch-black existential despair." Wesley Morris of *The Boston Globe* agreed. "*The Honeymooners* is a kindergartner's movie. It's loaded with Cedric's and Epps's exaggerated (not to mention crudely filmed) expressions and one inane pratfall after the next." Teresa Wiltz of *The Washington Post* complimented the assembled talent, but added, "Too bad it's left to fend for itself against a raging mechanical bull of a script. They mug maniacally, tap-dancing around one-liners on cue, but never manage to elicit real belly laughs." A. O. Scott of *The New York Times* was vaguely complimentary, writing, "Superfluous though it may be, *The Honeymooners* is not so bad." And Roger Ebert of *The Chicago Sun-Times* found himself pleasantly surprised by the film. "Sometimes you walk into a movie with quiet dread and walk out with quiet delight."

Jill Hamilton

CREDITS

Ralph Kramden: Cedric the Entertainer

Ed Norton: Mike Epps

Alice Kramden: Gabrielle Union

Trixie Norton: Regina Hall

Dodge: John Leguizamo

Kirby: Jon Polito

William Davis: Eric Stoltz

Alice's Mom: Carol Woods

Vivek: Ajay Naidu

Quinn: Kim Chan

Origin: USA

Language: English

Released: 2005

Production: David T. Friendly, Marc Turtletaub, Eric C. Rhone, Julie Durk; Deep River; released by Paramount Pictures

Directed by: John Schultz

Written by: Don Rhymer, Barry W. Blaustein, David Sheffield, Danny Jacobson, Barry W. Blaustein

Cinematography by: Shawn Maurer
Music by: Richard Gibbs
Sound: Kieran Horgan
Music Supervisor: Jennifer Hawks
Editing: John Pace
Art Direction: Colman Corish
Costumes: Joan Bergin
Production Design: Charles Wood
MPAA rating: PG-13
Running time: 90 minutes

REVIEWS

Boxoffice Online. June, 2005.
Chicago Sun-Times Online. June 9, 2005.
Entertainment Weekly Online. June 8, 2005.
Los Angeles Times Online. June 10, 2005.
New York Times Online. June 10, 2005.
Premiere Magazine Online. 2005.
Variety Online. June 9, 2005.
Washington Post Online. June 10, 2005, p. WE33.

QUOTES

Ralph Kramden: "One of these days, you're gonna push me too far."
Alice Kramden: "The only thing that could push you is a bulldozer!"

TRIVIA

Alice's mom says the line "Who does he think he is, Fred Flintstone?" when Alice tells her that Ralph is at the lodge—a reference to the fact that the TV show *The Flintstones* was actually based on the original *The Honeymooners* (1955).

HOSTAGE

Would you sacrifice another family to save your own?
—Movie tagline

On March 11th there will be no negotiation.
—Movie tagline

The opening scene of *Hostage* is so by-the-numbers, it almost seems like a joke. Jeff Talley (Bruce Willis) is a scraggly, bearded hostage negotiator in the midst of a tense standoff. The in-theater contrast between watching ads for popcorn, then suddenly being in the midst of life-or-death hostage negotiations is so abrupt, that it seems unreal, as though at any moment, Willis will turn to the camera and say, "Live from New York! It's Saturday Night!" Alas, he does not, and the movie hammers on.

Talley makes a crucial miscalculation in his negotiations, which leads to a child being killed. The death deeply affects Talley and he relocates to quiet Ventura County, cuts his long hair and takes a job as chief of police. There is also the most sketchily related side story of Talley having a troubled relationship with his wife, Jane (Serena Scott Thomas) and daughter, Amanda (Rumer Willis, Willis's real-life daughter with Demi Moore).

Forces conspire, as they do, to bring Talley back into the thick of things. Two brothers, Dennis and Kevin Kelly (Jonathan Tucker and Marshall Allman), along with their frighteningly unbalanced friend, Mars Krupcheck (Ben Foster), decide that they will add some excitement to their lives by chasing a girl, Jennifer Smith (Michelle Horn), who rejects their flirtations at a convenience store.

Somehow it ends up that a cop is killed and the guys end up ensconced in Jennifer's hillside mansion. While she and her little brother, Tommy (Jimmy Bennett) cower in fear, her father, middle-aged accountant Walter (Kevin Pollack), tries to calmly negotiate with his captors. It does not work and Walter is put out of commission, to be revived only when plot points force him to wake up briefly. (As Roger Ebert of *The Chicago Sun-Times* put it, "I would love to examine his medical charts during these transitions.")

Talley is called in and the situation gets more complex, and not in a particularly good way, when he finds out that Walter is the accountant for some sort of shady underworld group. Walter has a DVD that the bad guys simply must have and Talley is ordered to recover it or else. The "or else" in this case is that Talley's wife and daughter have been kidnapped and bad things will befall them if Talley does not get that DVD.

To fill the remaining time in the film, various things happen, none of them horribly interesting. Mars decides that Jennifer is his soulmate and follows her around creepily. Dennis and Kevin bicker over just how psycho their friend Mars really is. And little Tommy crawls all through the house's extensive duct system chatting with Talley on the phone and generally being helpful.

A fire is set, glass breaks and people fall from balconies. It is hard to believe that this amount of action could be boring, but somehow it is. Perhaps the most amazing thing about this film is how it makes such a tense situation seem non-interesting and slow-moving. Aficionados of HGTV may derive the most excitement from the numerous shots of the house's luxe interiors.

Willis tries his darndest but even he is powerless against the tedium of the plot and video game director Florent Siri's direction. The studio apparently saw this too. *Hostage* was hastily screened for critics at the last minute and given little fanfare. It was probably all for the best.

Ty Burr of *The Boston Globe* was feeling kindly toward the film and wrote, "Here's what I like about Bruce Willis, though: He acts like this functional swill is as good as *Pulp Fiction.* The man's got exhausted capability down to a science. Yes, he's been playing variations on this role for going on two decades now, but he still hasn't started phoning it in, and I believe this is what is known as professionalism." Stephen Holden of *The New York Times* felt less kindly and wrote, "More than sad, it's slightly sickening to consider the technology, talent and know-how squandered on *Hostage,* a pile of blood-soaked toxic waste dumped on to the screen in an attempt to salvage Bruce Willis's fading career as an action hero." And Michael Wilmington of *The Chicago Tribune* wrote, "Good action movies live on style and excitement. But they also need credibility, and in *Hostage,* almost a good genre piece, plausibility keeps getting slaughtered."

Jill Hamilton

CREDITS

Jeff Talley: Bruce Willis
Walter Smith: Kevin Pollak
Mars: Ben Foster
Dennis: Jonathan Tucker
Tommy Smith: Jimmy Bennett
Laura: Tina Lifford
The Watchman: Kim Coates
Jane Talley: Serena Scott Thomas
Kevin: Marshall Allman
Jennifer Smith: Michelle Horn
Wil: Rob Knepper
Amanda Talley: Rumer Willis
Carol Flores: Marjean Holden
Mr. Jones: Johnny Messner
Lt. Leifitz: Glenn Morshower
Bobby Knox: Chad Smith
Origin: USA
Language: English
Released: 2005
Production: Bruce Willis, Arnold Rifkin, Mark Gordon, Bob Yari; Cheyenne Enterprises; released by Miramax
Directed by: Florent Emilio Siri
Written by: Doug Richardson
Cinematography by: Giovanni Fiore Coltellacci
Music by: Alexandre Desplat
Sound: Peter J. Devlin, Phillip W. Palmer
Music Supervisor: Richard Glasser
Editing: Olivier Gajan
Art Direction: Keith Cunningham
Costumes: Elisabetta Beraldo
Production Design: Larry Fulton
MPAA rating: R
Running time: 113 minutes

REVIEWS

Boxoffice Online. March, 2005.
Chicago Sun-Times Online. March 11, 2005.
Entertainment Weekly Online. March 9, 2005.
Los Angeles Times Online. March 11, 2005.
New York Times Online. March 11, 2005.
Premiere Magazine Online. March 14, 2005.
Variety Online. March 6, 2005.
Washington Post Online. March 11, 2005, p. WE35.

HOUSE OF D

See the world a little differently.
—Movie tagline

You never know who your angel's gonna be.
—Movie tagline

House of D is told primarily as a flashback. It begins In Paris where Tom Warshaw (David Duchovny), an American artist who has lived in France for 30 years, is about to reveal a secret to his son on his 13th birthday. But before we can know the secret we have to know the past so back the story goes to 1973 and Greenwich Village New York. Tom is now 13 year-old Tommy (Anton Yelchin) who lives with his mother (Tea Leoni) who is still grieving the recent death of Tommy's father. Tommy's best friend is Pappass (Robin Williams) a mentally challenged 41-year-old man who works as a janitor at Tommy's school and with whom he works as a delivery boy for a local meat market. Because Pappass' alcoholic father takes their tips, they bury them outside a nearby women's prison called the House of D (as in House of Detention).

Tommy is having his share of adolescent trouble. He has a crush on a young girl, Melissa (Zelda Williams, Robin's daughter) who teases him after he insults her, his efforts in French class consist primarily of trying to get his teacher accidentally to say obscene words, and he spends his time in religion class drawing on the pages of the Bible, ripping them out and tossing them out the window. Since talking these problems over with Pappass is out of the question—especially his girl woes—Tommy ends up discussing them with an inmate in the House of D whose window overlooks their secret cache. Lady Bernadette (Erykah Badu) gives him insights into the woman's mind and even teaches him a dance strategy using a lamp post as a stand-in for his date.

Of course Tommy's infatuation with Melissa makes Pappass jealous and on the night of the school dance he breaks into a store and steals a bike, digs up their hidden tips and throws the money into the river. The theft gets Pappass fired from his janitorial job so Tommy takes the blame after a purposeful misunderstanding of the statement "he stole it for me" with Reverend Duncan (Frank Langella). (Did he steal it to give to Tommy or did Tommy ask him to steal it for him? When Pappass says it he means the first, but when Father Duncan repeats it thinking the second, Tommy does nothing to correct the mistake.) With this, Tommy is expelled from school, but it is going to get worse for the young man. His inconsolable mother overdoses on sedatives and ends up brain dead in the hospital.

Tommy is now basically alone. Fearing his only relatives—a cousin of his mother's from Canada—will send him off to military school he goes to Lady Bernadette for advice. "Be free!" she tells him. And that's exactly what he's going to do. But first he must take care of some unfinished business. He goes to the hospital to say goodbye to his mother, unplugs her life support, then gets Pappas to pose as his father as the thirteen-year-old buys an airplane ticket and flies off to France. The story now flashes forward to present day Paris and the night that started the film. The grown up Tom spends the whole night telling his wife and sleeping son his life's story, his secret. She concludes that the emptiness she's always seen in him can only be cured by his going back to New York City and starting over.

David Duchovny made a name for himself as the haunted, unorthodox FBI agent Fox Mulder on television's The *X-Files*. While he did direct a few of that series' episodes, *House of D*, for which Duchovny also wrote the screenplay, is his theatrical directorial debut. It is obvious that Duchovny has a great deal of affection for his material, that it reflects his personal philosophy of life and his love of New York City where he grew up. (Michael Chapman's cinematography is one of the film's true assets as is Lester Cohen's production design.)

The acting, especially that of Anton Yelchin as the young Tommy who is wise beyond his years, is fine…with one exception. Robin Williams seems to have a penchant for sentimental characters who mug their way through a film (think 1998's *Patch Adams* and 1999's *Jacob the Liar*). Here again he gets to tug our hearts while trying to make us laugh and since his character is mentally challenged it just doesn't quite ring true.

Duchovny's heartfelt coming-of-age story contains some wonderful details and attempts to be a tender treatment of a young life touched by too much pain, but on the whole it is basically unbelievable and at times overly sentimental and slow.

Beverley Bare Buehrer

CREDITS

Tom Warshaw: David Duchovny
Tommy: Anton Yelchin
Lady Bernadette: Erykah Badu
Pappas: Robin Williams
Melissa: Zelda Williams
Coralie Warshaw: Magali Amadel
Mrs. Warshaw: Tea Leoni
Reverend Duncan: Frank Langella
Odell Warshaw: Harold Cartier
Superfly: Orlando Jones
Mrs. Brevoort: Alice Drummond
Origin: USA, France
Language: English
Released: 2004
Production: Richard B. Lewis, Bob Yari, Jane Rosenthal; Tribeca Productions; released by Lions Gate Films
Directed by: David Duchovny
Written by: David Duchovny
Cinematography by: Michael Chapman
Music by: Geoff Zanelli
Sound: William Sarokin
Music Supervisor: Amanda Scheer Demme, Buck Damon
Editing: Suzy Elmiger
Art Direction: Teresa Mastropierro
Costumes: Ellen Luter
Production Design: Lester Cohen
MPAA rating: PG-13
Running time: 96 minutes

REVIEWS

Boxoffice Online. April, 2005.
Chicago Sun-Times Online. April 28, 2005.
Entertainment Weekly Online. April 13, 2005.
Los Angeles Times Online. April 15, 2005.
New York Times Online. April 15, 2005.
Premiere Magazine Online. April 15, 2005.
Variety Online. May 10, 2004.

HOUSE OF WAX

Prey. Slay. Display.
—Movie tagline

Sharing the name of the Vincent Price film in 1953, *House of Wax* is the latest edition to the young adult slasher feature cashing in on a classic. The 1970's was a time for fresh ideas in horror. Several classics were born during that decade. *Halloween*, *The Texas Chainsaw Massacre,* and *Friday the 13*th stand as paragons that promoted the notion that there is more to a movie than a substantial special effects budget and flashy well known screen stars. John Carpenter only had Donald Pleasance for a couple days of filming and the killer, Michael Meyers, wore a distorted William Shatner mask. The simple yet eerie music Carpenter composed could arguably stand as the momentum for the *Halloween's* status as an upper tier work of horror. The numerous series launched by these examples serve to show that the film industry strives to find a safe bet, whether by title, familiar characters, or similar storylines. Clone flicks, however, rarely overshadow their originals.

Perhaps in honor of this notion, director Jaume Collet-Serra's 2005 version of *House of Wax,* starts with a flashback to a disturbing, portentous scene taking place in a 1974 kitchen of a rural nuclear family. Flash-forward to the present and we are introduced to a two-car convoy traveling from the University of Florida to an important football game against LSU in Baton Rouge, Louisiana. Caught in a traffic jam, the students decide to take a detour and wind up in an area that doesn't even register on their GPS. Deciding to camp for the night in a dark, isolated forest clearing, the group encounters a pungent odor and are interrupted by a pickup that converges on their campsite, flooding them with its headlights in ominous, motionless silence. This should be their first clue to leave. One of the group, Nick (Chad Michael Murray), throws a beer bottle at it, successfully shattering one of the truck's headlights. Second clue to leave. The following morning, a broken fan belt is discovered in one of the cars. Too late to leave. Nick's sister Carly (Elisha Cuthbert) and her boyfriend, Wade (Jared Padalecki) unwisely decide to accept a ride into the closest town for a replacement belt from a man they find dumping road kill into a pit loaded with rotting carcasses.

Ambrose is a town caught in a wormhole, off the map and abandoned by time. The current film featured on the movie theater's marquee is *Whatever Happened to Baby Jane?* Wade and Carly interrupt what appears to be a funeral service and are drawn to the town's chief structure, a house literally composed of wax. The plot drones on at a predictable pace with grisly murder following grisly murder, executed by such gory methods as shearing an Achilles tendon in half, decapitation, supergluing victims' lips shut, and severing their fingers. Prior to the killing of Paige (Paris Hilton) she is allowed to give a seductive dance and to flee from her killer (perhaps mistaking her for the girl he saw in an erotic coupling on the Internet) in satin panties.

In a slight deviation from the genre, the serial killing pair turns out to be twins who are locked in a deadly battle with fraternal twins Nick and Carly (Nick transforms into the heroic bad boy). As in the original, victims are encased and preserved in a sheath of wax and frozen in a particular setting. Carly's beau received a deluxe wax finish while alive and remained so for a while, only able to move his eyes. The climax spirals into the ridiculous and inane as the House undergoes a meltdown with the remaining cast plodding through rivers of molten wax. While some may see the film to catch the infamous Paris Hilton in her much criticized film debut, it may be somewhat disappointing. While she is no Stella Adler protégé, there have been far worse performances. After all, she did get that Burger King gig.

David Metz Roberts

CREDITS

Carly: Elisha Cuthbert
Nick: Chad Michael Murray
Bo/Vincent: Brian Van Holt
Wade: Jared Padalecki
Dalton: Jon Abrahams
Blake: Robert Ri'chard
Paige: Paris Hilton
Origin: USA, Australia
Language: English
Released: 2005
Production: Joel Silver, Robert Zemeckis, Susan Levin, Herbert W. Gains, Steve Richards, Bruce Berman; Village Roadshow Pictures, Dark Castle Entertainment; released by Warner Bros.
Directed by: Jaume Collet-Serra
Written by: Carey Hayes, Chad Hayes
Cinematography by: Stephen Windon
Music by: John Ottman
Sound: Paul Brincat
Editing: Joel Negron
Art Direction: Nicholas McCallum
Costumes: Alex Alvarez, Graham Purcell
Production Design: Graham Walker
MPAA rating: R
Running time: 113 minutes

REVIEWS

Boxoffice Online. May, 2005.
Chicago Sun-Times Online. May 5, 2005.
Entertainment Weekly Online. May 4, 2005.
Los Angeles Times Online. May 6, 2005.

New York Times Online. May 6, 2005.
Premiere Magazine Online. May 6, 2005.
Variety Online. April 26, 2005.
Washington Post Online. May 6, 2005, p. C01.

AWARDS

Golden Raspberries 2005: Worst Support. Actress (Hilton)

Nomination:

Golden Raspberries 2005: Worst Picture, Worst Remake/Sequel.

HOWL'S MOVING CASTLE

(Hauru no ugoku shiro)

Box Office: $4.7 million

Howl's Moving Castle is the latest animated film from Hayao Miyazaki, the undisputed and renowned king of Japanese animation, and the follow-up to his Oscar winning feature *Spirited Away* (2003), and his first film to be based on foreign source material. In this case a novel by popular British fantasy author Diana Wynne Jones also titled *Howl's Moving Castle.* Although loosely following the Jones narrative, Miyazaki adds his own elements of an underlying anti-war theme with somewhat noticeably mixed results.

As with many of his films, this one follows the story of a lonely little girl, here named Sophie, who works in her family's hat shop. While out walking one day, she comes across a handsome young man who will change her life forever. His name is Howl, and he has many secrets. He is a wizard with the power of flight, which is a trait that comes in handy on their first meeting as he rescues her from slimy military men and then literally slimy (and oozing) creatures that chase them through an alleyway.

The jealous and spiteful Witch of the Waste does not take kindly to this and so she visits Sophie in her home one night and casts a spell that turns Sophie into an old woman. Unrecognizable to her family and friends, and cursed with the inability to tell them her true identity, Sophie leaves town in search of Howl hoping that he can help reverse the spell. Along the way, she comes across a one-legged scarecrow lying in a field. She helps stand him up and in return for her kindness he offers to guide her to the elusive traveling castle. Once inside, she comes upon the sentient fire demon named Calcifer, who is the mystical power source and engine of the castle. The sarcastic and flammable entity recognizes the spell she is under and offers to reverse it as long as she finds the secret to removing his own spell and free him. But finding the secret will take time (he is also cursed with the inability to reveal his secret), so she becomes the cook and maid of the castle in hopes of gradually learning the secrets of it as well as the denizens that inhabit it.

It turns out that Howl is also a shape-shifter who can change from his handsome human form into that of a feathered warrior of doom. He is a pacifist though, and though he hates war, he becomes embroiled in one between two factions that want him for their own ends. One of them is his old mentor, a snobby female wizard named Suliman, who is now working for one of the two governments and is hell-bent on capturing Howl, lest he be enlisted by the other side. She summons her former pupil along with the Witch of the Waste for a meeting with her boss King Sariman. But unbeknownst to her, Howl has also been summoned by the head of the other government as well. Sensing a trap, Howl sends Sophie to meet with Suliman and the King in his place, resulting in one of the films funniest and most inspired scenes, as Sophie (now dubbed Grandma Sophie) and the Witch of the Waste find themselves in a slow agonizing race up the steps of the King's palace.

This chain of events propel the film to its unfortunately confusing and seemingly rushed conclusion as Sophie and Howl find themselves falling in love while they conspire to thwart her evil Suliman's plans and end an unnecessary war in the process.

All the welcome Miyazaki staples are here including the fantastically realized and inventive visuals one would expect, such as the 19th century, cobble-stoned European towns, and expansive and sumptuous grassy fields under beautiful blue skies. The fantastic creatures and living objects with quirky and perky (but not obnoxious) personalities, include a sarcastic talking flame that doesn't take kindly to being denied his insatiable hunger for wood, to a scarecrow that travels the countryside by bouncing pogo-stick style. And then there is a mechanical walking castle that appears to have been constructed of spare parts from an avante garde junkyard that walks on impossibly thin legs.

The film is sumptuously beautiful to behold (as one has come to expect from Miyazaki), full of complexities lacking in the latest batch of Western animated fare, but is saddled with a story that, in the end, is hard to grasp. But while not on the level of his previous work, this film is nonetheless, a great piece of art that any fan of Miyazaki should see. And it is light years ahead of recent Western animated journeys into bombastic obnoxiousness such as *Madagascar* (2005) and *Robots* (2005). Even though *Howl's Moving Castle* stumbles in the end, it is clear that he respects the intelligence of his audience.

David E. Chapple

CREDITS

Sophie: Chieko Baisho (Voice)
Howl: Takuya Kimura (Voice)
Witch of the Waste: Akihiro Miwa (Voice)
Calcifer: Tatsuya Gashuin (Voice)
Markl: Ryunosuke Kamiki (Voice)
Servant: Mitsunori Isaki (Voice)
Prince: Yo Oizumi (Voice)
King of Ingary: Akio Otsuka (Voice)
Heen: Daijiro Harada (Voice)
Madam Suliman: Haruko Kato (Voice)
Origin: Japan
Language: Japanese
Released: 2004
Production: Toshio Suzuki; Studio Ghibli; released by Toho Films
Directed by: Hayao Miyazaki
Written by: Hayao Miyazaki
Cinematography by: Atsushi Okui
Music by: Joe Hisaishi
Sound: Shuji Inoue
Editing: Takeshi Seyama
Art Direction: Yozi Takeshige, Noboru Yoshida
MPAA rating: PG
Running time: 120 minutes

REVIEWS

Boxoffice Online. June, 2005.
Chicago Sun-Times Online. June 9, 2005.
Entertainment Weekly Online. June 8, 2005.
Los Angeles Times Online. June 10, 2005.
New York Times Online. June 10, 2005.
Premiere Magazine Online. June 15, 2005.
Variety Online. September 8, 2004.
Washington Post Online. June 10, 2005, p. WE36.

QUOTES

Howl: "I finally found someone worth protecting with my life. You."

TRIVIA

Hayao Miyazaki ended up as director when Mamoru Hosoda, originally set to direct the film, abruptly dropped out.

AWARDS

L.A. Film Critics 2005: Orig. Score
N.Y. Film Critics 2005: Animated Film

Nomination:

Oscars 2005: Animated Film
Broadcast Film Critics 2005: Animated Film.

HUSTLE & FLOW

Everybody gotta have a dream.
—Movie tagline

The music will inspire them. The dream will unite them. This summer get crunk.
—Movie tagline

Box Office: $22.2 million

The power of creativity and invention overcome social and moral destitution in Craig Brewer's *Hustle & Flow.* We find DJay (Terrence Howard), a drug dealing pimp runs affairs for his three "tricks." Lexus (Paula Jai Parker), his hooker/stripper/mother girlfriend, Shug (Taraii P. Henson), his formerly prosperous, now pregnant "number one" hooker, and Nola, a country girl stripper who DJay loves like a "brother," all live in a North Memphis residence together. DJay's days consist of picking up drugs from a local convenience store clerk to sell on the street, sitting in his car with Nola, waiting for the next John to show up, and picking up Lexus at night from her job at the local strip club. DJay has found himself in a rut. He is stuck, stagnant and frustrated with his present station in life.

One night after picking up Lexus from the strip club, one of his drug patrons offers to trade a small keyboard for some dope. When he sees the cheap synthesizer, DJay reminisces about his youth and his days as a real disc jockey at Westwood High School. Skinny Black, a now prolific hip-hop artist, disc jockeyed at Booker T. Washington High School across town. DJay takes the keyboard home and begins to play. We instantly witness the transformational potential of music as Lexus's crying son is pacified by the melodies and the beats.

The next day, DJay runs into an old high school friend, Key "Clyde" (Anthony Anderson), in the convenience store where DJay purchases his narcotics. Clyde reminds him of the days when DJay would "flow" and when no one could match his lyrical skills. Clyde, now employed as a sound technician and a small-time music producer, takes DJay and Nola to his gig that day: recording an opera singer at a church. The song moves DJay profoundly and he weeps. Later, he admits to Nola that he is having a "midlife crisis." He is scared and lost. He decides to change his life. Again, we see the revitalizing power of music.

Clyde is eating dinner with his wife, Yevette (Elise Neal), when DJay shows up at his door with Nola, Lexus and Shug and his new keyboard. DJay has a "flow" to share with Clyde. Though Yevette is not happy with the presence of the hookers, Clyde and DJay decide to form a musical alliance. They construct a makeshift studio with drink holders for sound-proofing in a room at DJay's residence. DJay tells Clyde that sometimes he feels a beat, and that beat puts him in the "mode." It is that "mode," that zone that inspires his lyrical explosions. Steadily, DJay grows disinterested with pimping and writes lyrics all day. Again, we see the ability of music to transform the spirit. It is music that pulls DJay away from the negative aspects of his life.

One day, Clyde's friend Shelby (DJ Qualls), shows up at DJay's house. Shelby is not the typical individual that one might find in DJay's rough, run-down neighborhood. He is a skinny, white, electronically adept church piano player. However, we soon find that even the most seemingly dissimilar individuals can be united by the altering force of music. Shelby sees music as a "right." Every man, he says, has the "right to sing his verse." And, though his day job consists of restocking vending machines, he can put together a fierce beat. Success, however, seems a distant dream as DJay and Clyde's personal relationships take a toll on their musical chemistry. Yevette is disconcerted that Clyde spends all his time in a house full of "whores" and DJay has a falling out with Lexus and kicks her and her son, literally, to the curb. Yet, when Shug brings in a lava lamp to a frustrating, unsuccessful studio session, Shelby sees it as an omen. Shug is asked to sing the hook for the song they have been working on. She has an amazing voice. Where formerly we had seen a pregnant, devastated hooker, we now see an artist. Music's revolutionary power now begins to trick the viewer's perception.

They finally cut the big track: "Whoop That Trick." DJay plans to give a copy of it to Skinny Black who is coming into town and will be at Arnel's, a club named after its owner (Isaac Hayes) who is a friend of DJay's. Arnel has discovered a way to introduce DJay to Skinny. DJay will give Skinny a bag of highly powerful marijuana. When DJay meets Skinny he slides his cassette tape across the table. Skinny is instantly respectful of the old school recording and shows DJay respect. They converse as old friends as the night goes on. Their commerce of conversation and old stories of Memphis is like music in itself. A bond is obviously formed.

Skinny, however, is wasted and stumbles to the bathroom. DJay, after thanking Arnel for the connection, decides to go to the bathroom before he leaves the club. There, he finds Skinny sprawled on the ground in front of a stall with his pants around his ankles. DJay helps him to straighten himself out but Skinny instantly collapses again. DJay notices his cassette tape in the toilet but does not know if Skinny intentionally threw it in there or if he simply dropped it. When Skinny suggests that DJay suck on his penis, DJay is goes into a rage and pummels Skinny who pulls a gun. DJay grabs the gun and shoots one of Skinny's posse who enters the bathroom. DJay leaves the club surrounded by gunfire and escapes toward home. The police are already waiting and DJay is dragged away and imprisoned.

Though Clyde is stuck recording court depositions and Shelby continues with his vending machine job, Nola takes up DJay's cause and goes to every radio station in town with DJay's track. Finally, it becomes a smash hit. The dedication, the bond between friends, the trust and the resolve, in the end, pay off.

Simple, undiluted story and a lack of humor pull down several fine performances. Terrence Howard is phenomenal and deserves the highest acclaim for his emotional clarity and silent communicative abilities. The message, too, remains clear and compelling. The music giveth and the music taketh away.

Nick Kennedy

CREDITS

Djay: Terrence DaShon Howard
Nola: Taryn Manning
Shug: Taraji P. Henson
Lexus: Paula Jai Parker
Yevette: Elise Neal
Arnel: Isaac Hayes
Shelby: DJ Qualls
Skinny Black: Ludacris
Key: Anthony Anderson
Origin: USA
Language: English
Released: 2005
Production: John Singleton, Stephanie Allain; Crunk Pictures, Homegrown Pictures; released by Paramount
Directed by: Craig Brewer
Written by: Craig Brewer
Cinematography by: Amelia Vincent
Music by: Scott Bomar
Sound: Andrew Black
Editing: Billy Fox
Costumes: Paul Simmons
Production Design: Keith Brian Burns
MPAA rating: R
Running time: 114 minutes

REVIEWS

Boxoffice Online. July, 2005.
Chicago Sun-Times Online. July 22, 2005.
Entertainment Weekly Online. July 20, 2005.

Los Angeles Times Online. July 22, 2005.
New York Times Online. July 22, 2005.
Premiere Magazine Online. July 26, 2005.
Variety Online. January 24, 2005.
Washington Post Online. July 22, 2005, p. WE32.

QUOTES

Key: "There are two types of people: those that talk the talk and those that walk the walk. People who walk the walk sometimes talk the talk but most times they don't talk at all, 'cause they walkin'. Now, people who talk the talk, when it comes time for them to walk the walk, you know what they do? They talk people like me into walkin' for them."

TRIVIA

Paramount Pictures/MTV Films purchased distribution rights for the film at the 2005 Sundance Film Festival for a festival record $9 million.

AWARDS

Oscars 2005: Song ("It's Hard Out Here for a Pimp")
Natl. Bd. of Review 2005: Breakthrough Perf. (Howard)
Broadcast Film Critics 2005: Song ("Hustle and Flow")

Nomination:

Oscars 2005: Actor (Howard)
British Acad. 2005: Actor (Howard)
Golden Globes 2006: Actor—Drama (Howard)
Ind. Spirit 2006: Actor (Howard)
Screen Actors Guild 2005: Cast.

I

THE ICE HARVEST

Thick Thieves. Thin Ice.
—Movie tagline
'Twas the night before Christmas...
—Movie tagline

Box Office: $9 million

Harold Ramis's *The Ice Harvest* is something of a departure from the feel-good comedies he is best known for, most notably the sophisticated *Groundhog Day* (1993) and the popular *Analyze This* (1999). Starring John Cusack and Billy Bob Thornton, *The Ice Harvest* has some laughs, but they are dark, befitting the desperate characters, their nefarious plans, and the violent deeds that drive their schemes. Punctuated by feelings of small town boredom and bursts of violence and set against a cold and miserable Christmas Eve, the heist plot indulges in noir turns that hardly evoke the holiday spirit.

Cusack plays Charlie Arglist, a mob lawyer trying to abscond with more than two million dollars from his boss, Bill Guerrard (Randy Quaid), and make a getaway before the money is discovered missing. But inclement weather and other unforeseen roadblocks keep delaying his departure. Adapting Scott Phillips's novel, Richard Russo and Robert Benton do not give much dramatic shape to Charlie's misadventures and wanderings among the lowlife hangouts of the Wichita, Kansas, underworld. Until the climax, when the double-crosses and killings start piling up, the film suffers from a very loose, unfocused structure, and, while the characters are generally entertaining, the screenplay does not have the sharp wit and enough snappy dialogue to make it a truly memorable neo-noir.

Charlie's partner in crime is Vic Cavanaugh (Thornton), who plays it low-key most of the time, trying to get Charlie to stay calm when they fear one of Bill's goons, Roy Gelles (Mike Starr), is after them. Charlie obviously carries a torch for Renata (Connie Nielsen), who runs one of the town's strip clubs. He helps her acquire a photo that will enable her to blackmail a councilman—a plot detail that does little beyond establishing his desire to please Renata. With her bright red lips and husky voice, she is the sexy, world-weary femme fatale, a woman Charlie should be wary of.

Giving the film a burst of comic energy is Oliver Platt as Pete Van Heuten, a friend who becomes Charlie's companion for a while after drinking too much and making a fool of himself in a bar. Cusack's Everyman persona is a solid anchor for the craziness swirling around Charlie, and Platt's Pete is a buoyant, loud foil for Charlie, who is trying to call as little attention to himself as possible. Pete is married to Charlie's ex-wife, and a stop at a family dinner where they are clearly unwelcome and where Pete's loutish behavior gets them kicked out, is a very funny, if inconsequential, scene. Indeed, just as Charlie is trapped by the freezing-cold weather and has to bide his time before he and Vic can make a run for it, so does the film feel like it is biding its time with such random incidents until the crime caper really kicks in.

Once Charlie arrives at Vic's house and discovers that he has Roy locked in a trunk, the heist plot takes center stage; it seems that Roy killed Vic's wife when he would not reveal where the stolen money was hidden, and then Vic got the upper hand on him. Vic is a fairly underdeveloped character, but Thornton does what he can with him, and, when the normally laconic Vic suddenly beats the trunk with a golf club, the violence is startling and very funny. This sequence is a comic highlight as the prisoner does his best to communicate through the locked trunk by screaming and desperately trying to plant the seeds of doubt in Charlie's head, claiming that Vic was really the one who killed his wife and is planning to kill Charlie as well. Once they drag the trunk to a dock to toss it into the lake, Vic finally kills Roy, but the dock collapses, plunging both Vic and Roy into the icy water. By this time, however, Charlie is suspicious of Vic's true intentions and lets him freeze to death, even throwing his wife's body into the lake to accompany him. As dark as this plot turn sounds, it has actually been softened somewhat from the novel, in which Charlie actively pushes Vic into the water. Perhaps the filmmakers did not want to make Charlie too much of an antihero and risk losing our sympathy. Indeed, one of Cusack's strengths is making us like Charlie and root for him despite the bad things he does.

With Vic out of the way, Charlie decides to pursue Renata, and, in a tense standoff, saves her from Bill, who has taken her prisoner to lure Charlie. Finally killing Bill in a bloody showdown, Charlie thinks that he can realize his dream of running away with Renata, but, when he finds the two million dollars in her home, he figures out that she was in cahoots with Vic all along. Charlie shoots her just as she is about to stab him. The rush of betrayals, revelations, and violence gives *The Ice Harvest* an exciting finish, which rescues it from a lackluster start.

The film ends rather optimistically (fitting for a Ramis comedy but puzzling for film noir) as Charlie flees with Pete in tow, leaving us to wonder what kind of future these two could possibly have together and where they will go with the money. Moreover, this finish is such a departure from the novel's harsh sensibility that it feels awkward. In Phillips's conclusion, Charlie is accidentally killed on his way out of town after doing a favor for a stalled driver; in a double irony, it is not only one of the few decent things he does but a deed that inadvertently leaves the loot in a complete stranger's hands. In the film, Charlie does the good deed (but for a friend, not a stranger) and narrowly escapes the brush with death.

But if the ending feels like a bit of a copout, it is indicative of a certain tepidness characterizing the film as a whole. Individual scenes have a grimly funny edge, and the chilly, seedy atmosphere beautifully evokes the dead-end feeling of a bleak town on what should be a joyous night. But the screenplay's meandering quality—the random visits to the strip clubs, bars, and middle-class homes that comprise Charlie's yuletide odyssey—robs the plot of momentum, of the sense of a perfect crime spiraling out of control. Perhaps it is unfair to compare *The Ice Harvest* to *Fargo* (1996), a neo-noir masterpiece with dark comedy and indelible characters, but the icy milieu, crime scheme gone awry, and quirky characters practically invite comparison and remind us how such material can be turned into classic filmmaking.

Peter N. Chumo II

CREDITS

Charlie: John Cusack
Vic: Billy Bob Thornton
Renata: Connie Nielsen
Bill Guerrard: Randy Quaid
Peter Van Heuten: Oliver Platt
Origin: USA
Language: English
Released: 2005
Production: Albert Berger, Ron Yerxa; Focus Features, Bona Fide; released by Focus Features, Pyramide Distribution
Directed by: Harold Ramis
Written by: Richard Russo, Robert Benton
Cinematography by: Alar Kivilo
Music by: David Kitay
Sound: Scott D. Smith
Editing: Lee Percy
Costumes: Susan Kaufmann
Production Design: Patrizia Von Brandenstein
MPAA rating: R
Running time: 88 minutes

REVIEWS

Boxoffice Online. November, 2005.
Chicago Sun-Times Online. November 23, 2005.
Entertainment Weekly Online. November 22, 2005.
Los Angeles Times Online. November 23, 2005.
New York Times Online. November 23, 2005.
Variety Online. September 14, 2005.
Washington Post Online. November 25, 2005, p. WE39.

QUOTES

Charlie Arglist: "As Wichita falls...so falls Wichita Falls."

ICE PRINCESS

Big things happen to those who dream big.
—Movie tagline

From small town Mathlete, to big time Athlete.
—Movie tagline

Box Office: $24.4 million

Ice Princess is the movie equivalent of comfort food. It tells a pleasing story that is enjoyable enough to watch. The drama level in the film is high enough to keep the story moving along, but not so high as to cause undue anxiety. Lessons are learned, people change, and there is some engaging ice skating to watch.

This Walt Disney Pictures film features Casey Carlyle (Michelle Trachtenberg) as a high school student who is gifted in physics. As any high schooler, or former high schooler, can attest, that alone is enough to place Casey firmly in the nerd group, despite her beauty and kindness. Casey needs to come up with an idea for the big physics competition to help her gain entry to Harvard. Her mother, Joan (Joan Cusack), an intellectual teacher, dreams of Casey going to Harvard, and Casey is going along with the plan. For her project, Casey decides to apply the principles of physics to ice skating, and she discovers a previously undiscovered passion for the sport. She sets up cameras at the local rink where former ice skating champ, Tina Harwood (Kim Cattrall), is molding her daughter, Gen (Hayden Panettiere), into a figure skating champion.

Making herself the subject of her studies, Casey enrolls in a skating class and discovers that she is a talented skater. But she has to keep her activities secret from her mother because, for some reason, her mother has an extreme distaste for skating. Her mother, an ardent feminist, says she objects to the skimpy outfits and the emphasis on physical appearance, but as it turns out, it is really because she is a bitter ugly duckling who is still "jealous" of the popular girls. (A film school grad student could create an extensive essay hypothesizing on why this movie has such a surprisingly harsh and negative attitude against feminists and intellectuals.)

At the rink, Casey gets involved with new dramas that seem a lot more exciting to her than her old life as a physics student. She has a tame flirtation with Tina's cute son, Teddy (Trevor Blumas), who drives the Zamboni. She thinks she might be getting accepted by the popular Gen. She has to figure out if she has the skills to compete as a skater. And she has to engage in such dialogue with her mother as this: Mother: "You can't do this, Case. You're giving up on your dream." Casey: "No, mom, I'm giving up YOUR dream."

The skating—courtesy of Panettiere, Trachtenberg and some stunt doubles—is believable. The competitors Nikki (Kirsten Olson), a fiery youngster and Zoey (Juliana Cannarozzo), a punk rocker, are played by real life skaters, and they are obviously more talented, but not enough to ruin the movie for anyone.

Cattrall is at her catty best as the ambitious skating coach who is so desperate for Gen to succeed that she is willing to cheat. Panettiere's Gen yearns to be a normal girl who can eat french fries and see her boyfriend on the weekends. Trachtenberg is suitably bland and perhaps it is for the best. The fewer personality traits she has, the easier it is for the target audience of preteen girls to identify with her. She is matched, or perhaps bested, in blandness by Blumas, who seems to have nothing to do other than stand around and stare at her supportively.

Many critics seemed pleased that they did not hate the movie. Roger Ebert of *The Chicago Sun-Times* wrote, "I started by clicking off the obligatory scenes, and then somehow the film started to get to me, and I was surprised how entertained I was." Kevin Thomas of *The Los Angeles Times* wrote, "Although this is the kind of entertainment designed to send its audience home happy, *Ice Princess* has its share of stinging moments and has a good deal more edge than one might have expected." Mick LaSalle of *The San Francisco Chronicle* wrote, "The script, within the limits of the sports movie formula—a creative straightjacket—finds minor flourishes and turns to keep even a jaded adult (who has seen 8,000 variations on this theme) watching contentedly." Stephen Holden of *The New York Times* was less entranced and wrote, "You can feel this niche-marketed tweener fantasy of athletic glory frantically trying to balance a decent sense of values against a market-savvy awareness."

Jill Hamilton

CREDITS

Casey Carlyle: Michelle Trachtenberg
Joan Carlyle: Joan Cusack
Tina Harwood: Kim Cattrall
Gen Harwood: Hayden Panettiere
Teddy Harwood: Trevor Blumas
Nikki: Kirsten Olson
Nikki's Mom: Connie Ray
Zoey Bloch: Juliana Cannarozzo
Brian Boitano (Cameo)
Michelle Kwan (Cameo)
Origin: USA
Language: English
Released: 2005
Production: Bridget Johnson; released by Buena Vista
Directed by: Tim Fywell
Written by: Hadley Davis, Meg Cabot
Cinematography by: David Hennings
Music by: Christophe Beck
Sound: Robert F. Scherer
Music Supervisor: Lisa Brown

Editing: Janice Hampton
Costumes: Michael Dennison
Production Design: Lester Cohen
MPAA rating: G
Running time: 92 minutes

REVIEWS

Boxoffice Online. March, 2005.
Chicago Sun-Times Online. March 18, 2005.
Entertainment Weekly Online. March 16, 2005.
Los Angeles Times Online. March 18, 2005.
New York Times Online. March 18, 2005.
Premiere Magazine Online. March 17, 2005.
Variety Online. March 16, 2005.
Washington Post Online. March 18, 2005, p. WE47.

IMAGINARY HEROES

People are never who they seem to be.
—Movie tagline

In 25-year-old writer/director Dan Harris' first film, *Imaginary Heroes*, we spend a year with the dysfunctional Travis family: relentless dad Ben (Jeff Daniels), sarcastic housewife mom Sandy (Sigourney Weaver), college-age daughter Penny (Michelle Williams), and diffident high school senior Tim (Emile Hirsch), who serves as the film's narrator. In the prologue, which is set in the fall, we see Tim's golden boy elder brother, Matt (Kip Pardue), at a swim meet, which he wins handily (harangued by Ben from the sidelines). Tim informs us that Matt hates the attention his athletic prowess earns him but more than the attention, he actually hates to swim. One morning, Tim discovers his brother's dead body—Matt has blown his brains out with a handgun. (What is shown is a shocked Tim coming into the kitchen and a trail of bloody footprints—an effective method of telegraphing the tragedy.)

A nightmare wake at the family's home finds Ben drinking too much, Sandy walking around in a fog, and Tim unable to stand the mourners' awkward sympathetic gestures. Tim, who has always been close to his mother, will later tell her that "People are so stupid I can't stand to live around them anymore." Sandy, considering, replies: "And they only get worse. You just have to find the one quality that makes them bearable." Tim, who feels he's the family misfit, is a slight, floppy-haired kid with no athletic ability and a teenager's hyper-sensitivity; he generally hangs around with quasi-girlfriend Steph (Suzanne Santo) and his best friend, Kyle Dwyer (the appealing Ryan Donowho), the stoner who lives next door. Sandy has a long-running feud with Kyle's mom, Marge (Deirdre O'Connell), the origins of which will be gradually revealed.

Steph discovers Tim's body is covered with old bruises when they make out at a party. Humiliated, he hides out in Kyle's car but the boys get into a drunk-driving accident on their way home. Tim winds up in the hospital with a broken leg and later meets fellow patient Vern (Jay Paulson), who has tried to kill himself. The duo have a discussion about heroes and Vern opines that meeting one of your heroes is always disappointing because they will either turn out to be jerks or completely ordinary. Sandy, who is coping with her grief by alternating pot with her constant cigarette smoking, also learns about Tim's bruises. Steph blames loser high school bully Jack and a stoned Sandy goes to have a talk with him that will have later repercussions. Meanwhile, Ben has become even more distracted and distant from his marriage and his children.

By winter, Tim is regularly taking a variety of recreational drugs from his dad's various prescriptions and whatever Kyle has to supply. Sandy gets busted trying to buy more pot and Ben spends his days sitting on park benches in a funk. When Penny returns home for Christmas, the family goes to a neighbor's awkward holiday party and Penny flirts with fellow guest Vern, the would-be suicide who has decided to live after all. During a very unhappy New Year's, Tim and Kyle get high on Ecstasy and wind up at midnight in Kyle's bedroom where they kiss. It's vague, but the implication is that they had some kind of sexual encounter as well. Whatever happened, it breaks up the boys' friendship.

In the spring, Sandy finally discovers that Ben has taken a leave of absence from work and is spending his days sitting on park benches. She doesn't believe him when he says he still loves her. Talking with Tim, Sandy tells him that Ben blames himself for Matt's suicide. She decides it's time to move on and clears out Matt's room. When Jack goes after Tim in a school bathroom, Kyle retaliates by threatening him and Kyle and Tim resume their friendship. We learn that the Dwyer feud started when Sandy had an affair with Kyle's long-gone dad and Marge told Ben. However, Marge comes to Sandy's aid when she finds Sandy passed out on the porch and takes her to the hospital. The Travis's are afraid that she has lung cancer. A worried Tim asks his sister: "What am I going to do for the rest of my life? Suddenly it matters." Penny advises him to do something he loves and we soon learn that Tim, a piano prodigy who stopped playing, has been writing music.

As it turns out, Sandy has benign lung tumors and pneumonia. The family doctor advises Ben that he needs to start looking out for his family and Ben works to revive his relationship with his wife. She thinks they also need to come clean with Tim and Sandy informs her son about her affair and that Randall Dwyer is his biological father. Shocked, Tim gets drunk and into an argument with Ben, who finally breaks down and tells the teenager that he always loved him even if Ben had been unable to show it.

At summer's high school graduation, the two families listen as Tim plays an original composition for the ceremony. While he plays, Tim has flashbacks of Matt and we see that it was his brother who had been beating him. We also watch Tim pass Matt's bedroom and see his brother with the handgun. Tim tells Kyle that Matt was always so angry but that one day he asked for Tim's help and he refused. Kyle calmly replies: "Not everyone can be a hero."

Imaginary Heroes is an attenuated stroll through a suburban family's angst, which is also clouded by grief, with first-timer Harris stuffing too many subplots and revelations into his story. That Sandy had an affair (and with a next-door neighbor), which still affects her marriage is one thing, but that Tim is the product of that affair is a revelation that weakens the family bonds. It's too easy to explain Tim's feelings of not fitting in as the result of him not being Ben's biological son and Sandy's saying that Ben and Matt treated Tim differently because of this knowledge (it's unclear if Penny knows or not). Why can't Tim feel like the family outsider (a common teenage lament) without the trite biological excuse? And has Kyle learned that he and Tim are half-brothers? If so, how did they reconcile whatever drug-fueled dalliance happened in Kyle's bedroom?

Before we know of Tim's parentage, Weaver's character makes a comment to her son that they are alike and find it difficult to fit in anywhere. It is the relationship between mother and son that is the strongest part of Harris's film. Sandy is an edgy, intelligent woman who is frustrated and confused over the way her life has turned out. It's not what she expected, not what she would have chosen. Tim is as much her lifeline as she is his and she offers her son her unconditional, if sometimes unconventional, love. Ben, who has neglected everyone in his obsession with Matt, is only too aware that the couple has little to bind them together but their grief and remaining children (though Penny is a negligible figure). Can they survive as a couple when they have that empty nest? Ben is also finally aware of his shortcomings as a father to Tim and they struggle towards a tentative and fragile bond. Both Weaver and Daniels are strong in their roles as is Hirsch, who refrains from overdoing the sorrow and guilt his character deadens with drugs and inappropriate actions. Harris, who first found success as a screenwriter, appears to be putting every idea he had into his debut feature; some judicious pruning would have make a stronger picture but this initial effort is nothing to scorn.

Christine Tomassini

CREDITS

Sandy Travis: Sigourney Weaver
Tim Travis: Emile Hirsch
Ben Travis: Jeff Daniels
Penny Travis: Michelle Williams
Matt Travis: Kip Pardue
Marge Dwyer: Deirdre O'Connell
Kyle Dwyer: Ryan Donowho
Vern: Jay Paulson
Steph Connors: Suzanne Santo
Origin: USA
Language: English
Released: 2005
Production: Illana Diamant, Gina Resnick, Denise Shaw, Art Linson, Frank Hubner; QI Quality Intl.; released by Sony Pictures Classics
Directed by: Daniel P. "Dan" Harris
Written by: Daniel P. "Dan" Harris
Cinematography by: Tim Orr
Music by: John Ottman, Deborah Lurie
Sound: Stuart Deutsch
Editing: James Lyons
Art Direction: Mila Khalevich, Heesoo Kim
Costumes: Michael Wilkinson
Production Design: Rick Butler
MPAA rating: R
Running time: 112 minutes

REVIEWS

Boxoffice Online. December, 2004.
Chicago Sun-Times Online. February 25, 2005.
Entertainment Weekly Online. February 16, 2005.
Los Angeles Times Online. December 17, 2004.
New York Times Online. December 17, 2004.
Variety Online. September 16, 2004.
Washington Post Online. March 11, 2005, p. WE34.

IN GOOD COMPANY

Box Office: $45.2 million

In Good Company, the solo effort of writer/director Paul Weitz, whose frequent collaborator, younger brother Chris, serves as a co-producer, is a serviceable dramedy as much about surrogate fathers and male bonding as it is about corporate life and family life and the complications inherent to both. Dennis Quaid and Topher Grace are well-worth spending time with as a dinosaur and a hot-shot trying to bridge the gap between two generations, both professionally and personally.

Dan Foreman (Quaid) is a 51-year-old top ad exec with a 20-year career at a successful New York sports weekly called *Sports America* that is about to be bought out by mega-corporation Globecom. He's got a happy marriage to 40-something beauty Ann (Marg Helgenberger) and is an over-protective father to his two teen daughters, one of whom, Alex (Scarlett Johansson), is the apple of her father's eye. In contrast is 26-year-old Carter Duryea (Grace), a business grad whiz kid whose claim to fame is successfully marketing dinosaur cell phones to children. While everyone at Sports America worries about job security, Carter is promoted way out of his comfort zone and abilities to head the ad sales division—he becomes a disbelieving Dan's new boss and gets his corner office.

Carter is not completely unaware of his predicament. He meets cute with Alex in the elevator and tells her that he is starting a new job, blurting out "I have no idea what I'm doing." Meanwhile, Dan grits his teeth and accepts his demotion to Carter's "wingman" because Ann has just told him she's pregnant (Dan worries he's too old to be a father again) and Alex has just transferred to NYU. Carter has celebrated his promotion by buying a top-of-the-line Porsche, which he promptly crashes. When he gets home, his wife Kim (Selma Blair) informs him that their seven-month-old marriage is over and she is moving out.

Carter's first day on the job is little better; socially inept and over-caffeinated, his meeting with his staff starts out badly when he announces that they must increase ad revenue by 20 percent. Carter regains confidence as he babbles corporate-speak about synergy and cross-promotion. Dan's skeptical, especially when he learns that Carter must immediately cut costs by firing a number of Dan's longtime sales force. The lonely, workaholic Carter even calls a staff meeting for Sunday, where a tired Dan accidentally invites his new boss home with him for dinner. Carter is overly ingratiating with the family and pretends that he and Alex are meeting for the first time. When they have a moment alone, he again blurts out the truth, saying that he is unhappy, and she is unexpectedly charmed. After his divorce, Carter moves into an apartment and runs into Alex at a coffee shop, telling her "My career is pretty much what I have in my life." He also tells her that although his mother is proud of him, he grew up without a father (can you just feel the foreshadowing). They keep their burgeoning relationship a secret although Dan gets worried when Alex starts ignoring his phone calls.

In the meantime, Carter has to fire more staff and continually consolidate his office space. At Dan's 52nd surprise birthday party, he spots Alex and Carter together and later confronts them at a restaurant. Dan punches Carter, who suddenly proclaims his love for Alex, and walks out in disgust. Later, Carter goes to Alex's dorm room and she tells him she's not ready for a big commitment and breaks up with him. Ann has a pregnancy scare and Alex and her father reconcile at the hospital. Dan admits that it's hard for him to see Alex grow up and become independent. She tells him he doesn't have to change but he tells her that he knows that he does.

Showy Globecom chairman Teddy K (an unbilled cameo by Malcolm McDowell) shows up at the office for a corporate confab and spouts a lot of buzzwords that have an irritated Dan asking pointed questions about current business tactics. When Dan is about to get fired for overstepping the boundaries of corporate hierarchy, Carter puts himself on the line and announces that he and Dan have a big ad deal pending that only they can close. With both their jobs at stake, Dan takes Carter to a former client, Mr. Kalb (Philip Baker Hall), and sells him on buying a lot of advertising by intimating that Carter's all-too obvious black eye has come from Dan taking umbrage at being called a dinosaur by his much-younger boss. He cockily tells Carter that the successful sale is because the older Kalb liked the idea of an "old fart beating the crap out of a young punk half his age." Carter realizes that Dan really loves his work and is doing it for more than perks and a paycheck.

Which is a good thing since, when they return to the *Sports America* office, they learn that Globecom has unexpectedly sold the magazine. Now it's Carter who's out of a job and Dan has been promoted again to the head of advertising and has his old corner office back. A month later, Dan calls Carter into the office and offers him a job as *his* second-in-command. Carter turns him down, admitting "I don't know what I want to do with my life." Carter thanks Dan for teaching him a few things and Dan reassures the younger man that he will be okay (they hug). Carter meets Alex in the lobby and they say a final goodbye and wish each other well. Dan becomes the proud father to another daughter.

There are some funny situations in *In Good Company* (mainly Dan's fatherly outrage) but what seemed to be touted as a comedy in the ads turns out to be unexpectedly dramatic, if sentimental. Mergers and buyouts and firings and their consequences are not played for laughs (although the management speak is both silly and frighteningly realistic). Dan is upset and uncomfortable when he has to fire two people he's worked with for years and even Carter learns about the human cost behind the trite phrase "being let go." The romance between Alex and Carter is sweet but secondary and serves more to insinuate Carter into Dan's personal life than anything else. He envies what the older man has and the happiness Dan derives from his personal life—something Carter has no experience with. Carter is, indeed, *In Good Company*, with Dan as his not-so-reluctant guide to becoming a responsible man.

Christine Tomassini

CREDITS

Dan Foreman: Dennis Quaid
Carter Duryea: Topher Grace
Alex Foreman: Scarlett Johansson
Ann Foreman: Marg Helgenberger
Morty: David Paymer
Steckle: Clark Gregg
Eugene Kalb: Philip Baker Hall
Kimberly: Selma Blair
Corwin: Frankie Faison
Enrique Colon: Ty Burrell
Lou: Kevin Chapman
Alicia: Amy Aquino
Jana: Zena Grey
Receptionist: Colleen Camp
Origin: USA
Language: English
Released: 2004
Production: Paul Weitz, Chris Weitz; Depth of Field; released by Universal
Directed by: Paul Weitz
Written by: Paul Weitz
Cinematography by: Remi Adefarasin
Music by: Stephen Trask
Sound: David Wyman
Editing: Myron Kerstein
Art Direction: Sue Chan, Fred Kolo
Costumes: Molly Maginnis
Production Design: William Arnold
MPAA rating: PG-13
Running time: 131 minutes

REVIEWS

Boxoffice Online. December, 2004.
Chicago Sun-Times Online. January 14, 2005.
Entertainment Weekly Online. January 12, 2005.
Los Angeles Times Online. December 29, 2004.
New York Times Online. December 29, 2004.
Premiere Magazine Online. January 13, 2005.
Variety Online. December 10, 2004.
Washington Post Online. January 14, 2005, p. WE32.

QUOTES

Dan Foreman: "Hello, this is Mr. Foreman. If you give my daughter an alcoholic beverage or a joint, I will hunt you down and neuter you."

TRIVIA

Ashton Kutcher had originally been cast in the role of Carter but dropped out due to creative differences. Since the studio wanted someone from the cast of *That '70s Show* in the role, Topher Grace auditioned and got the part.

IN HER SHOES

Friends. Rivals. Sisters.
—Movie tagline

Adapted by Susannah Grant from Jennifer Weiner's best-selling chick-lit novel, *In Her Shoes* tells the story of two wildly different sisters, their often contentious relationship, and their struggles to find a measure of happiness for themselves. From the opening title sequence, which cuts between Maggie's (Cameron Diaz) hard-partying, promiscuous life to Rose's (Toni Collette) hardworking drudgery as a lawyer, director Curtis Hanson spells out in broad strokes the different paths the Feller sisters have taken. We know from the moment Rose is called to pick up a drunken Maggie at her 10-year high school reunion that these sisters have assumed certain roles in the family, and, during the course of the film, they will clash with each other and try to break out of their timeworn, suffocating routines.

Hanson may not seem like an obvious choice for this material, primarily because his most acclaimed works, *L.A. Confidential* (1997), *Wonder Boys* (2000), and *8 Mile* (2002) focus on the world of men and their relationships, often in a gritty, hard-edged world. But these films demonstrate such a broad range that it should not be too surprising he would go in a different direction. Moreover, whether Hanson is delving into the world of the Los Angeles police, elite academia, or Detroit rap, he always captures the milieu and local color and makes us feel that we are seeing that world from the inside, which he does again in *In Her Shoes*, from the disparate lives of two Philadelphia sisters to a Miami retirement community.

While no other Hanson film has focused so thoroughly on women's relationships, he has always been drawn to character-driven material, and that is the main strength he brings to this film, observing the way these sisters develop and take on unexpected life challenges. It all adds up to a fairly entertaining story, a worthy entry in Hanson's recent string of character studies, buoyed by fine acting but too often weighed down by the predictable character trajectories as well as some unwieldy plotting along the way. Indeed, at two hours and 10 minutes, *In Her Shoes* is too long, stuffing in so many plot details in what is, at heart, a modest tale of sibling rivalry and personal maturation.

Maggie has never held a steady job for very long and always relies on her family to bail her out of tough scrapes. After her reunion debacle, her stepmother, Sydelle (Candice Azzara), insists that she move out, forcing her to stay with Rose, who is used to Maggie's assortment of troubles but puts up with her anyway. Barely able to read and relying on her looks to get what she wants, the slender and beautiful Maggie has been a magnet for guys her whole life, while Rose is plain and heavy, although Collette could only be considered heavy by Hollywood standards of beauty. Nevertheless, she has a frumpy look and an often harried manner that denotes her inferiority to her sister in overall attractiveness and confidence. Rose is exceedingly patient with Maggie's irresponsibility and recklessness, but, when she crosses the line and seduces the man Rose is in love with, the betrayal cuts to her core, and, showing her rage in all its raw fury, she practically throws Maggie out on the street.

At this point, the two stories diverge, and the sisters are forced to reevaluate where their lives are taking them. This is also the point where the screenplay makes a major divergence from the novel. In Weiner's story, Maggie travels from Pennsylvania to New Jersey and hides out on the Princeton campus, sleeping in odd places like the library and undergoing an intellectual transition as she sits in on classes and discovers that she has a taste for poetry. When it looks like she may be found out, she calls her widowed grandmother, Ella, whom she just discovered, and travels to Florida to stay with her. In the film, however, the whole Princeton section is scuttled, and Maggie makes a trip directly to see Ella (Shirley MacLaine).

Meanwhile, Rose takes a leave of absence and reinvents herself as a dog walker and errand runner. Soon she is beginning a romance with a former colleague, Simon Stein (Mark Feuerstein), who is very persistent in winning her affection even though she is, at first, not interested in him. Although Collette is a strong actress, Rose's initial transition from high-powered attorney to neighborhood dog walker is not persuasive. It happens too quickly in the film and is more believable in the novel because we understand Rose's torturous thought processes leading her to walk away from the law, at least for a while. Her romance with the slightly nebbishy Simon, however, works in the film because Collette is very adept at showing how Rose, appreciated in a way she has never felt before, gradually moves from indifference to acceptance of a man who is clearly smitten with her. As the sounding board Rose can vent her feelings to, Brooke Smith nicely fills out Rose's world as Amy, the sardonic best friend always ready with a witty retort.

The heart of the Florida sojourn is Maggie getting to know her long-lost, maternal grandmother, whom the girls' father, Michael (Ken Howard), shut out of their lives after their troubled mother committed suicide. In staying with Ella, Maggie receives some of the guidance she never had growing up and even finds work, first helping to tend to the shut-ins of the community and then using her fashion expertise to become a clothing consultant and personal shopper for some of the old ladies.

The excision of Maggie's days at Princeton feels like a loss since these chapters are among the novel's funniest, charting the attempt of the least likely Ivy Leaguer to blend into college life. They are also among the most touching, with Maggie discovering an academic side of herself she did not know she had. And yet including this section would have taken a screenplay already unnecessarily long and swollen it to epic proportions. But screenwriter Grant has found a smart, economical way of including Maggie's intellectual growth, transferring the novel's classroom foray to her relationship with a retired, blind professor (nicely played by Norman Lloyd), who becomes an informal tutor of poetry during her visits. The relationship is doubly satisfying because it also shows the normally selfish Maggie starting to change, reaching out to someone else and making a connection without expecting something in return.

The essential theme, then, embodied in the titular shoe metaphor, is that each sister gets to live for a while in the role the other has always occupied, and, in the process, each blooms. No longer beholden to cleaning up Maggie's messes, Rose gets to live for herself, and her budding romance with Simon becomes the reward, culminating in a wedding proposal. It is a bigger stretch to think that Maggie, spoiled adolescent all her life, could suddenly lurch into responsibility, but MacLaine's delicate performance as Ella helps us believe that Maggie could be guided to a fresh start. Feeling guilty that she was not there for her granddaughters when they needed her, Ella is trying to make up for the past but not in a desperate way, and MacLaine makes Ella the loving yet firm maternal figure Maggie always needed. And Ella's own friends give the story just the right dash of comic relief—Mrs. Lefkowitz (Francine Beers), the wise, spunky lady who helps Ella relate to Maggie, and Lewis (Jerry Adler), Ella's ardent admirer.

In Her Shoes is pleasing as a twin tale of personal development, but it lacks a strong structure and narrative drive. It is a shaggy-dog story with little crises and detours along the road to fulfillment, such as the thoughtless Sydelle showing unflattering pictures of Rose at her wedding shower or Simon reconsidering the wedding itself because he does not believe that Rose is opening up to him emotionally. Moreover, when Rose is finally invited down to Florida, the reunion is anticlimactic, and the reconciliation feels rather obligatory—Maggie's old betrayal is hardly an issue—since all the big life changes have already happened with the sisters apart, which is, of course, the only way they really could have happened. There are also reminiscences with Ella about the mother they barely knew, but this, too, feels like the perfunctory tying up of loose ends. Old family grudges are eventually healed as well (all too easily) between Michael and Ella, and the movie concludes with Rose's wedding when Maggie supplies both the wedding dress and a reading of a poem, a fitting, poignant ending that highlights her newfound talents.

The journeys Rose and Maggie take have their share of plot contrivances, as do the resolutions; nobody could really turn their lives around so quickly (even by meeting such wonderful people as Simon and Ella) and then bring the whole family together as well. But this is, after all, a story of hope, and the actors deliver the emotions with such conviction that it is easy to accept and even rejoice in the characters' newfound happiness.

Peter N. Chumo II

CREDITS

Maggie Feller: Cameron Diaz
Rose Feller: Toni Collette
Ella Hirsch: Shirley MacLaine
Simon Stein: Mark Feuerstein
Michael Feller: Ken Howard
Sydelle Feller: Candice Azzara
Mrs. Lefkowitz: Francine Beers
The Professor: Norman Lloyd
Lewis Feldman: Jerry Adler
Amy: Brooke Smith
Jim Danvers: Richard Burgi
Todd: Anson Mount
Origin: USA
Language: English
Released: 2005
Production: Ridley Scott, Curtis Hanson, Carol Fenelon, Lisa Ellzey; Scott Free/Deuce Three; released by 20th Century-Fox
Directed by: Curtis Hanson
Written by: Susannah Grant
Cinematography by: Terry Stacey
Music by: Mark Isham
Sound: Petur Hliddal
Editing: Craig Kitson, Lisa Zeno Churgin
Art Direction: John Warnke
Costumes: Sophie de Rakoff
Production Design: Dan Davis
MPAA rating: PG-13
Running time: 129 minutes

REVIEWS

Boxoffice Online. October, 2005.
Chicago Sun-Times Online. October 7, 2005.
Entertainment Weekly Online. October 5, 2005.
Los Angeles Times Online. October 7, 2005.
New York Times Online. October 7, 2005.
Premiere Magazine Online. October 7, 2005.
Variety Online. September 14, 2005.

QUOTES

Maggie Feller: "Shoes like this should not be locked up in a closet! You should be living a life of scandal. You should be getting screwed in an alley behind a club by a billionaire while his wife waits in the car and he told her he just forgot his wallet!"

TRIVIA

The author of the original book, Jennifer Weiner, her sister, grandmother, and agent all appear in the movie.

AWARDS

Nomination:

Golden Globes 2006: Support. Actress (MacLaine).

IN MY COUNTRY
(Country of My Skull)

A South African Story of Truth, Love and Reconciliation.
—Movie tagline

There must be some kind of a mistake here. How can a director as talented as John Boorman (*Deliverance, Hope and Glory*) and actors as good as Samuel L. Jackson and Juliette Binoche be responsible for something as dreadfully unwatchable as *In My Country?*

Answer: The road to cinematic hell is paved with good intentions. And the idea of dramatizing the healing process in post-apartheid South Africa with a fictionalized account of that country's Truth and Reconciliation Commission series was no doubt a noble one. Under Nelson Mandela's leadership, the new South African government in the mid-1990s decided that the best way to heal the wounds from the apartheid era was to let both victims and their relatives and those accused of murder and torture testify at open hearings. The commission decided the fate of regime collaborators and ended up exonerating many who apologized and proved convincingly that they were only following orders.

A straightforward documentary about the reconciliation commission's work would undoubtedly have proven more effective than this dramatized account, adapted by screenwriter Ann Peacock from the book *Country of My Skull* by Antjie Krog. Peacock, a white South African who opposed the apartheid regime, quite obviously pours her own political sentiments into the character played by Binoche, an Afrikaner poet named Anna Malan. Malan, defying the wishes of her family who want her to have nothing to do with cooperating with the black-run government, is assigned to cover the hearings for the South African public radio network. The result is a veritable orgy of white liberal guilt and excessive handwringing that nonetheless strives to be evenhanded, and occasionally succeeds.

Films made for political reasons—in this case, to show the stirring triumph of a politics based on peace, tolerance, and justice over violence and racial hatred—often come off as more didacticism than drama, and *In My Country* is a prime example of the dangers of excessive earnestness. It is dripping with piety and drenched with gripping moral lessons for both Anna and her fellow journalist Langston Whitfield (Jackson), an American reporter for the *Washington Post.* Langston, who is a caricature of American black pride out of touch with the conditions on the ground in Africa, can't understand why anyone would have the impulse to listen to, much less excuse or justify, any collaborators with apartheid.

These two aren't real characters, they're part of a set-up, pawns on a scriptwriter's checkerboard. A sincere white Afrikaner who wants sincerely to do the right things is paired up with a proud black American who knows little of African culture. (Even the name of Jackson's character is hackneyed.) Their meeting and struggles suggest, very obviously, a clash of cultures. And their ability to overcome their initial suspicions and hatred and join forces is an obvious metaphor for the racial healing process that the commission hearings are helping the country to embrace. But this film does not need metaphors; it needs some plot, tension, and action.

Peacock can't deliver those, and neither Boorman nor his stars can spin gold out of straw. Binoche and Jackson are hamstrung by a script that turns their disdain into love without providing anything other than political reasons to do so. You know right from the start that they are going to end up as lovers, but the two veteran actors fail to cook up any chemistry between them. When they finally fall in bed together they do so at what seems merely a convenient point in the script, and not out of any discernible personal attraction or any emotional development or watershed. Their romance is something to wince at. And that's a measure of how poorly their characters are written, because these are two normally compelling actors.

Stuck with snatches of wooden dialogue and speeches that are overwritten and obvious, Binoche and Jackson seem adrift in a swamp of good intentions that lack definition. Binoche plays her character with such dogged earnestness that she has all the appeal of a schoolmarm. Jackson sleepwalks through his part, trying to milk comic riffs out of the deadwood he's been dealt for lines.

For all its shortcomings, however, this clunky romance is the only thing that keeps the plot moving at all. Scene after scene of commission testimony doesn't advance the story or the tension, it just lays on more gruesome details about torture. Witnesses speak of unspeakable acts for such wholesome reasons that watching the film is like being tortured by righteousness.

What happened under apartheid should not be turned into a vehicle for entertainment. There is no need to concoct artificial drama to add to the stories of the victims; there is much more power in the truth than in a fictionalized version of it. *In My Country* fails as entertainment because of the nature of its subject matter and the cardboard cutout characters (including Brendan Gleeson as a bloated villain) that Peacock has substituted for believable real people. It fails as political propaganda because its points are lost in a muddle of pointless scenes. For impact, this movie depends on gruesome accounts of torture, but everything else melts away in a ridiculous concoction of badly played moralizing.

In the end, even the affair between the two principal characters must be cast into the crucible of reconciliation politics, cleansed by the rhetoric that says disclosure is good for the soul. Speaking the truth and bearing witness to unspeakable acts can be, of course, salutary experiences, but instead of moral depth *In My Country* turns the entire post-apartheid process into an easily digestible homily.

Boorman, who has not made a major film in some time, seems hopelessly adrift here, unable to give the predictable, punchless screenplay the shape and impact it needs. Except for Gleeson's torturer, everyone in the movie is a saint of some sort, or a redeemed sinner. In place of human complexity is the whitewash of politically correct sentiment.

Outside the United States, *In My Country* was released as *The County of My Skull,* a much more distinctive title. The film was shot on location in and around

Cape Town, and there's some beautiful cinematography. Unfortunately it's lost amid the forest of overcooked sentiment.

Michael Betzold

CREDITS

Langston Whitfield: Samuel L. Jackson
Anna Malan: Juliette Binoche
De Jager: Brendan Gleeson
Dumi Mkhalipi: Menzi "Ngubs" Ngubane
Anderson: Sam Ngakane
Elsa: Aletta Bezuidenhout
Edward Morgan: Lionel Newton
Boetie: Langley Kirkwood
Rev. Mzondo: Owen Sejake
Albertina Sobandla: Harriet Manamela
Willem Malan: Louis Van Niekirk
Old man in Wheelbarrow: Jeremiah Ndlovu
Felicia Rheinhardt: Fiona Ramsay
British reporter: Charley Boorman
Origin: USA, Great Britain, Ireland
Language: English
Released: 2004
Production: Robert Chartoff, Mike Medavoy, John Boorman, Lynn Hendee; Studio Eight, Country Merlin; released by Sony Pictures Classics
Directed by: John Boorman
Written by: Ann Peacock
Cinematography by: Seamus Deasy
Sound: Tom Johnson, John Fitzgerald
Music Supervisor: Philip King
Editing: Ron Davis
Art Direction: Emelia Roux-Weavind
Costumes: Jo Katsaras
Production Design: Derek Wallace
MPAA rating: R
Running time: 100 minutes

REVIEWS

Boxoffice Online. March, 2005.
Chicago Sun-Times Online. April 1, 2005.
Entertainment Weekly Online. March 9, 2005.
Los Angeles Times Online. March 11, 2005.
New York Times Online. March 11, 2005.
Variety Online. February 8, 2004.
Washington Post Online. April 1, 2005, p. WE45.

QUOTES

Anna Malan: "Because of you this land no longer lies between us but within."

IN THE REALMS OF THE UNREAL

In the Realms of the Unreal is a profoundly odd documentary directed by Jessica Wu that describes a man named Henry Darger, who joins the ranks of the outsider artists who tightrope their way across their mundane lives with balance beams of a wildly imaginative inner life. Except for the fact that he didn't murder anyone, Darger is akin to the 19th Century visionary artist, Richard Dadd in that both artists were immersed in worlds of imaginary fantasy. This film chronicles Darger's life from birth to death in his beloved Chicago—from the abandonment by his father at an early age (he never knew his siblings), his consignment to several drab and abusive workhouses and institutions such as the "Lincoln Asylum for Feeble-Minded Children," his short term as a draftee, his final decades in several rooming houses, until his death in 1972. He had few friends, aside from a boyhood pal and a sympathetic landlord. He rarely spoke, kept to himself, demonstrated no interest in sex and society, never changed his mood, and conducted imaginary conversations in multiple voices behind the closed door of his room. (In the documentary Dakota Fanning, who starred in *Dreamer* later in 2005, provides the voice of Henry Darger.) Henry Darger led a double life, bland and blunted on the outside, and exotically fantastic and disturbing on the inside. Paralleling his paranoia of authority, his obsession with little girls, his love for the narratives of Henty, Baum's Oz books, and Tarkington's "Penrod" stories are the hundreds of drawings on butcher paper (on both sides, no less!) and the thousands of pages he produced in his solitary hours. Here was the great epic of his interior life, *In the Realms of the Unreal*, a sprawling narrative of love and war, of armies of little girls (called "The Vivien"), bleeding children, malevolent soldiers all locked in the embrace of love and war. Enormous butterflies, nude children (especially transsexual "girls"), maniacal soldiers, winged demons all dance and rage across the sprawling drawings. As he lay dying in a Chicago hospital, cared for by his kindly landlady, Darger replied to inquiries about any assistance needed with the words, "Too late." It was only after his death that the landlady discovered that his room was stacked and crammed with scrapbooks, paintings (some of them 12 feet long), paint boxes, and typescripts.

His story is told through the testimonies of the landlady, Kiyoko Lerner, a sympathetic neighbor, the voice of a little girl (the actress Dakota Fanning, as noted above), and other voices that narrate and characterize the many adventures of his stories and drawings. As the camera pores minutely over the crudely typed manuscript pages, the drawings come to life. They cavort and dance against newsreel footage of Chicago (there are two sequences in which newsreels boast of Chicago's prosperity and all-American hustle). It's as if Henry's dream life, confined and stiffened to pages and typescript, at last can come out and play in all its delicately disturbing whimsy.

Apparently Henry harbored the desire to adopt a child. One winces at the prospect. A child himself, who professed the wish never to grow up, Henry might have been the best or the worst of parents. Were his preoccupations with little girls benign or did they conceal a dangerous pedophilia? And what do we make of his testimony one day to his landlady that he was raped by a 17-year old girl? His fascination with the Oz books and the Penrod stories (we see a bruised and tattered row of Oz books on his shelf) make a peculiar kind of sense. In secret, Tarkington's 12-year old Penrod wrote his own exotic adventures of the bandit "Ramirez"; and Baum's fables reflected their author's own secret and lively imagination. Particularly in the latter instance, the Oz stories are populated by androgynous characters, like the boy Tip who turns out to be the Princess Ozma, by armies of children and gnomes locked in endless battles, by bizarre creatures with names Henry appropriated for his own characters.

The real paradox here is that an "outsider" artist lived so long and earnestly on the "inside" of his imagination.

John C. Tibbetts and James M. Welsh

CREDITS

Origin: USA
Language: English
Released: 2004
Production: Susan West, Jessica Yu; Diorama Films; released by Wellspring Media
Directed by: Jessica Yu
Written by: Henry Darger (writings), Jessica Yu
Music by: Jeff Beal
Sound: Jeff Beal
Editing: Jessica Yu
MPAA rating: Unrated
Running time: 82 minutes

REVIEWS

Boxoffice Online. January, 2005.
Entertainment Weekly Online. January 12, 2005.
Los Angeles Times Online. January 21, 2005.
New York Times Online. December 22, 2004.
Variety Online. January 20, 2004.
Washington Post Online. February 4, 2005, p. C05.

THE INTERPRETER

The truth needs no translation.
—Movie tagline

Box Office: $72.5 million

It is not hard to interpret the final shot of *The Interpreter.* Director Sydney Pollack's latest film fades on a view of a New York skyline with the United Nations Headquarters but sadly without the twin towers of the World Trade Center. It juxtaposes an admirable coalescence to foster communication, understanding and peaceful coexistence with a site famously reduced to rubble by those opting for incendiary violence and destruction. Words or weapons—that is the choice. Both are capable of making a powerful statement with awesome, reverberating repercussions. "Words and compassion are the better way, even if it is slower than a gun," it is stated in the film. "The human voice is different from other sounds. Even the lowest whisper can be heard over armies when it's telling the truth." While Pollack is always cognizant of the fact that his primary objective is to entertain, he is clearly aiming to combine thoughtfulness and thrills.

Speaking of low whispering, that is what sets the plot—of *The Interpreter* and of some dark, unseen force—in motion. It is accidentally overheard by Silvia Broome (Nicole Kidman), a U.N. interpreter who was raised in the African nation of Matobo where they speak Ku. The language was created for the film, and Matobo, run by liberator-turned-genocidal dictator Edmund "The Teacher" Zuwanie (Earl Cameron), cannot be found on any map but bares a striking and unmistakable resemblance to Robert Mugabe's Zimbabwe.

Before Silvia is introduced, the film acquaints viewers with the wanton, bloody malevolence of Zuwanie's rule in the first of three major, sit-up-and-take-notice sequences which *The Interpreter* has to offer. Three men arrive at an eerily-deserted soccer stadium, and two proceed inside. One turns out to be Silvia's brother Simon and the other a rebel leader named Ajene Xola (Curtiss Cook). They are greeted by some boys who offer to take them to see a stash of wretched-smelling corpses buzzing with flies. Suddenly, another youngster appears, takes out a gun, and swiftly and rather startlingly adds the two men to the dead. "The Teacher says good day to you," the boy says with an icy boldness before finishing one of the men off with a blast to the brain.

It is this kind of shocking brutality that has made Zuwanie a hated man who many would like to see brought before the International Criminal Court at The Hague. Grudgingly aware that some image-polishing is now essential, Zuwanie is coming to the U.N. to address the General Assembly and put the best face he can on things going on in Matobo. (He will assert that his strong-armed tactics are necessary evils to combat destabilizing terrorist elements.) Late one night before his arrival, Silvia pops in to the deserted translator's booth to retrieve some things she had left there during an evacuation earlier that day caused by a security scare.

She happens to pick up her headset, and hears voices from somewhere down in the darkened, cavernous room below threaten in Ku to cut short both Zuwanie's upcoming speech and his life. The lights in her booth flicker on, and she becomes terrified that whoever she heard has seen her and will now seek to silence the woman who knows too much.

The next day, Silvia does the right thing and reports this apparent assassination plot. Secret Service Agent Tobin Keller (Sean Penn) and his partner Dot Woods (Catherine Keener) are called in to investigate. Now world-weary Keller will have to focus on the words Silvia heard in addition to those spoken by his wife on their answering machine, which he forlornly listens to over and over again. He immediately has doubts about Silvia's story. Maybe she just wants attention. Perhaps she wants to prevent Zuwanie's speech from taking place. After all, would anyone have really chosen to discuss such a plot on the floor of the microphone-laden General Assembly, even at night when the lights are down and few people are likely to be around? What are the chances, he wonders, of one of the few people around who can understand Ku being the one to overhear this supposed threat in that obscure language? It seems to Keller that he is being asked to swallow a fairly formidable helping of implausibility and coincidence, and if viewers stop and think about it, so are they. Still, that is the way the story has been scripted, and audience members, unlike Keller, will have witnessed this case of far-fetched movie-machinated happenstance, including Silvia's unsettled reaction to whatever it was she heard.

Silvia admits she does not like Zuwanie, but if she had approved of anyone killing him she would have kept silent. She asserts her belief in the U.N.'s mission of peaceful change, putting her faith in the making of persuasive points instead of the pointing of deadly guns. Keller labels her a liar, and senses, as viewers will, that if she is telling the truth it is not the whole truth. He would like to know exactly what she is withholding, but, just as her job requires, Silvia is maddeningly careful about what comes out of her mouth. Actually, both are keeping some painful personal information inside. Silvia is not sharing that she fears her brother may be part of the plot. (She remains unaware that her brother has been murdered.) Keller is basically a walking wound, churning inside because his estranged wife, planning to return to him, was recently killed in a car driven by her lover. Keller and Silvia are evenly matched in the tense verbal fencing they do as the agent tries to get to the bottom of things. He is tough, and offends her. She is guarded, and frustrates him.

As *The Interpreter* slowly unfolds, intriguing tidbits of information about Silvia's past reveal someone quite likely to want Zuwanie dead. There is the painful fact that her parents and sister were killed by one of his landmines when she was just entering her teens. A photograph surfaces which shows her to have at one time been a supporter of Xola. She is eventually revealed to have once killed someone out of necessity before renouncing violence. During a polygraph test administered by Zuwanie's white security chief Nils Lud (Jesper Christensen), she looks quite ill at ease. Keller is certain that Silvia needs watching, but he cannot figure out if that is because she is in trouble or in the process of making it.

The Interpreter's most dramatic and suspenseful scene is the one in which Silvia boards a city bus to gutsily grill exiled Matoban rebel figure Kuman-Kuman (George Harris) about her brother's possible whereabouts. Pollack cuts back and forth between what is transpiring inside the bus and Keller's desperate, horrified attempt to get everyone off before a bomb (brought on by one of Zuwanie's men) blows everyone sky high. Silvia happens to get off in the knick of time, but everyone else perishes in a spectacular fireball. This loss of life makes Keller finally lose patience with Silvia, and he blows up at her with a forcefulness rivaling that of the bus explosion. She finally relents, coming clean about her desperate concern for her brother. Standing amongst the carnage, he puts his arm around her and she eases into him, closing her eyes. It is not a sign of burgeoning love but of empathetic human compassion, comfort that they both are needing.

Aside from this scene, *The Interpreter* is generally unspectacular and never intensely gripping in an on-the-edge-of-your-seat type of way. It is, however, interesting as a law enforcement procedural, showing how the authorities go about trying to piece the puzzle together, even as Zuwanie steps to the podium. However, having already reached its eye-popping peak, what remains seems somewhat anticlimactic by comparison. Its final portion, which reveals that Lud had cooked up a fake plot to create sympathy for his boss, is intriguing because Silvia, tormented upon finally learning she has lost yet another family member to Zuwanie, deviates from her nonviolent path and holes up in a locked safe room with the man and a loaded gun. There are multiple implausibilities here, but there is a nice amount of tension created as Keller talks her out of doing something no one could blame her for wanting to do but which she would deeply regret. The suspense is marred by the fact that no one will worry a bit about Zuwanie, as well as that viewers' feelings for Silvia (and Keller for that matter) never transcend curiosity into concern for how things pan out. The film itself is intelligent, well-acted, admirably made, and fairly interesting without being acutely or satisfyingly involving. The talky ending, showing that both Silvia and Keller have found a degree of healing on the road they have traveled together, is weak. (The original one was discarded due to test audience disapproval.)

"I began the picture without a script," said Pollack, "which is a lousy way to make a movie." At least five writers labored on it. It shows. Made on a budget of $80 million, the film grossed $72.5 million. Critical reaction was mixed. For 1959's *North by Northwest,* director Alfred Hitchcock also envisioned murder and mayhem committed within the walls of the world's bastion of peace. There was only one hitch for Hitch: the U.N. refused to let anyone film inside their headquarters, and it has refused numerous requests in the years since until Pollack's lobbying convinced U.N. Secretary-General Kofi Annan to allow filming of *The Interpreter.* The location turns out to be the most potent, memorable presence in the film. Nowhere near as engaging as Pollack's *Three Days of the Condor* (1975), his *Interpreter,* like the U.N. itself, aims high, concerns itself with serious material, is not quite as effective as one wishes it would be, and can cause head-scratching incredulity. It is certainly not perfect, but then there are some far less palatable alternatives out there.

David L. Boxerbaum

CREDITS

Silvia Broome: Nicole Kidman
Tobin Keller: Sean Penn
Dot Woods: Catherine Keener
Nils Lud: Jesper Christensen
Philippe: Yvan Attal
Marcus: Michael Wright
Zuwanie: Earl Cameron
Kuman-Kuman: George Harris
Luan: Tsai Chin
Police Chief Lee Wu: Clyde Kusatsu
Simon Broome: Hugo Speer
Mo: Maz Jobrani
Rory Rob: Eric Keenleyside
Jonathan Williams: Christopher Evan Welch
Charlie Russell: David Zayas
Jay Pettigrew: Sydney Pollack
Ajene Xola: Curtiss Cook
Jean Gamba: Byron Utley
Origin: USA
Language: English
Released: 2005
Production: Tim Bevan, Eric Fellner, Kevin Misher; Working Title Productions; released by Universal
Directed by: Sydney Pollack
Written by: Charles Randolph, Scott Frank, Steven Zaillian
Cinematography by: Darius Khondji
Music by: James Newton Howard
Sound: Danny Michael
Editing: William Steinkamp
Art Direction: Tom Warren
Costumes: Sarah Edwards
Production Design: Jon Hutman
MPAA rating: PG-13
Running time: 128 minutes

REVIEWS

Boxoffice Online. April, 2005.
Chicago Sun-Times Online. April 22, 2005.
Entertainment Weekly Online. April 20, 2005.
Los Angeles Times Online. April 22, 2005.
New York Times Online. April 22, 2005.
Premiere Magazine Online. April 21, 2005.
Variety Online. March 30, 2005.
Washington Post Online. April 22, 2005, p. WE35.

QUOTES

Silvia Broome: "Vengeance is a lazy form of grief."

TRIVIA

This is the first film ever to be shot inside the United Nations Headquarters complex.

INTO THE BLUE

Treasure Has Its Price.
—Movie tagline
Hold your breath.
—Movie tagline

Probably the most shocking plot twist involved with *Into the Blue* was that critics did not dislike it as much as they might have. After all, a movie starring the highly attractive actors Paul Walker and Jessica Alba doing underwater diving and chasing treasure is not exactly the stuff that Oscar nominations are made of. If these elements had combined to form a big, important movie, it would have upset the Hollywood order completely.

Director John Stockwell, who also helmed the nautically-themed *Blue Crush,* follows the traditional moviemaking path, which dictates, in part, that if one has actors like Walker and Alba, said actors must spend much of the movie half-dressed, or, even better, in bathing suits. Writer Matt Johnson gives the actors plenty of reason to wear few clothes. The film is set on a Bahamian island where Jared (Walker), a scuba diver, hopes to make a living finding buried treasure. His girlfriend Sam

(Alba) takes care of the sharks at the local version of a Sea World. They sleep on Jared's dilapidated boat and, as the movie points out many times, live on love instead of money.

When Jared's old buddy Bryce (Scott Caan) flies into town with his club kid girlfriend Amanda (Ashley Scott), who he met the night before, Jared may get a chance to follow his dream. The two couples go on a dive and discover what might be the remains of a famous old ship, the Zephyr. According to Bahamian law, they can stake claim to the wreckage if they find an artifact that has the name of the wrecked ship on it.

But there is something else down there, too. The four find a small airplane that is filled with hundreds of tightly wrapped packages of cocaine. Bryce, a sleazy high-powered lawyer, and his girlfriend vote to take the cocaine. In their minds, there is nothing wrong with any plan that allows them free drugs and a chance to make a huge fortune. Sam, on the other, wants nothing to do with the drugs and, to prove her point, slices open one of the packages and dumps the contents into the sea. Jared is conflicted. He agrees with Sam, but how is he going to stake a claim on the Zephyr unless he can buy the right equipment to go through the wreckage? Would it really be so bad if they just took a package or two, just this once?

Things are further complicated by Bates (Josh Brolin), a local shipwreck-finder who, unlike Jared, has been successful. Is he going to jump in and claim the Zephyr? And what about the person who was sending the drugs? Are they going to notice the plane is gone and look for their cargo? It sounds like there are a lot of moral dilemmas and questions in *Into the Blue*, and there are—sort of. There are these issues, but most of the movie is dedicated to lovely shots of the ocean, both above and below, and to Walker and Alba, again, both above and below. The actors seem able to hold their breath way longer than the laws of physics would dictate, but they look good when doing it. Walker and Alba do not swim through the water so much as undulate through it. Such beautifully shot footage guarantees that while the movie might not sometimes be horribly interesting, at least it is not painful to watch.

Critics gave the film middling reviews. Wesley Morris of *The Boston Globe* explained plainly why he liked the film. "All the snorkeling, scuba diving, breath holding, and emergency mouth-to-mouth is sexy," he wrote. Colin Covert of *The Minneapolis Star-Tribune* was less excited and gave the movie one out of four stars. "It is an extraordinary cinematic achievement to take a story combining pirate treasure, drug runners, killer sharks, an airplane crash, car chases and Jessica Alba in a bikini, and turn it into an exercise in tedium." Roger Ebert of *The Chicago Sun-Times* liked the film, saying it offered "modest pleasures." He wrote, "The movie is written, acted and directed as a story, not as an exercise in mindless kinetic energy." Manohla Dargis of *The New York Times* had some odd praise for the film. "This undiluted nonsense is best suited to DVD-rental desperation. Still, aficionados of cheap cinematic thrills involving beautiful and stupid young people will be happy to learn that while the film fizzles far more than it sizzles, its director, John Stockwell, is a connoisseur of the female backside which he displays to great and frequent advantage."

Jill Hamilton

CREDITS

Jared: Paul Walker
Sam: Jessica Alba
Bryce: Scott Caan
Amanda: Ashley Scott
Bates: Josh Brolin
Reyes: James Frain
Primo: Tyson Beckford
Origin: USA
Language: English
Released: 2005
Production: David A. Zelon; Mandalay Pictures; released by Sony Pictures Entertainment
Directed by: John Stockwell
Written by: Matt Johnson
Cinematography by: Shane Hurlbut
Music by: Paul Haslinger
Sound: David Kirschner
Editing: Nicolas De Toth
Art Direction: David Klassen
Costumes: Leesa Evans
Production Design: Maia Javan
MPAA rating: PG-13
Running time: 110 minutes

REVIEWS

Boxoffice Online. September, 2005.
Chicago Sun-Times Online. September 30, 2005.
Entertainment Weekly Online. September 28, 2005.
Los Angeles Times Online. September 30, 2005.
New York Times Online. September 30, 2005.
Premiere Magazine Online. September 30, 2005.
Variety Online. September 29, 2005.
Washington Post Online. September 30, 2005, p. WE40.

QUOTES

Sam: "Ask yourself, What do you want in life that money won't get you?"

TRIVIA

The GPS indicates that the location of the wreck is at Latitude 24° 58' 250" North and Longitude 77° 18' 596", which is the location of an island near the Bahamas.

AWARDS

Nomination:

Golden Raspberries 2005: Worst Actress (Alba).

THE ISLAND

They don't want you to know what you are.
—Movie tagline

Plan Your Escape.
—Movie tagline

You Have Been Chosen.
—Movie tagline

In a summer filled with remakes (*Willie Wonka and the Chocolate Factory, War of the Worlds,* and even *Bewitched* and *The Dukes of Hazzard*) it is good to see an original film, but then again, maybe director Michael Bay's *The Island* isn't as original as one would think.

The plot involves a futuristic society in which the Earth has become so contaminated that its few survivors must live in a totally enclosed environment. There is, however, one untainted spot that is just referred to as "The Island" where one can while away one's time surrounded by untainted splendor. Of course, there's not room enough on The Island for everyone so a lottery is held every now and then and the winner gets a ticket to paradise. In the meantime people lead lives that are highly controlled: everyone wears white, health is constantly monitored, diet is tightly regulated, education allowed up to a point, and sex drives all but eliminated because the Rules of Proximity are strictly enforced.

Now one would think that what comes next would be a plot spoiler, but since DreamWorks studio has made a point of mentioning this in it's advertising, it should come as no surprise to most. The catch to "The Island" is that it doesn't exist. It's just the ploy Merrick Industries uses when it wants to cull the herd. And why would it want to do this? To harvest their organs. For, you see, all the people in this tightly controlled environment are clones, or "products" as Merrick (Sean Bean) calls them. In the year 2019 all one has to do is pay Merrick $5 million and a "sponsor" will have available to him on a moment's notice any part of his body that needs to be replaced. Of course sponsors don't realize these spare parts will be coming from clones that are complete humans. They believe it is just the organs that are being cloned because the Eugenics Law of 2015 has made cloning conscious beings illegal. However, in typical big business fashion, Merrick found that without consciousness the organs didn't survive, so he's doing an end run around the law assuming that the sponsors—which even include the president—would do anything to survive, even look the other way if it came to that. So in defense of his enormous profits, Merrick keeps his clones in underground shafts surrounded by holographic images of a world they can never visit.

But Merrick's control is about to be challenged when one of the clones, Lincoln Six Echo (Ewan McGregor) starts doing the unthinkable. He asks questions. His curiosity eventually gets the better of him and soon he's exploring places clones aren't allowed and developing friendships with people he shouldn't such as a tech services worker named McCord (Steve Buscemi). Eventually Lincoln realizes the truth about The Island and when his best friend, Jordan Two Delta (Scarlett Johansson) wins the lottery, he knows they have to try and escape before it is too late.

This ends part one of Michael Bay's movie. The part where important social and ethical questions are posed. Where one could examine the reality of profit over morality. Or what it means to be a human being. Where it could have done what science fiction does so well, commenting on the present by looking at it through the prism of the future. And considering the current political climate and discussions about stem cell research, these could all be important and thought-provoking ideas.

But director Bay has no time to plumb these ideas, for he's off into the second part of the movie, the part that consists of big, loud, fast chases and lots of special effects and crashes and explosions. From his past endeavors, this is the part he prefers and has done well and sometimes not so well in the past (*Armageddon, Pearl Harbor, Bad Boys II*). This section is breathtaking and exhausting. But when the film's all over, one is left frustrated that the intelligent plot of part one has been sacrificed on the altar of action.

What we are left with is a movie that itself is a sort of clone. Think *Logan's Run* on steroids. Throw in a bit of *Coma*, a dash of *THX-1138*, and a few parts *The Matrix* and *Total Recall* and one ends up with *The Island.*

This is not to say, however, that *The Island* isn't enjoyable. The acting is first rate, the music appropriately pounding, and the special effects fascinating. It has all the makings of a good summer movie. If it had kept the promise offered in the first half of the film it could have been a great one.

Beverley Bare Buehrer

CREDITS

Lincoln Six Echo/Tom Lincoln: Ewan McGregor
Jordan Two Delta/Sarah Jordan: Scarlett Johansson
Albert Laurent: Djimon Hounsou
McCord: Steve Buscemi

Starkweather: Michael Clarke Duncan
Suzie: Shawnee Smith
Merrick: Sean Bean
Jones Three Echo: Ethan Phillips
Carnes: Max Baker
Charles Whitman: Kim Coates
Origin: USA
Language: English
Released: 2005
Production: Walter F. Parkes, Michael Bay, Ian Bryce; Parkes/McDonald; released by DreamWorks
Directed by: Michael Bay
Written by: Caspian Tredwell-Owen, Alex Kurtzman, Roberto Orci
Cinematography by: Mauro Fiore
Music by: Steve Jablonsky
Sound: Peter J. Devlin
Editing: Paul Rubell, Christian Wagner
Art Direction: Jon Billington, Sean Haworth, Martin Whist
Costumes: Deborah L. Scott
Production Design: Nigel Phelps
MPAA rating: PG-13
Running time: 136 minutes

REVIEWS

Boxoffice Online. July, 2005.
Chicago Sun-Times Online. July 22, 2005.
Entertainment Weekly Online. July 20, 2005.
Los Angeles Times Online. July 22, 2005.
New York Times Online. July 22, 2005.
Premiere Magazine Online. July 22, 2005.
Variety Online. July 10, 2005.
Washington Post Online. July 22, 2005, p. WE33.

QUOTES

Tom Lincoln: "Don't shoot! He's my clone!"

TRIVIA

Though some shots are purportedly Los Angeles, the city of Detroit was the main location for filming. Notable landmarks include the Johnny Rocket's restaurant on Woodward Avenue across from Comerica Park, the giant building mural of Detroit Red Wings captain Steve Yzerman, the U.S. Federal Building, and the People Mover.

IT'S ALL GONE PETE TONG

The Legend of Frankie Wilde—the Deaf DJ.
—Movie tagline

Touted as *This Is Spinal Tap* for the rave/electronica set, *It's All Gone Pete Tong* is a mockumentary in the style of the Rob Reiner classic but takes a more dramatic and realistic turn mid-way through this tale of a British DJ who goes completely deaf. Real-life British dance DJ Pete Tong, who appears in this semi-biographical film, had the dubious distinction of having his name turned into Cockney rhyming slang, meaning "It's all gone wrong," which turns out to be the case for the film's hero Frankie Wilde, and his fall from fame. Canadian director Michael Dowse revisits the music-themed comedy found in his cult hit *Fubar* (2002) but adds significant heart as the cartoonish Wilde grows into an actual, three-dimensional person by the film's sweet ending.

Told in flashback, the film begins with interviews from various parties talking about the dubious fate of the famous British DJ Frankie Wilde and then flashes back to happier times one year previous. Looking like a cross between Pete Townsend and Seth Green and boasting a set of choppers Austin Powers would be appalled at, Paul Kaye plays the hot, Ibiza-based dance DJ who has it all. The spectacular opening sequences show Frankie in his element, spinning wildly at the club where he holds court—at one point sliding from the ceiling onto the dance floor on a cable, dressed Jesus-like with a crown of thorns. Subsequent shots in the opening credits montage further chronicle the hedonistic lifestyle of the aptly-named Wilde, who, when not indulging in the excesses of the club, can be seen heartily indulging his penchant for whiskey and cocaine on the beautiful Mediterranean island beaches surrounded by scantily clad girls and being interviewed by a lovely reporter.

A small portion of the film is devoted to his continuing rise: Frankie gets a gig producing his own album with a couple of Austrian mates and he marries the glamorous and very promiscuous Sonja (Kate Magowan), who has a cute young son from a previous relationship. Ensconced in a posh villa, Frankie and Sonja play tennis, snort vast amounts of cocaine, and engage in swinging sex sessions until one day Frankie realizes his hearing is starting to go. Deeply in denial, his way of coping with the problem is to ingest greater quantities of his pet drug. Dowse physically manifests his addiction onscreen as a giant black and white stuffed bear (the "monkey" on his back, as it were) wearing a frilly apron who menaces Wilde every time he tries to lay off cocaine. Sinking into despair, the oblivious Sonya busies herself by hiring people to redecorate the villa while Wilde's insensitive manager, complete with omnipresent Bluetooth headset, advises him to "eat some fruit and vegetables" and get some sun.

No longer able to mask his growing deafness, Wilde finally seeks professional help. The doctor tells the appalled DJ that he was born with a defect in both ears and that surgery is not an option. He is completely deaf in one ear and has twenty-five percent hearing left in the other. He can, however, prolong the time when he will eventually be completely without hearing by not exposing himself to loud noises and only wearing the hearing aid he is given when absolutely necessary. Back in the recording studio, the outraged Austrians hear the god-awful mix that their deaf producer has unknowingly come up with and begin to trash the place. With hearing aid in place to try and rectify his mistake, he unfortunately has his headphones on with the level on high just as one of the Austrians smashes an amp with his guitar. A tortuous scene shows Wilde writhing in agony on the floor with a blood pouring out of his last good ear.

The film somewhat moves away from the strict faux documentary style as Wilde descends into a sort of madness. With Sonja long-gone, he tapes up his ears, boards up the windows of his villa, and spends his days lying in bed, drinking and doing cocaine. After many weeks ending in a hilariously attempted pseudo-suicide, Wilde finally comes to his senses and manages to kick his coke habit, squaring off with the large bear (which actually turns out to be himself in a bear suit) and shooting it dead. Emerging from his self-imposed quarantine, Wilde again seeks professional help. He seeks out a lip-reading service for the blind and meets the spunky and attractive speech therapist Penelope (Beatriz Batarda), who is also profoundly deaf as well as sharing his love of whiskey.

The movie turns into a love story and an inspirational overcoming the odds saga. While figuring out what to do with his new life and depressed by his options as a deaf man, Frankie finds, while attending a flamenco dance concert with his new love Penelope, that he can "feel" the music as well as hear it as the dancer's stomping feet shakes his whiskey glass. This leads him to the bright idea of strapping speakers onto his feet and buying a machine that visually illustrates the sound waves so he can also "see" the music. He turns out a brilliant mix (the very *Spinal Tap*-like titled, "Hear No Evil") much to the delight of his overjoyed manager. He returns victoriously to the club he left in disgrace for one last gig which is a huge success. His subsequent disappearance leading to all sorts of conclusions, we see Frankie in a new city, living a quiet life with Penelope and their young child.

A former stand-up comedian, Kaye brings Frankie brilliantly to life with explosive energy and expressive eyes that capture the pain of addiction and physical ruin as well as a touching vulnerability. With his all profanity-laced gravelly barking, Wilmot is perfect as the greedy manager. The eye candy that is the Ibiza locales are another reason to watch, highlighted, naturally with a variety of appropriately adrenaline-inducing, thumping dance tracks.

Hilary White

CREDITS

Frankie Wilde: Paul Kaye
Penelope: Beatriz Batarda
Max Hagger: Mike Wilmot
Alfonse: Paul J. Spence
Sonia: Kate Magowan
Horst: Dave Lawrence
Origin: Great Britain, Canada
Language: English
Released: 2004
Production: Jamie Richardson, Alan Niblo, Elizabeth Yake; True West Films
Directed by: Michael Dowse
Written by: Michael Dowse
Cinematography by: Balasz Bolygo
Music by: Graham Massey
Sound: Michael McCann
Editing: Stuart Gazzard
Art Direction: Emily Straight
Production Design: Paul Burns
MPAA rating: R
Running time: 88 minutes

REVIEWS

New York Times Online. April 15, 2005.
Premiere Magazine Online. April 15, 2005.
Variety Online. September 17, 2004.

QUOTES

Frank Wilde: "Maybe I should write a book. That might take years though, perhaps a pamphlet or brochure."

TRIVIA

The title is Cockney rhyming slang for "it has all gone wrong."

THE JACKET

Terror has a new name.
—Movie tagline

When you die, all you want to do is come back.
—Movie tagline

I was 27 years old the first time I died.
—Movie tagline

Box Office: $6.3 million

In British director John Maybury's disturbing thriller *The Jacket,* Adrien Brody plays an American Gulf War veteran who may or may not be experiencing post-traumatic stress disorder (including bouts of amnesia), who may or may not have killed a policeman, who may or may not be subjected to mind-altering experiments in a hospital for the criminally insane, and who may or may not be able to travel to the future, beyond his death, and have a romance with the grown-up version of a little girl he befriended years before. How you interpret the film depends on your perspective, and that's part of the fun. Screenwriter Massy Tadjedin has concocted a challenging, original, and neatly constructed plot that borrows from sources as diverse as *One Flew Over the Cuckoo's Nest, Memento* and *Eternal Sunshine of the Spotless Mind,* but nonetheless is wholly original.

The film is compelling from the start, and Maybury employs a wrenching, mind-churning style that emphasizes the physical and emotional pain of central character Jack Starks's strange journey. Very much in your face, Maybury uses horror-movie-style flashing images to scream out the disturbing gaps and rips in the fragile and bombarded psyche of his beleaguered main character. In the film's opening sequence, tinted green to look like military night-vision video, Starks is an American soldier in the Gulf War who tries to befriend an Iraqi boy, but the boy shoots him. At first given up for dead in the military's battlefield hospital tent, Starks comes back to life, but is diagnosed as being susceptible to amnesia.

A year later, released from the hospital, he is hitchhiking along the back roads of snowy Vermont when he comes upon a young girl and her mother next to their stalled truck. The mother is incoherent, obviously drug-addicted, and barely able to stay awake, much less speak, but the young girl, whose name is Jackie, is cute and competent. Jack gets the car started, Jackie asks if he can have his dog tags, and the mother, Jean, then chases Jack away, mistakenly believing he is a dangerous pedophile because she sees him hug Jackie.

Later that day, Jack hitches a ride with a ne'er-do-well (Brad Renfro) who is apparently running from the law. When they are stopped by a policeman, the cop is gunned down, and the driver wipes the gun and leaves it next to Jack, who's been wounded. Confused and unable to defend himself from murder charges, Starks is found not guilty by reason of insanity. He's sentenced to Alpine Grove, a forensic psychiatric facility that seems barely a step removed from the Inquisition. There, Starks quickly becomes prey for Dr. Becker (Kris Kristofferson), a psychiatrist whose outlandish treatment methods say a lot about his own obvious mental instability. With the help of a skinnier but no less scarier clone of *Cuckoo's Nest*'s Nurse Ratched, and a burly thug of an orderly, Becker subjects Starks to injections of experimental drugs augmented by an extreme sensory deprivation experiment: Starks is straight-jacketed, placed on a table, and put inside a morgue-like drawer in a basement room for hours at a time.

When he is first put in the jacket and shelved away, the experience is nightmarish for Jack—and for us. Displayed on close-ups of Brody's frightened eyes in the dark are quick flashes of his wartime experience and other traumas and psychic tortures. Maybury focuses his camera on Jack's screaming mouth and effectively, and disturbingly, illustrates the assault of these mental images on Jack's brain. Starks comes out of the experiment barely conscious—but, according to Becker, that's better than anyone else who has undergone the trauma of the jacket experiment.

Jack sees something else when he's inside the jacket—he is transported to a future time, 2007, where he meets a grown-up Jackie. He cannot control the duration of his visits, but eventually Jack is concocting displays of insane misbehavior that will get him back into the jacket and back to the future, where he can not only romance Jackie, but discover more clues to the death that Jackie reports he will have experienced in a few more days at Alpine Grove. Among his allies is a sympathetic doctor (Jennifer Jason Leigh) who is critical of Becker's methods but also distrustful of Jack's reports of his psychic leaps through time.

Under Maybury's frenzied hand, *The Jacket* is a taut, harrowing thriller that only thins out a little as the dimensions of the plot come into focus, and Jack's quest becomes both more preposterous and more gripping. Perhaps the film could have been directed with more subtlety, but the pounding scenes provide a frightening glimpse into Jack's soul. Brody is highly compelling and sympathetic; watch how his Jack Starks hides his intelligence until it is necessary, how he displays his raw humanity despite how it's been crushed, how valiantly he clings to his sanity, and how willing he is to sacrifice his safety for his unusual quest. Brody has a natural affinity for a hangdog, cornered look, but he has infused this performance with the same kind of empathy he used so well in his Oscar-winning role in *The Pianist.*

As the grown-up Jackie, rising ingenue Keira Knightley is surprisingly nuanced and disturbing with her own brand of nervous insanity. She almost chews on a glass as she eyes the captive Brody, gnaws on her lips as she ponders whether he is a threat or an erotic godsend, and displays a remarkable vulnerability. Kristofferson is brilliantly villainous as the off-kilter, haunted mad doctor, and Leigh is attractive, intelligent, and highly believable as a medical professional caught between her convictions and her humanity.

Although other films have played with the themes *The Jacket* probes, few have duplicated its edgy, offbeat, frightening directness. This is a very original screenplay and a story confidently and bravely told. Though parts of Knightley's character's actions and dialogue start to sound contrived and mundane near the end, Tadjedin provides a satisfying conclusion to a plot that seems like it might unravel with the final revelations. And there's a tremendously compelling and unexpected scene at the end, with Jackie's mother awakening from her stupor to the plain wonder and joy of her daughter. The film's like a slap in the face, telling us all to wake up to the present regardless of what we know or think we fear about the future.

Michael Betzold

CREDITS

Jack Starks: Adrien Brody
Jackie: Keira Knightley
Dr. Becker: Kris Kristofferson
Dr. Lorenson: Jennifer Jason Leigh
Jean: Kelly Lynch
Stranger: Brad Renfro
Mackenzie: Daniel Craig
Nurse Harding: MacKenzie Phillips
Origin: USA
Language: English
Released: 2005
Production: Peter Guber, George Clooney, Steven Soderbergh, Peter E. Strauss, Ori Marmur, Ben Cosgrove, Jennifer Fox, Todd Wagner; Warner Independent Pictures, Mandalay Pictures; released by Warner Independent Pictures
Directed by: John Maybury
Written by: Massy Tadjedin
Cinematography by: Peter Deming
Music by: Brian Eno
Sound: Colin Nicolson
Music Supervisor: Andy Richards
Editing: Emma E. Hickox
Costumes: Doug Hall
Production Design: Alan Macdonald
MPAA rating: R
Running time: 102 minutes

REVIEWS

Boxoffice Online. March, 2005.
Chicago Sun-Times Online. March 4, 2005.
Entertainment Weekly Online. March 2, 2005.
Los Angeles Times Online. March 4, 2005.
New York Times Online. March 4, 2005.
Premiere Magazine Online. March 4, 2005.
Variety Online. January 24, 2005.
Washington Post Online. March 4, 2005, p. C01.

TRIVIA

Colin Farrell and Mark Wahlberg were both considered for the role of Jack Starks before Adrien Brody was cast.

JARHEAD

Welcome To The Suck.
—Movie tagline

Box Office: $62.3 million

I wanted a thankless mission; I wanted poor odds and likely death; I wanted to give myself over to beliefs that were more complex than base beliefs of the infantry grunt. The grunt dies for nothing, for fifteen thousand poorly placed rounds; the sniper dies for that one perfect shot.

***—Anthony Swofford from his book,** Jarhead: A Marines Chronicle of the Gulf War And Other Battles*

In Sam Mendes' *Jarhead,* marked differences and diversions from Swofford's book are made in the screenplay written by William D. Broyles Jr. Significantly whittled down, the movie is only a shard of light into the layered, poignant memoir whose nonlinear structure freely skips around the canvas of Swofford's life from boyhood, boot camp, sniper training, and attending a friend's funeral following his Gulf War experience. The departures from the book are significant in that it does not explore Swofford's familial interactions and romances nor his reintegration into society after his military career.

The historical events unfold as follows: in August, 1990, Iraq invaded its tiny neighbor, Kuwait, resulting in a global uproar. The United Nations failed in negotiating with Saddam Hussein's regime. The United States (Under President George Herbert Walker Bush) led a smaller United Nations force to free Kuwait. Ignoring UN ultimatums, Iraq maintained occupation of Kuwait. Desert Shield transitioned into Desert Storm. An air war of unprecedented power obliterated Iraqi forces with around-the-clock bombing. Meanwhile, more than half a million US troops were amassed in Saudi Arabia awaiting the ground war component to the operation. After a month of bombing, the ground war was unleashed on February 23, 1991. It lasted four days, four hours and one minute. A cease-fire ensued on February 27, and Iraq complied with UN terms on March 3.

Mendes' movie focuses on the tedious time spent by young Marines waiting their turn for their cut of the glory of war. There are no battle scenes in *Jarhead.* The conflict for these grunts is one not often portrayed in war movies: men trained to kill with no one to kill. Swofford (Jake Gyllenhaal) is a 20-year-old Marine sniper when he is deployed with his platoon to Saudi Arabia. He often finds himself at odds with his obvious gift towards intellect (implied by carrying around a copy of *The Iliad* in his rucksack) and ethical regard contrasted with a blood lust cultivated from his devil dog training as well as an esprit de corps instilled in the men by mass viewings of such Vietnam war flicks like *Apocalypse Now, Full Metal Jacket,* and *The Deer Hunter.* Sniper teams are composed of a trigger man and a spotter. Swofford's spotter is Troy (Peter Sarsgaard) who also becomes his best friend. Later in the movie, we learn that Troy was killed in a car accident in Greenville, Michigan and was given a burial in civilian clothes. The reason for portraying Troy's funeral with former platoon brothers attending (also in civilian clothing) is unclear. In the memoir, Troy is given a full military burial in uniform; Swofford and other Marines also attend in uniform.

During their wait, the platoon continues to train, they simulate combat while wearing heavy warfare gear and are required to ingest pills (that may or may not have dangerous long term side effects) in the event they are exposed to chemical weapons. Rehydration is ongoing in the above 100-degree heat. They play a football game in chemical garb for the American press that ends up in the rowdy soldiers participating in a simulated gang rape witnessed by the horrified media and career Marine Staff Sergeant Sykes' (Jamie Foxx). They drink awful desert hooch when available and patrol the desert. During one such patrol, the platoon encounters eight Arabs. Five are riding camels. Tension mounts as Swofford meets up with one of them and for a short time it looks like the language barrier might result in open fire. The mood simmers down immediately when it is finally discovered that they are only complaining about three of their camels being shot.

The climax of the anxiety that has brewed for six months finally arrives during the short ground war and Swofford and his spotter Troy are given a long-awaited assignment. Once Swofford has the target in his crosshairs, the mission is abruptly aborted and relegated to an air strike instead. Troy goes into a pathological temper tantrum: "Let him take the shot!" He screams rolling and pounding his fists on the ground. The scene best exemplifies the increasing futility and sense of uselessness the men feel. While they hate being there most of the time but they want to kill because that is specifically what they have been trained to do.

The acting in this movie is superb, but the screenplay is a disappointment and exudes a sense of anticlimax. The message of the book is clear: Swofford conveys the idea, time and time again in different ways, that once a Marine, always a Marine. Becoming a

Marine completely changes one's life forever and that being a Marine is a thing unto itself, aside from politics or even which war is being fought. It is an internal change, one which the film has trouble conveying and *Jarhead* vacillates in its efforts to stand apart from the standard war genre movie and encompass it as well. The end result is that Swofford's simple truth is lost in the mix.

David Metz Roberts

CREDITS

Tony "Swoff" Swofford: Jake Gyllenhaal
Troy: Peter Sarsgaard
Kruger: Lucas Black
Fergus: Brian Geraghty
Cortez: Jacob Vargas
Escobar: Laz Alonso
Fowler: Evan Jones
Pinko: Ivan Fenyo
Lt. Col. Kazinski: Chris Cooper
Major Lincoln: Dennis Haysbert
D.I. Fitch: Scott MacDonald
Staff Sgt. Sykes: Jamie Foxx
Foster: Jamie Martz
Welty: Kareem Grimes
Doc John: Peter Gail
Julius: Jocko Sims
Origin: USA
Language: English
Released: 2005
Production: Douglas Wick, Lucy Fisher; released by Universal
Directed by: Sam Mendes
Written by: William Broyles Jr.
Cinematography by: Roger Deakins
Music by: Thomas Newman
Sound: Willie Burton
Editing: Walter Murch
Costumes: Albert Wolsky
Production Design: Dennis Gassner
MPAA rating: R
Running time: 122 minutes

REVIEWS

Boxoffice Online. November, 2005.
Chicago Sun-Times Online. November 4, 2005.
Entertainment Weekly Online. November 2, 2005.
Los Angeles Times Online. November 4, 2005.
New York Times Online. November 4, 2005.
Premiere Magazine Online. November 3, 2005.
Variety Online. October 27, 2005.
Washington Post Online. November 4, 2005, p. C01.

QUOTES

Anthony "Swoff" Swofford: "Every war is different, every war is the same."

TRIVIA

Jamie Foxx's character, Staff Sgt. Sykes, originally had a tattoo of a panther on the back of his shaved head. Foxx sported the makeup at all times, even during his award sweeps for *Ray* (2004). However, the tattoo was later digitally removed in post-production by director Sam Mendes, who felt it made the character too "hard core."

JIMINY GLICK IN LALAWOOD

How a legend was born.
—Movie tagline

Martin Short, along with the fat suit that envelops him, plays the obnoxious titular entertainment reporter, which, over the years, could be seen interviewing a host of celebrities on his Comedy Central show, *Primtime Glick.* As is the case with many TV sketch characters, including a host from *Saturday Night Live*, the jump to the big screen proves too much for Glick. This showbiz sendup is only as mildly and sporadically funny as its lead character, a puzzling mix of fawning toady, caustic shark, androgynous everyman, and savvy entertainment insider, shifting from one to another as quickly as his impossibly high falsetto voice swoops back down to a serious bass and back again.

Directed by Vadim Jean and written by Short and longtime collaborator Paul Flaherty, the premise has the Butte, Montana celebrity interviewer taking his first trip to the Toronto Film Festival. The lisping, effeminate reporter heads north with wife Dixie (Jan Hooks) and the hilariously named twins Matthew (Landon Hansen) and Modine (Jake Hoffman). There is a mix-up in the hotel bookings and the Glicks end up staying in a seedy hotel inhabited, however, by director David Lynch (also played by Short) who is working on a film about a celebrity interviewer much like Glick himself who finds himself entangled in a murder.

Life imitates art as Glick does, indeed, believes he has murdered the alcoholic movie star Miranda Coolidge (Elizabeth Perkins), at the festival promoting her new film, a lesbian take on *The African Queen* entitled *The Queens of Africa.* How he winds up in such an unlikely scenario is all due to his natural ineptitude. Falling asleep at the fest's screening of the film *Growing Up Ghandi* about the young Mahatma as a champion boxer, Glick gives the awful film it's sole positive review. Suddenly, he's granted an interview by the film's popular star Ben diCarlo (Corey Pearson) who hasn't talked to a reporter in five years. Jiminy is rocketed to fame after his exclusive with the star. He's now attending parties with the likes of Coolidge, her press agent Dee Dee (Janeane Garofalo), and manager husband Andre (John Michael Higgins) where he is slipped a mickey. When Glick wakes up with Miranda's blood-covered handkerchief, he believes that his dream that he murdered the legendary star is actually true. The rest of the film is devoted to Glick making like Sherlock Holmes to unravel the mystery.

Largely improvised from a 40-page outline, Short is at his best playing Glick doing his off-the-cuff interviews he's perfected with the stars he meets in Toronto, including Whoopi Goldberg, Steve Martin and Kurt Russell, with whom he has an interesting discussion about Elvis. There is a very funny bit where poor little Jiminy struggles to get the attention of Kiefer Sutherland. Although Short's impression of Lynch is impressive, the antics of Glick merely seem stifled by the contrived murder plot, which, it is presumed, was only injected to stretch the action into this funny but forgettable feature-length film.

Hilary White

CREDITS

Jimmy Glick/David Lynch: Martin Short
Dixie Glick: Jan Hooks
Miranda Coolidge: Elizabeth Perkins
Andre Devine: John Michael Higgins
Natalie Coolidge: Linda Cardellini
Dee Dee: Janeane Garofalo
Barry King: Carlos Jacott
Ben DiCarlo: Corey Pearson
Matthew Glick: London Hansen
Modine Glick: Jake Hoffman
Gunner "Mc Gun" Jorge: Aries Spears
Jay Schiffer: Robert Trebor
Randall "Big Phallus" Bookerton: Gary Anthony Williams
Haygood Lewkin: Larry Joe Campbell
Sharon: Mo Collins
Mario "Fa Real" Greene: DeRay Davis
Kiefer Sutherland (Cameo)
Whoopi Goldberg (Cameo)
Steve Martin (Cameo)
Kevin Kline (Cameo)
Sharon Stone (Cameo)
Forest Whitaker (Cameo)
Susan Sarandon (Cameo)
Kurt Russell (Cameo)
Rob Lowe (Cameo)
Origin: USA, Canada
Language: English
Released: 2005
Production: Paul Brooks, Bernie Brillstein, Martin Short, Peter Safran; Gold Circle Films, Brillstiein-Grey; released by Equinox Films
Directed by: Vadim Jean
Written by: Martin Short, Paul Flaherty
Cinematography by: Mike J. Fox
Music by: David Lawrence
Sound: William Skinner
Editing: Matt Davis
Costumes: Loraine Carson
Production Design: Tony Devenyi
MPAA rating: R
Running time: 90 minutes

REVIEWS

Boxoffice Online. May, 2005.
Chicago Sun-Times Online. May 5, 2005.
Entertainment Weekly Online. May 4, 2005.
Los Angeles Times Online. May 6, 2005.
New York Times Online. May 6, 2005.
Variety Online. September 19, 2004.

JUNEBUG

Box Office: $2.7 million

Phil Morrison takes on a daunting task for his debut feature, *Junebug*: to fashion a social comedy from lives in which nothing happens. Like other unassuming American filmmakers of his generation, most notably Gregg Mottola with *The Daytrippers* (reviewed in the 1997 volume), Morrison steers clear of contrivance, even at the risk of courting narrative stasis. However, through finely nuanced acting and cinematography, his film remains riveting as a character study. If anything, Morrison would have to stand accused of transforming the simplemindedness of his Southern folk into motifs (and not very dramatic ones at that) for his filmic canvas.

As it happens, art (as painting) is very much the subject at the core of his film. It forms the mainstay in the life of Madeleine (Embeth Davidtz), a British expatriate who, with her husband George (Alessandro Nivola), owns an art gallery in Chicago. When we first see them they are a successful attractive, sexually hyperactive young couple. The catalyst in their lives turns out to be Wark (Frank Hoyt Taylor), an unknown painter in the boonies of North Carolina. Madeleine is convinced that his peculiar brand of folk art will be the next big thing on the high priced circuit.

The cause of art then begins to shape her life when she finds that to pull in her catch she will need to stay in the nearby town where, coincidentally, George's family live. Madeleine thus moves in full of cheer for the in-laws she has never met. This allows Morrison to use Madeleine as the outsider who throws the eccentricities of George's family into sharp relief.

The one to form the closest bond with Madeleine is the pretty Ashley (Amy Adams), the lumbering pregnant daughter who is all agog and can't get enough of her sister-in-law's urbane sophistication. At the opposite end of the spectrum is her husband, the scatter-brained, taciturn Johnny (Benjamin McKenzie), a dark continent to everyone. He works at a china factory while completing high school in his spare time. The father, Eugene (Scott Wilson), a retiree, keeps himself busy with his woodwork and is content to remain silent.When we see his wife Peg (Celia Weston), we know why. As a domineering virago, she waddles around illustrating the dictum that home is where the hurt is, making it clear for us why George had to escape his domestic roots.

Madeleine's stay is peppered with the uneventful flow of everyday life. There's a prolonged scene in which Ashley does her nails while the two exchange secrets about their mates. At the baby shower that shows Madeleine has blended into the homely scene, Wark and Sissy (Joanne Pankow), his sister, intrude to corner her with the news that a New York art gallery has made him a more generous offer. Madeleine has to plead with them to allow her time to come up with a better one.

A different strain is now gradually introduced into this bucolic rhapsody: the bedrock of Christian faith. It first surfaces when Ashley tells Johnny that Jesus loves him too much to allow him to remain as he is. It develops at a social gathering when the young Pastor (R. Keith Harris) voices a prayer for George and Madeleine's marriage to be a "spirit filled union" through which they realize "the impermanence of this world." The family members (all except for Johnny) pray along with their eyes closed. Madeleine too closes her eyes but that inner conviction that the others share, George included, seems to be missing. Then as George sings a hymn, his voice displaying the training of a singer in a choir, Madeleine looks on in rapt wonder, as if this was a side of him she had never known.

In a remarkable twist, this religious feeling takes on a dimension of purity and simplicity that shows up Madeleine's own lack of inner fortitude. When she attempts to help Johnny with a term paper, sitting up with him late at night, he misconstrues her gesture as condescending. Then when she apologizes, holding him close in affection, he takes it as a sexual overture. Madeleine promptly withdraws, whereupon he verbally abuses her and her inborn air of superiority that he hates in George as well. Owing to the context from which it springs, Johnny's anger takes on a resonance that suddenly reveals a socio-political rift in contemporary American society of seismic proportions. At the end of the scene, Madeleine is left silently aghast to question her own motives for being there.

The conflict between the old-fashioned life she has been leading with George's family and the professional commitment her work demands comes to a head when Ashley goes into labor. The event coincides with Madeleine coming to know that Wark has decided to sign with their rival in the bidding war. George feels she should be at Ashley's side out of a sense of devotion to the family; Madeleine however wants a stab at wooing Wark back.

Here again, she comes up against what to her is a brick wall of religious faith. When she says that she feels a "personal, spiritual connection" to Wark's paintings, he answers that he's "a collaborator with God" and that he's preparing himself to leave behind this "vale of tears." His only wish is a special fruit basket of the kind he hasn't been able to find. Madeleine promises him that, after which he looks into her eyes and gets her to commit herself to doing Jesus's work on earth. Madeleine's religious wheeling and dealing leads to her leaving with his signature where she wants it.

Her joy however evaporates when she learns from George on the phone that Ashley's boy was stillborn. George says he will remain with Ashley and tells her to take a cab back from Wark's place. In a moving scene, Ashley breaks down and confides to George how her faith in medical science has been shaken, along with her faith in nature and God. The name "Junebug" was to have been the name of her child.

When George returns home, Johnny expresses his rage by throwing a wrench at him, injuring him in the forehead. Like a true Christian, George merely walks away. The next morning he whisks Madeleine off, not allowing her to meet Ashley. On the open highway, Madeleine stares ahead, emotionally shaken. We then see her reaching out to feel the back of George's head, as if to assure him that their bond is stronger than that of blood.

Vivek Adarkar

CREDITS

Madeleine: Embeth Davidtz

George: Alessandro Nivola

Ashley: Amy Adams
Peg: Celia Weston
Johnny: Ben(jamin) McKenzie
Eugene: Scott Wilson
David Wark: Frank Hoyt Taylor
Sissy: Joanne Pankow
Origin: USA
Language: English
Released: 2005
Production: Mike S. Ryan, Mindy Goldberg; Epoch Films
Directed by: Phil Morrison
Written by: Angus MacLachlan
Cinematography by: Peter Donahue
Music by: Yo LaTengo
Sound: Jeffree Bloomer
Editing: Joe Klotz
Costumes: Danielle Kays
Production Design: David Doernberg
MPAA rating: R
Running time: 107 minutes

REVIEWS

Boxoffice Online. August, 2005.
Chicago Sun-Times Online. August 12, 2005.
Entertainment Weekly Online. August 3, 2005.
Los Angeles Times Online. August 3, 2005.
New York Times Online. August 3, 2005.
Premiere Magazine Online. August 5, 2005.
Variety Online. February 9, 2005.

QUOTES

Ashley: "God loves you just the way you are, but He loves you too much to let you stay that way."

AWARDS

Ind. Spirit 2006: Support. Actress (Adams)
Natl. Soc. Film Critics 2005: Support. Actress (Adams)
Broadcast Film Critics 2005: Support. Actress (Adams)

Nomination:

Oscars 2005: Support. Actress (Adams)
Ind. Spirit 2006: First Screenplay
Screen Actors Guild 2005: Support. Actress (Adams).

JUST FRIENDS

Some friends are just friends. Others you get to see naked.
—Movie tagline

Moments like this have been ruining friendships for centuries.
—Movie tagline

He loves her. She loves him not.
—Movie tagline

Box Office: $30.6 million

Ryan Reynolds is a decent actor who, after the modestly successful *Van Wilder* (2002), has starred in a number of depressingly bad movies. Although certainly not his breakout film, *Just Friends* is a likeable enough romantic comedy that, while not very sophisticated, has its charms. Directed by *The Sweetest Thing* helmer Roger Kumble and written by relative newcomer Adam "Tex" Davis, the film clips along at a good pace and balances the over-the-top comic characters with more dimensional ones with a script that boasts contemporary comic savvy.

Ryan Reynolds, sporting a patently fake fat suit, plays Chris Brander, who is a frizzy-haired, overweight New Jersey circa 1995 teenager when the picture opens. Chris is in love with Jamie Palamino (Amy Smart) a pretty cheerleader who is smart and sweet Chris's friend but who doesn't stand a chance with her, romantically speaking. Unfortunately, his true feelings for her are embarrassingly revealed and Chris flees town in shame, vowing to make something of himself.

Fast forward ten years, where Reynold's Chris, sans fat suit, has made good on his promise. He has become a successful Hollywood music executive, an accomplished hockey player and, most importantly, a lean and mean womanizer. He is, in fact, flying to Paris on a private jet with music video star Samantha James, played by Anna Faris in an over-the-top version of her ingénue character in *Lost in Translation.* A monster in high heels, the attractive but talentless Sam develops an obsession with Chris, who is trying to keep her at bay personally but woo her professionally.

Chris is forced to go face-to-face with his past when a fire on board the plane forces them to make an emergency landing in New Jersey. When he meets up with Jamie on Christmas Eve, all the old feelings come rushing back but now he is confident that he can win her over. It's not as easy as he thinks, however, and in a clever twist finds a rival for her love in another high school "Cinderfella" story, Dusty Dinkleman (Chris Klein). The once acne-ridden loser has turned into a handsome acoustic guitar player who seduces women with his sensitive, New Agey act. Also, it is clear the once sweet and sensitive Chris has changed inside as well as out, compromising himself for success. Now, he'll have to have a makeover of a different kind in order to win Jamie. He also must deal with the savagely territorial Sam who's hot on his heels.

The humor is mostly palatable but can be a bit crude at times. Reynolds is well-cast and able in his portrayal of the nerd who has his day but doesn't turn out to be what he thought it would. Smart is sweet and likeable in her girl-next-door turn and Klein is funny as Chris's geek-to-chic competition. It is Faris, however, howlingly funny as the narcissistic freak Sam who, in a brilliant move, can be heard during the closing credits singing her single, "Forgiveness."

Hilary White

CREDITS

Chris Brander: Ryan Reynolds
Jamie Palamino: Amy Smart
Samantha James: Anna Faris
Carol Brander: Julie Hagerty
Mike Brander: Christopher Marquette
KC: Stephen (Steve) Root
Dusty Dinkleman: Chris Klein
Clark: Fred Ewanuick
Origin: USA
Language: English
Released: 2005
Production: Chris Bender, JC Spink, William Vince, Bill Johnson, Michael Ohoven; Benderspink, Cinezeta Production; released by New Line Cinema
Directed by: Roger Kumble
Written by: Adam "Tex" Davis
Cinematography by: Anthony B. Richmond
Music by: Jeff Cardoni
Sound: Michael McGee
Music Supervisor: Patrick Houlihan
Editing: Jeff Freeman
Art Direction: Russell Moore
Costumes: Alexandra Welker
Production Design: Robb Wilson King
MPAA rating: PG-13
Running time: 94 minutes

REVIEWS

Boxoffice Online. November, 2005.
Chicago Sun-Times Online. November 23, 2005.
Entertainment Weekly Online. November 22, 2005.
Los Angeles Times Online. November 23, 2005.
New York Times Online. November 23, 2005.
Variety Online. November 17, 2005.
Washington Post Online. November 23, 2005, p. C10.

QUOTES

Mike: "You'll always be fat to me!"

TRIVIA

It took four hours just to make the 12 pound face Ryan Reynolds wore.

JUST LIKE HEAVEN

It's a wonderful afterlife.
—Movie tagline
Love will bring you back.
—Movie tagline

Box Office: $48.3 million

It begins with the camera drifting down through the clouds and revolving around a pretty lady serenely seated amidst a lush, beautiful garden. It ends with the camera ascending skyward amidst a welling-up of lovely, dreamy music as the same woman and her soul mate have their big smooch in another flowery setting. To those either not in the mood for or perhaps chromosomally allergic to such romantic gooeyness, *Just Like Heaven* must already sound like hell. However, if viewers are interested in and open to a rather charming fantasy which induces a modest amount of chuckles and sniffles, then the film is well worth seeing.

Emergency room doctor Elizabeth Martinson (Reese Witherspoon) is a driven, highly efficient workaholic bucking hard for the position of attending physician by tackling shifts that stretch from one day into the next. She is propelled through her demanding duties by plucky ambition and an awful lot of caffeine. Tap her on the shoulder during a much-needed catnap and she is back in action. Call out to her while she is in the restroom and she comes running. While the adorable doctor skillfully juggles the innumerable tasks her job entails, she shows far less aptitude when it comes to healthily counterbalancing her successful professional life with a fulfilling personal one. Her female coworkers, trying to eke out time for hot dates or grappling with the responsibility of children, are aware of Elizabeth's romantic and sexual inactivity, and one goes so far as to assert she is "so lucky that all you have to worry about is work." Elizabeth tells her concerned sister Abby (Dina Waters), who aims to set her up with a friend of a friend, that she is capable of meeting men on her own. "I know," says Abby, "I just want you to meet one who's not bleeding." Later that night, Elizabeth, thrilled to have won the coveted position, relents to the blind date and heads off to her sister's house through dark, rain-slicked San Francisco streets. Just as things are looking up, she looks down to adjust the radio and smashes head-on into a truck.

Cut to landscape architect David Abbott (Mark Ruffalo), a heartbroken young widower looking for an apartment to lease. Nothing the real estate agent shows him is quite to his liking. Then a windswept flier persists in plastering itself to various parts of his body no matter how many times he tries to toss it aside. David finally peels the paper off his face and reads about the availability of Elizabeth's beautiful apartment for a month's sublet. He finds himself strangely drawn to it, finds it warm and comfy, and is impressed with its sensational rooftop view of the city.

David spends too much time forlornly slouched on the couch, drinking and munching and watching his wedding video. It is clear he is a mess, and he is rapidly making Elizabeth's place into one, as well. He is jolted out of his sad sack reverie by Elizabeth's sudden appearance. She is as perplexed as he is but outraged as well, demanding to know exactly what he thinks he is doing in her apartment. David says he lives there. She says he most certainly does not. Elizabeth surmises he has broken in to steal her things, or at least ruin them with an obliviousness to coasters and trashcans. "It's like a pig moved into my house!" she fumes mightily. "A filthy pig!" Then, just as abruptly as she showed up, she disappears.

David does not know what to make of this strangely illusive and intrusive harpy. He wonders if perhaps his mind is playing tricks on him due to depression or drink. Visiting with psychiatrist pal Jack (Donal Logue), David uneasily discloses that he is "seeing someone." Assuming this means David's protracted emotional hibernation is finally coming to an end, Jack supportively proclaims, "This is the world. Join it!" Not quite sure what is going on, David tries changing the locks. It does no good.

Gradually, this dispirited man realizes he is dealing with a very spirited spirit, and *Just Like Heaven* successfully generates laughs as the two battle to occupy the same space. David tries to convince Elizabeth she is dead, and encourages her to "walk into the light." She feistily scoffs that she would certainly know if she were dead and is not going anywhere. Elizabeth keeps materializing in the bathroom, so David simply starts taking semi-clothed showers. When he goes to get a beer, she appears in the refrigerator and snidely chides his alcohol consumption. She sings "Tomorrow" to try and drive him out and he turns up the volume on the television to try and drown her out. He gets various ghostbusters and then finally resorts to an exorcism. When the priest throws holy water around, an unfazed Elizabeth merely retorts to David, "you're mopping that up." Finally, a slightly wacky slacker named Darryl (Jon Heder, memorable in 2004's *Napoleon Dynamite*) who works in an occult bookstore offers the sobering opinion that this woman who seems just like a ghost is actually the detached soul of a woman who is still alive. (Darryl can feel Elizabeth's presence, but cannot see her.)

The film shows its unevenness most during the lukewarm stretch in which Elizabeth and David hopscotch around town trying to figure out who she is (she cannot remember), what is actually happening to her, and why only he can see her. Eventually, they wind up at the hospital where Elizabeth worked, and learn the shocking truth: she has been lying there in a coma for three months since the accident. Thus, *Just Like Heaven* reveals itself to be the story of two wounded people who need to come back to life. Elizabeth realizes her "unfinished business" has been to help David do so, and he vows to do anything to save her. She really does need saving, too, because Abby has been approached to shut off her sister's life support machinery. Elizabeth—and their love—could both be doomed.

By the time Elizabeth and David have become taken with each other, most viewers will be sufficiently taken with them to care that they find some way to get together. So when David and Jack race to execute a desperate plan to abscond with Elizabeth's body, most will accept the far-fetched silliness. When viewers learn that David was the blind date Elizabeth was on her way to meet that fateful night, and that Jack is the old friend of Abby's who had helped set them up, most will be able to swallow it all. When Elizabeth miraculously awakens during their abortive effort and not only has no recollection of David whatsoever but is disconcerted by his ardor, everyone will feel for the poor guy. After a relatively brief, teasing delay, a satisfying resolution comes in the rooftop garden David has selflessly created for her enjoyment. Everything comes flooding back to Elizabeth as they kiss, and while tears will not come flooding into everyone's eyes, there will probably be some of those aforementioned sniffles.

Made on a budget estimated to be $58 million, *Just Like Heaven* grossed $48.2 million. Critical reaction was mixed. Based upon the popular 2000 novel by Marc Levy, it was not as well received as director Mark Waters' last two efforts, *Freaky Friday* (2003) and *Mean Girls* (2004). (Incidentally, the actress who plays Abby is his wife.) Witherspoon, enjoyably zesty and charming, is effective as a presence with presence. She sparkles even when the material does not quite do so. As David, Ruffalo's sweet, hangdog sensitivity nicely balances her peppery pushiness. The character's affliction and his eventual devotion are palpable and touching. When David says he will do whatever it takes to rescue her, the look on his face alone clearly tells how deeply he means it. Admittedly, *Just Like Heaven* does not have a *Ghost* (1990) of a chance of being as well remembered as that potently affecting, supernatural-tinged love story between Patrick Swayze and Demi Moore. However, it has its own pleasing charms which, unlike Elizabeth's spirit, will be visible to many.

David L. Boxerbaum

CREDITS

Eilzabeth: Reese Witherspoon
David: Mark Ruffalo
Jack: Donal Logue
Brett: Ben Shenkman
Abby: Dina Waters
Darryl: Jon Heder
Katrina: Ivana Milicevic
Fran: Rosalind Chao
Dr. Walsh: Ron Canada
Origin: USA
Language: English
Released: 2005
Production: Laurie MacDonald, Walter F. Parkes; released by DreamWorks
Directed by: Mark S. Waters
Written by: Peter Tolan, Leslie Dixon
Cinematography by: Daryn Okada
Music by: Rolfe Kent
Sound: Douglas Axtell
Editing: Bruce Green
Art Direction: Maria Baker
Costumes: Sophie de Rakoff
Production Design: Cary White
MPAA rating: PG-13
Running time: 101 minutes

REVIEWS

Boxoffice Online. September, 2005.
Chicago Sun-Times Online. September 16, 2005.
Entertainment Weekly Online. September 14, 2005.
Los Angeles Times Online. September 16, 2005.
New York Times Online. September 16, 2005.
Premiere Magazine Online. September 16, 2005.
Variety Online. September 8, 2005.
Washington Post Online. September 16, 2005, p. C01.

QUOTES

Elizabeth Masterson, after remembering that she was a doctor: "I may have been a home-wrecking slut, but I saved lives!"

TRIVIA

The film was shot using the apartment where co-writer Leslie Dixon used to live.

K

KICKING & SCREAMING

All his life Phil Weston has dreamed of being on a winning team. Phil...your time has come.
—Movie tagline

Box Office: $52.6

It's on the verge of becoming a reliable Hollywood formula: Team an edgy but bankable younger comedian with a venerable older dramatic actor in a family comedy and you get *Meet the Parents, Meet the Fockers* and *Kicking and Screaming.* With a box office receipts at a respectable $52 million, *Kicking,* directed by Jesse Dylan (*How High, American Wedding*) doesn't touch the Focker franchise, which grossed well over $100 per movie, but the result is similarly fresh and funny. Instead of the *Meet the's* dash of romantic comedy, however, *Kicking* employs a well-cast group of kiddies on a losing soccer team, ala *Bad News Bears.*

Will Ferrell plays Phil Weston, and just as the Gregory "Gaylord" Focker character is a nurturing, non-athletic male nurse, Phil is a nurturing, non-athletic vitamin salesman, not to mention bearing less-than-macho monikers. Instead of De Niro, it is the just-as-respected American icon Robert Duvall who is willing to riff on his tough guy image as Phil's father, sporting the studly name of Buck (De Niro's character was named Jack). Clearly a send-up of his Bull Meechum character in *The Great Santini* (1979), Buck, who owns a sporting goods store, is a strict disciplinarian who is only interested in sports and winning, keeping his young son on the bench during the big soccer championships. Cut to the now college-aged Phil, a determined but woefully incapable "athlete" stumbling over the hurdles and hurling himself a mere 15 inches in the long jump. Still, Phil manages to meet the girl of his dreams, Barbara (Kate Walsh) only to once again be upstaged by his old man, who gets engaged on the same day to the young, exotic Janice (Musetta Vander). To add insult to injury, both sire sons, born on the same day, with Buck's son coming out slightly bigger, naturally.

When the Weston children are both old enough to enter in the family tradition of soccer, Buck, who coaches the winning Gladiators team, keeps Phil's son Sam (Dylan McLaughlin) on the bench, just like he did to Phil, while turning his own son, young Bucky (Josh Hutcherson), into the team's star. When Buck then decides to "trade" Sam to the last-place Tigers (he casually mentions he didn't actually get anything in return), Phil decides enough is enough and it's time to stand up to his old man for the first time in his life.

The Tigers need a new coach, and Phil steps up to the plate, recruiting Buck's neighbor and long-time nemesis Mike Ditka (playing himself) as assistant coach in order to more effectively compete with his dad. Ditka's first coaching duty is turning the timid and sweet Phil into a ruthless winning machine. His first order of business? Getting the more holistically inclined Phil to start drinking coffee. It is one of the film's funniest running gags, with the now-caffeine addicted Phil buying a humongous, elaborate coffee machine that sits regally atop the Tigers bench at every game, the kids huddling in the few remaining inches of space.

The Tigers team is made up by an ensemble of challenged athletes, including the sarcastic and precocious Mark Avery (Steven Anthony Lawrence), with a delightfully comical mug and a tiny, bespectacled Asian child named Byong Sun (Elliott Cho), always addressed by his full name in another of the film's effective running jokes. In a nice reversal of the typical soccer-mom image, Byong Sun has two mommies, Ann Hogan (Rachael Harris) and Donna Jones (Laura Kightlinger). Both very caring and involved in their child, the mothers tell the flustered Phil that Byong Sun is shy, handing him a book to read called "My Child is Shy." There is also one child that proudly eats worms and a goalie who is half-blind.

The perfectly cast Ditka then works his next bit of magic, recruiting two young Italian children from the butcher shop he frequents. Though they don't speak a word of English, Massimo (Allesandro Ruggiero) and Gian Piero (Francesco Liotti) are virtual ringers, looking like young extras from *Bend it Like Beckham.* The Tiger's new strategy for winning is "Pass it to the Italians," which kicks off the team's winning streak and chance at the finals, up against (who else?) Buck's Gladiators.

Ditka's now thoroughly deranged protégé Phil, who now sports the former Bears coach's Blu Blockers, eclipses Ditka himself in the "must-win" department and scenes with Ferrell debasing children from the losing teams and delivering his maniacal inspirational speeches are hilarious. When, on the verge of an important game, the Italians are summoned back to the butcher shop for a big job by their uncle who owns the shop (his credo is the oft-repeated line, "Meat comes first"), a frantic Phil rushes the entire team over to the shop to speed things up. Armed with a chainsaw, Phil and the boys lay into the animal carcasses with abandon. In one of the film's set-pieces, a speeding meat truck spins out onto the field, and the back door opens amid a cloud of dust revealing the seriously blood-spattered Tigers looking like something out of a horror flick, causing the other team to immediately forfeit and flee in terror.

The championship game arrives and Phil shows up clad in a hilarious tiger suit which he has sewn just for the occasion. In a previous scene, Phil has bet Buck that if the Tigers win, Buck must hand over his prized Pele soccer ball that Buck brags he caught during a game. A flashback reveals that young Phil actually had a hold of the Pele ball first, but the larger Buck easily got it away and claimed credit. Hell-bent on proving his father wrong and winning back the ball, Phil has unthinkingly benched Sam for the last few games. Phil, busy berating little Byong Sun for trying to take a shot at goal, doesn't even notice that Sam hasn't shown up at all for the championship. Janice points this out to her husband when she arrives with Sam after talking him into going, sans uniform, to support his team. Phil steps back and realizes that he's been taking this way too seriously and is committing the sins of his father. He doffs his silly "tiger" jacket and tells the boys to do the opposite of what he's been telling them to do all along. The boys then use their own unique skills (including a worm-eating ploy) to win the game, with both Byong Sun, Mark, and Sam proving heroes. Phil not only gains the long-awaited respect of his father but joins forces with him in business, as well, with Buck allowing Phil to sell his vitamins at the sporting goods store. The last shots of "King" Buck and "Prince" Phil and the kids starring in the amateurish commercials for the family business underscore the big, happy family message of this effective family comedy.

Hilary White

CREDITS

Phil Weston: Will Ferrell
Buck Weston: Robert Duvall
Mark Avery: Steven Anthony Lawrence
Janice Weston: Musetta Vander
Byong Sun: Elliot Cho
Bucky Weston: Josh Hutcherson
Sam Weston: Dylan McLaughlin
Ann Hogan: Rachael Harris
Donna Jones: Laura Kightlinger
Ambrose: Eric Walker
Connor': Dallas McKinney
Hunter: Jeremy Bergman
Barbara Weston: Kate Walsh
Gian Piero: Francesco Liotti
Massimo: Alessandro Ruggiero
Mike Ditka (Cameo)
Origin: USA
Language: English
Released: 2005
Production: Jimmy Miller; Mosaic Media Group; released by Universal
Directed by: Jesse Dylan
Written by: Leo Benvenuti, Steve Rudnick
Cinematography by: Lloyd Ahern II
Music by: Mark Isham
Sound: Jose Antonio Garcia
Editing: Stuart Pappe
Art Direction: Clayton Hartley
MPAA rating: PG
Running time: 95 minutes

REVIEWS

Boxoffice Online. May, 2005.
Chicago Sun-Times Online. May 12, 2005.
Entertainment Weekly Online. May 11, 2005.

Los Angeles Times Online. May 13, 2005.
New York Times Online. May 13, 2005.
Variety Online. May 8, 2005.
Washington Post Online. May 13, 2005, p. C01.

QUOTES

Phil Weston: "I was born a baby..."

TRIVIA

Many of the names on the kids' jerseys are those of crew members. The child who attacks Will Ferrell during the last soccer game has the name "Apatow" on the back of his jersey, which is the last name of the executive producer and frequent Ferrell collaborator, Judd Apatow.

AWARDS

Nomination:

Golden Raspberries 2005: Worst Support. Actor (Ferrell).

THE KID & I

Get a little action.
—Movie tagline

When It Comes To Heroes, Size Doesn't Matter.
—Movie tagline

Saving The World Is Serious Business.
—Movie tagline

If there were some sort of contest for coming up with the most absurd script idea, the premise for *The Kid & I* would be the sure winner. It is about a rich kid, Aaron (Eric Gores), with cerebral palsy who dreams of being an actor. The kid idolizes the film *True Lies* and, in particular, its sidekick star, Tom Arnold. Aaron's dad offers Arnold a job making the film and Arnold accepts.

Not only is that a real premise, but it is somewhat based on a true story. Arnold lives next door to Eric and his rich father did indeed fund the picture. In interviews, Arnold has said that he took on the project because he was so taken with Eric's spunk and drive. He must have been quite charmed because his assignment was tricky. Before shooting, Eric laid out several stipulations. He wanted a movie to be an action-adventure in the vein of *True Lies*. He wanted to save animals. And he wanted to kiss a girl in a hot tub, preferably model Arielle Kebbel.

It is a credit to Arnold that he not only incorporated these elements, but managed to make a movie that almost hangs together. There are some good, funny moments in *The Kid*, mostly involving Arnold's self-deprecating humor, but there are too many other moods going on at the same time.

In the film, Bill Williams (Arnold), is a washed-up actor whose heyday was his costarring role years ago in *True Lies*. At the beginning of the film, Bill is meticulously setting up his suicide. He uses up the last of his toiletries, mails an obituary to the *Los Angeles Times* and gives his clothes away to a homeless man, Guy (Richard Edson). He neatly makes up his bed and wonders idly if he will make the montage of dead people at the Academy Awards.

But his suicide plans are foiled when Guy takes most of the pills and liquor Bill had laid out to take. The next morning, Bill's agent (Henry Winkler) shows up with an offer of $450,000 for a movie writing job. Bill, now homeless, without clothes and being reported dead by the *Times*, takes the job. When he finds out that the job is a vanity project for a rich kid with cerebral palsy, he balks, but eventually starts working on a film called *Two Spies*. As he works on the film, he gets more excited about it and develops a real fondness for the plucky Aaron, aka A-Dog. The two guys talk about girls and movies and fight off the local bullies.

Bill, who starts envisioning the film as his big comeback, is crushed when he finds out that the film will only be shown at Aaron's 18th birthday celebration. But all will be well because, as Williams puts it, "There's more important things in life than money. You guys taught me that." Such a speech would be one of those things that is not so good about the movie.

What is good is Arnold's performance. This is his *Lost in Translation*—not so much quality-wise, but the idea of an aging comedian playing a worn-down, depressive middle-ager. The funniest moments in the film come from Arnold's resigned acceptance about his place in life. When Aaron assigns himself the lovely Kebbel for movie girlfriend material, he suggests Rosie O'Donnell for Bill. Bill knowing that he has to please his young rich patron, agrees, saying with false cheer, "Yeah! She's hot!" The words come easily for Bill. He is used to such indignities.

The Kid & I also boast a host of celebrity appearances. Joe Mantegna is Aaron's father, Linda Hamilton is Bill's ex-wife, and Shannon Elizabeth is Aaron's stepmother. *Wayne's World* director, Penelope Spheeris plays herself as the director of *Two Spies* (she is also the real director of *The Kid*). Shaquille O'Neal makes an appearance and even Arnold's old costars Jamie Lee Curtis and Arnold Schwarzenegger show up.

The Kid & I was not a critical favorite but did have a few fans. Stephen Holden of *The New York Times* most definitely did not like the film and wrote, "A chore to watch, *The Kid & I* is self-congratulatory, excruciatingly sentimental and sloppily written and directed." Christy Lemire of *Associated Press* felt similarly and wrote, "With a look that's stiff and slapped-together, plus a preachy and heavy-handed tone, this is a public service announcement masquerading as a movie." Roger Ebert of *The Chicago Sun-Times* wrote, "*The Kid & I* is not a great film, but you know what? It achieves what it sets out to achieve, and it isn't boring and it kept me intrigued and involved." Kevin Thomas of *The Los Angeles Times* commended Spheeris' role in the film and wrote "It is difficult to imagine anyone but Spheeris pulling off this movie, undercutting all mawkishness, bringing to it nuance and shading, not to mention wit."

Jill Hamilton

CREDITS

Bill Williams: Tom Arnold
Johnny Bernstein: Henry Winkler
Guy: Richard Edson
Davis Roman: Joe Mantegna
Shelby: Shannon Elizabeth
Arielle: Arielle Kebbel
Bonnie: Brenda Strong
Cameo: Penelope Spheeris
Aaron Roman: Eric Gores
Origin: USA
Language: English
Released: 2005
Production: Penelope Spheeris, Tom Arnold; Wheels Up, The Kid and I Production; released by Slow Hand Releasing
Directed by: Penelope Spheeris
Written by: Tom Arnold
Cinematography by: Robert E. Seaman
Editing: Jan Northrop, John Whitton Wesley
Art Direction: Nanci B. Roberts, Harry Snodgrass, Gary Gelfand, Mark Piskorski
Production Design: Linda Spheeris
MPAA rating: PG-13
Running time: 93 minutes

REVIEWS

Chicago Sun-Times Online. December 2, 2005.
Entertainment Weekly Online. November 30, 2005.
New York Times Online. December 2, 2005.
Variety Online. December 1, 2005.

TRIVIA

Arnold Schwarzenegger's first movie since being elected governor of California.

KING KONG

The eighth wonder of the world.
—Movie tagline

Box Office: $142.7 million

Paraphrasing Charlie Denham, the film-director protagonist who captures King Kong, "a lot of people are going to pay to see this thing." That was a sure bet as Oscar-winner Peter Jackson realized a lifelong dream by making a big-budget, spectacular remake of *King Kong.* A colossal, extravagant blockbuster of a movie with a budget reportedly over $200 million, the new *Kong* was seeking to fill some mighty big shoes: the original is one of the most universally recognized stories that cinema has ever brought to the world, featuring a gorilla that has become a pop-culture myth worldwide.

Jackson has said the original *King Kong* inspired him to be a filmmaker, and he had wanted to do a remake for his entire career. But not until the previously virtually unknown director proved himself a formidable beast with the *Lord of the Rings* trilogy, sweeping the Academy Awards for 2004 with the epic finale *Return of the King,* did the doors open wide for his dream. And, only a year after the release of *Return of the King,* he came through on his dream, producing another incredible labor of love—a *King Kong* told on a massive scale, with a three-hour running time, a more complete and complex story than the original, and a island full of fantastic creatures, feverish action, and harrowing escapes. Without a doubt, Jackson has expanded upon yet remained faithful to the original film he is paying homage to. And there is also no doubt that Jackson has set a new standard for seamlessly realized computer-graphic-aided creatures that horrify, fight, and loom large and realistic.

Some critics, in fact, ventured to say that Jackson had done the impossible and topped *Lord of the Rings,* at least in terms of special effects and the intensity of the action. Almost everyone hailed his wizardry and spectacle. A minority of critics, however, felt the spectacle was overdone, with the sheer size and breadth of it overwhelming the audience; in essence, they said, it was a 1,000-pound gorilla of a movie.

For sheer entertainment, however, it's hard to think of a movie beyond *Lord of the Rings* that can compare to this—especially if you like action, monstrous creatures, and sharply focused sentiment. The only question is whether the story and the characters stand up to this gargantuan treatment. The original *King Kong* was a bizarre little fable that set the standard for all "monster movies" to come, changed the lexicon of pop culture, and inspired endless jokes about male-female relationships. Written and directed by Merian Cooper, the 1933 *Kong* was epic for its time, and Willis O'Brien's incredible stop-motion animation techniques made the title character not just frightening but sympathetic, and in doing so made Kong a shorthand for machismo beastliness and Ann Darrow (Fay Wray) an enduring symbol for vulnerable yet feisty femininity. It was an adventure story, a love story, and a parable about human greed and lust for fame and fortune.

But for all that, it was not the kind of sprawling epic that Tolkien wrote in *Lord of the Rings*. Also the material here is iconic, it is not deep and broad. Jackson expands the story with few missteps into something that strains to be an epic of its own. And the special effects are so dazzling that at times the audience can become more entranced by the effects than immersed in the movie. And that is a dangerous thing: spectacle can be distancing. Yet Jackson also expands the heart of this story, deepening our sympathy for Kong and Ann by making each of them more complex, sharpening the critique of mass exploitation embodied in the character of Denham, setting the fable squarely in its era (the Depression), and making audiences ache with sentiment for the lonely and entrapped beast. Yet Jackson's intent sometimes seems so obvious and so manipulative that it left some viewers uncomfortable.

A lot of your reaction to this film depends on what you think of the Kong story. If you're in love with its beauty-and-the-beast anguish, you'll be swept away. If, on the other hand, you think of this as merely the ultimate monster story, and a rather contrived and dated one at that, your reaction might be more of a "gee-whiz" appreciation than one of being blown away.

One thing that's clearly to Jackson's credit is that he has wisely resisted most impulses to update the story to soften some elements that now seem politically incorrect. His opening sequences, set in Depression-era New York, are a signal that this is a story not just set in the past, but firmly rooted in the sensibilities of that long-ago era. So Jackson doesn't flinch from making Skull Islanders' natives into fearsome, loathsome, barely human savages, and as a result he took flak from some PC critics. Neither did Jackson make an effort to improve Ann Darrow too much in terms of feminist ideals or human abilities: she's no ass-kicking Charlie's Angel, and she's no woman seeking to change the world or triumph over men. But with a pitch-perfect performance by Naomi Watts, she's no helpless damsel in distress either. She screams, she dangles, she is repeatedly plucked from peril, but she has a heart and a brain to go with her beauty, and she employs them throughout the film.

There's not a hint of satire or camp in Jackson's retelling. It is a clearly honest effort to faithfully honor the original story while improving it in every possible way, especially visually. And visually, it is stunning. The first and last quarters of the movie, taking place in New York City, portray Manhattan as a gleaming, crowded, chaotic human stage, full of many compelling characters, even some who have only one line of dialogue or none—and a city sharply divided between rich and poor. The shipboard second quarter gives us cramped cabins, budding romances and mutinies, and images of a lonely tramp steamer heading to unknown regions on wide expanses of lonely seas. And the biggest quarter of the movie—the hour spent on Skull Island itself—is a tour de force of memorably frightening confrontations between would-be heroes and savage predators.

Throughout this film, Jackson has the heat set on high. Even the quietest encounters are supercharged, and Jackson uses perhaps too many disorienting visual techniques and swelling something-scary-is-coming snatches of score to shout to audiences that danger looms or characters are teetering on the edge of sanity. These are most overdone during the shipboard sequences, when at times it seems like Jackson is lapsing into melodramatic overkill. There are moments when the director is shouting at you when he doesn't need to: more subtlety might indicate more confidence in the story to carry its own weight.

But everything is extravagant here: the spectacle *and* the emotion. Once the party of adventurers lands on Skull Island, it seems as if Jackson worries that if a second goes by without a threat, a fright, or a fight, somebody might walk out of the theater. It's like going to a modern pro sports event, where there is never a moment for contemplation, and every second is filled with noisy announcements, actions, or advertisements. Even the quiet scenes, when Ann and Kong are looking out over the beauty of the jungle landscape, are anything but subtle: they shout out their message of a peaceful paradise about to be forever spoiled.

Setting the tone right from the start is the questionable casting of Jack Black as Denham. On the one hand, Black, with his wild-eyed mania, is a perfect pitchman, a soulless moviemaker who doesn't matter what the damage is as long as he gets his shot, who shrugs off the deaths of colleagues, and always has his eye on the bottom line: entertainment. On the other, Jack Black is an actor who does not sink into a character; he's always Jack Black playing a role, and his mania borders on the cartoonish, because his acting range has trouble shifting out of satirical gear. He provides some laughs, but sometimes seems on the edge of shattering Jackson's solemn tone and making this *Kong* into a Monty Python movie.

Jackson had to be aware, in making the film, that the story about Denham's quest to shoot an epic film, to stage a spectacle, is itself a shorthand for the very thing Jackson is trying to pull off in making a movie about that quest. And the central question with this remake is whether Jackson is guilty of the same thing Denham is: keeping his eyes so focused on spectacle that he misses the human element, or, more precisely, makes every human encounter into its own spectacle.

Brody is another questionable choice as a leading romantic man. He is perpetually wearing a hangdog expression, as usual, and his character is a loveable, tentative kind of guy who is shy about courting Ann and unsure whether he has the power to capture her. Of course, Jack Driscoll should embody those doubts as a counterpoint to Kong's total lack of doubt about his masculine powers and mission. But Brody is too much of a postmodern man, and too stuck, for better or worse, in his look of vulnerable and downtrodden angst, to be believable when he plays the superhero in the quest for the captured Ann. When he takes off after her in the jungle, urging the others on and finally going off on his own, you think—there's *Adrien Brody* in the jungle, poor guy. Brody has neither leading-man dash nor heroic demeanor, and he's far more believable as King Kong's whipping boy than his conqueror.

Jackson also has plenty of minor characters that seem dangerously close to lifeless stereotypes. Among them are Kyle Chandler as fake-heroic swashbuckling actor Bruce Baxter, Evan Parke and Jamie Bell as the hulking quiet hero and the teenager who wants to be an action man, and Thomas Kretschmann as grizzled ship's captain Englehorn, looking and acting like he just stepped out of a German U-boat movie.

More delightful is Andy Serkis as Lumpy, the cook, a Popeye-the-sailor-man who steals every scene he's in with his cockeyed certitude, and who is one of the few actors who has ever gotten to play a character who gets his head swallowed up to the neck by a giant worm. Of course, Serkis's greater accomplishment in this movie is that he "plays" Kong, just as he played Gollum in *Lord of the Rings*, by acting the scenes in gorilla character and providing the expressive and physical motion template for the giant ape.

He and Watts are the real stars of the film, and their interaction is genuinely moving and comical. Watts is gorgeous as a flapper-era movie star and dauntless thespian who figures out that she can amuse Kong by doing vaudeville bits. She can also scream and dangle with the best of them. And, after being thrown around like a rag doll, she never looks any the worse for wear. The problem with her, though, is that she has to settle for Adrien Brody after losing her manly stud of a gorilla.

The other stars are the WETA studio's animatronics teams, and the legions of other technical artists who created Kong and an island full of dinosaurs that make *Jurassic Park* look like a Disney cartoon. For the film's meaty middle hour, Jackson has great fun first in staging the encounter with the natives and the sacrifice of Ann to Kong, and then in setting Kong and Ann and their pursuers into every conceivable encounter with creatures of the imaginative wild. There's a dinosaur stampede that is thunderous and bracing and that ends with a fleshy pile-up that is splendid to watch, there's the aforementioned worms and mollusks and lobster-like swamp creatures that set upon the hunting party, there are giant spiders and insects that are menacing and icky, and there are ravenous dinosaurs that fight Kong. The fight, which ends in a canyon of twisting vines, is one of the most amazing sequences ever filmed.

Yet this is the part of *King Kong* where the story gets overwhelmed most by the action. You can do nothing but let your mouth drop in amazement. But sometimes less is more. After Ann is tossed into the air for the umpteenth time and saved by Kong's outstretched paw or foot, the thrill wears off. You are watching a breathtaking special effects tour de force, but whether you are involved and captured by the movie is debatable.

In the end, you are left with many spectacular, memorable, and even haunting images, including natives pogo-sticking hundreds of feet above rocky chasms, Kong slipping off the top of the Empire State Building and plunging sickeningly to his death, and Kong straining at his shackles on a Times Square stage. And you are also left with a strong parable about rapacious human beings subduing nature for the sake of cheap and profitable entertainment. Jackson's wrestled with his gorilla, his lifelong dream writ large, and the question is whether he has caged his spirit or let it free once again to roam in the primitive corners of our collective psyche.

Michael Betzold

CREDITS

Ann Darrow: Naomi Watts
Carl Denham: Jack Black
Jack Driscoll: Adrien Brody
Capt. Englehorn: Thomas Kretschmann
Preston: Colin Hanks
Jimmy: Jamie Bell
Hayes: Evan Dexter Parke
Bruce Baxter: Kyle Chandler
Kong/Lumpy the Cook: Andy Serkis
Choy: Lobo Chan
Origin: USA, New Zealand
Language: English
Released: 2005
Production: Fran Walsh, Peter Jackson, Jan Blenkin, Carolynne Cunningham; Wingnut Films; released by Universal
Directed by: Peter Jackson
Written by: Peter Jackson, Fran Walsh, Philippa Boyens
Cinematography by: Andrew Lesnie

Music by: James Newton Howard
Sound: Hammond Peek
Editing: Jamie Selkirk, Jabez Olssen
Art Direction: Simon Bright, Joseph Bleakley
Costumes: Terry Ryan
Production Design: Grant Major
MPAA rating: PG-13
Running time: 187 minutes

REVIEWS

Boxoffice Online. December, 2005.
Chicago Sun-Times Online. December 13, 2005.
Entertainment Weekly Online. December, 2005.
Los Angeles Times Online. December 12, 2005.
New York Times Online. December 13, 2005.
Premiere Magazine Online. December 9, 2005.
Variety Online. December 6, 2005.
Washington Post Online. December 14, 2005, p. C01.

QUOTES

Hayes: "The beast looked upon the face of beauty. Beauty stayed his hand, and from that moment he was as one dead."

TRIVIA

The 1933 New York set was a mere four blocks across and one story high. The rest of the painstakingly detailed set, added digitally, included 90,000 separate buildings.

AWARDS

Oscars 2005: Sound, Visual FX
British Acad. 2005: Visual FX

Nomination:

Oscars 2005: Art Dir./Set Dec.
British Acad. 2005: Sound
Golden Globes 2006: Director (Jackson), Orig. Score
Broadcast Film Critics 2005: Director (Jackson), Film.

KINGDOM OF HEAVEN

Box Office: $47.3 million

Director Ridley Scott knows his way around big scenes and historical pieces as well. From 1977's *The Duellists,* which was set during the Napoleonic Wars, to *Alien* (1979), *Blade Runner* (1982), *Thelma & Louise* (1991), *1492: Conquest of Paradise* (1992), the Oscar-winning *Gladiator* (2000), and *Black Hawk Down* (2001), among others, Scott is not afraid to take a chance. So, since the director wanted to do a picture about a knight, well, why not do a picture about the Crusades and set it in Jerusalem. And why not give Christianity and Islam an equal voice? After all, Scott, who is a knighted Englishman, started planning his film before 9/11, before President George W. Bush made the word "crusade" a byword for his war on terrorism, before the United States invaded Iraq, and before fundamentalists of all persuasions made religion such a very, very touchy subject.

The film starts in France in 1184 at a crossroads where a gravedigger lays to rest the body of a young woman who committed suicide—a mortal sin in Christian belief so she cannot be buried in consecrated ground. A small band of Crusaders come down the road to the blacksmith shop where a young man is working. The baron in charge is Godfrey of Ibelin (Liam Neeson), who is looking for his illegitimate son, Balian (Orlando Bloom), who is the village blacksmith. Godfrey politely asks forgiveness for the way he treated Balian's mother (she didn't give her consent to their—ummm—union but he loved her "in my fashion") and asks the young man to return with him to Jerusalem. Balian refuses his request. Godfrey tells his son they are on their way to the port of Messina if he cares to follow them.

Balian's mind remains unchanged until the village priest (Michael Sheen) taunts him that his dead wife (the suicide) is in hell and that he should go to Jerusalem so that he can expiate her sins. In a fury, Balian kills him and rides to join his father's camp in the forest. He says he has committed murder and asks, "Is it true that in Jerusalem I can erase my sins and those of my wife?" Godfrey reassures him that Jerusalem is the "center of the world for asking forgiveness" and that in Jerusalem "you're not what you were born but what you have it in yourself to be." That night they are ambushed by the local sheriff who has come after Balian and Godfrey is wounded by an arrow. (This whole battle in the woods scene seems very reminiscent of *Gladiator* albeit on a much smaller scale.) They make it to the pilgrim camp at Messina where Godfrey, before dying, knights Balian and makes him promise to serve the king of Jerusalem and has him swear an oath to protect the people of the city.

Balian's troubles don't stop there. His ship is wrecked and he is washed up on a beach, the only survivor except for one horse that promptly runs away. When Balian finds the horse at an oasis, he attracts the attention of two men, one of who claims the horse is his. Balian fights for the animal, kills one man, but spares the other—a soldier named Nasir (Alexander Siddig) who serves the great Saracen leader, Saladin. Nasir guides Balian to Jerusalem where he spends the night at Golgotha, the place where Christ was crucified. Hoping to find solace, he sadly realizes that "God does not speak to me." This will be a central theme for Balian; he has lost his faith and hopes to earn God's forgiveness for his sins. Later that day, Balian meets the rest of Godfrey's knights and the impetuous Princess Sibylla (Eva Green).

The Christian crusaders have held Jerusalem since the First Crusade in 1099 and there has been an uneasy alliance for some six years between King Baldwin IV and Saladin. Baldwin allows both Christians and Muslims to worship in the city, much to the disgust of the Knights Templar, a religious and military sect who are agitating for a holy war against the infidels. Balian is taken to the Office of the Marshall of Jerusalem, Tiberius (Jeremy Irons), who leads the rival Knights Hospitalers, and who tries to provide a moderating influence. Balian is formally introduced to Sibylla and her noxious husband, Guy de Lusignan (Marton Csokas), the leader of the Templars. Sibylla, in turn, takes Balian to meet her brother, Baldwin (Edward Norton), who is dying. He suffers from leprosy and hides his disfigured face behind a silver mask. Baldwin asks that Balian protect the pilgrim road that lies outside his property at Ibelin as his father did.

Sibylla comes to visit Balian at Ibelin, complains of her arranged marriage, and reassures Balian that she is neither "bored or wicked" but is truly attracted to him (which leads to a *very* abbreviated love scene). Meanwhile, Guy and his bloodthirsty second in command, Reynald de Chatillon (Brendan Gleeson), attack a Saracen caravan and break the fragile peace. Tiberius informs Baldwin that Saladin has crossed the Jordan with 200,000 men and is on his way to attack Kerak Castle, Reynald's holding. Baldwin decides he will lead the army but sends Balian ahead to Kerak to protect the villagers. Balian and his knights are badly outnumbered against Saladin's cavalry but Nasir, who admires him as a worthy foe, spares Balian's life. Fortuitously, King Baldwin's army appears and the King and Saladin broker another peace when Baldwin promises to punish Reynald.

Tiberius has instructed Balian to come to Jerusalem where he is asked to take command of the army from Guy. The King asks Balian if he would marry Sibylla if she were free, intimating that Guy will be killed as a traitor. But Balian cannot go against his conscience and later refuses Sibylla herself, saying he could not sell his soul. She replies that he may have to "do a little evil for a greater good." When her brother dies, Sibylla is crowned Queen of Jerusalem and must crown Guy king. Meanwhile, Balian returns to Ibelin, where Guy sends men to kill him (they fail). Guy also releases Reynald from prison so they may start their holy war. Guy decides to take the army out of Jerusalem and go to meet Saladin's forces while Tiberius and Balian are left to defend the city. A lack of water weakens Guy's troops and they are badly defeated. Saladin kills Reynald but tells Guy that "a king cannot kill a king"; he does hold him prisoner. (Guy gets paraded on a donkey for Saladin's troops to jeer at and then is not seen again.) Balian and Tiberius ride out to view the slaughter on the battlefield and Tiberius tells the younger man "first I thought we were fighting for God. Then I realized we were fighting for greed and land." Disgusted, Tiberius informs Balian that he and his knights are heading for Cyprus—"God be with you. He's no longer with me."

Balian returns to Jerusalem and reinforces the city's defenses. He asks the people (in the first of several rallying speeches), which of the city's sites is more holy—the wall, sacred to Judaism; the mosque, sacred to Islam; the Holy Sepulcher, sacred to the Christians? All are equally to be revered but what is most important is to protect the people within Jerusalem's walls. Saladin has amassed his forces and begins a siege of the city. Balian knows he cannot win but he wants to hold on long enough to force Saladin to offer terms. The battle continues for several days (your basic arrows, siege towers, and boiling oil) until the Muslims break through a weakened gate. At dusk, amidst the carnage, Saladin sends up a white flag to arrange a parley with Balian. He asks him to yield the city but Balian replies that "before I lose it, I will burn it to the ground. ...I swear to God that to take this city will be the end of you." Saladin finally offers safe passage to everyone within the walls that wishes to leave and Balian agrees. He informs the Patriarch of Jerusalem (Jon Finch) that "If this is the kingdom of heaven, let God do with it what he wills." Sibylla asks what she should do; Balian replies that if she decides not be a queen, he will come to her. When Saladin enters Jerusalem, Balian also sees Nasir who tells him "...if God does not love you, how could you have done all the things you have done?" As the refugees leave, the Muslim crescent is raised over the city in place of the Christian cross. Balian notices Sibylla is just another person in the crowd and takes her hand.

They return to his village in France and Balian is taking a last look around when another band of Crusaders make their way to his blacksmith shop, looking for the man who defended Jerusalem. Balian responds, "I am a blacksmith." Their leader replies: "And I am the King of England." (He is, in fact, Richard I, the Lionheart.) But Balian replies again that he is only a blacksmith and then rides off with Sibylla, past the crossroads where the story began. An end title informs that Richard crusaded for three years and obtained only an uneasy peace with Saladin. (Richard and his allies led the Third Crusade, which actually began in 1189.)

Kingdom is an epic that doesn't feel, well, epic. At 145 minutes it moves quickly enough but something seems to be missing. Scott has stated in interviews that his first cut of the film came in at three hours and 40 minutes and that he hopes to release a director's cut on DVD. Maybe this will help fill in the blanks, especially in terms of character development. Because except for Balian's quest for forgiveness, there isn't any. In fact, most of the secondary characters pass through so fast that you can scarcely remember their names. Neeson, Irons, and David Thewlis (as a Hospitaler knight) offer various forms of fatherly advice to the callow Balian, only to depart the scene much too quickly; Green is beautiful but her character is something of a cipher. You don't know why Sibylla is so quickly attracted to Balian, other than the fact that her marriage is horrible and her would-be love is Orlando Bloom. Who's gorgeous. Bloom, who worked with Scott in *Black Hawk Down,* is given his first chance at a leading role after successful runs in supporting roles in *The Lord of the Rings* trilogy, *Pirates of the Caribbean,* and *Troy.* Critics complain he's a lightweight (especially in comparison to *Gladiator*'s Russell Crowe) but this seems unfair since Bloom is still in his mid-twenties (13 years younger than Crowe) and the character of Balian isn't a hardened warrior (you do wonder where he learned his sword skills if he's a simple blacksmith and he seems to be something of an engineer as well). His very sincerity works for the character.

Scott does make the much-maligned Knights Templar into the film's bogeymen. They are fanatical Christians and there is something disturbingly familiar about their rhetoric (whether this was intended or not). The characters of Guy and Reynald are also one-dimensionally evil. In opposition, Syrian actor Ghassan Massoud offers an impressive presence as the Muslim leader Saladin, firm in his belief that it is Allah's will that he fight but magnanimous to those he has defeated (however, his English is somewhat difficult to understand). Lastly, it can't be easy to act behind a mask but Edward Norton makes King Baldwin a tragic yet commanding figure. *Kingdom* also looks gorgeous as photographed by John Mathieson from locations in Spain and Morocco. And Sir Ridley certainly knows how to stage a fight scene—whether Balian is fighting one warrior or many. (King Mohammed VI of Morocco loaned some 1,500 of his soldiers as extras and CGI did the rest.)

Naturally, the film has been criticized for playing with the facts. Although Balian is an historical figure, little is known about him, but he was born a baron not a blacksmith. And you can't really tell about the passage of time in Scott's film. Baldwin IV died in 1185 and was briefly succeeded by his nephew and then by Guy de Lusignan, who ruled from 1186–1192 (he *was* married to Sibylla who died in 1190). Saladin defeated the Crusaders and entered Jerusalem in 1187. In the end, how much does this matter? *Kingdom of Heaven* isn't really about capturing Jerusalem or whether one religion is better than another—it's about personal honor. It's about following what your conscience dictates, whether you believe that inner voice directing your actions comes from God or not. It's about giving your word and standing by it, no matter what the consequence.

Christine Tomassini

CREDITS

Balian: Orlando Bloom
Sibylla: Eva Green
Godfrey: Liam Neeson
Tiberias: Jeremy Irons
Hospitaler: David Thewlis
Reynald: Brendan Gleeson
Guy de Lusignan: Marton Csokas
Priest: Michael Sheen
King Baldwin: Edward Norton
Nasir: Alexander Siddig
English Sergeant: Kevin McKidd
Patriarch: Jon Finch
Saladin: Ghassan Massoud
Almaric: Velibor Topi
Templar Master: Ulrich Thomsen
Village Sheriff: Nikolaj Coster-Waldau
Richard Coeur de Lion: Iain Glen
Origin: Great Britain, Spain, USA, Germany
Language: English
Released: 2005
Production: Ridley Scott; Scott Free; released by 20th Century-Fox
Directed by: Ridley Scott
Written by: William Monahan
Cinematography by: John Mathieson
Music by: Harry Gregson-Williams
Sound: David Stephenson
Music Supervisor: Marc Streitenfeld
Editing: Dody Dorn
Art Direction: John King, Gianni Giovagnoni, Alessandro Alberti, Maria Teresa Barbasso
Costumes: Janty Yates
Production Design: Arthur Max
MPAA rating: R
Running time: 145 minutes

REVIEWS

Boxoffice Online. May, 2005.
Chicago Sun-Times Online. May 5, 2005.
Entertainment Weekly Online. May 4, 2005.

Los Angeles Times Online. May 6, 2005.
New York Times Online. May 6, 2005.
Premiere Magazine Online. May 5, 2005.
Variety Online. May 1, 2005.
Washington Post Online. May 6, 2005, p. C01.

QUOTES

Balian: "Be without fear in the face of your enemies. Safeguard the helpless, even if it leads to your death; that is your oath. Rise a knight…rise a knight!"

TRIVIA

All the characters in the film, except Godfrey, existed in real life.

KINGS AND QUEEN

(Rois et reine)

Arnaud Desplechin's intellectual woman's picture from France, *Kings and Queen*, pits two major forces in contemporary French life—the elite classicism of a bygone era and the headlong mad rush of hi-tech at various levels of existence—in order to produce an engrossing, emotional and at times irresolvable narrative dilemma. Despite its unwieldly length, the film could well rank as the most powerful psychological exploration we have seen this year.

As his title would imply, Desplechin keeps his narrative focused on Nora (Emmanuelle Devos), a sophisticated owner of a small Parisian art gallery. However, Nora's plight is framed within filmic terms not at all customary for the film culture Desplechin is working within. As writer-director, he is bold enough to hint that no matter how complicated and depressing aspects of Nora's life turn out to be, what redeems her existence is (believe it or not) good old-fashioned American sensibility.

It's interesting to note how films from Europe, from countries that at one time used to pride themselves on their indigenous musical motifs, are now reaching for American pop standards to underscore the emotional quotient of their films. Henry Mancini's "Moon River" is performed in a Spanish translation in Pedro Almodovar's *Bad Education* (reviewed in the 2005 volume) and figures prominently in its narrative. Desplechin uses its plaintive strains to introduce the stylish veneer of Nora's life.

When we first see Nora, she introduces herself through her voiceover narration: she's 35 and has a 10 year old son from a first marriage who is the center of her life. At her own gallery, she picks up a painting of "Leda and the Swan" which she plans to present to her father in Grenoble. The myth of the Swan being the love-stricken Zeus in disguise, it will become clear, will serve to illustrate the film's title with Nora as the Queen and each of the important men in her life as kings within their domain, and each unable to live without her.

As Nora leaves for Grenoble, we catch a glimpse of Jean-Jacques (Olivier Rabourdin), her soft-spoken lover and a successful businessman. On the train, Nora's voiceover tells us about Ismael, her second husband, from whom she separated because of him treating their relationship as an affair rather than one based in "a sound commitment."

We find her son Elias is staying with her father but is away at a day camp. Louis (Maurice Garrel), the father, is a shriveled old man racked by the pain of an abdominal rot. No one knows the extent of his illness at this stage, only that it appears more moving since he's an intellectual; who is still writing. His growing dependence on Nora, however, will become the chief factor to create a dent in her insouciance. To counterpoint this is the joy she feels at being reunited with Elias (Valentin Lelong), who loves her despite her being away from him.

As Nora resigns herself to the surgery that will be needed to deal with her father's perforated ulcer, Desplechin switches emotional gears to focus on the frenetic life of the mentally unbalanced Ismael (Mathieu Amalric). We catch him just as he's being hauled away by force to a mental institution where he's held down and sedated. The fact of both Nora's and Ismael's predicaments being bound to hospitals allows Desplechin to foreground the thematic contrast between the increasingly helpless Nora and the amusingly feisty Ismael.

In a cold tone, Nora is informed that Louis has been nursing a case of cancer which has progressed to the point that he has at most ten days to live. Ismael, in a straitjacket, is visited by his parents who feel that a hospital stay is just what he needs. We also come to know that the other side to his violent behavior is his musical talent that has allowed him to play the viola in a string quartet and that, though not a threat to the community, he has been incarcerated at the request of his sister. Dr. Vasset (Catherine Deneuve in a cameo), the psychiatrist in charge, is willing to listen to Ismael's side of the story but finds herself embroiled in a philosophical debate when he claims that women do not have souls. When he flares up in her office his chances of being discharged worsen. Nora that night breaks down as she relates the news of their father to the younger Chloe (Nathalie Boutefeu) over the phone. The latter, a student, is more concerned with the fact that she hasn't received her remittance from Louis. Nora pleads with her that she's all alone and is even prepared to send her a ticket but Chloe insists on hitching her way.

While waiting within the whiteness of a hospital corridor, Nora receives a visitation in a dream from the kindly Pierre (Joachim Salinger), her husband who has been dead ten years. She assures him of their son he never got to see and how Elias found a father in Louis whose impending death will hurt Elias more than her. As he tries to comfort her, she says, "But you're dead!," caressing his face. He merely smiles.

Once the stylish veneer of its heroine has cracked, the film takes on a sprawling form; the cracks deepen but the scenes that follow do not progress in dramatic intensity, such as those that have set up her story. Ismael's attempts to prove his sanity in his psychiatric sessions and his stabs at happiness serve to individuate him as a character, but nothing more. His story becomes bound with Nora's when Elias makes it clear that he would rather live with Ismael than Jean-Jacques whom he seems to hate. It is our identifying with Nora's efforts to prove herself a loving mother in her son's eyes that turns the film into a woman's picture, though not a weepie. The film's dramatically uneven omniscience is redeemed only in its final section when it casts off its melodramatic quotient to reveal a shocking truth we would never have suspected.

Till that point the film remains entertaining owing to the surprises it throws up in relation to contemporary French mores. Ismael's lawyer, Mamanne (Hippolyte Girardot) advises him that it would prove more profitable for him to be classified insane even if he wasn't, since that would allow him to evade the fortune he owes in back taxes. In return for his convoluted strategy to free him, Ismael helps Mamanne to raid the hospital pharmacy so that the high-strung lawyer can get his non-prescription treats.

When Nora tells Elias about his grandfather's condition, he curses her as if it was her fault and runs from her. She does however manage to get him from the care of the camp counselor. She then races against time to leave him in Paris with Jean-Jacques (who has hired a nurse for him) and return to Grenoble. Her mad rush, though guided by her assistant in Paris via cell phone, results in her missing the only flight out. She then rushes to the nearest train station only to find that she has missed the last train to Paris as well. Rather than spend the night at a hotel, as her assistant advises, she decides to drive the distance. From this test of her devotion to her son and father comes a cheerful little twist. Elias, no doubt seeing all the effort she's making for him, forgives her with a smile and assures her that she has been a dutiful mom.

Ismael's life takes a pleasing turn as well. His own open compassionate stance to the world results in his striking up a liaison with the lively Arielle (Magali Woch), a graduate student in Sinology who has been brought in after a suicide attempt. While she feels drawn to more intimacy, Ismael is forthright and tells her he would like to keep the sex on hold. When Nora comes to see him at the clinic, it becomes clear how their opposing sensibilities must have fuelled the attraction between them. Now it is only the contradiction that has survived. Nora tries to bridge the gap by telling him how Jean-Jacques smokes marijuana every night and does heroin on weekends and furthermore, that she's quite comfortable with it. Even so, Ismael shirks from the responsibility of being a father once again to Elias.

For Nora, the harrowing ordeal of watching her father die at home stirs up the repressed memory of how Pierre died. She now relives the flashback where he shoots himself in front of her in order to escape the drudgery of being a father-to-be. Unable to bear her father's pain, she administers an overdose of painkillers that kill him.

Yet even this depth of despair is topped by what turns everything around as Nora reads the letter to her that comprises the closing pages of her father's memoirs. Desplechin shows Louis in an unwavering black-and-white medium shot, seated on a stool, against a grey wall, as if he were posing for one last portrait. With a calm voice, he conveys his rage against her "monstrous" egoism and pride which has turned into bitterness. He ends his diatribe of hate with the words, "I wish you would die instead of me …."

Shattered as this leaves Nora, she picks up the pieces to begin a no doubt wiser life with Jean-Jacques. Ismael explains life to Elias and prepares to start anew with Arielle. The continuity within the film's two narrative trajectories is now underscored by two different forms of popular music, both American. For Ismael, it is the profligate energy of hip-hop while for Nora it is the lyricism of a solitary guitar plucking the melody of "Moon River" with which the film opened.

Vivek Adarkar

CREDITS

Nora: Emmanuelle Devos

Ismael: Mathieu Amalric

Psychiatrist: Catherine Deneuve

Arielle: Magali Woch

Jean-Jacques: Olivier Rabourdin

Louis: Maurice Garrel

Chloe: Nathalie Boutefeu

Pierre: Joachim Salinger
Mamanne: Hippolyte Girardot
Origin: France
Language: French
Released: 2004
Production: Pascal Caucheteux; Why Not Productions, France 2 Cinema, Rhone Alps Cinema
Directed by: Arnaud Desplechin
Written by: Arnaud Desplechin, Roger Bohbot
Cinematography by: Eric Gautier
Sound: Jean-Pierre Laforce, Christian Monheim
Editing: Laurence Briaud
Costumes: Nathalie Raoul
Production Design: Dan Bevan
MPAA rating: Unrated
Running time: 150 minutes

REVIEWS

Boxoffice Online. May, 2005.
Chicago Sun-Times Online. May 26, 2005.
Entertainment Weekly Online. May 18, 2005.
Los Angeles Times Online. May 20, 2005.
New York Times Online. October 6, 2004.
Variety Online. September 10, 2004.

QUOTES

Nora: "There are four men I loved. I killed two of them."

TRIVIA

Valeria Bruni Tedeschi was initially considered for the role of Nora.

KING'S RANSOM

Big Man. Big Plan. Big Mistake.
—Movie tagline

Box Office: $4 million

Malcolm King (Anthony Anderson) is a self-centered, arrogant millionaire owner of a marketing company whose employees hate him, whose wife Renee (Kellita Smith) is divorcing him, and whose personal secretary, Miss Gladys (Loretta Devine), has to constantly keep Malcolm from self-destructing. Because Malcolm spends more time in the office dallying with his ditzy girlfriend/employee Peaches Clark (Regina Hall) than he does in running the business, day-to-day affairs are actually being taken care of by Angela Drake (Nicole Parker) who expects to be promoted to vice president for her efforts, but is passed over when the job is given to Peaches.

Corey (Jay Mohr) is a hapless sucker who lives with his chain-smoking, deaf grandmother, has just lost his job as a "hamburger" advertising a fast food restaurant, and whose step-sister has just escaped from prison and demanding money from Corey or she'll tell the police about his string of convenience store robberies.

As the major characters watch the news—waiting for the lottery numbers to be read—they all hear about a local kidnapping and ransom case. Inspiration strikes. Everyone sees this as a way out of their problems. Angela will kidnap King out of spite, Corey out of desperation for money, and even King, himself, thinks that staging his own kidnapping will get him out of the clutches of his nasty, money-grubbing wife. Even Renee considers kidnapping her husband, but she never gets around to it.

Of course things will go wrong. King's plan goes afoul when Peaches' ex-con brother Herb (Charlie Murphy) mistakenly kidnaps car valet, Andre (Donald Faison) who is pretending to be the wealthy King to impress the ladies. Angela's plan involves her boyfriend, King's stuttering chauffeur to kidnap him, and King goes along with it believing it is his own plan, only to have the car break down on the road. At this point Corey steps in and kidnaps King again who still believes it is his own plan in action and goes along with it willingly and stupidly believing Corey is Peaches' brother. The only person taking the kidnapping seriously is Miss Gladys who immediately heads off to the police who seem as inept as the kidnappers.

Directed by Jeff Byrd, a Spike Lee protégé and music video director, *King's Ransom* is Anderson's first starring vehicle, but his character is so dislikable that the movie does not serve his career well. Similarly, Jay Mohr, who showed such comedic promise in his early career, seems incapable lately of finding a vehicle in which to shine.

But worst of all, with the exception of Loretta Devine's Miss Gladys, the characters, both major and minor, in *King's Ransom* are incredibly offensive and stereotypical. With far too much booty wagging and way too few laughs, this film doesn't offer a story or characters that are worth spending any time with, even if it is only 97 minutes

Beverley Bare Buehrer

CREDITS

Malcolm King: Anthony Anderson
Corey: Jay Mohr
Renee King: Kellita Smith
Angela Drake: Nicole Ari Parker

Peaches Clarke: Regina Hall
Miss Gladys: Loretta Devine
Andre: Donald Adeosun Faison
Herb Clarke: Charlie Murphy
Raven: Lisa Marcos
Brooke Mayo: Brooke D'Orsay
Kim Baker: Leila Arcieri
Grandma: Jackie Burroughs
Origin: USA
Language: English
Released: 2005
Production: Daryl Taja; Catch 23's Alter Ego Production; released by New Line Cinema
Directed by: Jeff Byrd
Written by: Wayne Conley
Cinematography by: Robert McLachlan
Sound: Patrick Rousseau
Editing: Jeff Cooper
Art Direction: Jean Kazemirchuk
Costumes: Rita S. McGhee
Production Design: Kalina Ivanov
MPAA rating: PG-13
Running time: 97 minutes

REVIEWS

Los Angeles Times Online. April 25, 2005.
New York Times Online. April 23, 2005.
Variety Online. April 22, 2005.

KISS KISS BANG BANG

SeX. MurdEr. MyStery. Welcome to the party.
—Movie tagline

A bad week in a tough town.
—Movie tagline

Box Office: $4.1 million

Kiss Kiss Bang Bang is a miraculously wicked little low-budget film noir that came out of nowhere and caught the Postmodern critics at the BFI by surprise. Enraptured, they gave it cover treatment in the December 2005 issue of *Sight and Sound*, the critical organ of the British Film Institute, and the longest-established, most prestigious film periodical published in English. On the other hand, the coverage, like the film itself, was schizoid, in that the *Sight and Sound* review in the back of the book was at qualitative odds with the enthusiastic cover story and interview with debut director Shane Black, whose name would only be recognized by movie buffs who read and then memorize movie credits. Problem is, most viewers are not so well informed.

Shane Black broke into the Industry in 1987, when, at the age of 22, he wrote the script that was fated to become the legendary blockbuster directed by Richard Donner, *Lethal Weapon*, starring Mel Gibson and Danny Glover. Logically enough, he would later also script *Lethal Weapon 2* for Donner and the boys, but he wanted to kill off the Mel Gibson character at the end, which would have made further sequels awkward. Although he was not invited back to write the subsequent sequels, it was Black who first imagined the Gibson role as a manic, suicidal cop, which made the series click. The series was pitched as "*Dirty Harry* meets *The Odd Couple*, with an interracial twist," according to *Sight and Sound.* After experimenting with a creature-feature called *The Monster Squad* in 1987, Black moved on to write the scripts for other successful action features: *The Last Boy Scout* for Tony Scott in 1991, *The Long Kiss Goodnight* for Renny Harlin in 1996, and a draft for John McTiernan's *Last Action Hero*, which was a relative flop (too clever by half, it was) for Arnold Schwarzenneger in 1993. Black also found work as an actor for John McTiernan in *Predator* in 1987, and other roles would follow: *Dead Heat* (1988), *RoboCop* (1992), *As Good As It Gets* (1997), and *A.W.O.L.* (1999). Black's Ŭbercool Postmodern movie-savvy verbal style is typically represented by Bruce Willis when he remarks in *The Last Boy Scout* "This is the 1990s—you don't just go around punching people; you have to say something cool first." Now that brand of "cool" worked well enough up until *The Last Action Hero* failed at the box-office, according to Kim Newman in *Sight and Sound.* Therefter, Shane Black became increasingly in need of a second chance. So maybe he and Robert Downey, Jr., and Val Kilmer could tread the comeback trail together?

Kiss Kiss Bang Bang, a hell of a title for a movie, stolen from Pauline Kael, who stole it from a campy Italian movie poster, teams smart-alec petty thief Harry Lockhart (Robert Downey Jr., in one of his very best roles) with Perry Van Shrike (Val Kilmer), a supercool private eye who also happens to be gay and works as a Hollywood studio advisor. This is a winning combination. Both Downey and Kilmer have traveled through more than their share of rough patches and have had careers on the skids. Downey has had the more serious problem with substance abuse; Kilmer has been criticized for "being difficult to work with," according to *Time* magazine. *Kiss Kiss Bang Bang*, then, is potentially a work of redemption and second chances for them, archly informed by Shane Black's Postmodern wit and way too many insider jokes—such as Kilmer being confused with a lesser talented actor, Michael Beck, from *Xanadu* (1980) and *The Warriors* (1979). But Black is also spoofing film noir conventions and traditions, wonderfully through Downey's knowing, first-person narration that is generally convoluted and out-of-control, often given to a halfwit protagonist whose brain is driven by other, lower organs. To reiterate, *Kiss Kiss Bang Bang* is a second-chance comeback vehicle for Shane Black as well as for Kilmer and Downey. That became part of the studio's promotional story.

The provenance of Black's screenplay was explained in the December 2005 issue of *Sight and Sound* cover story by Kim Newman. Black credits his screenplay as being "based in part" on the Brett Halliday novel *Bodies Are Where You Find Them* (1941), and Harry Lockhart keeps stumbling over corpses that mysteriously appear. "Brett Halliday," whose *real* name was novelist Davis Dresser (1904-1977), wrote over sixty potboilers involving Miami-based private eye Michael Shayne, who was played on screen by Lloyd Nolan in the 1940s. In *Kiss Kiss Bang Bang* Halliday becomes pseudonymous author "Jonny Gossamer," whose pulp fiction "inspires" Harry Lockhart and his Hoosier high school sweetheart Harmony Faith Land (Michelle Monaghan). *Kiss Kiss Bang Bang* plays like a loop of *noir* "homage." Chapter headings pay tribute to Raymond Chandler, e.g., recalling "The Simple Art of Murder," "Lady in the Lake," and "Farewell, My Lovely." But what on earth is all this clever trivia going to mean to current filmgoers, who are not the film buffs of yesteryear?

In typical noir fashion, the plot is bound to confuse. After a flashback to bucolic rural Indiana, circa 1980, with a young Harry Lockhart attempting to work magic on a very young Harmony Lane, who aspires to be an actress, and seems to have the lungs for it. Twenty-five years later petty criminal Harry Lockhart comes running into a New York City loft while trying to escape from the police. In classic film noir, the men are not very bright, and the police are especially stupid. All of a sudden, Harry finds himself being accidentally auditioned for a big movie role. Harry is so edgy and convincing (think of a really trippy Robert Downey trying to improvise in this context) that he gets sent to Hollywood for a screen test, hoping to play a private detective in a feature film. At Veronica Dexter's Birthday Party, thrown by her devious father, Harlan Dexter (Corbin Bernsen), Harry is happily reunited with childhood sweetie Harmony Lane (Michelle Monagham), who is still an aspiring actress, but at least now in Hollywood. (A Movie Buff Alert should here be inserted to let readers know that *Harmony Lane* was the title of a 1935 romanticized composer biopic, sweetening the life and exploiting the music of that sentimental American favorite, Stephen Foster [1826-1864]. Perhaps Shane Black would want you to know that.)

To get valuable private-eye experience, Harry goes to work with Perry Van Shrike (Kilmer), nicknamed "Gay Perry." Perry is smarter than Harry, so of course Harry gets to narrate the film: "My name is Harry Lockhart," he says, "and I'll be your narrator." Harry and Perry are spotted while watching a woman's body being thrown into a lake (hence, "The Lady in the Lake") by the killers, oddly named Mr. Frying Pan (Dash Mihok) and Mr. Fire (Rockmond Dunbar). The corpse, who turns out to be Heiress Veronica Dexter, turns up in Harry's room. Perry helps Harry dispose of it, and they become true pals and now partners in crime. Harmony, who thinks that Harry is a real detective, wants to hire him to look into her sister's suicide. Mr. Frying Pan and Mr. Fire attempt to ambush and assassinate Perry in MacArthur Park in Los Angeles. Mr. Frying Pan is killed in the ensuing shoot-out and Harry kills Mr. Fire. Eventually, Harry discovers that Harlan Dexter concealed Veronica in a clinic and that Veronica's double, who appeared in public to assist in the illusion that her lawsuit had been settled, was the corpse that turned up in Harry's room. Later on, Harry and Perry intercept Dexter at the clinic before he can cremate the real Veronica's body. In a shoot-out Harry has to kill Dexter and his gunsels in order to save (or to maintain) Harmony, but, alas, Perry is apparently shot dead. But, no, this *noir* fantasy ends with a really goofy reversal that shows Perry still very much alive and ready to hire Harry as his partner.

In typical Black (which, in this case, is to say *noir*) formula fashion, then, *Kiss Kiss Bang Bang* is an ironic buddy film with an "odd couple" pairing a loser with an "Other." About the plot one can only say that Mr. Black tends to give precedence to cuteness and cleverness over coherence. *Kiss Kiss Bang Bang* begs comparison to another *film noir* spoof released only a few weeks earlier, *The Ice Harvest* but in that case, though the plot was certainly and amusingly convoluted, there was a sense of narrative clarity and coherence. Both films place dumb "buddies" (John Cusack and Billy Bob Thornton in *The Ice Harvest*, directed by Harold Ramis, from a Richard Russo screenplay) in a jokey killer-thriller with an improbable plot. Both films involved a potentially repulsive mixture of Christmas murder and mayhem. Oh, what fun! *Time* critic Joel Stein judged the film "off-putting, absurdist, [and] uncomfortable funny," however, and went so far as to describe the pairing of Downey and Kilmer as a punk reincarnation of Bob Hope and Bing Crosby. In fact, Stein might be on to something. Anthony Lane's *New Yorker* review described Downey's Harry as a "low-grade Bogart cut with shreds of Bob Hope."

Ultimately, *The Ice Harvest* was more dumb fun than *Kiss Kiss Bang Bang* which pushes the envelope of taste and tolerance too far. That's why Anthony Lane wrote that the film "should be the most annoying movie of the year," which seems an accurate assessment. Reckless in minding his plot points, Shane Black is "not aiming to make sense," as Anthony Lane noted. But it's easy to be won over by the engaging performances and seduced by the wit, shallow though it may be. (Lane liked the film, despite himself, however, claiming the film "is not a bust." But it's a qualified endorsement.)

So, has Shane Black managed to come back "with a 'Bang,'" to quote a *Washington Post* headline intended to hype the film? Certainly the film was well received at Cannes and Toronto, and that should enable Black to shake the "hack" label that had been affixed to him during his slump period of the 1990s, his nine-year dry spell. This time around *Lethal Weapon* producer Joel Silver saved his bacon by helping Black get the $15 million funding from Warner Bros. he needed to make the film. But A.O. Scott of the *New York Times* wasn't buying the comeback with a "Bang" story. Scott was not impressed or misled by the first-time director's "slick, dexterous self-confidence," adding "you can almost convince yourself that something interesting is going on." Yes, almost. The likable actors and the energetic acting create momentum that the director jams to a halt through a jerky editing style that seems to stop the projector and then reel backwards. But for A.O. Scott this film was merely an "empty stylistic exercise," not the sort of achievement that will get Shane Black invited to join the Academy of Motion Picture Arts and Sciences anytime soon. Surely Black's main talent is still as a writer, but it would be unfair to dismiss him as being merely a hack. The verbal dexterity of this screenplay (if not the narrative logic and the consistently self-conscious voice-over narration) is often impressive.

James M. Welsh

CREDITS

Harry Lockhart: Robert Downey Jr.
Gay Perry: Val Kilmer
Harmony Faith Lane: Michelle Monaghan
Harlan Dexter: Corbin Bernsen
Mr. Frying Pan: Dash Mihok
Dabney Shaw: Larry Miller
Pink Hair Girl: Shannyn Sossamon
Flicka: Angela Lindvall
Mr. Fire: Rockmond Dunbar
Origin: USA
Language: English
Released: 2005
Production: Joel Silver; Silver Pictures; released by Warner Bros.
Directed by: Shane Black
Written by: Shane Black
Cinematography by: Michael Barrett
Music by: John Ottman
Sound: Stephen A. Tibbo
Music Supervisor: Randall Poster
Editing: Jim Page
Art Direction: Erin Cochran
Costumes: Christopher J. Kristoff
Production Design: Aaron Osborne
MPAA rating: R
Running time: 103 minutes

REVIEWS

Boxoffice Online. October, 2005.
Chicago Sun-Times Online. October 21, 2005.
Entertainment Weekly Online. October 19, 2005.
Los Angeles Times Online. October 21, 2005.
New York Times Online. October 21, 2005.
Premiere Magazine Online. October 21, 2005.
Variety Online. May 13, 2005.
Washington Post Online. November 11, 2005, p. WE44.

QUOTES

Harry Lockhart: "This is every shade of wrong."

TRIVIA

Renowned action writer (*Lethal Weapon,* 1987) Shane Black's directorial debut.

KUNG FU HUSTLE

(Gong fu)

A new comedy unlike anything you have seen before.
—Movie tagline

Box Office: $17.1 million

Orson Welles had his stock company of trusted players in "The Mercury Theatre" that he used in many of his radio plays and films. Christopher Guest has his independent company of players, and in Hong Kong director, actor, and comedian Stephen Chow has his well-oiled group. What all three these directors have in common is the singular passion to bring their inspiration to the screen that only they uniquely could, while never hogging the spotlight and having the confidence to allow the rest of the cast to show their gifts as well.

Stephen Chow came to the American general public's attention with the release (long delayed by Miramax) of his previous high-energy kinetic comedy *Shaolin Soccer* (2003). He and his group return for another high-octane comedy this time in *Kung Fu Hustle,* which opens on a surreal Shanghai that belies reality, and signals to the audience that this film will take place in a hyper-cartoon reality that only can be seen in Chow's live-action cartoon world.

The opening five minutes combine the ultra violent content of a straight kung-fu action flick, with John Woo-esque visual violence, while at the same time takes the opportunity for a musical number montage illustrating the growing gangland takeover of most of China by a top-hatted, axe wielding gang. This is the basic M.O. of the film: Bang-bang violence followed by a punchline.

The gang is called the Axe gang for obvious reasons (it is the weapon of choice as their chief enforcement tool). And in the opening sequence the Axes are shown to be a formidable force to be reckoned with as they take out the local mob in violent, gruesome, and only in a chow film, humorous methods. If this sounds like an impossible and bizarre mix, you would usually be right, were it not for the fact that this is a Stephen Chow film. His films always seem to straddle a balance between implausible violent action and outright buffoonery, that makes the viewer feel as if he is watching a live-action version of a Warner Bros. cartoon. If you've ever seen one of those classic cartoons where Daffy Duck gets a shotgun in the face by Elmer Fudd time and time again, you will begin to understand the structure of a Stephen Chow film.

After the opening credits we are introduced to the denizens of Pig Sty Alley, a neighborhood so low rent and full of the seemingly ineffectual, that it is the only place that has not been taken over by the Axe Gang, because there is just no need to. The first time we meet Sing (Stephen Chow), he is standing in a dirt field on the outskirts of Pig Sty Alley, watching neighborhood kids playing a soccer game. Perceived audience expectations that he is a one-trick-pony are directly addressed. For anyone that has been wondering if *Shaolin Soccer* was the only two-toned ball in his comedic net, he quickly stomps on that notion while exclaiming, "No more soccer!" This is a filmmaker who does not rest on his laurels (even if his characters do).

Sing and his friend (Lam Tze Chung) are an inept Laurel and Hardy pair who come to Pig Sty Alley with the purpose of conning the residents out of their money by posing as Axe Gang members. But the residents don't believe them, and the town leader Landlady (Yuen Qiu), a more than middle-aged woman who seems to have never met a cigarette she didn't like soon confronts them for their transgressions. Throughout most of the film, she is dressed in a frumpy cotton nightgown, curlers in her hair, and always has a cigarette hanging from her mouth. She is tougher than she looks though, as the Axe Gang soon finds when the news of the counterfeit gang members reaches them and they come to the town to find the culprits and teach the residents a lesson in obedience.

The Axe gang members and the audience discover that the denizens of Pig Sty Alley are not exactly what they seem. But the arrogant gang members find out too slow and suffer an embarrassing and incredibly painful defeat at the hands of three of the unlikeliest townspeople (courtesy of fight choreographer Yuen Wo Ping). It is during this scene that one is reminded of a similar melee in *Matrix Reloaded* (2003), also choreographed by Ping, where Keanu Reeves' character Neo takes on hundreds of bad guys with the help of state of the art CGI, that ultimately felt boring and lifeless to the viewer. Here however, Chow understands that context is key and brings fun and exhilaration to the scene. Here he is able to show the heroism of his characters as they fight off odds and physics that cannot be overcome in real life, and they do it with such giddy energy and abandon that the similar scene in *Matrix Reloaded* reveals its smugness and lifelessness in comparison.

Embarrassed by the defeat, the leader of the Axe gang Brother Sum (Chan Kwok Kwan) seeks retribution on the town and sends a pair of professional assassins to reap vengeance on the three martial arts masters that handed the Axe gang their proverbial hats. The pair of mysterious robed men arrive with their main weapon of choice, a cello sized stringed harp instrument that when strummed creates deadly mystical (and CGI) knives and swords, and when they prove ineffective, finally attack with knife and sword wielding ghosts.

How this scene plays out is both exhilarating and poignant with moments of absurd but fitting (for this film) high humor. During the fight for example, the Landlady opens her window causing the assassins to temporarily stop playing. She berates the two by yelling at them to be quiet. When another resident tells her to shut up and die, she responds with one of the biggest laugh-lines in the film, "What, die in this racquet?" It is moments like these that a filmgoer can be thankful for the comedic genius of Stephen Chow. Because in any other film, that line may have garnered a groan, but here it works just fine.

The battle ends in a stalemate and Brother Sum and Landlady agree to a truce. But Sum's boss has no intention of abiding by it. Desperate and having been kicked out of Pig Sty Alley, Sing agrees to work for Sum in breaking out the "Beast" (Leung Siu Lung) from a high security prison. He is told that the Beast is known as the most insane and unbeatable fighter throughout China, and the Axe gang plans to use him to "clean up" Pig Sty Alley once and for all. But the Beast has his own plans and agenda. He is not concerned with the Axe gang or their plans, he only wants to defeat the greatest opponent ever, or be defeated by him.

David E. Chapple

CREDITS

Sing: Stephen (Chiau) Chow
Landlord: Yuen Wah
Brother Sam: Chan Kwok Kwan
Crocodile Gang Boss: Feng Xiao Gang
Axe Gang Vice-head: Lam Suet
The Beast: Leung Siu Lung
Donut: Dong Zhi Hua
Tailor: Chiu Chi Ling
Landlady: Yuen Qui
Coolie: Xing Yu
Fong: Huang Sheng Yi
Sing's Sidekick: Lam Tze Chung
Origin: China, Hong Kong
Language: Cantonese
Released: 2004
Production: Stephen Chow, Chui Po-Chu, Jeff Lau; Columbia Film Production Asia, Huayi Brothers & Taihe Film Investment Co.; released by Sony Pictures Classics
Directed by: Stephen (Chiau) Chow
Written by: Stephen (Chiau) Chow, Kan-Cheung (Sammy) Tsang, Chan Man-keung, Lola Huo
Cinematography by: Poon Hang-Seng
Music by: Raymond Wong
Sound: Leung Chi-tat
Editing: Angie Lam
Art Direction: Second Chan
Costumes: Shirley Chan
Production Design: Oliver Wong
MPAA rating: R
Running time: 99 minutes

REVIEWS

Boxoffice Online. April, 2005.
Chicago Sun-Times Online. April 22, 2005.
Entertainment Weekly Online. April 6, 2005.
Los Angeles Times Online. April 8, 2005.
New York Times Online. April 8, 2005.
Premiere Magazine Online. April 21, 2005.
Variety Online. September 19, 2004.
Washington Post Online. April 22, 2005, p. WE35.

QUOTES

Landlady: "You may know kung fu...but you're still a fairy."

TRIVIA

Surpassed *Shaolin Soccer* (2001) in February 2005 to become the highest-grossing Hong Kong-made movie in Hong Kong.

L

LAST DAYS

In his newest film, *Last Days*, Gus Van Sant continues a trend he began with *Gerry* and *Elephant* as he distances himself from, perhaps even declares war on, traditional notions of narrative filmmaking and character development. Imposing very little (if any) plot or structure on his material, Van Sant has been creating a stripped-down kind of cinema that some critics find innovative and even mesmerizing (indeed, *Elephant*, by far the most intriguing and focused of these experiments, employs its minimalism to good effect), but more often the results are painfully dull and off-putting.

All of these films have their roots in true stories ending in death, which Van Sant has used as jumping-off points for his own musings. *Last Days* is ostensibly a speculative work imagining the final days of grunge rocker Kurt Cobain, who died of a self-inflicted gunshot wound in 1994. Playing a singer named Blake, Michael Pitt—with his long, stringy, blond hair; scraggly, unshaven face; and blank demeanor—is meant to resemble the tragic singer-songwriter, to whom the film is dedicated. But while Pitt nails Cobain's look, he is never given a chance to embody Cobain's soul. There is no insight into Blake's inner torment, and, if the audience did not bring its knowledge of Cobain's troubled life to the film as well as its preconceptions about the alienation fame can engender, this movie would make no sense at all.

Last Days is composed of seemingly disconnected sequences revolving around Blake, who, on more than one occasion, wanders at length through the woods near his dilapidated mansion while mumbling to himself. In the film's opening, he strips and crosses a body of water; later, he builds a fire to warm himself. In another scene, he pours himself a bowl of cereal, and we are treated to the whole kitchen ritual, punctuated by the supposedly funny detail of Blake putting the box of cereal in the refrigerator. A Yellow Pages salesman (Thadeus A. Thomas) visits, and Blake hardly seems to understand what he is talking about. As the man is wrapping up his sales pitch, Blake is falling asleep. The "actor," however, is a real Yellow Pages salesman who just happened to come to Van Sant's office one day—why that chance meeting should warrant an appearance in this film other than to fill time is anybody's guess. Two Mormon missionaries also visit, and they talk to Scott (Scott Green), who seems to live in the mansion but whose precise relationship to Blake is never explained.

Another acquaintance of Blake, Donovan (Ryan Orion), is apparently concerned about him and comes to the estate with a private investigator (Ricky Jay), whose big moment is telling Donovan the strange story of Billy Robinson, a vaudeville performer who masqueraded as a Chinese magician and died when he failed to catch a fired bullet in his teeth. Jay himself is a professional magician who tells such historical anecdotes in his shows and was asked to improvise his bit for the film. Perhaps the story is meant as vague foreshadowing of Blake's death, but it really does not say anything relevant and feels like one more random digression. Moreover, because the conversation takes place in a car and is shot from outside, the glare from the window makes it almost impossible to see the actors' faces, making the whole scene more distracting than enlightening.

The most substantive encounter in the film involves a record executive (Sonic Youth's Kim Gordon), who tries to talk some sense into Blake, chastising him for being a rock-and-roll cliché and trying to invoke his daughter as a way of pulling him out of his stupor. Her efforts to wake him up prove fruitless, and this short scene, the film's one attempt to get inside Blake's psyche, goes nowhere.

But practically everything in *Last Days* feels superfluous, including Blake's acquaintances, who make his house their own and seem to have a standing invitation. These hangers-on do not interact much with the lonely Blake and serve no function in his story, such as it is. Luke (Lukas Haas) asks Blake for help on a demo tape; later, he and Scott go upstairs to a bedroom, undress, and make out in a scene that bears no relationship to anything other than the fact that Van Sant is a gay director known for his themes of homoeroticism involving young men.

Stylistically, Van Sant's work in *Last Days* is characterized by lengthy, meandering takes of Blake wandering around the woods (often shot from the back) or Blake stumbling around his property in his efforts to elude human contact. The scenes are interminable and often nonsensical. Blake, for example, turns on a television set on which is playing a music video by R&B group Boyz II Men, whose lush love songs are obviously antithetical to Blake's raw sound. But why the camera continues to linger on the TV to see the video to its completion (long after Blake has lost interest) is just one more puzzling detail.

For a film ostensibly about rock and roll, there is actually very little music in *Last Days*. Blake performs two solo pieces that go on too long and, given the camera setup, are static. One is shot from outside the house, with the camera slowly pulling back so that we can barely see Blake through the window as he plays different instruments and emits a wailing scream. The other is a guitar solo, "Death to Birth," which Pitt wrote himself but which does nothing to shed light on the character and pales next to Cobain's work. Shot in one long take with Blake strumming his guitar and singing inaudibly, it only goes further in alienating the audience.

Eschewing a completely linear chronology, Van Sant at times shows the same event twice but from different points of view. This method made a certain amount of sense in *Elephant*, which follows several students through a single school day on the way to a horrific shooting. The technique of trailing characters down corridors and circling back in time to see different kids going about their business at the same moment not only heightens the tension but also lends itself to the idea that we are examining a community from different angles. In *Last Days*, however, the device feels like a gimmicky attempt to add a layer of complexity, to make us feel that something of importance is happening when, in fact, nothing is happening.

Like its protagonist, the movie rambles along, finally reaching its inevitable conclusion. We are spared seeing the actual act that ends Blake's life, but a scene of a naked Blake, his spirit, rising out of his clothed body and climbing an invisible ladder feels like an awkward attempt to give the conclusion a quasi-mystical dimension. Nothing up to this point suggests that redemption or transcendence fits the story.

By the time the authorities arrive to take away the corpse, it is hard to fathom what Van Sant is trying to say about Blake, Cobain, or a rock-and-roll tragedy more generally. Blake remains as elusive at the end as he did at the beginning, and Van Sant's pretentious, self-indulgent style does not give any shape or meaning to his life, his creativity, or even his untimely demise.

Peter N. Chumo II

CREDITS

Blake: Michael Pitt
Luke: Lukas Haas
Asia: Asia Argento
Detective: Ricky Jay
Guy in Club: Harmony Korine
Scott: Scott Green
Nicole: Nicole Vicius
Donovan: Ryan Orion
Record Executive: Kim Gordon
Elder Friberg #1: Adam Friberg
Elder Friberg #2: Andy Friberg
Yellow Book Salesman: Thadeus A. Thomas
Tree Trimmer: Chip Marks
Origin: USA
Language: English
Released: 2005
Production: Dany Wolf; Meno Films
Directed by: Gus Van Sant
Written by: Gus Van Sant
Cinematography by: Harris Savides
Sound: Felix Andrew
Art Direction: Tim Grimes
Costumes: Michelle Matland
MPAA rating: R
Running time: 97 minutes

REVIEWS

Boxoffice Online. July, 2005.
Chicago Sun-Times Online. July 22, 2005.

Entertainment Weekly Online. July 20, 2005.
Los Angeles Times Online. July 22, 2005.
New York Times Online. July 22, 2005.
Premiere Magazine Online. July 22, 2005.
Variety Online. May 13, 2005.
Washington Post Online. August 5, 2005, p. WE30.

LAYER CAKE

Box Office: $2.3 million

Matthew Vaughn's *Layer Cake,* based on the book by J. J. Connelly, is the latest offering in a long line of British gangster flicks. Here, Vaughn takes the viewer away from the gritty, London streets and hinterworld of his earlier collaborations with Guy Ritchie (*Lock, Stock and Two Smoking Barrels* and *Snatch*), into the uptown world of today's modern drug dealers. The world of the *Layer Cake* is inhabited by clever, calculating Armani-wearing wise guys who approach the drug trade like any legitimate business. Vaughn, a producer of the aforementioned Ritchie-directed films, moves into the director's chair and the product he gives us is a slick, stylized film that stacks character upon character, and story line upon story line, until it reaches critical mass.

The film's unnamed central character (XXXX in the credits) is played by Daniel Craig, who doubles as the narrator of this often overly complex mixture. XXXX sees himself as an interlocutor, simply bringing together buyer and product. He is no gangster, in fact, he abhors violence which gives his character a fresh and unexpected vulnerability. Craig navigates all the treachery thrown his way with Steve McQueen cool. Craig has a more than passing resemblance to the *Bullitt* actor and Vaughn plays the McQueen angle for all it's worth, placing Craig in a dizzying array of iconic shots, including one close-up of Craig prowling around with a long barreled pistol pointed skyward, ala James Bond.

The film opens with a lush, well-crafted montage that gives viewers a condensed history of drugs in England, from the simple good-time 1960s filled with hippies and hookahs to the inevitable mix of gangsters and businessmen that make up today's "recreational drugs P.L.C. " These entrepreneurs look at the criminalization of drugs as a sort of modern day prohibition. In their eyes, with all the money to be made in recreational drugs it's just a matter of time before it all becomes legal. XXXX is the suave, cocaine-dealing middle-man who seems to have it all worked out: a respectable business front (real estate), a crooked banker to launder the $1 million he's managed to stash away, a flat in a smart part of town, and plan in place for early retirement. However, as Pacino famously quipped in *The Godfather: Part III,* "Just when I thought that I was out they pull me back in," proving that walking away is easier said than done.

XXXX and his two mates, Morty (George Harris) and Gene (Colm Meaney), are unexpectedly summoned to a meeting with their boss Jimmy Price (Kenneth Cranham) who has two delicate jobs for them. One: find the missing daughter of Jimmy's old friend, business tycoon and proper blueblood Eddie Temple (Michael Gambon), who has run off with her addict boyfriend. And two: Broker a deal for one million high-octane ecstasy pills that have been hijacked from the warehouse of a sadistic Serbian warlord who demands the heads, literally, of those who cross him. This seems like an odd task for a mere middleman like XXXX but Jimmy brushes it all aside by saying "Every now and then we are asked to do something above and beyond the call of duty. It's called sacrifice, son. Ask Gene, ask Morty."

The pills have been pinched by a hair-trigger, two-bit gangster named Duke (Jamie Foreman) who has no idea of the kind of people he has crossed to obtain this windfall. He just knows the stuff is top-notch and he has lots of it to sell: it must be worth millions. Morty, Gene, and XXXX track down The Duke and in a tense exchange, XXXX calmly explains how this sort of commerce works. There are many matters to consider, including currency fluctuations, broker fees, and the problem of finding someone who can handle this sort of volume. Just the sort of dialogue one would expect to find in any corporate negotiation, only this is no boardroom and the players are armed to the teeth.

For the job of finding Eddie's daughter Charlie (Nathalie Lunghi), XXXX employs a couple of slick con men, Cody (Dexter Fletcher) and Tiptoes (Steve John Shepherd). Their sleuthing takes them to the seedy section of London, King's Cross, where they find the body of Charlie's boyfriend Kinky (Marvin Benoit) but no sign of Charlie, who has apparently gone into hiding—where she stays for the rest of the film. The Charlie ploy merely serves as a vehicle to introduce Eddie, Tiptoes and Cody who all have more to do later in the film.

Harris' character Morty is more than just a large man in a sharp suit, as we find out when he bumps into an old acquaintance in a tearoom over breakfast. As the two converse, Morty's blood begins to boil and instead of breakfast, he serves up a savage beating to his old mate who we later find out is responsible for sending Morty to prison for ten years. The camera work in this scene places the viewer right in the middle of the action and inside the victim's eyes. The combination of deft camera work and the restrained use of XTC's "Making

Plans for Nigel" make this the film's most indelible moment.

When we are finally introduced to Eddie Templeton, things really get complicated, as the plot begins to double back on itself, and, as is so often the case, everything presented prior is not quite what it seems. XXXX's eyes are opened to the truth about Jimmy Price and that Eddie Temple is, in fact, the top of the "layer cake." Eddie wants the pills for himself, offering a very attractive price. It is an offer XXXX cannot refuse. Now it is up to XXXX to craft a plan to sidestep the Serbs, come to grips with the revelations about Jimmy, and extract the pills from Duke without getting himself killed, or worse. All of this makes for a very tense second half of the movie, one that is filled with so many twists and turns that it is often on the verge of spiraling out of control. Somehow, Vaughn manages to pull it all together and make it all work out with a very clever ending that involves XXXX's love interest Tammy, (Sienna Miller) and the danger at even the very lowest level of the layer cake.

The characters and settings may have changed but many of the elements from the earlier Ritchie collaborations and the genre in general remain. It is these elements that serve as a stepping-off point for Vaughn. He brings some fine cinema work, engaging characters, and wonderful locations to the mix. But in the end it is Daniel Craig's powerful performance that makes *Layer Cake* special.

Michael White

CREDITS

XXXX: Daniel Craig
Gene: Colm Meaney
Jimmy Price: Kenneth Cranham
Mr. Mortimer, "Morty": George Harris
JD, "Duke": Jamie Foreman
Eddie Temple: Michael Gambon
Terry: Tamer Hassan
Sidney: Ben Whishaw
Gazza: Burn Gorman
Slasher: Sally Hawkins
Tammy: Sienna Miller
Shanks: Stephen Walters
Larry: Jason Flemyng
Dragan: Dragan Micanovic
Cody: Dexter Fletcher
Tiptoes: Steve John Shepherd
Kinky: Marvin Benoit
Origin: Great Britain
Language: English
Released: 2005
Production: Matthew Vaughn, Adam Bohling, David Reid; released by Sony Pictures Classics
Directed by: Matthew Vaughn
Written by: J.J. Connolly
Cinematography by: Benjamin Davis
Music by: Lisa Gerrard, Ilan Eshkeri
Sound: Matthew Collinge
Editing: Jon Davis
Art Direction: Stephen Carter
Costumes: Stephanie Collie
Production Design: Kave Quinn
MPAA rating: R
Running time: 105 minutes

REVIEWS

Boxoffice Online. May, 2005.
Chicago Sun-Times Online. May 19, 2005.
Entertainment Weekly Online. May 11, 2005.
Los Angeles Times Online. May 13, 2005.
New York Times Online. May 13, 2005.
Premiere Magazine Online. May 12, 2005.
Variety Online. September 28, 2004.
Washington Post Online. May 27, 2005, p. C05.

QUOTES

XXXX: "My name? If I told you that, you'd be as clever as me."

TRIVIA

Guy Ritchie was originally set to direct but had to drop out due to other commitments.

THE LEGEND OF ZORRO

Box Office: $45.3 million

The Legend of Zorro is the long-gestating sequel to 1998's *The Mask of Zorro*, a PG-13 rated romp that starred Anthony Hopkins as the aging Zorro, Banderas as his protégé, and a then little-known Zeta-Jones as the love interest and a woman who was pretty handy with a sword herself; British actor Stuart Wilson played your basic foreign villain. The successful venture was directed by Martin Campbell and was intended as much for adults, who probably remembered Zorro in his previous incarnations (books, movies, and television), as for the younger crowd. Campbell returns for *Legend* as does Banderas, the first Spanish-speaking actor to play the part, and the now Oscar-winning (for 2002's *Chicago*) Zeta-Jones. British actor Rufus Sewell plays your basic foreign villain and young Mexican actor Adrian Alonso joins the cast as Zorro and Elena's son, Joaquin. This PG rated adventure is strictly family fare although a more adult audience won't be too bored (they may fear for their hearing because of the loudness of the sound effects however).

It's 1850 and California is voting on a constitution to make it the 31st state in the union. Before the votes can be taken to the governor's mansion, they are snatched by xenophobic "preacher" Jacob McGivens (Nick Chinlund) and his band of scum. But Zorro (Banderas) comes to the rescue, fighting the many and saving the day. Maybe it's because of the MPAA rating but he doesn't leave a lot of bodies behind so the bad guys live to fight him again. Unfortunately, Zorro is unmasked during the action and his identity is revealed to a couple of suspicious gentlemen (Shuler Hensley and Michael Emerson). Zorro finally gets home after all his adventures and is greeted by Elena (Zeta-Jones), who is thrilled because her husband had promised to hang up the cape and mask once statehood was achieved. After ten years of fighting, she wants him to go back to being just Don Alejandro de la Vega and pay some attention to her and their son. Zorro doesn't really want to give up the action and a fed-up Elena kicks him out of the house.

The next day, Elena is accosted by the same two suspicious gentlemen and before you know it, Zorro is being served with divorce papers. Three months pass, with Zorro drinking himself into a stupor every night, before he attends a party at the vineyard hacienda of French newcomer Count Armand (Sewell), an old friend of Elena's who has been romancing her. The trio's meeting doesn't go well. Meanwhile, McGivens has been threatening Zorro's friend Cortez because he's determined to get the deed to the Cortez farm. Although Zorro rides to his aid, Cortez is killed and McGivens delivers the deed to Armand, who needs the land to complete a railway line onto his own property. When Elena comes to Armand's for dinner, a jealous Zorro follows her. She breaks into a locked chapel while Zorro breaks into the library; she discovers a telegraph machine and a strange message about a meeting with Orbis Unum while Zorro finds a map detailing Armand's holdings and the railway line. In order to deflect Armand's suspicions, Elena agrees to marry him.

Young Joaquin is a chip off the old block when it comes to getting into trouble. Curious about nasty McGivens, the boy sneaks onto a mining site and steals a bar of soap from a cargo intended for Armand. Zorro rescues him and notices the boxes are stamped Orbis Unum. He learns from his friendly priest (Julio Oscar Mechoso) that Orbis Unum (One World) is an ancient brotherhood of knights who are the power behind many of the thrones of Europe. Now they are worried that the American government is usurping their influence and seek to stop it by encouraging an early victory for the Confederates when the country eventually goes to war. (Forget all the historical inaccuracies.) Zorro is drugged and thrown into prison by Elena's suspicious gentlemen, who turn out to be Pinkerton detectives who have been blackmailing her (to keep her husband's identity as Zorro a secret) so she will get close to Armand and discover his plans. You wonder why a bright woman like Elena couldn't have just revealed that she was being blackmailed but Zorro is a macho sort of guy and probably would have gotten his sword out first and thought about the consequences later.

Joaquin breaks his dad out of jail; Zorro takes him to safety at the church and then heads for Armand's where Elena is trying to discover the details of his plot. They both learn that the soap, which is pure glycerin, is being used to make nitroglycerin. The liquid explosive is then hidden in the wine bottles from Armand's vineyard. McGivens kidnaps Joaquin and takes him to Armand, who has finally discovered that Elena is a spy. Zorro gets captured and Joaquin learns that his dad and his hero are the same guy. Armand packs Joaquin and Elena onto the train while McGivens is charged with killing Zorro who finishes him off instead and then rides to his family's rescue. The train has, naturally, gone out of control and Zorro battles with Armand while Elena tries to get Joaquin to safety. She battles Armand's evil henchman after Joaquin gets off the train, only the kid notices that the train has taken the wrong rail line, so he grabs his father's horse and rides to the rescue. Meanwhile, Armand and Zorro are still fighting (on top of the train, on the side of the engine, on the front of the engine—both the actors and the stunt men really earned their pay for these sequences). Joaquin manages to divert the train, Elena vanquishes the henchman, Zorro defeats Armand, and the reunited twosome get off the train just before it blows up. The statehood documents are officially signed, Zorro and Elena remarry, Joaquin is happy his dad is Zorro and not some aristocratic wimp, and Elena agrees that Zorro has to go on being heroic because "it's who we are."

The Legend of Zorro is like some old-fashioned serial intended for Saturday matinees. There's a lot of acrobatic action (and a certain amount of slapstick) and the plot needn't make much sense as long as there are bad guys to defeat and Zorro gets to dress all in black and cut a few *Zs* into things. Banderas and Zeta-Jones still have a lot of chemistry together and you believe that the characters love and exasperate each other in equal measure. And Elena is just as feisty as ever and can still handle herself in a fight, although how she manages in those long, corseted gowns is anyone's guess. There's no subtlety to anything displayed onscreen, which was filmed on location in San Luis Potosi, Mexico, and happens to look very good thanks to the cinematography of Phil Meheux. There's also considerable violence for a PG rating, although the blood is kept to a strict minimum, and director Campbell keeps the story moving briskly. But, at more than two hours, the film could have used some additional editing. (The kids are definitely going to fidget.) *Legend*'s opening weekend boxoffice was modest, but if the studio does decide to make another sequel they shouldn't wait so long—unless Banderas passes on Zorro's mask to his onscreen offspring.

Christine Tomassini

CREDITS

Zorro/Alejandro: Antonio Banderas
Elena: Catherine Zeta-Jones
Armand: Rufus Sewell
Jacob McGivens: Nicholas Chinlund
Frey Felipe: Julio Oscar Mechoso
Pike: Shuler Hensley
Harrigan: Michael Emerson
Joaquin: Adrian Alonso
Origin: USA
Language: English
Released: 2005
Production: Walter F. Parkes, Laurie MacDonald, Lloyd Phillips; Amblin Entertainment; released by Sony Pictures Entertainment
Directed by: Martin Campbell
Written by: Roberto Orci, Alex Kurtzman
Cinematography by: Phil Meheux
Music by: James Horner
Sound: Tateum Kohut, Bill W. Benton, Jeffrey J. Haboush
Editing: Stuart Baird
Costumes: Graciela Mazon
Production Design: Cecilia Montiel
MPAA rating: PG
Running time: 129 minutes

REVIEWS

Boxoffice Online. October, 2005.
Chicago Sun-Times Online. October 28, 2005.
Entertainment Weekly Online. October 26, 2005.
Los Angeles Times Online. October 28, 2005.
New York Times Online. October 28, 2005.
Premiere Magazine Online. October 28, 2005.
Variety Online. October 23, 2005.
Washington Post Online. October, 2005.

QUOTES

Elena: "When I said we were never meant to be together…I meant it."

Zorro (before kissing Elena): "Finally, we agree on something!"

TRIVIA

Zorro's horse (played by Adriaan), a Frisian horse from Holland, was chosen because they are relatively small making Antonio Banderas seem bigger in comparison.

THE LONGEST YARD

It was hard to put a team together…until they found out who they were playing.
—Movie tagline

If you can't get out, get even.
—Movie tagline

It's time to even the score.
—Movie tagline

Hit hard or go home.
—Movie tagline

Box Office: $158 million

The Longest Yard is a remake of the 1974 sports comedy, directed by Robert Aldrich, which focused on a pro quarterback (played by Burt Reynolds) who gets sent to prison and is forced to make a rag-tag group of fellow cons into football players to take on the prison guards in a fixed game. It was R-rated and pretty brutal and profane and, most of all, funny, and Reynolds brought an effortless charm and cool to his part. Adam Sandler is not cool and "charm" isn't something he's associated with, "obnoxious," a better choice, probably. It's also hard to see him as anyone's idea of a quarterback unless it's some pick-up game in the park. But this PG-13 remake is surprisingly ingratiating—sports clichés and all—and it's still quite brutal and profane so our standards have definitely loosened up.

Sandler stars as Paul "Wrecking" Crewe, an NFL quarterback who was banned from the league for shaving points on a game and who's currently on probation. He's also currently drinking himself into a stupor at the designer home of his rich bitch girlfriend Lena (an unbilled Courtney Cox). Lena expects Paul to make an appearance at her party while he just wants to continue drinking and watching football. She threatens to throw him out, he locks him in her walk-in closet, takes her Bentley, and goes on a drunken joy-ride. She reports the car stolen, Paul gets into a cop-car chase, causes a multi-vehicle accident, and winds up with a three-year federal prison sentence. Now he's on his way to dusty West Texas and the confines of Allenville Federal Penitentiary where Warden Hazen (James Cromwell) is a football fanatic.

Warden Hazen has a semi-pro guard team, led by Captain Knauer (William Fichtner), that hasn't won the state championship in five years. The warden wants Paul to get his team into shape, which doesn't please Knauer.

Paul is essentially forced into going along with Hazen's demands and his first suggestion is that the guards need a tune-up game, so he's told to assemble an inmate team to play against the guards in a month's time. Paul's new friend, motor-mouthed facilitator Caretaker (Chris Rock), has arranged for try-outs but they attract only the most inept prisoners. The cons also have only a dusty, weed-patch field and fourth-hand equipment to work with but Paul perseveres. His first break is when aging inmate Nate Scarborough (Burt Reynolds) literally walks out of the sunset and informs Paul that he will coach the team. Nate won the Heisman Trophy and knows what he's doing and he's also got a beef with Hazen. They decide to go recruiting: "We may not have the most talented team but we will definitely have the meanest." Their next break is when black inmate Meggert (rapper Nelly), who's a fast runner, joins as tailback. Soon, other inmates with actual athletic ability are joining as a chance for payback against the guards, and the team starts to come together.

Hazen, who has ambitions of running for governor, has agreed to allow ESPN to televise the game as a human interest story. Since Crewe is giving him grief, he decides to let firebug con Unger (David Patrick Kelly), who's been the warden's snitch, teach the cons a lesson. Unger rigs a firebomb in Paul's cell but it kills Caretaker the day before the big game. This tragedy just makes the cons even more determined. They suit up (in uniforms tagged the Mean Machine) and get ready to do some damage in front of a hostile crowd at the Rio Grande High School Stadium. At first it looks like the warden will have nothing to worry about; the cons are so eager to fight the guards that they're not actually playing any football and the guards take an early lead. But then Paul gives them a pep talk and by the end of the first half the score is tied.

The warden is not happy. During half-time he threatens to make Paul an accessory to Caretaker's death unless he throws the game; he then tells Knauer that the guards should be as brutal as possible. In the second half, Paul deliberately fumbles and complains of being injured, taking himself out of the game. Then he sees how the guards are playing, gets disgusted with himself for being a wuss, and goes back in. There's six seconds left, the cons are down by seven, but they get a last second play by Scarborough of all people (and yes, the 60-something Reynolds did insist on running the football himself). Now it's up to Paul to win the game and—well, what do you think happens? Captain Knauer congratulates Paul on the game, tells him not to worry about the warden, and Paul gets in the last word with Hazen.

The Longest Yard is a lot of fun to watch, especially if you're looking for the silly and the familiar. And the actual game, which takes up at least the last third of the movie's run time, is never boring, even though you know what's going to happen. Director Peter Segal, who also worked with Sandler on *Anger Management* and *50 First Dates,* recruited a number of former NFL players (especially on the guards' side) so the game looks professional and since Sandler (who's an acquired taste) isn't carrying the movie alone, you don't get tired watching him. And Burt—well, Burt is still cool.

Christine Tomassini

CREDITS

Paul Crewe: Adam Sandler
Nate Scarborough: Burt Reynolds
Caretaker: Chris Rock
Warden Hazen: James Cromwell
Meggert: Nelly
Unger: David Patrick Kelly
Brucie: Nicholas Turturro
Captain Knauer: William Fichtner
Ms. Tucker: Tracy Morgan
Guard Garner: Brian Bosworth
Duane: Ed Lauter
Lynette: Cloris Leachman
Guard Dunham: Steve Austin
Switowski: Bob Sapp
Turley: Dalip Singh
Torres: Lobo Sebastian
Lena (uncredited): Courtney Cox
Punky: Rob Schneider
Origin: USA
Language: English
Released: 2005
Production: Jack Giarraputo; Happy Madison Productions, MTV Films; released by Paramount Pictures
Directed by: Peter Segal
Written by: Sheldon Turner
Cinematography by: Dean Semler
Music by: Teddy Castellucci
Music Supervisor: Michael Dilbeck
Editing: Jeff Gourson
Art Direction: Domenic Silvestri
Production Design: Perry Andelin Blake
MPAA rating: PG-13
Running time: 113 minutes

REVIEWS

Boxoffice Online. May, 2005.
Chicago Sun-Times Online. May 27, 2005.
Entertainment Weekly Online. May 25, 2005.

Los Angeles Times Online. May 27, 2005.
New York Times Online. May 27, 2005.
Variety Online. May 22, 2005.
Washington Post Online. May 27, 2005, p. WE37.

QUOTES

Cheeseburger Eddy: "You gotta protect your McNuggets!"

TRIVIA

The film was shot in a closed down part of the New Mexico State Penitentiary called "Old Main," the site of one of the worst prison riots in U.S. history in February 1980.

AWARDS

Nomination:

Golden Raspberries 2005: Worst Support. Actor (Reynolds).

LOOK AT ME

(Comme une image)

Box Office: $1.7 million

Agnes Jaoui and Jean-Pierre Bacri are the married filmmakers that have created and are featured in the remarkable *Look at Me,* a bitingly witty and incisive look at fame and ego. Both accomplished actors, Jaoui and Bacri began to write their own material in order to have better parts to act in and Jaoui made her directorial debut with 1999's *The Taste of Others*, which they wrote and starred in together. In *Look at Me* (*Comme une image* in France) they create memorable and realistic dialogue spoken by realistic and memorable characters all somehow engaged in the quest for fame, wealth, and love.

Central in the narrative is Etienne Cassard (writer Bacri), an acclaimed author and publisher who attracts a host of sycophants despite the fact that he has a severe case of writer's block and hasn't actually published anything in a long time. The other main character is Etienne's daughter, the ironically-named Lolita (Marilou Berry), an overweight struggling actress-turned singer who is nearly as bitter as her famous father. The film's title is a double entendre, referencing the quest for fame that many of the characters embark on as well as representing Lolita's stifled cry to her dismissive and inattentive father. The reasons Etienne has trouble dealing with his "big girl," which is meant affectionately but inadvertently cutting as well, is not completely clear. He mentions later in the film that Lolita's mother never loved him and he never loved her, for that matter, and they split when Lolita was still very young. Her size does not help matters either, Etienne's new trophy wife a picture of trim, Hollywoodesque proportion. Their cute new daughter, Lolita's stepsister, also better fits Etienne's view of a picture-perfect life.

With material that could well have come off as clichéd, the filmmakers relentlessly work to keep their characters real. Sure Karine (Virginie Desarnauts) is beautiful and slender (with an implied eating disorder) but she is no heartless mannequin; she loves Lolita and tries to be friends with her, even after Lolita rejects her. Lolita is a more sympathetic character than her father but she is not the typical shy, overweight girl that is usually presented in film. She is outspoken, avidly pursues her goals, and despite a healthy reserve of hostility and resentment, appreciates a good time. She has also learned to be suspicious of everyone who is interested in her, as most merely want to use her to get to her famous father. Sebastien (Keine Bouhiza), an attractive boy Lolita encounters, is not such a one, however, but Lolita is blind to the fact that he is actually interested in her for her until the very end of the film.

Lolita's brusque singing teacher's interests are not so pure, however. Sylvia (writer/director Jaoui) is mildly interested in Lolita's classical singing talents at the outset but becomes much more involved with her career after finding out that her hero Cassard is Lolita's father. Sylvia supports a husband who happens to be an author struggling to get published and soon Sylvia and husband Pierre (Laurent Grevill) are joining the Cassards in the country for a holiday. In no time, Pierre's book is published to much acclaim.

Not everyone is having a great time in the country, however. Lolita finds out her handsome boyfriend is a philandering user which she takes out on the hapless Sebastien, whom she has brought along in order not to be alone. Ignored by Lolita who is involved in her own drama, Sebastien sulks around depressed, planning to leave on the first train out and eliciting the bon mot from Etienne, "There's cyanide in the bathroom." Lolita resents Karine being nice to her and despite her good qualities, is on the verge of becoming more like her caustic father every day. Karine begins to resent Etienne's casual dismissal of her, as well, whose cutting and condescending comments aimed at her in front of the guests begin to grate. Sylvia, and Lolita for that matter, is bothered by Pierre's blatant toadying around Etienne while Pierre sees Sylvia as a nag. Only Etienne's sidekick, the loyal Vincent (Gregoire Oestermann), seems content, his timid, placid ways the perfect complement to the brash, narcissistic Etienne.

Lolita, in fact, has a beautiful classical voice and is a talented singer, despite suspicions otherwise from

Etienne. Still desperate to please him, Lolita has given him a tape made in class to prove that her singing lessons are not in vain, as perhaps some of her previous career choices. The tape does nothing more than gather dust on Etienne's impressive bookshelf. Greatly annoyed by the fact her father has never heard her sing, Lolita nonetheless invites him along with the whole extended family to her concert and the film's set piece. It another film, one might expect Etienne to attend and be suitably moved by his long-disregarded daughter's impressive talent. The filmmaker's wisely keep Etienne true to his nature, and after noticing a pretty girl singing alongside his daughter, he leaves after a few moments into Lolita's spotlight piece, suddenly and very selfishly, inspired to write.

The elated Lolita, fielding compliments left and right at her afterparty, did not realize her father was not there for the entire concert but has noticed he hasn't said a word to her about her performance. At evening's end, when Etienne compliments the pretty girl in the choir about her talent and mentioning she'll go far in the business, it is Sylvia—who interestingly enough is the only one Lolita does not suspect of using her to get to Etienne—that steps in and confronts Etienne about his obsession with looks and dismissal of his own daughter's great talent. The petulant Etienne storms out while Lolita sulks upstairs where Sebastien attempts to console her and lets it out that Etienne left the concert almost from the start. She misinterprets his sympathy for Karine's kindness toward her, wrongly thinking he has taken a job her father had offered him and buckled under like all the others. Etienne finds a dejected Lolita moping on the front porch, noting his contempt for Sebastien for refusing his generous offer of a job. The evening ends as the elated Lolita chases down Sebastien to apologize and Sylvia leaves the obsequious Pierre at the Cassard's, making sure to put Lolita's tape into the cassette player at full blast before exiting.

Bacri shows his range as the normally boorish, self-important author who, momentarily shows great vulnerability during his brief comeuppance when Karine leaves him (although she quickly returns) and tells him the truths no one else that surrounds him would dare. Berry's character is especially demanding, walking a fine line between sympathetic, whiney, and abrasive and pulling it off beautifully aided by the gorgeous vocal music backdrop of Mozart, Handel, Monteverdi, and Schubert, among others.

Hilary White

CREDITS

Sylvia: Agnes Jaoui
Etienne: Jean-Pierre Bacri
Pierre: Laurent Grevill
Lolita: Marilou Berry
Karine: Virginie Desarnauts
Sebastien: Keine Bouhiza
Vincent: Gregoire Oestermann
Origin: France
Language: French
Released: 2004
Production: Christian Berard, Jean-Philippe Andraca; Les Films A4, StudioCanal, France 2 Cinema, Lumiere, Eyescreen; released by Mars Distribution
Directed by: Agnes Jaoui
Written by: Agnes Jaoui, Jean-Pierre Bacri
Cinematography by: Stephanie Fontaine
Music by: Philippe Rombi
Sound: Jean-Pierre Duret, Gerard Lamps, Nadine Muse
Editing: Francois Gedigier
Costumes: Jackie Budin
Production Design: Olivier Jacquet
MPAA rating: PG-13
Running time: 110 minutes

REVIEWS

Boxoffice Online. April, 2005.
Chicago Sun-Times Online. April 22, 2005.
Entertainment Weekly Online. March 30, 2005.
Los Angeles Times Online. April 1, 2005.
New York Times Online. April 1, 2005.
Variety Online. May 16, 2004.
Washington Post Online. April 29, 2005, p. WE45.

QUOTES

Lolita Cassard: "I'm hopeless!"
Sebastien: "We all are...."
Lolita Cassard: "Yes, but me more than others."

TRIVIA

Contains a clip from *Blood on the Moon* (1948).

LORD OF WAR

The first and most important rule of gun-running is: never get shot with your own merchandise.
—Movie tagline

Got guns?
—Movie tagline

Where There's A Will, There's A Weapon.
—Movie tagline

He Sells Guns...And He's Making A Killing.
—Movie tagline

Box Office: $24.1 million

The illegal arms market has been one of the most venomous elements of post-World War II international relations. The criminal sale of weapons to despots, dictators and savage rebels is one of the gravest matters faced by peace-oriented nations and governmental bodies for over half a century. The issue is serious and, in the current context of underground resistance and fanaticism that stretches from West Africa to Indonesia, must be treated with utter earnestness. *Lord of War* deals with this momentous, stern and grim global phenomenon. Yet, instead of attacking the horrendous aspects of the practice of the black market weapons economy outright, writer and director Andrew Niccol satirizes the entire globo-political structure.

Comedy is the means of sensitization to the horrific nature of the business from the beginning. Yuri Orlov (Nicolas Cage) works for his family's restaurant in Little Odessa; the Ukrainian sector of Brooklyn, New York. It is 1982 and gang warfare is rampant and unavoidable. One day, Yuri witnesses a gruesome shootout while out running an errand. Yuri, however, is not shocked and appalled by the sight of the murders. Rather, he sees a logical business plan take form. People desire bullets and their delivery systems. Yuri will become the middleman. He won't make the guns but he will move them. Besides, he admits has always had "and instinct for smuggling contraband." Violence, he reasons, is a part of nature. Even in the remains of skulls of the earliest humans, one can find spear tips. Such a natural process needs actualization. Yuri, of course, never sees the brutality. It's always a bottom line. For example, in 1984, he "sold guns to everyone possible." In fact, he was the main supplier to "eight of the top ten war zones." The more dreadful the conflict, the better Yuri's financial status became.

In 1989, before being boarded by Interpol agents led by Jack Valentine (Ethan Hawke) off the coast of Columbia, Yuri quickly has the name and flag on his pirated ship changed to give the show of integrity. When the agents board the dilapidated, rusted excuse for a ship, they find Yuri in his power suit and sunglasses: Just an honest businessman, not a smuggler. What would ever give them that idea?

His fortunes and deceit allow him to achieve his wildest fantasies. After setting up a fake photo shoot and renting an entire hotel, he seduces his long-time object of lust: international supermodel Ava Fontaine (Bridget Moynahan). In the face of such a show of wealth and flood of gifts, she cannot choose but submit. He whisks her back to New York on a "private" jet with the name "Orlov" painted on its tail. However, when taking off, we see the painted name streak away with the wind. The plane was only a rental. Yuri's entire life has become based on deceit and charades: hilarious deceit and charades. He always holds the cards.

In 1991, Yuri and Ava get married, though Yuri's "business" is always a secret, and they have a son together. When their son is learning to walk Yuri is not there to witness the feat. He is in his bedroom kissing the televised image of Gorbechov as he discovers that the Cold War has ended. In Yuri's words, "The arms bazaar was open." Fortunately for him, his uncle Dmitri (Yevgeny Lazarev) was a Ukrainian general with warehouses and fields of recently deserted Russian arms including thousands of AK-47s, tanks and a squadron of assault helicopters. He looks at his new commodities as "profitable," never destructive. When Jack Valentine and his Interpol agents catch him trying to load the helicopters onto a freight ship, Yuri has the guns taken off the wings and claims they are for "humanitarian" purposes.

In 2000, over Sierra Leone, Interpol, with the aid of fighter jets, intercepts Yuri's plane in midair. They instruct him to put down at the airport. Knowing the jets cannot land on a dirt highway, Yuri instructs his pilots to put the cargo plane down immediately on a road filled with heavy pedestrian traffic. The pilots flee as the plane is still filled with hundreds of tons of illegal arms and Interpol on the way. Yuri, however, decides to have a giveaway. He calls the pedestrians to the plane and gives away everything on board. When Interpol shows up, the plane is empty.

When Ava finds out from Valentine what his actual occupation is, Yuri goes clean for six months. But when the President of Sierra Leone shows up at his New York apartment, he is back in the game. Yuri asks his brother Vitali (Jared Leto) to watch his back during this dangerous assignment. They take a shipment of weapons to a small rebel group outside of a refugee camp. But when Vitali discovers the weapons will be used to slaughter the refugees, he tries to blow up the entire supply. He is killed but Yuri completes the deal. In the meantime, in New York, Ava has discovered Yuri's storage unit and his identity is revealed to the world and to Jack Valentine. Yuri is arrested but quickly released as a shadowy, elite U.S. official in full brass intervenes. It appears, at the end of the film, that the U.S. government has been supporting Yuri the entire time. It's a dark, unexpected twist that serves this tremendous satire incredibly well.

Nick Kennedy

CREDITS

Yuri Orlov: Nicolas Cage
Vitali Orlov: Jared Leto
Ava Fontaine: Bridget Moynahan
Simeon Weisz: Ian Holm
Valentine: Ethan Hawke
Baptiste Senior: Eamonn Walker
Baptiste Junior: Sammi Rotibi
Dmitri: Yevgeny Lazarev
Origin: USA
Language: English
Released: 2005
Production: Philippe Rousselet, Andrew Niccol, Nicolas Cage, Norm Golightly, Andy Grosch, Chris Roberts; Saturn Films, VIP Medienfonds 3, Ascendant Pictures; released by Lions Gate Films
Directed by: Andrew Niccol
Written by: Andrew Niccol
Cinematography by: Amir M. Mokri
Music by: Antonio Pinto
Sound: Derek Mansvelt
Music Supervisor: John Bissell
Editing: Zach Staenberg
Art Direction: Stephen Carter
Costumes: Elisabetta Beraldo
Production Design: Jean-Vincent Puzos
MPAA rating: R
Running time: 122 minutes

REVIEWS

Boxoffice Online. September, 2005.
Chicago Sun-Times Online. September 16, 2005.
Entertainment Weekly Online. September 14, 2005.
Los Angeles Times Online. September 16, 2005.
New York Times Online. September 16, 2005.
Premiere Magazine Online. September 16, 2005.
Variety Online. September 6, 2005.
Washington Post Online. September 16, 2005, p. C01.

QUOTES

Yuri Orlov: "There are over 550 million firearms in worldwide circulation. That's one firearm for every twelve people on the planet. The only question is: How do we arm the other 11?"

TRIVIA

The filmmakers had to inform NATO before they shot the scene where tanks were lined up for sale, lest they think a real war was being started when viewing satellite images of the set.

LORDS OF DOGTOWN

They came from nothing to change everything.
—Movie tagline

Based on the true story of the legendary Z-Boys.
—Movie tagline

They never thought they'd be famous, but they always thought they'd be friends.
—Movie tagline

Box Office: $11 million

When Penelope Spheeris scripted and directed a compellingly haunting fable in 1984 about a group of throwaway, counterculture youth *(Suburbia)* she made a definitive point in casting the genuine articles. Punks as actors, not actors as punks, was her mandate, her rationale being that it would be next to impossible to replicate screen stars as their tortured real life counterparts of the disaffected punk generation. The result was an absorbing tale of a band of disowned kids' unraveling descent into tragedy. A good film, albeit one sorely lacking in ability to convey human emotions convincingly. Talented actors in a film polish raw events and evoke greater sympathy from the audience. It is an idea clearly espoused by director Catherine Hardwicke and veteran skateboard professional turned industry historian and documentarian Stacy Peralta, who penned this script with a melodramatic spin for their film, *Lords of Dogtown.*

This film, chronicling the tribal skate gurus growing up in the stretch of suburbia from Venice Beach to Santa Monica in balmy Southern California, employs acting that promotes rather than flattens the emotional impact of the scintillating lives these testosterone saturated, often hedonistically driven grommets led. Stacy Peralta archived facts from his 2001 documentary, *Dogtown and Z-Boys* and weaves them in with fictitious elements to craft a fascinating story revolving around life on a coastal slum, rife with broken families, budding teen angst and the seemingly spontaneous catapult from anonymity and poverty into exponential fame in the nascent, pre-X Games skate culture. In 1975, Peralta (played by John Robinson with perfect blonde locks sans the split ends), Jay Adams (Emile Hirsch), and Tony Alva (Victor Rasuk) are running wild, full of adrenalin-laden bravado, recklessly rolling down steep city streets at death-wish speeds throughout the Venice surf ghetto. Life is comprised of one passion for this future triumvirate: surfing. This they often accomplished by stormtrooping the dilapidated Pacific Ocean Park pier, which was condemned in 1967. Here, they rode swells as allowed by the grizzled, territorial chieftains who aggressively enforced the "locals only" code for their breaks.

When waves were deemed ankle-slappers, too small to ride, the clan exclusively skated within the corridors of suburban sprawl. Two marked events served as catalysts in propelling the surf-spawned skate culture: the invention and introduction of urethane wheels that gave the boards superior traction that allowed for a plethora of new tricks and a southwestern drought that led to nonessential water use restrictions. Suddenly, the Southland was a skater's nirvana full of empty swimming pools waiting to be conquered. One of the group's haunts was at the Zephyr Surf Shop owned and run by Skip (superbly played by Heath Ledger whose performance could pass as an homage to Val Kilmer's portrayal of *The Doors'* frontman, Jim Morrison). Skip's speech is disjointed and appearance stiff and stuporous. Throughout the movie, he appears to be in a marijuana- and alcohol-induced haze. But this self-serving dipsomaniac had a vision: sponsoring and coaching a team culled from the local talent. The Z-Boys were born. Initially, Stacy is not picked to be on the roster, as he is erroneously perceived by Skip to be an outsider due to his holding a part-time job. They enter a tournament in Del Mar and very quickly are off to the races, becoming trade poster boys and are soon surrounded by high-end sponsors wishing to exploit the crew with Faustian fervor.

Peralta emerges as the shining star, riding the corporate gravy train with product endorsements and global tours and even appearing on an episode of *Charlie's Angels.* Yet with their ascent, their idyllic youth vanishes as skateboarding becomes a promotional sport instead of a kinetic art. Jay Adams, never at ease in the spotlight, remains the most obstinate and seems more concerned for his mother (Rebecca De Mornay) whose fast track living of excessive partying and volatile relationships with aging beach bums have begun to take their toll.

Cinematographer Elliot Davis keeps the film rolling with its snappy skate and surf sequences. Towards the end, the three reunite in order to visit fellow Z-Boy, Sid (Michael Angarano) who is wheelchair bound and is succumbing to the final stages of brain cancer. In perhaps the film's most poignant moment, they wheel Sid into the deep end of the empty swimming pool and inundate his senses as they skate along its walls as a send off to their brother-in-arms. Commenting on the film's style, Kevin Thomas from the *Los Angeles Times* sums it up succinctly: "*Lords of Dogtown* isn't nostalgic—it's too clear eyed for that; it's happening right now."

David Metz Roberts

CREDITS

Skip: Heath Ledger
Jay: Emile Hirsch
Tony: Victor Rasuk
Stacy: John Robinson
Kathy Alva: Nikki Reed
Sid: Michael Angarano
Philaine: Rebecca De Mornay
Topper Burks: Johnny Knoxville
Origin: USA
Language: English
Released: 2005
Production: John Linson; Linson Films; released by Sony Pictures
Directed by: Catherine Hardwicke
Written by: Stacy Peralta
Cinematography by: Elliot Davis
Music by: Mark Mothersbaugh
Music Supervisor: Liza Richardson
Editing: Nancy Richardson
Art Direction: Seth Reed
Production Design: Chris Gorak
MPAA rating: PG-13
Running time: 107 minutes

REVIEWS

Boxoffice Online. June, 2005.
Chicago Sun-Times Online. June 2, 2005.
Entertainment Weekly Online. June 1, 2005.
Los Angeles Times Online. June 3, 2005.
New York Times Online. June 3, 2005.
Premiere Magazine Online. June 7, 2005.
Variety Online. May 26, 2005.
Washington Post Online. June 3, 2005, p. WE49.

QUOTES

Stacy: "So have any of you guys skated with Tony lately?"
Jay: "Yeah, he's competing today with the sun for the center of the universe."

TRIVIA

Stacy Peralta is the announcer at the last skate competition, while the real Jay Adams makes a cameo appearance during the scene of the party at Jay Adams's mother's house.

A LOVE SONG FOR BOBBY LONG

The heart is a lonely hunter.
—Movie tagline

The genre is family melodrama, a sort of bittersweet comedy, set in the Deep South, with colorful characters who nurse literary aspirations that might have been imagined by Tennessee Williams on a bad day. This is a movie involving boozy writers, a fine young woman in search of her past, ruined lives in search of redemption, and a bucketload of Southern, sentimental claptrap, packaged to be sold on the revived reputation of John Travolta, lacking this time a clever shot of *Pulp Fiction* to pull him through an embarrassing acting ordeal. Well, the star does his best and even has a turn or two on the dance floor of a New Orleans juke joint, but the actor has to overcome a gabby and flabby screenplay that seems at times uncertain about how to tell his story. One moment Travolta seems to be playing something akin to the lovable goober he created for Mike Nichols in *Primary Colors* (1998), the next he resembles the melancholy lawyer from *A Civil Action* (1998), but here motivated by sentimentality rather than idealism.

Bobby Long (Travolta) was at one time an English literature professor at an Alabama college (apparently Auburn University, if the man can be judged by his T-shirt); but one night Bobby got drunk at a campus party, came to the aid of his teaching assistant Lawson Pines (Gabriel Macht) in a brawl, got his face smashed, neglected to pick up his child (who subsequently was killed in a hit-and-run accident), and was turned out of house and home by his enraged and grief-stricken wife. So of course Bobby and his loyal graduate student assistant light out for New Orleans to start a new life and set up housekeeping with Lorraine Will, a red-hot mama who sings at a jazz club, in (or near?) the French Quarter. This would seem to indicate that the relationship between Lawson and Bobby is not gay, since apparently Lorraine shares her affections with both of these failed people. But, then, her judgment was seriously flawed. She wrote letters to her distant and separated daughter, whom she abandoned to her mother, but Lorraine lacked the courage to send those letters; and she also seemed to have had a problem with addiction.

The film, directed and written by Shainee Gabel, was "inspired" by a novel entitled *Off Magazine Street*, by Ronald Everett Capp. Lawson Pines has spent the past ten years in an alcoholic stupor writing the book that will be published before the film is over, entitled (no surprise!) *A Love Song for Bobby Long*. Bobby has no doubts whatsoever about Lawson's abilities or about the eventual success of the book, but, then, Bobby is a delusional, self-indulgent lush. But he believes he may be redeemed by Lawson's book, which may enable his children to understand him. As David Rooney summarized the relationship in his *Variety* review, Bobby believes (on scanty evidence) that Lawson's "book about his mentor will immortalize both of them."

However, this expectation seems more than a little presumptuous. Bobby's main talents seem to involve quoting famous writers, prodigious drinking, and playing his guitar under the influence. The music is comforting and atmospheric, but, then, almost everything about this movie is comforting and atmospheric. Whenever something interesting is said, it's likely to be Bobby or Lawson tossing off ponderous quotations from Robert Browning, Charles Dickens, George Sand, or Moliere to impress each other, or perhaps the viewer. The main problem is that their literary banter seems about sixty years outmoded, behind the curve of the New Criticism, semiotics, feminism, structuralism, post-modernism, queer theory, and all the other trends that seemed to consume the minds of those charged with the responsibility of teaching literature. In their cups, which is to say most of the time, Bobby and Lawson can do no more than to mix and match sometimes obscure quotations. It's recycled wit, cornpone style, more pathetic than convincing.

The film picks up their story after Lorraine Will dies in 2002. Her daughter, Purslane (Scarlett Johansson, given the cute nickname "Pursy," which gets the good ol' boys in stitches as they mirthfully ponder her name, in her presence and at her expense), arrives in New Orleans from Panama City, Florida, a few days too late for her mother's funeral. Why was she late? Because her thoughtless cracker boyfriend neglected to tell her that Bobby Long had tried to call her about her mother's death. Pursy had been raised by her grandmother and hardly had any memories of Lorraine. Bobby tells Pursy that Lorraine has left the house to the three of them, whereas in fact it belongs entirely to Pursy, who at least shows some pride of ownership and paints the house in colors her mother had chosen. So the good-hearted and gullible Pursy moves in with these two boozers and attempts to reform them. Meanwhile, they also try to reform her after Bobby decides that the 18-year-old girl needs to get her high-school diploma, take the SATs and get into college. Plucky Pursy isn't at first convinced, but she agrees to try if the boys will try to control their drinking, and, by the end of the story she seems to be enrolled at the University of New Orleans. Good for her.

While attempting to reclaim her past, Pursy is also in the process of escaping from it. Finally, she finds a packet of letters her mother wanted to send her but didn't have the courage to put in the mail and makes the film's big plot discovery: Bobby Long turns out to be her father, but by that time he is having symptoms of the diseases that will kill him: blood in the urine (prostate cancer?) and an infected toe (diabetes?). Before Bobby dies, however, Pursy graduates from high school (after having assimilated the kind of literary trivia she can learn from Bobby and Lawson, knowing, for certain, for example, that Willa Cather was from Nebraska), and the celebration that follows gives an excuse for Bobby and Pursy to dance off into the sunset, literally.

At the very end, we see Pursy walking the colorful streets of New Orleans, carrying a book bag that suggests that she is now enrolled at the University of New Orleans. Her trajectory follows the same path that Bobby had taken, bottle in hand, behind the film's opening credits. She is walking to the cemetery to pay her respects to her parents, now buried side by side: Lorraine Will, 1962-2002, and Bobby Long, 1955-2004. Between the graves she places the flower (or weed?) she is named for, along with the song her mother wrote for her, tucked into a copy of Lawson Pines's book, *The Love Song of Bobby Long*. A passage from the book is voiced over, telling us that "It was the invisible people Bobby wanted to live with." Lawson describes Bobby's mind as being "both crippled and exalted by too many stories and the path he chose to become one. Bobby Long's tragic flaw was his romance with all that he saw." So, the film is verbal at the end and to the end, right down to the epitaph from Robert Frost that ornaments Bobby's tomb stone: "I had a lover's quarrel with the world." But is the screenwriting up to the task? Can a film end well with a sentence as lame as this one: "And I guess if people want to believe in some form of justice, then Bobby Long got his for a song." *Variety* objected to "newcomer Shainee Gabel's flowery dialogue and pedestrian direction." But the writing is sometimes pedestrian, too.

What comes close to saving the picture is really strong casting, though, as *Variety* noted, John Travolta and Scarlett Johansson are both "playing roles neither of them probably were born to play." It's hard to believe that such a healthy looking actor might have one foot in the grave because of a dissolute lifestyle, and Gabriel Macht's Lawson looks even healthier, though *Variety* gave the actor credit for striking a "fragile balance between numbed resignation and galvanizing self-disgust." Despite these performances, the film tanked at the box office and went quickly and quietly to video after its initial release in September of 2004. Ultimately the film suffers from terminal torpor and lassitude, making it less than illuminating Faulkner lite. But the New Orleans atmosphere, from the French Quarter to the levee to sites presumably "off Magazine Street," certainly adds some overheated Cajun charm. The viewer is left with some confusion about Lorraine's singing career. At one point it seems that she performed at a jazz club (in keeping with the New Orleans setting), but the ballad she wrote seems soaked with country-and-western anguish. She is more of a puzzle than even Bobby Long.

James M. Welsh

CREDITS

Bobby Long: John Travolta
Pursy: Scarlett Johansson
Lawson: Gabriel Macht
Georgianna: Deborah Kara Unger
Earl: Sonny Shroyer
Cecil: Dane Rhodes
Origin: USA
Language: English
Released: 2004
Production: R. Paul Miller, David Lancaster; Crossroads Films, Bob Yari Production
Directed by: Shainee Gabel
Written by: Shainee Gabel
Cinematography by: Elliot Davis
Music by: Nathan Larson
Sound: Pud Cusack
Music Supervisor: James Black
Editing: Lee Percy, Lisa Fruchtman
Art Direction: Adele Plauche
Costumes: Jill Ohanneson
Production Design: Sharon Lomofsky
MPAA rating: R
Running time: 119 minutes

REVIEWS

Boxoffice Online. January, 2005.
Chicago Sun-Times Online. January 28, 2005.
Entertainment Weekly Online. January 19, 2005.
Los Angeles Times Online. December 29, 2004.
New York Times Online. December 29, 2004.
Premiere Magazine Online. January 4, 2005.
Variety Online. September 7, 2004.
Washington Post Online. January 28, 2005, p. WE39.

M

MADAGASCAR

Someone's got a zoo loose.
—Movie tagline

The lemurs: They're cute. They're cuddly. They're deranged.
—Movie tagline

They weren't born in the wild...They were shipped there.
—Movie tagline

Box Office: $193.2 million

DreamWorks's *Madagascar* is a modestly entertaining, computer-animated adventure whose main problem may be that, in an era of increasingly sophisticated animated features, especially Pixar's string of successes and DreamWorks's own *Shrek* series (2001 and 2004), it takes more than bright colors, some amusing characters, and a few funny gags to make a lasting impression. Directed by Eric Darnell and Tom McGrath, *Madagascar* has a great premise, a strong beginning, and a lively score by Hans Zimmer but loses its sense of invention, not to mention a strong plotline, just when it should be taking off.

The movie opens in the Central Park Zoo and follows the daily routine of a group of animals who reside there. The screenplay imagines them as stars who not only give grand, elaborate performances but pose for photos and then are pampered at the end of the day. Alex the lion (voiced by Ben Stiller) is the king of the zoo, a great mixture of vanity, ego, and good-heartedness, who loves his job and gives a snow globe featuring himself to his friend Marty the zebra (voiced by Chris Rock) for his birthday, just the latest of many Alex-centric souvenirs he has given. But Marty has grown dissatisfied with life in the zoo, yearning to see life outside the gates, even go to the wild, or at least Connecticut. Alex, on the other hand, thinks that life could not be better as it is and that his buddy is crazy. Rounding out the group are two friends who barely register—Melman the giraffe (voiced by David Schwimmer), the perpetual worrier and hypochondriac of the group, and Gloria the hippopotamus (voiced by Jada Pinkett Smith), whose levelheadedness makes her the voice of reason among these eccentrics but also the least interesting character.

The most original and memorable animals, however, are a band of supporting characters, the zoo's penguins, depicted as a group of commandos who are working on an escape plan as if they were prisoners in a POW camp. Burrowing their way out by using spoons and Popsicle sticks left by the zoo's visitors, they know that their life of confinement is unnatural and hope to get to Antarctica. They are led by the gung ho Skipper (voiced by McGrath), whose refrain of "cute and cuddly" is a great deadpan reminder to his cohorts to mask their true motives and maintain a benign appearance. Their dream inspires Marty to bust out, and soon he is bouncing through Times Square to the beat of "Stayin' Alive."

When his friends realize that Marty is gone, they go after him, causing a near riot at Grand Central Station (a hilarious sequence in which an old lady roughs up Alex), where police converge on the errant animals, who are packed up in crates for shipping to Africa. Knocking out the crew and essentially commandeering the ship, the no-nonsense penguins head for Antarctica, but, in the process, the crates fall overboard, and Alex and his friends end up washed ashore on the island of Madagascar.

Zoo animals living the celebrity life is a clever idea, and the penguins as an elite military squad are standouts, but once the four friends are in the wild, the movie loses its sense of fun and energy. They meet a tribe of lemurs who, under the leadership of the goofy King Julien XIII (voiced by Sacha Baron Cohen), seem to be throwing a nonstop party (their dance scene is cute and very funny), but they also live in fear of the predatory fossas. The story's main conflict, however, is internal, that is, Alex coming to terms with his own true nature, which starts to surface now that he is far away from city life. Where food was once brought to him, now Marty looks like food, and the question becomes whether the domesticated Alex can overcome his primal urges. But this is fairly dark material for a light animated film. Moreover, not only does it seem out of place after the initial frivolity, but the dilemma grows repetitive and does not play out in a very original or compelling way.

Without much of a story to anchor the action, the writers rely on quoting other films to generate laughs. *Madagascar* includes visual references to *Chariots of Fire* (1981), *Cast Away* (2000), *Planet of the Apes* (1968), and *American Beauty* (1999), with steaks instead of a rose-petaled teenager as Alex's fantasy, but rather than feeling especially original or witty, these jokes come across as a forced way to get a laugh, counting on the audience's film savvy and affection for the original movies. It also feels like an obvious, easy appeal to adults—giving them cultural references they will easily recognize but that will, unfortunately, go over the heads of most children.

Afraid of his newly discovered wild instincts, Alex exiles himself, but, when the fossas go on the attack, he comes to his friends' rescue. Somehow he is able to overcome his own innate longings and save their lives, but how he does this is never made clear, thus skirting the real tension instead of addressing it. By this time, the penguins, who, in a great throwaway bit, hate the blistering cold of Antarctica, have returned with the ship, just in time to end the film with their characteristic wry humor.

The main disappointment of *Madagascar* is that the New York scenes are so clever (Marty getting a taste of freedom and ice-skating at Rockefeller Center, for example) that the big African adventure falls short by comparison. The screenplay, credited to Darnell and McGrath as well as Mark Burton and Billy Frolick, flirts with something dark, even disturbing—what it means to be a wild animal who has lived a soft life and is now literally thrown into the wild—but since we know that Alex ultimately will not turn on his friends, the plot has no real suspense or drive. In the end, *Madagascar* has an underdeveloped feeling, starting strong and containing some funny sequences but ultimately going nowhere.

Peter N. Chumo II

CREDITS

Alex the Lion: Ben Stiller (Voice)
Marty the Zebra: Chris Rock (Voice)
Gloria the Hippo: Jada Pinkett Smith (Voice)
Melman the Giraffe: David Schwimmer (Voice)
Maurice: Cedric the Entertainer (Voice)
Mort: Andy Richter (Voice)
King Julien: Sacha Baron Cohen (Voice)
Origin: USA
Language: English
Released: 2005
Production: Mireille Soria; PDI, DreamWorks; released by DreamWorks
Directed by: Eric Darnell, Tom McGrath
Written by: Eric Darnell, Tom McGrath, Billy Frolick, Mark Burton
Music by: Hans Zimmer
Sound: Robert Renga, Craig Heath
Editing: H. Lee Peterson
Art Direction: Shannon Jeffries
Production Design: Kendal Cronkhite-Shaindlin
MPAA rating: PG
Running time: 80 minutes

REVIEWS

Boxoffice Online. May, 2005.
Chicago Sun-Times Online. May 26, 2005.
Entertainment Weekly Online. May 25, 2005.
Los Angeles Times Online. May 27, 2005.
New York Times Online. May 27, 2005.
Premiere Magazine Online. May 26, 2005.
Variety Online. May 22, 2005.
Washington Post Online. May 27, 2005, p. WE39.

QUOTES

Marty the Zebra: "The penguins are going, so why can't I?"
Alex the Lion: "Marty, the penguins are psychotic."

TRIVIA

Gwen Stefani, Madonna, and Jennifer Lopez were all considered for the voice of Gloria the Hippo before the role finally went to Jada Pinkett Smith.

MAIL ORDER WIFE

Because no one wants to be alone.
—Movie tagline

No Refunds, No Exchanges
—Movie tagline

Mail Order Wife will bemuse as much as it will amuse. This satire about the mail-order bride industry takes its chances but does not completely fulfill its promise (or is that proposal?).

Co-writer-directors Huck Botko and Andrew Gurland, known for their controversial 1998 documentary *Frat House* again employ a documentary format but this time tell a fictional story about a filmmaker, Andrew (Gurland), who probes the business of buying foreign wives by showing how Adrian (Adrian Martinez), a lonely man from Queens, New York, seeks, finds, and sends for an Asian spouse, Lichi (Eugenia Yuan), through a mail-order service advertising in the back of a magazine.

During the course of the shooting, Andrew realizes he has formed an attachment to Lichi and happily stops his project when Lichi walks out on Adrian, who seems to have only wanted Lichi to perform as his servant. Andrew helps Lichi move in with him and plans to get her a job as a chef, but Lichi fails the cooking audition and eventually becomes bored with Andrew, who does not always treat her respectfully.

Lichi returns to Adrian only to become used in Adrian's sexually explicit porn films. Andrew again rescues Lichi and promises to marry her, so she moves in again with Andrew but then leaves him one more time when he angrily refuses to father her child.

During the next several months, Andrew longs for Lichi and yearns to be with her. But when Adrian informs Andrew that Lichi is again advertising to be a mail-order bride, both men feel duped and plot to catch her during her next "courtship." With the help of his cinematographer's father, who impersonates a wealthy potential husband, Andrew schemes to reunite with Lichi, while Adrian simply wants revenge.

Just as with *The Blair Witch Project, Mail Order Wife* attempts to trick viewers into thinking they are seeing a cinema verite documentary (of course, the characters in the drama are also constantly duping each other). Cynics will immediately note how both *Blair Witch* and *Bride* include routine narrative plot contrivances and isolate the most dramatic incidents rather conveniently. Still, whether fooled or not, spectators will probably continue watching these movies to their conclusions—if only to learn just what happens.

The primary potency of *Mail Order Wife* is the bleakly amusing way it undercuts expectations: Andrew's verite "expose" stops before it really gets going; the naive, waiflike bride turns out to be a loud shrew, or maybe a grifter (or maybe both or maybe neither); the heroic White Knight Andrew turns out to be almost as repugnant as the creepy Adrian; the "revenge" scheme goes awry. And so on.

Mail Order Wife additionally benefits from consistently naturalistic performances by Eugenia Yuan (who is really American-born and recently starred in *Hulk* and *Memoirs of a Geisha*) and Adrian Martinez, whose blend of desperation, despair and general "ickyness" is concurrently moving and disgusting. Director Andrew Gurland is almost as good playing (one hopes) an unpleasant version of his actual self.

Paradoxically, what makes *Mail Order Wife* enthralling also makes it disturbing. Here is a topic (the mail-order bride phenomenon) that warrants a real expose, but this mockumentary sidesteps the industry's secret practices and abuses because it is so intently focused on the three-character drama. In the same vein, *Mail Order Wife* stacks the deck against Lichi's character by barely showing the abuses, misuses, and neglect by Adrian and Andrew. Clearly, we are supposed to have more sympathy for the men, while Lichi remains an exotic enigma (*The Devil is a Woman* in stereo).

Reviews for the film were polite but mixed. Ned Marten in *The New York Times* (on March 11, 2005) wrote, "The narrative manages 30 solid minutes of ingenuity, before breaking into a version of Charlie Kaufman-style absurdity."Nick Sylvester in the March 9, 2005 *Village Voice* saw other references: "*Mail Order Wife* is an aimlessly symbolic critique of the whole documentary-making process. While an empowered Lichi goes Nietzsche (yawn), Andrew learns he's as revolting as Adrian, possibly an oblique reference to Rodney Dangerfield's own epiphanies in *Back to School* and, debatably, *Ladybugs*. Deep inside the stacks of this nesting doll is, cough, no respect." Ruthe Stein in *The San Francisco Chronicle* (on March 25, 2005) expressed the most reservation: "Botko and Gurland, who wrote the script, let their imaginations run wild. But it's hard to laugh at bizarre situations knowing that anything is possible when a lonely man sends away for a mate out of a catalog."

So like a Wayans Brothers' or Farrelly Brothers' movie, *Mail Order Wife* wants to be politically correct and incorrect simultaneously. The net product is watchable, but, like a shot-gun wedding, will probably cause at least a few regrets.

Eric Monder

CREDITS

Andrew: Andrew Gurland

Lichi: Eugenia Yuan

Adrian: Adrian Martinez
Deborah: Deborah Teng
Origin: USA
Language: English
Released: 2004
Production: Avram Ludwig, Kendall Morgan, Andrew Weiner, Nina Yang; Hypnotic; released by Dada Films
Directed by: Huck Botko, Andrew Gurland
Written by: Huck Botko, Andrew Gurland
Cinematography by: Luke Geissbuhler
Sound: Chen Harpaz
Music Supervisor: Mark Wike
Editing: Kevin Napier
Costumes: Jennifer Galvelis
Production Design: Jon Nissenbaum
MPAA rating: R
Running time: 92 minutes

REVIEWS

Entertainment Weekly Online. March 30, 2005.
Los Angeles Times Online. March 11, 2005.
New York Times Online. March 11, 2005.
San Francisco Chronicle. March 25, 2005.
Variety Online. November 2, 2004.
Village Voice Online. March 9, 2005.

THE MAN

One guy walks the walk. The other talks and talks.
—Movie tagline
Only one of them can be...
—Movie tagline

Box Office: $8.3 million

The Man, a comic crime film directed by Les Mayfield and starring the unlikely combination of Eugene Levy and Samuel L. Jackson as accidental partners on a police investigation, mines just about every cliché imaginable in the buddy cop picture. Devoid of originality, whatever goodwill the film engenders stems from Levy's comic gifts as an appealing fish-out-of-water character, a decent guy thrust into a dangerous situation. He plays Andy Fiddler, a nebbishy dental supplies salesman attending a business convention in Detroit, which might as well be another planet to his sheltered world in Wisconsin. Jackson plays Derrick Vann, an ATF agent investigating a weapons heist that took the life of his partner. To make matters worse for Vann, who is already tightly wound, Internal Affairs Agent Peters (Miguel Ferrer) suspects that he may be dirty like his late partner. When the fates of Andy and Vann inadvertently collide on the mean streets of Detroit, it is not hard to guess where the film is headed.

True to the cop formula, Vann plays by his own rules and never lets proper police procedure get in the way of his work. Determined to stop the sale of the stolen weapons, he decides to go undercover and arranges a meeting with the bad guys. Unfortunately, Andy happens to be in the wrong place at the wrong time and is mistaken for Vann, who saves the hapless Andy from himself but now needs him to pretend to be the undercover agent.

Levy and Jackson play the ultimate mismatched pair. Andy is the mild-mannered innocent who always looks for the best in people and takes pride in his wife and children, while Vann is the streetwise cop who swears profusely, runs roughshod over everyone (including his informant), is divorced from his wife, and spends little time with his daughter. Jackson essentially does what he has done in previous films but plays his violent, menacing cop as straight man for Levy, whose amusing dialogue and befuddled expressions give the movie a jolt of life.

Indeed, were it not for Andy's sense of wide-eyed wonder and unstoppable optimism, the film would be a complete waste. There is one funny sequence in which Andy chastises Vann for his penchant for swearing and suggests a way for him to overcome the problem. It is a cute moment not just because Andy is very earnest, but, because Jackson is known for spewing four-letter words throughout his cinematic career, the very idea of telling Vann to curb his foul language is hilarious.

But the plot is so pedestrian, one wonders why the writers, Jim Piddock, Margaret Oberman, and Steve Carpenter, could not come up with something even a little more interesting. For the first part of the film, for example, Andy, who is essentially kidnapped by law enforcement, keeps fouling up his job of dropping off some money so that Vann can initiate the purchase. The weapons dealers, led by Joey (Luke Goss), are standard movie gangsters with nothing at all distinctive about them.

Much of *The Man* simply does not work, like a ridiculous scene in which Andy, alone in a car and handcuffed in the passenger seat, actually tries to drive. Other moments ring completely false, like milquetoast Andy actually trying to turn tough guy when he meets Joey and taking charge of the operation. He even gives Joey the half million dollars that Vann borrowed from headquarters and told Andy merely to use as flash money. We are supposed to believe that calling the shots is a giant step forward for Andy's self-confidence when it is really just another potentially fatal blunder. And the heartwarming material is just as hokey. Devoted family man Andy tries to get Vann to be a better father by having him attend his daughter's ballet recital—right in the middle of the investigation, which is hardly likely to happen. And the film's indulgence in flatulence humor (Andy gets an upset stomach when he eats red meat) feels like sheer desperation, an attempt to fill up an empty plot with the lowest kind of humor possible.

And yet, given all of these problems, the biggest is the plot itself, which grows more nonsensical as it progresses. Joey and his gang finally meet with Vann and Andy, who is now acting (very unpersuasively) like the leader of the operation with Vann as his underling, but a scene in which the thugs have the heroes standing in a swimming pool, as if they are prisoners, comes out of nowhere and is just baffling.

By the end, so hackneyed is the script that we are actually treated to the obligatory scene of Vann's superior, Lt. Rita Carbone (Susie Essman), forcing him to surrender his badge and gun after his informant is killed and Vann is under suspicion. This scene is so familiar to moviegoers, it could now only work as a parody, and the fact that the crusty, no-nonsense superior is played by a woman does not make the scene any less of a cliché.

By the time the big showdown with Joey occurs in a huge warehouse, Agent Peters, convinced that Vann is dirty, has Andy wearing a wire, and Lt. Carbone thinks Andy himself is an IA agent. Vann and Andy are more suspicious of each other than ever, but, despite all their antagonism and true to the formula, they quickly work things out in time to dispose of the villains.

Sorely lacking any original twist that might make this familiar story intriguing and fresh, *The Man* slavishly follows the narrative trajectory we would expect. Take two men (one naïve and the other street-smart), plunge them in the middle of a criminal investigation, and force them to play off each other until they grudgingly put aside their differences and emerge victorious. In the end, trite elements like stolen weapons, mistaken identity, and generic gangsters are not enough for the talented Levy to hang his funny shtick on.

Peter N. Chumo II

CREDITS

Derrick Vann: Samuel L. Jackson
Andy Fiddler: Eugene Levy
Joey/Kane: Luke Goss
Agent Peters: Miguel Ferrer
Booty: Anthony Mackie
Diaz: Horatio Sanz
Dara Vann: Rachael Crawford
Lt. Rita Carbone: Susie Essman
Kate Vann Montgomery: Tomorrow Baldwin
Origin: USA
Language: English
Released: 2005
Production: Rob Fried; Meradin Prods; released by New Line Cinema
Directed by: Les Mayfield
Written by: Jim Piddock, Margaret Grieco Oberman, Stephen Carpenter
Cinematography by: Adam Kane
Music by: John Murphy, Dana Sano
Sound: Bruce Carwardine
Editing: Jeffrey Wolf
Art Direction: James McAteer
Costumes: Delphine White
Production Design: Carol Spier
MPAA rating: PG-13
Running time: 79 minutes

REVIEWS

Boxoffice Online. September, 2005.
Chicago Sun-Times Online. September 9, 2005.
Entertainment Weekly Online. September 7, 2005.
Los Angeles Times Online. September 9, 2005.
New York Times Online. September 9, 2005.
Variety Online. September 5, 2005.

QUOTES

Andy Fiddler: "You shot me!"
Special Agent Derrick Vann: "I grazed you."
Andy Fiddler: "Well, that's still shooting me!"

TRIVIA

One of the working titles for this film was *El Maninator.*

MAN OF THE HOUSE

Protecting witnesses is a challenge. Living with them is impossible.
—Movie tagline

Box Office: $19.1 million

Tommy Lee Jones is making a career out of playing the same character: a rugged, rough, unrelenting, tough-as-nails, quick-witted, quick-reacting, desensitized, and determined enforcer of the law. *The Fugitive, U.S. Marshals* and the *Men In Black* movies have afforded Jones the practice needed to insert this character into a variety of different contexts. His deadpan demeanor and immaculate, bitter sense of comic and ironic timing make this character a delight to watch. He has been provided, in his past incidences of cinematic success, with fine counterpoints to his glacial portrayals. His bungling troops in *The Fugitive* and *U.S. Marshals* contrasted strongly with his indomitable, unwavering characterization. Jones collaborated finely with Will Smith in the *Men In Black* films to create an enchanting straight-man/funny-man, good cop/bad cop dichotomy. The formula has been a winner financially and professionally. Such formulas work well for certain actors. Minor contextual variations often make available a host of outwardly fresh, seemingly unique comedic moments. Such is the case with Sony Pictures' release of *Man Of The House*.

Jones is cast as Texas Ranger Lieutenant Roland Sharp: the severe, demanding, indefatigable, clever, rapid-retorting, gritty, and resolute character one comes to expect from Jones. Roland Sharp is so committed to his career that he has lost his wife and has a slight if detectable relationship with his daughter, Emma (Shannon Marie Woodward). At the outset, Sharp and his partner Maggie Swanson (Liz Vassey) are on the hunt for Morgan Ball (Curtis Armstrong), a witness to the crimes of John Portland, the head of a major meth cartel. Sharp receives information on the witness's whereabouts from an ex-con turned preacher Percy Stevens, played by Cedric the Entertainer. When they locate Ball and take him in to custody, all hell breaks loose. An unknown sniper wounds Maggie and Morgan Ball who somehow wanders away onto the streets of downtown Austin where he narrowly escapes being hit by the sniper driving a Ford Bronco and meanders into an alleyway behind a building where the University of Texas Cheer Squad is holding a rally. Five of the girls are on a break and are freshening up in the bathroom next to the alley. They spot the wounded man and someone "coming to help him." However, their assumption is wrong and Morgan Ball is shot dead by an unknown assailant, who we later find out to be a duplicitous and treacherous federal law enforcement officer working with Sharp on the Morgan Ball case but also operating in cahoots with criminal John Portland. The five cheerleaders—Anne (Christina Milian), Teresa (Paula Garces), Evie (Monica Keena), Heather (Vanessa Ferlito), and Barb (Kelli Garner)—become the next target of John Portland and his double-dealing friend in the feds. They need protection around the clock. Roland Sharp, whose partner is now in the hospital, is assigned to the case. He takes up residence with them in their near-campus house and becomes the *Man Of The House* and poses as their assistant cheer coach.

The main thrust of the comedic plot revolves around the coarse, tenacious Sharp and his struggle to deal with the feisty, energetic, strong-willed coeds. Roland Sharp is from the old school and the girls are expectedly wild and anti-traditional. They each have their own specific new age diet that they follow while Sharp still eats whatever tastes good. They dress predominantly in sports bras, spandex shorts, and tiny skirts. After Sharp's attempts to verbally establish a proper, tactful dress code, he purchases an industrial strength air conditioning unit in order to physically force the girls to dress according to his conservative tastes. When one of the girls has her period it is Sharp who must make the trip to the drugstore for a stare down between man and tampon worthy of an old western. Another time, the girls want to go to the Cactus Café to watch a band. Sharp reasserts that they cannot leave the house. When they attempt to physically force their way out, Sharp is forced to use the standard practices of law enforcement in order to restrain them.

Over time, however, the relationship between sharp and the girls proves not wholly caustic. Sharp begins to learn from the girls. He receives advice on how to talk to his daughter and about what her personal needs and desires might be; information which before had been unobtainable due to his impenetrability. Sharp meets one of the girls' Introduction to English teachers, Molly McCarthy, (Anne Archer) and is immediately smitten and he asks her to come to the house for dinner. The girls decide that Sharp is not physically presentable for a date and decide to give him a makeover including eyebrow plucking, a full manicure, and a facial mask. When the date arrives, the girls have employed Sharp's audio and video surveillance tools to assist him with the intricacies of dating success.

There are actually a few good belly laughs to be had by everyone while watching *Man Of The House* despite its ridiculous ending and absurd predictability, yet for this Longhorn Alumni (also director Stephen Herek's alma mater), the most powerful asset of the movie was the town of Austin itself. From the Mangia's Pizza delivery boy to Threadgill's Restaurant to Buffalo Billiards to the East Mall fountain and the statue of Martin Luther King Jr. to the tens of thousands at Memorials Stadium to the Hex Rally on the steps of the Tower, and a cameo by real-life Texas governor Rick Perry, *Man Of The House* undoubtedly satisfied my taste of nostalgia. Hook 'Em.

Nick Kennedy

CREDITS

Roland Sharp: Tommy Lee Jones

Percy Stevens: Cedric the Entertainer

Anne: Christina Milian
Teresa: Paula Garces
Evie: Monica Keena
Heather: Vanessa Ferlito
Barb: Kelli Garner
Prof. Molly McCarthy: Anne Archer
Eddie Zane: Brian Van Holt
Ranger Holt: Shea Whigham
Captain Nichols: R. Lee Ermey
Binky: Paget Brewster
Maggie Swanson: Liz Vassey
Morgan Ball: Curtis Armstrong
Ranger Riggs: Terry Parks
Emma Shannon: Marie Woodward
James Richard Perry (Cameo)
Origin: USA
Language: English
Released: 2005
Production: Steven Reuther, Todd Garner, Allyn Stewart; released by Sony Pictures Entertainment
Directed by: Stephen Herek
Written by: Robert Ramsey, Matthew Stone, John McLaughlin
Cinematography by: Peter Menzies Jr.
Music by: David Newman
Sound: John Pritchett
Music Supervisor: G. Marq Roswell
Editing: Chris Lebenzon
Art Direction: Kevin Constant
Costumes: Betsy Heimann
Production Design: Nelson Coates
MPAA rating: PG-13
Running time: 99 minutes

REVIEWS

Boxoffice Online. February, 2005.
Entertainment Weekly Online. March 2, 2005.
Los Angeles Times Online. February 28, 2005.
New York Times Online. February 26, 2005.
Variety Online. February 25, 2005.
Washington Post Online. February 26, 2005, p. C05.

QUOTES

Captain Nichols: "The girls have been fawning over mugshot books I now know the hottie rating of every ex-convict in the western United States."

TRIVIA

This is the first film with permission to use the full and actual name of the University of Texas at Austin.

MARCH OF THE PENGUINS

In the harshest place on Earth, love finds a way.
—Movie tagline

Box Office: $77.4 million

March of the Penguins was released to theaters in hopes of its becoming a success along the lines of *Winged Migration* (2001). While Jacques Perrin's soaring look at the migratory pattern of birds constantly offers startling images, Luc Jacquet's penguin documentary is more down-to-earth. While less varied visually than *Winged Migration, March of the Penguins* effectively chooses to emphasize the emotional side of the penguins' lives.

Jacquet and cinematographers Laurent Chalet and Jerome Maison spent months following the mating rites of a clan of emperor penguins in the South Pole. Each March, the adult penguins leave their oceanside homes to walk, slip, and slide seventy miles across the frozen tundra to their mating grounds. Narrator Morgan Freeman explains that there is no explanation for this behavior. They cannot breed closer to home simply because this is the way they have done things for centuries.

Once the hundreds of penguins reach the breeding grounds, they take several days to choose their mates before breeding. After the egg is hatched, the female transfers it to the male. Because the female has lost a third of her body weight and must find food for the newborn chick, she makes a return seventy-mile journey, leaving the male to guard the precious egg. When the female returns, the chicks have hatched, and the males, who have gone 120 days without eating, are a tad famished. They too march home and back again. By the fall, all the penguins return home to await the resumption of the cycle in the spring.

Jacquet, of course, presents much more drama. While the females are gone, the males gather in an enormous circle to help each other survive the harsh temperatures of the most intense cold on the planet. Some eggs, for various reasons, do not make it. Back at the home front, the females must elude such predators as leopard seals, and the chicks are sometimes the victims of winged predators. The narration, adapted by Jordan Roberts from the screenplay by Jacquet and Michel Fessler, never deigns to explain too much and does not even identify the albatross seen attacking a helpless chick.

Jacquet is selling *March of the Penguins* as a love story, stressing the emotional attachment of the parents and their chick at the expense of a better-rounded, more scientific approach. It's just entertainment, folks. It is a bit jarring, then, when the parents not only abandon their young at the end of the film but each other as well. The following March, they will seek new mates.

Jacquet's penguin march began with his response to a 1991 advertisement in a French newspaper for a biologist willing to spend fourteen months in Antarctica. Jacquet, who had just earned a Master's degree in animal biology from Lyons University, soon found himself at the French scientific research station in the Terre Adelie territory, following penguins around with a 35mm camera. A few years later, he wrote a screenplay about the mating ritual, received funding from the National Geographic Society, and returned to Antarctica in 2001 with Chalet and Maison for thirteen months of filming. The surprising success of another French nature documentary, *Microcosmos* (1996), made the financing possible.

They shot 140 hours of land footage and another thirty hours underwater. Jacquet decided not to make his film in 35mm or IMAX but in Super 16mm because of easy maneuverability, allowing them to get closer to the penguins. As a result, some of *March of the Penguins* is grainy, though there are still many breathtaking shots of the blue-and-white landscape and the beautiful black-and-white creatures. The close-ups of the birds reveal the intricate texture of their featured bodies.

Because Jacquet sees *March of the Penguins* as a love story and wants the audience to know what the birds are experiencing, the French version features actors (Charles Berling, Romane Bohringer, and Jules Sitruk) as the voices of the penguins. When Warner Independent Pictures acquired the American rights to the film, it jettisoned this narration in favor of Freeman's more stately version. Emilie Simon's sentimental score was replaced by Alex Wurman's, which suggests at times New Age mood music.

Such documentaries were once relegated to television, but with *Microcosmos, Winged Migration*, and the general boom in documentaries, there is clearly a market for nature films with unusual stories and images. *March of the Penguins* made $12 million in France, and in its first weekend of release in the United States, it averaged $26,000 per screen, the most of any film, with *The War of the Worlds* trailing with a distant $11,000 average. While Jacquet may have overstated the love story angle, the sight of the cute, cuddly creatures experiencing emotions to which humans can relate is fascinating.

Michael Adams

CREDITS

Origin: USA
Language: English
Released: 2005
Production: Yves Darondeau, Christophe Lioud, Emmanuel Priou; Bonne Bloche, National Geographic Feature Film
Directed by: Luc Jacquet
Written by: Jordan Roberts
Cinematography by: Laurent Chalet, Jerome Maison
Sound: Gerard Lamps, Laurent Quaglio
Editing: Sabine Emiliani
MPAA rating: G
Running time: 80 minutes

REVIEWS

Boxoffice Online. July, 2005.
Chicago Sun-Times Online. July 8, 2005.
Entertainment Weekly Online. June 15, 2005.
Los Angeles Times Online. June 24, 2005.
New York Times Online. June 24, 2005.
Premiere Magazine Online. June 23, 2005.
Variety Online. June 21, 2005.
Washington Post Online. July 1, 2005, p. WE31.

AWARDS

Oscars 2005: Feature Doc.
Natl. Bd. of Review 2005: Feature Doc.
Broadcast Film Critics 2005: Feature Doc.
Nomination:
British Acad. 2005: Cinematog., Film Editing.

MATCH POINT

Passion, Temptation, Obsession.
—Movie tagline
There are no little secrets.
—Movie tagline

Woody Allen fans have been longing for a return to form since his last true masterpiece, *Hannah and Her Sisters* (1986). The amazingly productive writer-director turns out a film a year, but most of his efforts since the mid-1980's have been disappointments or interesting failures. While some reviewers heralded *Melinda and Melinda* (2005) as a comeback, Allen failed to find the right balance between comedy and drama, a failing magnified by unconvincing characters and stiff dialogue, a common Allen weakness in recent years.

Even more reviewers have hailed *Match Point* as the real thing. While masterpieces such as *Annie Hall* (1977) and *Manhattan* (1979) are comedies with bittersweet dramatic moments, *Match Point* is a serious film with surprising comic touches. Unlike ponderously dreary psychological studies such as *Interiors* (1978) and *Another Woman* (1988), *Match Point* is a psychological film married to a genre film. It is a truly remarkable achievement after so many missteps, but is it truly a Woody Allen film?

Allen's first film set in England focuses on Chris Wilton (Jonathan Rhys Meyers), an Irish tennis player who has abandoned touring to become a teaching pro at a club. One of his wealthy students, Tom Hewett (Matthew Goode), invites Chris to his family's country estate. Tom's sister, Chloe (Emily Mortimer), falls instantly for the visitor, who seems more interested in a mysterious young American, Nola Rice (Scarlet Johansson), who turns out to be Tom's fiancée.

The ambitious Chris is torn between Chloe's sweet goodness (and money) and the sensuality of Nola, an unsuccessful actress. Before he knows it, Chris has been given an executive position in the corporation of Alec Hewett (Brian Cox) and is engaged to Chloe. Chris is surprisingly good at his job, despite frequent absences to be with the luscious Nola. When the American is suddenly dumped by Tom and discovers she is pregnant, what is Chris to do?

As a tale of class differences, ambition, and murder, *Match Point* has numerous literary and cinematic influences, beginning with Theodore Dreiser's *An American Tragedy* (1925) and George Stevens' film version, *A Place in the Sun* (1951). Allen inverts Dreiser's character dynamics from a man caught between his mousy, poor wife and a seemingly unattainable rich girl to one torn between a good, rich wife and a very attainable poor girl. Like Dreiser, Allen uses his characters to explore the consequences of fate. The remarkable, atypical for Allen, opening of *Match Point,* with a tennis ball going back and forth over a net in slow motion only to freeze on the verge of clearing or bouncing back from the net, sets the film's tone as a sophisticated, self-conscious look at how fate governs lives.

Match Point also has elements recalling Fyodor Dostoevsky's *Crime and Punishment* (1867); Alfred Hitchcock's *Strangers on a Train* (1951), from the 1950 novel by Patricia Highsmith; Highsmith's Tom Ripley novels, especially *The Talented Mr. Ripley* (1955); and Hitchcock's *Dial M for Murder* (1954). A scene featuring ghostly apparitions brings to mind William Shakespeare's *Hamlet* (1601) and *Macbeth* (1606). Chris and Chloe attend a performance of Andrew Lloyd Webber's *The Woman in White* (2004), and its source, the 1860 Wilkie Collins novel, also has plot elements similar to those of Allen's film. The characters attend the opera, and passages from operas by Georges Bizet, Gaetano Donizetti, Carlos Gomes, and Giuseppe Verdi, including *Macbeth* (1847), seem to be commenting ironically on the action.

Several reviewers have compared *Match Point* to Allen's *Crimes and Misdemeanors* (1989), and while the earlier film has a darker plot featuring a murder, its serious half melds awkwardly with its comic scenes. *Match Point* is most remarkable as a completely unified work, with no extraneous scenes, with the possible exception of Chris's bemoaning his dilemma to a friend (Rupert Penry-Jones). Many of Allen's films seem to have been written in haste and lack narrative cohesiveness, but *Match Point* is as tightly wound as Chris's psyche. Despite the leanness of the narrative, it is Allen's longest film, running about twenty minutes longer than his average. Notoriously rough on his work, Allen has said that this is a film he is proud of.

While Allen sometimes strains to inject seriousness into his comedies, his comic moments in *Match Point* come effortlessly. Chris is shown reading *Crime and Punishment* and the Cambridge University Press companion to the novel at the same time. The audience first thinks he is a serious young man, but he is a calculator, reading Dostoevsky only to impress Alec. Allen injects slapstick humor into the film's most emotionally intense scene by having a killer fumblingly assemble a gun before committing murder. Following the murder, seemingly innocent remarks become ironic comments about what has transpired. Such subtle dark humor keeps *Match Point* from being a cold intellectual exercise.

The film's characters, plot, and tone recall yet another film: the darkly satirical *Nothing But the Best* (1964), with Frederic Raphael, in his prime, adapting Stanley Ellin's novel and direction by Clive Donner, whose next film was *What's New, Pussycat* (1965), from Allen's first screenplay. Alan Bates plays an ambitious young man with his eye on his boss's daughter. He will do anything, including murder, to achieve his goals. Chris Wilton is like a combination of this character, Tom Ripley, and Montgomery Clift's George Eastman from *A Place in the Sun.*

Say what you will about Allen, but he has consistently gotten good performances throughout his career. Penelope Wilton is an excellent stage and television actress who has not had a meaty film role before sinking her teeth into Chloe and Tom's surprisingly feisty mother. James Nesbitt is charming as an extremely decent police detective, recalling the inspectors played by John Williams in *Dial M for Murder* and Alec McCowen in Hitchcock's *Frenzy* (1972).

Johansson, playing her first true grown-up, continues to grow astonishingly. Her Nola is sultry and smart, and it's obvious why Chris cannot help himself. Rhys Meyers has also grown considerably as a performer, with his work here matching his indelible portrait of the king of rock and roll in the miniseries *Elvis* (2005). With his penetrating eyes, Rhys Meyers creates an engaging antihero both intense and unsure of himself, much like the characters played by Clift.

But is *Match Point,* a radical departure for Allen, a fluke? It is a true Allen film for its expert mixing of humor with a philosophical inquiry into the nature of relations between the sexes. Many of Allen's films have touches of self-analysis, even self-flagellation at times.

With his deeply flawed protagonist, is the filmmaker exploring the depths of his psyche, his sense of guilt over his failures as a man and an artist? It does not matter. *Match Point* is such a smoothly running engine that it should entrance even those who have never heard of Woody Allen.

Michael Adams

CREDITS

Nola Rice: Scarlett Johansson
Chris Wilton: Jonathan Rhys Meyers
Chloe Hewett Wilton: Emily Mortimer
Tom Hewett: Matthew Goode
Alec Hewett: Brian Cox
Eleanor Hewett: Penelope Wilton
Inspector Dowd: Ewen Bremner
Detective Banner: James Nesbitt
Henry: Rupert Penry-Jones
Mrs. Eastby: Margaret Tyzack
Origin: Great Britain
Language: English
Released: 2005
Production: Letty Aronson, Lucy Darwin, Gareth Willey; BBC Films, HanWay, Thema Production SA, Jada Production
Directed by: Woody Allen
Written by: Woody Allen
Cinematography by: Remi Adefarasin
Sound: Peter Glossop
Editing: Alisa Lepselter
Art Direction: Diane Dancklefsen, Jan Spoczynski
Costumes: Jill Taylor
Production Design: Jim Clay
MPAA rating: R
Running time: 124 minutes

REVIEWS

Entertainment Weekly Online. December 23, 2005.
Los Angeles Times Online. December 28, 2005.
New York Times Online. December 28, 2005.
Variety Online. May 12, 2005.

QUOTES

Chris Wilton: "The innocent are sometimes slain to make way for grander schemes. You were collateral damage."

TRIVIA

Woody Allen's first film to be shot entirely in Britain.

AWARDS

Nomination:
Oscars 2005: Orig. Screenplay
Golden Globes 2005: Director (Allen)
Golden Globes 2006: Film—Drama, Screenplay, Support. Actress (Johansson).

ME AND YOU AND EVERYONE WE KNOW

Box Office: $3.9 million

An art house darling and recipient of a Special Jury Prize for Originality of Vision at this year's Sundance Film Festival, *Me and You and Everyone We Know* captured critics' attention for embodying many of the qualities often valued in independent films—an offbeat sensibility, edgy material, and an attempt to grapple with big themes (in this case, loneliness and the sometimes odd and painful ways people try to reach out to one another). Written and directed by performance artist Miranda July, the film is also one of the most frustrating of the year. While it is clear that there is a distinctive talent at work behind the camera, July's unique vision is ultimately in service of one more indie look at a group of sad sacks trying to overcome their alienation from each other and the world at large. For a film ostensibly about connection, moreover, July's feature debut employs so many arch, contrived, and seemingly shocking situations that we end up feeling distanced from her characters rather than being drawn in to empathize with their plight.

July plays Christine Jesperson, an aspiring multimedia artist who makes ends meet as a driver for an elder cab company. Her counterpart in loneliness and emotional dislocation is Richard Swersey (John Hawkes), a shoe salesman who is undergoing a separation from his wife and trying, in his own weird way, to be a good father to his sons, teenage Peter (Miles Thompson) and little Robby (Brandon Ratcliff).

But while both Christine and Richard are potentially sympathetic, each displays an oddity that is more off-putting than endearing. Richard finds a peculiar way to commemorate the separation by setting his hand on fire—a trick he once learned from his uncle—but, forgetting to use alcohol instead of lighter fluid, he ends up burning his hand very badly and wearing a bandage for much of the film. And yet, even after doing something so dangerous and idiotic, he still, inexplicably enough, gets to share custody of his sons. He says that he is ready "to be swept off my feet" and is "prepared for amazing things to happen," declarations that are probably meant to create a slightly surreal atmosphere as well as highlight the character's sense of optimism but that are really just a hint of the movie's overly self-conscious dialogue.

If glimpses of Christine's performance art, in which she plays all the characters and does the sound effects as well, were not an indication of her own eccentricity, then a scene in which she observes a goldfish in a baggie accidentally left on a car roof confirms it. Because the fish is almost certain to face death when the car stops, she is moved to say a few words of tribute, as if the prospect of a fish teetering on the brink of annihilation were a profound existential moment. July is seeking to find the transcendent in the ordinary. Think of the scene featuring the plastic bag fluttering in the breeze in *American Beauty* (1999), but where that moment punctuated a key theme of the film, July multiplies such moments to the point where they become ridiculous—her film becomes a series of epiphanies with no plot or character development supporting them.

When Christine pays a visit to Richard's shoe department and he examines her feet and learns that her shoes rub against her ankles, he sympathizes, "You think you deserve that pain, but you don't," as if this were yet another profound moment and he were peering deep into her soul. Such stylized, quasi-philosophical dialogue might work if it were engaging and helped create a world of its own, but it pops up at random moments and is more distracting than enlightening.

Christine, nonetheless, takes his concern very seriously and, seeing a soul mate, practically becomes a stalker. In one of the film's most highly discussed and praised scenes, they walk down the street together and frame the journey as a metaphor for their life together even though they barely know each other, with the inevitable parting of the ways at the end representing their separation by death. It is, admittedly, an original piece of writing but so abstract that one puzzles over the idea that two relative strangers are talking in such terms. After they depart, she finds him moments later and gets in his car (calling this portion of the relationship the afterlife), thus establishing that this woman is more scary than endearing. Another quirky scene has them gluing the mirror back in a compact and having to stand together and hold it in place for two minutes, as if this mundane event were a symbol for something greater, like commitment or dedication to a relationship.

But the bizarre mating ritual of Richard and Christine is just one part of the film, as the all-encompassing title suggests. Much of the screenplay focuses on the children of the neighborhood, who are also searching for a connection. Peter and Robby, for example, left alone most of the day, spend a lot of time on the Internet and are soon in a chat room where little Robby carries on a sexually charged, scatological exchange with a horny stranger. Meanwhile, two teenage girls, Rebecca (Najarra Townsend) and Heather (Natasha Slayton), begin a risky flirtation with would-be pervert Andrew (Brad Henke), Richard's coworker. At first, the girls and Andrew just talk, but soon he is taping on his window obscene notes declaring the sexual activities he would like to do with them. They, in turn, get competitive about who has the better oral skills and decide to use Peter as their guinea pig to get an objective opinion. He, of course, is only too happy to comply. Although these subplots are often played for laughs, they are also genuinely disturbing in a way that the film never confronts, as if July were venturing into taboo areas of adolescent and even childhood sexuality to make us squirm and see how far we will go with her. Ultimately, it feels gratuitous and distasteful to use children in such a way, especially when the stories do not add up to much, except perhaps July's attempt to show off her indie credentials by crossing the line, venturing to places where mainstream American films generally dare not go.

The sweetest and saddest child in the film is a little girl named Sylvie (Carlie Westerman), already preparing for her marriage by buying household appliances and accessories to furnish her future home and stashing them away in a hope chest. She comes across both wise beyond her years and yet very melancholy at the same time, establishing a wistful bond with Peter, who takes an unlikely interest in her. She, too, is venturing into adulthood before her time but without the sexual dimension of the other children. This child-woman is a fascinating character with a hint of depth lacking in many of the others, but the screenplay does not do enough with her.

Indeed, none of these stories have very much momentum or a compelling conclusion. When Rebecca and Heather finally take a bold step and go to Andrew's door, he cowers in fear, unable to try to get what he has supposedly wanted all along. Robby arranges a meeting with his chat room partner, and it turns out to be Nancy Harrington (Tracy Wright), the strange, dour curator of a museum where Christine lobbies to get her work shown. Nancy, we discover, is just one more isolated person yearning for human contact and getting an unexpected result, thus belaboring the point that everyone is searching for an ever elusive intimacy. By the end, Christine and Richard seem to have a chance at a future together, although given the fact that all of their encounters are more metaphor than realism, it is hard to figure out if theirs is even a match worth rooting for.

Despite July's attempt at a whimsical, romantically loopy tone, creeping into *Me and You and Everyone We Know* is an air of condescension, as if these desperate people, especially the children, were being examined for our amusement. While she does not veer into the outright contempt and bitterness of Todd Solondz, another filmmaker with a fascination with losers in disquieting situations and disturbing peeks into childhood sexuality (especially in 1998's *Happiness*), it is nonetheless hard to care about July's characters. Her overarching theme of the ways sad, lonely people try to find meaningful connections with each other is ultimately devoid of fresh insight and executed in such a random way that, after a while, it feels like just about any weird slice of life could fit in. With the exception of Hawkes, who brings a certain poignancy to Richard, and Westerman's portrayal of the sad but hopeful Sylvie, the actors do not lift their characters beyond abstractions. July's artiness ultimately drains out most of their humanity so that, by the end, it is hard to feel that we know them any better than we did at the beginning.

Peter N. Chumo II

CREDITS

Richard: John Hawkes
Sylvie: Carlie Westerman
Christine: Miranda July
Peter: Miles Thompson
Robby: Brandon Ratcliff
Heather: Natasha Slayton
Rebecca: Najarra Townsend
Origin: USA, Great Britain
Language: English
Released: 2005
Production: Gina Kwon; released by IFC Films
Directed by: Miranda July
Written by: Miranda July
Cinematography by: Chuy Chavez
Music by: Michael Andrews
Sound: Yehuda Maayan
Editing: Andrew Dickler
Art Direction: John Wyatt
Costumes: Christie Wittenborn
Production Design: Aran Mann
MPAA rating: R
Running time: 95 minutes

REVIEWS

Boxoffice Online. June, 2005.
Chicago Sun-Times Online. June 24, 2005.
Entertainment Weekly Online. June 15, 2005.
New York Times Online. June 17, 2005.
Variety Online. February 1, 2005.

MELINDA AND MELINDA

Life can be a comedy or a tragedy, it all depends on how you look at it.
—Movie tagline

Box Office: $3.8 million

Melinda and Melinda has been greeted by many reviewers as a return to form for Woody Allen as a director and screenwriter. The critical consensus is that he has not made a completely successful film since *Hannah and Her Sisters* and that most of the eighteen films since are disappointing or worse. *Melinda and Melinda* is much better than *Celebrity* (1998) and *Hollywood Ending* (2002), though much inferior to *Manhattan Murder Mystery* (1993) and *Sweet and Lowdown* (1999). Though it never quite comes to life, it has its moments and is of most interest in how it fits into Allen's enormous body of work.

The conceit of *Melinda and Melinda* is telling two versions of the same story. Two playwrights are having dinner in a Greenwich Village restaurant when they hear an anecdote about a young woman who drops in unexpectedly on a dinner party. Sy (Wallace Shawn), who writes comedies, then explains how this story can evolve into a romantic comedy, while Max (Larry Pine), a more serious writer, takes a darker spin. *Melinda and Melinda* alternates scenes from two parallel lives, with Melinda (Radha Mitchell), the only common character in each version.

In the more serious story, Melinda arrives from out of town to the apartment of Laurel (Chloe Sevigny), one of her best friends when they were in college. Laurel, from a wealthy Park Avenue family, teaches music but apparently lives off her inheritance. Lee (Jonny Lee Miller), her husband, is a failed actor dissatisfied with his life. The very nervous and distracted Melinda is soon revealed to be retreating from a failed marriage and a disastrous affair. Laurel and another college friend, Cassie (Brooke Smith) want to help Melinda find some stability by setting her up with a stable man. Instead, Melinda falls for a musician, Ellis (Chiwetel Ejiofor), she meets at a party. Complications arise when Ellis and Laurel become attracted.

In the comic version, Melinda barges into a dinner party in a neighboring apartment after taking too many sleeping pills. There she meets Susan (Amanda Peet), a filmmaker, and her husband, Hobie (Will Ferrell), another failed actor. While Susan tries to find a man for Melinda, Hobie finds himself increasingly drawn to his neighbor. Hobie searches for a way to get Melinda without hurting Susan.

Melinda and Melinda has all the qualities that Allen haters hate. All the characters are self-centered, privileged types in the arts or professions who take their privileges too much for granted. Allen's films are especially misleading about the ease of obtaining good tables in upscale Manhattan restaurants. The characters live in apartments or townhouses real people like themselves could probably not afford. Allen has perhaps drifted too far away from the days when his character in *Manhattan* was forced to move into a cheaper apartment.

More damningly, Allen's characters continue to talk and act like those in his 1970's films. Even though most of the characters are in their thirties, their diction and cultural references are those of earlier generations. Allen has written and continues to write funny dialogue, but his serious talk seems strained. Melinda describes herself as resembling "the Wreck of the Hesperus," and other characters quote Cole Porter instead of more likely references like Kurt Cobain.

Even younger characters talk like this in Allen's previous film, *Anything Else* (2003), but this reworking of the plot of *Annie Hall* (1977) has surprising charm. The anachronistic dialogue and references coming out of the mouths of characters in their twenties makes the film seem like a student tribute to Allen.

Anything Else works well when the young cast seems to believe in the characters' flawed views of life. *Melinda and Melinda* also works best when the actors make the characters believable. A great responsibility is thus placed upon Mitchell, and she lives up to it. Melinda is a variation on all the neurotic Allen characters played by Diane Keaton and Mia Farrow, with a great deal of the depressed character played by Charlotte Rampling in the underrated *Stardust Memories* (1980). Allen and his male protagonists seem to be drawn to such women not despite their insecurities and instabilities but because of them.

Melinda could easily be a cliché, but Mitchell brings her vulnerability and self-destructive selfishness to life. Best known as the object of Ally Sheedy's affection in *High Art* (1998) and as Johnny Depp's wife in *Finding Neverland* (2004), Mitchell even looks like Mia Farrow in a few shots. Melinda is a part that seems to call either for overacting or for a subdued performance in hopes of making the character more sympathetic. Yet Mitchell is never hysterical, nor does she ever sentimentalize Melinda. Because she believes in the character, the audience also accepts Melinda's behavior as credible.

Sevigny also makes the relatively underwritten Laurel believable. While she, Mitchell, and Smith make Allen's artificial dialogue sound almost natural, most of the rest of the cast have problems. Miller, burdened with the least sympathetic character and the most ponderous lines, struggles, and while Ejiofor has considerable presence, his Ellis speaks as if the actor is trying to rationalize the character's behavior. His timing also seems a bit off at times. Miller and Ejiofor, as Britons, may have been hampered by concentrating on their American accents, though this does not seem to be a problem for the Australian Mitchell.

As with John Cusack in *Bullets Over Broadway* (1994), Kenneth Branagh in *Celebrity*, and Jason Biggs in *Anything Else*, Ferrell is saddled with dialogue that would sound much more natural coming from its creator's distinctive voice. While Ferrell is not as handcuffed by the Allen persona as was Branagh, he does not seem too comfortable in the role, adopting bug eyes and an awkward posture to make sure the audience realizes Hobie is a comic character. Melinda's falling for Hobie is fitting for ending the comic half of the film, but it strains credibility.

Melinda and Melinda represents three notable departures for Allen. All his films are crammed with jazz and classical music, but in a gesture toward the characters' age group, Allen includes some electronic pop and a bit of Barry White. Allen has been widely criticized for ignoring New York's racial and ethnic diversity, with the prostitute played by Hazelle Goodman in *Deconstructing Harry* (1997) the only significant African American character. *Melinda and Melinda*, however, offers two black characters: Ellis and Billy (Daniel Sunjata), Hobie's main rival for Melinda.

Few critics have commented on how Allen's visual style varies from film to film. While much of his oeuvre is stylistically simple, with little camera movement and cutting within scenes, there are always subtle differences, perhaps having to do with the cinematographer with whom he is collaborating. Since departing from longtime colleague Gordon Willis after *The Purple Rose of Cairo* (1985), Allen has worked with a variety of cinematographers, including many from Europe and Asia. Having Vilmos Zsigmond as his director of photography is a bit unusual since Zsigmond has specialized in thrillers such as *Blow Out* (1981) and outdoor films like *McCabe & Mrs. Miller* (1971) and *The Deer Hunter* (1978). The result is more camera movement and occasional odd, for Allen, camera angles. For perhaps the first time in any of his films is a scene with tight close-ups. By focusing on the faces of Laurel and Ellis when they discover they are in love, Allen demonstrates how the two have shut out everything else.

Examining serious themes is nothing new for Allen, who began introducing such elements into his comedies as early as *Love and Death* (1975) and made the first of several mostly serious films with *Interiors* (1978). Like *Melinda and Melinda, Crimes and Misdemeanors* (1989) alternates between serious and comic stories, but in both films, the serious side is not that engrossing. While Max calls his version tragic, it is not. Melinda's eventual crackup is obvious from the start. At the end, Sy does a lovely job of explaining how the thin line between happiness and despair is what life is all about, but this theme is not as clearly elucidated by the rest of the film.

What remains is the performance of Mitchell, who finds more shadings of character than the screenplay provides.

Michael Adams

CREDITS

Melinda: Radha Mitchell
Laurel: Chloe Sevigny
Lee: Jonny Lee Miller
Hobie: Will Ferrell
Susan: Amanda Peet
Ellis: Chiwetel Ejiofor
Sy: Wallace Shawn
Origin: USA
Language: English
Released: 2005
Production: Letty Aronson; released by 20th Century-Fox
Directed by: Woody Allen
Written by: Woody Allen
Cinematography by: Vilmos Zsigmond
Sound: Gary Alper
Editing: Alisa Lepselter
Art Direction: Tom Warren
Costumes: Judy Ruskin
Production Design: Santo Loquasto
MPAA rating: PG-13
Running time: 99 minutes

REVIEWS

Boxoffice Online. March, 2005.
Chicago Sun-Times Online. March 23, 2005.
Entertainment Weekly Online. March 16, 2005.
Los Angeles Times Online. March 23, 2005.
New York Times Online. March 18, 2005.
Premiere Magazine Online. March 17, 2005.
Variety Online. September 19, 2004.
Washington Post Online. March 25, 2005, p. WE33.

MEMOIRS OF A GEISHA

Box Office: $13.2 million

Arthur Golden's *Memoirs of a Geisha* was a hit with critics and readers in 1997. Reviewers praised the novel's historical detail, compelling narrator/protagonist, and insight into a foreign culture little understood by Westerners. The book sold more than four million copies in English and was translated into thirty-three languages. Steven Spielberg snapped up the film rights and planned to direct the project. After many delays, *Memoirs of a Geisha* was eventually assigned to Rob Marshall, the former choreographer fresh off the critical and commercial success of his first theatrical film, *Chicago* (2002). The resulting film skims the surface of Golden's novel without ever truly coming to life.

In a poor Japanese fishing village in the 1920's, a desperate, widowed father (Mako) sells his young daughters, Chiyo (Suzuka Ohgo) and Satsu (Samantha Futerman). The girls are taken to a village near Osaka and are separated, with the nine-year-old Chiyo becoming trained by the dictatorial Mother (Kaori Momoi) to become a geisha. With her friend Pumpkin (Zoe Weizenbaum), Chiyo learns to perform the duties of a geisha, including dancing and the tea ceremony. After a kindly gesture by a wealthy businessman known only as the Chairman (Ken Watanabe), Chiyo becomes obsessed with him.

As she grows older, the girl is renamed Sayuri (Ziyi Zhang) and is tutored by the older geisha Mameha (Michelle Yeoh). Sayuri learns that a geisha's virginity is to be auctioned off to the highest bidder and that each geisha comes under the protection of a wealthy man. Mameha's protector is the Baron (Cary-Hiroyuki Tagawa), who has eyes for Sayuri, as do all the men she encounters. Sayuri develops an attachment to the Chairman's friend Nobu (Kôji Yakusho). Mameha convinces Sayuri that because Nobu's face has been badly scarred during the conflict between Japan and China, no other geisha will become jealous and try to interfere in her life.

Sayuri's main rival is the older geisha Hatsumomo (Gong Li), who has resented her since she was a little girl. Hatsumomo, aging and losing her influence, takes out her frustrations on Sayuri whenever possible. Meanwhile, Pumpkin (Youki Kudoh), while pretending to be Sayuri's friend, also becomes resentful and plots against her. All Sayuri wants is some attention from the Chairman, but her life, seen through the end of World War II, is never that simple.

Screenwriters Robin Swicord, whose most notable credit is for Gillian Armstrong's excellent *Little Women* (1994), and Doug Wright streamline Golden's novel, hitting all the high points and eliminating Sayuri's later life, which includes moving to New York with her son. As with too many adaptations of novels, what is missing is Sayuri's narrative voice, though it is heard in voiceover a few times, and any psychological depth. With the exception of Mameha and Nobu, none of the characters are more than two dimensional.

As with the screenplay, Marshall's direction is serviceable but unimaginative, moving steadily from scene to scene without really saying anything about the period, the place, or the people, a complaint some have also had about the vastly overrated Chicago. Like that film, *Memoirs of a Geisha*, as many reviewers pointed out, is all about sets and costumes. While Marshall stages Sayuri's one extended dance number quite well, the theatrical effects, with flowing fabrics and flashing lights, seem to owe less to the period than to contemporary Broadway.

Dion Bebe, who shot *Chicago*, as well as the more artful *Collateral*, lights the film beautifully. He and Marshall shoot several street scenes from overhead, much in the style of such Asian directors as Akira Kurosawa and Yimou Zhang. Some painterly effects, especially in the closing scene, are a tad too self-consciously pretty.

Speaking of Zhang, Ziyi Zhang (no relation) and Li fare much better in his films than they do here. *Memoirs of a Geisha* has received some criticism for casting two Chinese and a Malaysian (Yeoh) instead of Japanese performers. Marshall and the producers apparently felt that since the protagonists would be speaking in English, nationality did not matter, and these three actresses have been acclaimed for work quite popular outside Asia. But compare Zhang's performance here to her sensitive work in the thematically similar *2046* to see what is missing in Sayuri. Zhang captures the surface emotions but not the depth. Li, a truly great actress in such films as *Raise the Red Lantern* (1991) and *Farewell, My Concubine* (1993), is reduced to playing a clichéd dragon lady. Both actresses have worked in English before, Zhang in *Rush Hour 2* (2001) and Li in *Chinese Box* (1997), but they seem at a loss. Poor Li sounds like she has rocks in her mouth. Despite the success of such films *as Crouching Tiger, Hidden Dragon* (2002), starring Zhang and Yeoh, the producers did not have the courage to make *Memoirs of a Geisha* in Japanese with subtitles, almost dooming it to artistic failure to start with.

Yeoh, who speaks English quite well in *Tomorrow Never Dies* (1997), fares much better, investing the underwritten character with dignity and pathos. Watanbe, who has appeared memorably in *The Last Samurai* (2003) and *Batman Begins* (2005), conveys the Chairman's sensitivity, though the character is primarily a symbol of Sayuri's ambitions. Best known for *Shall We Dance?* (1996) and *The Eel* (1997), Yakusho is working in English for the first time but is outstanding at displaying how Nobu's self-pitying gruffness is slowly melted by being with Sayuri.

Stripped of its essence, *Memoirs of a Geisha* resembles the Hollywood soap operas of the 1930's, 1940's, and 1950's in which the point was to put the heroine, often played by Bette Davis, Joan Crawford, Barbara Stanwyck, or Jane Wyman, through various trials before she finally gets her man. *Memoirs of a Geisha*, unfortunately, has the same type of conventional, seemingly tacked-on, conclusion.

Michael Adams

CREDITS

The Chairman: Ken(saku) Watanabe
Mameha: Michelle Yeoh
Nobu: Koji Yakusho
Pumpkin: Youki Kudoh
Aunti: Tsai Chin
The Baron: Cary-Hiroyuki Tagawa
Hatsumomo: Gong Li
Dr. Crab: Randall Duk Kim
Sakamoto: Mako
The General: Kenneth Tsang
Sayuri Narrator: Shizuko Hoshi
Sayuri: Ziyi Zhang
Mother: Kaori Momoi
Chiyo: Suzuka Ohgo
Mr. Bekku: Thomas Ikeda
Young Pumpkin: Zoe Weizenbaum
Origin: USA
Language: English
Released: 2005
Production: Lucy Fisher, Douglas Wick, Steven Spielberg; Columbia Pictures, Dreamworks Pictures, Spyglass Entertainment, Amblin Entertainment, Red Wagon Films, Inc.; released by Sony Pictures Entertainment
Directed by: Rob Marshall
Written by: Robin Swicord
Cinematography by: Dion Beebe
Music by: John Williams
Sound: John Pritchett
Editing: Pietro Scalia
Art Direction: Patrick M. Sullivan Jr.
Costumes: Colleen Atwood
MPAA rating: PG-13
Running time: 137 minutes

REVIEWS

Boxoffice Online. December, 2005.
Chicago Sun-Times Online. December 16, 2005.
Entertainment Weekly Online. December 7, 2005.
Los Angeles Times Online. December 9, 2005.
New York Times Online. December 9, 2005.
Premiere Magazine Online. December 9, 2005.
Variety Online. November 20, 2005.
Washington Post Online. December 16, 2005, p. C01.

QUOTES

Mameha: "A true geisha can stop a man in his tracks with a single look."

TRIVIA

Steven Spielberg Brett Ratner, Spike Jonze and Kimberly Peirce, all considered directing this film.

AWARDS

Oscars 2005: Art Dir./Set Dec., Cinematog., Costume Des.
British Acad. 2005: Cinematog., Costume Des., Orig. Score
Golden Globes 2006: Orig. Score
Natl. Bd. of Review 2005: Support. Actress (Li)
Broadcast Film Critics 2005: Orig. Score

Nomination:

Oscars 2005: Sound, Orig. Score
British Acad. 2005: Actress (Ziyi), Makeup
Golden Globes 2006: Actress—Drama (Ziyi)
Screen Actors Guild 2005: Actress (Ziyi)
Broadcast Film Critics 2005: Film, Soundtrack.

THE MERCHANT OF VENICE

(William Shakespeare's The Merchant of Venice)

Box Office: $3.7 million

Michael Radford's *The Merchant of Venice* is right at home sitting next to a compendium of other Shakespearean *adaptations.* On that shelf you may also find Baz Luhrman's energetic *Romeo + Juliet* (1996), *O* (adaptation of *Othello*; 2001); or *10 Things I Hate About You* (adaptation of *Taming of the Shrew;* 1999). Radford's *Merchant of Venice* includes Shakespearean trained actors such as Jeremy Irons (*Richard II* for the Royal Shakespeare Company) and Joseph Fiennes (*Troilus and Cressida* for the RSC) as opposed to teen stars. In fact, over all the film looks and sounds more "Shakespearean," so why is it that these adaptations (*Romeo + Juliet* containing twenty-five percent of the text and the others containing no verse at all) and Radford's *The Merchant of Venice* are in the same camp?

The Merchant of Venice opens with sinister monks who look like they've just returned from the auto-da-fe gliding through Venetian waters. Then in grand George Lucas style, the formidable words scroll up the screen, "Intolerance of the Jews was a fact of 16th century life even in Venice, the most powerful and liberal city-state in Europe." We are given a further history lesson on intolerance, this time about the Jewish ghettos. Though this certainly gives us a setting and a mood for the story, it has little to do with Shakespeare's problem comedy.

Then the story finally begins: a Venetian merchant (Antonio played by a craggy Jeremy Irons) is asked by his young friend Bassanio (Joseph Fiennes) to help finance a romantic adventure. The father of a rich heiress named Portia (Lynn Collins) has died. In his will he has left explicit demands on how she is to be married. Three caskets of gold, silver, and "base" lead are to be chosen by the intended suitor. In one casket contains Portia's picture (that means marriage), and other two (well, not so good.) But Bassanio has been a bit liberal with his moneys and needs 3,000 ducats to approach the contest. Antonio's ships are at sea, but they decide to borrow from Shylock, a Jewish usurer. Shylock will lend the money on one condition that the forfeiture will be a pound of Antonio's flesh, nearest his heart.

The film continues to Antonio, who already looks suicidal, uttering the words, "In truth, I know not why I am so sad." Note: Shakespeare's opening line is, "In sooth, I know not why I am so sad." We then are introduced to another bold choice on the part of Radford: a homosexual relationship between Antonio and Bassanio.

Now this is by no means a new idea: hundreds of stage productions have alluded to Antonio and Bassanio being better than great mates. But Radford doesn't let the suspense build. He does not allow for there to be a possibility of a relationship on the brink of sexual fruition, or that a consummation is out of the question. Instead we see Bassanio and Antonio kiss in the first scene, a kiss that will never be mentioned or used again in the film. (Note: Observe Trevor Nunn's *Merchant of Venice* where David Bamber's Antonio seductively toys with Bassanio, but is never bold enough to kiss him.)

We are then introduced to Lynn Collins Portia who appears to have two facial expressions: a large smile or large eyes that convey dense confusion. Lynn Collins has a certain vitality and warmth on the screen, but none of Portia's intellect. As with many of Shakespeare's great heroines, Portia begins as a naïve girl and ends as a mature woman. Lynn Collins does not appear to grow throughout the story.

Then there is Al Pacino's Shylock, a shabby fellow in long robes and impressive hat, in meeting Bassanio at what appears to be a meat market (the cleverest choice in the film). Pacino is a grouchy, hunched, mumbling Shylock who rarely conveys guile, desperation, or rage. Even when Pacino delivers the famous "Hath not a Jew eyes" passage, his eyes tend to wander as though he were reading off of cue cards.

Pacino is not helped by the fact that Shakespeare's Shylock is unrecognizable in delivery. Here are a few of many textual changes:

Shakespeare: Sufficient Radford: good credit
Shakespeare: supposition Radford: question

Shakespeare: baned	Radford: killed
Shakespeare: carrion flesh	Radford: human flesh

Especially in the last example, the meaning is twisted to a point of breaking. Carrion is decaying flesh a much stronger image than human flesh, which could be healthy, or not. There is a great misunderstanding that Shakespeare wrote in Old English (i.e. Chaucer) but this is not the case. Although some words may be archaic, Shakespeare actually wrote in Modern English.

Great verse speaking in Shakespeare has been often compared to great jazz. Both have a form that can be twisted, turned, and changed almost to breaking point. When Pacino speaks Shakespeare in this film he constantly is breaking the natural rhythms in the text (and Shylock speaks quite a bit of prose!) Lengthy "Pinteresque" pauses (for which Pacino is a main offender) are placed throughout the film, a prime example used in many of the trailers.

"Shylock......................."

"…….is my name."

Radford (best know for the film *Il Postino*) has shot a beautiful film. There are gorgeous views of the palaces of Belmont, the claustrophobic atmosphere of the market and the trial scene, and a beautiful feel of the 16th century throughout. Yet there is something hollow about the overall effect. Beautiful Italian costumes and period settings do not make up for the lack of clarity and an overall sluggishness in the storytelling. Lack of subtlety and clumsy comedy in the treatment of Old Gobbo (a character often cut, though played with simple honesty by Shakespearean Ron Cook) add to a desired sentimentality in the film. Yet the lack of subtlety that could be attributed to these extremely multi-dimensional characters, creates an adverse effect. The film becomes long, tedious, and screaming for us to cry and feel for these characters. Radford really strikes his gold only when Shylock's daughter stares at her ring in the closing shots as she overlooks Belmont waters. But showing Al Pacino being locked into the Jewish ghetto destroys so many possibilities: maybe he committed suicide, maybe he's rousing the troops, maybe he attempted to flee the country? Shakespeare lets our "imaginary forces work," Radford does not.

Shakespeare's story is by no means easy: anti-Semitism and prejudice are a major part of the play. Yet Radford even makes this too easy: by heralding that the Christians are the "bad guys" to Shylock from the word "go." Since Pacino's Shylock never appears to be of much of a threat (they even spit on him during the trial scene, when he has a knife to their friends neck!) we are manipulated into feeling bad for Shylock because he is a Jew in an unjust society and angry with the dour, homosexual Antonio for making him a Christian. This conclusion is helped by antithetical shots of praying Jews with whoring Christians.

By the time we have made it to the famous "trial" scene in which Shylock attempts to extract his grisly bond, the film has already lost interest. When Shylock is forced to become a Christian (one of the plays most chilling moments), Al Pacino's classical yarmulke is nonchalantly knocked to the ground by one of the many blustering Christians on his way off the set. This moment, like many others in Michael Radford's *The Merchant of Venice,* just don't seem to have very high stakes.

Richard Baird

CREDITS

Shylock: Al Pacino
Antonio: Jeremy Irons
Bassanio: Joseph Fiennes
Jessica: Zuleikha Robinson
Gratiano: Kris Marshall
Nerissa: Heather Goldenhersch
Salerio: John Sessions
Lancelot Gobbo: Mackenzie Crook
Solanio: Gregor Fisher
Old Gobbo: Ron Cook
Tubal: Allan Corduner
The Duke: Anton Rodgers
Portia: Lynn Collins
Lorenzo: Charlie Cox
Origin: USA
Language: English
Released: 2004
Production: Cary Brokaw, Barry Navidi, Jason Piette, Michael Cowan; Spice Factory; released by Sony Pictures Classics
Directed by: Michael Radford
Written by: Michael Radford
Cinematography by: Benoit Delhomme
Music by: Jocelyn Pook
Sound: Brian Simmons, Paul Davies
Editing: Lucia Zucchetti
Costumes: Sammy Sheldon
Production Design: Bruno Rubeo
MPAA rating: R
Running time: 138 minutes

REVIEWS

Boxoffice Online. January, 2005.
Chicago Sun-Times Online. January 21, 2005.
Entertainment Weekly Online. January 5, 2005.

Los Angeles Times Online. December 29, 2004.
New York Times Online. December 29, 2004.
Premiere Magazine Online. February 10, 2005.
Variety Online. September 6, 2004.
Washington Post Online. January 28, 2005, p. WE36.

QUOTES

Shylock: "If you prick us, do we not bleed? If you poison us, do we not die? And if you wrong us, shall we not revenge?"

TRIVIA

Ian McKellen was originally cast as Antonio, but was forced to drop at the last minute due to scheduling conflicts. Cate Blanchett was set to play Portia, but had to drop out after discovering she was pregnant and Dustin Hoffman was contacted director Michael Radford about playing Shylock, but Al Pacino had already been cast.

MILK & HONEY

Modern marriage looks pretty curdled and bitter in *Milk & Honey*, a flawed but well-meaning "indie." Joe Maggio's sophomore directing effort lacks the impact of his first feature, the ultra low-budget *Virgil Bliss,* though the new film at least starts out well.

Milk & Honey centers on Rick Johnson (Clint Jordan), a New York stockbroker who emerges from a recent mental collapse by throwing a party with his wife of ten years, Joyce (Kirsten Russell). Unfortunately, during the fete with his friends, Rick's mental insecurity reappears when he aggressively and publicly re-proposes marriage to Joyce and she politely declines.

The proposal incident abruptly ends the party and the couple's guests leave. What follows is an all-night, all-day journey for both Rick and Joyce. First, Rick storms out of the apartment and drops in on his former girlfriend, Katie (Eleanor Hutchins). But Katie also argues with Rick when Rick becomes jealous about another man she is dating. Later, Rick sees his therapist, Dudley (Greg Amici), but instead of having a productive session, Rick steals a bottle of gin and leaves. Finally, after a few drinks, Rick contemplates jumping off the Queensboro bridge.

In the meantime, Joyce tries desperately to find Rick, but has little luck. She begins by asking her good friend, Maud, to help. During their search, Joyce confesses to Maud about her affair with a musician named Patrick, which had earlier caused problems in her marriage. In addition, Patrick's recent death had triggered even more heartache for Joyce; thus, she is shocked when she goes to a party with Maud and sees a man, Tony (Anthony Howard), who looks like Patrick. Joyce is so taken with Tony, she momentarily stops her search for Rick and goes home with Tony for a night of passion.

At the same time, Rick requests a stranger he meets in a diner, Moses (Dudley Findlay, Jr.), to kill him. In return, Rick promises to pay Moses with the expensive engagement ring Joyce rejected earlier. Moses agrees to the plan, but instead mugs Rick and flees. Later, Rick is mugged again by another man and taken to a nearby hospital. At the facility, Rick notices an elderly woman dying in her bed; the woman turns out to be Moses's mother!

The next morning, Joyce attempts to duplicate her romance with Patrick through Tony, but quickly realizes her mistake when Tony's young girlfriend shows up and Tony doesn't even remember Joyce's name. Joyce races back to her apartment, where she reunites with Rick—and considers holding on to their love and their marriage.

In *Virgil Bliss,* writer-director Maggio displayed a strength for developing down-and-out characters trying to make their lives better. In the same vein, Joyce and Rick are clearly troubled, even unpleasant, but they elicit audience sympathy and understanding. With the aid of actors Clint Jordan and Kirsten Russell, Maggio neatly illustrates a rounded, incisive portrayal of a marriage at crisis point..

Sadly, Maggio doesn't seem to trust his audience with the simple idea of closely examining this complicated union, because he weighs down *Milk & Honey* with gratuitous supporting characters and wild, unlikely plot twists and turns. If the film had been a simple, though agonizing, character study in the tradition of Bergman's classic, *Scenes from a Marriage*, then *Milk & Honey* might have been worthwhile. But this melodramatic, high-pitched work owes itself more to Stanley Kubrick's over-stuffed *Eyes Wide Shut,* only without the gothic ambiance and claustrophobic intensity. Did Maggio add so many narrative elements because he didn't feel audiences today wouldn't tolerate a straight chamber piece? Perhaps, he should have looked other two-character, urban-based male-female studies, like Tom Noonan's *What Happened Was....*

While critics found elements to appreciate about the Kubrick and Noonan films, very few could recommend *Milk & Honey.* Ed Gonzalez in *Slant Magazine.com* wrote: "The film aspires to Greek tragedy, and while the unfortunate events that happen to Rick and Joyce do give way to some kind of catharsis, it's not a revelation that feels particularly earned or eye-opening." In the March 13, 2005 *Film Threat,* Merle Bertrand agreed: "Strangely, as improbably interconnected as all these events eventually become, *Milk & Honey* isn't nearly as confusing as it might sound. Unfortunately, it's not quite as interesting as it sounds either, despite sterling performances from its ensemble cast."

Stylistically *Milk & Honey* recalls another indie feature, Woody Allen's *Husbands and Wives,* as Maggio and cinematographer Gordon Chou use the once-fashionable shaky camerawork style that made that flawed Woody Allen film challenging to watch (without getting dizzy). Renowned indie director Hal Hartley contributed the music to the film (along with Yo La Tengo and Fischerspooner), but the score hardly saves the picture.

Milk & Honey endorses a noble purpose and offers a few genuine moments, but never becomes a noble or genuine film.

Eric Monder

CREDITS

Rick Johnson: Clint Jordan
Joyce Johnson: Kirsten Russell
Katie: Eleanor Hutchins
Moses Jackson: Dudley Findlay Jr.
Tony: Anthony Howard
Dudley: Greg Amici
Origin: USA
Language: English
Released: 2003
Production: Thierry Cagianut, Matthew Myers; released by Wellspring Media
Directed by: Joe Maggio
Written by: Joe Maggio
Cinematography by: Gordon Chou
Music by: Hal Hartley, Yo La Tengo
Editing: Seth Anderson
Art Direction: Nick Stavrides
Production Design: Bryce (Paul Mama) Williams
MPAA rating: Unrated
Running time: 91 minutes

REVIEWS

New York Times Online. March 18, 2005.
Variety Online. February 2, 2003.
Village Voice Online. March 15, 2005.

MILLIONS

Can anyone be truly good?
—Movie tagline

Box Office: $6.5 million

Millions is an unlikely film coming from screenwriter Frank Cottrell Boyce and director Danny Boyle, whose previous efforts have a much harder edge than this childhood whimsy. *Millions* is an inventive, charming film that turns sappy a bit toward its conclusion.

Young brothers Damian (Alexander Nathan Etel) and Anthony (Lewis Owen McGibbon) move to a new home in the north of England with their father, Ronnie (James Nesbitt), after the death of their mother. They quickly adapt to new surroundings and a new school, with Anthony, the older brother, showing Damian how to use their mother's death to get sympathy and free stuff.

Damian gets much more than he expects while playing near the neighboring railway when a large bag of money lands at his feet. After counting the £229,370, the brothers decide to keep the loot secret, but they must do something with it soon because the euro is about to displace the pound. They have only seventeen days to spend or convert the money.

Another option is to give it away. This possibility appeals strongly to Damian because of his obsession with Catholic saints. He wants to do good and hopes to see his late mother become a saint, too. With perfect innocence, Damian asks strangers if they are poor and buys them food or tries to give them money.

Damian is dismayed to learn that the money, destined to be burned, was stolen from a train. When the thief (Christopher Fulford) who was supposed to have picked up the bag arrives, Damian thinks he is another poor person, only for Anthony to see the evil his brother is immune to.

Eventually, the truth is discovered by Ronnie and his new lady friend, Dorothy (Daisy Donovan), who decide to convert as much of the money as they can before the deadline. The four protagonists and the thief come together at a nativity pageant at Damian and Anthony's school.

Millions is full of small, delightful moments, as when the neighborhood policeman (Pearce Quigley) explains, with considerable clumsiness, that Ronnie and his neighbors can expect to be robbed during the holiday season. Then there are Damian's encounters with St. Clare (Kathryn Pogson), St. Francis (Enzo Cilenti), St. Nicholas (Harry Kirkham), St. Peter (Alun Armstrong), and St. Joseph (Nasser Memarzia). Damian, whose visions are inspired both by his reading and by his encounters with adults, is somewhat surprised that saints smoke and curse. There is a lovely moment when Damian disappears from the nativity play and Joseph steps in to play himself.

Millions, like *In America* (2002), benefits enormously through the casting of realistic, unmannered child actors.

Etel, who resembles the young Jerry Mathers, effortlessly conveys Damian's naivety and bewilderment. He has considerable presence, and Boyle composes many shots around the boy's expressive face. Anthony Dod Mantle, whose credits include Boyle's *28 Days Later* (2002) and Lars von Trier's *Dogville* (2003), alternates between naturalistic and fanciful lighting, creating some shots that resemble the muted tones of 1950's British films. This effect adds to the film's otherworldly qualities.

In addition to *28 Days Later,* Boyle has also directed *Shallow Grave* (1994) and *Trainspotting* (1996), all seemingly worlds away from that of *Millions.* Yet this film resembles Boyle's other work in juggling several characters and constantly shifting between humor and other emotions. *Millions* also shows Boyle's skill at pacing a film and employing odd compositions. Boyle uses unusual camera angles occasionally to underscore the psychology of the characters.

Boyce is best known for such adult fare as *Welcome to Sarajevo* (1997), *Hilary and Jackie* (1998), and *24 Hour Party People* (2002). The father of seven children, he was inspired by stories he made up for one of his sons. Boyce, who appears as the teacher responsible for the nativity play, has also published *Millions* as a children's book.

It is misleading to characterize *Millions* as a children's film because much of it is likely to be frightening or, at least, confusing for younger children, and Damian does discover his father and Dorothy in bed together. While the adventure of the loot and the mixture of realistic and whimsical touches should appeal to children, the extremely well handled theme of lost innocence is more likely to resonate with adult viewers.

Michael Adams

CREDITS

Damian: Alex(ander Nathan) Etel
Anthony: Lewis Owen McGibbon
Ronnie: James Nesbitt
The Man: Christopher Fulford
St. Peter: Alun Armstrong
St. Clare: Kathryn Pogson
Himself: Leslie Phillips
Dorothy: Daisy Donovan
Community Policeman: Pearce Quigley
Mum: Jane Hogarth
St. Francis: Enzo Cilenti
St. Joseph: Nasser Memarzia
St. Nicholas: Harry Kirkham
Gonzaga: Cornelius Macarthy
Ambrosio: Kolade Agboke
Language: English
Released: 2005
Production: Graham Broadbent, Damian Jones, Andrew Hauptman; Mission Pictures; released by Pathe, Fox Searchlight
Directed by: Danny Boyle
Written by: Frank Cottrell Boyce
Cinematography by: Anthony Dod Mantle
Music by: John Murphy
Sound: Dennis Cartwright
Editing: Chris Gill
Costumes: Susannah Buxton
Production Design: Mark Tidesley
MPAA rating: PG
Running time: 97 minutes

REVIEWS

Boxoffice Online. March, 2005.
Chicago Sun-Times Online. March 18, 2005.
Entertainment Weekly Online. March 9, 2005.
Los Angeles Times Online. March 11, 2005.
New York Times Online. March 11, 2005.
Variety Online. September 13, 2004.
Washington Post Online. March 18, 2005, p. WE45.

QUOTES

Damian Cunningham (voiceover): "The French have said au revoir to the franc. The Germans have said auf widersehn to the mark."

MINDHUNTERS

For seven elite profilers, finding a serial killer is a process of elimination. Their own.
—Movie tagline

Quarter to Death.
—Movie tagline

They are America's best. Their identities are protected. Their missions are highly classified. Can they survive the final assignment?
—Movie tagline

The killer isn't any smarter than they are. That's because it's one of them.
—Movie tagline

Box Office: $4.5 million

In 1939 famed mystery writer Agatha Christie wrote a little gem of a story titled *Ten Little Indians.* It has been the inspiration for many other adaptations since, and one can easily see its influence in this latest film from director Renny Harlin.

The story involves the final exercise of a group of FBI profiler trainees who are taken by their unpleasant instructor Jake Harris (Val Kilmer) to remote Oniega island where, amongst the seedy storefronts and mannequins of a fake main street USA, he has prepared a serial killer simulation called "The Puppeteer." At the last minute, as Harris and his seven students board the helicopter to the now-abandoned, one-time navy operated island, there is one more addition, Detective Gabe Jensen (LL Cool J) of the Philadelphia Police Department who is unknown to all of them and is supposedly there to observe the exercise only and not to participate in it.

Harris shows his charges around the island then takes the helicopter leaving them, as one character states, "isolated, alone and forgotten; like the mind of a sociopath." Before the exercise can even begin, however, something strange happens: a dead cat is found hanging in the washroom with a badge pinned onto its bloody chest and a clock set for ten stuck into it. The group doesn't understand its importance, however, and begins exploring the fake town looking for the fake killer's next pretend victim. They soon find her, a mannequin dangling from fishhooks and ropes in the ceiling of a toy store. As they examine the scene of the fake crime a tape recorder begins playing music and when lead profiler J.D. Reston (Christian Slater) turns it off, he begins a Rube Goldberg cascade of falling dominoes and rolling ball bearings that eventually knock the top of a canister of liquid propane that is aimed directly at J.D., freezing him solid in seconds and sending him crashing to the floor, dead. And it is ten o'clock. It would appear the simulation has suddenly turned very real.

Back at headquarters the group finds another clock and it is set for 12. Quickly they race to the sole boat on the island only to have it explode when they set off a trip wire on the pier. It's not yet noon when they get back to headquarters to discuss their situation over nice, warm cups of coffee...which have been drugged. It is noon when they all pass out and after five when they wake up. Although they believe they have missed the 12 o'clock deadline of death, they suddenly realize another one of them has been drained of his blood and decapitated while they were sleeping. And then they find two watches and they're both set for six o'clock.

One by one, the future profilers are killed off and watches found to indicate when the next ingenious murder will take place. Soon the profilers are suspecting and profiling each other only to eventually grasp that the killer is profiling them and inventing a death that plays on each of their weaknesses or strengths: the leader, the go-to guy, the smoker, the guy who won't give up his gun, the one afraid of water. And when they are told that wild-card Gabe is really with the department of Justice and is investigating Harris and his teaching techniques, they are also soon wondering if Harris actually left the island after all.

There are certain inevitable questions audiences try to answer as this type of story unfolds. In what order will the characters die (and at least *Mindhunters* breaks convention by getting rid of its most well known actors early), who might appear dead or missing but isn't really, and will show up again when least expected, and who's the killer and why is he killing. There are a lot of good red herrings in the film from the scientific (DNA matches) to the historic (a clue referring to the lost colony of Roanoke's last message CROATOAN invisibly written letter-by-letter on their backs), but even after sifting them out, viewers will probably feel cheated because there is no way they can figure out who the killer is and what his/her motives are until the killer actually presents him/herself and explains.

It is unfortunate that scriptwriters Wayne Kramer and Kevin Brodbin took an intriguing premise and instead of emphasizing the intelligence and technique that would be necessary to solve this story instead just used it as an excuse for blood, gore and action. And although the murders are, indeed, quite ingenious, one begins to realize how thoroughly impossible it would be for anyone to set them up with the complexity and precision required in the brief time allotted.

Mindhunters was on the Miramax/Dimension shelves for a long time. It saw three release dates come and go, was released overseas first, and seemed destined to go straight to video in America. This kind of history would lead one to believe that no one had any faith in the film and that's why it was dumped into theaters one week before the last *Star Wars* episode swatted all weak movies off their screens. While there is a lot of mindlessness to *Mindhunters,* taken for what it is, a violent, improbable story acted out by interchangeable actors, then one won't be disappointed.

Beverley Bare Buehrer

CREDITS

Jake Harris: Val Kilmer

J.D. Reston: Christian Slater

Gabe Jensen: LL Cool J

Bobby Whitman: Eion Bailey

Vince Sherman: Clifton (Gonzalez) Collins Jr.

Rafe Perry: Will(iam) Kemp

Lucas Harper: Jonny Lee Miller

Sara Moore: Kathryn Morris

Nicole Willis: Patricia Velasquez

Origin: USA, Great Britain, Netherlands, Finland

Language: English
Released: 2005
Production: Jeffrey Silver, Robert Newmyer, Cary Brokaw, Rebecca Spikings; Weed Road Pictures; released by Miramax
Directed by: Renny Harlin
Written by: Wayne Kramer, Kevin Brodbin
Cinematography by: Robert Gantz
Music by: Tuomas Kantelinen
Sound: Marcel DeHoogd
Music Supervisor: Joe Rangel
Editing: Paul Martin Smith, Neil Farrell
Art Direction: Marco Rooth
Costumes: Louise Frogley
Production Design: Charles Wood
MPAA rating: R
Running time: 106 minutes

REVIEWS

Boxoffice Online. May, 2005.
Chicago Sun-Times Online. May 12, 2005.
Entertainment Weekly Online. May 11, 2005.
Los Angeles Times Online. May 13, 2005.
New York Times Online. May 13, 2005.
Premiere Magazine Online. May 13, 2005.
Variety Online. May 4, 2005.
Washington Post Online. May 13, 2005, p. C05.

QUOTES

Harris: "Here we are. Crimetown USA. Where all the residents are dead...or about to be."

TRIVIA

J.D. is the name of the character played by Christian Slater and also the name of his character in *Heathers* (1989).

MISS CONGENIALITY 2: ARMED AND FABULOUS

Box Office: $48.4 million

Gracie Hart returns. Although it's been five years since Sandra Bullock did the original *Miss Congeniality* (back in 2000), it's only three weeks in movie time. Gracie, having saved the day at the Miss United States beauty pageant, is back at FBI headquarters in New York involved in an undercover operation on a gang of bank robbing housewives. Only Gracie's cover gets blown when she is recognized and things go bad (although not too bad since this is a comedy). Soon Gracie's boss McDonald (Ernie Hudson) is telling the agent that she's too famous for field work and she has a choice—either take a desk job or become the official face of the FBI. She also meets her petite new nemesis, Agent Sam Fuller (Regina King), who's been transferred for anger management issues. They take an immediate and physically aggressive dislike to each other. Gracie's day just gets worse when her would-be beau, Agent Eric Matthews (played by Benjamin Bratt in the first flick), breaks up with her over the phone and she finds out he's been transferred.

Depressed, Gracie tells McDonald that she'll become an "FBI Barbie" and even gets her own swishy style consultant, Joel (Diedrich Bader), to remind her not to snort, hit, or chew with her mouth open. Ten months later, Gracie is indeed plastic perfection as a ghostwritten bestseller on her exploits has her appearing on talk shows, including chatting with Regis Philbin who gets on the wrong end of a self-defense lesson given by Agent Fuller. But Gracie's rejuvenated when she learns that her best friend Cheryl Frazier (Heather Burns), the reigning Miss United States, and pageant host Stan Fields (William Shatner), have been kidnapped in Las Vegas. McDonald sends Gracie out to handle publicity with Fuller as her very unhappy bodyguard (along with the ever-present Joel).

Gracie isn't exactly welcomed with open arms at the FBI office in Vegas, which is headed by the slickly officious Walter Collins (Treat Williams) who doesn't want Gracie to actually help solve the crime but just to smile and schmooze the press. He assigns her Agent Jeff Foreman (Enrique Murciano), a milquetoast firmly under the control of his girlfriend and fellow agent Janet (Elisabeth Rohm), as her liaison. However, Gracie can't leave the investigation alone and gets a clue about a limo driver and a drag Dolly Parton, which leads to Gracie chasing the real Dolly Parton through a hotel lobby (one of the many by-the-numbers scenes) and embarrassing the bureau. Collins takes Gracie off the case and tries to send her and Sam back to New York.

By now, Gracie has figured out that Stan (who owes money to loan sharks) was the real target of the kidnappers, a couple of muscle-bound brothers named Karl (Nick Offerman) and Lou (Abraham Benrubi). She sends Foreman into the FBI office to get more info and he not only blows the assignment but also learns that his girlfriend Janet has been fooling around with Walter. Collins once again tries to send Gracie and Sam back to New York and once again they have their own agenda. This time it involves talking to fake Dolly at the Oasis drag club, which also involves Sam dressing up as Tina Turner and Gracie in a yellow showgirl costume, complete with a lot of flowing boas (when Bullock shakes her tailfeather, she has lots of feathers to shake), as her back-up singer. (The costume makes no particular sense for the scene as it's hardly something someone working for Tina Turner would wear for a performance but, of course, the costume is important for other reasons). They then have to perform a lip-synched version of "Proud Mary" before they can actually get any information. This leads Gracie and Sam to the Treasure Island hotel, which lives up to its name by featuring a nightly pirate attack and a sinking ship in the hotel's outside lagoon. The kidnappers have tied Cheryl and Stan below the deck so they'll drown (they never really wanted the money but were after revenge for being fired by the hotel—yada, yada, yada).

Gracie and Sam kick brotherly butt in the casino and Gracie learns where Cheryl and Stan are being held and goes to the rescue with Collins belatedly getting to the scene. Stan and Cheryl get free (as—oh no!—the water inside the hull of the pirate ship rises ever higher) but that darned boa on her costume traps Gracie. Naturally, Sam rescues her in the nick of time since they've now bonded over the fact that they're really both just tough chicks out to do their job. Gracie takes care of the smarmy Collins by accidentally pushing him into the hotel lagoon; goofy Foreman bonds with the good-hearted Cheryl; Stan promises to stop gambling; and McDonald makes Gracie and Sam official partners. And then there's a really useless end scene about Gracie and a public school visit and being true to yourself and the movie could have ended at least 10 minutes earlier, no harm done.

Which it really needed to do because this is one draggy (and not just in the dressing-up sense) action/female buddy/comedy. Time may have been kind to Bullock herself (she certainly doesn't look five years older) but it hasn't been kind to the sequel. It's as klutzy as Gracie herself and even the ever-amiable Bullock has to work hard to get any laughs. The 5-foot-8 Bullock and the 5-foot-3 King have a certain oddball visual charm in their scenes together, especially since King's character is the human equivalent of a pit bull, and they bond in a believable girl-power fashion. Even if you can see all of that coming from their first scene. Writer/producer Marc Lawrence, who also worked with Bullock on the first *Miss Congeniality* as well as on *Forces of Nature* and *Two Weeks Notice*, has nothing new to offer the audience. And even the talented Bullock can't carry this load of Hollywood mediocrity.

Christine Tomassini

CREDITS

Gracie Hart: Sandra Bullock
Sam Fuller: Regina King
Jeff Foreman: Enrique Murciano
Stan Fields: William Shatner
McDonald: Ernie Hudson
Cheryl: Heather Burns
Joel: Diedrich Bader
Collins: Treat Williams
Lou Steele: Abraham Benrubi
Karl Steele: Nick Offerman
Janet: Elisabeth Rohm
Origin: USA
Language: English
Released: 2005
Production: Sandra Bullock, Marc Lawrence; Fortis Films; released by Warner Bros.
Directed by: John Pasquin
Written by: Marc Lawrence
Cinematography by: Peter Menzies Jr.
Sound: Marc Weingarten
Music Supervisor: John Houlihan
Editing: Garth Craven
Art Direction: Andrew Max Cahn, Greg Richman
Costumes: Deena Appel
Production Design: Maher Ahmad
MPAA rating: PG-13
Running time: 115 minutes

REVIEWS

Boxoffice Online. March, 2005.
Chicago Sun-Times Online. March 24, 2005.
Entertainment Weekly Online. March 22, 2005.
Los Angeles Times Online. March 24, 2005.
New York Times Online. March 24, 2005.
Premiere Magazine Online. March 23, 2005.
Variety Online. March 20, 2005.
Washington Post Online. March 24, 2005, p. C04.

MR. & MRS. SMITH

Box Office: $186.3 million

Big-budget Hollywood summer films always get tons of pre-release publicity: newspaper and magazine stories, television interviews with the stars, commercials, etc. All this is to ensure that everyone from Portland, Maine, to Portland, Oregon, is aware of the product. Then there is the unpredictable: unexpected, often negative, publicity. Such occurs when a film tests badly with a preview audience and undergoes reediting or reshooting. Or when the tabloids go crazy because of alleged romantic hanky-panky on the set.

Such, alas, is the fate of *Mr. & Mrs. Smith*. In the great tradition of Elizabeth Taylor and Richard Burton in *Cleopatra* (1963) and Meg Ryan and Russell Crowe in *Proof of Life* (2000), *Mr. & Mrs. Smith* received considerable attention for the supposed romance between the stars. Almost always when on-set love overshadows a film's content, that film is a dog. While *Mr. & Mrs. Smith* has a few virtues, it is ultimately a disappointment.

John Smith (Brad Pitt) and Jane Smith (Angelina Jolie) have been married for five or six years. (John's inability to know for sure is a running joke.) He is a construction engineer; she runs an office temp agency. Or so each thinks. Neither seems suspicious that they met in Colombia right in the middle of a drug war. The truth is that each is an assassin for vague government agencies. When these agencies learn that these killers are a married couple, the Smiths are assigned to kill each other.

This plotting is rather clumsily handled in Simon Kinberg's screenplay. It is often difficult to be certain what is happening and for what reasons. Let's just say that a government so inefficient that it takes six years to discover that two employees share the same address deserves what it gets.

Jane and John are willing to kill each other because their marriage has grown rather stale. The film opens cleverly with the couple talking to an unseen marriage counselor. Jane comes off as sincere, while John, who cannot remember when they met, is a bit of a jerk. In terms of their being assassins, Jane seems coolly efficient, and John is a frat boy. When he goes to a remote desert location to intercept a target, he accidentally urinates on his boots. The audience believes Jane is a killer and wonders how John can keep from shooting himself.

Still, these early scenes are the best part of *Mr. & Mrs. Smith,* slowly revealing the emptiness of the Smith marriage, showing occasional humor, as with the counseling scene, and the Smiths' hiding places for their weapons: his are under the garage, hers beneath the stove. And Jolie and Pitt have chemistry and charm enough to keep the film going as it lumbers awkwardly from scene to scene.

Once their identities have been discovered, Jane and John set about trying to kill each other, shooting and throwing things at each other in their luxurious suburban house. This mayhem, ironically, revitalizes their affection for each other.

Kinberg and director Doug Liman do not quite make clear whether their skills with guns and knives—they do keep missing each other, after all—unlock their passions or whether they are simply turned on by the violence, but whatever the case, they are soon making love, despite all the cuts, scratches, and bruises. The humor and sex appeal of this scene are reduced by including on the soundtrack a dreadful version of Bob Dylan's "Lay Lady Lay" by Magnet. The bad arrangement and singing undercut the scene.

This shootout in the suburbs is, unfortunately, only the first of three extended action scenes. The second occurs when goons blow up the Smith residence and chase the couple out of the suburbs. The chase makes up for what it lacks in originality by going on and on and on. This scene leads to the final shootout with the government agents in a huge home-and-garden store, which, strangely enough, also sells clothing so that our heroes can change outfits. This confrontation also goes on and on.

While logic and consistency cannot be expected of big-budget action films, *Mr. & Mrs. Smith* is unusually sloppy. At home, the Smiths fire dozens of bullets at each other and always miss. On the road and in the store, they never miss, and their opponents cannot hit anything. The film ends with Jane and John returning happily to the counselor, all their problems solved. But are their agencies still not after them? They have killed thirty or forty poor anonymous souls, but there are certainly more where they came from.

Mr. & Mrs. Smith has been compared with Danny DeVito's *The War of the Roses,* and it could have worked as a satire of a sterile suburban marriage. The Smiths' too-perfect home and their vacuous neighbors are only a means to an end: men with guns blowing up stuff. Although the Smiths live somewhere in the greater New York metropolitan area, probably Westchester County, a road sign indicating the distance to Los Angeles is plainly visible during the chase scene. It could have easily been digitally altered, but almost everything about *Mr. & Mrs. Smith* indicates the filmmakers' low regard for the audience.

What is most infuriating about *Mr. & Mrs. Smith* is the involvement of Liman, who has directed three very good films. *Swingers* (1996) is a low-key character study with tons of charm. *Go* (1999) is a truly original, comic look at a drug deal gone bad. *The Bourne Identity* (2002) takes well-worn material that should not have worked but does and becomes perhaps the best espionage film since the genre's heyday in the 1960's.

Each of these films is stylish in different ways, showing a masterly touch in terms of the composition of shots and pacing. None of this skill is evident in *Mr. & Mrs. Smith.* In addition to the publicity about the stars' apparent romance, there were also reported tensions between Liman and others, especially Jolie, and stories about delays resulting from the director's inability to make up his mind. Production had to be halted so that Pitt could leave to make *Ocean's Twelve* (2004), but scenes were still being reshot or added weeks before *Mr. & Mrs. Smith* was released. Each of Liman's films has gotten progressively more action oriented. *Mr. & Mrs. Smith* is just too big and too loud.

Jolie has become a star, even won an Oscar, without ever actually appearing in a good film, with *Pushing Tin* (1999) being the best of a mediocre lot. For all its many flaws, *Mr. & Mrs. Smith* is watchable when she is on the screen. She has presence, and something always seems to be going on behind her eyes. Pitt is likable in a role that requires little acting effort. Their star appeal and the curiosity inspired by all the tabloid stories made the film a box-office success, once again proving to the big studios that quality is irrelevant, especially during the summer.

Another problem is that *Mr. & Mrs. Smith* is unusually under-populated. Besides the protagonists, the only other characters of note are Benjamin Diaz (Adam Brody), a callow young agent used as a pawn to set up the Smiths, and Eddie (Vince Vaughn), John's partner. Vaughn, who specializes, like Bruce Dern and Jeff Goldblum, in offbeat line readings, provides much-needed comic relief as an assassin who lives in a ramshackle dwelling with his mother.

More touches like the latter would have enlivened *Mr. & Mrs. Smith* considerably. Reviewers compared the film to John Huston's comic masterpiece *Prizzi's Honor* (1985) because it is also about killers who marry only to have their work interfere with their romance. The big difference between the two is that Huston's film is a character study. In addition to the two protagonists, there are several well-drawn supporting characters, and when Jack Nicholson kills Kathleen Turner, there is an emotional payoff. *Prizzi's Honor* emphasizes the romantic angle more than the violence. *Mr. & Mrs. Smith* is all about the killings and explosions; that the main characters are married is almost an afterthought.

Michael Adams

CREDITS

John Smith: Brad Pitt
Jane Smith: Angelina Jolie
Benjamin Danz: Adam Brody
Eddie: Vince Vaughn
Jasmine: Kerry Washington
Martin Coleman: Chris Weitz
Father: Keith David
Suzy Coleman: Rachael Huntley
Origin: USA
Language: English
Released: 2005
Production: Arnon Milchan, Akiva Goldsman, Lucas Foster, Patrick Wachsberger, Eric McLeod; New Regency Pictures, Summit Entertainment, Weed Road Pictures; released by 20th Century-Fox
Directed by: Doug Liman
Written by: Simon Kinberg
Cinematography by: Bojan Bazelli
Music by: John Powell
Sound: Steve Cantamessa
Music Supervisor: Julianne Jordan
Editing: Michael Tronick
Art Direction: Keith Neely
Costumes: Michael Kaplan
Production Design: Jeff Mann
MPAA rating: PG-13
Running time: 119 minutes

REVIEWS

Boxoffice Online. June, 2005.
Chicago Sun-Times Online. June 9, 2005.
Entertainment Weekly Online. June 8, 2005.
Los Angeles Times Online. June 10, 2005.
New York Times Online. June 10, 2005.
Premiere Magazine Online. June 9, 2005.
Variety Online. May 29, 2005.
Washington Post Online. June 10, 2005, p. WE33.

QUOTES

John Smith: "Come to Daddy."
Jane Smith, *she beats and kicks him*: "Who's your Daddy now?"

TRIVIA

A risqué sex scene between leads Brad Pitt and Angelina Jolie was relegated to the cutting room floor in order to get a wider PG-13 audience.

MRS. HENDERSON PRESENTS

Nudity - Variety - High Society.
—Movie tagline

The show must go on, but the clothes must come off.
—Movie tagline

The delightful *Mrs. Henderson Presents* has a sweet, old-fashioned appeal, telling the familiar story of a group of people putting on a show and battling the forces of adversity to survive and flourish in hard times. Judi Dench stars as Laura Henderson, a plucky widow who, in 1937, finds herself alone and not sure what to do without her husband. When embroidery and charity work do not agree with her, this charmingly eccentric woman buys the old, dilapidated Windmill Theatre in London's West End with the intention of fixing it up and producing live shows even though she has no entertainment experience. She hires a general manager, in essence an artistic director, named Vivian Van Damm (Bob Hoskins, also the film's executive producer), who is every bit the pragmatist that she is, thus beginning a productive, creative, yet contentious relationship.

Directed by Stephen Frears from a screenplay by Martin Sherman, *Mrs. Henderson Presents* is, as the opening tells us, "Inspired by true events," words that almost always guarantee that many liberties have been taken in the translation from real life to the screen. Anchored by a good-hearted love-hate relationship between its two leads, the film has a terrific opening section, a fun, fast-paced theatrical romp full of backstage comedy. The screenplay later becomes a bit clunky, however, taking on subplots that feel underdeveloped and then shifting uneasily to a more serious mood once World War II begins. But Dench and Hoskins, by the very force of personality, make their characters very endearing and thus smooth over the film's rough patches.

Van Damm's musical revues are entertaining, vaudeville-style variety shows called *Revudeville*, whose main innovation is that they run all day. Their main problem, ironically, is their success. Because they are so popular, other theatres copy the format, forcing Mrs. Henderson to try something different. Inspired by the French, she hits on the idea of featuring female nudity in her shows—a revolutionary idea for England at the time—but must get the permission of the Lord Cromer (Christopher Guest), who grants it on the condition that the actresses on stage remain as still as nudes in a painting, thus giving the production a connection to the art world and making it more palatable to polite society. The tableaux vary from the American West to mermaids, and the shows are a resounding success.

The role of Mrs. Henderson seems tailor-made for Dench, who brings her trademark imperiousness to the role, but she also shows a softer, vulnerable side. Mrs. Henderson may have a tart tongue and display loads of gumption, but there is a melancholy center to her, best glimpsed when she is visiting the cemetery in France where her son, a soldier killed in World War I, is buried, or when, in her more pensive moments, she rows out alone to the middle of a river. Hoskins is quite good in being both the hard-driving theatrical director as well as the father figure who genuinely cares about the showgirls, some of whom are understandably nervous about appearing nude and have to be convinced of the artistry involved. Most important, his cautiousness is an ideal foil for Mrs. Henderson's daring and mischievousness. They may do battle, but there is always an underlying affection and respect in their feisty relationship.

But if *Mrs. Henderson Presents* has a major flaw, it is in the screenplay's structure—once the nude show becomes a hit, there are really no obstacles to be overcome, and the film has to manufacture crises to keep the story moving. Mrs. Henderson, for example, becomes jealous and hurt when she learns that Van Damm is married (apparently she was growing very fond of him, although this aspect of her character is not developed at all). But when she vows not to enter the theatre anymore and then resorts to disguises—attending a show in a Chinese costume and auditioning in a polar bear suit—so that she can see what is going on inside, it becomes a petty, silly, and, thankfully, short-lived feud.

The arrival of World War II and the blitz over London bring more challenges and a radical shift in tone from the bubbly, jovial celebration of vaudeville-style naughtiness that animates the first part of the film. The main subplot here involves a key performer named Maureen (a very appealing Kelly Reilly), whom Mrs. Henderson, playing matchmaker, fixes up with an admiring, shy soldier. The romance is very sketchily drawn since we barely know Maureen (no pun intended), and then the romance is cut short when he must go off to the front. Maureen gets pregnant, and the soldier returns to his girlfriend. Then the story ends tragically when a distraught Maureen ventures outside the theatre and is killed during an air raid. Unfortunately, we are meant to interpret the episode as the fault of Mrs. Henderson for meddling, as if she should have foreseen what would happen by encouraging Maureen to take a chance on love. It is a rather odd sequence, a very awkward and unfair way of highlighting Mrs. Henderson's supposed shortsightedness.

The final crisis finds the government trying to close the beloved Windmill because, as a place where people congregate en masse, it is vulnerable to attack. But such a threat prompts a rousing speech from Mrs. Henderson in which she reveals what has been motivating her all along. After her son died in the war, she discovered hidden in his room a French postcard of a naked woman and found it sad that he died without probably ever seeing one in real life. She concludes that the Windmill exists so that other boys going off to war will not have that same misfortune. In another actress's hands, this could be a very corny speech tying a nude musical revue to a sense of patriotism, but Dench delivers it with such compassion and authority that it is actually quite moving, even stirring. Her words win the day, the shows continue, and the Windmill gains fame as the only theatre that never closed during the war.

Mrs. Henderson Presents has such a crowd-pleasing energy and warm feelings of nostalgia that one is willing to forgive its narrative shortcomings and surrender to its show-must-go-on verve. Scenes of auditions, rehearsals, and beautiful musical numbers (not to mention beautiful, naked women) are not only spunky and fun but are refreshing in their innocence. While the film winks at being naughty, it actually has a wholesome feeling. Indeed, were it not for the nudity (always tastefully rendered) and an occasional verbal sexual reference, the film could have been made in Mrs. Henderson's own era. It may be uneven dramatically and indulge in a bit of sentimental uplift, but it does not get weighed down by it, and Dench and Hoskins keep the story grounded with the determination and spirit they bring to their characters. *Mrs. Henderson Presents* is a tribute to the joys of musical theatre and a reminder of how art, even so-called lowbrow entertainment, has the power to touch people's lives.

Peter N. Chumo II

CREDITS

Laura Henderson: Judi Dench
Vivian Van Damm: Bob Hoskins
Lord Cromer: Christopher Guest
Maureen: Kelly Reilly
Bertie: Will Young
Lady Conway: Thelma Barlow
Origin: Great Britain
Language: English
Released: 2005
Production: Norma Heyman; Pathe Pictures, BBC Films, Weinstein Company, U.K. Film Council, Future Films; released by Weinstein Co.
Directed by: Stephen Frears
Written by: Martin Sherman
Cinematography by: Andrew Dunn
Music by: George Fenton
Sound: Peter Lindsay
Editing: Lucia Zucchetti
Art Direction: Tony Woollard
Costumes: Sandy Powell
Production Design: Hugo Luczyc-Wyhowski
MPAA rating: R
Running time: 102 minutes

REVIEWS

Boxoffice Online. December, 2005.
Entertainment Weekly Online. December 7, 2005.
Los Angeles Times Online. December 9, 2005.
New York Times Online. December 9, 2005.
Variety Online. September 9, 2005.

AWARDS

Natl. Bd. of Review 2005: Cast
Nomination:
Oscars 2005: Actress (Dench), Costume Des.
British Acad. 2005: Actress (Dench), Costume Des., Orig. Screenplay, Orig. Score
Golden Globes 2006: Actress—Mus./Comedy (Dench), Film—Mus./Comedy, Support. Actor (Hoskins)
Screen Actors Guild 2005: Actress (Dench)
Broadcast Film Critics 2005: Actress (Dench).

MONDOVINO

Jonathan Nossiter's film *Mondovino* documents the debate between globalization versus individualism in the world's wine industry and how the former is slowly crushing the latter, much like the grapes that provide their livelihood. Four years in the making, Nossiter has crafted a compelling thesis that strips bare the inner workings of an industry that prides itself on quality and personality while at the same time fights for homogeneity. From three continents and seven countries Nossiter assembles hundreds of hours of interviews with participants in the wine business with varying opinions of what it means to be a winemaker, what makes a good wine, and what is best for the future of the industry, that are as varied as the grapes they cultivate. Pared down to just over two hours, *Mondovino* makes for an entertaining, engrossing and compelling study of an industry in turmoil.

Nossiter, a former sommelier and unabashed wine lover, certainly has a point of view. He feels that the industry is in trouble and is too much focused on the quest for wealth. He bookends his film first with a tribe in Northeastern Brazil who make coconut wine just for their village, and finally a man in Tolombon, Argentina who cultivates a tiny field of grapes just to put food on his table, for $60 a month. In between, Nossiter focuses on who he considers the main culprits of this change from a business that has for 2000 years been a localized, artisanal, tradition into a world of mega-conglomerates, ubiquitous wine consultants, and wine critics, who with a good or bad rating could make or break a wine producer. The end result of this alliance is that the wines all have the same plainness and lack of personality, unlike the people.

With his digital camera and small crew, he is allowed access to many of the world's most influential and famous vintners as well as the people who have become indispensable to them. Nossiter first travels to France where he rides along with Michel Rolland, a jocular wine consultant who calls himself a "flying winemaker" who has clients all over the world, visiting them on a regular basis seemingly always advising them that the best way to improve their wine is to "micro-oxygenate" it. It is a term that he knows half of his clients don't understand what it means, and some that don't really care, but they do what he says anyway because he is the expert. They know he knows what good wine is because he is good friends with wine critic Robert Parker, a wine writer for the magazine *Wine Advocate* whose influential rating is coveted in the industry and a good or bad rating could make or break a vintage. The value of Parker to the industry is so important that his nose and palate are insured for one million dollars. In contrast to the view of Rolland, that good saleable wine can be produced through technology, and Parker, who feels that a wine should be familiar, is that of the family wine producers of France and Italy who have held onto their land for generations and feel that wine should have a distinctive taste and personality of the place where it comes from. They feel that wine is the relationship between man and nature and that a true wine maker should not give in to the distractions of the "phantom's of progress."

One of the main culprits of progress is that of the mega-corporation Robert Mondavi Winery in Napa Valley, California. Producing millions of bottles of wine a year, and selling them all over the world, has made millions for their stockholders, who are always looking over their shoulders for the latest profit-to-loss reports, putting pressure on the bottom line which in turn perpetuates a cycle of a quest for profit. Competition is so fierce that the Mondavi family feels the need to grab as much land for their grapes as possible. When one town refuses to let them in, they find a way to get into it anyway. And after they're in, Michel Rolland is there to tell them how to make the wine taste the best, enabling critic Robert Parker to approve it, enabling the vicious circle to continue that Nossiter argues will inevitably smother the industry that he loves.

The director is hardly noticeable in the film, choosing to forego narration, and using a small hand-held camera to shoot his interviews, allowing the participants to tell their own story. The camerawork is non-traditional; its curious gaze often veering from the main subjects to observe the daily workers in the field and the chauffeurs of the rich revealing a subtle commentary on the class structure. But generally, it is most easily distracted by dogs. Some of them very territorial.

David E. Chapple

CREDITS

Origin: USA

Language: English, French, Italian, Portuguese, Spanish

Released: 2004

Production: Jonathan Nossiter, Emmanuel Giraud; Goatworks Films, Diaphana Films, Les Films de la Croisade, Sophie Dulac Prods., Ricardo Preve Films

Directed by: Jonathan Nossiter

Cinematography by: Jonathan Nossiter, Stephanie Pommez

Sound: Nostradine Benguezzou, Juan Pittaluga

Editing: Jonathan Nossiter

MPAA rating: PG-13

Running time: 131 minutes

REVIEWS

Boxoffice Online. March, 2005.

Entertainment Weekly Online. March 23, 2005.

Los Angeles Times Online. April 29, 2005.

New York Times Online. March 23, 2005.

Premiere Magazine Online. March 31, 2005.

Variety Online. May 14, 2004.

MONSIEUR N

History says that Napoleon Bonaparte spent the last six years of his life under British house arrest on St. Helena, an island in the middle of the South Atlantic, before dying of cancer in 1821. *Monsieur N*, written by Rene Manzor and directed by Antoine de Caunes, takes a more romantic view of the deposed emperor's final days. Much more than a biographical film, *Monsieur N* examines why Napoleon remains so compelling.

Most of the film is seen from the point of view of Basil Heathcote (Jay Rodan), a young lieutenant charged with verifying that Napoleon (Phillippe Torreton) remains on the grounds of Longwood, his estate in the center of the island. Heathcote is commanded by St. Helena's governor, Sir Hudson Lowe (Richard E. Grant), a pompous, jealous autocrat who resents Napoleon's relative freedom. Heathcote delivers notes from the governor addressed to General Napoleon only for the recipient to refuse to open them because Lowe does not call him emperor.

Napoleon is surrounded by loyal officers who have voluntarily followed him into exile, and they live much as they would at any military encampment. The toadying General Montholon (Stephane Freiss) will do anything to remain in Napoleon's favor in hopes of being rewarded in his will. He achieves this goal less out of his loyalty than because his beautiful wife, Albine (Elsa Zylberstein) is the latest in a long line of imperial mistresses. Albine prefers the rugged Napoleon to her spineless husband.

Betsy Balcombe (Siobhan Hewlett), a young Englishwoman who lives with her parents, truly loves Napoleon. When Betsy is not being playful, calling him "Boney," she tries to get Napoleon to admit that he loves her as well. Heathcote falls in love with Betsy at first sight, but she ignores him.

Napoleon's supporters in Brazil hatch a plot to rescue him, communicating by a code in the crossword puzzle of a London newspaper. When the conspirators arrive and storm the beach, however, Napoleon not only refuses to go but betrays them to the British. He explains to Lowe that escaping would be admitting that he is a prisoner.

Far from delusional, Napoleon wants to end his exile on his terms. After sending Betsy away in 1818, he is not clearly seen by his jailers for the last three years of his life. If, that is, he in fact died in 1821. The filmmakers' speculation about this matter, which leads Heathcote to Baton Rouge, Louisiana, in 1840, after Napoleon's body has supposedly been returned to Paris, brings *Monsieur N* to an immensely satisfying conclusion.

Except for Abel Gance's magnificent *Napoleon* (1927), one of the greatest silent films, big-screen treatments of the failed world conqueror have not been that impressive. Marlon Brando offers a highly idiosyncratic Napoleon in *Desiree* (1954), a guilty pleasure of a soap opera. More recently, *The Emperor's New Clothes* (2001) presents a comic view of Napoleon's exile. *Monsieur N* may be the best Napoleon film since Gance's because de Caunes and Manzor treat their subject not as a towering historical figure but as a soul tormented by more than his military and political failings. Imagine a Richard M. Nixon with presence and a sense of humor, and that is this Napoleon.

Monsieur N benefits enormously from a wonderful performance by the charismatic Torreton, the star of Bertrand Tavernier's *Capitaine Conan* (1996). Swarthy and, of course, short, Torreton resembles a cross between Jose Ferrer and the English character actor Kenneth Cranham. Despite his ordinary looks, however, Torreton has a star's commanding authority, drawing the eye to him regardless of what else is going on within a frame. When he disappears from sight, the viewer looks for him as intently as does Heathcote.

Torreton is matched by the unconventionally beautiful Hewlett, whose Betsy matures from a coquettish girl to a woman experiencing the pains of an impossible love. A long scene in which Napoleon and Betsy hold each other while she tries to force him to admit that he loves her is the film's apex. Torreton betrays the emperor's feelings without words, almost bursting to tell her how he feels. This scene is more emotionally charged and erotic than much more explicit scenes in any recent commercial film. Such subtlety makes *Monsieur N* a small treasure.

Michael Adams

CREDITS

Napoleon Bonaparte: Philippe Torreton
Hudson Lowe: Richard E. Grant
Basil Heathcote: Jay Rodan
Albine de Montholon: Elsa Zylberstein
Cipriani: Bruno Putzulu
General Montholon: Stephane Freiss
General Gourgaud: Frederic Pierrot
Marshal Bertrand: Roschdy Zem
Betsy Balcombe: Siobhan Hewlett
Origin: Great Britain, France
Language: English, French
Released: 2003
Production: Marie-Castille Mention-Schaar, Pierre Kubel; released by Mars Distribution
Directed by: Antoine de Caunes
Written by: Rene Manzor
Cinematography by: Pierre Aim
Music by: Stephan Eicher
Sound: Dominique Levert, Didier Lozahic
Editing: Joelle Van Effenterre
Costumes: Carine Sarfati
Production Design: Patrick Durand
MPAA rating: Unrated
Running time: 127 minutes

REVIEWS

Los Angeles Times Online. March 11, 2005.
New York Times Online. January 21, 2005.
Premiere Magazine Online. 2005.
Variety Online. February 10, 2003.

MONSTER-IN-LAW

She met the perfect man. Then she met his mother.
—Movie tagline

He gave her a ring. His mom gave her a finger.
—Movie tagline

This relationship is going to be a real mother.
—Movie tagline

Box Office: $82.9 million

Watching Jane Fonda return to motion pictures after a fifteen year absence in *Monster-in-Law* is like bumping into a long-lost, treasured friend who is in the midst of a dreadful case of the flu: one is happy to see the person again, but sure wishes it were under better circumstances. With work in her much-honored past like that in *Klute* (1971), *Julia* (1977), and *Coming Home* (1978), how regrettable that hopes for some sort of remarkable, triumphant return to the silver screen have been dashed by her reemergence in such forgettable fare. Fonda's own advice for enjoying this romantic comedy was,

"Don't think too much," but even uncritical viewers willing to simply grab the popcorn and let the intermittently amusing film wash over them are still likely to notice the things that hobble this *Monster* and, towards the end, suddenly, completely and ridiculously defang it.

The two-time Oscar-winner actually gets second billing to the more contemporary Jennifer Lopez, who takes yet another stab at portraying a bona-fide sweetheart ripe for a meet cute. In introducing her Charlotte "Charlie" Cantilini, there is such bending over backwards to get across what a doll she is that chiropractics may have been necessary. She has an upbeat, genuine, unaffected air about her, smiles warmly, loves animals, and cannot bound out the front door to dogwalk without first kissing framed pictures of loved ones. Her personality is sunny, her hair is sun-kissed, and she is bathed in sunlight. It is a wonder that someone worthwhile has not come along so far to snatch her up, yet there she is, the only interaction with males seeming to be chats with her gay pal Remy (Adam Scott) and quick, upbeat words exchanged with an elderly man handing her his urine sample at the doctor's office where she temps. Clearly, it is time for that meet cute. Finally and fatefully, she repeatedly runs into handsome Dr. Kevin Fields (Michael Vartan), only to have a jealous rival for his affections lie to her that he is gay. Once Kevin and Charlie have comedically ironed out that confusion, close-ups filled with warmth and wonderment seem to point in the direction of happily ever after.

Nowhere near as happy is Kevin's mother Viola (Fonda), a legendary newswoman who has just learned she is being replaced by some neophyte to attract that highly sought after younger demographic. Viola erupts like Vesuvius, spouting off in irate disbelief and attempting to break anything she can get her hands on. One of those things is the neck of the final person she interviews live on the air, lunging for the throat of a trashy-looking numbskull nymphet who infuriatingly giggles about never having read a newspaper and thinks that Roe v. Wade was a boxing match. Despite the fact that Viola's long and storied career has come to a sudden, ego-crushing, ignominious end, this immediate swing into such extreme, unrestrained behavior unfortunately stamps her as more of an unstable nut than a distinguished news icon whose outrage viewers feel completely comfortable sharing.

Cut to Viola's release from what is referred to here as "the funny farm." Even after her stay there, it is clear that all the clinic's doctors and all the clinic's meds could not quite put Viola back together again. With barely a foot out of the place, she already appears to be relapse-bound upon learning from her loyal but incorrigibly acid-tongued assistant Ruby (scene-stealing Wanda Sykes) that her beloved son the doctor has gotten quite serious about someone who is, in Viola's eyes, a totally unsuitable choice. The two things that had always sustained her were her career and her son, and now, having already lost one and feeling as though she is about to lose the other, Viola may completely lose her grip while trying to hang on to Kevin.

While this boy of Viola's is said to be a brilliant surgeon, one cannot help wondering almost from the beginning about his stunning lack of judgment and perception. For starters, he strangely chooses to spring a marriage proposal on Charlie in front of his still-recuperating mother, and just minutes after introducing the two women to each other. Although Charlie happily accepts, a broad-humored look at what is going on in Viola's head behind feigned delight (she imagines repeatedly slamming the young woman's face into a cake) clearly indicates what a discombobulating jolt this is to her. Charlie senses Viola's true feelings, but utterly oblivious Kevin soothes, "Trust me, she loves you."

Kevin's popping the question sends Viola into imperfectly concealed panic, rifling though the medicine cabinet for anything containing alcohol and ranting about the "dogwalking slut" who has outrageously gotten the well-to-do, fabulous physician in her clutches. Maybe no one would ever have been good enough, but Viola's current state of affairs and current state of mind make her react ferociously toward the idea of Kevin marrying charming Charlie. So this inwardly threatened and outwardly outraged woman vows to "save my son." She throws a lavish engagement party and invites all sorts of illustrious VIPs and assorted glitterati so that Charlie will feel painfully out of place. At an al fresco luncheon where the ladies wear pearls (Charlie orders a burger and fries), the young woman is dismayed when Viola announces with fevered enthusiasm that she is planning what will be a truly ostentatious wedding. When Charlie politely takes the reins back into her own hands (many will think of Lopez's role in 2001's *The Wedding Planner*), Viola swoons and is briefly hospitalized. Before she is discharged, a concerned doctor warns Kevin that his mother may be precipitously on the verge of a true psychotic break. Amazingly, the apple of his mother's eye says nothing about canceling his trip to a medical conference. Once again, this supposedly gifted man's obliviousness is quite unbelievable and off-putting, and many viewers will wonder how great a catch he actually is as he continually fails to catch on.

So Viola's care falls to Charlie, and the former's craziness nearly drives the latter insane. Clearly, scheming Viola would settle for driving her away. However, when Charlie finds out that Viola's pills are merely

Vitamin C tablets and her Dr. Chamberlain (Stephen Dunham) is not really a doctor, it becomes time for some payback. That includes Charlie triumphantly drugging her tormented tormentor so that the woman plops face-first into a plateful of disgusting tripe. Both women now have their claws out to do battle, although Viola's roars clearly trump Charlie's piqued meows. While what follows cannot be dismissed as mere tripe, it is rarely more than tepidly humorous.

Throughout *Monster-in-Law*, Fonda seems strenuously determined to make the material shine, passionately sinking her teeth into her role. However, what comedic bite Jane has created along with wisecracking Wanda and the arrival of the always-formidable Elaine Stritch as Viola's own monster-in-law Gertrude, instantaneously disappears during a finale which transforms this catfight into a paper tiger. For when Viola has a sudden epiphany that she has been as miserable and disparaging to Charlie as Gertrude has always been to her, the film's tone changes with incredible abruptness from hawkish to mawkish. Viewers may get whiplash from the way the screenplay (written by first-timer Anya Kochoff) slams the breaks on all the purposeful nastiness and then proceeds with an utterly incredible and gooey laying-down-of-arms which feels wholly forced and false. Everything is absolutely hunky-dory by the time the credits roll, although whether surviving it all to wed a bland, doofus dreamboat was actually worth it is open to debate. That is, of course, if anyone really cared enough to do so.

Fonda's return, along with the prospect of seeing old Hollywood duke it out with new, enabled *Monster-in-Law* (made on a budget of approximately $60 million) to gross $82.9 million. Critical reaction, however, was not nearly as positive. Periodically enjoyable but utterly unmemorable, the film is a disappointing trifle which, for Fonda fans, is more than a trifle disappointing. It is sincerely hoped by those fond of Fonda that she soon enjoys a better marriage of talent and material than exists in *Monster-in-Law*.

David L. Boxerbaum

CREDITS

Viola Fields: Jane Fonda
Charlie Cantilini: Jennifer Lopez
Kevin Fields: Michael Vartan
Ruby: Wanda Sykes
Kit: Will Arnett
Remy: Adam Scott
Morgan: Annie Parisse
Fiona: Monet Mazur
Gertrude: Elaine Stritch
Dr. Chamberlain: Stephen Dunham
Origin: USA
Language: English
Released: 2005
Production: Paula Weinstein, Chris Bender, JC Spink; Benderspink, Spring Creek Productions; released by New Line Cinema
Directed by: Robert Luketic
Written by: Anya Kochoff
Cinematography by: Russell Carpenter
Music by: David Newman, Dana Sano
Sound: Steve Cantamessa
Editing: Kevin Tent
Art Direction: James F. Truesdale
Costumes: Kym Barrett
Production Design: Missy Stewart
MPAA rating: PG-13
Running time: 100 minutes

REVIEWS

Boxoffice Online. May, 2005.
Chicago Sun-Times Online. May 12, 2005.
Entertainment Weekly Online. May 11, 2005.
Los Angeles Times Online. May 13, 2005.
New York Times Online. May 13, 2005.
Premiere Magazine Online. May 12, 2005.
Variety Online. May 5, 2005.
Washington Post Online. May 13, 2005, p. C01.

TRIVIA

Monster-in-Law is Jane Fonda's return to film after a 15-year hiatus.

AWARDS

Nomination:

Golden Raspberries 2005: Worst Actress (Lopez).

MUNICH

The world was watching in 1972 as 11 Israeli athletes were murdered at the Munich Olympics. This is the story of what happened next.
—Movie tagline

Box Office: $9.5 million

Steven Spielberg may be the most schizophrenic director in film history. He can make both wonderful entertainments such as *Jaws* (1975), *Indiana Jones and the Last*

Crusade (1989), and *Catch Me If You Can* (2002), as well as more serious-minded efforts such as *Empire of the Sun* (1989), *Schindler's List* (1993), and *Saving Private Ryan* (1998). Despite considerable storytelling and technical skills, he can also make clumsy, embarrassing failures such as *1941* (1979), *Hook* (1991), and *The Terminal* (2004). He can contradict himself, as by presenting beings from outer space as benevolent in *Close Encounters of the Third Kind* (1977) and *E.T.: The Extra-Terrestrial* (1982) and as nightmarish creatures in *War of the Worlds* (2005). Spielberg can be sloppy, sentimental, and heavy-handed, even in his best films. Fortunately, these defects are kept to a minimum in *Munich*, one of his most admirable achievements.

Munich is inspired by the true story of how Israeli agents tracked down and killed those responsible for the deaths of eleven Israeli athletes and coaches at the 1972 Olympics in Munich. The film opens with members of the Black September terrorist group sneaking into the Olympic village and taking the hostages, followed by how television covered the event, mixing in footage of ABC sportscaster Jim McKay and others forced into the world of hard news.

Afterward, Israel must have revenge, so Prime Minister Golda Meir (Lynn Cohen) asks Avner Kauffman (Eric Bana), an agent with the Mossad, the Israeli secret police, to form a team to track down those responsible for the massacre. The catch, as he is told by Ephraim (Geoffrey Rush), his case officer, is that he will have to resign from Mossad, losing all his benefits, and that his operation, even his existence, will be denied by the government. Despite having a wife (Ayelet Zurer) seven months pregnant, Avner, the son of an Israeli hero, agrees.

Departing from the usual procedure, Spielberg does not show how Avner assembles his team but simply presents a get-acquainted meeting. The others are Hans (Hanns Zischler), an antiques dealer and expert in forging documents; Robert (Mathieu Kassovitz), a toymaker who knows about bombs; Carl (Ciarán Hinds), who refuses to disclose his background but is an expert at cleaning up messes; and Steve (Daniel Craig), a hothead with an itchy trigger finger.

To find their targets, Avner enlists the aid of Louis (Mathieu Amalric), a member of a mysterious French group that despises all governments. Avner's colleagues are constantly suspicious of Louis, fearing he is setting them up for failure or worse. As the team travels from city to city in Europe, with a notable detour to Beirut, they shoot and blow up their targets, becoming, especially Avner, increasingly soured by their revenge. Can they even be sure that their targets are connected to Munich? Is the Mossad, through Louis, using them to attack other targets?

Such moral qualms make *Munich* more than a just-the-facts docudrama or a suspenseful thriller. The screenplay by Eric Roth, who deals with similar moral territory in *The Insider* (1999), and Tony Kushner, the award-winning author of *Angels in America* (1991-1992), who presents themes related to *Munich* in his play *Homebody/Kabul* (2001), wants the audience to contemplate the ethical ramifications of revenge. Though each tension-filled episode of violence is excitingly staged, Avner's team worries about their actions afterward, often over meals prepared by their leader, who uses cooking as a respite from his work. The film's moral ambiguity is accentuated by emphasizing the humanity of Avner's first three targets.

The political content of *Munich* has made it one of the most controversial films of 2005. It has been called anti-Israeli for implying that Israel loses moral authority through acts of revenge. Ehud Danoch, the Israeli consul general in Los Angeles, objected to the idea that the Olympic terrorists and the Israeli government are ethically equivalent. Spielberg's friend Rabbi Marvin Hier, founder of the Simon Wiesenthal Center, accused the filmmaker of supporting a kind of blind pacifism. Spielberg has answered his critics by saying, "I worked very hard so this film was not in any way, shape or form going to be an attack on Israel."

On the other hand, Abraham Foxman, national director of the Anti-Defamation League, does not interpret *Munich* as an indictment of Israel's actions. Ironically, Mohammed Daoud, the Palestinian who planned the Munich attack, complained that Spielberg did not use him as a consultant. By doing so, according to Daoud, the film's point of view would have been more balanced. Daoud made these comments prior to seeing *Munich*. The film also invites American outrage for claiming that the CIA protected Black September. Three apparent CIA agents pose as drunken tourists in Paris to keep a terrorist from being assassinated.

Adapting George Jonas' book *Vengeance* (1984), previously the source of the made-for-television *Sword of Gideon* (1986), Kushner and Roth bring their intentions into focus by having Louis send Avner's team to a Greek safe house at the same time as a Palestinian group. Pretending to be Basque separatists, the avengers discover they can get along with the enemy. In a scene reminiscent of the quiet interlude spent listening to a phonograph in a deserted village in *Saving Private Ryan,* Steve and a Palestinian have a mild dispute over what music to listen to on the radio, ending with the discovery that everyone can agree about Al Green.

Similar Spielbergian sentimentality occurs as blowing up a target in Paris has to be postponed when the man's young daughter unexpectedly returns to their apartment. The scene is meant to be painfully tense, but the audience knows Spielberg will not kill a child. Other examples of the director's penchant for the sentimental include Avner's defying orders to return to Israel for the birth of his daughter, his hearing her, months later, say "Dada" during a telephone call, and having a dying female victim clutch for her cat.

Spielberg's films are sometimes full of gaps of logic, of going from point A to point C while completely ignoring point B. Thankfully, *Munich* is not guilty of any especially grievous sins, this coming after the supposedly dead son miraculously reappears at the end of *War of the Worlds*, in which the director sets a personal record for the illogical. Spielberg's staging of the massacre at the Munich airport, however, is questionable. The terrorists appear to be standing in plain view of the German sharpshooters yet still have all the time in the world to kill their hostages.

Spielberg's legendary heavy handedness comes into play in this scene, appearing near the end of the film, by cutting back and forth between Avner having sex with his wife and the flashback to the massacre. The point is that Avner is a tormented soul, but would he not be more obsessed by his own deadly actions? Bret Stephens, a member of the editorial board of *The Wall Street Journal*, claimed the scene suggests Black September was responding to Israeli atrocities and trivializes the murders of the hostages.

The last scene of *Munich* is a soul-searching conversation between Avner and Ephraim on a Brooklyn waterfront, with the twin towers of the World Trade Center looming in the background of the final shot. Many reviewers and commentators have complained that Spielberg is being too openly didactic here by overselling his point about the consequences of revenge and possible connections between the events of the film and the Bush administration's war on Iraq, but the image does have a haunting effect.

Several critics have said that even if they have problems with *Munich* as an essay in geopolitics, it works as a thriller, much in the same way as *Minority Report* (2002). Spielberg's major model is clearly *The Day of the Jackal* (1973). The two films have similar episodic structures, and Spielberg uses European streets in the manner of Fred Zinnemann in the earlier film. Casting one of the stars of *The Day of the Jackal,* Michael Lonsdale, as Louis' father is an acknowledgement of this debt.

Munich has some of the best performances of any Spielberg film. There is excellent work by Cohen, Hinds, Kassovitz, Gila Almagor as Avner's mother and conscience, and Marie-Josée Croze as an assassin. Bana, star of such weak efforts as *Hulk* (2003) and *Troy* (2004), is a revelation. Resembling a cross between Tom Cruise and Luke Wilson, Bana is called upon to alternate constantly between determination and uncertainty. Avner is torn between loyalty to his country, his family, his men, and his true nature. Bana conveys wonderfully how his character's soul is being ripped apart.

The best performance of all is that of the great Lonsdale, appearing in only three scenes. This veteran international character actor, who has worked with Luis Buñuel, Louis Malle, François Truffaut, and Orson Welles and even played the villain in a James Bond film, *Moonraker* (1979), transforms what could have been a world-weary cynic by investing the character with great humanity. The leader of Louis' organization, he longs for a better world but knows such is hopeless. Regardless of what *Munich* is saying politically, ethically, and emotionally, it is worth seeing just for Lonsdale's magnificent work.

Michael Adams

CREDITS

Avner: Eric Bana
Steve: Daniel Craig
Carl: Ciarán Hinds
Robert: Mathieu Kassovitz
Hans: Hanns Zischler
Ephraim: Geoffrey Rush
Papa: Michael (Michel) Lonsdale
Louis: Mathieu Amalric
Golda Meir: Lynn Cohen
Jeanette: Marie Josée Croze
Wael Zwaiter: Makram Khoury
Andreas: Moritz Bleibtreu
Avner's Mother: Gila Almagor
Mike Harari: Moshe Ivgi
Tony (Andreas' Friend): Yvan Attal
Marie Claude Hamshari: Hiam Abbass
Sylvie: Valeria Bruni-Tedeschi
Yvonne: Meret Becker
Daphna: Ayelet Zurer
Mahmoud Hamshari: Igal Naor
Ali: Omar Metwally
Hussein Abad Al-Chir: Mostefa Djadjam
Origin: USA
Language: English
Released: 2005
Production: Kathleen Kennedy, Steven Spielberg, Colin Wilson, Barry Mendel; Amblin Entertainment, Alliance

Atlantis Communications, Barry Mendel, Kennedy/Marshall; released by Universal, DreamWorks
Directed by: Steven Spielberg
Written by: Tony Kushner, Eric Roth
Cinematography by: Janusz Kaminski
Music by: John Williams
Sound: David Stephenson
Editing: Michael Kahn
Art Direction: Tony Fanning, Andrew Menzies, Iain McFadyen, Janos Szaboics, Ino Bonello, David Swayze
Costumes: Joanna Johnston
Production Design: Rick Carter
MPAA rating: R
Running time: 164 minutes

REVIEWS

Boxoffice Online. December, 2005.
Chicago Sun-Times Online. December 23, 2005.
Entertainment Weekly Online. December 14, 2005.
Los Angeles Times Online. December 23, 2005.
New York Times Online. December 23, 2005.
Premiere Magazine Online. December 22, 2005.
Variety Online. December 9, 2005.
Washington Post Online. December 23, 2005, p. C01.

QUOTES

Golda Meir: "Every civilization finds it necessary to negotiate compromises with its own values."

TRIVIA

Originally, Steven Spielberg planned a 2003 or 2004 release for this film but began work on *War of the Worlds* (2005) when Tom Cruise became available instead.

AWARDS

Nomination:

Oscars 2005: Adapt. Screenplay, Director (Spielberg), Film, Film Editing, Orig. Score
Directors Guild 2005: Director (Spielberg)
Golden Globes 2006: Director (Spielberg), Screenplay
Broadcast Film Critics 2005: Director (Spielberg).

MURDERBALL

Box Office: $1.5 million

Universally acclaimed documentary is certainly one of the year's best, detailing the dramas of the athletes who compete in quadriplegic rugby during a two-year period. Every bit as competitive as any professional sport not played in a wheelchair, quad rugby utilizes the rules of traditional rugby, played in specially designed wheelchairs on a standard indoor basketball court. With the ruggedly-made chairs constantly crashing into each other and the ferocity of the players, the sport was originally invented in Canada and dubbed murderball but, as one of the film's central characters Mark Zupan succinctly summed up, "You can't market 'murderball' to corporate sponsors." The characters are so compelling and situations caught by directors Henry Alex Rubin and Dana Adam Shapiro are so riveting that it is sometimes hard to believe that this is, in fact, not a scripted affair but real-life drama unfolding.

Produced by MTV, the film opens with U.S. Paralympic quadriplegic rugby star Mark Zupan, muscular, heavily tattooed and sporting a goatee that makes him look like he could be the lead singer in the heavy metal band that can be heard throughout the film's soundtrack. Zupan's will be the first, and most dramatic, in the series of stories of how these young men became disabled. In 1993, while drinking with best friend Christopher Igoe, the then 18-year-old Zupan wandered out to sleep in the back of Chris's truck. Unaware that Zupan was in the back, Igoe drove home that night and accidentally crashed the truck, sending Zupan flying into a canal where he clung to a branch for 13 hours until his rescue. Causing a rift in their friendship, the film captures the process by which Zupan and Igoe are able to overcome the tragedy and become best friends once again. Zupan, who began playing the sport in 1996, became the leader of the U.S. Paralympic team and official spokesperson.

Amid the central plot device of the fierce competition between the Canadian and U.S. wheelchair rugby teams, the various players tell their stories, interspersed with candid interviews with family, friends, and onlookers. Scott Hogsett's spinal cord was snapped in a fistfight. Bob Lujano contracted a deadly childhood disease which robbed him of his legs and lower arms and there is a moving animated sequence, courtesy of artists Damon Ciarelli and David Egan, which illustrates his recurring dream where he can fly. After watching the interaction between these intensely capable players, one forgets they are wheelchair-bound as they drink, curse, play practical jokes, and discuss women as any other macho team of tough guys.

Perhaps the toughest and most macho among them is Joe Soares, the film's other central character. Afflicted with polio during childhood, the extremely charismatic Soares became one of the sport's best players, leading the American team until, in his 40's, age caught up with him and, due to his slowing times, he was cut. The enraged player then decides to coach the Canadian team, dubbed a Benedict Arnold by many former teammates and openly despised by Zupan: "If he were on fire, I wouldn't piss on him to put it out." The huge wall of trophies and medals he won is a testament to his fervent dedication to the sport, even to the exclusion of his adolescent son who does well in school and plays the viola but isn't much of an athlete. His father is hard on him and hard on his players but believes that instilling discipline is the only way to win.

This is a sport where winning is the ultimate goal, as Hogsett reminds viewers after someone mistakenly thought he was competing in the Special Olympics. Nothing could be farther from the truth: "We're not going for a hug, we're going for the gold medal," he quips. The film opens at the 2002 World Championships in Sweden where quad teams from 12 countries, including Australia, Great Britain, Belgium, and Japan, gather to compete. The players are given rankings based on their degree of upper-body mobility beginning with .5 to a high of 3.5, allowing the less mobile players to participate alongside the more abled, who score most of the goals. A team can only have a total of 8 points on the court at one time. As the refs, many who are wheelchair-bound, explain, of the last 11 championship games, the U.S. has won ten. Joe intends to reverse this and in a tense, profanity-laced match, leads his Canadians to victory in the final seconds of the game. The rematch will be at the 2004 Paralympic Games in Athens, Greece.

In the ensuing two years we follow the players, many who have girlfriends, in their everyday lives. One issue the film deals with in particular is the subject of sex and the quadriplegic. Most of the athletes are able to vigorously participate in regular intercourse, and the filmmakers show graphic clips from an instructional sex video given to quads during the rehabilitation.

Shortly before the Paralympic Games, Joe suffers a serious heart attack and we watch as he undergoes surgery at the hospital. He recovers and as his Portuguese family back in New York exclaim, he has become a different person. He seems to have a different perspective on life and tells his son he loves him on the phone, rushing home to see his viola recital. Despite all his macho blustering, Joe emerges as a hugely sympathetic figure in the film, with his can-do attitude, commitment to the sport, and dedication to his family. He resumes coaching the Canadians who lose the match to the U.S. that determines their rank going into the games. However, in a surprising upset, New Zealand wins the gold medal in Athens, with Canada getting the silver and the U.S. receiving the bronze medal.

The film winds down with Keith Cavill, who broke his neck in a 2003 Motocross event and is freshly out of rehabilitation, being introduced to the sport by Zupan. The enthusiasm is evident as he wheels around in the tough-looking rugby chair that looks like it's covered with gladiator shields. An intriguing post-script brings Joe back to the fore, however, as it notes he was fired as the Canadian coach and is applying to be the coach of the U.S. team.

Hilary White

CREDITS

Origin: USA
Language: English
Released: 2005
Production: Jeffrey Mandel, Dana Adam Shapiro; Eat Film; released by ThinkFilm
Directed by: Henry Alex Rubin, Dana Adam Shapiro
Cinematography by: Henry Alex Rubin
Music by: Jamie Saft
Sound: Patrick G. Donahue
Music Supervisor: Tracy McKnight
Editing: Geoffrey Richman
MPAA rating: R
Running time: 85 minutes

REVIEWS

Boxoffice Online. July, 2005.
Chicago Sun-Times Online. July 22, 2005.
Entertainment Weekly Online. July 6, 2005.
Los Angeles Times Online. July 8, 2005.
New York Times Online. July 8, 2005.
Premiere Magazine Online. July 8, 2005.
Variety Online. January 23, 2005.
Washington Post Online. July 22, 2005, p. WE32.

MUST LOVE DOGS

The hardest trick is making them stay.
—Movie tagline

Box Office: $43.9 million

Chick flick. If these words don't strike terror into your heart (and you are not a grumpy middle-aged male critic), you will probably enjoy this harmless romantic comedy despite its various clichés and its frequently ornate dialogue (John Cusack came up with a number of his own tongue-twisting ad-libs). This is a story about life after divorce. Preschool teacher Sarah Nolan (Diane Lane) has been divorced eight months and her large Irish-American family stage an intervention to push her back into the dating pool. They all have various friends they are eager to set her up with but the very thought gives Sarah the heebie-jeebies. Then there's Jake Anderson (Cusack). His divorce has just been finalized and his best friend and lawyer Charlie (Ben Shenkman) also thinks Jake should date or at least find a chick to have sex with. Jake's an aggressively articulate guy who builds wooden racing boats that no one buys and is very reluctant to have his heart broken again.

One suggestion is that Sarah meet a single guy at the grocery store—instead she has to explain, somewhat hysterically, to the butcher that she wants only one chicken breast because "I'm divorced. I eat alone—usually standing over the kitchen sink. I don't want a bunch of chicken hanging around!" Sarah does have somewhat of a prospect in the separated dad of one of her young students—Bob Connor (Dermot Mulroney) takes the time to notice that Sarah is attractive and flirts with her. Meanwhile, Jake is repeatedly watching his favorite movie—*Doctor Zhivago*—and enjoying the yearning and suffering. Sarah is finally pushed into dating by her bossy older sister Carol (Elizabeth Perkins) who puts Sarah's profile on an online dating service. When Sarah meets her first blind date, it turns out to be her own twinkly widowed father Bill (Christopher Plummer) who's looking for a little companionship. Sarah then goes on a series of really, really bad dates that only make her want to stay home in her pajamas eating ice cream.

Carol tries another profile for Sarah with "must love dogs" as a requirement (maybe the guys seem more trustworthy if they love dogs). Sarah doesn't actually own a dog and borrows her brother's huge Newfoundland, Mother Teresa, to meet the aforementioned Jake at a dog park. Jake, who's borrowed Charlie's aggressive little West Highland terrier, is extremely nervous and intense so he makes a generally bad first impression. Meanwhile, Bill has met three-time divorcee Dolly (Stockard Channing), who lives in a trailer park. At least while meeting her father's lady friend, Sarah also runs into flirty Bob, who's moved into the same park with his son. Carol encourages her to go after Bob, if for no other reason than he's got a "great ass."

Jake has not been able to get Sarah out of his mind and arranges another evening out. He wonders how anyone could have let Sarah go and she finally admits that her ex simply "stopped loving me." They wind up back at her house but minus a condom. After a frantic, and rather silly, trip to various stores, Sarah admits to Jake that the moment has passed. Sarah also reluctantly admits to Carol that she likes Jake because he's emotional and talkative: "I don't want to do random dating. I want to be in love." Jake is also singing Sarah's praises to Charlie. Naturally, this would-be romance has to have some frustrations—and that would be Bob once again. Through an unfortunate coincidence, Jake shows up at Sarah's house just when Bob is kissing her. Jake is upset. While Sarah spends Thanksgiving with her meddling family, Jake and Charlie spend it at a strip club where Jake decides to date every bimbo Charlie can set him up with in order to get over Sarah. Sarah has also decided to take Dolly's advice and puts up fake profiles on various dating websites, which only result in another series of really bad dates.

Sarah then decides to call Bob and winds up spending the night with him, only to realize that he is Mr. Wrong. Jake wallows in *Doctor Zhivago,* trying to forget "dog park girl." In a meet cute scene—while we head into the romantic home stretch—Jake unknowingly chats with Sarah's dad about finding and losing that special girl. Sarah manages to put two and two together and tracks Jake to the river where he has gone rowing. She hunts him down in a seriously over-the-top moment and they agree to give it one more try. Sarah goes grocery shopping and doesn't have to settle for one chicken breast because Jake is with her. While the film started with various singles explaining their dating strategies, it ends with various members of Sarah's family explaining how they got together, including a happy Jake and Sarah.

Must Love Dogs is based on the bestselling 2002 chick lit book by Claire Cook. It is written and directed by TV sitcom (*Family Ties, Spin City)* veteran Gary David Goldberg as if a laugh track was ready to be inserted in case the audience needed any help. The beautiful Lane, who received an Oscar nomination for the romantic thriller *Unfaithful* (2002) and who also played a shaken divorcee in the romantic dramedy *Under the Tuscan Sun* (2003), actually comes across as a little too worldly and intense for the froth of the material. This is a Meg Ryan in her heyday of romantic comedies part. It needs someone wounded but basically optimistic and Lane is filled with Irish melancholy. In contrast, Cusack seems like an older version of his immortal teen heartthrob Lloyd Dobler (1989's *Say Anything*)—decent, sensitive, and a little neurotic but a real mensch. Channing makes the most of what could be a brassy one-note character by emphasizing Dolly's romantic awareness; Perkins is the perfect exasperating but loving older sister; and Plummer does a Irish brogue, recites Yeats, and juggles romantic opportunities with aplomb.

There are some extraneous characters and plots that could have easily been done away with to make the somewhat sluggish film move a little faster—Sarah's gay confidante is superfluous as is Dolly's dating crisis, and the one date we see Jake go on is with a young blonde ditz (although winningly played by Jordana Spiro); there's also a number of familiar love-themed songs in the film, including the Linda Ronstadt opener "When Will I Be Loved," that are appropriate but sometimes intrusive. And while the dogs are a mere plot contrivance, they are completely appealing and don't appear in the film nearly enough.

Christine Tomassini

CREDITS

Sarah: Diane Lane
Jake: John Cusack
Bob: Dermot Mulroney
Bill: Christopher Plummer
Dolly: Stockard Channing
Carol: Elizabeth Perkins
Charlie: Ben Shenkman
June: Julie Gonzalo
Stanley: Brad Hall
Leo: Brad Henke
Christine: Ali Hillis
Vinnie: Steve Schirripa
Marcia: Laura Kightlinger
Sherry: Jordana Spiro
Origin: USA
Language: English
Released: 2005
Production: Suzanne Todd, Jennifer Todd, Gary David Goldberg; Team Todd, UBU; released by Josephine Ward, Warner Bros.
Directed by: Gary David Goldberg
Written by: Gary David Goldberg
Cinematography by: John Bailey
Music by: Craig Armstrong
Sound: David M. Kelson
Editing: Eric A. Sears, Roger Bondelli
Art Direction: Kevin Kavanaugh
Costumes: Florence-Isabelle Megginson
Production Design: Naomi Shohan
MPAA rating: PG-13
Running time: 98 minutes

REVIEWS

Boxoffice Online. July, 2005.
Chicago Sun-Times Online. July 29, 2005.
Entertainment Weekly Online. July 27, 2005.
Los Angeles Times Online. July 29, 2005.
New York Times Online. July 29, 2005.
Premiere Magazine Online. July 29, 2005.
Variety Online. July 22, 2005.
Washington Post Online. July 29, 2005, p. C01.

TRIVIA

The dog named Mother Theresa was played by two 6-month old Newfoundland puppies named Molly and Maeve and adopted at the end of filming by director Gary David Goldberg.

MY MOTHER'S SMILE

(L'ora di religione: Il sorriso di mia madre)

(The Religion Hour)

The Vatican's Film List includes some odd and oddly liberal choices (Pasolini, for goodness sake!), but the Italian-produced *My Mother's Smile* will probably not make it there and director Marco Bellocchio shouldn't wait for an audience with the Pope. Bellocchio's dark melodrama defies church dogma, although it tells its tale in mostly an ordinary way. Failings and all, *My Mother's Smile* (also known as *The Religion Hour* or *L'Ora di religione: Il sorriso di mia madre*) takes chances through its confrontational stance.

My Mother's Smile starts with Ernesto (Sergio Castellitto), a famous local painter, finding out for the past three years that his family has been assisting the Vatican in nominating his murdered mother for canonization. Ernesto, a husband and father and devout atheist, has uneasy feelings about his discovery because he believes his mother was an ignorant, aloof, uncaring person, not worthy of the tribute.

While his family tries to take advantage of the prospective sainthood his mother, Ernesto throws a monkey wrench into the process: he demands that his mother's killer, Ernesto's own deranged sibling, be canonized as well. The Church hierarchy dislikes Ernesto's ultimatum, which prompts Ernesto to reject their many demands. A looming battle is circumvented by the Pope himself, a deus ex machina, if there ever was one.

Marco Bellocchio has provoked the Roman Catholic Church many times before: even his first film, *Fists in the Pocket*, in 1965, was condemned as "blasphemous"; his best known film, *China Is Near*, in 1967, was not appreciated by many religious Italians; and *Devil in the Flesh*, in 1986, was banned in some places for its graphic sex scenes. Still, many Bellochio characters often yearn for spiritual enlightenment (Ernesto is no exception), and the writer-director's style looks conventional next to the cinematically self-reflexive heresy of Luis Bunuel or Italy's own Pier Paolo Pasolini; Bellocchio's straightforward approach (even in odd and over-the-top narrative moments) is far too low key (let alone darkly lit) to shock or stun.

Nevertheless, the very idea of critiquing the Catholic Church could be considered iconoclastic—the elders' brutish conduct becomes apparent immediately, and this is not a Monty Python-style parody. Note, for instance, the sequence where the priests force African youths to climb steep stairs on their knees.

Sadly (since it is not a spoof), some of *My Mother's Smile* goes a bit haywire—e.g. a scene with a conservative royalist politico challenging Ernesto to a duel at dawn, Ernesto's romance with his son's religion instructor (who may not really exist), and a conclusion that frustrates through vagueness and compromise.

On the other hand, the film is thoughtful and well produced (cinematographer Pasquale Mari highlights the interior chiaroscuro). Among the cast members, Sergio Castellitto (of 2001's *Mostly Martha*) stands out with his lovely performance as the headstrong but tormented Ernesto and Alberto Mondini leaves a memorable impression as Ernesto's inquisitive son. Best of all, *My Mother's Smile* is almost as brave as its protagonist in tackling both the politics of the Catholic Church and the duplicity of organized religion.

The critics were divided, though many mainstream newspapers and journals skipped reviewing the film altogether. The January 1, 2005 *Hollywood Reporter* dismissed the entire production with, "The movie never gives us much reason to sympathize with its hero's plight. Emotionally cut off from all but his son, he seems rather ineffectual in his protests against the canonization and mostly is as confused about his past as his present.... The actors, including Chiara Conti as a mysterious blonde, deliver strong performances, but their characters are so thin that it feels like everyone is playing a different subtext. Dramatic music by Riccardo Giagni and Pasquale Mari's moody cinematography evoke an atmosphere of heightened melodrama that the story and characters fail to live up to."

The 2002 *Slant Magazine* review by Ed Gonzalez was far more favorable (the film was completed and shown at several festivals in 2002, where it won many awards): "The man's strange experiences (a commercial photo op, a surreal religious gathering) bring to mind Tom Cruise's road to fidelity in *Eyes Wide Shut* to Italian opera. Bellocchio has a way of spelling everything out for the audience; nonetheless, the film's intellectualism is both provocative and remarkably playful." Elvis Mitchell's October 4, 2002 *New York Times* review was also mixed but typical: "Though the narrative is spotty, and occasionally confounding, there is an epic warmth in the way it's rendered."

My Mother's Smile deserves an audience (okay, maybe not with the Pope), but the film still seems like an opportunity missed to really go after its subject.

Eric Monder

CREDITS

Ernesto: Sergio Castellitto
Irene: Jacqueline Lustig
Diana: Chiara Conti
Leonardo: Alberto and Ernesto Mondini
Filippo Argenti: Gianni Schicchi
Cardinal Piumini: Maurizio Donadoni
Ettore: Gigio Alberti
Origin: Italy
Language: Italian
Released: 2002
Production: Marco Bellocchio, Sergio Pelone; RAI, Filmalbatros; released by Istituto Luce
Directed by: Marco Bellocchio
Written by: Marco Bellocchio
Cinematography by: Pasquale Mari
Music by: Riccardo Giagni
Sound: Maurizio Argentieri
Editing: Francesca Calvelli
Costumes: Sergio Ballo
Production Design: Marco Dentici
MPAA rating: Unrated
Running time: 103 minutes

REVIEWS

Boxoffice Online. February, 2005.
Hollywood Reporter. January 1, 2005.
New York Times Online. October 4, 2002.
Slant Magazine. 2002.
Variety Online. April 18, 2002.

MY SUMMER OF LOVE

The most dangerous thing to want is more.
—Movie tagline

Box Office: $1 million

In his review of *My Summer of Love*, A. O. Scott of *The New York Times* wrote, "The story *My Summer of Love* tells is modest; looking back on it, you may be surprised at how little has actually happened." In the film, directed by Polish-born, British director Pawel Pawlikowski, how the story is told is just as important as the story itself. The phrase "mood piece" came up in many reviews of the film. The film is shot at a languid pace that makes the 87 minute film seem like it accurately conveys the feel of a long lazy summer.

The story is based on the novel by Helen Cross, although Cross's novel contained many elements like a miner's strike and some murders that are not present here. Instead of using a standard 120 page script, Pawlikowski used the novel as a base and a 37 page "shooting document" that he wrote with Michael Wynne. The story takes place in the Yorkshire countryside in midsummer. Mona (Nathalie Press) is lying in a field after an aimless drive on her engine-lacking moped. She is startled to see the face of Tasmin (Emily Blunt) hovering above her. Tasmin is astride a horse and, to Mona, appears to be something of her knight in shining armor. Tasmin is a rich girl home for the summer. She reports coolly that she has been kicked out of school for being a bad influence. Tasmin invites Mona to drop by her sprawling stone manor any time she is feeling bored.

Mona heads over right away, happy to escape her own life. Her older brother, Phil (Paddy Considine), is a felon who has recently been released from prison. In order to cope with his own evil instincts, he has become a born-again Christian. He turns the family pub, The Swan, into a religious fellowship hall. He no longer sees Mona as his little sister, but as someone who he needs to speak to about Jesus. "I want my brother," Mona pleads with her brother. "He used to be real." While Phil is busy on a project to build a huge wooden cross to erect on a hill over the town, Mona has plenty of time to slip away to see Tasmin.

Tasmin seems glamorous, exotic and a bit dangerous. She shows Mona around her self-described "creepy" house, including her sister's bedroom. It has remained unchanged since her beautiful sister's tragic death from anorexia, reports Tasmin. Her mother is absent and her father is spending a lot of time with his pretty young assistant. Mona is fascinated. Tasmin takes Mona under her wing and instructs her on things she feels Mona should know about like the works of Nietzsche, Edith Piaf and Freud.

The girls spend time doing picturesque things like trying on elaborate formal gowns, riding the moped (now with a motor) across the English countryside, and swimming in isolated ponds, complete with a lovely waterfall. They goad each other on to make bold gestures. Mona heads home one day and tells her brother baldly, "God is dead." When Tasmin cries over seeing her father's car parked in his lover's driveway, Mona picks up a stone and tosses it through his car window. Soon the two girls are sharing a bed and developing the kind of obsessive teenage love relationship that involves many pledges of undying love forever and ever. Such a heated, heady relationship probably can not come to a good end, and indeed it does not. There are some twists, which give the film a nice punch at the end.

Critics appreciated the lyrical qualities of the film. Glenn Whipp of *The Los Angeles Daily News* wrote, "Pawlikowski's beautifully shot, sensual movie puts you at the heart of all these strong emotions and secrets in this self-contained world where rapture and delusion are intertwined and ambiguity is the name of the game. You won't forget these girls any time soon." Ty Burr of *The Boston Globe* gave kudos to cinematographer Ryszard Lenczewski, writing, "Here, it's as though he has reinvented how to see the world. He injects an impatient, hormonal heat into the camera angles and woozy colors—the cinematographic equivalent of an adolescent's diary." And Kenneth Turan of *The Los Angeles Times* commended director Pawlikowski, writing that he "has the knack of getting his people to act dramatically, unexpectedly and always believably. He's created a most provocative love story, about two people who will never forget each other, but not for anything like the reasons they initially imagine."

Jill Hamilton

CREDITS

Tamsin: Emily Blunt
Phil: Paddy Considine
Mona: Nathalie Press
Ricky: Dean Andrews
Ricky's wife: Michelle Byrne
Tamsin's father: Paul Antony-Barber
Tamsin's mother: Lynette Edwards
Sadie: Kathryn Sumner
Origin: Great Britain
Language: English
Released: 2005
Production: Tanya Seghatchian, Chris Collins; Take Partnerships; released by ContentFilm
Directed by: Pawel Pawlikowski
Written by: Pawel Pawlikowski, Michael Wynne
Cinematography by: Ryszard Lenczewski
Music by: Alison Goldfrapp, Will Gregory
Sound: John Pearson
Editing: David Charap
Art Direction: Netty Chapman
Costumes: Julian Day
Production Design: John Stevenson
MPAA rating: R
Running time: 85 minutes

REVIEWS

Boxoffice Online. June, 2005.
Chicago Sun-Times Online. June 17, 2005.
Entertainment Weekly Online. June 15, 2005.
Los Angeles Times Online. June 17, 2005.
New York Times Online. June 17, 2005.

Variety Online. August 23, 2004.
Washington Post Online. June 17, 2005, p. WE34.

MYSTERIOUS SKIN

Gregg Araki's film *Mysterious Skin* opens with colored bits of something falling through a white space. Then we see the face of a dark-haired, smiling boy and realize that the bits are neon-colored cereal. An intertitle switches to "Brian Lackey Summer 1981" and we hear a voiceover by Brady Corbet (as the teenaged Brian) stating: "The summer I was eight years old, five hours disappeared from my life...lost, gone without a trace." We see another boy hiding in a cellar—small, blonde, with oversized glasses and a baseball uniform. He also has a bloody nose. The young Brian (George Webster) begins having nightmares and suffering from nosebleeds and blackouts. That same summer Brian also believes he sees a UFO hovering over his house.

"Neil McCormick Summer 1981" Neil (Chase Ellison) is the dark-haired boy of the first scene. His father is unknown and his single, hard-drinking mother, Ellen (Elisabeth Shue), has a string of boyfriends. The teenaged Neil (as voiced by Joseph Gordon-Levitt) states: "The summer I was eight years old, I came for the first time" after observing his mom having sex with her latest conquest; Neil is watching the man's reaction, not his mother.

Neil and Brian know each other slightly from Little League in their small Kansas communities of Hutchinson and nearby Little River. Brian is completely unathletic—Neil just the opposite. All that matters to Neil is making his handsome, mustachioed Coach (Bill Sage) proud. Neil is Coach's favorite and they spend a lot of time together at Coach's house; he has videogames and snacks and soda. In a queasy kitchen scene (featuring cereal) that is also unexpectedly tender, Coach seduces the needy Neil.

By October of 1983, Neil has met his best friend and soul mate, Wendy, noting that if he wasn't queer, he would want to marry her. That same Halloween, Brian is attacked by bullies and runs away, losing his glasses. He faints after seeing a vague figure and wakes up remembering nothing except "All I knew was it was somehow linked to the other time—the night I woke up in the cellar. ...I knew I had to find out what had happened to me. I had to find an answer to the mystery." By November of 1987, 15-year-old Neil is hanging out at the local playground, hustling older men. Wendy (Michelle Trachtenberg) is worried that he'll trick with the wrong guy and she'll "find pieces of you everywhere."

In the fall of 1991 (the film will remain in that year with flashbacks), Brian is now a geeky introvert who has become convinced that he was abducted by aliens. He learns of a fellow abductee who lives nearby: a woman named Avalyn (Mary Lynn Rajskub) who talks about missing chunks of time. Brian wants to meet her. Meanwhile, Wendy is moving to New York and warns new friend Eric (Jeffrey Licon), who is infatuated with Neil, to be careful: "...you have to understand one thing, where normal people have a heart, Neil McCormick has a bottomless hole. And if you don't watch out, you can fall in and get lost forever."

Brian dreams about aliens and writes about them in his journal. He goes to visit Avalyn and shares the fact that he remembers himself and a dark-haired boy wearing their Little League uniforms—and a tall alien hovering over them both. Avalyn suggests Brian concentrate on figuring out who the other boy is. Brian finds a Little League team picture but Neil is only identified as "N. McCormick." When Brian manages finally tracks down the right McCormick, he learns that Neil has just left to join Wendy in New York. Instead, he is befriended by Eric.

In November and December of 1991, Eric is writing to Neil about meeting Brian and that Brian has concluded both he and Neil were abducted by aliens when they were eight. Brian, whom Eric has described as asexual, freaks out when Avalyn tries to seduce him and breaks off their friendship. Neil has continued hustling in New York but has begun to question his choice of profession. Wendy is the only one who knows about Neil and Coach. He confesses to her: "What happened that summer is a huge part of me. No one ever made me feel that way before or since. I was special, you know?"

Brian turns 19; Eric notices that he has drawn an alien wearing baseball cleats. Neil is coming home for Christmas. Wendy has gotten him a legit job in a sub shop but that doesn't stop him from picking up a trick. Only the guy is violent and Neil is badly beaten; he cries for the first time. Neil finally meets Brian on Christmas Eve after his return home. Remembering just who Brian is, he takes the teenager with him to Coach's former house. Brian recognizes the blue light that has also haunted him as the house's porch light. The family is away and Neil breaks into the house. As they move through the rooms, Neil wants to know why Brian is searching for answers now. He replies: "I want to dream about something else for a change."

As they sit on the couch in the living room, Neil feels Coach's presence as he recounts what happened the day of the baseball game. There was a rainout and Brian had no way home so he accompanied Neil to Coach's house. Neil explains: "Any time there was another boy involved it was always the same. Coach used me as a prop to pull you in." Brian listens, numb, as Neil graphically recalls the sexual details of the afternoon. He puts his head in Neil's lap and begins to cry as Christmas carolers come to the door.

Araki's camera slowly pans up from the boys sitting on the couch, their figures getting smaller and smaller, surrounded by darkness, as we hear Neil's final speech: "As we sat there listening to the carolers, I wanted to tell Brian it was over now and everything would be okay but that was a lie. I wish there was someway to go back and undo the past but there wasn't. There was nothing we could do, so I just stayed silent and tried to telepathically communicate how sorry I was about what had happened. I wished with all my heart we could just leave this world behind and rise like two angels in the night and magically disappear."

Araki, a landmark director of the New Queer Cinema of the 1990s, was so moved by Scott Heims' 1995 novel *Mysterious Skin* that he made it the first work he ever adapted as well as directed. The film has a fearless candor as it follows the parallel lives of Brian and Neil and how their sexual experience as eight-year-olds has damaged them both, albeit in different ways. The asexual Brian is scared of sexual contact and is socially shy and awkward; his blonde hair in bangs, his face half-hidden behind his glasses, frequently clothed in long-sleeved shirts and sweater vests. The gay Neil is physically promiscuous while emotionally detached; his skinny body frequently on display, an insolent sneer and a cigarette hanging from his mouth. He seems to enjoy the temporary power and pleasure he has over the older men he favors but his only love is for his long-lost Coach. Quick edits and close-ups make for some unnerving seduction sequences in this character-driven narrative that is also highlighted by a dreamy ambient soundtrack created by Robin Guthrie and Harold Budd. While the two teenagers lives crosscut, they only (finally!) meet for the devastating end sequence, an acting tour de force by both Corbet and Gordon-Levitt that is both moving and disturbing in its depiction of the lingering devastation that child abuse can cause.

Christine Tomassini

CREDITS

Brian: Brady Corbet
Neil: Joseph Gordon-Levitt
Wendy: Michelle Trachtenberg
Mrs. McCormick: Elisabeth Shue
Eric: Jeffrey Licon
Avalyn Friesen: Mary Lynn Rajskub
Mr. Lackey: Chris Mulkey
Charlie: Richard Riehle
Mrs. Lackey: Lisa Long
Zeke: Billy Drago
Young Brian: George Webster
Young Neil: Chase Ellison
Coach: Bill Sage
Origin: USA
Language: English
Released: 2004
Production: Mary Jane Skalski, Jeff Levy-Hinte, Gregg Araki; Antidote Film, Desperate Pictures, Fortissimo Films
Directed by: Gregg Araki
Written by: Gregg Araki
Cinematography by: Steve Gainer
Music by: Harold Budd, Robin Guthrie
Sound: Trip Brock
Editing: Gregg Araki
Costumes: Alix Hester
Production Design: Devorah Herbert
MPAA rating: NC-17
Running time: 103 minutes

REVIEWS

Boxoffice Online. May, 2005.
New York Times Online. May 6, 2005.
Variety Online. September 3, 2004.

N-O

THE NEW WORLD

Once discovered, it was changed forever.
—Movie tagline

Daring to cross the Earth's second-largest expanse of open water in creaking, wooden, wind-powered vessels at the dawn of the 17th Century, the Englishmen who laid eyes on the breathtakingly beautiful and bountiful shores of this continent must surely have felt their long, sometimes challenging journey had been worthwhile. Most viewers will feel the same way about Terrence Malick's lovely, lengthy, and somewhat amorphously told *The New World.* It presents perfectly glorious material in an imperfect but mesmerizing and generally successful manner. The film flows along with slow but steady grace, providing arresting, intoxicating, utterly sublime images of natural splendor for those willing to let it all wash over them. The soundtrack not only features exquisite music but is also alive with the sound of water, wind, birds and insects. This sumptuously sensuous, dreamily-unfolding style is admittedly not for everyone, including filmgoers who require a conventional narrative presentation and, more particularly, those who demand booming, explosive action served up at a breakneck clip. For those who do not need to be bombastically shaken in order to be stirred, however, *The New World* has much to offer.

In what is only his fourth film in the past thirty-one years, writer-director Malick not only tells of the legendary love between Pocahontas and Captain John Smith but also of the consequential collision of their respective cultures. Viewers cannot help but marvel at the explorers' courage and know that their small, vulnerable settlement at Jamestown will eventually lead to a vast, powerful, glorious nation. However, it is also made abundantly clear that their arrival in what they felt was a "Promised Land" bestowed upon them by God himself was anything but a blessing to those who already called it home, Native Americans to whom this so-called "New World" was a very old and venerated one. There is a definite, palpable, and haunting elegiac tone to the film, a mourning of magnificence forever altered, of Paradise lost.

Malick fittingly first introduces the indigenous people, and immediately emphasizes how they were at one with their surroundings. Underwater shots show them gliding amidst the fish and fauna, unifying nature and those who the settlers will aptly refer to as "the naturals." Into an existence which has remained relatively unchanged for millennia come white men on white-sailed ships, which the natives watch from shore with curiosity and awe more than with the wariness that time will soon teach them. Captain Christopher Newport (Christopher Plummer) instructs his men to avoid offending them, as their help may very well be needed. The Englishmen are astonished by the seemingly infinite resources, with one exclaiming exultantly, "We'll live like kings!" Those who already live there sniff the newcomers and fix them with inquisitive stares, as if not quite sure what to make of them. These first encounter scenes seem wholly authentic.

Recognizing that the daunting task of founding a colony will call for intrepidness as well as skill, Newport gives a last-second commutation of the death sentence imposed upon insubordinate soldier-of-fortune Smith (an admirable Colin Farrell). During initial exploration,

Smith catches sight of Pocahontas (Q'Orianka Kilcher) amongst waving fields of tall grass. He stares in wonder and disbelief at the striking young beauty who seems like some sort of otherworldly, enchanting creature, which, of course, she is. It is obvious that she finds him just as captivating.

In fairly short order, the settlers both fail to acclimate to their surroundings and succeed in alienating their new neighbors, so Newport taps Smith for the dangerous mission of seeking assistance from the great Algonquin Chief Powhatan (August Schellenberg). It is during this expedition that Smith is captured and about to be killed by Powhatan's order when Pocahontas, the chief's youngest and favorite daughter, throws herself upon him and spares his life. Thereafter, Malick begins to provide scenes which show their growing fascination with each other. Much of the film's most revealing and romantic dialogue is provided in hushed voiceovers which can unfortunately be difficult to hear. Smith says that he loves Pocahontas (although she is never actually called by that name), but it is potent reverence more than something pantingly carnal, a lot of whole-hearted marveling but no making love. (It should be noted that historians say she was actually around twelve years old and he more than twice that.) Smith is clearly spellbound by this radiant spirit, utterly untainted, lovely, and endlessly intriguing, the personification of the world she inhabits. He seems to her to be "a God." The two nuzzle each other and share tender caresses, blissfully lying or swimming together in beautiful surroundings. The comment is made that they are no longer two but now one, an ideal, harmonious, mutually-satisfying commingling of cultures.

Alas, Smith must dutifully return to the fort, and when he does it is an exceedingly harsh jolt back to reality. Whereas he was previously shown luxuriating with Pocahontas, laughing and wrestling with the robust men, and in general feeling rather comfortably at home in the serene, verdant wilderness, he and those watching are now confronted with bleak images of discord, despair, sickness and starvation. Smith describes the time he shared with Pocahontas as a dream. "Now," he says grimly, "I am awake." He wonders if he should go back. She comes to help him and the remaining settlers with not only food to sustain them through the winter but also seed for crops which will allow the English themselves to put down roots come Spring. Powhatan finds out Pocahontas has put her heart above the best interests of her people, disowns her, and banishes forever the daughter he calls "the light of my life." This cleaving is clearly agonizing for the characters to endure, and is difficult to watch. Having driven her away, the chief's tribe attempts to drive the colonists away by attacking the fort in dramatic fashion.

When Pocahontas had mercifully and boldly dared to give comfort to the enemy, Smith seems to feel guilty over having gotten this girl in too deep for her own good. "Don't trust me," he had said, a warning one remembers when he disappears to lead a prestigious, potentially lucrative expedition and leaves behind the instructions to wait two months and then tell her he has perished. Perhaps he wanted her told this to help her move on. However, when Pocahontas, already feeling deserted since his departure, learns of his supposed demise it is a cruel, crushing blow. Although Kilcher (with looks and poise which belie her fourteen years) was excellent as the spellbinding, spirited nymph, her performance from this point on is even richer and more affecting as a more mature young woman in quiet, dignified mourning. Now living amongst the settlers, her Pocahontas is seen trying to get used to shoes, dresses, and a host of other unfamiliar things, including the new name given to her at baptism of Rebecca. No wonder she seems to be "broken, lost."

The most involving portion of *The New World*'s story is the final one in which kindhearted, gentlemanly John Rolfe (a perfectly-pitched Christian Bale) hesitantly and respectfully intrudes upon Pocahontas' silent sorrow to express sincere caring for her. Having lost a wife and child, he obviously sees her as a wondrous, dispirited kindred spirit. Watching his patience, understanding, and openness in courting her is bittersweet (as so much of the film is), especially when Pocahontas' voiceover makes clear that her heart remains spoken for. "Why can I not feel as I should?" she wonders, praying to a higher power to "take out the thorn" that prevents her heart from healing. She enters into marriage with Rolfe and they have a child, but their growing closeness is endangered when Pocahontas learns that Smith is alive and residing in London. She is soon there herself, invited to be a guest before the King and Queen, and it is now her turn to make an awed arrival in a strange land. During the regal ceremony, a formally attired Pocahontas peers at a small, bewildered animal on display in a cage, ripped from its natural surroundings in the New World and now a curiosity for the Old. Few will miss the comparison being drawn between the creature and Pocahontas. While in London, a final meeting with Smith provides her with closure, a scene of less concern to viewers at this point than the subsequent one of particular poignancy in which Rolfe's constancy is finally rewarded. That their search for contentment is over makes Pocahontas' death at just past twenty years old from a respiratory ailment seem especially tragic. Rolfe sails back to America with their small child, and as the ship floats across the frame, one cannot help but think of other majestic things that have passed.

Many critics admired *The New World* and marveled at Kilcher, although some complained the film lacks sufficient focus and is too soporific. Made on a budget estimated to be $30 million, *The New World* grossed over $4 million in limited release Malick (who never does interviews) reportedly wrote the screenplay some twenty-five years ago. In addition to Malick himself, particular praise must go to cinematographer Emmanuel Lubezki (who shot entirely within Virginia), production designer Jack Fisk, costume designer Jacqueline West, and the much-heralded composer James Horner. *The New World* is lyrical, atmospheric, and contemplative. It might best be described as evocative, cinematic poetry.

David L. Boxerbaum

CREDITS

Captain Smith: Colin Farrell
Captain Newport: Christopher Plummer
John Rolfe: Christian Bale
Powhatan: August Schellenberg
Opechancanough: Wes Studi
Wingfield: David Thewlis
Captain Argall: Yorick Van Wageningen
Ben: Ben Mendelsohn
Tomocomo: Raoul Trujillo
Lewes: Brian F. O'Byrne
Pocahontas' Mother: Irene Bedard
Savage: John Savage
Emery: Jamie Harris
Patawomeck's Wife: Alex Rice
Rupwew: Michael Greyeyes
Selway: Noah Taylor
King James: Jonathan Pryce
Pocahontas: Q'orianka Kilcher
Parahunt: Klanai Queypo
Queen Anne: Alexandra Malick
Origin: USA
Language: English
Released: 2005
Production: Sarah Green; released by New Line Cinema
Directed by: Terrence Malick, Jack Fisk
Written by: Terrence Malick
Cinematography by: Emmanuel Lubezki
Music by: James Horner
Sound: Jose Antonio Garcia
Editing: Richard Chew, Hank Corwin, Saar Klein, Mark Yoshikawa
Art Direction: David Crank, Sara Hauldren
Costumes: Jacqueline West
MPAA rating: PG-13
Running time: 160 minutes

REVIEWS

Boxoffice Online. December, 2005.
Los Angeles Times Online. December 23, 2005.
New York Times Online. December 23, 2005.
Variety Online. December 12, 2005.

TRIVIA

Writer/director Malick actually finished the script in the late 1970s, but production did not get underway until 2004.

AWARDS

Natl. Bd. of Review 2005: Breakthrough Perf. (Kilcher)

Nomination:

Oscars 2005: Cinematog.

NORTH COUNTRY

All She Wanted Was To Make A Living. Instead She Made History.
—Movie tagline

Box Office: $18.1 million

According to publicity and to captioning in the film itself, *North Country* is "inspired by true events." It is very loosely based on the book *Class Action: The Story of Lois Jenson and the Landmark Case that Changed Sexual Harassment Law* (by Clara Bingham and Laura Leedy Gansler), which chronicles the long and difficult struggle of Lois Jenson as she endured the nation's first class-action sexual harassment lawsuit against the Minnesota mining company that employed her in the mid-1970s. *North Country* is actually more inspired by the landmark case itself, rather than the details of the historical facts surrounding it. In the film, real-life Lois Jenson is replaced by the character of Josey Aimes, played by Charlize Theron, and the time frame in which she suffers cruel harassment in the workplace is moved forward so that what was really a multi-decade experience is condensed for dramatic purposes, culminating in 1991. Although *North Country* does deviate in significant ways from the "true" story, it is an emotionally compelling, effectively constructed film that tells a story that is important both socially and personally in its reflections on the need to take courageous stands against injustice and evil, even when the stakes are high.

The film is structured so that the courtroom proceedings in the timeline's present act as a frame for the real story, the struggle Josey faces when she finds herself in the hostile environment of a workplace where men outnumber women thirty to one. Josey's story is told in a series of flashbacks, beginning with her return home to a small town in northern Minnesota town after leaving a physically abusive husband. Unfortunately, from the outset she does not receive much sympathy.

When she arrives home with her two children, Sammy (Thomas Curtis) and Karen (Elle Peterson), her father Hank (Richard Jenkins) actually questions whether Josey might have played some role in provoking the violence from her husband: "He catch you in bed with another man?" Hank's attitude is an early sign of the seemingly prevalent attitude toward women in this setting.

Josey starts a job at a hair salon but has little hope of making ends meet on such a paycheck. However, she soon meets Glory (Frances McDormand), an old friend who tells her that she could earn six times as much working in the iron mines, where she herself works. Josey eagerly takes on the job, even though both her father and mother are opposed to the idea (according to Hank, it is a "man's job").

Right away, the harassment begins from male coworkers, who believe that women do not belong in the mines and who claim that the female workers are taking jobs away from men who need to support their families. At first it comes in the form of obscene joking, demeaning language, and pranks such as putting sex toys in lunch boxes. The other women in the mine, afraid of losing their much-needed jobs if they complain, weather the humiliation and verbal abuse as best as they can (they have all been told to "take it like men"). The situation seems to intensify for Josey, however, who is subjected to more torment than the other women and who faces especially despicable conduct from Bobby Sharp (Jeremy Renner), a supervisor with whom Josey had a relationship in high school. Obscenities, sexual slurs, and pranks evolve into fondling and groping. Graffiti appears on the walls of the women's locker room, written in human feces. When Josey complains to management, without the backing of any of the other women, matters only worsen. Eventually she is attacked and almost raped by Bobby, at which point she decides she has had enough.

She turns to sympathetic lawyer Bill White (Woody Harrelson), who helps her launch a class-action sexual harassment suit against the mining company. Unlike most of the other males in the story, Bill is a kind and decent man who respects Josey and wants to help. He also sees it as an opportunity to make a name for himself by initiating a case that could lead to new laws. The trial eventually becomes the focus of the film but, somewhat unsatisfactorily insofar as the developing drama, does not reach a resolution during the course of the story. Titles at the end of the film explain the eventual outcome of the lawsuit, which set the groundwork for current laws regarding harassment in the workplace.

While the film's story is an important and emotionally-charged one, much of the direction of the plot is fairly predictable even if one is not acquainted with the history of the actual lawsuit. The nature of the harassment the women suffered may be surprising—and to the extent that it is, the film achieves a significant level of social enlightenment—but the trial scenes proceed much as trial scenes in movies often do, and by this time in the film's progression, a more dramatic turn of events (and a clearer resolution for the characters) would be a more effective direction for the story. The film is revelatory in its exposition of the treatment of women in this particular setting (and prompts one to wonder how often such harassment may still occur) and also in the way that those who are put on the defensive actually attempt to blame the victims, a ploy that is most certainly used in defense of many other acts of injustice around the world.

Theron plays the role of Josey with a believability that makes her plight even more affecting. Likewise, the powerful performances of several other actors also help lift the story from potential slips into mediocrity. Frances McDormand and Sean Bean (who plays Glory's gentle and caring husband Kyle) give their characters a unique kind of strength that provides a needed balance against the antagonists whose behavior engenders so much anger, though Bean's appearance is rather brief. Thomas Curtis delivers a very realistic and empathetic performance as a son who loves his mother but is torn by shame when she takes on such a negative public image; he also brings deep emotion to a scene in which Josey reveals to him the identity of his real father. Richard Jenkins also achieves psychological depth in his portrayal of the very conflicted Hank, who eventually comes to understand the reality of his daughter's struggle and begins to come to terms with his own fears and failures as well as his love for Josey.

Aside from the performances and the compelling story itself, the musical score, production design, and cinematography all work together to effectively create a sad, often gloomy atmosphere that serves as an appropriate backdrop for the darkness and the hatred that Josey must face. However, what is perhaps most memorable about *North Country* is not only the moral and political battles it depicts and the significant issues therein, but the underlying theme of courage in the face of monstrous and seemingly unbeatable enemies, a courage that will drive one forward to fight for what is right despite the personal cost.

David Flanagin

CREDITS

Josey Aimes: Charlize Theron
Glory: Frances McDormand

Kyle: Sean Bean
Hank: Richard Jenkins
Bobby Sharp: Jeremy Renner
Sherry: Michelle Monaghan
Bill White: Woody Harrelson
Alice: Sissy Spacek
Big Betty: Rusty Schwimmer
Peg: Jillian Armenante
Sammy: Thomas Curtis
Karen: Elizabeth Peterson
Leslie Conlin: Linda Emond
Young Josie: Amber Heard
Young Bobby: Cole Williams
Origin: USA
Language: English
Released: 2005
Production: Nick Weschler; Nick Weschler; released by Warner Bros.
Directed by: Niki Caro
Written by: Michael Seitzman
Cinematography by: Chris Menges
Music by: Gustavo Santaolalla
Sound: William Sarokin
Editing: David Coulson
Art Direction: Greg Hooper
Costumes: Cindy Evans
Production Design: Richard Hoover
MPAA rating: R
Running time: 123 minutes

REVIEWS

Boxoffice Online. October, 2005.
Chicago Sun-Times Online. October 21, 2005.
Entertainment Weekly Online. October 19, 2005.
Los Angeles Times Online. October 21, 2005.
New York Times Online. October 21, 2005.
Premiere Magazine Online. October 21, 2005.
Variety Online. September 12, 2005.
Washington Post Online. October 21, 2005, p. C01.

TRIVIA

The lawsuit that inspired this film was settled in 1998, ten years after it was first filed and more than 20 years after the harassments began.

AWARDS

Nomination:

Oscars 2005: Actress (Theron), Support. Actress (McDormand)

British Acad. 2005: Actress (Theron), Support. Actress (McDormand)

Golden Globes 2006: Actress—Drama (Theron), Support. Actress (McDormand)

Screen Actors Guild 2005: Actress (Theron), Support. Actress (McDormand)

Broadcast Film Critics 2005: Actress (Theron), Support. Actress (McDormand).

NOVEMBER

The truth lies outside the frame.
—Movie tagline

Shot for a mere $150,000 in a quick 15 days, Greg Harrison's *November* is a puzzle movie, one that plays an elaborate game challenging the audience to figure out what is real and what is made up, imagined, or possibly even dreamed. Recent years have seen a spate of such twisty films that play with our perceptions of reality and traditional narrative logic, a noir subgenre that encompasses Bryan Singer's *The Usual Suspects* (1995), Christopher Nolan's *Memento* (2000), and David Lynch's masterful *Mulholland Drive* (2001). *November*, penned by Benjamin Brand, does not have the visceral punch or narrative sophistication of the best of these films, and it is too restrained and cold to draw us in completely in its labyrinth, but, if one is willing to follow the clues and watch closely, *November* can still be appreciated as a cerebral exercise, just not as a very thrilling mystery.

Looking very dour and serious in glasses and an unglamorous hairstyle, Courteney Cox plays Sophie Jacobs, a photographer who seems to be on the verge of unraveling. She is plagued by headaches and is undergoing a serious trauma involving her relationship with her boyfriend, Hugh (James Le Gros). Running a relatively brief 73 minutes, the film is broken into three parts, each telling a variation on the basic story, which revolves around a convenience store robbery on November 7, and each named for a different response to death—"Denial," "Despair," and "Acceptance."

In "Denial," Hugh is shot and killed in the store while making an impromptu stop to satisfy Sophie's craving for chocolate after dinner. Sophie is, naturally enough, distraught in the aftermath, her feelings of grief compounded by her guilt for having cheated on him with her coworker, Jesse (Michael Ealy). She visits a psychiatrist, Dr. Fayn (Nora Dunn), has lunch with her mother (Anne Archer), and even seeks the help of an investigator, Officer Roberts (Nick Offerman), when a slide showing the exterior of the convenience store on the fateful night mysteriously turns up in her carousel during a photography class she teaches. The slide was developed only two days after the robbery, but when the officer discovers that the photo is hers, she cannot understand what has happened. Because she does not remember taking it, her already tenuous grip on reality grows more fragile.

"Despair" puts a very different spin on the crime. Instead of Hugh, Sophie is in the store and taking photos when the crime occurs. She survives the shooting when the robber, having already killed the store's proprietors, finds himself out of bullets when he faces her. This section deals head-on with Sophie's infidelity and its consequences. Hugh is suspicious of her behavior, and, after she confesses to cheating, he leaves her.

"Acceptance" finds Sophie and Hugh reconciling after their split. Sophie has ended her affair, and her mental health, as revealed in her meeting with her psychiatrist, seems much improved. But in this chapter's version of the robbery, not only is Hugh killed but so is Sophie after she hears the initial gunfire and races inside the store.

November is structured around repetitions, especially certain scenes—the robbery, the visit with the psychiatrist, the photography class, and lunch with the mother—that are replicated in each scenario but with slight variations to suggest a different state of mind. Even a small detail like a glass of wine that spills in the first scene with Sophie's mother and spreads on the tablecloth like blood is transformed in the later chapters. A lighter-colored drink spills in the second scenario, and, in the third, Sophie stops the glass from spilling at all. The progression suggests that the wine is a psychological substitute for blood, which Sophie literally spills when she is shot and killed at the end. For ultimately the accumulation of details and clues suggests that "Acceptance" is the true story and "Denial" and "Despair" are psychological projections, alternate realities that Sophie envisions at the moment she is dying. In this way, *November*'s closest filmic relative is *Mulholland Drive*, which turns on a similar twist.

But such a comparison highlights the weaknesses of *November*. Lynch's film has a dreamy, seductive, and mysterious atmosphere that draws the viewer into its surreal landscape, making *November* seem anemic by comparison. Ultimately, Sophie's hallucinations, her psychological responses to her own demise, are not especially gripping, and the film's dark look, while creating a certain mood, is rather pretentious and not very imaginative.

Moreover, Naomi Watts's mesmerizing, multidimensional performance as the dying heroine fantasizing a different life for herself in *Mulholland Drive* was a revelation. Courteney Cox does an admirable job of conveying Sophie's perpetual glumness and sense of disconnection from her life, but the character itself feels one-dimensional and is written more as a device for the plot to unfold around than as a real character with whom we can identify. Because she and Hugh are not very well developed, we never feel a real rooting interest in whether they stay together. Aside from a flashback to their cute meeting in her studio when she takes his picture and he flirts with her—one scene that gives them a human spark—there is little interaction that makes us care about their fates, either together or apart. Even their deaths, while tragic, are just a plot point to be figured out.

November has the rudimentary elements for a solid mind teaser but lacks the ingenuity, texture, and character development to shape them into an intriguing mystery. The joys of these puzzle films are untangling the details to uncover what is really going on or simply losing oneself in the elaborate gamesmanship. But, in *November*, as the same essential story is spun out in three different ways, the repetitions become rather tedious, and trying to uncover the truth becomes more of a chore than a delight.

Peter N. Chumo II

CREDITS

Sophie Jacobs: Courteney Cox
Hugh: James LeGros
Dr. Fayn: Nora Dunn
Carol Jacobs: Anne Archer
Jesse: Michael Ealy
Officer Roberts: Nick Offerman
The Shooter: Matthew Carey
Origin: USA
Language: English
Released: 2005
Directed by: Greg Harrison
Written by: Benjamin Brand
Cinematography by: Nancy Schreiber, Nancy Schreiber
Music by: Lew Baldwin
Costumes: Danny Glicker
Production Design: Tracey Gallacher
MPAA rating: R
Running time: 73 minutes

REVIEWS

Boxoffice Online. July, 2005.
Chicago Sun-Times Online. August 5, 2005.
Entertainment Weekly Online. July 20, 2005.
Los Angeles Times Online. July 22, 2005.
New York Times Online. July 22, 2005.
Washington Post Online. August 11, 2005, p. WE35.

OLDBOY

End of confrontation, one must die.
—Movie tagline

15 years forced in a cell, only 5 days given to seek revenge.
—Movie tagline

Oldboy is the latest film from South Korean director Park Chan-Wook and was the winner of the Grand Jury Prize at the 2004 Cannes Film Festival. Sharing a similar aesthetic with Quentin Tarantino's *Kill Bill Parts 1* and *2* (2004, 2005), that of the bloody revenge thriller, it comes as no surprise that Tarantino was the presiding juror on that panel and the films biggest fan. Park's film however, is as much concerned with the brutal violence as he is with examining the cost of vengeance on the human psyche and the cause-and-effect karmic circle of past misdeeds on the offender and the offended. It is also a film that is as much a brutal, stylish revenge thriller as it is a Greek tragedy.

Choi Min-Sik is a Seoul businessman named Oh Dae-Su who, after getting drunk one night on the way to his daughter's birthday party, is taken into police custody for disorderly conduct. He is bailed out of jail by a friend and after calling his wife from a phone booth, disappears. He wakes up the next morning in what appears to be a run-down hotel room that is sparsely furnished except for a bed, desk, and a television. He attempts to leave but the door is locked from the outside. There is a slot in the door that he uses to scream out for help and demands to be set free. Nobody answers him. He remains in this "prison" for fifteen years, never being told why. His captors deliver his meals through the slot in the door and pump sleeping gas into his room periodically in order to bathe him and extract some of his blood.

He has no contact with the outside world except for the television where he learns that he has been declared the main suspect in his wife's murder, his blood having been discovered at the scene. Hoping to figure out who imprisoned him and why, he begins writing a journal naming everybody that he has wronged. One morning he finds himself on a grass covered rooftop having been set free. Filled with rage he determines to find out the mystery of his imprisonment, who did it, and why.

Shortly, he is caught in a street fight and through his emotionless narration he states that, "From television I learned many things, including how to fight, but not curse words, because television does not teach those." Because of his imprisonment, he has missed out on a lot of things, and he does not have the ability to express himself. That part of him is missing and he doesn't know how to get it back. Because of his lack of human contact during his isolation, and his reliance on television, he has forgotten how to think for himself. The only thing he knows, the only thing he has that's his, is the insatiable need for vengeance.

He makes his way to a local sushi bar that he has heard of from television and he meets the beautiful Mido (Gang Hye-Jung) who is the chef. He passes out after consuming a live squid and wakes up in Mido's apartment. He tells her his story and together they begin to try to unravel the mystery of his imprisonment. Why she takes him in so quickly and believes his story is as much due to her instincts as the machinations of the man behind the curtain.

Soon Oh Dae-Su finds the place where he was held, and in a gruesome tooth-extracting scene reminiscent of *Marathon Man* (1976) he "interrogates" the main jailor as to who ordered his incarceration, using the claw end of a hammer. He doesn't get a name (for security purposes the jailer never uses clients' names) but he does get another clue.

All this leads to a conclusion that is as disturbing as it is inevitable. His captor is revealed, his identity going back to Oh Dae-Su's childhood. When he finally meets his captor, Oh Dae Su asks him the inevitable question as to why he imprisoned him for 15 years. His captor, in turn, answers this with another question. It is not so much why he imprisoned him for 15 years, but why he released him after 15 years.

The climax of the film is quite gruesome and may have viewers averting their heads in one scene in particular during the final confrontation between Oh Dae-Su and his captor. But the viewer may want to remain for the closing credits just for their own cathartic release from this nightmare world.

In *Oldboy*, Park Chan-Wook has crafted a film that is a stylish and brutal character study of a man made monster living in his world of hate and redemption that is as brilliant in its execution as it is mesmerizing in its energy. The philosophical journey of Oh Dae-Su from an unfocused father and alcoholic to a man focused in hate and back again is a tour de force in acting from Choi Min-Sik.

David E. Chapple

CREDITS

Dae-su Oh: Mink-sik Choi
Woo-jin Lee: Yu Ji-tae
Mido: Gang Hye-jeong
Origin: South Korea
Language: Korean
Released: 2003
Production: Kim Dong-ju; Show East; released by Show East
Directed by: Park Chan-wook
Written by: Park Chan-wook, Hwang Jo-yun, Lim Jun-hyeong
Cinematography by: Jeong-hun Jeong

Music by: Yeong-wook Jo, Shim Hyeon-jeong, Lee Ji-su, Choi Sung-hyeon
Sound: Lee Sang-wook, Lee Seong-cheol
Editing: Kim Sang-Beom
Production Design: Yu Seong-heui, Jo Sang-gyeong
MPAA rating: R
Running time: 120 minutes

REVIEWS

Boxoffice Online. March, 2005.
Chicago Sun-Times Online. March 25, 2005.
Entertainment Weekly Online. March 23, 2005.
Los Angeles Times Online. March 25, 2005.
New York Times Online. March 25, 2005.
Premiere Magazine Online. March 22, 2005.
Variety Online. January 7, 2004.
Washington Post Online. April 8, 2005, p. WE45.

QUOTES

Oh Dae-Su: "Even though I'm no more than a monster—don't I, too, have the right to live?"

TRIVIA

Min-sik Choi lost twenty pounds and trained for six weeks to get in shape for the role of Dae-su. He also did most of his own stuntwork.

OLIVER TWIST

Box Office: $2 million

There can be little doubt that Roman Polanski is one of the few genius directors of the 20th Century who is still working in the 21st Century, but, unfortunately, to be gifted is not necessarily to be popular. *Oliver Twist*, Polanski's most recent adaptation after the tremendous success of *The Pianist* (2002), was not a popular success, even though Polanski was working with much the same screenwriter (Ronald Harwood), cinematographer (Pawel Edelman), editor (Herve De Luze), and crew that had generated seven Academy Award nominations in 2003 and had won awards for best director (from the Directors Guild) and best film at the Cannes Festival. In its issue of January 9, 2006, *Variety* listed the "Domestic Top 250 of 2005." Polanski's film made the list, but, at number 217, it was nearly in the lower ten percent. By the end of 2005 *Oliver Twist* had only grossed just over $2 million.

Oliver Twist was published in 1837-1838, the first success of young Charles Dickens, who, according to screenwriter Ronald Harwood, eventually fixed a particular image of life in 19th Century England in the imagination of his later readers. Oliver Twist (played by Barney Clark) is the name given to an orphan of unknown parentage, born and raised in a miserable workhouse, where he is mistreated by the parish beadle, Mr. Bumble (Jeremy Swift plays this Bumble-beadle). Sold as an apprentice into conditions that are not much better to work for a conniving undertaker, Mr. Sowerberry (Michael Heath), Oliver is whipped after an altercation with another boy who makes disparaging comments about Oliver's mother.

Thereafter, Oliver runs away to London, where is falls in with bad company, a juvenile gang of thieves trained by Fagin (Sir Ben Kingsley), a caricatured Jewish villain, to work as a pickpocket with his more experienced colleagues, the "Artful Dodger" (Harry Eden) and Charley Bates (Lewis Chase). More dangerous than Fagin, however (who is somewhat humanized by Polanski's treatment, though still a Dickensian caricature) is the burglar Bill Sikes (Jamie Foreman) and his "fierce dog," since Sikes is a psychopath who brutalizes both Oliver and his companion, Nancy (Leanne Rowe), presented as a "fallen angel."

While in training as a pickpocket, Oliver is pursued and arrested after his gang attempts to rob the kindly Mr. Brownlow (Edward Hardwicke) at a London bookstall. Captured by the authorities and brought before a cruel magistrate, Oliver faints, eventually causing Mr. Brownlow to take pity on him. The bookseller who witnessed the robbery attempt exonerates Oliver as being innocent, and Mr. Brownlow, who recognizes an innate goodness and innocence in the boy, takes Oliver home, apparently intending to adopt him. "I feel strongly disposed to trust you," Brownlow tells Oliver after asking him "How would you like to grow up a clever man?" Later sent on an errand to the bookseller with a £5 note, Oliver betrays that trust, but through no fault of his own. He is recognized by Bill Sikes and Nancy, kidnapped by them, and taken back to Fagin.

Oliver is later forced by Sikes, at gunpoint, to assist the criminals in breaking into Mr. Brownlow's home. Brownlow is warned in time, however, and manages to chase the thieves away, but in the course of doing so, Oliver is wounded. Further complications and complicated relationships abound in the novel, but these were purposefully simplified by the screenplay. In a "special feature" about the film's making, Ronald Harwood explains that the "phenomenal variety of characters" found in the world of this Dickens novel had to be condensed, as well as the far-fetched complications of the subplots, particularly Brownlow's relationship to Oliver as Dickens imagined it. Instead, Harwood choose to focus on the Oliver plot, starting with Oliver at the age of nine. Harwood described this simplified version as follows: "It's about a boy, a little boy, who takes charge of his own life, escapes from terrible trials and dangers, and emerges triumphant." Dickens purists should not have been offended, given the atmospheric beauty of the visualization and the integrity of the reimagined characterizations.

Polanski explained his own motives for making this film after *The Pianist* by saying simply that he wanted to make a film for his children. Drawing on his own childhood experiences, moreover, Polanski could well understand this story of survival. "I was a hungry orphan [for] quite a while during the way, when my parents were taken off to the concentration camps," Polanski explained in the DVD "special feature" on the making of the film.

It's hardly surprising that, after having adapted Thomas Hardy's *Tess of the D'Urbervilles* in 1979 (and winning three Oscars), director Roman Polanski would eventually turn his talents toward adapting Charles Dickens's first novel to the screen, even if that meant following in the wake of one of England's greatest directors, David Lean, who adapted *Oliver Twist* in 1948 with a cast that included Alex Guinness as Fagin, Robert Newton ad Sikes, and John Howard Davies as Oliver. Indeed, the 1948 David Lean adaptation constitutes the gold standard for film adaptations of this Dickens classic. In the Lean treatment, Fagin's juvenile gang and Bill Sikes's unrelieved psychopathy are presented as diametrically opposed to Mr. Brownlow's benevolence, as if representing two autonomous worlds. Lean used Expressionist camera angles and lighting techniques to contrast the darkness of the underworld with the cozy whiteness of the Brownlow sequences. Polanski takes a similar approach. Mr. Brownlow's home is ordinarily bathed in sunshine and seems to be located on the bucolic edge of Oliver's London, where the mise-en-scene is often drab and gloomy and where brown tones dominate.

The David Lean adaptation was so controversial for its characterization of Fagin that, according to *Variety*, "its U.S. release was delayed for three years." George C. Scott would later play Fagin for director Clive Donner's 1982 adaptation, and Ron Moody was Fagin for Carol Reed's 1968 musical adaptation, *Oliver!*, which captured six Oscars. Sir Ben Kingsley took the challenge for the Polanski adaptation and was certainly capable of doing justice to the role, even though the rest of the cast fell short of including another actor of his fame and magnitude. Without question, Kingsley's Fagin would be familiar to anyone who had read the Dickens description: "a very shriveled old Jew, whose villainous-looking and repulsive face was obscured by a quantity of matted red hair."

Even so, Polanski's approach to Fagin was quite the opposite of the Lean/Guinness treatment, according to Todd McCarthy's evaluation for *Variety*: "Kingsley and Polanski appear most interested in attempting to humanize him, to argue that, even though he takes advantage of his boys and makes them break the law, this might be preferable to their fates if they were left to their own devices on the streets." As a consequence, Kingsley's Fagin exudes "a certain feebleness and insecurity that makes him more pathetic than hateful." Moreover, the film ends with Oliver visiting Fagin on an errand of mercy and forgiveness before that "wretched" man's execution. And it is certainly a good trick to present Fagin as a "lovable" villain. Kingsley saw Fagin as a magician: "I put him on like a dirty old mitten," he explained, colorfully.

The film begins and ends with a black-and-white evocation of Dickensian England visualized through a series of apparent etching, which slowly fade into the color cinematography of the film proper. Polanski intended to suggest the visualizations of etchings by 19th Century book illustrator Paul Gustave Doré (1832-1883), while Ronald Harwood explains that for most of us Victorian London is essentially Dickensian London, as seen and described by the era's greatest novelist. In fact, however, no "real" London (or even British) locations were used. The entire movie was shot with English actors in Prague at Barrandov Studio, but the work is meticulously done. The visual details all seem to fit, appropriately.

Polanski himself, born in 1933 and about Oliver's age at the time of the Nazi invasion, could contextualize the Dickens story of survival. Polanski's previous film, *The Pianist* was also a story of survival, though involving an older protagonist. Within a few months of the film's American release, the PBS television network was to feature an 8-hour "Masterpiece Theatre" miniseries based on yet another Dickens classic, *Bleak House*. This latter adaptation, fabricated by screenwriter Andrew Davies, was praised for having done "supreme justice" to the source novel. Roman Polanski's collaborator, Ronald Harwood, who had touched the ceiling by adapting his own play *The Dresser* to the screen as an Albert Finny vehicle in 1983, was no less gifted. The Polanski film was praised by *New York Times* reviewer A.O. Scott as a "wonderful new adaptation." So what went wrong?

Wall Street Journal reviewer Joe Morgenstern considered "the young hero's passivity" a "dramatic problem inherent in any adaptation" of this novel. Morgenstern criticized actor Barney Clark not only for being passive, but also "bleak in the bargain." Morgenstern stopped short of writing that the performances were bad, complaining "only that they lack luster." Hence Ben Kingsley's Fagin and Jamie Foreman's Bill Sikes "manage to make villainy a bit of a bore." Kingsley's Fagin is "grubby and ugly, but recessive and diminished, a nutty old victim in his own right," which is certainly true of the last glimpse Polanski gives us of him, while Bill Sikes is reduced to "a slightly tedious psychopath." Reviewers seemed to agree composer Rachel Portman's score was overly obvious and overly insistent. But for Variety reviewer Todd McCarthy, the film's main flaw was obvious: the picture "conveys the impression of Polanski coasting through this one, rather than investing much of himself or injecting it with the unmistakable personal touches that reliably marked his earlier work."

In his *New Yorker* review, Anthony Lane found another problem in the way Harwood's screenplay had cut the melodramatic heart out of the novel by its simplifications of plot and character relationships: "Harwood has chopped out the awkward coincidences, notably those surrounding Oliver's parentage, on the assumption that such melodramatic dovetailing would offend the taste of modern viewers. But is he right to assume as much," Lane wanted to know. Clearly not, by implication, but Lane was also offended by the anti-Semitic nastiness attached to the Dickens descriptions of Fagin, a "hideous old man [who] seemed like some loathsome reptile, engendered in the slime and darkness through which he moved: crawling forth, by night, in search of some rich offal for a meal." For a director who had lost his mother to Auschwitz to even think of approaching such material, Lane implies, could be tantamount to a betrayal; but can such carping be fairly applied to the director who made *The Pianist*? One might prefer to think merely that the treatment is tedious, tiresome, and clichéd, even if one would prefer not to agree with Morgenstern. If we consign Fagin to the ash-heap of politically-correct obsolescence, should Shakespeare's Shylock follow a similar fate? Of course, there could be a more troublesome reason for the film's box-office failure—that classic Dickens no longer appeals to an ignorant audience of uneducated non-readers. Now, *that* assumption would be hard to digest and accept.

James M. Welsh

CREDITS

Fagin: Ben Kingsley
Bill Sykes: Jamie Foreman
Artful Dodger: Harry Eden
Nancy: Leanne Rowe
Mr. Brownlow: Edward Hardwicke
Mr. Limbkins: Ian McNeice
Toby Crackit: Mark Strong
Mr. Bumble: Jeremy Swift
Mrs. Bedwin: Frances Cuka
Magistrate Fang: Alun Armstrong
Dining Hall Master: Peter Copley
Old Woman: Liz Smith
Oliver Twist: Barney Clark
Mr. Sowerberry: Michael Heath
Mrs. Sowerberry: Gillian Hanna
Workhouse Master: Andy De La Tour
Origin: Great Britain, Czech Republic, France, Italy
Language: English
Released: 2005
Production: Robert Benmussa, Alain Sarde, Roman Polanski; released by Sony Pictures Entertainment
Directed by: Roman Polanski
Written by: Ronald Harwood
Cinematography by: Pawel Edelman
Music by: Rachel Portman
Sound: Jean-Marie Blondel
Editing: Herve De Luze
Costumes: Anna Sheppard
Production Design: Allan Starski
MPAA rating: PG-13
Running time: 130 minutes

REVIEWS

Boxoffice Online. September, 2005.
Chicago Sun-Times Online. September 30, 2005.
Entertainment Weekly Online. September 21, 2005.
Los Angeles Times Online. September 23, 2005.
New York Times Online. September 23, 2005.
Premiere Magazine Online. September 23, 2005.
Variety Online. September 11, 2005.
Washington Post Online. September 30, 2005, p. WE38.

TRIVIA

Due to the set's massive size, director Roman Polanski rode around it on a motorized scooter.

P

THE PACIFIER

Prepare for bottle.
—Movie tagline

Box Office: $113 million

The training to become a Navy SEAL is notoriously grueling, but what results from such rigorous training are some of the most disciplined, resolute, and startlingly skilled members of our armed forces. One of these powerfully built, specially trained individuals is the focus of the lightweight and less-than-special effort entitled *The Pacifier*. In this negligible family fare from Disney, hilarity is supposed to ensue when a brawny SEAL is turned into a sitter for a family full of unruly kids, the older ones spewing unhappy, angry words while the littlest let loose their own equally formidable eruptions. While the acronym SEAL indicates that members of this elite fighting force can handle anything on sea, air, or land, this fish out of water finds himself floundering, which the film itself does throughout.

The initial scene introduces SEAL Shane Wolfe (Vin Diesel) as a fearless and commanding presence, calmly giving orders which other men listen to with rapt attention before carrying them out as specified. He intrepidly announces that there is only "my way—no highway option" as a daring marine rescue is attempted of a kidnapped professor whose invention the bad guys are dying to get their hands on. The bold, throbbing music which accompanies his actions leaves no doubt who the hero is here. Unfortunately, the professor dies during all this derring-do, and Shane is wounded, as well. What the Serbian terrorists get off the slain scientist is useless without the all-important but unaccounted-for "Ghost" computer program, and so everyone makes it their mission to find it.

While Shane's colleague Capt. Bill Fawcett (Chris Potter) jets off with the dead man's widow (Faith Ford) to rummage for vital information within a safety deposit box in Switzerland, Shane is given the task of protecting the Plummer's five challenging children, including headstrong and hormonal handful Zoë (Brittany Snow), sullen Seth (Max Thieriot), sparkplug Lulu (Morgan York), incontinent Peter (twins Kegan and Logan Hoover) and tiny Tyler (twins Bo and Luke Vink). As if they are not enough to keep Shane busy, he must also try to find the pivotal program around the house, perhaps tucked behind the couch or maybe stashed in a drawer amongst someone's underwear.

When Shane arrives at the Plummers' home, one would in no way blame the intrepid man for having trepidations. His training has enabled him to overpower, outmatch and outwit his adversaries, artfully dodging whizzing bullets and surviving poison gas attacks. However, Shane finds himself ill equipped to master this unhappy and uppity brood and all their formidable whizzing and gas. Once the family's freakish foreign nanny (Carol Kane) takes a kid-induced dive down a flight of stairs and beats a hasty retreat, Shane must go it alone. His "top priority" mission is hardly top-drawer entertainment. As the film goes on, things get a tad saccharine. Sometimes they get just plain weird.

As take-charge, efficient Shane endeavors to instill order and discipline, expecting respect and complete compliance, it is abundantly clear that those currently under his command could not care less. The authoritative whistle he initially employs is only slightly more shrill than the kids' cries of "Stay out of my life!" and "Bite me!" (which the family's equally unmanageable pet duck actually does to Shane's ear). Nothing goes quite right. When Shane dutifully sticks up for Seth on the school playground, the embarrassed boy yells at him for interceding. When the new security system he has installed warns of intruders, Shane hustles off to bust some heads but only breaks up a tryst between Zoe and her boyfriend. (Needless to say, the girl is not pleased.) She disposes of the tracking device he has made for her, sending Shane on a frantic wild-goose chase rescue mission into the sewers, sloshing around in revolting sludge. Lulu, feeling Shane treats her too much like a baby, rails at him about being disrespected. Meanwhile, the smallest Plummers add their own scatological challenges. "We hate you and you hate us," Shane is told, "so why not leave us alone?"

The children's utter distaste for Shane's presence evaporates quickly with the arrival of the bad guys, who for some reason are now Asian martial artists. After Shane performs his heroics, using toys and a barrage of baby powder, the highly relieved kids look a tad sheepish and instantly become more docile and cooperative. "You listen to me and I'll listen to you," he says soothingly, and the film starts a shift in tone: less trouble, more treacle. So Shane gets Zoe to open up, and each cathartically reveals inner torment about their father's death. Tearful hugs ensue. Shane loosens up enough to sing and dance so Peter can contentedly drift off to sleep (after sweetly calling Shane "Daddy"). (Prepare to cringe during Diesel's rendition of the Peter Panda Dance.) In *The Pacifier*'s cutest moments, Shane teaches Lulu and her fellow Firefly Girls how to gustily fend off a group of boys who keep trying to intimidate them. The boys may have broken the girls' cookies, but, thanks to Shane, the punks will never succeed in breaking their spirits. Seth's sudden and disturbing penchant for Nazi garb turns out to only mean that the lad ardently longs for a career on the stage, and is trying out for his school's production of *The Sound of Music.* Seth is tonally challenged, and Leisel von Trapp may be rendered incapable of crossing the Alps to safety if he keeps dropping her with a thud at every rehearsal, but Shane consoles the boy, takes over direction of the play, and all is well. Shane also develops a barely palpable romance with Principal Claire Fletcher (highly-talented Lauren Graham, with little to do).

All is certainly not well in the scenes featuring creepy Vice Principal Murney (a way-over-the-top Brad Garrett), who doubles as wrestling coach and is clearly wrestling with some deep-seated personal issues. This peculiarly aggressive buffoon is present in the film to incite derisive laughter but he comes off as more than a little disturbing, such as when he nastily needles Seth about leaving the wrestling team. This leads Shane to hit the mats with Murney (literally) in the school gym, a scene which features moves like "the nipple crippler" and misses hilarity by a wide margin. The sight of Murney in a tight, too-skimpy wrestling uniform makes Zoe cover her little brother's eyes, and many viewers will wish that someone would do the same for them.

Finally, in the climactic showdown with turncoat Fawcett and the Asian terrorists (who turn out to be the Plummers' Korean neighbors), the film gets wholeheartedly ridiculous. Apparently the kids' late father had been able to surreptitiously dig impressive, intricately booby-trapped catacombs underneath the family's garage to house his all-important invention. The enemy is defeated when everybody (including recently-returned mom) works harmoniously with Shane, a clear message to the kiddies in the audience about the importance of cooperation. This loopy lameness leads to a sappy, everything-tied-up-neatly-in-a bow denouement, in which everyone is so filled with love, happiness and fulfillment they could burst.

Made on a budget of $56 million, *The Pacifier* grossed over $113 million from moviegoers desirous of family-friendly fare. Critical reaction was generally negative. Like Shane, the filmmakers appear to have known what their goal was but found themselves ill equipped to accomplish the task at hand. *The Pacifier* aims to travel a familiar trajectory from friction to fuzzy and warm emotions, from consternation to cooperation, but there is nothing palpably charming, especially creative, or particularly compelling here to make that predictable path an enjoyable one to take. Diesel, whose action film credentials would seem to make him a suitable choice to fill (and fill out) such a role, comes off as rather wooden. One has to give him credit for having the guts to poke fun at his own tough-guy image (like Arnold Schwarzenegger before him), making a good-natured but still sinewy stretch beyond the adrenaline-infused, testosterone-soaked material that made him a star. When the big man nearly loses his lunch while changing a dirty diaper (gingerly utilizing tongs, no less), dealing with noisily emitted odiferous baby fumes, or exasperatedly fending off persistent queries about his "boobs," kids will surely titter. The sight of a supremely capable and confident, muscle-bound Titan being thrown off his game by his potent young charges will likely make them feel empowered. Most adults, on the other hand, will occasionally smile but find much less charm in the proceedings Except for trying to keep their children mildly mollified for an hour and a half, grown-ups will have little use for *The Pacifier.*

David L. Boxerbaum

CREDITS

Shane Wolfe: Vin Diesel
Principal Claire Fletcher: Lauren Graham
Julie Plummer: Faith Ford
Zoe: Brittany Snow
Seth: Max Thieriot
Capt. Bill Fawcett: Chris Potter
Lulu: Morgan York
Director: Scott Thompson
Helga: Carol Kane
Vice Principal Murney: Brad Garrett
Howard Plummer: Tate Donovan
Mr. Chun: Denis Akiyama
Mrs. Chun: Mung-Ling Tsui
Origin: USA
Language: English
Released: 2005
Production: Roger Birnbaum, Gary Barber, Jonathan Glickman; Roger Birnbaum, Gary Barber; released by Buena Vista
Directed by: Adam Shankman
Written by: Robert Ben Garant
Cinematography by: Peter James
Music by: John Debney
Sound: Glen Gauthier
Editing: Christopher Greenbury
Art Direction: Arv Grewal
Costumes: Kirston Mann
Production Design: Linda DeScenna
MPAA rating: PG
Running time: 95 minutes

REVIEWS

Boxoffice Online. March, 2005.
Chicago Sun-Times Online. March 4, 2005.
Entertainment Weekly Online. March 9, 2005.
Los Angeles Times Online. March 4, 2005.
New York Times Online. March 4, 2005.
Premiere Magazine Online. March 4, 2005.
Variety Online. March 2, 2005.
Washington Post Online. March 4, 2005, p. WE43.

QUOTES

Shane Wolfe: "I'm never gonna be able to remember your names because there's not enough time so you're Red One, you're Red Two, you're Red Three, and you're Red Baby."

PALINDROMES

"Say what you will about Solondz,"wrote Carina Chocano in *The Los Angeles Times,* "He's an artist with a worldview. And it's not rosy." Todd Solondz, the filmmaker behind such non-cheery fare as *Welcome to the Dollhouse, Happiness* and *Storytelling,* may not make rosy films, but they are also thought-provoking, and often, haunting. *Palindromes* is his most haunting film yet. It is quite dark, and covers uncomfortable—to say the least—topics like a messed-up abortion, murder, and pedophilia, yet Solondz finds a certain hypnotic quality in his doomed, pitiful characters. The odd and unsettling film lingers in the brain.

Palindromes starts with a nod to fans of *Welcome to the Dollhouse.* It begins at the funeral of Dawn Wiener, the awkward high school outcast of *Dollhouse* who has committed suicide after getting pregnant. After the funeral, her 13-year-old cousin Aviva (Emani Sledge), is in tears in her bedroom because Dawn's sister compared Aviva to Dawn. Her mother, Joyce Victor (Ellen Barkin), comforts the little girl with, "You are the cutest little bundle of love in the whole world, no matter what anyone says." Aviva takes this all in and decides that her solution will be to get pregnant so that there will always be someone to love her. On a visit to friends of the family, she propositions their pudgy teenage son, Judah (Robert Agri). After doing the deed, which Solondz naturally films in all its awkward, unsexy real-time glory, she gets her wish and indeed becomes pregnant.

Aviva's parents force her to get an abortion, which leaves Aviva accidentally infertile. This sets the girl off on a journey which includes meeting and having sex with a guilty, young girl-liking trucker, Earl (Stephen Adly Guirgis), and a stint with Mama Sunshine (Debra Monk), a born-again Christian who runs a house for handicapped children.

Besides the subject matter, one of the things that makes *Palindromes* seem so off-kilter is Solondz's decision to have eight different actors play Aviva. At different points in the film, the young teen is played by a boy (Will Denton), a 43-year-old (Jennifer Jason Leigh), and a morbidly obese African-American woman (Sharon Wilkins). It is a casting gimmick but oddly affecting too. Aviva is such a well-formed character—with her halting, quiet speech and downcast eyes—that it is not at all disconcerting to see her played by different people. Owen Gleiberman of *Entertainment Weekly* wrote that it almost was as though her identity were "a ghost passing through different bodies." And each Aviva actor brings out a different aspect of the character. One of the most eloquent performances is by Wilkins. The large woman is so dense in physical body size, but she perfectly conveys the wispiness of Aviva's personality. She seems as though she might float away at any moment.

The other stylistic quirk that makes *Palindromes* such an odd experience is that it does not have an easily discernible point of view. Is it disparaging the views of Aviva's upper middle class Jewish family? Or is it making fun of Mama Sunshine and her band of misfits? Solondz films the scenes of the Christian household with an unblinking eye. There is a scene in which a boy with Down's Syndrome comments at the dinner table, "My name is Skippy! Like the peanut butter!" He, and his family laugh uproariously at this joke. Is Solondz making fun of the family? Or is he making fun of the viewer for being cynical?

Solondz is master of the uncomfortable scene and this film is filled with them. The most memorable is after Aviva and her trucker have a one-night stand. The morning after in their seedy hotel room, the trucker is obviously looking to beat a hasty retreat. Aviva, oblivious, lolls about in bed replaying the night. She gushes about how beautiful it had been and plans future rendezvous. The whole thing is just painful.

Critics were divided as to whether the film was an artful provocation or just tasteless titillation. Owen Gleiberman of *Entertainment Weekly* wrote, "Solondz, who seems to have entered his avant-garde outlaw phase, has made a movie that demands to be seen because it's like nothing you've seen before...*Palindromes* isn't flawless, yet it's an experience to love, to hate, to fight with and to meld your mind with." A.O. Scott of *The New York Times* wrote, "The real problem, it seems to me, is not that Mr. Solondz goes too far, but that he seems to have no particular direction in mind, no artistic interest beyond the limitless ugliness of humanity." Andrew O'Hehir of *Salon.com* wrote, "I've seen some whacked-out movies in my time—but I've never seen anything crazier than *Palindromes*. You can read that as praise if you're that sort of person, but I don't mean it that way. I watched Todd Solondz's new film with a kind of horrified fascination: It's like seeing a fatal car accident happen in slow motion."

Jill Hamilton

CREDITS

Aviva: Jennifer Jason Leigh
Joyce Victor: Ellen Barkin
Steve Victor: Richard Masur
Mama Sunshine: Debra Monk
Aviva: Emani Sledge
Aviva: Valerie Shusterov
Aviva: Hannah Freiman
Aviva: Rachel Corr
Aviva: Will Denton
Aviva: Shayna Levine
Aviva: Sharon Wilkins
Joe/Earl/Bob: Stephen Adly Guirgis
Mark Wiener: Matthew Faber
Dr. Fleischer: Steve Singer
Dr. Dan: Richard Riehle
Judah: Robert Agri
Judah: John Gemberling
Peter paul: Alexander Brickel
Bo Sunshine: Walter Bobbie
Origin: USA
Language: English
Released: 2004
Production: Mike S. Ryan, Derrick Tseng; An Extra Large Pictures
Directed by: Todd Solondz
Written by: Todd Solondz
Cinematography by: Tom Richmond
Music by: Nathan Larson
Sound: Christof Gebert
Editing: Millie Goldstein, Kevin Messman
Costumes: Victoria Farrell
Production Design: David Doernberg
MPAA rating: Unrated
Running time: 100 minutes

REVIEWS

Boxoffice Online. April, 2005.
Chicago Sun-Times Online. April 28, 2005.
Entertainment Weekly Online. April 13, 2005.
Los Angeles Times Online. April 15, 2005.
New York Times Online. October 15, 2004.
Premiere Magazine Online. April 14, 2005.
Variety Online. September 7, 2004.
Washington Post Online. April 29, 2005, p. WE45.

PARADISE NOW

(Al-Jenna-An)

From the most unexpected place, comes a bold new call for peace.
—Movie tagline

Box Office: $1 million

Political cinema attains a milestone with Hany Abu-Assad's deceptively simple action thriller from Palestine, *Paradise Now.* In this subgenre it deserves to take its place alongside Gillo Pontecorvo's controversial classic *The Battle of Algiers* (1965). Both films strive to lend credence to the adage that today's terrorists are tomorrow's freedom fighters. Pontecorvo, however, was recreating history. Abu-Assad is presenting a contemporary phenomenon, that of the suicide bomber and so, no matter how wide his scope, his effort is bound to be found wanting in the light of today's headlines. Wisely, therefore, the director and his co-scenarist adopt the opposite tack. They remain focused on a specific geographical context. In so doing, it is left to their audience to supply the macrocosmic factors missing from their microcosm.

Paradise Now thus emerges as an earnest human document, shorn of any art house gimmickry or formal cleverness, about a global threat whose origins remain inexplicable to those who do not share the ideological convictions from which it has grown. This is because Abu-Assad treats his audience as mere witnesses, not those who need to be converted. Nothing is explained because nothing needs to be in the film's scheme of things.

The film's geographical setting, the city of Nablus, is central to its action and since the film has been shot on location, the backgrounds provide an authenticity, as well as a panoply of everyday life, not seen in news coverage. Allowing the much-disputed land to be a co-star, Abu-Assad aspires to an omniscient perspective.

The film opens with the attractive young Suha (Lubna Azabal), a martyr's daughter, at a checkpost on the outskirts of town. The checking of her documents and the inspection of her bag brings alive the distrust and the tenseness in the air before she's allowed to pass. The film then cuts to a comic scene at an auto repair shed where a customer is fuming to Said (Kais Nashef), a mechanic, that his fender is still crooked. Khaled (Ali Suliman), a hotheaded co-worker, points out that it looks that way because the ground is crooked. The customer then insults Said's father, whereupon Khaled loses it and twists the fender for good. Said's day, however, livens up when Suha brings in her classy car for repair.

It is only when we see the two mechanics on a hillside above the city, sharing a water pipe after a day's work, that their personalities emerge. Through astute casting, they look a globally appealing twosome, given the imperialism of Hollywood. Said resembles as well as exudes the laid back air of David Duchovny while Khaled transmits the familiarity of Billy Crystal with a thick beard. Though Khaled is the energetic one, ready to paint the town, it is Said who has won the heart of Suha, which in turn provides the narrative with its romantic thread. It is a late afternoon like any other. The sound of an explosion from the city below is ignored as if it were just a fact of life.

That evening, however, Said is accosted by the middle-aged Jamal (Amer Hlehel), a resistance fighter, and told that he and Khaled have been selected for a suicide mission that will take place tomorrow. Without so much as a twitch, Said says that he's ready. The moment speaks volumes about how heroism is perceived when religion merges with politics. The sacrificing of one's life in an ongoing struggle for political independence is not seen as an act reflecting individual courage but merely a religious duty fulfilling the will of God. It becomes clear to us that Said, like his numerous shadowy brethren, must have thought about this moment for months, but never feared it.

The film then places Said's impending self-sacrifice within the fabric of his everyday life. Jamal must spend the night at Said's house, so Said's Mother (Hiam Abbass), kept in the dark about the mission, welcomes him. Said himself greets his mother with a kiss on the cheek. We then see Said sitting by himself in his room. It is a moment of tiredness and nothing more. He then tells his mother that Jamal has been able to get him a work permit and that he'll be leaving for Tel Aviv the next day. At dinner, Jamal compliments the mother on her cooking. The film then cuts to Said in bed, awake, with Jamal fast asleep beside him.

On what is to be the last night of his life, Said slips out to Suha's house. He is about to slip her car keys under her door when she opens it. Though it is four in the morning, she invites him in. Like Said's mother, she also does not suspect a thing. The economic disparity between their respective social spheres becomes evident in their inconsequential nervous chatter. When Suha says that Said's life "is like a minimalist Japanese film," Said replies that he doesn't go to the movies because there isn't a movie theater in Nablus. When their conversation touches upon the political, Said remarks that since the Palestinian people cannot retaliate with military might, they have to find alternatives. In his shy manner, Said takes his leave without breaking through to any intimacy. He then runs back through the deserted streets, presumably because of the curfew.

The next morning, the only gesture out of the ordinary that Said makes is to speak to his mother about his father who was executed for being a collaborator. Then he's off with Jamal. On the way, as they walk past a war torn neighborhood in ruins, Jamal spouts his radical rhetoric: "Whoever fights for freedom can die for it!" but we can see it is only preaching to the converted.

As Said is reunited with Khaled within the concrete walls of the hideout, they embrace each other tight. Said says proudly, "Now it's our turn!" Khaled is the first one to be videographed as he holds up a submachine gun and delivers a lengthy speech to the camera about how as a martyr he's not afraid of death. His fervor is wasted when he has to do it again because of technical glitches. This time, he adds an aside to his mother in which he tells her where she can find the brand of water filters she has been looking for. When it's Said's turn, he too curses "the never-ending occupation."

The two are then given haircuts, shaven clean and made to change into business suits. Without his beard, Khaled is almost unrecognizable; Said just looks a yuppie version of himself. For their last meal, the seating resembles Da Vinci's "The Last Supper." Then the belts of explosives are taped to their waists. Jamal makes it clear that if they try to remove the belt it will go off, and that only his men will be able to undo the tapes. Once ready to leave, they are shown posters glorifying them.

Now enters the figure who is clearly at the top of this chain of underground power. Abu Karem (Ashraf Barhoum) tells the two that their families will be well protected while they "ascend to heaven." He adds that this is the first such operation in two years and that "the world will be impressed."

In the car, they are told that once they cross the fence, a contact will take them to the location. Jamal gives them money and fake ID's which they have to memorize. Said asks, "What happens afterwards?" Jamal answers, "Two angels will pick you up."

As the two wait in the tall grass for a signal from Jamal, Said is struck by doubt. "Are we doing the right thing?" he asks. Khaled answers, "In one hour we will be with God."

It is only after the plan goes askew that the film becomes a taut action thriller. As a patrol car approaches, the car meant to pick them up goes off without them. The two then separate and scamper, dodging gunfire. Khaled returns to Jamal while Said crosses onto a road with a bus stop. Khaled and Jamal meet with Abu Karem at the hideout. He fears they could be betrayed by Said and so, could be hit by a rocket at any moment.

As Khaled drives frantically around Nablus looking for Said, the latter makes his way into a washroom in the marketplace. He sits on a toilet seat and carefully wipes the blood from under the belt. We hear a voiceover in his own voice saying, "It is God's will. You cannot alter your fate!"

At the garage, Said meets Suha, who still doesn't suspect anything. She in fact gives Said a lift. This time he kisses her before stepping out. It is only when Suha sees that Khaled too has changed his appearance that the truth dawns on her. She lashes out at him, crying that there's no difference in their killing and the Israelis killing. "There is no Paradise!" she screams. "It's all in your head!" Khaled merely answers, "In this life, we're dead anyway." They at last track down Said near his father's grave.

Said is then taken to see Abu Karem. It is here that Said explains why he has to fulfill his destiny as a suicide bomber, of how he was born in a refugee camp, grew up almost imprisoned in one, and after his father was executed, he became convinced that this was the only way to deliver his message, that he was being forced to be a murderer. Abu Karem silently acquiesces to a second attempt.

This time, after Khaled turns back at the last minute, Said proceeds by himself. The film ends with him seated on a bus in upscale Tel Aviv with armed Israeli soldiers standing nearby. The camera tracks in to an extreme close-up of his lifeless eyes before the screen bleaches out.

Vivek Adarkar

CREDITS

Suha: Lubna Azabal
Said's mother: Hiam Abbass
Said: Kais Nashef
Khaled: Ali Suliman
Jamal: Amer Hlehel
Abu-Karem: Ashraf Barhoum
Origin: France, Germany, Netherlands, Isreal
Language: Arabic
Released: 2005
Production: Bero Beyer; Lama Films, Razor Film
Directed by: Hany Abu-Assad
Written by: Hany Abu-Assad, Bero Beyer
Cinematography by: Antoine Heberle
Sound: Uve Haussig, Matthias Lempert
Editing: Sander Vos
Art Direction: Bahir Abu-Rabia
Costumes: Walid Maw'ed
Production Design: Oliver Meidinger
MPAA rating: PG-13
Running time: 90 minutes

REVIEWS

Boxoffice Online. November, 2005.
Chicago Sun-Times Online. November 4, 2005.
Entertainment Weekly Online. October 26, 2005.
Los Angeles Times Online. October 28, 2005.
New York Times Online. October 28, 2005.
Variety Online. February 15, 2005.
Washington Post Online. November 4, 2005, p. WE44.

AWARDS

Golden Globes 2006: Foreign Film
Ind. Spirit 2006: Foreign Film
Natl. Bd. of Review 2005: Foreign Film

Nomination:

Oscars 2005: Foreign Film

Broadcast Film Critics 2005: Foreign Film.

PEACE, PROPAGANDA & THE PROMISED LAND

Brief but scorching, *Peace, Propaganda & The Promised Land* unveils something few individuals ever get to see or hear: the Arab side to the Middle Eastern conflict. Naturally, this feature will anger those sympathetic strictly to the Israeli perspective, but for free-thinking types (and agnostics), this is essential viewing.

Peace, Propaganda & The Promised Land delivers the basic but convincing polemic that the western media has been co-opted by Israeli's propaganda industry, which has skillfully persuaded a majority of Americans for decades that the Palestinians of the West Bank and Gaza are the evil antagonists in the endless regional war. The documentary also shows how and why the media and most politicians have aided and abetted this single-sided misinformation campaign. Most specifically, the film examines the U.S. government's fixation with oil and military base security, as well as the underlying issues of racism and xenophobia (Europe vs. Muslim, light skin vs. dark skin, et al.).

Directors Bathsheba Ratzkoff and Sut Jhally (both professors from the University of Massachusetts) question several leading experts from a variety of backgrounds, including MIT academic Noam Chomsky, Palestinian politician and activist Hanan Ashrawi, publisher Michael Lerner, and news reporter Alisa Solomon.

In 2004, Ratzkoff and Jhally co-directed another, even better documentary, *Hijacking Catastrophe: 9/11, Fear & the Selling of American Empire,* about how the current Bush administration craftily and deviously used the tragedy of the 2001 World Trade Center bombing to launch the war in Iraq and develop the U.S. military behemoth.

There are quite a few similarities to the *Hijacking Catastrophe* (in addition to the slicker documentaries, *Outfoxed,* a critique of the Fox News Channel, and *Control Room,* about Al-Jazeera's media): in-depth reporting on suppressed or little-known information and statistics; a lucid view of a seemingly complicated state of affairs; and fundamental but proficient filmmaking technique. Both films also hurt themselves with verbose, unwieldy titles. At one early point in *Peace, Propaganda & The Promised Land,* the screen reads, "American Media: Occupied Territory." This could have been a far superior (or at least much catchier) title, but in a bitterly ironic way, the choice of *Peace, Propaganda...*etc. for the marquee illustrates what the movie itself says is the very dilemma with the Palestinian cause: poor public relations!

Expectedly, mainstream critics were divided: in the January 28, 2005 *New York Post,* Russell Scott Smith wrote, "There's only one smoking gun—a CNN memo instructing reporters to refer to the Israeli West Bank settlements as 'neighborhoods.' This semantic change legitimizes the settlements, filmmakers say...Incidentally, if words like 'semantic' make your eyes glaze over, this is definitely one to miss. The movie has none of the Michael Moore-style humor or razzle-dazzle that might have made it more accessible...Often, the movie feels like sitting through a college lecture class... "

But Joshua Land in the January 24, 2005 *Village Voice* countered, "The result may be better suited for classroom viewing than for theatrical exhibition, but that's a tribute to the movie's instructive value. The schematic PowerPoint structure highlights seven 'PR Strategies' used by pro-occupation groups to dominate American news coverage of the region. No new ground is broken, but examples of media outrages abound..."

And a few reviewers tried to balance what they viewed as imbalanced in their writing. Phil Hall of the February 8, 2005, *Film Threat* wrote, "...the film ignores a very long history of Palestinian terrorism which included gruesome violence well beyond the borders of the Holy Land. It also ignores the venal and corrupt leadership of Yasser Arafat, who enriched himself to shameless lengths while his people were forced to live in squalor (though in fairness, the depth of Arafat's shenanigans received greater coverage in the British media than in the American press)...But clearly, the quality of American news coverage from the Middle East is weak and unbalanced—to the point that only four percent of network news reports from the West Bank and Gaza even bothers to mention the territories are under a nearly four-decade military occupation, the longest in modern history and a complete a violation of international law."

Those who feel defensively about Israel, of course, will question much about this documentary, from the data and sources of the data offered to the archival footage shown (including excessive Israeli army violence toward the Palestinians) to the choice of "talking head" subjects (mainly pro-Palestinian, though several are Jewish). The Noam Chomsky segments are typical; at one point Chomsky says, "When Israelis in the occupied territories now claim that they have to defend themselves, they are defending themselves in the sense that any military occupier has to defend itself against the population they are crushing...You can't defend yourself when you're militarily occupying someone else's land. That's not defense. Call it what you like, it's not defense."

But *Peace, Propaganda & The Promised Land* won't change the thinking of those committed to the status quo. Instead, the film is aimed at those interested in little-known stories, the stories behind the stories, and alternate points of view.

Eric Monder

CREDITS

Origin: USA
Language: English
Released: 2004
Production: Bathsheba Ratzkoff; Media Education Foundation
Directed by: Sut Jhally, Bathsheba Ratzkoff
Cinematography by: Kelli Garner
Music by: Thom Monahan
Editing: Kenyon King, Bathsheba Ratzkoff
MPAA rating: Unrated
Running time: 80 minutes

REVIEWS

Film Threat. February 8, 2005.
New York Times Online. January 28, 2005.
San Francisco Chronicle Online. March 11, 2005.
Variety Online. March 13, 2005.
Village Voice Online. January 24, 2005.

THE PERFECT MAN

The story of a family that wanted it all. Never settle.
—Movie tagline
Is it all too good to be true?
—Movie tagline

Box Office: $16.3 million

Hilary Duff fluff. This PG-rated comedy isn't meant for anyone over the age of 14—and that may be pushing it. It's more TV movie territory than big screen as well (as is its cast despite everyone's best efforts). The teenaged Duff stars as 16-year-old Holly Hamilton who, in this mother-daughter role reversal flick, is the responsible one in the family. Desperate-not-to-be-single single mom Jean (Heather Locklear, trying to turn down her own hottie quotient and quite compatible to the blonde Duff in looks) is a baker who specializes in fancy cakes; what she also specializes in is loser relationships. And every time she breaks up with another loser, Holly hears Patsy Cline singing "I Fall to Pieces" and knows that she and seven-year-old Zoe (Aria Wallace who's cute but negligible to the story) will be packing up and moving again.

Since Holly is a 21st century teen, she maintains a blog under the name Girl on the Move so she can record her latest laments: "We're starting off on another big adventure. That's my mom's word for running away." This time the move is from Wichita to Brooklyn where Jean has a job with old friend, Dolores (Kym Whitley), and Holly is once again the new girl at school. At least she immediately makes a friend, contrasting brunette Amy (Vanessa Lengies), and finds a cute and soulful guy, cartoonist Adam (Ben Feldman), who's interested in her. Mom is also making new friends—there's co-worker Gloria (Caroline Rhea), who's just gotten engaged, and bread guy, Lenny (Mike O'Malley). Lenny is a well-meaning doofus who uses incredibly bad lines to flirt with Jean. Which is just what Holly is worried about. As she tells Amy—if the perfect man for her mom doesn't come along within two weeks, she'll hook up with some loser. Although Holly won't admit it to Jean, she's fed up with moving around.

Amy introduces Holly to her Uncle Ben (Chris Noth), a suave restaurateur who owns a place called the River Bistro. He flatters Holly and she hits him up for romance advice; he thinks orchids are the perfect thing to send to that special lady. So that's what Holly does—sends an orchid to Jean from her "secret admirer." Which isn't Lenny, although Jean has agreed to go out with him. His idea of a big date is to drive up in his restored 1980 Trans-Am (she has to take her shoes off to sit in it) and take her to a concert by a Styx tribute band. Holly's appalled when Jean says, unconvincingly, that she had fun. Quick! Time to find mom the perfect guy before that dork wins by default. Holly goes to ask Ben for more advice: what makes a perfect man perfect? Well, even if he were half way around the world, he would rather be with her "because life is better by her side." Awwwww.

Next, Holly sends Jean a romantic letter; she's touched but confused by all the secrecy. She wants to at least know what the guy looks like so Amy and Holly send her a photo of Ben with a message that he's opening a restaurant in China so they can't actually meet. Instead, they can email: Brooklyn Boy to Passionate Baker. But this time, Holly has dragged Adam into her scheme by borrowing his home computer so her mom won't get suspicious. Adam is willing because he really likes Holly; he even draws her as a multi-armed fantasy babe named Princess Holly. The email thing is working great and Holly learns a lot of unexpected stuff about her mom, such as she admits she's made a lot of mistakes and that her kids have suffered for it. Jean's so thrilled by Ben's attention that she breaks up with Lenny.

Too bad that Gloria's bridal shower is at the River Bistro. This means that Amy and Holly must create a diversion so Ben and Jean can't meet. It's extreme though when Holly decides to set off the restaurant's sprinkler system. It's taken a while but Holly finally realizes that Ben would really be the perfect man for her mom. The problem is how can she get around all her lies? She decides to ask Adam to break up with Jean via phone call but when Jean says "Ben" makes her so happy, he thinks about how much he likes Holly and just can't do it. Worse is to come when Lenny decides to ask Jean to marry him. Since Ben shows no sign of turning up, Jean's actually considering his proposal, much to Holly's horror. She fakes another phone call, supposedly from Ben's secretary, and arranges a meeting at the park under the Brooklyn Bridge.

Now she just has to get Ben to agree. So she prints out the emails that Brooklyn Boy and Passionate Baker have been exchanging and tracks Ben to a wedding, which she interrupts when she thinks Ben is the groom—where she got her mistaken idea isn't important and he's the best man anyway. Holly makes a big speech and hands him the emails and then goes to meet her mother and finally confesses to her charade. Jean is crushed. Then Holly gets into a fight with Adam and goes home to ask Jean to move: "We've moved more times for you than I can count and just this once I want to move for me."

Adam goes to their apartment to talk but Holly isn't home. He hands Jean a drawing he's made—Princess Holly and her prince who says he'll always be by her side. Since fair is fair in interfering, Jean secretly emails Adam, who *really* doesn't want Holly to run away. Jean tells her daughter that she's changed her mind about moving: "running away is good for avoiding things. Problem is you end up avoiding yourself, avoiding the people you love. You end up avoiding life." They decide to stick it out and Jean finally gives Lenny back his ring. Ben has finally gotten around to reading the emails and decides he really wants to meet Jean and they agree to have dinner, and Holly finally gets to dress up and go to her first school dance (Adam gives her an orchid corsage). "Can you believe it? The teenage gypsy has finally settled down."

Really, no adult should judge this movie. It's ridiculous and frequently demeaning to adult eyes. Jean is as selfish as Holly accuses her of being and it takes a long time for her to realize how her desperate actions have affected her daughters. She's not exactly a role model although she apparently looks after her kids pretty well. Since this is PG territory, it's not as if Jean's hanging out at bars and bringing home one-night stands. She and Lenny kiss once. Even Holly and Adam get to do that much. And Holly does some very reckless and foolish things as her lies pile on top of each other; she's also easily forgiven since things work out okay for everyone in the end. Hey, but this is tweenie wish fulfillment and no one really expects anything as dreary as reality to intrude into Duff's shiny, happy world.

Christine Tomassini

CREDITS

Holly Hamilton: Hilary Duff
Jean Hamilton: Heather Locklear
Ben Cooper: Christopher Noth
Amy Pearl: Vanessa Lengies
Zoe Hamilton: Aria Wallace
Adam Forrest: Ben Feldman
Lenny Horton: Michael O'Malley
Gloria: Caroline Rhea
Dolores: Kym E. Whitley
Origin: USA
Language: English
Released: 2005
Production: Marc Platt, Dawn Wolfrom, Susan Duff; Marc Platt; released by Universal Pictures
Directed by: Mark Rosman
Written by: Gina Wendkos
Cinematography by: John R. Leonetti
Music by: Christophe Beck
Sound: Greg Chapman
Music Supervisor: Billy Gottlieb
Editing: Cara Silverman
Art Direction: Anastasia Masaro
Costumes: Marie-Sylvie Deveau
Production Design: Jasna Stefanovich
MPAA rating: PG
Running time: 100 minutes

REVIEWS

Boxoffice Online. June, 2005.
Chicago Sun-Times Online. June 17, 2005.
Entertainment Weekly Online. June 15, 2005.
Los Angeles Times Online. June 17, 2005.
New York Times Online. June 17, 2005.

Variety Online. June 16, 2005.
Washington Post Online. June 16, 2005, p. WE36.

AWARDS

Nomination:

Golden Raspberries 2005: Worst Actress (Duff).

POOH'S HEFFALUMP MOVIE

There's something new in the Hundred Acre Wood.
—Movie tagline

Heffa nice day.
—Movie tagline

Box Office: $18.1 million

Pooh's Heffalump Movie follows in the footsteps of Walt Disney Pictures' *The Tigger Movie* (2000) and *Piglet's Big Movie* (2003). Each is a new, feature-length movie based on the popular A.A. Milne characters. This movie could have been made in 1975 as easily as 2005. The characters are drawn in their familiar, comforting way. They act and sound the same as always. And the Hundred-Acre Woods remains the same gentle place. The timelessness of Pooh's world is not a bad thing.

The movie has a similar idea to *Piglet's Big Movie*. In both, a small fellow is deemed too little for important jobs, but ends up being the most important one of all. To tiny viewers, this is likely a most pleasing message. In this film, the creatures of the forest get scared after hearing the sound of a distant Heffalump. They organize an expedition to the scary Heffalump Hollow to capture the creature. Much to his disappointment, little Roo (voiced by Nikita Hopkins) is left behind. But he sets out on his own to prove that he can find a Heffalump too.

While Pooh (Jim Cummings), Tigger (Cummings), Piglet (John Fiedler) and Rabbit (Ken Sansom) are still trying to drag all their luggage, including a grandfather clock and unicycle, along the trail, Roo has already found a Heffalump. He ties a rope loosely around little Lumpy's (Kyle Stanger) neck and declares, as Rabbit taught him, "In the name of the Hundred Acre Wood, you are captured." Lumpy seems agreeable to this. Roo is surprised to discover that Lumpy is not the fearsome, horned creature that had been described to him but rather a sweet, little elephant-like creature. Likewise, Lumpy's fellow Heffalumps have told him many stories about the horrible creatures that populate the Hundred Acre Woods. As they wander the woods, Lumpy and Roo do things like frolic in the water and have a food fight while Carly Simon tunes play tastefully in the background.

When Roo introduces Lumpy to Rabbit and the rest of the gang, they react with fear and chase him away. Their preconceived notions about him are so strong, they cannot see the reality of the situation—that this is a gentle, shy creature. And, that, of course, would be the lesson of the whole thing. It is only after Lumpy and his mother (Brenda Blethyn) save Roo from danger that they realize that they had been wrong about Heffalumps.

The movie, written by Brian Hohlfeld and Evan Spiliotopoulos, has the usual kind of gentle humor of Pooh stories, with plenty of wordplay and physical mishaps. When Rabbit tells Roo he will not be able to go on the expedition, Rabbit explains "It's fraught with danger! And you can't argue with a word like fraught." And while Piglet is carefully leaving a trail of pink jelly-beans for the expeditioners, Pooh is just as methodically picking them up and eating them. There is also the old favorite of a character getting stuck in a hole and having to be pushed on their behind.

Pooh purists might have a gripe or two. As Eleanor Ringel Gillespie of *The Atlanta Journal-Constitution* points out, the movie is only very loosely based on Milne's work. In the books, Heffalumps were only something that Pooh had imagined. The idea was that the imagination can be a powerful thing. "Apparently the Disney folks don't even bother with A.A. Milne anymore," wrote Gillespie, "They just borrow his characters and do with them what they will—which mostly means cramming toy stores with plush Poohs, Piglets and Eeyores."

Otherwise, critics were mostly charmed by the film. Billy Heller of *The New York Post* wrote, "While kids older than eight may be too jaded to sit through this cute flick, at just over an hour, it may be the perfect fit for first-time filmgoers." Kevin Crust of *The Los Angeles Times* wrote, "An innocuous introduction to diversity for the preschool set, *Pooh's Heffalump Movie* features some charming songs by Carly Simon and is warmly animated so as to evoke nostalgia in parents." Anita Gates of *The New York Times* wrote that "adults as well as children may fall in love with Lumpy, partly because he's a sort of roly-poly lavender baby elephant but even more because of the endearing voice and infectious laugh of Kyle Stanger." And Liz Braun of *The Toronto Sun* wrote, "*Pooh's Heffalump Movie* is quick, witty and lovely to look at; children laugh with delight in all the right places. Too bad the basic message of understanding had to be underlined with those overwrought Carly Simon songs, but what can you do?"

Jill Hamilton

CREDITS

Winnie the Pooh/Tigger: Jim (Jonah) Cummings (Voice)
Piglet: John Fiedler (Voice)
Roo: Nikita Hopkins (Voice)
Kanga: Kath Soucie (Voice)
Rabbit: Ken Sansom (Voice)
Eeyore: Peter Cullen (Voice)
Mama Heffalump: Brenda Blethyn (Voice)
Lumpy: Kyle Stanger (Voice)
Origin: USA
Language: English
Released: 2005
Production: Jessica Koplos-Miller; DisneyToon Studios; released by Buena Vista
Directed by: Frank Nissen
Written by: Brian Hohlfield, Evan Spiliotopolos
Music by: Joel McNeely
Sound: Donald J. Malouf
Editing: Anthony F. Rocco, Robert Fisher Jr.
Art Direction: Tony Pulham
MPAA rating: G
Running time: 63 minutes

REVIEWS

Boxoffice Online. February, 2005.
Entertainment Weekly Online. February 9, 2005.
Los Angeles Times Online. February 11, 2005.
New York Times Online. February 11, 2005.
Variety Online. February 10, 2005.
Washington Post Online. February 11, 2005, p. C05.

TRIVIA

More than 900 children, many of them actors, auditioned in the U.S. for the voice of Lumpy. Auditions were later held in the U.K. where the team found their Lumpy in five-year-old Kyle Stanger, who had never acted before.

PRETTY PERSUASION

Revenge is a bitch.
—Movie tagline

Revenge knows no mercy.
—Movie tagline

In an episode of *The Simpsons*, Homer Simpson is watching Garrison Keillor's *A Prairie Home Companion* on TV. "Be funnier," he says pleadingly. Audience members may well be thinking the same thing about *Pretty Persuasion*. The film boasts a group of talented actors and touches upon so many audacious topics that it seems like the makings of a sharp, edgy satire are here. But writer Skander Halim and director Marcos Siega are not able to pull it all together to make the film what it could have been. What they end up with is a collection of provocative topics trotted out, but not handled in any kind of definitive way. Among the racy subjects covered are racism, pedophilia, and manipulative sex.

Kimberly Joyce (Evan Rachel Wood) is a 15-year-old aspiring actress attending a posh Beverly Hills high school. Her father, Hank (James Woods), is a businessman of some sort who conducts business in his bathrobe in between snorts of cocaine and conversations with a phone sex professional. He does not talk so much as spew out a constant stream of anti-Semitic commentary. He has a trophy wife, Kathy (Jaime King), who Kimberly taunts with vulgar comments about her supposed actions with the family dog.

Kimberly is a cynical, manipulative teen. She takes on a new Palestinian friend, Randa (Adi Schnall), because she thinks she will look comparatively more attractive to the shy girl. Kimberly informs Randa, that she respects all the races, but she is "glad to be white." She then lists what races she would like to be, in order from best to worst. Asian would be good, she reports, because men like Asian woman. And black would be okay, too, if she had Caucasian features "like Halle Berry." Arab, she informs Randa, is last on her list. She follows this with a crude joke about Arab sexual relations. Randa listens to this silently and unblinkingly. It is the same way she reacts to Kimberly's lessons on bulimia and pornography.

The main action in the story revolves around Kimberly's plan to accuse the school English and drama teacher, Percy Anderson (Ron Livingston), of sexual harassment. She enlists Randa and her "best friend" Brittany (Elisabeth Harnois) to agree to testify that Percy has made sexual overtures to them. The girls are happy to go along with it because they each have resentment against the teacher. Randa is angry because Percy bluntly criticized her writing ability and Brittany was humiliated by an embarrassing acting exercise Percy forced her into. This teacher is a canny choice of victim on Kimberly's part because, although he is technically innocent of these charges, he is not without a certain sexual strangeness to the female students. For his wife's (Selma Blair) birthday, he buys her a gray skirt just like the students wear. He has her try it on, then asks her to read one of Kimberly's essays aloud.

As Kimberly had hoped, her plan has soon affected the whole town. A local TV reporter, Emily (Jane Krakowski), who has been assigned to do a puff piece on the school, is delighted when she finds a juicy sexual harassment story to pursue. As part of Kimberly's elaborate plan, she seduces the reporter to make she that she is portrayed in a sympathetic light.

Kimberly is a devious, bad kid, who does and says bad things and, well…that's about it. After all its posturing and revealing of dark, seamy things, *Pretty Persuasion* does not seem to have much of a point. The satire does not quite hit the mark and instead, just seems like meanness for meanness sake.

Critics split on the film. Janice Page of *The Boston Globe* wrote, "*Pretty Persuasion* isn't so much awful as it is self-conscious, overdone, shallow, and just not up to the level of its star." Stephen Holden of *The New York Times* wrote, "An obscene, misanthropic go-for-broke satire, *Pretty Persuasion* is so gleefully nasty that the fact that it was even made and released is astonishing. Much of it is also extremely funny. Any satire worth its salt should not be afraid to offend, and *Pretty Persuasion* flings mud with a fearless audacity." Roger Ebert of *The Chicago Sun-Times* wrote, "The material in *Pretty Persuasion* needed to be handled as heavy drama, or played completely for comedy, and by trying to have it both ways, the movie has it neither way." And David Denby of *The New Yorker* wrote, "Relentlessly barbed and often ice-cold, *Pretty Persuasion* is not a nice movie, and it's not as funny as it should be. But it's a fresh achievement: a dirty-minded poison-pen to a country swollen with self-esteem."

Jill Hamilton

CREDITS

Kimberly Joyce: Evan Rachel Wood
Percy Anderson: Ron Livingston
Hank Joyce: James Woods
Emily Klein: Jane Krakowski
Brittany: Elisabeth Harnois
Grace Anderson: Selma Blair
Roger Nicholl: Danny Comden
Troy: Stark Sands
Headmaster Meyer: Michael Hitchcock
Larry Horowitz: Robert Joy
Kathy Joyce: Jaime (James) King
Randa: Adi Schnall
Joe: Alex Desert
Origin: USA
Language: English
Released: 2005
Production: Matthew Weaver, Todd Dagres, Carl Levin, Marcos Siega
Directed by: Marcos Siega
Written by: Skander Halim
Cinematography by: Ramsay Nickell
Music by: Gilad Benamram
Sound: Robert C. Jackson
Music Supervisor: Janet Billig Rich, Elissa Marshall
Editing: Nicholas Erasmnus
Costumes: Danny Glicker
Production Design: Paul Oberman
MPAA rating: Unrated
Running time: 104 minutes

REVIEWS

Boxoffice Online. August, 2005.
Chicago Sun-Times Online. August 26, 2005.
Entertainment Weekly Online. August 10, 2005.
Los Angeles Times Online. August 12, 2005.
New York Times Online. August 12, 2005.
Variety Online. January 24, 2005.

QUOTES

Brittany Wells, mistaking the word 'pedophile': "Mr. Anderson's kind of weird. Especially around girls. We think he's a podiatrist."

PRIDE AND PREJUDICE

A romance ahead of its time.
—Movie tagline

Sometimes the last person on earth you want to be with is the one person you can't be without.
—Movie tagline

The first thought upon hearing about *Pride & Prejudice* is why? Have there not already been enough film adaptations of Jane Austen's most popular novel? Actually, there has been only one previous, faithful big-screen version, the dreary 1940 adaptation with Greer Garson and Laurence Olivier, much too old to play the protagonists. British television has adapted it several times, with the 1995 version widely considered the best dramatized Austen. Then there are *Pride and Prejudice* (2003), updated to contemporary America, *Bride & Prejudice* (2004), the Bollywood version, and *Bridget Jones's Diary* (2001), a loose, modern retelling. Austen's novel is only one of the best, best-loved, and most influential of all time. Another big-screen version seems called for only if something new can be offered, and *Pride & Prejudice* does that.

Written by Deborah Moggach and directed by Joe Wright, both of whom had worked previously only in television, the film is not as faithful as the beloved 1995 miniseries because time restrictions necessitate that something has to be left out. Moggach, whose credits include the excellent *Love in a Cold Climate* (2001), has done an exceptional job of deciding what to omit, and Wright, who directed *The Last King,* makes Austen's tale more visually spectacular than previous versions.

In Georgian England, Mr. Bennet (Donald Sutherland) and Mrs. Bennet (Brenda Blethyn) are burdened with five unmarried daughters. When the wealthy Mr. Bingley (Simon Woods) moves into nearby Netherfield Hall, Mrs. Bennet becomes intent upon his marrying Jane (Rosamund Pike), her oldest daughter. While the two fall for each other instantly, the same cannot be said for Elizabeth Bennet (Keira Knightley) and Bingley's friend, Mr. Darcy (Matthew MacFayden), after Elizabeth overhears his snobbish remarks at a ball. It will take approximately two hours of screen time for the two to overcome their prejudices and discover they are meant for each other.

Elizabeth's other problems with Darcy include her belief that he has dissuaded Bingley from pursuing Jane. She is also told by Wickham (Rupert Friend), who grew up on Darcy's estate, that Darcy has prevented him from receiving the post as a clergyman promised by Darcy's late father. Matters are further complicated because without a son Mr. Bennet cannot pass on his property to his children. The heir is a distant relative, Mr. Collins (Tom Hollander), a rather inept parson who shocks Elizabeth by proposing. Instead, Elizabeth's closest friend, the sensible Charlotte Lucas (Claudie Blakley) shocks her even more by becoming Mrs. Collins. Then the powerful Lady Catherine de Bourg (Judi Dench), Darcy's aunt, takes a dislike to Elizabeth.

All these machinations come to a head when Elizabeth's silliest sister, Lydia (Jena Malone), runs off to marry the dastardly Wickham. As a result, Elizabeth finally learns of Darcy's true nature, and everyone begins drifting toward the inevitable happy ending.

Moggach streamlines Austen through such means as drastically reducing the roles of the three youngest Bennet sisters and generally cutting everything but the Elizabeth-Darcy relationship. Austen purists, especially members of the Jane Austen Society of North America, have voiced objections to liberties taken by the filmmakers, especially having chickens and a huge pig roaming inside the Bennet home and the lengthy barefoot kissing scene that ends the film.

These critics are correct that *Pride & Prejudice* is less of a traditional, lightly satirical comedy of manners than most film and television adaptations of Austen. It is not quite *Lust & Prejudice,* but Moggach and Wright have made it somewhat sexier than some would like. They are clearly trying to appeal to modern sensibilities that find concepts like comedy of manners meaningless.

Though the film remains faithful to the general spirit and intent of the book, there are moments, as with a helicopter shot of a forlorn Elizabeth perched on the edge of a cliff and a disheveled Darcy emerging slowly from the mist, that closely resemble Emily Brontë's *Wuthering Heights* (1847) more than anything by Austen. Wright and cinematographer Roman Osin emphasize the landscape more than in any other Austen film, with the possible exception of Ang Lee's *Sense and Sensibility,* as if to stress that the characters are part of a larger world outside their rather insular little group.

Another complaint of Austen enthusiasts and reviewers of the film is that McFayden is no Colin Firth, who became a star with his Darcy in the 1995 miniseries and repeated his role, sort of, in *Bridget Jones's Diary.* While Firth adds a touch of lovable insecurity to Darcy, McFayden, in the spirit of Brontë's Heathcliff, is more melancholy and brooding. (McFayden plays Hareton Earnshaw in a splendid 1998 television version of *Wuthering Heights.*) With his sonorous voice, McFayden, best known to American audiences as the star of the British spy series shown in the U.S. as *Spooks* (2002-), makes Darcy a more sexual creature.

Reviewers of *Pride & Prejudice* have made much of the Firth/McFayden contrast while ignoring Jennifer Ehle's equally wonderful Elizabeth in the miniseries. Ehle presents the character as both more sensible and headstrong than does Knightley, who also broods a bit. At first, Knightley seems too young for the role, but Wright has toned down the actress's trademark goofy, adolescent grin. Knightley is at her best when she is simply thinking, especially in a long take of Elizabeth staring at herself in a mirror, trying to make sense of her confused state.

Mr. Collins is usually presented as a bumptious fool, but Hollander, an expert comic performer, finds sensitivity behind the clergyman's awkward façade. Kelly Reilly gives a solidly arch performance as Bingley's snooty sister. All the performances are good with the notable exception of Blethyn. She is not exactly bad; she is just repeating the nervous, flighty shtick she has done way too many times. The problem is less Blethyn herself than whoever rather unimaginably decided to cast her. (Dench has also done this I-am-not-amused aristocrat a bit too often, and her character would never sport such a tan.)

Critics invariably praise overacting or mistake a good part for a good performance. Reviewers of *Pride & Prejudice* neglected the excellent work of Sutherland, who transforms Mr. Bennet from a cliché to a well-rounded character. While Blethyn jumps around and screams, Sutherland commands the screen by remaining still, conveying Bennet's level-headed strength with subtle gestures. He is outstanding when Elizabeth reveals she has rejected Collins and again when he sheds a small tear at the eventful resolution of all the crises. This, rather than shouting and twitching, is what good film acting should be about.

Michael Adams

CREDITS

Elizabeth Bennet: Keira Knightley
Darcy: Matthew MacFadyen
Mrs. Bennet: Brenda Blethyn
Mr. Bennet: Donald Sutherland
William Collins: Tom Hollander
Lady Catherine de Bourg: Judi Dench
Jane Bennet: Rosmund Pike
Lydia Bennet: Jena Malone
Caroline Bingley: Kelly Reilly
Charlotte Lucas: Claudie Blakley
Mr. Gardiner: Peter Wight
Mrs. Gardiner: Penelope Wilton
Charles Bingley: Simon Woods
Lt. Wickham: Rupert Friend
Kitty Bennet: Carey Mulligan
Mary Bennet: Talulah Riley
Georgiana Darcy: Tamzin Merchant
Origin: France, Great Britain
Language: English
Released: 2005
Production: Tim Bevan, Eric Fellner, Paul Webster; Working Title Productions; released by UIP, Focus Features
Directed by: Joe Wright
Written by: Deborah Moggach
Cinematography by: Roman Osin
Music by: Dario Marianelli
Sound: Danny Hambrook, Catherine Hodgson, Paul Hamblin
Music Supervisor: Nick Angel
Editing: Paul Tothill
Costumes: Jacqueline Durran
Production Design: Sarah Greenwood
MPAA rating: PG
Running time: 127 minutes

REVIEWS

Boxoffice Online. November, 2005.
Chicago Sun-Times Online. November 11, 2005.
Entertainment Weekly Online. November 9, 2005.
Los Angeles Times Online. November 11, 2005.
New York Times Online. November 11, 2005.
Premiere Magazine Online. November 11, 2005.
Variety Online. September 11, 2005.
Washington Post Online. November 11, 2005, p. C01.

QUOTES

Elizabeth Bennet: "Believe me, men are either eaten up with arrogance or stupidity."

TRIVIA

Emma Thompson did an uncredited and unpaid re-write of the script for which she received a "Special Thanks" credit at the end of the film.

AWARDS

Nomination:

Oscars 2005: Actress (Knightley), Art Dir./Set Dec., Costume Des., Orig. Score

British Acad. 2005: Actress (Knightley), Adapt. Screenplay, Costume Des., Makeup, Support. Actress (Blethyn)

Golden Globes 2006: Actress—Mus./Comedy (Knightley), Film—Mus./Comedy

Broadcast Film Critics 2005: Actress (Knightley).

PRIME

A therapeutic new comedy.
—Movie tagline

Box Office: $22.7 million

Prime is a vastly different movie for director Ben Younger whose only other film was 2000's *Boiler Room,* the gritty story of Wall Street hustlers. *Prime* is a romance. Actually, it's a story of a mismatched romance. The leading lady is Rafi Gardet (Uma Thurman) who is an affluent, 37-year-old, recent divorcee who makes her living in the fashion industry. The leading man is David Metzger (Bryan Greenberg), a 23-year-old artist in the making who still lives with his grandparents. But age and lifestyle are not the only obstacles in the way of this pair who fall in love at first sight. For example, David is Jewish, while Rafi is a lapsed Catholic. And unfortunately, while these two characters obviously have been raised in different times, the cultural references that could be so alien between the two isn't mined for its comic potential. However, it does soon become apparent that the major question in this romance is, is love enough?

That's pretty much it for the basic plot of *Prime,* but there is one twist. Rafi, being recently divorced, has been seeing a psychologist, Lisa (Meryl Streep), in order to work out her fear of intimacy. She continues to tell all her secrets to Lisa even after she begins a torrid relationship with David. The twist is that Lisa is David's mother. Now Lisa is torn between her responsibilities to her patient and the conflict of interest that comes with not telling her the truth. Imagine her squirming as she hears about her son's prowess in bed. Oh, and Lisa is also very upset with David because he's dating a non-Jewish girl.

In reality, between the two story lines, the one between Lisa and Rafi is probably the more interesting to watch develop. Although it does take a bit of rationalization to justify why Lisa doesn't immediately stop and tell Rafi that she is David's mother, it's just a small suspension of disbelief in order to enjoy the comedy that ensues.

The cast of *Prime* is talented and good-looking. The characters are interesting and not too stereotypical. Well, maybe Lisa is a little too much the "Jewish Mama," but it is a comedy, after all. Most appealing of all is that Rafi is not portrayed as a desperate or pathetic character. Ten or twenty years ago she would have been, but a woman's options in respect to marriage and even children have changed a lot since then and Rafi's character reflects that maturity.

Many critics have compared this film, with its heavy New York City ambience, to those of Woody Allen. In a way it is similar to those, it's just not as sharp or intelligent. As a romantic comedy, *Prime* is likable enough and has some genuinely funny moments but in the long run it's fairly forgettable.

Beverley Bare Buehrer

CREDITS

Lisa Metzger: Meryl Streep
Rafi Gardet: Uma Thurman
David Bloomberg: Bryan Greenberg
Morris: Jon Abrahams
Randall: Zak Orth
Katherine: Annie Parisse
Origin: USA
Language: English
Released: 2005
Production: Suzanne Todd, Jennifer Todd; Team Todd, Younger Than You; released by Universal
Directed by: Ben Younger
Written by: Ben Younger
Cinematography by: William Rexer
Music by: Ryan Shore
Sound: Tod A. Maitland
Music Supervisor: Jim Black
Editing: Kristina Boden
Art Direction: Paul Kelly
Costumes: Melissa Toth
Production Design: Mark Ricker
MPAA rating: PG-13
Running time: 105 minutes

REVIEWS

Boxoffice Online. October, 2005.
Chicago Sun-Times Online. October 28, 2005.
Entertainment Weekly Online. October 26, 2005.
Los Angeles Times Online. October 28, 2005.
New York Times Online. October 28, 2005.
Premiere Magazine Online. November 2, 2005.
Variety Online. October 12, 2005.
Washington Post Online. October 28, 2005, p. WE42.

QUOTES

Rafi Gardet: "Your mother now knows intimate details."
David Bloomberg: "Well, she better not use that to get me home for Thanksgiving."

TRIVIA

Originally rated R by the MPAA, the film was re-rated PG-13 on appeal.

THE PRIZE WINNER OF DEFIANCE, OHIO

The true story of how a mother raised ten kids on twenty-five words or less.
—Movie tagline

In the midst of daunting hardship, only the most determined of optimists could not only see their glass as half-full but act as if it is overflowing. One such person was Evelyn Ryan (Julianne Moore), whose true story is told in *The Prize Winner of Defiance, Ohio.* Using her wits and wittiness and possessing an amazing strength of character, she refused to let misery make her miserable. While trying to raise ten children with little help from her alcoholic husband, it was impossible to be oblivious or blind to the harsh realities of her existence. However, Evelyn chose to focus through rose-colored glasses on, and wholeheartedly delight in, the good stuff in life. How appropriate that this dignified, indomitable spirit lived in a town called Defiance.

Based upon Terry "Tuff" Ryan's loving 2001 memoir about her mother (who died in 1998), the film is a winning little gem about a woman whose winnings from the jingle contests so popular in the 1950's and early 1960's kept her large family afloat. Evelyn's bitter, volatile husband, Kelly (Woody Harrelson), routinely liquidated the paychecks from his dead-end factory job into six-packs of beer and bottles of whiskey, a fair amount of which was already consumed by the time he crossed the threshold. Thus, it was hard to pay the milkman, afford groceries, or buy the multitude of other things the family needed. So Evelyn found a way, using her way with words. She sent in a steady stream of clever little rhymes extolling the virtues of Dial Soap, Parkay Margarine, Maidenform Bras, and countless other products (in her own name and those of her sizeable brood), and what flowed back to her included cash and prizes like a car, trips, a washer and dryer, toasters, bikes and a slew of other items they could otherwise not have afforded. Numerous scenes show the enjoyment and satisfaction Evelyn got out of crafting her entries, but any ego boost she got was secondary to the financial boost which would benefit her children. It is clear that they were not just her top priority but her purpose in life. "That's where my prayers went," she says. "That's where they all went."

Today, many women would not put up with such trying circumstances, grabbing the kids and leaving. However, Evelyn's struggles have to be viewed in the context of that time. When she and Kelly go to the bank to sign a mortgage, she begins to take her gloves off to do so but is told that all they are looking for is her husband's signature. When Kelly listens to a baseball game on the radio with a bellyful of booze and his temper flares, he ends up swearing and screaming and struggling mightily to push the big new freezer she has won out the door. Failing at that, he opts to bash it in with a frying pan. When the police come, they merely stand around talking sports with Kelly and tell Evelyn he just needs to sleep it off. Later, when she seeks counsel from their priest, the man points out her wifely responsibility to create a happy home and advises her to try a little harder in that department. (One of her little ones notes that his breath smells "just like dad's.") Clearly, there is no help there either, and the look on Evelyn's face shows she feels let down, trapped, but not defeated. "I'm tired of this day. I need a new one," she says, picking herself up and heading off to bed with a determination to press on.

Throughout *Prize Winner*, one is not only continuously filled with admiration and awe concerning Evelyn's resourcefulness and ability to roll with the (figurative) punches, but also with the understanding she shows toward Kelly. She knows—and the film shows—that his disconcerting, disruptive, and verbally abusive meltdowns are born of frustration, self-loathing, and that ever-present bottle. When he is sober, Kelly is jovial, kind, fatherly, helpful, thoughtful and good intentioned. He vows to fill up the freezer even if it takes a year for him to do so, the very same freezer he attacks in the drunken rage which makes the wary kids steer clear. In one scene, Evelyn speaks directly to the audience (as she periodically does throughout the film to cleverly and often entertainingly provide background or explanation) about how he had been "loads of fun" and they had been a "perfect match" when the two met years before on the verge of adulthood. An aspiring band crooner, Kelly's singing voice and career aspirations were suddenly taken away from him due to injuries sustained in a car accident. Evelyn sympathetically points out how devastating it must have been for him to suddenly have to lower his sights and settle for an ordinary life. As the prize winner continually brings in what the traditional breadwinner fails to provide, shots of him carefully capture a mixture of resentment, mortification, and shame. Kelly feels emasculated, but knows full well it is his own fault. Later in the film, he accidentally makes Evelyn fall, causing the two glass bottles of milk she is holding to smash upon the floor and cut her. He is obviously horrified, and sobbingly apologetic. Another time, before Evelyn goes on a breakneck shopping spree she has won, she asks Kelly what he would especially like and remembers to pick up a shrimp cocktail. When she arrives back, overflowing with cheerfulness and all sorts of expensive, exotic goods, an inebriated Kelly sniffles and sulks and opts for plain old Spam. With a warm and patient manner, she is able to talk him down from his snit, a disruptive, troubled eleventh child with whom she must deal. "I don't need you to make me happy," she says at one point in the film with weary honesty rather than anger. "I just need you to leave me alone when I am."

Perhaps the time the audience sees Evelyn at her happiest is when teenaged Terry (impressive Ellary Porterfield) drives her eighty-five miles to the home of Dortha Schaefer (delightfully vivid Laura Dern), another avid contester who has become her pen pal. As they drive along with sunny-drenched, green farmland stretching on either side of them, it is lovely to watch an exhilarated Evelyn getting away from it all for the very first time, thoroughly enjoying—both figuratively and literally—a breath of fresh air. It is warm inside the car and the engine even hotter, forcing them to stop at a gas station, but Evelyn could not care less. Before they are able to proceed, Evelyn and Terry have their first of two tender, telling talks. Terry earns her "Tuff" nickname with a brutally honest assessment of her mother's life, one which she thinks "stinks," is "not fair," and would make her "angry all the time." Evelyn says such feelings would do no one any good, and asserts her choice—her conviction—to not let the bad in life keep her from filling herself up joyously with the good. Later, when Evelyn talks shop with Dortha and the other ladies in her contesting club, she is delightedly in her element, spilling over with that joy.

As Evelyn's prizes keep arriving to solve each crisis that arises, there is some diminution of suspense but not of interest. In the final portion, the out-of-the-blue coming-due of a second mortgage Kelly never told Evelyn about threatens to force them out of their home and necessitate sending some of the children to live with other people. It is powerful to finally see Evelyn thrown, dispirited and crying. Then, a lucrative first-prize win from Dr. Pepper comes in, just in the nick of time. Viewers will rejoice in this victory along with the beleaguered Ryans, but a quieter instance of greater potency lies ahead. The real Ryan siblings appear as themselves in a scene following Evelyn's death. Terry lovingly caresses her mother's old typewriter, lost in thought about the woman who used it and all the good that sprang from it. Suddenly, Moore's Evelyn leans into the frame and gives Terry a comforting kiss on the cheek. It is a powerfully moving, transcendent moment.

Made on a budget of $12 million, *The Prize Winner of Defiance, Ohio* only grossed $626,310 in limited release. However, the film received positive reviews from Roger Ebert, *Variety, The New York Times,* and others. It was adapted and directed by Jane Anderson in her feature film debut. She nicely captures the era in question, and clearly has tremendous affection, admiration, and respect for Evelyn Ryan. Moore is excellent, and one is reminded of her extraordinary work as trapped housewives in *The Hours* (2002) and *Far from Heaven* (2003). She deservedly received high praise in many reviews for this performance, as well. Moore's skillful, warm, vibrant, wholly convincing performance is the key to this *Prize Winner*'s success.

David L. Boxerbaum

CREDITS

Evelyn Ryan: Julianne Moore
Kelly Ryan: Woody Harrelson
Dortha Schaefer: Laura Dern
Bruce Ryan at 16: Trevor Morgan
Ray the Milkman: Simon Reynolds
Origin: USA
Language: English
Released: 2005
Production: Jack Rapke, Steve Starkey, Robert Zemeckis; Imagemovers; released by Go Fish Pictures
Directed by: Jane Anderson
Written by: Jane Anderson
Cinematography by: Jonathan Freeman
Music by: John Frizzell
Sound: Bruce Carwardine
Editing: Robert Dalva
Art Direction: Andrew Stearn
Costumes: Hala Bahmet
Production Design: Edward T. McAvoy
MPAA rating: PG-13
Running time: 99 minutes

REVIEWS

Boxoffice Online. September, 2005.
Chicago Sun-Times Online. September 30, 2005.
Entertainment Weekly Online. September 28, 2005.
Los Angeles Times Online. September 30, 2005.
New York Times Online. September 30, 2005.
Premiere Magazine Online. September 29, 2005.
Variety Online. September 22, 2005.

QUOTES

Evelyn Ryan: "So far three of my chicks have found their nests, and I am so very proud of them."

THE PRODUCERS

Box Office: $6.6 million

The 2005 version of *The Producers* has taken a unique route to the screen. Its genesis is in the 1968 Mel Brooks comedy about a crooked Broadway producer and the hapless accountant (memorably played by Zero Mostel and Gene Wilder, respectively), who connive to steal a fortune by engineering the biggest theatrical flop in history. Funnyman Brooks won an Academy Award for his screenplay, and, 33 years later, he reconceived the project as a Broadway musical, writing the songs himself and collaborating on the book with Thomas Meehan. Under Susan Stroman's direction and choreography, the show was an instant commercial success and went on to win a record-breaking 12 Tony Awards. With the release of the film version of the musical, *The Producers* has come full circle. The spirit of the Broadway show is intact, as is much of the cast, most notably Nathan Lane as Max Bialystock, the scheming producer, and Matthew Broderick as Leo Bloom, the timid, neurotic accountant who lives out all his fantasies of showbiz success under Max's tutelage.

Making her directorial debut for the screen, Stroman has not reimagined the stage show for a different medium but instead has essentially transferred the production to film. The direction does not employ elaborate camera moves or spectacular shots; indeed, Stroman tends to shoot the musical numbers at a medium distance as if we were watching a stage. While this is not a visually innovative musical in the tradition of *Moulin Rouge* (2001) or *Chicago* (2002), it is nonetheless very entertaining—a joyful, gleeful adaptation bursting with life and laughter. Lane gives an oversized, highly stylized performance that some would argue is probably better suited to the stage than the intimacy of film, but to give anything less would not be *The Producers*. Throwing himself into the part with gusto and throwing himself all over the screen with physical abandon, Lane is a natural ham who loves to mug for the camera. Even though he is playing a con artist, he always retains an essential likeability, making Max a scoundrel we can root for.

At the same time, to watch this version is to realize what a long shadow the original film casts. The first meeting between Leo and Max, during which Leo casually mentions the potential profitability of a Broadway flop—how a crooked producer could raise more money than he needs and then abscond with the excess once the show bombs—plays very much like the lengthy opening in the 1968 version. Broderick seems to have internalized Wilder's nervous tics, including the physical business with the blue security blanket, to such an extent that it sometimes feels like an impersonation.

But the musical also deepens the character of Leo in the song "I Wanna Be a Producer." We see his dull life as an accountant and the dreary firm where all the accountants sit in rows like drones and pound on their adding machines while singing about how unhappy they are. Then Stroman segues into a rapturous fantasy sequence in which Leo imagines himself with a bevy of chorus girls as he lives out his dream of being a producer. It is the first of several larger-than-life numbers that make this version of *The Producers* a grand entertainment, a showbiz musical that, in such inspired moments, hearkens back to the classic *Singin' in the Rain* (1952).

Max and Leo embark on a quest to find a guaranteed theatrical disaster, and their dreams come true when they read a script called *Springtime for Hitler*, a goofy tribute to the Führer himself. If some audiences wonder why we need yet another version of *The Producers*, the answer may be more controversial than the sight of storm troopers singing and dancing across a Broadway stage—the new film is actually an improvement over the original. Many fans and critics would contest this idea; Roger Ebert of the *Chicago Sun-Times*, for example, while giving the remake a positive review, admits being unable to give it a fair appraisal because the original looms so large in his mind. And yet, while the 1968 version has garnered a reputation as one of the funniest films ever made, it is not readily acknowledged that it is also weighed down with many dull, tedious moments. Nothing should be taken away from Mostel's and Wilder's indelible performances, but the rhythms are often slow for a manic comedy, and some elements are painfully flat. In particular, Dick Shawn's portrayal of L.S.D., the actor who plays Hitler, is an unfunny parody of the hippie movement and feels hopelessly dated, stopping the action in its tracks every time he appears. He was wisely excised from the musical version, both on stage and film, making the production of *Springtime for Hitler* much more exuberant and fun.

Moreover, the supporting actors bring an added spark to the 2005 *Producers*. Where Kenneth Mars is a bit demented as Nazi playwright Franz Liebkind in the original and his scenes grow tiresome, Will Ferrell is hilarious. Wearing a German Army helmet and lederhosen, he conveys his own oddball charm and enthusiasm, playing this delusional Nazi as an overgrown boy who talks to his pigeons and seems to live in his own cracked universe. And Uma Thurman is an absolute joy as Ulla, the Swedish sexpot who becomes the boys' receptionist, an actress in their show, and, ultimately, Leo's love interest. The part has been greatly expanded from the original film, in which Ulla is a mere sex object, the blonde who can barely speak English and dances a little in a bikini. In the musical version, Ulla's flirtatiousness brings sexual tension to the story as well as an added dimension to Leo, who develops a romantic persona he did not have in the first film and ends up winning the beautiful girl. And, last but not least, Thurman herself is a complete delight, radiating sex appeal, luminousness, and even a touch of sweetness in a role that could have been a stereotype. Ulla's rendition of "When You Got It, Flaunt It" is a brassy, high-energy solo number, while her duet with Leo, "That Face," is a lovely Astaire-and-Rogers type of song and dance that encapsulates their relationship—from Leo's initial resistance to his pursuit of Ulla and her pursuit of him, concluding with a romantic kiss.

But the movie is filled with big productions, including "Keep It Gay," an extravaganza of humorous gay stereotypes led by Broadway's worst director and flaming cross-dresser, Roger De Bris (Gary Beach), recruited by Max to helm his fiasco, and Roger's strange, lisping manservant or "common-law assistant," Carmen Ghia (Roger Bart). Finally, Max has to make a foray into Little Old Lady Land, which means having to sleep with old ladies to get them to sign over huge sums of money to finance his dream. The resulting number, "Along Came Bialy," gives the film a chance to leave the soundstage as Max leads a virtual parade of walker-toting old ladies down Fifth Avenue through Central Park. But no matter how hard Max works, his plot ultimately backfires when his Nazi musical, in all its garish bad taste, garners hearty laughter from an appreciative opening-night audience and is misinterpreted as wicked satire.

The movie loses some of its energy after "Springtime for Hitler," such a comic high point in every version of *The Producers* that trying to wrap things up in its aftermath is almost impossible to do. And certainly at two hours and 14 minutes, the remake has an almost epic length for its fairly simple premise and too many endings. Leo runs off to Rio with Ulla, leaving Max to take the fall on his own, leading to a jailhouse number, "Betrayed," in which Max recaps the entire show—a dazzling song, to be sure, but one that, on film, stops the momentum when the story should be racing to a big finish. Leo returns to testify on behalf of his friend in "'Til Him," a very sweet tribute to the way this rapscallion changed Leo's life for the better, which sends both of them to prison until they face a reversal; the governor commutes their sentences, allowing them to take the show they were rehearsing in Sing Sing, *Prisoners of Love*, all the way to Broadway.

As humor has gotten cruder and more outrageous since 1968, the notion of swindling old ladies and mounting a Nazi play to make an easy fortune may not seem as wild and risky as it once did, especially with World War II a more distant memory. But if *The Producers* has lost some of its satiric bite since its first incarnation, in its place is a grand showbiz musical, full of big backstage laughs, romance, and crowd-pleasing shtick. The new film may not be on the cutting edge of comedy, but it proudly boasts the nostalgic feel of an old-fashioned Broadway classic being preserved for all time with two great stars immortalizing the performances that made them icons of the Great White Way.

Peter N. Chumo II

CREDITS

Max Bialystock: Nathan Lane
Leo Bloom: Matthew Broderick
Ulla: Uma Thurman
Franz Liebkind: Will Ferrell
Carmen Ghia: Roger Bart
Hold Me-Touch-Me: Eileen Essell
Judge: David Huddleston
Prison Trustee: Michael McKean
Lick Me-Bite-Me: Debra Monk
Kiss Me-Feel-Me: Andrea Martin
Mr. Marks: Jon Lovitz
Roger De Bris: Gary Beach
Origin: USA
Language: English
Released: 2005
Production: Mel Brooks, Jonathan Sanger; Brooksfilms; released by Universal Pictures, Columbia Pictures
Directed by: Mel Brooks, Susan Stroman
Written by: Mel Brooks, Thomas Meehan
Cinematography by: John Bailey, Charles Minsky
Music by: Mel Brooks
Sound: Tod A. Maitland
Editing: Steven Weisberg
Art Direction: Peter Rogness
Costumes: William Ivey Long
Production Design: Mark Friedberg
MPAA rating: PG-13
Running time: 129 minutes

REVIEWS

Boxoffice Online. December, 2005.
Chicago Sun-Times Online. December 16, 2005.
Entertainment Weekly Online. December 14, 2005.
Los Angeles Times Online. December 16, 2005.
New York Times Online. December 16, 2005.
Premiere Magazine Online. December 22, 2005.
Variety Online. December 9, 2005.
Washington Post Online. December 24, 2005, p. C01.

QUOTES

Mr. Marks: "Bloom, where do you think you're going? You've already had your toilet break!"

Leo Bloom: "I'm not going into the toilet! I'm going into show business!"

TRIVIA

The byline for a terrible newspaper review for the show that Bialystock produces at the beginning of the film is Addison DeWitt, the acerbic theater critic played by George Sanders in *All About Eve* (1950).

AWARDS

Nomination:

Golden Globes 2006: Actor—Mus./Comedy (Lane), Film—Mus./Comedy, Song ("There's Nothing Like a Show on Broadway"), Support. Actress (Ferrell).

PROOF

The biggest risk in life is not taking one.
—Movie tagline

Box Office: $7.5 million

Director John Madden and actress Gwyneth Paltrow last collaborated in the blockbuster *Shakespeare in Love,* which won acclaim and an Academy Award for it's pedigreed, blond star. *Proof,* with it's own impressive pedigree as an adaptation of David Auburn's Pulitzer Prize-winning play, while appealing to a more narrow audience than the former film, is an intelligent and well-written drama that heavily relies on Paltrow in the lead to carry off the central theme. Echoing Ron Howard's *A Beautiful Mind,* the main character is the daughter of a brilliant mathematician who may or may not have inherited his genius and his madness, forming the crux of the plot. With such an inward-looking theme, termed "something of a psychological whodunit," by the *New York Times'* Manohla Dargis, *Proof* has more than a few obstacles to overcome in its transformation from play to film and largely does so with an exceptional performance by its female lead.

Paltrow reprises the role of 27-year-old Catherine which she played on the London stage directed, once again, by Madden, who has recently lost her famous father Robert (Anthony Hopkins). Having descended into madness long before his death, Robert is attended to in his final years by his devoted daughter who has all but given up her own life and promising math career in the process. Friendless and rudderless, Catherine is left alone to grapple with the demons in her own mind. Rambling around the large old family home near the University of Chicago where most of the film takes place, the rumpled and confused Catherine has frequent conversations with Robert, who appears as alive as his youngest daughter but whom we know is, in fact, quite deceased.

Catherine's more practical and infinitely more socialized older sister Claire (Hope Davis) arrives from New York for the funeral and the interaction between the two polar opposites forms a fine extension of the family drama first introduced in the Robert/Catherine relationship. In this four-person ensemble, in fact, it is these two women, playing off each other's strengths and weaknesses, that are the perfectly cast standouts. It is clear that Catherine is the one who takes after their father, while Claire tries to help the sister she doesn't understand find her way back to the land of the living.

The quartet is complete when Hal enters into the equation. A former student of Robert's played by Jake Gyllenhaal, Hal doesn't suffer from the brilliance of his mentor but is, however, ambitious. He has come to pour through the 103 notebooks Robert filled with his compulsive scribblings to see if they actually contain anything lucid, or indeed, groundbreaking. The already paranoid Catherine is naturally suspicions about the handsome, young professor's intentions as he tries to get closer to her. She weaves back and forth in her mind about whether to trust Hal and whether she can still trust her own judgement. The two consummate their relationship after the funeral and Catherine hands him the key to a drawer containing a 40-page mathematical proof that may or may not be a breakthrough in the field. This leads to yet another of the story's mysteries: who actually wrote the proof, Catherine or her father?

The film, with its screenplay by Auburn and Rebecca Miller, goes wrong in a few key areas. Blunting the play's sharp humor, *Proof* becomes an overly sober drama onscreen. Though injecting his character with his trademark puppy-eyed sweetness, Gyllenhaal is sorely miscast as a serious math geek. The story can't overcome it's stage roots, either, and feels static as a film.

Where the film succeeds, however, is the wise choice to focus more on the family drama and less on the world of mathematics that is, however, the oeuvre of three of the film's central characters. Hopkins is a natural in the role of a mad genius who haunts his daughter from beyond the grave. Davis, also appearing in 2005's *Duma,* shows her talents are far-ranging as Catherine's chatty, bourgeois but also sympathetic big sister. It is Paltrow, however, who owns this film in a multifaceted, nuanced performance. *Proof* allows her to display the edge she showed in films like *Flesh and Bone* and channels aspects of her portrayals as the depressed child genius in *The Royal Tenenbaums* and the depressed titular poet in *Sylvia.*

Hilary White

CREDITS

Catherine: Gwyneth Paltrow
Robert: Anthony Hopkins
Hal: Jake Gyllenhaal
Claire: Hope Davis
Prof. Bhandari: Roshan Seth
Prof. Jay Barrow: Gary Houston
Origin: USA
Language: English
Released: 2005
Production: Jeffrey Sharp, John Hart, Robert Kessel, Alison Owen; Hart Sharp Entertainment; released by Miramax Films
Directed by: John Madden
Written by: David Auburn
Cinematography by: Alwin Kuchler
Music by: Stephen Warbeck
Sound: Peter Lindsay
Editing: Mick Audsley
Art Direction: Keith Slote
Costumes: Jill Taylor
Production Design: Alice Normington
MPAA rating: PG-13
Running time: 99 minutes

REVIEWS

Boxoffice Online. September, 2005.
Chicago Sun-Times Online. September 23, 2005.

R

RACING STRIPES

His stripes made him an outcast. His heart made him a hero.
—Movie tagline

Cheer 'til you're horse!
—Movie tagline

He's the wrong sort of horse with the right sort of friends.
—Movie tagline

Kiss my tail!
—Movie tagline

Box Office: $49.2 million

Garnering frequent and not unwarranted comparisons to *National Velvet* and *Babe*, *Racing Stripes*—about an abandoned zebra living on a humble farm who dreams of becoming a racehorse—doesn't reach those lofty echelons of children's entertainment that manage to please both kids and adults but is a sturdy, effective addition to the genre. The best thing about this live-action zebra tale directed by Frederik Du Chau and written by David F. Schmidt is that it boasts a barnyard full of top notch voice talent, including Dustin Hoffman as a curmudgeonly Shetland pony, Whoopi Goldberg as a wise goat, and Joe Pantoliano as a pelican hiding from the mob as well as David Spade and Steve Harvey as a pair of hilarious horseflies. Contains a fine message, gentle humor, and adorable talking animals but not much in the way of originality or more adult-friendly material in the mix.

A dramatic and well-executed opening scene shows a traveling circus caravan caught in the pouring rain stopping to change a tire. The animals are redistributed among the wagons and a baby zebra is accidentally left in a basket on the side of the road in the fray. A passing truck stops to investigate and the young zebra is rescued by the driver, Nolan Walsh (Bruce Greenwood) who happens to own a nearby farm. His daughter Channing (Hayden Panettiere) immediately falls for the adorable little foal, whom she names Stripes (voice of Frankie Muniz), and he is quickly brought into the fold of the rest of the animals in the Walsh's Kentucky barn which happens to overlook a racetrack. The aforementioned pony Tucker (voice of Hoffman), particularly, takes Stripes under his wing and encourages his racing potential. Franny the goat (voice of Goldberg) is always there for no nonsense advice and to straighten out the other animals from time to time, including the wacky rooster Reggie (voice of Jeff Foxworthy) and a clumsy, wiseguy pelican on the lam named Goose (voice of Joe Pantoliano). Snoop Dogg is surprisingly unmemorable as the lazy hound ironically named Lightning.

Next door, at a state-of-the-art horse training facility run by the wicked Clara Dalrymple (Wendie Malick), things are not so friendly. As Stripes playfully but determinedly races with the mail truck each day to varying degrees of success (some days he actually doesn't run into the tree), two racehorses from across the fence, Trenton's Pride (voice of Joshua Jackson) and Ruffshodd (Michael Rosenbaum) relentlessly tease the ambitious zebra, who doesn't actually know that that he's not a racehorse himself, never having seen another zebra. They are nothing compared with their rigid, black stallion father, however, Sir Trenton himself (voice of Fred Dalton Thompson) who sounds exactly like a drill sergeant and intensely dislikes the little zebra who would be a racehorse. There is one sympathetic soul on the other side of the fence, however, a little filly named Sandy (voice of Mandy Moore). A champion jumper who has traveled the world, Sandy respects Stripes ambitions and is the only one who knows that he is, in fact, a zebra.

Although relegated to the position of plough horse, Stripes' racing skills and ambitions grow along with him over the ensuing three years on the farm along with Channing's desire to race a horse. It is then revealed that Nolan used to be a champion horse trainer working for Clara until a terrible riding accident that killed Nolan's jockey wife, Channing's mother, and her horse. Emotionally crippled, the defeated Nolan retired to the farm and refused to let Channing follow in her mother's ill-fated footsteps. Girl and zebra must both overcome the odds: Stripes to race despite his small stature and strength next to a horses' and Channing to convince her father that she must fulfill her dreams. And of course, Nolan must overcome his fear and face life again. Which of course, all happens in the course of events after the requisite setbacks for dramatic purposes.

The day of the big race, The Kentucky Open, arrives and Stripes manages to gain entrée in the prestigious race jockeyed by Channing, of course. Not without a fight from the bullying thoroughbreds next door, however, who menace Stripes and kidnap Sandy, threatening to hurt her if Stripes goes through with the race. Stripes' barnyard buds, however, go to the rescue aided by the comic horseflies Buzz (voice of Harvey) and Scuzz (voice of Spade). Then, it's off to the races where more last-minute drama is injected when a newly confident Nolan bets the overly confident Clara that if Stripes wins, she must give him Sandy. Clara agrees only on the condition that if Stripes loses, he go back to work for her *forever* ("a lifetime contract"). Hardly likely, Nolan nonetheless agrees to her evil terms. Despite the dirty tactics of the other jockeys and aided once again by the bantering horseflies and sage advice from Tucker, Stripes miraculously prevails.

Of the humans, Greenwood comes across as an earnest dad while Panettiere is appealing, although a tad saccharine, and Malick too one-dimensionally evil. As in *Babe*, all the animals (except the computer generated horseflies) are real and are made to look like they can talk with CGI lip movements that are generally well done but a tall order to make look convincing throughout a feature-length film. The dialogue is simple but smart, with much of the adult humor coming from the horseflies witty repartee and Goose's *Godfather* gangland references while children will like the broad physical comedy found throughout. Uplifting story is echoed in the amiable soundtrack, featuring original tunes "Taking The Inside Rail" co-written and performed by Sting and "It Ain't Over Yet" by Bryan Adams which should both please little girls everywhere who will see this movie.

Hilary White

CREDITS

Nolan Walsh: Bruce Greenwood
Channing Walsh: Hayden Panettiere
Woodzie: M. Emmet Walsh
Clara Dalrymple: Wendie Malick
Stripes: Frankie Muniz (Voice)
Sandy: Mandy Moore (Voice)
Clydesdale: Michael Clarke Duncan (Voice)
Trenton's Pride: Joshua Jackson (Voice)
Reggie: Jeff Foxworthy (Voice)
Goose: Joe Pantoliano (Voice)
Ruffshod: Michael Rosenbaum (Voice)
Buzz: Steve Harvey (Voice)
Scuzz: David Spade (Voice)
Lightning: Snoop Dogg (Voice)
Sir Trenton: Fred Dalton Thompson (Voice)
Tucker: Dustin Hoffman (Voice)
Franny: Whoopi Goldberg (Voice)
Origin: USA
Language: English
Released: 2005
Production: Andrew A. Kosove, Broderick Johnson, Edward L. McDonnell, Lloyd Phillips; Alcon Entertainment; released by Warner Bros.
Directed by: Frederick Du Chan
Written by: Frederick Du Chan, David F. Schmidt
Cinematography by: David Eggby
Music by: Mark Isham
Sound: Nico Louw
Music Supervisor: Deva Anderson
Editing: Tom Finan
Art Direction: Jonathan Hely-Hutchinson
Costumes: Jo Katsaras
Production Design: Wolf Kroeger
MPAA rating: PG
Running time: 102 minutes

REVIEWS

Boxoffice Online. January, 2005.
Chicago Sun-Times Online. January 14, 2005.
Entertainment Weekly Online. January 12, 2005.
Los Angeles Times Online. January 14, 2005.
New York Times Online. January 14, 2005.
Variety Online. January 9, 2005.

QUOTES

Lightning: "Well, like my momma used to say, you can put your boots in the oven, but that won't make 'em biscuits."

REBOUND

A comedy where old school...meets middle school.
—Movie tagline

Box Office: $16.8 million

Scientists in the field of cloning would do well to study *Rebound.* It is a near perfect replica of countless coaching films that came before it. A lackluster coach takes on a ragtag team of young kids on a losing team. The coach inspires the kids, the kids inspire the coach and lessons are learned. Sometimes the coach is a strict disciplinarian (as in *Coach Carter*), sometimes the coach is bumbling (*The Bad News Bears*), but always the results are the same: the team of losers becomes a team of winners. Rob Blackwelder of *SplicedWIRE*, wrote that the film was "so predictable that director Steve Carr doesn't even bother with scenes of its basketball team of 13-year-old misfits discovering their skills and a love of the game. He just assumes you know the formula."

In *Rebound*, the coach is of the bumbling variety. Roy McCormick (Martin Lawrence) is a successful college coach who has lost touch with the joys of coaching. He misses parts of his team's games for magazine photo shoots, he endorses any product that will pay him well enough and probably knows more about the features of his fancy SUV than his players' stats. Roy's job is already in danger, but when, during another temper tantrum, he accident kills the vulture mascot of an opposing team, he is banned from coaching college ball. His slimy agent, Tim Fink (Breckin Meyer), figures that the best way to get Roy back into the good graces of the league officials is to have Roy perform some public service in the form of coaching a team of middle schoolers at Mount Vernon Junior High. It is even better that Mount Vernon is the coach's alma mater.

The Mount Vernon team is, of course, bad. Losses of a hundred points or more are not uncommon for them. At first Coach Roy is unconcerned, expect to feel disgust for just how bad they are. Screenwriter John J. Strauss seemed not to go beyond brief character sketches when he devised the players on the team. There is Ralph (Steven Anthony Lawrence), a character whose main trait is that he often vomits. Goggles (Gus Hoffman) cannot see very well. In Roy's first inkling of coaching interest, he recruits the school's bully, Big Mac (Tara Correa), because she is mean. "You have five fouls,"he advises her. "Don't be afraid to use them." He also recruits the shy, quiet Wes (Steven C. Parker), because he is tall.

In a bit of movie magic, Roy starts caring and the kids start winning. They do not simply improve. They go from losing by huge margins to beating the best teams in the league. The movie does not give much reason for this, short of a few of Roy's coaching tips such as putting Ben Gay in the players' arm pits to make sure they keep their hands up.

Any humorous presence that Lawrence might have is completely unused in this film. He appears briefly as a crazy preacher friend of Roy's but the character is both not funny and out of left field. Like Roy, Lawrence seems to be appearing in the film only to do the bare minimum to keep his high-paying career afloat. Other underused characters floating about in the film are the school principal, Principal Walsh (Megan Mullally), and a type-A opposing coach, Larry Burgess (Patrick Warburton). Jeanie Ellis (Wendy Raquel Robinson), the protective mother of hotshot player Keith (Oren Williams), has a mild romance with Roy but as Wesley Morris of *The Boston Globe* wrote, "The writing doesn't break a sweat trying. He's single. So is she." Perhaps the faults of the film also lie with director Carr, who has showed a taste for bland, middlebrow fare with his other films, *Daddy Day Care* and *Doctor Doolittle 2.*

Critics either disliked the film or gave it only the mildest of praise. Roger Ebert of *The Chicago Sun-Times* wrote, "I can't recommend the movie except to younger viewers, but I don't dislike it. It's *Coach Carter* Lite, and it does what it does." Michael Booth of *The Denver Post* wrote, "Parents may feel a need to shrug off the most predictable moments in *Rebound*, but there's a good summer family movie hiding behind the worst clichés." Stephen Holden of *The New York Times* wrote, "*Rebound* is a children's sports movie that runs on almost no adrenaline.... At times the movie, directed by Steve Carr, seems so bored with itself that it dozes off while still on its feet."

Jill Hamilton

CREDITS

Roy McCormick/Preacher Don: Martin Lawrence
Ralph: Steven Anthony Lawrence
Mr. Newirth: Horatio Sanz
Principal Walsh: Megan Mullally
Larry Burgess Sr.: Patrick Warburton
Jeanie Ellis: Wendy Raquel Robinson
Tim Fink: Breckin Meyer
Late Carl: Fred Stoller
Keith Ellis: Oren Williams
One Love: Eddy Martin

Amy: Alia Shawkat
Wes: Steven Christopher Parker
Fuzzy: Logan McElroy
Goggles: Gus Hoffman
Big Mac: Tara Correa
Annie: Amy Bruckner
Origin: USA
Language: English
Released: 2005
Production: Robert Simonds; Robert Simonds, Runteldat Entertainment; released by 20th Century-Fox
Directed by: Steve Carr
Written by: Jon Lucas, Scott Moore
Cinematography by: Glen MacPherson
Music by: Teddy Castellucci, Spring Aspers
Sound: David Obermeyer
Editing: Craig Herring
Art Direction: Bruce Crone
Production Design: Jaymes Hinkle
MPAA rating: PG
Running time: 103 minutes

REVIEWS

Boxoffice Online. July, 2005.
Chicago Sun-Times Online. July 1, 2005.
Entertainment Weekly Online. June 29, 2005.
Los Angeles Times Online. July 1, 2005.
New York Times Online. July 1, 2005.
Variety Online. June 30, 2005.
Washington Post Online. July 1, 2005, p. C05.

RED EYE

Fear Takes Flight.
—Movie tagline

Box Office: $57.9 million

Red Eye is one of the best thrillers to emerge from Hollywood in quite some time, anchored by yet another fine, nuanced performance by Rachel McAdams, who continues to demonstrate a broad range in a variety of genres. She plays Lisa Reisert, who, on a flight home from her grandmother's funeral, finds herself virtually taken hostage on a red-eye flight by a psychopath with the ominous-sounding name of Jackson Rippner (Cillian Murphy). Director Wes Craven, working from a script by Carl Ellsworth, delivers a fast-paced, suspenseful story that builds to a tense conclusion.

It would be easy to take for granted the pleasure of *Red Eye*. After all, it does not break new ground and tends to follow many of the familiar beats we would expect in this kind of film. But it is rare to see all of the elements come together so well, from lead performances to the taut script to the precise camerawork, courtesy of Robert Yeoman, that keeps us involved despite the fact that we are cooped up in an airplane for much of the running time.

Lisa is the type of person who remains cool under fire, a hotel manager who can solve, via cell phone, customer complaints that would frazzle just about anyone else even as she is rushing to the airport to catch her flight home. When the flight is delayed and she is stranded, she strikes up an airport friendship with Jackson, who flirts with her and sometimes flirts with being a bit forward. But all the while his seeming concern in the wake of her grandmother's death is just a ploy to soften her up for his bigger plan. Once they board the plane, Lisa discovers that she is sitting right next to Jackson and soon learns that this is no coincidence at all. Jackson works for some nameless group that is plotting to kill Deputy Secretary of Homeland Security Charles Keefe (Jack Scalia). He and his family are staying at Lisa's hotel, and, if she does not make a phone call to have the Keefes' room changed, then her father, Joe (Brian Cox), will be killed.

Lisa faces a serious moral dilemma, and the bulk of the film revolves around her attempts to outsmart Jackson—placing a note in a book she gives another passenger (a Dr. Phil fan who provides some comic relief), pretending to make the call when the phone signal is really down, and writing a distress message with soap on a bathroom mirror. Jackson foils each attempt and even knocks her out at one point, thus raising the tension in their game of cat and mouse.

The film's great achievement is in its use of the plane's tight quarters and the way the two principals carry the film through basic two-shots and close-ups. McAdams, her beauty masking a fierce tenacity, always lets the audience see the subtle shifts in Lisa's thoughts, even as she turns from vulnerability to determination in a moment. Lisa, after all, is used to handling crises but never one where so much is at stake. And Murphy is quietly menacing in the way that Jackson controls the situation, using verbal and physical threats to control his captive. Murphy has an offbeat, androgynous look that can be attractive but also borders on creepiness and contrasts nicely with McAdams's wholesome good looks.

Lisa finally makes the phone call, but, upon learning that not just Keefe but his family is targeted as well, she strengthens her resolve to outsmart her captor. When the plane lands, she stabs Jackson in the throat with a pen she stole from another passenger. The wound, nonetheless, is not fatal, and, in an improbable turn that is nonetheless expected in this genre (we have to suspend our disbelief to some extent), Jackson chases her through the airport. Lisa, however, is able to foil the assassination by making the call that evacuates the Keefes just one step ahead of the killers' firing the missile at their room.

Lisa makes it to her home, where she drives a vehicle right into the killer stationed outside her father's house, but somehow Jackson makes it there as well. The chase sequences through the airport and then the house are not quite as compelling as the heart of the movie on the airplane, probably because they seem more familiar, but Craven nonetheless does an expert job of building to a thrilling climactic battle. It is also to the film's benefit that Lisa does not become a superhero but remains a scared yet steadfast woman using whatever resources and cunning are at her disposal. She has a scar from a mugging, and her vow never again to be a victim drives her to persevere. Putting up an incredible fight and enduring a lot of abuse, she even takes a tumble down a flight of stairs, but, just when it looks like Jackson is moving in for the kill, her father shoots him.

Although she appears in only a few scenes, Jayma Mays as Cynthia, Lisa's assistant at the hotel, is quite memorable in her feature film debut. Whether she is panicking and needing Lisa's help in dealing with an unforeseen problem or maintaining, with her own loopy charm, an air of professionalism after the missile has ripped through the building and left devastation in its wake, Cynthia is the harried employee eager to do the right thing and maintain a positive outlook. The results are often comic, which is just what *Red Eye* needs from time to time, and Lisa and Cynthia's camaraderie in handling troublesome customers in the final scene is a great capper after all they have been through.

Craven's direction is masterful throughout *Red Eye*, but it helps that he is working from a great, economical script and with two expressive actors who can communicate a breadth of emotion with their faces. Nothing is extraneous or wasted, and each character, even the nameless passengers on board, plays a pivotal part in the film's tight narrative.

Peter N. Chumo II

CREDITS

Lisa Reisert: Rachel McAdams
Jackson Rippner: Cillian Murphy
Joe Reisert: Brian Cox
Cynthia: Kyle Gallner
Rebecca: Brittany Oaks
Charles Keefe: Jack Scalia
Wes Craven (Cameo)
Carl Ellsworth (Cameo)
Origin: USA
Language: English
Released: 2005
Production: Chris Bender, Marianne Maddalena; Benderspink; released by Dreamworks Pictures
Directed by: Wes Craven
Written by: Carl Ellsworth, Dan Foos
Cinematography by: Robert Yeoman
Music by: Marco Beltrami, Marco Beltrami
Sound: James Steube
Editing: Patrick Lussier, Stuart Levy
Art Direction: Andrew Max Cahn
Costumes: Mary Claire Hannan
Production Design: Bruce Alan Miller
MPAA rating: PG-13
Running time: 85 minutes

REVIEWS

Boxoffice Online. August, 2005.
Chicago Sun-Times Online. August 19, 2005.
Entertainment Weekly Online. August 17, 2005.
Los Angeles Times Online. August 19, 2005.
New York Times Online. August 19, 2005.
Premiere Magazine Online. August 18, 2005.
Variety Online. August 14, 2005.
Washington Post Online. August 19, 2005, p. WE37.

QUOTES

Jackson Rippner: "Sometimes bad things happen to good people."

TRIVIA

First time screenwriter Carl Ellsworth was the only screenwriter to work on the movie script, a rarity in Hollywood.

RENT

No day but today.
—Movie tagline

Box Office: $28.8 million

Hopes were sky high for the screen adaptation of the hit Broadway show that was not only a huge success but also helped to define the musical genre for an entire generation. Chris Columbus was tasked with bringing this beloved musical from the stage to the silver screen. He struck me as an odd choice for the job. Director of such light comedies as *Home Alone*, *Mrs. Doubtfire*, and *Adventures in Babysitting*, I was hoping he would be capable of setting aside his usual sunny, feel-good disposition to truly capture the gritty and harsh realities of the artists of *Rent* who struggle to survive in an unforgiving city. Let's just say I was skeptical to say the least. I actually had the privilege of seeing the nationally touring Broadway production in the recent past and fell in love with the music and the complex, textured characters. I cringed at the thought of what might have been adapted to make the bleak musical seem a little more "mainstream" for the big screen.

To my pleasant surprise, six of the eight original cast members were involved in the film. That fact alone made me want to tap dance with joy on my way to my seat in the front of the theatre. But, the look I got from the greasy-faced, adolescent taking the tickets persuaded me to play it cool and passively slurp my six-dollar soda.

At any rate, this story takes place in New York City in the late 1980s. A time when the AIDS epidemic was reaching it's peak in America. The narrative follows a group of starving artists that are forced to deal with a variety of unfortunate circumstances. Personal loss, homelessness, disease, and drug addiction are just a few of the hurdles encountered by this young collection of characters in a city that affords the perfect circumstances by which an ambitious artist can become a star, but just as easily wind up swallowed in a pool of identity dissolution.

Benny (Taye Diggs) was once a member of this aspiring group, but his marriage to the daughter of a corporate developer has altered his perspective on life. He now finds himself poised to evict Mark (Anthony Rapp) and Roger (Adam Pascal) unless they agree to help him foil a protest rally headed by Mark's ex-girlfriend Maureen (Idena Menzel). The rally is geared towards preventing the developer from constructing a new building that would level Maureen's performance space and displace a tent city for the homeless in the community. Mark and Roger's former roommate, Tom Collins (Jesse L. Martin) is on his way over to celebrate Christmas Eve when he is suddenly and violently mugged. Fortunately for Tom, he is discovered by Angel, (Wilson Jermaine Hedia) a passing transsexual who nurses Tom back to health and robustness. They reveal to each other that they each have AIDS and a bond forms which leads to a triumphant, non-judgmental relationship. Tragedy and triumph mingle in this well concocted narrative fraught with contradiction and extremity.

The spirit of the original musical remains intact with Mr. Columbus adding some interesting visual twists that could only be delivered through film. However, I was disappointed that a handful of my favorite musical numbers from the original stage production didn't survive the editing process.

The film is well timed though. It follows in the footsteps of recent successful Hollywood musicals such as *Moulin Rouge* and *Chicago.* Overall, I thought this was a marvelous adaptation of the original, with powerful musical numbers and performances by all. Anthony Rapp brings an amazing performance to the screen, capturing the essence of the downtrodden and apathetic Mark with poise and precision.

Nick Kennedy and Jeff Sullivan

CREDITS

Mark Cohen: Anthony Rapp
Roger Davis: Adam Pascal
Mimi Marquez: Rosario Dawson
Benjamin Coffin III: Taye Diggs
Tom Collins: Jessie L. Martin
Angel Dumont Schunard: Jermaine Heredia Wilson
Maureen Johnson: Idina Menzel
Joanne Jefferson: Tracie Thoms
Origin: USA
Language: English
Released: 2005
Production: Jane Rosenthal, Robert De Niro, Chris Columbus, Mark Radcliffe, Michael Barnathan; Revolution Studios, Tribeca Productions, 1492 Pictures; released by Sony Pictures Entertainment
Directed by: Chris Columbus
Written by: Taye Diggs
Cinematography by: Stephen Goldblatt
Music by: Rob Cavallo
Sound: Nelson Stoll
Music Supervisor: Matt Sullivan
Editing: Richard Pearson
Art Direction: Nanci Starr Noblett
Costumes: Aggie Guerard Rodgers
Production Design: Howard Cummings
MPAA rating: PG-13
Running time: 128 minutes

REVIEWS

Boxoffice Online. November, 2005.
Chicago Sun-Times Online. November 23, 2005.
Entertainment Weekly Online. November 22, 2005.
Los Angeles Times Online. November 23, 2005.
New York Times Online. November 23, 2005.
Premiere Magazine Online. November 22, 2005.
Variety Online. November 20, 2005.

QUOTES

Mark, sung: "To love attention, no pension, to more than one dimension, to starving for attention hating convention hating pretension, not to mention of course, hating dear old Mom and Dad."

TRIVIA

The first half of the movie takes place in the winter and since it was filmed in San Francisco and New York during the spring and summer, all of the visible breath coming from the mouths of the actors was added digitally in post-production.

THE RING TWO

Fear comes full circle.
—Movie tagline
The dead don't sleep.
—Movie tagline

Box Office: $75.9 million

Part of what makes horror horrifying is the element of surprise. *The Ring Two* did not have that advantage. It came after the 1998 Japanese thriller *Ringu,* which spawned a mini-cottage industry of sequels and spinoffs, including the popular American remake, 2002's *The Ring.* To raise interest in *The Ring Two,* Hideo Nakata, director of *Ringu,* was brought in to direct. (Adding to the *Ring* family tree confusion, Nakata also directed the Japanese sequel to *Ringu,* which was completely different from this sequel.) The disturbing images and ideas in *The Ring* helped make it a huge hit, but repeated in this sequel, they become more familiar and lose some of their power to frighten.

Another part of a successful horror movie is the scary thrill of trying to figure out exactly what is happening, why it is happening, and who is behind it. In *The Ring Two* those questions have already pretty much been answered, so there is little to do but just dole out some more killings. Here, *The Ring* veterans, Rachel (Naomi Watts) and her son, Aidan (David Dorfman), are back for more punishment. After their unfortunate time in Seattle, they have moved to a small town in Oregon to start anew. Rachel takes a job at a small town newspaper and the two try to forget about being terrorized by a dead girl, Samara (Daveigh Chase) who comes and gets people through VCR tapes. (Those who have adopted DVD technology, apparently, are safe.)

It seems as though a terror-free life will not be so easy since Rachel soon finds herself investigating the case of a teenager's suspicious death. His face bears the telltale twisted death grimace that means Samara probably had something to do with it. Soon it becomes apparent that what Samara actually wants is to take over the body of Aidan and enjoy life as Rachel's child.

Rachel catches on to this concept quickly but other adults are not so sure about the idea. Her handsome coworker, Max (Simon Baker), is sincere in wanting to help but he does not seem to get it. A psychologist at the hospital, Dr. Emma Temple (Elizabeth Perkins), where Aidan is being treated for low body temperature, thinks Rachel is abusing the boy. At her most desperate, she contacts Samara's one-time adoptive mother, Evelyn (Sissy Spacek), who now lives in a mental institution. The encounter involves a lot of emoting and a truly frightening wig on Spacek's part, but little useful information for Rachel to use. "Be a good mother!" Evelyn hisses unhelpfully.

Samara's hairy man arms and weird double-jointed lurching retain their power of creepiness, but the rest of the thrills in the film are none too thrilling. Samara attacks poor Aidan in his bath, a carpet gets soaked with water, and Rachel has to go in Samara's scary well. The strangest scene is one in which Rachel and Aidan drive down a country road and get attacked by a herd of really angry deer. It does not make much sense in the context of the movie, but credit should go to Nakata for making the scene scarier than it deserves to be.

Dorfman is spooky in the way of a less talented Haley Joel Osment. He conveys the same sense of knowing too much at too young an age. And Watts should get a few kudos for not laughing (or crying) through lines like, "You can't have him, Samara! You're going back where you came from!" Or the audience favorite, "I'm not your (bleeping) mommy!"

Critics were not scared by the film and they were not afraid to say it. Michael Wilmington of *The Chicago Tribune* wrote, "Despite the scene change, there's not much mystery, unless you've forgotten the first movie and aren't paying attention this time." Wesley Morris of *The Boston Globe* wrote, "The movie's torpid pacing and blocks of dead space will leave plenty of time for a bored and frustrated audience to yell obscenities at the screen." Mick LaSalle of *The San Francisco Chronicle* wrote that there was "nothing terrifying about the movie and nothing to root for either." Manohla Dargis of *The New York Times* wrote, "Despite Mr. Nakata's track record and the radiant presence of its star, Naomi Watts, *The Ring Two* is a dud."

Jill Hamilton

CREDITS

Rachel Keller: Naomi Watts
Max Rourke: Simon Baker
Aidan: David Dorfman
Dr. Emma Temple: Elizabeth Perkins
Martin Savide: Gary Cole
Evelyn: Sissy Spacek
Jake: Ryan Merriman
Emily: Emily Van Camp
Samara: Daveigh Chase
Betsy: Kelly Overton
Evil Samara: Kelly Stables

Doctor: James Lesure
Origin: USA
Language: English
Released: 2005
Production: Walter F. Parkes, Laurie MacDonald; Parkes/McDonald; released by DreamWorks
Directed by: Hideo Nakata
Written by: Ehren Kruger, Hideo Nakata
Cinematography by: Gabriel Beristain
Music by: Henning Lohner, Martin Tillman
Sound: David MacMillan
Editing: Michael N. Knue
Art Direction: Christa Munro
Costumes: Wendy Chuck
Production Design: James Bissell
MPAA rating: PG-13
Running time: 111 minutes

REVIEWS

Boxoffice Online. March, 2005.
Chicago Sun-Times Online. March 18, 2005.
Entertainment Weekly Online. March 16, 2005.
Los Angeles Times Online. March 18, 2005.
New York Times Online. March 18, 2005.
Premiere Magazine Online. March 17, 2005.
Variety Online. March 13, 2005.
Washington Post Online. March 18, 2005, p. WE45.

TRIVIA

To promote the film, copies of the "Cursed Tape" were left in public places. About five minutes into the footage, the viewer is directed to the movie's website.

THE RINGER

Special has been redefined.
—Movie tagline

Box Office: $13.6 million

What sounds like the ultimate exercise in offensiveness and poor taste—the guy from MTV's *Jackass* rigs the Special Olympics for profit—actually turns out to be a likeable, high concept comedy with as much heart as laughs. Produced by Peter and Bobby Farrelly, the kings of low-brow humor and the warped minds behind such royally successful comedies as *Dumb and Dumber* and *There's Something About Mary,* the film was given the seal of approval by the Special Olympics after the brothers relentlessly wooed the board and, amazingly, granted them final say on the script and the option to cut any ad-libbed scenes from the final cut. Boasting the most intellectually disabled actors and athletes ever assembled in a feature film—about 150—the film is indeed what producer Peter Farrelly dubbed "groundbreaking." Striving to break the mold of the overly-sentimental way such stories are usually handled, the Farrellys—longtime volunteers with Best Buddies, a mentoring program for the intellectually disabled—along with director Barry Blaustein (*Beyond the Mat* [1999]) and screenwriter Ricky Blitt (TV's *The Family Guy*) create a film that portrays people with intellectual disabilities as fun and multidimensional as well as living up to the film's tagline: Special has been redefined.

A somewhat shaky setup introduces Steve Barker (Johnny Knoxville), a mild-mannered, low-level office worker with ambition, as evidenced in the motivational tapes he diligently listens to at his desk. The self-help speaker (Jesse Ventura) barks at him to take action, prompting him to confront his pompous, dismissive boss who promotes him on the spot just so Steve can fire the company's janitor Stavi (Luis Avalos). Steve heads to the men's room to undertake the odious task made all the more difficult by the fact that Stavi loves his job—cleaning toilets seems to be an especial favorite—and that Stavi is a widower with five young children to support. Stavi also likes to talk about himself in the third-person, which may be the reason he is being fired. Nonetheless, Steve softens the blow by offering him a job mowing lawns at his apartment complex, along with a raise and medical benefits, which Steve will have to provide for Stavi out-of-pocket. Of course, Steve does not get Stavi any insurance (the fact that he is an illegal alien doesn't help either) so it is clear what must happen next and it does. Investigating a stalled lawnmower, Stavi, in a pure Farrelly touch, gets multiple fingers chopped off. Steve rushes Stavi to the hospital with a Ziploc baggie full of ice and Stavi's dismembered digits. The doctor informs Steve that the $40,000 required to reattach the fingers is required upfront so he only has two weeks to come up with the fee before the fingers become unsewable.

What Steve must do to get the money becomes clear very quickly thereafter. *His* idea is to call in some outstanding loans from friends and relatives and his first stop is uncle Gary (Brian Cox) to collect a $1,000 loan. *Uncle Gary,* who is also being tapped—albeit much more forcefully—by the mob to call in a small fortune in gambling loans, has a different an idea that will get them both the money they need after the mobster loanshark leaning on him mentions his love of the Special Olympics' seven-time winning star athlete Jimmy (Leonard Flowers, a long-time Special Olympian) who even appears on a Wheaties cereal box (in real-life, as well). Remembering that Steve was a former track and field star in high school as well as a frustrated actor, Gary cooks up a scheme to enter Steve in the Special Olympics while betting a bundle against Jimmy with the mobster. Thoroughly disgusted with the idea but eager to save his friend Stavi—whose children forlornly give him the new Stavi "wave," that looks like the Hawaiian hang-loose signal of the thumb and pinky only going back and forth—Steve agrees.

After a period of researching his role (which includes the videos of *Rain Man, Forrest Gump* and *The Best of Chevy Chase*), Steve comes up with the lame, disabled alter-ego Jeffy and he and Uncle Gary head to The Games. On the verge of heading right back home again when faced with the reality of the situation, the two are greeted by a pretty, perky blond S.O. volunteer Lynn (Katherine Heigl) which gets Steve's attention and he is once again eager to participate in the fraud just to be close to her. When prompted for his last name, Gary hilariously comes up on the spot with Dahmer—"with an 'O'" of course. All signed in, Jeffy Dahmor then heads to the dormitories where he'll be living for the duration of the games.

It is here Jeffy meets his colorful teammates in the games. He immediately clashes with his roommate Billy (Edward Barbanell, a longtime Special Olympian in his film debut), busy on his computer when Jeffy arrives, when he accidentally scratches one of Billy's CDs and will, henceforth, always be reminded of that fact. The others, including smart alec Glen (Jed Rees, *Galaxy Quest*), sweet, rotund Thomas (Bill Chott, *Dude, Where's My Car*), Mark (Leonard Earl Howze, *Antwone Fisher, Barbershop*), Winston (Geoffrey Arend, *Garden State*), and music buff Rudy (John Taylor, *The Seventh Sign*) greet him with a mixture of skepticism, scorn, and indifference. In his frustration with the foreign surroundings and the constant teasing by his teammates, "Jeffy" reverts to "Steve" more than a few times prompting suspicion from the gang by his change in language and demeanor. Ready to ditch the charade, Steve readily confesses that he is indeed not disabled when confronted by the angry group. Surprisingly, the boys take an unexpected and comic tack when faced with Steve's honesty, urging him to stay and beat seven time Special Olympics champ Jimmy (a wonderful turn from longtime Special Olympic champion Leonard Flowers), who has become an industry unto himself, arriving in a limo complete with a posse, a bevy of high-paying endorsements, and outrageous attitude. Steve's teammates then take it upon themselves to train the lazy, out-of-shape imposter for this task—waking him at the crack of dawn and forcing him to run, hurdle, get chased by angry dogs, and, just for laughs, get punched in the stomach a lot.

Although the boys are now in on the ruse, Lynn is still blissfully unaware that Jeffy's not special at all. She does take a shine to the very ingratiating athlete, however, and invites him to lunch. What Steve doesn't know, however, is that it's a setup, with Lynn bringing along another special person for Jeffy as well as her own fiancé David. Although Yolie (Nicole Bradley) is attractive and funny, Steve is more in love with the virtuous Lynn than ever and hates the fact that David (longtime Farrelly favorite Zen Gesner) is such a smarmy womanizer (he flirts with the waitress while she's in the loo). David gets his comeuppance, however, when Steve sneaks the boys out to the movies one night to see *Dirty Dancing*—which is prohibited by their curfew—and David is caught making out with the aforementioned waitress. David drives the boys home where a worried Lynn is waiting up for the missing athletes only to be told by Jeffy about David's indiscretion. This opens the door for Steve who then takes a fun-filled trip with Lynn to Costco, where they sing and joke until Steve sees the picture of Lynn's brother, now dead, who was "also" special which presumably, causes Steve to reevaluate his behavior. That, and the fact that he has grown to care about and respect his teammates as athletes and people.

The games begin, however, and Steve manages to be in a virtual tie with Jimmy after the hurdles, long jump, high jump, and shot put. The remaining race will decide the winner, with Steve clearly out front in the final stretch. When Jimmy twists his ankle and falls, however, Steve and many other concerned teammates race over to help him up at the expense of the win. Glen actually wins the race and the games overall. At the medal ceremony, silver-medallist Jeffy blows his own cover in front of shocked and disgusted fans and Lynn (who slaps him on his way out), while Thomas then wins a medal by default, with Jimmy in third. Because Gary only bet on the fact that Jimmy would lose, not that Jeffy would win, however, Gary gets out of gambling debt and Stavi is able to get his operation.

Cut to six months later, where Steve has taken a job as an acting teacher for the disabled that includes many of his former teammates. The scene includes a wonderful performance by Barbanell doing a monologue from *Romeo and Juliet* (learning this monologue from an acting teacher is what prompted Barbanell to act and has appeared in regional productions of the play). Lynn unknowingly wanders in to find Steve, whom she has finally forgiven after learning about Stavi (who is now complete with fingers) and the two reunite.

While most of the film is gently humorous veering toward the uplifting, there are some priceless bits, especially the ones involving Stavi and his unfortunate accident. The Stavi "wave" for example, and when Uncle Gary shows up at the games holding up a giant foam hand bearing three fingers sporting the phrase "We miss you Stavi" to urge Steve on to victory.

Knoxville is wonderfully vulnerable as the guilt-ridden Steve and has a definite chemistry with all the supporting actors. Cox, always entertaining, makes the odious Uncle Gary mischievously funny as the mastermind behind thc twisted scheme. Gesner, too, makes his bad-guy character fun to watch as he tries to smooth-talk everything in sight while Heigl is the least compelling character, perpetually upbeat and sweet but completely proficient.

It's Jeffy's teammates that makes this movie so much fun, with it's compelling mix of able and disabled actors that all bring something special and unique to the table.

Hilary White

CREDITS

Steve Barker: Johnny Knoxville
Gary Barker: Brian Cox
Lynn Sheridan: Katherine Heigl
Winston: Geoffrey Arend
Mark: Leonard Earl Howze
Glen: Jed Rees
Rudy: John Taylor
Billy: Edward Barbanell
Thomas: Bill Chott
Jimmy: Leonard Flowers
Origin: USA
Language: English
Released: 2005
Production: Peter Farrelly, Bradley Thomas, Bobby Farrelly; Fox Searchlight, Conundrum Entertainment; released by 20th Century-Fox
Directed by: Barry W. Blaustein
Written by: Ricky Blitt
Cinematography by: Mark Irwin
Music by: Mark Mothersbaugh
Sound: Jonathan Stein
Music Supervisor: Tom Wolfe, Manish Raval
Editing: George Folsey Jr.
Art Direction: Arlan Jay Vetter, John Frick
Costumes: Lisa Jensen
MPAA rating: PG-13
Running time: 94 minutes

REVIEWS

Boxoffice Online. December, 2005.
Chicago Sun-Times Online. December 23, 2005.
Entertainment Weekly Online. December 23, 2005.
Los Angeles Times Online. December 23, 2005.
New York Times Online. December 23, 2005.
Variety Online. December 21, 2005.
Washington Post Online. December 23, 2005, p. C05.

TRIVIA

The film was actually endorsed by the Special Olympics.

ROBOTS

Repair for adventure!
—Movie tagline
Riveting in IMAX
—Movie tagline

Box Office: $128.2 million

As computer animation has rather quickly supplanted traditional animation, thanks to the amazingly consistent success of Pixar Animation Studios and films like *Shrek* and *Shrek 2*, a phenomenon has appeared that is akin to the pitfalls associated with the technological advancement of special visual effects in "live action" movies. Film critics and general audiences have all observed the tendency for the makers of many big-budget, high-concept films to be more concerned with dazzling, jaw-dropping special effects than on well-developed, meaningful stories. The growth of computer animation lends itself almost naturally to the same kind of tendency, one that is perfectly illustrated in *Robots*. This film suffers from the same type of flaws evidenced in its makers' previous animated feature, *Ice Age* (2002), a movie that made money even though it was thin on story. For awhile at least, *Robots* is interesting to look at because of its stylish design and its eerie but other-worldly realism, yet it quickly becomes tedious and dull because the filmmakers have focused on creating a visual extravaganza at the expense of crafting a compelling and emotionally resonant story.

Robots takes place in an ambiguous other-world apparently populated only by robots. Oddly, the robots appear to be pieced together from spare parts of machines, appliances, or vehicles from our human world. Perhaps the filmmakers intended this to be creative, and it does contribute to an offbeat, almost surreal visual design, but it also seems awkward and inexplicable. The beginning of the film introduces this robotic world and sets up some of the background for understanding their society and how the robots grow and reproduce. The first characters to be introduced are a husband and wife, Mr. and Mrs. Copperbottom (voices of Stanley Tucci and Dianne Wiest), who are ecstatic to share the news that they are having a baby. Of course it turns out that they must construct a child from a "Build a Baby" kit. The baby is a boy they name Rodney (adult voice of

Ewan McGregor). As time passes, Rodney "grows" by being upgraded with new parts. However, since the Copperbottoms live on a modest income (Herb is a dishwasher at a local restaurant), they cannot afford new parts, so Rodney gets hand-me-downs from cousins and other relatives.

Growing up, Rodney develops an interest in inventing new gadgets and idolizes the famous inventor Mr. Bigweld (voice of Mel Brooks), "the greatest robot in the world," a huge, round robot whose company provides parts for robots everywhere. Bigweld's motto is "You can shine no matter what you're made of," which is obviously supposed to be one of the central themes of the story, and that thought inspires Rodney to dream big dreams. His father, who early in life abandoned his own dreams of becoming a musician, encourages Rodney to leave Rivet Town and head to Robot City to try to get a job for Bigweld. "Never give up," he says to his son. So off Rodney goes to the metropolis of Robot City, hoping to fulfill his dreams.

Unfortunately, when Rodney arrives at Bigweld's headquarters in Robot City, he discovers that Bigweld himself is nowhere to be found. In his place is the shiny, sleek Ratchet (voice of Greg Kinnear), a greedy robot who has assumed Bigweld's position as head of the company. Ratchet, who has much bigger plans in store for the company, has no time for Rodney's intrusion and has the young robot thrown out of the complex.

Ratchet unveils to company executives his plan for increasing profits. The company will no longer supply spare parts for "outmodes" but will now only market a new line of sleek upgrades. Bigweld's old motto will be replaced by a new one: "Why be you, when you can be new?" Any poor robots who cannot afford the upgrades will be destined for the junk pile—or worse, for the "Chop Shop," run by Ratchet's wicked, scheming mother, Madame Gasket (voice of Jim Broadbent), where they will be melted down and used to manufacture new parts. Unfortunately, no one has the courage to object to Ratchet's plan, not even the very concerned Cappy (voice of Halle Berry), who does not like what she is hearing.

Meanwhile, Rodney teams up with a small family of oddball robots and tries to encourage them to help him learn the whereabouts of Bigweld. His quest gets sidetracked, however, when ailing robots in the city, who can no longer buy spare parts but cannot afford upgrades, learn that he has the skills to repair them. Long lines of them show up to beg for his help, and he graciously agrees to do so. Before long, word reaches Madame Gasket and Ratchet that someone is repairing outmodes, and they vow to find the culprit and destroy him.

After Rodney and his wacky friend Fender (voice of Robin Williams) crash a big annual party that is supposed to be hosted by Bigweld, only to learn that the big robot is not in attendance, Cappy decides to take Rodney to the place where Bigweld has sequestered himself. There Rodney is discouraged to learn that Bigweld has given up and no longer seems to believe in his old motto, thinking he has grown too old and powerless. This, by the way, is one extremely weak element of the plot that lacks much sense; the story does not explain why Bigweld came to feel this way or why he let Ratchet take over, and clearly all the other robots still respect him—even Ratchet, who fears him.

Disheartened, Rodney returns to Fender's family and thinks about giving up. Predictably, though, Bigweld himself shows up, having had a change of heart, and they all team up to stop Ratchet and his mother. The climax of the story comes in the form of a big battle inside Madame Gasket's Chop Shop. Not surprisingly, Rodney sees his dream fulfilled when Bigweld makes him his "right-hand man" and names him as his successor.

Robots has good intentions, at least in the themes it attempts to convey. The film's obvious messages are that people should be happy with who they are and should not be afraid to pursue their dreams. Those themes are borne out in an obvious, superficial way, but the plot itself does not focus on developing them. Instead, they are more stated than they are illustrated, and ultimately the messages almost seem as if they are not much more than token themes, present only because the filmmakers thought an animated film like this needed something to say to young audiences.

The plot itself is fairly thin, full of too many forced comic moments and even more forced action sequences that are apparently meant to be visually impressive. The humor, even when coming from comical characters, often seems contrived. The central character intended to make the audience laugh is Fender, a wisecracking robot who is constantly falling apart. Fender has his funny moments, but he has no real depth beyond his incessant joking. Considering Robin Williams' zany and lovable contributions to past animated films, most notably *Aladdin* in 1992, the character of Fender is disappointingly flat and perhaps even pointless. The character of Aunt Fanny (voice of Jennifer Coolidge) is supposed to be funny because she has an enormous rear-end that knocks objects over when she moves, but there is no logic as to why a robot would even have such an oversized part, so there is little humor in the situation; essentially, it just seems silly.

Action sequences (including some filled with slapstick humor) are so numerous in *Robots* that they quickly become tiresome. When Rodney arrives in Robot City, for example, he meets Fender and then finds himself caught up in a strange transportation system that seems inspired by a cross between a roller coaster and a pinball machine. The journey to their destination is evidently supposed to be visually exciting, but the sequence lasts far longer than it should and ultimately defies common sense anyway, in that the transportation system seems more dangerous than useful or practical. It is one of many instances in which the filmmakers attempt to take the viewer on a stunning trip through an animated but realistic wonderland, yet it is overdone and done too often. The final sequences of the film leading up to the resolution of the climax are all like this—a series of chase scenes, rescue attempts, and chaotic battles that rapidly grow uninteresting. Ultimately, the entire story could have been told in a much shorter timeframe if these sequences were trimmed (without detrimental impact on the plot).

The emphasis on visual spectacle and contrived comedy swallows the potential for an effective story. Some films manage to rise above mediocrity even when their stories are overshadowed by special effects, elevated to better-than-average stature because of strong characters, excellent performances, or truly breathtaking, unprecedented accomplishments in visual effects. Unfortunately that is not the case with *Robots*, a film that is lacking in all those other elements. Ironically, while the story is about technology with a message about staying true to one's heart, the technology of the film itself gets in the way so that *Robots* ultimately is short on enough substance to actually touch the heart.

David Flanagin

CREDITS

Rodney Copperbottom: Ewan McGregor (Voice)
Cappy: Halle Berry (Voice)
Fender: Robin Williams (Voice)
Ratchet: Greg Kinnear (Voice)
Bigweld: Mel Brooks (Voice)
Crank Casey: Drew Carey (Voice)
Madame Gasket: Jim Broadbent (Voice)
Piper Pinwheeler: Amanda Bynes (Voice)
Aunt Fanny: Jennifer Coolidge (Voice)
Herb Copperbottom: Stanley Tucci (Voice)
Mrs. Copperbottom: Dianne Wiest (Voice)
Tim the Gate Guard: Paul Giamatti (Voice)
Loretta Geargrinder: Natasha Lyonne (Voice)
Mr. Gasket: Lowell Ganz (Voice)
Mr. Gunk: Dan Hedaya (Voice)
Water Cooler: Jackie Hoffman (Voice)
Voice Box at hardware store: James Earl Jones (Voice)
Lug: Harland Williams (Voice)
Bigmouth Executive/Forge: Stephen Tobolowsky (Voice)
Jack Hammer: Alan Rosenberg (Voice)
Fire Hydrant: Jay Leno (Voice)
Broken Arm bot: Terry Bradshaw (Voice)
Watch: Paula Abdul (Voice)
Origin: USA
Language: English
Released: 2005
Production: Jerry Davis, John C. Donkin, William Joyce; Blue Sky Productions; released by 20th Century-Fox
Directed by: Chris Wedge
Written by: Lowell Ganz, Babaloo Mandel, David Lindsay-Abaire
Music by: John Powell
Sound: Sean Garnhart, Paul Massey, D.M. Hemphill
Music Supervisor: Becky Mancuso-Winding
Editing: John Carnochan
Art Direction: Steve Martino
Production Design: William Joyce
MPAA rating: PG
Running time: 91 minutes

REVIEWS

Boxoffice Online. March, 2005.
Chicago Sun-Times Online. March 11, 2005.
Entertainment Weekly Online. March 9, 2005.
Los Angeles Times Online. March 11, 2005.
New York Times Online. March 11, 2005.
Premiere Magazine Online. March 10, 2005.
Variety Online. March 6, 2005.
Washington Post Online. March 11, 2005, p. WE33.

QUOTES

Fender: "It's a combination of Jazz and funk…called 'Junk!'"

ROCK SCHOOL

Teaching kids the basics: Power chords, head banging, and being a rock star.
—Movie tagline

The arrival of *Rock School* into theaters was overshadowed by the similarly titled and earlier debuting *School of Rock. School of Rock*, a big studio movie starring Jack Black was a fictionalized account of a former musician and wild child who teaches kids how to play rock music. *Rock School* is a documentary about Paul Green, a former musician and wild child who teaches kids how to play rock music. How closely the fiction was inspired by the nonfiction was something that was left to lawyers to figure out. Whether of not the makers of *School of Rock* literally stole ideas from *Rock School*, they certainly stole quite a bit of its thunder. As Owen Gleiberman of *Entertainment Weekly* put it, "the novelty of kids learning to play rock & roll in a structured setting, absorbing a 'devil chord"as systematically as a Bach triad, no longer carries the same zing."

Paul Green runs an after-school music program in Philadelphia called, as only Green would have it, the Paul Green School of Rock. The program, established in 1988, takes kids 8 to 18 and has them study things like the more difficult works of Frank Zappa. There are now several Paul Green schools scattered about the country, but it is difficult to imagine how they must function without Green. That is because, at least in the way Don Argott portrays it, Green's school consists mostly of Green hectoring his students.

The film is about one-fifth about kids and their experience with a serious pursuit with rock stardom and four-fifths about Green yelling and occasionally talking. Green is the kind of guy who so strongly imprinted his self-image during adolescence, that he finds it difficult to move on, despite unmistakable evidence that he is, indeed, aging. If he had not started the school, it is easy to imagine him working in a record store, offering loud and unwanted commentary on customers' purchases. Rather than rock music prowess, Green seems determined to instill his entire rock and roll ethos into the tots. Thus one of his rants toward an unwitting kid includes "Do you love this song? Do you love Dio? Do you love Satan?" His tirades are sometimes fun and clever, but other times just seem abusive, especially since he is the lone authority figure at the school (at least in the film). "Don't &%$#ing make mistakes!" he shouts at a hapless kid.

Green embraces a teaching philosophy that is not exactly in vogue any more. "You know how the trend is not to compare people? I don't do that. I'll say, 'She's better than you,'" he says. Most likely Green envisions himself as a cool older brother showing his young sibling the ropes and teaching them bad words. He is more like a mean older brother who would twist an arm just to hear a hissed, "Uncle," but his method does seem to get results. The movie's climax at the annual East German Frank Zappa festival, Zappanale, shows that the students have acquired the chops to play alongside grown-ups. They play the difficult Zappa piece, "Inca Roads," and earn the respect of ex-Zappa player Napoleon Murphy Brock. It is telling that as the kids are getting their well-deserved applause, Green rushes onstage to claim the credit.

It is a pity that more time is not devoted to some of the more interesting students. CJ Tywoniak is the prodigy of the school. The 12 year-old can whip out Carlos Santana solos with ease and has a fierce work ethic combined with an amiable star quality. Asa and Tucker Collins are 9 year-old twins who, with their spiky blonde hair certainly look the part, but seem supremely untalented musically. Their mother seems to want them to be rockers simply because she likes rock so much. And the most poignant character is Will O'Connor, a depressive teenager. He has been labeled slow by the educational system, but offers some of the most insightful comments in the film. Characteristically, Green treats him with his usual teasing and abuse, even naming a "Will O'Connor Award for Student Most Likely to Kill Himself."

Critics found the film entertaining enough. Ty Burr of *The Boston Globe* wrote, "As a portrait of a dysfunctional pedagogy, it's both refreshing and more than a little terrifying." Manohla Dargis of *The Los Angeles Times* expressed a similar sentiment, calling the film "alternately hilarious and alarming." Peter Hartlaub of *The San Francisco Chronicle* wrote, "That Green gets some positive results—along with the inevitable destruction in his path—makes for an occasionally thoughtful and very entertaining movie, with just enough over-the-top *The Great Santini*-style rants to distract audiences from all the unanswered questions about the school and the teacher's life."

Jill Hamilton

CREDITS

Origin: USA
Language: English
Released: 2005
Production: Sheena M. Joyce; released by Newmarket Films
Directed by: Don Argott
Cinematography by: Don Argott
Sound: Efrain Torres
Music Supervisor: Charles Raggio
Editing: Demian Fenton
MPAA rating: R
Running time: 93 minutes

REVIEWS

Boxoffice Online. June, 2005.
Chicago Sun-Times Online. June 2, 2005.
Entertainment Weekly Online. June 1, 2005.
Los Angeles Times Online. June 3, 2005.
New York Times Online. June 3, 2005.

Variety Online. July 7, 2004.
Washington Post Online. June 3, 2005, p. C05.

QUOTES

Paul Green: "Do you love Dio? Do you love Satan?"

ROLL BOUNCE

Box Office: $17.3 million

Roll Bounce takes place in the summer of 1978 and it seems entirely possible that the film was actually made that year. Director Malcolm D. Lee perfectly captures the feel of that era and the brief period of time when dancing on roller skates, aka roller boogie, was a cool thing to do. Lee's film has the characters wearing exactly the right clothes, making exactly the right cultural references and even drinking Pepsi from that era's can design.

This is the strength of the film. It throws the viewer into an immediate visceral timewarp. The soundtrack alone, including cuts by Chic, the Ohio Players and K.C. and the Sunshine Band, is enough to conjure memories of a time when having a huge comb at the ready in one's back pocket was de rigueur and a "couple's skate" was the height of romance. Even the banter in the film sounds like it could have come from a lost episode of "Welcome Back, Kotter."

The period accuracy is also the weakness of the film. In it, there is plenty of roller boogying and people striving to become fabulous at the art of it. With the wisdom of hindsight, it is hard not to yell at the screen to warn the characters to pursue a more lasting form of excellence. In the year 2005, when the film came out, being Lord of the Skating Rink was not exactly a ticket to social success.

Xavier, or X (Bow Wow), and his group of fellow South Side skaters, Junior (Brandon T. Jackson), Naps (Rick Gonzalez), Mixed Mike (Khleo Thomas) and Boo (Marcus T. Paulk), are despondent when their local rink closes. They are the best skaters around and skating gives them status and joy. The group, along with new neighbor Tori (Jurnee Smollett) decide to brave the bus ride and cultural shock to go to Sweetwaters, a fancier rink on the north side of town. There they encounter Sweetness (Wesley Jonathan), the alpha male of the rink who is always surrounded by a trio of disco-clad ladies and some obsequious minions. X also sees former girlfriend, Naomi (Meagan Good), an estranged friend who has become quite beautiful. Also at the rink, needlessly, is Bernard (Nick Cannon), a guy who works being the skate rental counter and sports a Jimi Hendrix hairdo. (Cannon is barely in the film, but due to his popularity ranks a prime position on the DVD box.)

To no one in the audience's surprise, there is a big Skate-Off coming up with a grand prize of $500. It will also not surprise anyone that Sweetness's gang and the South Side gang will be the two top contenders.

To balance the fluff, there is also a backstory about X's troubled family life. His mother died the year before and the family is still struggling with it. X's engineer father, Curtis (Chi McBride), has lost his job, but is too ashamed to tell his family. Instead he takes his hostility out on X. McBride should be commended for doing an excellent job in a pretty silly movie.

Also populating the movie are Mike Epps and Charlie Murphy as comedic garbage men and Wayne Brady as a not-particularly comedic emcee. Kellita Smith is Tori's comely and newly divorced mother who has a bit of a crush on Curtis.

Critics found *Roll Bounce* a sweetly innocent period piece and mostly gave it favorable reviews. Michael Phillips of *The Chicago Tribune* gave the film three out of four stars and wrote, "The movie is a thing of honey and gloss, yet there's just enough heart in the central father/son relationship, and in the teenagers' ensemble interactions, to make it glide by." Mike Clark of *USA Today* wrote, "With severe tightening, good nature alone would turn the picture into a bona fide sleeper. Yet even as is, *Roll Bounce* rates a friendly nod. If it doesn't exactly kick out the jams, it does move them around a little bit." John Anderson of *Newsday* wrote, Malcolm D. Lee pays such affectionate homage to skating and "70s B-movies that you almost think they were, well, Peter Frampton or something." Manohla Dargis of *The New York Times* was less taken with the film and wrote that it had "some nifty roller-skating and about a half an hour's worth of sitcom shenanigans stretched to a ruinously overlong 107 minutes."

Jill Hamilton

CREDITS

Xavier "X" Smith: Bow Wow
Curtis: Chi McBride
Byron: Mike Epps
Sweetness: Wesley Jonathan
Vivian: Kellita Smith
Naomi Phillips: Meagan Good
Mixed Mike: Khleo Thomas
Bernard: Nick Cannon
Naps: Rick Gonzalez
Tori: Jurnee Smollett
Victor: Charlie Murphy

D.J. Johnny Feelgood: Wayne Brady
Boo: Marcus T. Paulk
Junior: Brandon T. Jackson
Troy: Paul Wesley
Dee: Darryl "DMC" McDaniels
Origin: USA
Language: English
Released: 2005
Production: Robert Teitel, George Tillman Jr.; State Street Pictures; released by 20th Century-Fox
Directed by: Malcolm Lee
Written by: Norman Vance Jr.
Cinematography by: J. Michael Muro
Music by: Stanley Clarke
Sound: Scott D. Smith
Editing: George Bowers, Paul Millspaugh
Art Direction: Gary Baugh
Costumes: Danielle Hollowell
Production Design: William Elliott
MPAA rating: PG-13
Running time: 107 minutes

REVIEWS

Boxoffice Online. September, 2005.
Chicago Sun-Times Online. September 23, 2005.
Entertainment Weekly Online. September 21, 2005.
Los Angeles Times Online. September 23, 2005.
New York Times Online. September 23, 2005.
Premiere Magazine Online. September 22, 2005.
Variety Online. September 15, 2005.

QUOTES

Sweetness: "I'm the king of this here flo', ya dig?"

TRIVIA

Ten percent of the movie's opening weekend gross was donated to the victims of Hurricane Katrina.

RORY O'SHEA WAS HERE

(Inside I'm Dancing)

Live life like you mean it.
—Movie tagline

Rory O'Shea (James McAvoy) is a free-spirit, who sports a spiked, blond Billy Idol haircut and a maverick attitude to match, who longs to escape from his dependence on others and gain his own independence. But he feels trapped in his body taken over by muscular dystrophy that has cruelly left him with the full power of speech, but the use of only a few fingers of one hand.

He arrives at the Carrigmore Home For The Disabled (telling himself that this time it will only be a temporary stay), whose residents seemingly live out their lives in front of the television or on the streets begging for donations to help keep the facility they call home in business. He soon meets Michael Connoly (Steven Robertson), who is suffering from cerebral palsy, and who has been left with speech that no one, including the facility's staff and residents, can understand. Michael has long passed the point of frustration to the point of resignation.

But one day, during a decidedly one-sided conversation with another resident, he is surprised to find that Rory understands him perfectly and they become fast friends. On "National Collection Day" the residents of Carrigmore are brought to city and assigned the task of holding collection buckets in their laps on street corners as passersby drop spare change into them. Rory takes this as an opportunity to sneak away from the group and show Michael a good time by using the money for barhopping, getting drunk, and picking up some girls.

By introducing him to joys of Guinness and girls, Rory begins to show Michael the joys of the outside world that Michael had never thought existed outside Carrigmore, and begins to stir in him the same feelings of independence that he himself long for. Rory desperately wants to break the bonds of perpetual institutional living and applies for an Independent Living grant from the government, but is rejected by the board of supervisors who feel his attitude of recklessness and his disability are too difficult to overcome.

Always a man with a plan, Rory convinces Michael that he should apply for the grant, and accompanies him to the board interview as his translator. The board grants Michael Independent Living status, to which Rory offers that of course he should be granted the same status because Michael will need a translator. A fact that the board can hardly argue against. The two move out of Carrigmore but find that apartment hunting is more difficult than they thought, so Rory convinces Michael that he should contact his father who is a high ranking, and wealthy, government official, for help. In a poignant scene both full of pain and triumph, the two boys visit the father at his government office and soon make a deal with him that will provide them with an apartment, as long as there are no familial strings attached.

In contrast to Michael's inattentive father who has enough to help his son, but is too busy to try, Rory's father, a working class bloke, visits him on a regular basis, always apologizing for not having enough to provide his son with what he feels he needs. After moving in to their new spacious flat, Michael and Rory soon realize that they will need a caregiver. They interview many obviously unacceptable prospects (that one hopes are not based on the reality of the state of qualified home-care providers) and are about to give up when, they come across a beautiful blonde girl, Siobhan (Romola Garai) in a grocery store. They remember meeting her in the bar earlier and offer her the job of caregiver. She is a little hesitant (she has no experience at such things), but she takes an instant liking to the boys and one can presume that she in some way feels trapped in her present situation as well, so she accepts.

Things become complicated when Michael begins to fall in love with Siobhan, who truly cares about the boys, but not in the same way. When after a Halloween party, Michael finally tells her how he feels, she rejects him in one the films best acted and realistic scenes, reminding the audience that you can't choose whom another person will love. It is another of many scenes in which the filmmakers ground this story and these characters in reality, where life is tough and there are no easy answers, for anybody.

The performances in the film by these three young actors are top-notch. After the film it was a surprise to find out that both James McAvoy and Steven Robertson were both able-bodied. In fact although Michael's speech does not change, his performance is so good, that you begin to fell that you could be his translator as well. While Romola Garai's character in lesser hands, could have been written a typical movie-nurse (completely self-sacrificing and perfect) is played with sincerity, while staying in the reality of an attractive woman in her early twenties that is desperately searching for her own path in life.

This is no disease of the week or message film about the need to change the way society treats people with disabilities or even about two people that overcome the impossible odds handed to them. It is refreshing that Director Damien O'Donnell and writers Jeffrey Caine and Christian O'Reilly chose to ground their story in reality. While it is indeed a drama, it is never heavy handed. There is plenty of humor in the movie and it seems natural to the situations while never being forced. This is essentially a small film about three characters that come into orbit around each other and the profound effect that has upon each of them.

David E. Chapple

CREDITS

Michael Connolly: Steven Robertson
Rory O'Shea: James McAvoy
Siobhan: Romola Garai
Eileen: Brenda Fricker
Fergus Connolly: Gerard McSorley
Con O'Shea: Tom Hickey
Annie: Ruth McCabe
Origin: Ireland, Great Britain, France
Language: English
Released: 2004
Production: James Flynn, Juanita Wilson; WT2 (Squared), Octagon; released by Momentum Pictures
Directed by: Damien O'Donnell
Written by: Jeffrey Caine
Music by: David Julyan
Sound: Jon Stevenson
Music Supervisor: Nick Angel
Costumes: Lorna Marie Mugan
Production Design: Tom Conroy
MPAA rating: R
Running time: 104 minutes

REVIEWS

Boxoffice Online. February, 2005.
Chicago Sun-Times Online. February 18, 2005.
Entertainment Weekly Online. February 2, 2005.
Los Angeles Times Online. February 4, 2005.
New York Times Online. February 4, 2005.
Variety Online. September 2, 2004.
Washington Post Online. February 18, 2005, p. WE42.

RUMOR HAS IT...

Based on a true rumor.
—Movie tagline

Box Office: $7.5 million

Rumor Has It... is a middling romantic comedy which suffers from too few yuks and too much yuck. Heavy on star power but lightweight nonetheless, the film is periodically amusing but mainly whiffs while clearly swinging for the fences. What it does contain is an underlying, inescapable and somewhat off-putting ick-factor which mars the proceedings. One would be hard-pressed to find another film in which the words "blunt testicular trauma" signal ardor ahead, especially between a young woman and a man she was hoping until just seconds before was her biological father. Yet it is the learning of one mighty kick to the groin during a long-ago soccer game which kicks off her affair with him, and he is someone she knows not only had sex with her mother but also with her grandmother, to boot. Yech. While this sterile guy is definitely not impotent, *Rumor Has It...* too often is.

It is an intriguing idea from which the film springs. Screenwriter T.M. Griffin wondered what might have happened to the characters in Mike Nichol's resonant classic *The Graduate* (1967) after the credits and thirty years rolled by. Griffin was set to make his directorial debut with the material he came up with but was replaced by vet Rob Reiner just ten days into the shoot. Although Reiner successfully cast a spell over audiences with films like *When Harry Met Sally...* (1989) and *The American President* (1995), this *Graduate* sequel of sorts generally fails to do so. At one point, the aforementioned young lady says she does not feel what she thinks she is supposed to be feeling, a sentiment which unfortunately is shared throughout most of the film by most of those watching. *Rumor Has It...* is akin to watching admittedly gifted painters trying mightily to create something noteworthy without having been afforded the proper paints, brushes and other necessary materials.

Like Dustin Hoffman's Benjamin Braddock, Jennifer Aniston's Sarah Huttinger is at a significant crossroads in life and uncertain of how best to proceed. Things are literally up in the air for unsettled Sarah when she first appears onscreen, nervously enduring a turbulent flight back home to Pasadena with her new fiancé, Jeff Daly (Mark Ruffalo) in 1997. Visits there apparently always throw her for a loop, as she feels she has little in common with her family in that well-to-do, conservative enclave where the lawns are as well manicured as the residents themselves. It seems that Sarah finds it a stilted and stifling place, a trap she is determined to avoid. The couple will attend the wedding there of her younger and exceedingly bouncy sister Annie (Mena Suvari), which is stirring up additional anxiety within Sarah now that her marriage to Jeff is on the horizon. She is terrified that her plans to settle down may involve settling. It is bad enough, Sarah seems to feel, that her journalistic career has stalled at the level of writing wedding announcements and obituaries, but now she worries that the man whose proposal she has accepted is maybe more of an Ashley Wilkes than the dazzling, swoon-inducing Rhett Butler type. However, it is a little hard to understand why she frets so, considering that the paper she writes for is *The New York Times* and that Jeff is handsome, sweet, kind, understanding, patient and in general quite a catch. He is a nice guy, clearly no milquetoast. Nevertheless, when she wants to soothe her jangled nerves with bathroom sex on the plane, he suggests hot tea. (Decaffeinated, one hopes.) Jeff fairly quickly agrees to her request for some lavatory loving, but he and the cramped surroundings are both simply a tad too uncomfortable, and Sarah disappointedly returns to her seat without having been ravaged. That she was not pawed with abandon gives her pause.

Although Sarah's mother is dead, her grandmother Katherine (Shirley MacLaine) is exceedingly alive. The woman reminds one of the downing of tequila: salty and potently alcoholic. From Katherine, Sarah learns that her late mom's cold feet had her running off to Cabo San Lucas just before entering into what Sarah feels was a dull marriage which tied her mother down to a dear but less-than-exciting man. Then Jeff does the math and points out that Sarah's mother must have gotten pregnant prior to getting married. She surmises that she is the result of a pre-wedding liaison south of the border, which would explain why she seems so unlike the rest of the Huttinger clan. After going to visit her Aunt Mitzi (an unbilled Kathy Bates), Sarah comes to a startling realization: her family inspired Charles Webb's 1963 book *The Graduate* which in turn inspired the iconic film. Her grandmother was the saucily-seductive Mrs. Robinson portrayed by Anne Bancroft, her mother was the Robinsons' daughter portrayed by Katharine Ross, and a classmate of her mom's named Beau Burroughs (Kevin Costner) was immortalized by Webb as Braddock. With Jeff's loyal support, Sarah heads off to get the truth out of her mother and grandmother's old Beau.

As Sarah begins her journey of self-discovery, viewers will most likely care that the poor girl gets the answers she needs to stop feeling so uncomfortable. Having her played by such a likeable actress helps here. However, when she confronts Beau (now a highly-successful Internet guru) with her newfound knowledge is when many will start feeling a tad uncomfortable themselves. After the man admits all, Sarah indelicately inquires if he had worn condoms at the time, and wonders anyway if they could have busted or slipped off while he made vigorous love to mom. Then Beau uncomfortably shares that he could not possibly be her father due to that "blunt testicular trauma," a phrase which, despite Aniston's numerous repetitions of it thereafter, is not likely to take its place next to the oft-quoted "Mrs. Robinson, you're trying to seduce me." He kindly tries to cheer her up with dancing and drink, and on a dime he changes in her eyes from papa to paramour. She learns details of her mom's three glorious days in Cabo frolicking with Beau in both the surf and the sack, and somewhat-soused Sarah's burgeoning passion is astonishingly not doused by getting the mental image of him making tender love to her very own mother. So when the handsome, worldly man says she is very beautiful and reminds him of her mother, the tipsy young woman dives in with gusto for a passionate kiss. Next thing Sarah knows she awakens in his bed, staring incredulously at his monogrammed pillowcases.

In one charismatic, well-dressed, well-heeled, and only somewhat faded package, Beau obviously represents the illusive, glamorous excitement and adventure Sarah feels has been missing from her life, something she thinks would top what she already has. As he pilots his own aircraft to take her here and there for boisterous galas and quiet, tender moments alone, Beau asserts reassuringly to Sarah that "Life should be a little nuts." The look on her besotted face shows that his words have resonated. However, Jeff thinks things have gone more than a little nuts when he reappears on the scene to observe May smooching December. Suddenly Sarah's feelings do a 180° turn as she tries to explain away her sudden, hard-to-swallow detour from their previously-agreed-upon path to the altar. She professes her love to Jeff, but when he demands she prove it with an official "I do," Sarah maddeningly remains mum. He stalks off, exasperated and wounded, and few viewers will blame him for losing patience with her teary-eyed, whiny, befuddled vacillation over which side of the fence has greener grass.

From then on, Reiner offers up a series of mildly meaningful, fairly mawkish conversations Sarah has with Annie, Katherine, Beau, her father, and, finally, Jeff. Exactly when her inevitable epiphany occurs is hard to ascertain. Viewers will likely be curious but not emotionally invested in who Sarah eventually chooses, and when she gives her clichéd "I wouldn't blame you for not taking me back but I hope you do" speech, more than a few will find themselves feeling protective of Jeff and wanting something better for him. The final scene drags out his predictable forgiveness and their reunification. As in this year's *Just Like Heaven*, love certainly can be rough on Ruffalo, but he gets the film's funniest line to wrap things up: "If we have a daughter, Beau Burroughs is not coming within a thousand miles of her!"

Made on an undisclosed budget, the mildly amusing *Rumor Has It...* only managed a disappointing gross of about $42 million. Critical reaction was not kind. An accomplished cast and the public's reservoir of good will toward Aniston were not enough to save a forced affair which dares to follow in the footsteps of Nichol's film and seems all the more wan and wanting by comparison. The best way to enjoy *Rumor Has It...* is to watch *The Graduate* instead.

David L. Boxerbaum

CREDITS

Sarah Huttinger: Jennifer Aniston
Beau Burroughs: Kevin Costner
Katherine Richelieu: Shirley MacLaine
Jeff Daly: Mark Ruffalo
Earl Huttinger: Richard Jenkins
Roger McManus: Christopher McDonald
Annie Huttinger: Mena Suvari
Scott: Steve Sandvoss
Origin: USA
Language: English
Released: 2005
Production: Paula Weinstein, Ben Cosgrove; Village Roadshow Pictures, Section 8/Spring Creek; released by Warner Bros.
Directed by: Rob Reiner
Written by: T.M. Griffin
Cinematography by: Peter Deming
Music by: Marc Shaiman
Sound: Steve Cantamessa
Music Supervisor: Chris Douridas
Editing: Robert Leighton
Art Direction: Thomas P. Wilkins
Costumes: Kym Barrett
Production Design: Tom Sanders
MPAA rating: PG-13
Running time: 96 minutes

REVIEWS

Boxoffice Online. December, 2005.
Chicago Sun-Times Online. December 23, 2005.
Entertainment Weekly Online. January 3, 2006.
Los Angeles Times Online. December 23, 2005.
New York Times Online. December 23, 2005.
Variety Online. December 18, 2005.
Washington Post Online. December 24, 2005, p. C01.

QUOTES

Sarah Huttinger: "You've slept with my mother and my grandmother. Maybe every girl in my family has to sleep with you!"

Beau Burroughs: "Well, I don't know if they have to, but they certainly have."

TRIVIA

Writer Ted Griffin (*Ocean's Eleven, Matchstick Men*) was to make his directorial debut with this film, but was replaced with Rob Reiner for undisclosed reasons.

S

SAHARA

Dirk Pitt. Adventure has a new name.
—Movie tagline

Adventure has a new destination.
—Movie tagline

Box Office: $68.8 million

In *Sahara*, that arid African region is shown to be a place where few plants grow but implausibility flourishes. The film's interminably calm, cool and collected hero, Dirk Pitt (Matthew McConaughey), is game for any problem the screenplay can throw his way, what with his astounding combination of luck, timing and imperviousness to defeat. It is no wonder this handsome charmer is so insouciantly confident, endlessly flashing his megawatt grin and never getting worked up about it all. The problem is that as Dirk remains so unflappably cool and continues to beat the odds in a plot that holds about as much water as a mirage, the audience can never be expected to sweat much about anything that happens to anyone in *Sahara*.

Sahara aims to follow in the tradition of escapist fare like the *Indiana Jones* films, but it has little in characterization and content which made those noteworthy works so engaging and exhilarating. Directed by Breck Eisner (son of Disney head Michael), *Sahara* energetically packs a great deal into a running time that feels overlong, a lot of motion eliciting exceedingly little emotion. It begins many miles and years removed from present-day Africa, aboard an embattled Confederate ironclad containing rare gold coinage during the U.S. Civil War. As the opening credits roll following this brief introductory scene, newspaper clippings and historical artifacts effectively acquaint viewers with dashing adventurer/treasure hunter Dirk and his long-time, got-your-back buddy Al Giordino (Steve Zahn), the film's periodically successful comic relief. (Zahn is a startling casting choice for those who remember Cussler's description of Al as a broad shouldered "beefy little Italian.") Both men work for the National Underwater and Marine Agency, under the direction of cigar-chomping Admiral Jim Sandecker (William H. Macy).

It seems that Dirk has a theory: that the aforementioned 19th Century warship may have somehow (and for some unfathomable reason) chugged thousands of miles across open ocean waters to Northern Africa, where it could now lay buried, valuable coins and all. It seems some old texts speak vaguely of a strange, cursed "ship of death" which arrived there 140 years before and brought sickness to countless souls. Al (and the audience) is not sure he can buy into all this, but goes along anyway because that is what sidekicks do. Meanwhile, fetching World Health Organization doctor Eva Rojas (unconvincing Penelope Cruz) is all seriousness as she endeavors to poke around the same area of Africa trying to solve another mystery: the source of a baffling and oh-so-deadly plague.

Dirk and Eva's paths fatefully cross in Lagos, Nigeria, when some brutal thugs try to stop both her investigation and her breathing. A buff, shirtless Dirk, pausing just long enough to give female viewers a chance to ogle his physique and then be revived, rises from the ocean and chivalrously fends off her attackers. Upon regaining consciousness after her ordeal, Eva and Dirk begin exchanging smiles and gazing into each other's eyes. (McConaughey's choppers look especially white when set off by an orangish tan/makeup which sometimes makes him look like he should cut way back on carrot consumption.) Despite the fact that McConaughey and Cruz became an item during the filming of *Sahara*, their real-life passion for each other never translates to much palpable onscreen chemistry.

Since Dirk and friends, including geeky scientist Rudi Gunn (Rainn Wilson), happen to be going the same way as Eva and colleague Dr. Frank Hopper (Glynn Turman), the former offer the latter a ride up the Niger to civil war-torn Mali, where the two groups split up on their separate missions. Their presence makes murderous warlord Zateb Kazim (Lennie James) uneasy and unhappy, and so he dispatches a band of ominous-looking soldiers with powerful-looking weapons, this time to not only snuff out Eva but also Dirk and the other good guys. This allows the film to set up its rip-roaring, kitchen-sink action sequences (complete with a steroidally-pumped-up soundtrack of classic rock tunes), in which Dirk can show off.

Most of what transpires is a leave-your-disbelief-at-the-door mix of prowess and preposterousness. When Kazim's forces blast away at Dirk's boat from land and on the water, countless bullets miss their mark. Even when Dirk leaps between his boat and that of the enemy, vigorous attempts to shoot, stab or at least give him a paper cut end in failure and frustration. A tricky escape maneuver demolishes their own (or actually Sandecker's) boat, but Dirk and company end up victorious and unhurt. It is like that for most of *Sahara*. When Eva is stranded at the bottom of a well while Kazim and his men shoot up everything and everyone (including Frank) above her, Dirk appears in a most timely fashion. He strolls through the mayhem, disarming a soldier or two and giving them a good thrashing in the process. He cannot keep himself from hot dogging it just a little, swinging around on a camel's neck while beating one man senseless. "I need a little help here," Dirk calls out to Al, who runs through a hail of bullets without incident. Finally, Eva shoots a man when he is just about to do the same to Dirk, using a gun that fell very conveniently into the well from which she was somehow able to extricate herself.

More scenes follow which will excruciatingly strain the credulity of anyone still intensely caught up in it all. When a ball Al is casually kicking around happens to roll down into just the right cave where drawings shed light on both the ironclad and plague mysteries, viewers' eyes will likely roll, too. There is also the scene in which Dirk, chained with Al in the back of a truck carting them off to certain death, is able to grunt and push and finally disengage the bed liner while the armed men up front continue to drive off none the wiser. Still handcuffed to each other and attached to the liner, the two drag it along until they happen upon some plane wreckage. Despite their arduous trek across a great expanse of sun-baked terrain without any food or water, Dirk and Al doctor-up the wreckage and feel fit enough to gleefully wind surf it across the desert. It is startlingly unbelievable even for Dirk, and the mood (and music) is so lighthearted that one cannot feel any sense of urgency whatsoever about their plight. There is no way that enjoyable, gut-tightening, breath-holding suspense can be created when the results of his endeavors are never even the least bit in doubt.

Even when it is revealed that massive amounts of toxic waste from a remote solar energy plant run by French meanie Yves Massarde (Lambert Wilson) are causing all the deaths and threaten to spread unparalleled and unspeakable environmental horrors across our planet, it is impossible to feel like much is at stake here. As usual, there is little concern for Dirk when he takes a plunge off the plant's colossal tower while doing battle with Massarde, and little surprise when he makes an absurdly far-fetched reappearance, scampering up the immense structure's moving solar panels to heroically rescue Eva. By the time they find the Confederate warship and its riches buried in the desert and triumph over Kazim's encroaching forces by successfully shooting off the boat's rusty old cannonballs, even the film's characters are uttering lines like "No way that should've worked!" As the film ends, Dirk and Eva are seen happily frolicking on a beautiful beach, which will mean a great deal to no one.

Even if what transpires in films like *Sahara* is not meant to be taken too seriously, the absence of captivating characters and a compelling script to make viewers marvel and thrill makes for much less enjoyable, detached viewing. One person who definitely got worked up over what was in *Sahara* was Clive Cussler, the best-selling author of the 1992 novel upon which this movie was based (and over a dozen other books featuring Dirk Pitt). Upset over numerous and "significant" changes to his story that made it into the script over his strenuous objections, Cussler filed a multi-million dollar lawsuit against Crusader Entertainment and went public with his displeasure. Crusader turned around and sued Cussler for trying to sabotage *Sahara* and endangering what the company had hoped would turn into a profitable franchise. While legal wrangling never helps at the box office, it was the $130 million film's own shortcomings which made it struggle to gross half of that (critical reaction was generally tepid), ensuring a dearth of Dirk for the foreseeable future.

David L. Boxerbaum

CREDITS

Dirk Pitt: Matthew McConaughey
Al Giordano: Steve Zahn
Ana Rojas: Penelope Cruz
Yves Massarde: Lambert Wilson
Dr. Frank Hopper: Glynn Turman
Admiral Sandecker: William H. Macy
Carl: Delroy Lindo
Gen. Kazim: Lennie James
Rudi Gunn: Rainn Wilson
Ambassador Polidori: Patrick Malahide
Origin: USA
Language: English
Released: 2005
Production: Howard Baldwin, Karen Baldwin, Mace Neufeld, Stephanie Austin; Kanzaman S.A., J.K. Livin, Paramount Pictures, Bristol Bay Prods.; released by Paramount Pictures
Directed by: Breck Eisner
Written by: John C. Richards, Thomas Dean Donnelly, Joshua Oppenheimer, James V. Hart
Cinematography by: Seamus McGarvey
Music by: Clint Mansell
Sound: Chris Munro
Music Supervisor: Lindsay Fellows
Editing: Andrew MacRitchie
Art Direction: Giles Masters, Anthony Reading
Costumes: Anna Sheppard
Production Design: Allan Cameron
MPAA rating: PG-13
Running time: 127 minutes

REVIEWS

Boxoffice Online. April, 2005.
Chicago Sun-Times Online. April 8, 2005.
Entertainment Weekly Online. April 6, 2005.
Los Angeles Times Online. April 8, 2005.
New York Times Online. April 8, 2005.
Premiere Magazine Online. April 7, 2005.
Variety Online. April 3, 2005.
Washington Post Online. April 8, 2005, p. WE46.

QUOTES

Al Giordino: "I am so tired of being shot at!"

TRIVIA

The cast had to take camel-riding lessons during which they would have to ride the camel at full gallop alongside a moving train.

SARABAND

Ingmar Bergman is one of the greatest film directors. With films such as *Smiles of a Summer Night* (1955), *Wild Strawberries* (1957), *Persona* (1966), *Shame* (1968), and *Cries and Whispers* (1972), Bergman has created a large body of films whose explorations of serious, adult themes is matched by the sophistication of his visual style and the brilliance of the performances he elicits. Following a final masterpiece, *Fanny and Alexander* (1982), Bergman announced he would no longer make films only to write and direct *After the Rehearsal* (1984) and several other moderately scaled films for television and write a few screenplays directed by others.

When Liv Ullmann was directing Erland Josephson in *Faithless* (2000), from a Bergman screenplay, they discussed revisiting the characters they play in Bergman's *Scenes from a Marriage* (1973), still the most devastating film portrait of a married relationship. They sent a videotape of what they had in mind to Bergman, and he was inspired to write *Saraband.* Speaking after a showing of the result at the 2004 New York Film Festival, Ullmann joked that she and Josephson envisioned *Saraband* as a comedy and were surprised at the rather dire screenplay Bergman produced. While *Saraband,* which the director insists is absolutely his final film, is not as intense as might have been expected, it still packs an emotional wallop.

Since *Fanny and Alexander,* Bergman has devoted most of his creative energies to the stage, and *Saraband* opens like a play. Marianne (Ullmann) sits at a table covered with photographs and talks directly to the audience about herself and Johan (Josephson), who have not seen each other in thirty years. The next scene is her arrival at Johan's summer house, a photograph of which is the summer house Bergman grew up in. She walks around a room, looking at and commenting on various objects, just like a character in a play. Marianne peeks out at Johan dozing on a veranda and tells the audience she has been watching him for ten minutes, when the actual time has been less than a minute. She says she will go out to him in one minute and counts down the seconds. This scene establishes Marianne's playful nature and humanity and that she is no longer the angry woman seen in *Scenes from a Marriage.*

After this opening, the film becomes less self-consciously stagy and more cinematic. Bergman, who was eighty-five when he made the film, is a master at pacing scenes and knowing when to punctuate an emotional encounter with a close-up. He knows just how long to linger on an actor's face after the dialogue has ended, when to prolong a shot to underscore an emotion, and when to cut away to avoid sinking into bathos.

It is quite unusual for Bergman to make allusions to the films of others because he is the master that other directors, Woody Allen in particular, usually quote. It is a bit surprising, therefore, when Johan's granddaughter, Karin (Julia Dufvenius), runs away from an argument with her father, Henrik (Borje Ahlstedt), into the woods in her nightdress and tumbles down an embankment, as with the suicidal protagonist of Robert Bresson's *Mouchette* (1967). Another shot begins with Karin and her cello against a stark white background, and the camera quickly puts back until they disappear. This shot recalls the nightmare sequences in Alfred Hitchcock's films.

In an age when filmmakers, playwrights, and novelists seek to enlarge their themes by imposing social and medical issues into their art, it is always refreshing to see an artist who realizes that the quiet desperation of ordinary lives provides enough drama without resorting to easy emotional shortcuts. Bergman has always been such an artist and remains so for most of *Saraband* before making the hints of incest about the relationship between Karin and Henrik more overt. While this element is in keeping with Bergman's stern treatment of parent-child relations, it makes these characters too specific, losing the universality which has made him one of the world's greatest filmmakers.

Johan has always been disappointed by Henrik, a failure as a musician and an academic. In the film's most brutal scene, he tells his son, from Johan's first marriage, how much he hates him. Such tempestuous relationships, spurred by the harsh treatment Bergman received from his father, occur periodically in his films and serve as the focus of *Autumn Sonata* (1978), in which the mother played by Ingrid Bergman thoroughly humiliates the daughter played by Ullmann.

Guilt-ridden by what she has absorbed at Johan's, Marianne, in the film's coda, decides to visit the middle-aged, mentally retarded daughter (Gunnel Fred) neither she nor Johan have seen in years. This scene is awkward because of Marianne's conflicting emotions, and this awkwardness provides the film with an anticlimactic conclusion. *Saraband* is three-fourths a great film, with serious thematic and structural problems at the end. If only Bergman could have ended his great career with more of a bang instead of this whimper.

Michael Adams

CREDITS

Johan: Erland Josephson
Marianne: Liv Ullmann
Henrik: Borje Ahlstedt
Karin: Julia Dufvenius
Martha: Gunnel Fred
Origin: Sweden, Italy, Germany, Finland, Denmark, Austria
Language: English, German, Swedish
Released: 2003
Production: Pia Ehrnvall; Swedish TV
Directed by: Ingmar Bergman
Written by: Ingmar Bergman
Cinematography by: Raymond Wemmenlov, Sofi Stridh, P.O. Lantto
Sound: Borje Johansson
Editing: Sylvia Ingemarsson
Art Direction: Goran Wassberg
Costumes: Inger E. Pehrsson
MPAA rating: R
Running time: 107 minutes

REVIEWS

Boxoffice Online. August, 2005.
Chicago Sun-Times Online. August 5, 2005.
Entertainment Weekly Online. July 6, 2005.
Los Angeles Times Online. July 8, 2005.
New York Times Online. October 15, 2004.
Variety Online. November 30, 2003.

TRIVIA

With the title derived from Bach's cello suites, which are dances for couples, the film mimics the shape of the dance, with a couple in a conversation that can be described as a dance.

SAW II

We Dare You Again...
—Movie tagline
Oh Yes, There Will Be Blood.
—Movie tagline

Box Office: $86.9 million

The best thing that can be said about *Saw II* is that, unlike many sequels, it does not merely repeat the basic plot of its predecessor, which was released last year to surprisingly strong box office. An attempt is made to take the basic idea of *Saw*, a demented killer teaching moral lessons to people who do not appreciate the value of life, and do something a bit different with it, mainly by focusing on the villain himself. It should also be noted that the sequel, helmed by Darren Lynn Bousman and written by Bousman and Leigh Whannell (the costar and cowriter of the first film), does not feel as amateurish as *Saw* often did. While *Saw II* has a washed-out look and at times resorts to frenetic cutting and a bombastic soundtrack, the basic filmmaking nonetheless is better, and the story tighter than in the original. Having noted these improvements, however, it is impossible to overlook the fact that all the technique in the world cannot redeem the sadistic, nihilistic story in which relentless brutality is passed off as entertainment.

The creepy Jigsaw (Tobin Bell) escaped at the end of the first film and is captured pretty quickly at the outset of the sequel. But just as the capture of John Doe in 1995's *Seven* (a far superior film that has clearly influenced the *Saw* series) does not neutralize the threat but takes the cat-and-mouse game to a new level, so too does Jigsaw's capture merely initiate a new game of survival for his hapless victims. He has locked a group of eight people in a house where a nerve agent seeping in through the vents will kill them in two hours if they do not find the antidote, which has been hidden in various rooms. To complicate their efforts, the house is rigged with deadly booby traps. One of the prisoners is Daniel (Erik Knudsen), a teenager who has a troubled relationship with his father, Detective Eric Matthews (Donnie Wahlberg), with whom Jigsaw wants to toy. Once Jigsaw, whose real name is John, is captured in his lair, the film cuts between his exchanges with Detective Matthews and scenes of the victims, whose actions the law enforcement team can view on a series of video monitors.

The prisoners are an assortment of ex-convicts who have a common bond; all were arrested by Matthews, a dirty cop who planted evidence to seal their fates. Thus, the situation could turn even uglier for Daniel if they learn his identity. The prisoners are not well drawn, but deep or even marginally interesting characters are not what the *Saw* films are about. One familiar face is Amanda (Shawnee Smith), an ex-junkie and the sole survivor of Jigsaw's deadly games in the first film, who, it seems, is being forced to play again.

But the main interest of the movie is not character or even suspense but rather grotesque traps and human suffering—a gun that fires unexpectedly when a door is unlocked, a crematory oven that closes on a man and then kills him, a pit of dirty syringes that Amanda is forced to scrounge through to find an important key, a glass box that traps a woman's hands in its openings and then tears at her wrists as she writhes in pain. The movie plods along on its predictable, tedious, and sickening path as some victims fall prey to Jigsaw's traps and one in particular, the psychotic Xavier (Franky G), finally turns on the others in his desperate attempt to secure the antidote for himself (in an especially gruesome scene, he cuts off a piece of flesh from his neck to find a clue).

The only nod in the direction of character development is the back story of Jigsaw himself, who began his cruel tests of the morally reckless after he was diagnosed with cancer and had the revelation that a person does not appreciate his life until he is about to lose it. But this extra dimension does not make the story any more profound, and, while Bell has a ghostly, eerie quality, Kevin Spacey's John Doe in *Seven* was far more chilling. Moreover, Jigsaw's pseudo-philosophical discussions about the value of life are not very compelling, even when he is taunting Matthews with the idea that he only cares about his son now that his life is hanging in the balance.

Matthews is finally fed up with Jigsaw's preaching and demands to be taken to the crime scene, thus setting up the climax. The police backup follows but winds up at the wrong house—a steal from 1991's *The Silence of the Lambs* (the high point for this genre); interestingly enough, *Saw II* is the second film this year after *The Edukators* to use this plot device. But the bigger twist is that everything going on with Jigsaw's victims has already happened and the police were actually watching a videotape, not a live feed. Daniel survived the ordeal and was locked in a safe in Jigsaw's lair the whole time. The scheme itself was set up to lure Matthews to the house, where he is captured in the filthy lavatory that was the primary setting of the first film and where he is now primed to be the first victim for a new villain—Amanda, who, in the film's big surprise, is revealed as Jigsaw's protégé. Ever since she survived his test in the first film, she has dedicated her life to continuing his work after his imminent death.

Despite the sheer moral hollowness of a movie that wallows in torture and the grisliest of deaths, it is hard not to have at least some grudging respect for an ending that has the power to shock, especially when we hear Amanda's voice on the final tape-recorded message—Jigsaw's usual way of communicating with his victims—and see her adopting the mantle of serial killer and self-proclaimed teacher of life lessons. Unfortunately, the clever ending just about guarantees that this ugly and depraved franchise is sure to continue.

Peter N. Chumo II

CREDITS

Jigsaw/John: Tobin Bell
Amanda: Shawnee Smith
Eric Matthews: Donnie Wahlberg
Daniel Mathews: Erik Knudsen
Xavier: Franky G.
Jonas: Glenn Plummer
Laura: Beverley Mitchell
Kerry: Dina Meyer
Addison: Emmanuelle Vaugier
Origin: USA

Language: English
Released: 2005
Production: Gregg Hoffman, Oren Koules, Mark Burg; released by Lions Gate Films
Directed by: Darren Lynn Bousman
Written by: Darren Lynn Bousman, Leigh Whannell
Cinematography by: David Armstrong
Music by: Charlie Clouser
Sound: Richard Penn
Music Supervisor: Jonathan McHugh, Jonathan Platt, Jonathan Miller
Editing: Kevin Greutert
Art Direction: Michele Brady
Costumes: Alex Kavanagh
Production Design: David Hackl
MPAA rating: R
Running time: 93 minutes

REVIEWS

Boxoffice Online. October, 2005.
Entertainment Weekly Online. October 26, 2005.
Los Angeles Times Online. October 28, 2005.
New York Times Online. October 28, 2005.
Premiere Magazine Online. October 28, 2005.
Variety Online. October 20, 2005.
Washington Post Online. October 28, 2005, p. WE42.

QUOTES

John: "Those who do not appreciate life do not deserve life."

TRIVIA

The entire film was shot in a single building in 25 days.

SCHIZO

(Shiza)

In fights without rules, there is no rule that says: "Until first blood!"
—Movie tagline

Schizo sounds like a grade-B Hollywood horror movie, but it is as far afield from that type of film as possible. Rather, this Kazakhstan-produced melodrama examines poverty's effects on the human condition, a worthy theme skillfully executed.

In her directorial debut, Guka Omarova creates a raw, realistic version of an old-fashioned boxing movie, another Hollywood genre staple: one where a nice guy must decide whether to confront or condone a corrupt syndicate (remember *The Set-Up* and *Body and Soul?*).

With *Schizo,* the focus isn't on a boxer but a recruiter, Mustafa (played by the charming newcomer, Olzhas Nusuppeav), who is called Schizo because he behaves erratically at his school in rural Kazakhstan. The teenage Schizo helps his single mother with the household finances by assisting her mobster boyfriend, Sakura (Eduard Tabyschev), to locate fighters to box in an illegal, subterranean operation.

After one of Schizo's discoveries, Ali, dies during a bout, Schizo experiences guilt and decides to visit the man's home to convey the bad news personally. When Schizo meets Ali's wife, Zina (Olga Landina), and her child, Sanzhik (Kanagat Nurtay), and notices they are even poorer than his own family, he hands over the money Ali earned to Zina but hesitates telling her she is now a widow.

Finally, Schizo tells Zina about Ali, and, despite her initial outrage, Zina decides to let Schizo into her home. Later, Zina and Schizo warm to each other; with Sanzhik, they form an unexpected but loving family of their own. Nevertheless, Schizo faces the dilemma of continuing as an organizer of unsafe boxing exhibitions or trying to begin a new life with his new family. Schizo's decision leads to a battle with Sakura—and a test of courage for the man-child.

Schizo's allure comes from the fashion writer-director Omarova and co-writer-co-producer Sergey Bodrov expand their conventional, linear storyline. Like Francois Truffaut's *400 Blows* (1959) and the Dardenne Brothers' equally trenchant *La Promesse* (1995), the naturalism of the screenwriting, direction, performances, and production design is sustained throughout the film, so what would have been hackneyed seems completely real and persuasive. *Schizo* grabs viewers with heartfelt emotion, and, except for the pat, overly simplistic conclusion, feels quite genuine.

For an economically produced first directing job, *Schizo* is impressive without ever seeming trendy or cynical. The fact the narrative is set in Kazakhstan adds an aspect of cultural richness not often present in this genre, and, despite the questionable choice of titles, Omarova smartly avoids turning her feature into an exotic travelogue or envelope-pushing attention-getter (to be fair, the film was also released under the name, *Schiza*).

Schizo clearly shows how economics play a critical and everlasting part in the lives of citizens. From this story and its treatment one understands Schizo's participation in an illegal and brutal profession, but one can also comprehend the choices of all the characters, even the repugnant Sakura.

The 2005 reviewers reactions were not entirely praiseworthy. In the March 15 *Village Voice,* Michael Atkinson wrote, "Unfortunately, *Schizo*'s familiar trials could have, and have, played out anywhere else. Some Central Asian movie could put this dead-empire-skeleton geography to use as a spectacularly metaphoric film set, but we haven't seen it happen yet." But Andrew O'Hehir in the March 17 *Salon.com* was more favorable: "Although it's told in a more elliptical manner than your typical Hollywood actioner, *Schizo* is in its way a taut and exciting thriller, featuring gunplay and violence, a beautiful girl, a posse of ominous thugs and a Mercedes won in a midnight bare-knuckle boxing match." Finally, A.O. Scott in the March 18 *New York Times* was the most positive: "This modest neo-realist film from Kazhakstan is both tough and tender, and it illuminates the lives of its characters with bracing clarity and understated empathy." One of the few flaws of *Schizo* is that it lacks comic relief but what is missing in humor, it compensates with dramatic truth.

Eric Monder

CREDITS

Schizo: Olzhas Nusuppaev
Sakura: Eduard Tabychev
Zinka: Olga Landina
Jaken: Bakhytbek Baymukhanbetov
Doctor Viktor: Soukhorukov
Kulyash: Gulnara Jeralieva
Sunzhik: Kanagat Nurtay
Origin: Russia, France, Germany
Language: Russian
Released: 2004
Production: Sergei Bedrov, Sergei Selyanov, Sergei Azimov; CTB, Kazakh Film, Le Petite Lumieres, Kinofabrika GmbH
Directed by: Gulshad Omarova
Written by: Sergei Bodrov, Gulshad Omarova
Cinematography by: Hassanbek Kidirialev
Music by: Sig
Sound: Andrei Vlaznev
Editing: Ivan Lebedav
Production Design: Talgan Asirankulov
MPAA rating: Unrated
Running time: 86 minutes

REVIEWS

Los Angeles Times Online. April 1, 2005.
New York Times Online. March 18, 2005.
San Francisco Chronicle Online. April 22, 2005.
Variety Online. May 26, 2004.

SCHULTZE GETS THE BLUES

It's never too late to retune your soul.
—Movie tagline

Schultze Gets the Blues is a low-budget, offbeat counterpoint to Alexander Payne's extremely bleak view of life after retirement in *About Schmidt* (2002). While Jack Nicholson's Schmidt stumbles about in despair, Horst Krause's Schultze is determined to do something with his life.

The film, the first from writer-director Michael Schorr, opens with Schultze and two friends (Karl Fred Muller and Harald Warmbrunn) facing early retirement from their jobs in a German salt mine. None of them know quite what to do with themselves. Schultze lives alone in a strange little L-shaped shack beside a brutally ugly slag heap. Schultze imposes some order on this bleak landscape by growing a large garden and polishing his garden gnomes. The rest of the time, he hangs out with his friends in their neighborhood bar in a Saxony village and visits his senile mother (Loni Frank) in a nursing home.

Schultze eventually picks up his apparently neglected accordion and halfheartedly plays a polka. Unable to sleep one night, he hears a Zydeco tune on the radio by chance and becomes intrigued with this style of Cajun music. Soon, he is playing the one song he knows for his friends, for his mother and her fellow patients, and for his local music club, which greets his effort rudely.

Zydeco represents not just a release for Schultze's energies but as a sign that life has more to offer than what he has been used to. His new interest is encouraged by Frau Lorant (Rosemarie Deibel), his mother's rather flamboyant roommate, and by Lisa (Wilhelmine Horschig), an even more colorful young waitress, who gives Schultze a book about the Louisiana bayous.

Eventually, the music club sends Schultze to a German music festival in his town's sister city, New Braunfels, Texas. Once in the United States, Schultze travels from the Texas river town into Louisiana's bayous, drifting aimlessly in an old swamp boat. He finally hears and dances to live Zydeco and befriends an African-American woman and her young daughter.

Schultze Gets the Blues is a charming, low-key film that may be too low-key for some tastes. Much of it seems unscripted, and after Schultze gets to America, not much happens. Schorr simply puts his star in real settings amid real people and follows him around with his static camera. Schorr's training as a documentary filmmaker is obvious. This approach is effective up to a point but can also be painfully artless but avoids the sentimental pathos the material could have easily had, as with the similar *Brassed Off* (1997). The film's odd quirkiness contributed to its winning awards at the San Marco, Stockholm, and Venice film festivals.

The film's studied artlessness extends to Krause's performance. Because much of his performance involves sitting and staring at the actions of others, Krause seems like a nonprofessional, yet *Schultze Gets the Blues* is his sixty-eighth film or television credit. A lathe operator before becoming an actor when he was twenty-three, Krause is perfect for the role of a man who has learned to react more than act. Within his minimalist approach, there are a handful of wonderful moments, such as the intrigued expression on his face when Schultze first hears Zydeco.

With his Michelin Man build and doughy face, Krause resembles a cartoon character. An Internet Movie Database user compares him to Peter Griffin in *Family Guy*. His sweet passivity also makes him resemble the bemused hero of *Wallace & Gromit*. Krause's delightfully deadpan approach gives this gentle film its main appeal.

Michael Adams

CREDITS

Schultze: Horst Krause
Jurgen: Harald Warmbrunn
Manfred: Karl-Fred Muller
Manfred's wife: Hannelore Schubert
Gatekeeper: Wolfgang Boos
Frau Lorant: Rosemarie Deibel
Lisa: Wilhelmine Horschig
Aretha: Anne V. Angelle
Jurgen's wife: Ursula Schucht
Josephine: Alozia St. Julien
Origin: Germany
Language: English, German
Released: 2003
Production: Jens Korner, Thomas Riedel, Oliver Niemeier; Filmcombinat
Directed by: Michael Schorr
Written by: Michael Schorr
Cinematography by: Axel Schneppat
Music by: Thomas Wittenbecher
Sound: Christian Lerch
Editing: Tina Hillmann
Costumes: Constanze Hagedorn
Production Design: Natascha E. Tagwerk
MPAA rating: PG
Running time: 114 minutes

REVIEWS

Boxoffice Online. February, 2005.
Chicago Sun-Times Online. March 11, 2005.
Los Angeles Times Online. February 18, 2005.
New York Times Online. February 18, 2005.
Variety Online. September 8, 2003.
Washington Post Online. March 4, 2005, p. WE41.

QUOTES

Captain Kirk, while hooking up Schultze's boat: "I'm captain Kirk."

SEPARATE LIES

Separate Lies opens with a dramatic hit-and-run accident that happens on a quiet road in the English countryside as a speeding SUV sideswipes a man riding his bicycle and he is knocked off the road. The SUV speeds on as if nothing had happened. The victim is the husband of the housekeeper of the upper middle-class British couple whose lives, and that of their aristocratic neighbor, will take a dramatic turn in light of the tragic event. Julian Fellowes, who won an Academy Award for his screenplay for *Gosford Park,* makes his directorial debut with a drama that explores morality, ethics, and class.

All three actors are excellent in their portrayals, representing different class-levels of British society. Tom Wilkinson is the priggish, wealthy lawyer James Manning, a perfectionist whose condescending air pervades the household he shares with wife Anne (Emily Watson), who likes their upper class lifestyle but hates the way he makes her feel so inadequate. The marriage, long sterile, is now threatening disintegration. Their new neighbor Bill Bule (Rupert Everett) is a divorced, aristocratic snob from one of the town's leading families. Playing the type to a tee, Everett's Bill has the pedigree and money that allows him to indulge his indolent lifestyle, which consists mainly of drinking and playing video games at the family's estate with his young sons.

When Anne spies the appealing young Bule lolling about the grounds, she suddenly announces to her much older husband that they should invite the neighbors over for drinks. James has a natural aversion to the aristocracy in general, and Bule in particular after, invited in for a drink, he turns up his blueblood nose at a portrait the Mannings have in their home. "One should never hang bad paintings," Bule imperiously intones.

James is forced to miss a party Anne is giving one night, as he has business in London. Bule drives Anne at the train station the next day to meet her husband, who is more than a little annoyed to see his unwelcome neighbor there. It is revealed that the accident happened on the night of Anne's party. The Manning's housekeeper Maggie (Linda Bassett), whose husband was hit and later died at the hospital, turns out to be a witness to the crime and who may be able to identify the driver. The film, however, doesn't so much plumb the mystery of who the hit-and-run driver was as much as why they did it, how they feel about it, and what they're going to do about it.

The police investigation into the death leads them to talk to the Mannings and Bule to help gather information. James, however, immediately suspects Bule as the driver, further corroborated by a new dent in his Range Rover. Over lunch, James confronts him and it is not long until Bule confesses to the crime with James ordering him to turn himself in to the police. Bule, however, is merely covering up the fact that he and Anne are having an affair and that she was the one actually driving his SUV when the crime occurred. Anne confesses this to James and wants to go to the police. James, however, mindful of the scandal that would ensue, begins to weave an elaborate alibi. He discovers that Maggie used to work for Bule's family, and that Bule himself actually helped convict her on a charge of theft. Her reputation ruined, Anne was the only one in town willing to give her a second chance. If Maggie i.d.'s Bule, he can use that fact to his advantage, claiming Maggie merely fingered him as a way of getting revenge. The film, here, asserting that the separate lies of the title are further proliferating and weaving into one another.

The most compelling aspect of the drama is the way in which events change the lordly James from arrogant know-it-all to humbled cuckold. Anne reveals that there is much more to her character than just an obedient, bourgeois housewife. Bill, despite the fact that he was willing to take the blame to protect his lover, remains the same unlikable effete that he was at the film's start. It's merely his presence that is required, however, as a device to effect the machinations of the Manning's complicated and fascinating relationship that drive this drama through the weaker whodunit bits.

Hilary White

CREDITS

James Manning: Tom Wilkinson
Anne Manning: Emily Watson
William Bule: Rupert Everett
Maggie: Linda Bassett
Inspector Marshall: David Harewood
Lord Rawston: John Neville
Priscilla: Hermione Norris
Origin: Great Britain
Language: English
Released: 2005
Production: Steve Clark-Hall, Christian Colson; Celador Films; released by 20th Century-Fox
Written by: Julian Fellowes
Cinematography by: Tony Pierce-Roberts
Music by: Stanislas Syrewicz
Sound: Chris Munro
Editing: Alex Mackie, Martin Walsh
Art Direction: Niall Moroney
Costumes: Michele Clapton
Production Design: Allison Riva
MPAA rating: R
Running time: 87 minutes

REVIEWS

Boxoffice Online. October, 2005.
Chicago Sun-Times Online. October 7, 2005.
Entertainment Weekly Online. September 14, 2005.
Los Angeles Times Online. September 30, 2005.
New York Times Online. September 16, 2005.
Premiere Magazine Online. September 15, 2005.
Variety Online. September 15, 2005.

SERENITY

Can't stop the signal.
—Movie tagline
They aim to misbehave.
—Movie tagline
The future is worth fighting for.
—Movie tagline

Box Office: $25.3 million

In the 26th century, humans have run out of resources here on planet Earth and have gone on to explore and terraform planets in new solar systems. Some of these colonies are glistening and modern while others are more primitive both in assets and in law. Think metropolis vs. the wild west. These new worlds, the United Planets, are controlled by the Alliance, which wants to bring order to all colonies. But as its tentacles of control spread out into the outer colonies, some have decided to take a stand against the Alliance. A War for Unification is fought, but the rebels fighting for independence lose.

Fighting on the side of the losing rebels was Captain Malcolm Reynolds (Nathan Fillion) and his second-in-command, Zoe (Gina Torres) who are now marginalized into trying to eke out a living on the edges of the Alliance-controlled system. They have taken the rusty hulk of a space ship named "Serenity" (which is of the Firefly class of interplanetary cargo vessels) and take on any odd job—from robbing banks to transporting questionable passengers and cargo—that might bring in income. The rest of Mal's crew consists of Wash (Alan Tudyk) who is Zoe's husband and Serenity's pilot, Jayne (Adam Baldwin) a mercenary with a heart of fool's gold, Kaylee (Jewel Staite) the ship's extremely adept mechanic, Dr. Simon Tam (Sean Maher) the ship's physician, and his psychic and maybe psychotic sister River (Summer Glau).

Simon and River came late to the ship's crew. They started as passengers who were running from the Alliance because the gifted River had been subjected to painful mind experiments and her loving brother has kidnapped her from their control. The problem is, River has been exposed to some compromising Alliance secrets and has abilities even she doesn't realize yet. Consequently the Alliance wants her back and they will do anything to accomplish this including sending out "the Operative" (Chiwetel Ejiofor) a menacing, way-too-calm and almost courtly killer.

Gradually, River begins to act even more strangely than normal. For example, although she usually wanders around the ship like a fragile, lost ghost, one day while in a bar something on a television screen triggers her into becoming a fighting machine who takes on everyone in the bar…and wins. What has the Alliance done to her? And how dangerous is she to Mal and his crew? To make matters worse, River is constantly getting mental flashes of a modern city where something very, very bad has happened. And it's because River knows this information that the Alliance has sent the Operative out to eliminate her and anyone else who gets in their way. River knows something that challenges their claim that they are creating a utopian world.

The movie *Serenity* is based on the television show *Firefly*. It was shown on the Fox network in the fall of 2002 but was cancelled before all the episodes were aired. In fact, only 11 of the 14 were shown and they weren't even shown in order! But the creator of *Firefly* is Joss Whedon of *Buffy the Vampire Slayer* and *Angel* fame, and there are many, many fans of his work. Although *Firefly* fans—called "brown coats" after the Alliance rebels in the TV show—protested vehemently about the show's cancellation, Fox refused to reinstate it. But when the episodes were released on DVD, its sales were so impressive that Whedon got the go-ahead from Universal to make a big screen episode. And to further please the brown coats, just before the feature-length version was released, the original episodes repeated on the Sci-Fi Channel

Serenity is very true to the original spirit and wit and feel of the television show and is bound to give *Firefly* fans more than their share of fulfilling moments, however it is not necessary to have seen the television show to enjoy this exuberant space western. Whedon has gathered together all the original, engaging cast from the alienated, reluctant hero Mal to the mysterious and spiritual Shepherd Book (Ron Glass) and they all seem to realize that this is a story in which to have fun…no matter how scary it gets when the torturing, flesh-eating Reavers arrive.

Although this is Whedon's big screen directorial debut he has done enough television work that there's nothing of the novice about what visually hits the screen. And anyone who is a fan of his trademark quick, unique dialogue with its offbeat humor and unexpected punchlines will be well pleased.

While *Serenity* has great and gritty special effects, that's not what the movie is about. In fact, guns shoot bullets not light rays, people get around on horses as often as flying craft, and with the exception of the Reavers—who, it turns out are really humans turned into cannibals—there are no strange looking aliens. What *Serenity* is about is telling a good, solid story with more than a bit of humor and featuring likeable, well-drawn characters. It is a genuine space western blessed with a great story, fast pacing, lots of action, strong characters who are well acted, and lots of just plain fun.

Beverley Bare Buehrer

CREDITS

Capt. Malcolm "Mal" Reynolds: Nathan Fillion
Zoe: Gina Torres
Wash: Alan Tudyk
Jayne: Adam Baldwin
Simon: Sean Maher
Shepherd Book: Ron Glass
The Operative: Chiwetel Ejiofor
Inara: Morena Baccarin
Kaylee: Jewel Staite
River: Summer Glau
Origin: USA
Language: English
Released: 2005
Production: Barry Mendel; released by Universal Pictures
Directed by: Joss Whedon
Written by: Joss Whedon
Cinematography by: Jack N. Green
Music by: David Newman
Sound: Art Rochester
Editing: Lisa Lassek
Art Direction: Barry Chusid
Costumes: Ruth E. Carter
MPAA rating: PG-13
Running time: 119 minutes

REVIEWS

Boxoffice Online. September, 2005.
Chicago Sun-Times Online. September 30, 2005.

Entertainment Weekly Online. September 28, 2005.
Los Angeles Times Online. September 30, 2005.
New York Times Online. September 30, 2005.
Premiere Magazine Online. September 30, 2005.
Variety Online. August 22, 2005.
Washington Post Online. September 30, 2005, p. WE38.

TRIVIA

In an unusual move, Universal Studios allowed early previews of the unfinished film and on May 5, 2005 previews were held in 10 cities; on May 26, 2005 previews were held in 20 cities; and on June 23, 2005 the film previewed in 35 cities. An early screening was also held on the Gold Coast, Queensland, Australia on July 22, 2005.

SHOPGIRL

Relationships don't always fit like a glove.
—Movie tagline

Box Office: $10 million

Shopgirl is based on the best-selling 2000 Steve Martin novella of the same name. There are differences between the book and film, but Martin, who wrote the screenplay, imbues the film with the same kind of sparse melancholy. When writing about the film, many critics used words like "elegant," "exquisitely tailored," and "tasteful." Oddly, a different set of words were also used. Words like "creepy" and "dirty old man." *Shopgirl* is all of these things simultaneously. It is muted, understated, a little fusty and maybe a touch perverted.

The movie has the feel of an older film. There is a narrator, Ray Porter (Martin), a sweeping soundtrack and lovely wardrobe choices. Porter introduces us to Mirabelle Buttersfield (Claire Danes), whose very name is tastefully old-fashioned, a young woman who works behind the glove counter at the Saks Fifth Avenue in Beverly Hills. The glove department is rarely frequented, as it does not sell gloves to keep hands warm, but rather gloves one might wear as a lark. Mirabelle wishes to be an artist, but instead stands behind her counter, frequently shifting her weight in order to stay alert, lest a manager walk by. After a day's work, she drives home in her beat-up pickup truck to her depressing Silver Lake apartment. She occasionally goes on cheap and awkward dates with Jeremy (Jason Schwartzman), a young slacker who designs fonts for rock and roll amplifiers. He borrows money and begins dates by honking his car's horn, expecting Mirabelle to run outside.

Ray, a wealthy, older gentleman, is the dating opposite of Jeremy. He shows up in the glove department, buys a pair of gloves, then has them delivered to Mirabelle's apartment, along with an invitation to dinner. Thus begins an affair. Ray selects Mirabelle to be his lover the same way he might have selected a particular piece of art for his house or a new sofa. She is a tasteful choice. The two might have had a deeper connection, but Ray is only prepared for an unemotional arrangement. He showers Mirabelle with gifts and she provides him with companionship. Ray tells Mirabelle that he is not looking for commitment, but Mirabelle does not really believe him.

It is strange to see Martin in a role that amounts to being a sugar daddy. In his career, he has created a jovial, light and almost sexless persona, and it is jolting to see him coveting a much younger woman, and being a bit of a cad about it all. However, Martin does bring a nice sense of melancholy to the role. It is an interesting contrast to see his familiar friendly face saying some not so friendly things. "He had hurt them both, and he cannot justify his actions except that, well, it was life," narrates Ray dispassionately.

Shopgirl is a slow movie. Director Anand Tucker films everything very exactly and precisely. Ray's apartment is all cool surfaces and tasteful minimalism. Mirabelle's apartment is claustrophobic and uncomfortable. Whenever she walks to enter her apartment door, she is subjected to the tyranny of poor design. She must first go up one staircase and then down another. Ray's wealth insulates him from such discomforts of real life. In shots of Mirabelle behind the glove counter, Tucker keeps the camera at a discreet distance, as if creating a still life.

The film is not satisfying in the way film romances usually are. Claire could end up with Ray or Jeremy, but neither coupling would have a sense of complete rightness about it. Still, there is something that lingers about the film. It is not so much the story as the odd, crisply depressive feeling about it. It is a small movie, but Tucker and Martin have given it close attention and an artistic touch.

Critics generally found the film flawed yet enjoyable. David Ansen of *Time* wrote, "*Shopgirl* isn't seamless...but it has a plaintive emotional delicacy that gets under your skin. It's a trio for three instruments that have to struggle to play in tune." Carina Chocano of *The Los Angeles Times* wrote, "*Shopgirl* is like *Pygmalion* for the upper-middle-brow business class flier. Which isn't to say it's bad. On the contrary, it's smart, spare, elegant and understated." A. O. Scott of *The New York Times* wrote, "*Shopgirl* is a resolutely small movie, finely made and perhaps a bit too fragile." Andrew O'Hehir of *Salon* was one who disliked the film calling it "an aging celebrity's unpleasant fantasy." He wrote, "There's so little sexual chemistry between the actors in this film that it seems like a kind of accomplishment. I've seen shows on C-SPAN that were hotter than this."

Jill Hamilton

CREDITS

Ray Porter: Steve Martin
Mirabelle Buttersfield: Claire Danes
Jeremy: Jason Schwartzman
Lisa Cramer: Bridgette Wilson-Sampras
Dan Buttersfeild: Sam Bottoms
Catherine Buttersfield: Frances Conroy
Christie Richards: Rebecca Pidgeon
Loki: Samantha Shelton
Del Rey: Gina Doctor
Mr. Agasa: Clyde Kusatsu
Loan Officer: Romy Rosemont
Origin: USA
Language: English
Released: 2005
Production: Ashok Amritraj, Jon Jashni, Steve Martin; released by Buena Vista
Directed by: Anand Tucker
Written by: Steven M. Martin
Cinematography by: Peter Suschitzsky
Music by: Barrington Pheloung
Sound: Edward Tise
Editing: David Gamble
Art Direction: Sue Chan
Costumes: Nancy Steiner
Production Design: William Arnold
MPAA rating: R
Running time: 116 minutes

REVIEWS

Boxoffice Online. October, 2005.
Chicago Sun-Times Online. October 28, 2005.
Entertainment Weekly Online. October 19, 2005.
Los Angeles Times Online. October 21, 2005.
New York Times Online. October 21, 2005.
Premiere Magazine Online. October 21, 2005.
Variety Online. September 11, 2005.
Washington Post Online. October 28, 2005, p. C05.

QUOTES

Mirabelle: "I guess I have to choose whether to be miserable now, or miserable later."

TRIVIA

In the first shot of the scene where Jeremy and Luther are shopping at Best Buy, in the foreground, somewhat out of focus, are rows and rows of DVD sets for *My So-Called Life* (1994) and *Saturday Night Live* (1975) in a nod to stars Danes and Martin, respectively, who were featured on the shows.

SIN CITY

(Frank Miller's Sin City)

Walk down the right back alley in Sin City and you can find anything.
—Movie tagline

She smells like angels ought to smell.
—Movie tagline

Hell of a way to end a partnership.
—Movie tagline

Beautiful and merciless.
—Movie tagline

Skinny little Nancy Callahan. She grew up. She filled out.
—Movie tagline

You're gonna love this, baby.
—Movie tagline

Do I take this cop down and risk it all?
—Movie tagline

There is no justice without sin.
—Movie tagline

Deadly little Miho.
—Movie tagline

Box Office: $74.1 million

Based on the steamy, gritty graphic novels of Frank Miller, *Sin City* is both graphic and novel. Robert Rodriguez's latest project achieves a stunning visual style that bends the boundaries between live action and caricature, as did 2004's *Sky Captain and the World of Tomorrow.* Like that film, *Sin City* is preoccupied with creating a memorable look that is nonetheless highly derivative—a homage to a particular artistic genre. But both films—shot entirely on empty sound stages and using computer-drawn backdrops—are so preoccupied with style that they squander their chances for much emotional impact.

Some critics of *Sin City* skewered Rodriguez, saying that the film failed to capture the hard-boiled film noir of old tough-guys-and-dames movies that it sends up. They missed the point. Rodriguez wasn't trying to pay homage to film noir; he was trying to be faithful to the look, feel, and mood of Miller's intricate and sophisticated modern comic books.

It's fascinating that as technology and ingenuity allow moviemakers to produce cartoons that look incredibly realistic (such as *The Incredibles* and the live-action-to-animation transformations of Richard Linklater's rotoscoped features *Waking Life* and *A Scanner Darkly*), some of the same computer-aided creativity and special effects wizardry allows live-action films to look like cartoons. Such is the canvas that Rodriguez has achieved. The film is primarily shot in black and white, but colors (primarily red) are painted onto women's dresses and lips–and used for the enormous quantities of blood that splatter the characters in the many gruesome fights that are the core of the film's unrelenting gore.

The world of Miller's vivid imagining—a souped-up noir fantasyland which would make Humphrey Bogart's head spin—allows Rodriguez to portray excessive and sometimes graphic violence. His film is not for the squeamish, but since everyone and everything in it is so over-the-top cartoonish, it's hard to feel much emotion even as body parts fly across the screen. Still, if your repulsion at decapitation, dismemberment, vampirism, cannibalism, and gunshot orgies is so strong that even caricatured displays of it turn your stomach, *Sin City* is not the film for you. And, with its well-deserved R rating for its gruesome scenes, so vividly depicted, it poses a real dilemma for parents of teenage and preteen children who'll want to see it. This is as hard-boiled a film as can be imagined, but it's several steps removed from impactful realism.

The film unwinds as four stories, stacked around each other like an elaborate puzzle box, whose pieces begin to fit together only at the end. It's a wild, distinctive ride, all emanating from the twisted mind of Miller, whose popular works have never gotten full treatment until now. Rodriguez gives both Miller and his mentor and friend Quentin Tarantino a share of directorial credit.

The film starts and ends with a cryptic sequence involving a mysterious hit man (Josh Hartnett); the opening scene, with the suave gunman on a rooftop with one of the film's ubiquitous femme fatales (there is no other kind of femme in this world except fatales), establishes the film's primary visual motifs: black-and-white with splotches of feminine red; occasional reversed-out white-outlined characters on black backgrounds, and noirish, exaggerated camera angles scanning the fictional "Basin City," a dark metropolis in which Miller's grotesque fantasies play out. After this prologue, we get the first half of a story involving an honest cop with a heart problem named Hartigan (Bruce Willis), who on his last mission is trying to save a young girl from a brutal rapist who turns out to be the son of a powerful politician. Immediately we discover that this is the sort of film in which people are repeatedly shot at point-black range but survive; the bodies in *Sin City* are living in a universe of pen and ink in which parts of them can be skewered, lopped off, and blown away, but somehow the inhabitants survive. This becomes a kind of running visual gag.

The second, longer sequence involves the elaborate revenge-taking of Marv (Mickey Rourke), a square-faced, ugly, brutal ex-con with a heart of gold, who is seeking to find the killer of a hooker named Goldie (James a.k.a. Jaime King), who was killed after a rare and puzzling night of drunken sex with Marv. Marv's the kind of man who is not usually favored by beautiful women but who defends them with a chivalry worthy of a knight from days of old (as the Miller/Rodriguez script needlessly reminds us). After slaughtering his way up the food chain, Marv finds Goldie's twin sister Wendy and traces Goldie's stalker to a notorious farmhouse haunted by a malevolent rapist and cannibal who is played by Elijah Wood and looks like something out of a twisted nightmare version of a Harry Potter movie—he's a weird geek, and a pretty laughably creepy villain. Marv dispatches him by turning the villain's relish for mutilation back on him full force and, after saturated with more gore and blood, works his way up to a higher authority behind the conspiracy that used Goldie. This would be compelling were it not so terribly unsubtle.

The final extended story, which is by far the best of the three, involves Dwight (Clive Owen), who has made the mistake of hooking up with a barmaid named Shellie (Brittany Murphy), whose boyfriend is a brutal abusive creep named Jackie Boy (Benicio Del Toro). After Dwight gives Jackie his comeuppance—partially drowning him in a toilet filled with Jackie's own urine—he follows Jackie to Old Town, a part of Sin City ruled by gun-toting supervixen hookers led by the statuesque Gail (Rosario Dawson), who of course turns out to be an old flame of Dwight. When Jackie pulls a gun on an Old Town regular named Becky (Alexis Bledel), he incurs the righteous wrath of the girls, who descend on him and his buddies in a fury. Then they find out too late that Jackie is a cop, and his killing will mean the end of the uneasy truce between the Sin City authorities and the Old Town ladies of the night. A complicated and occasionally clumsy but always entertaining escape, chase, and rescue operation ensues, pitting Dwight and Gail against a panoply of mercenaries, cops, and turncoats.

Deftly, the film then returns to Hartigan's story. Eight years later, the girl he saved has turned into a classy stripper named Nancy (Jessica Alba), and Hartigan must again save her from the clutches of her tormentor, who has been medically restored into some kind of freakish yellow, foul-smelling demon—the only point at which the film seems to take leave of its gritty noir roots and fly off into bad science fiction. The other problem with this sequence is that it's basically rehashing the same plot as the first sequence. There seems to be a limit to Miller's imagination.

The film is terrifically entertaining in its astonishing visuals and its penchant for going way over the top with gruesome comic excesses. And there's a terrific stable of actors turning in some fine performances. Del Toro is oily and enchanting, then hilarious as the ghost of the slain cop; Rourke is astonishingly transformed into a monstrous brute; Willis is fine, though not convincingly decrepit, as the old cop Hartigan. Many of the female actors chafe and strain, however, against the restraints of their roles—they all have to be tough-as-nails dames with hearts of gold.

While the language ranges from unintentionally to intentionally cliched, the combination of irony and homage wears thin after awhile. Though it couldn't have been more skillfully shot, even the style wears thin after awhile as Rodriguez employs the same techniques over and over. And the mayhem becomes predictable too: how many body parts can be chopped or bitten off, severed or blown away with various weapons, how many faces can be splattered with blood, before the effect becomes enervating? The characters and story lines are also repetitive. Cops and the authorities are corrupt, the heroes are brutal but chivalrous and highly protective of female honor, the women are daringly sexual and dangerous but also ridiculously vulnerable. The protagonists—the men who saved the women from extreme predation—are themselves chaste or romantic, old and beaten down, and will be betrayed and framed for the very heinous crimes they are trying to prevent.

The extremes of the carnage and the brilliance of the style are both entertaining and off-putting, keeping you at a distance. These people aren't real, they're exaggerated archetypes, and Miller doesn't even seem to a large variety of character types. Ingenuity and imagination are more surface than deeply embedded in the themes. *Sin City,* like all good entertainment, doesn't require too much of the viewer, and it was, especially with the generation of younger readers who eat up graphic novels rather than the meatier prose kind. Clever but in a limited way, this tour de force pulls no punches with its images but leaves the viewer hungry for the complexities of richer psychological territory, more intricate characters, and something more tangible and human to connect with.

Michael Betzold

CREDITS

Nancy: Jessica Alba
Miho: Devon Aoki
Becky: Alexis Bledel
Gail: Rosario Dawson
Jackie Boy: Benicio Del Toro
Manute: Michael Clarke Duncan
Lucille: Carla Gugino
The Man: Josh Hartnett
Cardinal Roark: Rutger Hauer
Goldie/Wendy: Jaime (James) King
Bob: Michael Madsen
Shellie: Brittany Murphy
Dwight: Clive Owen
Marv: Mickey Rourke
Roark Jr./Yellow Bastard: Nick Stahl
Hartigan: Bruce Willis
Kevin: Elijah Wood
The Customer: Marley Shelton
Senator Roark: Powers Boothe
Stuka: Nicky Katt
Nancy, age 11: Makenzie Vega
Murphy: Arie Verveen
Weevil: Tommy Nix
Commissioner Liebowitz: Jude Ciccolella
Origin: USA
Language: English
Released: 2005
Production: Elizabeth Avellan, Robert Rodriguez, Frank Miller; released by Dimension Films
Directed by: Robert Rodriguez, Frank Miller
Cinematography by: Robert Rodriguez
Music by: Robert Rodriguez, Graeme Revell, John Debney
Sound: John Pritchett
Art Direction: Jeanette Scott
Costumes: Nina Proctor
MPAA rating: R
Running time: 124 minutes

REVIEWS

Boxoffice Online. March, 2005.
Chicago Sun-Times Online. March 30, 2005.
Entertainment Weekly Online. March 30, 2005.
Los Angeles Times Online. April 1, 2005.
New York Times Online. April 1, 2005.
Premiere Magazine Online. April 1, 2005.
Variety Online. March 26, 2005.
Washington Post Online. April 1, 2005, p. WE43.

QUOTES

Marv: "I love hitmen. No matter what you do to them, you don't feel bad."

TRIVIA

Robert Rodriguez, a longtime fan of the comic, filmed a secret "audition" piece for a chance to direct this film which he then showed to writer Frank Miller. Shot in early 2004, the footage featured Josh Hartnett and Jamie King acting out the *Sin City* short-story "The Customer is Always Right." Up until that point, Miller had refused to relinquish the movie rights to any of his comic works, *Sin City* in particular, after a bad Hollywood experience in the early 1990s. Miller, however, approved of the footage and the film was underway.

THE SISTERHOOD OF THE TRAVELING PANTS

Laugh. Cry. Share the pants.
—Movie tagline

Box Office: $39 million

Tibby (Amber Tamblyn), Lena (Alexis Bledel), Carmen (America Ferrera), and Bridget (Blake Lively) have been friends since before birth because all four of their mothers took the same pre-natal exercise class and all four girls were born the same week. The girls are now 16 years old and preparing for a summer in which they will be apart for the very first time.

Lena, the shy artist of the group, is off to Greece to visit her grandparents. Carmen, the half Puerto Rican writer-to-be, will be spending some quality time with the father (Bradley Whitford) who abandoned her and her mother when she was young. Bridget, the take-charge first born of the quartet, will be expending her summer energy at a soccer camp in Baja, Mexico. Only cynical filmmaker Tibby will be staying home, working at the local Megamart to make money for the film equipment required for the "suckumentary" she is filming on the lives of the losers she sees around her.

Before they part ways, however, the foursome does a little shopping, and, as incredible as it sounds, in a thrift store they run across a pair of pants that perfectly fits all four girls from supermodel thin Lena to ample Carmen. Believing that this must make the pants magical, the girls decide to share the jeans. Each girl will wear them for a week then send them on to the next girl and so on until each girl has had the jeans twice and they are all home together again.

The first to have possession of the jeans is Lena, but the only magical thing they seem capable of doing is almost getting her drowned when she falls into the water surrounding the island of Santorini. She is, however, rescued by a most handsome young man who turns out to be from a family involved in a long feud with Lena's grandparents. So off the pants go to their next recipient.

For Bridget the pants seem to give her the confidence (as if she needed any more) to try and seduce a totally off-limits coach. For Carmen they are a touch of acceptance in a world which seems to be totally rejecting her as her father has not told her that their summer together will be shared with his perfectly WASPy fiancée Lydia (Nancy Travis) and her two perfectly WASPy children. For Tibby, the jeans just bring an annoying little kid, Bailey (Jenna Boyd), who worms her way into helping Tibby make her film.

After each girl has had the jeans once, even though it doesn't seem as if anything magical has actually taken place in their lives, the pants begin their rounds again. For reserved Lena this time the pants give her the courage to fall in love with her Greek Montague and stand up to her Capulet grandparents. Bridget comes to the sad realization that seducing her coach has not made up for the emptiness she feels because of an emotionally distant father and a mother who committed suicide. Tibby will soon come to realize that Bailey, who always seems so interested in and even likes all the so-called losers they are filming, not only may have a life-view superior to Tibby's cynicism, but is also gravely ill. As for Carmen, the pants will eventually help her to heal her rift with her father.

Director Ken Kwapis has done a charming job of bringing the very popular Ann Brashares' novel *The Sisterhood of the Traveling Pants* to the screen, He has maintained the integrity of the story which will be sure to please Brashares' legion of teen fans while still making a film that is engaging even for adults. It doesn't resort to the usual tired clichés of teen-angst films and instead gives us the stories of four highly individual characters and their own very human problems. Because there are four stories being told here none of them begins to wear thin, yet even in this abbreviated telling each story unfolds and resolves in a most satisfying manner. Similarly, by alternating between the four stories our attention never wanders. And when one adds the beautiful cinematography of John Bailey and the scenic splendor of Santorini it is as engaging to watch as it is to hear.

The five actresses who share the screen for this film all imbue their characters with credible individuality and make us care about the challenges and growth they go through. Like the magical pants that seem to embrace and absolve all physical limitations of the girls, Kwapis and his actors allow us to embrace these characters and watch as they absolve themselves of their own problems.

Beverley Bare Buehrer

CREDITS

Carmen: America Ferrera

Tibby: Amber Tamblyn

Lena: Alexis Bledel

Bailey: Jenna Boyd
Bridget: Blake Lively
Al: Bradley Whitford
Lydia: Nancy Travis
Carmen's mother: Rachel Ticotin
Eric: Mike Vogel
Kostas: Kyle Schmid
Origin: USA
Language: English
Released: 2005
Production: Di Novi Pictures, Debra Martin Chase; released by Warner Bros.
Directed by: Ken Kwapis
Written by: Delia Ephron, Elizabeth Chandler
Cinematography by: John Bailey
Music by: Cliff Eidelman
Sound: Jason George
Music Supervisor: Dawn Soler
Editing: Kathryn Himoff
Art Direction: Kevin Humenny, Helen Jarvis
Costumes: Lisa Jensen
Production Design: Gae Buckley
MPAA rating: PG
Running time: 119 minutes

REVIEWS

Boxoffice Online. June, 2005.
Chicago Sun-Times Online. June 1, 2005.
Entertainment Weekly Online. June 1, 2005.
Los Angeles Times Online. June 1, 2005.
New York Times Online. June 1, 2005.
Premiere Magazine Online. May 31, 2005.
Variety Online. May 29, 2005.

QUOTES

Lena: "We may have been wrong about the pants."

TRIVIA

Blake Lively, who plays Bridget, and Ernie Lively, who plays Bridget's dad, are real life father and daughter.

THE SKELETON KEY

It can open any door.
—Movie tagline
You will believe.
—Movie tagline
Fearing Is Believing.
—Movie tagline

Box Office: $47.8 million

The Skeleton Key, a ghost story set in ultra-steamy Louisiana bayou country, may elicit more perspiration in viewers than trepidation. Many watching will start to actually feel a little clammy due to the film's remarkably palpable evocation of the area's thick, sticky sultriness. That is quite different, however, from leaving audiences in a satisfying cold sweat, the primary objective of such spooky thrillers.

The film's protagonist is Caroline Ellis (competent Kate Hudson), a hospice worker who is shown to sincerely care about the people she cares for. She is appalled by her colleagues' casual and callous disposition of the dead and their personal effects. As a result, she decides to go solo, and finds a surprisingly well-paying live-in job at an elderly couple's plantation mansion in the dark recesses of the bayou. Both the house and its owners have clearly seen better days. Caroline's African-American friend Jill (Joy Bryant) has heard enough about that area's immersion in Hoodoo, a dark, disturbing form of African-based folk magic, to be troubled by her pal's move. However, Caroline is undeterred by her friend's unease, the less-than-welcoming signs outside the property that read "No Admittance" and "Keep Out," and that vague, ominous something that hangs in the humid air all around her like the Spanish moss upon the bayou's majestic, imposing trees.

In keeping with a convention of similar films set in this region, Caroline chooses to stop for gas at an out of the way, fly-infested, shocking shack adorned with alligator heads and attended by suddenly-appearing, otherworldly women and men who eat oysters with great big knives. Arriving at her destination, a rocking chair on the porch moves to and fro on its own, and the statues and paintings within seem rather scary in the dark. Out in the garden, Caroline meets her wizened patient, Ben Devereaux (John Hurt), left paralyzed and mute from a stroke. His wife, the proud, ultra-formidable Violet (Gena Rowlands, relishing every minute of it), is a force to be reckoned with, even more so than is initially apparent. With a decided lack of Southern hospitality and charm, she greets the young New Jersey native with pointed skepticism. "She wouldn't understand the house," Violet tells the couple's suave, handsome, and strangely omnipresent lawyer, Luke Marshall (Peter Sarsgaard). Caroline learns that all the caretakers who preceded her decided to quit. If she had any sense, she would point her little Volkswagen back toward New Orleans and not pick her foot off the accelerator until she gets there, but Caroline pluckily stays put.

Soon after her arrival, Caroline becomes part Florence Nightingale and part Nancy Drew. Like so many horror heroines before her, the young woman cannot help snooping around alone in the exact places she should avoid, creeping up the dark staircase to the upper reaches of the mansion while clutching the skeleton key Violet gave her. Her inquiring mind wants to know: why have all the house's mirrors been banished to the attic? What else is up there, particularly behind the door to an inner room which rattles and thumps as if something or someone wants out? When Caroline finally enters that chamber, it looks like a one-stop-shopping place for all one's Hoodoo needs, filled with things like monkey skulls, pickled body parts, disquieting dolls, and old, scratchy recordings of an aged African-American man reciting something alarmingly titled "Conjure of Sacrifice."

It is all quite baffling and troubling, as are the intense, anguished, pleading looks Ben gives Caroline that strangely vanish the instant his wife enters the room. Caroline wonders if Ben could have some reason to be afraid of his own wife, and might be begging for deliverance. Then, on a suitably stormy night, Caroline is horrified to find that her supposedly paralyzed patient has climbed out his bedroom window and taken a header off the roof, leaving a frantically-scrawled appeal for help on one of his bed sheets. Hurt is rather riveting whenever on screen, skillfully conveying without words an agony and terror so overwhelming that they are likely beyond words anyway.

At this point, Caroline (and the audience) thinks it is high time someone filled in some blanks. Violet grudgingly agrees to do so after Caroline reveals she has seen the hair-raising room where, surely not coincidentally, Ben had suffered his stroke. Violet tells of an incident which took place on a pitch-black night ninety years before, when a banker and his drunken party guests lynched husband and wife servants Papa Justify (Ronald McCall) and Mama Cecile (Jeryl Prescott Sales) after finding them conducting a Hoodoo ceremony in that very room with the rich man's children. A powerful flashback depicting the events of that long-ago night is highly disturbing, using black and white spooky images, disorienting camerawork, and quick, agitated cutting to effectively portray the headlong, horrific violence. Violet discloses that the ghosts of Papa Justify and Mama Cecile are still in the house and are seen in the mansion's mirrors. (Sure enough, Ben convulses apoplectically when Caroline has him look into a compact mirror.) "Now you'll leave like all the rest of 'em," Violet says to Caroline. However, the young woman, remembering how her own father died without her comforting, soothing assistance (he had kept his illness a secret), stays to pour her caring into distressed and defenseless Ben. One clearly senses that Caroline cares too much for her own good.

Caroline hypothesizes that Ben's condition is merely psychosomatic: he is only paralyzed because he thinks Hoodoo has got him under its spell. To try and help him, she attempts to bone up on her Hoodoo. Learning about Justify's notoriously-prodigious powers would alone justify fearful flight. Still, Caroline conducts a ceremony to "uncross" this supposed spell, and Ben is just able to croak, "Caroline, help me!" This proves to her that it was all in his head, but it apparently never registers that it could also have proved there was indeed a spell to dispel. Caroline continually insists with seemingly rock-solid rationality that she does not buy into such beliefs, and is told while visiting those who know about such things that Hoodoo cannot touch those who do not believe. "I suggest," warns the African-American girl who last worked for the Devereauxs, "you leave before you do!" Her words are drenched with dire foreshadowing, but Caroline remains focused on her mission of mercy.

Certain that Violet has done something dreadful to Ben but unsure exactly what, Caroline prepares to do battle with the battle-ax and get him to safety. Amidst lightning flashes from yet another of the film's innumerable storms, this showdown marks a full-throttle degeneration into fevered, hackneyed fare. When Caroline attempts to put Violet out of commission by injecting something into the sugar cubes and putting a dash or two in her tea, the elderly woman falls to the floor, twirling and twitching like an overturned beetle trying mightily to right itself, and alternately screaming out Hoodoo and less than genteel things like "Whore!" The sight is unintentionally giggle-inducing, as is Violet's subsequent "I believe you broke my legs" as she drags herself ridiculously along the floor after a particularly ungainly tumble over a banister and down a flight of stairs.

Caroline deposits Ben in her car and tries unsuccessfully to bash their way out through the property's mysteriously-locked gates. Stashing him for safekeeping in a garden shed, she paddles a canoe into the bayou while a gun-toting Violet shoots and shouts from shore. Caroline thinks Luke will offer her a helping hand, but instead he uses both hands to strangle her into unconsciousness and transports her back to Violet. (It is a shocking moment, although there was some earlier telegraphing which pointed to his true nature.) It turns out that Justify's Conjure of Sacrifice offers immortality by enabling souls to periodically abandon bodies that have passed their prime and jump into young, vibrant ones. Caroline realizes that this is Violet's plan for her, and begins to think that she may have given the whole Hoodoo business short shrift. Even as she continues to proclaim that she does not believe, Caroline opts to use a host of Hoodoo tricks to try and keep the seemingly indomitable Violet and Luke at bay. The whole finale seems breathlessly ludicrous, leading viewers to connect the dots and realize that Papa Justify and Mama Cecile have successfully passed from the banker's offspring to Violet and Ben and now to the bodies which used to belong to Caroline and Luke. *The Skeleton Key* bows out after an arresting shot of horrified Caroline and Luke, now trapped within the paralyzed bodies of Violet and Ben, staring helplessly at each other in the back of the ambulance called to cart them away.

The Skeleton Key was written by Ehren Kruger, whose previous work in this vein includes *Scream 3* (2000), *The Ring* (2002), and that film's unfortunate sequel. Made on a budget of $43 million, *The Skeleton Key* succeeded in grossing over $47 million. Critical reaction skewed toward the negative. Yes, the film has atmosphere galore, is generally intriguing, eerie, and sometimes startling, but it seldom pushes viewers beyond mere unsettled curiosity into genuine, potent concern or dread. It is somewhat clichéd and sometimes confusing. A middling mixture of horror, Hoodoo, humidity, and just plain hooey, *The Skeleton Key* intermittently loses its grip on the audience, and when it veers toward B-movie ridiculousness, seems to be just plain losing its grip.

David L. Boxerbaum

CREDITS

Caroline: Kate Hudson
Luke: Peter Sarsgaard
Violet: Gena Rowlands
Ben: John Hurt
Jill: Joy Bryant
Origin: USA
Language: English
Released: 2005
Production: Iain Softley, Michael Shamberg, Stacey Sher; Double Feature Films; released by Universal Pictures
Directed by: Iain Softley
Written by: Ehren Kruger
Cinematography by: Dan Mindel
Music by: Ed Shearmur
Sound: Peter J. Devlin
Music Supervisor: Sara Lord
Editing: Joe Hutshing
Art Direction: Drew Boughton
Costumes: Louise Frogley
Production Design: John Beard
MPAA rating: PG-13
Running time: 104 minutes

REVIEWS

Boxoffice Online. August, 2005.
Chicago Sun-Times Online. August 12, 2005.
Entertainment Weekly Online. August 10, 2005.
Los Angeles Times Online. August 12, 2005.
New York Times Online. August 12, 2005.
Variety Online. July 22, 2005.
Washington Post Online. August 11, 2005, p. WE35.

QUOTES

Violet: "We've been waiting for you, Caroline."

SKY BLUE

(Wonderful Days)

A fantastic journey to the future begins.
—Movie tagline
Wonderful days are coming...
—Movie tagline

Sky Blue has been taken seriously in some quarters while being ballyhooed as the first major Korean animated feature (at a record $10 million production cost), but the producer's American-style makeover mars an already flawed anime project.

Originally titled *Wonderful Days, Sky Blue* took seven years to make and was actually finished two years ago (in 2003). Thus, one might expect the technical side of the film to look already dated, yet it is the animation (at least of the backgrounds and details) that provide the true aesthetic pleasures of the work.

Sky Blue takes place in 2140, following a worldwide environmental destruction that has nearly ended human civilization. In Ecoban, the only standing city, Jay, a young patrol officer, is assigned to fight off invaders by Simon, the head of security who loves her. But when Jay witnesses Simon and her other bosses commit an egregious environmental crime, her world turns upside down. Now feeling betrayed, Jay considers joining the opposition, an underground operation trying to take over the city, and helping make the city pollution-free.

To her delight, Jay discovers that her childhood love, Shua, is the leader of the rebel group plotting the coup against Ecoban's leaders. From Shua, Jay also learns all about how Ecoban's main energy source is powered by pollutants and that her former employers are trying to obtain more of the hazardous materials. Jay and Shua join forces—nearly getting killed in the process—to put a halt to the pollution and topple Ecoban's evil officials.

Sky Blue obviously comes from South Korea as a not-so-veiled indictment of corrupt and megalomaniacal dictators; it is not so surprising that the western world, including the U.S., would embrace this feature, given the west's consistent demonization of North Korea's leader, Kim Jong-il, as a corrupt and megalomaniacal dictator.

Whatever the real world political theater behind this release, *Sky Blue* carries a blatantly liberal western message that is both anti-totalitarian and eco-friendly. Naturally, one must be mindful that *Sky Blue* has been given a English-language renovation, with new dialogue translations (by Howard Rabinowitz, Park Sunmin, and Jeffrey Winter), new line readings (including David Naughton providing the voice of Dr. Noah, a guru for the rebels, Catherine Cavadini "ghosting" Jay, and Marc Worden dubbing Shua), and even some re-editing (by Michael McCusker, who worked on *The Day After Tomorrow*). So the message may have changed slightly during the Americanization (fans on the Web of the Korean version assert the original is superior).

One could hardly object to *Sky Blue* 's morality tale, but the film is hardly new in its storytelling, exposition, or character development. More surprisingly, the sketches of the characters evoke American Saturday-morning cartoons of the 1970s and '80s, with their flat dimensions and Caucasian features (didn't anyone of color survive the environmental holocaust of the backstory?). Not one of the characters resembles even the more rounded and life-like figures of classic or recent Disney blockbusters. It's a wonder that the film has been given such an auspicious reception at such venues as the Sundance and Venice Film Festival (both in 2004).

Still, just around and behind *Sky Blue*'s 2D characters are the sumptuous 3D backgrounds, which are superbly designed and executed, from the noirish futuristic settings (quoting Fritz Lang's *Metropolis* and Ridley Scott's *Bladerunner*) to the live-action miniatures that make *Final Fantasy* (and everything before that high-tech rotoscope feature) look not fully realized. By imagining this futuristic universe so opulently and completely, kudos go to directors Moon-Saeng Kim (a former TV commercial helmer) and Park Sunmin and their animation team—art directors Yoon-cheol Jung and Suk-Young Lee, special effects artist Sung-Ho Hong, and visual effects artist Young-Min Park.

More than a few reviewers noted the disparity between the beauty of the background and banality in the foreground. In the February 15, 2005 *Village Voice*, Ed Park wrote: "...the self-sufficient, energy-sucking city of Ecoban reveals itself at moments as a nightmare of sudden abysses, inscrutable floating cubes, and elevator doors designed to look like mazes. Unfortunately, these eye-openers share time with indifferently imagined characters whose visual flatness clashes with the more detailed backgrounds." Likewise, Stephen Holden wrote in the February 18, 2005 *New York Times*, "*Sky Blue* teeters unsteadily between dystopian fable and Saturday-morning cartoon." And Sheri Linden summed up in the December 30, 2004 *Hollywood Reporter* that "The relative flatness of the characters—conventional anime figures—is a jarring contrast to the meticulously wrought setting."

For those who love state-of-the-art computer animation, special effects, and production design, *Sky Blue* will satisfy as entertainment—or at least as an object d'art. Those seeking something lively or interesting to watch in the story will be disappointed.

Eric Monder

CREDITS

Origin: USA, South Korea
Language: Korean
Released: 2003
Production: Kyeong hag Lee, Kay Hwang, Sunmin Park; Tinhouse, Maxmedia, Masquerade Films
Directed by: Moon Sang Kim
Written by: Sunmin Park
Cinematography by: Sun Kwan Lee
Music by: Sam Spiegel
Sound: Suk-Won Kim
Art Direction: Youn-Cheol Jung
Production Design: Il Won, Soug-Youn Lee
MPAA rating: Unrated
Running time: 86 minutes

REVIEWS

Boxoffice Online. February, 2005.
Entertainment Weekly Online. February 23, 2005.
Los Angeles Times Online. December 31, 2004.
New York Times Online. February 18, 2005.
Variety Online. February 1, 2004.
Washington Post Online. March 4, 2005, p. WE43.

SKY HIGH

Brains, Brawn And Beyond.
—Movie tagline

Saving The World... One Homework Assignment At A Time.
—Movie tagline

Box Office: $63.9 million

It is no longer enough for a movie superhero to bend beams of steel, leap tall buildings in a single bound, and so forth. A modern movie superhero must also have a sense of irony about his or her particular line of work.

The success of *The Incredibles* and *Spy Kids* meant that subsequent superhero movies marketed to the preteen audience must be not only exciting but funny, too.

Sky High understands the rules and does a good job following them. There is plenty of excitement and cool feats of strength, but the film is also light, lively and full of fun, over-the-top performances. The Sky High of the title refers to a secret school for fledgling superheroes. It is hidden in a cloud bank atop a chunk of land held aloft by an antigravity machine. Will Stronghold (Michael Angarano) is a natural for the school. His parents, the Commander (Kurt Russell) and Josie Jetstream (Kelly Preston), are the most famous superheroes around (by day they dabble in real estate.) Will's parents assume that he will inherit either his father's super strength or his mother's ability to fly, or even both. But Will's big secret is that, so far, he has not inherited any powers. As the school nurse (Cloris Leachman) tells him, he might get a superpower or he might not. Lacking a handy vat of toxic waste to jumpstart his superpower, Will heads for school, hoping for the best.

Instead of geeks, jocks and cheerleaders, the kids at Sky High are divided into heroes or sidekicks, or as the sidekicks are more politely called, "hero support." On the first day of school, each freshman is called up to the stage by tough Coach Boomer (cult star Bruce Campbell) and asked to demonstrate their superpower in front of the rest of the kids. Kids who can clone themselves, turn into a rock monster or spew toxic spit go on the superhero track. Those with more minor powers, such as the ability to shape-shift into a hamster, like Magenta (Kelly Vitz), are deemed sidekicks. Will is promptly placed into the latter group. He finds friends among the sidekicks, including Zach (Nicholas Braun), an Eninem wannabe whose power is glowing slightly in the dark, and Ethan (Dee Jay Daniels), who can transform himself into a pile of goo. His pretty childhood friend, Layla (Danielle Panabaker), has the nice superpower of being able to control plants, but she does not believe in performing on demand and gets placed in the sidekick group. She is also harboring a big crush on Will.

Will faces the same high school challenges that any kid in a Disney film might. He has an archenemy, Warren Peace (Steven Strait), who wants to make his life miserable. And he does not know how to deal with the school's bullies. When Gwen Grayson (Elizabeth Winstead), the school's most popular girl, starts showing an interest in Will, he is so dazzled by his newfound social status that he neglects his old friends.

Part of the fun of the film is watching the actors ham it up. Russell demonstrates good comic timing as the self-satisfied superhero. And Campbell captures the steroidal, slightly sadistic edge that can mark gym teachers. *Kids in the Hall* alums Dave Foley and Kevin McDonald make appearances, too. Foley is Mr. Boy, the Commander's forgotten former sidekick who now teaches hero support at Sky High. McDonald is Mr. Medulla, who sports a gigantic skull and teaches mad science. Also fun is seeing all the superpowers and how they are used. The school bullies use super speed and flexible rubber body parts in order to round up victims to flush in the toilet. Gwen is a "technopath," that is, someone who can control technology with her thoughts. She uses her power to build a freezing ray gun, but can also fix household appliances. Even the school nurse uses her x-ray vision for patients' exams.

Critics were mildly entertained by the film. Jane Horwitz of *The Washington Post* called the film, "slight, but sure-footed" and said that the director "pillages the great 2004 computer-animated lark *The Incredibles*...but in forgivable, unassuming fashion." Wesley Morris of *The Boston Globe* called it "a squeaky clean, family-friendly comedy." And Carrie Rickey of *The Philadelphia Inquirer* wrote, "*Sky High* is a diverting family comedy that at its best aims to be a live-action *Incredibles* and at its middling a live-action episode of 'Kim Possible.'"

Jill Hamilton

CREDITS

Will Stronghold: Michael Angarano
Steve Stronghold/The Commander: Kurt Russell
Josie Stronghold/Jetstream: Kelly Preston
Coach Boomer: Bruce Campbell
Principal Powers: Lynda Carter
Mr. Boy: Dave Foley
Layla: Danielle Panabaker
Gwen Grayson: Mary Elizabeth Winstead
Warren Peace: Steven Strait
Ron Wilson, Bus Driver: Kevin Heffernan
Zach: Nicholas Braun
Mr. Medulla: Kevin McDonald
Nurse Spex: Cloris Leachman
Ethan: Dee-Jay Daniels
Magenta: Kelly Vitz
Mr. Grayson: Jim Rash
Lash: Jake Sandvig
Speed: Will Harris
Penny: Malika Khadijah
Royal Pain: Patrick Warburton (Voice)
Origin: USA
Language: English
Released: 2005
Production: Andrew Gunn; GUNNFilms; released by Buena Vista

Directed by: Mike Mitchell
Written by: Robert Schooley, Mark McCorkle, Paul Hernandez, Paul Amundson
Cinematography by: Shelly Johnson
Music by: Michael Giacchino
Sound: Paul Ledford
Music Supervisor: Lisa Brown
Art Direction: Bruce Robert Hill, William Hawkins
Costumes: Michael Wilkinson
MPAA rating: PG
Running time: 100 minutes

REVIEWS

Boxoffice Online. July, 2005.
Entertainment Weekly Online. July 27, 2005.
Los Angeles Times Online. July 29, 2005.
New York Times Online. July 29, 2005.
Premiere Magazine Online. July 29, 2005.
Variety Online. July 27, 2005.
Washington Post Online. July 29, 2005, p. C05.

QUOTES

Layla: "What's embarrassing him in front of the entire class going to prove? That is so unfair."

Will Stronghold: "Yeah, well if life were to suddenly get fair, I doubt it would happen in high school."

TRIVIA

Lynda Carter was originally given gold bracelets to wear in the film as an homage to her 1970s Wonder Woman role. However, Warner Bros., who owns copyright to the Wonder Woman character, didn't agree to the bracelets being portrayed in a Disney movie and they were subsequently removed from Carter's wardrobe.

SON OF THE MASK

Who's next?
—Movie tagline

The next generation of mischief.
—Movie tagline

Box Office: $17 million

"Surely this is a sign of the time of the coming of Ragnarock (The End of All Things)!" "Nay, 'tis but only the release of *Son of the Mask.*"

Son of the Mask is the dreadful and unnecessary sequel to the 1994 hit *The Mask* (originally based on the popular Dark Horse comic series of the same name) that insured Jim Carrey's status as one of the most malleable and bankable comedic actors in Hollywood. That film was a perfect vehicle for the high-energy Carrey that ably melded his own rubber-bodied shtick seamlessly with the highest-grade computer effects available to filmmakers at that time.

Audiences who enjoyed that film will sadly, but not unpredictably, leave the theater with the same feelings. The energy of Carrey that propelled the audiences through is sorely lacking in the actor who has been handed the torch, or mask in this case, although the level of CGI technology retains its 1994 standards.

This time around Jamie Kennedy is the unwitting recipient of the mask. He plays Tim Avery, an aspiring animator who just wants his shot at pitching a character he's been working on to the Walt Disney like boss Daniel Moss (Steven Wright). We are told that the boss is hard to get a hold of, even though he is seen in film sharing the lunch cafeteria with the rest of the general staff. While at the same time he is treated in the film as an intimidating and almost mythological figure at the company who has an office on the second floor, that to the staff might as well be Asgard. While Tim struggles to get a pitch meeting with Moss, or even just a sideways glance, he works in the Disney like park dressed in a cumbersome turtle suit (presumably echoing his slow career pace) while thanklessly guiding public tours through the animation studios. At this point in the film the audience is supposed to sympathize with him and his situation, and begin to have a rooting interest in achieving his goal. But his character, while closely resembling Carrey's nebbish bank employee in the first film, Kennedy's character is written and acted as the company whiner who manages to engender nothing but annoyance from the audience.

Kennedy's character is named Tim Avery, presumably named after the famous animator Tex Avery, who is credited with creating many of the famous MGM and Warner Bros. Cartoon characters including Daffy Duck, Chilly Willy, and Droopy, as well as with the creation of Bugs Bunny's personality and his famous line, "What's up, Doc?" Naming a character after a famous animator would be a clever and fitting homage (especially in a film that promotes itself as a live-action cartoon), were it not for the fact that it occurs in this film. It is more of an insult and a slap in the face to a truly talented creator than anything else, and should have been saved for a better film.

Traylor Howard plays Tim Avery's wife Tonya, the current breadwinner of the household who longs for a baby, but Tim doesn't think he is financially or emotionally ready for such commitment. And throughout the film he unintentionally proves himself right. While preparing to attend a company Halloween party, Tim, realizing he is lacking a mask for his costume, is given

The Mask by his dog Otis, who had been the first one to find it earlier in the film, and who had felt its effects in several unfunny (but well advertised) scenes. Just before going into the party Tim puts the Mask on and is transformed into a white-toothed, green-faced mirthful prankster that becomes the life of the party. The audience is obviously supposed to see this scene as the equivalent of the big musical number in the first film. But Jamie Kennedy never pulls it off. He lacks the necessary commitment, exuberance and imagination that Jim Carrey brought to that scene.

Tim leaves the party and arrives home where, still possessed by the mask gives his unsuspecting wife her "best night ever." Soon the wife finds that she is pregnant, with what later turns out to be the "Son of the Mask." After the baby is born, the wife is called out of town, which leaves Tim to take care of the baby while at the same time finish his character proposal for his boss. It seems that the boss who was at the Halloween party was so enamored by the green faced character that he wants to give that character his own animated series. And he wants Tim to deliver a proposal to the board ASAP. But he finds it impossible to work without the Mask, which he seems to have lost. Furthermore, the baby has become more than he can handle. Frustrated and in order to work without distractions, Tim does what any able-minded parent would do in this situation, and sets the baby in front of the television set where the baby (and the audience) has a chance to watch the only funny scene in the film: the classic Warner Bros. Cartoon "One Froggy Evening" (1965) that introduced the character (and WB Network mascot) Michigan J. Frog. The following scene (which the filmmakers somehow thought would be funny) in which the baby does a dead-on song-and dance imitation of the musical number from that cartoon, is possibly one of the most bizarre and creepiest moments in cinema history.

Meanwhile, it turns out Otis has had the mask all along ever since the night of the party and had hid it away in his doghouse. This gives the animators a chance for a scene involving the dog wearing the Mask and planning several Wily Coyote style attacks on the baby that he feels jealous of. These scenes are obviously meant to be funny, in the style of the classic Road Runner Wily Coyote cartoons, but the fact that one is a dog and one is a baby removes any humor from them.

During all of this, Loki (Alan Cumming), the Norse God of mischief (and original owner of the Mask) has been searching for the Mask. He soon finds out that there is now a Son of the Mask, and in an odd homage to the Terminator films, Loki goes door to door looking for the Avery baby, checking off a list of names that he found in a phone book. All of this while constantly being hounded by the voice of Odin (Bob Hoskins) whose only job seems to be finding several different ways to yell the name "Loki!" Throughout this film one is reminded of the camp 1950s classic *Attack of the 50 Foot Woman,* which had a women searching for her cheating husband while constantly yelling his name "Harry!"

While obviously not on a level of Carrey, Kennedy is a talented actor who usually can at least be counted on for an adequate and honest portrayal, but here he seems to know that this film was a bad idea, and has the look of a man who feels guilty for picking up his paycheck. Steven Wright, whose trademark stand-up routines are a wondrous journey into ironic lethargy, must have seen his character as a clever twist on the mega-corporation head, but it just doesn't work here, because he never comes into contact with the only contrasting character Loki, that would make his character funny. He seems to be channeling nothing more than Walt Disney, post-freezer.

The first film, while not perfect, was a brilliantly funny and energetic story about a person gaining self-confidence by shedding the physical and emotional masks of insecurity, thus giving that film its heart. This film on the other hand isn't about anything but an unpleasant endless stream of bad slapstick, tasteless violence, bathroom humor, ugly camerawork, and pre-1995 CGI effects.

As in mythology, Odin shows up with one eye missing. Forced to sit through *Son of the Mask,* this reviewer would gladly hand the god two replacements.

David E. Chapple

CREDITS

Tim Avery: Jamie Kennedy
Loki: Alan Cumming
Tonya Avery: Traylor Howard
Daniel Moss: Steven Wright
Alvey: Liam Falconer
Alvey: Ryan Falconer
Kal Penn
Odin: Bob Hoskins
Origin: USA
Language: English
Released: 2005
Production: Erica Huggins, Scott Kroopf; Radar Pictures, Dark Horse Entertainment; released by New Line Cinema
Directed by: Lawrence (Larry) Guterman
Written by: Lance Khazei
Cinematography by: Greg Gardiner
Music by: Randy Edelman
Editing: Malcolm Campbell, Debra Neil Fisher
Costumes: Mary Vogt

MPAA rating: PG
Running time: 86 minutes

REVIEWS

Boxoffice Online. February, 2005.
Chicago Sun-Times Online. February 18,2005.
Entertainment Weekly Online. February, 2005.
Los Angeles Times Online. February 18, 2005.
New York Times Online. February 18, 2005.
Premiere Magazine Online. February 17, 2005.
Variety Online. February 10, 2005.

TRIVIA

The dog's name in the first movie, *The Mask,* was Milo. In *Son of the Mask,* its name is Otis, a reference to *The Adventures of Milo and Otis.*

AWARDS

Golden Raspberries 2005: Worst Remake/Sequel

Nomination:

Golden Raspberries 2005: Worst Picture, Worst Actor (Kennedy), Worst Support. Actor (Cumming, Hoskins), Worst Director (Guterman), Worst Screenplay.

A SOUND OF THUNDER

Evolve or die.
—Movie tagline
Some Rules Should Never Be Broken.
—Movie tagline

Box Office: $1.9 million

Director/cinematographer Peter Hyams is no stranger to the science fiction genre, helming such films as *Capricorn One, End of Days, The Relic, 2010* and *Timecop* while Ray Bradbury, on whose classic short story this film is based, is certainly one of the best writers in the Sci-Fi field. Even with the eminent Ben Kingsley in a leading role, however, what sounds like a good idea on paper just doesn't come across onscreen. Where it goes wrong, however, it goes rather spectacularly wrong with its $52 million budget apparently not enough to buy the convincing special effects that this cautionary time-travel tale requires. The uneven pacing and jumbled storyline is either the byproduct of or the reason for what appears to have been an extensive editing job. And then there's the ridiculous white pompadour wig Kingsley is forced to wear in his role as the greedy corporate CEO whose business is to send people back in time on dinosaur safaris. All this makes for a certain kind of entertainment, although undoubtedly not of the nature the filmmakers intended. Grossing a dismal $1.8 million, on DVD *A Sound of Thunder* may enjoy a certain cult celebrity.

In the year 2055, Kingley's Charles Hatton runs the successful Time Safari company, a fairly literal moniker for a Chicago-based operation that sends people back in *time,* approximately 65 million years, for a disasaur *safari,* for a small fortune, of course. Dr. Travis Ryer (Edward Burns) leads these expeditions and dreams of reviving species of the earth's wild animals that have long since been wiped out. The only problem with Hatton's racket is that he has stolen the time-travel technology from physicist Dr. Sonia Rand (Catherine McCormack) who fears that in the wrong hands might have catastrophic repercussions.

Hatton thinks he's covered his bases by cleverly coming up with a way for his clients to kill dinosaurs and not actually change history. The dinosaurs are chosen because they are to die at any moment anyway and frozen liquid nitrogen bullets are used that will kill the beast but evaporate and leave no trace afterward. He's also created some basic time travel rules. Participants are not allowed to change anything in the past, leave any trace of evidence behind, and not supposed to bring anything back with them as any of these forbidden actions could seriously affect evolution.

As expected, someone eventually breaks the rules, bringing a small object back to the future. The repercussions Dr. Rand feared are now visited upon a hapless present day Chicago, which goes through a series of "time waves" that result in the Windy City being transformed into a prehistoric-looking jungle complete with all manner of dinosaurs, overly large bugs, and creepy giant bats. The main plot revolves around the adventures of Travis and Sonia, who travel back in time to try and fix what went wrong.

Apparently, much went wrong during the making of the doomed film, as well. Plagued by floods while on location in Prague, *A Sound of Thunder's* original production company also went bankrupt during post-production, thus delaying the film's release in order that money could be found to finish it. The lack of funds is perhaps one of roots of the film's problems but certainly not the only one.

Kingsley's performance ranges from over-the-top to phoned in. Burns and McCormack merely suffice. None of the actors are aided by the ridiculous dialogue they are often called upon to spew.

There has been much said in the press about the lack of quality of the film's FX. Roger Ebert of *The Chicago Sun-Times* said that the look of a particular effect "scarcely improves on the original *King Kong*" before devoting an entire paragraph to the multitude of other FX sins. *Variety* noted that the "chintzy special effects often make it appear the actors have been dropped into the middle of a video game" while the Los Angeles Times noted simply that "everything on the screen looks patently fake." However, unlike many other reviewers, Ebert did admit that there was "something endearing about the clunky special effects and clumsy construction" and that while he couldn't recommend the film, he could "appreciate it."

Hilary White

CREDITS

Travis Ryer: Edward Burns
Sonia Rand: Catherine McCormack
Charles Hatton: Ben Kingsley
Jenny Krase: Jemima Rooper
Clay Derris: August Zirner
Christian Middleton: Corey Johnson
Tech Officer Payne: David Oyelowo
Dr. Andrew Lucas: Wilfried Hochholdinger
Origin: Germany, USA, Czech Republic
Language: English
Released: 2005
Production: Moshe Diamant, Howard Baldwin, Karen Baldwin; Scenario Lane, Jericho; released by Warner Bros.
Directed by: Peter Hyams
Written by: Thomas Dean Donnelly, Joshua Oppenheimer, Gregory Poirier
Cinematography by: Peter Hyams
Music by: Nick Glennie-Smith
Sound: Manfred Banach
Editing: Sylvie Landra
Art Direction: Keith Pain
Costumes: Esther Walz
Production Design: Richard Holland
MPAA rating: PG-13
Running time: 102 minutes

REVIEWS

Boxoffice Online. September, 2005.
Chicago Sun-Times Online. September 2, 2005.
Entertainment Weekly Online. September 7, 2005.
Los Angeles Times Online. September 2, 2005.
New York Times Online. September 2, 2005.
Premiere Magazine Online. September 2, 2005.
Variety Online. September 1, 2005.

TRIVIA

Originally set for a 2003 release, production was slowed by the great floods of 2002 in Prague where filming took place.

THE SQUID AND THE WHALE

Joint Custody Blows.
—Movie tagline

Box Office: $4.8 million

The Squid and the Whale is about the pain of divorce, especially how it affects children. Written and directed by Noah Baumbach, the autobiographical film is miles away from the way this topic, usually relegated to dreary made-for-television movies, is commonly treated. Baumbach shows how his parents' separation affected him and his younger brother with wit, insight, and a dollop of self-pity.

In 1986, Bernard Berkman (Jeff Daniels) and Joan Berkman (Laura Linney) live in Brooklyn's Park Slope. This neighborhood of brownstones gives a terrific performance as Boston in Steven Spielberg's *The War of the Worlds* (2005). Bernard is a novelist who teaches at an unnamed college, while Joan is an aspiring writer. One of the many irritating details in about *The Squid and the Whale* includes showing Bernard meeting with his creative-writing class, while Joan does not seem to do anything. Only late in the film is it revealed that both have doctorates in literature. Does Joan teach, too?

Such an omission may be the result of filtering most of the film through the sensibility of Walt (Jesse Eisenberg), the Berkmans' teenaged son, for whom Joan has a minimal presence. Walt is very much his father's boy and is deeply resentful when he learns that Joan has had affairs, including one with the father of his best friend. The much younger, more sensitive and vulnerable Frank (Owen Kline) sides with his mother. Walt parrots Bernard's opinions about writers, including those he has not actually read. He tries to impress his classmate Sophie (Halley Feiffer) by saying Franz Kafka's *Metamorphosis* is Kafkaesque.

Bernard and Joan resemble the protagonists of *A Star Is Born* (1937, 1954, 1976). Bernard's career is going downhill. He claims he fired his agent because the man dared to disparage the New York Knicks, and he cannot interest a new one in his latest manuscript, a fact he keeps secret from everyone. At the behest of a former student, he gives a reading at the State University of New York at Binghamton, and only a handful of students show up. He moves into a shabby house because it is the best he can afford. When he accompanies Walt and Sophie to a restaurant and she offers to pay her share, he takes the money without hesitation, one of several splendid gestures handled perfectly by Daniels.

Meanwhile, Joan, who has only recently begun writing fiction, has a novel accepted for publication, with an excerpt in *The New Yorker*. Bernard finds out about her success only when it is mentioned casually by one of his students, Lili (Anna Paquin). The revelation shocks Bernard into even deeper despair. Baumbach's parents are Georgia Brown, once a *Village Voice* film critic, and Jonathan Baumbach, a novelist and critic who taught for many years at Brooklyn College.

Bernard is a humorless, pompous snob who refers to Fyodor Dostoevsky as one of his predecessors and belittles those who cannot appreciate foreign films. He says Elmore Leonard is the "fillet" of crime fiction and describes his new house as being the "fillet" of the neighborhood. When Bernard learns that Walt's high school class is reading Charles Dickens' *A Tale of Two Cities* (1859), he wonders why schools insist upon inflicting the lesser works of major writers upon their students. In this instance, however, he is right.

Bernard's overly critical manner has infected his sons. Walt tells Sophie that she has too many freckles, and Frank, who loves his mother, nevertheless tells her she is ugly. Walt wants a shortcut to success, and when he performs a Pink Floyd song in a school talent show, he passes it off as his composition. Frank's pain over the divorce leads to drinking beer and masturbating. Frank lightens up a bit after Ivan (William Baldwin), his tennis instructor, becomes his mother's new boyfriend. The goofy, laid-back Ivan is a breath of fresh air amid the self-absorbed, uptight Berkmans.

The Squid and the Whale is not quite as good as *Kicking and Screaming* (1995), the first film written and directed by Baumbach. That comedy about recent college graduates uncertain over what to do with their lives captures a good slice of the confusion experienced by young people in the 1990's. Baumbach co-wrote Wes Anderson's *The Life Aquatic with Steve Zissou* (2004), and Anderson serves as the producer of *The Squid and the Whale*. Baumbach's characters here more closely resemble the conflicted family in Anderson's *The Royal Tenenbaums* (2001). As with Anderson's work in general, as well as Woody Allen's, the Berkmans may strike some as unsympathetically neurotic. While some viewers may want to pinch their ears and tell them to shape up, this family is an accurate portrayal of what passes for life in portions of middle-class America.

Baumbach writes witty, perceptive dialogue, and the film is full of wonderful touches. On Walt's wall is a poster for Jean Eustache's *The Mother and the Whore* (1973), a sign of his pretentiousness and his viewing his mother as a slut. Like the Jean-Pierre Leaud character in Eustache's film, Walt is torn between two quite different women: the innocence Sophie and the manipulative Lili. Walt also has a poster of Alfred Hitchcock's *Psycho* (1960), again reflecting his negative view of his mother.

Bernard lusts after Lili, whom he takes in as a boarder. Daniels played Paquin's father in *Fly Away Home* (1996), making Bernard's request for fellatio, interrupted by Walt, a tad unsettling. Baumbach has a wonderful shot of Bernard and Walt gazing longingly at Lili with the same expression but unfortunately repeats it later.

As with *Kicking and Screaming*, Baumbach proves he has a good touch with actors. Kline, son of Phoebe Cates and Kevin Kline, is quite natural as the very messed-up Frank. (Kline's sister Greta appears briefly as Sophie's sister.) Eisenberg, the nephew from *Roger Dodger* (2002), conveys Walt's awkward intensity. Feiffer provides Sophie with a mixture of confidence and uncertainty. The career of Baldwin, no longer known as Billy, has been downhill since *Backdraft* (1991), but he is a revelation here, making Ivan's relaxed charm a delight. Daniels, in a role once intended for Bill Murray, is the film's center. A likeable but bland actor whose career highpoint is *Something Wild* (1986), Daniels is an unlikely choice for such an empty monster, but he is terrific. Daniels always shows Bernard's selfish mind at work and his subtle squirming at his dissatisfaction with himself.

The film's title refers to the display of a whale and a squid wrapped in conflict at the Museum of Natural History. (The display did not actually exist until 2000.) Walt says it frightened him as a child, but he was nevertheless fascinated by it. Baumbach intends the title to reflect both the characters' pain and the way he hopes audiences will respond to the film.

Michael Adams

CREDITS

Bernard: Jeff Daniels
Joan: Laura Linney
Walt: Jesse Eisenberg
Frank: Owen Kline
Lili: Anna Paquin
Ivan: William Baldwin
Sophie: Halley Feiffer
Carl: David Benger
Origin: USA
Language: English
Released: 2005
Production: Wes Anderson, Peter Newman; Clara Markowicz, American Empirical Pictures, Peter Newman-Interal
Directed by: Noah Baumbach
Written by: Noah Baumbach
Cinematography by: Robert Yeoman
Music by: Britta Phillips, Dean Wareham
Sound: Allan Byer
Editing: Tim Streeto
Costumes: Amy Westcott
Production Design: Anne Ross
MPAA rating: R
Running time: 88 minutes

REVIEWS

Boxoffice Online. October, 2005.
Chicago Sun-Times Online. November 4, 2005.

Entertainment Weekly Online. October 5, 2005.
Los Angeles Times Online. October 14, 2005.
New York Times Online. October 5, 2005.
Premiere Magazine Online. October 6, 2005.
Variety Online. January 25, 2005.

TRIVIA

The title refers to esteemed displays at the American Museum of Natural History.

AWARDS

L.A. Film Critics 2005: Screenplay
Natl. Bd. of Review 2005: Screenplay
N.Y. Film Critics 2005: Screenplay
Natl. Soc. Film Critics 2005: Screenplay

Nomination:

Oscars 2005: Orig. Screenplay
Golden Globes 2006: Actor—Mus./Comedy (Daniels), Actress—Mus./Comedy (Linney), Film—Mus./Comedy
Ind. Spirit 2006: Actor (Daniels), Actress (Linney), Director (Baumbach), Film, Screenplay, Support. Actor (Eisenberg)
Writers Guild 2005: Orig. Screenplay.

STAR WARS: EPISODE III—REVENGE OF THE SITH

Box Office: $380.2 million

There are two points of view to consider in this review of *Star Wars: Episode III—Revenge of the Sith.* There is that of the fan who wants to rave about how wonderfully the film completes the circle, which is contrasted with that of the cynical reviewer who needs to dissect the film for its cinematic validity. Examining the film on the basis of its merits and then briefly touching on its place within the Star Wars canon is perhaps the best way to reconcile these approaches.

Revenge of the Sith (third in the prequel trilogy of the larger six-film saga) manages to recapture some of the excitement of the first incarnation of *Star Wars,* yet never achieves the whimsicality of its predecessors. While it is closer to the film fans have wanted since George Lucas began revisiting the *Star Wars* universe in 1997, it is perhaps best suited for fans reared on the prequels (*The Phantom Menace* and *Attack of the Clones*) than those yearning to relive the good old days of the original trilogy. *Revenge of the Sith* is arguably the most accomplished of the more recent films (it may even rival *Return of the Jedi* for some fans). However, as has become the norm for Lucas, it still comes up short in two rather important categories—acting and writing. While neither have been utilized particularly well in any film in the entire series, the films of the earlier trilogy compensated with engaging characters and harrowing action scenes. Though *Revenge of the Sith,* like the other prequels, has its share of impressive sequences, there is ultimately no pertinent reason to pay attention until the next space battle or lightsaber duel.

This installment begins not long after the events of *Attack of the Clones.* The galaxy is being torn apart by the war between the Republic and the Separatists led by Count Dooku (Christopher Lee) and the droid commander, General Grievous. Chancellor Palaptine (Ian McDiarmid) has been kidnapped by Grievous, prompting a rescue by Anakin Skywalker (Hayden Christensen) and Obi-Wan Kenobi (Ewan McGregor) during which they have a final confrontation with Dooku. The film then begins to slow as various plot points are introduced: Padmé (Natalie Portman), to whom Anakin is secretly married, is pregnant with his child; the Jedi Council is having their doubts about the honesty of the Supreme Chancellor; Anakin, who is becoming increasingly impatient with his development as a Jedi is having recurring dreams foretelling Padmé's death; and the Chancellor has been poisoning Anakin against the Jedi. After several battle sequences, a few lightsaber duels, and a few too many expositional scenes, all this ultimately results in Anakin's conversion to the Dark Side of the Force and his transformation into Darth Vader.

The film excels in many production aspects. Trisha Biggar's costumes are simply amazing. As in the other prequels, Biggar's work bestows a tangible identity to the whims of George Lucas. The special effects work is impressive as well. There is something happening in every corner of every frame of the film. As A. O. Scott writes in the *New York Times,* "the sheer beauty, energy and visual coherence of *Revenge of the Sith* is nothing short of breathtaking." The score by *Star Wars*-stalwart John Williams utilizes elements of the original trilogy's music to link the two series in a subtle yet emotionally evocative way. Unfortunately, such fine production elements cannot compensate for a film lacking a concise, coherent narrative that services likeable characters.

The *Star Wars* saga is at its best when the action is fast and relentless. Whereas the delivery of such thrills in the original films was tightly structured, the prequels have achieved this only sporadically. *Sith* does succeed far more on that level than either *Phantom Menace* or *Attack of the Clones,* both of which were mired in far too many scenes of exposition (though *Revenge of the Sith* has its share of such scenes). The plot does not offer up dramatic tension so much as give a connect-the-dots story arc designed to bring the prequel trilogy to a close, tie up all loose ends, and lead directly into the original trilogy. That is a real problem for the film as there is simply too much information crammed into two-and-a-half hours. Breaking up the copious exposition with effects-laden action sequences does not change the fact that a lot of this information could have been played out in earlier films in a far more economical and satisfying way. Lucas's writing has not improved with experience. He purportedly enlisted the help of Tom Stoppard with this script, but the results are not there. The dialogue is witless and often downright silly. The characters are little more than vehicles used to get from one Industrial Light & Magic effect to another.

The lack of endearing characters has been a recurring problem in the prequels. A major reason for this is the inclusion of far too many characters in each film. While the original trilogy was confined to the exploits of Luke, Han, Leia, Chewbacca, and, to a lesser extent, R2-D2 and C-3PO, the prequels introduce new characters in every other scene. There are no central characters whose fate the audience can actually care about. In *Star Wars,* these characters were introduced and put in one perilous situation after another. The film was essentially a series of escapes. In the two subsequent films, those established characters were placed in increasingly dangerous, although sometimes separate, situations. The audience was emotionally attached to these essential characters. This is not the case with the new trilogy. There are so many characters and narrative strands, that the simplistic adventure stories which *Star Wars* once paid homage to are completely gone.

To say that the characters in *Revenge of the Sith* (and the other two prequels) are wooden is to do them a disservice as no one has ever gone to see a *Star Wars* film for the acting. The spectacle is the attraction. However, a certain amount of characterization is required to further the story along. Although the too-often referenced archetypes of Lucas's universe are present, the emotional climax of the story, the tragedy of Anakin Skywalker and his ascension to Darth Vader is handled so matter-of-factly that there is really very little emotional impact (with the possible exception of the nostalgia felt by an older fan remembering the first time they saw the original *Star Wars*). Only Ian McDiarmid as Palpatine and Samuel L. Jackson as Mace Windu are able to overcome the lackadaisical script and chew some scenery with any real bravado. While it is open to debate whether Lucas or the actor himself is to blame for Hayden Christensen's bland portrayal of Anakin in *Attack of the Clones* and *Revenge of the Sith,* Christensen does manage to breath some life into the character once he turns to the dark side. Perhaps Lucas was more comfortable directing him as the lord of an evil empire than as a confused young man.

When the original *Star Wars* premiered in 1977 (the title was later changed to *Episode IV—A New Hope* in conjunction with subsequent installments), Vincent Canby noted in the *New York Times* that when seeing the film, one should not "expect a film of cosmic implications or to footnote it with so many references that one anticipates it as if it were a literary duty." Rather, he concluded that the film was a "breathless succession of escapes, pursuits, dangerous missions, [and] unexpected encounters." That is the allure of *Star Wars,* at least to its intended audience. However, there seems to be a schism between those who feel the films still adhere to this principle and those who feel that Lucas lost his way at some point. It is disappointing that the same audience that finds nostalgia in such lines as "But I was going into Tosche Station to pick up some power converters!" grimace in dismay when similar, yet equally inept lines are delivered in the new films. The sad fact may be that the audience has grown up whereas the films have not. While the generation that came of age during the original trilogy may not feel that the same cultural resonance exists in *Revenge of the Sith* as it did in *A New Hope, The Empire Strikes Back,* or *Return of the Jedi,* that does not mean that those growing up with the current trilogy do not feel the same affection for the prequels. Indeed, fans are a devout yet surprisingly open-minded lot. As Kenneth Turan notes in the *Los Angeles Times*: "It's a tribute to the power and durability of the universe Lucas and company created in the first three *Star Wars* movies that we want to see this episode despite the tedium of the previous two." Perhaps the validity of the prequels and, for that matter, the "cultural resonance" of the entire *Star Wars* saga cannot be viewed without bias until a later, more objective, generation weighs in.

Although *Revenge of the Sith* is not a bad movie, it certainly is not as good as it could, or should, have been. Perhaps Ty Burr's theory, as put forth in the *Boston Globe,* holds true. He wrote that the first two films in the prequel trilogy were "so dramatically inept, so stiffly played, so humorlessly locked into its maker's private mythology that anything would look better in comparison." Indeed, through a series of exhilarating action sequences, the film mimics the excitement of the earlier trilogy, but a lack of understanding as to what made those films great—characters and a sense of fun—make for less than satisfying entertainment. In 1977 Vincent Canby applauded George Lucas for being able "to recall the tackiness of the old comic strips and serials he loves without making a movie that is, itself, tacky."

Unfortunately, that is precisely what the franchise has become—a tacky version of itself.

Michael J. Tyrkus

CREDITS

Obi-Wan Kenobi: Ewan McGregor
Anakin Skywalker: Hayden Christensen
Padme: Natalie Portman
Mace Windu: Samuel L. Jackson
Supreme Chancellor Palpatine: Ian McDiarmid
Chewbacca: Peter Mayhew
Senator Bail Organa: Jimmy Smits
R2-D2: Kenny Baker
C-3PO: Anthony Daniels
Count Dooku: Christopher Lee
Jar Jar Binks: Ahmed Best
Sio Bibble: Oliver Ford Davies
Commander Cody: Temuera Morrison
Queen of Naboo: Keisha Castle-Hughes
Tion Medon: Bruce Spence
Ki-Adi-Mundi & Nute Gunray: Silas Carson
Captain Typho: Jay Laga'aia
Governor Tarkin: Wayne Pygram
Mas Amedda: David Bowers
Yoda: Frank Oz (Voice)
Darth Vader: James Earl Jones (Voice)
General Grievous: Matthew Wood (Voice)
Origin: USA
Language: English
Released: 2005
Production: Rick McCallum; Lucasfilm Ltd.; released by 20th Century-Fox
Directed by: George Lucas
Written by: George Lucas
Cinematography by: David Tattersall
Music by: John Williams
Sound: Paul Brincat
Editing: Roger Barton, Ben Burtt
Art Direction: Ian Gracie, Phil Harvey
Costumes: Trisha Biggar
Production Design: Gavin Bocquet
MPAA rating: PG-13
Running time: 140 minutes

REVIEWS

Boxoffice Online. May, 2005.
Chicago Sun-Times Online. May 16, 2005.
Entertainment Weekly Online. May 18, 2005.
Los Angeles Times Online. May 15, 2005.
New York Times Online. May 16, 2005.
Premiere Magazine Online. May 10, 2005.
Variety Online. May 5, 2005.
Washington Post Online. May 18, 2005, p. C01.

QUOTES

The Emperor: "Anakin Skywalker, you are one with the Order of the Sith Lords. Henceforth, you shall be known as...Darth Vader."

TRIVIA

Both George Lucas and his son have cameos. General Grievous' coughing is actually George Lucas's own coughing, recorded after the director came down with a bad cough during production. Lucas's son Jett turns up as a young Jedi that rushes from the Temple towards Bail Organa's speeder during the Jedi Purge.

AWARDS

Golden Raspberries 2005: Worst Support. Actor (Christensen)
Nomination:
Oscars 2005: Makeup.

STAY

Between the worlds of the living and the dead there is a place you're not supposed to stay.
—Movie tagline

Box Office: $3.6 million

Ewan McGregor walking around looking confused in high-water pants is just one of the signs, but arguably the most interesting, that things are not really as they seem in *Stay*, an overly elaborately conceit from Swiss/German director Marc Forster (*Finding Neverland, Monster's Ball*) and writer David Benioff (*Troy*). Other dead giveaways that something weird is going on within this psycho-thriller include a suspicious number of twins and triplets among the extras, never-ending staircases, angled camera shots aplenty, people suddenly morphing into other people, and a blind Bob Hoskins who is miraculously cured near the film's twist ending that is supposed to explain all the aforementioned nonsense but merely serves to annoy. As Shlomo Schwartzberg summed up in his *Boxoffice* review, "Like David Lynch's *Mullholland Drive,* but to considerably less effect, *Stay* is interested in blurring the boundaries between reality and fantasy."

The basic plot within the gloomy, dark-and-forebodingness of it all, is a New York psychiatrist, Sam Foster (McGregor) who tries to prevent the death of a highly suicidal patient Henry Letham (Ryan Gosling).

Henry sees his death as inevitable and even knows the exact time and place (Saturday, The Brooklyn Bridge) where he will do the deed. Sam is able to track down the college student attending a lecture, and tries to reason with him. For his part, the guilt-wracked Henry says he indeed wants to live yet he must, in fact, take his own life because, he confesses, he is responsible for the death of his parents. When Henry disappears again, Sam is under the gun to find this troubled boy in the big city before he is able to go ahead with his plan to kill himself. Sam and Henry seem to be wearing very similar outfits at times as they move through scenes where the aforementioned twins and triplets, also dressed alike, loom ominously.

Complicating matters is Sam's girlfriend and former patient Lila (Naomi Watts), an artist who bears the scars of her own attempted suicide. She takes a deep interest in Sam's latest patient, urging Sam to "Tell him there's too much beauty to quit." A dreamy scene shows the multitude of paintings she is keen on are, in fact, by a Henry Latham—another good reason why Henry simply mustn't snuff it. When she actually starts calling Sam "Henry" and Sam starts reliving recent events over and over again, Sam starts to wonder if he's the one that's insane. When Sam tracks down Henry's mother (Kate Burton), she too mistakes him for Henry but Sam is informed later that Henry's mother is long deceased and Sam is, literally, at another dead end. There is also a waitress/actress named Athena (Elizabeth Reaser) that Sam finds who knew Henry and may hold some key to his disturbance but this weak subplot only serves as a device to allow Sam to ominously fall down an endless stairway after seeing her.

Insane or not, Sam is still determined to get to Henry. On the way to the bridge on the predestined evening, Henry pops up just long enough to claim that Sam's friend, the blind Dr. Leon Patterson (Hoskins) is actually his dead father, much to Sam and Leon's surprise. Leon wanders out into the rain where he is suddenly able to see again. Sam rushes to the bridge and all the plots loose ends are apparently tied together with the revelation that Henry and his family and girlfriend were killed in a car accident that actually happened at the beginning of the film and Henry is in sort of a netherworld between life and death. All the people in the film's plot, Sam, Lila, and the various bit players, are in fact onlookers at the site of the car crash that Henry, ala Dorothy in *The Wizard of Oz,* injected into his fantasy world where they became completely different characters. If he wasn't in such bad shape, you might expect him to sit up and say, "And you were there, and you, and you. Sam, I think I'll miss you the most." This also explains Sam's pants being too short: Sam is squatting down trying to help Henry, therefore Henry's laying-on-the-ground P.O.V. sees his pants ride up a few inches exposing his bare ankles. This, however, doesn't explain many of the other events that must merely get brushed under the "suspension of disbelief" banner.

Supports do what they can, and Hoskins certainly throws himself valiantly into his thankless role. Janeane Garofalo, as Sam's associate Dr. Beth Levy, was apparently directed to just act whacked-out on drugs and is convincingly dazed. The three talented lead actors, especially McGregor, do their best with the material they are given but unless handed a pen for a rewrite, are as hopelessly stuck as the not-quite-dead Henry within the flawed framework of *Stay.*

Hilary White

CREDITS

Sam Foster: Ewan McGregor
Lila Culpepper: Naomi Watts
Henry Latham: Ryan Gosling
Dr. Beth Levy: Janeane Garofalo
Dr. Ren: B.D. Wong
Dr. Leon Patterson: Bob Hoskins
Mrs. Letham: Kate Burton
Officer: Michael Gaston
Business Man: Mark Margolis
Athena: Elizabeth Reaser
Security: Sherriff Kennelly
Origin: USA
Language: English
Released: 2005
Production: Arnon Milchan, Tom Lassally, Eric Kopeloff; New Regency; released by 20th Century-Fox
Directed by: Marc Forster
Written by: David Benioff
Cinematography by: Roberto Schaefer
Music by: Asche & Spencer
Sound: James Sabat
Editing: Matt Chesse
Art Direction: Jonathan Arkin
Costumes: Frank Fleming
Production Design: Kevin Thompson
MPAA rating: R
Running time: 99 minutes

REVIEWS

Boxoffice Online. October, 2005.
Chicago Sun-Times Online. October 21, 2005.
Entertainment Weekly Online. October 19, 2005.
Los Angeles Times Online. October 21, 2005.

New York Times Online. October 21, 2005.
Variety Online. October 20, 2005.

QUOTES

Sam Foster: "If this is a dream, the whole world is inside it."

TRIVIA

Director Marc Forster revealed in an interview with MTV.com that the reason why Sam's trousers are always shown as too short is because Henry's view of Sam is when he is crouching down, thus causing his trousers to pull up.

STEALTH

Fear The Sky.
—Movie tagline

In *The Fast and the Furious*, director Rob Cohen showed that he understood action in a way that few directors did. His action sequences were indeed both fast and furious, capturing the excitement of being behind the wheel in a street race (or at least, what most of us imagine it to be.) In *Stealth*, it is as though he has forgotten everything he knew.

It is not that he lacks the raw materials. He has the usual good looking cast, with Josh Lucas, Jessica Biel and Jamie Foxx onboard. And the subject matter, fast navy planes, certainly seems ripe for *Fast and Furious* treatment. But somehow Cohen gets bogged down in slow moving scenes with boring exposition (and it is not like the story is that complex in the first place), romance between two pilots and even a half-hearted debate about the ethics of video game-like warfare. Probably most of the target audience for *Stealth* would be happy to see two hours of planes flying fast and blowing things up. Anything that is not that is just taking up wasted space. The movie runs nearly two hours long, indicating that Cohen should have spent a lot more time in the editing room.

The plot, by W. D. Richter, concerns an elite group of stealth fighter pilots, Lt. Ben Gannon (Lucas), Kara Wade (Biel) and Henry Purcell (Foxx). The expert trio, led by manly Captain George Cummings (Sam Shepard), fly around the world on secret missions, doing things like blowing up wayward scud missiles and killing various warlords.

Their happy gang is threatened when Cummings announces that a new member will be added to the team. The new member turns out to be EDI (pronounced Eddie), a high-tech non-manned robotic plane. EDI talks in that preternaturally calm, yet vaguely ominous computer voice that movie computers since *2001's* HAL tend to have.

Gannon has a "bad feeling" about EDI and, since the higher-ups seem to entrust many matters of national security to Gannon's gut, they should listen to him on this one too. But alas they do not. EDI gets hit by lighting and turns evil. It would seem that such an advanced plane, one that can easily withstand enemy fire, could also deal with a little weather, but apparently not. It not only downloads "all" the songs from the Internet, but also decides it will start taking out targets on its own. Foxx, being a black guy in a movie (the movie was pre-*Ray* fame), is the first to go.

Now Gannon and Wade must contend with saving the world from this plane, and equally important, figure out their relationship. They are enamored with each other, but do not want to jeopardize their jobs by fraternizing. This leads to an improbable and semi-upsetting scene where Gannon risks a nuclear war just to save his beloved Wade. Yes, it is romantic, but still...

There is a bit of discussion in the film about the morality of warfare that resembles a video game. (Gannon thinks it is bad.) But the words ring hollow given what happens in the film. Exotic locales (and the people living there), including spots in Alaska, North Korea and Rangoon, are blown up with barely a thought to the lost lives. When a cloud of radioactive dust covers a poor peasant village, Wade, the emotional one (she is a woman, after all), helpfully suggests that some medics will need to be sent there. Presumably, they can just rinse off the radioactivity with some antiseptic wipes. In a rare passionate outburst from a critic, who tends to keep things light and apolitical, Ty Burr of *The Boston Globe*, wrote, "For a movie to pretend, in the face of the deaths of tens of thousands of Iraqi men, women, and children directly or indirectly caused by our presence there, that we can wage war without anyone *really* getting hurt isn't naive, or wishful thinking, or a Jim-dandy way to spend a Saturday night at the movies. It's an obscenity."

Most other critics did not like the film either. Roger Ebert of *The Chicago Sun-Times*, wrote, "*Stealth* is an offense against taste, intelligence and the noise pollution code" adding, "It might be of interest to you if you want to see lots of jet airplanes going real fast and making a lot of noise, and if you don't care that the story doesn't merely defy logic, but strips logic bare, cremates it and scatters its ashes." Manohla Dargis of *The New York Times* wrote that Cohen "has almost extinguished all the good will he built up from *The Fast and the Furious*." And Christian Toto of *The Washington Times* was a rare critic with a kind word for the movie, writing blissfully of the "big, bold action. Beautiful stars who could double for Bally's 'after' models. Dialogue that will never make it into any AFI quotation list."

Jill Hamilton

CREDITS

Lt. Ben Gannon: Josh(ua) Lucas
Lt. Henry Purcell: Jamie Foxx
Lt. Kara Wade: Jessica Biel
Capt. George Cummings: Sam Shepard
Capt. Dick Marshfield: Joe Morton
Keith Orbit: Richard Roxburgh
Lt. Aaron Shaftsbury: Ian Bliss
Executive Officer: Nicholas Hammond
EDI: Wentworth Miller (Voice)
Origin: USA
Language: English
Released: 2005
Production: Laura Ziskin, Mike Medavoy, Neal H. Moritz; released by Sony Pictures Entertainment
Directed by: Rob Cohen
Written by: W.D. Richter
Cinematography by: Dean Semler
Music by: BT (Brian Transeau)
Sound: David Lee
Music Supervisor: Bob Badami
Editing: Stephen E. Rivkin
Art Direction: Richard Hobbs
Production Design: J. Michael Riva, Jonathan Lee
MPAA rating: PG-13
Running time: 121 minutes

REVIEWS

Boxoffice Online. July, 2005.
Chicago Sun-Times Online. July 28, 2005.
Entertainment Weekly Online. July 27, 2005.
Los Angeles Times Online. July 29, 2005.
New York Times Online. July 29, 2005.
Premiere Magazine Online. July 29, 2005.
Variety Online. July 28, 2005.
Washington Post Online. July 29, 2005, p. C01.

QUOTES

Lt. Kara Wade: "Just tell me you love me, you pussy."

STEAMBOY

Katsuhiro Otomo's *Akira* (1988) was one of the most influential Japanese animated films of the 20th century and one of the first anime films to be brought to the states. It has enjoyed cult status for many years and people have been looking forward to Otomo's follow-up film with anticipation. Although he's been mainly a screenwriter for other animated films including *Metropolis* (2002), he has been working on his latest feature for the past ten years and returns to the director's seat with *Steamboy* after sixteen years. The results however are unfortunately mixed.

The film is undeniably beautiful to watch. The mixture of traditional hand-drawn 2-D animation with modern computer animation mesh together seamlessly. The rendering of 19th century Victorian England which is the film's setting is so well detailed and awe-inspiring in its depth of field it is a testament to Otomo's artistry and talent. The production design is as mesmerizing as it is at the same time overblown. It soon becomes clear however, that he has spent years slavering over the visual detail and look of the film to the detriment of its story.

The film opens in a cave in Alaska: Russian America, where Lloyd Steam and his son Edward are preparing to mine and capture a pure form of steam energy. A group of dark suited men watch with anticipation from scaffolding. There is an explosion and Edward is severely injured. The setting moves to Manchester, England and a title card reveals that the year is 1866. We are introduced to a young boy mechanical genius named Ray Steam who is the son Edward and grand son of Lloyd, both of whom are thought to be working on research in the United States. A package arrives at the house of Ray's mother, a box containing a strange round metal object and blueprints to some mysterious device. It also contains a note. It is a warning from Lloyd, telling Ray that he must prevent the "steam ball" and blueprints from falling into the wrong hands, at all costs. The "wrong hands" turn up in the form of two burly men dressed in black, who want to take the "steam ball" and blueprints to their boss at the O'Hara Foundation. Ray's grand father Lloyd shows up at the house, quickly tells Ray that Edward is dead and urges Ray to run. He tells him that there is somebody waiting for him on the train passing through town. (Whether Lloyd was actually at the house at that moment is made confusing in a scene later in the film and may make the viewer wonder if this was a continuity mistake.)

Ray runs and the bad guys chase him in what will be one the films many spectacular, but overlong and noisy set pieces. Ray jumps into his favorite mode of transportation, a steam-powered gyroscope unicycle contraption and a chase ensues. Ray makes his way to a moving train, closely followed by the two O'Hara Foundation men in a souped up steam powered car. The car it seems can ride the rails and soon Ray has to abandon his unicycle as it is crushed between the car and train engine. He climbs aboard "Indiana Jones" style as the bad guys are thrown into the water by the locomotive, and finds himself in one of the passenger cars sitting across from a man named Robert Stevenson. Turns out that Stevenson was a colleague of Lloyds and was coming here to meet with him. In the note, Ray was told to give the "steam ball" to Stevenson. Just as he is about to hand it over a zeppelin with a giant mechanical claw rips the roof off the train car and takes Ray and the "steam ball" to parts unknown.

He is taken to the London headquarters of the O'Hara Foundation where he is re-united with his father Edward, alive, but now half-man half machine. Displaying a mental instability and megalomanical personality disorder of Darth Vader proportions, he takes Ray on a tour of the complex he calls the "Steam Palace" via an art deco elevator. Coming along for the ride is the president of the O'Hara Foundation, a blond girl Ray's age named Scarlett. (Scarlett O'Hara must have been a funny joke that Otomo just couldn't resist, but her character is never developed beyond the obnoxiousness than her name suggests, and has no real reason to be in the film.) As the open air elevator travels toward the top of the palace Edward explains to his son that he and Lloyd have spent years working together with the O'Hara Foundation to find a stable energy source. Three years ago they finally succeeded in confining steam pressure. And with that energy, they could power an entire city.

They arrive at the top where a beautiful panorama of London can be seen from the observation dome. As they all gaze at the amazing vista, the father reveals (in a speech evoking Dr. Evil crossed with any Bond villain) that he wants to release man from nature's energy and that man has finally conquered nature, and with the Steam Palace he can now use science to control the world and propel civilization forward. The God metaphor is helpfully backed up as Edward gives his speech while becoming a human eclipse, blocking the sun with his body, causing sun rays to shine off his back. But just to make sure the message wasn't missed, Otomo helpfully cuts to a shot of a cross patch worn by a British military official.

But he didn't bring Ray up here to here him wax on, turns out he needs his help too. He tells him that even though he and Lloyd spent years working on the palace together, Lloyd has abandoned Edward leaving him without someone talented enough in steam engineering to help him finish it. He wants to finish it time for the Great Exhibition at the Crystal Palace in London just a few days away. Ray agrees to help his father get the "Steam Palace" ready. However, as Ray is checking on a malfunctioning valve in the heart of the complex, he finds his grandfather Lloyd who is trying to sabotage it. He tells Ray that this is a machine of mass destruction that Edward plans on selling to the highest bidder at the Exhibition and was not the original intended purpose. He tells Ray that he Edward were duped by the O'Hara Foundation in creating it. That the O'Hara Foundation is a military arms producer and they have built weapons using the steam technology that he and Edward help perfect. He also tells Ray that Edward has lost his mind and that he may destroy London with this palace unless something is done to stop it.

Meanwhile, outside, Robert Stevenson has gathered the British armed forces to attack the O'Hara Foundation and take the weapons he knows they have stored inside. He launches an attack and The O'Hara Foundation answers with a counter-attack using some of their new weapons. It's also an opportunity for military representatives from several major powers to se the new products, in case they want to purchase them. The doors of the Foundation building open up and out come steam powered soldiers to steam powered flying machines that drop bombs. A mini-war with Britain has begun.

This causes Edward to put the final part of his master plan in motion: he will use the "Steam Palace" to destroy London and show everyone the power of science. The façade Foundation walls collapse and fall away revealing a giant metal and steel behemoth several stories high and several blocks wide. It releases large amounts of steam allowing it to float above the city as it heads towards the Exhibition.

What follows is a protracted forty minutes of noise and images that look spectacular and are amazing to behold, as the Behemoth destroys most of the London cityscape while the British military tries to stop its rampage. During all of this Ray and his grandfather try to shut down the engines before it explodes. As exciting as it is, after the first ten minutes of this carnage the eye becomes distracted and bored. In addition Lloyd and Edward carry on a debate on the dangers of science being used for warfare. Amid the beautifully realized animated noise and fury of explosions, the heavy-handed anti-war message is drowned out by Otomo's glorification of it.

In the end, Lloyd and Edward go down with their creation, allowing time for Ray and Scarlett to escape. They watch from a rooftop as the behemoth sinks to the bottom of the Thames. But Otomo plays it safe, showing that Lloyd and Edward have escaped and are safe. This negates any notion of those characters sacrificing themselves, allowing for their redemption (presumably having destroyed millions of dollars worth of property and killing man Londoners), and turns it into a Darth Vader escape. The message would have been more clear (if not less loud) if their deaths were left ambiguous.

David E. Chapple

CREDITS

James Ray Steam: Anne Suzuki (voice)
Dr. Eddie Steam: Masane Tsukayama (voice)

Dr. Lloyd Steam: Katsuo Nakamura (voice)
Scarlett O'Hara: Manami Konishi (voice)
Robert Stephenson: Kiyoshi Kodama (voice)
David: Ikki Sawamura (voice)
Freddie: Susumu Terajima (voice)
Origin: Japan
Language: English, Japanese
Released: 2005
MPAA rating: PG-13
Running time: 126 minutes

REVIEWS

Boxoffice Online. March, 2005.
Chicago Sun-Times Online. March 18, 2005.
Entertainment Weekly Online. March 22, 2005.
Los Angeles Times Online. March 18, 2005.
New York Times Online. March 18, 2005.
Premiere Magazine Online. March 17, 2005.
Variety Online. September 29, 2004.
Washington Post Online. March 25, 2005, p. C01.

TRIVIA

With a budget of roughly $20 million, the most expensive Japanese animated film to date.

SWIMMING UPSTREAM

The pride of a nation. The heart of a champion.
—Movie tagline

Dora Fingleton, a long-suffering mother of five, sits dejectedly on the site of a beached shipwreck on the Brisbane shore trying to comfort her son Tony, lately berated by his father, her abusive, alcoholic husband. The shipwreck is an apt visual parallel for the dysfunctional Fingleton family, who nonetheless manage to succeed despite the constant challenges arising from the alcoholism and bullying of the family patriarch. Much more than a sports drama, this true story about Australian swimming champion Anthony Fingleton is an engaging family saga produced and adapted by Fingleton from the autobiography written by himself and his sister Diane Fingleton. Best known for directing videos for the likes of Elton John, AC/DC, and Duran Duran, helmer Russell Mulcahy, who also directed 1986's *Highlander*, proves himself able in the realm of complex character portrayal films.

The second eldest among five children growing up in the 1950s, the young Tony (played by Mitchell Dellevergin) differentiates himself from his three other brothers by being an accomplished pianist and favorite of his mother Dora (Judy Davis). This leads to bullying and beatings by his older brother Harold Jr. (Kain O'Keefe as a child and David Hoflin as a teenager)—an accomplished footballer and favorite of their dad—and derision from his macho, longshoreman father Harold (Geoffrey Rush). Tony, desperate but at a loss at how to please his surly dad, invites Harold to join him at the local pool where he and the brother he's closest with, John (Thomas Davidson), spend most of their free time. The pool offers a sort of cleansing for Tony and an escape from his troubled home life. A place where he and the sympathetic John share the disgust at their father's behavior as well as a special handshake they developed in their camaraderie. And it is there that Harold accidentally discovers that Tony has real potential as a backstroke swimmer. Tony fatefully points out that John is probably an even better swimmer than he is, and Harold immediately takes them both on for proper training. Harold, however, clearly favors John and it is he whom he "chooses" to be the champion.

Jesse Spencer plays the handsome teenage Tony and Tim Draxl the teen John, who have now been training together with their demanding father for a number of years. Harold has built a virtual shrine to John's swimming accomplishments over the years—erecting a heraldic portrait of him on the wall towering over his trophies and medals with Tony's accomplishments all but ignored. Harold has long since resumed the drinking career he temporarily put on hold when he fathered his five children, leading to violent rows occurring regularly in the Fingleton home, with Dora the punching-bag of choice. Loyal in the extreme, she rationalizes his behavior with the knowledge of Harold's nightmarish upbringing, the child of a sometime prostitute who was forced to witness his mother with her various customers and allusions to Harold being abused by these men as well. He was also prevented from playing football for Australia in his younger days due to the Depression, which all contributes to his pushing his boys to athletic excellence but also resenting the success of Tony. Dora protects her children as best she can against these drunken outbursts but begins to lose the battle as she attempts suicide with an overdose of pills. She is rescued by her children who tell her she can't go because they need her. Later, Tony gets the full brunt of Harold's anger, telling him he wished he'd never been born. Confused and hurt, Dora says to Tony "You have to be strong. Up here." gesturing to her head. His entire life his father encouraged physical strength but his mother gave him the key to real strength. In that touching scene on the shore, Tony tells Dora that she's his hero—a term boys usually reserve for their fathers but one that his mother amply deserves.

The numerous swimming contests that occur between John and Tony are normally friendly, beginning with their usual good luck handshake, but Harold abruptly switches John to the backstroke—Tony's forte—and trains John privately now in a manipulative strategy to get John to win, unbeknownst to Tony. Competing in high level tournaments all over Australia with the likes of notable Aussie swim champs Murray Rose (Remi Broadway) and Dawn Fraser (Melissa Thomas), who also appear in cameos in the film, the boys both excel but Tony is the one with the drive to succeed. John takes time off from training, partly in arrogance that no one can beat him and partly because he's just sick of it at times. Tony, however, never falters and continues to rigorously train himself alone, eventually excelling over John regularly now. Despite that fact, Harold still ignores Tony's victories and refuses to attend Tony's swim meets now that John has all but given up the sport. The friction that Harold has fostered between his once close-knit sons is increasingly apparent as the friendly handshakes evaporate, much to the chagrin of the sensitive Tony.

Strong throughout the first two thirds of the film, it loses steam in the final act. Tony becomes the number one backstroke swimmer in the country but Harold still refuses to give him the approval he craves. After a particularly bad fight, Dora decides enough is enough and kicks Harold out for good. Wisely taking his mother's advice about becoming strong mentally, Tony opts for a full scholarship at Harvard, the alma mater of his hero John F. Kennedy, rather than a chance to compete in the 1964 Olympics. The film ends on a triumphant note, with a jubilant Tony getting his fastest time ever in the Harvard pool. In a postscript, it is also noted that Harold, on the road to recovery at the time of Tony's departure to the States, won his battle with alcohol and remained friends with Dora although the two never reconciled.

The talented, chameleon-like Rush takes to the role of a regular, working class Aussie like a fish to water and shows glimpses of the better man he might have been if only he had not been so scarred by his childhood. Davis plays the put-upon Dora with characteristic strength and depth. Spencer and Draxl have believable brotherly chemistry that turns a bit sour in the end, with Spencer especially able to convey the hurt his father inflicts upon him without resorting to overacting. Brother Ronald Fingleton (Robert Quinn and later Craig Horner) and sister Diane (Keeara Byrnes and later Brittany Byrnes) ably lend support, mostly in the form of cheering Tony on in his live and televised matches.

Fingleton went on to produce the films *Drop Dead Fred* (1991) and *Blood Bath* (1976) before mining his own story for this effective and moving account of his early life. Filmed by award-winning Australian cinematographer Martin McGrath, production designer Roger Ford and costumer Angus Stathie all add to the picture's striking and believable 1950s/60s look.

Hilary White

CREDITS

Harold Fingleton: Geoffrey Rush
Dora Fingleton: Judy Davis
Tony Fingleton: Jesse Spencer
Billie: Deborah Kennedy
Tommy: Mark Hembrow
Dawn Fraser: Melissa Thomas
John Fingleton: Tim Draxl
Harold Fingleton Jr.: David Hoflin
Ronald Fingleton: Craig Horner
Diane Fingleton: Brittany Byrnes
Young Tony: Mitchell Dellevergin
Young John: Thomas Davidson
Young Harold Jr.: Kain O'Keefe
Young Ronald: Robert Quinn
Young Diane: Keeara Byrnes
Mack: Des Drury
Dawn Fraser's coach: Dawn Fraser
Murray Rose: Remi Broadway
Reporter: Murray Rose
Origin: Australia
Language: English
Released: 2003
Production: Howard Baldwin, Karen Baldwin, Andrew Mason, Paul Pompian; Crusader Entertainment; released by Hoyts Distribution
Directed by: Russell Mulcahy
Written by: Anthony Fingleton
Cinematography by: Martin McGrath
Music by: Reinhold Heil, Johnny Klimek
Sound: Andrew Plain, Greg Burgmann
Editing: Marcus D'Arcy
Art Direction: Laurie Faen
Costumes: Angus Strathie
Production Design: Roger Ford
MPAA rating: PG-13
Running time: 113 minutes

REVIEWS

Boxoffice Online. February, 2005.
Los Angeles Times Online. February 4, 2005.
New York Times Online. February 4, 2005.
Variety Online. November 5, 2002.

SYRIANA

Everything is connected.
—Movie tagline

Box Office: $30.4 million

The complicated process through which American companies acquire oil rights in the Middle East may not seem a likely topic for a commercial American film, but writer-director Stephen Gaghan turns this subject into an engrossing thriller with *Syriana.* By showing how the interests of wealthy Arabs, American businessmen, and the United States government intertwine, Gaghan offers a compelling morality tale. Like Steven Soderbergh's *Traffic* (2000), written by Gaghan, *Syriana* is an illustrated civics lesson but has more emotional impact than the earlier film.

In loosely adapting *See No Evil: The True Story of a Ground Soldier in the CIA's War on Terrorism* (2002) by former Central Intelligence Agency officer Robert Baer, Gaghan juggles several interrelated stories. The most prominent plot revolves around Bob Barnes (George Clooney), an aging, overweight CIA agent in the Middle East first seen selling two missiles to Arabs for reasons that never become completely clear. His bosses back in Langley, Virginia, consider Barnes a loose cannon and try unsuccessfully to tie him down to a desk job.

Bryan Woodman (Matt Damon), an energy analyst for a company based in Switzerland, makes a deal with Prince Nasir (Alexander Siddig), a reformer who wants the American military and oil companies out of Kazakhstan. Nasir's scheming younger brother, Prince Meshal (Akbar Kurtha), tries to undercut his efforts in favor of a big payoff from the merging oil companies run by Jimmy Pope (Chris Cooper) and Leland Janus (Peter Gerety). The unscrupulous Pope is pure evil, hunting exotic animals on his Texas ranch.

Washington lawyer Bennett Holliday (Jeffrey Wright) seems at first to have a conscience. Working for Pope, Holliday is made uneasy by the moral equivocations and back-stabbings involved in smoothing the way to the merger only to find scapegoats to take the raps for the sins of others. Holliday's alcoholic father (William Charles Mitchell) keeps popping up to remind the lawyer—and the audience—of his failings. Gaghan constantly jumps back and forth between ethically gray areas and clear-cut cases of black and white, with most of the businessmen—and they are all men—and government employees on display easily finding justifications for their often despicable actions. One group of businessmen claims it be devoted to restoring Iran to freedom when clearly all it wants is the country's oil reserves.

The most controversial aspect of *Syriana* is the story of Wasim Khan (Mazhur Munir), a young Pakistani immigrant who, along with his father (Shadid Ahmed), loses his job in a Middle Eastern oil field—Gaghan can be frustratingly vague about geography—and slowly becomes an Islamic fundamentalist and, eventually, a terrorist. Though some have criticized Gaghan for trying to grapple with why such people become terrorists, he is clearly attempting to put a human face on a devotion to faith and politics that most Westerners have difficulty understanding. This is not quite the same as justifying acts of terrorism. Regardless, this strand of the plot, though sincere, seems more mechanical and arbitrary than the rest of the film.

Several reviewers, notably David Edelstein of the online journal Slate, have complained that *Syriana* is difficult to follow. Gaghan presents most of his narrative in short scenes conveying bits of information about the role of big business in the world of geopolitics and about the characters' complex motivations, with perhaps too much about the families of Barnes and Woodman, with his too obviously symbolic name. There have been a plethora of American films since the mid-1970's, with *Forrest Gump* perhaps being the worst offender, that bombard the viewer with images, ideas, and emotions like a Rorschach test into which almost anything can be read. It is not clear whether the foggy aspects of *Syriana* are the result of Gaghan's ineptness, though Traffic is fairly easy to follow, significant details lost as the film was edited down to two hours and six minutes—many scenes end abruptly—or the filmmaker's deliberate intent to keep the viewer off balance until matters come into sharp, deadly focus at the end.

Again as with Traffic, *Syriana* is blessed with excellent performances. Clooney famously gained thirty pounds to make Barnes seem more like a put-upon everyman. He gives Barnes a shambling walk, almost a waddle, to emphasize the burden under which the agent operates. Clooney sustained a serious back injury during one of the film's most devastating scenes, when Barnes is brutally tortured. Once again, exactly why he is being tortured is not all that clear. Barnes calls his tormentor (Mark Strong) Jimmy, but the man, who speaks with an American accent, calls himself Mussawi. Is he an Arab, an Arab-American, or a CIA agent or former agent? He has obviously worked with Barnes in the past.

Damon's Woodman is a variation on the rather naïve man caught up in a whirlwind of chaos he does so well in *The Bourne Identity* (2002) and *The Bourne Supremacy* (2004). With his tightly wound attorney, Wright offers the exact opposite of his effusive neighbor from *Broken Flowers* (2005). William Hurt makes a strong impression as Barnes' friend and advisor. Though it is somewhat lazy casting Christopher Plummer as the sinister head of Holliday's legal firm, the actor does such oily villains better than almost anyone.

The outstanding performance is that of Siddig, who plays a similar idealistic Arab prince in *A Dangerous Man: Lawrence After Arabia* (1990). Siddig, whose uncles include a former Sudanese prime minister and actor

Malcolm McDowell, effortlessly portrays Nasir's disgust at his family's eagerness to ignore the best interests of their people. With his intense, penetrating eyes, Siddig makes Nasir the film's true moral center.

As a cynical look at how business and government subvert morality to achieve goals they convince themselves are ethically justifiable, *Syriana* is a throwback to those paranoid thrillers of the 1970's: *The Conversation* (1974), *The Parallax View* (1974), *Three Days of the Condor* (1975), *and All the President's Men* (1976). With the exception of the somewhat contrived *The Parallax View*, these films are thought-provoking and entertaining, as is *Syriana*. Even those who object to its political message cannot deny that in its final scenes it humanizes some complex issues, but it does require some effort to stick with Gaghan's narrative emotionally and intellectually to get to the bitter, pessimistic payoff. Yet in an era when not only filmmakers but even serious novelists seem to give in and explain things to ill-informed audiences with short attention spans, Gaghan's belief in his viewers' ability to rationalize is admirable.

Michael Adams

CREDITS

Bob Barnes: George Clooney
Bryan Woodman: Matt Damon
Bennett Holiday: Jeffrey Wright
Jimmy Pope: Chris Cooper
Stan: William Hurt
Danny Dalton: Tim Blake Nelson
Julie Woodman: Amanda Peet
Dean Whiting: Christopher Plummer
Prince Nasir Al-Subaai: Alexander Siddig
Prince Meshal Al-Subaai: Akbar Kurtha
Robby Barnes: Max Minghella
Donald: David Clennon
Tommy Barton: Robert Foxworth
Mussawi: Mark Strong
Wasim Khan: Mazhar Munir
Saleem Ahmed: Khan Shadid Ahmed
Bennett's Father: William C. Mitchell
Farooq: Dadral Sonnell
Leland Janus: Peter Gerety
Division chief: Jayne Atkinson
Terry: Jamey Sheridan
Origin: USA
Language: English, Arabic
Released: 2005
Production: Jennifer Fox, Michael Nozik, Georgia Kacandes; Section Eight, Participant Production, 4M Film; released by Warner Bros.
Directed by: Stephen Gaghan
Written by: Stephen Gaghan
Cinematography by: Robert Elswit
Music by: Alexandre Desplat, Cynthia Weil
Sound: Petur Hliddal
Editing: Tim Squyres
Art Direction: Laurent Ott, Alan Hook, Andrew Menzies, Daran Fulham
Costumes: Louise Frogley
MPAA rating: R
Running time: 126 minutes

REVIEWS

Boxoffice Online. December, 2005.
Chicago Sun-Times Online. December 9, 2005.
Entertainment Weekly Online. November 22, 2005.
Los Angeles Times Online. November 23, 2005.
New York Times Online. November 23, 2005.
Premiere Magazine Online. November 23, 2005.
Variety Online. November 30, 2005.
Washington Post Online. December 9, 2005, p. C01.

QUOTES

Bryan Woodman: "It's running out, and 90 percent of what's left, is in the Middle East. This is a fight to the death."

TRIVIA

George Clooney, due to the 35 pounds he gained for the film, suffered a spinal injury during a stunt that caused him severe migraine headaches (which prevented him from doing publicity for *Ocean's Twelve* (2004)), and had him bedridden for a month. The injury was eventually corrected with surgery, and Clooney has since publicly regretted his weight gain.

AWARDS

Oscars 2005: Support. Actor (Clooney)
Golden Globes 2006: Support. Actor (Clooney)
Natl. Bd. of Review 2005: Adapt. Screenplay
Nomination:
Oscars 2005: Orig. Screenplay
British Acad. 2005: Support. Actor (Clooney)
Golden Globes 2006: Orig. Score
Screen Actors Guild 2005: Support. Actor (Clooney)
Writers Guild 2005: Adapt. Screenplay
Broadcast Film Critics 2005: Support. Actor (Clooney), Cast.

T

THREE...EXTREMES

From the Nightmares of 3 Horror Masters.
—Movie tagline

Three...Extremes (2005) is a compilation of three short horror films from three of the hottest film directors in Asia, and is a sequel to the similar compilation film *Three* (2002). The newest version brings directors from Hong Kong, South Korea and Japan to tell 40 minute horror stories that attempt to raise the bar on the current state of Asian horror to the extreme, and go beyond the expectations of genre fans of the Asian Horror movement. It is a trilogy of terror that is intended to shock the most jaded horror fan, and may be too much for the rest. And while each of these films is extreme in its subject matter, they all share the same common passion, artistry, and commitment that is sorely lacking in contemporary Western horror films, and further proves why American audiences are gravitating to Asian horror to a great degree. Each film (examining the monster within) while different in tone, adheres to rule uncommon in its Western counterparts, there can be no horror without meaning.

In "Box" Japanese director Takashi Miike turns in a creepy tale centering on a young Japanese novelist (Kyoko Hasegawa) suffering from recurring nightmares of being buried alive on a snow covered hilltop. The dreams always stop at the same moment, as she is being buried she claws at the thick clear plastic that covers her entire body. Things change one morning when, after handing her latest hand-written manuscript to her agent he rewards her with a vintage music box. After he leaves she opens the box and while the music plays, she sees a young Japanese girl standing in the darkened corner of the room, who she thinks is the ghost of her young twin sister Shoko, who died tragically when they were kids. It is at this point where Kyoko's horrifying past begins to catch up with her.

Miike's tale is the more restrained of the bunch, and straddles the line between familiar Japanese horror film creepiness, and art-house melodiousness. The film is quite different than his seminal horror work "Audition" (1999), absent of much of the gruesome visuals, replaced with more psychological themes, nonetheless is just as horrifying in its implications. It is Miike's most subtle and meditative film to date.

Subtlety, however is not a word one would use to describe the second film, "Dumplings" by Chinese director Fruit Chan. This segment could at its core, be considered a social commentary on the desperate pursuit of youth, and the lengths that some women will go to regain and retain it. Miriam Yeung is an aging actress who is having difficulty finding work and a husband who no longer desires her. In fact he barely hides the fact that he is constantly having affairs with much younger women. She seeks out Mei (Bai Ling) who she has heard makes dumplings with a secret ingredient that will restore her youthful features and make her husband desire her again. What the secret ingredient is a disturbing indictment on the childbirth restrictions in China and while sound design was not a major factor in the Miike's tale; here Chan's film finds it an absolute necessity. The over cranked sound effects of Yeung crunching down on each dumpling is quite chilling and may have some filmgoers walking out of the theatre, especially when they find out what she is actually eating (and later addicted to).

The third film "Cut" by South Korean director Park Chan-wook, is a self-reflexive and gruesome examination of the theme of revenge that Park has visited many times before, most notably in his stunning feature *Oldboy* (2004). A popular director of horror films wakes up one morning on the set of his latest film, bound to a wall by a giant red rubber band while his wife is bound and also gagged, her hands glued to the piano she sits in front of. A little girl is also in the room, bound, gagged, and blindfolded, and whimpering on the couch. Turns out the person holding them hostage is a disgruntled former extra that wants to teach the wealthy and successful director a depraved lesson in humility. He gives the director a choice: strangle the little girl or every five minutes he will cut off one of his wife's fingers, who is a famous and successful concert pianist. As the husband struggles with the variation of his "Sophie's Choice," director Park seeps in the theme of class struggle amid the blood, to give this Poe-ish psychodrama a deeper resonance.

David E. Chapple

CREDITS

Mei ("Dumplings"): Ling Bai
Li's Maid ("Dumplings"): Paulina Lau
Lee ("Dumplings"): Tony Leung Ka Fai
Connie ("Dumplings"): Meme Tian
Ching ("Dumplings"): Miriam Yeung Chin Wah
Old Hairdresser ("Dumplings"): Sum-Yeung Wong
Vomiting Woman ("Dumplings"): Kam-Mui Fung
Nurse ("Dumplings"): Wai-Man Wu
Wang ("Dumplings"): Chak-Man Ho
Kate ("Dumplings"): Miki Yeung
Kate's Mother ("Dumplings"): So-Fun Wong
Gynaecologist ("Dumplings"): Kai-Piu Yau
Director ("Cut"): Byung-hun Lee
Stranger ("Cut"): Won-Hee Lim
Director's Wife ("Cut"): Hye-jeong Kang
Actor in School Girl Uniform ("Cut"): Dae-yeon Lee
Assistant Director ("Cut"): Gene Woo Park
Kyung-Ah ("Cut"): Mi Mi Lee
Old Man Mannequin ("Cut"): Gyu-sik Kim
Vampire Actress ("Cut"): Jung-ah Yum
Kyoko ("Box"): Kyoko Hasegawa
Yoshii/Higata ("Box"): Atsuro Watabe
Kyoko (Age 10, "Box"): Mai Suzuki
Shoko (Age 10, "Box"): Yuu Suzuki
Circus Member ("Box"): Mitsuru Akaboshi
Origin: Hong Kong, Japan, South Korea
Language: Japanese, Korean
Released: 2004
Production: Peter Chan, Fumio Inoue ("Box"), Naoki Sato ("Box"), Shun Shimizu ("Box"), Ahn Soo-Hyun ("Cut"); Applause Pictures Limited
Directed by: Fruit Chan ("Dumplings"), Takashi Miike ("Box"), Chan-wook Park ("Cut")
Written by: Haruko Fukushima ("Box"), Lilian Lee ("Dumplings"), Chan-wook Park ("Cut"), Bun Saikou ("Box")
Cinematography by: Christopher Doyle ("Dumplings"), Jeong-hun Jeong ("Cut"), Koichi Kawakami ("Box")
Music: Kwong Wing Chan ("Dumplings"), Koji Endo ("Box")
Editing: Fruit Chan ("Dumplings"), Jae-beom Kim ("Cut"), Sang-Beom Kim ("Cut"), Yashushi Shimamura ("Box")
Art Direction: Pater Wong ("Dumplings")
Costumes: Sang-gyeong Jo ("Cut"), Dora Ng ("Dumplings")
MPAA rating: R
Running time: 126 minutes

REVIEWS

Boxoffice Online. October, 2005.
Chicago Sun-Times Online. October 28, 2005.
Entertainment Weekly Online. October 26, 2005.
Los Angeles Times Online. October 18, 2005.
New York Times Online. October 28, 2005.
Variety Online. January 11, 2005.
Washington Post Online. October 28, 2005, p. C01.

QUOTES

Mei: "You're rich but I'm free."

3-IRON
(Bin-jip)

Kim Ki-duk's quixotic dark comedy from South Korea, *3-Iron,* offers a refreshing variation on contemporary filmic realism and its preoccupation with mirroring the tangled technologies of today's urban landscape. By eschewing surface elements that would particularize its narrative as taking place in modern-day Seoul, Ki-duk's film attains an universal stature.

Such transcendence permeated his previous film to be released in the U.S., *Spring, Summer, Autumn, Winter and Spring* (reviewed in the 2005 Annual), which was set in and around a Buddhist monastery in the middle of an unbelievably tranquil landscape. *3-Iron* however manages to convey a magically real plane of experience not so much by representing it but by presenting its essence filmically. This must be the first romantic comedy ever in which the couple in love never say a word to each other. More important, they don't feel the need to. We come away from the film feeling that the technologies of instant communication which are rapidly developing are taking us further away from communicating in a meaningful manner. Ki-duk's two leads speak to each other through their charged silences, gestures and facial expressions.

Such a narrative and stylistic approach takes the film onto a terrain that becomes the cinematic correlative for the seemingly vacuous plays of Samuel Beckett. The German critic Adorno pointed out that those plays did not require a metaphysical content, since their very form and substance was metaphysical. The same argument would apply to *3-Iron*. But Ki-duk seems to be drawing upon yet another theatrical tradition also, that of the medieval Noh drama, in which the aim was to directly raise the consciousness of the audience, who were assumed to have come into the theater with their minds buffeted by the pace of the world outside. The Noh literally slowed down the action, so that a mere movement of the hand could take a few minutes. The text of the play, comprising the words spoken, could thus be very short, but more importantly, each play evoked a transcendent plane of reality linked to the flow of seasons, whose essence was reflected in the story of the play. No matter what the human dilemma, it was seen as part of a flow. Not coincidentally, Ki-duk's previous film, from its title on down, was structured along these lines. *3-Iron* also moves through the essences of various seasons.

The marvel that Ki-duk achieves is to translate this abstract ideal into the concereteness of a filmic narrative, so that one leaves the hall directly affected by the film's formal impact before one has had a chance to mull over the thematic aspects of its narrative.

The film's title can be seen to be derived from a type of golf club used for long lateral strokes that the protagonist, Tae-suk (Jae Hee), a rootless aspiring golfer uses for practice. The strokes wielded intersect with life and so the title can also be taken to mean three nodal points and a triangular flow of power between them. Tae is clearly at the apex of this triangle since he is the only one who is free to pursue his whims and desires. His only possession in life, it would appear, is his flashy motorcycle.

The film opens with Tae sticking restaurant flyers onto the front doors of houses in an upscale neighborhood. Tae's strategy of acquiring power is simple but original. After the affixing, Tae returns to see which stickers are still in place, taking that to mean that the occupants of the house must be away. Tae is never wrong as he then gets to work cracking the lock and treating himself to the delights of the elite life, if only for a few fleeting moments.

In one such house, we watch, intrigued, as Tae does his thing in silence. First he checks the answering machine in order to know just how long the occupants will be away. He then brushes his teeth, showers, takes what fits him from the closet, fixes himself a sandwich from what he finds in a well-stocked fridge. After snapping a picture of himself with his own digital camera, he falls asleep watching a large-screen TV. We then see him washing his clothes on the bathroom floor, then hanging them up to dry on a balcony. Before the occupants can return to find an intruder on their property, Tae is out of there.

The jolt to Tae's modus operandi does not come from the law or any hi-tech security system but from the second nodal point in the flow of power that the film sets out to depict. Sun-hHwa (Lee Seung-yeon) is a young, beautiful photographer's model trapped in a dead-end marriage. She is suffering in silk when she upsets Tae's mental equilibrium just as he thinks there's no one in the opulent house he has broken into. Through mere glances, they find themselves on the same side, having to fight the third nodal point of the triangle, Lee Min-kyu (Kwon Hyuk-ho), Sun's bespectacled businessman-husband on the cusp of middle age. As Tae spies on Lee mistreating Sun, he lures Lee out onto his backyard where he aims golf balls at him to the point that Lee is knocked to the ground and writhing in pain. Sun then uses the opportunity to run off with Tae.

As Tae and Sun proceed to follow the housebreaking template that has proven so successful, the elite niches that they inhabit take on a metaphorical significance, representing a hi-tech world shorn of its users. Their romance blossoms through the most subtle of means. As they are silently sipping tea in a house in the Chinese quarter of town, Sun extends her foot to rub it against his. Tae then responds by kissing her.

As a counterpoint to their intimacy, the theme of violence now intrudes as a force from within Tae as well as from the world around him. First, a golf ball he hits strikes the windshield of a car, giving the female occupant a bloody face. Tae looks on, as a bystander, as shocked as we are by what he's done. Then, in a decrepit building, Tae and Sun break into a hovel to find an old man lying dead on the kitchen floor, a pool of blood near his head. Tae and Sun tie him up in a ceremonial shroud and give him a decent burial in the yard. For doing so, Tae gets charged with murder. An autopsy soon reveals that the victim had died of lung cancer.

However, Tae's nemesis now takes the form of the corrupt Detective Cho (Joo Jin-mo) who releases Tae from police custody by abandoning him, handcuffed, under a bridge, where Lee is waiting to strike him with golf balls. When Cho tries to taunt Tae further, the latter chokes him, using his handcuffs. For this offense, Tae is put into prison. Worse, the violence erupting from within him results in him being thrown into solitary confinement.

The film now takes off in a mystical direction. Tac starts to practice his own brand of exercises energizing his mind, body and spirit. More specifically, he tries to turn into a ghost of himself, attempting to contract his presence into a kind of ethereality that would allow him to fly like a martial arts expert. Tae's aim, as becomes evident, is not to inflict harm upon the enemy as much as to be able to hide under his very nose. He first tries it out on a guard, hiding behind him when he enters the cell. The guard is bewildered until Tae's shadow gives him away. Tae then suspends himself from a skylight, only to be brought down by repeated strikes from a baton.

Sun also embarks on a quasi-mystical pursuit of her own. She returns to a house she had broken into with Tae in the Chinese quarter. This time, in the presence of the occupants, she makes herself comfortable on an ornate sofa and goes to sleep. The kindly couple who live there can only watch in disbelief mixed with a trace of wonder. Ki-duk cuts to a close-up of a vat of water lilies, linking the tranquility emanating from Sun to that in nature.

When Tae is released, he proceeds to get his back on those who have been cruel to him, most notably Detective Cho. As the latter gets out of his car in a parking lot building, Tae gets him with a volley of golf balls so that Cho is struck down and left whimpering. Lee, who has been warned of Tae's release, prepares to confront the young man he last saw, not the ghost that Tae has become.

As Sun sneaks out of bed in the middle of the night, Lee gets up and goes after her. After having turned away from him repeatedly, she now turns round and says to Lee: "I love you!" Lee, on his part, is overjoyed and embraces her. He cannot see that Tae is right behind him and that Sun is kissing him literally behind his back. At breakfast the next morning, Tae is right behind Lee, sharing the food without Lee having a clue. When Lee rushes off to work, Tae and Sun once again have the place to themselves.

A closing image shows their feet together on a weighing scale indicating their weight as zero, a testament to the weightlessness of their conjoined desire. The film ends with a title that could well serve as a credo for its magic realism: "It is hard to tell whether the world we live in is a reality or a dream."

Vivek Adarkar

CREDITS

Detective Cho: Ju Jin-mo
Sun-hwa: Lee Seung-yeon
Tae-suk: Jae Hee
Min-kyu: Kwon Hyuk-ho
Jailer: Choi Jeong-ho
Son of Old Man: Lee Jo-suk
Origin: South Korea, Japan
Language: Korean
Released: 2004
Production: Kim Ki-duk Film; Chungeorahm Film, Cineclick Asia, Happinet Pictures; released by Sony Pictures Classics
Directed by: Kim Ki-duk
Written by: Kim Ki-duk
Cinematography by: Jang Seung-baek
Sound: Kim Yong-hun
Editing: Kim Ki-duk
Art Direction: Ju Jin-mo
Costumes: Gu Jae-hyeon, Jeong Jin-uk
MPAA rating: R
Running time: 95 minutes

REVIEWS

Boxoffice Online. May, 2005.
Entertainment Weekly Online. May 4, 2005.
New York Times Online. April 29, 2005.
Variety Online. September 12, 2004.

TRIVIA

Director Kim Ki-duk wrote this screenplay in a month, filming lasted 16 days, and the editing was done in 10 days.

THUMBSUCKER

Box Office: $1.3 million

Mike Mills stylish but tedious feature directorial debut delves into the overly familiar territory of family dysfunction and addiction in suburban America. With its Freudian title, this unsure mix of drama and comedy is agonizingly slow paced with drawn out montages of teen angst set to the dark, introspective songs of Elliott Smith. Written by Mills from a novel by Walter Kirn, the dialogue is often fake and forced with many one-liners attempting to answer life's big questions, often from the overly self-aware teenagers at the film's center. Eventually, the whole thing sinks into a feel-good coming-of-ager as clichéd as any big Hollywood blockbuster as the once angst ridden teen meets cute on the way to his bright new destiny at the film's close. The film is not without its pleasures, however, and cineastes will appreciate the carefully crafted shots and enviable attention to production design, generally good performances all-around, and the film's biggest surprise, Keanu Reeves stealing every scene he's in with his best role in years.

The film starts promisingly enough in the neat suburban Oregon home of Justin Cobb (Lou Taylor Pucci), a quirky teen with a quirky habit. Long-haired, shy, and sensitive, Justin self-soothes by indulging in the nasty titular habit even at age 17. It's easy to see why when we meet his self-absorbed parents, whom he addresses by their first names. His mother Audrey, a nurse, is quietly concerned about Justin while currently obsessed with winning a contest on the back of a cereal box: a date with TV star Matt Schramm (Benjamin Bratt). His father Mike (Vincent D'Onofrio) is a failed football hero turned sporting goods store manager who humiliates Justin whenever he finds him engaging in his infantile pasttime. At school, Justin is suitably ostracized but he's entranced by his fellow debate-team member, the comely Rebecca (Kelli Garner), whose pale complexion and pouty lips perfectly mirror Justin's. Despite some innocent teasing, she sees him as merely a friend.

Justin finds help kicking his habit in an unlikely place: the orthodontist. The long-haired, New Ager Dr. Perry Lyman (Keanu Reeves) guesses at the source of Justin's angst and offers to hypnotize the boy to cure him of his addiction to his thumb. It's one of the film's comic highlights, as Reeves riffs on his own image, deadpanning that Justin find his inner "power animal" for strength. The fact that the timid teen's power animal looks exactly like Bambi is not a shock. "You don't need your thumb and your thumb doesn't need you," Lyman's whispery, soothing voice intones. It turns out he's right: Justin is miraculously cured...for awhile. His method for dealing with stress now stymied, Justin's angst becomes even worse.

The troubled teen turns from holistic to more traditional medicine when he is diagnosed at school with having Attention Deficit Disorder (ADD) and put on medication. His parents are wary about medicating their son on a regular basis, but Justin sees this as the easy answer to all his personality problems. Happily popping pills daily, Justin immediately shows a dramatic change, reading *Moby Dick* in one sitting. In no time, Justin, now amazingly studious and articulate, becomes the star of the debate team and pride of its teacher, Mr. Geary (Vince Vaughn). Conversely, Rebecca has quit the team and become involved with the school's chief stoner.

Winning debate trophy after trophy, the now overly-ambitious Justin, who has gone from his usual grungewear to a button-down shirt and tie, turns into a monster, taking a condescending tone with his parents and teachers alike. The film goes awry here too, with the medicated Justin suddenly much too interested in his parents relationship as well as his mother's new job that has her working at a celebrity rehab clinic that currently houses the recovering Matt Schramm. Acting like a self-actualized 35-year-old, he's constantly probing his parents for the key to their motivations, speculating on their personal history for the explanations.

Another highly improbable plot point involves Justin's relationship with Rebecca. Realizing his current state of mind is more than a tad unhealthy, Justin ditches the prescription meds and lets Rebecca introduce him to her drug of choice, marijuana. Soon the two are happily stoned and experimenting with sex until the petulant and manipulative Lolita explains he's just a pawn in what she dubs her "teenage experiment" to become more sexually experienced.

Justin has other things on his mind, however, and is convinced his mother is having an affair with Schramm after he finds a signed picture of him thanking Audrey for "saving his ass." In a disgusting flashback, we, along with the surprised Justin, find this quote is quite literal as the hippie-like Schramm meets up with Justin to clear things up. What Justin eventually learns through all his experiences is that everyone's got an addiction, whether it's a thumb, or drugs, or celebrity, or just an idea.

Justin's life takes a final unexpected turn when he's accepted to New York University, where he sent a highly fictionalized application during his brief with overachievement. Visiting Dr. Lyman before his big move East, Justin finds him completely changed, as well. His holistic tendencies are as thoroughly discarded as his New Agey views on life. The chain-smoking orthodontist now tells Justin that he was all wrong about everything and that "The trick is living without an answer."

Borrowing heavily from the likes of Wes Anderson and Jared Hess, instead of an outsider teen tale like *Rushmore* or *Napolean Dynamite,* Mill's promising but ultimately muddled *Thumbsucker* comes off more like an arty after-school special.

Hilary White

CREDITS

Justin Cobb: Lou Taylor Pucci
Audrey Cobb: Tilda Swinton
Mr. Geary: Vince Vaughn
Mike Cobb: Vincent D'Onofrio
Dr. Perry Lyman: Keanu Reeves
Matt Schramm: Benjamin Bratt
Rebecca: Kelli Garner

Joel Cobb: Chase Offerle
Origin: USA
Language: English
Released: 2005
Production: Anthony Bregman, Bob Stephenson; This Is That Cinema Go-Go
Directed by: Mike Mills
Written by: Mike Mills
Cinematography by: Joaquin Baca-Asay
Music Supervisor: Brian Reitzell
Editing: Angus Wall, Haines Hall
Art Direction: Walter Cahall
Costumes: April Napier
Production Design: Judy Becker
MPAA rating: R
Running time: 97 minutes

REVIEWS

Boxoffice Online. September, 2005.
Chicago Sun-Times Online. September 23, 2005.
Entertainment Weekly Online. September 14, 2005.
Los Angeles Times Online. September 16, 2005.
New York Times Online. September 16, 2005.
Premiere Magazine Online. September 15, 2005.
Variety Online. January 28, 2005.

QUOTES

Justin Cobb: "We have to overcome the idea that everyone is the same."

TRIVIA

Scarlett Johansson was originally set to play Rebecca Crane but dropped out shortly before filming began.

TIM BURTON'S CORPSE BRIDE

(Corpse Bride)

Rising to the occasion.
—Movie tagline
There's been a grave misunderstanding.
—Movie tagline

Box Office: $53.3 million

Isn't it about time for Tim Burton to stop brand-naming his own movies eponymously? *Tim Burton's Corpse Bride* follows squarely in the tradition of *Tim Burton's The Nightmare Before Christmas,* and both title attributions are wholly unnecessary. Would we want *Macbeth* to be titled *William Shakespeare's Macbeth?* I don't see why. No one else is doing the kind of thing Tim Burton is doing, at least not with any credibility, so Tim, give your self-referentiality a rest.

Besides, *Corpse Bride* is plenty innovative on its own. Its look returns to the combination of grotesquery and frivolity, the mix of mild terror and sentimentality, that Burton skewered together in *The Nightmare Before Christmas,* and that are really a hallmark of all his films, including *Edward Scissorshands, Big Fish,* and *Charlie and the Chocolate Factory.* But this story, cobbled together by a squadron of screenwriters and animated with the help of co-director *Mike Johnson,* defies comparison to any other movies. And so does the visual style and execution. It's quite enchantingly unique.

As in many of Burton's films, the main characters here live in a world that looks like Victorian England on a gloomy day, or like something out of the dark and dreary palette of *The Cabinet of Dr. Caligari.* And they are almost all grotesques in appearance—most of them with stick-figure arms and legs and various distorted bodies. Some of them also, as is the custom of the current era of animation, suggest in some ways a facial caricature of the actors who voice them. Thus, Victor Van Dort, with his slicked-back dark hair and moody, sullen appearances, looks a lot like Johnny Depp. No wonder he talks like him too.

With a splendid opening ditty by the remarkable Danny Elfman (a frequent Burton collaborator, as is most of the cast), the bones of the nice little plot are made clear from the get-go: Victor is to be wedded to a woman he's never met, Victoria Everglot (voice of Emily Watson), in an arranged marriage designed to give both sets of parents what they want: the Van Dorts, a fish-market owner and wife by trade, a chance at fame by association with aristocracy, and the Everglots, who are land-rich and cash-poor, a needed infusion of capital to better match their social status. It's an amusing conceit that the fallen-on-hard-times nobility can't match the earning power of the fishmongers.

Victoria's parents are a match of opposites: an imposingly tall, not to say statuesque, and witch-faced dominatrix of a mother, with a hairdo that looks like a flamethrower; and a little rubber ball of a rotund, wizened father, who don't look at all like Joanna Lumley and Albert Finney, who voice them. Tracey Ullman and Paul Whitehouse play Victor's parents, who are also a match of a big, loudmouthed woman and a cowering man.

And they are all puppets, given life and movement by the time-consuming process of stop-action animation. It's completely unexpected that, in the year 2005, the *Corpse Bride* was released just weeks before *Wallace and Gromit: The Curse of the Were-Rabbit,* two films using difficult techniques of animation that were in use long before anyone dreamed of computers. Sharp eyes will catch a tribute of sort on a piano nameplate that Depp's Victor plays early in the film: Harryhausen, a reference to stop-motion pioneer Ray Harryhausen. It's one of many cinematic references sprinkled throughout this flick, as Burton likes to do. There's the Victor/Victoria pairing, most obviously, and a Jiminy Cricket sort of conscience that's actually a maggot in the Corpse Bride's head, a delightfully macabre twist on Disney cartoon animal sidekicks.

The Bride appears, in standard horror-movie fashion, by rising up out of the ground. She does so because the inept and ridiculous Victor, who has repeatedly muffed his vows at his wedding rehearsal, successfully recites them in the woods at night, using a tree branch as a prop, but the branch turns out to be the skeletal extension of the Corpse Bride's arm. Suddenly the mild-mannered, innocuous, and bumbling Victor finds himself transported into the nether world, where a rollicking wedding party of skeletons is holding forth at a place that somehow reminds you of the bar from *Star Wars.*

It's strange that the Corpse Bride (voiced by Helena Bonham Carter) has no name, but it's also strange and good fun that her world of the dead is inhabited by jive-talking, music-playing, dancing and singing skeletons, and others that are pirates and other fairly recognizable cartoon characters—or caricatures of common cartoon characters—along with a head waiter who is nothing but a detachable head. With Elfman spinning out a couple more numbers, Burton dazzles with his morbid, hilarious imagination, and somehow manages to spin a rather creaky, implausible plot into something of a minor miracle.

The rules for going back and forth between the real world and the Corpse Bride's realm are a little fuzzy and inconsistent, and so is the belated discovery by the elder of the underworld, himself nothing more than a head with a scraggly beard and reading glasses, that Victor's marriage is not official until he makes the vow in the land of the living and pledges himself to commit suicide and join his bride in death for all eternity. Don't try to make logical sense of any of this, but it works surprisingly well, as Victoria ends up in the clutches of the same villain who was responsible for the Corpse Bride's plight, a wed-'em-and-slay-'em evildoer who is in it for the money. I'm not giving anything away that any sharp-eyed ten-year-old wouldn't grasp immediately. It's clear who the villain is, because he looks like a standard vaudeville villain.

The result of all this machination is a delightful mess of entertainment that is part vaudeville, part melodrama, completely outrageous, and somehow sweetly endearing. In other words, a Tim Burton tour de force. But unlike the excesses that plague some of his other efforts, which drag on too long and end up in murky mawkishness, the *Corpse Bride* wraps up in a snappy 76 minutes, just right for an animated feature, and at the first signs of flabbiness or extravaganza it moves smartly along to the next scene or musical number. The last half of the movie could have used another Elfman number or two, but that's a minor complaint; Burton is sure-footed here, avoiding some of his customary traps, and even his usual sentimentality here is somehow miraculous: he manages to make audiences care about the three central characters even though the entire undertaking is ridiculous and unnerving, and one of the women is, after all, a corpse.

Maybe this welcome economy was due to budgetary and time constraints, for Burton used virtually the same ensemble as *Charlie and the Chocolate Factory,* which was filmed and released in close proximity to this movie. But then Watson, Carter, Depp, and some of the others involved here are part of Burton's usual acting stable anyway. *Corpse-Bride* avoids completely the curse of *Charlie:* that of taking a minor trifle of a story and taking it much too seriously. Here, Burton takes his eerie, fantastic, little snatch of a story for what it is—a small romp through the world of grotesque imagination. The stop-motion animation is fluid and wondrous to behold, the backgrounds are rich and spare by equal turns, and a few of the scenes will remind the cinephile of silent motion picture scenes. And in many ways, the *Corpse Bride* is a homage to the history of film, especially the kind of movies made in the days before special effects made everything possible, the kind of film that uses exaggeration, melodrama, and all these lost dramatic arts to concoct the fantastic out of the ordinary.

Michael Betzold

CREDITS

Victor Van Dort: Johnny Depp (Voice)
Corpse Bride: Helena Bonham Carter (Voice)
Victoria Everglot: Emily Watson (Voice)
Nell Van Dort/Hildegarde: Tracey Ullman (Voice)
Maudeline Everglot: Joanna Lumley (Voice)
Finnis Everglot: Albert Finney (Voice)
Barkis Bittern: Richard E. Grant (Voice)
Elder Gutnecht: Michael Gough (Voice)
Paster Galswells: Christopher Lee (Voice)
Black Widow Spider/Mrs. Plum: Jane Horrocks (Voice)
General Bonesapart: Deep Roy (Voice)
Bonejangles: Danny Elfman (Voice)

William Van Dort/Mayhew/Paul the Head Waiter: Paul Whitehouse (Voice)
Maggot/Town Crier: Enn Reitel (Voice)
Emil: Stephen Ballantyne (Voice)
Solemn Village Boy: Lisa Kay (Voice)
Origin: Great Britain, USA
Language: English
Released: 2005
Production: Tim Burton, Allison Abbate; Laika Entertainment; released by Warner Bros.
Directed by: Michael Johnson, Tim Burton
Written by: John August, Caroline Thompson, Pamela Pettler
Cinematography by: Pete Kozachik
Music by: Danny Elfman
Sound: Sandy Buchanan, Paul Langwade, Rupert Coulson
Editing: Chris Lebenzon, Jonathan Lucas
Art Direction: Nelson Lowry
Production Design: Alex McDowell
MPAA rating: PG
Running time: 75 minutes

REVIEWS

Boxoffice Online. September, 2005.
Chicago Sun-Times Online. September 23, 2005.
Entertainment Weekly Online. September 14, 2005.
Los Angeles Times Online. September 16, 2005.
New York Times Online. September 16, 2005.
Premiere Magazine Online. September 16, 2005.
Variety Online. September 7, 2005.

QUOTES

Elder Gutknecht: "Why go up there when people are dying to get down here?"

TRIVIA

The first stop-motion feature to be edited using Apple's Final Cut Pro.

AWARDS

Natl. Bd. of Review 2005: Animated Film.

TOUCH THE SOUND

Among other things, *Touch the Sound* challenges the accepted belief that film emphasizes the visual over the aural. This cinematic study of sound, music, and rhythm is far from ideal, but it is much more engaging and enlightening than many narrative features about music or musicians.

Thomas Riedelsheimer (director of 2001's *Rivers and Tides,* about nature-artist Andy Goldsworthy) employs a minimal story as the "glue" to many striking set-pieces. Riedelsheimer follows the Scottish-born percussionist Evelyn Glennie as she travels from Manhattan to Scotland to California and other locations in a quest for sounds that inspire her to write and perform her unique style of music. During her visit to her ancestral home in Scotland, Glennie discusses her childhood, when she became hearing-impaired, and how her early difficulties guided, informed, and determined her life and career choices. Along the way, Riedelsheimer interviews many of Glennie's friends, colleagues, and music students.

For all its heartfelt charms, *Touch the Sound* may disappoint musicians and non-musicians alike. Those without an appreciation for music will chafe at the film's slow, pensive pace and the generously protracted instrumental passages. On the other hand, the musically inclined will not necessarily welcome how Riedelsheimer "distracts" from the performances by cutting away to lovely visual images of nature (it is as if the director didn't quite trust the music or the performances to carry the day).

Still, this "sound journey" (as the subtitle of the film dubs it) features much to praise and recommend. Glennie makes an interesting if somewhat peculiar object of study and her return to her family farm halfway through the film is surprisingly moving (it is there she talks about her troubled childhood while looking at old photos). More significantly, Glennie's vocational pursuit is absorbing—both in theory and practice. Glennie seems to asking whether or not all sounds should be considered some form of music. And, if not, she questions when a sound become music. These are but two areas Glennie explores through her work. Abetting the philosophical conundrums, Glennie's experimental pieces are often distinctive and intricate, and the climactic composition she performs in a cavernous loft-workspace is both poignant and haunting (though her work is categorized as "classical" and has won a Grammy Award, it blends both popular and alternative motifs).

Touch the Sound begins with an equally striking sequence, as the soundtrack heightens and highlights the various noisy objects and the dissonant New York City street sounds evolve into a harmonious symphony. This introduction compares favorably with the breathtaking opening to Rouben Mamoulian's *Love Me Tonight* (1932), where the hustle-and-bustle sounds of Paris at dawn produce a comparable effect.

Despite all the movie's artistic highpoints, the 2005 critical response was mixed, though Stephen Holden's September 7 review in *The New York Times* was favorable: "*Touch the Sound* concludes with a sustained meditation for percussion and guitar, in which Mr. Frith, stationed on an elevated platform on the other side of the room, elicits plaintive, shivery cries from an electric guitar while Ms. Glennie taps out a deep, quiet, musical prayer on the marimba. This is synergy of a high order." Likewise, Kenneth Turan called the film "potent and imaginative" in his September 7 *Los Angeles Times* review, but Shlomo Schwartzberg's *Box Office On-line* blurb of September was mixed: "[Glennie's] music, often using found objects, is similarly one-note; Riedelsheimer indulges her with overly lengthy—and tiresome—scenes of her performing. *Touch the Sound's* virtues lie in his superb direction, expertly using sound and image to show how a deaf person would relate to the world. It's a cinematically masterful portrait even if its subject falls short of expectations." Finally, Joshua Kosman's September 23 *San Francisco Chronicle* review was an out-and-out pan: "...there is a maddening sense of dislocation through much of the movie—a feeling that genuinely fascinating questions have been squeezed out by woo-woo philosophizing and material (like Glennie's brief return to the family farm) of only minor import."

Actually, if there is any real flaw in the film, it is that there is just too much background and talkiness. Sure, without this *Touch the Sound* might not have ended up feature length, but so what? Shouldn't the music speak for itself, once the premise is established? Also, on a technical level, the close-ups of Glennie are just too tight at times, chopping off sections of her head and face. Otherwise, Riedelsheimer admirably directs, photographs and edits this non-fiction work, which may be overly niche to impatient audiences but charming and gratifying to others.

Eric Monder

CREDITS

Origin: Germany, Great Britain
Language: English
Released: 2004
Production: Stefan Tolz, Leslie Hills, Trevor Davies; Skyline Production
Directed by: Thomas Riedelsheimer
Cinematography by: Thomas Riedelsheimer
Music by: Evelyn Glennie, Fred Frith
Sound: Marc von Stuerier, Gregor Kuschel, Christoph von Schoenburg, Hubertus Rath
Editing: Thomas Riedelsheimer
MPAA rating: Unrated
Running time: 107 minutes

REVIEWS

Boxoffice Online. September, 2005.
Chicago Sun-Times Online. October 14, 2005.
Los Angeles Times Online. September 9, 2005.
New York Times Online. September 7, 2005.
Variety Online. October 12, 2004.

TRANSAMERICA

Life is more than the sum of its parts.
—Movie tagline

Life is a journey. Bring an open mind.
—Movie tagline

It is undeniable that Felicity Huffman's performance in *Transamerica* is the kind that justifiably garners critical acclaim and year-end recognition. Playing a preoperative male-to-female transsexual, Huffman is virtually unrecognizable in the role of Bree (formerly Stanley), a soon-to-be woman trying desperately to put her life in order and be the person she feels she was meant to be. The fact that the role itself is physically extreme and almost seemingly calculated to garner awards, however, should not detract from what Huffman achieves and the risk she was taking. In a lesser actress's hands or under the wrong direction, the character could have been a freak, a one-dimensional joke, and the actress playing her could have looked silly in the role. But the physical aspect of the performance is only part of what makes it great. Just as important is the textured inner life—the heart, intelligence, and deadpan wit—that Huffman gives the character.

As mesmerizing as she may be, however, the film is not. Lacking a strong narrative drive, the meandering screenplay by first-time writer-director Duncan Tucker is only sporadically engaging and, in the end, does not add up to a full emotional experience worthy of its unique protagonist.

Just a week before the final surgery that will complete the transformation that Bree has already begun with electrolysis, various operations, hormone treatment, and extensive practice in talking and behaving like a woman, she discovers that she has a teenage son, fathered years ago from a one-time college encounter. Her therapist, Margaret (Elizabeth Peña), insists that she seek him out and resolve this issue. So Bree heads from Los Angeles to New York and bails the 17-year-old boy, Toby (Kevin Zegers), out of the youth jail. His mother is dead, and he has become a tough, streetwise kid doing dope and turning tricks to survive. Bree offers Toby a ride to Los Angeles, which he accepts, all the while believing that Bree is a do-gooder Christian missionary out to help juvenile delinquents.

True to many road films, *Transamerica* has a loose, episodic structure, which is always a risk, especially when many of the episodes are not very compelling dramatically. Bree's attempt to reunite Toby with his stepfather, for example, goes badly when she learns that he sexually abused the boy, a revelation that feels like a cliché to explain why Toby became a wayward youth. A stop in Dallas to visit a friend who just happens to be hosting a party for transsexuals is neither funny nor enlightening; it also strains credulity that, even after such an encounter, Toby would not discern that Bree is one herself. After all, this kid is no innocent—he is a male prostitute who has presumably encountered many kinds of people—and Bree's physical features should be a giveaway.

During their drive across America, which, incidentally, does not have the lush cinematography of the best road movies, Bree tries to instill some kind of discipline in Toby and broaden his horizons. Despite the fact that she works in a Mexican restaurant and does some telemarketing at home, Bree is highly educated and bright. She corrects his language skills and introduces him to some knowledge from fields like archaeology, which she has studied. While Bree is not really a missionary, she does adopt that role to some extent, trying to discourage Toby from doing drugs and prostituting himself, essentially trying to get him to aim higher in his life. And because she carries herself in a prim fashion, always self-consciously trying to be feminine and ladylike, stressing pinks and lavenders in her clothing, the church alias somehow fits. The role is obviously a challenge, from the awkward gait and the deep voice to the swirl of feelings attendant in dealing with a long-lost son while holding onto deep secrets. Despite some emotionally charged scenes, however, Huffman also imbues Bree with a degree of equanimity and grace, turning her into a person who has made a certain peace with herself but one who must still concentrate on how to present herself to the world and always be wary of people's reactions. It is a unique character worthy of a better film.

Indeed, it is too bad that Tucker does not provide a sense of dramatic momentum or, at the very least, encounters on the road that are as complex as Bree. But there are no big obstacles along the way or major life lessons to be learned, and the only real suspense is wondering when Toby will figure out Bree's secrets and how he will react. When he accidentally sees Bree's male anatomy, his response is to embarrass her at a souvenir stand in the desert, as if he were personally betrayed.

A dull episode in which a hitchhiker steals their car is mere time filler leading to the film's only charming interlude, in which Bree strikes up a friendship with an Indian named Calvin (Graham Greene), an easygoing fellow who takes an instant liking to her. It is a sweet sequence simply because her in-between kind of state more often prompts curious stares than kindness and admiration.

But a visit with Bree's family relies on broad character types constituting a dysfunctional family the likes of which we have seen many times before, straddling the fine line between wacky screwball clan and a genuine source of pain. Her father, Murray (Burt Young), is a passive sort ruled over by the domineering mother, Elizabeth (Fionnula Flanagan), who is not hesitant to show her revulsion at her daughter's gender status while fawning over the grandson she is meeting for the first time. Rounding out the picture is the younger sister, Sydney (Carrie Preston), who at least brings a welcome sarcastic wit to the dinner table.

But the story suddenly takes a very bizarre turn when Toby, somehow still not figuring out that Bree is his father, makes a pass at her, kissing her on the mouth and even proposing marriage. Not only is this incestuous turn icky, but, because this attraction comes out of nowhere, it is also unbelievable. Ultimately, this grotesque plot turn is just a strange, melodramatic way to force a confrontation that, by this point, should not be necessary. When Bree is forced to reveal that she is his father, Toby knocks her down and runs away in a fit of rage.

By the end, Bree has her surgery but feels a void and a tinge of guilt from Toby's disappearance. Now living in California and making a gay porn film, he visits her one night, but we are still left to wonder what good the journey might have done or what kind of relationship, if any, they might have. Toby is not living a better life than he had been (unless making porn is considered marginally safer than hustling on the streets), and the screenplay does not confront or really even recognize the sordidness of his situation. *Transamerica* is worth seeing for Huffman's rich, layered performance, but, unfortunately, it is surrounded by a disjointed, tepid story that, despite spanning the continent, ends up going nowhere.

Peter N. Chumo II

CREDITS

Bree: Felicity Huffman
Toby: Kevin Zegers
Elizabeth: Fionnula Flanagan
Margaret: Elizabeth Peña
Calvin: Graham Greene
Murray: Burt Young
Sydney: Carrie Preston
Origin: USA
Language: English
Released: 2005
Production: Linda Moran, Rene Bastian, Sebastian Dungan; Belladonna

Directed by: Duncan Tucker
Written by: Duncan Tucker
Cinematography by: Stephen Kazmierski
Music by: David Mansfield
Sound: Griffin Richardson
Music Supervisor: Doug Bernheim
Editing: Pam Wise
Costumes: Danny Glicker
Production Design: Mark White
MPAA rating: R
Running time: 104 minutes

REVIEWS

Boxoffice Online. December, 2005.
Entertainment Weekly Online. November 30, 2005.
Los Angeles Times Online. December 2, 2005.
New York Times Online. December 2, 2005.
Variety Online. February 21, 2005.
Washington Post Online. December 23, 2005, p. C05.

QUOTES

Bree: "I got a phone call last night from a juvenile inmate of the New York prison system. He claimed to be Stanley's son."
Margaret: "No third-person."
Bree (brief pause): "My son."

TRIVIA

This is the first non-Miramax film to be acquired by Harvey and Bob Weinstein.

AWARDS

Golden Globes 2006: Actress—Drama (Huffman)
Ind. Spirit 2006: Actress (Huffman), First Screenplay
Natl. Bd. of Review 2005: Actress (Huffman)

Nomination:

Oscars 2005: Actress (Huffman), Song ("Travelin' Thru")
Golden Globes 2006: Song ("Travelin' Thru")
Ind. Spirit 2006: First Feature
Screen Actors Guild 2005: Actress (Huffman)
Broadcast Film Critics 2005: Actress (Huffman), Song ("Travelin' Thru").

TRANSPORTER 2

The Best In The Business Is Back In The Game.
—Movie tagline

Box Office: $43.1 million

When *The Transporter* came out, it did poorly at the box office. However, when it was released on DVD, strong word of mouth helped sell over 3 million copies. Those are sequel-worthy numbers and, indeed, a sequel was quickly put in the works. Director Louis Leterrier was not particularly eager to do the sequel, but became convinced when he figured out an angle. He decided that, Frank Martin (Jason Statham), the well-dressed and suave hero would be gay. He did not change the movie, but rather his own perception of the film. It was like a joke to himself. "Action fans in general are pretty homophobic," he said in an interview with *The Los Angeles Times*. "You see these tough guys who say, '*The Transporter*, that's such a great movie!' If only they knew they're really cheering for a new kind of action hero."

Whether or not Leterrier was having a little joke on the audience or the *Times* reporter about the hidden subtext is not entirely clear. But he did come up with an action film that is a bit better than others of its ilk. It is the sort of enjoyably bad film that might be in a similar category with a film like *The Fast and the Furious*. It is fun to look at, moves briskly, and has an engaging main character.

In this film, the dapper Martin has moved from France to Southern Florida. Instead of transporting dangerous cargo, he has taken on a month-long stint as a chauffeur for little Jack Billings (Hunter Clary). Jack is the son of U.S. drug czar/neglectful husband and father Mr. Billings (Matthew Modine) and beautiful/neglected Audrey Billings (Amber Valletta).

There are the usual action elements such as a kidnapping, a darkly handsome European villain, and a vial of stuff that can destroy the world. In this case, the victim of the kidnapping is of Jack. The bad Euro guy, Gianni (Alessandro Gassman), takes Jack to infect him with a virus that will, in turn, infect his father and his fellow drug czars around the world at a big upcoming conference. Martin must get a hold of the antidote, get Jack back safely, and fend off the amorous advances of Jack's lonely mother.

Naturally, it is not plot that fills theater seats, but action, and *Transporter 2* has plenty of that. Frank Martin specializes in the same kind of over-the-top, unbelievable, bordering-on-comical-in-their-complexity stunts that James Bond does. He does not seem to carry a gun and instead relies on martial arts and random objects that might be lying about, such as a jet ski, a hose, and a pipe. In one sequence, he cleverly removes a bomb that is attached to the bottom of his car by launching his car off a pier, turning so that his car is flying sideways and swiping the bomb off with a handy crane hook. Seconds later, the bomb explodes.

Part of the film's charm is just how coolly competent Martin is. No matter how dire the situation gets, he scarcely changes his demeanor. Indeed, he seems more concerned about staining his shirt than losing his life. After one particularly rattling sequence, his shirt is torn and covered in blood. He pops open his trunk and coolly pulls out a fresh shirt and tie that are crispy wrapped in plastic.

Critics disagreed whether the first film or the second was the superior mindless fluff. Gregory Kirschling of *Entertainment Weekly* gave the film a C+ and wrote, "*Transporter 2* betrays the legacy of the first *Transporter*, if such a thing is possible…In place of the original's straight-faced ridiculousness, this one plays like pure parody." David Germain of the *Associated Press* called the film "insufferable" and "laughably awful" and cited as proof "car stunts that would be beyond belief in a Looney Tunes short." And Wesley Morris of *The Boston Globe* called the film "a sequel that makes it clear that the outrageous antics of the first movie had a one-time-only charm." But Kevin Thomas of *The Los Angeles Times* called it a "slick, modern thriller that has the timeless, edge-of-your-seat appeal of a classic cliffhanging serial." And Laura Kern of *The New York Times* thought the sequel better than the original. She wrote, "Purely shallow, but never dull, the film wisely pushes the limits of absurdity to the extreme, making it easier to submit to its sheer camp."

Jill Hamilton

CREDITS

Frank Martin: Jason Statham
Gianni: Alessandro Gassman
Audrey Billings: Amber Valletta
Mr. Billings: Matthew Modine
Dimitri: Jason Flemyng
Stappleton: Keith David
Lola: Kate Nauta
Tarconi: Francois Berleand
Vasily: Jeffrey Chase
Jack Billings: Hunter Clary
Origin: USA, France
Language: English
Released: 2005
Production: Luc Besson; Europacorp, TF-1 Films; released by Europacorp, 20th Century-Fox
Directed by: Louis Leterrier
Written by: Luc Besson, Robert Mark Kamen
Cinematography by: Mitchell Amundsen
Music by: Alexandre Azaria
Sound: Dominique Lacour, Cyril Holtz, Alexandre Widmer, Aymeric Devoldere, Francois Joseph Hors
Editing: Vincent Tabaillon, Christine Lucas Navarro
Costumes: Bobbie Read
Production Design: J. Mark Harrington
MPAA rating: PG-13
Running time: 88 minutes

REVIEWS

Boxoffice Online. September, 2005.
Chicago Sun-Times Online. September 2, 2005.
Entertainment Weekly Online. September 2, 2005.
Los Angeles Times Online. September 2, 2005.
New York Times Online. September 2, 2005.
Premiere Magazine Online. September 6, 2005.
Variety Online. August 3, 2005.
Washington Post Online. September 2, 2005, p. C05.

QUOTES

Frank Martin: "I'm afraid that your flight's been canceled."
Gianni: "I'm afraid that *you* have been canceled!"

TRIVIA

It was unclear if there would be a sequel to the first *Transporter* movie, but strong DVD sales assured that this sequel was greenlit.

THE TROUBLES WE'VE SEEN: A HISTORY OF JOURNALISM IN WARTIME

(Veillees d'armes)

Eleven years after its European release, *The Troubles We've Seen: A History of Journalism in Wartime* opened in America, mainly in art house theatres. This newest masterwork from Marcel Ophuls deserves a wider exposure.

As the lengthy title states, the 1994 non-fiction feature traces the history of journalism and war, although the Serbian conflict was the most urgent and relevant during the January 1993 principal photography of *The Troubles…*. Thus, Marcel Ophuls starts his investigation with interviews he filmed around that time (including his heated debate with Slobodan Milosevic, prior to the ex-leader's war crimes trial at the Hague). In the fashion of his earlier documentaries, including the seminal *Sorrow and the Pity* (1970) and *Hotel Terminus* (1988), Ophuls questions his subjects in probing, intellectual cat-and-mouse style. Ophuls relentlessly seeks answers, especially from those who have committed moral or legal offenses.

Yes, those yearning for the obstinate Nazi hunter in Ophuls, may be somewhat frustrated to see him mingling with more neutral subjects—e.g. *New York Times* reporter John Burns and CNN's Christiane Amanpour, plus less celebrated journalists and photographers from French and British media. Philippe Noiret represents one of the outsiders, as the French actor expounds on the hypocrisy of the French press claiming independence while taking marching orders from President Francois Mitterand. French philosopher Bernard-Henri Lévy also observes the ironies and conundrums of war with wit and candor. But no one gets the third degree.

Still, many charged exchanges occur about reportage ethics and principles. In one debate, Ophuls questions a reporter as to whether he should help someone in trouble or merely get his story. In another argument, Ophuls asks a photographer about the morality of staging a shot, even moving around a corpse, for the sake of enhancing a story. In these passages, Ophuls presents a vital, lively history lesson (Thomas Brady's Civil War tableaux and Robert Capa's Spanish Civil War photos are scrutinized—and Capa is strongly defended by former war correspondent and the former Mrs. Ernest Hemingway, Martha Gelhorn, a striking figure); Ophuls also creates a suspenseful screen drama, particularly since Sarajevo snipers are firing from the rooftops during many of the interviews! Credit cinematographers Pierre Boffety and Pierre Milon for bravery as well as skill.

Yes, at 224 minutes, *The Troubles We've Seen* lasts nearly four hours, but tolerant, inquisitive viewers will be pleased with the expansive and multi-layered investigation. Those not familiar with Ophuls' deliberate pacing and building-block technique might be irritated by the protracted running time and ostensibly chaotic structure; or they may be confused by the inclusion of such old movie excerpts as Warner Bros.' *Yankee Doodle Dandy* (1942) during an interview with an amputee. Other clips are more direct and on-target, such as the anti-war Marx Bros. comedy, *Duck Soup* (1930) and Marcel Ophuls' own father Max Ophuls' *From Mayerling to Sarajevo* (1940), which is interpolated more for irony than illustration since his father's film, released just before WWII, re-enacts the 1914 assassination that triggered WWI in the same region (later, in *The Troubles…*, Marcel Ophuls sighs, "History never ends"). One other potential source of frustration may be Ophuls' privileging primarily Anglo, Western journalists—a real lapse for the filmmaker, despite his naming his film after a slave spiritual (leftist yes, multi-cultural no!).

Back in 1994, when the film was shown at the New York Film Festival, Janet Maslin wrote in the October 6 *New York Times*: "Working on his usual vast canvas, Mr. Ophuls constructs another brave, enveloping inquiry into a compelling subject, reveling in the investigative process as he presents it imaginatively on screen. The topics here range from journalistic ethics to survival tactics to grace under pressure. And a leisurely four-hour running time lets Mr. Ophuls explore them in rambling, frequently surprising ways."

During the recent North American release, the reviewers were even more enthusiastic: David Sterritt of the *Christian Science Monitor* wrote in the November 2005 *Cinemateque Ontario* program, "Lucid and lacerating, a bitterly funny and sometimes infuriating work, *Troubles* caused controversy from the moment it debuted at the Cannes film festival. Ophuls traveled to Sarajevo four times to make this scathing essay on war journalism and its role in the history of our century." And Phil Hall of *Film Threat* (August 12, 2005) called the film, "an extraordinary achievement on every possible intellectual and emotional level."

The Troubles We've Seen is indeed a special event, which should have been seen in the United States a long time ago. This is not so much because Americans needed clarity about the complex Bosnian-Serbian war as much as the film articulates so powerfully how news coverage of war can affect and influence battles, cultures, and even history itself.

Eric Monder

CREDITS

Origin: France, Germany, Great Britain
Language: French
Released: 1994
Production: Frederic Bourboulon, Bertrand Tavernier; Little Bear, Canal Plus, Premiere, BBC
Directed by: Marcel Ophuls
Written by: Marcel Ophuls
Cinematography by: Pierre Milon, Pierre Boffety
Editing: Sophie Brunet
MPAA rating: Unrated
Running time: 224 minutes

REVIEWS

New York Times Online. October 6, 1994.
Variety Online. June 10, 1994.

2046

Box Office: $1.4 million

If the vibrant style of *Chungking Express* (1994) first brought Hong Kong's Wong Kar-Wai to international attention, the ripe romanticism of *In the Mood for Love* (2000) made it obvious that he is a major filmmaker. *2046*, the long-awaited sequel to his greatest success, offers more of the same but with variations on his rhythms and themes.

In the Mood for Love found Chow (Tony Leung Chiu-Wai) in a reluctant but passionate affair with Su Li Zhen (Maggie Cheung) after their mates run off with each other. In *2046*, Chow leaves Singapore for Hong Kong in 1966 to work as a newspaperman and write pulp novels. He recognizes Lulu (Carina Lau) from his past and becomes infatuated with her hotel room, number 2046, after Lulu is stabbed there and he takes the room next door, 2047. 2046 is also the number of the hotel room where Chow and Su consummate their affair in *In the Mood for Love*. Chow and Lulu are introduced in Wong's *Days of Being Wild* (1991), with Lulu as a main character and Chow first appearing in the odd coda that ends the film.

Chow is drawn to 2046's next occupant, Bai Ling (Ziyi Zhang), a young prostitute. While Bai slowly falls in love with Chow, he never allows himself to see her as anything other than a sexual partner. Meanwhile, Wang (Wang Sum), owner of the Oriental Hotel, refuses to allow his daughter, Jing Wen (Faye Wong), to continue her relationship with Tak (Takuya Wong) because of Japan's violence against the Chinese during World War II. When Tak returns to Japan, Chow helps Jing Wen carry on a secret correspondence and uses their love as the inspiration for *2046*, a futuristic love story. Chow does not recognize that his novel's unrequited-love theme has a real-life parallel involving him and Bai. Jing Wen also has literary aspirations and collaborates with Chow on a martial-arts novel.

While these two subplots dominate the film, a third introduces another Su Li Zhen (Gong Li), a professional gambler who helps Chow regain the money he has lost. The mysterious Su, who wears a lone black glove, clearly develops feelings for Chow, which he again cannot recognize. Chow has an actively romantic sensibility but is too passive and self-centered to understand the depth of the emotions of the women in his life. His referring to himself, in a voiceover, as "an expert ladies' man" is ironic.

The plot of *2046*, as with most of Wong's films, is far from linear, constantly jumping about in time and place, with several shots repeated. Wong begins his films without a script and writes while a film is in production, reportedly taking five years on and off to make *2046*, in part because of the SARS epidemic, the creation of *In the Mood for Love* overlapping for two of these. Like a painter or writer, he constantly reworks his films until he is satisfied.

While many critics and cinephiles have acclaimed Wong as a genius, there have been some dissenters. In *The New Yorker*, for example, Anthony Lane objected to Wong's impassive approach to passion, calling *2046* "a near-death experience." Wong's defenders can point out that his narrative style is not obtuse but an effort to force the viewer to pay attention, to become more engaged in the process, seeing how the fragmented elements fit together. Wong attempts to merge style and content, his fragmented narrative reflecting the fragile psychological state of his characters.

Wong is also notable for trying to appeal to as many senses as possible in his films. The sound of a key entering a lock is accentuated, as is the clatter of Chow's spoon as he tries to get every last morsel of food from a bowl. As Chow and Bai make love, the soundtrack music suddenly stops to reveal the sounds of sexual passion. Characters are constantly touching people, clothing, and objects. A shot of a woman's leg emerging from a black slit skirt is repeated, carrying a different identity and meaning each time.

The principal sense, of course, is sight, and Wong once again has the acclaimed Christopher Doyle as his primary cinematographer. Because of the way Wong made *2046*, Doyle was not available for the entire shoot, and parts of the film were shot by Yiu-Fai Lai, who did *Infernal Affairs* (2002) in Doyle's style, and Pung-Leung Kwan. As with *In the Mood for Love*, *2046* has a mixture of soft and dark colors, with saturated greens and reds breaking through essentially black and gray frames. Wong repeats shots of characters lounging beside the sign atop the Oriental Hotel, the sky in the background a different shade each time, reflecting the characters' moods and contrasting strongly with the neon blue-green of the sign. The sign represents the stability of artificial reality, the fluctuating sky the tentativeness of emotional truth.

Working in widescreen for the first time, Wong jams the characters, whose lives are out of balance, into the corners of frames. Once again, there are numerous slow-motion shots, often of women smoking or crying, and Wong's women are certainly given to crying. This seemingly arbitrary use of slow motion is especially annoying to Wong's detractors. As with his earlier films, there are constant shots of the narrow hallways and staircases that seem to confine the characters' lives. Wong does, however, play down the rain that threatens to drown *In the Mood for Love*, with only one shot of a forlorn Chow standing in a downpour.

Music is extremely important in Wong's films. The stylishness of *In the Mood for Love* is enhanced by his use of Spanish-language songs from Nat King Cole's *Mis Mejores Canciones*. Cole is also present in *2046*, singing

Mel Torme's "The Christmas Song" to underscore Chow's loneliness on three successive Christmas Eves. The soundtrack also features songs by Connie Francis and Dean Martin, arias from Vincenzo Bellini's *Norma* (1831), and the Latin rhythms of Xavier Cugat, repeating the latter from *Days of Being Wild.* The exotic score by Shigeru Umebayashi and Peer Raben, who composed the music for many Rainer Werner Fassbinder films, blends several styles to evoke the changing moods of Chow and his women. Wong, who has also directed music videos, says he has been strongly influenced by Fassbinder's use of music.

Some reviewers complained about Chow's transformation from the shy, reticent lover of *In the Mood for Love* to a womanizer. Since the two films skip from 1962 to 1966, Chow's experiences in the interim are left to the imagination. Obviously, the pain of his affair with the first Su, who appears briefly in two flashbacks, has changed him. Wong gives Chow a pencil moustache and a swinger's wardrobe to underscore his metamorphosis, but Leung, one of Asia's best actors, uses his expressive eyes to convey the melancholy beneath this slick façade.

Wong's women rarely have much to say, leaving Li, Zhang, and Faye Wong to create their characters through longing glances. Faye Wong is especially good not only as the hotel owner's daughter but as a lovesick android in Chow's futuristic tale. Zhang, star of *Crouching Tiger, Hidden Dragon* (2000), *Hero* (2002), and *House of Flying Daggers* (2004), shows she is capable of excellent work beyond costume dramas. When Bai realizes Chow is not going to love her, Wong leaves the camera on her as Zhang expresses shock, pain, and resignation, all in a few seconds.

Even reviewers who praised *2046*, as most did, felt it is not quite as good as *In the Mood for Love.* While the earlier film is much more cohesive and emotionally involving, the artist in Wong clearly made him want to try something different, and no one blends images, sounds, music, and romantic disappointment in quite the way he does.

Michael Adams

CREDITS

Chow Mo Wan: Tony Leung Chiu-Wai
Su Li Zhen: Gong Li
Tak: Takuya Kimura
Wang Jingwen/wjw 1967: Faye Wong
Bai Ling: Ziyi Zhang
Lulu/Mimi: Carina Lau
cc 1966: Chang Chen
slz 1960: Maggie Cheung
Mr. Wang/Train captain: Wang Sum
Ping: Lam Siu-ping
Bird: Thongchai McIntyre
Wang Jiewen: Dong Jie
Origin: China, Hong Kong, France, Germany
Language: Chinese, Japanese
Released: 2004
Production: Wong Kar-wai; Jet Tone Film
Directed by: Wong Kar-Wai
Written by: Wong Kar-Wai
Cinematography by: Christopher Doyle, Lai Yiu-fai, Kwan Pun-leung
Music by: Peer Raben, Shingeru Umebayashi
Sound: Claude Letessier, Tu Duu-chih
Editing: William Chang
Art Direction: Alfred Yau
Costumes: William Chang
Production Design: William Chang
MPAA rating: R
Running time: 129 minutes

REVIEWS

Boxoffice Online. August, 2005.
Chicago Sun-Times Online. September 2, 2005.
Entertainment Weekly Online. August 3, 2005.
Los Angeles Times Online. August 5, 2005.
New York Times Online. August 5, 2005.
Premiere Magazine Online. July 5, 2005.
Variety Online. May 21, 2004.

QUOTES

Chow Mo Wan: "Everyone who goes to 2046 has the same intention, they want to recapture lost memories. Because in 2046 nothing ever changes. But, nobody knows if that is true or not because no one has ever come back."

TRIVIA

This is the first Wong Kar-Wai film to be photographed in widescreen (2.39:1 projected aspect ratio), and the first to be photographed using anamorphic lenses.

AWARDS

N.Y. Film Critics 2005: Cinematog.
Natl. Soc. Film Critics 2005: Cinematog.

TWO FOR THE MONEY

Gambling on sporting events has long been an American obsession, but this phenomenon has been mostly ignored by filmmakers. John Sayles' look at the 1918 Chicago Black Sox scandal in *Eight Men Out*

(1988) is probably the most notable exception. *Two for the Money* is not, however, really interested in gambling for its own sake so much as how it twists the personalities and lives of those who run the industry.

Brandon Lang (Matthew McConaughey) is a college quarterback with dreams of professional glory until a devastating knee injury ends his playing career. Six years later, he is a poorly paid Las Vegas telemarketer called upon to substitute for a colleague who offers odds on football games only to discover he is a master at predicting outcomes. His success comes to the attention of Walter Abrams (Al Pacino), who summons him to New York to make some big bucks. Abrams offers sports-betting advice on cable television and has a small army of "salesmen" who convince "clients" to wager large sums with their local bookies in exchange for a cut of their winnings.

An innocent in the big city, despite his Las Vegas background, Lang is slowly seduced into becoming Abrams' star prognosticator. Lang grew up being schooled in the finer points of sports by his alcoholic father (Gary Hudson) until he, his mother (Denise Galik), and his younger brother (James Kirk) were abandoned when he was nine. Abrams tries to become a substitute father and succeeds, manipulating his protégé with both praise and criticism. At first, Lang is a huge success, attracting the business of a high roller (Armand Assante) Abrams has been after for years. Then things begin to fall apart, and Abrams and his devoted wife, Toni (Rene Russo), start battling for the young man's soul.

Though most reviewers greeted *Two for the Money* with either a shrug or hostility, it is slickly presented by screenwriter Dan Gilroy and director D. J. Caruso, whose *Taking Lives* (2004) is much worse and *The Salton Sea* (2002) is much grittier and better. *Two for the Money* offers a realistic, compelling glimpse of a glamorous yet decadent world of gambling. Unlike many sports films, it also gets the details of football, especially televised football, right. Despite occasional clichéd storytelling, as when the young woman (Jaime King) Lang picks up in a restaurant turns out to be a prostitute hired by Abrams, the film is engrossing until a weak, sentimental conclusion. That this sentimentality is underscored by a truly awful piece of conventional music by composer Christophe Beck only makes the ending more disappointing.

The performances make up for many of the film's weaknesses. Assante, whose career has plummeted since *The Mambo Kings* (1992), is truly frightening as the vicious high roller. Jeremy Piven provides his usual excellent, slightly off-kilter work as Lang's jealous colleague. Russo finds considerable poignancy in Toni's tug-of-war between her love for and exasperation with her husband. McConaughey, though a decade older than his character, offers his patented good-old-boy charm, though he fades a bit in his scenes with Piven, Russo, and Pacino.

Pacino has been down this road many times before, with his corrupt mentors to naïve young men in *City Hall* (1996), *The Devil's Advocate* (1997), and *The Recruit* (2003). Though many reviewers dismissed his work here as yet another of the unfortunately bombastic performances to which he is prone, his Abrams is engrossing as a master manipulator, and the actor does not shout as much as might be expected. The way Pacino can subtly shift his expression from joy to disappointment to sorrow within seconds carries the film.

Michael Adams

CREDITS

Walter Abrams: Al Pacino
Brandon Lang: Matthew McConaughey
Toni Morrow: Rene Russo
Novian: Armand Assante
Jerry: Jeremy Piven
Alexandria: Jaime (James) King
Southie: Kevin Chapman
Milton: Gedde Watanabe
Tammy: Carly Pope
Herbie: Gerard Plunkett
Origin: USA
Language: English
Released: 2005
Production: Jay Cohen; Morgan Creek Productions; released by Universal
Directed by: D.J. Caruso
Written by: Dan Gilroy
Cinematography by: Conrad W. Hall
Music by: Christophe Beck
Sound: David Husby
Music Supervisor: John Houlihan
Editing: Glen Scantlebury
Art Direction: Willie Heslup
Costumes: Marie-Sylvie Deveau
Production Design: Tom Southwell
MPAA rating: R
Running time: 124 minutes

REVIEWS

Boxoffice Online. October, 2005.
Chicago Sun-Times Online. October 7, 2005.
Entertainment Weekly Online. October 5, 2005.
Los Angeles Times Online. October 7, 2005.
New York Times Online. October 7, 2005.
Premiere Magazine Online. October 7, 2005.
Variety Online. October 6, 2005.
Washington Post Online. October 7, 2005, p. WE39.

QUOTES

Walter Abrams: "After the therapy, and the psychiatry, and the meetings, you know what it all comes down to? You're all f***** up."

TRIVIA

When the film debuted, the phone number featured on Walter's television show (1-800-BET ON IT) was the number of a real sports advice service.

U-V

UNDEAD

Prepare Yourself.
—Movie tagline

Crazy has come to town for a visit!
—Movie tagline

Twin brothers Michael and Peter Spierig from Queensland, Australia emerge on the cinematic landscape with their zombie movie, *Undead.* A crossbred product, the film splices several different genres and inventively melds them together along a plot resulting in a goulash composed of science fiction, horror, and the spaghetti western with a sprig of slapstick.

In the tranquil, rustic fishing town of Berkeley in Queensland, a mysterious meteor shower bombards the community with celestial rocks that bore through some citizens, immediately transforming them into groaning, barely ambulatory quasi-living corpses afflicted with the requisite drive to consume unaffected human flesh. The cosmic debris has also contaminated the town's water supply, which results in the same living death metamorphosis. Abiding with zombie lore, a small group of humans survive the initial onslaught and are forced to lock themselves away from the hordes of preternatural flesh eaters.

Undead's hodge-podge of survivors include Berkeley's reigning beauty pageant winner, Rene, who has been crowned "Miss Catch of the Day." This mantle entitles her image to be displayed on numerous products at various local bait and tackle shops. Rene (Felicity Mason) has been forced to leave Berkeley and her prestigious beauty queen status behind following the foreclosure of her recently deceased parents' house. Rene's efforts are stymied as a pile of wrecked cars blocks her exit. She meets and joins forces with a local bush pilot, Wayne (Rob Jenkins) and his pregnant wife, Sally-anne (Lisa Cunningham), who looks like her water is going to break in two minutes. Two inept cops of the Keystone ilk join the trio: the profane Harrison (Dirk Hunter) and his austere and shy partner, Molly (Emma Randall).

The argumentative quintet seek sanctuary at the homestead of the local eccentric, Marion (Mungo McKay). Reclusive and reticent, Marion is Berkeley's resident weirdo who tells of his own close encounter of alien abduction when he was visited by a spaceship (apparently Berkeley is Australia's Roswell) which beams him up following his fight with a reanimated fish he recently caught which attacked him with a flying launch to the throat. It would seem that regardless of specie, any animal imbued with zombie life ubiquitously craves human flesh. An impressive acrobat, Marion's weapons include a pair of spurs as well as three shotguns harnessed together enabling him to blast a zombie in half leaving a pair of legs, bereft of a torso, navigating about aimlessly complete with a jagged jutting spine.

Trapped in a steel enforced concrete underground concrete shelter constructed by Marion, the group must resurface as Marion failed to supply the room with food and water. This they succeed in doing in a display of slow motion aerial gunplay. Risky last minute escapes are abundant in this film, which takes a drastic turn with the inexplicable appearance of benevolent extraterrestrials. Towards the end, thousands of humans are suspended in mid-air in traditional yet eerie columns of light flooding down from several spacecraft which later converge into a puzzling mothership.

Initially starting off at a fast pace, *Undead* nestles into a slumbering crawl with few original surprises from any genre. Kevin Thomas from the *Los Angeles Times* accurately observes: "Peter and Michael Spierig's *Undead* is an ambitious but murky and overlong zombie picture that borrows from *Night of the Living Dead, Close Encounters of the Third Kind, ET* and other movies. However visually striking, this Australian film is ultimately as tedious as it is striking."

David Metz Roberts

CREDITS

Rene: Felicity Mason
Marion: Mungo McKay
Sallyanne: Lisa Cunningham
Harrison: Dirk Hunter
Molly: Emma Randall
Agent: Steve Greig
Chip: Noel Sheridan
Aggie: Gaynor Wensley
Ruth: Eleanor Stillman
Wayne: Rob Jenkins
Origin: Australia
Language: English
Released: 2005
Production: Peter Spierig, Michael Spierig; Spierigfilm; released by Imagine Entertainment
Directed by: Michael Spierig, Peter Spierig
Written by: Michael Spierig, Peter Spierig
Cinematography by: Andrew Strahorn
Music by: Cliff Bradley
Sound: Michael Spierig
Art Direction: Jan Culverhouse
Costumes: Chintamani Aked
Production Design: Matthew Putland
MPAA rating: R
Running time: 100 minutes

REVIEWS

Boxoffice Online. July, 2005.
Chicago Sun-Times Online. July 8, 2005.
Entertainment Weekly Online. June 29, 2005.
Los Angeles Times Online. July 1, 2005.
New York Times Online. July 1, 2005.
Variety Online. June 16, 2005.
Washington Post Online. July 8, 2005, p. WE40.

QUOTES

Marion: "...time is short. So you gotta ask yourself: Are you a fighter, Fish Queen, or are you zombie food?"

TRIVIA

More than 150 gallons of fake blood was used for special effects during filming.

UNDERCLASSMAN

A Comedy About Upholding The Law And Disturbing The Peace.
—Movie tagline

Get Ready To Be Schooled.
—Movie tagline

Box Office: $5.6 million

Underclassman is a movie that is not afraid to trot out any filmic stereotype across the screen. When there is a young African-American male, it is a sure thing that he is a poor student but one heck of a basketball player. When there is a group of criminals, they are inexplicably compelled to gather and discuss their evil plan, thus explaining to the audience what is going on. When there is a young cop, he is sure to be a renegade that does not play by the rules. At the end of the second act, said cop will be kicked off the force, only to solve the crime by himself, and be reinstated just before the credits roll.

It's all there in *Underclassman.* Tracy Stokes (Nick Cannon), a poor student, good basketball player, and renegade cop, reaches his own second act moment when LAPD Captain Delgado (Cheech Marin) says to him, "You're reckless and you're dangerous and you're kicked off the force." But it takes Tracy (and the audience) two long acts to get to this point. Viewers must first learn that Tracy's father was a legendary Los Angeles cop and that Tracy dreams only of following in those footsteps. The audience must see Captain Delgado give Tracy the prime assignment of going undercover in a local posh prep school where a murder has been committed, even though Tracy was a poor student and is quickly proving himself to be an equally inept police officer.

Once enrolled in the school, the series of improbable events continues to unfold. Tracy's Spanish teacher, Karen Lopez (Roselyn Sanchez), is movie star beautiful and does not seem adverse to flirting with, and offering private tutoring to, one of her students. When Tracy starts work on uncovering a car theft/drug ring, not only do all of his hunches prove to be correct, he is such a gifted cop that he is able to do a quite serviceable job in a high speed chase with a souped-up sports car—while on foot. Even when Tracy makes stunningly bad decisions, such as having his (unarmed) buddy drive a car straight through the wall of a warehouse where a bunch of armed—and soon to be very angry—bad guys are making a deal, it all works out okay in the end. And when a group of the bad students, led by Rob Donovan

(Shawn Ashmore), comes into an old shed to talk about their plan, Tracy just happens to be hiding in that exact shed. It is all either stunningly good luck on Tracy's part, or stunningly bad writing on writers David T. Wagner and Brent Goldberg's part. Lines like this from Captain Delgado: "Every time I see that kid, I think of his father—all passion, no procedure," tip the scales to side of the latter possibility.

Cannon himself came up with the concept for the film, but he has done himself no favors. Actually, the concept is not that bad, it is the way it is executed that finally does this movie in. It is difficult for a movie to work when its hero, upon being offered a crab cake, is forced to say such lines as, "In my old neighborhood, getting crabs meant something totally different." Cannon has done good work on TV and in his feature film *Drumline*, but here his charm is stifled and he seems to be trying to be an Eddie Murphy-type character. The combination of the lame writing, the lackluster direction and Cannon seeming not to have a good handle on his character, all work together to make the movie a tiresome bore.

Such an uninspired retread inspired a vast majority of critics to write caustic reviews. Lisa Schwarzbaum of *Entertainment Weekly* gave the film a D grade and wrote that it was a "loserville teen comedy" that seemed "like a student project sloppily cribbed from other kids' notes." Ty Burr of *The Boston Globe* wrote that Cannon is "not even a third-string Wayans brother" and that he "preens and wisecracks with a maximum of sass and nothing that remotely resembles charm." Roger Ebert of *The Chicago Sun-Times* objected to the many clichés and lamented, "Did anyone think to create an African-American character who was an individual and not a wiseass standup with street smarts?" And A.O. Scott of *The New York Times* wrote that the film "plays like the longest episode of '21 Jump Street' ever made."

Jill Hamilton

CREDITS

Tracy Stokes: Nick Cannon
Rob Donovan: Shawn Ashmore
Karen Lopez: Roselyn Sanchez
Lisa Brooks: Kelly Hu
Det. Gallecki: Ian Gomez
Headmaster Powers: Hugh Bonneville
Capt. Victor Delgado: Richard "Cheech" Marin
Ms. Hagery: Mary Pat Gleason
David Boscoe: Angelo Spizzirri
Des: Kaylee DeFer
Origin: USA
Language: English
Released: 2005
Production: Peter Abrams, Robert Levy, Andrew Panay; Tapestry Films; released by Miramax Films
Directed by: Marcos Siega
Written by: David T. Wagner, Brent Goldberg
Cinematography by: David Hennings
Music by: BT (Brian Transeau)
Sound: Doug Arnold
Editing: Nicholas C. Smith
Art Direction: Oana Bogdan
Production Design: Gary Frutkoff
MPAA rating: PG-13
Running time: 95 minutes

REVIEWS

Boxoffice Online. September 2, 2005.
Chicago Sun-Times Online. September 2, 2005.
Entertainment Weekly Online. August 31, 2005.
Los Angeles Times Online. September 2, 2005.
New York Times Online. September 2, 2005.
Variety Online. September 1, 2005.
Washington Post Online. September 2, 2005.

TRIVIA

This film, originally set for a 2004 release, stayed in Miramax vaults unreleased until the infamous Disney and Miramax split was complete.

AN UNFINISHED LIFE

Every secret takes on a life of its own.
—Movie tagline

Former pretty-boy actor Robert Redford is not only playing his age but looks it as crusty Wyoming rancher Einar Gilkyson in director Lasse Hallstrom's *An Unfinished Life*. It was nearly the unseen film, sitting on the studio shelf for two years, caught in the maelstrom of the Weinstein brothers/Miramax/Disney split. Not that the delay would much change the film's low-key storytelling or reception, although Morgan Freeman's wise best friend role might have seemed fresher before its near-clone in 2004's *Million Dollar Baby* opposite grizzled Clint Eastwood.

The film opens with a bear and not just any bear but a huge grizzly (played by Bart II) roaming the outskirts of Einar's rundown ranch. This bear is Einar's personal nemesis, having severely mauled best friend and ranch hand Mitchell Bradley (Freeman) nearly to death. Now Einar cares for the crippled Mitch, administering a daily shot of morphine to ease the man's constant pain.

Einar goes bear hunting but is prevented from shooting the animal by sheriff Crane Curtis (Josh Lucas); instead the grizzly is captured and taken to a local animal park where he's herded into a bare steel cage.

Meanwhile, abused Jean Gilkyson (Jennifer Lopez), Einar's widowed daughter-in-law, is stoically enduring the pathetic justifications of boyfriend Gary (Damian Lewis) for hitting her while Jean's 11-year-old daughter Griff (Becca Gardner) looks on. Griff reminds her mother that she promised they would leave if the abuse continued and they take off in Jean's rattletrap car, which naturally breaks down on a lonely stretch of highway. Jean, short of cash, is forced to take Griff to the grandfather she was told was dead. They walk up to Einar's door only to be greeted by his hostility. "I don't want you here," he tells the despised Jean, but grudgingly relents when he learns that Griff is his granddaughter (named for her deceased father, Griffin, Einar's only child). Jean insists they will only stay until she can scrape together enough money to get them on the road again.

Einar may be a senior citizen but he's more than a manly match for a couple of drunken young cowpokes harassing diner owner Nina (Camryn Manheim), who will conveniently become Jean's new employer and confidante. This is after the attractive woman meets the handsome sheriff when she gives him a police report about her worthless boyfriend. They take a shine to each other but Griff resents her mother's latest romantic involvement.

Einar checks out the bear at the roadside zoo while Griff and Mitch get to know each other. Einar later visits his son's grave, overlooking the ranch; the gravestone reads "an unfinished life." While Griff adjusts to ranch life, Einar snarls at Jean, still blaming her for his son's death in a car crash in which she was driving. Mitch tries in vain to reason with Einar, telling him "They call them accidents because they're nobody's fault." Mitch is also worried about the bear and insists that Einar and Griff go to the zoo and feed him some fresh meat. And lest we forget Jean's past, Gary shows up. When Einar learns about Gary's presence, he takes his shotgun to frighten the lowlife out of town.

Though Einar has been warming to Griff—teaching her to rope, ride, and drive his old pickup—he and Jean continue to argue even as Jean admits that she still feels guilty every day. However, Jean tells Einar that she "tried to keep living and you didn't." Fed up, Jean takes Griff and moves into Nina's while Einar begins hitting the booze again. Griff soon insists upon moving back to the ranch (alone) while Nina plays peacemaker, telling Jean "We're not supposed to outlive our children. You have to understand that about Einar."

Still worried, Mitch now insists upon visiting the caged bear himself and, dismayed by the animal's condition, he asks Einar to set the bear free. Einar has also mellowed enough to ask Jean to come back to the ranch. That same night, Einar and Griff steal a cage and go to free the bear but the plan doesn't work as expected and the grizzly gets loose and takes a swipe at Einar before running off. Griff drives Einar to the hospital and calls her mother to stay with them. Mitch hears a noise and when he goes outside he sees the bear prowling around, but this time the bear retreats instead of attacking him. Sneaking out of the hospital, the threesome return to the ranch the next morning in time for Gary to turn up. He forces Griff into his car so Jean will come away with him, but Einar gets that trusty shotgun, shoots up the car, and beats Gary to a pulp.

Jean and Griff settle happily into their new lives, Griff makes nice with Sheriff Crane, the bear wanders safely up in the hills, and Einar and Mitch are jawing on the porch as usual. Mitch asks: "Would you bury me next to Griffin?" and Einar indignantly replies: "Where else would I bury you. It's where my family lies."

While the grizzly is impressive, his symbolic presence is overwhelming. Though Mark Spragg adapted his own novel, along with wife Virginia Korus Spragg, you have to wonder if the bear as metaphor worked better on the page than on screen. No matter, it's really Redford and Freeman's movie anyway—their two characters squabble and fuss with each other like a couple married for 40 years, so much so that outspoken Griff (the tomboyish solemn Gardner is a real find) blurbs out a question about their being a gay couple, earnestly assuring them that it's okay if they are. (This drew a big laugh not only from the characters but the audience as well.) The philosophical musings of Freeman's Mitch sometimes go over-the-top but the actor delivers them with a firm sincerity while Redford lets his vanity go to play a surly grump who, at the end, remains only a slightly mellower grump.

Lopez has surprisingly little to do—she's the catalyst to bring the story's ideas about anger, guilt, forgiveness, and acceptance into play but she never makes a strong impression; nor does Josh Lucas as your standard small town, nice guy sheriff. Damien Lewis's Gary could have never re-entered the plot after Jean's flight and it would have made little difference, which is no reflection on the actor's talents at playing a psycho. His character is actually a distraction since the viewer waits impatiently for him to show up and get what's coming to him. There's lots of panoramic shots of Einar's ranch and various scenic foothills and trails supplied—as usual—by British Columbia substituting for Wyoming but *An Unfinished*

Life feels more like a well-done Hallmark television drama than a big screen effort.

Christine Tomassini

CREDITS

Einar Gilkyson: Robert Redford
Mitch: Morgan Freeman
Jean Gilkyson: Jennifer Lopez
Crane: Josh(ua) Lucas
Gary: Damian Lewis
Nina: Camryn Manheim
Griff Gilkyson: Becca Gardner
Origin: USA
Language: English
Released: 2005
Production: Leslie Holleran, Alan Ladd Jr., Kellian Ladd; Ladd Company; released by Miramax, Buena Vista
Directed by: Lasse Hallstrom, Andrew Mondshein
Written by: Mark Spragg, Virginia Korus Spragg
Cinematography by: Oliver Stapleton
Music by: Christopher Young
Sound: Rudy Zasloff
Art Direction: Karen Schulz Gropman, James Steuart
Costumes: Tish Monaghan
Production Design: David Gropman
MPAA rating: PG-13
Running time: 107 minutes

REVIEWS

Boxoffice Online. September, 2005.
Chicago Sun-Times Online. September 9, 2005.
Entertainment Weekly Online. September 7, 2005.
Los Angeles Times Online. September 9, 2005.
New York Times Online. September 9, 2005.
Premiere Magazine Online. September 2, 2005.
Variety Online. August 21, 2005.
Washington Post Online. September 9, 2005, p. C05.

QUOTES

Mitch Bradley: "They call 'em accidents cause it's nobody's fault."

TRIVIA

Filmed in Kamloops, British Columbia, Canada.

UNLEASHED
(Danny the Dog)

Serve no master.
—Movie tagline

On April 8th, the collar comes off.
—Movie tagline

Chained by Violence. Freed by Music.
—Movie tagline

Box Office: $24.5 million

Unleashed is an action film that could have fallen flat on its well-traveled genre feet, but ultimately walks a successful and satisfying line that is rarely seen in Hollywood these days. Perhaps that is, in part, because the filmmakers were from France, Britain, and Hong Kong. Or just as likely the reason for its success is the fact that it is a story well told, one that respects its audience. Or perhaps because it is written by Luc Besson, who always brings an emotional core to his films and is never satisfied with simply showing his audience a good time surface level action film. Working outward from an obvious metaphor, this is the rare action film that not only works on a visceral level, but also on a deep emotional one as well. All these combined factors come together to make *Unleashed* one of the best action films to come out in the last few years, and is also the best martial arts film to come out of France and Britain. And the best film outside China to star Jet Li. It also serves as a nice return for Bob Hoskins who played a similar role in his first film *The Long Good Friday* (1980).

The attack dog for mob boss Bart (Bob Hoskins), Jet Li plays Danny, who lives caged in the basement of the bosses' warehouse. There he is given food and water in bowls and the only thing he owns is the teddy bear hanging above his head, much like the vague childhood memories that lie just out of reach in his dreams. In a scene in the beginning of the film, Bart and his gang confront a group of men who are late on their payments. Bart shows them the error of their ways by removing Danny's metal collar and whispering in his ear the go words, "Kill them." Danny springs into primal kung-fu action that is as violently brutal as it is a wonder to watch. Jet Li almost seems too fast for the cameras here and one is reminded of an earlier experience of Bruce Lee's during the filming of a fight scene in the original *Green Hornet* television series where after he had finished a fight, the director had to take him aside and tell him to slow down his skills so the camera could actually see what he was doing.

The fight scene is quite brutal and it was a surprise and delight to find out that the fight choreographer Yuen Wo Ping is the same person who did a similar job on *Kung Fu Hustle.* While that films action was more based in comedy, this films purpose is to show the violent brutality, and is definitely not played for laughs. It is credit to his talent and diversity that while both films are quite different in tone, both share in exhilaration of great choreography. Each film has its own style and tone and Ping adapts to that requirement with the seamless ease befitting his experience. It is also a credit to director Louis Leterrier who has the confidence of letting the camera observe the action and not rely on editing tricks to convey the kinetic energy of the fight and allow the choreography to speak for itself. Also by allowing the audience to observe what is actually going in the scene helps to illustrate the brutal lengths that Bart will go in pushing his "dog" and how the action helps tell the story and giving it meaning and soul, while not allowing the audience to shy away from the realism of the bloody brutality of an unleashed dog loosed on an outmatched group of thugs.

Jet Li also gets more to do in this film than just show he still has his kung-fu chops as he spends the first thirty minutes without uttering a single line of dialog. He is able therefore to show his subtle emotional range as an actor through nothing but his facial expressions. When he finally does speak, the audience feels sympathy for him and realizes that he has been suppressing his emotions much like an abused child would in front of a parent that could strike at any time. It is an act of courage that he feels allowed to speak when he receives his first bit of kindness from a blind piano tuner named Sam (Morgan Freeman).

Danny does not fear physical violence whenever he fights or even when violence erupts around him. He only fears the wrath of his master, and so when he begins to speak to Sam and later his stepdaughter Victoria (Kerry Condon) he starts to feel real humanity that is the real heart of the film. It this deeper meaning and examinations beyond the metaphor of a dog and his master that separates this film from most blockbuster Hollywood action pictures and places *Unleashed* in a category of the intelligent action film that is scarcely populated, but always full of life. This film has a soul. The film continually delves deeper into the metaphor of what it means to be a free man, unleashing himself first from the person that would control him, but also himself from his own perceptions and past, and ultimately what it means to be human. All in the context of the action film milieu.

David E. Chapple

CREDITS

Danny: Jet Li
Sam: Morgan Freeman
Bart: Bob Hoskins
Wyeth: Michael Jenn
Victoria: Kerry Cordon
Infirmier: Christian Gazio
Maddy: Carole Ann Wilson
Origin: USA, France, Great Britain, Hong Kong
Language: English
Released: 2005
Production: Luc Besson, Pierre Ange Le Pogam; TF-1 Films; released by Europacorp
Directed by: Louis Leterrier
Written by: Luc Besson
Cinematography by: Pierre Morel
Music by: Massive Attack
Sound: Vincent Tulli, Cyril Holtz, Francois Joseph Hori
Costumes: Olivier Beriot
Production Design: Jacques Bufnoir
MPAA rating: R
Running time: 102 minutes

REVIEWS

Boxoffice Online. May, 2005.
Chicago Sun-Times Online. May 12, 2005.
Entertainment Weekly Online. May 11, 2005.
Los Angeles Times Online. May 13, 2005.
New York Times Online. May 13, 2005.
Variety Online. February 8, 2005.
Washington Post Online. May 13, 2005, p. C04.

QUOTES

Wyeth, referring to Bart's turning a man into a dog: "How did you do that?"

Bart: "Like my saint of a mum used to say, 'Get 'em young, and the possibilities are endless.'"

TRIVIA

This film features Jet Li's longest action sequence.

UP FOR GRABS

Chronicling the legal battle that erupted over San Francisco Giant Barry Bonds's 73rd home run ball in the 2001 baseball season, Michael Wranovics's *Up for Grabs* captures a piece of the zeitgeist of American sports culture today. If it is not a pretty picture, it is nonetheless very funny as two fans go to extremes to lay claim to a baseball that could potentially net millions of dollars for its owner. In zeroing in on the media circus and the peculiarly American notion of getting rich quick by being in just the right place at the right time, Wranovics's documentary turns a bemused, often satiric eye on our national obsession with sports, the greed that leads grown men to act like fools, and, ultimately, the sheer absurdity of the battle over a souvenir.

The 2001 baseball season saw Bonds break the single-season home run record, just a scant three years after Mark McGwire of the St. Louis Cardinals had broken Roger Maris's long-standing record, set in 1961. (Of course, recent charges of steroid use call into question the legitimacy of both McGwire's and Bonds's achievements, but a disclaimer at the film's beginning tells us that is a subject for a different movie.) To give his story historical perspective and to suggest how times have changed, Wranovics interviews Sal Durante, the fan who caught Maris's record-setting ball, and shows archival material of the young man smiling with Maris. At the time, Durante was offered $5,000 for the memento. The genuine good feelings of the moment and the price, not to mention the era's innocence, will seem quaint as the events of 2001 unfold.

Before the final game of the season on October 7, 2001, Bonds had broken McGwire's record, but everyone knew that the last home run ball would be the most valuable. The swarm of spectators at San Francisco's Pac Bell Park awaiting the chance to catch a ball is staggering, and, when Bonds belts out number 73, a cameraman named Josh Keppel captures the moment on tape, which shows a fan named Alex Popov catching the ball in his glove. A melee ensues, and soon another fan, Patrick Hayashi, emerges with the prize. What happened in between these two pivotal moments forms the dispute at the core of the film. Emboldened by the footage (called the "Keppel tape" and affectionately compared to the Zapruder film), Popov files a lawsuit for recovery of the ball, which he believes was taken from him in the mad scramble.

A spinmeister who does not miss a chance to drive the media engine, Popov is clearly the heart of the film and its most colorful personality. Thriving in the spotlight, he loves to work a crowd and tell his story to everyone. But, as the film progresses, a sense of desperation develops around him. At first, he seems like a man robbed of what was rightfully his, but he soon comes across as someone whose claims become more dubious, including his alleged injuries, which do not prove to be very persuasive in court. He revels in his high profile and plays up his public image as he turns his quest for the ball into a full-time job, but, as one observer notes, he ultimately becomes "a media curiosity." Hayashi, on the other hand, is much cooler, but then again, since he gained possession of the ball, he does not have anything to prove.

Wranovics has assembled a group of talking heads, including witnesses who describe what they think happened that day and Bay Area sportswriters and broadcasters who try to make sense of it all. From a series of witnesses in court demonstrating Popov's catch to interviews with everyday San Franciscans weighing in on the controversy to a panel of law professors debating the legal issues, it is clear that the combination of sports, the promise of easy wealth, and our litigious society are a potent mix in capturing everyone's imagination. While all of this commentary puts the conflict into perspective, however, it also makes the tale seem more important than it really is. But maybe that is the point—people are so in love with sports and celebrity that they turned a relatively small event into a big deal. Nonetheless, even at a fast-paced 88 minutes, the film feels a bit padded, as if Wranovics were, at times, straining to fill out a simple story to feature length.

A court decision does not come down until December 18, 2002, when a judge declares that the ball be sold and the proceeds divided equally between the claimants. On June 25, 2003, the ball sells at auction for $450,000, a far lower price than what had been hoped for, probably because it had been tainted and now symbolized greed more than Bonds's achievement. The result is devastating for Popov, whose $225,000 share cannot cover his $640,000 in legal bills. All of a sudden, the smile disappears from the face of this narcissist, whose arrogance led him to the courtroom in the first place. (Ironically enough, Barry Bonds, generally not known for his wisdom or tact, emerges as the unlikely voice of reason—his admonition early on that the two men should split the profits before the lawyers get involved turns out to be solid advice.)

While it is questionable whether justice was served since Hayashi's claim seemed stronger, the story does end on a note of poetic justice. Popov, refusing to pay his legal team, is embroiled in yet another lawsuit. There is a restraining order on his winnings, none of which he has seen. Hayashi's lawyers, on the other hand, waive their fee, and he is given the opportunity to pursue his M.B.A.

If the fight over a baseball seems like a slight subject for a feature documentary, at times it is, but overall, first-time filmmaker Wranovics has created a compelling drama around an unlikely subject. The whole farcical notion of how a baseball is imbued with such worth and the way the dream of instant wealth leads grown men to act irrationally make *Up for Grabs* an entertaining and hilarious little morality tale of our national pastime.

Peter N. Chumo II

CREDITS

Origin: USA

Language: English

Released: 2005

Production: Michael Wranovics; Crooked Hook Productions

Directed by: Michael Wranovics
Written by: Michael Wranovics
Cinematography by: Zack Richard, Josh Keppel
Editing: Dave Ciaccio
MPAA rating: Unrated
Running time: 88 minutes

REVIEWS

Los Angeles Times Online. May 13, 2005.
New York Times Online. May 6, 2005.
San Francisco Chronicle Online. April 15, 2005.
Variety Online. April 21, 2005.

THE UPSIDE OF ANGER

Sometimes what tears us apart helps us put it back together.
—Movie tagline

...is the person you can become.
—Movie tagline

Box Office: $18.7 million

Mike Binder's *The Upside of Anger* is both oddly charming and strangely annoying. This unconventionally plotted domestic comedy-drama has moments of high originality and admirable reach amid stretches of sitcom banality. The writer-director makes unusual choices that create a unique set of challenges for lead actress Joan Allen.

Playing suburban Detroit housewife and mother of four Terry Wolfmeyer, Allen has to carry a heavy emotional load without the object of her rage being ever present on screen. This turns her anger into something difficult to evaluate and digest. In most cases, a Hollywood filmmaker would have given us some early scenes of Terry's husband and their four girls' father to anchor his character—or at least some flashbacks. A more conventional approach would have revealed Gray Wolfmeyer as, perhaps, a doting father, a loving but distant husband, and a liar and cheater.

Instead, we know nothing of Terry's collapsed marriage except its wreckage—the anger she has left when her husband disappears. We don't know whether their marriage was stormy or mundane, whether he was a work-obsessed charlatan or a dutiful man suddenly swept away by emotions or crisis. Allen has to play the movie opposite a cipher—a man she blames for leaving her and making a ruin of her life—but we have to take it on faith that the fault was all his.

Allen wallows and wails in the aftermath of a storm that we never saw happen. According to the narrative supplied by her youngest daughter, Popeye (Evan Rachel Wood), she once was a sweet, happy woman; now she's become a snarling, nasty, shriveled cauldron of boiling emotions. Allen's Terry emerges full-blown in her rage, grief, despair, and self-centeredness.

Tearing pictures off the wall and snapping at her daughters for failing to appreciate sufficiently the depth of her pain, Terry is a prototypical "mad housewife" and woman wronged. Both Allen and Binder nicely walk a fine line here between honoring the righteousness of Terry's wrath and revealing how self-absorbed and shrunken and unfair she can be. So does Kevin Costner, who plays Denny Davies, an ex-baseball hero and talk radio host, who tiptoes around Terry's rage while trying to get her in the sack. Costner employs his usual understatement, but this time he is not using it to downsize and humanize a larger-than-life character, and it's of better use this way: Costner makes his more ordinary failure of a man into an enormously appealing and realistic figure.

The plot and attitude almost sound like the set-up for a dour John Cassavetes or Ingmar Bergman film, and there are many moments when we get to see the tawdry underside of Terry's despair and wrath. Allen is unafraid to look worn, spent, disgusted, or put out, and it's one of those performances—glamorous leading lady turned sour—that Oscar voters like to honor with a nomination. And that she has to stew in her juices without the physical release of the presence of the real object of her wrath makes the performance all the more remarkable.

Binder takes his rather brave and daring pretense—the full cleverness of which is not revealed until a major plot twist at the end—and occasionally tries to stretch Terry's plight into a statement on the universal human condition. This motif plays out in a video assignment young Popeye is doing for class, which deals with violence, war, misunderstanding, and tragedy as outgrowths of humans' inability to transcend their anger. Yet the suggestion at film's end is that the crucible of such anger can be cleansing.

You have to admire Binder for stretching outside the boundaries of convention. But it's also worth noting that the laudable ambition of his film is often dragged down by his subservience to the very convention he seeks to defy. Instead of giving us a zinger into the heart of darkness, Binder wants to charm and amuse audiences with the banter of sitcom land. To begin with, his Terry appears never to have worked a day in her life, and the characters live in a fairyland of upper-middle-class suburban privilege. Her life and her character lack grit, and you can't help but feel how spoiled Terry is, and how much her complaints amount to whining.

The four daughters are probably two too many. They serve mainly to provide Binder easy fodder for rather stilted domestic vignettes that highlight Terry's pain and her parenting dilemmas—as well as her character's short-sightedness, insensitivity and inflexibility. The oldest daughter, college-age Hadley (Alicia Witt), is cool to her mother, and Terry feels powerless with her, scolding her for having her own life apart from the drama at home. Control-freak Terry also freaks when daughter Andy (Erika Christensen) announces she isn't going to college and is getting a job instead. Mother also she does not honor the artistic achievements of daughter Emily (Keri Russell), whom she scolds for going to a "New Age" arts school rather than a top university. Popeye is not the object of any significant maternal foible—she's just constantly scolded for being young.

The impact of Binder's central dilemma of the wronged wife is frittered away in these mother-daughter spats and contrived and inessential subplots. Popeye wants to win the affections of Gordon (Dane Christensen), a boy who insists he is gay. She doesn't get into any trouble (and the thwarted teen romance serves no plot purpose). Andy's headstrong nature roils the waters when she takes a job with Denny's producer, Shep (played by Binder—note the character's name obviously denotes a buffoon). Shep is a 40-something sleazeball who likes to date women, like Andy, who are half his age, and when they becomes lovers, Terry has another reason to stew—and to blame Denny. Terry's antipathy toward both Hadley and Emily is less easy to explain or understand, and when she lashes out at them you recoil in horror and pity.

Terry drinks heavily, and that helps her forge a bond with Denny, a sluggish ne'er-do-well who doesn't want to talk about what his radio audience wants to hear about—his bygone glory days in baseball. He is ashamed of his own lack of direction in middle age and is attracted to the domestic fullness of Terry's life, as screwed up as it is. As he explains, while his house has nothing but a void and mementos of the past, her house is full of smells—the daughters seem constantly to be cooking up some huge dinner, while their mother seems incapable of helping.

Then Terry suddenly stops drinking, as the plot offers up some clumsy rebukes—a neglected daughter gets very sick (a lazy plot devise), and Denny loses his patience in an explosive scene of anger. It's not clear why these events don't plunge Terry into a deeper spiral of alcoholism and self-pity, but her character's arc relies on a three-year "time heals all wounds" explanation that doesn't completely wash.

Allen is awesome in her righteousness and pitiable in her wounded pride and excessive absorption in her own victimization. Binder's attitude is interestingly ambivalent—both honoring her plight and at times making it look ridiculous. The surprise ending throws everything into a new light, but instead of deepening the contradictions, Binder chooses a happy-ever-after ending that seems more than a bit contrived.

The Upside of Anger is mildly bizarre: you get a few shocking twists in otherwise predictable territory, like taking a packaged tour and having the tour bus break down in the middle of a dangerous place. But for the most part we're firmly on the bus, stuck in movie-suburbia land, stranded among standard family squabbles, and marooned at the climax. Is Terry's anger to be mourned, pitied, celebrated, or laughed away? It's all bottled up in her provincial life and attitude, and you get a sense of a privileged character suffocating in insular torments. Terry is all electricity in a closed circuit, sparking off bits of malevolent energy but usually failing to reach or transform those around her.

Costner, Allen, and Wood turn in fine performances—with Costner's being one of the most endearing he's had in quite awhile. In the end, Binder's venture becomes more of a puzzle than a satisfying exploration of the murky depths of human emotion. It's not clear what he's getting at, and he doesn't have the courage to follow through his observations and arrive at a really controversial destination. Are we supposed to applaud Terry for her integrity, despise her for her shallowness, or simply revel in the comfy landing spot of movie climaxes: life gives hard lessons, but all's well that ends well? I'll take a charitable explanation, and give credit for the film's unusual ambivalence about its protagonist.

Michael Betzold

CREDITS

Terry Wolfmeyer: Joan Allen
Denny: Kevin Costner
Andy Wolfmeyer: Erika Christensen
Popeye Wolfmeyer: Evan Rachel Wood
Emily Wolfmeyer: Keri Russell
Hadley Wolfmeyer: Alicia Witt
Adam "Shep" Goodman: Mike Binder
Gordon: Dane Christensen
Origin: USA
Language: English
Released: 2005
Production: Alex Gartner, Jack Binder, Sammy Lee; Sunlight; released by New Line Cinema
Directed by: Mike Binder
Written by: Mike Binder
Cinematography by: Richard Greatrex

Music by: Alexandre Desplat, Steve Edwards
Sound: Brian Simmons, Matthew Desorgher
Editing: Robin Sales
Art Direction: Tim Stevenson
Costumes: Deborah Scott
Production Design: Chris Roope
MPAA rating: R
Running time: 118 minutes

REVIEWS

Boxoffice Online. March, 2005.
Chicago Sun-Times Online. March 18, 2005.
Entertainment Weekly Online. March 9, 2005.
Los Angeles Times Online. March 11, 2005.
New York Times Online. March 11, 2005.
Variety Online. January 22, 2005.
Washington Post Online. March 18, 2005, p. C05.

TRIVIA

Director/writer Mike Binder said that Kevin Costner's character is a mixture of baseball players Kirk Gibson and Denny McLain (where the character gets his first name).

VALIANT

Some pigeons eat crumbs, others make history.
—Movie tagline
Featherweight Heroes.
—Movie tagline

Box Office: $19.4 million

Valiant, produced by England's Vanguard Animation and distributed by Disney, is the cheerful, good-natured tale of a little pigeon who wants nothing more than to be a member of the Royal Homing Pigeon Service, an elite squad carrying messages for the Allies during World War II. Determined and brave, Valiant (voice of Ewan McGregor) may be small, but, as he himself proudly declares, "It's not the size of your wingspan. No, it's the size of your spirit." Hewing to the well-trodden formula of the underdog who proves his worth against a formidable foe, this CG-animated feature, directed by Gary Chapman from a screenplay by Jordan Katz, George Webster, and George Melrod, also delivers some funny lines and high-flying adventure but does not create as richly imagined a world as we have seen in the cutting-edge work done in recent years by Pixar and DreamWorks. Interestingly enough, John H. Williams, who produced *Shrek* (2001) and *Shrek 2* (2004) for DreamWorks, shepherded this project at Vanguard, whose goal was to make *Valiant* for roughly half the money and in half the time it takes other studios to produce such a movie.

Inspired by a recruiting film (cleverly presented in the style of an old-time, grainy newsreel), Valiant yearns to join the service despite the fact that everyone tells him he is too little. On his way, he meets a pigeon named Bugsy (voice of Ricky Gervais), a self-styled ladies' man, fast talker, and con man who inadvertently enlists along with Valiant in order to escape some angry crows he recently swindled. Later searching for a way to get out, he says, "Maybe I'm not that conscientious, but I do object"—a witty line that sums up his quick-thinking wordplay. Gervais, who improvised much of his dialogue and based his character on Bob Hope's screen persona, is perfect as the swaggering, seemingly cowardly bird who ultimately becomes a loyal friend and hero.

Valiant is relatively short, even by standards of other animated films, and it is a shame that more time was not spent filling out this world and the relationships between the pigeons. Nonetheless, some offbeat avian humor helps fill in the gaps between the characters. Valiant's mother, for example, facing his pending enlistment, recalls that he was such a cute egg and then holds up a photo of the egg as if it were a baby picture. Insisting that he eat something before leaving home, she regurgitates a worm for him. Valiant's flirtation and little romance with a pretty nurse dove named Victoria (voice of Olivia Williams), feels fairly perfunctory—apart from his brief medical visits, the screenplay does not make time for a genuine rapport to develop—but one surprising scene finds him bringing her a flower and her eating the bug inside it before tossing aside the flower. Such is romance in the bird world.

The villains of the film are falcons with German accents led by the powerful Von Talon (voice of Tim Curry, almost unrecognizable except for his deep, hearty laugh). A pigeon named Mercury (voice of John Cleese) has become his prisoner of war, and scenes of Von Talon trying to get him to talk (torture by yodeling, truth serum) are fun at first but grow a bit tedious and go nowhere.

Valiant and his small band of fellow recruits undergo tough training under Sarge (voice of Jim Broadbent), which includes lifting weights (consisting of an apple on each end of a stick) and learning to make aerial formations. It is characteristic of the film's lack of depth that the rest of the tiny squad is given short shrift and is composed of characters who are not very well developed. Together they are a bit of a hapless band called into duty before they are truly ready when another squad fails its mission. Led by the legendary Wing Commander Gutsy (voice of Hugh Laurie), Valiant's squad receives its orders to fly into occupied France and bring back an important message that will determine the outcome of the war.

Valiant rises to the occasion as leader of the mission and contacts the mouse division of the French Resistance, led by the cute and aptly named Charles De Girl (voice of Sharon Horgan). Bugsy retrieves the message but is captured by the falcons when he saves Valiant during a thrilling chase. Because everyone else in the squad is too big to sneak into Von Talon's fortified bunker, Valiant becomes the hero—getting the message and rescuing Bugsy as well. But Von Talon chases Valiant all the way back to England, where Valiant traps his nemesis in a climactic confrontation at an old mill and then goes on to deliver the message, which, in a great finish, leads to the Normandy invasion. We are told at the film's end that animals really did make contributions to the Allied war effort and were given the Dickin Medal for their efforts. Pigeons, with 32 awards, were the most celebrated.

Compared to other recent animated features that have more sophisticated characters and more complex plots, *Valiant* is rather thin, but its sweet story and bits of sly humor are nonetheless very appealing. Despite its computer-generated imagery, *Valiant* is an unabashedly old-fashioned kind of family entertainment; devoid of irony and pop culture references, it is full of good humor, bright colors, exciting derring-do, and a message about never giving up on one's dream.

Peter N. Chumo II

CREDITS

Valiant: Ewan McGregor (Voice)
General Von Talon: Tim Curry (Voice)
Sergeant: Jim Broadbent (Voice)
Gutsy: Hugh Laurie (Voice)
Tailfeather: Daniel Roberts (Voice)
Mercury: John Cleese (Voice)
Felix: John Hurt (Voice)
Lofty: Pip Torrens (Voice)
Bugsy: Ricky Gervais (Voice)
Toughwood: Brian Lonsdale (Voice)
Victoria: Olivia Williams (Voice)
Cufflingk: Rik Mayall (Voice)
Charles De Girl: Sharon Horgan (Voice)
Origin: Great Britain, USA
Language: English
Released: 2005
Production: John H. Williams, Shuzo John Shiota; Odyssey Entertainment, Take Film Partnerships, Baker Street Finance; released by Buena Vista, Touchstone Pictures, Vanguard Animation
Directed by: Gary Chapman
Written by: Jordan Katz, George Webster, George Melrod
Cinematography by: John Fenner
Music by: George Fenton
Editing: Jim Stewart
Art Direction: Carl Jones
MPAA rating: G
Running time: 80 minutes

REVIEWS

Boxoffice Online. August, 2005.
Entertainment Weekly Online. August 17, 2005.
Los Angeles Times Online. August 19, 2005.
New York Times Online. August 19, 2005.
Premiere Magazine Online. August 18, 2005.
Variety Online. March 31, 2005.

QUOTES

Valiant: " It's not the size of your wingspan that counts, no, it's the size of your spirit."

TRIVIA

The film took more than two years to complete.

WAITING...

No one's gonna make it big here.
—Movie tagline

This is not what I ordered.
—Movie tagline

*Never F*** with the people that serve you food!*
—Movie tagline

What happens in the kitchen ends up on the plate.
—Movie tagline

Chicken flied steak, anyone?
—Movie tagline

Box Office: $16.1 million

Perhaps the legacy of *Waiting...* will be that it inspires a generation of filmgoers to treat waitstaffers much more courteously. *Waiting...* shows graphically, most would probably say too graphically, exactly what happens in the kitchen to the food of complaining customers. Suffice it to say that it is mighty gross. Customers whose food is tossed onto the kitchen floor to provide "floor flavoring" are the lucky ones.

The movie takes place in a restaurant called Shenaniganz, a theme restaurant along the lines of Bennigan's, TGI Friday's, Chili's, Applebee's, ad nauseum. Production designer Devorah Herbert should get kudos for the way she so perfectly captures the feel of such restaurants. There is the dark green and wood color scheme, the brass railings and the corporate-issued bits of whimsical signs and photos crowding the walls. Such restaurants grew popular in the 1980s and Shenanigans is starting to show its wear.

The film takes place over the period of one day. First time writer and director Rob McKittrick attempt to capture the boredom, humor and desperation of college age (and older) kids working a restaurant. The job is low-status, there are long hours and little hope for a good future. The way they cope with all this is by becoming romantically involved with each other fueled by nightly afterwork parties with plenty of beer.

McKittrick, who himself spent six years working in similar restaurants, surely had enough material to make a witty, *Clerks*-like film, but somehow does not end up with such a film. Instead of using the humor inherent in such a recognizable work place like *Clerks* and *Office Space*, *Waiting...* instead goes in the direction of gross-out humor, homophobic jokes, and the hilarity of lusting after underage sexual conquests.

The audience's tour guide into this world is Monty (Ryan Reynolds), a long-timer who is supposedly training new guy Mitch (John Francis Daley). Monty seems a bit older than the rest of the crew, and he is looked to as the alpha male. He is a master of schmoozing customers and getting the prettiest girlfriends. (Although, as the movie explains in a typically offensive line of dialogue, being the coolest guy at Shenaniganz is akin to being the smartest guy at the Special Olympics.) Monty spends most of his time with Mitch explaining the many varieties of a complex game that the workers have devised that involves getting other workers to inadvertently look at their genitals.

Dean (Justin Long) is a former high school honors student who is taking classes at a community college and trying to figure out what to do with his life. When the buffoonish manager, Dan (David Koechner), offers

Dean the assistant manager job, he has to figure out whether taking the job would eventually condemn him to a life sentence in the food service industry. Naomi (Alanna Ubach) is a tightly wound waitress who has been working in the restaurant too long. The best (and only) joke around her character is that, as shrill and horrible as she is in the kitchen, once she is at her table, she is all friendly, obsequious smiles. There is also the Bishop (Chi McBride), an older dishwasher who dispenses surprisingly wise advice to employees who come sit with him. Calvin (Patrick Benedict) is a virgin who has a shy bladder and leaves way too many messages on his would-be girlfriend's answering machine. Also along are Luiz Guzman as a cook who is a little bit too into putting gross things into the customers' food and Anna Faris as Monty's sharp ex-girlfriend. Hilarious stand-up phenom Dana Cook is a standout in his all too brief stint as assistant cook Floyd.

Most critics did not like the movie. Roger Ebert of *The Chicago Sun-Times* did not care for the film and wrote, "The characters in *Waiting...* seem like types, not people. What they do and say isn't funny because someone real doesn't seem to be doing or saying it." Stephen Holden of The New York Times wrote, "*Waiting...*, a witless farce about working at a chain restaurant, belongs in a circle of gross-out hell somewhere below *Porky's* and slightly above the recent Jenny McCarthy debacle, *Dirty Love*." Ty Burr of *The Boston Globe* called it a "friendly but poorly made timewaster that confuses frat-house crudity and shock gags with actual humor. Teenage boys will be in heaven. All others: Check, please." Representing the minority of critics who did like the film was Peter Hartlaub of *The San Francisco Chronicle* who wrote, "This movie's two goals are to be over-the-top funny and remind audiences what it feels like to be in your early 20s without a plan, and it's a complete success in both areas."

Jill Hamilton

CREDITS

Monty: Ryan Reynolds
Serena: Anna Faris
Dean: Justin Long
Dan: David Koechner
Raddimus: Luis Guzman
Bishop: Chi McBride
Naomi: Alanna Ubach
Natasha: Vanessa Lengies
T-Dog: Max Kasch
Floyd: Dane Cook
Danielle: Jordan Ladd
Tyla: Emmanuelle Chriqui
Monty's mom: Wendie Malick
Mitch: John Francis Daley
Amy: Kaitlin Doubleday
Calvin: Robert Patrick Benedict
Nick: Andy Milonakis
Origin: USA
Language: English
Released: 2005
Production: Jeff Balis, Jay Rifkin, Rob Green, Stavros Merjos, Adam Rosenfelt; Eden Rock Media, Element Films, Wisenheimer Films; released by Lions Gate Films
Directed by: Rob McKittrick
Written by: Rob McKittrick
Cinematography by: Matthew Irving
Music by: Adam Gorgoni
Sound: Scott Sanders, Stew Bernstein, Richard Dwan
Music Supervisor: Pete Soldinger
Editing: Andy Blumenthal, David Finfer
Art Direction: Morgan Blackledge
Costumes: Jillian Kreiner
Production Design: Devorah Herbert
MPAA rating: R
Running time: 93 minutes

REVIEWS

Boxoffice Online. October, 2005.
Chicago Sun-Times Online. October 7, 2005.
Entertainment Weekly Online. October 5, 2005.
Los Angeles Times Online. October 7, 2005.
New York Times Online. October 7, 2005.
Premiere Magazine Online. October 6, 2005.
Variety Online. October 3, 2005.

QUOTES

Floyd: "We almost had to move it up to the 10 second rule!"

WALK THE LINE

Love is a burning thing.
—Movie tagline

Box Office: $89 million

Coming a year after *Ray* (2004), *Walk the Line* faces comparisons because the subjects of the two films are so similar. Both Ray Charles and Johnny Cash had brothers who died young, leaving the survivor haunted by guilt. Both experienced years of difficulties with alcohol and drugs while becoming America's most popular rhythm and blues and country singers, respectively, before finally overcoming these demons. Both films are also similar in being rather conventional narratives, except for the flashbacks to Charles's boyhood. With just a few changes, either could be a made-for-television biopic. Yet both overcome these flaws to some degree through the force of their performances. In addition to Jamie Foxx's indelible portrayal of Charles, Ray offers excellent work by almost everyone in a large cast. *Walk the Line* is carried by its lead performers, with several outstanding performances among the supporting cast.

The life of Cash (Joaquin Phoenix) is followed from the death of his beloved brother, Jack (Lucas Till), in 1944, to his days in the Air Force in Germany in the early 1950s, to the beginnings of his musical career in Memphis, and on to success and chaos. Cash's alcoholic father, Ray (Robert Patrick), blames him for Jack's death and never has a kind word for him, even after Cash becomes famous. When Cash sees a newsreel about California's Folsom Prison while in the service, he identifies with the convicts because he is imprisoned emotionally. An impulsive marriage to the constantly nagging Vivian (Ginnifer Goodwin) only increases his sense of isolation.

Vivian wants Cash to be a success as a door-to-door salesman, but he pursues a singing career and enlists two auto mechanics (Larry Bagby and Dan John Miller) as his band. When the trio auditions for Sun Records' Sam Phillips (Dallas Roberts) with a gospel number, Phillips is not impressed and suggests Cash sing something that conveys his true feelings. He responds with "Folsom Prison Blues," which he composed in response to the newsreel, and history, as they say, is made. This scene corresponds to a similar moment in the television miniseries Elvis, when the young Presley struggles to find his true voice at the instigation of a prodding Phillips.

Performing on the road, Cash's eye is caught by the spunky June Carter (Reese Witherspoon), a recent divorcee who rejects his advances. The rest of *Walk the Line* consists of Cash pursuing June and her holding him off despite her attraction to him. This storyline is complicated by Cash's use of amphetamines, which the film blames on Elvis (Tyler Hilton). Insecure about performing on stage, Cash is told that Elvis pops pills, so he does as well. An irony of the situation is that Cash abuses drugs because June will not love him, and she cannot return his affections because of the pills and the drinking.

If Cash were not such a tormented soul, however, his music would not have the emotional impact it has for his fans. Cash reads fan letters from convicts and decides to record a live concert at Folsom. This is the highpoint of his career, propelling him on to greater popularity. Again, there is a parallel with Elvis and the acoustic television special that launched Presley's comeback.

Director James Mangold, who co-wrote the screenplay with Gill Dennis, is at his best with individual scenes, as with Cash's confrontation with the suits at Columbia Records over the live Folsom album. A good moment comes when a tentative Cash goes into an alley to sneak a peek at a Presley recording session at Sun only for an unsympathetic Phillips to close the door in his face. Another moving scene has June innocently shopping only for a stranger to tell her she is going to the devil for being divorced. The best moment occurs when the Folsom warden (James Keach, producer of the film) tells Cash not to sing anything that will remind the prisoners of where they so and the singer tears into "Cocaine Blues."

Though predictable and occasionally a bit sluggish, *Walk the Line* is nevertheless made enthralling by its performances. If Phoenix's Cash is not quite the tour-de-force Foxx's Charles is, it is still impressive. Beefed up from his previous roles, swaggering in Cash's trademark black clothing, Phoenix resembles Michael Madsen but seems influenced by James Dean and Marlon Brando in his portrait of a misunderstood man tormented by inner demons. Pain and insecurity flood from Phoenix's eyes.

Just as June battled her doubts about her singing talents by doing a comedy act, Witherspoon has had much more success in comedies than in dramas. She ably conveys June's mixed emotions about Cash, though the screenplay does not make clear why June would be attracted to him other than good girls like bad boys. Given the limitations of the role, Witherspoon, an extremely appealing actress, is terrific.

Waylon Malloy Payne steals every scene he is in as Jerry Lee Lewis. The son of country singer Sammi Smith, of "Help Me Make It Through the Night" fame, and Willie Nelson guitarist Jody Payne, the actor conveys Lewis's cocky wildness more convincingly than does Dennis Quaid in *Great Balls of Fire* (1989). Payne is named for his godfather Waylon Jennings, and Jennings' son Shooter plays his father in *Walk the Line.* In addition to Cash, Presley, Lewis, and Jennings, Carl Perkins (Johnny Holiday) and Roy Orbison (Johnathan Rice) are also depicted, though Lewis' role is the only one of substance.

Roberts gives a subtle performance as the legendary Phillips. (While Ray Charles's shift from the record label that gives him his break to a bigger company is significant in Ray , Cash's leaving Sun for Columbia is not shown because it is not part of his ongoing trauma.) Ridge Canipe, who resembles Phoenix, is quite good as the young Johnny, displaying the boy's sorrow over his brother's death and his sadness at being blamed. Patrick, a dependable character actor, gives Ray Cash an explosive edge that shows Johnny is truly his father's son. Patrick is softer, more contained as Virgil Presley in Elvis.

While Foxx does not do his own singing in *Ray,* Witherspoon and Phoenix, who underwent six months of training, do and perform ably. Phoenix lowers his natural voice several registers to approximate Cash's distinctive bass growl. While Phoenix appears to have more of a rock edge than the real Cash, the singer began his Sun career as a rockabilly artist in the manner of Presley, Perkins, and Lewis. In many of his songs, Cash married a rock-and-roll attitude to country lyrics. The film's musical highlight is Phoenix and Witherspoon's spirited duet of Bob Dylan's "It Ain't Me, Babe."

Though Cash and Carter died in 2003, they were involved in the early stages of the film's productions and approved of Mangold's interpretation of their lives. Cash invited Phoenix to dinner because of his admiration of the young actor's work in *Gladiator* (2000) and approved of his casting. Though Phoenix is much shorter than the singer, he wonderfully conveys the singer's stature and intensity.

Michael Adams

CREDITS

John R. Cash: Joaquin Rafael (Leaf) Phoenix
June Carter: Reese Witherspoon
Vivian Cash: Ginnifer Goodwin
Ray Cash: Robert Patrick
Sam Phillips: Dallas Roberts
Marshall Grant: Larry Bagby
Luther Perkins: Dan John Miller
Carrie Cash: Shelby Lynne
Elvis Presley: Tyler Hilton
Jerry Lee Lewis: Waylon Malloy Payne
Shooter Jennins: Waylon Jennings
Origin: USA
Language: English
Released: 2005
Production: Cathy Konrad, James Keach; Catfish Productions; released by 20th Century-Fox, Tree Film, Line Film
Directed by: James Mangold
Written by: James Mangold, Gill Dennis
Cinematography by: Phedon Papamichael
Music by: T-Bone Burnett
Sound: Peter Kurland
Editing: Michael McCusker
Art Direction: Rob Simons
Costumes: Arianne Phillips
Production Design: David J. Bomba
MPAA rating: PG-13
Running time: 135 minutes

REVIEWS

Boxoffice Online. November, 2005.
Chicago Sun-Times Online. November 18, 2005.
Entertainment Weekly Online. November 16, 2005.
Los Angeles Times Online. November 18, 2005.
New York Times Online. November 18, 2005.
Premiere Magazine Online. November 17, 2005.
Variety Online. September 5, 2005.
Washington Post Online. November 18, 2005, p. C01.

QUOTES

Johnny Cash: "June, I've asked you to marry me 40 different ways, and I'm waiting for a fresh answer!"

TRIVIA

Producers worked for four years to secure the rights to the story from James Keach who is a friend of Johnny Cash and his family. After Keach agreed, it took another four years to get the film made.

AWARDS

Oscars 2005: Actress (Witherspoon)
British Acad. 2005: Actress (Witherspoon), Sound
Golden Globes 2006: Actor—Mus./Comedy (Phoenix), Actress—Mus./Comedy (Witherspoon), Film—Mus./Comedy
N.Y. Film Critics 2005: Actress (Witherspoon)
Natl. Soc. Film Critics 2005: Actress (Witherspoon)
Screen Actors Guild 2005: Actress (Witherspoon)

Nomination:

Oscars 2005: Actor (Phoenix), Costume Des., Film Editing, Sound
British Acad. 2005: Actor (Phoenix)
Screen Actors Guild 2005: Actor (Phoenix).

WALLACE & GROMIT: THE CURSE OF THE WERE-RABBIT

Something bunny is going on...
—Movie tagline

Wallace=Master, Gromit=Mind
—Movie tagline

Something wicked this way hops.
—Movie tagline

Box Office: $55.7 million

Sixteen years ago a young Nick Park finally finished his graduate project. It had taken him six years to hand craft the characters that would populate his stop-action, short feature *A Grand Day Out.* It paid off, though, for it was nominated for an Oscar in 1990, only to lose to another Nick Park entry, *Creature Comforts.* But the main characters of *A Grand Day Out* would go on to star in two more short features, *The Wrong Trousers* in 1994 and *A Close Shave* in 1996. These features again garnered Oscar nominations for Park, and both of them won. So, with three nominations and two wins under their belts, it is no wonder that the characters featured in all three would go on to star in a feature-length movie of their own.

For those not familiar with Park's work, they are missing out on two wonderful characters, Wallace and Gromit. Wallace is the optimistic, cheese-loving inventor of contraptions that would make Rube Goldberg quite proud. Gromit is Wallace's unflappable, intelligent canine who never says a word but speaks volumes with his eyebrows. While Wallace cheerfully invents his way into mess after mess, Gromit is stoically resigned to constantly having to clean up after him. They are a duo worthy of Abbott and Costello or Laurel and Hardy comparisons, and a duo who have won the hearts of millions of animation fans worldwide.

In 2000, Park's Aardman Features released its first animated feature, a co-production with DreamWorks called *Chicken Run.* It was a critical and popular success, but it didn't feature Wallace and Gromit. *The Curse of the Were-Rabbit,* Aardman and DreamWork's second co-production rectifies that situation.

Set in an idyllic English village circa the 1950s, *Wallace and Gromit: The Curse of the Were-Rabbit* is a delightful horror-romance that contains no gore or sex. In fact, Park calls it the first vegetarian horror film, and that should tell one a lot about Park's off-kilter sense of humor.

In this village everyone is preparing for the Giant Vegetable Competition, which has been sponsored by Lady Tottingham's (voice of Helena Bonham Carter) family since the middle ages. The prize is the Golden Carrot, but there is a threat to the British gardeners' prize veggies...rabbits. So to protect their crops the people of the village have hired Wallace (voice of Peter Sallis) and Gromit to keep their gardens free of the furry pests. Their business is called, appropriately and punnily enough, Anti-Pesto, which watches over the plots via a gnome surveillance system. When rabbits are spotted, Wallace and Gromit sweep in with their Bunny-Vac 6000, which humanely sucks them up at a rate of 125 RPMs (rabbits per minute). They are then taken back to Wallace's basement where they are well cared for. In fact, Wallace wonders if maybe he can't rehabilitate the rabbits by using his latest invention, the Mind Manipulation-O-Matic, which extracts unwanted thoughts from one's brain. He tries it out on himself and a rabbit, but it doesn't seem to work...or does it?

But all is not well for the bunnies, for also wanting to rid the borough of its rabbits is one Lord Victor Quartermaine (voice of Ralph Fiennes) who wants nothing more than to blast them into oblivion. Victor has an obsession with hunting and an obsession with winning the hand of the eccentric but desirable Lady Tottingham. Not so much because he loves her as he wants her name, her prestige, her lands, and her money. The pompous cad Victor, however, will also soon have a suitor for Lady Tottingham's affections. When she calls in Wallace to rid her estate of some pesky rabbits, Wallace is immediately smitten and Victor immediately threatened.

It's not long before there is a terrible night of vegetable carnage and not even Anti-Pesto seems able to stop this new and monstrous vegetable predator, the were-rabbit. Luckily the local vicar has a book detailing how to get rid of a were-rabbit, and it involves a bullet of pure gold, 24 carat, naturally. So now it becomes a race between Wallace who promises Lady Tottingham to trap the rabbit and Victor who would love nothing more than to shoot it.

Wallace and Gromit: The Curse of the Were-Rabbit is a whimsical and funny romp that will appeal to both old and young. It has enough physical humor to appeal to the kids and more than enough wit and pun—both in the foreground and the background—to appeal to the adults. There is a real aerial dogfight between two dogs, Wallace's Gromit and Victor's bulldog Philip. There are books in the library with titles like *East of Edam* and *Fromage to Eternity.* There is a vegetable shop named "Harvey's" (after Jimmy Stewart's invisible rabbit), a barbershop called "A Close Shave" (after Park's own feature) and one that springs up when needed called "Angry Mob Supplies." There is an hysterical exchange between Victor and Wallace concerning the homonyms "toupee" and "to pay" and "hairs" and "hares." That monster book the vicar refers to is written by Claude Savagely, and the label on the box a naked Wallace finds himself dressed in at one point is too funny to be ruined here.

This is a film that is not only a funny and witty lampoon of old horror films, it is also a world of the gentle and the kind. There is a distinct optimism to Wallace's can-do spirit and even to Lady Tottingham's bubbly eccentricities. And it looks and sounds great, too. With music by Julian Not and wonderfully hand-crafted plasticine characters, it is a sheer pleasure to watch. And if one pays close enough attention, one can find that the humanity of the characters and the story is remarkably reflected in the occasional fingerprint that appears on a character's body.

Beverley Bare Buehrer

CREDITS

Wallace: Peter Sallis (Voice)
Victor Quartermaine: Ralph Fiennes (Voice)
Lady Campanula Tottington: Helena Bonham Carter (Voice)
Reverend Clement Hedges: Nicholas C. Smith (Voice)
Mrs. Mulch: Liz Smith (Voice)
PC Mackintosh: Peter Kay (Voice)
Origin: Great Britain
Language: English
Released: 2005
Production: Claire Jennings, Carla Shelley, David Sproxton, Peter Lord, Nick Park; Aardman Production; released by DreamWorks
Directed by: Nick Park, Steve Box
Written by: Nick Park, Steve Box, Bob Baker, Mark Burton
Cinematography by: Tristan Oliver, Dave Alex-Riddett
Music by: Julian Nott, Hans Zimmer
Editing: Dave McCormick, Gregory Perler
Production Design: Phill Lewis
MPAA rating: G
Running time: 85 minutes

REVIEWS

Boxoffice Online. October, 2005.
Chicago Sun-Times Online. October 7, 2005.
Entertainment Weekly Online. October 5, 2005.
Los Angeles Times Online. October 5, 2005.
New York Times Online. October 5, 2005.
Premiere Magazine Online. October 5, 2005.
Variety Online. September 16, 2005.

QUOTES

Wallace, to Gromit, while he's holding a carrot and has fluffy rabbit-ears: "What's up, Doc?"

TRIVIA

The Latin motto of the Tottington family inscribed on the manor house translates roughly as "Manure Liberates Us All."

AWARDS

Oscars 2005: Animated Film
L.A. Film Critics 2005: Animated Film
Broadcast Film Critics 2005: Animated Film.

WAR OF THE WORLDS

They're already here.
—Movie tagline

This Summer, the last war on Earth won't be started by humans.
—Movie tagline

Box Office: $234 million

In Steven Spielberg's new version of the H.G. Wells classic, *War of the Worlds*, human beings are clueless dupes. They've done nothing to provoke the enmity of another race, but suddenly they are under attack by an enemy so powerful and so advanced that there seems no hope of survival. From an apparently omnipotent narrator's perspective, Morgan Freeman solemnly tells us how unprepared civilization is for what is about to befall it. Freeman is the new James Earl Jones when it comes to voice-of-God cinematic needs. Steven Spielberg is confident enough of his ability to carry an apocalyptic mood that he doesn't bother to ease into the story. Not only does Freeman tell us the world is in trouble, it seems that Americans are the last to catch on.

What's worse, the film's protagonist, Ray Ferrier (played by a bug-eyed, nearly over-the-top Tom Cruise) clearly has trouble with responsibility. He won't work an extra shift at the docks, citing union rules but not because he's a union man, just because he's making excuses. Then he's a half-hour late receiving the handoff of his two kids, the surly Robbie (Justin Chatwick) and the adorably precocious Rachel (the ubiquitous Dakota Fanning), from their mom and his ex, Mary Ann (Miranda Otto, who proved in *Return of the King* that she's certainly up to any challenge). And his refrigerator is empty. He tries to interact with his son by playing catch, but it's more like they're each lobbing balls of venom at each other. It's the antithesis of the father-son game of catch in *Field of Dreams*: these two aren't reconnecting, they're at war. Not much later, Ray takes a nap and tells the poor kids to order out. OK, Spielberg, we get the point—he's a bad father, but only because he hasn't really been paying much attention.

Then something awakens his interest: a storm unlike anything anyone's ever seen. It comes up out of the ocean, with scary black clouds and frequent lightning, but no thunder. (This proves to be doubly strange when it's later revealed the lightning is a stairway to underground battle stations for the aliens; so why would it be striking over water?) In an evocative, memorable scene, Ray and his neighbors, who live in Brooklyn right under the Brooklyn Bridge, stand in their tiny fenced-off back yards, one potential victim after another, and stare at the phenomenon, transfixed. Only Rachel has the sense to run inside the house.

Ray and many other Brooklynites prove to be a curious bunch indeed. They run out of their homes and apartments after the lightning strikes are over to survey the damage. They gather around an intersection where a fissure is opening in the asphalt. Even when the fissure becomes a menacing crack, and the street falls in and there's a huge crater, Ray and his buddies and neighbors simply stay at the edge of the hole and gape. And even when a giant tripod monster emerges from the hole in the street, they don't all run.

The tripod, the size of a very tall building, starts blasting the fleeing citizens with vaporizing rays of lights. Panic ensues—and not a second too late. Ray rushes home, somehow eluding the tripod (he proves quite adept at this, or lucky). He somehow figures he's only got a couple minutes to spare, gathers up his kids and some provisions, and takes them to the local auto repair shop. The lightning strikes have rendered all the cars immobile (a television report in the background says something about EMP, electromagnetic pulse), but Ray has figured out this can be overcome through the installation of a solenoid, and he's instructed his mechanic buddy to do so. In short order, he's commandeered what's apparently the only functioning car in the whole borough, invited his mechanic friend to come along and then watched him be vaporized as he refuses.

And so this broken family starts out on what becomes a road trip from hell, a nightmarish journey through crowds of dazed survivors and into landscapes of deeper and more widespread devastation. This is not a standard science-fiction movie: it's more like a horror movie played on a grand scale. And it also has the cruel and unrelenting tenor of Spielberg's most emotionally difficult movies, *Saving Private Ryan* and *Schindler's List.*

Cruise's protagonist and his kids go through increasingly harrowing trials by fire. Hiding in the basement of his ex-wife's house, they see a blinding flash and then surface to discover a plane has crashed outside the house. Somehow they can drive right out of the debris (the film requires plenty of suspension of disbelief). The plan is to get to Boston, where his ex-wife and her husband have gone to visit her parents. But when they try to cross the Hudson River upstream on a ferry near Albany, they find a horde of people so desperate they are willing to fight and even kill just to get possession of a car.

In this disaster movie, there is nothing except unexplained disaster. Soldiers occasionally rush past, and a news crew at the plane crash gives Ray—and us—a better grasp of the scope of the alien attack. It soon becomes clear there is virtually no place to run and hide from the tripods. But we don't get scenes of generals in control, or command centers. Instead, as the devastation becomes more vast, the film becomes claustrophobic. Robbie, who apparently has an inexplicable urge to be a fighter on the front lines (a desire that seems totally at odds with his slacker character), leaves and joins up with the soldiers in tanks who seem to be hilariously mismatched. We don't see him again until film's end.

Ray and Rachel end up holed up in a basement with a crazed survivalist played with eerie craziness by Tim Robbins. There we are treated to an excruciating game of hide-and-seek involving the aliens and their machines, including a long sequence where a snake-like mechanical imager is eventually eluded by means of a mirror. This is where the movie stops being about a war against aliens and shifts into a psychological study of the fear of being discovered. The film focuses on Ray's ingeniousness and his overwhelming desire to protect and defend his daughter. It raises the question of character: How far would you go to protect yourself and your family in a time of war?

Spielberg's forte is the use of iconic imagery to drive home the emotional impact of his storyline, and *War of the Worlds* is a virtually non-stop display of that talent. Special effects have never been used with such skill (with the possible exception of the *Lord of the Rings* trilogy) to marry fearsome images to the projection of unending and overwhelming peril. Spielberg's alternating use of broad landscapes to reveal the attacks and the extent of destruction and his close-ups of Ray and the kids tells the story of a global attack in highly personal terms.

Quite a few reviewers (including David Denby in the *New Yorker*) expressed dismay that Spielberg's film is almost completely devoid of secondary characters and subplots. At times Spielberg seems to toy with that possibility, at one point introducing a character during the ferry crossing that may be a girlfriend of Ray, but she is quickly destroyed along with the others. Perhaps the film has more impact precisely because it's so direct and unrelenting, but much of that depends on your tolerance for Cruise and Fanning and your ability to identify with their characters.

Cruise gives a performance that's fairly comfortable for him: the ordinary guy awakened to his reservoir of inner heroism (for him, this dates all the way back to *Risky Business*). He's a metaphor for an entire generation of American men who remained trapped in a perpetual adolescence until challenged to be a man, and Ray fits squarely into this motif. He has even to earn the respect of his son, who appears to have more guts than he does (though even less sense). Cruise's performance does not seem effortless, however; instead, it seems strained and overdone, full of the actor's obvious efforts to disappear into his role. He does not succeed: he's basically Tom Cruise fighting aliens.

At her young age, Fanning is also already in danger of disappearing into a stereotyped character she's played before (*Man on Fire, Hide and Seek*): the precocious young girl in great peril. Spielberg makes every effort to emphasize her vulnerability and emotion, but after awhile it's a little absurd. When Ray must meet his biggest challenge as a man—whether he is capable of killing another man to save his family—he blindfolds Rachel and she blocks her ears. But she's already seen people incinerated on a bloody battlefield, so presumably she's been emotionally prepared.

War of the Worlds is Spielberg at his best and his worst. His tripods are spectacularly menacing, especially looming over a hill above a village full of frightened citizens trapped between them and a ferry that is leaving the docks. The world eventually becomes draped in bloody threads of root systems that are the filament of fertilization by the aliens. The scenes are powerful, if sometimes in a glorified B-movie kind of way. But Spielberg seems to want to sample all of his movies—there are visual references to *E.T., Jurassic Park, Saving Private Ryan*, and others. And he can't resist the impulse to make his menacing aliens both reptilian and a tad cute.

What's most frustrating is that the film provides no solid and coherent explanation for the timing of the arrival of the aliens and the motives for their attack, nor does it explain why they eventually meet their demise. It has something to do with their intolerance for the human climate, which is a bit absurd considering their power. (The film has probably the most unsatisfying and least credible happy ending in disaster movie history.) It's almost as if the details of the plot are uninteresting to the filmmaker, and that's what's most disturbing about Spielberg's vision. Rachel early on asks her father if these are terrorists, and since the family is living in New York City, it's clear what wellsprings of emotion Spielberg is exploiting.

He fits his panorama of unremitting terror—and even the senselessness of it—into the current sources of civic uneasiness just as surely as the 1950s sci-fi movies tapped into the fear of nuclear weapons. What Spielberg seems to be asking is this: Who among this current population of irresponsible grown-up juvenile men has the guts and the brains to figure out how to survive the terror of all-out, unprovoked attack? Hell, he even gives us Robbins as a survivalist who doesn't have what it takes just to serve as a foil for Cruise.

Is this exploitive? It surely is. Spielberg is the unchallenged master at exploiting basic human emotions, and *War of the Worlds* is one long manipulation of our deep-seated fears of a terror attack. On the other hand, perhaps the success of Spielberg in this quest proves that he is a great moviemaker, for he is focused and unrelenting in his pursuit of the impact of panic. Stripped of pretense and diversions, *War of the Worlds* is perhaps Spielberg's most focused movie since *Jaws*. He's hitting the same tone, over and over, and there is nothing complex about his message. It's a tour de force of an uncomplicated (though not very original) idea.

Michael Betzold

CREDITS

Ray Ferrier: Tom Cruise
Rachel Ferrier: Dakota Fanning
Mary Ann: Miranda Otto
Ogilvy: Tim Robbins
Robbie Ferrier: Justin Chatwin
Vincent: Rick Gonzalez
Tim: David Alan Basche
Julio: Yul Vazquez
Manny the Mechanic: Lenny Venito
Bartender: Lisa Ann Walter
Grandmother: Ann (Robin) Robinson
Grandfather: Gene Barry
Narrator: Morgan Freeman (Narrated)
Origin: USA
Language: English
Released: 2005
Production: Kathleen Kennedy, Colin Wilson; Amblin Entertainment, Cruise-Wagner Productions; released by Paramount
Directed by: Steven Spielberg
Written by: David Koepp, Josh Friedman
Cinematography by: Janusz Kaminski
Music by: John Williams
Sound: Ronald Judkins
Editing: Michael Kahn
Art Direction: Doug Meerdink, Andrew Menzies, Norman Newberry
Costumes: Joanna Johnston
Production Design: Rick Carter
MPAA rating: PG-13
Running time: 118 minutes

REVIEWS

Boxoffice Online. June, 2005.
Chicago Sun-Times Online. June 29, 2005.
Entertainment Weekly Online. June 29, 2005.
Los Angeles Times Online. June 29, 2005.
New York Times Online. June 29, 2005.
Premiere Magazine Online. June 28,2005.
Variety Online. June 28, 2005.
Washington Post Online. June 29, 2005, p. C01.

QUOTES

Ogilvy: "They've been planning this for a million years. And these are only the first. They'll keep coming."

TRIVIA

A *Jaws* (1975) movie poster hangs on one of the walls in Ray's house that can be seen at the beginning of the film.

AWARDS

Nomination:

Oscars 2005: Sound, Visual FX

Golden Raspberries 2005: Worst Actor (Cruise).

THE WEATHER MAN

...bring an umbrella
—Movie tagline

Box Office: $12.5 million

Think of one of those bleak winter days, the dark, dreary sky only occasionally brightening to a shade that is still rather gray, and you will know what *The Weather Man* is like. It is a low-key, predominantly overcast but quite effective character study of a Chicago TV weather forecaster who must find a way to make peace with life's distressing unpredictability and disappointments. Bearing the vaguely irritating professional name of Dave Spritz (well-cast Nicolas Cage), he tries desperately, persistently, often misguidedly, sometimes angrily, often with good intentions, and really rather poignantly to get his footing. However, while some sizeable success in his career seems to be just around the corner, the stability and satisfaction he yearns for in his personal life seems to always lie more than a few stumbling blocks down the road.

The Weather Man sets its chilly, gloomy tone with a desolate, frigid shot of Lake Michigan, undulating and ice-covered beneath the looming Chicago skyline. (There is excellent, crystalline cinematography throughout by Phedon Papamichael.) Dave's current on-air position there is a successful and lucrative cakewalk. He cheerfully delivers weather predictions others come up with for him because he never got around to getting a meteorological degree. He spends a lot of time planted next to the water cooler. Aside from the fact that some disgruntled weather-watchers persistently pelt him on the street with jumbo-sized beverages and other sloppy fast-food menu choices, the hardest thing about his job is that his viewers expect him to be the smiling, affable man they see on the news when they come up to him for information or autographs. Dave would much rather that they left him alone, and when he brushes them off they assume he thinks he is someone special. Actually, Dave thinks of himself as anything but superior, and his simmering frustration and dispiriting sense of inadequacy sometimes come up to the surface in less-than-attractive ways. For unfortunately, just like the difference between the climate-controlled studio and the ever-changing environment outside, Dave's success at his less-than-taxing job is a far cry from his trying and turbulent life off-camera.

Dave's wife Noreen (Hope Davis) has divorced him and is now getting serious with Russ (Michael Rispoli). His rather vague, stubby 12-year-old daughter Shelly (Gemmenne de la Pena) is sullen, clandestinely smoking, and being called something rude and obscene at school due to her too-tight pants. His troubled teenage son Mike (Nicholas Hoult, so good in 2002's *About A Boy*) is just emerging from rehab. Sometimes, Dave parks his car outside the beautiful home he once shared with his family and wonders how things could possibly have gone so wrong. Now Dave's father Robert (Michael Caine), an aloof, illustrious, award-winning novelist and a hard act for his son to follow, is undergoing tests that point toward a very grim prognosis. The accomplished man Dave looks up to seems to look at him with chagrined disappointment, and these pained glances hurt Dave terribly.

"I'm not just a hill of beans," Dave asserts in his voiceover. "I have a plan." He is waiting for good news which he feels would enable everything in his life to fall into place. Dave has applied for the big-time weatherman position on the New York-based national morning show "Hello, America," hosted by Bryant Gumbel (who plays himself in a cameo). If only he could land this prestigious, enviable position, then his father would not die thinking of him as a pathetic screw-up. Maybe Noreen would be impressed enough to take him back, and the reunited family could move to New York for an exhilarating fresh start. At one point Dave has a dream in which he, Noreen, Mike and Shelly are on a float in the Macy's Thanksgiving Day Parade, all waving, all smiles, all together. It is an awfully tall order.

It seems unlikely that Dave will get exactly what he wants out of life, partly because of life's stubborn refusal to precisely conform to one's plans and partly because of Dave himself. Sometimes he is clearly and maddeningly his own worst enemy. He is apt to exasperatedly erupt at people with biting bursts of profanity. In a telling flashback to his marriage that combines humor and hurt, viewers see how Dave's weirdly-wandering mind while running an errand to get tartar sauce leads to his empty-handed return and a loud, destructive blow-up. When visiting Noreen, he playfully hurls a snowball at her and smashes the unsuspecting, incredulous woman in the face. Later, she agrees to Dave's request for couples counseling, during which each is asked to write down a secret complaint about the other person, exchange notes, and then vow to never look at what was written. This exercise is supposed to foster trust, but Dave cannot stop himself from reading what she wrote anyway, thinking the information might help guide him in his quest for a second chance. He learns that Noreen thinks the science fiction novel he has been working on for four years is a stupid, embarrassing waste of time. Dave's hurt turns into open fury, and her understandable outrage at his transgression leads her to deliver more crushing blows to his already wounded pride. He unquestionably brings on some of his own troubles, acting in such a way that viewers could be tempted to dismiss him as a ridiculous jerk or loser. However, throughout *The Weather Man*, there are ample scenes which allow those watching to not only understand what makes Dave tick and sometimes blow, but also to feel for and like him.

The film clearly gets across that Dave sincerely cares about his children, wants them to be happy, and would like a good relationship with them. He invites Shelly to his employer's family-oriented Winterfest to help them bond, but she tearfully hobbles away from a potato sack race with torn ligaments. Feeling guilty and on edge upon dropping her off, Dave gets into a curse-laden confrontation with Noreen and Russ. He meant well, anyway. When Shelly seems interested in archery, he pays for equipment and a slew of lessons. He is patient, helpful and encouraging, even though she shows no aptitude whatsoever. (Actually, Shelly thought it would just be fun to be able to shoot and kill animals.) Things turn out better when she accompanies her father and grandfather to New York for the former's interview and the latter's medical tests, and a sweet bonding scene shows Shelly delightedly trying on nicer, better-fitting clothing as Dave warmly gives her positive reinforcement. Both sweet and humorous is the scene involving Dave's gentle discussion with Shelly to see if the poor kid understands the meaning of her vulgar sexual nickname at school. She does not and he leaves it that way, glad to keep her innocence intact a while longer. Mike, in a disturbing subplot, is nearly sexually assaulted by his trusted counselor Don (a creepy Gil Bellows). The man was previously shown telling the boy to take off his shirt and then practically drooling while snapping countless photographs. When Don lies and gets Mike charged for supposedly trying to mug him, Dave's ferocious indignation leads him to exact physical retribution on his son's behalf. Mike is clearly impressed by, and grateful for, his father's actions.

There are two other scenes memorable for moments of particular poignancy. Both occur on the day a "living funeral" is held for Robert so that he can see everyone before he goes and enjoy their final, meaningful expressions of how they feel about him. The first is when Dave is crushed by one of those small hot apple pies. Nicely dressed and armed with a carefully prepared eulogy, which will express things from the heart that he has wanted to but never said, Dave is struck by the dessert from a passing car. Humiliated, livid, and dripping with slop on his way to his momentous moment, Dave dashes after his snickering detractor and shoves the pie remains in the man's startled face. Left standing, at a loss, in the middle of traffic, Dave looks down at his embarrassingly-marred formal attire in disbelief and cries out in affecting consternation that he now has to go and face his entire family looking that way. It is truly painful to watch.

The other scene is the ceremony itself. Dave proudly announces to Noreen that he has been offered the job, and hopes that the news will win her over. His devastation is clear when she breaks news of her own: she is marrying Russ. Dave walks out to the car, grabs the bow and arrow with which he, unlike his daughter, has become quite skilled, and aims at some nearby trees as a form of release. For a suspensefully-held moment, a frustrated Dave looks across the lawn and aims instead at the man who has supplanted him in Noreen's life. Perhaps he thinks better of it, perhaps it is because he is called to make his speech, but Dave never lets the arrow fly. He begins his tribute with obvious high hopes, drawing a parallel between his dad and words from the Bob Seger hit, "Like A Rock." The power goes off. When it comes back on forty minutes later, Dave says in his voiceover that no one seemed to remember he had ever begun.

Made on a budget $35 million, *The Weather Man* grossed just under $12.5 million. Critical reaction was mixed, with many emphasizing the film's dreariness. *Variety* labeled it "one of the biggest downers to emerge from a major studio in recent memory." Directed by Gore Verbinski, widely known for *The Ring* (2002) and *Pirates of the Caribbean: The Curse of the Black Pearl* (2003), this work, to use Cage's description, belongs more in the category of "edgy, thought-provoking, independent-spirited films." When it ends, Robert is gone, Noreen and Russ are together, but Dave, working in New York, finally feels a degree of self-worth, peace and contentment. The fact that his life is not all that he wanted is not an easy pill for Dave to swallow, but as his father sagely points out late in the film as they come to understand each other better, "Easy doesn't enter into grownup life." The words are insightful but not especially cheerful—just like *The Weather Man.*

David L. Boxerbaum

CREDITS

David Spritz: Nicolas Cage

Robert Sprizel: Michael Caine

Noreen: Hope Davis
Shelly: Gemmenne de la Pena
Mike: Nicholas Hoult
Russ: Michael Rispoli
Don: Gil Bellows
Lauren: Judith McConnell
Origin: USA
Language: English
Released: 2005
Production: Todd Black, Steve Tisch, Jason Blumenthal; Escape Artists; released by Paramount
Directed by: Gore Verbinski
Written by: Steve Conrad
Cinematography by: Phedon Papamichael
Music by: Hans Zimmer
Sound: Lee Orloff
Editing: Craig Wood
Art Direction: Patrick Sullivan
Costumes: Penny Rose
Production Design: Tom Duffield
MPAA rating: R
Running time: 102 minutes

REVIEWS

Boxoffice Online. October, 2005.
Chicago Sun-Times Online. October 28, 2005.
Entertainment Weekly Online. October 26, 2005.
Los Angeles Times Online. October 28, 2005.
New York Times Online. October 28, 2005.
Premiere Magazine Online. October, 2005.
Variety Online. October 20, 2005.
Washington Post Online. October 28, 2005, p. C01.

QUOTES

David Spritz: "Always fast food. Fast food. Things that people would rather throw out than finish. It's easy, it tastes all right, but it doesn't really provide you any nourishment. I'm fast food."

TRIVIA

Although Paramount Pictures wanted the production be shot in Canada, as a substitute for Chicago, Gore Verbinski and Nicolas Cage both insisted that the film be shot in Chicago for authenticity.

WEDDING CRASHERS

Hide your bridesmaids.
—Movie tagline
Life's a party. Crash it.
—Movie tagline

Box Office: $209 million

Wedding Crashers, directed by David Dobkin and written by Steve Faber and Bob Fisher, is one of the most entertaining films of the summer, an exuberant, outrageous comedy anchored by a terrific twosome, Vince Vaughn and Owen Wilson, who have such an ease and chemistry together, one would think that they have been a team for years. The premise is simple but inventive. Divorce mediators and self-styled ladies' men John Beckwith (Wilson) and Jeremy Grey (Vaughn) are long-time buddies who revel in wedding season—to them, it is like Christmas time for a child—so they can crash nuptials and pick up women who will be easy prey for their charm. Assuming fake identities and phony back stories to ingratiate themselves in any setting, they consider wedding crashing to be practically an art with specific rules that Jeremy has internalized to the point that they might as well be religious dogma for him.

A raucous, fast-paced montage demonstrating their technique has them at a variety of celebrations, a Jewish wedding, an Irish wedding, even a Chinese wedding. Striving not only to fit in but to become the life of the party, they put themselves at the center of the action, toasting the happy couple, dancing with all the beautiful women, and, by the end of the evening, going to bed with them.

Vaughn and Wilson play perfectly off of each other. True to the persona he has cultivated over the course of his career, Vaughn is the confident motormouth, quick on his feet with a sharp-witted reply for every potentially awkward situation. (Jeremy's rapid-fire monologue on why he does not like to date is hilarious.) He is also the classic overgrown adolescent who embraces life to the fullest and barely thinks of the consequences of his actions. Wilson, on the other hand, is expert at playing the laid-back friend. John can party as hard as Jeremy, but, even at the outset, is beginning to have moral qualms about the games they are playing. To Jeremy, these are the fun times of their youth, but, as John wryly observes, "We're not that young."

The main plot kicks in when Jeremy persuades John to take on their biggest wedding yet, the nuptials of the daughter of the Secretary of the Treasury, William Cleary (Christopher Walken), even though John is tired and would really like to take a break for a while. But when he sees the bride's sister, Claire (Rachel McAdams), for the first time, he is completely disarmed by her sweetness and beauty. It does not hurt that they click right away and that she is also bright and lots of fun to be around. Jeremy faces a bigger challenge at the wedding when another Cleary sister, the bubbly Gloria (Isla Fisher), sets her sights on him and falls for him instantly. Their sexual romp on the beach obviously means a lot to her, and, when the clinging Gloria tells him that this was her first time, she sends the usually in-control Jeremy into a panic. But John, truly smitten with Claire, does not want to leave the reception; on the contrary, he wants to stay as long as possible, and the obsessed Gloria, throwing a tantrum to get her way, makes certain that John and Jeremy have invitations to spend time vacationing with her family.

John faces some unexpected obstacles in his pursuit of Claire—from fending off the sexual advances of her mother, Kathleen (Jane Seymour), who tells him to call her "Kat" and wants him to feel her new breasts, to contending with Claire's obnoxious and belligerent boyfriend, Sack (Bradley Cooper), a bit of a cliché as the odious rich kid with an overweening sense of entitlement. And Jeremy has to endure not only the attentions of Gloria but also the interest of the Cleary brother, Todd (Keir O'Donnell), who is gay and at least somewhat mentally unbalanced. It says something about the eccentricity of this modern-day screwball clan, which also includes a rude, foulmouthed grandmother (Ellen Albertini Dow), that, with the exception of McAdams, Walken, generally known for his odd characters, actually plays the most normal of the Clearys.

As great as Vaughn and Wilson are together, the women complement them quite nicely. After strong turns in last 2004's *Mean Girls* and *The Notebook*, the gorgeous McAdams is demonstrating quite a range. The part of Claire is fairly thin—why, for example, would a woman who could have practically any man settle for a jerk like Sack?—but the actress makes her sympathetic and engaging. Claire is forthright but also has an appealing vulnerable streak, and it is not hard to see why John would fall for her immediately. And Isla Fisher, who can be adorable, bratty, and even scary in just a twinkle of an eye as Gloria, delivers a star-making performance. She continuously reins Jeremy in when she thinks that his interest in her is wavering, forcing this dedicated womanizer into a new role as the hunted, not the hunter. Jeremy's suggestion that they take things slowly and get to know each other is very funny because we know that he would never say such things to any other woman. But then again, no other woman has ever pursued him with such single-minded passion. Ultimately, Gloria is his perfect match because she is a game player like him; far from being a sexual neophyte, she turns out to be a nymphomaniac who claimed to be a virgin only because she thought that is what men like to hear. When she fondles his crotch under the dinner table at a very proper family gathering and Jeremy squirms with a mixture of delight and discomfort, it is a comedic high point.

If Gloria's fixation on Jeremy produces the most laughs, then John's courtship of Claire is the emotional heart of the film. In one of their sweetest scenes together, he talks about his dreams, declaring that he may fulfill them yet because he is still young, to which she gently replies, "You're not that young." It is a line that echoes his early doubts to Jeremy about their extended bachelorhood, emphasizing that he needs to grow up and that she is the one who will help him.

But once the wedding crashers are exposed as frauds, their vacation comes to an abrupt end, forcing John to figure out how to get back into Claire's good graces and prove that he is not the scoundrel everyone thinks he is. At this point, however, as the emotionally bereft John falls into a downward spiral, fueled also by his jealousy that Jeremy is still with Gloria and actually falling for her, the movie loses some of its manic sense of fun and goes on way too long. The tension between John and Jeremy feels forced, as if the screenwriters are biding their time and unsure how to tie all the storylines together for a satisfying finish. But built into the ending is another problem. The very process of growing up, of a wedding crasher redeeming himself and changing his ways, while central to John's arc as well as necessary to the overall plot, is simply not as much fun to watch as the crazy and carefree bachelor life.

By the time John pays a visit to the legendary Chazz (an uncredited Will Ferrell), the king of the wedding crashers, who passed his secrets on to Jeremy, the screenplay is foundering. Chazz is an odd man-child who still lives with his mother and yet scores with the hot ladies anyway. As a would-be playboy, he is pathetic but not very funny, and a little of Chazz goes a long way. It may have been a fun cameo for Ferrell, but, as a plot device meant to sober up John and show how sad his life would be as a perpetual crasher, it is superfluous since John has already turned over a new leaf through his wooing of Claire.

Moreover, when Chazz introduces John to the dubious joys of funeral crashing and the widow's grief inspires him to want the kind of relationship that she presumably had with her late husband, it is just hammering home a transformation that has already happened. Taking a serious, sentimental turn, while far from ruinous, defuses much of the film's comic energy. We simply want John to win Claire, which he finally does by crashing Jeremy's wedding to Gloria and making a big speech declaring his love—a routine romantic-comedy climax unworthy of a movie punctuated by so many witty, clever scenes.

Despite its lengthy denouement and overt stabs at heart-tugging emotion, *Wedding Crashers* is nonetheless one of the most entertaining of 2005's summer films. Neither a sequel nor a remake, this high-spirited, cheerfully raunchy comedy is a rare example of a fun script married to actors who seem to be having a blast embodying their characters with gusto. Wilson and Vaughn are a natural comedy team and make us feel as if their characters really are longtime best friends. But it is a tribute to the talent in the film that McAdams and Fisher nearly steal the movie just as they steal the hearts of the inveterate wedding crashers themselves.

Peter N. Chumo II

CREDITS

John Beckwith: Owen C. Wilson
Jeremy Grey: Vince Vaughn
Claire Cleary: Rachel McAdams
Secretary Cleary: Christopher Walken
Kathleen Cleary: Jane Seymour
Chaz Reingold: Will Ferrell
Grandma Mary Cleary: Ellen A. Dow
Gloria Cleary: Isla Fisher
Sack Lodge: Bradley Cooper
Randolph: Ron Canada
Father O'Neil: Henry Gibson
Todd Cleary: Keir O'Donnell
Mr. Kroeger: Dwight Yoakam
Mrs. Kroeger: Rebecca De Mornay
Trap: David Conrad
Best Man: Larry Joe Campbell
Christina Cleary: Jennifer (Jenny) Alden
Craig: Geoff Stults
Origin: USA
Language: English
Released: 2005
Production: Peter Abrams, Robert Levy, Andrew Panay; Tapestry Films; released by New Line Cinema
Directed by: David Dobkin
Written by: Bob Fisher, Steve Faber
Cinematography by: Julio Macat
Music by: Rolfe Kent, Rolfe Kent
Sound: Mark Ulano
Editing: Mark Livolsi
Art Direction: Kevin Constant
Costumes: Denise Wingate
Production Design: Barry Robison
MPAA rating: R
Running time: 119 minutes

REVIEWS

Boxoffice Online. July, 2005.
Chicago Sun-Times Online. July 15, 2005.
Entertainment Weekly Online. July 13, 2005.
Los Angeles Times Online. July 15, 2005.
New York Times Online. July 15, 2005.
Premiere Magazine Online. July 18, 2005.
Variety Online. July 7, 2005.
Washington Post Online. July 15, 2005, p. WE31.

QUOTES

John Beckwith: "I'm not asking you to marry me. I'm asking you *not* to marry *him!*"

THE WEDDING DATE

Love doesn't come cheap.
—Movie tagline

Box Office: $31.6 million

When people speak of chick flicks, they are talking about movies exactly like, *The Wedding Date.* Perhaps the best evidence of this is that most of the movie takes place in scenic England, in the kind of houses that would not be out of place in a Merchant-Ivory film. Or maybe it is that its heroine, Kat Ellis (Debra Messing), is not particularly charming or interesting, but still she gets her man. Or it might be that the love interest, Nick (Dermot Mulroney), is a male escort who is not only not sleazy at all, but also happens to have a degree in Comparative Literature from Brown. He is also, not unimportantly, quite hunky. Everything in this film that will make certain members of a particular gender swoon will be exactly the same things that make others cringe.

Based on a novel by Elizabeth Young called *Asking for Trouble* and directed by Clare Kilner, *The Wedding Date* picks up on Kat's life after she is invited to her sister Amy's (Amy Adams) wedding. Amy's fiancee Edward Fletcher-Wooten (Jack Davenport) is British, so there are plot-driven reasons for the footage of the lovely country manors, picturesque games of rounders and such. Kat's caddish ex-fiance, Jeffrey (Jeremy Sheffield), is going to be the best man and Kat, wanting to impress both him and her family, hires a male escort to attend the wedding with her. Kat instructs Nick to pretend that he is madly in love with her.

Nick shows up and is gorgeous, understanding and has a knack for tossing about interesting psychological theories such as, "Every woman has the exact love life they want." Kat should fall madly in love with him right then and there, but the movie must spend time going through its required motions. Kat sports a wide variety of attractive clothing. There are lovers' betrayals and misunderstanding. And Nick and Kat must figure out that they are in love.

The elements for a successful genre film are all there, but *The Wedding Date* never quite gels. This has a lot to do with Messing. The actress is well-cast and well-used in her role on the popular TV show, *Will and Grace,* but here, her character is not as appealing. She has some good moments, like when Kat wakes up after sleeping on an airplane, talks to Nick, then is horrified when she checks herself in the mirror and discovers her terribly disheveled face. But her character is supposed to be likable—someone whom the audience wants to get the guy. She is not really unlikable, but she never demonstrates any characteristics that make her someone to root for. After all, Kat is supposed to be someone so irresistible that a seasoned escort and expert with women would fall for her. Mulroney, to his credit, holds up his end of the film. He has a certainty about himself and a sharp masculinity that harkens back to a romantic lead like Rhett Butler rather than the tamer, modern romantic heroes played by actors like Tom Hanks or Hugh Grant. Stephanie Zacharek of *Salon* wrote, "His features are handsome in a way that's neither too soft nor rugged. He represents the perfect intersection of civilization and wilderness—untamed Alaska and urbane Paris in just one guy."

The movie also fails in that it brings up the rather provocative topic of male escorts, but does not delve very deep into it. There is an inevitable scene in which Kat and Nick have sex and there is discussion whether Kat should pay or not, but the movie pretty much breezes over the issue.

Mostly critics did not care for this film and their distaste united them across their gender divide. Lisa Swartzbaum of *Entertainment Weekly* gave the film a C- and wrote, "So many body parts from other engineered romantic comedies have been crudely harvested and stitched together in the making of this weird robotic lark that *Maid of Honor of Frankenstein* might be more useful a nickname." Roger Ebert of *The Chicago Sun-Times* wrote, "I have so many questions about the movie's premise that it seems, in memory, almost entirely composed of moments when I was shaking my head in disbelief." Wesley Morris of *The Boston Globe* wrote, "The cast seems discouraged from doing anything witty or madcap—especially the movie's star, who looks lost, ordinary, and more than a little sorry. Messing should know this is precisely the kind of movie Grace would ridicule Will for dragging her to see."

Jill Hamilton

CREDITS

Kat Ellis: Debra Messing
Nick Mercer: Dermot Mulroney
Amy: Amy Adams
Edward Fletcher-Wooten: Jack Davenport
Jeffrey: Jeremy Sheffield
Victor Ellis: Peter Egan
Bunny: Holland Taylor
TJ: Sarah Parish
Woody: Jolyon James
Bike Messenger: C. Gerod Harris
Teenager: Martin Barrett
Male Flight Attendant: Jay Simon
Harry: Stephen Lobo
Origin: USA
Language: English
Released: 2005
Production: Paul Brooks, Nathalie Marciano, Michelle Chydzik Sowa, Jessica Bendinger; released by Universal
Directed by: Clare Kilner
Written by: Dana Fox
Cinematography by: Oliver Curtis
Sound: Martin Trevis
Music Supervisor: Randy Gerston, Randy Gerston
Editing: Mary Finlay
Art Direction: Astrid Sieben
Costumes: Louise Page
Production Design: Tom Burton
MPAA rating: PG-13
Running time: 90 minutes

REVIEWS

Boxoffice Online. February, 2005.
Chicago Sun-Times Online. February 4, 2005.
Entertainment Weekly Online. February 2, 2005.
Los Angeles Times Online. February 4, 2005.
New York Times Online. February 4, 2005.
Premiere Magazine Online. February 4, 2005.
Variety Online. February 2, 2005.
Washington Post Online. February 4, 2005, p. WE39.

QUOTES

Nick Mercer: "I'd rather fight with you than make love to anybody else."

WEEPING MEADOW

(Trilogia: To Livadi pou dakryzei) (Trilogy: The Weeping Meadow) (Eleni) (La Sorgente del fiume) (La Terre qui pleure)

Master Greek filmmaker Theo Angelopoulos's stirring historical saga, *The Weeping Meadow,* captures twenty-five years of suffering from 1910 to 1945 through the experiences of a family of refugees. In both content and form, Angelopoulos's humanism seeks as wide a domain as can be encompassed within the constraints of a theatrical feature film. The family is presented as part of a larger community having to endure what someone calls an "omnipotent curse" that wrecks their lives from political as well as geophysical forces. In so doing, Angelopoulos, with his uncompromising filmic stance, affirms his unique position in the history of cinema at being able to use the medium to convey the durational aspect of human experience. As the year's most serious film, *The Weeping Meadow,* on its part, demands a concomitant sensibility from its viewers, lacking which its unwieldy length could prove ponderous.

History on film, rendered as domestic suffering (the most notable recent example being Roman Polanski's *The Pianist* (reviewed in the 2003 volume), is made palatable by drawing us into a psychological sphere of identification with members of a family. Angelopoulos reverses this template with a detachment that suffuses his filmic form, clearly appealing to our social conscience. Understandably, his films have enjoyed only an art house reputation. Perhaps one of the few committed filmmakers still working in the medium, this has not led him to change his style. His masterwork, *The Travelling Players* (1975) used the background of the political changes his country has had to endure to tell the story of an indomitable theater troupe. *Meadow* similarly uses the leitmotif of a group of courageous musicians who are caught in the crossfire between the fascists and the leftists. In unexpected and often poetic ways, artistic expression continues to rear its humble head, thereby signaling a collective invincibility in the face of political might.

While presenting his still unreleased *The Suspended Step of the Stork* at the New York Film Festival of 1991, Angelopoulos put across his philosophical view that life was all about crossing borders. *Meadow* thus opens with a prolonged mid-long shot that concretizes the notion, which the film's narrative will then illustrate, on geographical, political, domestic and aesthetic levels.

Spyros (Vassilis Kolovos) leads a group of refugees across a vast uninhabited plane. The notable members of his family will turn out to be Alexis, a little boy at this time and Eleni, an orphaned little girl the family has adopted. The group comes to a halt beside a river as Spyros recounts their travails to an unseen voice of authority. They are Greeks who had to flee the burning city of Odessa destroyed by the Red Army. After disembarking at the nearby port of Thessaloniki, they were told they could settle on the land they have now reached.

After the first part of its prologue the film leaps a decade and a half to show a thriving town mostly of shanties, except for Spyros's two-storey house, into which a teenage Eleni is being led after having given birth to twins, who have been put into a foster home. Alexis assures her from below her window that he loves her but the poor girl doesn't know what to think. It is only when we see a fully grown Eleni (Alexandra Aidini) that the narrative proper begins. Spyros, as a widower who has planned to marry her, is left in the lurch on his wedding day as Eleni runs off with Alexis (Nikos Poursandis), now a talented accordionist. In Thessaloniki, Alexis and Eleni (still in her bridal gown) are taken under the wing of the fatherly Nikos the Fiddler (Giorgos Armenis) and his small troupe of musicians. The romantic couple is given a room in the attic of a large theater in which other refugees have strung their washing across the stage.

As life unfolds, Spyros remains a continuing threat. After he comes hunting for them one night, screaming Eleni's name, the couple has to move into a rickety shanty on the outskirts of town. Nikos tells Alexis that there's "gold in your hands" but when he arranges a gig for the group, they find the restaurant is closed.

Despite their travails, the romance between Alexis and Eleni remains alive. The beautiful deserted seaside provides an escape for them both. It is here that Alexis's dream of America is expressed and where it will ultimately be tested. This is also where they are united with their twins, Yannis and Yorgos, who have now grown into healthy young boys. Like the horizon on a clear day, Alexis's dream becomes more real as a prospect when Nikos introduces him to Markos, a talent scout who is forming a troupe to take to America.

The political tumult, however, catches up with everyone. Bitterness ensues when an agitation organized by the leftist Popular Front is mercilessly put down by the rightist military. In a bold gesture of defiance, Nikos organizes a dance in an abandoned warehouse. No one shows up, until the band starts to play their catchy melodic refrain, after which couples appear and dancing fills the place, thereby affirming the solidarity of the people. The event is marred by the intrusion of Spyros who, after dancing with Eleni, is so overcome with emotion that he has a fatal collapse. When Alexis and Eleni return to what is justly their family home, a harrowing sight awaits them: each of Spyros's sheep has been hung from a nearby tree as a gesture of protest against his elite status.

A third force now assails the community of refugees, a force they cannot possibly oppose. The river they have been living beside overflows its banks in a massive flood that drowns the shanties. Peasants flee from their roofs while Alexis, Eleni and the twins get onto a rowboat from the second floor of their house. That night, as the women pray around a fire, one of them calls their fate "an omnipotent dark curse that has yet to run its course."

In the midst of the severe crackdown on the leftists, Alexis and Eleni have no place to hide except in the shanty they had left behind, leaving the twins in a foster home. On their first morning of freedom, they hear a familiar musical strain from the midst of a mass of white sheets that have been hung to dry. Nikos is playing his fiddle beside the river along with his group of musicians. Then Nikos too is gunned down by "the general's men."

Fate however bestows another benefactor on Alexis. Markos at last comes through with his plan of taking a troupe to America. Alexis on his part vows to send for Eleni as soon as he's settled. By the same seafront, as he takes her leave, she shows him an incomplete sweater she has been knitting for him. As he walks away in the direction of the huge steamer waiting near the pier, he takes the woolen thread, allowing it to stretch between them as a poetic promise of their battered love.

Their separation allows the film to skim over years of history in an epistolary form. From the letters Eleni receives we learn that Markos's group was soon to disband, leaving Alexis no option but to join the U.S. Army so as to become a citizen. She is told the next letter she receives from him was found near his dead body on an island in the Pacific.

Eleni herself is first imprisoned, then released when it is discovered that one of her sons is fighting in the Greek army. Yannis, we subsequently come to know, has joined the rebels in the Civil War of 1942. When Eleni is taken to claim Yannis's body, which has been thrown by the river, she collapses beside it, wailing.

The Eleni we see after this is a broken, deranged woman. As she is being looked after by two women, episodes out of the historical past all appear to merge together in her mind. With her eyes closed, she cries out to imaginary guards for water, soap and paper with which to write letters to her sons. The guards, whether in grey, black or German green, all represent the same persecution.

When Eleni recovers, one of the women who has been nursing her claims to have witnessed a battle in which both of her sons died. She takes Eleni to the embankment where what the woman saw is recreated. Yannis with a white cloth tied over the end of his rifle, advances into enemy territory calling out Yorgis's name. When they meet, they take off their caps and throw down their rifles. When Yannis tells Yorgis the news that their mother has died in prison, they embrace each other in solace. The woman then points out where Yorgis lies dead. Eleni, disregarding the patrols, runs to find her son.

As Eleni rows to a flooded house to find Yorgis's body beside the water, we hear Alexis's voiceover in which he relates in his last letter a dream he had of discovering the source of the river in dewdrops from a meadow, falling from the wild grass like tears.

The film's final shot shows a bereft Eleni crying that now she has no one left for her to even think about. She then lets out a primal wail. It is significant that Angelopoulos does not capture her from the front, which would have foregrounded her personal tragedy. Instead, we see her from the side, as if representing the tragic history of her homeland and her people. The camera then leaves her and rises, allowing the murky river to fill the screen.

Vivek Adarkar

CREDITS

Eleni: Alexandra Aidini
Spyros' Son: Nikos Poursanidis
Nikos, the Fiddler: Yorgos Armenis
Spyros: Vasilis Kolovos
Cassandra: Eva Kotamanidou
Woman in Coffee House: Toula Stothopoulou
Zissis the Clarinetist: Mihalis Yannatos
Danae: Thalia Argyriou
Teacher: Grigoris Evangelatos
Origin: Germany, France, Italy, Greece
Language: Greek
Released: 2004
Production: Theo Angelopoulos, Fivi Ekonomopoulos; Theo Angelopoulos, Greek Film Center, Attica Art Prods, Hellenic Broadcastering, BAC Films Ltd.; released by Arte France Cinema
Written by: Tonino Guerra, Petros Markaris, Giorgio Silvagni
Cinematography by: Andreas Sinani
Music by: Eleni Karaindrou
Sound: Marinos Athanasopoulos
Editing: Yorgos Triantafyllou
Art Direction: Yorgos Patsas, Kostas Dimitriadis
Costumes: Ioulia Stavridou
MPAA rating: Unrated
Running time: 168 minutes

REVIEWS

Boxoffice Online. September, 2005.
New York Times Online. September 14, 2005.
Variety Online. February 12, 2004.

WHERE THE TRUTH LIES

A young, ambitious journalist tries to unravel a showbiz mystery from long ago in *Where the Truth Lies,* the lurid, clever, and admittedly convoluted thriller from art house favorite Atom Egoyan. While a noir thriller might not be what we would expect from the double Oscar nominee behind *The Sweet Hereafter* (1997), he has skillfully brought Rupert Holmes's dense and complex whodunit to the screen while retaining a surprising amount of the plot details and imbuing it with his own distinctive signature.

Lanny Morris (Kevin Bacon) and Vince Collins (Colin Firth) are a Martin-and-Lewis-like entertainment act, nightclub headliners who command the love of a nation and the attention of practically any woman they want. It is 1957, and the duo is riding high when a mysterious crime changes their fates forever—a beautiful woman from Miami, Maureen O'Flaherty (Rachel Blanchard), turns up dead in the bathtub of their New Jersey hotel suite just as they are coming off of their triumphant Veterans Day telethon for polio. While Maureen's murder was never solved, both men were cleared because they had solid alibis. Due to circumstances that were never explained, however, the team soon splits up.

The main story pivots around aspiring writer Karen O'Connor (Alison Lohman), who, in 1972, is trying to get Vince's cooperation to write a book on his life. She wants to get to the heart of the mystery involving Maureen, but it is clear that, while Vince wants to sell his story for a million dollars, he does not want to revisit the past. At the same time (and by sheer coincidence), Karen meets Lanny and has a one-night stand.

Aside from scuttling the novel's humor and deleting certain plot points while telescoping others, Egoyan's major change is to create a connection between Karen and the team of Morris and Collins. Unbeknownst to both men, as a little girl, she had polio and appeared on the telethon that aired right before their breakup. Karen thus carries feelings of girlhood hero worship and admiration, which she will be forced to reassess, especially when the men begin revealing their seamy side.

Another shrewd change from the novel is that, in the film, Karen and Maureen bear a striking similarity—both are young, beautiful blondes who want to write about Vince and Lanny (Maureen was a waitress hoping to interview the guys for her college paper when she died), so that, through Karen's own history with the team and her resemblance to Maureen, there is a sense of the past coming back to haunt them. Lohman brings the right blend of innocence and experience to the role, as if Karen still had some of the little girl in her who idolized Lanny and Vince, and yet she is also a savvy young adult determined to make a name for herself.

Bacon and Firth play very well off each other in the love-hate relationship that holds these men together and ultimately divides them. Bacon expertly reveals the dark side behind the goofball comic—when Lanny admits that "Having to be a nice guy is the toughest job in the world when you're not," we understand that being a star means having to act all the time. Bacon makes us wonder where the star persona ends and the real Lanny begins or if there is even such a distinction. And Firth, although playing a less flashy role, brings just the right combination of charm, menace, and loneliness to the suave British straight man who, in a surreal sequence worthy of David Lynch, uses a girl dressed as Alice in Wonderland (Kristin Adams) to put Karen in a sexually compromising situation so that he can blackmail her into not asking questions about the death of Maureen.

Ironically enough, while Egoyan appears to be embracing subject matter that could attract a wider audience than he is used to and is certainly using bigger-name actors, an explicit sex scene, a ménage à trois that holds the key to the mystery, earned the film an NC-17 rating, thus limiting its box office potential. (Losing its ratings appeal with the MPAA, the film was released unrated but intended for adults only.) While Lanny was having sex with Maureen, Vince joined in the fun and got too sexually intimate with Lanny, thus revealing his homosexual feelings for his partner, who recoiled at the advance. In the aftermath, Maureen saw an opportunity to blackmail the boys, but, as Karen finally discovers, Maureen was thwarted when Lanny's loyal valet, Reuben (David Hayman), killed her.

Where the Truth Lies may be considered lightweight, sordid material for Egoyan, who usually has loftier goals than penetrating the hypocrisies of celebrities and exploring the underbelly of showbiz, but, despite its sleazy packaging, the story is a good fit that actually resonates with Egoyan's techniques and themes—multiple narrators and thus multiple perspectives (Lanny and Karen alternate in telling the story in voice-over), a fragmented narrative structure, a search for an elusive truth that has remained hidden, and a confrontation with dark sexual secrets.

Moreover, *Where the Truth Lies* also has a surprising emotional heft, especially in its depiction of a mourning parent, Maureen's mother (Deborah Grover), which recalls the feelings of loss in *The Sweet Hereafter*. Karen visits her twice. The first time Mrs. O'Flaherty discusses how she deals with grief and offers very poignant thoughts on the afterlife. When Karen visits again at the end and reveals that she cannot explain to the world why Maureen died because it would hurt someone still living (all Karen can say is that Maureen learned something about Vince), there is an implicit understanding that the person hurt would be Mrs. O'Flaherty herself, who desperately needs to believe in the idea of her daughter as a good girl and could not bear to know otherwise.

But the ending is doubly moving because, now that her illusions about her one-time idols have been smashed, Karen is also in mourning—for herself as a little girl. When, during the Veterans Day telethon, Lanny shed a tear, it was, seemingly, a private moment just for her but seen by a nationwide audience. Through her investigation, however, she now knows that Lanny was not crying for her but rather for the death of Maureen. Unlike the novel, which concludes in marriage to a redeemed Lanny, the film ends on a melancholy note with Karen alone bearing the weight of her new-found knowledge.

The notion of secrets and traumas of the past impinging on the present animates much of Egoyan's work, as do serpentine plots, deception, and morally ambiguous characters. The irony is that, while Egoyan here presents these challenging themes in the service of an accessible, entertaining, and scintillating film noir, complete with a beautiful, haunting score by Mychael Danna that recalls Bernard Herrmann, the movie still did not find the audience it deserved.

Peter N. Chumo II

CREDITS

Lanny Morris: Kevin Bacon
Vince Collins: Colin Firth
Karen O'Connor: Alison Lohman
Maureen O'Flaherty: Rachel Blanchard
Reuben: David Hayman
Sally Sanmarco: Maury Chaykin
Alice: Kristin Adams
Bonnie: Sonja Bennett
Mrs. O'Flaherty: Deborah Grover
Jack Scaglia: Beau Starr
Origin: USA
Language: English
Released: 2005
Production: Robert Lantos; Robert Lantos; released by ThinkFilm
Directed by: Atom Egoyan
Written by: Atom Egoyan
Cinematography by: Paul Sarossy
Music by: Mychael Danna
Sound: Chris Munro
Music Supervisor: Liz Gallacher
Editing: Susan Shipton
Art Direction: Craig Lathrop, Lucy Richardson
Costumes: Beth Pasternak
Production Design: Phillip Barker
MPAA rating: Unrated
Running time: 107 minutes

REVIEWS

Boxoffice Online. October, 2005.
Chicago Sun-Times Online. October 28, 2005.
Entertainment Weekly Online. October 12, 2005.
Los Angeles Times Online. October 14, 2005.
New York Times Online. October 14, 2005.
Variety Online. May 13, 2005.

TRIVIA

Various cuts were made to the film, including an orgy scene, in a failed attempt to challenge the NC-17 rating given by the MPAA. Distributor ThinkFilm has since announced that the version shown in US theaters is the same as the one shown at the Cannes Film Festival.

THE WHITE COUNTESS

The White Countess is the final Merchant-Ivory film. Producer Ismail Merchant died May 25, 2005, ending his four-decade collaboration with director James Ivory. From early, low-budget films set in India such as *The Householder* (1963) and *Shakespeare Wallah* (1965) to a series of adaptations of Henry James novels beginning with *The Europeans* (1979) to such popular triumphs as *A Room with a View* (1985), *Howards End* (1992), and *The Remains of the Day* (1993), the duo became known for the dependable literary qualities of their films. Interspersed with these films were almost as many of considerably lesser quality, including such embarrassments as *The Wild Party* (1975), *Slaves of New York* (1989), and *Le Divorce* (2003). Because of such failures, Merchant Ivory films represent for many, especially reviewers, tasteful predictability and dullness. Alas, *The White Countess* is in this unfortunate tradition.

The screenplay by Kazuo Ishiguro, who previously adapted his novel, *The Remains of the Day,* is set in 1936-1937 Shanghai and is centered around the blind American Jackson (Ralph Fiennes), a former diplomat. Jackson spends much of his time in seedy bars and longs for an ideal nightclub. When he comes into some money at the racetrack, he finances his dream, hiring Sofia (Natasha Richardson), as his hostess.

The White Countess divides its narrative equally between Jackson and Sofia and her family. Sofia is an exiled Russian countess, who has been working as a dance hostess in one of the clubs Jackson frequents, and he names his club the White Countess after her. Sofia lives in genteel poverty with her daughter, Katya (Madeleine Daly), mother-in-law, Olga (Lynn Redgrave), sister-in-law, Greshenka (Madeleine Potter), aunt, Sara (Vanessa Redgrave), and Sara's husband, Peter (John Wood). Sara and Peter are the Princess and Prince Belinsky. The most frustrating aspect of *The White Countess* is sorting out all these relationships, which takes over half the film. Matters are not helped by the close resemblance between Greshenka and Katya as a result of Potter and Daly being mother and daughter.

The White Countess ever so slowly follows the developing tenderness between Jackson and Sofia. At first, he wants them to exist only within the club and is not interested in her private life or sharing his. In one of the best scenes, Sofia and Katya pass Jackson at a sidewalk café, and while the mother honors his wishes by ignoring him, the irrepressible daughter charges right into his privacy. This encounter leads to a softening of the Jackson-Sofia relationship, and he eventually explains how he lost both his family and his eyesight in separate incidents.

The other significant person in Jackson's life is Matsuda (Hiroyuki Sanada), a mysterious Japanese visitor with whom the American shares his vision of the White Countess. When Jackson expresses his desire for the club to have a political component, Matsuda arranges for Chinese communists, Chinese army officers, and Japanese sailors to mix in with the usual clientele of Americans, Europeans, and wealthy Chinese. Everything begins to change as China's political climate darkens and the Japanese, who already occupy the northern part of the country, eventually make their way to Shanghai and throw everything into chaos.

Until its final half hour, *The White Countess* is slow and tedious. Ishiguro's novels are delicate mood pieces, and he obviously intends the same here. The screenplay has the structure of a novel, carefully, perhaps too carefully, introducing the characters, setting, and themes. The scenes are too long, and the visual style too static. Ivory is dealing with material somewhat similar to that explored by Wong Kar Wai in such films as *In the Mood for Love* (2000) and *2046* (2005), but he never comes close to approximating the romantic rhythms typical of Wong's style, rhythms so desperately needed here. Jackson tells Matsuda he wants his club to be erotic and tragic, but Ivory is the least erotic of filmmakers, to which the absurd orgy scene in *The Wild Party* testifies.

The static visuals are surprising given the presence of Christopher Doyle, Wong's usual cinematographer and one of the greatest lighting artists. The notoriously feisty Doyle has said in interviews that he had difficulty communicating with the director and producer, as the generally flat results indicate. While the scenes within *The White Countess* have a seductive orange glow, the other scenes are photographed rather drably. Only with beautiful shots of the sails on the boats fleeing the city at the end does Doyle's style seem in effect.

The last portion of *The White Countess*, with Jackson desperately trying to find Sofia and Sofia searching for Katya as the Japanese bombs fall all around them, is handled much better than the rest of the film. There is almost no violence in Merchant Ivory films, but they seem to need a war to knock them out of their doldrums. The final scenes have considerable energy and are almost good enough to save the film from failure.

Ivory, as always, excels at eliciting good performances. While *The White Countess* is an historic occasion, with the Redgrave sisters and Richardson, Vanessa's daughter, working together for the first time, the Redgraves have little to do. Lynn Redgrave, however, has one brief splendid moment when the imperious Olga essentially kicks Sofia out of the family. Richardson always seems to be a faint echo of her famous mother, with a similar voice and the same pause-laden deliver. Here, she eliminates most of her usual mannerisms, though Sofia, and this is mostly the fault of the script, does not quite have the majestic allure she should have. While Potter, in her fourth Ivory Merchant effort, however, is even more irritatingly mannered than usual, Daly is remarkably free of such self-consciousness, delivering one of the best child performances in recent years. Sanada, best known for *Ring* (1998) ably conveys the conflicts within Matsuda. When Jackson finally learns that his friend is probably the most dangerous person in China and expresses his outrage at this betrayal of their friendship, Sanada displays a complex range of emotions. In misleading Jackson, Matsuda has committed a shameful act.

In 2005, Fiennes had a remarkable year, with outstanding performances in *The Constant Gardener, Wallace and Gromit: The Curse of the Were-Rabbit,* and *Harry Potter and the Goblet of Fire.* His Jackson is a subtle variation on his widowed husband in *The Constant Gardener,* with both characters bitter and repressed in different ways. Fiennes apparently realized that his usual actorish tics (the nervous laugh, the slow smile, the squint) would be inappropriate for a blind man who responds to his environment quite differently, and he keeps most of them in check. Fiennes's Jackson is a man who wants to limit his world to what he can control, a man who searches for small pleasures in mundane places. Not caring what others think of him, Jackson delights himself by jumping from the steps leading from his house. Fiennes is especially wonderful at showing Jackson's consuming joy when hearing a jazz tune on his radio. By giving the character depth and feeling mostly missing from the screenplay, Fiennes gives a triumphant performance.

Michael Adams

CREDITS

Todd Jackson: Ralph Fiennes
Countess Sofia Belinsky: Natasha Richardson
Aunt Sara: Vanessa Redgrave
Matsuda: Hiroyuki Sanada
Olga: Lynn Redgrave
Samuel: Allan Corduner
Kao: Ying Da
Antoine Jacquier: Jean-Pierre Lorit
Crane: Lee Pace
Greshenka: Madeleine Potter
Uncle Peter: John Wood
Katya: Madeleine Daly
Frenchman: Dan Herzberg
Russian Singer: Pierre Seznec
Liu: Luoyong Wang
Origin: USA
Language: English
Released: 2005
Production: Ismail Merchant; Merchant-Ivory Productions, VIP Medienfonds 3, Shanghai Film Group Corp; released by Sony Pictures Entertainment
Directed by: James Ivory
Written by: Kazuo Ishiguro, John Bright
Cinematography by: Christopher Doyle
Music by: Richard Robbins
Sound: Bob Hein
Editing: John David Allen
Art Direction: Steve Simmonds, Yu Baiyang, Chen Shaomian
Production Design: Andrew Sanders
MPAA rating: PG-13
Running time: 138 minutes

REVIEWS

Boxoffice Online. December, 2005.
Chicago Sun-Times Online. December 21, 2005.
Los Angeles Times Online. December 21, 2005.
New York Times Online. December 21, 2005.
Variety Online. November 27, 2005.

TRIVIA

Stock footage from Seabiscuit (2003) is used in the racing scene.

WHITE NOISE

The dead are trying to get a hold of you.
—Movie tagline

There are nearly 7 billion audio and video recording devices in homes around the world. Everyone of them is a portal.
—Movie tagline

The voices of the dead are all around you.
—Movie tagline

Box Office: $55.9 million

Critics and moviegoers showed just how different they were in January, 2005, when *White Noise* arrived in theaters. Critics gave the film overwhelmingly poor reviews, but enough moviegoers were interested in the film to make it the number two movie the week it came out. The movie might have been helped by the fact that *White Noise* was the main major release opening that weekend. And it did not have much lingering competition since January is traditionally the time that movie studios put out their worst material. Then, too, the trailers for *White Noise* were quite frightening. They offered a short, eerie lesson in EVP, or Electronic Voice Phenomenon. EVP occurs when the sound of voices come through white noise, or the static between stations on electronic devices like radios and TVs. According to this film, and believers in EVP, those voices are not just random scraps of sound from the ether, but the voices of the dead. The trailer for *White Noise* featured several staticky examples of the dead speaking through EVP saying such creepy things as, "I will see you no more." Why a dead person would bother using their big chance on EVP to say something as non-informative as "I will see you no more"—they are dead, after all, and that should be presumed—is a mystery that the movie does not tackle.

White Noise has a lot going for it. Its subject matter is spooky enough, and although it was not apparent from trailers, the star of the film is Michael Keaton. The director, Geoffrey Sax, fresh from the BBC, is gifted at creating well-lit yuppie environments. But somehow it does not work. Perhaps the fault lies with writer, Niall Johnson. Johnson seems to have no idea how to exploit EVP for maximum frights, and instead turns the film into a crime-solving drama with little urgency. Also, with the prevalence of digital radio and cable TV, electronic static is not a phenomenon that younger viewers might be familiar with. Perhaps these ghosts could modernize and try using IMs.

Jonathan Rivers (Keaton) becomes interested in EVP after his author wife, Anna (Chandra West), dies suddenly. A mysterious Brit, Raymond Price (Ian McNeice), convinces Jonathan that EVP can help him communicate with his wife. At Raymond's dusty, cluttered house filled with electronics (in an older movie, it would have been a dusty metaphysical bookstore), Jonathan meets Sarah Tate (Deborah Kara Unger), a comely widow who uses EVP to speak with her late husband.

Soon Jonathan has set up a mess of wires, recorders and TVs in his own stylish loft apartment (completely ruining the feng shui) and is spending his evenings hunched over the screens, obsessively searching for messages from Anna. (It is not apparent how he manages to retain his day job.) He gets some messages from Anna that say things though the static like, "Jon-a-than." Those messages are nice and creepy. Also intriguing is the fact that some of messages are from unfriendly spirits who bark out threats. But the script does not exploit the foreboding mood that it has built up. Jonathan starts receiving messages from people who are not yet dead. They give him clues so that he can stop crimes before they occur. The movie becomes dreary at exactly the moment when Jonathan becomes a supernatural crime solver. One of the unintentionally funny things about the film is how Jonathan is always around when someone has just been killed, but the dense police officer never seems to suspect Jonathan of any wrong doing.

Critics were happy to see Keaton starring in a film again, but their good will did not translate into good reviews. Elizabeth Weitzman of *The New York Daily News* wrote "The unhappy dead populated Geoffrey Sax's third-rate thriller *White Noise* like a pre-Christmas crowd at a suburban mall. This is a shame, since they are neither scary nor sad, and less likely to haunt an audience than simply bore them to death." Scott Brown of *Entertainment Weekly* gave the film a C- and wrote, "In lieu of satisfying answers, we get crude, gee-whizzikers scares, cribbed from the horror cannon." Manohla Dargis of *The New York Times* called it, "a film worthy neither of Mr. Keaton's talents nor even a desperate horror fan's attention." And Wesley Morris of *The Boston Globe* called it "a moronic exercise in supernatural claptrap."

Jill Hamilton

CREDITS

Jonathan Rivers: Michael Keaton
Anna Rivers: Chandra West
Sarah Tate: Deborah Kara Unger
Raymond Price: Ian McNeice
Jane: Sarah Strange
Mike Rivers: Nicholas Elia
Detective Smits: Mike Dopud
Origin: USA
Language: English
Released: 2005
Production: Paul Brooks, Shawn Williamson; White Noise UK, Brightlight Pictures; released by Universal
Directed by: Geoffrey Sax
Written by: Niall Johnson
Cinematography by: Chris Seager
Music by: Claude Foisy
Sound: William Skinner
Editing: Nick Arthurs
Art Direction: Greg Venturi
Costumes: Karen Matthews
Production Design: Michael Bolton
MPAA rating: PG-13
Running time: 101 minutes

REVIEWS

Boxoffice Online. January, 2005.
Entertainment Weekly Online. January 5, 2005.
Los Angeles Times Online. January 7, 2005.
New York Times Online. January 7, 2005.
Premiere Magazine Online. January 7, 2005.
Variety Online. January 6, 2005.

QUOTES

Mirabelle Keegan: "(after reading Jonathan's palm) The spirits don't want you here…"

TRIVIA

The recording in the film that is attributed to Stanley Searles is thought to be the "ghostly" voice of Searles himself, a former politician who died in 2002. The recording was reportedly made by Searles' daughter, well-known Electronic Voice Phenomenon (EVP) researcher Karen Mossey.

THE WILD PARROTS OF TELEGRAPH HILL

Box Office: $3 million

Deceptively simple, *The Wild Parrots of Telegraph Hill* is more than a movie about birds.

It is easy to get caught up in this documentary about a drifter who cares for some unusual winged creatures; the man-and-bird story becomes progressively eye-opening and emotionally affecting.

Judy Irving keeps the focus of her non-fiction feature on Mark Bittner, a "Bohemian St. Francis" and one-time street musician who protects and feeds a flock of green-and-red colored parrots that lives both in and outside his temporary residence in the lush San Francisco hills.

Bittner informs the audience about each bird: for example, we learn that Connor, an azure-topped conure, guards the other birds while maintaining his aloof nature. We also observe the mating, feeding, and fighting rituals of the red-crowned flock, including Mingus, Picasso, Sophie, Pushkin, and Tupelo.

Several San Francisco residents provide explanations for how this odd, wild bird species came into the vicinity. Irving interviews natives Ivan Stormgart, Maggie McCall, Gary Thompson, Elizabeth Wright, and Jamie Yorck, whose stories range from one about a pet-shop owner letting her flock loose to another about the accidental release of a bird cargo by an airline employee.

Unexpected drama occurs when Mark Bittner's landlords ask him to leave his apartment so that they can renovate the dwelling. Bittner realizes he must say goodbye to his birds and reluctantly gives his indoor birds to a sanctuary. After a final feeding, he sadly witnesses his outdoor birds fly away. Later, Bittner finds out that several hawks in the area have killed Connor and some of the others in the group. A surprise ending makes the news slightly less traumatic but still bittersweet.

Judy Irving's film lacks the technical pizzazz of other recent "bird" documentaries, including 2002's *Winged Migration* and 1998's *The Life of Birds*, both of which promoted super high-speed photography for slow-motion stroboscopic effects. *The Wild Parrots of Telegraph Hill* doesn't even include many close-ups of its colorfully-feathered and hooded stars.

Still, while this documentary falls short in up-to-the-minute pyrotechnics, it compensates with a heartfelt sense of humanitas. Interestingly, Mark Bittner does not appear as a lovable character at the outset, but his rapport and bond with the parrots becomes so entrancing and poignant that *The Wild Parrots of Telegraph Hill* quickly develops the warmth, humor and tragic sorrow of a fine fictional film narrative.

Two small complaints: while the "surprise" ending is pleasantly unforced, it dulls the shock of the devastating news about Bittner's sorrowful eviction and Connor's death; moreover, the event that occurs at this ending, which the film's publicists do not want revealed, causes one to question the real relationship between filmmaker and subject and whether the viewer should know more sooner. Also, Chris Michie's original music score is flat and forgettable, offering little to the overall work.

Most critics who reviewed *Wild Parrots* liked it. In the February 8 *Village Voice*, Ed Park wrote: "Several sharp jolts give the doc its dramatic shape, and one episode in particular, caught with a neighbor's lens, will make you gasp with grief. The conures' shadowy origins are explored, but pale next to the fundamental mysteries of the friendship between man and bird. The fate of the flock is, necessarily, left up in the air, and though there's a quite surprising resolution for the humans in this film, we're free to imagine the fate of the conures outside the frame—cryptically darting en masse to some unknown goal, their bodies the same green as the leaves on the trees."

In the March 2 *Entertainment Weekly*, Lisa Schwarzbaum concurred: " *Wild Parrots* has something of a molting look and an excess of watch-the-birds music. But in watching the birds and the man with an affectionate, curious eye, the filmmaker builds a story of surprising emotional resonance."

Finally, Sura Wood, in the February 9 *Hollywood Reporter* found a greater meaning in the piece: "On another level, *Wild Parrots* is a nostalgic tale of an almost vanished San Francisco, where elderly Italian ladies in alley bistros handed out free pastries and cappuccinos to those in need and Jack Kerouac and Allen Ginsberg prowled the streets. Caught somewhere between the dreary narcissism of the Beats and the spaced-out hippies, Bittner finds his way with a little help from his friends."

The Wild Parrots of Telegraph Hill surely won't win over cynical industrialists, let alone non-animal lovers. In fact, environmentalists may not be so pleased, either, since their lone reference makes them into unseen villains, ready to kill the "foreign" parrots for invading the area and disrupting the lives of the local birds. Nevertheless, Judy Irving's peek into this unique world will reach those who care about any of nature's more precious creatures.

Eric Monder

CREDITS

Origin: USA

Language: English

Released: 2003

Production: Judy Irving; Pelican Media

Directed by: Judy Irving

Cinematography by: Judy Irving

MPAA rating: G

Running time: 83 minutes

REVIEWS

Boxoffice Online. March, 2005.

Entertainment Weekly Online. March 2, 2005.

Hollywood Reporter. February 9, 2005.

Los Angeles Times Online. March 4, 2005.

New York Times Online. February 11, 2005.

Variety Online. April 30, 2004.

Village Voice. February 8, 2005.
Washington Post Online. March 11, 2005, p. WE37.

WINTER SOLSTICE

In the good old days of 1970's Hollywood, *Winter Solstice* would have been a major studio release. Today, this quiet, contemplative family melodrama is illustrative of independent cinema, the kind of film that provides an alternative to Tinseltown's mainstream products.

First-time director director Josh Sternfeld obviously likes the kinds of narratives that emphasize exploration of character and place. His original screenplay features more awkward silence than dramatic dialogue, but that is completely appropriate considering that his main characters are emotionally paralyzed.

Anthony LaPaglia (the star of CBS-TV's *Without a Trace*) plays Jim Winters, a shy but tense suburban landscape gardener who still silently grieves five years after his wife died suddenly in a car accident. Jim lives with his two teenage sons, Gabe (Aaron Stanford) and Pete (Mark Webber), though their lives together are far from harmonious. The three often fight or keep to themselves, while Gabe prepares to leave his loyal girlfriend (Michelle Monaghan) and the town itself, and his younger brother abuses alcohol and pays little attention to his school work. A house-sitter in town (Allison Janney) takes a liking to Jim, which upsets the uneasy calm of the all-male household. Finally, the men confront each other about their grief, which leads to a rapprochement of sorts. Gabe still leaves the family, but now with greater hope, if just as much uncertainty, about the future.

Winter Solstice is aptly named for its story is about people frozen emotionally by external events. Winters is also the surname of the main characters—father and sons. Unfortunately, several other recent films bear the same title, including a 2004 short subject, a 2003 TV movie (based on a book by Rosamunde Pilcher), and a 2000 short subject, so it could be easy to get confused. Yet, this *Winter Solstice* is worth seeking out.

Sternfeld never panders to his audience, delaying the explanation for the men's strife (i.e. the death of Mrs. Winters) until the climax of the story (though attentive viewers will probably figure it out earlier). Some will be reminded of earlier intimate family dramas, like Bart Freundlich's *Myth of Fingerprints* (1997), though *Winter Solstice* is far less elliptical and darkly humorous. Another influence seems to be Robert Redford's *Ordinary People* (1980), with its character study of those affected by the death of a beloved family member.

Sternfeld's craftmanship is less skilled than Freundlich and Redford's, and there is a first-time filmmaker's aura about *Winter Solstice* (Harlan Bosmajian's cinematography is just routine and the film stock looks oddly dated). Also dated, in a more positive way, is John Leventhal's musical score—a decided throwback to that 70s cinema the film emulates.

But what distinguishes the film above everything else are the performances. LaPaglia is excellent as the patriarch, a time bomb ready to go off; newcomers Stanford and Webber are completely convincing as the troubled brothers; Monaghan makes a definite impression in her small role (she can also be seen in *Syriana* in 2005); and even Allison Janney does a commendable job as the likable new neighbor, making you almost forget about her weekly West Wing gig and the fact her character is a little too tolerant of the Winters family and its bad behavior. Others in small roles do fine work, including Ron Livingston as Pete's high school history teacher.

Roger Ebert in the April 14 *Chicago Sun-Times* appreciated the film's open-endedness: "When *Winter Solstice* is over we sit and look at the screen and wonder what will happen to them all. We don't expect dramatic developments; these lives don't seem on a course for tragedy or happiness, but for a gradual kind of acceptance. Maybe the movies do us no service by solving so many problems, in a world with so few solutions." David Edelstein in the April 15 *Slate Magazine* was even more impressed: "For the first 20 minutes or so, I was impatient with the longeurs, but then it became clear that the movie is one long longeur, and that each still frame is bursting with emotional desperation. You can feel your inner rhythms slow as the film takes hold—enough for you to take in the details of the houses, yards, garages, and basements. I found myself almost in tears over a minor item in the cellar—a Calphalon box on a crowded shelf, maybe a piece of kitchen equipment bought by the mother and now stowed away, unused. (It's worth singling out the production designer, Jody Asnes.) (Actually, it's often worth singling out production designers—we don't do it enough.)" And Laura Sinagra in the April 5 *Village Voice* also taken with the film: "What makes *Winter Solstice,* a nice little Jersey vignette about a widower and his two teenage sons, so striking is writer-director Josh Sternfeld's respect for the verbal shorthand of family interaction. The low-key plot—grieving dad tentatively starts dating again, his older son prepares to leave home, his younger struggles through school—is less important than the way families speak, the codes hammered out over time, the lived-in language of grunts and fragments."

Those who do not enjoy slow-paced stories or require many plot twists should avoid *Winter Solstice.* Others will admire this moving, adult drama.

Eric Monder

CREDITS

Jim Winters: Anthony LaPaglia
Gabe Winters: Aaron Stanford
Pete Winters: Mark Webber
Molly Ripkin: Allison Janney
Stacey: Michelle Monaghan
Mr. Bricker: Ron Livingston
Robbie: Brandon Sexton III
Steve: Ebon Moss-Bachrach
Origin: USA
Language: English
Released: 2004
Production: John M. Limotte, Doug Bernheim, George Paaswell, Anthony LaPaglia, Jodi Peikoff; Sound Pictures
Directed by: Josh Sternfeld
Written by: Josh Sternfeld
Cinematography by: Harlan Bosmajian
Music by: John Leventhal
Sound: Brian Miksis
Editing: Plummy Tucker
Costumes: Paola Weintraub
MPAA rating: R
Running time: 90 minutes

REVIEWS

Boxoffice Online. April, 2005.
Chicago Sun-Times Online. April 14, 2005.
Entertainment Weekly Online. April 6, 2005.
Los Angeles Times Online. April 8, 2005.
New York Times Online. April 8, 2005.
Premiere Magazine Online. April 15, 2005.
Slate Magazine. April 15, 2005.
Variety Online. May 4, 2004.
Village Voice. April 15, 2005.

WITH FRIENDS LIKE THESE...

*With Friends Like These...*was finished in 1998 and became a straight-to-video release, which begs the question: why was the film shown in movie theaters in 2005? This spoof of Hollywood gamesmanship would have seem dated the first time around, making one wonder who would want to watch it, let alone pay good money to view it in a movie house.

Writer-director Philip Frank Messina invades Robert Altman's *The Player* territory with a parody of behind-the-scenes movieland casting tricks concerning four character actors who are best friends but discover they are competing for the same role—the part of Al Capone—in director Martin Scorsese's latest gangster epic.

The premise is enticing as Johnny (Robert Costanza), Steve (Adam Arkin), Armand (David Straithairn), and Dorian (Jon Tenney) all attempt to outmaneuver each other throughout the tryouts and screentests. While the casting call tests the friendships, few of the fellow thespians hesitate to stab each other in the back; nonetheless, they are surprised and upset by each other's actions to land the coveted part.

With Friends Like These... relies on audiences reveling in insider commentary on commercial filmmaking practices, ala *Entertainment Tonight,* yet this feature avoids the black humor of Billy Wilder's *Sunset Boulevard* or Altman's *The Player* and the riotous screwball comedy of Preston Sturges' *Sullivan's Travels* or Blake Edwards' *S.O.B.* Instead, Philip Frank Messina imitates a typical TV sitcom style, featuring an overwhelmed father figure (i.e. Costanza's Johnny), whining or worried wives, cute or clever children, and dialogue chock-full of forced humor. Only some dark lighting in a few of the interior scenes suggests something other than a family-hour television program.

Next to *Friends & Lovers,* the last theatrical film with the word "Friends" in the title, which happened to star a beautiful but inept model-turned-actor (Claudia Schiffer), *With Friends Like These...* (featuring Elle Macpherson) may seem like a masterwork, but that's not exactly a suggestion to see this abysmal entry.

Even those who relish backstage jokes and anecdotes may find themselves bewildered. For instance, a mention of Kate Moss as excessively thin couldn't have seemed very witty in the late 1990s; today, would viewers even recall Kate Moss (a supermodel, who, gratefully, never attempted acting)? A few members of the film's ensemble (e.g. Amy Madigan, Adam Arkin, Laura San Giacomo) also bring to mind another era when their Hollywood stock was much higher. Here, they just seem like *has-beens* desperate for work. Likewise, the pre-*Sopranos* "goombah" gags aren't exactly fresh and up-to-date.

Of course, Scorsese the Great finally shows up (as the story promises) and Bill Murray makes a lackadaisical cameo (not as himself but a blasé producer). Still, even for a low-budget outing, *With Friends Like These...* is bereft of guest appearances. After all, even the worst of these kind of movies usually get a boost from a parade of celebrities making fun of themselves. To wit, the misbegotten *Burn, Hollywood, Burn* and the dreary *The Muse* featured (and relied on) several key Tinseltown personalities popping up—including Scorsese as himself again in the latter!

The critics were notably harsh: in his February 25, 2005, *New York Post* review, Lou Lumenick wrote,"*With Friends Like These...*, an inside-baseball show-business comedy that's been available on video since 2001, has a solid cast bogged down in the broad script and lethargic direction of one Philip Messina." Peter L'Official's February 22, 2005, *The Village Voice* piece was even more severe: "Messina's characters gripe at being typecast as goombah hit men, yet the director seems blissfully unaware that he dooms them to the very fate they protest by painting them with such prosaic, uninspired strokes. Even a few strong strands of acting from David Strathairn aren't enough to stitch the threadbare script in this cheap mohair suit of a movie, where plot and characterization are drawn strictly off the rack. Only a mook could love it, and if you don't know what a mook is, go see *With Friends Like These...* and be found—I mean find out."

One positive exception came from Ray Greene's February 2005 *Box Office Magazine* review: "Perhaps the reason *With Friends Like These...* works so well is that the actors in its cast are all playing a predicament they can relate to. As an extended and richly detailed industry prank, *With Friends Like These...* may be a bit too "inside" for some audiences. But the great thing about a well-crafted indie project created on the cheap is that it really doesn't have to speak to everybody to turn a profit."

The fact *With Friends Like These...* got a chance with movie audiences seven years after it was completed is itself a Cinderella story, but it looks like the clock struck midnight for this cinematic pumpkin, and it went quickly back to the video bins in 2005.

Eric Monder

CREDITS

Steve Hersh: Adam Arkin
Johnny DiMartino: Robert Costanzo
Theresa Carpenter: Beverly D'Angelo
Samantha Mastandrea: Elle Macpherson
Hanna DiMartino: Amy Madigan
Armand Minetti: David Strathairn
Dorian Mastandrea: Jon Tenney
Yolanda Chin: Lauren Tom
Nino DiMartino: Carmine Costanzo
Frank Minetti: Garry Marshall
Dr. Maxwell Hersh: Michael McKean
Marissa DiMartino: Ashley Peldon
Rudy Ptak: Jon Polito
Babette: Heather Stephens
Maurice Melnick: Bill Murray
Scorsese: Martin Scorsese
Joanne Hersch: Laura San Giacomo
Head Mob Guy: Tom La Grua
Dr. Puccini: Armando Pucci
Trent Rabinowitz: Andrew Schaifer
Origin: USA
Language: English
Released: 1998
Production: Robert Greenhut, Amy Lemisch; Parkway Productions, Quadrant
Directed by: Philip Messina
Written by: Philip Messina
Cinematography by: Brian Reynolds
Editing: Claudia Finkle
Costumes: Mary Kay Stolz
Production Design: Beth DeSort
MPAA rating: R
Running time: 105 minutes

REVIEWS

Boxoffice Online. February, 2005.
New York Post. February 25, 2005.
New York Times Online. February 25, 2005.
Variety Online. March 20, 1998.
Village Voice Online. February 22, 2005.

X-Z

XXX: STATE OF THE UNION

Prepare for the next level.
—Movie tagline

The greatest threat to our nation comes from within.
—Movie tagline

Box Office: $26.1 million

First, in 2002, there was director Rob Cohen's *XXX,* starring Vin Diesel as a top-secret government agent who operated outside the rules. Next, in 2005, came the sequel, *XXX: State of the Union,* with a new director, New Zealand transplant Lee Tamahori, and a new XXX, Ice Cube. At the end of the sequel, there's a strong suggestion there will be another sequel, with a different XXX. Don't say you haven't been warned.

The winning appeal of ex-rapper Ice Cube, who somehow is loveable even when he's playing a soulless thug, is what saves *XXX: State of the Union* from its own determined mediocrity. Ice Cube, who was memorable in the Gulf War drama *Three Kings,* strikes just the right tone in this throwaway action thriller: studied indifference and detached snide humor. He's a bad-ass who doesn't need to raise his voice to be credible as a street fighter you'd hate to tangle with on any turf.

Strangely, this *XXX* franchise has decided to rotate its star protagonist from film to film. In extra footage from the first film, released only on the DVD version, Diesel's XXX is killed. The one character who's a holdover from the first film, the star-crossed agent Augustus Gibbons (Samuel L. Jackson), has confidence in his new pick, who's been rotting in prison after their last fiasco together. But Gibbons's computer-hacker second lieutenant, Toby (Michael Roof), starts out belittling the new XXX, listing the old hero's accomplishments: "The last XXX could ski, surf, and do all kinds of stuff." But Darius Stone, Ice Cube's character, can do all kinds of stuff too, and soon proves his worth, mostly by blowing things up.

Director Tamahori, who made such a huge impact internationally with his semidocumentary movie about violence among his native Maori people, *Once Were Warriors,* and followed up with the even more mesmerizing Hollywood noir drama, *Mulholland Falls,* has stumbled badly in the ten years since. There's no sign in *XXX* that this talented director is attempting to rise above the mundane material of the script. This film looks and feels like a series of video game moments held together by implausible connective tissues. Scenes seem to exist independently of each other, and there's little coherence to the film. For most of the film, we don't even know what's at stake, we only know that Darius Stone is going to be a bad-ass.

In the film's opening scenes, a group of unknown assailants raids a futuristic undergrounder bunker that houses a cadre of super-secret agents working for the U.S. government's National Security Agency. The bunker is underneath an idyllic horse farm. Gibbons, the leader of the crew, makes an improbable escape, and the others are killed. During the fight, the assailants employ flying pods that look like something out of a *Star Wars* movie. The savvy Toby tells Gibbons that these devices are ten generations ahead of the government's technology. But then not another word is said about the devices, and they are never seen again, and the raiders morph confusingly into a group that looks like a bunch of frat boys in suits; their leader, Kyle Steele (Scott Speedman), turns out, in the end, to be a good guy, but it's not clear how.

The real bad guy is Willem Dafoe—who else? Dafoe, who's made a nice career out of playing sneering, cynical, soft-spoken villains, here takes an easy duplicate of his standard role, playing a Department of Defense secretary planning to assassinate the president and all other officials above him in the line of succession during a State of the Union address. We're asked to believe that his character is staging a coup because the president is telling the nation that it must compromise and court our enemies and in so doing cut the military budget. It's hard to know what scenario is most farfetched in this film.

But for a long time, we don't know of Dafoe's plans, it's not clear exactly what Gibbons is hiring Stone to do, and it's far from clear how Steele's group ends up changing allegiances. In between, there are plenty of references to past battles that the viewer has no clue about, including one in which Gibbons's face got burned. And there are the kind of women characters that commonly populate a film like this: a bad white bitch, Charlie (Sunny Mabrey), who betrays Stone, and a good black ex-lover who helps Darius with his ultimate getaway car. Nona Gaye's aptly named Lola dresses like a hooker for her job running an upscale chop shop, and she and Stone never actually have sex, but just talk about it. In this genre of film, sex might rob the action hero of his strength.

Completing the cast is Roof's Toby, who wears sweater vests and for most of the film is known as "College Boy," Peter Strauss as a president who makes *The West Wing's* Martin Sheen president look like a right-winger, and Xzibit, another rapper who made a much bigger impact in two other 2005 films, *Crash* and *Derailed.* His character is an old homey of Stone who gathers his crew to help in the final assault on the Capitol Building to prevent the planned assassination. Their idea of protection is to drive tanks through back alleys and then launch rockets at the House and Senate.

There are a few tongue-in-cheek lines strewn amid the dialogue that almost make you think the filmmakers are spoofing their enterprises, but the level of knowingness doesn't rise that high; mostly characters ridicule other characters' cliched inspirational talks. Otherwise, the material is below standard fare, but it includes plenty of inexplicable talk about cars and an action rescue finale that takes place on a bullet train for no logical reason.

In between, plenty of things go boom. Not once, but twice, does XXX win the day by spewing gasoline on pursuers' vehicles and launching them on fire. Not once, but twice, is a key character rescued improbably by helicopter. Otherwise, even the action scenes are mundane. The disinterest of the actors and the crew on this film is almost palpable. It's like everyone knows they are churning out formulaic material, but nobody cares.

XXX: State of the Union is a marketing ploy that has little chance of succeeding. In a key scene, Ice Cube's Stone must convince Xzibit's character that he and his homeboys should rise to the defense of the nation by preventing the Defense Secretary's planned coup. XXX tries to convince his friend that he should care, because if he doesn't intervene he'll be robbed of his freedom to hijack and chop up cars. Similarly, the intent of the entire movie hinges on this argument, which is a weak one: That fans of gangsta rap and violent exploitation action films should care about a drama about a military takeover of the nation. It's like writers took two separate movies and cobbled them together into a hybrid that can neither move nor think on its own.

This film would have been much better if it had abandoned its silly pretenses and just became the action movie that it is, with no pauses for ridiculous speeches that even the film's characters ridicule. Tamahori, who should know much more about the origins of violence and the ridiculous arguments for it, needs to come to grips with whether to play this paltry material as a semi-spoof, but too much of the script combines a wooden seriousness with a few knowing winks and nods.

Despite all its flaws, *XXX: State of the Union* is enjoyable only because we get to spend so much time with Ice Cube on screen, and the more he preens and postures, the more enjoyable he is. His low-key, smirking role-playing struck some critics as one-dimensional, but in fact he's the only actor in the movie who seems to know how to inhabit his character and strike the right self-mocking tone. Dafoe and Jackson seem lost and miserable in roles they know are beneath them, and everyone else in the film is nothing more than a prop. Ice Cube, however, rises above the muck, and by all rights should earn some better roles for so doing.

Michael Betzold

CREDITS

XXX/Darius Stone: Ice Cube

Augustus Gibbons: Samuel L. Jackson

Sec. of Defense George Deckert: Willem Dafoe

Agent Kyle Steele: Scott Speedman

President Sanford: Peter Strauss

Lola: Nona Gaye

Toby Lee Shavers: Michael Roof
Charlie: Sunny Mabrey
Zeke: Xzibit
Lt. Alabama "Bama" Cobb: John G. Connolly
Origin: USA
Language: English
Released: 2005
Production: Neal H. Moritz, Arne L. Schmidt; Original Film; released by Sony Pictures Entertainment
Directed by: Lee Tamahori
Written by: Simon Kinberg
Cinematography by: David Tattersall
Music by: Marco Beltrami
Sound: Willie Burton
Music Supervisor: Laura Z. Wasserman, Darren Higman
Editing: Mark Goldblatt, Steven Rosenblum, Todd E. Miller
Art Direction: Bradford Ricker
Costumes: Sanja Milkovic Hays
Production Design: Gavin Bocquet
MPAA rating: PG-13
Running time: 94 minutes

REVIEWS

Boxoffice Online. April, 2005.
Chicago Sun-Times Online. April 28, 2005.
Entertainment Weekly Online. May 2, 2005.
Los Angeles Times Online. April 29, 2005.
New York Times Online. April 29, 2005.
Premiere Magazine Online. 2005.
Variety Online. April 27, 2005.
Washington Post Online. April 29, 2005, p. C05.

TRIVIA

Vin Diesel and Rob Cohen were originally attached to the project before the original film opened, but left.

YES

Created by writer/director Sally Potter as a response to the pessimism of the post-9/11 world, *Yes* is not so much a study in affirmation and acceptance but a celebration of the fact that we are still here—even after we die, she suggests, we leave a permanent imprint on the earth that can never be erased. This and other weighty postulations fill the screenplay which is spoken by the characters in rhymed iambic pentameter. The themes covered by her overly-ambitious film—religion, culture, class, racism, politics, beauty, chemistry, love—are as diverse as the characters themselves: a pale Irish research scientist and a swarthy Lebanese surgeon cum chef known simply as She and He, who meet and fall in love in London. Though visually striking and emotionally packed, Potter crams too many messages in a film that is also stacked with a plethora of tricky visual effects that confuse rather than clarify the love story that is at the film's heart.

Stuck in a now loveless marriage, She (Joan Allen) is a native of Ireland who came to the United States at age ten and now lives in London with her British politician husband, Anthony (Sam Neill). The film opens with the sound of a vacuum cleaner and out-of-focus dust particles flying about, eventually introducing the unhappy couple's housekeeper (a wonderfully expressive Shirley Henderson) who muses that although she is the best at her craft, there are always traces of dirt left behind: "Cleanliness is an illusion. Those of us that clean as a profession know." She knows the couple's secrets by the various secretions left behind and muses that people think those of her profession are invisible. Potter expands on the theme of class distinction by scattering many such cleaning women throughout the film, who often wordlessly stare directly into the camera after the main characters have passed them by.

As She and her husband wordlessly sit elegantly in the back of limo bound for a formal dinner, Her thoughts of rage at her husband cheating on her, in their own house even, are heard in voiceover. At the party, She meets He (Simon Abkarian) who works in the kitchen and doubles as a waiter. He immediately notices her and wastes no time in a poetic flirtation which leads to an overhead shot—that look suspiciously like a security camera P.O.V.—that reveals the two exchanging numbers. They secretly meet in his brightly colored flat amid breathy confessions of love and desire mingled with longing looks. The curry-colored walls of His apartment contrast with the spare, white minimalism of Her home with Anthony, where the whirring of a vacuum is virtually omnipresent and appearance is everything. Set at Christmastime, even the couples's tree is white bearing all-white lights. A research scientist, She also is faced with a clinical work environment and it is clear why she would fall for the messy immigrant who is given to dancing on tables at the drop of a hat.

They exchange stories of violence and turmoil in their respective homelands. He left Beirut after performing a life-saving operation on a patient only to witness him being immediately shot dead. Born in Belfast, She also knows about violence in the name of religion. She also chose to leave her homeland and not look back, loathe to visit the elderly aunt she left behind in Ireland.

The kitchen in which He works is a sort of microcosm of the larger world, populated with an Irish atheist and a devout Christian Jamaican, among others.

Normally a place for lively debate about women and the like, a political/religious discussion breaks out leading to an angry Irish co-worker lumping Him in with the terrorists due to his being a Muslim, and a nasty confrontation ensues when the enraged co-worker rushes at him with a makeshift weapon, causing Him to reach for his knife. He is immediately fired and begins to see that his life in London is not so idyllic after all. He begins to embrace his Arabic, Muslim roots which serve to alienate She, who represents all the problems he associates with the Western world. He is now determined to end their illicit affair and return to his homeland where he can be seen as a viable, respected person once again, declaring her culture has "unmanned" him in a one of the film's most effective scenes in a parking garage.

During their argument in which they spew raw insults like "Terrorist" "Bitch" and "Bigot," She receives a call that her aunt in Belfast (Sheila Hancock) is dying and she is forced to abruptly leave Him to fly to her side. This is another of the film's best scenes, as the feisty, dying aunt's thoughts are heard in voiceover. It is revealed she is a communist who idealizes Castro and has always dreamed of living in Cuba. "Cuba" becomes her last word, in fact, which she whispers to She who immediately recognizes that this may be the unlikely place where She and He, who is now in Beirut, could finally be happy together. The movie bears this out, and they—now both foreigners in a strange land—reunite amid the pale, blue, green, and pink Caribbean tones of the island: a happy medium between his color-saturated life and her bare, stark white one. The last shot of the lovers is of them frolicking on the beach in slow-motion.

Potter, who directed *Orlando* and adapted the screenplay from the novel by Virginia Woolf, employs the same lush visuals and color found in her earlier film. Her style firmly in the art-house niche, Potter employs too much avante garde filmic gimmickry here. Awash in angled shots, poetry and symbolism, the film feels too self-consciously arty. There is much to appreciate within the film, though. None of the characters are one-dimensional, even the uptight British snob Anthony is shown grooving to the blues music he loves. Performances are universally strong, including supporting roles by Samantha Bond as Kate, a friend of both She and Anthony who is secretly sleeping with him as well, and Stephanie Leonidas as Kate's daughter and the couple's goddaughter. And much of the poetic dialogue is beautiful. While alone in Cuba, wondering if He will indeed leave Beirut and join her there, she muses in a videotaped "confession" to God, "Now all I was is turned to ash and doubt. Love has tasted me and spat me out."

The film comes full circle at the end, completing its meditation on cleaning and life. Comparing the constant presence of dirt to the impression humans leave on the world—even after death—on an atomic and sub-atomic level, Henderson has the final word, speaking the film's title and last line with, "No does not exist. There's only yes."

Hilary White

CREDITS

She: Joan Allen
He: Simon Abkarian
Anthony: Sam Neill
Cleaner: Shirley Henderson
Aunt: Sheila Hancock
Kate: Samantha Bond
Billy: Gary Lewis
Whizzer: Raymond Waring
Grace: Stephanie Leonidas
Virgil: Wil Johnson
Origin: USA
Language: English
Released: 2004
Production: Christopher Sheppard, Andrew Fierberg; Adventure Pictures
Directed by: Sally Potter
Cinematography by: Alexei Rodionov
Music by: Sally Potter
Sound: Jean-Paul Mugel
Editing: Daniel Goddard
Art Direction: Carlos Conti, Claire Spooner
Costumes: Jacqueline Durran
MPAA rating: R
Running time: 99 minutes

REVIEWS

Boxoffice Online. July, 2005.
Chicago Sun-Times Online. July 8, 2005.
Entertainment Weekly Online. June 29, 2005.
Los Angeles Times Online. June 24, 2005.
New York Times Online. June 24, 2005.
Variety Online. September 8, 2004.
Washington Post Online. July 29, 2005, p. WE27.

QUOTES

Cleaner: "...In fact I think I'd guess/That 'no' does not exist. There's only 'yes.'"

YOURS, MINE & OURS

18 kids. 2 families. 1 force of nature.
—Movie tagline

Rock The House!
—Movie tagline

Box Office: $48.3 million

It was a near certainty that the success of *Cheaper by the Dozen* would spawn some similar fare. And indeed, the end of 2005 brought not only *Cheaper by the Dozen 2* but the similarly kid-infested *Yours, Mine & Ours. Yours, Mine & Ours* is based on the moderately well-liked 1968 comedy starring Lucille Ball and Henry Fonda. That movie was based on a true story—about a military man with eight children marrying a widow with ten children—that was widely publicized in the early 1960s. This version of the story proves the adage that each copy of something becomes yet a paler version of the original. One can only imagine the 2064 remake of the story.

Surely there was plenty of drama and humor inherent in the real life courtship of Helen North and Frank Beardsley and their subsequent eighteen-child family. But writers Ron Burch and David Kidd and director Raja Gosnell do not seem interested in discovering what those might have been. Instead they layer on tiresome clichés, obligatory slapstick and predictable plot beats. As Roger Ebert of *The Chicago Sun-Times* put it, "Consider the outing on the sailboat. The *moment* Admiral Frank warns everybody that the boom can swing around and knock you overboard, I would have given 19-to-1 odds that the person knocked overboard would be...but you already know."

It seems that casting Dennis Quaid and Rene Russo to play the leads amid the chaos would add a touch of class, and, to a certain extent, it does. As former high school sweethearts who are reunited many years and children later, Quaid and Russo put real feeling into their roles. The story of a middle-aged rekindled love, especially between two such well-preserved midlife actors, would have made for a nice film of its own, but unfortunately there is the matter of those eighteen kids and the food fights that they must have.

After courting for the briefest of time, Frank and Helen impulsively decide that they will elope and blend their two large broods. It would be a rare pack of children that would immediately embrace such a plan, but the situation is complicated by the fact that Frank and Helen subscribe to completely different parenting philosophies. Frank, an admiral in the United States Coast Guard, orders his eight children around like they are his soldiers. He is fond of charts, blowing a whistle and has even been known to employ a bit of corporal punishment. Helen, with her multicultural blend of adopted and biological children, is an artistic handbag designer who says things like, "Homes are places for free expression, not first impressions." Frank's home is shipshape; Helen's has a potbellied pig running around. (That the filmmakers felt the need to include a pig when there was already quite enough going on is a fine example of the kind of overkill and gracelessness they used when making this film.)

When the kids are first forced to move in together, they aim their powers of destruction toward each other. But they quickly come to the conclusion that to break up their parents' marriage, they must pool their resources and work together. It is not hard to imagine that such cooperative efforts just might lead to new closeness and respect among the children. (And with so many children—not to mention various and sundry pets—onscreen, they do remain "the children" instead of a bunch of individuals. Some of the less noticeable kid actors are practically extras in their own films.)

It was difficult to find a critic that liked the film. Ty Burr of *The Boston Globe* wrote, "*Yours, Mine & Ours* is the movie equivalent of a box of generic macaroni and cheese: bland, easily digested, comforting, forgettable." Robert K. Elder of *The Chicago Tribune* wrote, "Think of it as a reverse *Parent Trap*, only with more schmaltzy life lessons than a full season of *7th Heaven* and half the charm...*Yours, Mine & Ours* isn't so much a movie as it is scene after scene of Quaid getting pelted with paint, food and other associated goo. But even as slapstick, it's a major snoozefest." Roger Ebert of *The Chicago Sun-Times* wrote that it was as if director Gosnell "is checking off obligatory scenes and wants to get home in time for the lottery drawing." And finally, there was Steve Rhodes on www.InternetReviews.com whose review of the film was headlined simply, "Gag."

Jill Hamilton

CREDITS

Frank Beardsley: Dennis Quaid
Helen North: Rene Russo
Commandant Sherman: Rip Torn
Mrs. Munion: Linda Hunt
Max: Jerry O'Connell
Darrell: David Koechner
William Beardsley: Sean Faris
Christina Beardsley: Katja Pevec
Michael Beardsley: Tyler Patrick Jones
Phoebe North: Danielle Panabaker
Dylan North: Drake Bell
Joni North: Miranda Cosgrove
Harry Beardsley: Dean Collins
Kelly Beardsley: Haley Ramm
Ely Beardsley: Brecken Palmer
Otter Beardsley: Bridger Palmer
Ethan Beardsley: Ty Panitz
Naoko North: Miki Ishikawa
Mick North: Slade Pearce
Jimi North: Little JJ
Lao North: Andrew Vo

Bina North: Jennifer Habib
Marisa North: Jessica Habib
Aldo North: Nicholas Roget-King
Origin: USA
Language: English
Released: 2005
Production: Robert Simonds; Paramount Pictures, MGM, Nickelodeon, Columbia Pictures; released by Paramount
Directed by: Raja Gosnell
Written by: Ron Burch, David Kidd
Cinematography by: Theo van de Sande
Music by: Christophe Beck
Sound: David Wyman
Music Supervisor: Spring Aspers
Editing: Stephen A. Rotter, Bruce Green
Art Direction: Jim Nedza
Costumes: Marie-Sylvie Deveau
Production Design: Linda DeScenna
MPAA rating: PG
Running time: 90 minutes

REVIEWS

Boxoffice Online. November, 2005.
Chicago Sun-Times Online. November 23, 2005.
Entertainment Weekly Online. November 22, 2005.
Los Angeles Times Online. November 23, 2005.
New York Times Online. November 23, 2005.
Variety Online. November 20, 2005.
Washington Post Online. November 25, 2005, p. WE39.

QUOTES

Dylan North: "Mom gets married, we get drafted."

TRIVIA

The band that plays at the party in the movie is Christian alternative rock band Hawk Nelson.

ZATHURA

A New Adventure From the World of Jumanji.
—Movie tagline

Adventure Is Waiting.
—Movie tagline

Box Office: $28 million

In a children's action adventure market filled with the wizardry of high-tech computer imagery, it's a wonder *Zathura* got made. This film about a couple of brothers who play a board game that turns into a science-fiction fantasy is a throwback in many ways—not only because the special effects are old-fashioned and hardly special at all, but because the story itself isn't full of gimmicks or gadgetry.

In 1995, a movie of Chris Van Allsburg's book *Jumanji,* starring Robin Williams, sent viewers along with the children who played a board game that opened up portals to a spectacular, and frightening, jungle universe. *Zathura* follows exactly the same plot, and it's based on a book by the same author, except this time the board game sends its players into outer space. But while *Jumanji* was loud and strenuous, thanks to lush graphics and the outsized antics of Robin Williams, this film, despite its equally exotic location, is quieter and more contemplative and, if you're in the right frame of mind, even more satisfying. But in order to enjoy it, you might want to forget everything about *Jumanji,* because this film is not just derivative, it's an exact copy, complete with an older adult version of one of the game players who appears on the scene during the course of the game.

As the film opens, Tim Robbins plays a harried divorced father who is trying to juggle working-at-home responsibilities with caring for his two sons, ten-year-old Walter (Josh Hutcherson) and six-year-old Danny (Jonah Bobo), who are bored and constantly vying for his attention. Walter dislikes Danny because he's young and stupid and doesn't know how to play sports or compete in a game without cheating. Danny is trying to do something, anything, that Walter approves of, but he can't find how to hold his interest. As Walter explains, "I'm in fourth grade. I have a girl friend." Walter has no time anymore for little kids' stuff. Walter would rather watch ESPN; he treats his little brother as an annoyance.

Frankly, both these boys are a bit too annoying to be objects of audience rooting interest. Walter is off-putting, a kid who wants to act like a grown-up and is both cruel and inattentive to his little brother. Bobo plays Danny as a little younger than his reported six-and-three-quarter years; he can't read, is given to frequent bouts of whining and pouting, and seems as wide-eyed and naive as a four-year-old. These kids are fine actors, and they handle their transformations reasonably well through the movie, it's just that they are not playing the most compelling of characters.

But perhaps it's fine that they aren't all that sympathetic. You know this is the kind of movie that will test their mettle and morals, and force them to bond in new ways or die for lack of effort. The boys, even though they're competing with one another, must learn to function as a team, and help each other out. Danny must learn winning isn't worth cheating, and Walter must learn that his little brother has something to offer.

There are moral lessons aplenty, and none of them are surprises or particularly unexpected. What happens in *Zathura* is not that new ground is broken in terms of plot points, character development, or ethical lessons, and there's certainly not new territory to be covered in terms of sophisticated imagery. When the house is sent off into outer space, it simply floats around there, anchored for some reason to a hunk of earth that's been torn up along with it, and it looks ridiculous. But it also looks funny, like something we'd see in an old television show.

Can generations used to their frontiers being expanded to realms beyond casual imagination be willing to accept a house floating around in space? Will they ask about air supply and weightlessness and other scientific matters that don't seem to matter in the world of this fantasy? *Zathura* will be a real test of a child's capacity to accept the kind of old-fashioned suspension of disbelief that used to be mandatory in almost every children's film, but now has been blown away by high-tech realizations of fantastic worlds.

The reason *Zathura* works is that director Jon Favreau (*Elf,* 2003) uses a light touch that is halfway between an old television episode of *Lost in Space* and a sort of live-action version of *The Incredibles* (2005). There's a slight bit of tongue-in-cheek humor here, but there's no attempt to be either overly campy or needlessly sardonic; the movie has just the right tone of slack-jawed whimsy and careless serendipity. OK, flesh-eating Zorgons are attacking, so why not hide in the fireplace?

For all that might be going against it, *Zathura* is simply funny and pleasantly entertaining. The game itself is flawlessly rendered: two clunky metal spaceships advance by some hidden mechanism along a metal track that leads to the planet Zathura. A key is turned, a number rolls up on a counter, and it looks like some sort of rudimentary pinball machine crossed with a board game. Whoever designed this obviously lived through the 1950s, when family games were clunky and clever at the same time.

Inexplicably, on each turn the game spits out an instruction card. The cards are priceless examples of literary economy. The first one, drawn by Walter, says simply: YOUR ROBOT IS DEFECTIVE. And soon Walter's robot appears, and its defectiveness is readily transparent: it's trying to attack its owner. A violent struggle ensues. The kids have to figure out how to deal with unexpected events that arise, and Walter has to insist—a few times too many—that Danny keep playing the game.

A pleasant little wild card in the deck is the boys' older sister, a teenager named Lisa (Kristen Stewart), who is holed up in her room, with music plugged into her ears, sleeping off a late night. She's supposed to be watching the boys after dad has left the house for a meeting, but of course she's not. The fact that the house comes unmoored and is sent into outer space while she is trying to shut out all traces of her siblings' existence is funny enough; the fact that she is first transformed into ice for five turns leads to some other wacky comic moments. Stewart is goofily convincing in the part.

Eventually, the boys must RESCUE STRANDED ASTRONAUT. The astronaut (Dax Shepard) ends up doing most of the rescuing, explaining to the boys how to hide from the dangerous flesh-eating Zorgons who are hunting them down. Between the Zorgons, a defective robot in the basement, and a brush or two with some dangerous gravitational fields, the boys have a wild ride that teaches them about courage and mutual aid.

It's disappointing that Van Allsburg's book is so similar to *Jumanji* that it doesn't allow the director of this film much new turf to navigate in terms of plot, characters, or themes. This is basically *Jumanji* minus the steroids of Robin Williams. Robbins is understated and convincing in his small part, but otherwise the game's the thing. Expect low-budget but effectively rendered space creatures and a spinning house in space that looks like something from the days of early television. It might turn out that parents who grew up in the 1950s and 1960s will enjoy *Zathura* more rather than their sophisticated children or grandchildren.

Michael Betzold

CREDITS

Danny: Jonah Bobo
Walter: Josh Hutcherson
Astronaut: Dax Shepard
Lisa: Kristen Stewart
Dad: Tim Robbins
Voice of Robot: Frank Oz (Voice)
Origin: USA
Language: English
Released: 2005
Production: William Teitler, Scott Kroopf, Michael De Luca; Radar Pictures, Teitler Film, Michael De Luca; released by Columbia Pictures
Directed by: Jon Favreau
Written by: David Koepp, John Kamps
Cinematography by: Guillermo Navarro
Music by: John Debney
Sound: Mark Ulano
Editing: Dan Lebental
Art Direction: Richard F. Mays
Costumes: Laura Jean Shannon
Production Design: J. Michael Riva

MPAA rating: PG
Running time: 113 minutes

REVIEWS

Boxoffice Online. November, 2005.
Chicago Sun-Times Online. November 11, 2005.
Entertainment Weekly Online. November 9, 2005.
Los Angeles Times Online. November 11, 2005.
New York Times Online. November 11, 2005.
Premiere Magazine Online. November 11, 2005.
Variety Online. October 27, 2005.
Washington Post Online. November 11, 2005, p. C05.

QUOTES

Danny: "Zorgons are the lizardmen. They eat meat and we are MEAT!"

List of Awards

Academy Awards

Film: *Crash*
Animated Film: *Wallace & Gromit: The Curse of the Were-Rabbit*
Director: Ang Lee (*Brokeback Mountain*)
Actor: Philip Seymour Hoffman (*Capote*)
Actress: Reese Witherspoon (*Walk the Line*)
Supporting Actor: George Clooney (*Syriana*)
Supporting Actress: Rachel Weisz (*The Constant Gardener*)
Original Screenplay: Paul Haggis, Robert Moresco (*Crash*)
Adapted Screenplay: Larry McMurtry, Diana Ossana (*Brokeback Mountain*)
Cinematography: Dion Beebe (*Memoirs of a Geisha*)
Editing: Hughes Winborne (*Crash*)
Art Direction: John Myhre, Gretchen Rau (*Memoirs of a Geisha*)
Visual Effects: Joe Letteri, Brian Van't Hul, Christian Rivers, Richard Taylor (*King Kong*)
Sound: Christopher Boyes, Michael Semanick, Michael Hedges, Hammond Peck (*King Kong*)
Makeup: Howard Berger, Tami Lane (*The Chronicles of Narnia: The Lion, the Witch, and the Wardrobe*)
Costume Design: Colleen Atwood (*Memoirs of a Geisha*)
Original Score: Gustavo Santaolalla (*Brokeback Mountain*)
Original Song: "It's Hard Out Here for a Pimp" (Jordan Houston, Cedric Coleman, Paul Beauregard, *Hustle & Flow*)
Foreign Language Film: *Tsotsi*
Documentary, Feature: *March of the Penguins*

Directors Guild of America Award

Director: Ang Lee (*Brokeback Mountain*)

Writers Guild of America Awards

Original Screenplay: Paul Haggis, Robert Moresco (*Crash*)
Adapted Screenplay: Larry McMurtry, Diana Ossana (*Brokeback Mountain*)

Golden Globes

Film, Drama: *Brokeback Mountain*
Film, Musical or Comedy: *Walk the Line*
Director: Ang Lee (*Brokeback Mountain*)
Actor, Drama: Philip Seymour Hoffman (*Capote*)
Actor, Musical or Comedy: Joaquin Phoenix (*Walk the Line*)
Actress, Drama: Felicity Huffman (*Transamerica*)
Actress, Musical or Comedy: Reese Witherspoon (*Walk the Line*)
Supporting Actor: George Clooney (*Syriana*)
Supporting Actress: Rachel Weisz (*The Constant Gardener*)
Screenplay: Larry McMurtry, Diana Ossana (*Brokeback Mountain*)
Score: John Williams (*Memoirs of a Geisha*)
Song: "A Love That Will Never Grow Old" (Gustavo Santaolalla, Bernie Taupin; *Brokeback Mountain*)
Foreign Language Film: *Paradise Now*

Independent Spirit Awards

Film: *Brokeback Mountain*
First Film: *Crash*
Director: Ang Lee (*Brokeback Mountain*)
Actor: Philip Seymour Hoffman (*Capote*)
Actress: Felicity Huffman (*Transamerica*)
Supporting Actor: Matt Dillon (*Crash*)
Supporting Actress: Amy Adams (*Junebug*)
Screenplay: Dan Futterman (*Capote*)

First Screenplay: Duncan Tucker (*Transamerica*)
Cinematography: Robert Elswit (*Good Night, and Good Luck*)
Foreign Language Film: *Paradise Now*
Documentary: *Enron: The Smartest Guys in the Room*

Los Angeles Film Critics Awards

Film: *Brokeback Mountain*
Director: Ang Lee (*Brokeback Mountain*)
Actor: Philip Seymour Hoffman (*Capote*)
Actress: Vera Farmiga (*Down to the Bone*)
Supporting Actor: William Hurt (*A History of Violence*)
Supporting Actress: Catherine Keener (*The 40-Year-Old Virgin, Capote, The Ballad of Jack and Rose*, and *The Interpreter*)
Screenplay: Dan Futterman (*Capote*)
Cinematography: Robert Elswit (*Good Night, and Good Luck*)
Score: Joe Hisaishi (*Howl's Moving Castle*)
Animated Film: *Wallace & Gromit: The Curse of the Were-Rabbit*
Foreign Language Film: *Cache (Hidden)*
Documentary: *Grizzly Man*

National Board of Review Awards

Film: *Good Night, and Good Luck*
Director: Ang Lee (*Brokeback Mountain*)
Actor: Philip Seymour Hoffman (*Capote*)
Actress: Felicity Huffman (*Transamerica*)
Supporting Actor: Jake Gyllenhaal (*Brokeback Mountain*)
Supporting Actress: Gong Li (*Memoirs of a Geisha*)
Foreign Language Film: *Paradise Now*
Documentary: *March of the Penguins*

National Society of Film Critics Awards

Film: *Capote*
Director: David Cronenberg (*A History of Violence*)
Actor: Philip Seymour Hoffman (*Capote*)
Actress: Reese Witherspoon (*Walk the Line*)
Supporting Actor: Ed Harris (*A History of Violence*)
Supporting Actress: Amy Adams (*Junebug*)
Cinematography: Christopher Doyle, Pung-Leung Kwan, Yiu-Fai Lai (*2046*)
Foreign Language Film: *Gegen die Wand*

New York Film Critics Awards

Film: *Brokeback Mountain*
Director: Ang Lee (*Brokeback Mountain*)
Actor: Heath Ledger (*Brokeback Mountain*)
Actress: Reese Witherspoon (*Walk the Line*)
Supporting Actor: William Hurt (*A History of Violence*)
Supporting Actress: Maria Bello (*A History of Violence*)
Screenplay: Noah Baumbach (*The Squid and the Whale*)
Cinematography: Christopher Doyle, Pung-Leung Kwan, Yiu-Fai Lai (*2046*)
Foreign Language Film: *2046*
Documentary: *Grizzly Man* and *White Diamond*
Animated Film: *Howl's Moving Castle*

Screen Actors Guild Awards

Actor: Philip Seymour Hoffman (*Capote*)
Actress: Reese Witherspoon (*Walk the Line*)
Supporting Actor: Paul Giamatti (*Cinderella Man*)
Supporting Actress: Rachel Weisz (*The Constant Gardener*)
Ensemble Cast: *Crash*

Obituaries

Anthony Patrick Adams (February 15, 1953–October 22, 2005). Producer Tony Adams was born in Dublin, Ireland, and grew up running the family's theater alongside his siblings. He served as an assistant on the set of *Deliverance* and star Burt Reynolds introduced him to director Blake Edwards. After attending Pepperdine University, Adams became the associate producer on Edwards' *The Return of the Pink Panther* (1975) and went on to produce five more installments in the series, including the last, *Son of the Pink Panther* (1993). He also worked on the Edwards' films *10* (1979), *S.O.B.* (1981), *Victor/Victoria* (1982), and *The Man Who Loved Women* (1983). Other credits included *A Fine Mess* (1986), *Sunset* (1988), and *Switch* (1991).

Don Adams (April 13, 1923–September 25, 2005). Born Donald James Yarmy in New York City, Adams changed his named when he began his career as a comic in the 1940s. He became typecast for his role as bumbling Maxwell Smart, Agent 86, in the sitcom Get Smart (1965–70), earning three Emmys. He reprised the role in the 1980 film *The Nude Bomb*, the 1989 TV movie *Get Smart Again,* and the brief 1995 revival series. He also voiced the title character in the animated *Inspector Gadget* series and his voice was heard as the Brain in the 1999 live-action film version. Other screen credits included *Jimmy the Kid* (1982) and *Back to the Beach* (1987).

Mason Adams (February 26, 1919–April 26, 2005). Born in Brooklyn, New York, the character actor worked on radio in the 1940s, including the title role in *Pepper Young's Family*, and taught speech. With his distinctive voice, Adams served as the spokesman for the J.M. Smucker Company for more than 30 years and played managing editor Charlie Hume on the TV series *Lou Grant* (1977–82), earning three Emmy nominations. Film credits included *A Shining Season* (1979), *The Final Conflict* (1981), *Adam* (1983), *F/X* (1986), *Houseguest* (1994), and *From the Earth to the Moon* (1998).

Mousstapha Akkad (July, 1930–November 11, 2005). Born in Aleppo Syria, the director and producer died of wounds sustained in a terrorist bombing in Jordan. He came to America in 1950 to study filmmaking and was the producer for all eight *Halloween* films, beginning in 1978. Akkad was also the producer and director of the films *The Message* (1976) and *Lion of the Desert* (1981).

Eddie Albert (April 22, 1906–May 26, 2005). Born Edward Albert Heimberger in Rock Island, Illinois, the actor studied drama at the University of Minnesota but left to join a singing trio and do radio and stage work. His first Broadway role was 1935's *O Evening Star.* Albert made his movie debut recreating his stage role in the Warner Bros. film *Brother Rat* (1938). He served in the Navy during WWII and used his experience with military training films to launch Eddie Albert Productions in 1946, making industrial and educational films, returning to Hollywood in *Smash-Up: The Story of a Woman* (1947). Albert was nominated for two supporting actor Academy Awards for *Roman Holiday* (1953) and *The Heartbreak Kid* (1972). While continuing his movie and stage work, Albert found TV success in the comedy series *Green Acres* (1965–71) and also co- starred in *Switch* (1975–78). Among Albert's other screen credits were *The Fuller Brush Girl* (1950), *Carrie* (1952), *I'll Cry Tomorrow* (1955), *Oklahoma!* (1955), *The Teahouse of the August Moon* (1956), *The Sun Also Rises* (1957), *Beloved Infidel* (1959), *The Longest Day* (1962), *Captain Newman, M.D.* (1963), *7 Women* (1966), *The Longest Yard* (1974), *Escape to Witch Mountain* (1975), *The Concorde: Airport '79* (1979), *Dreamscape* (1984), *Brenda Starr* (1986), and *The Big Picture* (1989).

Keith Andes (July 12, 1920–November 11, 2005). Born John Charles Andes in Ocean City, New Jersey, the actor graduated from Temple University and studied voice at the Philadelphia Conservatory of Music, performing in USO shows during WWII. Andes was working on Broadway when Darryl F. Zanuck saw him perform and offered the actor a minor role in the 1944 film *Winged Victory.* Screen credits included *The Farmer's Daughter* (1947), *Blackbeard the Pirate* (1952), *Clash by Night* (1952), *Away All Boats* (1956), *Back from Eternity* (1956), *Tora! Tora! Tora!* (1970), and *The Ultimate Imposter* (1979).

Leon Askin (September 18, 1907–June 3, 2005). Born Leo Aschkenasy in Vienna, Austria, the actor began his career on stage in 1926. He was an actor and director at the Dumont Playhouse in Vienna but was thrown out in 1933 for being Jewish. Askin fled to Paris and emigrated to the United States in 1940, serving with the Army Air Corps in WWII. He worked as a drama teacher as well as acting and directing on Broadway before breaking into films with 1952's *Assignment Paris.* Ironically, Askin was best-known for his TV role as Nazi Gen. Albert Burkhalter in *Hogan's Heroes* (1965–71). In 1994, Askin returned to Vienna and worked in cabaret and in opera. Other screen credits included *Road to Bali* (1952), *The Robe* (1953), *Valley of the Kings* (1954), *One, Two, Three* (1961), *The Terror of Dr. Mabuse* (1962), *Double Trouble* (1967), *The Perils of Pauline* (1967), *The Maltese Bippy* (1969), *The World's Greatest Athlete* (1973), *Airplane II: The Sequel* (1982), and *Odd Jobs* (1986).

George Atkinson (1935–March 3, 2005). Born in Shanghai, China, Atkinson was a pioneer in the video rental industry. He and his family spent two years in a Japanese prison camp during WWII before emigrating to Canada and later moving to Los Angeles. Atkinson worked as a stand-in and stunt-double before starting Home Theater Systems, which rented Super 8 movies and projectors. When the first consumer VCRs came on the market in 1975, Atkinson decided to expand his business and began renting videos from his new franchise, Video Station, in 1977, the first video-rental store. At its peak, Video Station had more than 550 affiliated stores. Atkinson was inducted into the Video Hall of Fame in 1991.

Anne Bancroft (September 17, 1931–June 6, 2005). Born Anna Maria Louisa Italiano in the Bronx, New York, the actress studied at the American Academy of Dramatic Arts in 1948 and began acting on TV in 1950 under the name Anne Marno. Signed to a 20th Century Fox contract in 1952, she chose her new stage name from a studio list. Bancroft appeared in a number of B-movies, including *Treasure of the Golden Condor* (1953), *Demetrius and the Gladiators* (1954), *Gorilla at Large* (1954), *Nightfall* (1956), and *The Girl in Black Stockings* (1957) before returning to Broadway to star in *Two for the Seesaw* (1958), which earned Bancroft her first Tony. She then starred as Annie Sullivan in *The Miracle Worker* (1952), opposite Patty Duke, and won her second Tony. When the play was made into a film in 1962, both Duke and Bancroft won Academy Awards. Bancroft received Oscar nominations for *The Pumpkin Eater* (1964), her iconic role as Mrs. Robinson in *The Graduate* (1967), *The Turning Point* (1977), and *Agnes of God* (1985). Bancroft was studying at the Actors Studio when she met Mel Brooks; the two married in 1964 and worked together in *Silent Movie* (1976) and *To Be or Not to Be* (1983). Other screen credits included *Young Winston* (1972), *The Prisoner of Second Avenue* (1974), *The Bell Jar* (1979), *The Elephant Man* (1980), *Fatso* (1980, also directed), *Garbo Talks* (1984), *84 Charing Cross Road* (1986), *'Night Mother* (1986), *Torch Song Trilogy* (1988), *Broadway Bound* (1992), *How to Make an American Quilt* (1995), *G.I. Jane* (1997), *Up at the Villa* (2000), and *The Roman Spring of Mrs. Stone* (2003).

Ronnie Barker (September 25, 1929–October 3, 2005). Born in Bedford, England, the writer and comedian was best known for his partnership with Ronnie Corbett. The two first worked together on the David Frost shows *The Frost Report* and *Frost On Sunday* in the 1960s and went on to star in the 1971 TV series *The Two Ronnies*, which lasted more than 13 years and for which he wrote most of the sketches under the pseudonym Gerald Wiley. Barker also starred in the series' *Porridge* and *Open All Hours.* Barker's film roles were few but included *The Man Outside* (1968), *Robin and Marian* (1976), *The Gathering Storm* (2002), and *My House in Umbria* (2003). He also authored the memoir *Dancing in the Moonlight.*

Barbara Bel Geddes (October 31, 1922–August 8, 2005). The actress was born in New York City, the daughter of industrial designer and architect Norman Bel Geddes, who used his contacts to get Barbara a job in summer stock. Her first important role on Broadway was in *Deep Are the Roots* (1945) and in 1946, Bel Geddes signed a contract with RKO; her first film was 1947's *The Long Night.* She received an Academy Award nomination as best supporting actress for *I Remember Mama* (1948). Dropped by RKO after four years, Bel Geddes returned to Broadway as the original Maggie in *Cat on a Hot Tin Roof* (1955) and starred in *Mary, Mary* (1961). Bel Geddes played matriarch Miss Ellie from 1978–90 on the TV series *Dallas,* receiving an Emmy in 1980. Other screen credits included *Blood on the Moon* (1948), *Caught* (1949), *Panic in the Streets* (1950), *Vertigo* (1958), *The Five Pennies* (1959), *Summertime* (1971), and *The Todd Killings* (1971).

Belita (October 21, 1923–December 18, 2005). Born Gladys Olive Jepson-Turner at Garlogs in Nether Wallop, England, the ice-skater had a brief acting career. At the age of 12, Belita was selected to compete in a skating contest at the 1936 Olympics. She turned professional at age 14 and came to America in 1938 on an exhibition tour, remaining throughout WWII. She appeared in 1941's *Ice-Capades* and signed a contract with Allied Artists. Among her films were *Silver Skates* (1943), *Lady Let's Dance* (1944), *Suspense* (1946), *The Gangster* (1947), *The Hunted* (1948), *The Man on the Eiffel Tower* (1950), *Never Let Me Go* (1953), and *Invitation to the Dance* (1956). Belita retired from the rink in 1956 and from show business three years later.

Lloyd Bochner (July 29, 1924–October 29, 2005). Born in Toronto, Ontario, Bochner started as a child actor on radio and the stage. He began working in New York in 1951 and moved to Los Angeles in 1960 to co-star in the TV series *Hong Kong.* Among his other TV credits were a two-year role as Cecil Colby in the series *Dynasty.* Screen credits included *The Night Walker* (1964), *Point Blank* (1967), *Tony Rome* (1967), *The Detective* (1968), *The Dunwich Horror* (1970), *Ulzana's Raid* (1972), *The Lonely Lady* (1983), *Naked Gun 2: The Smell of Fear* (1991), *Morning Glory* (1993), *Bram Stoker's The Mummy* (1997), *Before I Say Goodbye* (2003), and *The Commission* (2003).

Thomas Ross Bond (September 16, 1926–September 24, 2005). Born in Dallas, Texas, Bond began his career at the age of six working for Hal Roach studios in the *Our Gang* serials, playing Tommy from 1932 to 1934 and then bully Butch from 1937 to 1940. He appeared in 27 of the shorts. He later appeared with Carl "Alfalfa" Switzer in the 1947 *Gas House Kids* films, as Joey Pepper in *The Five Little Peppers* serials, and as cub reporter Jimmy Olsen in the 1948 and 1950 *Superman* serials. He retired from acting in 1951 and turned to television production. Bond published his memoir, *You're Darn Right It's Butch!*, in 1993.

James Booth (December 19, 1927–August 11, 2005). Born David Geeves-Booth in Croyden, Surrey, England, the character actor left school at 17 and joined the army. After his military service, Booth won a place at RADA (Royal Academy for Dramatic Arts) and then joined the Theatre Workshop at Stratford East and later the Royal Shakespeare Company. One of his best-known film roles was as Private Henry Hook in the 1964 film *Zulu*. Other acting credits included *The Trials of Oscar Wilde* (1960), *Sparrers Can't Sing* (1962), *French Dressing* (1964), *Robbery* (1967), *The Bliss of Mrs. Blossom* (1968), *That'll Be the Day* (1973), *Zorro, the Gay Blade* (1981), and *Bad Guys* (1986). Booth was living in Los Angeles, working as a writer, when he took the role of Ernie Miles in TV's *Twin Peaks*. His writing credits included *Sunburn* (1979), *Pray for Death* (1985), *Avenging Force* (1986), and *American Ninja 2* (1987).

Dorris Bowdon (December 27, 1915–August 9, 2005). Born in Coldwater, Mississippi, the actress was spotted by a scout while attending Louisiana State University and signed to a contract at 20th Century Fox. Bowdon had bit roles before being cast in two films directed by John Ford: *Drums Along the Mohawk* and *Young Mr. Lincoln* (both 1939). She then played Rose-of-Sharon in Ford's classic *The Grapes of Wrath* (1940). Bowdon married the film's screenwriter, Nunnally Johnson, and retired in 1943 after appearing in *The Moon Is Down*, also written by Johnson.

John Box (January 27, 1920–March 7, 2005). Born in London, England, and raised in Ceylon, the art director and production designer received his architectural degree from the University of London but became a draftsman for London Films, moving into art direction by the mid-1950s. He won Academy Awards for *Lawrence of Arabia* (1962), *Doctor Zhivago* (1965), *Oliver!* (1968), and *Nicholas and Alexandra* (1971), and was nominated for *Travels With My Aunt* (1972) and *Passage to India* (1984). Among Box's other credits were *The Million Pound Note* (1953), *Zarak* (1956), *The Inn of the Sixth Happiness* (1958), *Our Man in Havana* (1960), *The World of Suzie Wong* (1960), *A Man for All Seasons* (1966), *The Great Gatsby* (1974), *Rollerball* (1975), *Black Beauty* (1994), and *First Knight* (1995).

Jocelyn Brando (November 18, 1919–November 27, 2005). Born in San Francisco, California, the actress was the older sister of actor Marlon Brando. Marlon followed Jocelyn to New York and it was she who introduced him to the Stella Adler acting studio. Jocelyn made her Broadway debut in 1942, but her best-known stage role was in 1948's *Mister Roberts*. Her first film was 1953's *China Venture* and Jocelyn acted with her brother in the films *The Ugly American* (1963) and *The Chase* (1966). Other screen credits included *Big Heat* (1953), *Ten Wanted Men* (1955), *Nightfall* (1957), *Bus Riley's Back in Town* (1965), *Movie Movie* (1978), and *Mommie Dearest* (1981).

Donald Brooks (January 10, 1928–August 1, 2005). Born Donald Marc Blumberg in New Haven, Connecticut, the costume designer studied at the Fashion Institute of Technology and Parsons School of Design. Brooks began his career as a fashion designer and opened his own business in the early 1960s and also began designing for Broadway, beginning with 1962's *No Strings*. Brooks branched into film work with *The Cardinal* (1963) and received the first of his Academy Award nominations; he was also nominated for *Star!* (1968) and *Darling Lili* (1970). Other credits included *The Third Day* (1965), *The Detective* (1968), *The Terminal Man* (1974), *The Bell Jar* (1979), *Scruples* (1981), *Belizaire the Cajun* (1986), and *The Two Mrs. Grenvilles* (1987).

Argentina Brunetti (August 31, 1907–December 20, 2005). Born in Buenos Aires, Argentina, the character actress followed her mother, Sicilian actress Mimi Aguglia, into the theater by the age of three. She signed a contract with MGM in 1937 and appeared uncredited in various films before her first credited role as Mrs. Martini in 1946's *It's a Wonderful Life*. Brunetti appeared in some 90 movies and 60 television shows and was a founding member of the Hollywood Foreign Press Association. Screen credits included *Holidays in Havana* (1949), *The Lawless* (1950), *The Great Caruso* (1951), *My Cousin Rachel* (1952), *When in Rome* (1952), *The Caddy* (1953), *The Brothers Rico* (1957), *Duel at Apache Wells* (1957), *The George Raft Story* (1961), *Fatso* (1980), and *The 4th Tenor* (2002). Her autobiography, *In Sicilian Company*, was published in 2005.

Hamilton Camp (October 30, 1934–October 2, 2005). The folksinger, comic, and actor was born in London, England, and moved with his family to Canada and later to California after WWII. He appeared in more than 100 films and television shows, beginning with the 1946 film *Bedlam*. Camp also formed a folk duo with Bob Gibson in the early 1960s, working clubs in New York and Chicago, but they broke up when Camp joined Chicago's Second City comedy troupe. Camp later moved to Los Angeles to pursue his acting career; screen credits included *Eating Raoul* (1982), *Under Fire* (1983), *Meatballs 2* (1984), *Lots of Luck* (1985), *Arena* (1989), *Almost Heroes* (1997), *Joe Dirt* (2001), and *Hard Four* (2005).

J.D. Cannon (April 24, 1922–May 20, 2005). Born John Donovan Cannon in Salmon, Idaho, the character actor graduated from the American Academy of Dramatic Arts. Between 1960 and 1991, Cannon appeared on more than 85 TV shows, including a regular role in the NBC series *McCloud* (1970–77). Among his screen credits were *Cool Hand Luke* (1967), *Cotton Comes to Harlem* (1970), *Lawman* (1971), *Scorpio* (1973), *Raise the Titanic* (1980), *Death Wish 2* (1982), and *Street Justice* (1989). The actor retired in 1991.

Robert I. Clarke (June 1, 1920–June 11, 2005). The actor was born in Oklahoma City, Oklahoma, and moved to Los Angeles in 1942, signing a contract with RKO. Clarke became a cult favorite for his work in such genre films as *The Body Snatcher* (1945), *Zombies on Broadway* (1945), *The Man from Planet X* (1951), *Sword of Venus* (1953), *The Astounding She-Monster* (1958), *Hideous Sun Demon* (1959), *Beyond the Time Barrier* (1960), *Terror of the Bloodhunters* (1962), *Attack from Mars* (1988), and *Aliena-*

tor (1989). In recognition, Clarke titled his 1996 autobiography, *To 'B' or Not to 'B'.*

Henry Corden (January 6, 1920–May 19, 2005). The character and voice actor was born in Montreal, Quebec, and moved to New York as a child. Corden was already working in radio when he moved to Hollywood in the 1940s and made his screen debut in *The Secret Life of Walter Mitty* (1947). Adept at dialects, he was frequently typecast as villains in films and on TV. Corden moved into cartoon voice work in the 1960s, including *The Jetsons, Jonny Quest, The Atom Ant Show, Scooby-Doo,* and others before taking over as the voice of Fred Flintstone in 1977. Film credits included *The Asphalt Jungle* (1950), *The Black Castle* (1952), *Viva Zapata!* (1952), *Jupiter's Darling* (1955), and *The Ten Commandments* (1956).

George P. Cosmatos (January 4, 1941–April 19, 2005). Born in Florence, Italy, the director graduated from the London Film School and got his start as an assistant director on Otto Preminger's *Exodus* (1960). Cosmatos' own directorial debut came with *Restless* (1971). He was known for his ability to handle tough action shoots and fix troubled film projects. Directorial credits included *Massacre in Rome* (1973), *The Cassandra Crossing* (1976), *Escape to Athena* (1979), *Of Unknown Origin* (1983), *Rambo: First Blood Part II* (1985), *Cobra* (1986), *Leviathan* (1989), *Tombstone* (1993), and *The Shadow Conspiracy* (1996).

Joseph Patrick Cranshaw (June 17, 1919–December 28, 2005). Born in Bartlesville, Oklahoma, the character actor appeared in dozens of films and had a late-career success as elderly frat boy Blue in the raucous 2003 comedy *Old School.* Cranshaw (frequently billed as Pat or Patrick Cranshaw) made his screen debut as a bartender in 1955's *Texas Lady.* Other screen credits included *The Seventh Commandment* (1960), *Bonnie and Clyde* (1967), *Pee-Wee's Big Adventure* (1985), *The Beverly Hillbillies* (1993), *The Hudsucker Proxy* (1994), *Everyone Says I Love You* (1996), *Almost Heroes* (1998), *Best in Show* (2000), *Herbie: Fully Loaded* (2005), and *Air Buddies,* which is expected to be released in 2006.

Constance Cummings (May 15, 1910–November 23, 2005). Born in Seattle, Washington, the actress came to Hollywood at 20 and was signed to a contract at Columbia Pictures. Her screen debut came in 1931's *The Criminal Code* and she made 10 films for the studio in two years. She married in 1933 and Cummings and her husband, British playwright Benn Wolfe Levy, returned to England where the actress concentrated on her stage career, appearing in numerous plays either written and/or directed by her husband, although she did act in a few films. Film credits included *American Madness* (1932), *Movie Crazy* (1932), *Night After Night* (1932), *Broadway Through a Keyhole* (1933), *Remember Last Night?* (1935), *Busman's Honeymoon* (1940), *The Foreman Went to France* (1942), *This England* (1942), *Blithe Spirit* (1945), *John and Julie* (1945), *The Intimate Stranger* (1956), and *The Battle of the Sexes* (1959).

Richard Earl Cunha (March 4, 1922–September 18, 2005). Born in Honolulu, Hawaii, the director and cinematographer made his name in low-budget genre films. Cunha served as an aerial photographer for the Army Air Corps during WWII and made military training films, newsreels, and documentaries at Hal Roach Studios. He was best-known for a quartet of films: *Frankenstein's Daughter* (1958), *Giant from the Unknown* (1958), *She Demons* (1958), and *Missile to the Moon* (1959). Cunha formed a production company that made TV commercials and industrial films and he worked as a cameraman for a number of early TV shows.

Ossie Davis (December 18, 1917–February 4, 2005). The actor, writer, and director was born Raiford Chatman Davis in Cogdell, Georgia. His parents called him R.C. but the county clerk registering his birth misheard the name as "Ossie," which it remained. Davis left Howard University (where he studied drama) in 1939 and moved to Harlem, joining the Rose McClendon Players; he served in the Special Services in WWII. Davis made his Broadway debut in 1946's *Jeb,* in which he meet actress Ruby Dee, whom he married in 1948. Davis made his screen debut in 1950's *No Way Out,* which also featured Dee. Among their other collaborations was the 1961 Davis-written play, *Purlie Victorious* in which they both starred; Davis adapted it for the screen as *Gone Are the Days* (1963). It was turned into the Broadway musical *Purlie* in 1970 and nominated for a Tony as best musical. Davis co-starred on the TV shows *The Defenders* (1963–65) and *Evening Shade* (1990–94). His directorial credits included *Cotton Comes to Harlem* (1970), *Kongi's Harvest* (1971), *Black Girl* (1972), *Gordon's War* (1973), and *Countdown at Kusini* (1976). Davis was featured in six films by director Spike Lee: *School Daze* (1988), *Do the Right Thing* (1989), *Jungle Fever* (1991), *Malcolm X* (1992), *Get On the Bus* (1996), and *She Hate Me* (2004). Other credits included *A Man Called Adam* (1966), *The Scalphunters* (1968), *Roots* (1977), *King* (1978), *All God's Children* (1980), *Harry & Son* (1984), *Grumpy Old Men* (1993), *The Stand* (1994), *I'm Not Rappaport* (1996), *Miss Evers Boys* (1997), *Twelve Angry Men* (1997), *Dr. Doolittle* (1998), and *Bubba Ho-Tep* (2003). He and Dee published their joint memoir, *With Ossie & Ruby: In This Life Together,* in 1998, and both received Kennedy Center honors for their lifetime achievements in the arts in 2004.

Sandra Dee (April 23, 1942–February 20, 2005). Born Alexandra Zuck in Bayonne, New Jersey, the actress was the perky blonde, All-American teenager next door in the late 1950s and early 1960s. Dee attended the Professional Children's School in New York and began modeling as a child; she was signed to a Universal contract by producer Ross Hunter and renamed by the studio. Dee made her screen debut in *Until They Sail* (1957). She starred as teen surfer *Gidget* in 1959 and made a number of romantic comedies, including *The Reluctant Debutante* (1958), *Tammy Tell Me True* (1961), *Tammy and the Doctor* (1963), and *Take Her, She's Mine* (1963). Other screen credits included *Imitation of Life* (1959), *A Summer Place* (1959), *Portrait in Black* (1960), *Come September* (1960), *Romanoff and Juliet* (1961), *If a Man Answers* (1962), *That Funny Feeling* (1965), *Rosie!* (1968), *The Dunwich Horror* (1970), and *Lost* (1983). She had suffered from anorexia and drug and alcohol problems that effectively ended her career. Dee married fellow teen idol Bobby Darin in 1960; they divorced in 1967. Her son, Dodd Darin, wrote about his parents' lives in the 1994 biography, *Dream Lovers: The Magnificent Shattered Lives of Bobby Darin and Sandra Dee.*

Tonino (Antonio) Delli Colli (November 20, 1923–August 17, 2005). The cinematographer was born in Rome, Italy, and began working at Cinecitta Studios in 1938, learning his profession on the job. Delli Colli shot over 130 movies, beginning with 1943's *Finalmente Si,* and including Italy's first color movie *Toto a Colori* (1952). Other credits included *Accatone!* (1961), *Mamma Roma* (1962), *The Gospel According to Matthew* (1964), *The Good, the Bad, and the Ugly* (1967), *Once Upon a Time in the West* (1968), *Spirits of the Dead* (1968), *The Decameron* (1970), *Lacome Lucien* (1975), *Salo, or the 120 Days of Sodom* (1975), *Seven Beauties* (1976), *Once Upon a Time in America* (1984), *The Name of the Rose* (1986), *Intervista* (1987), *Bitter Moon* (1992), and *Death and the Maiden* (1994). He retired after the film *Life Is Beautiful* (1997).

Bob Denver (January 9, 1935–September 2, 2005). Born in New Rochelle, New York, the actor was typecast for his title character on the TV comedy *Gilligan's Island* (1964–67) although he had already played beloved beatnik Maynard G. Krebs in *The Many Love of Dobie Gillis* (1959–63). Denver also voiced Gilligan in two animated series and starred as the character for three made-for-TV movies. Denver's interest in acting began at Loyola University and he acted with the Del Ray Players in Los Angeles, also working as a teacher and mailman before making his screen debut with a small role in *A Private's Affair* (1959). Other film credits included *Who's Minding the Mint?* (1967), *Wackiest Wagon Train in the West* (1977), *High School USA* (1984), and *Back to the Beach* (1987).

James Montgomery Doohan (March 3, 1920–July 20, 2005). Born in Vancouver, British Columbia, the actor served in the Canadian Army during WWII, took acting classes in Toronto, and later won a scholarship to study at the Neighborhood Playhouse in New York. Doohan guest-starred in a number of TV shows before being cast as Lt. Cmdr. Montgomery "Scotty" Scott on *Star Trek* (1966–69) and in seven feature *Star Trek* films. Doohan tried a number of different accents before deciding on the familiar Scots brogue for his character. Doohan eventually resigned himself to being typecast and made appearances at numerous fan conventions, including his last in 2004. He even entitled his 1996 autobiography, *Beam Me Up, Scotty.* Fittingly, per Doohan's request, his ashes will be sent into space in early 2006.

Richard Eastham (June 22, 1916–July 10, 2005). Born Dickinson Swift Eastham in Opelousas, Louisiana, the singer/actor studied at the American Theatre Wing in New York and appeared on Broadway in *Call Me Madam, South Pacific* and other shows. Eastham also had regular roles on the TV series *Tombstone Territory* (1957–59), *Wonder Woman* (1976–79), and *Falcon Crest* (1982–83). His first film was *There's No Business Like Show Business* (1954); other credits included *Man on Fire* (1957), *Toby Tyler* (1960), *That Darn Cat!* (1965), *Not With My wife, You Don't!* (1966), *McQ* (1974), *The Missiles of October* (1974), and *A Wedding on Walton's Mountain* (1982).

Dana Elcar (October 10, 1927–June 6, 2005). The actor was born Ibson Dana Elcar to Danish immigrants who lived on a farm in Ferndale, Michigan. Elcar had a long television career, including series roles on *Baretta* (1975), *Black Sheep Squadron* (1976–78), and as Peter Thornton on *MacGyver* (1985–92). Elcar struggled with glaucoma and went blind after four seasons with the series; the producers adapted his character to match Elcar's medical condition. Film credits included *The Fool Killer* (1965), *The Learning Tree* (1969), *Soldier Blue* (1970), *The Sting* (1973), *Missiles of October* (1974), *The Nude Bomb* (1980), *Forbidden Love* (1982), *All of Me* (1984), *2010* (1984), *Toughlove* (1985), and *Inside Out* (1991).

Stephen Elliott (November 27, 1918–May 21, 2005). Born Elliott Pershing Stitzel in New York City, the actor studied at the Neighborhood Playhouse and made his Broadway debut in *The Tempest* in 1945, after serving as a merchant marine. Elliott often played patrician or authority figures, both on TV and in films. He appeared on *Beacon Hill, Falcon Crest,* and *Chicago Hope* among other series. Screen credits included *The Hospital* (1971), *Death Wish* (1974), *The Hindenburg* (1975), *Betrayal* (1978), *Arthur* (1981), Cutter's Way *(1981), Beverly Hills Cop* (1984), *Arthur 2: On the Rocks* (1988), and *Taking Care of Business* (1990).

Morris Engel (April 8, 1918–March 5, 2005). Born in Brooklyn, New York, the still photographer and independent filmmaker was a Naval combat photographer during WWII, later working as a photojournalist. His Oscar-nominated (for best screenplay) film *The Little Fugitive* (1953) was made for $30,000, using a hand-held, 35-millimeter camera that Engel helped design. Engel and his wife, Ruth Orkin, also made the independent features *Lovers and Lollipops* (1956) and *Weddings and Babies* (1958). Engel soloed on the feature *I Need a Ride to California* (1968), which was never released, and the video documentaries *A Little Bit Pregnant* (1993) and *Camelia* (1998).

Jason Evers (January 2, 1922–March 13, 2005). The actor was born Herb Evers in New York City. After serving in the Army in WWII, Evers started acting in repertory companies. His first break came as the star of the western series *Wrangler* (1960) and he was a regular on *Channing* (1963–64) and *The Guns of Will Sonnett* (1967–69) besides guest-starring on numerous TV series through the 1980s. Evers starred in the cult sci-fi film *The Brain That Wouldn't Die* (1963); other credits included *Pretty Boy Floyd* (1960), *The Rebellion* (1967), *The Green Berets* (1968), *The Illustrated Man* (1969), *A Man Called Gannon* (1969), *Escape from the Planet of the Apes* (1971), *A Piece of the Action* (1977), *Barracuda* (1978), and *Basket Case 2* (1990).

John Fielder (February 3, 1925–June 25, 2005). Born in Platteville, Wisconsin, the character actor was the high-pitched voice of timid Piglet, beginning with the animated Disney film *Winnie the Pooh and the Blustery Day* (1968) through *Piglet's Big Movie* (2003), *Winnie the Pooh: Springtime with Roo* (2004), and *Pooh's Heffalump Movie* (2005). Fielder also did voice work on the animated Disney features *Robin Hood* (1973), *The Rescuers* (1977), *The Fox and the Hound* (1981), and *The Emperor's New Groove* (2000). He joined the Neighborhood Playhouse in the late 1940s and made his stage debut in 1954's *The Sea Gull.* Screen credits included *Twelve Angry Men* (1957), *A Raisin in the Sun* (1961; Fielder had also appeared in the Broadway production), *That Touch of Mink* (1962), *Kiss Me, Stupid!* (1964), *The Odd Couple* (1968), *True Grit* (1969), *Cannonball Run* (1981), and *Sharkey's Machine* (1981).

Geraldine Fitzgerald (November 24, 1913–July 17, 2005). Born in Dublin, Ireland, the actress debuted as a teenager at Dublin's Gate Theatre. She made her U.S. stage debut in 1938's *Heartbreak House*, which led to a contract at Warner Bros. Her Warner's screen debut was in 1939's *Dark Victory* and that same year she co-starred in *Wuthering Heights*, for which Fitzgerald received an Academy Award nomination as best supporting actress. She had a number of strong roles in the 1940s, including *Watch on the Rhine* (1943), *Wilson* (1944), *Nobody Lives Forever* (1946), *O.S.S.* (1946), and *Three Strangers* (1946) but constantly battled Jack Warner over her roles and the studio's refusal to let her do stage work and was frequently on suspension. Later in her career, Fitzgerald return to the stage, including as the director for *Mass Appeal* (1982) for which she received a Tony nomination. Additional screen credits included *A Child is Born* (1940), *The Gay Sisters* (1942), *So Evil My Love* (1948), *Ten North Frederick* (1958), *The Pawnbroker* (1964), *Rachel, Rachel* (1968), *The Last American Hero* (1973), *Harry and Tonto* (1974), *Arthur* (1981), *Easy Money* (1983), *Poltergeist 2: The Other Side* (1986), and *Arthur 2: On the Rocks* (1988).

Suzanne Flon (January 28, 1918–June 15, 2005). Born in Le-Kremlin-Bicetre, Val-de-Marne, France, the actress got her start as the secretary to singer Edith Piaf. She then worked at the Etoile music hall and began her celebrated stage career with *Antigone* (1944). Screen credits included *Moulin Rouge* (1952), *Mr. Arkadin* (1955), *Thou Shalt Not Kill* (1961), *The Trial* (1962), *The Train* (1964), *Mr. Klein* (1976), *Children of the Marshland* (1999), and *La Fleur du Mal* (2003). Flon won Cesar awards for *One Deadly Summer* (1983) and *The Dragon* (1990).

Elisabeth Fraser (January 8,1920–May 5, 2005). Born in Brooklyn, New York, the actress began her career on stage in *There Shall Be No Night* (1940), which earned her a contract with Warner Bros. Screen credits included *The Man Who Came to Dinner* (1941), *One Foot in Heaven* (1941), *All My Sons* (1948), *Hills of Oklahoma* (1950), *Death of a Salesman* (1951), *Young at Heart* (1954), *Ask Any Girl* (1959), *Two for the Seesaw* (1962), *A Patch of Blue* (1965), *The Graduate* (1967), *Tony Rome* (1967), and *Nine to Five* (1980). Fraser was a regular on TV's *The Phil Silvers Show* (as Sgt. Bilko's girlfriend) and on *Fibber McGee and Molly* besides doing numerous guest-star roles.

Devery Freeman (February 18, 1913–October 7, 2005). Born in Brooklyn, New York, the writer attended Brooklyn College and wrote television scripts before moving to California to become a staff writer at MGM. Freeman participated in the first negotiations between the Screen Writers Guild and the studios to determine writing credits and was instrumental in its 1954 reorganization, which created the Writers Guild of America. Freeman's credits included *Main Street Lawyer* (1939), *The Fuller Brush Man* (1948), *Miss Grant Takes Richmond* (1949), *Watch the Birdie* (1950), *The Yellow Cab Man* (1950), *Francis Joins the WACs* (1954), *Francis in the Navy* (1955), and *The Girl Most Likely* (1957). Freeman was also the author of the novel *Father Sky,* which was made into the 1981 movie *Taps.*

Christopher Fry (December 18, 1907–June 30, 2005). Born in Bristol, England, the dramatist was also a screenwriter. Fry began writing in the mid-1930s but his best-known work was 1948's *The Lady's Not for Burning,* which was filmed in 1987. Fry did an uncredited rewrite on William Wyler's 1959 epic *Ben-Hur*. Other film credits included *Barabbas* (1962), *The Bible* (1966), and *The Brontes of Haworth* (1973).

Vance Gerry (August 21, 1929–March 5, 2005). Born in Pasadena, California, the animation story artist joined Walt Disney Studios in 1955 after studying at the Chouinard Art Institute. Gerry first worked in the story department on *The Jungle Book* (1967) and contributed to *The Aristocats* (1970), *Robin Hood* (1973), *The Many Adventures of Winnie the Pooh* (1977), *The Rescuers* (1977), *The Fox and the Hound* (1981), *The Great Mouse Detective* (1986), *Oliver & Company* (1988), *Pocahontas* (1995), and *Hercules* (1997) among others, adapting books, developing original ideas, doing storyboards, and working on visual development and character design.

Alexander Golitzen (February 28, 1908–July 26, 2005). Born in Moscow, Russia, the art director and his family fled the Russian Revolution, eventually settling in Seattle. Golitzen moved to Los Angeles after graduating from the University of Wisconsin and began at MGM in 1933, working for Alexander Toluboff. Golitzen joined Universal in 1942 and acted as supervising art director at the studio for three decades. He received Academy Awards for *Phantom of the Opera* (1943), *Spartacus* (1960), and *To Kill a Mockingbird* (1962), and received nominations for *Foreign Correspondent* (1940), *Sundown* (1941), *Arabian Nights* (1942), *The Climax* (1944), *Flower Drum Song* (1961), *That Touch of Mink* (1962), *Gambit* (1966), *Thoroughly Modern Millie* (1967), *Sweet Charity* (1969), *Airport* (1970), and *Earthquake* (1974).

Frank Gorshin (April 5, 1933–May 17, 2005). The impressionist and actor was born in Pittsburgh, Pennsylvania, and got his first professional job at 17 after winning a talent contest. After serving in the Korean War, Gorshin worked as a comedian and character actor before gaining TV fame in 1966 on *Batman* as the Caped Crusader's nemesis, The Riddler. Screen credits included *Dragstrip Girl* (1957), *Invasion of the Saucer Men* (1957), *Where the Boys Are* (1960), *The Great Imposter* (1961), *That Darn Cat* (1965), *Batman* (1966), *12 Monkeys* (1995), *Beethoven's 3rd* (2000), and *Manna from Heaven* (2005).

Guy Green (November 5, 1913–September 15, 2005). Born in Frome, England, the director and cinematographer entered the British film industry at 20, working his way up from camera assistant to director of photography. Green's first film as a cinematographer was 1944's *The Way Ahead* and he won an Oscar for 1946's *Great Expectations.* Other cinematography credits included *Carnival* (1946), *Oliver Twist* (1948), *Captain Horatio Hornblower RN* (1951), *The Story of Robin Hood and His Merrie Men* (1952), *The Dark Avenger* (1955), and *I Am a Camera* (1955). Green switched to directing in the mid-1950s; credits included *Sea of Sand* (1958), *The Angry Silence* (1960), *The Mark* (1961), *Light in the Piazza* (1962), *Diamond Head* (1963), *A Patch of Blue* (1965), *Pretty Polly* (1967), *The Magus* (1968), *Walk in the Spring Rain* (1970), *Luther* (1974), *Once Is Not Enough* (1975), and *Strong Medicine* (1984).

Kevin Hagen (April 3, 1928–July 9, 2005). The character actor was born in Chicago, Illinois, and began his career working on numerous television shows in the 1950s, often appearing as a villain. He had a continuing role in the 1958 series *Yancy Derringer* but was best known on the small screen for his role as kindly Doc Baker in *Little House on the Prairie* (1974–83). Hagen's film credits included *The Light in the Forest* (1958), *Pork Chop Hill* (1959), *Shenandoah* (1965), *The Last Challenge* (1967), *The Hunter* (1980), and *The Ambulance* (1990).

Kayo Hatta (March 18, 1958–July 20, 2005). Born Lori Kayo Hatta in Honolulu, Hawaii, the filmmaker died in a drowning accident. She graduated from Stanford University and received a master's degree in film from the University of California, Los Angeles. Her first film was the 1988 short *Otemba* and she directed and co-wrote the independent feature *Picture Bride* (1995) and had just completed the short, *Fishbowl* (2005).

June Haver (June 10, 1926–July 4, 2005). The singer/actress was born June Stovenour in Rock Island, Illinois; the Haver name came from her stepfather. She worked on radio as a child and sang in dance bands before signing a contract with 20th Century Fox. Haver made her debut as a hatcheck girl in 1943's *The Gang's All Here* and went on to appear in such films as *Home in Indiana* (1944), *Irish Eyes Are Smiling* (1944), *The Dolly Sisters* (1945), *Where Do We Go from Here?* (1945), *Three Little Girls in Blue* (1946), *Look for the Silver Lining* (1949), *Oh, You Beautiful Doll* (1949), *The Daughter of Rosie O'Grady* (1950), and *The Girl Next Door* (1953). Haver married Fred MacMurray in 1954 and retired from acting.

Paul Henning (September 16, 1911–March 25, 2005). Born in Independence, Missouri, Henning was best-known for creating the TV series *The Beverly Hillbillies* (1962–71) and writing its theme song. Although he graduated from law school, the producer started writing for radio, including *Fibber McGee and Molly* and *The George Burns and Gracie Allen Show.* Henning also created, produced and wrote the TV comedy *The Bob Cummings Show* (1955–59) and created *Petticoat Junction* (1963–70). Henning was a screenwriter for the 1964 film *Bedtime Story* and its 1988 remake, *Dirty Rotten Scoundrels,* which later became a Broadway musical.

Debra Hill (November 10, 1950–March 7, 2005). Born in Haddonfield, New Jersey, the producer started her Hollywood career as a production assistant, script supervisor, and assistant director before meeting John Carpenter in 1975. Hill worked as script supervisor on the director's 1976 film *Assault on Precinct 13* and was the co-writer and co-producer of *Halloween* (1978). Hill also worked with Carpenter on *The Fog* (1980, 2005 remake), *Escape from New York* (1981), *Halloween 2* (1981), *Halloween 3* (1982), *Halloween 5* (1989), *Halloween: The Curse of Michael Myers* (1995), *Escape from L.A.* (1996), *Halloween: H20* (1998), and *Halloween: Resurrection* (2002). Hill also produced *The Dead Zone* (1983), *Clue* (1985), *Head Office* (1985), *Adventures in Babysitting* (1987), *Heartbreak Hotel* (1988), *Gross Anatomy* (1989), *The Fisher King* (1991), and *Crazy in Alabama* (1999).

Joel Hirschhorn (1938?–September 18, 2005). Born in the Bronx, New York, the songwriter and his longtime collaborator, Al Kasha, earned best song Academy Awards for "The Morning After" for 1973's *The Poseidon Adventure* and "We May Never Love Like This Again" from 1975's *The Towering Inferno.* They were also nominated for the song "Candle on the Water" and the original score of *Pete's Dragon* (1977). They had met at Columbia Records and wrote music for Broadway and television as well as the books *If They Ask You, You Can Write a Song* (1979), *Notes on Broadway: Conversations With the Great Songwriters* (1985), and *Reaching the Morning After* (1986). Hirschhorn also wrote for various publications, including *Songwriter, Variety,* and *Video Times.*

Gregg Hoffman (1963?–December 4, 2005). Born in Phoenix, Arizona, the producer graduated from the American University and started as an assistant at the independent production company PRO Filmworks after moving to Hollywood in the late-1980s. Hoffman joined the Walt Disney Co. in 1995, eventually becoming a senior vice president of production, and was also a producer on 1997's *George of the Jungle.* He joined Evolution Entertainment in 2003 and was the producer of the successful horror films *Saw* (2004) and *Saw II* (2005).

Evan Hunter (October 15, 1926–July 6, 2005). The novelist was born Salvatore Lombino in New York City, but changed his name in 1952 to avoid discrimination. He started writing stories while serving in the Navy during WWII and later graduated from Hunter College. Hunter's 1954 novel *The Blackboard Jungle* was filmed in 1955. Hunter used the pseudonym of Ed McBain for the 55 novels in his 87th Precinct detective series, which began with *Cop Hater* in 1956; several of the novels were filmed with Hunter's screenplays, including *Cop Hater* (1958), *The Mugger* (1958), *The Pusher* (1960), and *Fuzz* (1972). Hunter also adapted his novels *Strangers When We Meet* (1960), *The Young Savages* (1961), *Mister Buddwing* (1966), *Last Summer* (1969), and *Every Little Crook and Nanny* (1972) and wrote the screenplay for Alfred Hitchcock's *The Birds* (1963).

Ruth Hussey (October 30, 1911–April 19, 2005). Born Ruth Carol O'Rourke in Providence, Rhode Island, the actress took her mother's maiden name professionally and began her career as a fashion commentator on radio, worked as a model in New York, and toured with stage companies. A performance in Los Angeles got Hussey a contract with MGM and her first film was an uncredited role in 1937's *Big City.* Hussey was nominated for a best supporting actress Oscar for *The Philadelphia Story* (1940). Other screen credits included *Blackmail* (1939), *Within the Law* (1939), *Flight Command* (1940), *Northwest Passage* (1940), *Susan and God* (1940), *Our Wife* (1941), *Tennessee Johnson* (1943), *The Uninvited* (1944), *Bedside Manner* (1945), *I, Jane Doe* (1948), *The Great Gatsby* (1949), *That's My Baby* (1951), *Stars and Stripes Forever* (1952), and *The Facts of Life* (1960). Hussey also worked on the stage and on television.

Gordon Kay (September 6, 1916–March 8, 2005). The producer was born in Montreal, Quebec, and grew up in New York and Massachusetts. Kay worked as a reader on Broadway before landing a job as a gofer at Republic Pictures in 1939, working his way up to producing 26 Allan "Rocky" Lane westerns from 1947's *The Wild Frontier* to 1951's *Wells Fargo Gunmaster.* Kay worked for 12 years at

Universal, beginning in 1955, producing seven westerns starring Audie Murphy as well as such films as *Unguarded Moment* (1956), *Man Afraid* (1957), *Day of the Bad Man* (1958), *Twilight for the Gods* (1958), *Voice in the Mirror* (1958), *Fluffy* (1965), and *The Young Warriors* (1967).

John Ulick Knatchbull, 7th Baron Brabourne (November 9, 1924–September 22, 2005). The film and television producer, who was credited as John Brabourne, was born in Bombay, India, where his father was governor and later viceroy. At age 10, he was sent to England to be educated and he served in the Coldstream Guards during WWII and became an aide to Lord Louis Mountbatten. Brabourne learned his craft working for several producers in the 1950s and his first production was 1957's *Harry Black and the Tiger.* Among his other credits were *Sink the Bismarck!* (1959), *HMS Defiant* (1961), *Othello* (1965), *The Mikado* (1966), *Up the Junction* (1967), *The Dance of Death* (1968), *Romeo and Juliet* (1968), *Tales of Beatrix Potter* (1971), *Murder on the Orient Express* (1974), *Death on the Nile* (1978), *The Mirror Crack'd* (1980), *Evil Under the Sun* (1982), *A Passage to India* (1984), and *Little Dorrit* (1987).

Gavin Lambert (July 23, 1924–July 17, 2005). The screenwriter and author was born in East Grinsted, England, and began his career writing scripts for commercials shown in movie theaters. In 1948, he collaborated with friend Lindsay Anderson in founding the film journal, *Sequence*, and Lambert edited *Sight and Sound* from 1950 to 1956. He then moved to the U.S. to work with director Nicholas Ray on *Bitter Victory* (1957). Lambert received Oscar nominations for *Sons and Lovers* (1960) and *I Never Promised You a Rose Garden* (1977). Additional credits included *Another Sky* (1956), *The Roman Spring of Mrs. Stone* (1961), *Sweet Bird of Youth* (1989), and *Dead on the Money* (1991). Lambert wrote about Hollywood in a 1959 short story collection, *The Slide Area: Scenes of Hollywood Life*, and in the novel *Inside Daisy Clover*, which he adapted for the 1965 Natalie Wood film; he also wrote the biography/memoir *Mainly About Lindsay Anderson* (2000) and the 2004 biography, *Natalie Wood: A Life* among other works.

Frances Langford (April 4, 1913–July 11, 2005). Born in Lakeland, Florida, the singer and actress began in vaudeville and moved into radio, including the popular 1940s comedy *The Bickersons*. Langford also traveled frequently on tours with Bob Hope during WWII and was known as the "Sweetheart of the Fighting Fronts." Film credits included *Every Night at Eight* (1935), *Born to Dance* (1936), *Palm Springs* (1936), *Hollywood Hotel* (1937), *Dreaming Out Loud* (1940), *Too Many Girls* (1940), *Yankee Doodle Dandy* (1942), *Dixie Jamboree* (1944), *Girl Rush* (1944), *Deputy Marshal* (1950), and *The Glenn Miller Story* (1954). Langford left Hollywood after her second marriage in 1955.

Alberto Lattuada (November 13, 1914–July 3, 2005). The director was born in Milan, Italy, to composer Felice Lattuada, and broke into films in 1933 as a set decorator. His first film was 1942's *Giacomo L'Idealista/Giacomo the Idealist.* Other credits included *La Freccia Nel Fianco/The Arrow* (1944), *Il Bandito/The Bandit* (1946), *Il Delitto Di Govanni Espiscopo/Flesh Will Surrender* (1946), *Senza Pieta/Without Pity* (1948), *Anna* (1951), *Il Cappotto/The Overcoat* (1952), *Amore in Citta/Love in the City* (1953), *La Spiaggia/The Beach* (1953), *Tempest* (1958), *Cosi Come Sei/Stay As You Are* (1978), and *La Cicala/The Cricket* (1980).

Marc Lawrence (February 17, 1910–November 28, 2005). Born Max Goldsmith in New York City, the sinister-looking actor had a 60-year career in villainous roles. Lawrence went to Hollywood in 1932 and played small parts in numerous movies (his first was an uncredited bit in 1932's *If I Had a Million*) as a freelancer before signing a contract with Columbia Pictures. Screen credits included *Dr. Socrates* (1935), *Johnny Apollo* (1940), *The Shepherd of the Hills* (1941), *This Gun for Hire* (1942), *Cloak and Dagger* (1946), *Key Largo* (1948), and *The Asphalt Jungle* (1950). Lawrence was blacklisted by 1951 and moved his family to Italy where he continued his career; his return to Hollywood in 1959 was as a television director. Lawrence returned to screen roles with 1963's *Johnny Cool.* Later credits included *Diamonds Are Forever* (1971), *The Man With the Golden Gun* (1974), *Marathon Man* (1976), *Foul Play* (1978), *The Big Easy* (1987), *Ruby* (1992), *From Dusk Till Dawn* (1996), *Gotti* (1996), and *Looney Tunes: Back in Action* (2003). Besides acting, Lawrence wrote, directed, and produced the films *Nightmare in the Sun* (1964) and *Daddy's Dead Darling* (1972). His 1991 autobiography was entitled *Long Time No See: Confessions of a Hollywood Gangster.*

Gordon Lee (October 25, 1933–October 16, 2005). Born Eugene Lee in Fort Worth, Texas, the child actor was credited as Eugene "Porky" Lee for his character in the popular *Our Gang* shorts of the 1930s. His adoptive parents later called him Gordon after Lee's frequent director Gordon Douglas and he kept the name as an adult. Lee appeared in 42 shorts from 1935 to 1939 as Spanky's younger brother who mispronounced "okay" as "otay." Lee was forced to retire from the series when he grew taller and thinner and never acted again; he became a teacher but began making appearances at *Our Gang* reunions in the 1980s and attended film festivals and autograph shows.

Ernest Lehman (December 8, 1915–July 2, 2005). Born in New York City, the screenwriter began his career freelancing for popular magazines before supplying tidbits to gossip columnists while working for press agent Irving Hoffman. Lehman used his experiences to write the 1950 novella *Tell Me About It Tomorrow*, which he co-scripted with Clifford Odets as the 1957 film *Sweet Smell of Success.* Lehman received an Academy Award nomination for his only original script, 1959's *North by Northwest* and for his adaptations of *Sabrina* (1954), *West Side Story* (1961), and *Who's Afraid of Virginia Woolf?* (1966). As a producer, Lehman received Oscar nominations for *Woolf* and *Hello, Dolly!* (1969). Other screenplay credits included *Executive Suite* (1954), *The King and I* (1956), *Somebody Up There Likes Me* (1956), *The Sound of Music* (1965), *Family Plot* (1976), and *Black Sunday* (1977). In addition, Lehman produced, adapted, and directed the 1972 film *Portnoy's Complaint.*

Julian "Bud" Lesser (January 18, 1915–March 22, 2005). The producer was born in San Francisco, California, the son of Sol Lesser, the producer of the Tarzan film series. Bud's first production job was as an assistant on 1948's *Tarzan and the Mermaids.* Other credits included *Michael*

O'Halloran (1948), *Massacre River* (1949), *Jungle Headhunters* (1951), *Whispering Smith Hits London* (1951), *Death of an Angel* (1952), and *The Saint's Girl Friday* (1953).

Sid Luft (November 2, 1915–September 15, 2005). Born in New York City, the producer became the third husband of Judy Garland (from 1952 to 1965) and helped revive her career with 1954's *A Star Is Born*. Luft moved to Hollywood in the late 1930s, launching a custom car company, and worked briefly as a talent agent before producing the low-budget pictures *Kilroy Was Here* (1947) and *French Leave* (1948).

Richard Lupino (October 29, 1929–February 9, 2005). Born in Hollywood, he acted as a child and made his film debut in 1940's *Just William*. Other credits included *Rhapsody* (1954), *The Marauders* (1955), *Never So Few* (1959), *Midnight Lace* (1960), and *Avengers of the Reef* (1973). Lupino also acted on the stage and on television and wrote several television scripts with his cousin, actress and director Ida Lupino.

Bruce Malmuth (February 4, 1934–June 28, 2005). The director was born in Brooklyn, New York, and began his career making documentaries while serving in the Army. Directorial credits included *Foreplay* (1975), *Nighthawk* (1981), *The Man Who Wasn't There* (1983), *Where Are All the Children?* (1985), *Hard to Kill* (1989), and *Pentathlon* (1994).

Barney Martin (March 3, 1923–March 21, 2005). Born in Queens, New York, the character actor served in the Air Force during WWII and was a New York police detective for 20 years while writing for comedy shows on the side. His first screen role was in 1968's *The Producers* and he appeared in *Charley* (1968), *Hot Stuff* (1979), *Arthur* (1981), *Arthur 2: On the Rocks* (1988), and *Deadly Weapon* (1989). Martin also appeared in several Broadway musicals, including the original production of the musical *Chicago* (1975), in which he played murderer Roxie Hart's husband, Amos, and introduced the song "Mr. Cellophane." Martin was also familiar to television viewers, including his role as Morty Seinfeld on *Seinfeld*; he was the third and last actor to play the part, remaining with the series until its 1998 finale.

Virginia Mayo (November 30, 1920–January 17, 2005). Virginia Clara Jones was born in St. Louis, Missouri, and took the name "Mayo" from the boss of the vaudeville act she joined in 1937. The actress was performing in a revue when she was offered a contract as a Goldwyn Girl in 1942, making her screen debut in 1943's *The Story of Jack London*. Although frequently appearing in musicals and comedies, Mayo had memorable dramatic turns as the unfaithful wife in *The Best Years of Our Lives* (1946) and as gangster James Cagney's abused spouse in *White Heat* (1949). Additional screen credits included *The Princess and the Pirate* (1944), *Wonder Man* (1945), *The Kid from Brooklyn* (1946), *The Secret Life of Walter Mitty* (1947), *A Song Is Born* (1948), *Colorado Territory* (1949), *The Flame and the Arrow* (1950), *Along the Great Divide* (1951), *Captain Horatio Hornblower* (1952), *The Iron Mistress* (1952), *She's Working Her Way Through College* (1952), *King Richard and the Crusaders* (1954), *The Silver Chalice* (1954), *Great Day in the Morning* (1956), and *Jet Over the Atlantic* (1959). Mayo's screen career faded in the 1960's although she had small roles in films and appeared on television and the stage.

Lon McCallister (April 17, 1923–June 11, 2005). Born Herbert Alonzo McCallister Jr. in Los Angeles, the actor's first role (uncredited) was at 13 in *Romeo and Juliet* (1936). Other credits included *The Adventures of Tom Sawyer* (1938), *Judge Hardy's Children* (1938), *Stage Door Canteen* (1943), *Home in Indiana* (1944), *Winged Victory* (1944), *The Red House* (1947), *Scudda Hoo! Scudda Hay!* (1948), *The Big Cat* (1949) and *The Story of Seabiscuit* (1949). McCallister quit acting at 30 and began a career in real estate investment.

Pat McCormick (June 30, 1927–July 29, 2005). Born in Lakewood, Ohio, the comedian and comic writer began writing material for television and nightclub performers, including Jonathan Winters, Henny Youngman, Merv Griffin, Red Skelton, and Phyllis Diller, before he joined TV's *The Jack Parr Show* as a writer. McCormick also made frequent appearances as a comedian on *The Tonight Show Starring Johnny Carson*, *Candid Camera*, and *The Gong Show*. McCormick played Big Enos Burdette in the three *Smokey and the Bandit* movies (1977, 1980, 1983) and also appeared in *Buffalo Bill and the Indians* (1976), *A Wedding* (1978), *Under the Rainbow* (1981), *Doin' Time* (1985), and *Chinatown Connection* (1990).

Matthew McGrory (May 17, 1973–August 9, 2005). Born in West Chester, Pennsylvania, the seven-foot- six actor starred as Karl the Giant in Tim Burton's *Big Fish* (2003). Other credits included *Bubble Boy* (2001), *Men in Black 2* (2002), *House of 1000 Corpses* (2003), and *The Devil's Rejects* (2005). McGrory had been filming a biography of wrestler-turned-actor Andre the Giant at the time of his death.

Ismail Merchant (December 25, 1936–May 25, 2005). Born Ismail Noormohamed Abdul Rehman in Bombay, India, the producer and occasional director met James Ivory in 1961 and their partnership, Merchant Ivory Productions, made more than 40 films. Merchant came to study at New York University in 1958 and earned a business degree; he produced his first film, the Oscar-nominated short *The Creation of Woman*, in 1961. Merchant's first directorial effort was also a short, 1974's *Mahatma and the Mad Boy*; his feature debut was 1993's *In Custody*. Other directorial credits included *The Proprietor* (1996), *Cotton Mary* (1999), and *The Mystic Masseur* (2001). The first Merchant Ivory collaboration was 1963's *The Householder* and their subsequent films earned 31 Oscar nominations, including best picture nominations for *A Room With a View* (1986), *Howard's End* (1992), and *The Remains of the Day* (1993). Merchant's last film as a producer was 2005's *The White Countess*.

Arthur Miller (October 17, 1915–February 10, 2005). Born in New York City, the playwright studied writing at the University of Michigan. Miller's first commercial success on Broadway was 1947's *All My Sons* (filmed 1948 and 1986). *Death of a Salesman* opened in 1949, won a Pulitzer and a Tony, and was filmed in 1951 (also for television in 1995 and 2000). 1953's *The Crucible* (another Tony winner) became the French feature *Les Sorcieres de Salem* in 1957 and was remade under its original title in 1996. His 1955 play *A View from the Bridge* became the 1961 French feature, *Vu du Pont*. Television productions were also done of the plays *Incident at Vichy* (1973), *After the Fall* (1974), *The American Clock* (1993), and *Broken Glass* (1996). Miller married actress Marilyn Monroe in 1957 and wrote the screenplay for her 1961 western, *The Misfits*; they divorced the same year. His autobiography, *Timebends: A Life*, was published in 1987.

Sir John Mills (February 22, 1908–April 23, 2005). Born Lewis Ernest Watts Mills in Felixstowe, Suffolk, England (some sources say North Elham, Norfolk), the actor made more than 100 films. He christened himself John when he began his career as a chorus boy in 1929; Mills made his screen debut in 1932's *The Midshipman*. Substantial roles came to Mills after he was invalided out of the army, including *Cottage to Let* (1941), *In Which We Serve* (1942), *We Dive at Dawn* (1943), *This Happy Breed* (1944), *Waterloo Road* (1944) and *The Way to the Stars* (1945). Other credits included *Great Expectations* (1946), *Scott of the Antarctic* (1948), *The History of Mr. Polly* (1949), *The Rocking Horse Winner* (1950), *The Long Memory* (1952), *Hobson's Choice* (1953), *Above Us the Waves* (1955), *The End of the Affair* (1955), *The Baby and the Battleship* (1956), *Town On Trial* (1957), *Dunkirk* (1958), *Ice Cold in Alex* (1958), *Tiger Bay* (1959), *Tunes of Glory* (1960), *King Rat* (1965), *The Wrong Box* (1966), *Lady Hamilton* (1967), *Oh! What a Lovely War* (1969), *Lady Caroline Lamb* (1972), *Young Winston* (1972), *The 39 Steps* (1978), *Ghandi* (1982), *Who's That Girl* (1987), *Hamlet* (1996), *Bean* (1997), and *Bright Young Things* (2003). Mills won a best supporting actor Oscar for 1970's *Ryan's Daughter*, and he directed one film, *Sky West and Crooked* (1965), which was written by his wife Mary Hayley Bell and starred their daughter, Hayley. Daughter Juliet is also an actress and son Jonathan is a screenwriter. Mills' autobiography, *Up In the Clouds, Gentlemen Please*, was published in 1981.

Brigitte Mira (April 20, 1910–March 8, 2005). Born in Hamburg, Germany, the actress started her career as a singer in operettas and cabaret before working in films beginning in the 1950s. Mira was best-known for her work with director Rainer Werner Fasbbinder, whom she met in 1972. She played the lead in *Ali: Fear Eats the Soul* (1974) and also appeared in Fassbinder's *Fear of Fear* (1975), *Fox and His Friends* (1975), *Mother Kusters Goes to Heaven* (1976), *Berlin Alexanderplatz* (1980), and *Lili Marleen* (1981).

Constance Moore (January 18, 1920–September 16, 2005). Born in Sioux City, Iowa, the actress started as a singer and was signed to a contract in 1937 by Universal Studio. Moore starred opposite Buster Crabbe in the 1939 *Buck Rogers* serial and opposite W.C. Fields in the 1939 film *You Can't Cheat an Honest Man*. Other screen credits included *Framed* (1940), *I Wanted Wings* (1941), *Take a Letter, Darling* (1942), *Atlantic City* (1944), *Show Business* (1944), *Delightfully Dangerous* (1945), *Earl Carroll Vanities* (1945), *In Old Sacramento* (1946), and *Hit Parade of 1947* (1947). Moore retired in 1947 except for some guest-star roles on television.

Noriyuki "Pat" Morita (June 28, 1932–November 24, 2005). Born in Isleton, California, the comedian and actor, whose parents were migrant fruit pickers, spent much of his childhood in a sanitarium (where he got his nickname) with spinal tuberculosis. Then, during WWII, his family was sent to a Japanese internment camp in Arizona. Morita began doing standup comedy (as "The Hip Nip") and he made his screen debut in a small role in 1967's *Thoroughly Modern Millie*. His first big break came on TV, playing the role of malt shop owner Arnold on *Happy Days*. Then came the screen role of philosophical martial arts teacher Mr. Miyagi, opposite Raph Macchio, in 1984's *Karate Kid* (for which he received an Oscar nomination) and its 1986, 1989, and 1994 sequels. Other screen credits included *Collision Course* (1990), *Honeymoon in Vegas* (1992), *Even Cowgirls Get the Blues* (1994), *Spy Hard* (1996), *Mulan* (1998), and *The Center of the World* (2001).

Howard Morris (September 4, 1919–May 21, 2005). Born in New York City, the comic actor and director served in the Army's entertainment unit during WWII. He joined Sid Caesar, Imogene Coca, and Carl Reiner on TV's *Your Show of Shows* from 1951 to 1954 and also made a lasting impression with fans as Ernest T. Bass on *The Andy Griffith Show*, though the character only appeared in five episodes. Morris also appeared in character roles in *40 Pounds of Trouble* (1962), *The Nutty Professor* (1963), *High Anxiety* (1977), *History of the World, Part 1* (1981), *Splash* (1984), and *Life Stinks* (1991). He also directed numerous TV shows and such films as *Who's Minding the Mint?* (1967), *With Six You Get Eggroll* (1968), *Don't Drink the Water* (1969), and *Goin' Coconuts* (1978).

Lyle "Spud" Murphy (August 19, 1908–August 5, 2005). The film composer was born in Berlin, Germany, but moved to the U.S. age the age of four. He went to New York in 1933 and became known for creating arrangement for bandleaders, working with Benny Goodman among others. Moving to California in the late 1930s, Murphy worked for Columbia Pictures; by the late 1940s, he was teaching his method of composing, arranging, and orchestrating, which he called the Equal Interval System, which is still widely used by professional musicians.

Robert Frederick Newmyer (May 30, 1956–December 12, 2005). The independent film producer was born in Washington, D.C., and was a graduate of Swarthmore College and Harvard Business School. Newmyer went to work at Columbia Pictures, eventually becoming a vice president of production and acquisitions, before he and Jeffrey Silver formed Outlaw Productions in 1987. Their first hit was 1989's *sex, lies and videotape*. Other productions included *Don't Tell Mom the Babysitter's Dead* (1991), *Mr. Baseball* (1992), *Indian Summer* (1993), *The Santa Clause* (1994), *Don Juan DeMarco* (1995), *How to Be a Player* (1997), *Three to Tango* (1999), *Gossip* (2000), *Training Day* (2001), *The Santa Clause 2* (2002), *National Security* (2003), *Mindhunters* (2004), and *The Thing About My Folks* (2005). Newmyer had a number of films in production at the time of his death from a heart attack, which are expected to be released in 2006, including *Breach, The Lost Boys of Sudan, Phat Girlz,* and *The Santa Clause 3*.

Sheree North (January 17, 1933–November 4, 2005). Born Dawn Bethel in Los Angeles, the actress worked as a dancer in nightclubs before making her film debut in the 1951 comedy *Eat My Dust*. North was groomed as a glamour girl by 20th Century Fox and was never able to shake her bombshell image (often compared to Marilyn Monroe.). Screen credits included *Living it Up* (1954), *How to Be Very, Very Popular* (1955), *The Best Things in Life Are Free* (1956), *The Organization* (1971), *Charley Varrick* (1973), *The Outfit* (1973), *The Shootist* (1976), *Women in White* (1978), *Portrait of a Stripper* (1979), *Marilyn: The Untold Story* (1980), *Defenseless* (1991), and *Dying to Get Rich* (1998). North made numerous television appearances beginning in the 1950s and received Emmy nominations for her work on *Marcus Welby M.D.* and *Archie Bunker's Place*; she also had a recurring role on *Seinfeld* as Kramer's mother, Babs.

Dan O'Herlihy (May 1, 1919–February 17, 2005). The character actor was born in Wexford, Ireland, and took acting parts to pay for his architectural studies at the National University of Ireland. O'Herlihy was spotted at the Gate Theatre by director Carol Reed, who cast him in *Odd Man Out* (1947). He received a best actor Oscar nomination for his starring role in 1954's *The Adventures of Robinson Crusoe*. Screen credits included *Kidnapped* (1948), *Macbeth* (1948), *At Sword's Point* (1952), *Invasion USA* (1952), *Soldier's Three* (1952), *Bengali Brigade* (1954), *The Black Shield of Falmouth* (1954), *Imitation of Life* (1959), *A Terrible Beauty* (1960), *The Cabinet of Caligari* (1962), *Fail-Safe* (1964), *MacArthur* (1977), *Halloween 3: Season of the Witch* (1982), *The Last Starfighter* (1984), *The Dead* (1987), *RoboCop* (1987), *RoboCop 2* (1990), and *The Rat Pack* (1998).

Jean Parker (August 11, 1915–November 30, 2005). Born Lois May Green in Deer Lodge, Montana, the actress moved to California in the early 1930s and got a contract with MGM, making her debut in 1932's *Rasputin and the Empress*. Parker played Beth in 1933's *Little Women* and was the solo star of 1934's *Sequoia* in which she played a girl living near a national forest who raises an orphaned fawn and a mountain lion. Other films included *Gabriel Over the White House* (1933), *Lady for a Day* (1933), *The Secret of Madame Blanche* (1933), *Operator 13* (1934), *The Ghost Goes West* (1936), *The Texas Rangers* (1936), *The Flying Deuces* (1939), *Beyond Tomorrow* (1940), *Bluebeard* (1944), *Dead Man's Eyes* (1944), *Detective Kitty O'Day* (1944), *One Body Too Many* (1944), *The Gunfighter* (1950), *Those Redheads from Seattle* (1953), *A Lawless Street* (1955), and *Apache Uprising* (1966). Parker also appeared on stage and later became an acting teacher.

Brock Peters (July 2, 1927–August 23, 2005). Born George Fisher in Harlem, New York, Peters decided on his acting career as a child and began as a teenager on Broadway in the 1943 revival of *Porgy and Bess*. Known for his deep, rich bass voice, Peters had a 60-year career but is best remembered for the role of Tom Robinson, the black man wrongly accused of rape in 1962's *To Kill a Mockingbird*. Additional credits included *Carmen Jones* (1954), *Porgy and Bess* (1959), *The L-Shaped Room* (1962), *Heavens Above!* (1963), *The Pawnbroker* (1965), *The Incident* (1967), *Slaughter's Big Rip-Off* (1973), *Soylent Green* (1973), *Lost in the Stars* (1974), *Two-Minute Warning* (1976), *Roots: The Next Generation* (1979), *Ghosts of Mississippi* (1996), and *The Locket* (2002). Peters also maintained a following for his roles in *Star Trek IV: The Voyage Home* (1986), *Star Trek VI: The Undiscovered Country* (1991), and in the series *Star Trek: Deep Space Nine*.

Otto Plaschkes (September 13, 1929–February 14, 2005). Born in Vienna, Austria, the film producer arrived in England in 1939 as one of the Jewish children of the kindertransport. Plaschkes studied at Cambridge and Oxford and found work at Ealing Studios as a production assistant. Among his productions were *Georgy Girl* (1966), *The Bofors Gun* (1968), *A Separate Peace* (1972), *The Homecoming* (1974), *Galileo* (1975), *In Celebration* (1975), *Butley* (1976), *The Sailor's Return* (1978), *Hopscotch* (1980), *The Holcroft Covenant* (1985), and *Shadey* (1985).

Charles A. Pratt (October 17, 1923–April 27, 2005). Born in Chicago, Illinois, the film producer worked in advertising before joining Bing Crosby Productions. The firm's first release was *Willard* (1971). Other productions included *Ben* (1972), *Walking Tall* (1973), *Walking Tall, Part 2* (1975), *Walking Tall: The Final Chapter* (1977), and *The Great Santini* (1979). Pratt retired from filmmaking in 1985.

Richard Pryor (December 1, 1940–December 10, 2005). The controversial comedian and actor was born in Peoria, Illinois, and grew up in his grandmother's brothel. After two years in the Army, Pryor began his stand-up career in nightclubs and on variety shows in the 1960s. He made his screen debut with 1968's *The Busy Body* and also appeared in such films as *Lady Sings the Blues* (1972), *The Mack* (1973), *Uptown Saturday Night* (1974), *The Bingo Long Traveling All-Stars and Motor Kings* (1976), *Car Wash* (1976), *Silver Streak* (1976), *Greased Lightning* (1977), *Blue Collar* (1978), *California Suite* (1978), *The Wiz* (1978), *The Muppet Movie* (1979), *Richard Pryor—Live in Concert* (1979), *Stir Crazy* (1980), *Wholly Moses* (1981), *Richard Pryor—Live on the Sunset Strip* (1982), *The Toy* (1982), *Superman III* (1983), *Brewster's Millions* (1985), *Harlem Nights* (1989), *See No Evil, Hear No Evil* (1989), *Another You* (1991), and *Lost Highway* (1997). Pryor was severely burned in 1980 in a suicide attempt, but used his ordeal—and drug and alcohol addictions—in his routines; he had also suffered with multiple sclerosis since 1986. He co-wrote 1974's *Blazing Saddles* with Mel Brooks and starred, directed, co-wrote, and co-produced the loosely autobiographical 1985 film *Jo Jo Dancer, Your Life is Calling*. Pryor won Grammys for his concert albums *Bicentennial Nigger* and *That Nigger's Crazy* and, in 1998, he received the first Mark Twain Prize for humor from the John F. Kennedy Center for the Performing Arts. His autobiography, *Pryor Convictions and Other Life Sentences*, was published in 1995.

Amrish Puri (June 22, 1932–January 12, 2005). Born in India, the character actor, known for his villainous roles, made more than 200 films but had relatively minor roles (he debuted in 1971's *Reshma Aur Shera*) until he was cast as Mogambo in Shekhar Kapur's *Mr. India* (1987). Puri had previously worked on stage and in radio. He had parts in a few English-language movies, including *Ghandi* (1982) and *Indiana Jones and the Temple of Doom* (1984).

Ford Rainey (August 8, 1908–July 25, 2005). Born in Mountain Home, Idaho, the actor made his Broadway debut in 1939 and began on television in 1952, including regular roles on *Window on Main Street* (1961–62) and *The Richard Boone Show* (1963–64). Rainey made his screen debut in an uncredited part in 1949's *White Heat*. Additional screen credits included *Flaming Star* (1960), *The Sand Pebbles* (1966), *My Sweet Charlie* (1970), *The Parallax View* (1974), *Babe!* (1975), *Mountain Man* (1977), *The Cellar* (1990), and *Bed & Breakfast* (1992).

Ron Randell (October 8, 1918–June 11, 2005). Born in Sydney, Australia, Randell began his career in radio and moved on to stage roles, which lead to a film contract in Hollywood. He made his debut in *It Had to Be You* (1947). Additional credits included *Bulldog Drummond at Bay* (1947), *Bulldog Drummond Strikes Back* (1947), *The Loves of Carmen* (1948), *Kiss Me, Kate* (1953), *The Girl in Black Stockings* (1957), *The She-Creature* (1957) *The Story of Esther Costello* (1957), *King of Kings* (1961), *The Longest Day* (1962), and *Follow the Boys* (1963).

Joe Ranft (March 13, 1960–August 16, 2005). Born in Pasadena, California, the writer and story artist died in a car accident. Ranft joined Walt Disney Studio in 1980 as a story artist, working on *Oliver & Company* (1988), *Who Framed Roger Rabbit?* (1988), *Beauty and the Beast* (1991), *The Lion King* (1994), and *Fantasia 2000* (2000) as well as doing story work on the Disney-distributed *The Nightmare Before Christmas* (1993) and *James and the Giant Peach* (1996). He joined Pixar Animation Studios and was one of the Oscar-nominated writers on 1995's *Toy Story*. Ranft worked on the stories and also voiced Heimlich the caterpillar in *A Bug's Life* (1998) and Wheezy the Penguin in *Toy Story 2* (1999).

Jocelyn Rickards (July 29, 1924–July 7, 2005). The costume designer and artist was born in Melbourne, Australia, went to art school, and moved to London in 1949. She got film work as a set decorator before working as the costumer on the films *Look Back in Anger* (1958) and *The Entertainer* (1960). Additional credits included *From Russia With Love* (1963), *The Knack* (1965), *Blow-Up* (1966), *Mademoiselle* (1966), *Morgan* (1966), *The Sailor from Gibraltar* (1967), *Alfred the Great* (1969), *Ryan's Daughter* (1970), and *Sunday, Bloody Sunday* (1971). Rickards married director Clive Donner in 1970 and retired from costume designing in the 1970s; her memoir, *The Painted Banquet: My Life and Loves*, was published in 1987.

Charles Rocket (August 24, 1949–October 7, 2005). Born Charles Claverie in Bangor, Maine, the comedian and actor committed suicide. He was a reporter and news anchor under the name Charles Kennedy in the 1970s before making his TV debut on *Saturday Night Live* in 1980 as the mock anchor of "Weekend Update"; he was fired in 1981 for uttering an unscripted obscenity during a skit. Among his screen credits were *Earth Girls Are Easy* (1989), *How I Got Into College* (1989), *Dances With Wolves* (1990), *Hocus Pocus* (1993), *Wild Palms* (1993), *Dumb & Dumber* (1994), *It's Pat: The Movie* (1994), *Steal Big, Steal Little* (1995), *Father's Day* (1996), and *Shade* (2003).

Patsy Rowlands (January 19, 1934–January 22, 2005). Born in London, England, the actress appeared in the popular *Carry On* comedies from 1969's *Carry On Again Doctor* to 1975's *Carry On Behind*. Rowlands began her career on stage at 15 and besides her stage roles was also frequently seen on television, including a regular role on *Bless This House*. Other screen credits included *Over the Odds* (1961), *A Kind of Loving* (1962), *Tom Jones* (1963), *Joseph Andrews* (1977), *Tess* (1970), *Little Lord Fauntleroy* (1980), *Vanity Fair* (1998), and *The Cazalets* (2001).

Nipsey Russell (October 13, 1924–October 2, 2005). Born in Atlanta, Georgia, the comedian settled in New York after serving in WWII and began a nightclub act in the 1950s. Russell was a frequent television guest star, beginning in 1959, and was known for humorous four-line poems. He had a regular role in 1961–62 on the series *Car 54, Where Are You?* and also appeared in the 1994 film version. Russell played the Tin Man in *The Wiz* (1978) and also appeared in *Nemo* (1984), *Wildcats* (1986), and *Posse* (1993).

Maria Schell (January 15, 1926–April 26, 2005). Born in Vienna, Austria, the actress was the older sister of actor Maximilian Schell and was the subject of his 2002 documentary *Meine Schwester Maria/My Sister Maria*. The family moved to Switzerland in 1938 and Maria made her screen debut in 1942's *Der Steinbruch/The Quarry*. She studied drama in Zurich and did not make another film until 1948's *Der Engel Mit der Posaune/The Angel With the Trumpet*. Schell received the best actress award at the 1954 Cannes film festival for *Die Letzte Brucke/The Last Bridge*. Other screen credits included *Napoleon* (1955), *The Brothers Karamazov* (1958), *The Hanging Tree* (1959), *Cimarron* (1960), *The Mark* (1961), *The Odessa File* (1974), *Voyage of the Damned* (1976), *Superman* (1978), *Inside the Third Reich* (1982), *Christmas Lilies of the Field* (1984), and *Samson and Delilah* (1984).

Vincent Schiavelli (November 10, 1948–December 26, 2005). The character actor with the droopy eyes and gloomy demeanor was born in Brooklyn, New York, studied acting at New York University's School of the Arts, and appeared in some 150 movie and television productions. Screen credits included *One Flew Over the Cuckoo's Nest* (1975), *The Frisco Kid* (1979), *Fast Times at Ridgemont High* (1982), *Night Shift* (1982), *The Adventures of Buckaroo Banzai* (1984), *Amadeus* (1984), *Ghost* (1990), *Batman Returns* (1992), *A Little Princess* (1995), *The People vs. Larry Flynt* (1996), *Tomorrow Never Dies* (1997), *Milo* (1998), *American Virgin* (2000), *Death to Smoochy* (2002), and *The 4th Tenor* (2002). Schiavelli also wrote three cookbooks and numerous food articles for magazines and newspapers.

Robert J. "Bob" Schiffer (September 4, 1916–April 26, 2005). Born in Seattle, Washington, the makeup artist got his first job working on the 1932 Marx Brothers comedy *Horse Feathers*. Schiffer worked at RKO, Columbia Pictures, MGM, and spent 33 years at Walt Disney Studios, retiring in 2001. His association with Rita Hayworth included such films as *Cover Girl* (1944), *Gilda* (1946), and *The Lady from Shanghai* (1948), and Schiffer's films with Burt Lancaster included *Elmer Gantry* (1960), *Judgment at Nuremberg* (1961), *The Young Savages* (1961), *The Leopard* (1962), and aging the actor from 18 to 80 for *The Birdman of Alcatraz* (1962). Among Schiffer's other films were *Becky Sharp* (1935), *Mutiny on the Bounty* (1935), *Captains Courageous* (1937), *The Good Earth* (1937), *Only Angels Have Wings* (1939), *The Wizard of Oz* (1939), *Here Comes Mr. Jordan* (1941), *The Magnificent Ambersons* (1942), *Death of a Salesman* (1951), *From Here to Eternity* (1953), *Marty* (1955), *Pal Joey* (1957), *Auntie Mame* (1958), *Cleopatra* (1963), *My Fair Lady* (1964), *The Trouble With Angels* (1966), *Bedknobs and Broomsticks* (1971), *The Shaggy*

D.A. (1976), *Pete's Dragon* (1977), *Tron* (1982), *Something Wicked This Way Comes* (1983), *and Splash* (1984).

Debralee Scott (April 2, 1953–April 5, 2005). Born in Elizabeth, New Jersey, the actress made her first screen appearances in *Dirty Harry* (1972) and *American Graffiti* (1973). She also appeared in *Deathmoon* (1978), *Our Time* (1979), *Just Tell Me You Love Me* (1980), *Police Academy* (1984), and *Police Academy 3: Back in Training* (1986). Scott had recurring roles on the television series *Welcome Back Kotter* (1975–76), *Mary Hartman, Mary Hartman* (1976–77), and *Angie* (1979–80).

Mildred Shay (September 26, 1911–October 15, 2005). Born in Cedarhurst, New York, the five-foot-two actress was nicknamed "Hollywood's Pocket Venus" by columnist Walter Winchell. She was well-known for her headline-making personal life, featuring such men as Errol Flynn, Victor Mature, Cecil B. De Mille, and Louis B. Mayer. Her father was a studio lawyer and got Shay a screen test at MGM; she made her debut in 1932's *The Age of Consent.* Other screen appearances included *Roman Scandals* (1933), *All Women Have Secrets* (1939), *Balalaika* (1939), *The Women* (1939), and *In Old Missouri* (1940). Shay married a British Army captain in 1941, moved to London, and retired for some 25 years before returning to appear in such films as *Star!* (1968), *The Great Gatsby* (1974), *Valentino* (1976), and *Parting Shots* (1999).

Simone Simon (April 23, 1911–March 22, 2005). Born in Bethune, France, the actress made her stage debut in 1931 and her screen debut the same year in *Le Chanteur Inconnu/The Unknown Singer*, although Simon's first major role was in Jean Renoir's *La Bete Humaine/The Human Beast* (1938). Darryl Zanuck brought Simon to Hollywood in the late 1930's and she appeared in *Love and Hisses* (1937) and *Josette* (1938) before making four films for RKO: *All That Money Can Buy* (1941), *Cat People* (1942), *The Curse of the Cat People* (1944), and *Mademoiselle Fifi* (1944). Simon returned to Europe in 1950; additional credits included *La Ronde* (1950), *La Plaisir* (1952), and *Femme en Bleu* (1973).

Lane Smith (April 29, 1936–June 13, 2005). Born in Memphis, Tennessee, the character actor studied at the Actors Studio in New York and made his stage debut in 1959. Lane made his screen debut with *Maidstone* (1970) and moved to Los Angeles in 1978 to concentrate on film and television work, including playing Richard Nixon in the 1989 docudrama *The Final Days* and irascible Daily Planet editor Perry White in the series *Lois and Clark: The New Adventures of Superman* (1993–97). Other screen credits included *Prison* (1988), *Air America* (1990), *The Distinguished Gentleman* (1992), *The Mighty Ducks* (1992), *My Cousin Vinny* (1992), *Son-in-Law* (1993), *The Hi-Lo Country* (1998), and *The Legend of Bagger Vance* (2000).

John Spencer (December 20, 1946–December 16, 2005). Born John Speshock in New York City, the actor was a student at the Professional Children's School and took Spencer as his stage name when he began his career as a teenager. Spencer landed his first television role as a recurring character on *The Patty Duke Show* (1964–65) but he established himself as a character actor on stage, winning a 1981 Obie Award for *Still Life*. He also had regular roles on the TV series *L.A. Law* (1990–94) and played Leo McGarry on *The West Wing* from 1999 until his death, winning an Emmy for the role in 2002. Spencer made his film debut in 1983's *WarGames*. Other screen credits included *Black Rain* (1989), *Sea of Love* (1989), *Green Card* (1990), *Presumed Innocent* (1990), *Caf, Society* (1995), *Forget Paris* (1995), *Albino Alligator* (1996), *The Rock* (1996), *Cop Land* (1997), *Lesser Prophets* (1997), *The Negotiator* (1998), *Twilight* (1998), and *Ravenous* (1999).

Wendie Jo Sperber (September 15, 1958–November 29, 2005). Born in Los Angeles, the actress appeared in many supporting roles in both television and film. Film credits included *I Wanna Hold Your Hand* (1978), *1941* (1979), *Used Cars* (1980), *Bachelor Party* (1984), *Back to the Future* (1985), *Moving Violations* (1985), *Stewardess School* (1986), *Back to the Future, Part 3* (1989), and *Mr. Write* (1992). Sperber also had recurring roles on TV's *Bosom Buddies* (1980–82) and *8 Simple Rules* (2002–05). Sperber had been diagnosed with breast cancer in 1997 and founded the weSPARK Cancer Support Center in 2001.

Harold J. Stone (March 3, 1913–November 18, 2005). Born Harold Hochstein in New York City, he was a third-generation actor and made his debut opposite his father at age six in the Yiddish play *White Slaves.* Stone's uncredited film debut came in 1946's *The Blue Dahlia.* Additional film credits included *The Harder They Fall* (1956), *The Wrong Man* (1956), *The Invisible Boy* (1957), *Spartacus* (1960), *The Greatest Story Ever Told* (1965), *The Big Mouth* (1967), *Which Way to the Front?* (1970), and *Hardly Working* (1980). Stone retired in 1980.

Herbert L. Strock (January 13, 1918–November 30, 2005). Born in Boston, Massachusetts, the producer and director moved to Los Angeles with his family at 13 and by 17 was working for Fox Movietone News. He began producing television shows in the 1940s and also worked as a film editor and producer before taking over as the uncredited director of the 1953 science fiction films *The Magnetic Monster* and *Riders to the Stars.* Strock also directed such low-budget genre features as *Gog* (1954), *Blood of Dracula* (1957), *I Was a Teenage Frankenstein* (1957), and *How to Make a Monster* (1958), and was the writer/director of *The Crawling Hand* (1963), *Brother on the Run* (1973), and *Monster* (1979). Strock quit directing in 1980; he published his memoir *Picture Perfect* in 2000.

Beverly Tyler (July 5, 1927–November 23, 2005). The actress was born Beverly Jean Saul in Scranton, Pennsylvania, and signed a contract with MGM at the age of 14. Tyler had minor roles in a couple of films, including 1943's *Best Foot Forward*, until co-starring in *The Green Years* (1946). She was featured in a series of B movies but made her last film, *Toughest Gun in Tombstone*, in 1958. Other credits included *My Brother Talks to Horses* (1947), *The Fireball* (1950), *The Palomino* (1950), *The Battle at Apache Pass* (1952), *The Cimarron Kid* (1952), *Night Without Sleep* (1952), *Chicago Confidential* (1957), *Voodoo Island* (1957), and *Hong Kong Confidential* (1958).

Pastor Vega (February 12, 1940–June 2, 2005). Born in Havana, Cuba, the filmmaker began his career as an actor in 1958 with the Teatro Estudio but soon preferred writing and directing. Vega was the assistant director of several documentaries before directing 1961's *The War*. His first feature-length film was 1979's *Portrait of Teresa*. Other credits included *Habanera* (1984), *Love in a Minefield* (1987), *On the Air* (1988), *Parallel Lives* (1993), and *Amanda's Prophecies* (1999). In addition, Vega ran the Festival of New Latin American Cinema from 1979 through 1990.

John Vernon (February 24, 1932–February 1, 2005). Adolphus Raymondus Vernon Agopsowicz was born in Zehner, Saskatchewan, and became interested in acting while in high school. Vernon was a graduate of the Royal Academy of Dramatic Arts and began his career on the English stage in the 1950s; he also did the voice of Big Brother in the 1956 British film *1984*. After returning to Canada, Vernon worked on stage and television, including the 1966 series *Wojeck*. The character actor played many tough guy roles but is most familiar as Dean Wormer in 1978's *National Lampoon's Animal House*. Additional credits included *Point Blank* (1967), *Tell Them Willie Boy Is Here* (1969), *Topaz* (1969), *Dirty Harry* (1971), *Charley Varrick* (1973), *Brannigan* (1975), *The Outlaw Josey Wales* (1976), *Herbie Goes Bananas* (1980), *Fraternity Vacation* (1985), *I'm Gonna Git You Sucka* (1988), *Killer Klowns from Outer Space* (1988), *Mob Story* (1990), and *Malicious* (1995).

Jacques Villeret (February 6, 1951–January 28, 2005). Born in Loches, France, the comedic actor moved to Paris in 1968 and began working on the stage. Villeret won the Cesar Award for best supporting actor in 1979 for *Robert et Robert* (1978) and the best actor award in 1999 for *Le Diner de Cons/The Dinner Game* (1998); he was nominated as best supporting actor in 1984 for *Garcon!* (1983). Other credits included *Rien Ne Va Plus* (1979), *Danton* (1983), *The Children of the Marshlands* (1999), *Actors* (2000), *Malabar Princess* (2004), *Viper in the Fist* (2004), and *Les Parrains* (2005).

George D. Wallace (June 8, 1917–July 22, 2005). Born in New York City, the actor worked in the coal mines, was a lumberjack, served in the Navy, and was a bartender in Hollywood when he was discovered by gossip columnist Jimmie Fidler. Wallace's first major role was as Commando Cody in the 1952 serial *Radar Men from the Moon*. Among his other films were *Forbidden Planet* (1956), *Defending Your Life* (1991), *A Rage in Harlem* (1991), *Diggstown* (1992), *Bicentennial Man* (1999), *Nurse Betty* (2000), and *Minority Report* (2002). The baritone singer also had an extensive stage career, including *Pipe Dream, The Pajama Game, Jennie,* and *New Girl in Town.*

Kay Walsh (August 27, 1914–April 16, 2005). Kathleen Walsh was born in London, England, and began her career in the chorus of West End music halls. She made her screen debut in *How's Chances?* (1932). Additional credits included *Get Your Man* (1934), *Secret of Stamboul* (1936), *Keep Fit* (1937), *I See Ice* (1938), *In Which We Serve* (1942), *This Happy Breed* (1944), *Vice Versa* (1947), *Oliver Twist* (1948), *Last Holiday* (1950), *Stage Fright* (1950), *Meet Me Tonight* (1952), *Young Bess* (1953), *Lease of Life* (1954), *Cast a Dark Shadow* (1957), *Tunes of Glory* (1960), *80,000 Suspects* (1963), *The Beauty Jungle* (1964), *The Witches* (1966), *Connecting Rooms* (1970), *Scrooge* (1970), *The Ruling Class* (1972), and *Night Crossing* (1982).

Ruth Warwick (June 29, 1916–January 15, 2005). Born in St. Joseph, Missouri, the actress began working on radio in the late 1940s. Orson Welles cast Warwick as his wife in 1941's *Citizen Kane*, which lead to a contract with RKO. Additional credits included *The Corsican Brothers* (1942), *Journey Into Fear* (1942), *Mr. Winkle Goes to War* (1944), *Arch of Triumph* (1948), *Great Dan Patch* (1949), *Three Husbands* (1950), and *One Too Many* (1951). Warwick created the role of Phoebe Tyler Wallingford on the soap opera *All My Children* in 1970 and made her final appearance at the show's 35th anniversary episode on January 5, 2005. Warwick entitled her autobiography, *The Confessions of Phoebe Tyler*.

Mel Welles (1924–August 19, 2005). Born in New York City, the character actor was best-known for his role as florist Gravis Muchnik in Roger Corman's 1960 comedy *The Little Shop of Horrors*. Among his other credits were *Abbott and Costello Meet the Mummy* (1955), *Attack of the Crab Monsters* (1957), *Rock All Night* (1957), *The Undead* (1957), *The Brothers Karamazov* (1958), *High School Confidential!* (1958), *The She-Beast* (1965), *Body and Soul* (1981), *Chopping Mall* (1986), and *Rented Lips* (1989). Welles also directed B-movies in Europe, did voice work, and was a script supervisor, among other careers.

Onna White (March 24, 1922–April 8, 2005). The choreographer was born in Inverness, Nova Scotia, and began her career as a dancer. White worked with choreographer Michael Kidd on *Finian's Rainbow* and later became his assistant. Her own first show was 1958's *The Music Man* for which White received the first of eight Tony nominations. White received a special Oscar for her work on the 1969 film *Oliver!* She also choreographed the film versions of her stage productions *The Music Man* (1962), *1776* (1972) and *Mame* (1974) as well as the films *Bye Bye Birdie* (1963), *The Great Waltz* (1972), and *Pete's Dragon* (1977).

Thelma White (December 4, 1910–January 11, 2005). Born Thelma Wolpa in Lincoln, Nebraska, the actress was the daughter of carnival performers and started in vaudeville as a child. White signed a contact with RKO in 1928 and was cast in such movies as *A Night in a Dormitory* (1930), *Ride 'Em Cowboy!* (1930), *Sixteen Sweeties* (1930), *Hey, Nanny Nanny* (1933), and *Never Too Late* (1935) before being cast in the now-notorious exploitation film, *Reefer Madness* (1936). Later credits included *Wanted by the Police* (1938), *Spy Train* (1943), and *Bowery Champs* (1944). White was struck with a crippling illness while touring as a USO performer during WWII; after her recovery, she became an agent and producer.

Paul Winchell (December 21, 1922–June 24, 2005). The ventriloquist and voice actor was born in New York City and began working on radio at the age of 13. Winchell worked with his ventriloquist dummies—Jerry Mahoney and Knucklehead Smith—on numerous variety and children's shows beginning in the late 1940s. He created the voice of Tigger the Tiger for Walt Disney's 1968 animated short *Winnie the Pooh and the Blustery Day* and continued through 1999's *Winnie the Pooh: Seasons of Giving*. Winchell also did voice work for the Disney features *The Aristocats* (1970) and *The Fox and the Hound* (1981) as well as such animated TV series as *The Jetsons* and *The Smurfs*.

Robert Wise (September 10, 1914–September 14, 2005). Born in Winchester, Indiana, the director followed his brother to Hollywood in 1933 and got a job at RKO. Wise learned sound effects and music and film editing and was eventually hired by Orson Welles to edit *Citizen Kane* (1941), for which he received an Oscar nomination for editing; he also did the studio edit of 1942's *Magnificent Ambersons*, which the director denounced as a mutilation. Wise took over as director on 1944's *The Curse of the Cat People* and had a long and prolific career in the field, earning both director and producer Academy Awards for *West Side Story* (1961) and *The Sound of Music* (1965). Other credits included *The Body Snatcher* (1945), *Born to Kill* (1947), *The Set-Up* (1949), *Three Secrets* (1950), *The Day the Earth Stood Still* (1951), *The House on Telegraph Hill* (1951), *The Desert Rats* (1953), *Executive Suite* (1954), *Somebody Up There Likes Me* (1956), *I Want to Live!* (1958), *Run Silent, Run Deep* (1958), *Odds Against Tomorrow* (1959), *Two for the Seesaw* (1962), *The Haunting* (1963), *The Sand Pebbles* (1966), *Star!* (1968), *The Andromeda Strain* (1971), *The Hindenburg* (1975), *Audrey Rose* (1977), *Star Trek: The Motion Picture* (1979), and *Rooftops* (1989). Wise received the D.W. Griffith Award for career achievement from the Directors Guild of America in 1988 and the American Film Institute's life achievement award in 1998.

Robert Wright (September 25, 1914–July 27, 2005). Born in Daytona Beach, Florida, the composer and lyricist met his collaborator, George "Chet" Forrest, in the late 1920s and they worked together more than 70 years on some 2,000 compositions for revues, musicals, and motion pictures. While under contract to MGM, the duo received best song Oscar nominations for "Always and Always" from *Mannequin* (1938), "It's a Blue World" from *Music in My Heart* (1940), and "Pennies for Peppino" from *Flying With Music* (1942). Wright and Forrest also worked extensively on Broadway and won Tony awards for the score of 1953's *Kismet* and received Tony nominations for their last stage musical, 1989's *Grand Hotel*.

Teresa Wright (October 27, 1918–March 6, 2005). Born Muriel Teresa Wright in New York City, the actress dropped her first name after finding another Muriel Wright registered with Actors' Equity. She began acting in summer stock and went to Broadway where producer Samuel Goldwyn offered her a film contract. Wright was nominated for Oscars for her first three films: best supporting actress for *The Little Foxes* (1941), best actress for *The Pride of the Yankees* (1942), and best supporting actress (she won) for *Mrs. Miniver* (1942). However, Goldwyn terminated Wright's contract in 1948 for refusing to do glamour girl publicity for her films. She continued as an independent and additional credits included *Shadow of a Doubt* (1943), *Casanova Brown* (1944), *Best Years of Our Lives* (1946), *Pursued* (1947), *Enchantment* (1948), *The Capture* (1950), *The Men* (1950), *California Conquest* (1952), *Somewhere in Time* (1980), *The Good Mother* (1988), and *John Grisham's The Rainmaker* (1997). Wright also worked on Broadway and in television, receiving three Emmy nominations for her work in *The Miracle Worker* (1957), *The Margaret Bourke-White Story* (1960), and *Dolphin Cove* (1989).

Selected Film Books of 2005

Adelman, Kim. *The Ultimate Guide to Chick Flicks.* Broadway Books, 2005.
The 10 elements of what makes a chick flick and a compendium of movies for every emotional occasion.

Alda, Alan. *Never Have Your Dog Stuffed: And Other Things I've Learned.* Random House, 2005.
A memoir by the stage, television, and film actor.

Anderson, D. Brian. *The Titanic in Print and on Screen: An Annotated Guide to Books, Films, Television Shows and Other Media.* McFarland & Company, Inc., 2005.
Bibliography surveys the various materials that depict the shipwreck, including documentaries, narrative films, books, plays, articles, websites, songs, and other material.

Aquino, John T. *Truth and Lives on Film: The Legal Problems of Depicting Real Persons and Events in a Fictional Medium.* McFarland & Company, Inc., 2005.
Considers the legal issues surrounding the fictionalization of real events and people, including a number of courtroom dramas.

Bacall, Lauren. *By Myself and Then Some.* Harper Entertainment, 2005.
Bacall updates her 1978 autobiography *By Myself.*

Barbas, Samantha. *The First Lady of Hollywood: A Biography of Louella Parsons.* University of California Press, 2005.
Chronicles the life of the gossip columnist for the Hearst newspapers, including her feud with rival Hedda Hopper.

Beck, Jerry. *The Animated Movie Guide.* Chicago Review Press, 2005.
Covers more than 300 films over an 80-year period, including Japanese animation, computer graphics, and stop-motion techniques.

Bellin, Joshua David. *Framing Monsters: Fantasy Film and Social Alienation.* Southern Illinois University Press, 2005.
Situates representative fantasy films such as *King Kong, The Wizard of Oz, Aliens, X-Men, The Lord of the Rings,* and others within their cultural moments.

Bernard, Jami, editor. *The X List: The National Society of Film Critics' Guide to the Movies That Turned Us On.* Da Capo, 2005.
Essays from numerous film critics cover classics, musicals, thrillers, love stories, and more.

Bogle, Donald. *Bright Boulevards, Bold Dreams: The Story of Black Hollywood.* One World, 2005.
Focuses on African-American involvement in the movie business from the silent era to the 1960s, including independent studios, actors, and residential segregation.

Boland, Michaela and Michael Bodey. *Aussiewood: Australia's Leading Actors and Directors Tell How They Conquered Hollywood.* Allen & Unwin, 2005.
Interviews with such performers as Nicole Kidman, Hugo Weaving, Geoffrey Rush, Phillip Noyce and others on how they've encountered and dealt with Hollywood success.

Brettell, Andrew et al. *Cut! Hollywood Murders, Accidents, and Other Tragedies.* Barron's, 2005.
Eight film historians compiled this anthology of more than 250 Hollywood obituaries, arranged in sections by causes of death, from early stars such as John Barrymore to contemporary actors such as Christopher Reeve.

Briggs, Joe Bob. *Profoundly Erotic: Sexy Movies That Changed History.* Universe, 2005.
A collection of essays on sex in films from cult movies to Hollywood blockbusters.

Chandler, Charlotte. *It's Only a Movie: Alfred Hitchcock, A Personal Biography.* Simon & Schuster, 2005.
Biography of the filmmaker with many reminiscences from his family and collaborators, including actors and technicians.

Chandler, Charlotte. *Nobody's Perfect: Billy Wilder, A Personal Biography.* Applause Books, 2005.
Interviews with director/writer Wilder over a 20-year period and with many of the people who worked with him.

Christopher, Robert J. *Robert and Frances Flaherty: A Documentary Life, 1883–1922.* McGill-Queen's University

Press, 2005.
Examines the early career of the documentary filmmaker and the contributions his wife made to it.

Churchwell, Sarah. *The Many Lives of Marilyn Monroe.* Holt/Metropolitan, 2005.
Focuses on the phenomena of Monroe and why so much has been written about the actress and her image.

Coleman, Terry. *Olivier.* Henry Holt, 2005.
Biography of Sir Laurence Olivier that accesses his private papers and correspondence and those of his family.

Decherney, Peter. *Hollywood and the Culture Elite: How the Movies Became American.* Columbia University Press, 2005.
Examines links between the movie business and various cultural institutions such as universities and museums, including Columbia University's film studies program, the Museum of Modern Art's curator Iris Barry, and philanthropist Nelson Rockefeller.

Dissanayake, Wimal. *Melodrama and Asian Cinema.* Cambridge University Press, 2005.
Examines the importance of melodrama in the film traditions of Japan, India, China, Indonesia, the Philippines, and Australia.

Drate, Spencer and Judith Salavetz. *The Independent Movie Poster Book.* Abrams, 2005.
Showcases posters from the films of such independent filmmakers as David Lynch, Quentin Tarantino, Spike Lee, Jean-Luc Godard, and Pedro Almodovar. Taken from the collection of the Posteritati Gallery in New York.

Dumont, Herve. *Frank Borzage: The Life and Films of a Hollywood Romantic.* McFarland & Company, Inc., 2005.
Eighteen chapters offer a reevaluation of Borzage's career and the more than 100 films he made.

Duralde, Alonso. *101 Must-See Movies for Gay Men.* Advocate Books, 2005.
The good, the bad, and the outrageous—film analysis, importance, production notes, credits, and availability.

Ebert, Roger. *The Great Movies II.* Broadway Books, 2005.
Film critic Ebert's second collection of 100 essays on great movies.

Edwards, Gwynne. *A Companion to Luis Bunuel.* Tamesis Books, 2005.
Guide to the filmmaker's career from 1929 to 1977.

Epstein, Edward Jay. *The Big Picture: The New Logic of Money and Power in Hollywood.* Random House, 2005.
Examines the structure, personalities, and connections between the six media companies that control the majority of motion picture entertainment and the process of how a film is made and where the money goes.

Eyman, Scott. *Lion of Hollywood: The Life and Legend of Louis B. Mayer.* Simon & Schuster, 2005.
Biography of Mayer from his early career selling scrap metal to his days as founder and studio head of MGM.

Finstad, Suzanne. *Warren Beatty: A Private Man.* Harmony, 2005.
Candid interviews with family, friends, and associates on the differences between the actor/filmmaker's public and private persona.

Fleischer, Richard. *Out of the Inkwell: Max Fleischer and the Animation Revolution.* University Press of Kentucky, 2005.
The animator's son looks at his father's innovative career and the creation of such characters as KoKo the Clown, Betty Boop, Popeye the Sailor, and Superman.

Fleming, E.J. *Carole Landis: A Tragic Life in Hollywood.* McFarland & Company, Inc., 2005.
Examines the actress's life and career in Hollywood.

Fonda, Jane. *My Life So Far.* Random House, 2005.
Autobiography of the actress/activist's life from her rocky childhood with father Henry Fonda through her marriages, film roles, and exploits as a Vietnam War radical.

Frascella, Lawrence and Al Weisel. *Live Fast, Die Young: The Wild Ride of Making Rebel Without a Cause.* Simon & Schuster/Touchstone, 2005.
An overview of the Warner Bros. classic focuses first on script problems, casting, and rehearsals before providing a detailed chronology of the actual filming and what went on behind the scenes.

Frayling, Christopher. *Mad, Bad and Dangerous? The Scientist and the Cinema.* Reaktion Books, 2005.
An extensive survey depicting the scientist in films from the silent era onwards.

Frayling, Christopher. *Once Upon a Time in Italy: The Westerns of Sergio Leone.* Abrams, 2005.
Illustrated history illuminates the director's life as well as his visual style and his way of telling stories.

Fryer, Paul. *The Opera Singer and the Silent Film* McFarland & Company, Inc., 2005.
Examines the relationship between operatic stars and the developing motion picture industry primarily between 1895 and 1926.

Funnell, John. *Best Songs of the Movies: Academy Award Nominees and Winners, 1934–1958.* McFarland & Company, Inc., 2005.
Examines the 160 nominated songs, including how each song was presented and performed, lyrics and melody, and historical and biographical insights.

Garner, Joe. *Life is Like a Box of Chocolates...And Other Motherly Wisdom from the Movies: A Tribute to Mom.* Andrews McMeel, 2005.
Highlights memorable film moments by moms on such themes as love, forgiveness, and respect. Includes a DVD.

Garr, Terri. *Speedbumps: Flooring It Through Hollywood.* Hudson Street Press, 2005.
The actress discusses her career, family, and living with multiple sclerosis.

Gehring, Wes. *James Dean: Rebel with a Cause.* Indiana Historical Society Press, 2005.
Looks at the actor's life from growing up in Fairmount to his work on Broadway, television, and his three films.

Gerster, Carole and Laura W. Zlogar. *Teaching Ethnic Diversity with Film: Essays and Resources for Educators in History, Social Studies, Literature and Film Studies.* McFarland & Company, Inc., 2005.
Details methods for incorporating available films into middle school, high school, and undergraduate curriculums.

Goldman, Harry. *Kenneth Strickfaden, Dr. Frankenstein's Electrician.* McFarland & Company, Inc., 2005.
Biography of the man who developed special effects from the silent era to the television age.

Goldmark, Daniel. *Tunes for 'Toons: Music and the Hollywood Cartoon.* University of California Press, 2005.
Examines music written for Hollywood animated cartoons from the 1930s through the 1950s, focusing on classical music, opera, and jazz.

Grace, Maria. *Reel Fulfillment: A 12-Step Plan for Transforming Your Life Through Movies.* McGraw-Hill, 2005.
Self-help program that uses film metaphors and characters to recognize unhealthy behaviors and improve personal lives.

Greene, Doyle. *Mexploitation Cinema: A Critical History of Mexican Vampire, Wrestler, Ape-Man and Similar Films, 1957–1977.* McFarland & Company, Inc., 2005 Places the films within their historical and cultural context; features stills and posters.

Gross, Michael Joseph. *Starstruck: When a Fan Gets Close to Fame.* Bloomsbury, 2005.
The journalist examines the star system and changing celebrity culture from the viewpoint of fans, collectors, celebrities, and publicists.

Gural-Migdal, Anna and Robert Singer, editors. *Zola and Film: Essays in the Art of Adaptation.* McFarland & Company, Inc., 2005.
Collection of 13 essays discussing the adaptation of Emile Zola's work in films from the silent era to 1993's *Germinal.*

Gussow, Mel. *Michael Gambon: A Life in Acting.* Applause Books, 2005.
Interviews with the British actor cover his stage, television, and film career.

Hawn, Goldie. *A Lotus Grows in the Mud.* Putnam, 2005.
Hawn's memoir focuses as much on her private life and spiritual beliefs as it does on her career.

Hayes, Kevin J., editor. *Charlie Chaplin: Interviews.* University Press of Mississippi, 2005.
Gathers interviews Chaplin gave between 1915 and 1967.

Hearn, Marcus. *The Cinema of George Lucas.* Abrams, 2005.
Looks at four decades of director George Lucas's work using interviews and access to Lucasfilm archives.

Herzberg, Bob. *Shooting Scripts: From Pulp Western to Film.* McFarland & Company, Inc., 2005.
Looks at the adaptation of seven writers' pulp novels from print to screen.

Heylin, Clinton. *Despite the System: Orson Welles Versus the Hollywood Studios.* Chicago Review, 2005.
A re-examination of the six film Welles made within the Hollywood system gathered from shooting scripts, memos, correspondence, and the director's interviews and public lectures.

Highberger, Craig. *Superstar in a Housedress: The Life and Legend of Jackie Curtis.* Penguin/Chamberlain Bros, 2005.
Oral biography of the drag queen star, a friend and collaborator of Andy Warhol, who died of a drug overdose in 1985. Includes a DVD of the author's same-titled documentary.

Hillman, Roger. *Unsettling Scores: German Film, Music and Ideology.* Indiana University Press, 2005.
Examines the use of classical music in film, particularly in the New German cinema of the 1970s and early 1980s.

Hofler, Robert. *The Man Who Invented Rock Hudson: The Pretty Boys and Dirty Deals of Henry Wilson.* Carroll & Graf, 2005.
Looks at the ambitious agent of Rock Hudson, Tab Hunter, Troy Donahue and others as well as the studio star-making system.

Hogan, David J., editor. *Science Fiction America.* McFarland & Company, Inc., 2005.
Twenty-two essays on how issues in science fiction films from 1930 to 1999 reflected the prevailing concerns of their time.

Hogan, Ron. *The Stewardess Is Flying the Plane! American Films of the 1970s.* Bulfinch, 2005.
Hogan mentions more than 400 movies in various film genres in his narrative of '70s movies and includes numerous candid and promotional photographs.

Hunter, Stephen. *Now Playing at the Valencia: Pulitzer Prize-Winning Essays on Movies.* Simon & Schuster, 2005. *Washington Post* film critic Hunter celebrates the last decade of popular Hollywood pictures grouped by such genres as westerns, war, and sci-fi.

Hunter, Tab with Eddie Muller. *Tab Hunter Confidential: The Making of a Movie Star.* Algonquin Books, 2005.
The 1950s heartthrob talks about his career, having to hide his homosexuality to be successful, and his career revival as a gay icon.

Jewison, Norman. *This Terrible Business Has Been Good to Me: An Autobiography.* St. Martin's/Thomas Dunne, 2005.
The director looks at a career that spans 40 years, 12 Academy Awards, 46 nominations, and 25 films.

Kaveney, Roz. *From Alien to the Matrix: Reading Science Fiction Film.* Palgrave Macmillan, 2005.
Explores the history of science fiction film and literature, recurring themes and characters, the development of special effects technology, and science fiction movie franchises, including the *Terminator, Star Wars,* and *Alien* series.

Keel, Howard with Joyce Spizer. *Only Make Believe: My Life in Show Business.* Barricade, 2005.
The actor completed his autobiography shortly before his death in 2004, covering his career on the stage, in MGM musicals, and later on television.

Kinnard, Roy and Tony Crnkovich. *The Films of Fay Wray.* McFarland & Company, Inc., 2005.
Filmography is divided into discussions of Wray's early silent features, her leading lady period in the sound era, and her latter-day supporting roles.

Klossner, Michael. *Prehistoric Humans in Film and Television: 576 Dramas, Comedies and Documentaries, 1905–2004.* McFarland & Company, Inc., 2005.
Details productions that include depictions of human prehistory or prehistoric people in historical periods or extraterrestrial settings.

Klugman, Jack with Burton Rocks. *Tony and Me: A Story of Friendship.* Good Hill, 2005.

Brief memoir of the actor's longtime friendship with *Odd Couple* partner Tony Randall.

Kord, Susanne and Elizabeth Krimmer. *Hollywood Divas, Indie Queens, and TV Heroines: Contemporary Screen Images of Women.* Rowman & Littlefield, 2005.
Examines the representations of women in film from 1990 to 2003, particularly through the careers of Julia Roberts, Sandra Bullock, Meg Ryan, and Renee Zellweger.

Koszarski, Richard. *Fort Lee: The Film Town (1904-2004).* Indiana University Press, 2005.
Examines the cinematic history of Fort Lee, New Jersey, which was used by such studios as Paramount and Universal during the silent era.

Lascia, J.D. *Darknet: Hollywood's War Against the Digital Generation.* Wiley, 2005.
Examines the culture clash over digital distribution and remixing between amateurs and entertainment conglomerates.

Le Berre, Carole. *Truffaut at Work.* Phaidon Press, 2005.
A behind-the-scenes look at the director's career and filmmaking methods from 1959 to 1983.

Leamer, Lawrence. *Fantastic: The Life of Arnold Schwarzenegger.* St. Martin's, 2005.
Chronicles the life of the bodybuilder turned actor turned Republican governor of California, including his marriage to Maria Shriver.

Lee, Spike as told to Kaleem Aftab. *Spike Lee: That's My Story and I'm Sticking to It.* Norton, 2005.
Reverential biography arranged around the director's films from 1986 to 2004.

Leopold, David. *Irving Berlin's Show Business * Broadway * Hollywood * America.* Abrams, 2005.
Assemblage of photographs, drawings, posters, sets and costume designs, sheet music, and album covers of the popular songwriter.

Lewerenz, Spencer and Barbara Nicolosi, editors. *Behind the Scenes: Hollywood Insiders on Faith, Film and Culture.* Baker Books, 2005.
Essays on Hollywood, including a history of the movie industry's relationship with Christianity and how Christian writers working in film and television integrate their beliefs with their work.

Lewis, Jerry and James Kaplan. *Dean & Me (A Love Story).* Doubleday, 2005.
Lewis discusses his 10-year partnership with singer/straight man Dean Martin, including their nightclub, movie, and television performances.

Lewis, Leon, editor. *Robert M. Young: Essays on the Films.* McFarland & Company, Inc., 2005.
Compilation of 15 essays that analyze the elements of Young's work as director, writer, cinematographer, and producer.

Lisanti, Tom. *Hollywood Surf and Beach Movies: The First Wave, 1959-1969.* McFarland & Company, Inc., 2005.
Provides 32 examples of the teenage surf movie genre.

Long, Robert Emmet. *James Ivory in Conversation: How Merchant Ivory Makes Its Movies.* University of California Press, 2005.
Ivory speaks of his 40-year career as an independent filmmaker.

Maltin, Leonard. *Leonard Maltin's Classic Movie Guide.* Plume, 2005.
Capsule reviews of more than 7,000 classic movies, including availability on DVD.

Mann, William J. *Edge of Midnight: The Life of John Schlesinger.* Billboard Books, 2005.
Authorized biography of the openly gay director who won an Academy Award for the film *Midnight Cowboy.*

McGinn, Colin. *The Power of Movies: How Screen and Mind Interact.* Pantheon, 2005.
An entertaining look at film's hold on a viewer's imagination and the author's assertion that watching a movie is like seeing a dream turned into art.

McNeil, Legs with Jennifer Osbourne. *The Other Hollywood: The Uncensored Oral History of the Porn Film Industry.* Regan, 2005.
The darker side of the American adult-film industry from mob connections to murder, drugs, suicide, and various scandals.

McPherson, Edward. *Buster Keaton: Tempest in a Flat Hat.* Newmarket, 2005.
Examines the filmmaker's life and career from his two-reelers and feature films to his descent into alcoholism and the reissue of his silent classics that made him a cultural icon.

Meikle, Denis. *Johnny Depp: A Kind of Illusion.* Reynolds & Hearn, 2005.
Tracks the actor's career from his days as a teen idol to the present.

Mitchum, Petrine Day. *Hollywood Hoofbeats: Trails Blazed Across the Silver Screen.* Bowtie Press, 2005.
Chronicles the history of horses in the movies from 1894 to the present, including how stunts were done.

Mora, Carl J. *Mexican Cinema: Reflections of a Society, 1896-2003.* McFarland & Company, Inc., 2005.
Updated and revised edition, arranged chronologically, traces the development of Mexico's film industry, with particular attention to changes from 1990 to the present.

Morton, Ray. *King Kong: The History of a Movie Icon, From Fay Wray to Peter Jackson.* Applause Books, 2005.
Chronicles the making of the seven feature films in which King Kong has appeared.

Muir, John Kenneth. *Singing a New Tune: The Rebirth of the Modern Film Musical from Evita to De-Lovely and Beyond.* Applause Books, 2005.
Traces the rebirth of the film musical from the early 1990s to 2004.

Nemerov, Alexander. *Icons of Grief: Val Lewton's Home Front Pictures.* University of California Press, 2005.
Looks at the horror films Lewton made between 1942 and 1946 as commentaries on the American home front during WWII.

Noonan, Bonnie. *Women Scientists in Fifties Science Fiction Films.* McFarland & Company, Inc., 2005.

Draws on feminist literary and cultural theory to explore the role of women professionals in B-movie science fiction films.

Paietta, Ann C. *Saints, Clergy and Other Religious Figures on Film and Television, 1895–2003.* McFarland & Company, Inc., 2005.
Details over 900 films and TV series in which a religious figure plays a prominent or recurring role or a character poses as a religious figure.

Papadimitriou, Lydia. *The Greek Film Musical: A Critical and Cultural History.* McFarland & Company, Inc., 2005.
Examines the genre and its cinematic and historical aspects within the development of popular culture in a postwar Greece.

Pappas, Charles. *It's a Bitter Little World: The Smartest, Toughest, Nastiest Quotes from Film Noir.* F & W Publications, Inc., 2005.
Includes classic and contemporary quotes organized by theme and decades.

Parish, James Robert. *Katharine Hepburn: The Untold Story.* Advocate, 2005.
Revisionist biography posits that Hepburn had romantic liaisons with women and that her affairs with men were business-minded or publicity stunts.

Perry, George. *James Dean.* DK, 2005.
Overview of the actor's life, including interviews and previously unpublished photographs, many drawn from his family's collection.

Polish, Mark, Michael Polish and Jonathan Sheldon. *The Declaration of Independent Filmmaking: An Insider's Guide to Making Movies Outside of Hollywood.* Harcourt, 2005.
The Polish brothers offer personal and practical advice into writing, shooting, editing, scoring, promoting, and distributing short and feature films.

Pond, Steve. *The Big Show: High Times and Dirty Dealings Backstage at the Academy Awards.* Faber & Faber, 2005.
Chronicles Academy Awards history as well as campaigns and behind-the-scenes glimpses of the annual event over the past 15 years.

Raabe, Meinhardt. *Memories of a Munchkin: An Illustrated Walk Down the Yellow Brick Road.* Back Stage Books, 2005.
The 4-foot-7 actor discusses his life and career, including his work as the munchkin coroner on the 1939 film.

Radosh, Richard and Allis Radosh. *Red Star Over Hollywood: The Film Colony's Long Romance with the Left.* Encounter Books, 2005.
Covers radical political activity in the movie industry from the 1930s through the blacklist.

Read, Piers Paul. *Alec Guinness: The Authorized Biography.* Simon & Schuster, 2005.
Read was designated Guinness's biographer by his widow after the actor's death in 2000; this work focuses on the actor's personal life rather than his career.

Reisfield, Scott and Robert Dance. *Garbo: Portraits from Her Private Collection.* Rizzoli, 2005.
Includes a number of studio portraits taken by MGM's premier photographers as well as previously unseen family photos and candid shots. Reisfield is Garbo's grandnephew.

Rhodes, Gary D. and John Parris Springer, editors. *Docufictions: Essays on the Intersection of Documentary and Fictional Filmmaking.* McFarland & Company, Inc., 2005.
Eighteen essays examine the relationship between narrative fiction and documentary filmmaking and how they influence each other.

Richards, Andrea. *Girl Director: A How-To Guide for the First-Time Flat-Broke Film and Video Maker.* Ten Speed Press, 2005.
A guide to do-it-yourself filmmaking from a female perspective as well as a history of women filmmakers.

Riley, Christopher. *The Hollywood Standard: The Complete and Authoritative Guide to Script Format and Style.* Michael Wiese Productions, 2005.
Riley, a script proofreader, has designed a manual that presents formats for various screenplays from theatrical films to made-for-TV movies and series; includes a section on taking a script from first draft to production draft and sample script pages.

Robbins, Christopher. *The Empress of Ireland.* Thunder's Mouth, 2005.
A memoir of Brian Desmond Hurst, an openly gay filmmaker of some 25 films, begun in the 1970s when the director was in his 80s.

Roeper, Richard. *Schlock Value: Hollywood at Its Worst.* Hyperion, 2005.
The film critic offers essays and lists on various Hollywood subjects, including one-hit wonders, film clichés, bad accents, and awards ceremonies.

Schickel, Richard. *Elia Kazan: A Biography.* HarperCollins, 2005.
The *Time*'s movie critic works to restore the director's artistic achievements and discusses his controversial stand with HUAC.

Schifando, Peter and Jean H. Mathison. *Class Act: William Haines—Legendary Hollywood Decorator.* Pointed Leaf Press, 2005.
After his acting career faded, Haines remade himself into one of the film industry's most sought-after decorators.

Sheldon, Sidney. *The Other Side of Me: A Memoir.* Warner, 2005.
Besides his career as a bestselling novelist, Sheldon discusses his years in Hollywood as a screenwriter and director and his work in television and on Broadway.

Silver, Alain and James Ursini. *L.A. Noir: The City as Character.* Santa Monica Press, 2005.
A guide to noir and neo-noir films and their California settings.

Standish, Isolde. *New History of Japanese Cinema: A Century of Narrative Film.* Continuum, 2005.
Focuses on the historical development of Japanese film from 1896 and its position in Japanese society.

Stevens Jr., Steve. *So You Want to Be in Show Business.* Cumberland House Publishing, 2005.
A 50-year Hollywood veteran, talent agent Stevens provides basic information, including finding the right agent, reading the trades, meeting with casting directors, and other insider tips.

Stewart, Jacqueline Najuma. *Migrating to the Movies: Cinema and Black Urban Modernity.* University of California Press, 2005.
Focuses on black film culture in Chicago during the silent era, including cinematic representations of African-Americans and films made specifically for black audiences.

Stewart, James B. *DisneyWar.* Simon & Schuster, 2005.
Looks at the conflict-ridden tenure of Walt Disney Co. CEO Michael Eisner.

Stock, Dennis. *James Dean: Fifty Years Ago.* Abrams, 2005.
Photographer Stock professionally and privately shot the actor over a three-month period in 1954. Published on the 50th anniversary of Dean's 1955 death.

Suid, Lawrence H. and Delores A. Harerstick. *Stars and Stripes on Screen: A Comprehensive Guide to Portrayals of American Military on Film.* Scarecrow Press, 2005.
Portrayal of the armed services on film from 1898 to the present; covers more than 1000 feature films, 100 made for television movies, and 175 documentaries.

Summers, Anthony and Robbyn Swan. *Sinatra: The Life.* Knopf, 2005.
Comprehensive biography of singer/actor Frank Sinatra.

Tevis, Ray and Brenda Tevis. *The Image of Librarians in Cinema, 1917–1999.* McFarland & Company, Inc., 2005.
Chronological arrangement analyzes the stereotypical image of librarians primarily in American and British motion pictures.

Turtu, Tony. *Bad Girls: Film Fatales, Sirens and Molls.* Collectors Press, 2005.
Features B-movie bad girls from posters and publicity stills.

Vankin, Jonathan and John Whalen. *Based on a True Story*: Fact and Fantasy in 100 Favorite Movies *But with More Car Crashes.* Chicago Review, 2005.
Examines four decades of films purportedly based on fact and discovers what is true and what is fictional.

Vaz, Mark Cotta. *Living Dangerously: The Adventures of Merian C. Cooper, Creator of King Kong.* Villard, 2005.
Life and career of the producer/director from his work with partner Ernest Shoedsack on documentaries in the 1920s to his filming of the 1933 movie and his time as the head of RKO studios.

Vieira, Mark A. *Greta Garbo: A Cinematic Legacy.* Abrams, 2005.
Celebrates the centenary of the birth of the actress and chronicles Garbo's career from her American debut in 1926 to her film retirement in 1941.

Vincendeau, Ginette. *Stars and Stardom in French Cinema.* Continuum, 2005.
Analyzes the French star system and such popular stars as Jean Gabin, Brigette Bardot, Jeanne Moreau, Jean-Paul Belmondo, Alain Delon, Catherine Deneuve, and others.

Vogel, Michelle. *Children of Hollywood: Accounts of Growing Up as Sons and Daughters of Stars.* McFarland & Company, Inc., 2005.
Looks into the private lives of the children of such classic Hollywood icons as the Marx Brothers, Douglas Fairbanks, W.C. Fields, Boris Karloff, and others.

Von Dassanowsky, Robert. *Austrian Cinema: A History.* McFarland & Company, Inc., 2005.
Examines the influences of Austrian social-critical and comedy genres on international cinema from 1895 to the present.

Walker, John, editor. *Halliwell's Top 1,000: The Ultimate Movie Countdown.* HarperCollins UK, 2005.
Compiles the top 1,000 films and various top-10 lists from critics, directors, actors, and others in the industry.

Wallach, Eli. *The Good, the Bad, and Me: In My Anecdotage.* Harcourt, 2005.
The actor offers an engaging memoir of his life from his 1915 birth in Brooklyn through his work with the Actor's Studio and various stage and film roles.

Wasson, Haidee. *Museum Movies: The Museum of Modern Art and the Birth of Art Cinema.* University of California Press, 2005.
Traces the creation of MoMa's Film Library from 1935 as the first North American film archive and museum.

Watkins, Mel. *Stepin Fetchit: The Life and Times of Lincoln Perry.* Pantheon, 2005.
An examination of the life and career of African-American actor Perry (1902–1985) and his stereotypical subservient character, which was a fixture in early films.

Watts, Jill. *Hattie McDaniel: Black Ambition, White Hollywood.* Amistad, 2005.
Biography of the first African-American actress to win an Academy Award (in 1939) whose career was blighted by typecasting and racism.

Waxman, Sharon. *Rebels on the Backlot: Six Maverick Directors and How They Conquered the Hollywood Studio System.* HarperCollins, 2005.
Profiles Quentin Tarantino, Paul Thomas Anderson, David Fincher, Steven Soderbergh, David O. Russell, and Spike Jonze.

Wayne, Jane Ellen. *The Leading Men of MGM.* Carroll & Graf, 2005.
Filmographies, photos, and warts-and-all biographies of such figures as Clark Gable, Spencer Tracy, James Stewart, Frank Sinatra, Elvis Presley, and others.

Weaver, Tom. *Earth vs. the Sci- Fi Filmmakers: 20 Interviews.* McFarland & Company, Inc., 2005.
Interviews actors, directors, and others involved in horror and science fiction films of the 1950s and 1960s.

White, Raymond E. *King of the Cowboys, Queen of the West: Roy Rogers and Dale Evans.* University of Wisconsin Press/Popular Press, 2005.
Surveys the 60-year career of the duo in radio, film, recordings, television, and comic books.

Wilder, Gene. *Kiss Me Like a Stranger.* St. Martin's, 2005.
Memoir by the actor covering his life, including his marriage to the late Gilda Radner, and his career.

Wildermuth, Mark E. *Blood in the Moonlight: Michael Mann and Information Age Cinema.* McFarland & Company, Inc., 2005.
Critical examination of the films of Michael Mann and the recurring theme of modern communication and information and its effect on the individual and society.

Wranovics, John. *Chaplin and Agee: The Untold Story of the Tramp, the Writer, and the Lost Screenplay.* Palgrave Mac-

millan, 2005.
Examines the friendship of the author and the filmmaker, including Agee's work on a 1949 film script.

York, Michael. *Are My Blinkers Showing?: Adventures in Filmmaking in the New Russia.* Da Capo, 2005.
The actor discusses his adventures making an action film in present-day capitalist Russia, including language difficulties and what mysterious men's garment a blinker could be.

Zimmerman, Steve and Ken Weiss. *Food in the Movies.* McFarland & Company, Inc., 2005.
Covers more than 500 American and British films in which food played a prominent part.

Zone, Ray. *3-D Filmmakers: Conversations with Creators of Stereoscopic Motion Pictures.* Scarecrow Press, 2005.
Interviews with 21 industry pros, including directors, cinematographers, producers, and screenwriters.

Director Index

Screenwriter Index

Cinematographer Index

Editor Index

Art Director Index

Music Index

Performer Index

Stephen Adly Guirgis
Palindromes *301*

Donevan Gunia
Downfall *104*

Andrew Gurland
Mail Order Wife *248*

Luis Guzman (1956-)
Dreamer: Inspired by a True Story *106*
Waiting *405*

Jake Gyllenhaal (1980-)
Brokeback Mountain *47*
Jarhead *207*
Proof *317*

Maggie Gyllenhaal (1977-)
Happy Endings *158*

Lukas Haas (1976-)
Last Days *233*

Jennifer Habib
Yours, Mine & Ours *434*

Jessica Habib
Yours, Mine & Ours *434*

Matthias Habich (1940-)
Downfall *104*

Julie Hagerty (1955-)
Just Friends *211*

Catherine Lough Haggquist
Alone in the Dark *6*

Kathryn Hahn (1974-)
A Lot Like Love *1*

Sid Haig (1939-)
The Devil's Rejects *93*

Brad Hall (1958-)
Must Love Dogs *281*

Philip Baker Hall (1931-)
The Amityville Horror *7*
In Good Company *191*

Regina Hall (1971-)
The Honeymooners *177*
King's Ransom *226*

Nicholas Hammond (1950-)
Stealth *368*

Sheila Hancock (1933-)
Yes *433*

Perla Haney-Jardine
Dark Water *85*

Colin Hanks (1977-)
King Kong *218*

Gillian Hanna
Oliver Twist *296*

London Hansen
Jiminy Glick in LaLa Wood *208*

Daijiro Harada
Howl's Moving Castle *(V)* *183*

David Harbour
Brokeback Mountain *47*

Marcia Gay Harden (1959-)
The Bad News Bears *19*

Edward Hardwicke (1932-)
Oliver Twist *296*

Robert Hardy (1925-)
Harry Potter and the Goblet of Fire *160*

Dorian Harewood (1950-)
Assault on Precinct 13 *12*

Corinna Harfouch
Downfall *104*

Angie Harmon
The Deal *86*
Fun With Dick and Jane *140*

Elisabeth Harnois (1979-)
Pretty Persuasion *309*

Woody Harrelson (1962-)
North Country *291*
The Prize Winner of Defiance, Ohio *313*

C. Gerod Harris
The Wedding Date *417*

Ed Harris (1949-)
A History of Violence *172*

George Harris
The Interpreter *198*
Layer Cake *235*

Jamie Harris
The New World *289*

Kenneth "K.C." Harris
The Bad News Bears *19*

Rachael Harris
Kicking & Screaming *215*

Sean Harris
Asylum *15*

Steve Harris
Diary of a Mad Black Woman *94*

Will Harris
Sky High *357*

Mya Harrison
See Mya

Ian Hart (1964-)
Breakfast on Pluto *43*

Josh Hartnett (1978-)
Sin City *350*

Steve Harvey
Racing Stripes *(V)* *321*

Dave Harwood
Separate Lies *346*

Kyoko Hasegawa
Three ... Extremes *375*

Tamer Hassan
Layer Cake *235*

Anne Hathaway (1982-)
Brokeback Mountain *47*

Rutger Hauer (1944-)
Batman Begins *23*
Sin City *350*

Cole Hauser (1975-)
The Cave *60*

Ethan Hawke (1971-)
Assault on Precinct 13 *12*
Lord of War *241*

John Hawkes (1959-)
Me and You and Everyone We Know *256*

Sally Hawkins
Layer Cake *235*

Elizabeth Hawthorne
The Chronicles of Narnia: The Lion, the Witch and the Wardrobe *68*

Heidi Hayes
A History of Violence *172*

Isaac Hayes (1942-)
Hustle & Flow *184*

Miss Laura Hayes
Beauty Shop *28*

David Hayman (1950-)
Where the Truth Lies *420*

Dennis Haysbert (1955-)
Jarhead *207*

Lena Headey (1976-)
The Brothers Grimm *53*
The Cave *60*

Amber Heard
North Country *291*

John Heard (1946-)
The Deal *86*

Michael Heath
Oliver Twist *296*

Dan Hedaya (1940-)
Robots *(V)* *330*

Jon Heder
Just Like Heaven *212*

Garrett Hedlund
Four Brothers *139*

Jae Hee
3-Iron *376*

Leonard Earl Howze
The Ringer *328*

Kelly Hu (1967-)
Underclassman *394*

David Huband
Cinderella Man *71*

David Huddleston (1930-)
The Producers *315*

Ernie Hudson (1945-)
Miss Congeniality 2: Armed and Fabulous *268*

Kate Hudson (1979-)
The Skeleton Key *354*

Felicity Huffman (1962-)
Transamerica *383*

Bonnie Hunt (1964-)
Cheaper by the Dozen 2 *64*

Linda Hunt (1945-)
A Lot Like Love *1*
Yours, Mine & Ours *434*

Dirk Hunter
Undead *393*

Rachael Huntley
Mr. & Mrs. Smith *269*

Paige Hurd
Beauty Shop *28*

John Hurt (1940-)
The Skeleton Key *354*
Valiant *(V)* *402*

Mary Beth Hurt (1948-)
The Exorcism of Emily Rose *123*

William Hurt (1950-)
A History of Violence *172*
Syriana *372*

Danny Huston (1962-)
The Constant Gardener *75*

Josh Hutcherson
Kicking & Screaming *215*
Zathura *436*

Eleanor Hutchins
Milk and Honey *264*

Eugene Hutz
Everything is Illuminated *122*

Kwon Hyuk-ho
3-Iron *376*

Stanislav Ianevski
Harry Potter and the Goblet of Fire *160*

Ice Cube (1969-)
Are We There Yet? *8*
XXX: State of the Union *431*

Curtiss I'Cook
See Curtiss Cook

Thomas Ikeda
Memoirs of a Geisha *260*

Michael Irby
Flightplan *134*

Jeremy Irons (1948-)
Casanova *59*
Kingdom of Heaven *221*
The Merchant of Venice *262*

Amy Irving (1953-)
Hide and Seek *169*

Jason Isaacs (1963-)
Harry Potter and the Goblet of Fire *160*

Mitsunori Isaki
Howl's Moving Castle *(V)* *183*

Aysel Iscan
Head On *163*

Miki Ishikawa (1991-)
Yours, Mine & Ours *434*

Marcel Iures
The Cave *60*
Layer Cake *235*

Moshe Ivgi
Munich *277*

Ja Rule (1976-)
Assault on Precinct 13 *12*

Brandon T. Jackson
Roll Bounce *334*

Curtis "50 Cent" Jackson
Get Rich or Die Tryin' *144*

Dominique Jackson
The Hitchhiker's Guide to the Galaxy *175*

Joshua Jackson (1978-)
Cursed *83*
Racing Stripes *(V)* *321*

Samuel L. Jackson (1948-)
Coach Carter *74*
In My Country *195*
The Man *250*
Star Wars: Episode 3—Revenge of the Sith *364*
XXX: State of the Union *431*

Peter Jacobson
Domino *100*
Good Night, and Good Luck *146*

Carlos Jacott
Fun With Dick and Jane *140*
Jiminy Glick in LaLa Wood *208*

Jesse James (1989-)
The Amityville Horror *7*

Jolyon James
The Wedding Date *417*

Kevin James
Hitch *174*

Lennie James
Sahara *339*

Paul James
Cry_Wolf *81*

Pell James
Broken Flowers *50*

Allison Janney (1960-)
Winter Solstice *427*

Famke Janssen (1964-)
Hide and Seek *169*

Jesse Janzen
Cry_Wolf *81*

Agnes Jaoui (1964-)
Look at Me *240*

Ricky Jay (1948-)
Last Days *233*

Marc John Jefferies
Get Rich or Die Tryin' *144*

Carter Jenkins
The Bad News Bears *19*

Richard Jenkins
Fun With Dick and Jane *140*
North Country *291*
Rumor Has It… *336*

Michael Jenn
Unleashed *397*

Shooter Jennings
Walk the Line *406*

Julia Jentsch
The Edukators *113*

Choi Jeong-ho
3-Iron *376*

Gulnara Jeralieva
Schizo *344*

Yu Ji-tae
Oldboy *294*

Zhou Jianjun
Eros *120*

Dong Jie
2046 *387*

Ju Jin-mo
3-Iron *376*

Courtney Jines
Because of Winn-Dixie *30*

Lee Jo-suk
3-Iron *376*

Richard Kind (1956-)
Bewitched *36*

Jaime (James) King (1979-)
Cheaper by the Dozen 2 *64*
Pretty Persuasion *309*
Sin City *350*
Two for the Money *389*

Regina King (1971-)
Miss Congeniality 2: Armed and Fabulous *268*

Ben Kingsley (1943-)
Oliver Twist *296*
A Sound of Thunder *361*

Laurence Kinlan
Breakfast on Pluto *43*

Greg Kinnear (1963-)
The Bad News Bears *19*
Robots *(V)* *330*

Nikolai Kinski
Aeon Flux *4*

Guven Kirac
Head On *163*

Harry Kirkham
Millions *265*

Langley Kirkwood
In My Country *195*

Tory Kittles
Get Rich or Die Tryin' *144*

Burghart Klaussner
The Edukators *113*

Chris Klein (1979-)
Just Friends *211*

Kevin Kline (1947-)
Jiminy Glick in LaLa Wood *208*

Owen Kline
The Squid and the Whale *362*

Rob Knepper
Good Night, and Good Luck *146*
Hostage *179*

Lily Knight
The Assassination of Richard Nixon *11*

Matthew Knight
The Greatest Game Ever Played *150*

Keira Knightley (1985-)
Domino *100*
The Jacket *205*
Pride and Prejudice *310*

Don Knotts (1924-)
Chicken Little *(V)* *65*

Johnny Knoxville (1971-)
The Dukes of Hazzard *107*
Lords of Dogtown *243*
The Ringer *328*

Erik Knudsen
Saw II *342*

Mpho Koaho
Get Rich or Die Tryin' *144*

Motoki Kobayashi
The Great Raid *148*

Kiyoshi Kodama (1934-)
Steamboy *(V)* *369*

David Koechner
The Dukes of Hazzard *107*
The 40 Year Old Virgin *137*
Waiting *405*
Yours, Mine & Ours *434*

Juliane Koehler
Downfall *104*

Vasilis Kolovos
Weeping Meadow *418*

Rich Komenich
The Amityville Horror *7*

Manami Konishi (1978-)
Steamboy *(V)* *369*

Karin Konoval
Alone in the Dark *6*

Harmony Korine (1974-)
Last Days *233*

Scott Kosar
The Amityville Horror *7*

Eva Kotamanidou
Weeping Meadow *418*

Elias Koteas (1961-)
The Greatest Game Ever Played *150*

Hubert Kounde
The Constant Gardener *75*

Jeroen Krabbe (1944-)
Deuce Bigalow: European Gigolo *92*

Sammi Kraft
The Bad News Bears *19*

Jane Krakowski (1966-)
Pretty Persuasion *309*

Horst Krause
Schultze Gets the Blues *345*

Thomas Kretschmann (1962-)
Downfall *104*
King Kong *218*

Kris Kristofferson (1936-)
Dreamer: Inspired by a True Story *106*
The Jacket *205*

David Krumholtz (1978-)
Guess Who *152*

Youki Kudoh (1971-)
Memoirs of a Geisha *260*

Lisa Kudrow (1963-)
Happy Endings *158*

Chen Kun
Balzac and the Little Chinese Seamstress *21*

Akbar Kurtha
Syriana *372*

Mehmet Kurtulus
Head On *163*

Clyde Kusatsu (1948-)
The Interpreter *198*
Shopgirl *349*

Ashton Kutcher (1978-)
A Lot Like Love *1*
Guess Who *152*

Chan Kwok Kwan
Kung Fu Hustle *229*

Michelle Kwan
Ice Princess *188*

Tom La Grua
With Friends Like These *428*

Shia LaBeouf (1986-)
Constantine *77*
The Greatest Game Ever Played *150*

Jordan Ladd (1975-)
Waiting *405*

Jay Laga'aia
Star Wars: Episode 3—Revenge of the Sith *364*

Olga Landina
Schizo *344*

Forrest Landis
Cheaper by the Dozen 2 *64*

Diane Lane (1965-)
Must Love Dogs *281*

Nathan Lane (1956-)
The Producers *315*

Jessica Lange (1949-)
Broken Flowers *50*

Frank Langella (1940-)
Good Night, and Good Luck *146*
House of D *180*

Anthony LaPaglia (1959-)
Winter Solstice *427*

Agustin Lara
Downfall *104*

Ali Larter (1976-)
A Lot Like Love *1*

Lucy Liu (1968-)
Domino *100*

Blake Lively
Sisterhood of the Traveling Pants *353*

Ron Livingston (1968-)
Pretty Persuasion *309*
Winter Solstice *427*

LL Cool J (1968-)
Mindhunters *266*

Norman Lloyd (1914-)
In Her Shoes *193*

Luigi Lo Cascio
Best of Youth *34*

Stephen Lobo
The Wedding Date *417*

Heather Locklear (1962-)
The Perfect Man *306*

Robert Loggia (1930-)
The Deal *86*

Donal Logue (1966-)
Just Like Heaven *212*

Lindsay Lohan (1986-)
Herbie: Fully Loaded *167*

Alison Lohman (1979-)
Where the Truth Lies *420*

Nancy Lollar
The Amityville Horror *7*

Justin Long
Herbie: Fully Loaded *167*
Waiting *405*

Lisa Long
Mysterious Skin *286*

Nia Long (1970-)
Are We There Yet? *8*

Brian Lonsdale
Valiant *(V)* *402*

Michael (Michel) Lonsdale (1931-)
Munich *277*

George Lopez
The Adventures of Sharkboy and Lavagirl in 3-D *2*

Jennifer Lopez (1970-)
Monster-in-Law *275*
An Unfinished Life *395*

Jean-Pierre Lorit
The White Countess *422*

Patrick Louis
Cinderella Man *71*

Jon Lovitz (1957-)
The Producers *315*

Rob Lowe (1964-)
Jiminy Glick in LaLa Wood *208*

Elina Lowensohn (1967-)
Dark Water *85*

Josh(ua) Lucas (1972-)
Stealth *368*
An Unfinished Life *395*

Ludacris
Crash *80*
Hustle & Flow *184*

Joanna Lumley (1946-)
Tim Burton's Corpse Bride *(V)* *380*

Jacqueline Lustig
My Mother's Smile *283*

Jane Lynch
The 40 Year Old Virgin *137*

John Lynch (1961-)
The Bridge of San Luis Rey *46*

Kelly Lynch (1959-)
The Jacket *205*

Shelby Lynne
Walk the Line *406*

Natasha Lyonne (1979-)
Robots *(V)* *330*

Sunny Mabrey
XXX: State of the Union *431*

Bernie Mac (1958-)
Guess Who *152*

Cal Macaninch
Dear Frankie *88*

Cornelius Macarthy
Millions *265*

Norm MacDonald (1963-)
Deuce Bigalow: European Gigolo *92*

Scott MacDonald
Jarhead *207*

Andie MacDowell (1958-)
Beauty Shop *28*

Matthew MacFadyen
Pride and Prejudice *310*

Gabriel Macht (1972-)
A Love Song for Bobby Long *244*

Anthony Mackie
The Man *250*

Shirley MacLaine (1934-)
Bewitched *36*
In Her Shoes *193*
Rumor Has It… *336*

Peter MacNeill
A History of Violence *172*

Elle Macpherson (1964-)
With Friends Like These *428*

William H. Macy (1950-)
Sahara *339*

Amy Madigan (1957-)
With Friends Like These *428*

Michael Madsen (1959-)
Sin City *350*

Kate Magowan
It's All Gone, Pete Tong *203*

Sean Maher (1975-)
Serenity *347*

Sophie Main
Dear Frankie *88*

Mako (1933-)
Memoirs of a Geisha *260*

Khoury J. Makram
See Makram Khoury

Patrick Malahide (1945-)
Sahara *339*

Romany Malco
The 40 Year Old Virgin *137*

Robyn Malcolm
Boogeyman *40*

Alexandra Malick
The New World *289*

Wendie Malick (1950-)
Racing Stripes *321*
Waiting *405*

John Malkovich (1953-)
The Hitchhiker's Guide to the Galaxy *175*

Jena Malone (1984-)
The Ballad of Jack and Rose *20*
Pride and Prejudice *310*

Robert Mammone
The Great Raid *148*

Harriet Manamela
In My Country *195*

Tyler Mane
The Devil's Rejects *93*

Camryn Manheim (1961-)
Dark Water *85*
An Unfinished Life *395*

Gabriel Mann
A Lot Like Love *1*
Dominion: Prequel to the Exorcist *98*

Leslie Mann (1972-)
The 40 Year Old Virgin *137*

Taryn Manning (1978-)
A Lot Like Love *1*
Hustle & Flow *184*

Thongchai McIntyre
2046 *387*

Mungo McKay
Undead *393*

Michael McKean (1947-)
The Producers *315*
With Friends Like These *428*

Ian McKellen (1939-)
Asylum *15*
Emile *118*

Ben(jamin) McKenzie (1978-)
Junebug *209*

Kevin McKidd (1973-)
Kingdom of Heaven *221*

Dallas McKinney
Kicking & Screaming *215*

Craig McLachlan
The Great Raid *148*

Dylan McLaughlin
Kicking & Screaming *215*

Julian McMahon
Fantastic Four *129*

Ian McNeice (1950-)
The Hitchhiker's Guide to the Galaxy *(V)* *175*
Oliver Twist *296*
White Noise *424*

Marnie McPhail
The Greatest Game Ever Played *150*

Peter McRobbie
Brokeback Mountain *47*

Gerard McSorley
The Constant Gardener *75*
Rory O'Shea Was Here *335*

Colm Meaney (1953-)
Layer Cake *235*

Julio Oscar Mechoso
The Legend of Zorro *236*

Meghnaa
Bride & Prejudice *45*

Nasser Memarzia
Millions *265*

Ben Mendelsohn (1969-)
The New World *289*

Eva Mendes (1978-)
Hitch *174*

Natalie Mendoza
The Great Raid *148*

Idina Menzel
Rent *325*

Kad Merad
The Chorus *67*

Tamzin Merchant
Pride and Prejudice *310*

Ryan Merriman (1983-)
The Ring 2 *327*

Debra Messing (1968-)
The Wedding Date *417*

Johnny Messner
Hostage *179*

Charles Mesure
Boogeyman *40*

Omar Metwally
Munich *277*

Breckin Meyer (1974-)
Herbie: Fully Loaded *167*
Rebound *323*

Dina Meyer (1969-)
Saw II *342*

Dragan Micanovic
Layer Cake *235*

Alexander Michaletos
Duma *108*

Tracy Middendorf
The Assassination of Richard Nixon *11*

Tatsuya Mihashi (1923-)
Dolls *97*

Dash Mihok (1974-)
Kiss Kiss, Bang Bang *227*

Christina Milian (1981-)
Be Cool *26*
Man of the House *251*

Ivana Milicevic
Just Like Heaven *212*

Dan John Miller
Walk the Line *406*

Jonny Lee Miller (1972-)
Aeon Flux *4*
Melinda and Melinda *258*
Mindhunters *266*

Larry Miller (1953-)
Kiss Kiss, Bang Bang *227*

Omar Benson Miller
Get Rich or Die Tryin' *144*

Sienna Miller
Casanova *59*
Layer Cake *235*

Wentworth Miller
Stealth *(V)* *368*

Andy Milonakis (1976-)
Waiting *405*

Max Minghella
Bee Season *31*
Syriana *372*

Helen Mirren (1946-)
The Hitchhiker's Guide to the Galaxy *(V)* *175*

Ralph Misske
Head On *163*

Beverley Mitchell
Saw II *342*

Radha Mitchell (1973-)
Melinda and Melinda *258*

William C. Mitchell
Syriana *372*

Akihiro Miwa
Howl's Moving Castle *(V)* *183*

Matthew Modine (1959-)
Transporter 2 *385*

Jay Mohr (1970-)
Are We There Yet? *8*
King's Ransom *226*

Alfred Molina (1953-)
Steamboy *(V)* *369*

Kaori Momoi
Memoirs of a Geisha *260*

Michelle Monaghan
Kiss Kiss, Bang Bang *227*
North Country *291*
Winter Solstice *427*

Alberto Mondini
My Mother's Smile *283*

Mo'Nique
Domino *100*

Debra Monk (1949-)
Dark Water *85*
Palindromes *301*
The Producers *315*

Paolo Montalban (1973-)
The Great Raid *148*

Cesar Montano
The Great Raid *148*

Sheri Moon
The Devil's Rejects *93*

Julianne Moore (1961-)
The Prize Winner of Defiance, Ohio *313*

Mandy Moore (1984-)
Racing Stripes *(V)* *321*

Shemar Moore
Diary of a Mad Black Woman *94*

Chloe Grace Moretz
The Amityville Horror *7*

Debbi (Deborah) Morgan (1956-)
Coach Carter *74*

Subject Index

Title Index

This cumulative index is an alphabetical list of all films covered in the volumes of the *Magill's Cinema Annual.* Film titles are indexed on a word-by-word basis, including articles and prepositions. English and foreign leading articles are ignored. Films reviewed in this volume are cited in bold with an Arabic number indicating the page number on which the review begins; films reviewed in past volumes are cited with the *Annual* year in which the review was published. Original and alternate titles are cross-referenced to the American release title. Titles of retrospective films are followed by the year, in brackets, of their original release.

A

B

C

D

E

G

I

J

L

N

O

P

Q

R

U

V

W